GOD MATTERS

Readings in the Philosophy of Religion

* * *

RAYMOND MARTIN

Union College

CHRISTOPHER BERNARD

University of Maryland

Longman

New York   San Francisco   Boston
London   Toronto   Sydney   Tokyo   Singapore   Madrid
Mexico City   Munich   Paris   Cape Town   Hong Kong   Montreal

Vice President/Publisher: Priscilla McGeehon
Director of Marketing: Tim Stookesberry
Production Manager: Charles Annis
Project Coordination, Text Design, and Electronic Page Makeup: Shepherd, Inc.
Cover Designer/Manager: Nancy Danahy
Cover Illustration: Foreground image © Laurie L. Jarrell; background © PhotoDisc
Senior Print Buyer: Dennis Para
Printer and Binder: Hamilton Printing Co.
Cover Printer: Lehigh Press, Inc.

For permission to use copyrighted material, grateful acknowledgement is made to the copyright holders on pp. 559-561, which are hereby made part of this copyright page.

Library of Congress Cataloging-in-Publication Data

God matters : readings in the philosophy of religion / Raymond Martin,
Christopher Bernard.
      p. cm.
   Includes bibliographical references.
   ISBN 0-321-10365-3
   1. Religion—Philosophy. I. Martin, Raymond, 1941– II. Bernard,
   Christopher, 1972–
   BL51 .G683 2002
   210—dc21

                                          2002069437

Please visit our website at http://www.ablongman.com

ISBN 0-321-10365-3

1 2 3 4 5 6 7 8 9 10—HT—05 04 03 02

CONTENTS

Preface   ix
Introduction   1

PART I. THE NATURE OF GOD

OMNIPOTENCE
1. GOD IS ALL POWERFUL * *Thomas Aquinas*   5
2. SOME PUZZLES CONCERNING OMNIPOTENCE * *George I. Mavrodes*   7
   Harry Frankfurt, "The Paradox of the Stone"

OMNISCIENCE
3. GOD'S KNOWLEDGE * *Thomas Aquinas*   10
4. DIVINE KNOWLEDGE AND HUMAN FREEDOM * *Scott A. Davison*   12
   St. Augustine, "God's Foreknowledge Does Not Rule Out Freedom"
   Jonathan Edwards, "God's Foreknowledge Rules Out Libertarian Freedom"

GOD AND TIME
5. GOD IS OUTSIDE OF TIME * *Boethius*   24
6. ETERNITY * *Eleonore Stump and Norman Kretzmann*   26
   William Lane Craig, "Time: The Familiar Stranger"
   William J. Wainwright, "God's Compassion"

SUGGESTIONS FOR FURTHER READING   37

PART II. ARGUMENTS FOR THE EXISTENCE OF GOD

THE ONTOLOGICAL ARGUMENT
7. THE ONTOLOGICAL ARGUMENT * *Anselm and Gaunilo*   41
   Rene Descartes, "It Is Impossible to Think of God as Not Existing"
8. CRITIQUE OF THE ONTOLOGICAL ARGUMENT * *Immanuel Kant*   44
   William Rowe, "Anselm Begs the Question"
   Stephen Davis, "Existence Is a Predicate"

9. ANSELM'S ONTOLOGICAL ARGUMENTS ✶ *Norman Malcolm*　　49
　Alvin Plantinga, "The Hartshorne-Malcolm Version of the Ontological Argument"

THE COSMOLOGICAL ARGUMENT

10. THE FIVE WAYS ✶ *Thomas Aquinas*　　61
　Frederick Copleston, "A Hierarchy of Causes"
11. THE COSMOLOGICAL ARGUMENT ✶ *David Yandell and Keith Yandell*　　64
　Gottfried Leibniz, "Proving God"
　Bertrand Russell and Frederick Copleston, "The Russell-Copleston Debate"
12. CRITICISMS OF THE COSMOLOGICAL ARGUMENT ✶ *J. L. Mackie*　　77
　Elliot Sober, "The Birthday Fallacy"
　William Rowe, "An Argument Against the Principle of Sufficient Reason"
13. THE KALAM COSMOLOGICAL ARGUMENT ✶ *William Lane Craig*　　82
　Paul Davies, "Is the Universe a Free Lunch?"
　John D. Barrow and Frank J. Tipler, "The Anthropic Principle"
14. A CRITICAL EXAMINATION OF THE KALAM COSMOLOGICAL ARGUMENT ✶
　Wes Morriston　　95

THE DESIGN ARGUMENT

15. THE WATCH AND THE WATCHMAKER ✶ *William Paley*　　108
　Michael Denton, "Self-Duplication as Evidence of Design"
　Walter Bradley, "Complex Living Systems Are Evidence of Design"
16. CRITIQUE OF THE DESIGN ARGUMENT ✶ *David Hume*　　115
　George Smith, "Who Designed the Designer?"
　Robin Le Poidevin, "Evolution Explains Apparent Design"
17. GOD, DESIGN, AND FINE-TUNING ✶ *Robin Collins*　　119
　Richard Dawkins, "Atheism Before Darwin?"

THE MORAL ARGUMENT

18. THE MORAL ARGUMENT FOR THE EXISTENCE GOD ✶ *C. S. Lewis*　　135
19. CRITIQUE OF THE MORAL ARGUMENT ✶ *J. L. Mackie*　　139

SUGGESTIONS FOR FURTHER READING　　147

PART III. FAITH AND REASON

THE EVIDENTIAL CHALLENGE

20. THE PRESUMPTION OF ATHEISM ✶ *Antony Flew*　　151
　Michael Scriven, "Santa Claus and Belief in God"
21. A PASCALIAN REJOINDER TO THE PRESUMPTION OF ATHEISM ✶ *R. Douglas Geivett*　　162
22. RESPONSE TO R. DOUGLAS GEIVETT'S "A PASCALIAN REJOINDER
　TO THE PRESUMPTION OF ATHEISM" ✶ *Antony Flew*　　175

23. IT IS WRONG TO BELIEVE WITHOUT EVIDENCE * *William Clifford*   180

24. WHAT SHOULD WE EXPECT FROM THEISTIC PROOFS? * *George I. Mavrodes*   183

BELIEF WITHOUT EVIDENCE: A DEFENSE

25. PASCAL'S WAGER * *Blaise Pascal*   197
    William Lycan and George Schlesinger, "You Bet Your Life"

26. THE WILL TO BELIEVE * *William James*   199

27. RELIGIOUS BELIEF REQUIRES A LEAP OF FAITH * *Søren Kierkegaard*   202

28. KIERKEGAARD'S ARGUMENTS AGAINST OBJECTIVE REASONING IN RELIGION *
    Robert Merrihew Adams   209

29. REFORMED EPISTEMOLOGY AND THE RATIONALITY OF THEISTIC BELIEF *
    James F. Sennett   219
    Alvin Plantinga, "The Aquinas/Calvin Model"
    Alvin Plantinga, "The Great Pumpkin Objection"

30. REFORMED EPISTEMOLOGY: AN ATHEIST PERSPECTIVE * *Keith M. Parsons*   232
    Michael Martin, "Son of a Great Pumpkin"

31. RELIGIOUS BELIEF FOR THE REST OF US: REFLECTIONS ON REFORMED EPISTEMOLOGY *
    Sandra Menssen and Thomas D. Sullivan   244

REASON AND REVELATION

32. REASON AND REVELATION COMPLEMENT EACH OTHER * *Thomas Aquinas*   255

SUGGESTIONS FOR FURTHER READING   257

PART IV. THE PROBLEM OF EVIL

33. EVIL AND THE EXISTENCE OF GOD * *David Hume*   261
    An Author of Genesis, "Abraham and Isaac"

34. SOUL-MAKING THEODICY * *John Hick*   265
    Edward Madden and Peter Hare, "The Torturing Headmaster"
    Sarvepalli Radhakrishnan, "Karma and Freedom"

35. THIS IS THE BEST POSSIBLE WORLD * *Gottfried Leibniz*   277

36. MUST GOD CREATE THE BEST? * *Robert M. Adams*   280
    Tan Tai Wei, "Morality and the God of Love"

37. THE LOGICAL PROBLEM OF EVIL * *J. L. Mackie*   288

38. THE FREE WILL DEFENSE * *Alvin Plantinga*   295
    Richard Gale, "The Causal Compatibilist Objection"
    Richard Swinburne, "Free to Be Responsible for Others"

39. THE EVIDENTIAL ARGUMENT FROM EVIL * *Michael Martin*   315
    William Rowe, "The Inductive Argument from Evil"
    Paul Draper, "The Abductive Argument from Evil"

40. INDUCTION, ABDUCTION, AND THE ARGUMENT FROM EVIL * *Christopher Bernard*   323

SUGGESTIONS FOR FURTHER READING   338

PART V. RELIGIOUS EXPERIENCE

41. VARIETIES OF RELIGIOUS EXPERIENCE * *William James* 343
    Shankara, "The Mind"
    Laozi, "Dao De Jing"
42. IS NUMINOUS EXPERIENCE EVIDENCE THAT GOD EXISTS? * *Keith Yandell* 361
    Walpola Rahula, "Nirvana"
43. PERCEIVING GOD * *William P. Alston* 375
44. CRITIQUE OF THE ARGUMENT FROM RELIGIOUS EXPERIENCE * *Michael Scriven* 382

SUGGESTIONS FOR FURTHER READING 386

PART VI. MIRACLES

45. OF MIRACLES * *David Hume* 389
46. ON HUME'S PHILOSOPHICAL CASE AGAINST MIRACLES * *Daniel Howard-Snyder* 395
    C. S. Lewis, "Hume Begs the Question"
47. HISTORIANS ON MIRACLES * *Raymond Martin* 412
    Morton Smith, "Historical Method in the Study of Religion"
    Nancy Murphy, "The Historian as Philosopher"

SUGGESTIONS FOR FURTHER READING 427

PART VII. EVOLUTION

48. SCIENCE REFUTES RELIGION * *Richard Dawkins* 431
    Daniel Dennett, "Darwin's Dangerous Idea"
49. DARWINIST RELIGION * *Phillip E. Johnson* 434
    Alvin Plantinga, "The Grand Evolutionary Myth"
50. EVOLUTION IS NOT A THREAT TO RELIGION * *Phillip and Patricia Kitcher* 440

SUGGESTIONS FOR FURTHER READING 446

PART VIII. SURVIVAL OF BODILY DEATH

51. DEATH AND IMMORTALITY * *Plato* 449
    Sri Aurobindo, "The Nature of the Self"
    Shunryu Suzuki, "Zen Mind, Beginner's Mind"
52. EXPLORING THE CASE FOR LIFE AFTER DEATH * *J. P. Moreland* 456
    Peter van Inwagen, "Resurrection"
    Thomas Nagel, "Death"
    C. J. Ducasse, "Remembrances of Past Lives"

SUGGESTIONS FOR FURTHER READING 471

PART IX. RELIGION, ETHICS, AND THE MEANING OF LIFE

53. THE EUTHYPHRO DILEMMA * *Plato*   475
    Jiddu Krishnamurti, "Religion and Spirituality"
54. IS GOD THE SOURCE OF MORALITY? * *Sharon M. Kaye and Harry J. Gensler*   481
55. MY CONFESSION * *Leo Tolstoy*   488
    Adrienne Rich, "The Liar Fears the Void"
56. THE MYTH OF SISYPHUS * *Albert Camus*   494
    Robert Nozick, "Why Are Traces Important?"

SUGGESTIONS FOR FURTHER READING   498

PART X. RELIGIOUS PLURALISM

57. RELIGIOUS PLURALISM * *John Hick*   501
    Nancy Hartsock, "Feminist Revolution"
    Jiddu Krishnamurti, "Revolution"
58. A DEFENSE OF RELIGIOUS EXCLUSIVISM * *Alvin Plantinga*   510
    Peter van Inwagen, "Born into the Right Religion?"
59. EXCLUSIVISM, PLURALISM, AND ANARCHY * *Kevin Meeker*   524
    Ralph Waldo Emerson, "Choices"
60. RELIGIOUS DIVERSITY AND RELIGIOUS BELIEF * *Allen Stairs*   535
    Jane Flax, "Patriarchy"
    Naomi Goldenberg, "Women Preists"
61. RELIGION FROM AN AFRICAN PERSPECTIVE * *Kwasi Wiredu*   547

SUGGESTIONS FOR FURTHER READING   557

Credits   559

✦ PREFACE ✦

In the last quarter of the twentieth century, analytic philosophy of religion came of age. Previously a by-product of mainstream analytic epistemology and metaphysics, it became not only an autonomous field of investigation, but one of the most exciting in contemporary philosophy. However, from a pedagogical point of view, this progress has come at a price. Much of the most important recent literature in philosophy of religion is too technical for introductory students. As a result, those who teach introductory philosophy of religion courses are faced with a dilemma: either give students an outdated introduction to philosophy of religion which they can understand or an up-to-date one which they cannot.

God Matters has been designed to solve this dilemma. More than any other anthology currently on the market, it is both up-to-date and accessible. We accomplished this primarily by commissioning original, state-of-the-art, but user-friendly, essays by well-regarded contemporary philosophers to replace overly technical ones that are standard in other anthologies. In most cases, we have then included short excerpts from the essays being replaced to convey their flavor and to introduce important authors in their own words. The result is an anthology that is both state-of-the-art *and* user-friendly.

To further facilitate introducing students to the philosophy of religion, we have provided a variety of useful pedagogical features. These include, *for every selection:*

- A brief, partly biographical, partly thematic introduction
- A set of "Reading Questions" to facilitate basic, reading comprehension
- "Questions for Further Reflection"
- Boxed text to introduce related ideas and important thinkers, as well as to enhance diversity without diluting the main focus of the text

We provide 61 selections covering ten areas in contemporary philosophy of religion. These selections are representative of virtually every important development in the field. They will provide teachers with enough choice to easily structure their courses around the issues that they think are most salient.

The editors of this anthology have a great deal of expertise in philosophy of religion. Raymond Martin, formerly Professor of Philosophy and Distinguished Scholar Teacher at the University of Maryland-College Park, is now chair of the Department of Philosophy at Union College. He is the author of *The Elusive Messiah: A Philosophical Overview of the Quest for the Historical Jesus* (Westview, 1999), *Self-Concern: An Experiential Approach to What Matters in Survival* (Cambridge University Press, 1998), and co-author of *Naturalization of The Soul: Self and Personal Identity in the Eighteenth Century* (Routledge, 2000). Christopher Bernard, a Lecturer and Ph.D. candidate at the University of

Maryland, has a B.A. in philosophy from the University of Minnesota, an M.A. in philosophy from the University of Maryland, and an M.A. in New Testament from Luther Seminary. For the last several years he has taught the University of Maryland's main undergraduate course offering in philosophy of religion, as well as other courses.

We are grateful to Alex J. Coleman for valuable assistance in preparing this anthology and to all of the authors who so kindly contributed original material for this volume. Douglas Geivett was especially helpful in preparing material for the manuscript. Christopher Bernard is particularly grateful for the ongoing support and encouragement of his wife, Mary. Raymond Martin is grateful for the same to Dorothy Wang.

GOD MATTERS

✦ INTRODUCTION ✦

* Is there a God?
* If there is a God, what is God like?
* If God is all-powerful and wholly good, why is there evil?
* Has any human actually experienced God?
* Is God concerned with what humans do? Concerned enough to have a plan for humans?
* If God does have a plan for humans, how could we ever know what it is?
* If we *can* know what God's plan is for humans, what is it?
* Have miracles occurred—that is, has God ever suspended natural laws in order to intervene directly in human affairs?
* What is faith? What is reason? What is the relationship between the two?
* Is faith an appropriate way to arrive at one's beliefs?
* Psychologically, what is the function of religious beliefs? Socially, what is their function?
* Do religious beliefs bring people together or divide them? Do they promote peace, or conflict?
* Is it possible to live without any religious beliefs, either pro or con? If it were possible, would it be a good thing?
* What is the relationship between science and religion? Are they in competition with each other?
* What is the relationship between morality and religion? Does morality depend on religion?
* What will happen to me when I die?
* What, if anything, is the meaning of my life?

Questions such as these are the subject matter of the *philosophy of religion*. It is not *entirely* up to us whether we think about them. They tend to force themselves upon every thinking person.

Because you are reading this introduction, you probably have already asked yourself some of these questions. Probably you too cannot help but think about them. Perhaps, though, you can help how seriously you think about them. Does it matter how seriously you think about them? Yes, it seems to. How seriously you think about questions of philosophy of religion tends to importantly affect what sort of person you become. How seriously all of us think about them tends to importantly affect what sort of world we live in.

Many people, often with the encouragement of their religious authorities, simply accept those answers to questions about God and religious belief that have been handed down to them in their religious or cultural traditions. Usually there are powerful inducements not to question, and most people succumb to them. However, accepting without question what one has been told virtually guarantees that one's understanding will be shallow. It also guarantees that one will become a second-hand person.

Should you read this book? That all depends. It's very likely that reading it will affect how deeply you think about questions in the philosophy of religion. How deeply you think about such questions may well influence who you associate with, how you feel about associating with them, what you think about, what you read, who you marry (if you marry), how you raise your children (if you have children), who you vote for, what political and social causes you espouse, and so on. It may also influence how tolerant you become toward those who identify with cultural and religious traditions that differ from your own. Do you want these aspects of your life to be affected by your study of philosophy of religion? If you do, read on. If you do not, stop now.

If you are like most students who begin to think seriously about questions in the philosophy of religion, you crave answers. But in philosophy of religion, as in other areas of philosophy, answers are hard to come by—at least the kind of answers the craving for which typically brings us to philosophy in the first place. The reason for this is that answers—in philosophy, as in every field of inquiry—emerge only within a framework of assumptions. In other areas of inquiry—the sciences and historical studies, for instance—many such background assumptions are simply taken for granted. Their being taken for granted allows those who work in those fields, and those who learn of their discoveries, to arrive at answers. In philosophy, nothing is taken for granted. Thus, typically what emerges from the study of philosophy is not definite, noncontroversial answers but, rather, enhanced understanding. This enhanced understanding involves discovering what the relevant points of view are from which one can usefully examine an issue. It also involves figuring out which answers are most plausible when an issue is approached from various points of view. Whether one can reduce all legitimate points of view to just one and then demonstrate definite answers to the questions of philosophy of religion is itself a question in the philosophy of religion. It is a question about which reasonable people differ. Such differences of opinion are part of what makes the study of philosophy of religion exciting. We hope you enjoy it.

PART I

✦ THE NATURE OF GOD ✦

OMNIPOTENCE

1. GOD IS ALL POWERFUL * *Thomas Aquinas*
2. SOME PUZZLES CONCERNING OMNIPOTENCE * *George I. Mavrodes*

Harry Frankfurt, "The Paradox of the Stone"

OMNISCIENCE

3. GOD'S KNOWLEDGE * *Thomas Aquinas*
4. DIVINE KNOWLEDGE AND HUMAN FREEDOM * *Scott Davison*

St. Augustine, "God's Foreknowledge Does Not Rule Out Freedom"

Jonathan Edwards, "God's Foreknowledge Rules Out Libertarian Freedom"

GOD AND TIME

5. GOD IS OUTSIDE OF TIME * *Boethius*
6. ETERNITY * *Eleonore Stump and Norman Kretzmann*

William Lane Craig, "Time: The Familiar Stranger"

William J. Wainwright, "God's Compassion"

SUGGESTIONS FOR FURTHER READING

1. GOD IS ALL POWERFUL

Thomas Aquinas

Thomas Aquinas (1224–1274), born of Italian nobility, began his education in Naples where he became a Dominican monk. He later studied in Cologne under Albertus Magnus, the leading Aristotelian of the time. He then taught theology in Paris for a few years, where his principle duties consisted of lecturing on Peter Lombard's "Sentences." He eventually returned to Italy where he spent most of the rest of his life. In his own thought, Aquinas adapted and applied the philosophy of Aristotle and used it in service of Christian theology. He was a prolific writer. Although he lived less than 50 years, he wrote over 60 works. Towards the end of his life, he had a series of intense religious experiences. Although censured by the Church in his own time, he has since been dubbed "the angelic doctor." He is widely considered to be the greatest of medieval philosophers and theologians. In this selection, in which he explains what it means for God to be omnipotent, he argues that God's omnipotence does not imply that God can do absolutely anything.

READING QUESTIONS

1. Why does Aquinas think that God's power is limited to doing the logically possible?
2. What is the vicious circle that Aquinas mentions?
3. Why does Aquinas think that God's mercy demonstrates his omnipotence?

Objection 1. It seems that God is not omnipotent. For movement and passiveness belong to everything. But this is impossible with God, for He is immovable, as was said above. Therefore He is not omnipotent.

Objection 2. Further, sin is an act of some kind. But God cannot sin, nor "deny Himself" as it is said in 2 Tim. 2:13. Therefore He is not omnipotent.

Objection 3. Further, it is said of God that He manifests His omnipotence "especially by sparing and having mercy" (Collect, 10th Sunday after Pentecost). Therefore the greatest act possible to the divine power is to spare and have mercy. There are things much greater, however, than sparing and having mercy; for example, to create another world, and the like. Therefore God is not omnipotent.

Objection 4. Further, upon the text, "God hath made foolish the wisdom of this world" (1 Cor. 1:20), a gloss says: "God hath made the wisdom of this world foolish [Vulg.: 'Hath not God,' etc.] by showing those things to be possible which it judges to be impossible." Whence it would seem that nothing is to be judged possible or impossible in reference to inferior causes, as the wisdom of this world judges them; but in reference to the divine power. If God, then, were omnipotent, all things would be possible; nothing, therefore impossible. But if we take away the impossible, then we destroy also the necessary; for what necessarily exists is impossible not to exist. Therefore there would be nothing at all that is necessary in things if God were omnipotent. But this is an impossibility. Therefore God is not omnipotent.

On the contrary, it is said: "No word shall be impossible with God" (Lk. 1:37).

I answer that all confess that God is omnipotent; but it seems difficult to explain in what His omnipotence precisely consists: for there may be doubt as to the precise meaning of the word "all" when we say that God can do all things. If, however, we consider the matter aright, since power is said in reference to possible things, this phrase, "God can do all things," is rightly understood to mean that God can do all things that are possible; and for this reason He is said to be omnipotent. Now according to the Philosopher, a thing is said to be possible in two ways.

First in relation to some power, thus whatever is subject to human power is said to be possible to man.

Secondly absolutely, on account of the relation in which the very terms stand to each other. Now God cannot be said to be omnipotent through being able to do all things that are possible to created nature; for the divine power extends farther than that. If, however, we were to say that God is omnipotent because He can do all things that are possible to His power, there would be a vicious circle in explaining the nature of His power. For this would be saying nothing else but that God is omnipotent, because He can do all that He is able to do.

It remains therefore, that God is called omnipotent because He can do all things that are possible absolutely; which is the second way of saying a thing is possible. For a thing is said to be possible or impossible absolutely, according to the relation in which the very terms stand to one another, possible if the predicate is not incompatible with the subject, as that Socrates sits; and absolutely impossible when the predicate is altogether incompatible with the subject, as, for instance, that a man is a donkey.

It must, however, be remembered that since every agent produces an effect like itself, to each active power there corresponds a thing possible as its proper object according to the nature of that act on which its active power is founded; for instance, the power of giving warmth is related as to its proper object to the being capable of being warmed. The divine existence, however, upon which the nature of power in God is founded, is infinite, and is not limited to any genus of being; but possesses within itself the perfection of all being. Whence, whatsoever has or can have the nature of being, is numbered among the absolutely possible things, in respect of which God is called omnipotent. Now nothing is opposed to the idea of being except nonbeing. Therefore, that which implies being and nonbeing at the same time is repugnant to the idea of an absolutely possible thing, within the scope of the divine omnipotence. For such cannot come under the divine omnipotence, not because of any defect in the power of God, but because it has not the nature of a feasible or possible thing. Therefore, everything that does not imply a contradiction in terms, is numbered amongst those possible things, in respect of which God is called omnipotent: whereas whatever implies contradiction does not come within the scope of divine omnipotence, because it cannot have the aspect of possibility. Hence it is better to say that such things cannot be done, than that God cannot do them. Nor is this contrary to the word of the angel, saying: "No word shall be impossible with God." For whatever implies a contradiction cannot be a word, because no intellect can possibly conceive such a thing.

Reply to Objection 1. God is said to be omnipotent in respect to His active power, not to passive power, as was shown above. Whence the fact that He is immovable or impassible is not repugnant to His omnipotence.

Reply to Objection 2. To sin is to fall short of a perfect action; hence to be able to sin is to be able to fall short in action, which is repugnant to omnipotence. Therefore it is that God cannot sin, because of His omnipotence. Nevertheless, the Philosopher says that God can deliberately do what is evil. But this must be understood either on a condition, the antecedent of which is impossible—as, for instance, if we were to say that God can do evil things if He will. For there is no reason why a conditional proposition should not be true, though both the antecedent and consequent are impossible: as if one were to say: "If man is a donkey, he has four feet." Or he may be understood to mean that God can do some things which now seem to be evil: which, however, if He did them, would then be good. Or he is, perhaps, speaking after the common manner of the heathen, who thought that men became gods, like Jupiter or Mercury.

Reply to Objection 3. God's omnipotence is particularly shown in sparing and having mercy, because in this is it made manifest that God has supreme power, that He freely forgives sins. For it is not for one who is bound by laws of a superior to forgive sins of his own free will. Or, because by sparing and having mercy upon men, He leads them on to the participation of an infinite good; which is the ultimate effect of the divine power. Or because, as was said above the effect of the divine mercy is the foundation of all the divine works. For nothing is due to anyone, except on account of something already given him gratuitously by God. In this way the divine omnipotence is particularly made manifest, because to it pertains the first foundation of all good things.

Reply to Objection 4. The absolute possible is not so called in reference either to higher causes, or to inferior causes, but in reference to itself. But the possible in reference to some power is named possible in reference to its proximate cause. Hence those things which it belongs to God alone to do immediately—

as, for example, to create, to justify, and the like—are said to be possible in reference to a higher cause. Those things, however, which are of such kind as to be done by inferior causes are said to be possible in reference to those inferior causes. For it is according to the condition of the proximate cause that the effect has contingency or necessity, as was shown above. Thus is it that the wisdom of the world is deemed foolish, because what is impossible to nature, it judges to be impossible to God. So it is clear that the omnipotence of God does not take away from things their impossibility and necessity.

QUESTIONS FOR FURTHER REFLECTION

1. The question "Can God make a rock so heavy that He cannot lift it," seems to involve a paradox. If God can make the rock, then he cannot lift it. If He cannot make the rock, then there is something He cannot do. In fact, either way, there seems to be something God cannot do. Given what Aquinas says about God's omnipotence, what could he say in reply to this paradox?
2. Aquinas says that there is a sense in which God can be said to sin. Explain Aquinas's reasoning, in your own words.

2. SOME PUZZLES CONCERNING OMNIPOTENCE

George I. Mavrodes

George Mavrodes (1926–) is Professor Emeritus of philosophy at the University of Michigan where he taught for 33 years. The author of two books and almost one hundred articles, he has written on virtually every topic in the philosophy of religion. In this article, he argues that the paradox of the stone is not reason to think that God is not omnipotent.

READING QUESTIONS

1. What, according to Mavrodes, is Aquinas's solution to the paradox of the stone?
2. Mavrodes claims that there is an important difference between drawing a square circle and creating a rock so big that God cannot lift it. What, in his view, is the difference?
3. Why does Mavrodes think that "a stone too heavy for God to lift" is a contradiction?

The doctrine of God's omnipotence appears to claim that God can do anything. Consequently, there have been attempts to refute the doctrine by giving examples of things which God cannot do; for example, He cannot draw a square circle.

Responding to objections of this type, St. Thomas pointed out that "anything" should be here construed to refer only to objects, actions, or states of affairs whose descriptions are not self-contradictory.[1] For it is

---

[1]St. Thomas Aquinas, *Summa Theologiae*, 1a, q. 25, a. 3.

THE PARADOX OF THE STONE ∗ *Harry Frankfurt*

Suppose, then, that God's omnipotence enables Him to do even what is logically impossible and that He actually creates a stone too heavy for Him to lift. The critic of the notion of divine omnipotence is quite mistaken if he thinks that this supposition plays into his hands. What the critic wishes to claim, of course, is that when God has created a stone which He cannot lift He is then faced with a task beyond His ability and is therefore seen to be limited in power. But this claim is not justified.

For why should God not be able to perform the task in question? To be sure, it is a task—the task of lifting a stone which He cannot lift—whose description is self-contradictory. But if God is supposed capable of performing one task whose description is self-contradictory—that of creating the problematic stone in the first place—why should He not be supposed capable of performing another—that of lifting the stone. After all, is there any greater trick in performing two logically impossible tasks than there is in performing one?

If an omnipotent being can do what is logically impossible, then he can not only create situations which he cannot handle but also, since he is not bound by the limits of consistency, he can handle situations which he cannot handle.

From Harry Frankfurt, *The Philosophical Review* (1964).

only such things whose nonexistence might plausibly be attributed to a lack of power in some agent. My failure to draw a circle on the exam may indicate my lack of geometrical skill, but my failure to draw a square circle does not indicate any such lack. Therefore, the fact that it is false (or perhaps meaningless) to say that God could draw one does no damage to the doctrine of His omnipotence.

A more involved problem, however, is posed by this type of question: can God create a stone too heavy for Him to lift? This appears to be stronger than the first problem, for it poses a dilemma. If we say that God can create a stone, then it seems that there might be such a stone. And if there might be a stone too heavy for Him to lift, then He is evidently not omnipotent. But if we deny that God can create such a stone, we seem to have given up His omnipotence already. Both answers lead us to the same conclusion.

Further, this problem does not seem obviously open to St. Thomas' solution. The form "*x* is able to draw a square circle" seems plainly to involve a contradiction, while "*x* is able to make a thing too heavy for *x* to lift" does not. For it may easily be true that I am able to make a boat too heavy for me to lift. So why should it not be possible for God to make a stone too heavy for Him to lift?

Despite this apparent difference, this second puzzle *is* open to essentially the same answer as the first. The dilemma fails because it consists of asking whether God can do a self-contradictory thing. And the reply that He cannot does no damage to the doctrine of omnipotence.

The specious nature of the problem may be seen in this way. God is either omnipotent or not.[2] Let us assume first that He is not. In that case the phrase "a stone too heavy for God to lift" may not be self-contradictory. And then, of course, if we assert either that God is able or that He is not able to create such a stone, we may conclude that He is not omnipotent. But this is no more than the assumption with which we began, meeting us again after our roundabout journey. If this were all that the dilemma could establish it would be trivial. To be significant it must derive this same conclusion *from the assumption that God is omnipotent*; that is, it must show that the assumption of the omnipotence of God leads to a *reductio*. But does it?

On the assumption that God is omnipotent, the phrase "a stone too heavy for God to lift" becomes self-contradictory. For it becomes "a stone which cannot be lifted by Him whose power is sufficient for lifting anything." But the "thing" described by a self-contradictory

_____
[2]I assume, of course, the existence of God, since that is not being brought in question here.

phrase is absolutely impossible and hence has nothing to do with the doctrine of omnipotence. Not being an object of power at all, its failure to exist cannot be the result of some lack in the power of God. And, interestingly, it is the very omnipotence of God which makes the existence of such a stone absolutely impossible, while it is the fact that I am finite in power which makes it possible for me to make a boat too heavy for me to lift.

But suppose that some die-hard objector takes the bit in his teeth and denies that the phrase "a stone too heavy for God to lift" is self-contradictory, even on the assumption that God is omnipotent. In other words, he contends that the description "a stone too heavy for an omnipotent God to lift" is self-coherent and therefore describes an absolutely possible object. Must I then attempt to prove the contradiction which I assume above as intuitively obvious? Not necessarily. Let me reply simply that if the objector is right in this contention, then the answer to the original question is "Yes, God can create such a stone." It may seem that this reply will force us into the original dilemma. But it does not. For now the objector can draw no damaging conclusion from this answer. And the reason is that he has just now contended that such a stone is compatible with the omnipotence of God. Therefore, from the possibility of God's creating such a stone it cannot be concluded that God is not omnipotent. The objector cannot have it both ways. The conclusion which he himself wishes to draw from an affirmative answer to the original question is itself the required proof that the descriptive phrase which appears there is self-contradictory. And "it is more appropriate to say that such things cannot be done, than that God cannot do them."[3]

The specious nature of this problem may also be seen in a somewhat different way.[4] Suppose that some theologian is convinced by this dilemma that he must give up the doctrine of omnipotence. But he resolves to give up as little as possible, just enough to meet the argument. One way he can do so is by retaining the infinite power of God with regard to lifting, while placing a restriction on the sort of stone He is able to cre-

ate. The only restriction required here, however, is that God must not be able to create a stone too heavy for Him to lift. Beyond that the dilemma has not even suggested any necessary restriction. Our theologian has, in effect, answered the original question in the negative, and he now regretfully supposes that this has required him to give up the full doctrine of omnipotence. He is now retaining what he supposes to be the more modest remnants which he has salvaged from that doctrine.

We must ask, however, what it is which he has in fact given up. Is it the unlimited power of God to create stones? No doubt. But what stone is it which God is now precluded from creating? The stone too heavy for Him to lift, of course. But we must remember that nothing in the argument required the theologian to admit any limit on God's power with regard to the lifting of stones. He still holds that to be unlimited. And if God's power to lift is infinite, then His power to create may run to infinity also without outstripping that first power. The supposed limitation turns out to be no limitation at all, since it is specified only by reference to another power which is itself infinite. Our theologian need have no regrets, for he has given up nothing. The doctrine of the power of God remains just what it was before.

Nothing I have said above, of course, goes to prove that God is, in fact, omnipotent. All I have intended to show is that certain arguments intended to prove that He is not omnipotent fail. They fail because they propose, as tests of God's power, putative tasks whose descriptions are self-contradictory. Such pseudo-tasks, not falling within the realm of possibility are not objects of power at all. Hence the fact that they cannot be performed implies no limit on the power of God, and hence no defect in the doctrine of omnipotence.

QUESTIONS FOR FURTHER REFLECTION

1. Mavrodes assumes, without argument, that it does not count against an omnipotent being's power that it cannot do something that is self-contradictory. Does this assumption require an argument in its support? If so, how might Mavrodes argue for it?

---

[3]St. Thomas Aquinas, *Summa Theologiae.*
[4]But this method rests finally on the same logical relations as the preceding one.

3. GOD'S KNOWLEDGE

Thomas Aquinas

A brief biography of Aquinas appears on page 5. In this selection, Aquinas explains what it means for God to be omniscient. He notes that God's omniscience does not imply that God can know absolutely anything.

READING QUESTIONS

1. What, according to Aquinas, is the cause of all things?
2. Are there future contingents to God? Are there future contingents to us?
3. How does Aquinas think that God has knowledge of future contingents?

Objection 1. It seems that the knowledge of God is not of future contingent things. For from a necessary cause proceeds a necessary effect. But the knowledge of God is the cause of things known, as said above. Since therefore that knowledge is necessary, what He knows must also be necessary. Therefore the knowledge of God is not of contingent things.

Objection 2. Further, every conditional proposition of which the antecedent is absolutely necessary must have an absolutely necessary consequent. For the antecedent is to the consequent as principles are to the conclusion: and from necessary principles only a necessary conclusion can follow, as is proved in Poster. i. But this is a true conditional proposition, "If God knew that this thing will be, it will be," for the knowledge of God is only of true things. Now the antecedent conditional of this is absolutely necessary, because it is eternal, and because it is signified as past. Therefore the consequent is also absolutely necessary. Therefore whatever God knows, is necessary; and so the knowledge of God is not of contingent things.

Objection 3. Further, everything known by God must necessarily be, because even what we ourselves know, must necessarily be; and, of course, the knowledge of God is much more certain than ours. But no future contingent things must necessarily be. Therefore no contingent future thing is known by God.

On the contrary, It is written (Ps. 32:15), "He Who hath made the hearts of every one of them; Who understandeth all their works," that is, of men. Now the works of men are contingent, being subject to free will. Therefore God knows future contingent things.

I answer that, Since as was shown above, God knows all things; not only things actual but also things possible to Him and creature; and since some of these are future contingent to us, it follows that God knows future contingent things.

In evidence of this, we must consider that a contingent thing can be considered in two ways; first, in itself, in so far as it is now in act: and in this sense it is not considered as future, but as present; neither is it considered as contingent (as having reference) to one of two terms, but as determined to one; and on account of this it can be infallibly the object of certain knowledge, for instance to the sense of sight, as when I see that Socrates is sitting down. In another way a contingent thing can be considered as it is in its cause; and in this way it is considered as future, and as a contingent thing not yet determined to one; forasmuch as a contingent cause has relation to opposite things: and in this sense a contingent thing is not subject to any certain knowledge. Hence, whoever knows a contingent effect in its cause only, has merely a conjectural knowledge of it. Now God knows all contingent things not only as they are in their causes, but also as each one of them is actually in itself. And although contingent things become actual successively, nevertheless God knows contingent things not successively, as they are in their own being, as we do but simultaneously. The reason is because His knowledge is measured by eternity, as is also His being; and eternity being simultaneously whole comprises all time, as said above. Hence all things that are in time are present to God from eternity, not only because He has the types of things present within Him, as some say; but because His glance is carried from eternity over all things as they are in their presentiality. Hence it is manifest that contingent things are infallibly known by God, inasmuch as they are subject to the divine sight in their presentiality; yet they are future contingent things in relation to their own causes.

Reply to Objection 1. Although the supreme cause is necessary, the effect may be contingent by reason of the proximate contingent cause; just as the germination of a plant is contingent by reason of the proximate contingent cause, although the movement of the sun which is the first cause, is necessary. So likewise things known by God are contingent on account of their proximate causes, while the knowledge of God, which is the first cause, is necessary.

Reply to Objection 2. Some say that this antecedent, "God knew this contingent to be future," is not necessary, but contingent; because, although it is past, still it imports relation to the future. This however does not remove necessity from it; for whatever has had relation to the future, must have had it, although the future sometimes does not follow. On the other hand some say that this antecedent is contingent, because it is a compound of necessary and contingent; as this saying is contingent, "Socrates is a white man." But this also is to no purpose; for when we say, "God knew this contingent to be future," contingent is used here only as the matter of the word, and not as the chief part of the proposition. Hence its contingency or necessity has no reference to the necessity or contingency of the proposition, or to its being true or false. For it may be just as true that I said a man is an ass, as that I said Socrates runs, or God is: and the same applies to necessary and contingent. Hence it must be said that this antecedent is absolutely necessary. Nor does it follow, as some say, that the consequent is absolutely necessary, because the antecedent is the remote cause of the consequent, which is contingent by reason of the proximate cause. But this is to no purpose. For the conditional would be false were its antecedent the remote necessary cause, and the consequent a contingent effect; as, for example, if I said, "if the sun moves, the grass will grow."

Therefore we must reply otherwise; that when the antecedent contains anything belonging to an act of the soul, the consequent must be taken not as it is in itself, but as it is in the soul: for the existence of a thing in itself is different from the existence of a thing in the soul. For example, when I say, "What the soul understands is immaterial," this is to be understood that it is immaterial as it is in the intellect, not as it is in itself. Likewise if I say, "If God knew anything, it will be," the consequent must be understood as it is subject to the divine knowledge, that is, as it is in its presentiality. And thus it is necessary, as also is the antecedent: "For everything that is, while it is, must be necessarily be," as the Philosopher says in Peri Herm. i.

Reply to Objection 3. Things reduced to act in time, as known by us successively in time, but by God (are known) in eternity, which is above time. Whence to us they cannot be certain, forasmuch as we know future contingent things as such; but (they are certain) to God alone, whose understanding is in eternity above time. Just as he who goes along the road, does not see those who come after him; whereas he who sees the whole road from a height, sees at once all travelling by the way. Hence what is known by us must be necessary, even as it is in itself; for what is future contingent in itself, cannot be known by us. Whereas what is known by God must be necessary according to the mode in which they are subject to the divine knowledge, as already stated, but not absolutely as considered in their own causes. Hence also this proposition, "Everything known by God must necessarily be," is usually distinguished; for this may refer to the thing, or to the saying. If it refers to the thing, it is divided and false; for the sense is, "Everything which God knows is necessary." If understood of the saying, it is composite and true; for the sense is, "This proposition, 'that which is known by God is' is necessary."

Now some urge an objection and say that this distinction holds good with regard to forms that are separable from the subject; thus if I said, "It is possible for a white thing to be black," it is false as applied to the saying, and true as applied to the thing: for a thing which is white, can become black; whereas this saying, "a white thing is black" can never be true. But in forms that are inseparable from the subject, this distinction does not hold, for instance, if I said, "A black crow can be white"; for in both senses it is false. Now to be known by God is inseparable from the thing; for what is known by God cannot be known. This objection, however, would hold if these words "that which is known" implied any disposition inherent to the subject; but since they import an act of the knower, something can be attributed to the thing known, in itself (even if it always be known), which is not attributed to it in so far as it stands under actual knowledge; thus material existence is attributed to a stone in itself, which is not attributed to it inasmuch as it is known.

QUESTIONS FOR FURTHER REFLECTION

1. Why is the question of God's knowledge of the future so important? What are the consequences for free will based on the way this question is answered?
2. In his answer, Aquinas quotes the Bible. What role does the Bible play in Aquinas's answer? Is that role legitimate? Explain your answer.

4.   DIVINE KNOWLEDGE AND HUMAN FREEDOM

Scott A. Davison

Scott A. Davison earned a B.A. and M.A. in philosophy from Ohio State University before completing a second M.A. and a Ph.D. in philosophy from the University of Notre Dame. He taught courses in philosophy at Ohio State, Notre Dame, St. Mary's College, Indiana University at South Bend, and Calvin College before moving to Morehead State University, in Kentucky, where he is an Associate Professor of Philosophy. He is the author of several published papers in metaphysics and the philosophy of religion. In this selection, in order to consider various answers to the question, "Could God know what people will freely choose to do in the future," he first clarifies the notions of knowledge and freedom. Then, he develops several arguments for the conclusion that not even God could foreknow a future free action. He also considers responses to these arguments, including the ideas that God exists outside of time and that God knew before creation what every possible creature would do in every possible situation.

READING QUESTIONS

1. Why do incompatibilists think that it is impossible to be both free and determined at the same time?
2. Explain one reason why some people believe that not even God could foreknow a future free choice.
3. Why do some philosophers think that God's foreknowledge of a fact cannot be useful in God's providential governance of the world?

All of the major theistic religious traditions hold that God is omniscient, which means that God knows everything that can be known. And the vast majority of theists also hold that human beings act freely, at least sometimes. How can these two beliefs fit together? If God knows in advance everything that you are going to do, then how can you act freely? How can anything at all be up to you, if God already knows what the future holds? And if nobody ever acts freely, then how can people be properly praised or blamed for what they do?

In order to consider these questions carefully, it will be important to take a closer look at the nature of knowledge and the nature of freedom. Then it will be possible to consider the strengths and weaknesses of the main answers that people have suggested to these questions, and maybe even to make up our own minds about what to think. We will try to consider every possibility in order to keep our options open.

1. KNOWLEDGE

What does it mean to say that someone knows something? First of all, to know that something is the case, it must be *true*. For example, you can't know that the Washington Monument is full of circus peanuts because it isn't.

Second, you must have a *belief* about something before you can claim to know it. It is true that I buried my pet mouse in the back yard when I was a young child, but you could not have known that this was true until I told you so (because you did not have a belief about my pet mouse until I mentioned it).

So in order for people to know something, they must have a true belief concerning it. But that is not all. Just because you have a true belief, this does not necessarily mean that you have knowledge. There is such a thing as lucky true belief, which does not count as knowledge.

Suppose that my mischievous friend wants to lure me off campus for a surprise party, so he makes up a story and tells me that my dormitory room has been closed because of asbestos removal. Now imagine that by sheer coincidence, as I am walking off campus towards the surprise party, my dormitory room actually does become closed because of asbestos removal. At this point, I believe that my dormitory room is closed because of asbestos removal, and that is true, but I certainly don't have knowledge of it. My belief turned out to be true by accident.

What else is required, then, for knowledge, besides true belief? Philosophers who study Epistemology (the theory of knowledge and related topics) disagree quite a bit about how to answer this question, but they all agree that knowledge is belief that is *true in a non-accidental way*. In other words, if a person knows something, then it is not the case that this person's belief is true by accident, or that this person's belief could have turned out to be false just as easily as it turned out to be true. There must be some kind of appropriate connection between the person who has knowledge and the fact that is known, although it is hard to be more specific than that.

When we turn from knowledge in general to God's knowledge, we encounter some puzzles immediately. For instance, God is supposed to be omniscient, which means that God knows how many hairs you have on your head right now (for example). But how does God know this? In order for me to know how many hairs there are on your head, I would need to count them using my eyes or my fingers or something. But God has no eyes or fingers. In fact, God has no physical body at all, since God is a nonphysical spirit. So God has no sense organs. How then does God know things about the physical world?

Theists have suggested different answers to this question. One popular answer is that the world is created in accordance with perfect exemplars or ideas in God's mind. Since God knows those exemplars or ideas perfectly, God knows the world by extension.

Another popular answer is that God is so deeply connected to the world through creation that God knows first hand everything that occurs in the physical world. Most theists throughout history have claimed that God not only created the world at the first moment of time, but also that at every moment of time, God sustains the world in being and contributes actively to every event that occurs in it. If God is this closely connected to the physical world, then perhaps God's knowledge of the world is direct and immediate, so that it doesn't require any sense organs at all.

Of course, this solution to the question about God's knowledge of the physical world raises a different question about God's power. If God has no body, as we mentioned earlier, then how does God create a physical world or sustain it in being? How could a spiritual being cause things to happen in a physical world?

Theists throughout history have just said that God is the kind of agent who can bring about effects in the physical world without being physical. Although human beings manage to bring about effects in the physical world only through the use of their bodies, God is different. (For more on this, see Swinburne 1979.) God's power is unlimited, human power is limited. Is this a satisfactory answer? Well, it's a bit mysterious, but theists have always been happy to admit that there are aspects of God's nature that will always remain mysterious to our limited minds. So this mystery may

GOD'S FOREKNOWLEDGE DOES NOT RULE OUT FREEDOM * *St. Augustine*

Wherefore, although God foreknows our wills to be, it does not thereby follow that we do not will a thing by our will. You said about happiness that you could not become happy through yourself, and said it as if I would deny it. But I say, when you are going to be happy you are not going to be happy against your will, but wanting to be happy. When therefore, God foreknows your future happiness, it cannot come to pass otherwise than as He has foreknown it, else there is no foreknowledge; nevertheless we are not obliged to think what is most absurd and far removed from the truth, that you are going to be happy when you do not want to. Moreover, just as God's foreknowledge, which today is certain of your future happiness, does not take away your will for happiness when you shall have begun to be happy; so also a culpable will, if you are going to have one, will be none the less your own will because God foreknows that it is to be so . . .

For mark, I beg you, with what blindness it is said that if God has foreknown my future will, it is necessary that I will what He has foreknown, since naught can come to pass otherwise than as He has foreknown. But if it is necessary, it must be acknowledged that I will no longer by will, but by necessity. O strange unreason! How then could it not be otherwise than as God has foreknown, if that should not be a will which He foreknew would be a will? I pass over that equally monstrous thing which a little while ago I said was said by the same man: It is necessary that I so will—thus endeavoring to take away the will and to substitute necessity. For if it is necessary that He so will, how then does He will when there is no will? . . .

And so it comes about both that we do not deny God foreknows all that is to be, and that notwithstanding we may will what we will. For when He foreknows our will, it will be that very will that He foreknows. It will therefore, be a will, because His foreknowledge is of a will. Nor can it be a will if it is not in our power. Therefore, that power is not taken from me by His foreknowledge . . .

From *St. Augustine on Free Will*, trans. C. Sparrow
University of Virginia Studies (1947).

not trouble those who are theists already, but those who are not theists might wonder whether or not they can accept this approach to understanding God's power or knowledge.

2. FREEDOM

What does it mean to say that an action is free? At this moment, you are reading this chapter. But you could have been doing something else instead, right? Although you decided to read this chapter right now, you might decide to do something else in the next moment. (If this chapter doesn't get interesting fast, I might lose you, right?) Apparently you are reading this chapter now freely. Can we say anything more about the qualities of a free action in general?

First of all, one necessary ingredient in free decisions is that they are not compelled by any outside forces. This point was made first by Aristotle (384–322 B.C.), a student of Plato and the tutor of Alexander the Great. Imagine that you and I are visiting a museum, and that I push you into a display of very old vases, causing you to knock them over in order to break your fall. In that case, your knocking over the vases is not a free action because it was forced by an outside source.

After that, though, philosophers begin to disagree sharply about what else is necessary in order for an action to be free. Some philosophers insist that in order for an action to be free, it must not be determined in advance, so that at the time of choice, it was possible to do one thing and also possible to do something else. These philosophers are called *incompatibilists* because they believe that acting freely is incompatible with being determined to act by anything else. For example, although it may seem to you that you are now reading this chapter freely, what if a psychiatrist told you that were compelled by guilt and anxiety to read this chapter now? What if this psychiatrist also identified some chemical imbalance in your brain, and said that all of these factors together made it impossible for you to do anything else besides read this chapter now? If this were to happen, an incompatibilist would insist that your action of reading this chapter right now was not free after all, since it was determined by the factors just mentioned.

By contrast, compatibilists claim that acting freely and being determined are compatible, that it is possible to perform a free action and to be determined to perform that very action at the same time. Suppose that the psychiatrist mentioned above offers a completely different explanation as to why you are reading this chapter right now. Instead of saying that you suffer from guilt, anxiety, and chemical imbalances, the psychiatrist says that you are a perfectly normal person, and that you are reading this chapter just because you want to do so. Furthermore, the psychiatrist adds that given your desire to read this chapter, together with the fact that you don't have a stronger desire to do anything else right now, together with the fact that nothing is preventing you from reading, it follows that you are determined to pursue your desire to read. In other words, you are determined to read by your own strong desire to read. Since you are determined by your own desires, though, and not by anything outside of yourself, compatibilists would insist that you are reading freely now. Even though no other option is open to you, given your psychological and physical condition at the moment, they insist that you are acting freely in this situation.

Philosophers disagree sharply about whether or not we should be incompatibilists or compatibilists. This debate is very, very old, and there is no indication that it will stop any time soon. Since we want to know about the relationship between God's knowledge and human freedom, and there are these very two different accounts of freedom, we will need to consider them separately in order to see how their differences make a difference.

3. COMPATIBILISM AND GOD'S KNOWLEDGE

Let's consider first the compatibilist approach to freedom. Suppose that when a person performs an action freely, that action is determined at the same time.

Earlier we supposed that your action of reading this chapter right now was free. Could God have known long ago that you were going to be reading this chapter right now, even if you are currently reading freely?

As long as we accept the compatibilist's approach to freedom, there seems to be no reason to deny that God could have known long ago that you would freely read now. After all, this reading of yours is also determined, according to compatibilists, so by knowing what would determine you to read now God could have concluded that you certainly would read now. (In fact, anyone at all who knew enough about the world a long time ago could have concluded that you certainly would read now, if compatibilism is true.)

In terms of our discussion concerning the nature of knowledge, God could have a true belief about what you would do in the future, a belief that was appropriately connected to the future fact (through what would determine it to occur), a belief that was not true by accident. So if we are compatibilists about freedom, we can accept complete divine foreknowledge without the threat of any contradiction. (For some theists who are already strongly committed to God's complete omniscience, this result has become a reason to accept compatibilism about freedom.)

However, it is important to recognize the fact that some philosophers think that the compatibilist approach to freedom is mistaken. They insist that in order to perform an action freely, there must be some alternative action open to an agent. If an action is determined, they say, then it cannot be free, and vice versa. These days, there are several common arguments that are often offered for this conclusion.

To get our terminology straight, let's suppose that an event is *determined* when its occurrence is implied by a description of the past history of the world plus the laws of nature. When I drop a pencil on the floor, for instance, a description of my dropping the pencil in these circumstances, together with the law of gravity, implies that the pencil will fall towards the floor. So the falling of the pencil is a determined event.

The first common argument against compatibilism begins with the claim that you have no choice now about how past events turned out. (This is what people mean when they say that the past cannot be changed.) Then it adds the claim that you have no choice now about which laws of nature hold. Finally,

GOD'S FOREKNOWLEDGE RULES
OUT LIBERTARIAN FREEDOM   * *Jonathan Edwards*

To suppose the future volitions of moral agents not to be necessary events; or, which is the same thing, events which it is not impossible but that they may not come to pass; and yet to suppose that God certainly foreknows them, and knows all things; is to suppose God's knowledge to be inconsistent with itself.

For to say, that God certainly, and without all conjecture, knows that a thing will infallibly be, which at the same time he knows to be so contingent, that it may possibly not be, is to suppose his knowledge inconsistent with itself; or that one thing he knows, is utterly inconsistent with another thing he knows. It is the same as to say, he now knows a proposition to be of certain infallible truth, which he knows to be of contingent uncertain truth. If a future volition is so without all Necessity, that nothing hinders but it may not be, then the proposition which asserts its future existence, is so uncertain, that nothing hinders, but that the truth of it may entirely fail.

And if God knows all things, he knows this proposition to be thus uncertain. And that is inconsistent with his knowing that it is infallibly true; and so inconsistent with his infallibly knowing that it is true. If the thing be indeed contingent, God views it so, and judges it to be contin-

gent, if he views things as they are. If the event be not necessary, then it is possible it may never be: and if it be possible it may never be, God knows it may possibly never be; and that is to know that the proposition, which affirms its existence, may possibly not be true; and that is to know that the truth of it is uncertain; which surely is inconsistent with his knowing it as a certain truth.

If volitions are in themselves contingent events, without all Necessity, then it is no argument of perfection of knowledge in any being to determine peremptorily that they will be; but on the contrary, an argument of ignorance and mistake; because it would argue, that he supposes that proposition to be certain, which in its own nature, and all things considered, is uncertain and contingent. To say, in such a case, that God may have ways of knowing contingent events which we cannot conceive of, is ridiculous; as much so, as to say, that God may know contradictions to be true, for ought we know; or that he may know a thing to be certain, and at the same time know it not to be certain, though we cannot conceive how; because he has ways of knowing which we cannot comprehend.

From Jonathan Edwards, *Freedom of the Will* (1754).

---

it suggests that if you have no choice about *P* and *Q*, and if *P* and *Q* together imply a third proposition *R*, then you have no choice about *R*, either. These three claims together lead to the conclusion that if an action is determined, then nobody has any choice about it, which seems to show that determined actions cannot be free. (This argument is defended in detail in Van Inwagen 1983 and criticized in Dennett 1985.) This argument has been the source of lots of controversy, but many philosophers find it persuasive as a reason for rejecting compatibilism.

The second common argument against compatibilism that is often offered by incompatibilists has to

do with moral responsibility. It seems natural to say that if people freely perform actions, then they are morally responsible for doing so. But if all of our actions are determined, then how can anyone be held morally responsible for anything? If all of my actions are determined, then it will always be true to say that I could not have helped but do what I did; I could not do otherwise. And this suggests that I should be neither praised nor blamed for what I did. So if all of our actions are determined, then none of them are free, either. (A slightly different version of this argument is defended in Van Inwagen 1983, explored in Fischer 1986, and criticized in Dennett 1985.) Philosophers argue quite a bit about this argument too, but some of them find it to be a compelling reason for rejecting compatibilism.

The third common argument against compatibilism comes from a theistic perspective, and it concerns the problem of evil. Theists believe that God is all-powerful and perfectly loving, yet the world is full of creatures who perform evil actions. How can this be explained? Why isn't God responsible for the evil actions performed by these creatures?

The most common answer to this question is that these creatures are free to do as they please. It is good to have free creatures, even if they do bad things sometimes, and God cannot be blamed for the actions of free creatures because not even God could control free actions. (One version of this argument can be found in Plantinga 1974.) In fact, if God *could* control free actions, then God would be to blame for the evil actions of creatures. But if compatibilism is true, then God *can* control the free actions of creatures (since compatibilism includes the idea that free actions can be determined at the same time), so we must conclude that compatibilism is false (since God is not to blame for these free actions).

By way of conclusion: if compatibilism is the right account of freedom, then there is no problem with reconciling God's complete foreknowledge with human freedom. But compatibilism may not be the best account of freedom, and some philosophers think that incompatibilism is clearly better. So perhaps now we should consider the relationship between God's foreknowledge and human freedom as described by the incompatibilist.

4. INCOMPATIBILISM AND GOD'S KNOWLEDGE: ONE ARGUMENT

By way of reminder, incompatibilists believe that if an action is free, then it cannot be determined at the same time. If this is the correct approach to freedom, then what should we say about God's foreknowledge? Is it possible for God to know what a person will do freely in the future, even before the person has made a choice?

Many philosophers have argued that the answer to this question is "no," that not even God could know about a future, undetermined event such as a free choice. There are two main ways to argue for this conclusion. It will be helpful to consider each one carefully.

The first argument against the compatibility of God's knowledge and human freedom is very similar to the first argument against compatibilism discussed above, and it centers around the nature of freedom. It will be helpful to display it in the following format:

P1. You have no choice now about how events in the past turned out (this is the so-called "fixity" of the past).

P2. God knew long ago that you would read this chapter right now (for example) (this is the assumption of divine omniscience).

P3. You have no choice now about the fact that God knew long ago that you would read this chapter right now (from P1 and P2).

P4. If P implies Q and you have no choice about P, then you have no choice about Q.

P5. God's knowing long ago that you would read this chapter right now implies that you would read this chapter right now (by the definition of knowledge).

Conclusion. You have no choice now about reading this chapter right now (for example) (from P3, P4, and P5).

This argument attempts to show that if you assume that God knew long ago what you would do now (this assumption occurs in P2), then it follows that what you do now is not free. The argument can also be reversed: if we assume instead that what you do right now is free, then the argument attempts to show that it is not possible that God knew long ago what you would do now. Either way, the argument concludes that it is impossible for God to foreknow a free action. (This argument is defended in detail in Hasker 1989.)

Many philosophers find this argument compelling, but some philosophers think that it can be resisted. Is it true, for example, that it is impossible to change the past? Well, yes, it is impossible to change the past, in the sense that it is impossible to make the past be different from what it was. The phrase "the past" refers to what actually happened prior to the present moment, whatever that turns out to be. For the same reasons, it is impossible to change the future, since "the future" refers to whatever actually happens after the present moment, whatever that turns out to be. But is it possible to prevent the past? In other words, is it possible to perform an action now such that, were you to perform it, the past would have been different?

Let's consider again the suggestion that you are now freely reading this chapter. According to P2, God knew long ago that you would be reading right now. And if P1 is true, then you have no choice now about this fact concerning the past. But is that right? If you are really free right now in reading this chapter, then you could have decided not to read instead. And if you had decided not to read instead, then what would God have thought long ago? Presumably, if God knows the future, then God's past belief would have been different too. In other words, maybe we should say this: at this moment, you can do something (namely, stop reading) such that if you do it, then God's past beliefs about the future will have always been different from what they were in fact.

This reply to the argument seems to suggest that God's past beliefs "track" our future free choices, so that whatever we decide to do, then that is what God believed we would do. As St. Augustine noticed, typically we do not assume that whenever a person knows something in the present time, that person determines what is known. For example, I can know that you are reading right now without bringing it about that you are reading right now. In the same way, perhaps God knows what we are going to do in the future, without bringing it about that we will do those things. So God's foreknowledge may be compatible with our freedom after all. (See St. Augustine 1993.)

This seems to be the best reply to the argument, but to be honest, it's a strange reply. It's strange to think that we have this power now to do something such that if we did it, then the past would have been different always. However, philosophers who defend this idea often point out that independently of the question of God's knowledge, you already have the power to do something such that if you did it, then *it would have been true* always that you were going to do it. In other words, you have the same kind of "counterfactual power" over God's past beliefs as you do over past truths about the future. So maybe this is not so strange after all, although it still seems very puzzling.

Perhaps what makes it so puzzling is that it is hard to see *how* God could know in advance exactly what you are going to do right now, especially if what you decide is not determined in advance. In other words,

simply saying that God knows the future, without saying how, is very mysterious. But theists already have a certain amount of mystery to deal with (God is beyond our comprehension), so perhaps they will not be disturbed by the fact that there is no clear mechanism to explain God's complete knowledge of the future. In the end, this argument for the conclusion that God's knowledge of the future is incompatible with freedom is compelling, but not absolutely decisive.

5. INCOMPATIBILISM AND GOD'S KNOWLEDGE: A SECOND ARGUMENT

A second argument for the conclusion that God's foreknowledge is incompatible with freedom goes like this:

P1. God knew long ago that you would read this chapter right now (for example) (this is the assumption of divine omniscience).

P2. A person S knows something only if it is impossible for S to be mistaken about it in those circumstances.

P3. It is impossible for God to be mistaken in those circumstances about the fact that you would read this chapter right now (for example) (from P1 and P2).

P4. A person S acts freely only if it is possible for S to do something else in those circumstances (from the definition of incompatibilism).

Conclusion. You do not read this chapter freely right now (for example) (from P3 and P4).

As before, this argument starts with the assumption of divine foreknowledge and draws a conclusion about human freedom. But it could be reversed as well: if we assumed instead that a given choice was free, then we could argue that since the person in question could do something else in those circumstances, it follows that God's past belief could be mistaken, in which case God's past belief (even if it is true) would not count as knowledge. (One version of this argument is developed in detail in Davison 1991.)

The crucial question for this argument concerns P2: why should anyone accept it? Earlier we said that in order to have knowledge, a person's belief must be true in a nonaccidental way. But we did not say that a person must be unable to be wrong in the circumstances. Why should we believe this? Well, some philosophers have accepted P2 because of arguments like the following one.

Suppose that a fair lottery drawing will occur tomorrow, and that one hundred tickets have been sold. Only one ticket will win, and let's imagine you have bought one ticket for yourself. What are the odds in favor of your winning the lottery? A hundred to one, of course. So there is a 99 percent chance that you will lose. Suppose that you know that there have been one hundred tickets sold, and so you are very pessimistic about your ticket's chances of winning. In fact, let's say that you believe that your ticket will lose tomorrow.

To continue the story, let's imagine that tomorrow arrives, the drawing takes place, and your ticket loses, just like you believed it would. So far, you satisfy two of the criteria for knowing yesterday that your ticket would lose today: you believed that your ticket would lose, and it was true that your ticket would lose. However, should we go ahead and say that you *knew* that your ticket would lose? After all, there was some chance that you would win—you could have been wrong in believing that your ticket would lose. Because of this, many philosophers would say that you did not really know that your ticket would lose, even though your belief was very reasonable and actually turned out to be true. (This argument occurs in Dretske 1971.)

If this argument is correct, then it seems that the actual number of tickets in the lottery doesn't matter very much. As long as there is some chance that your ticket will win, you do not actually know that your ticket will lose. And this suggests strongly that in order to know something, it must be impossible for a person to be mistaken about it in the circumstances.

If we return to the case of God's foreknowledge, imagine how things look to God from the perspective of long ago. Imagine that God knows that at some future moment, you will be faced with the choice of either reading this chapter or not reading it, and God knows that your choice will be free. Suppose that God believes that you will read this chapter, and it turns out to be true. Should we say that God knew that you would read this chapter now? According to the lottery example, the answer here is "no," because God could have been mistaken. Even if the odds of your reading this chapter right now were high, there was still a chance that you would decide not to read now, in which case God's belief would be wrong. So even if

God's belief is true, and reasonable, it does not qualify as knowledge.

Does this argument show, then, that it is impossible even for God to foreknow human free actions? Not exactly. For one thing, not everyone will accept P2, despite the lottery argument developed above. And someone could try to argue that the circumstances mentioned in P2 are different from the circumstances mentioned in P4.

Still, this argument does bring into sharp focus the question about how God could foreknow the outcome of a future free choice, given the very real possibility that something else might happen instead. Once again, though, some theists are inclined to say that although it is mysterious to us, God somehow has a way of knowing what will happen in the future. Nontheists or those who are not impressed by the appeal to mystery will not find this move to be very plausible, of course. So it seems safe to say that this second argument for the conclusion that not even God could foreknow free actions is rather plausible.

6. COULD GOD BE OUTSIDE OF TIME?

So far, we have considered two arguments for the conclusion that it is impossible for God to foreknow free actions, when freedom is understood in the incompatibilist's way. Are there any arguments on the other side, arguments trying to show that God could foreknow free actions?

One popular suggestion throughout history is the idea that God exists outside of time altogether, which enables God to see past, present, and future events all at once. On this suggestion, it is misleading to say that God *foreknows* a future free action, because God's knowledge doesn't really occur *prior to* the free action in time, strictly speaking. After all, if God is outside of time altogether, then nothing belonging to God's essential nature occurs before, during, or after any event that occurs in time.

St. Thomas Aquinas used a famous analogy to describe God's relationship to time in a way that suggests a model for God's knowledge of free actions. (The analogy occurs in his *Summa Theologica*, Part 1, question XIV, article 13, reply to objection 3.) He imagines a wagon train passing through a valley, one wagon at a time. Passengers in the wagons can only see the wagons right in front of theirs, and the wagons right behind theirs. These passengers correspond to human beings, who live in time, and thus have access only to the present moment, the immediate past, or the immediate future.

In addition to the wagon train passing through the valley, in St. Thomas' analogy there is a person sitting on top of a mountain who is watching the entire wagon train from above. Unlike the passengers sitting on the wagons, who have a very limited view of the wagon train, this person can see all of the wagons together, including the relationships in which they stand to one another. This person represents God, of course. The idea is that since God is outside of time (not in between any two wagons), God can see all of history at once, including the distant past and the distant future.

Does this suggestion help? Does St. Thomas' analogy make sense? Does this approach provide a good reason for thinking that God could know what human persons will freely choose to do in the future?

In order to answer this question, we need to see whether or not the arguments we discussed earlier still apply to the suggestion that God exists outside of time altogether. The first argument stated that if God knew something in the past, and you had no choice now about the past, then you had no choice now about what God knew would happen in the future. If we now suggest that God is outside of time, then we can no longer talk about what God knew in the past. But we can talk instead about what God knows from the perspective of eternity. And now the argument can be restated:

P1. You have no choice now about how events look from the perspective of eternity.
P2. God knows from the perspective of eternity that you are reading this chapter right now (for example) (this is the assumption of divine omniscience).
P3. You have no choice now about the fact that God knows from the perspective of eternity that you are reading this chapter right now (from P1 and P2).
P4. If P implies Q and you have no choice about P, then you have no choice about Q.
P5. God's knowing from the perspective of eternity that you are reading this chapter right now implies that you are reading this chapter right now (by the definition of knowledge).

Conclusion. You have no choice now about reading this chapter right now (for example) (from P3, P4, and P5).

In this version of the argument, we have substituted "God knows from the perspective of eternity" for "God knew in the past." The main question here concerns P1: is it just as plausible as the premise that you have no choice now about how events in the past turned out?

It is hard to know what to say here. For some reason, it does seem that what is true from the perspective of eternity might be subject to my current choices in a way that the past is not. This suggests that viewing God as existing outside of time altogether might help to explain how God knows the future in every detail.

On the other hand, it seems very strange to say that what I freely decide to do tomorrow will bring it about that something is true from the perspective of eternity. If I myself haven't decided yet what to do tomorrow, for example, then how could God (or anyone else, for that matter) know what I will freely decide to do tomorrow, whether from the perspective of eternity or any other perspective? And if I were to do something else instead, so that God would believe something different from the perspective of eternity, then does this mean that I have some kind of power over what God thinks from the perspective of eternity? This is puzzling indeed.

Our second argument against the possibility that God knows in advance what people freely choose to do can also be recast in terms of the perspective from eternity:

P1. God knows from the perspective of eternity that you are reading this chapter right now (for example) (this is the assumption of divine omniscience).
P2. A person S knows something only if it is impossible for S to be mistaken about it in those circumstances.
P3. It is impossible for God to be mistaken in those circumstances about the fact that you are reading this chapter right now (for example) (from P1 and P2).
P4. A person S acts freely only if it is possible for S to do something else in those circumstances (from the definition of incompatibilism).
Conclusion. You do not read this chapter freely right now (for example) (from P3 and P4). This argument seems just as strong as the earlier version that involved God's past knowledge (instead of God's time-

less knowledge from the perspective of eternity). As we noted earlier, though, although this argument is plausible, it is not absolutely decisive. If there is some way to resist P2, or some way to argue that the circumstances mentioned in P2 and P4 are different, then perhaps this argument can be answered. So to some degree, our earlier arguments for the conclusion that God could not foreknow human free actions remain standing even under the assumption that God exists outside of time altogether.

Some philosophers have objected to the idea that God exists outside of time for reasons that are independent of our question. (For a helpful summary of these reasons, see Hasker 1989.) For example, some philosophers think that if God exists outside of time, then it makes no sense to say that God does things at particular times (like creating the world at the first moment of time, or causing things to happen in the world at particular times) or to say that God could be united with a human nature (as traditional Christians believe the second person of the Trinity was, in the person of Jesus of Nazareth) (see Davis 1983). Other philosophers argue that the idea of God existing outside of time seems to stem from Greek philosophical thought, whereas the idea of God existing in time is more faithful to the biblical depiction of God's nature (see Wolterstorff 1975). In other words, even though appealing to the idea that God exists outside of time altogether might help to answer the question of how God could know about the free choices of creatures in the future, it might introduce new problems of its own. (Exploring this question fully would take us beyond the scope of this essay.)

7. IS FOREKNOWLEDGE USELESS TO GOD?

As we noted at the beginning of this essay, all of the major theistic religious traditions hold that God is omniscient, which means that God knows everything that can be known. As a result, the vast majority of theists throughout history have held that God foreknows free human actions. But what good is it to know the future? Would having foreknowledge of human free actions help God to exercise providential control over the world, for example?

Many theists have believed so. The idea is that if God knows what the future holds, then it can be pre-

vented. However, a little reflection shows that this conclusion is mistaken.

In order to foreknow something, it must be a truth about the future. And the future is just whatever will in fact happen after the present moment. So if God (or anyone else) foreknows that something will happen, then it is too late to do anything about it. In particular, it is impossible to prevent anything that anyone foreknows will occur. (If it were prevented, then it would not actually have been part of the future, and so it could not have *ever* been foreknown, because it would have never been true in the first place.) (This argument is stated clearly in Hasker 1989.)

All major theistic traditions have held that God is omniscient, but they have also held that God is omnipotent (all-powerful) and provident. To be provident, God must exercise some degree of control over the world in order to achieve good purposes. (For more on this, see Davison 1999.) The argument just mentioned above shows that having foreknowledge of human free choices is not enough for providential planning. In order to determine the future (at least in part), God needs to have knowledge of *what would happen* if certain steps were taken, not just *what will actually happen* in the future.

It will be helpful to consider an example in order to make this point more clear. Suppose that I am playing with my new chemistry set and mixing chemicals at random. If I mix a certain combination of chemicals, then there will be an explosion that will kill me. God knows this, of course, and doesn't want me to die in this way. Suppose also that God knows what the future holds, so that God foreknows that I will (in fact) mix the chemicals and cause the explosion and die. If that is so, then it is too late even for God: since God knows that it is true, then it is true, and that's the end of it.

However, if God were to prevent me from mixing the chemicals, then God never could have foreknown that I was going to mix them together (since a person can foreknow only that which will in fact take place). What we want to say here is that God knows that *if* I am placed in certain circumstances, *then* I will choose freely to mix those chemicals together so as to cause the explosion to occur. Then God can make sure that I am never in those circumstances, and in this way God can prevent me from ever causing the explosion to occur. In other words, God needs to know not just what will in fact happen, but what would happen if free persons were placed in certain circumstances.

Luis de Molina, an influential Jesuit theologian (1535–1600 A.D.), realized that this was true, and so he formulated an account of God's knowledge that explained how God can foreknow free human actions and also how God can be provident. Molina's theory (often called "Molinism") involves distinguishing three different kinds of knowledge that God possesses. (For more on Molina, see Freddoso's introduction to Molina 1988, Craig 1987, and Flint 1988.)

Natural knowledge is God's knowledge of necessary truths, truths over which God has no control at all (such as "1 + 1 = 2," for instance). *Free knowledge* is God's knowledge of contingent truths over which God has complete control (such as "There exists a physical universe"). Finally, *Middle knowledge* is God's knowledge of contingent truths over which God has no control at all (such as "If you were to hear a siren right now, then you would freely stop reading this chapter and look out the nearest window instead").

Middle knowledge is so-called because it is "in between" natural knowledge and free knowledge: like free knowledge, it is contingent, and like natural knowledge, it is beyond God's control. According to Molina, God considers the items of natural knowledge and middle knowledge when deciding what kind of world to create. For instance, earlier we mentioned God's desire that I should not blow myself up with my new chemistry set. Molina would say that God knew (through middle knowledge) that if I were placed in some circumstances, then I would freely blow myself up, whereas if I were placed in other circumstances, I would freely not do this. God cannot choose which circumstances are the ones in which I would blow myself up or vice versa, though, because that depends upon what I would freely choose to do. In this regard, the items of God's middle knowledge are both contingent (that is, they could have been otherwise) and also beyond God's control.

So Molina thinks that God's middle knowledge includes knowledge of what every possible creature would do in every possible situation. This gives God a measure of control over a world containing free creatures, since God need only place them in the right circumstances in order to get the desired results. How-

ever, on Molina's account, God is also constrained to some degree by what free creatures would decide to do. For instance, it might just turn out that there are no circumstances in which I would freely do a certain thing, so God would be unable to bring it about that I do that thing freely. (God could bring it about directly that I do that thing, of course, but God could not bring it about that I do it *freely*: since we are talking about freedom in the incompatibilist's sense, it is impossible even for God to *make* someone do something *freely* in this sense. For more on this, see Plantinga 1974.)

Molina's picture also explains how God could have complete foreknowledge concerning the future, including the future free choices of human beings. Here is how it works: from middle knowledge, God would know what every possible creature would do in every possible situation. And from free knowledge, God would know in which future situations actual creatures would be placed. Finally, from these two things, God can infer what actual creatures will freely choose to do in those situations. Isn't this a neat explanation?

It certainly is. And since many philosophers accept the argument mentioned above for the conclusion that foreknowledge alone is useless for God's providence, many philosophers are tempted to embrace Molina's theory of middle knowledge. But it is important to realize that although Molina's theory can easily explain how God has foreknowledge of free human actions, it has a hard time explaining how God gets middle knowledge in the first place.

In order to see why this is so, let's consider again Molina's view of the nature of middle knowledge. Logically prior to the creation of the world, even if no free creatures actually exist, God still knows what every possible creature would freely do in every possible situation. But how does God know these things? Surely it is at least as puzzling (if not more so) to say that God knows what every possible creature would freely do in every possible situation than it is to say that God knows what actual creatures will freely do in the future. The argument against foreknowledge developed in section 5, for example, clearly applies here just as well as it did there.

Of course, it is always open to the theist to claim that God has this knowledge, even though we do not understand how it is possible. There are many mysterious things in life, and perhaps this is one of them. But nontheists are not likely to find this explanation very satisfying.

8. WHAT IF GOD DOESN'T KNOW?

On the basis of all of the arguments discussed above (and many others besides these), some philosophers who are theists have simply concluded that it is not possible for God to foreknow free actions. However, they do not regard this conclusion as unwelcome or unsettling. Instead, they argue that God is still omniscient (since God knows everything that it is possible to know) and that God is still provident. Many of these philosophers call their approach "The Open Future View" (see Rice 1985, Hasker 1989, Pinnock 1994, and Basinger and Basinger 1994, for example).

Proponents of the Open Future View like to emphasize the fact that according to their view, God still knows everything that is possible. And God also knows what will probably happen in the future. But God doesn't know every single detail. In particular, God doesn't know how free creatures will choose to act in specific circumstances. But God is very resourceful (this is an understatement, of course), and although creating free creatures involves taking a risk of sorts, God will not be taken off guard or be thwarted in the long run.

Most traditional theists view the Open Future View as a departure from the traditional way of thinking about God's knowledge and providence, but defenders of the Open Future View argue that this is a mistake. Who is right about this? Theists need to consider the arguments on both sides before making up their minds, but that task falls beyond the scope of this paper.

9. CONCLUSION

We have discovered that it is important to clarify the ideas of knowledge and freedom. Once those ideas become clear, it is obvious that God could foreknow the free actions of creatures in the compatibilist's sense of "free." However, there are several plausible arguments for the conclusion that God could not foreknow the free actions of creatures in the incompatibilist's sense of "free." These

arguments are not absolutely irresistible, though, and some theists think that an appeal to the timelessness of God or to God's middle knowledge will help to explain God's foreknowledge. These moves generate new puzzles of their own, though, so that in the end it is not clear whether they are worthwhile moves to make. Some theists say that God simply does not know the future free choices of creatures, but they are quick to add that their view is faithful to the major theistic traditions on all important points.

What conclusion should you draw from all of this? Now that you have finished reading this chapter freely, do you have a clearer idea? Do you think that God knew long ago that you would finish this chapter now, or not? Only you can decide for yourself what to believe.

REFERENCES

Aquinas, St. Thomas. *Summa Theologica* (available in many editions).

St. Augustine, *On Free Choice of the Will*, translated by Thomas Williams (Hackett Publishing Company, 1993).

David Basinger and Randall Basinger (editors), *Four Views on Sovereignty and Human Freedom* (InterVarsity Press, 1986).

William L. Craig, *The Only Wise God* (Baker Book House, 1987).

Stephen T. Davis, *Logic and the Nature of God* (William B. Eerdmans Publishing Company, 1983).

Scott A. Davison, "Divine Providence and Human Freedom" in Michael Murray (editor), *Reason for the Hope Within* (William B. Eerdmans Publishing Company, 1999), pp. 217–237.

Scott A. Davison, "Foreknowledge, Middle Knowledge, and 'Nearby' Worlds," *International Journal for Philosophy of Religion*, Volume 30, Number 1 (August 1991), pp. 29–44.

Daniel Dennett, *Elbow Room: The Varieties of Free Will Worth Wanting* (MIT Press, 1985).

Fred Dretske, "Conclusive Reasons" in *The Australasian Journal of Philosophy* 49 (1971), pp. 1–22, reprinted in *Knowledge: Readings in Contemporary Epistemology* (Oxford University Press, 2000), pp. 42–62.

John Martin Fischer (editor), *Moral Responsibility* (Cornell University Press, 1986).

Thomas P. Flint, "Two Accounts of Providence" in Thomas V. Morris (editor), *Divine and Human Action* (Ithaca: Cornell University Press, 1988), pp.147–81.

William Hasker, *God, Time, and Knowledge* (Cornell University Press, 1989).

J. L. Mackie, *The Miracle of Theism* (Oxford University Press, 1982).

Luis de Molina, *On Divine Foreknowledge* (Liberi arbitri cum gratiae donis, divina praescientia, providentia, praedestinatione et reprobatione concordia, Disputations 47–53), translated with an introduction by Alfred J. Freddoso (Ithaca: Cornell University Press, 1988).

Clark H. Pinnock (editor), *The Openness of God : A Biblical Challenge to the Traditional Understanding of God* (InterVarsity Press, 1994).

Alvin I. Plantinga, *God, Freedom, and Evil* (William B. Eerdmans Publishing Company, 1974).

Richard Rice, *God's Foreknowledge and Man's Free Will* (Bethany House Publishers, 1985).

William L. Rowe, *Philosophy of Religion* (Wadsworth Publishing Company, 1978).

Richard Swinburne, *The Existence of God* (Oxford University Press, 1979).

Peter van Inwagen, *An Essay on Free Will* (Oxford University Press, 1983).

Nicholas Wolterstorff, "God Everlasting" in Clifton J. Orlebeke and Lewis B. Smedes (editors), *God and the Good* (William B. Eerdmans Publishing Company, 1975).

Questions for Further Reflection

1. Do you agree with compatibilists, who say that it is possible to be both free and determined in what you do at the same time?
2. Do you find it troubling that theists are unable to explain how God knows the future?
3. Do you think that it is possible to know something when there is some chance, however small, that your belief could be mistaken?
4. If you discovered that God knew every single detail concerning the future, including every choice that you would ever make, would you feel that your freedom to choose was somehow not real?
5. If God knew the future in every detail, then would it be appropriate for God to hold people responsible for the good and bad things that they do? Would God be partly responsible for the good and bad things that people do, since God would have known about them in advance?

5. GOD IS OUTSIDE OF TIME

Boethius

Boethius (c. 480–524) was born near Rome. Orphaned at a young age, he was raised by a rich aristocrat whose daughter he later married. Boethius knew Greek and set out to translate and interpret the works of Plato and Aristotle. He did not complete much of that project. Accused of disloyalty to King Theodoric, he was imprisoned and then executed. While in prison awaiting his execution, he wrote *The Consolation of Philosophy* from which the following selection is taken. In this selection, he argues that God transcends time altogether. That is, he argues that God is not everlasting in the sense that he exists within time from beginning to end, but rather is eternal by being outside of time altogether.

Reading Questions

1. What, according to Boethius, is providence?
2. How does God view the timeline?
3. What two kinds of necessity does Boethius mention?
4. Does Boethius think that God knows the future *and* that humans have free will?

Since then all judgment apprehends the subjects of its thought according to its own nature, and God has a condition of ever-present eternity, His knowledge, which passes over every change of time, embracing infinite lengths of past and future, views in its own direct comprehension everything as though it were taking place in the present. If you would weigh the foreknowledge by which God distinguishes all things, you will more rightly hold it to be a knowledge of a never-failing constancy in the present, than a foreknowledge of the future.

Whence Providence is more rightly to be understood as a looking forth than a looking forward, because it is set far from low matters and looks forth upon all things as from a lofty mountain-top above all. Why then do you demand that all things occur by necessity, if divine light rests upon them, while men do not render necessary such things as they can see? Because you can see things of the present, does your sight therefore put upon them any necessity?

Surely not. If one may not unworthily compare this present time with the divine, just as you can see things in this your temporal present, so God sees all things in His eternal present. Wherefore this divine foreknowledge does not change the nature or individual qualities of things: it sees things present in its understanding just as they will result some time in the future. It makes no confusion in its distinctions, and with one view of its mind it discerns all that shall come to pass whether of necessity or not. For instance, when you see at the same time a man walking on the earth and the sun rising in the heavens, you see each sight simultaneously, yet you distinguish between them, and decide that one is moving voluntarily, the other of necessity.

In like manner the perception of God looks down upon all things without disturbing at all their nature, though they are present to Him but future under the conditions of time. Wherefore this foreknowledge is not opinion but knowledge resting upon truth, since He knows that a future event is, though He knows too that it will not occur of necessity. If you answer here that what God sees about to happen, cannot but happen, and that what cannot but happen is bound by necessity, you fasten me down to the word necessity, I will grant that we have a matter of most firm truth, but it is one to which scarce any man can approach unless he be a contemplator of the divine.

For I shall answer that such a thing will occur of necessity, when it is viewed from the point of divine knowledge; but when it is examined in its own nature, it seems perfectly free and unrestrained. For there are two kinds of necessities; one is simple: for instance, a necessary fact, "all men are mortal"; the other is conditional; for instance, if you know that a man is walking, he must be walking: for what each man knows cannot be otherwise than it is known to be; but the conditional one is by no means followed by this simple and direct necessity; for there is no necessity to compel a voluntary walker to proceed, though it is necessary that, if he walks, he should be proceeding.

In the same way, if Providence sees an event in its present, that thing must be, though it has no necessity of its own nature. And God looks in His present upon those future things which come to pass through free will. Therefore if these things be looked at from the point of view of God's insight, they come to pass of necessity under the condition of divine knowledge; if, on the other hand, they are viewed by themselves, they do not lose the perfect freedom of their nature. Without doubt, then, all things that God foreknows do come to pass, but some of them proceed from free will; and though they result by coming into existence, yet they do not lose their own nature, because before they came to pass they could also not have come to pass . . .

"What?" you will say, "can I by my own action change divine knowledge, so that if I choose now one thing, now another, Providence too will seem to change its knowledge?" No; divine insight precedes all future things, turning them back and recalling them to the present time of its own peculiar knowledge. It does not change, as you may think, between this and that alternation of foreknowledge. It is constant in preceding and embracing by one glance all your changes. And God does not receive this ever-present grasp of all things and vision of the present at the occurrence of future events, but from His own peculiar directness. Whence also is that difficulty solved which you laid down a little while ago, that it was not worthy to say that our future events were the cause of God's knowledge. For this power of knowledge, ever in the present and embracing all things in its perception, does itself constrain all things, and owes naught to following events from which it has received naught.

Thus, therefore, mortal men have their freedom of judgment intact. And since their wills are freed from all binding necessity, laws do not set rewards or punishments unjustly. God is ever the constant fore-knowing overseer, and the ever-present eternity of His sight moves in harmony with the future nature of our actions, as it dispenses rewards to the good, and punishments to the bad. Hopes are not vainly put in God, nor prayers in vain offered: if these are right, they cannot but be answered. Turn therefore from vice: ensue virtue: raise your soul to upright hopes: send up on high your prayers from this earth. If you would be honest, great is the necessity enjoined upon your goodness, since all you do is done before the eyes of an all-seeing Judge.

QUESTIONS FOR FURTHER REFLECTION

1. What is the relationship between God's time-lessness and God's unchanging or immutable nature? Why might one think that that if God is not timeless, then He is not unchanging?
2. If free will and divine foreknowledge were incompatible, so that you could have only one of them, which would you choose?

---

6. ETERNITY

Eleonore Stump and Norman Kretzmann

Eleonore Stump (1942–) is Robert J. Henle Professor of Philosophy at St. Louis University. She has published in the areas of medieval philosophy, the philosophy of religion, and metaphysics. She has also served as the president of the Society of Christian Philosophers.

Norman Kretzmann (1928–1998) was the Susan Linn Sage Professor of Philosophy and Humane Letters at Cornell University. He specialized in medieval philosophy and the philosophy of religion and wrote 14 books and 70 articles. In this article, Stump and Kretzmann defend the ability of a timeless God to relate to his creation by defending a new form of the simultaneity relation.

READING QUESTIONS

1. In what two ways is eternality commonly misunderstood?
2. What do Stump and Kretzmann think is the more natural reading of "illimitable"?
3. What is simultaneity?
4. What view of time is fundamental to the special theory of relativity?
5. What kind of activities can God not do if He is conceived of as an atemporal mind?

The concept of eternity makes a significant difference in the consideration of a variety of issues in the philosophy of religion, including, for instance, the apparent incompatibility of divine omniscience with human freedom, of divine immutability with the efficacy of petitionary prayer, and of divine omniscience with divine immutability; but, because it has been mis-understood or cursorily dismissed as incoherent, it has not received the attention it deserves from contemporary philosophers of religion. In this paper we expound the concept as it is presented by Boethius (whose definition of eternity was the *locus classicus* for medieval discussions of the concept), analyze implications of the concept, examine reasons for considering it incoherent, and sample the results of bringing it to bear on issues in the philosophy of religion.

Eternality—the condition of having eternity as one's mode of existence—is misunderstood most often in either of two ways. Sometimes it is confused with limitless duration in time—sempiternality—and sometimes it is construed simply as atemporality, eternity being understood in that case as roughly analogous to an isolated, static instant. The second misunderstanding of eternality is not so far off the mark as the first, but a consideration of the views of the philosophers who contributed most to the development of the concept shows that atemporality alone does not exhaust eternality as they conceived of it, and that the picture of eternity as a frozen instant is a radical distortion of the classic concept.

1. BOETHIUS'S DEFINITION

Boethius discusses eternity in two places: *The Consolation of Philosophy*, Book V, Prose 6, and *De trinitate*, chapter 4.[1] The immediately relevant passages are these:

> CP That God is eternal, then, is the common judgment of all who live by reason. Let us therefore consider what eternity is, for this makes plain to us both the divine nature and knowledge. Eternity, then, is the complete possession all at once of illimitable life. This becomes clearer by comparison with temporal things. For whatever lives in time proceeds as something present from the past into the future, and there is nothing placed in time that can embrace the whole extent of its life equality. Indeed, on the contrary, it does not yet grasp tomorrow but yesterday it has already lost; and even in the life of today you live no more fully than in a mobile, transitory moment. . . . Therefore, whatever includes and possesses the whole fullness of illimitable life at once and is such that nothing future is absent from it and nothing past has flowed away, this is rightly judged to be eternal, and of this it is necessary both that being in full possession of itself it be always present to itself and that it have the infinity of mobile time present [to it]. (422.5–424.31)

> DT What is said of God, [namely, that] he is always, indeed signifies a unity, as if he had been in all the past, is in all the present—however that might be—[and] will be in all the future. That can be said, according to the philosophers, of the heaven and of the imperishable bodies; but it can-

not be said of God in the same way. For he is always in that for him *always* has to do with present time. And there is this great difference between the present of our affairs, which is *now*, and that of the divine: our now makes time and sempiternity, as if it were running along; but the divine now, remaining, and not moving, and standing still, makes eternity. If you add "*semper*" to "eternity," you get sempiternity, the perpetual running resulting from the flowing, tireless now. (20.64–22.77)

The definition Boethius presents and explains in CP and elucidates in the earlier DT is not original with him, nor does he argue for it in those passages. Similarly, we mean to do no more in this section of our paper than to present and explain a concept that has been important in Christian and pre-Christian theology and metaphysics. We will not argue here, for instance, that there is an eternal entity or even that God must be eternal if he exists. It is a matter of fact that many ancient and medieval philosophers and theologians were committed to the doctrine of God's eternality in the form in which Boethius presents it, and our purpose in this section of the paper is simply to elucidate the doctrine they held.

Boethius's definition is this: *Eternity is the complete possession all at once of illimitable life.*

We want to call attention to four ingredients in this definition. It is clear, first of all, that anything that is eternal has life. In this sense of "eternal," then, it will not do to say that a number, a truth, or the world is eternal, although one might want to say of the first two that they are atemporal and of the third that it is sempiternal—that it has beginningless, endless temporal existence.

The second and equally explicit element in the definition is illimitability: the life of an eternal being cannot be limited; it is impossible that there be a beginning or an end to it. The natural understanding of such a claim is that the existence in question is infinite duration, unlimited in either "direction." But there is another interpretation that must be considered in this context despite its apparent unnaturalness. Conceivably the existence of an eternal entity is said to be illimitable in the way in which a point or an instant may be said to be illimitable: what cannot be extended cannot be limited in its extent. There are passages that can be read as suggesting that this second interpretation is

---

[1] E. K. Rand, ed., in H. F. Stewart, E. K. Rand, and S. J. Tester, *Boethius: The Theological Tractates and The Consolation of Philosophy* (London: Heinemann; Cambridge, Mass.: Harvard, 1973).

TIME: THE FAMILIAR STRANGER * *William Lane Craig*

Time, it has been said, is what keeps everything from happening at once. When you think about it, this definition is probably as good as any other. For it is notoriously difficult to provide any analysis of time that is not in the end circular. If we say, for example, that time is duration, then we shall want to know what duration is. And duration turns out to be some interval of time. So time is some interval of time—not very enlightening! Or if we say that time is a dimension of the world, the points or inhabitants of which are ordered by the relations *earlier than* and *later than*, we may ask for an analysis of those relations so as to distinguish them, for example, from similar relations such as *behind* and *in front of* or *less than* and *greater than*, only to discover that *earlier* and *later*, on pain of circularity, are usually taken to be primitive, or unanalyzable, terms. Perhaps we may define *earlier* and *later* in terms of the notions *past, present,* and *future*; but then this triad is irreducibly temporal in character. Even if we succeed in defining *past* and *future* in relation to the *present*, what is the present except for the time that exists (where "exists" is in the present tense)?

Still, it is hardly surprising that time cannot be analyzed in terms of nontemporal concepts, and the proffered analyses are not without merit, for they do serve to highlight some of time's essential features. For example, most philosophers of time would agree that the *earlier than/later than* relations are essential to time. It is true that in certain high-level theories of physics one sometimes speaks of "imaginary time" or "quantum physical time," which are not ordered by these relations; but it would be far less misleading simply to deny that the geometrical structures posited by the relevant theories really are time at all. Some philosophers of time who deny that the past and future are real or existent have also denied that events or things are related to one another as *earlier than* or *later than*; but such thinkers do affirm the reality of the present as an irreducible feature of time. These features of time are common to our experience as temporal beings, even if ultimately unanalyzable.

Time, then, however mysterious, remains "the familiar stranger." This is the import of St. Augustine's famous disclaimer, "What, then, is time? If no one asks me, I know; but if I wish to explain it to one who asks, I know not."

From William Lane Craig, *Time and Eternity* (2001).

what Boethius intends. In CP eternal existence is expressly contrasted with temporal existence described as extending from the past through the present into the future, and what is eternal is described contrastingly as possessing its entire life *at once*. Boethius's insistence in DT that the eternal now is unlike the temporal now in being fixed and unchanging strengthens that hint with the suggestion that the eternal present is to be understood in terms of the present instant "standing still." Nevertheless, there are good reasons, in these passages themselves and in the history of the concept of eternity before and after Boethius, for rejecting this less natural interpretation. In the first place, some of the terminology Boethius uses would be inappropriate to eternity if eternity were to be conceived as illimitable in virtue of being unextended. He speaks in CP more than once of the *fullness* of eternal life. In DT and in *The Consolation of Philosophy* immediately following our passage CP he speaks of the eternal present or an eternal entity as *remaining* and *enduring*. And he claims in DT that it is correct to say of God that he is *always*, explaining the use of "always" in reference to God in such a way that he can scarcely have had in mind a life illimitable in virtue of being essentially durationless. The more natural reading of "illimitable," then, also provides the more natural reading of these texts. In the second place, the weight of tradition both before and after Boethius strongly favors interpreting illimitable life as involving infinite duration, beginningless as well as endless. Boethius throughout the *Consolation* and especially in passage CP is plainly working in the Platonic tradition, and both Plato and Plotinus understand eternal existence in that sense.[2] Medieval philosophers after Boethius, who depend on him for their conception of eternity, also clearly understand "illimitable" in this way.[3] So, for both these sets of reasons, we understand this part of Boethius's definition to mean that the life of an eternal entity is characterized by beginningless, endless, infinite duration.

The concept of duration that emerges in the interpretation of "illimitable life" is the third ingredient we mean to call attention to. Illimitable life entails duration of a special sort, as we have just seen, but it would be reasonable to think that any mode of existence that could be called a life must involve duration, and so there may seem to be no point in explicitly listing duration as an ingredient in Boethius's concept of eternality. We call attention to it here, however, because of its importance as part of the background against which the fourth ingredient must be viewed.

The fourth ingredient is presented in the only phrase of the definition still to be considered: "The complete possession all at once." As Boethius's explanation of the definition in CP makes clear, he conceives of an eternal entity as atemporal, and he thinks of its atemporality as conveyed by just that phrase in the definition. What he says shows that something like the following line of thought leads to his use of those words. A living temporal entity may be said to possess a life, but, since the events constituting the life of any temporal entity occur sequentially, some later than others, it cannot be said to possess all its life *at once*. And since everything in the life of a temporal entity that is not present is either past and so no longer in its possession, or future and so not yet in its possession, it cannot be said to have the *complete* possession of its life. So whatever has the complete possession of all its life at once cannot be temporal. The life that is the

mode of an eternal entity's existence is thus characterized not only by duration but also by atemporality.

With the possible exception of Parmenides, none of the ancients or medievals who accepted eternity as a real, atemporal mode of existence meant thereby to deny the reality of time or to suggest that all temporal experiences are illusory. In introducing the concept of eternity, such philosophers, and Boethius in particular, were proposing two separate modes of real existence. Eternity is a mode of existence that is, on Boethius's view, neither reducible to time nor incompatible with the reality of time.

In the next two sections of this paper, we will investigate the apparent incoherence of this concept of eternity. We will begin with a consideration of the meaning of atemporality in this connection, including an examination of the relationship between eternity and time; and we will go on to consider the apparent incoherence generated by combining atemporality with duration and with life.

2. THE ATEMPORALITY OF AN ETERNAL ENTITY: PRESENTNESS AND SIMULTANEITY

Because an eternal entity is atemporal, there is no past or future, no earlier or later, *within* its life; that is, the events constituting its life cannot be ordered sequentially from the standpoint of eternity. But, in addition, no temporal entity or event can be earlier or later than or past or future with respect to the whole life of an eternal entity, because otherwise such an eternal life or entity would itself be part of a temporal series. Here it should be evident that, although the stipulation that an eternal entity completely possesses its life all at once entails that it is not part of any sequence, it does not rule out the attribution of presentness or simultaneity to the life and relationships of such an entity, nor should it. In so far as an entity *is*, or *has* life, completely or otherwise, it is appropriate to say that it has present existence in some sense of "present"; and unless its life consists in only one event or it is impossible to relate an event in its life to any temporal entity or event, we need to be able to consider an eternal entity or event as one of the *relata* in a simultaneity relationship. We will consider briefly the applicability of presentness to something

[2]See Plato, *Timaeus* 37D–38C; Plotinus, *Enneads* III 7.

[3]See, for example, Thomas Aquinas, *Summa Theologiae* I, q. 10. Augustine, who is an earlier and in general an even more important source for medieval philosophy and theology than Boethius and who is even more clearly in the Platonist tradition, understands and uses this classic concept of eternity (see, e.g., *Confessions*, book XI, ch. 11; *The City of God*, book XI, ch. 21); but his influence on the medieval discussion of eternity seems not to have been so direct or important as Boethius's.

eternal and then consider in some detail the applicability of simultaneity.

If anything exists eternally, it exists. But the existing of an eternal entity is a duration without succession, and, because eternity excludes succession, no eternal entity has existed or will exist; it *only* exists. It is in this sense that an eternal entity is said to have present existence. But since that present is not flanked by past and future, it is obviously not the temporal present. And, furthermore, the eternal, pastless, futureless present is not instantaneous but extended, because eternity entails duration. The temporal present is a durationless instant, a present that cannot be extended conceptually without falling apart entirely into past and future intervals. The eternal present, on the other hand, is by definition an infinitely extended, pastless, futureless duration.

Simultaneity is of course generally and unreflectively taken to mean existence or occurrence at one and the same time. But to attribute to an eternal entity or event simultaneity with anything we need a coherent characterization of simultaneity that does not make it altogether temporal. It is easy to provide a coherent characterization of a simultaneity relationship that is not temporal in case both the *relata* are eternal entities or events. Suppose we designate the ordinary understanding of temporal simultaneity *T-simultaneity*:

(T) T-simultaneity = existence or occurrence at one and the same time.

Then we can easily enough construct a second species of simultaneity, a relationship obtaining between two eternal entities or events:

(E) E-simultaneity = existence or occurrence at one and the same eternal present.

What really interests us among species of simultaneity, however, and what we need for our present purposes, is not E-simultaneity so much as a simultaneity relationship between two *relata* of which one is eternal and the other temporal. We have to be able to characterize such a relationship coherently if we are to be able to claim that there is any connection between an eternal and a temporal entity or event. An eternal entity or event cannot be earlier or later than, or past or future with respect to, any temporal entity or event. If there is to be

any relationship between what is eternal and what is temporal, then, it must be some species of simultaneity.

Now in forming the species T-simultaneity and E-simultaneity, we have in effect been taking the genus of those species to be something like this:

(G) Simultaneity = existence or occurrence at once (i.e., together).

And we have formed those two species by giving specific content to the broad expression "at once." In each case, we have spelled out "at once" as meaning at one and the same *something*—time, in the case of T-simultaneity; eternal present, in the case of E-simultaneity. In other words, the *relata* for T-simultaneity occur together at the same time, and the *relata* for E-simultaneity occur together at the same eternal present. What we want now is a species of simultaneity—call it *ET-simultaneity* (for eternal-temporal simultaneity)—that can obtain between what is eternal and what is temporal. It is only natural to try to construct a definition for ET-simultaneity as we did for the two preceding species of simultaneity, by making the broad "at once" in (G) more precise. Doing so requires starting with the phrase "at one and the same——" and filling in the blank appropriately. To fill in that blank appropriately, however, would be to specify a single mode of existence in which the two *relata* exist or occur together, as the *relata* for T-simultaneity coexist (or co-occur) in time and the *relata* for E-simultaneity coexist (or co-occur) in eternity. But, on the view we are explaining and defending, it is theoretically impossible to specify a single mode of existence for two *relata* of which one is eternal and the other temporal. To do so would be to reduce what is temporal to what is eternal (thus making time illusory) or what is eternal to what is temporal (thus making eternity illusory) or both what is temporal and what is eternal to some *third* mode of existence; and all three of these alternatives are ruled out. The medieval adherents of the concept of eternity held that both time and eternity are real and that there is no mode of existence besides those two.

Against this background, then, it is not conceptually possible to construct a definition for ET-simultaneity analogous to the definitions for the other two species of simultaneity, by spelling out "at once" as "at one and the same——" and filling in the blank ap-

GOD'S COMPASSION * *William J. Wainwright*

Anselm argued that God is compassionate in the sense that He acts *as if* He felt compassion although He doesn't actually do so. . . .

Bernard of Clairvaux (1090–153) maintains that while God can't grieve or suffer in His *own* nature, He became incarnate so that He might "learn by his own experience how to commiserate and sympathize with those who are . . . suffering and tempted.". . .

Thomas Aquinas (1225–1274) has a more adequate solution. Love and joy are pure perfections. Hence, God literally has them although the mode in which He loves and rejoices differs from the mode in which we do so. (Human love and joy are often partly voluntary. We willingly embrace what we love or rejoice in. But they are also "passions"— externally induced modifications of our animal nature over which we have little control. God has no animal nature. His love and joy are wholly active, an expression only of His will.)

Anger and sorrow differ from love and joy because they entail suffering. Hence, even when these emotions are appropriate, they are only mixed perfections. They can therefore only be ascribed to God metaphorically. Nevertheless, anger and sorrow aren't *equally* metaphorical. Anger is ascribed to God because He produces effects similar to those which an angry person might produce. But no internal modification of God corresponds to anger in us. By contrast, God "is said to be saddened in so far as certain things take place contrary to what He loves and approves." While god doesn't literally grieve, there is something *in* God (an internal modification of God) that we apprehend as sorrow, namely, His love. That is, when our awareness of God's love is coupled with our recognition that creatures disobey God and suffer, we construe that divine love as sorrow.

Like Bernard, Thomas implicitly recognizes that there is no compassion without sympathetic feelings or emotion. But unlike many modern theologians, Thomas thinks the emotion in question is simpley love—not tender sorrow. This has two advantages. Love is compatible with unalloyed joy while sympathetic sorrow is essentially a reaction rather than an action. Love thus coheres better with God's independence.

Thomas's solutions is superior to Anselm's and Bernard's. Whether it is fully satisfactory depends on whether a compassion that doesn't literally involve sympathetic suffering is really compassion and thus adequately meets the demands of religious consciousness.

From *Philosophy of Religion* (1988).

---

propriately. What is temporal and what is eternal can coexist, on the view we are adopting and defending, but not within the same mode of existence; and there is no single mode of existence that can be referred to in filling in the blank in such a definition of ET-simultaneity.

The significance of this difficulty and its implications for a working definition of ET-simultaneity can be better appreciated by returning to the definition of T-simultaneity for a closer look. Philosophers of physics, explaining the special theory of relativity, have taught us to be cautious even about the notion of temporal simultaneity; in fact, the claim that temporal simultaneity is relative rather than absolute is fundamental to the special theory of relativity.

For all ordinary practical purposes and also for our theoretical purposes in this paper, time can be thought of as absolute, along Newtonian lines. But, simply in order to set the stage for our characterization of ET-simultaneity, it will be helpful to look at a standard philosophical presentation of temporal simultaneity along Einsteinian lines. Imagine a train traveling *very* fast, at 6/10 the speed of light. One observer (the "ground observer") is stationed on the embankment beside the track; another observer (the "train observer") is stationed on the train. Suppose that two lightning bolts strike the train, one at each end, and suppose that the ground observer sees those two lightning bolts simultaneously. The train observer also sees the two lightning bolts, but, since he is traveling toward the light ray emanating from the bolt that strikes the front of the train and away from the bolt that strikes the rear of the train, he will see the lightning bolt strike the front of the train before he sees the other strike the rear of the train. "This, then, is the fundamental result: events occurring at different places which are simultaneous in one frame of reference will not be simultaneous in another frame of reference which is moving with respect to the first. This is known as *the relativity of simultaneity*."

We want to leave to one side the philosophical issues raised by this example and simply accept it for our present purposes as a standard example illustrating Einstein's notion of the relativity of temporal simultaneity. According to this example, the very same two lightning flashes are simultaneous (with respect to the reference frame of the ground observer) and not simultaneous (with respect to the reference frame of the train observer). If we interpret "simultaneous" here in accordance with our definition of T-simultaneity, we will have to say that the same two lightning flashes occur at the same time and do not occur at the same time; that is, it will be both true and false that these two lightning flashes occur at the same time. The incoherence of this result is generated by filling in the blank for the definition of T-simultaneity with a reference to one and the same time, where time is understood as one single uniform mode of existence. The special theory of relativity takes time itself to be relative and so calls for a more complicated definition of temporal simultaneity than the common, unreflective definition given in (T), such as this relativized version of temporal simultaneity:

(RT) RT-simultaneity = existence or occurrence at the same time within the reference frame of a given observer.

This relativizing of time to the reference frame of a given observer resolves the apparent incoherence in saying that the same two lightning flashes occur and do not occur at one and the same time. They occur at the same time in the reference frame of one observer and do not occur at the same time in the reference frame of a different observer.

Once this is understood, we can see that, if we persist in asking whether or not the two lightning bolts are *really* simultaneous, we are asking an incoherent

question, one that cannot be answered. The question is asked about what is assumed to be a feature of reality, although in fact there is no such feature of reality; such a question is on a par with "Is Uris Library *really* to the left of Morrill Hall?" There is no absolute state of being temporally simultaneous with, any more than there is an absolute state of being to the left of. We determine the obtaining of the one relationship as we determine the obtaining of the other, by reference to an observer and the observer's point of view. The two lightning flashes, then, are RT-simultaneous in virtue of occurring at the same time within the reference frame of the ground observer and not RT-simultaneous in virtue of occurring at different times within the reference frame of the train observer. And, Einstein's theory argues, there is no privileged observer (or reference frame) such that with respect to it we can determine whether the two events are *really* simultaneous; simultaneity is irreducibly relative to observers and their reference frames, and so is time itself. Consequently, it would be a mistake to think that there is one single uniform mode of existence that can be referred to in specifying "at once" in (G) in order to derive a definition of temporal simultaneity.

These difficulties in spelling out even a very crude acceptable definition for temporal simultaneity in the light of relativity theory foreshadow and are analogous to the difficulties in spelling out an acceptable definition of ET-simultaneity. More significantly, they demonstrate that the difficulties defenders of the concept of eternity encounter in formulating such a definition are by no means unique to their undertaking and cannot be assumed to be difficulties in the concepts of ET-simultaneity or of eternity themselves. Finally, and most importantly, the way in which we cope with such difficulties in working out a definition for RT-simultaneity suggests the sort of definition needed for ET-simultaneity. Because one of the *relata* for ET-simultaneity is eternal, the definition for this relationship, like that for E-simultaneity, must refer to one and the same present rather than to one and the same time. And because in ET-simultaneity we are dealing with two equally real modes of existence, neither of which is reducible to any other mode of existence, the definition must be constructed in terms of *two* reference frames and *two* observers. So we can characterize

ET-simultaneity in this way. Let "x" and "y" range over entities and events. Then:

(ET) For every x and for every y, x and y are ET-simultaneous if
  (i) either x is eternal and y is temporal, or vice versa; and
  (ii) for some observer, A, in the unique eternal reference frame, x and y are both present—that is, either x is eternally present and y is observed as temporally present, or vice versa; and
  (iii) for some observer, B, in one of the infinitely many temporal reference frames, x and y are both present—that is, either x is observed as eternally present and y is temporally present, or vice versa.

Given the concept of eternity, condition (ii) provides that a temporal entity or event observed as temporally present by some eternal observer A is ET-simultaneous with every eternal entity or event; and condition (iii) provides that an eternal entity or event observed as eternally present (or simply as eternal) by some temporal observer B is ET-simultaneous with every temporal entity or event.

On our definition, if x and y are ET-simultaneous, then x is neither earlier nor later than, neither past nor future with respect to, y—a feature essential to any relationship that can be considered a species of simultaneity. Further, if x and y are ET-simultaneous, x and y are not temporally simultaneous; since either x or y must be eternal, it cannot be the case that x and y both exist *at one and the same time* within a given observer's reference frame. ET-simultaneity is symmetric, of course, but, since no temporal or eternal entity or event is ET-simultaneous with itself, the relationship is not reflexive; and the fact that there are different domains for its *relata* means that it is not transitive. The propositions

(1) x is ET-simultaneous with y.

and

(2) y is ET-simultaneous with z.

do not entail

(3) x is ET-simultaneous with z.

And even if we conjoin with (1) and (2)

(4) x and z are temporal.

(1), (2), and (4) together do not entail

(5) x and z are temporally simultaneous.

(RT) and the Einsteinian conception of time as relative have served the only purpose we have for them in this paper, now that they have provided an introductory analogue for our characterization of ET-simultaneity, and we can now revert to a Newtonian conception of time, which will simplify the discussion without involving any relevant loss of precision. In the first place, at least one of the theological issues we are going to be discussing—the problem of omniscience and immutability—depends on the concept of an absolute present, a concept that is often thought to be dependent on a Newtonian conception of absolute time. But the concept of an absolute present which is essential to our discussion is not discredited by relativity theory. Every conscious temporal observer has an undeniable, indispensable sense of the absolute present, *now*, and that thoroughly pervasive feature of temporal consciousness is all we need. We do not need and we will not try to provide a philosophical justification for the concept of an absolute present; we will simply assume it for our present purposes. And if it must be said that the absolute present is absolute only within a given observer's reference frame, that will not affect our use of the concept here. In the second place, in ordinary human circumstances, all human observers may be said—*should* be said—to share one and the same reference frame, and distinguishing individual reference frames for our discussion of time in the rest of this paper would be as inappropriate as taking an Einsteinian view of time in a discussion of historical chronology.

3. IMPLICATIONS OF ET-SIMULTANEITY

If x and z are temporal entities, they coexist if and only if there is some time during which both x and z exist. But if anything exists eternally, its existence, although infinitely extended, is fully realized, all present at once. Thus the entire life of any eternal entity is coexistent with any temporal entity at any time at which that temporal entity exists. From a temporal standpoint, the present is ET-simultaneous with the whole infinite extent of an eternal entity's life. From the standpoint of eternity, every time is present, co-occurrent with the whole of infinite atemporal duration.

We can show the implications of this account of ET-simultaneity by considering the relationship between an eternal entity and a future contingent event. Suppose that Richard Nixon will die at noon on August 9, 1990, precisely sixteen years after he resigned the Presidency. Nixon's death some years from now *will be* present to those who will be at his deathbed, but it *is* present to an eternal entity. It cannot be that an eternal entity has a vision of Nixon's death before it occurs; in that case an eternal event would be earlier than a temporal event. Instead, the actual occasion of Nixon's dying is present to an eternal entity. It is not that the future preexists somehow, so that it can be inspected by an entity that is outside time, but rather that an eternal entity that is wholly ET-simultaneous with August 9, 1974, and with today, is wholly ET-simultaneous with August 9, 1990, as well. It is *now* true to say "The whole of eternity is ET-simultaneous with the present"; and of course it was true to say just the same at noon of August 9, 1974, and it will be true to say it at noon of August 9, 1990. But since it is one and the same eternal present that is ET-simultaneous with each of those times, there is a sense in which it is now true to say that Nixon at the hour of his death is present to an eternal entity; and in that same sense it is now true to say that Nixon's resigning of the Presidency is present to an eternal entity. If we are considering an eternal entity that is omniscient, it is true to say that that entity is *at once* aware of Nixon resigning the Presidency and of Nixon on his deathbed (although of course an omniscient entity understands that those events occur sequentially and knows the sequence and the dating of them); and it is true to say also that for such an entity both those events are present at once.

Such an account of ET-simultaneity suggests at least a radical epistemological or even metaphysical relativism, and perhaps plain incoherence. We *know* that Nixon is now alive. An omniscient eternal entity *knows* that Nixon is now dead. Still worse, an omniscient eternal entity also *knows* that Nixon is now alive, and so Nixon is apparently both alive and dead at once in the eternal present.

These absurdities appear to be entailed partly because the full implications of the concept of eternity have not been taken into account. We have said

enough to induce caution regarding "present" and "simultaneous," but it is not difficult to overlook the concomitant ambiguity in such expressions as "now" and "at once." To say that we know that Nixon is now alive although an eternal entity knows that Nixon is now dead does not mean that an eternal entity knows the opposite of what we know. What we know is that:

(6) Nixon is alive in the temporal present.

What an eternal entity knows is that

(7) Nixon is dead in the eternal present.

and (6) is not incompatible with (7). Still, this simple observation does nothing to dispel the appearance of incompatibility between (7) and

(8) Nixon is alive in the eternal present.

and, on the basis of what has been said so far, both (7) and (8) are true. But Nixon is temporal, not eternal, and so are his life and death. The conjunction of (7) and (8), then, cannot be taken to mean that the temporal entity Nixon exists in eternity, where he is simultaneously alive and dead, but rather something more nearly like this. One and the same eternal present is ET-simultaneous with Nixon's being alive and is also ET-simultaneous with Nixon's dying; so Nixon's life is ET-simultaneous with and hence present to an eternal entity, and Nixon's death is ET-simultaneous with and hence present to an eternal entity, although Nixon's life and Nixon's death are themselves neither eternal nor simultaneous.

These considerations also explain the appearance of metaphysical relativism inherent in the claim that Nixon's death is really future for us and really present for an eternal entity. It is not that there are two objective realities, in one of which Nixon's death is really future and in the other of which Nixon's death and life are really present; that *would* be incoherent. What the concept of eternity implies instead is that there is one objective reality that contains two modes of real existence in which two different sorts of duration are measured by two irreducibly different sorts of measure: time and eternity. Given the relations between time and eternity spelled out in section 2 of this paper, Nixon's death is really future or not depending on which sort of entity, temporal or eternal, it is being related to. An eternal entity's mode of existence is such that its whole life is ET-simultaneous with each and every temporal entity or event, and so Nixon's death, like every other event involving Nixon, is really ET-simultaneous with the life of an eternal entity. But when Nixon's death is being related to *us*, on [today's date], then, given our location in the temporal continuum Nixon's death is not simultaneous (temporally or in any other way) with respect to us, but really future.

4. ATEMPORAL DURATION AND ATEMPORAL LIFE

With this understanding of the atemporality of an eternal entity's existence, we want to consider now the apparent incoherence generated by combining atemporality with duration and with life in the definition of eternity.

The notion of atemporal duration is the heart of the concept of eternity and, in our view, the original motivation for its development. The most efficient way in which to dispel the apparent incoherence of the notion of atemporal duration is to consider, even if only very briefly, the development of the concept of eternity. The concept can be found in Parmenides, we think, but it finds its first detailed formulation in Plato, who makes use of it in working out the distinction between the realms of being and becoming; and it receives its fullest exposition in pagan antiquity in the work of Plotinus. The thought that originally stimulated this Greek development of the concept of eternity was apparently something like this. Our *experience* of temporal duration gives us an impression of permanence and persistence which an *analysis* of time convinces us is an illusion or at least a distortion. Reflection shows us that contrary to our familiar but superficial impression, temporal duration is only apparent duration, just what one would expect to find in the realm of becoming. The existence of a typical existent temporal entity, such as a human being, is spread over years of the past, through the present, and into years of the future; but the past is not, the future is not, and present must be understood as no time at all, a durationless instant, a mere point at which the past is continuous with the future. Such radically evanescent existence cannot be the foundation of existence. Being,

the persistent, permanent, utterly immutable actuality that seems required as the bedrock underlying the evanescence of becoming, must be characterized by genuine duration, of which temporal duration is only the flickering image. Genuine duration is fully realized duration—not only extended existence (even *that* is theoretically impossible in time) but also existence *none* of which is already gone and *none* of which is yet to come—and such fully realized duration must be atemporal duration. Whatever has atemporal duration as its mode of existence is "such that nothing future is absent from it and nothing past has flowed away," whereas of everything that has temporal duration it may be said that from it *everything* future is absent and *everything* past has flowed away. What has temporal duration "does not yet grasp tomorrow but yesterday it has already lost"; even today it exists only; "in a mobile, transitory moment," the present instant. To say of something that it is future is to say that it is not (yet), and to say of something that it is past is to say that it is not (any longer). Atemporal duration is duration none of which is not—none of which is absent (and hence future) or flowed away (and hence past). Eternity, not time, is the mode of existence that admits of fully realized duration.

The ancient Greek philosophers who developed the concept of eternity were using the word *aiōn*, which corresponds in its original sense to our word "duration," in a way that departed from ordinary usage in order to introduce a notion which, however counter-intuitive it may be, can reasonably be said to preserve and even to enhance the original sense of the word. It would not be out of keeping with the tradition that runs through Parmenides, Plato, and Plotinus into Augustine, Boethius, and Aquinas to claim that it is only the discovery of eternity that enables us to make genuinely literal use of words for duration, words such as "permanence" and "persistence," which in their ordinary, temporal application turn out to have been unintended metaphors. "Atemporal duration," like the ancient technical use of *aiōn* itself, violates established usage; but an attempt to convey a new philosophical or scientific concept by adapting familiar expressions is not to be rejected on the basis of its violation of ordinary usage. The apparent incoherence in the concept is primarily a consequence of continuing to think of duration only as "persistence *through time*."

Since a life is a kind of duration, some of the apparent incoherence in the notion of an atemporal life may be dispelled in rendering the notion of atemporal duration less readily dismissible. But life is in addition ordinarily associated with processes of various sorts, and processes are essentially temporal, and so the notion of an atemporal entity that has life seems incoherent. Now what Aquinas, for example, is thinking of when he attributes life to eternal God is the doctrine that God is a mind. (Obviously what is atemporal cannot consist of physical matter; we assume for the sake of the argument that there is nothing incoherent in the notion of a wholly immaterial, independently existent mind.) Since God is atemporal, the mind that is God must be different in important ways from a temporal, human mind. Considered as an atemporal mind, God cannot deliberate, anticipate, remember, or plan ahead, for instance; all these mental activities essentially involve time, either in taking time to be performed (like deliberation) or in requiring a temporal viewpoint as a prerequisite to performance (like remembering). But it is clear that there are other mental activities that do not require a temporal interval or viewpoint. Knowing seems to be the paradigm case; learning, reasoning, inferring take time, as knowing does not. In reply to the question "What have you been doing for the past two hours?" it makes sense to say "Studying logic" or "Proving theorems," but not "Knowing logic." Similarly, it makes sense to say "I'm learning logic," but not "I'm knowing logic." And knowing is not the only mental activity requiring neither a temporal interval nor a temporal viewpoint. Willing, for example, unlike wishing or desiring, seems to be another. Perceiving is impossible in any literal sense for a mind that is disembodied, but nothing in the nature of incorporeality or atemporality seems to rule out the possibility of awareness. And though *feeling* angry is impossible for an atemporal entity—if feelings of anger are essentially associated, as they seem to be, with bodily states—we do not see that anything prevents such an entity from *being* angry, a state the components of which might be, for instance, being aware of an injustice, disapproving of it, and willing its punishment. It seems, then, that the notion of an atemporal mind is not incoherent, but that, on the contrary, it is possible that such a mind might have a variety of faculties or activities. Our informal, incomplete consideration of that possibility is not even the beginning of an argument for such a conclusion, but it is enough for our purposes here to suggest the line along which such an argument might develop. The notion of an atemporal mind is not *prima facie* absurd, and so neither is the notion of an atemporal life absurd; for any entity that has or is a mind must be considered to be *ipso facto* alive, whatever characteristics of other living beings it may lack. . . .

6. OMNISCIENCE AND IMMUTABILITY

The doctrine that God is eternal is obviously of critical importance in the consideration of any issue involving the relationship of God to temporal entities or events. We will conclude our exploration of the concept of eternity by sampling its effect on three such issues concerning either God's knowledge or God's power in connection with the future, the past, and the present, respectively.

First, the short answer to the question whether God can foreknow contingent events is no. It is impossible that any event occur later than an eternal entity's present state of awareness, since every temporal event is ET-simultaneous with that state, and so an eternal entity cannot *fore* know anything. Instead, such an entity considered as omniscient knows—is aware of—all temporal events, including those which are future with respect to our current temporal viewpoint; but, because the times at which those future events will be present events are ET-simultaneous with the whole of eternity an omniscient eternal entity is aware of them as they are present.[4]

Second, the short answer to the question whether God can change the past is no. But it is misleading to

---

[4]What we present here is essentially Boethius's line against the suggestion that divine omniscience and human freedom are incompatible, a line in which he was followed by many medievals, especially Aquinas. On Aquinas's use of the Boethian solution, see Anthony Kenny, "Divine Foreknowledge and Human Freedom," in Kenny (ed.), *Aquinas: Collection of Critical Essays* (Garden City, N.Y.: Doubleday-Anchor, 1969), pp. 255–70; 264.

say, with Agathon, that not even God can change the past;[5] God *in particular* cannot change the past. The impossibility of *God's* changing the past is a consequence not of the fact that what is past is over and done with but rather of the fact that the past is solely a feature of the experience of temporal entities. It is just because no event can be past with respect to an eternal entity that an eternal entity cannot alter a *past* event.[6] An omnipotent, omniscient, eternal entity can affect temporal events, but it can affect events only as they are actually occurring. As for a past event, the time at which it was actually occurring is the time at which it is present to such an entity; and so the battle of Waterloo is present to God, and God can affect the battle. Suppose that he does so. God can bring it about that

Napoleon wins, though we know that he does not do so, because whatever God does at Waterloo is over and done with as we see it. So God cannot alter the past, but he can alter the course of the battle of Waterloo.[7]

QUESTIONS FOR FURTHER REFLECTION

1. What is the problem with relating a timeless entity with a temporal entity?
2. How does ET-simultaneity solve the problem of how a timeless being can relate to a temporal world?
3. Stump and Kretzmann define ET-simultaneity using "observation language." What consequences does this have for their definition?

---

[5]Aristotle, *Nicomachean Ethics* VI 2.

[6]Although the concept of *the* past, dependent on the concept of the absolute temporal present, has no application for an eternal entity, for an omniscient eternal entity there is the awareness of your past, your present, your future as of January 1, 1970, and of your past, your present, your future as of January 1, 1980, and so on for every temporal entity as of any date in its duration.

[7]These observations regarding God's relationship to the past might suggest further issues regarding petitionary prayer. It is obviously absurd to pray in 1980 that Napoleon win at Waterloo when one knows what God does not bring about at Waterloo, but it might not seem absurd—at least not in the same way—to pray in 1980 that Napoleon lose at Waterloo. After all, your prayer and the battle are alike present to God; why should your prayer not be efficacious in bringing about Napoleon's defeat? But, as a petition addressed to the will of God, a prayer is also an expression of the will of the one who prays it, and any temporal entity who prays in 1980, "Let Napoleon lose at Waterloo," is to that extent pretending to have atemporal knowledge and an atemporal will. The only appropriate version of that prayer is "Let Napoleon have lost at Waterloo," and for one who knows the outcome of the battle more than a hundred and fifty years ago, that prayer is pointless and in that

sense absurd. But a prayer prayed in ignorance of the outcome of a past event is not pointless in that way. (We are thus disagreeing with Peter Geach, when he claims that "A prayer for something to have happened is simply an absurdity, regardless of the utterer's knowledge or ignorance of how things went" [*God and the Soul* (London: Routledge & Kegan Paul, 1969), p. 90]; but we find much else to admire in his chapter "Praying for Things to Happen." On the hypothesis that there is an eternal, omniscient, omnipotent God, the praying of such a prayer would indeed qualify as "the only instance of behavior, on the part of ordinary people whose mental processes we can understand, designed to affect the past and coming quite naturally to us" [Michael Dummett, "Bringing about the Past," *The Philosophical Review*, 73; 3 (July 1964), pp. 338–59, p. 341]. We are grateful to members of the Sage School of Philosophy at Cornell for pointing out the relevance of Dummett's discussion. Dummett does not draw on the concept of divine eternality, but, if it is acceptable in its own right, its introduction would lead to a modification and strengthening of some of the claims he makes—for example, "I am not asking God that, even if my son has drowned, He should *now* make him not to have drowned; I am asking that, at the time of the disaster, He should then have made my son not to drown at that time" (342).

SUGGESTIONS FOR FURTHER READING

St. Augustine. *On Free Choice of the Will.* trans. Thomas Williams. Indianapolis and Cambridge: Hackett Publishing Company, 1993.

Flint, Thomas P. "Two Accounts of Providence" in *Divine and Human Action*, edited by Thomas V. Morris. Ithaca: Cornell University Press, 1988, pp.147–81.

Plantinga, Alvin I. *God, Freedom, and Evil.* Grand Rapids, MI: Eerdmans Publishing Company, 1974.

Hasker, William. *God, Time and Knowledge.* Ithaca: Cornell University Press, 1989.

PART II

◆ ARGUMENTS FOR THE EXISTENCE OF GOD ◆

THE ONTOLOGICAL ARGUMENT

7. THE ONTOLOGICAL ARGUMENT • *Anselm and Guanilo*
Rene Descartes, "It Is Impossible to Think of God as Not Existing"
8. CRITIQUE OF THE ONTOLOGICAL ARGUMENT • *Immanuel Kant*
William Rowe, "Anselm Begs the Question"
Stephen Davis, "Existence Is a Predicate"
9. ANSELM'S ONTOLOGICAL ARGUMENTS • *Norman Malcolm*
Alvin Plantinga, "The Hartshorne-Malcolm Version of the Ontological Argument"

THE COSMOLOGICAL ARGUMENT

10. THE FIVE WAYS • *Thomas Aquinas*
Frederick Copleston, "A Hierarchy of Causes"
11. THE COSMOLOGICAL ARGUMENT • *David Yandell and Keith Yandell*
Godfreid Leibniz, "Proving God"
Bertrand Russell and Frederick Copleston, "The Russell-Copleston Debate"
12. CRITICISMS OF THE COSMOLOGICAL ARGUMENTS • *J. L. Mackie*
Elliot Sober, "The Birthday Fallacy"
William Rowe, "An Argument Against the Principle of Sufficient Reason"
13. THE KALAM COSMOLOGICAL ARGUMENT • *William Lane Craig*
Paul Davies, "Is the Universe a Free Lunch?"
John D. Barrow and Frank J. Tipler, "The Anthropic Principle"
14. A CRITICAL EXAMINATION OF THE KALAM COSMOLOGICAL ARGUMENT • *Wes Morriston*

The Design Argument

15. The Watch and the Watchmaker * *William Paley*
Michael Denton, "Self-Duplication as Evidence of Design"
Walter Bradley "Complex Living Systems Are Evidence of Design"
16. Critique of the Design Argument * *David Hume*
George Smith, "Who Designed the Designer?"
Robin Le Poidevin, "Evolution Explains Apparent Design"
17. God, Design, and Fine-Tuning * *Robin Collins*
Richard Dawkins, "Atheism Before Darwin?"

The Moral Argument

18. The Moral Argument for the Existence of God * *C. S. Lewis*
19. Critique of the Moral Argument * *J. L. Mackie*

Suggestions for Further Reading

7. THE ONTOLOGICAL ARGUMENT

Anselm and Guanilo

Anselm (1033–1109) was born in a town in the Italian Alps. Unable to get along with his father he left home and set out to cross Mont Cenis by foot. At one point in the journey, he fainted from hunger and ate snow to regain his strength. Three years later he joined the Benedictine monastery at Bec in Normandy. There he studied philosophy and theology with the famous Lanfranc, who eventually left the monastery to become the Bishop of Canterbury. Anselm replaced him at the monastery as Prior. Years later, upon Lanfranc's death, Anselm was appointed Archbishop of Canterbury. He wrote several important works including *Molologion, Proslogion*, and *Cur deus homo*. His view of the doctrine of the atonement became the standard Christian view on the subject.

Gaunilo was an eleventh century monk best known for his debate with Anselm. In this selection from the *Proslogion* and *On Behalf of the Fool*, Anselm and Gaunilo debate the ontological argument for the existence of God.

READING QUESTIONS

1. What is Anselm's definition of God?
2. Where, according to Anselm, will even the fool admit that God exists?
3. Why does Anselm think that it is impossible for God to be conceived of as not existing?
4. Gaunilo tries to reduce Anselm's argument to absurdity by applying Anselm's argument in a different context. What is his argument and what analogy does he use to make this argument?

1. GOD TRULY EXISTS.

Therefore, O Lord, You who give understanding to faith, grant me to understand—to the degree You know to be advantageous—that You exist, as we believe, and that You are what we believe [You to be]. Indeed, we believe You to be something than which nothing greater can be thought. Or is there, then, no such nature [as You], for the Fool has said in his heart that God does not exist?[1]

But surely when this very same Fool hears my words "something than which nothing greater can be thought," he understands what he hears. And what he understands is in his understanding, even if he does not understand [i.e., judge] it to exist. For that a thing is in the understanding is distinct from understanding that [this] thing exists. For example, when a painter envisions what he is about to paint: he indeed has in his understanding that which he has not yet made, but he does not yet understand that it exists. But after he has painted [it]: he has in his understanding that

---

[1]Psalms 13:1 & 52:1 (14:1 & 53:1).

which he has made, and he understands that it exists. So even the Fool is convinced that something than which nothing greater can be thought is at least in his understanding; for when he hears of this [being], he understands [what he hears], and whatever is understood is in the understanding. But surely that than which a greater cannot be thought cannot be only in the understanding. For if it were only in the understanding, it could be thought to exist also in reality—something which is greater [than existing only in the understanding]. Therefore, if that than which a greater cannot be thought were only in the understanding, then that than which a greater *cannot* be thought would be that than which a greater *can* be thought! But surely this [conclusion] is impossible. Hence, without doubt, something than which a greater cannot be thought exists both in the understanding and in reality.

2. GOD CANNOT BE THOUGHT NOT TO EXIST

Assuredly, this [being] exists so truly [i.e., really] that it cannot even be thought not to exist. For there can be thought to exist something which cannot be thought not to exist; and this thing is greater than that which can be thought not to exist. Therefore, if that than which a greater cannot be thought could be thought not to exist, then that than which a greater cannot be thought would not be that than which a greater cannot be thought—[a consequence] which is contradictory. Hence, something than which a greater cannot be thought exists so truly that it cannot even be thought not to exist. And You are this [being], O Lord our God. Therefore, O Lord my God, You exist so truly that You cannot even be thought not to exist. And this is rightly the case. For if any mind could think of something better than You, the creature would rise above the Creator and would sit in judgment over the Creator—something which is utterly absurd. Indeed, except for You alone, whatever else exists can be thought not to exist. Therefore, You alone exist most truly of all and thus most greatly of all; for whatever else exists does not exist as truly [as do You] and thus exists less greatly [than do You]. Since, then, it is so readily clear to a rational mind that You exist most greatly of all, why did the Fool say in his heart that God does not exist?[2]—why [indeed] except because [he is] foolish and a fool!

3. HOW THE FOOL SAID IN HIS HEART THAT WHICH CANNOT BE THOUGHT

Yet, since to speak in one's heart and to think are the same thing, how did [the Fool] say in his heart that which he was unable to think, or how was he unable to think that which he did say in his heart? Now, if he truly [i.e., really]—rather, since he truly—both thought [what he did] because he said [it] in his heart and did not say [it] in his heart because he was unable to think [it], then it is not the case that something is said in the heart, or is thought, in only one way. For in one way a thing is thought when the word signifying it is thought, and in another way [it is thought] when that which the thing is is understood. Thus, in the first way but not at all in the second, God can be thought not to exist. Indeed, no one who understands that which God is can think that God does not exist, even though he says these words [viz., "God does not exist"] in his heart either without any signification or with some strange signification. For God is that than which a greater cannot be thought. Anyone who rightly understands this, surely understands that that [than which a greater cannot be thought] exists in such way that it cannot even conceivably not exist. Therefore, anyone who understands that God is such [a being] cannot think that He does not exist.

Thanks to You, good Lord, thanks to You—because what at first I believed through Your giving, now by Your enlightening I understand to such an extent that [even] if I did not want to believe that You exist, I could not fail to understand [that You exist].

4. GAUNILO'S REPLY

. . . For example, some people say that there is an island somewhere in the ocean. Some call it Lost Island because of the difficulty—or, rather, the impossibility—of finding what does not exist. They say that it abounds with inestimable plenitude of all riches

---

[2]Psalms 13:1 & 52:1 (14:1 & 53:1).

"IT IS IMPOSSIBLE TO THINK OF GOD AS NOT EXISTING" ✳ *Rene Descartes*

But now, if just because I can draw the idea of something from my thought, it follows that all which I know clearly and distinctly as pertaining to this object does really belong to it, may I not derive from this an argument demonstrating the existence of God? It is certain that I no less find the idea of God, that is to say, the idea of a supremely perfect Being, in me, than that of any figure or number whatever it is; and I do not know any less clearly and distinctly that an [actual and] eternal existence pertains to this nature than I know that all that which I am able to demonstrate of some figure or number truly pertains to the nature of this figure or number, and therefore, although all that I concluded in the preceding Meditations were found to be false, the existence of God would pass with me as at least as certain as I have ever held the truths of mathematics (which concern only numbers and figures) to be.

This indeed is not at first manifest, since it would seem to present some appearance of being a sophism. For being accustomed in all other things to make a distinction between existence and essence, I easily persuade myself that the existence can be separated from the essence of God, and that we can thus conceive God as not actually existing. But, nevertheless, when I think of it with more attention, I clearly see that existence can no more be separated from the essence of God than can its having its three angles equal to two right angles be separated from the essence of a [rectilinear] triangle, or the idea of a mountain from the idea of a valley; and so there is not any less repugnance to our conceiving a God (that is, a Being supremely perfect) to whom existence is lacking (that is to say, to whom a certain perfection is lacking), than to conceive of a mountain which has no valley.

But although I cannot really conceive of a God without existence any more than a mountain without a valley, still from the fact that I conceive of a mountain with a valley, it does not follow that there is such a mountain in the world; similarly although I conceive of God as possessing existence, it would seem that it does not follow that there is a God which exists; for my thought does not impose any necessity upon things, and just as I may imagine a winged horse, although no horse with wings exists, so I could perhaps attribute existence to God, although no God existed.

But a sophism is concealed in this objection; for from the fact that I cannot conceive a mountain without a valley, it does not follow that there is any mountain or any valley in existence, but only that the mountain and the valley, whether they exist or do not exist, cannot in any way be separated one from the other. While from the fact that I cannot conceive God without existence, it follows that existence is inseparable from Him, and hence that He really exists; not that my thought can bring this to pass, or impose any necessity on things, but, on the contrary, because the necessity which lies in the thing itself, that is the necessity of the existence of God determines me to think in this way. For it is not within my power to think of God without existence (that is of a supremely perfect Being devoid of a supreme perfection) though it is in my power to imagine a horse either with wings or without wings.

From Rene Descartes, *The Philosophical Works of Descartes* trans. by Elizabeth S. Haldene (1911).

and all delights—much more so than is reported of the Isles of the Blessed. Having no owner or inhabitant [it is said] to excel completely—because of the superabundant goods for the taking—all other lands in which men dwell. Now, should someone tell me that this is the case, I would easily understand what he said, wherein there is nothing difficult. But suppose he were then to add, as if it followed logically: "You can no more doubt that this island which is more excellent than all [other] lands truly exists somewhere in reality than you [can] doubt that [it] is in your understanding. And since [for it] to exist not only in the understanding but also in reality is more excellent [than for it to exist in the understanding alone], then, necessarily, it exists in reality. For if it did not exist [in reality], then whatever other land did exist in reality would be more excellent than it, and thus this [island], which has already been understood by you to be more excellent [than all other lands], would not be more excellent [than all others]." If through these [considerations] he wanted to prove to me regarding this island that it ought no longer to be doubted truly to exist, then either I would think he

were jesting or I would not know whom I ought to regard as the more foolish—either myself, were I to assent thereto, or him, were he to suppose that he had proved with any degree of certainty the existence of this island. For he would first have to prove that this island's excellence is in my understanding only as [is the excellence of] a thing which truly and certainly exists and not at all as [is the excellence of] a thing which is false or doubtfully real.

QUESTIONS FOR FURTHER REFLECTION

1. When I have an idea in my mind, say, of a bicycle does a bicycle exist in my mind? If not, then can Anselm really claim that God exists in the mind?
2. Why is it better to exist both in reality and in the understanding. In what sense is a bicycle that exists *both* in reality *and* in the understanding better than a bicycle that just exists in the understanding?
3. Are there any relevant differences between God and the greatest possible island that would make Gaunilo's analogy weak?

8. CRITIQUE OF THE ONTOLOGICAL ARGUMENT
Immanuel Kant

Immanuel Kant (1724–1804), widely regarded as one of the greatest philosophers of all time, was born in Königsberg (now Kaliningrad, Russia). His parents were Lutheran pietists. Teaching at the University of Königsberg for much of his life, Kant wrote three ground breaking works: *The Critique of Pure Reason, The Critique of Practical Reason*, and *The Critique of Judgment*. In *The Critque of Pure Reason*, from which this selection is taken, his central concern is whether metaphysics is possible. He limits knowledge to appearances or phenomena and rules out knowledge of noumena, or things-in-themselves. He thereby rules out the possibility of metaphysics, understood as the project of trying to acquire knowledge of things-in-themselves. In this selection, Kant offers one of the most historically and philosophically important criticisms of the ontological argument, criticizing it by questioning whether existence is a great-making predicate. He does this by arguing that existence isn't a predicate at all.

READING QUESTIONS

1. What are necessary judgments? Give some examples.
2. What does Kant mean by the word "predicate"?

3. What is the difference between a logical predicate and a real predicate?
4. Why does Kant think that being is not a real predicate? What example does he give to illustrate this point?

1. THE IMPOSSIBILITY OF AN ONTOLOGICAL PROOF OF THE EXISTENCE OF GOD

It is evident from what has been said, that the conception of an absolutely necessary being is a mere idea, the objective reality of which is far from being established by the mere fact that it is a need of reason. On the contrary, this idea serves merely to indicate a certain unattainable perfection, and rather limits the operations than, by the presentation of new objects, extends the sphere of the understanding. But a strange anomaly meets us at the very threshold; for the inference from a given existence in general to an absolutely necessary existence, seems to be correct and unavoidable, while the conditions of the *understanding* refuse to aid us in forming any conception of such a being.

Philosophers have always talked of an *absolutely necessary* being, and have nevertheless declined to take the trouble of conceiving whether—and how—a being of this nature is even cogitable, not to mention that its existence is actually demonstrable. A verbal definition of the conception is certainly easy enough; it is something, the nonexistence of which is impossible. But does this definition throw any light upon the conditions which render it impossible to cogitate the nonexistence of a thing—conditions which we wish to ascertain, that we may discover whether we think anything in the conception of such a being or not? For the mere fact that I throw away, by means of the word *Unconditioned*, all the conditions which the understanding habitually requires in order to regard anything as necessary, is very far from making clear whether by means of the conception of the unconditionally necessary I think of something, or really of nothing at all.

Nay, more, this chance-conception, now become so current, many have endeavored to explain by examples, which seemed to render any inquiries regarding its intelligibility quite needless. Every geometrical proposition—a triangle has three angles—it was said, is absolutely necessary; and thus people talked of an object which lay out of the sphere of our understanding as if it

were perfectly plain what the conception of such a being meant.

All the examples adduced have been drawn, without exception, from *judgments*, and not from *things*. But the unconditioned necessity of a judgment does not form the absolute necessity of a thing. On the contrary, the absolute necessity of a judgment is only a conditioned necessity of a thing, or of the predicate in a judgment. The proposition above-mentioned, does not enounce that three angles necessarily exist, but, upon condition that a triangle exists, three angles must necessarily exist—in it. And thus this logical necessity has been the source of the greatest delusions. Having formed an a priori conception of a thing, the content of which was made to embrace existence, we believed ourselves safe in concluding that, because existence belongs necessarily to the object of the conception (that is, under the condition of my positing this thing as given), the existence of the thing is also posited necessarily, and that it is therefore absolutely necessary—merely because its existence has been cogitated in the conception.

If, in an identical judgment, I annihilate the predicate in thought, and retain the subject, a contradiction is the result; and hence I say, the former belongs necessarily to the latter. But if I suppress both subject and predicate in thought, no contradiction arises; for there is *nothing* at all, and therefore no means of forming a contradiction. To suppose the existence of a triangle and not that of its three angles, is self-contradictory; but to suppose the nonexistence of both triangle and angles is perfectly admissible. And so is it with the conception of an absolutely necessary being. Annihilate its existence in thought, and you annihilate the thing itself with all its predicates; how then can there be any room for contradiction? Externally, there is nothing to give rise to a contradiction, for a thing cannot be necessary externally; nor internally, for, by the annihilation or suppression of the thing itself, its internal properties are also annihilated. God is omnipotent—that is a necessary judgment. His omnipotence cannot be denied, if the existence of a Deity is posited—the existence, that is, of an infinite being, the two conceptions being identical. But when you say, *God does not exist*, neither omnipotence nor any other predicate is affirmed; they must all disappear with the subject, and in this judgment there cannot exist the least self-contradiction.

You have thus seen, that when the predicate of a judgment is annihilated in thought along with the subject, no internal contradiction can arise, be the predicate what it may. There is no possibility of evading the conclusion—you find yourselves compelled to declare: There are certain subjects which cannot be annihilated in thought. But this is nothing more than saying: There exist subjects which are absolutely necessary— the very hypothesis which you are called upon to establish. For I find myself unable to form the slightest conception of a thing which, when annihilated in thought with all its predicates, leaves behind a contradiction; and contradiction is the only criterion of impossibility, in the sphere of pure a priori conceptions.

Against these general considerations, the justice of which no one can dispute, one argument is adduced, which is regarded as furnishing a satisfactory demonstration from the fact. It is affirmed, that there is one and only one conception, in which the nonbeing or annihilation of the object is self-contradictory, and this is the conception of an *ens realissimum*.[1] It possesses, you say, all reality, and you feel yourselves justified in admitting the possibility of such a thing. (This I am willing to grant for the present, although the existence of a conception which is not self-contradictory, is far from being sufficient to prove the possibility of an object.[2]) Now the notion of all reality embraces in it that of existence; the notion of existence lies, therefore, in the conception of this possible thing. If this thing is

annihilated in thought, the internal possibility of the thing is also annihilated, which is self-contradictory.

I answer: It is absurd to introduce—under whatever term disguised—into the conception of a thing, which is to be cogitated solely in reference to its possibility, the conception of its existence. If this is admitted, you will have apparently gained the day, but in reality have enounced nothing but a mere tautology. I ask, is the proposition, *this or that thing* (which I am admitting to be possible) *exists*, an analytical or a synthetical proposition? If the former, there is no addition made to the subject of your thought by the affirmation of its existence; but then the conception in your minds is identical with the thing itself, or you have supposed the existence of a thing to be possible, and then inferred its existence from its internal possibility—which is but a miserable tautology. The word *reality* in the conception of the thing, and the word *existence* in the conception of the predicate, will not help you out of the difficulty. For, supposing you were to term all positing of a thing, reality, you have thereby posited the thing with all its predicates in the conception of the subject and assumed its actual existence, and this you merely repeat in the predicate. But if you confess, as every reasonable person must, that every existential proposition is synthetical, how can it be maintained that the predicate of existence cannot be denied without contradiction—a property which is the characteristic of analytical propositions, alone.

I should have a reasonable hope of putting an end forever to this sophistical mode of argumentation, by a strict definition of the conception of existence, did not my own experience teach me that the illusion arising from our confounding a logical with a real predicate (a predicate which aids in the determination of a thing) resists almost all the endeavors of explanation and illustration. A *logical predicate* may be what you please, even the subject may be predicated of itself; for logic pays no regard to the content of a judgment. But the determination of a conception is a predicate, which adds to and enlarges the conception. It must not, therefore, be contained in the conception.

Being is evidently not a real predicate, that is, a conception of something which is added to the conception of some other thing. It is merely the positing of a thing, or of certain determinations in it. Logically, it is merely the copula of a judgment. The proposition, *God is omnipotent*, contains two conceptions, which

---

[1] Latin: "most real being."

[2] A conception is always possible, if it is not self-contradictory. This is the logical criterion of possibility, distinguishing the object of such a conception from the *nihil negativum*. But it may be, notwithstanding, an empty conception, unless the objective reality of this synthesis, by which it is generated, is demonstrated; and a proof of this kind must be based upon principles of possible experience, and not upon the principle of analysis or contradiction. This remark may be serviceable as a warning against concluding, from the possibility of a conception—which is logical, the possibility of a thing— which is real.

"ANSELM BEGS THE QUESTION" ✳ *William Rowe*

What we have just seen is that introducing *existing* or *nonexisting* into the definition of a concept has a very important implication. If we introduce *existing* into the definition of a concept, it follows that no nonexisting thing can exemplify that concept. And if we introduce *nonexisting* into the definition of a concept, it follows that no existing thing can exemplify that concept. No nonexisting thing can be a *magican* and no existing thing can be a *magico*.

But must some existing thing exemplify the concept *magican*? No! From the fact that *existing* is included in the definition of *magican* it does not follow that some existing thing is a *magican*—all that follows is that no nonexisting thing is a *magican*. If there were no magicians in existence there would be nothing to which the term *magican* would apply. This being so, it clearly does not follow merely from our definition of *magican* that some existing thing is a *maigican*. Only if magicians exist will it be true that some existing thing is a *magican*.

We are now in a position to help our friend see that, from the mere fact that God is defined as an existing, wholly perfect being, it will not follow that some existing being is God. Something of interest does follow from his definition: namely, that no nonexisting being can be God. But whether some existing thing is God will depend entirely on whether some existing thing is a wholly perfect being. If no wholly perfect being exists there will be nothing to which this concept of God can apply. This being so, it clearly does not follow merely from this definition of *God* that some existing thing is God. Only if a wholly perfect being exists will it be true that God, as our friend conceives of him, exists . . .

Our final critique of Anselm's argument is simply this. In granting that Anselm's God is a possible thing, we are in fact granting that Anselm's God actually exists. But since the purpose of the argument is to prove to use that Anselm's God exists, we cannot be asked to grant as a premise a statement which is virtually equivalent to the conclusion that is to be proved.

From William Rowe, *Philosophy of Religion* (1993).

have a certain object or content; the word *is*, is no additional predicate—it merely indicates the relation of the predicate to the subject. Now, if I take the subject (God) with all its predicates (omnipotence being one), and say, *God is*, or *There is a God*, I add no new predicate to the conception of God, I merely posit or affirm the existence of the subject with all its predicates—I posit the *object* in relation to my *conception*. The content of both is the same; and there is no addition made to the conception, which expresses merely the possibility of the object, by my cogitating the object—in the expression, it *is*—as absolutely given or existing. Thus the real contains no more than the possible. A hundred real dollars contain no more than a hundred possible dollars. For, as the latter indicate the conception, and the former the object, on the supposition that the content of the former was greater than that of the latter, my conception would not be an expression of the whole object, and would consequently be an inadequate conception of it. But in reckoning my wealth there may be said to be more in a hundred real dollars, than in a hundred possible dollars—that is, in the mere conception of them. For the real object—the dollars—is not analytically contained in my conception, but forms a synthetical addition to my conception (which is merely a determination of my mental state), although this objective reality—this existence—apart from my conception, does not in the least degree increase the aforesaid hundred dollars.

It does not matter which predicates or how many of them we may think a thing possesses, I do not make the least addition to it when we further declare that this thing exists. Otherwise, it would not be the exact same thing that exists, but something more than we had thought in the idea or concept; and hence, we could not say that the exact object of my thought

"EXISTENCE IS A PREDICATE" ✳ *Stephen Davis*

Let us return to the examples given by Kant and Malcolm. Kant knew, of course, that there is a difference between a real hundred thalers and the mere concept of them, but his point appears to be that the content of the two *concepts* must be identical. And it is obviously correct to claim that the two concepts do not differ in *number of thalers*. If the real hundred thalers contained a hundred thalers and the idea of them contained only ninety-nine, the one would not be the idea of the other. Fair enough. But that does not show that the concepts cannot differ in other ways. And surely they do.

Of the real hundred thalers, my concept of them includes the property of having-purchasing-power-in-the-real-world. My concept of the concept of a hundred thalers does not have that property.

Contrary to his linguistic intuitions, I think there are contexts in which Malcolm's sentence "My house will be a better house if it exists than if it does not" can make perfect sense. But then what about Malcolm's claim that "any person who satisfied A's description [of the most perfect chancellor] would *necessarily* satisfy B's description and *vice versa*? This does not appear to be true. There might be a character in a Dostoyevsky novel who satisfies all the attributes on B's list (knowledge, wit, resolution, etc.) but who, since he does not exist *in re*, fails to satisfy all the attributes on A's list (since "A included existence in his list of attributes"). Somebody who is dead—Charles De Gaulle, for instance—might satisfy all the requirements in B's list but not those in A's list. Accordingly, Malcolm is wrong—the lists *do* differ, and "exists" can be a real predicate.

If I am right, Kant's argument does not refute the . . . [ontological argument].

From Stephen Davis, God, Reason, and Theistic Proofs (1997).

exists. On the contrary, it exists with the same defect with which I have thought it, since otherwise what exists would be something different from what I thought. So when I think of a being as the highest reality, without any imperfection, the question still remains whether or not this being exists. For although, in my idea, nothing may be lacking in the possible real content of a thing in general, something is still lacking in its relation to my mental state; that is, I am ignorant of whether the object is also possible a posteriori. It is here we discover the core of our problem. If the question regarded an object of sense merely, it would be impossible for me to confuse the idea of a thing with its existence. For the concept of the object merely enables me to think of it according to universal conditions of experience; while the existence of the object permits me to think of it within the context of actual experience. However, in being connected with the content of experience as a whole, the concept of the object is not enlarged. All that has happened is that our thought has thereby acquired another possible perception. So it is not surprising that, if we attempt to think existence through the pure categories alone, we cannot specify a single mark distinguishing it from mere possibility.

Whatever be the content of our conception of an object, it is necessary to go beyond it, if we wish to predicate existence of an object. In the case of sensuous objects, this is attained by their connection according to empirical laws with some one of my perceptions; but when it comes to objects of pure thought, there is no means whatever of knowing of their existence, since it would have to be known in a completely a priori manner. But all our knowledge of existence (be it immediately by perception or by inferences connecting some object with a perception) belongs entirely to the sphere of experience—which is in perfect unity with itself—and although an existence out of this sphere cannot be absolutely declared to be impossible, it is a hypothesis the truth of which we have no means of discovering.

The idea of a supreme being is in many ways a very useful idea; but for the very reason that it is an idea, it is incapable of enlarging our knowledge with regard to the existence of things. It is not even sufficient to instruct us as to the possibility of a being which we do not know to exist. The analytical criterion of possibility, which consists in the absence of contradiction in propositions, cannot be denied it. But the connection of real properties in a thing is a synthesis of the possibility of which an a priori judgment cannot be formed, because these realities are not presented to us specifically; and even if this were to happen, a judgment would still be impossible, because the criterion of possibility of synthetical cognitions must be sought for in the world of experience, to which the object of an idea cannot belong. And thus the celebrated Leibniz has utterly failed in his attempt to establish upon a priori grounds the possibility of this sublime ideal being.

The celebrated ontological or Cartesian argument for the existence of a Supreme Being is therefore insufficient; and we may as well hope to increase our stock of knowledge by the aid of mere ideas, as the merchant to increase his wealth by adding a few zeros to his bank account.

QUESTIONS FOR FURTHER REFLECTION

1. Explain the difference between a predicate and a property.
2. Is Kant right when he claims there is no difference between 100 real dollars and 100 possible dollars?
3. Kant accuses proponents of the ontological argument of defining God into existence. They simply add the predicate existence or being to the list of things predicated of God. Is this what Anselm does? How could Anselm respond to this criticism?
4. What do you think that Kant means when he says that the idea of an absolutely necessary being, "serves merely to indicate a certain unattainable perfection."

9. ANSELM'S ONTOLOGICAL ARGUMENTS

Norman Malcom

Norman Malcolm (1911–1990) was a student and close friend of the philosopher Ludwig Wittgenstein, about whom he wrote a memoir (1958). Malcolm taught philosophy at Cornell University. He wrote on topics ranging from Wittgenstein and epistemology to medieval philosophy and the philosophy of religion. In this essay, he argues that there are actually two ontological arguments in Anselm's *Proslogion*. Philosophers have criticized the first one for relying on the notion that existence is a predicate. Malcolm argues that even if this criticism is right, it does not detract from the second argument, which depends instead on the notion that *necessary existence* is a predicate.

READING QUESTIONS

1. Why does Malcolm think Anselm believes that whatever is understood is in the understanding?
2. What doctrine underlies Anselm's view that what is something that exists both in the understanding and in reality is greater than something that exists in the understanding alone?
3. What two analogies does Malcolm offer against the view that existence is a real predicate?
4. About which "great making property" is Anselm concerned in his first argument? In his second?
5. What is J. N. Finlay's argument supposed to show?

I believe that in Anselm's *Proslogion* and *Responsio editoris* there are two different pieces of reasoning which he did not distinguish from one another, and that a good deal of light may be shed on the philosophical problem of "the ontological argument" if we do distinguish them. In Chapter 2 of the *Proslogion*[1] Anselm says that we believe that God is *something a greater than which cannot be conceived*. (The Latin is *aliquid quo nihil maius cogitari possit*. Anselm sometimes uses the alternative expressions *aliquid quo maius nihil cogitari potest*, *id quo maius cogitari nequit*, *aliquid quo maius cogitari non valet*.) Even the fool of the Psalm who says in his heart there is no God, when he hears this very thing that Anselm says, namely, "something a greater than which cannot be conceived," understands what he hears, and what he understands is in his understanding though he does not understand that it exists.

Apparently Anselm regards it as tautological to say that whatever is understood is in the understanding (*quidquid intelligitur in intellectu est*): he uses *intelligitur* and *in intellectu est* as interchangeable locutions. The same holds for another formula of his: whatever is thought is in thought (*quidquid cogitatur in cogitatione est*).[2]

Of course many things may exist in the understanding that do not exist in reality; for example, elves. Now, says Anselm, something a greater than which cannot be conceived exists in the understanding. But it cannot exist *only* in the understanding, for to exist in reality is greater. Therefore that thing a greater than which cannot be conceived cannot exist only in the understanding, for then a greater thing could be conceived: namely, one that exists both in the understanding and in reality.[3]

Here I have a question. It is not clear to me whether Anselm means that (a) existence in reality by itself is greater than existence in the understanding, or that (b) existence in reality and existence in the understanding together are greater than existence in the understanding alone. Certainly he accepts (b). But he might also accept (a), as Descartes apparently does in *Meditation III* when he suggests that the mode of being by which a thing is "objectively in the understanding" is *imperfect*.[4] Of course Anselm might accept both (a) and (b). He might hold that in general something is greater if it has both of these "modes of existence" than if it has either one alone, but also that existence in reality is a more perfect mode of existence than existence in the understanding.

In any case, Anselm holds that something is greater if it exists both in the understanding and in reality than if it exists merely in the understanding. An equivalent way of putting this interesting proposition, in a more current terminology, is: something is greater if it is both conceived of and exists than if it is merely conceived of. Anselm's reasoning can be expressed as follows: *id quo maius cogitari neguit* cannot be merely conceived of and not exist, for then it would not be *id quo maius cogitari neguit*. The doctrine that something is greater if it exists in addition to being conceived of, than if it is only conceived of, could be called the doctrine that *existence is a perfection*. Descartes maintained, in so many words, that existence is a perfection,[5] and presumably he was holding Anselm's doctrine, although he does not, in *Meditation V* or elsewhere, argue in the way that Anselm does in *Proslogion 2*.

When Anselm says, "And certainly, that than which nothing greater can be conceived cannot exist merely in the understanding. For suppose it exists merely in the understanding, then it can be conceived to exist in reality, which is greater,"[6] he is claiming that if I conceived of a being of great excellence, that being would be *greater* (more excellent, more perfect) if it existed than if it did not exist. His supposition that "it exists merely in the understanding" is the supposition that it is conceived of but does not exist. Anselm repeated this claim in his reply to the criticism of the

---

[1] I have consulted the Latin text of the *Proslogion*, of *Gaunilonis pro Insipiente*, and of the *Responsio editoris*, in S. Anselmi. *Opera Omnia*, edited by F. C. Schmitt (Secovii, 1938), vol. I. With numerous modifications, I have used the English translation by S. N. Deane: *St. Anselm* (LaSalle, Illinois, 1948).

[2] See *Proslogion 1* and *Responsio 2*.

[3] Anselm's actual words are: "Et certe id quo maius cogitari nequit, non potest esse in solo intellectu. Si enim vel in solo intellectu est, potest cogitari esse et in re, quo maius est. Si ergo id quo maius cogitari non potest, est in solo intellectu: id ipsum quo maius cogitari non potest, est quo maius cogitari potest. Sed certe hoc esse non potest." *Proslogion 2*.

[4] Haldane and Ross. *The Philosophical Works of Descartes*, 2 vols. (Cambridge, 1931). I. 163.

[5] *Op. cit.*, p. 182.

[6] *Proslogion 2*: Deane, p. 8.

monk Gaunilo. Speaking of the being a greater than which cannot be conceived, he says:

> I have said that if it exists merely in the understanding it can be conceived to exist in reality, which is greater. Therefore, if it exists merely in the understanding obviously the very being a greater than which cannot be conceived, is one a greater than which can be conceived. What, I ask, can follow better than that? For if it exists merely in the understanding, can it not be conceived to exist in reality? And if it can be so conceived does not he who conceives of this conceive a thing greater than it, if it does exist merely in the understanding? Can anything follow better than this: that if a being a greater than which cannot be conceived exists merely in the understanding, it is something a greater than which can be conceived? What could be plainer?[7]

He is implying, in the first sentence, that if I conceive of something which does not exist then it is possible for it to exist, and *it will be greater if it exists than if it does not exist.*

The doctrine that existence is a perfection is remarkably queer. It makes sense and is true to say that my future house will be a better one if it is insulated than if it is not insulated; but what could it mean to say that it will be a better house if it exists than if it does not? My future child will be a better man if he is honest than if he is not; but who would understand the saying that he will be a better man if he exists than if he does not? Or who understands the saying that if God exists He is more perfect than if He does not exist? One might say, with some intelligibility, that it would be better (for oneself or for mankind) if God exists than if He does not—but that is a different matter.

A king might desire that his next chancellor should have knowledge, wit, and resolution; but it is ludicrous to add that the king's desire is to have a chancellor who exists. Suppose that two royal councilors, A and B, were asked to draw up separately descriptions of the most perfect chancellor they could conceive, and that the descriptions they produced were identical except that A included existence in his list of attributes

of a perfect chancellor and B did not. (I do not mean that B put nonexistence in his list.) One and the same person could satisfy both descriptions. More to the point, any person who satisfied A's description would *necessarily* satisfy B's description and *vice versa!* This is to say that A and B did not produce descriptions that differed in any way but rather one and the same description of necessary and desirable qualities in a chancellor. A only made a show of putting down a desirable quality that B had failed to include.

I believe I am merely restating an observation that Kant made in attacking the notion that "existence" or "being" is a "real predicate." He says:

> By whatever and by however many predicates we may think a thing—even if we completely determine it—we do not make the least addition to the thing when we further declare that this thing *is.* Otherwise, it would not be exactly the same thing that exists, but something more than we had thought in the concept; and we could not, therefore, say that the exact object of my concept exists.[8]

Anselm's ontological proof of *Proslogion* 2 is fallacious because it rests on the false doctrine that existence is a perfection (and therefore that "existence" is a "real predicate"). It would be desirable to have a rigorous refutation of the doctrine but I have not been able to provide one. I am compelled to leave the matter at the more or less intuitive level of Kant's observation. In any case, I believe that the doctrine does not belong to Anselm's other formulation of the ontological argument. It is worth noting that Gassendi anticipated Kant's criticism when he said, against Descartes:

> Existence is a perfection neither in God nor in anything else; it is rather that in the absence of which there is no perfection. . . . Hence neither is existence held to exist in a thing in the way that perfections do, nor if the thing lacks existence is it said to be imperfect (or deprived of a perfection), so much as to be nothing.[9]

---

[7]*Responsio* 2: Deane, pp. 157–58.

[8]*The Critique of Pure Reason.* tr. by Norman Kemp Smith (London, 1929), p. 505.

[9]Haldane and Ross, II, 186.

I take up now the consideration of the second ontological proof, which Anselm presents in the very next chapter of the *Proslogion*. (There is no evidence that he thought of himself as offering two different proofs.) Speaking of the being a greater than which cannot be conceived, he says:

> And it so truly exists that it cannot be conceived not to exist. For it is possible to conceive of a being which cannot be conceived not to exist; and this is greater than one which can be conceived not to exist. Hence, if that, than which nothing greater can be conceived, can be conceived not to exist, it is not that than which nothing greater can be conceived. But this is a contradiction. So truly, therefore, is there something than which nothing greater can be conceived, that it cannot even be conceived not to exist. And this being thou art, O Lord, our God.[10]

Anselm is saying two things: first, that a being whose nonexistence is logically impossible is "greater" than a being whose nonexistence is logically possible (and therefore that a being a greater than which cannot be conceived must be one whose nonexistence is logically impossible); second, that *God* is a being than which a greater cannot be conceived.

In regard to the second of these assertions, there certainly is *a* use of the word "God," and I think far the more common use, in accordance with which the statements "God is the greatest of all beings," "God is the most perfect being," "God is the supreme being," are *logically* necessary truths, in the same sense that the statement "A square has four sides" is a logically necessary truth. If there is a man named "Jones" who is the tallest man in the world, the statement "Jones is the tallest man in the world" is merely true and is not a logically necessary truth. It is a virtue of Anselm's unusual phrase, "a being a greater than which cannot be conceived,"[11] to make it explicit that the sentence "God is the greatest of all beings" expresses a logically

necessary truth and not a mere matter of fact such as the one we imagined about Jones.

With regard to Anselm's first assertion (namely, that a being whose nonexistence is logically impossible is greater than a being whose nonexistence is logically possible) perhaps the most puzzling thing about it is the use of the word "greater." It appears to mean exactly the same as "superior," "more excellent," "more perfect." This equivalence by itself is of no help to us, however, since the latter expressions would be equally puzzling here. What is required is some explanation of their use.

We do think of *knowledge*, say, as an excellence, a good thing. If A has more knowledge of algebra than B we express this in common language by saying that A has a *better* knowledge of algebra than B, or that A's knowledge of algebra is *superior* to B's, whereas we should not say that B has a better or superior *ignorance* of algebra than A. We do say "greater ignorance," but here the word "greater" is used purely quantitatively.

Previously I rejected *existence* as a perfection. Anselm is maintaining in the remarks last quoted, not that existence is a perfection, but that *the logical impossibility of nonexistence is a perfection*. In other words, *necessary existence* is a perfection. His first ontological proof uses the principle that a thing is greater if it exists than if it does not exist. His second proof employs the different principle that a thing is greater if it necessarily exists than if it does not necessarily exist.

Some remarks about the notion of *dependence* may help to make this latter principle intelligible. Many things depend for their existence on other things and events. My house was built by a carpenter: its coming into existence was dependent on a certain creative activity. Its continued existence is dependent on many things: that a tree does not crush it, that it is not consumed by fire, and so on. If we reflect on the common meaning of the word "God" (no matter how vague and confused this is), we realize that it is incompatible with this meaning that God's existence should *depend* on anything. Whether we believe in Him or not we must admit that the "almighty and everlasting God" (as several ancient prayers begin), the "Maker of heaven and earth, and of all things visible and invisible" (as is said in the Nicene Creed), cannot be thought of as being brought into existence by anything or as depending for His continued existence on anything. To conceive of

---

[10]*Proslogion* 3; Deane, pp. 8–9.

[11]Professor Robert Calhoun has pointed out to me that a similar locution had been used by Augustine. In *De moribus, Manichaeorum* (Bk. II, ch. xi. sec. 24), he says that God is a being *quo esse aut cogitari melius nihil possit* (*Patrologiae Patrum Latinorum* ed. by J. P. Migne, Paris, 1841–1845, vol. 32: *Augustinus.* vol. 1).

"THE HARTSHORNE-MALCOLM VERSION OF THE ONTOLOGICAL ARGUMENT" * *Alvin Plantinga*

But of course there are many other versions of the argument. (And I wish to remark parenthetically that the existence of many importantly different versions makes most of the "refutations" one finds in textbooks look pretty silly.) Professors Charles Hartshorne and Norman Malcolm, for example, find two quite distinct versions of the argument in St. Anselm's writings. In the first of these St. Anselm holds that *existence* is a perfection; he holds some version of the view that a being is greater in a world in which it exists than it is in a world in which it does not. But in the second version, say Malcolm and Hartshorne, it is *necessary* existence that is said to be a perfection. What does *that* mean? Take a world like α and consider two things, A and B that exist in it, where A exists not only in α but in every other world as well while B exists in some but not all worlds. According to the doctrine under consideration, A is so far forth greater in α than B is. Of course B may have some other properties—properties that make for greatness—that A lacks. It may be that on balance it is B that is greater in α. For example, the number 7 exists necessarily and Socrates

does not; but it would be peculiar indeed to conclude that the number seven is therefore greater, in α, than Socrates is. The point is only that necessary existence is a great-making quality—it is one of the qualities that must be considered in comparing a pair of beings with respect to greatness. But then it is plausible to suppose that the maximum degree of greatness includes necessary existence—that is to say, a possible being has the maximum degree of greatness in a given world only if it exists in that world and furthermore exists in every other world as well. . . what this argument shows is that if it is even *possible* that God, so conceived exists, then it is true that he does and, indeed, necessarily true that he does. As it is stated, however, there is one fairly impressive flaw: even if an essence entailing *is maximally great in W* is exemplified, it does not so far follow that this essence entails *is maximally great in α*. For all we have shown so far, this being might be at a maximum in some world W, but be pretty insignificant in α, our world.

From Alvin Plantinga, *The Nature of Necessity* (1974).

anything as dependent upon something else for its existence is to conceive of it as a lesser being than God.

If a housewife has a set of extremely fragile dishes, then as dishes they are *inferior* to those of another set like them in all respects except that they are *not* fragile. Those of the first set are *dependent* for their continued existence on gentle handling; those of the second set are not. There is a definite connection in common language between the notions of dependency and inferiority, and independence and superiority. To say that something which was dependent on nothing whatever was superior to ("greater than") anything that was dependent in any way upon anything is quite in keeping with the everyday use of the terms "superior" and "greater." Correlative with the notions of dependence and independence are the notions of *limited* and

unlimited. An engine requires fuel and this is a limitation. It is the same thing to say that an engine's operation is *dependent* on as that it is *limited* by its fuel supply. An engine that could accomplish the same work in the same time and was in other respects satisfactory, but did not require fuel, would be a *superior* engine.

God is usually conceived of as an *unlimited* being. He is conceived of as a being who *could not* be limited, that is, as an absolutely unlimited being. This is no less than to conceive of Him as *something a greater than which cannot be conceived*. If God is conceived to be an absolutely unlimited being He must be conceived to be unlimited in regard to His existence as well as His operation. In this conception it will not make sense to say that He depends on anything for coming into or continuing in existence. Nor, as Spinoza observed, will it make sense to say that something could *prevent* Him from existing.[12] Lack of moisture can prevent trees from existing in a certain region of the earth. But it would be contrary to the concept of God as an unlimited being to suppose that anything other than God Himself could prevent Him from existing, and it would be self-contradictory to suppose that He Himself could do it.

Some may be inclined to object that although nothing could prevent God's existence, still it might just *happen* that He did not exist. And if He did exist that too would be by chance. I think, however, that from the supposition that it could happen that God did not exist it would follow that, if He existed, He would have mere duration and not eternity. It would make sense to ask, "How long has He existed?," "Will He still exist next week?," "He was in existence yesterday but how about today?" and so on. It seems absurd to make God the subject of such questions. According to our ordinary conception of Him. He is an eternal being. And eternity does not mean endless duration, as Spinoza noted. To ascribe eternity to something is to exclude as senseless all sentences that imply that it has duration. If a thing has duration then it would be merely a *contingent* fact, if it was a fact, that its duration was endless. The moon could have endless duration but not eternity. If something has endless duration it will *make sense* (although it will be false) to say that it will cease to exist, and it will make sense (although it will be false) to say that something will *cause* it to cease to exist. A being with endless duration is not, therefore, an absolutely unlimited being. That God is conceived to be eternal follows from the fact that He is conceived to be an absolutely unlimited being.

I have been trying to expand the argument of *Proslogion 3.* In *Responsio 1* Anselm adds the following acute point: if you can conceive of a certain thing and this thing does not exist then if it *were* to exist its nonexistence would be *possible.* It follows, I believe, that if the thing were to exist it would depend on other things both for coming into and continuing in existence, and also that it would have duration and not eternity. Therefore it would not be, either in reality or in conception, an unlimited being, *aliquid quo nihil maius cogitari possit.*

Anselm states his argument as follows:

> If it [the thing a greater than which cannot be conceived] can be conceived at all it must exist. For no one who denies or doubts the existence of a being a greater than which is inconceivable, denies or doubts that if it did exist its nonexistence, either in reality or in the understanding, would be impossible. For otherwise it would not be a being a greater than which cannot be conceived. But as to whatever can be conceived but does not exist: if it were to exist its nonexistence either in reality or in the understanding would be possible. Therefore, if a being a greater than which cannot be conceived, can even be conceived, it must exist.[13]

What Anselm has proved is that the notion of contingent existence or of contingent nonexistence cannot have any application to God. His existence must either be logically necessary or logically impossible. The only intelligible way of rejecting Anselm's claim that God's existence is necessary is to maintain that the concept of God, as a being a greater than which cannot be conceived, is self-contradictory or nonsensical.[14] Supposing that this is false, Anselm is right to deduce God's necessary existence from his characterization of Him as a being a greater than which cannot be conceived.

Let me summarize the proof. If God, a being a greater than which cannot be conceived, does not exist then He cannot *come* into existence. For if He did He would either have been *caused* to come into existence or have *happened* to come into existence, and in either case He would be a limited being, which by our conception of Him He is not. Since He cannot come into existence, if He does not exist His existence is

---

[12]*Ethics,* pt. I, prop. 11.

[13]*Responsio* 1: Deane. pp. 154–55.

[14]Gaunilo attacked Anselm's argument on this very point. He would not concede that a being a greater than which cannot be conceived existed in his understanding (*Gaunilonis pro Insipiente,* secs. 4 and 5; Deane. pp. 148–50). Anselm's reply is: "I call on your faith and conscience to attest that this is most false" (*Responsio* 1; Deane, p. 154). Gaunilo's faith and conscience will attest that it is false that "God is not a being a greater than which is inconceivable," and false that "He is not understood (*intelligitur*) or conceived (*cogitatur*)" (*ibid.*). Descartes also remarks that one would go to "strange extremes" who denied that we understand the words "*that thing which is the most perfect that we can conceive*; for that is what all men call God" (Haldane and Ross. II, 129).

impossible. If He does exist He cannot have come into existence (for the reasons given), nor can He cease to exist, for nothing could cause Him to cease to exist nor could it just happen that He ceased to exist. So if God exists His existence is necessary. Thus God's existence is either impossible or necessary. It can be the former only if the concept of such a being is self-contradictory or in some way logically absurd. Assuming that this is not so, it follows that He necessarily exists.

It may be helpful to express ourselves in the following way: to say, not that *omnipotence* is a property of God, but rather that *necessary omnipotence* is: and to say, not that omniscience is a property of God, but rather that *necessary omniscience* is. We have criteria for determining that a man knows this and that and can do this and that, and for determining that one man has greater knowledge and abilities in a certain subject than another. We could think of various tests to give them. But there is nothing we should wish to describe, seriously and literally, as "testing" God's knowledge and powers. That God is omniscient and omnipotent has not been determined by the application of criteria: rather these are requirements of our conception of Him. They are internal properties of the concept, although they are also rightly said to be properties of God. *Necessary existence* is a property of God in the *same sense* that *necessary omnipotence* and *necessary omniscience* are His properties. And we are not to think that "God necessarily exists" means that it follows necessarily from something that God exists *contingently*. The a priori proposition "God necessarily exists" entails the proposition "God exists," if and only if the latter also is understood as an a priori proposition: in which case the two propositions are equivalent. In this sense Anselm's proof is a proof of God's existence.

Descartes was somewhat hazy on the question of whether existence is a property of things that exist, but at the same time he saw clearly enough that *necessary existence* is a property of God. Both points are illustrated in his reply to Gassendi's remark, which I quoted above:

I do not see to what class of reality you wish to assign existence, nor do I see why it may not be said to be a property as well as omnipotence,

taking the word property as equivalent to any attribute or anything which can be predicated of a thing, as in the present case it should be by all means regarded. Nay, necessary existence in the case of God is also a true property in the strictest sense of the word, because it belongs to Him and forms part of His essence alone.[15]

Elsewhere he speaks of "the necessity of existence" as being "that crown of perfections without which we cannot comprehend God."[16] He is emphatic on the point that necessary existence applies solely to "an absolutely perfect Being."[17]

I wish to consider now a part of Kant's criticism of the ontological argument which I believe to be wrong. He says:

If, in an identical proposition. I reject the predicate while retaining the subject, contradiction results; and I therefore say that the former belongs necessarily to the latter. But if we reject subject and predicate alike, there is no contradiction; for nothing is then left that can be contradicted. To posit a triangle, and yet to reject three angles, is self-contradictory; but there is no contradiction in rejecting the triangle together with its three angles. The same holds true of the concept of an absolutely necessary being. If its existence is rejected, we reject the thing itself with all its predicates and no question of contradiction can then arise. There is nothing outside it that would then be contradicted, since the necessity of the thing is not supposed to be derived from anything external: nor is there anything internal that would be contradicted, since in rejecting the thing itself we have at the same time rejected all its internal properties. "God is omnipotent" is a necessary judgment. The omnipotence cannot be rejected if we posit a Deity, that is, an infinite being; for the two concepts are identical. But if we say, "There is no God," neither the omnipotence nor any other of its predicates is given: they are one and all rejected

---

[15]Haldane and Ross. II, 228.
[16]*Ibid*., I, 445.
[17]E.g., *ibid*., Principle 15, p. 225.

together with the subject, and there is therefore not the least contradiction in such a judgment.[18]

To these remarks the reply is that when the concept of God is correctly understood one sees that one cannot "reject the subject." "There is no God" is seen to be a necessarily false statement. Anselm's demonstration proves that the proposition "God exists" has the same a priori footing as the proposition "God is omnipotent."

Many present-day philosophers, in agreement with Kant, declare that existence is not a property and think that this overthrows the ontological argument. Although it is an error to regard existence as a property of things that have contingent existence, it does not follow that it is an error to regard necessary existence as a property of God. A recent writer says, against Anselm, that a proof of God's existence "based on the necessities of thought" is "universally regarded as fallacious: it is not thought possible to build bridges between mere abstractions and concrete existence."[19] But this way of putting the matter obscures the distinction we need to make. Does "concrete existence" mean contingent existence? Then to build bridges between concrete existence and mere abstractions would be like inferring the existence of an island from the concept of a perfect island, which both Anselm and Descartes regarded as absurd. What Anselm did was to give a demonstration that the proposition "God necessarily exists" is entailed by the proposition "God is a being a greater than which cannot be conceived" (which is equivalent to "God is an absolutely unlimited being"). Kant declares that when "I think a being as the supreme reality, without any defect, the question still remains whether it exists or not."[20] But once one has grasped Anselm's proof of the necessary existence of a being a greater than which cannot be conceived, no question remains as to whether it exists or not, just as Euclid's demonstration of the existence of an infinity of prime numbers leaves no question on that issue.

Kant says that "every reasonable person" must admit that "all existential propositions are synthetic."[21] Part of the perplexity one has about the ontological argument is in deciding whether or not the proposition "God necessarily exists" is or is not an "existential proposition." But let us look around. Is the Euclidean theorem in number theory, "There exists an infinite number of prime numbers," an "existential proposition"? Do we not want to say that in some sense it asserts the existence of something? Cannot we say, with equal justification, that the proposition "God necessarily exists" asserts the existence of something, in some sense? What we need to understand, in each case, is the particular sense of the assertion. Neither proposition has the same sort of sense as do the propositions, "A low pressure area exists over the Great Lakes," "There still exists some possibility that he will survive," "The pain continues to exist in his abdomen." One good way of seeing the difference in sense of these various propositions is to see the variously different ways in which they are proved or supported. It is wrong to think that all assertions of existence have the same kind of meaning. There are as many kinds of existential propositions as there are kinds of subjects of discourse.

Closely related to Kant's view that all existential propositions are "synthetic" is the contemporary dogma that all existential propositions are contingent. Professor Gilbert Ryle tells us that "Any assertion of the existence of something, like any assertion of the occurrence of something, can be denied without logical absurdity."[22] "All existential statements are contingent," says Mr. I. M. Crombie.[23] Professor J. J. C. Smart remarks that "Existence is not a property" and then goes on to assert that "There can never be any logical contradiction in denying that God exists."[24] He declares that "The concept of a logically necessary being is a self-contradictory concept, like the concept of a round square. . . . No existential proposition can be logically necessary," he maintains, for "the truth of a logically necessary proposition depends only on our symbolism, or to put the same

[18]Op. cit., p. 502.
[19]J. N. Findlay, "Can God's Existence Be Disproved?" New Essays in Philosophical Theology," ed. by A. N. Flew and A. MacIntyre (London, 1955), p. 47.
[20]Op. cit., pp. 505–6.

[21]Ibid., p. 504.
[22]The Nature of Metaphysics, ed. by D. F. Pears (New York, 1957), p. 150.
[23]New Essays in Philosophical Theology, p. 114.
[24]Ibid., p. 34.

thing in another way, on the relationship of concepts" (p. 38). Professor K. E. M. Baier says, "It is no longer seriously in dispute that the notion of a logically necessary being is self-contradictory. Whatever can be conceived of as existing can equally be conceived of as not existing."[25] This is a repetition of Hume's assertion, "Whatever we conceive as existent, we can also conceive as nonexistent. There is no being, therefore, whose nonexistence implies a contradiction."[26]

Professor J. N. Findlay ingeniously constructs an ontological *disproof* of God's existence, based on a "modern" view of the nature of "necessity in propositions": the view, namely, that necessity in propositions "merely reflects our use of words, the arbitrary conventions of our language."[27] Findlay undertakes to characterize what he calls "religious attitude," and here there is a striking agreement between his observations and some of the things I have said in expounding Anselm's proof. Religious attitude, he says, presumes *superiority* in its object and superiority so great that the worshiper is in comparison as nothing. Religious attitude finds it "anomalous to worship anything *limited* in any thinkable manner. . . . And hence we are led on irresistibly to demand that our religious object should have an *unsurpassable* supremacy along all avenues, that it should tower *infinitely* above all other objects" (p. 51). We cannot help feeling that "the worthy object of our worship can never be a thing that merely *happens* to exist, nor one on which all other objects merely *happen* to depend. The true object of religious reverence must not be one, merely, to which no *actual* independent realities stand opposed: it must be one to which such opposition is totally *inconceivable*. . . . And not only must the existence of *other* things be unthinkable without him, but his own nonexistence must be wholly unthinkable in any circumstances" (p. 52). And now, says Findlay, when we add up these various requirements, what they entail is "not only that there isn't a God, but that the Divine Existence is either senseless or impossible" (p. 54). For on the one hand, "if God is to satisfy religious claims and needs, He must be a being in every way inescapable, One whose existence and whose pos-

session of certain excellences we cannot possibly conceive away." On the other hand, "modern views make it self-evidently absurd (if they don't make it ungrammatical) to speak of such a Being and attribute existence to Him. It was indeed an ill day for Anselm when he hit upon his famous proof. For on that day he not only laid bare something that is of the essence of an adequate religious object, but also something that entails its necessary nonexistence" (p. 55).

Now I am inclined to hold the "modern" view that logically necessary truth "merely reflects our use of words" (although I do not believe that the conventions of language are always *arbitrary*). But I confess that I am unable to see how that view is supposed to lead to the conclusion that "the Divine existence is either senseless or impossible." Findlay does not explain how this result comes about. Surely he cannot mean that this view entails that nothing can have necessary properties: for this would imply that mathematics is "senseless or impossible," which no one wants to hold. Trying to fill in the argument that is missing from his article, the most plausible conjecture I can make is the following: Findlay thinks that the view that logical necessity "reflects the use of words" implies, not that nothing has necessary properties, but that *existence* cannot be a necessary property of anything. That is to say, every proposition of the form "*x* exists," including the proposition "God exists," must be *contingent*.[28] At the same time, our concept of God requires that His existence be *necessary*, that is, that "God exists" be a necessary truth. Therefore, the modern view of necessity proves that what the concept of God requires *cannot* be fulfilled. It proves that God *cannot* exist.

The correct reply is that the view that logical necessity merely reflects the use of words cannot possibly have the implication that every existential proposition must be contingent. That view requires us to *look at* the use of words and not manufacture a priori theses about it. In the Ninetieth Psalm it is said: "Before the mountains were brought forth, or

---

[25]*The Meaning of Life* Inaugural Lecture. Canberra University College (Canberra, 1957), p. 8.
[26]*Dialogues Concerning Natural Religion*, pt. IX.
[27]Findlay, *op. cit.*, p. 154.

---

[28]The other philosophers I have just cited may be led to the opinion by the same thinking. Smart, for example, says that "the truth of a logically necessary proposition depends only on our symbolism, or to put the same thing in another way, on the relationship of concepts" (*supra*). This is very similar to saying that it "reflects our use of words."

ever thou hadst formed the earth and the world, even from everlasting to everlasting, thou art God." Here is expressed the idea of the necessary existence and eternity of God, an idea that is essential to the Jewish and Christian religions. In those complex systems of thought, those "language-games," God has the status of a necessary being. Who can doubt that? Here we must say with Wittgenstein. "This language-game is played!"[29] I believe we may rightly take the existence of those religious systems of thought in which God figures as a necessary being to be a disproof of the dogma, affirmed by Hume and others, that no existential proposition can be necessary.

Another way of criticizing the ontological argument is the following. "Granted that the concept of necessary existence follows from the concept of a being a greater than which cannot be conceived, this amounts to no more than granting the a priori truth of the *conditional* proposition. 'If such a being exists then it necessarily exists.' This proposition, however, does not entail the *existence* of *anything*, and one can deny its antecedent without contradiction." Kant, for example, compares the proposition (or "judgment," as he calls it) "A triangle has three angles" with the proposition "God is a necessary being." He allows that the former is "absolutely necessary" and goes on to say:

> The absolute necessity of the judgment is only a conditional necessity of the thing, or of the predicate in the judgment. The above proposition does not declare that three angles are absolutely necessary, but that, under the condition that there is a triangle (that is, that a triangle is given), three angles will necessarily be found in it.[30]

He is saying, quite correctly, that the proposition about triangles is equivalent to the conditional proposition, "If a triangle exists, it has three angles." He then makes the comment that there is no contradiction "in rejecting the triangle together with its three angles." He proceeds to draw the alleged parallel: "The same holds true of the concept of an absolutely necessary being. If its existence is rejected, we reject the thing itself with

all its predicates; and no question of contradiction can then arise."[31] The priest, Caterus, made the same objection to Descartes when he said:

> Though it be conceded that an entity of the highest perfection implies its existence by its very name, yet it does not follow that that very existence is anything actual in the real world, but merely that the concept of existence is inseparably united with the concept of highest being. Hence you cannot infer that the existence of God is anything actual, unless you assume that that highest being actually exists; for then it will actually contain all its perfections, together with this perfection of real existence.[32]

I think that Caterus, Kant, and numerous other philosophers have been mistaken in supposing that the proposition "God is a necessary being" (or "God necessarily exists") is equivalent to the conditional proposition "If God exists then He necessarily exists."[33] For

[29]*Philosophical Investigations* (New York, 1953), sec. 654.
[30]*Op. cit.*, pp. 501–2.
[31]*Ibid.*, p. 502.
[32]Haldane and Ross, II. 7.
[33]I have heard it said by more than one person in discussion that Kant's view was that it is really a misuse of language to speak of a "necessary being," on the grounds that necessity is properly predicated only of propositions (judgments) not of *things*. This is not a correct account of Kant. (See his discussion of "The Postulates of Empirical Thought in General," *op. cit.*, pp. 239–56. esp. p. 239 and pp. 247–48.) But if he had held this, as perhaps the above philosophers think he should have, then presumably his view would not have been that the pseudo-proposition "God is a necessary being" is equivalent to the conditional "If God exists then He necessarily exists." Rather his view would have been that the genuine proposition " 'God exists' is necessarily true" is equivalent to the conditional "If God exists then He exists" (*not* "If God exists then he *necessarily* exists," which would be an illegitimate formulation, on the view imaginatively attributed to Kant).

"If God exists then He exists" is a foolish tautology which says nothing different from the tautology "If a new earth satellite exists then it exists." If "If God exists then He exists" were a correct analysis of " 'God exists' is necessarily true," then "If a new earth satellite exists then it exists" would be a correct analysis of " 'A new earth satellite exists' is necessarily true." If the *analysans* is necessarily true then the *analysandum* must be necessarily true, provided the analysis is correct. If this proposed Kantian analysis of " 'God exists' is necessarily true" were correct, we should be presented with the consequence that not only is it necessarily true that God exists, but also it is necessarily true that a new earth satellite exists: which is absurd.

how do they want the antecedent clause, "*If* God exists," to be understood? Clearly they want it to imply that it is *possible* that God does *not* exist.[34] The whole point of Kant's analysis is to try to show that it is possible to "reject the subject." Let us make this implication explicit in the conditional proposition, so that it reads: "If God exists (and it is possible that He does not) then He necessarily exists." But now it is apparent, I think, that these philosophers have arrived at a self-contradictory position. I do not mean that this conditional proposition, taken alone, is self-contradictory. Their position is self-contradictory in the following way. On the one hand, they agree that the proposition "God necessarily exists" is an a priori truth; Kant implies that it is "absolutely necessary," and Caterus says that God's existence is implied by His very name. On the other hand, they think that it is correct to analyze this proposition in such a way that it will entail the proposition "It is possible that God does not exist." But so far from its being the case that the proposition "God necessarily exists" entails the proposition "It is possible that God does not exist," it is rather the case that they are *incompatible* with one another! Can anything be clearer than that the conjunction "God necessarily exists but it is possible that He does not exist" is self-contradictory? Is it not just as plainly self-contradictory as the conjunction "A square necessarily has four sides but it is possible for a square not to have four sides"? In short, this familiar criticism of the ontological argument is self-contradictory, because it accepts *both* of two incompatible propositions.[35]

One conclusion we may draw from our examination of this criticism is that (contrary to Kant) there is a lack of symmetry, in an important respect, between the propositions "A triangle has three angles" and "God has necessary existence," although both are a pri-

ori. The former can be expressed in the conditional assertion "If a triangle exists (and it is possible that none does) it has three angles." The latter cannot be expressed in the corresponding conditional assertion without contradiction.

I turn to the question of whether the idea of a being a greater than which cannot be conceived is self-contradictory. Here Leibniz made a contribution to the discussion of the ontological argument. He remarked that the argument of Anselm and Descartes

> . . . is not a paralogism, but it is an imperfect demonstration, which assumes something that must still be proved in order to render it mathematically evident; that is, it is tacitly assumed that this idea of the all-great or all-perfect being is possible, and implies no contradiction. And it is already something that by this remark it is proved that, assuming that God is possible, he exists, which is the privilege of divinity alone.[36]

Leibniz undertook to give a proof that God is possible. He defined a *perfection* as a simple, positive quality in the highest degree.[37] He argued that since perfections are *simple* qualities they must be compatible with one another. Therefore the concept of a being possessing all perfections is consistent.

I will not review his argument because I do not find this definition of a perfection intelligible. For one thing, it assumes that certain qualities or attributes are "positive" in their intrinsic nature, and others "negative" or "privative," and I have not been able clearly to understand that. For another thing, it assumes that some qualities are intrinsically simple. I believe that Wittgenstein has shown in the *Investigations* that nothing is *intrinsically* simple, but that whatever has the status of a simple, an indefinable, in one system of concepts, may have the status of a complex thing, a definable thing, in another system of concepts.

I do not know how to demonstrate that the concept of God—that is, of a being a greater than which cannot be conceived—is not self-contradictory. But I

---

[34]When summarizing Anselm's proof (in part II, *supra*) I said: "If God exists He necessarily exists." But there I was merely stating an entailment. "If God exists" did not have the implication that it is possible He does not exist. And of course I was not regarding the conditional as *equivalent* to "God necessarily exists."

[35]This fallacious criticism of Anselm is implied in the following remarks by Gilson: "To show that the affirmation of necessary existence is analytically implied in the idea of God, would be . . . to show that God is necessary if He exists, but would not prove that He does exist" (E. Gilson, *The Spirit of Medieval Philosophy*, New York, 1940, p. 62).

[36]*New Essays Concerning the Human Understanding* Bk. IV. ch. 10: ed. by A. G. Langley (LaSalle, Illinois, 1949), p. 504.

[37]See *Ibid.*, Appendix X, p. 714.

do not think that it is legitimate to demand such a demonstration. I also do not know how to demonstrate that either the concept of a material thing or the concept of *seeing* a material thing is not self-contradictory, and philosophers have argued that both of them are. With respect to any particular reasoning that is offered for holding that the concept of seeing a material thing, for example, is self-contradictory, one may try to show the invalidity of the reasoning and thus free the concept from the charge of being self-contradictory *on that ground*. But I do not understand what it would mean to demonstrate *in general*, and not in respect to any particular reasoning, that the concept is not self-contradictory. So it is with the concept of God. I should think there is no more of a presumption that it is self-contradictory than is the concept of seeing a material thing. Both concepts have a place in the thinking and the lives of human beings.

But even if one allows that Anselm's phrase may be free of self-contradiction, one wants to know how it can have any *meaning* for anyone. Why is it that human beings have even *formed* the concept of an infinite being, a being a greater than which cannot be conceived? This is a legitimate and important question. I am sure there cannot be a deep understanding of that concept without an understanding of the phenomena of human life that give rise to it. To give an account of the latter is beyond my ability. I wish, however, to make one suggestion (which should not be understood as autobiographical).

There is the phenomenon of feeling guilt for something that one has done or thought or felt or for a disposition that one has. One wants to be free of this guilt. But sometimes the guilt is felt to be so great that one is sure that nothing one could do oneself, nor any forgiveness by another human being, would remove it. One feels a guilt that is beyond all measure, a guilt "a greater than which cannot be conceived." Paradoxically, it would seem, one nevertheless has an intense desire to have this incomparable guilt removed. One requires a forgiveness that is beyond all measure, a forgiveness "a greater than which cannot be conceived." Out of such a storm in the soul, I am suggesting, there arises the conception of a forgiving mercy that is limitless, beyond all measure. This is one important feature of the Jewish and Christian conception of God.

I wish to relate this thought to a remark made by Kierkegaard, who was speaking about belief in Christianity but whose remark may have a wider application. He says:

> There is only one proof of the truth of Christianity and that, quite rightly, is from the emotions, when the dread of sin and a heavy conscience torture a man into crossing the narrow line between despair bordering upon madness—and Christendom.[38]

One may think it absurd for a human being to feel a guilt of such magnitude, and even more absurd that, if he feels it, he should *desire* its removal. I have nothing to say about that. It may also be absurd for people to fall in love, but they do it. I wish only to say that there *is* that human phenomenon of an unbearably heavy conscience and that it is importantly connected with the genesis of the concept of God, that is, with the formation of the "grammar" of the word "God." I am sure that this concept is related to human experience in other ways. If one had the acuteness and depth to perceive these connections one could grasp the *sense* of the concept. When we encounter this concept as a problem in philosophy, we do not consider the human phenomena that lie behind it. It is not surprising that many philosophers believe that the idea of a necessary being is an arbitrary and absurd construction.

What is the relation of Anselm's ontological argument to religious belief? This is a difficult question. I can imagine an atheist going through the argument, becoming convinced of its validity, acutely defending it against objections, yet remaining an atheist. The only effect it could have on the fool of the Psalm would be that he stopped saying in his heart "There is no God," because he would now realize that this is something he cannot meaningfully say or think. It is hardly to be expected that a demonstrative argument should, in addition, produce in him a living faith. Surely there is a level at which one can view the argument as a piece of logic, following the deductive moves but not being touched religiously? I think so. But even at this level the argument may not be without religious value, for it may help to remove some philosophical scruples

---

[38] *The Journals*, tr. by A. Dru (Oxford, 1938), sec. 926.

that stand in the way of faith. At a deeper level, I suspect that the argument can be thoroughly understood only by one who has a view of that human "form of life" that gives rise to the idea of an infinitely great being, who views it from the *inside* not just from the outside and who has, therefore, at least some inclination to *partake* in that religious form of life. This inclination, in Kierkegaard's words, is "from the emotions." This inclination can hardly be an *effect* of Anselm's argument, but is rather presupposed in the fullest understanding of it. It would be unreasonable to require that the recognition of Anselm's demonstration as valid must produce a conversion.

QUESTIONS FOR FURTHER REFLECTION

1. Why does Malcolm think that Anselm's second argument is immune from Kant's criticism of the ontological argument?
2. Is "necessary existence" a real predicate? What arguments can be offered against this view?
3. In what important ways does Anselm's ontological argument differ from Descartes's?
4. According to Malcolm, Leibniz's tried to show that God's existence is possible. Why is this project important to the ontological argument?

10. THE FIVE WAYS

Thomas Aquinas

A brief biography of Aquinas appears on page 5. In this selection, from *Summa Theologica*, Aquinas offers five argument-sketches for the existence of God.

READING QUESTIONS

1. Why does Aquinas think that something cannot be both a thing that moves and a thing that is moved "in the same respect and same way"?
2. Why does Aquinas think there cannot be an infinite causal chain?
3. What is the difference between a necessary thing and a possible thing?
4. Where does Aquinas get the idea that "the maximum in any genus is the cause of all in that genus"?
5. Why does Aquinas think that natural objects, like rocks, act toward a goal?

The existence of God can be proved in five ways. The first and more manifest way is the argument from motion. It is certain, and evident to our senses, that in the world some things are in motion. Now whatever is in motion is put in motion by another, for nothing can be in motion except it is in potentiality to that towards which it is in motion; whereas a thing moves inasmuch as it is in act. For motion is nothing else than the reduction of something from potentiality to actuality. But nothing can be reduced from potentiality to actuality, except by something in a state of actuality. Thus that which is actually hot, as fire, makes wood, which is potentially hot, to be actually hot, and thereby moves and changes it. Now it is not possible that the same thing should be at once in actuality and potentiality in the same respect, but only in different respects. For what is actually hot cannot simultaneously be potentially hot; but it is simultaneously potentially cold. It is therefore impossible that in the same respect and in the same way a thing should be both mover and moved, that is, that it should move itself. Therefore, whatever is in motion must be put in motion by another. If that by which it is put in motion be itself put in motion, then this also must needs be put in motion by another, and that by another again. But this cannot go on to infinity, because then there would be no first mover, and, consequently, no other mover; seeing that subsequent movers move only inasmuch as they are put in motion by the first mover; as the staff moves only because it is put in motion by the hand. Therefore it is necessary to arrive at a first mover, put in motion by no other; and this everyone understands to be God.

"A HIERARCHY OF CAUSES" * Frederick Copleston

In the first argument, Aquinas supposes that movement or change is dependent on a "mover" acting here and now, and in the second argument, he supposes that there are efficient causes in the world which even in their causal activity are here and now dependent on the causal activity of other causes. That is why I have spoken of a "hierarchy" rather than of a "series." What he is thinking of can be illustrated in this way. A son is dependent on his father, in the sense that he would not have existed except for the causal activity of his father. But when the son acts for himself, he is not dependent here and now on his father. But he is dependent here and now on other factors. Without the activity of the air, for instance, he could not himself act, and the life-preserving activity of the air is itself dependent here and now on other factors, and they in turn on other factors . . . when Aquinas talks about an "order" of efficient causes he is not thinking of a series stretching back into the past, but of a hierarchy of causes, in which a subordinate member is here and now dependent on the causal activity of a higher member . . .

The meaning of the rejection of an infinite regress should now be clear. Aquinas is not rejecting the possibility of an infinite series as such. . . . We have to imagine, not a lineal or horizontal series, so to speak, but a vertical hierarchy, in which a lower member depends here and now on the present causal activity of the member above it. It is the latter type of series, if prolonged to infinity, which Aquinas rejects. And he rejects it on the ground that unless there is a "first" member, a mover which is not itself moved or a cause which does not itself depend on the causal activity of a higher cause, it is not possible to explain the "motion" or the causal activity of the lowest member. His point of view is this. Suppress the first unmoved mover and there is no motion or change here and now. Suppress the first efficient cause and there is no causal activity here and now. If therefore we find that some things in the world are changed, there must be a first unmoved mover, And if there are efficient causes in the world, there must be a first efficient, and completely nondependent cause. The word "first" does not mean first in the temporal order, but supreme or first in the ontological order.

From Frederick Copleston, *Aquinas*, (1961).

The second way is from the nature of the efficient cause. In the world of sense we find there is an order of efficient causes. There is no case known (neither is it, indeed, possible) in which a thing is found to be the efficient cause of itself; for so it would be prior to itself, which is impossible. Now in efficient causes it is not possible to go on to infinity, because in all efficient causes following in order, the first is the cause of the intermediate cause, and the intermediate is the cause of the ultimate cause, whether the intermediate cause be several, or only one. Now to take away the cause is to take away the effect. Therefore, if there be no first cause among efficient causes, there will be no ultimate, nor any intermediate cause. But if in efficient causes it is possible to go on to infinity, there will be no first efficient cause, neither will there be an ultimate effect, nor any intermediate efficient causes; all of which is plainly false. Therefore it is necessary to admit a first efficient cause, to which everyone gives the name of God.

The third way is taken from possibility and necessity, and runs thus. We find in nature things that are possible to be and not to be, since they are found to be generated, and to corrupt, and consequently, they are possible to be and not to be. But it is impossible for these always to exist, for that which is possible not to be at some time is not. Therefore, if everything is possible not to be, then at one time there could have been nothing in existence. Now if this were true, even now there would be nothing in existence, because that which does not exist only begins to exist by something already existing. Therefore, if at one time nothing was in existence, it would have been impossible for anything to have begun to exist; and thus even now nothing would be in existence—which is absurd. Therefore, not all beings are merely possible, but there must exist something the existence of which is necessary. But every necessary thing either has its necessity caused by another, or not. Now it is impossible to go on to infinity in necessary things which have their necessity caused by another, as has been already proved in regard to efficient causes. Therefore we cannot but postulate the existence of some being having of itself its own necessity, and not receiving it from another, but rather causing in others their necessity. This all men speak of as God.

The fourth way is taken from the gradation to be found in things. Among beings there are some more and some less good, true, noble and the like. But "more" and "less" are predicated of different things, according as they resemble in their different ways something which is the maximum, as a thing is said to be hotter according as it more nearly resembles that which is hottest; so that there is something which is truest, something best, something noblest and, consequently, something which is uttermost being; for those things that are greatest in truth are greatest in being, as it is written in Metaph. ii. Now the maximum in any genus is the cause of all in that genus; as fire, which is the maximum heat, is the cause of all hot things. Therefore there must also be something which is to all beings the cause of their being, goodness, and every other perfection; and this we call God.

The fifth way is taken from the governance of the world. We see that things which lack intelligence, such as natural bodies, act for an end, and this is evident from their acting always, or nearly always, in the same way, so as to obtain the best result. Hence it is plain that not fortuitously, but designedly, do they achieve their end. Now whatever lacks intelligence cannot move towards an end, unless it be directed by some being endowed with knowledge and intelligence; as the arrow is shot to its mark by the archer. Therefore some intelligent being exists by whom all natural things are directed to their end; and this being we call God.

QUESTIONS FOR FURTHER REFLECTION

1. How do the discoveries of Newtonian physics, with regard to motion, bear on the first way?
2. Why does the first cause, described in the second way, have to be God? Why can't it be the universe or some part of the universe?
3. In the third way, Aquinas claims that there is at least one point in time when a merely possible thing does not exist. Why think this is true? Couldn't an object be both merely possible and eternal? Couldn't there, at least in principle, be an eternal, indestructible piece of matter that did not exist necessarily?
4. In the fourth way, Aquinas contends that the "maximum in any genus is the cause of all in that genus" and that fire, for example, is caused by the greatest in the spectrum of hot things, namely, heat. Is this true? Can you think of examples of spectrums where the greatest in that spectrum is not the cause of everything else in the spectrum?
5. Aquinas argues at the end of each way that the being we are talking about is God. Even if we grant his arguments up to that point, do they prove that *God* exists? Suppose, Aquinas is right and there is first, uncaused cause. Is that uncaused cause God? Doesn't God have psychological characteristics like being loving that a mere uncaused cause doesn't have? Explain the apparent leap he makes at the end of each way.

11. THE COSMOLOGICAL ARGUMENT
AN APPRAISAL
David Yandell and Keith Yandell

David Yandell is Associate Professor of Philosophy at Loyola University of Chicago. He received his Ph.D. in Philosophy from the University of Wisconsin–Madison. He has published articles in several anthologies and journals, such as *History of Philosophy Quarterly* and *British Journal for the History of Philosophy*. The topics of these articles have included early modern metaphysics, philosophy of religion, and philosophical naturalism. Currently he is working on a book defending Cartesian dualism. A brief biography of Keith Yandell may be found on p. 361.

In this essay, the Yandells discuss what a cosmological argument is, and what it is intended to show. They consider versions of the argument based on the supposed impossibility of actually infinite series of contingent beings, but find these wanting. They then turn to versions based on the apparent need for an explanation of contingent or dependent reality, considering in some detail alternative forms of the Principle of Sufficient Reason on which such arguments are based. They explain and sketch a defense of a particular version of this type that they think is an especially strong one, though it too rests on a version of the Principle of Sufficient Reason that they concede they cannot prove on the basis of any more obviously true claim. Rejecting the Principle, however, leaves one in the puzzling position of claiming that there are perfectly meaningful questions for which there are no answers. It is not just that we don't know the answers (this would hardly be surprising), but that there literally *are* no answers; they say that this is a difficult position to justify. They close by briefly considering whether the notion of "best explanation" is a useful one in this context.

Reading Questions

1. What does it mean to say that something "might not have been"? What reason is there to think that this is true about some things?
2. What sort of things, if any, are contingent?
3. What does the Principle of Sufficient Reason claim?
4. Does something have to have necessary existence if it can explain the existence of other things in a way that satisfies the principle of sufficient reason?
5. Why can't the existence of abstract objects explain the existence of things that might not have existed?

1. INTRODUCTION

There are several important kinds of arguments leading to the conclusion that God exists, including those based on the order of the universe (the "teleological argument"), on the conceivability of God (the "ontological argument"), and on the existence and character of morality (the "moral argu-

ment").[1] This chapter will focus on another important kind of argument, called the "cosmological argu-

---

[1] In our discussion of the argument here, we draw on a number of previous treatments of it. These include writings of both historical figures (especially, but not only, Aquinas, Descartes, Spinoza, Leibniz, Clarke, and Hume) and contemporary philosophers (especially, but not only, William Rowe, Richard Swinburne, J. L. Mackie, and

ment." Like the others mentioned, the term "cosmological argument" refers not to a single argument but to a kind of argument offered as grounds for believing in the existence of God. For our purposes here, God is taken to be an all-powerful ("omnipotent"), all-knowing ("omniscient"), morally perfect ("omnibenevolent") creator and sustainer of the universe.[2]

Cosmological arguments are those that start with the existence of the objects with which we are acquainted and argue that there must be a causal or ontic ground for those objects. (An ontic ground is something such that its existence explains the existence of another thing.) Cosmological arguments conclude that God is either the only possible ground for, or at least the ground that best explains, the existence of the things that we experience. Traditionally, though not always, such arguments have taken the universe as a whole to be what needs explaining. Because of this, the arguments' name comes from the Greek words cosmos ("universe") and logos (here meaning "account"); cosmological arguments have traditionally tried to show that the belief that God exists is justified because God's existence and activity are the basis for the best or only account of the existence of the universe.

The cosmological argument has a very long history. The greatest of the ancient Greek philosophers whose writings have survived, Plato and Aristotle, both offer arguments for an uncaused first cause of the motion of the universe. Their accounts, however, do not claim that God exists in any sense recognizable by

the major monotheistic religions, though they have sometimes been treated as if they did by those wanting the support of Plato and Aristotle for their monotheistic views. So, these accounts are outside of the scope of the present discussion.

All three of the major "Western" monotheistic traditions (Judaism, Christianity, and Islam) developed versions of the argument drawing on Greek philosophy as well as on their own theological doctrines.[3] Probably independently, Indian monotheists crafted their own forms of the argument.[4] It seems that such an argument is at home in any of the major monotheisms. It has also been criticized from a range of different perspectives by theists, atheists, and agnostics alike. The purpose of this chapter, however, is not to trace the history of the argument, but to explain and to critically evaluate some forms of it in a way that casts light on whether the argument provides rational grounds for belief in God.

There are several major traditional varieties of the argument. We will discuss three of them, but much that applies to these types also bears on others. The first kind of the argument that we will discuss includes versions that are based on the alleged impossibility of an actual infinite. (We will explain what this means when we discuss the argument.) The second kind comprises versions based on the alleged contingency of created reality. The third kind is made up of versions that claim that God's existence and activity are the "best" explanation of allegedly dependent reality. We will also discuss the strongest formulation of the argument we are aware of, distinguishing it along the way from other versions and considering various criticisms.

William Lane Craig). See the works listed in the Suggestions for Further Reading for the contemporary authors. For philosophers from earlier centuries, including Aquinas, Spinoza, and Leibniz, a good place to start is Craig's The Cosmological Argument from Plato to Leibniz, which also shows the profound debt those who offer Christian forms of the argument owe to medieval Islamic thinkers. For Descartes's unusual versions, see Meditation III in Meditations on First Philosophy; the interesting critical exchanges that followed appear in the Objections and Replies to the Meditations. All of these can be found in the Descartes collection in the Suggestions. For Clarke, start with Clarke's Demonstration of the Being and Attributes of God and Rowe's The Cosmological Argument. Finally, for Hume, read his Dialogues Concerning Natural Religion and Keith Yandell's Hume's "Inexplicable Mystery."
[2]Obviously these are not all of the attributes God is said to have by one or more of the major monotheistic traditions. Some of the others are debated among orthodox members of one or more traditions. In any case, if one could show this much by the argument, most of its proponents would be satisfied.

[3]It seems a bit silly to call religions that developed in Southwestern Asia (Judaism, Christianity, and Islam) "Western" and ones that began in Southcentral Asia (Hinduism and Buddhism) "Eastern," but that is the custom. For the history of the "Western" development of the argument, it is useful to begin with Craig, The Cosmological Argument.
[4]Indian examples, combining cosmological and teleological elements, can be found in Sarvepalli Radhakrishnan and Charles A. Moore, eds., A Sourcebook in Indian Philosophy, pp. 379–85 and 401–3. For scholarly discussion of Indian arguments concerning God's existence, see Ninian Smart, Doctrine and Argument in Indian Philosophy, chapter 11.

2. THE GIST OF THE ARGUMENT

The cosmological argument for the existence of God, not very surprisingly, has this basic form: there is a world or cosmos, so God exists. Explaining the argument is a matter of filling in the premises fully enough so that together they entail, or at least justify accepting, the conclusion and so that one can see why an intelligent person might think the premises are true. Defending the argument is a matter of providing whatever support can be found for thinking the premises to be true.

3. TWO BASIC IDEAS

The cosmological argument begins by directing our attention to two things. One is that there exist things that might never have existed. Carrots, lady bugs, and pebbles might never have existed; there are possible worlds (possible ways that reality could have been) without them. The same holds for planets, stars, and galaxies. The other is that things do not seem just to come to exist; something brings their existence about.

4. THINGS THAT EXIST BUT MIGHT NOT HAVE EXISTED

To say that something "might not have existed" is to say that its existence is not logically necessary. That there might not have been carrots is a matter of *There aren't any carrots* not being self-contradictory. Of course *There aren't any carrots* is contradicted by the fact that there are carrots, in contrast to *There aren't any unicorns*, which isn't contradicted by there being unicorns. But *There are carrots*, unlike *Seven and one are eight* and *If William is enormous then William has size*, is not a necessary truth. So *There aren't any carrots* is not a necessary falsehood, and thus it might have been true. Since *There aren't any carrots* is not a necessary falsehood, there might not have been any carrots.

Once one has firmly in mind that *There exist things that might never have been*, it is time to ask how widely this class of things extends. How many of the things that do exist might never have graced our world? The answer is: all of the ones that we are likely to think of, unless we are inclined to a certain sort of abstract thought. Any material item, whether very big or very small or somewhere in between, might not have existed. In fact, for all materials things whatever, spread out over space and time, they might not have existed—there might never have been a material universe at all. If persons are wholly material, then, they might never have existed. On the alternative view that persons are essentially minds or souls, and that persons are not material, persons are typically still thought of as things that exist but might not have existed. So the idea of a thing that exists but might not have existed need not be limited to material things.

The standard term in philosophy for things that do exist but might not have existed is *contingent beings*. This is a somewhat unfortunate term, because it also has another meaning besides "things that do exist but might not have existed." It also means "things that so exist as to depend for their existence on something else." But "contingent being" here just means the former—a being that exists but might not have existed, with no implications about either possible or actual dependence. For clarity, we will refer to things that so exist as to depend on something else for their existence as *dependent beings*. We will return to the issue of whether a being that is contingent must also be dependent. (For those who can't wait, the answer to "Must a being that exists but might not have existed depend for its existence on something else?" is "No.")

5. ABSTRACT OBJECTS

Some philosophers, logicians, and mathematicians have reasoned along the following lines. There are necessarily true propositions—propositions like *Two and four are six*, *If there are cows then there are living things*, and *No one is taller than herself*. If there are necessarily true propositions, then there is something in virtue of which they are true—these propositions have "truth-makers." These "truth-makers" must exist necessarily. So something exists necessarily—something exists no matter what and in every possible world and in such a way that its nonexistence is not a possibility.

These truth-makers of necessary truths are thought of in various ways. There is no need to go into the details here. It is enough to note that the ways in which they are thought of come in two varieties: either the truth-makers are abstract objects or they are thoughts that a necessarily existing God necessarily has. Construe them in the latter way and one has the

"PROVING GOD" ✳ *Godfreid Leibniz*

Our reasons are founded on *two great principles, that of contradiction*, in virtue of which we judge that to be *false* which involves contradiction, and that *true*, which is opposed or contradictory to the false.

And *that of sufficient reason*, in virtue of which we hold that no fact can be real or existent, no statement true, unless there be a sufficient reason why it is so and not otherwise, although most often these reasons cannot be known to us.

There are also two kinds of truths, those of *reasoning* and those of *fact*. Truths of reasoning are necessary and their opposite is impossible, and those of fact are contingent and their opposite is possible. When a truth is necessary its reason can be found by analysis, resolving it into more simple ideas and truths until we reach those which are primitive. . . .

But there must also be a *sufficient reason for contingent truths*, or those *of* fact—that is, for the series of things diffused through the universe of created objects—where the resolution into particular reason might run into a detail without limits, on account of the immense variety of objects and the division of bodies *ad infinitum*.

And as all this *detail* only involves other contingents, anterior or more detailed, each one of which needs a like analysis for its explanation, we make no advance: and the sufficient or final reason must be outside of the sequence or *series* of this detail of contingencies, however infinite it may be.

And thus it is that the final reason of things must be found in a necessary substance, in which the detail of changes exists only eminently, as in their source; and this it is which we call God.

Now this substance, being the sufficient reason of all this detail, which also is linked together throughout, *there is but one God, and this God suffices*.

From *The Monadology* (1714).

---

material for an argument from necessary truth to the existence of God. That is an interesting argument that raises issues of its own, but it is not a version of the cosmological argument and we won't explore it here.

If one construes the truth-makers of necessary truths as abstract objects, then their existence is irrelevant to the cosmological argument. An abstract object is a necessarily existing item that has no spatial properties and exists eternally (timelessly) or everlastingly (at all times). An abstract object has no causal powers—it cannot bring anything about or make anything happen. It cannot, for example, bring it about that there exist things that there might not have been.

Note that there is no such thing as explaining how it is that abstract objects exist. The reason is that, if they exist at all, there is no possibility of their not existing. To explain the existence of something is a matter of *explaining its existing rather than not*. If it isn't an option that something *not* exist, then it also isn't an option that its existence be explained. It also is not possible that an abstract object *depend* for its existence on anything—there isn't any condition under which something could happen or something could be done that would undermine the existence of an abstract object. An abstract object enjoys what we can call existential security.

While we shall not focus on abstract objects in this essay, there are two things to be kept in mind. First, there being abstract objects can't be what explains there being things that do exist but might not have existed. There are two reasons for this. One is that they have no causal powers. The second is that, even if *per impossibile* they did have causal powers, since they lack intelligence and will, they could not decide whether to exercise them or not. If they could cause contingent things, they would inevitably do so—in fact, it would be a necessary truth that they did do. But if a necessarily existent item necessarily produces something, then the existence of the thing produced is itself necessary. But nothing that exists necessarily, of course, is a contingently existing thing—a thing that exists, but might not have existed. It wouldn't work to suggest that what abstract objects brought into existence might vary depending on the environment because on this account there will not *be* any environment other than that provided by what the abstract objects inevitably produce. Necessary beings cannot necessarily produce contingent beings.

The second thing to be kept in mind is that abstract objects have existential security—they cannot be put out of existence nor can they depend for existence on anything else. Being clear concerning the notion of existential security is crucial for understanding the cosmological argument.

It is worth mentioning here that there needn't be a *set* of all necessary truths or all abstract objects for the considerations noted here to be in order. Similarly, there need not even possibly be a set of all necessary truths in order for God to be omniscient. We can talk about all abstract objects, and about all necessary truths—"quantify over" such objects and truths, as logicians say—whether there is a set of all such or not. It is the case that all abstract objects are nonspatial, all propositions are true and false, and all necessary truths are consistent. If there cannot be a set of all abstract objects, propositions, or necessary truths, then there need not be such a set in order for these things to be the case.

6. THE PRINCIPLE
OF SUFFICIENT REASON

The cosmological argument requires some version of a principle of sufficient reason. Various formulations have been offered. "Reason" here means "explanation." "Explanation" here means "metaphysical explanation" as opposed to "epistemological explanation." The metaphysical explanation of the existence of some contingent being is whatever it is in virtue of which that being exists. Suppose God decides to create a rare flower that exists only in a tiny valley that no one will ever visit. Then the metaphysical explanation of the existence of that flower is that God created it. If no one discovers that this flower exists, then no one will offer an explanation of that fact, and so there will be no epistemological explanations. We can put the difference is this way: while *E is an epistemological explanation of* X entails *Someone, at some time, offers E*, by contrast *E is the meta-*

physical explanation of X does not entail *Someone, at some time, offers* E. An epistemological explanation, if it is correct, simply is a matter of someone actually offering the right metaphysical explanation. Incorrect epistemological explanations are simply explanations that are offered but do not express the correct metaphysical explanation. If there is no metaphysical explanation, then of course there is no correct epistemological explanation. The cosmological argument contends that the existence of contingent beings must have a metaphysical explanation—there must be something in virtue of which there are contingent beings, whether we know what that something is or not. Of course it also contends that we can know what that something is, and that the cosmological argument itself tells us what it is.

Some presenters of the cosmological argument have different things in mind than do others. Some of them think that there cannot have been an infinite series of caused and causing things. They think that there cannot be an "actual infinite"—a collection that is infinitely large or has an infinite number of members. This claim is central to their version of the argument. Other presenters of the cosmological argument have simply waived the question as to whether there can be an actual infinite or not. They have offered a version of the argument that is consistent with the existence of an actually infinite collection. The difference between these presenters of the cosmological argument centers on their offering diverse statements of the Principle of Sufficient Reason.

7. VERSION ONE
OF THE COSMOLOGICAL ARGUMENT:
THE "NO ACTUAL INFINITE" VERSION

One kind of cosmological argument is based on the alleged impossibility of an infinite series of finite causes.[5] It might be outlined like this:[6]

---

[5]For the fullest statement and defense of this argument, see William Lane Craig, *The Kalaam Cosmological Argument*.
[6]For the sake of convenience in stating the argument, we are speaking as if things had single causes. Of course in many cases, at least, there are several causes involved in the production of a thing according to most theories of causation. So, by "cause" here, we mean to include all of the immediate causes of the thing's existence.

1. There are contingent things.
2. The cause of a contingent thing must be either contingent or necessary.
3. If the cause is necessary, then the causal chain producing a contingent thing has a beginning, since necessary beings have no cause (outside, perhaps, of their own essences).[7]
4. If the cause is contingent, then it must in turn have a cause that is either necessary or contingent.
5. If this cause is necessary, then the causal chain . . . (see line 3).
6. If this cause is contingent, then it . . . (see line 4).
7. Therefore, all contingent things are the products either of causal chains beginning with a necessary thing or of an infinite chain of contingent causes.
8. There can be no infinite chains of contingent causes.
9. Therefore, all contingent things are the products of causal chains beginning with a necessary thing.

A few points about this kind of argument seem worth making. First, it presupposes a version of the Principle of Sufficient Reason, of roughly this sort: Each contingent thing has a cause.[8] Second, even if the argument is sound and valid, and therefore establishes its conclusion, this would show only that there are one or more necessary beings that serve as causal grounds for contingent reality. This does not seem to get us very close to proving that God exists. So a pair of supplementary arguments are needed: one to show that there can be (or at least is) only one such necessary being and one to show that such a necessarily existing causal ground would have to be omnipotent, omniscient, and omnibenevolent.[9] Third, line 8, *There can be no infinite chains of contingent causes*, is not obviously true. It is worthwhile to discuss this claim briefly before we move on to the other varieties of the argument.

There are several connected issues regarding claims about its being impossible that there be an actual infinite. Sometimes the claim is that the very idea of an actually infinite collection is contradictory. Various arguments are offered for this claim—for example, that when you "take away" some infinite series of numbers from any infinite series of numbers, you still have an infinite series of numbers. "Take away" the set of even whole integers from the set of all whole integers and you still "have left" the set of odd whole integers. The response would seem to be that while an infinite series is indeed a remarkable thing, there is nothing inconsistent in the idea that one infinite set contains another or in the fact that if one such set is "removed" from the other, an infinite set remains. There seem to be an actually infinite number of truths—say, the truths about the whole integers—and whether it is abstract objects or divine thoughts that are the "truthmakers" for these truths, there must be an infinite number of them. An infinite set—a set that has a subset whose members can be put into one-to-one correspondence with the members of the whole set—seems perfectly possible. The set of whole integers seems to be precisely such a set.

It might be argued in reply that the set of even integers does not actually exist; perhaps abstract objects such as sets and numbers merely subsist (since they are real but do not exist in time, or for some other reason) or perhaps they do not exist at all but are merely convenient fictions. This is not the place to argue over whether a realist or a conventionalist view of mathematical objects is true, so let us consider another example, one that the person offering a cosmological argument cannot so easily resist.

If God exists, then since God is omniscient, God knows every truth. There are infinitely many truths (just in the area of arithmetic, there are infinitely many truths about what numbers you get when you add 1 to other numbers). Thus, God knows infinitely many truths. Notice that this infinity is not of the mathematical objects themselves but rather of God's states of knowing. One might reply that God knows all things in a single mental act

---

[7]Causal chains can, of course, be very short. So if a necessary thing is the immediate cause of a contingent thing, this will count for present purposes as a causal chain.

[8]The Principle of Sufficient Reason in one form or another appears in all the arguments discussed. Whether one should accept some form(s) of it is considered near the end of the chapter.

[9]Or, one might offer this argument as further support for belief in God's existence after providing independent reason to warrant such belief. That is, one argument need not do all of the evidential work by itself. If we had other reasons for supposing that an omnipotent, omniscient, omnibenevolent creator exists, this argument might help warrant adding necessity to the list of divine attributes. Still, the fact remains that this argument as it stands does not clearly bear on God's existence.

"THE RUSSELL-COPLESTON DEBATE"
Bertrand Russell and Frederick Copleston

Frederick Copleston: . . . we know that there are at least some beings in the world which do not contain in themselves the reason for their existence. For example, I depend on my parents, and now on the air and food, and so on . . . secondly, the world is simply the . . . aggregate of individual objects, none of which contain in themselves alone the reason for their existence. There isn't any world distinct from the objects which form it, anymore than the human race is something apart from its members. Therefore, . . . [the world] must have a reason external to itself. That reason must be a being . . . this being is either the reason for its own existence, or it is not. If it is, well and good. If it is not, then we must proceed farther. But if we proceed to infinity in that sense, then there's no explanation of existence at all. So, . . . we must come to a being which contains within itself the reason for its own existence . . .

Bertrand Russell: . . . the best point at which to begin is the question of necessary being. The Word "necessary" . . . can only be applied significantly to propositions. And, in fact, only to such as are analytic—that is to say—such as it is self-contradictory to deny. I could only admit a necessary being if there were a being whose existence it is self-contradictory to deny . . . I don't admit the idea of a necessary being and I don't admit that there is any particular meaning in calling other beings "contingent."

These phrases don't for me have a significance . . .

Copleston: Do you . . . reject these terms because they won't fit in with what is called "modern logic"? . . .

Russell: Well, I can't find anything they could mean. The word "necessary," it seems to me, is a useless word . . .

Copleston: . . . the proposition that metaphysical terms are meaningless . . . [is] . . . based on an assumed philosophy. The dogmatic position behind it seems to be this: What will not go into my machine is nonexistent, or it is meaningless; it is the expression of emotion . . .

Russell: . . . I don't maintain the meaninglessness of metaphysics in general . . . I maintain the meaninglessness of certain particular terms— not on any general ground, but simply because I've not been able to see an interpretation of those particular terms. It's not a general dogma . . . but those points I will leave . . . and I will say that what you have been saying brings us back . . . to the ontological argument that there is a being whose existence is analytic. That seems to me to be impossible . . . I think a subject named can never be significantly said to exist but only as a subject described.

From Bertrand Russell & Frederick Copleston, "A Debate on the Existence of God" in *The Existence of God*, John Hick ed. (1964).

or state, perhaps a knowledge of all truths conjoined. However, that one state would itself then be an actually infinite state in the sense of a state whose content included an infinite number of truths. Moreover, if one knows *P* and *Q* and one knows the laws of inference and thereby sees that *R* is entailed by *P* and *Q*, it is at least very plausible to say that one knows *R*. So if God knows an infinitely long proposition containing all truths, it seems reasonable to infer that God (who, being omniscient, knows the laws of inference and is presumably very good at identifying which propositions follow from which others) also knows each of the truths contained in that proposition. If so, then God has infinitely many states of knowledge. But then if God exists, there is an actual infinite.

One might claim that God is not contingent and that therefore this example does not apply to the principle in question. (We will return to the question of God being contingent later.) Then one would need some reason weaker than the general claim that nothing actually infinite exists for claiming that there cannot be an infinite series of contingent causes. That is, one could grant that there can be actually infinite necessary things, but hold that there is something peculiar to contingent things that prevents them from instantiating infinity. It is hard to see what this would be however. One would have thought that an omnipotent being could create infinitely many finite things. If this is so, then there can be actual contingent instantiations of infinity. If it is not so, then the question is, why not? An omniscient being is one that can do anything that it is logically possible for that being to do. So if an omnipotent being cannot instantiate infinity in the contingent world, either instantiating infinity at all is impossible (which is ruled out by the counterexample of God's knowledge) or instantiating infinity in contingent things would involve some contradiction, or there is something about God that would in principle preclude God's instantiating infinity in contingent things. It is difficult to see, however, what is contradictory about a possible reality in which God exists and creates infinitely many marigolds (for example). Unless there is some general impossibility in instantiating infinity, where is the supposed contradiction?

Because of the difficulty of answering such questions, most defenders of this kind of argument have defended it by appeal to supposed paradoxes about the nature of instantiated infinity. These "paradoxes," however, do not seem insoluble. That they must have a solution is implied by the existence of counterexamples such as those discussed above.

A weaker claim actually would serve these presenters of the cosmological argument just as well. All they require is that there cannot be an infinite number of concrete things. But here too it is not clear why there cannot be. Why is it impossible that an omnipotent God create, say, an infinite number of material atoms at a given time? If the sorts of considerations that are alleged to show that the concept of an infinite series is inconsistent are unsuccessful, then there seems to be no reason why this would be impossible.

A weaker claim still would do. Consider the claim that there cannot be an infinite *successive* sequence of concrete things—a temporal series that goes on for an infinite amount of time. If this is true, then there cannot be an infinite past—it cannot be that before the present moment there have been an infinite number of past moments. So there must have been a first moment. There are contingent beings, and if there must have been a first moment, there must have been a moment at which, for the first time, there existed some contingent being.

There are two views of time—that time is atomistic and that time is continuous. If time is atomistic, then there are temporal minima. There are moments—bits of time than which no bit of time can be smaller. If time is continuous, then there are no temporal minima, no moments, no temporal bits than which no bit is smaller. For any unit of time measurement you like, there is a measurement half as large that one could use with just as much accuracy to time itself. The limits here are practical or technological, not ontological or metaphysical.

If time is continuous, then between any two times T1 and T2, there are in principle an infinite number of times specifiable by a sufficiently fine-tuned system of measurement. (Whether we can usefully apply it or not is irrelevant.) So by lasting as long as (say) a second, one traverses an infinite temporal series. Presumably, then, presenters of the cosmological argument who deny there can be an infinite series of successive contingent beings because there cannot be an infinite successive temporal series of any sort will have to hold that time is atomistic, not continuous.

But why can't time, even if it is atomistic, be infinite—why can't there be an infinite past? The basic argument offered for this conclusion is this: if there has been an infinite past series of contingent beings, then some such being or a series thereof has "traversed an infinite series" and that is impossible. Presumably if there can have been an infinite number of temporal atoms that have come and gone, then each could have been occupied by some one contingent being or some series of contingent beings, so the impossibility of "traversing an infinite series" applies to moments or temporal atoms as well as to a contingent being or series of contingent beings. Either both an infinite sequence of moments of time and an infinite succession of contingent beings are impossible, or neither is.

The idea that "an infinite series cannot be traversed" cannot be merely the notion that one cannot *construct* an infinite series—that if, say, we start counting from one to two to three and so on, one won't ever count to an infinite number. In order for the past to be infinite, we do not have to construct anything at all. The idea is that an infinite past is in itself impossible because no matter how far back we went, we'd never have traveled an infinite temporal distance, and so no matter how far we went forward from any past point we'd never have traveled an infinite temporal distance either. An infinite past could never have gotten to now.

Trying to focus one's thought on such propositions about an infinite past in such a manner as to be rightly confident that one's judgment is correct can be exquisitely difficult. Is the claim that there cannot be an infinite past true, as the first sort of presenter of a cosmological argument requires? Proponents of this claim don't seem to have offered an argument from premises more obviously true than this claim from which it follows. It is not clear that the supposed impossibility of an infinite past is any more securely grounded than the idea that you cannot still have an infinite series once you "take away" the whole even integers from all the whole integers. Presenters of the other version of the cosmological argument suggest that it is better to waive the whole dispute about whether there can be an infinite succession of one contingent being after another or one or more contingent beings that have an infinite past. Their position is: if you like, let's suppose there can be, and get on with the argument.

To sum up things regarding the first sort of cosmological argument, let's consider a brief statement of it as follows:

C1. There cannot be an infinite past series of successively existing contingent beings or one or more infinitely old contingent beings.
C2. There are contingent beings.
C3. If 1 and 2 are true, then there was a first time at which there existed a contingent being.
C4. There was a first time at which there existed a contingent being. (from 1–3)

C5. If 4, there is an explanation of there being a contingent being at that first time.
C6. There is an explanation of there being a contingent being at that first time. (from 4, 5)

The argument then continues in a fashion that we will explore when we discuss the second sort of cosmological argument. This continuing segment of argument is required by both versions. The presenter of the second version is unsure whether premise C3 is true because she is unsure about premise C1; or perhaps she simply rejects C1 and is unsure about C3, which might be true even if C1 is false. It might be the case that an infinite past succession of contingent beings or an infinitely old contingent being is possible, but in fact there was a first time at which such a thing existed. In any case, the presenter of the second version of the cosmological argument does not appeal to either C1 or to C2.

We said earlier that the presenter of the first version of the cosmological argument offers a different version of the Principle of Sufficient Reason than does the presenter of the second version. The first version requires some such principle as:

Principle of Sufficient Reason One (PSR1): There cannot be an infinite past series of successively existing contingent beings or one or more infinitely old contingent beings and if there was a first time at which there existed a contingent being, there is an explanation of its existing.

We have suggested reasons for doubting (PSR1).

8. VERSION TWO OF THE COSMOLOGICAL ARGUMENT: THE NO BRUTE FACT VERSION

Strictly, both versions of the cosmological argument deny that there are any brute facts, and the title of version two can properly be put as "The An Infinite Series Is OK but Brute Facts Are Not OK Version." A brute fact is a state of affairs that does obtain, though it might not have obtained, where it is possible that it have had an explanation and there is in fact no explanation of its obtaining. If a blueberry were just to "pop into" existence on top of your cereal tomorrow morning, that would be a brute fact—it might not have popped into existence, the existence of blueberries is explicable and there might have been an explanation of the existence of this one, but there happens not to be an explanation.

The cosmological argument is concerned with the *existence* of things that might not have existed. For the second version, it may well be true that there was no first time at which there existed a contingent being. Maybe every contingent being was caused to come to exist by some previously existing contingent being; perhaps one or more contingent beings has everlastingly existing. What matters here is this: *there are contingent beings*. There exist things that might not have existed and whose existence is possibly explicable. Note that one cannot explain there being contingent beings by there being contingent beings, any more than one can explain the fact that there are trees by the fact that there are trees or explain the fact that there are skunks by the fact that there are skunks. What is relevant is that *there are contingent beings at all*. When it comes to explaining that fact, there are just two options. One is that there being contingent beings is (metaphysically) explained by there existing beings of some other sort. The other is that it is just a brute fact that there are contingent beings.

We come now to the version of the Principle of Sufficient Reason favored by presenters of the second version of the cosmological argument. The gist of it is this claim: there are no brute existential facts. If there are contingent beings, then—since it possible that there be an explanation of this fact—there is an explanation of this fact. The cosmological arguer proposes that this explanation is that God created contingent beings.

9. A CRITICISM OF THE PRINCIPLE OF SUFFICIENT REASON

Probably the most perceptive critique of any attempt to develop this sort of argument goes as follows. Suppose God exists necessarily and necessarily chooses to create contingent beings. Then so-called contingent beings are actually necessary beings. The necessary cannot explain the existence of the contingent. Suppose that God is a contingent being. Then even if God creates other contingent beings, God too is a contingent being and there must be some explanation of God's existence. Hence, in contrast to what

monotheism holds, God's existence is explicable in terms of the existence of something else. This is a conclusion that most presenters of the cosmological argument will properly refuse to accept on the grounds that a being whose existence can be explained by reference to a another nondivine being cannot really be God.

This critique can be put succinctly as follows: the second version of the cosmological argument requires that *there being contingent beings* be explained. Whatever exists is either a necessary being or a contingent being. Necessary beings cannot explain the existence of contingent beings. Contingent beings are the things the existence of which is supposed to be explained. Neither way can *there exist contingent beings* be explained. But those are the only ways. So *there exist contingent beings* cannot be explained. So much for the cosmological argument.

10. A REPLY TO THE CRITIQUE

There is a reply to the critique. Suppose a being B has this feature: it is logically impossible that B be caused to exist. About it, the following is a necessary truth: *If B exists, then B is not caused to exist.* Most contingent beings do not have this feature. Possible contingent beings, at least, come in two brands: those that have this feature and those that do not. Let's call those beings, if any, that have this feature *contingent beings whose existence it is logically impossible to explain* in contrast to the typical case of *contingent beings whose existence it is logically possible to explain.* A properly constructed cosmological argument will explain the existence of contingent beings whose existence is it is logically possible to explain.

The crux of the critique is that the contingent can be explained only by reference to the contingent. But a free choice by a necessarily existing being is one that might not have been made. A contingent being whose existence it is logically impossible to explain nonetheless might not have existed. Reference to either of these as a means of explaining the existence of contingent beings whose existence it is possible to explain is a matter of explaining that existence by reference to the contingent. The same holds for a free choice of a contingent being whose existence it is logically impossible to explain.

11. THE PRINCIPLE OF SUFFICIENT REASON IN THE SECOND VERSION OF THE COSMOLOGICAL ARGUMENT

One part of the cosmological argument contends that the existence of contingent beings whose existence can be explained is to be explained by reference to the existence of things whose existence cannot be explained. Its version of the Principle of Sufficient Reason asserts:

(PSR2) If a being or collection of beings B exists, B might not have existed, and B's existence it is logically possible to explain, then there actually is an explanation of B's existence.

The argument goes like this:

A1. There exists a collection of contingent beings such that every member of it, as well as the collection itself, might not have existed, and whose existence it is logically possible to explain.

Note that one need not *infer* from the fact that each member of the collection might not have existed and that its existence logically possibly has an explanation to the fact that the collection itself has these features. The whole collection might not have existed and it is logically possible that the whole collection has an explanation, whether this fact follows from the corresponding things being true of the members of the collection or not.

A2. There exists a collection of contingent beings whose existence actually has an explanation. (From [PSR2] and A1.)

A3. No contingent being, or collection of contingent beings, whose existence it is possible to explain, can explain that there exists a collection of contingent beings whose existence it is possible to explain.

A4. The existence of a collection of contingent beings whose existence can be explained is explained by the existence of something whose existence cannot be explained. (From A2 and A3.)

The move from A2 and A3 to A4 is valid. Behind it lies the necessary truth that any being is either such that its existence is logically possible to explain or such that its existence is logically impossible to explain.

The next thing to consider is what sort of being it is whose existence it is logically impossible to explain. Anything that necessarily exists has this feature. As great a philosopher as Kant held that *only* necessarily existing things have it. In this, it seems, he was wrong. A being that existed contingently, but was omniscient, omnipotent, and morally perfect, would also enjoy existential security. As omnipotent, it would know of any threat, internal or external, to its existence; as omnipotent, it could only be put out of existence with its consent; as morally perfect, it would not consent to the ending of its morally perfect existence because no state of affairs could justify this. So the existence of such a being would be entirely secure. But a being whose existence was entirely secure does not depend for its existence on anything that might not exist. A being whose existence does not depend for its existence on anything that might not exist cannot be caused not to exist. In sum: *B is omnicompetent* (omnipotent, omniscient, and morally perfect) entails *B has existential security* entails *B's existence is impossible to explain.*

A further point should be mentioned. The existence of a being that has existential security for the reasons just described has that feature necessarily—not by happenstance or contingently, but in virtue of its nature. A being that has existential security, and has it necessarily, cannot be caused to exist. If something can be caused to exist, it can exist dependently; whatever is caused to exist depends for its existence on whatever caused it. Since a being that has necessary existential security cannot exist dependently, it cannot be caused to exist. So, even if it exists contingently, its existence is not explicable. Something's existence is a brute fact if it exists, it is logically possible that it not exist, and *it is logically possible that its existence be explained although in fact its existence has no explanation.* The existence of a being that enjoys necessary existential security, then, cannot be such that it is a brute fact.

Suppose God were to create a collie named Princess—a animal God decided to grant unending existence to protect no matter what. Princess would then be existentially secure. But her security would come by courtesy of the divine guarantee of her protection, come what may; she would not possess her existential security *necessarily, or by nature.* God possesses existential security by nature. Thus, as we have noted, God's existence cannot be explained, and hence God's existence cannot be a brute fact. (This is so whether or not God's existence is logically necessary.) Thus, just as some people say that the fact that the universe exists at all is a fact with no explanation, one offering this version of the cosmological argument says that the fact that God exists at all is a fat with no explanation. The difference is that the defender of this version has an explanation for why God's existence has no explanation: it cannot in principle have one.

A still further point, obvious but important, is that something that can explain the existence of contingent beings must have the power to produce contingent beings. What A4 requires, then, is that there exist something which either exists necessarily or exists contingently but has existential security, and has the power to cause contingent beings to exist whose existence is possibly explicable.

12. COSMOLOGICAL ARGUMENT AND TELEOLOGICAL ARGUMENT

The sheer existence of a being that has existential security (and so whose existence is thus impossible to explain) and the power to bring into existence contingent beings whose existence is possibly explicable of course is not enough to explain the existence of contingent beings whose existence is possibly explicable. It must also be contingently the case that this power to produce contingent beings is exercised.

Suppose, then, that an existentially secure God freely brings it about that there are contingent beings whose existence is possibly explicable, and that God has sufficient reason to do so—that such a choice is neither inevitable nor without adequate justification. If this reason or justification is of the proper sort, it will be logically impossible that it in turn requires further justification. One function of arguments concerning the purpose of there being contingent beings is to give an account of what sort of reason or justification is relevant here. Once that account is given, there remains nothing that might be explained that is not explained, and the Principle of Sufficient Reason has been satisfied.

We can put this last point in terms of a further element in the Principle of Sufficient Reason the second version of the cosmological argument embraces:

(PSR3) There is an existentially secure being that exercises its causal power to cause B to exist and that has sufficient reason for doing so.

The idea here is that what the relevant Principle of Sufficient Reason—the principle composed of (PSR2) and (PSR3) together—requires is this: *whatever can be explained regarding the fact that there exist contingent beings whose existence can be explained, actually has an explanation.*[10] The idea is that this principle is satisfied only if an existentially secure God has sufficient reason to create such beings, and does so.

Suppose, for example, that God freely decides to create, and that it would have been perfectly morally in order for God to create and perfectly morally in order for God not to create. God creates a world such that it is perfectly morally in order that the world that is created come to be. The idea here is not that God appears before some tribunal that judges God justified in choosing to create at all, and to create the world God does create, and then kindly grants God permission to proceed. The idea is rather that what God does is something for which God—"internally" so to speak—has eminently sufficient reason for doing. There can be cases in which either doing some specific thing or not doing it is perfectly justified, and if God for perfectly sufficient reason freely chooses to create, this is compatible with its being true that, had God decided not to create, God would have had perfectly sufficient reason for not creating. An "arbitrary" choice can be (1) one made without rationale or it can be (2) one made when there are equally good rationales for deciding to perform an action and for decided to refrain from performing it. Even if God's action in creating is "arbitrary" in virtue of satisfying (2), it can be true that there is an explanation of God's choosing to create such that, given that explanation, it not possible that there be anything more by way explanation when one says that an existentially secure God has freely chosen to create contingent beings whose existence is possibly explicable. (We do not suggest that there are not other ways of articulating the notion of God's having sufficient reason to create contingent beings whose existence is

---

[10]This issue is further discussed in Keith Yandell, *Philosophy of Religion*, pp. 91ff.

possibly explicable, and doing so, that are also compatible with the second sort of cosmological argument.)

Abstract objects have no such power to exercise. Any material thing, or collection thereof, can fail to exist, and its existence is possibly explicable. One quickly runs out of candidates for beings who have existential security and the power to produce contingent beings whose existence it is logically possible to explain. It is hard to see how an existentially secure being could contingently produce contingent beings whose existence is possible explicable other than by free choice, a choice entirely rationally justified but not inevitably made. (Hence the relevance of [PSR3].) Thus two things can be said regarding the second version of the cosmological argument: it is hard to see other alternative explanations of there being contingent beings whose existence is possibly explicable, and so if there is an explanation of there being such things, it is reasonable to suppose that the explanation is the freely creative and rationally justified activity of an existentially secure God.

Perhaps the basic question in evaluating this version of the argument is this: is the conjunct composed of (PSR2) and (PSR3) true? Is it true that:

(PSR*) If a being or collection of beings B exists, B might not have existed, and B's existence is logically possible to explain, then there actually is an explanation of B's existence, and there is an existentially secure being that exercises its causal power to cause B to exist and that has sufficient reason for doing so.

It is hard to find something more clearly true than (PSR*) from which it follows. It is also not just obvious that (PSR*) is true—it lacks the evident truth of *The number four is even* or *You cannot be a bachelor if you are married*. Perhaps the best defense of it is this: if one denies it, then there is a perfectly good question to which there might have been a perfectly good answer, to which in fact there is no answer at all. That question is *What explains the fact that there are contingent beings whose existence is possibly explicable?* If PSR* is false, then there is no answer to that question; the existence of such things is a brute fact. While some deny this, in fact it is not a necessary truth that there are any brute facts; indeed, if (PSR*) is true, there are no brute facts.

13. A THIRD SORT OF COSMOLOGICAL ARGUMENT

A third sort of cosmological argument uses the notion of a best explanation. It holds that the existence and creative activity of an existentially secure God is the best explanation of the fact that there are contingent beings. A full articulation of this argument will involve tackling some difficult notions. One such notion is that of explanation itself: what exactly is it for something A to be the explanation of something else B? Then there is the notion of a best explanation: what makes one explanation better than another? Must there always be a best explanation? Does "best" amount to "best possible" or only to "better than any alternative we can think of"? What are the competing explanations to the one the cosmological argument offers of there being contingent beings whose existence is explicable?

If it is correct that the alternative explanations reduce to (1) the free and rational creative activity of an existentially secure God or (2) the existence of contingent beings simply being a brute fact, then whether the cosmological argument offers the best explanation is easy: it offers the only explanation, and therefore easily offers the best explanation. The question then is whether there must be an explanation or not, and that is what the cosmological arguer and her opponent dispute over.

There is also, as we have seen, a dispute between presenters of versions of the cosmological argument concerning which version of the argument is best. This is tantamount to a dispute as to which version of the principle of sufficient reason is true. The best explanation is the one that appeals to the true version of that principle.

It is at least not easy to locate a genuinely distinct third version of the cosmological argument—one that does not simply amount to disputes already noted. The remainder of the content of the supposed third version is perhaps simply the general issues noted above concerning explanation and relatively better or even best possible explanation. These are general issues in philosophy—particularly, in metaphysics and philosophy of science—that apply to, but are not specific to, the cosmological argument.

1. What can be said on behalf of the Principle of Sufficient Reason? How does this vary according to which form of it one is considering?
2. Is it reasonable to accept brute facts of existence?
3. Would it matter to the cosmological argument if there were just one thing in the world that does exist but might not have existed?
4. Can anything be necessarily self-preserving but not necessarily morally perfect?
5. Why can't the creative act that a necessarily existing God necessarily performs be the explanation of the fact that there exist things that might never have existed?

12. CRITICISMS OF THE COSMOLOGICAL ARGUMENT

J. L. Mackie

After receiving his B.A. from the University of Sydney and his M.A. from Oxford University, J. L. Mackie (1917–1981) taught at the University of York (England), the University of Otago (New Zealand), and the University of Sydney (Australia), before becoming Reader in Philosophy at Oxford University. He wrote extensively in metaphysics, ethics, the philosophy of science, and the history of philosophy. *The Miracle of Theism*, from which this selection is taken, is considered by many to be a contemporary classic in the philosophy of religion. In what follows, Mackie criticizes the cosmological argument.

READING QUESTIONS

1. How does Mackie sum up his two criticisms of the Principle of Sufficient Reason?
2. Does Mackie agree with Kant's claim that the cosmological argument rests on the ontological argument?
3. What is a "brute fact"?
4. What kind of explanation does Plato suggest?
5. Does Mackie claim to have shown the Principle of Sufficient Reason to be false?

1. CONTINGENCY AND SUFFICIENT REASON

Leibniz gives what is essentially the same proof in slightly different forms in different works; we can sum up his line of thought as follows. He assumes the *principle of sufficient reason*, that nothing occurs without a sufficient reason why it is so and not otherwise. There must, then, be a sufficient reason for the world as a whole, a reason why something exists rather than nothing. Each thing in the world is contingent, being causally determined by other things: it would not occur if other things were otherwise. The world as a whole, being a collection of such things, is therefore itself contingent. The series of things and events, with their causes, with causes of those causes, and so on, may stretch back infinitely in time; but, if so, then however far back we go, or if we consider the series as a whole, what we have is still contingent and therefore requires a sufficient reason outside this series. That is, there must be a sufficient reason *for* the world which is *other than* the world. This will have to be a necessary being, which contains its own sufficient reason for existence. Briefly, things must have a sufficient reason for their existence, and this must be found ultimately in a necessary being. There must be something free from the disease of contingency, a disease which affects everything in the world and the world as a whole, even if it is infinite in past time.

This argument, however, is open to criticisms of two sorts, summed up in the questions "How do we know that everything must have a sufficient reason?" and "How can there be a necessary being, one that contains its own sufficient reason?" These challenges are related: if the second question cannot be answered satisfactorily, it will follow that things as a whole cannot have a sufficient reason, not merely that we do not know that they must have one.

2. DOES THE COSMOLOGICAL ARGUMENT ASSUME THE ONTOLOGICAL ARGUMENT?

Kant's criticism of the Leibnizian argument turns upon this second objection; he claims that the cosmological proof depends upon the already criticized ontological proof. The latter starts from the concept of an absolutely necessary being, an *ens realissimum* [most real being], something whose essence includes existence, and tries to derive from that concept itself alone the fact that there is such a being. The cosmological proof "retains the connection of absolute necessity with the highest reality, but instead of reasoning . . . from the highest reality to necessity of existence, it reasons from the previously given unconditioned necessity of some being to the unlimited reality of that being." However, Kant's claim that the cosmological proof "rests" or "depends" on the ontological one, that "the so-called cosmological proof really owes any cogency which it may have to the ontological proof from mere concepts" is at least misleading. The truth is rather this. The cosmological argument purports to show, from the contingency of the world, in conjunction with the principle of sufficient reason, that there must be something else which is not contingent, which exists necessarily, which is or contains its own sufficient reason. When we ask how there could be such a thing, we are offered the notion of an *ens realissimum* whose essence includes existence. . . .

Does this connection imply that successful criticism of the ontological proof undermines the cosmological one also? That depends on the nature of the successful criticism. If its outcome is that the very concept of something's essence including existence is illegitimate—which would perhaps have been shown by

Kant's thesis that existence is not a predicate, or by the quantifier analysis of existence in general, if either of these had been correct and uncontroversial—then at least the final step in the cosmological proof is blocked, and Leibniz must either find some different explanation of how something might exist necessarily and contain its own sufficient reason, or else give up even the first step in his proof, abandoning the search for a sufficient reason of the world as a whole. But if the outcome of the successful criticism of the ontological proof were merely that we cannot validly start from a mere concept and thence derive actual existence—if we allowed that there was nothing illegitimate about the concept of a being whose essence includes existence, and insisted only that whatever a concept contains, it is always a further question whether there is something that instantiates it—then the cosmological proof would be unaffected by this criticism. For it does offer something that purports independently to answer this further question, namely the first step, the claim that the contingency of the world shows that a necessary being is required. . . .

Consequently the cosmological proof is not undermined by the so far established weakness of the ontological, though, since Kant thought he had carried through a criticism of the first sort, it would have been consistent for him to say that the cosmological proof was at least seriously threatened by it, that Leibniz would need to find some other account of how there could be a necessary being.

But perhaps we can still make something like Kant's point, even if we are relying only on a criticism of the second sort. Since it is always a further question whether a concept is instantiated or not, no matter how much it contains, the existence even of a being whose essence included existence would not be self-explanatory: there might have failed to be any such thing. This "might" expresses at least a conceptual possibility; if it is alleged that this being none the less exists by a metaphysical necessity, we are still waiting for an explanation of this kind of necessity. The existence of this being is not logically necessary; it does not exist in all logically possible worlds; in what way, then, does it necessarily exist in this world and satisfy the demand for a sufficient reason?

It might be replied that we understand what it is for something to exist contingently, in that it would

"THE BIRTHDAY FALLACY" ✳ *Elliot Sober*

Another problem arises when we ask whether the argument shows that there is *precisely one* first cause, or instead shows only that there is *at least one*. Suppose we grant that each causal chain in nature has a first member. According to Aquinas, each of these first members must be caused by some event outside of nature. However, it does not follow that there is exactly one such event outside of nature that set all causal chains in the natural world in motion. Here it is important to see the difference between the following two propositions; the first is different from and doesn't deductively imply the second:

Every event in the natural world traces back to an event that occurs outside nature.

There is a single event outside of the natural world to which each event in nature traces back.

The difference here parallels the logical difference between the following two propositions, the first of which is true and the second false:

Every person has a birthday—a day on which he or she was born.

There is a single day that is everyone's birthday.

I want to give a name to the mistaken idea that the second proposition follows from the first. I'll call it the *Birthday Fallacy*.

So one problem with. . . [Aquina's] . . . arguments. . . is that they don't show there is exactly one first cause or unmoved mover; at best, they show that there is at least one. To think otherwise is to commit the Birthday Fallacy.

From Elliot Sober, *Core Questions in Philosophys*, 3rd ed., (2001).

not have existed if something else had been otherwise: to exist necessarily is to exist but not contingently in this sense. But then the premiss that the natural world as a whole is contingent is not available: though we have some ground for thinking that each part, or each finite temporal stretch, of the world is contingent in this sense upon something else, we have initially no ground for thinking that the world as a whole would not have existed if something else had been otherwise; inference from the contingency of every part to the contingency *in this sense* of the whole is invalid. Alternatively, we might say that something exists contingently if and only if it might not have existed, and by contrast that something exists necessarily if and only if it exists, but it is not the case that it might not have existed. In this sense we could infer the contingency of the whole from the contingency of every part. But once it is conceded, for reasons just given, that it is not logically impossible that the alleged necessary being might not have existed, we have no understanding of how it could be true of this being that it is not the case that it might not have existed. We have as yet no

ground for believing that it is even possible that something should exist necessarily in the sense required.

3. THE PRINCIPLE OF SUFFICIENT REASON

This criticism is reinforced by the other objection, "How do we know that everything must have a sufficient reason?" I see no plausibility in the claim that the principle of sufficient reason is known a priori to be true. Leibniz thought that reliance on this principle is implicit in our reasoning both about physics and about human behaviour: for example, Archimedes argued that if, in a symmetrical balance, equal weights are placed on either side, neither will go down, because there is no reason why one side should go down rather than the other; and equally a rational being cannot act without a motive. But what is being used by Archimedes is just the rule that like causes produce like effects. This, and in general the search for, and expectation of, causes and regularities and reasons, do indeed guide inquiry in many fields. But the principles used are

"AN ARGUMENT AGAINST THE PRINCIPLE OF SUFFICIENT REASON" * William Rowe

Let us introduce the idea of *a positive, contingent state of affairs* as follows: X is a positive, contingent state of affairs if and only if from the fact that X obtains it follows that at least one contingent being exists. That there are elephants, for example, is a positive, contingent state of affairs. For, from the fact that it obtains, it follows that at least one contingent being exists. That there are no unicorns, however, is not a positive, contingent state of affairs. That God knows there are elephants is a positive, contingent state of affairs, and this is so even on the assumption that God is not a contingent being . . .

Consider the general state of affairs *t* recorded by the proposition "There are positive, contingent states of affairs." Is *t* itself a contingent or a necessary state of affairs? It is reasonable, I think, to claim that *t* is a contingent state of affairs. For although contingent beings do exist, it does not seem to be necessary that contingent beings exist. . . . Of course, if every true contingent statement records an actual state of affairs, there is no possible world in which only necessary states of affairs obtain. Each possible world contains some contingent states of affairs. But a contingent state of affairs may obtain in a given world—for example, the state of affairs recorded by the proposition "There

are no centaurs"—without it being true that any contingent beings exist in that world. But if, as it seems reasonable to believe, there is a possible world in which no contingent beings exist, then *t* is a contingent state of affairs. For if that world were the actual world, the state of affairs *t* would not obtain—since if *t* did obtain it would follow that some contingent being exists. Unlike S (the state of affairs recorded by the proposition "There are contingent states of affairs"), *t*, it appears, is a contingent state of affairs.

Armed with the idea of a positive, contingent state of affairs, we may now reformulate the argument against . . . [the principle of sufficient reason, or PSR,] . . . is as follows:

1. *PSR implies that every state of affairs has an explanation either within itself or in some other state of affairs.*
2. *There are positive, contingent states of affairs.*
3. *If there are positive, contingent states of affairs, then there is some state of affairs for which there is no explanation.*
Therefore:
4. *PSR is false.*

From William Rowe, *The Cosmological Argument* (1998).

not known a priori, and Samuel Clarke pointed out a difficulty in applying them even to human behaviour: someone who has a good reason for doing either A or B, but no reason for doing one of these rather than the other, will surely choose one arbitrarily rather than do neither. Even if, as is possible, we have some innate tendency to look for and expect such symmetries and continuities and regularities, this does not give us an a priori guarantee that such can always be found. In so far as our reliance on such principles is epistemically justified, it is so a posteriori, by the degree of success we have had in interpreting the world with their help. And in any

case these principles of causation, symmetry, and so on refer to how the world works; we are extrapolating far beyond their so far fruitful use when we postulate a principle of sufficient reason and apply it to the world as a whole. Even if, within the world, everything seemed to have a sufficient reason, that is, a cause in accordance with some regularity, with like causes producing like effects, this would give us little ground for expecting the world as a whole, or its basic causal laws themselves, to have a sufficient reason of some different sort.

The principle of sufficient reason expresses a demand that things should be intelligible *through and through.* The simple reply to the argument which relies on it is that there is nothing that justifies this demand, and nothing that supports the belief that it is satisfiable even in principle. As we have seen in considering the other main objection to Leibniz's argument, it is difficult to see how there even could be anything that would satisfy it. If we reject this demand, we are not thereby committed to saying that things are utterly unintelligible. The sort of intelligibility that is achieved by successful causal inquiry and scientific explanation is not undermined by its inability to make things intelligible through and through. Any particular explanation starts with premises which state "brute facts," and although the brutally factual starting-points of one explanation may themselves be further explained by another, the latter in turn will have to start with something that it does not explain, *and so on however far we go.* But there is no need to see this as unsatisfactory.

A sufficient reason is also sometimes thought of as a final cause or purpose. Indeed, if we think of each event in the history of the world as having (in principle) been explained by its antecedent causes, but still want a further explanation of the whole sequence of events, we must turn to some other sort of explanation. The two candidates that then come to mind are two kinds of purposive or teleological explanation. Things are as they are, Plato suggested, because it is *better* that they should be so. This can be construed either as implying that (objective) value is in itself creative . . . or as meaning that some intelligent being sees what would be better, chooses it, and brings it about. But why must we look for a sufficient reason of either of these sorts? The principle of sufficient reason, thus understood, expresses a demand for some kind of absolute purposiveness. But if we reject this demand, we are not thereby saying that "man and the universe are ultimately meaningless." People will still have the purposes that they have, some of which they can fulfil, even if the question "What is the purpose of the world as a whole?" has no positive answer.

The principle of sufficient reason, then, is more far-reaching than the principle that every occurrence has a preceding sufficient cause: the latter, but not the former, would be satisfied by a series of things or events running back infinitely in time, each determined by earlier ones, but with no further explanation of the series as a whole. Such a series would give us only what Leibniz called "physical" or "hypothetical" necessity, whereas the demand for a sufficient reason for the whole body of contingent things and events and laws calls for something with "absolute" or "metaphysical" necessity. But even the weaker, deterministic, principle is not an a priori truth, and indeed it may not be a truth at all; much less can this be claimed for the principle of sufficient reason. Perhaps it just expresses an arbitrary demand; it may be intellectually satisfying to believe that there is, objectively, an explanation for everything together, even if we can only guess at what the explanation might be. But we have no right to assume that the universe will comply with our intellectual preferences. Alternatively, the supposed principle may be an unwarranted extension of the determinist one, which, in so far as it is supported, is supported only empirically, by our success in actually finding causes, and can at most be accepted provisionally, not as an a priori truth.

4. CONCLUSION

The form of the cosmological argument which relies on the principle of sufficient reason therefore fails completely as a demonstrative proof.

QUESTIONS FOR FURTHER REFLECTION

1. Mackie contends that there is no reason to think that the Principle of Sufficient Reason is true. What reasons can you offer to think it is true?

2. Is it sufficient for the critic to undermine the Principle of Sufficient Reason by arguing there is no good reason to accept it or does he have to show that it is false?

3. Mackie argues that there is no good reason to accept the Principle of Sufficient Reason. Are there other beliefs that we cannot give good reason to think are true but are nevertheless justified. Think about *modus ponens,* the problem of induction and beliefs based on sense perception. Are they similar to the Principle of Sufficient Reason in this regard?

13. THE KALAM COSMOLOGICAL ARGUMENT

William Lane Craig

William Lane Craig (1949–) is Research Professor of Philosophy at the Talbot School of Theology, in La Mirada, California. He pursued his undergraduate studies at Wheaton College and his graduate studies at Trinity Evangelical Divinity School. He possesses two earned doctorates, the first from the University of Birmingham (England), where he studied under John Hick, the second from the Universität München (Germany). He lives in Atlanta, Georgia, with his wife Jan and their two teenage children, Charity and John. In this selection, Craig defends the kalam cosmological argument.

READING QUESTIONS

1. What, in Russell's view is the answer to the question "what explains the existence of the universe?"
2. What is the difference between an actual infinite and a potential infinite?
3. How is the "big bang" supposed to show that the universe began to exist?
4. What two models of the big bang theory does Craig mention?
5. How is the second law of thermodynamics supposed to show that the universe had a beginning?

". . . The first question which should rightly be asked," wrote Gottfried Wilhelm Leibniz, is "Why is there something rather than nothing?"[1] Think about that for a moment. Why *does* anything exist at all, rather than nothing? Why does the universe, or matter, or anything at all exist, instead of just nothing?

Many great minds have been puzzled by this problem. For example, in his biography of the renowned philosopher Ludwig Wittgenstein, Norman Malcolm reports,

> . . . he said that he sometimes had a certain experience which could best be described by saying that 'when I have it, *I wonder at the existence of the world*, I am then inclined to use such phrases as "How extraordinary that anything should exist!" or "How extraordinary that the world should exist!" '[2]

Similarly, the Australian philosopher J. J. C. Smart has said, ". . . my mind often seems to reel under the im-mense significance this question has for me. That anything exists at all does seem to me a matter for the deepest awe."[3]

Why *does* something exist instead of nothing? Unless we are prepared to believe that the universe simply popped into existence uncaused out of nothing, then the answer must be: something exists because there is an eternal, uncaused being for which no further explanation is possible. But who or what is this eternal, uncaused being? Leibniz identified it with God. But many modern philosophers have identified it with the universe itself. Now this is exactly the position of the atheist: the universe itself is uncaused and eternal; as Russell remarks, ". . . the universe is just there, and that's all."[4] But are there reasons to think that the universe is not eternal and uncaused, that there is something more? I think that there are. For we

---

[1]G. W. Leibniz, "The Principles of Nature and of Grace, Based on Reason," in *Leibniz Selections*, ed. Philip P. Wiener, The Modern Student's Library (New York: Charles Scribner's Sons, 1951), p. 527.
[2]Norman Malcolm, *Ludwig Wittgenstein: A Memoir* (London: Oxford University Press, 1958), p. 70.

[3]J. J. C. Smart, "The Existence of God," *Church Quarterly Review* 156 (1955): 194.
[4]Bertrand Russell and F. C. Copleston, "The Existence of God," in *The Existence of God* (Problems of Philosophy Series), ed. with an Introduction by John Hick (New York: Macmillan, 1964), pp. 174, 176.

can consider the universe by means of a series of logical alternatives:

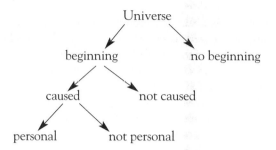

By proceeding through these alternatives, I think we can demonstrate that it is reasonable to believe that the universe is not eternal, but that it had a beginning and was caused by a personal being, and that therefore a personal Creator of the universe exists.

1. DID THE UNIVERSE BEGIN?

The first and most crucial step to be considered in this argument is the first: that the universe began to exist. There are four reasons why I think it is more reasonable to believe that the universe had a beginning. First, I shall expound two philosophical arguments and, second, two scientific confirmations.

The First Philosophical Argument

1. An actual infinite cannot exist.
2. A beginningless series of events in time is an actual infinite.
3. Therefore: a beginningless series of events in time cannot exist.

A collection of things is said to be actually infinite only if a part of it is equal to the whole of it. For example, which is greater? 1, 2, 3, . . . or 0, 1, 2, 3, . . . According to prevailing mathematical thought, the answer is that they are equivalent because they are both actually infinite. This seems strange because there is an extra number in one series that cannot be found in the other. But this only goes to show that in an actually infinite collection, a part of the collection is equal to the whole of the collection. For the same reason, mathematicians state that the series of even numbers is the same size as the series

of all natural numbers, even though the series of all natural numbers contains all the even numbers plus an infinite number of odd numbers as well. So a collection is actually infinite if a part of it is equal to the whole of it.

Now the concept of an *actual* infinite needs to be sharply distinguished from the concept of a *potential* infinite. A potential infinite is a collection that is increasing without limit but is at all times finite. The concept of potential infinity usually comes into play when we add to or subtract from something without stopping. Thus, a finite distance may be said to contain a potentially infinite number of smaller finite distances. This does not mean that there actually are an infinite number of parts in a finite distance, but rather it means that one can keep on dividing endlessly. But one will never reach an "infinitieth" division. Infinity merely serves as the limit to which the process approaches. Thus, a potential infinite is not truly infinite—it is simply indefinite. It is at all points finite but always increasing.

To sharpen the distinction between an actual and a potential infinite, we can draw some comparisons between them. The concept of actual infinity is used in set theory to designate a set which has an actually infinite number of members in it. But the concept of potential infinity finds no place in set theory. This is because the members of a set must be definite, whereas a potential infinite is indefinite—it acquires new members as it grows. Thus, set theory has only either finite or actually infinite sets. The proper place for the concept of the potential infinite is found in mathematical analysis, as in infinitesimal calculus. There a process may be said to increase or diminish to infinity, in the sense that the process can be continued endlessly with infinity as its terminus.[5] The concept of actual infinity does not pertain in these operations because an infinite number of operations is never actually made. According to the great German mathematician David Hilbert, the chief difference between an actual and a potential infinite is that a potential infinite is always something growing toward a limit of infinity, while an actual

---

[5]See Abraham A. Fraenkel, *Abstract Set Theory*, 2nd rev. ed. (Amsterdam: North-Holland Publishing Co., 1961), pp. 5–6.

"IS THE UNIVERSE A FREE LUNCH?" ✳ *Paul Davies*

We can . . . construct a cosmic scenario that reveals the astonishing scope of the new physics to explain the physical world. . . . Recent discoveries in particle physics have suggested mechanisms whereby matter can be created in empty space by the cosmic gravitational field, which only leaves the origin of spacetime itself as a mystery. But even here there are some indications that space and time could have sprung into existence spontaneously without violating the laws of physics. . . . In this remarkable scenario, the entire cosmos simply comes out of nowhere, completely in accordance with the laws of quantum physics, and creates along the way all the matter and energy needed to build the universe we now see. It thus incorporates the creation of all physical things, including space and time. Rather than postulate an unknowable singularity to start the universe off, the quantum spacetime model attempts to explain everything entirely within the context of the laws of physics. It is an awesome claim. We are used to the idea of "putting something in and getting something out," but getting something for nothing (or out of nothing) is alien. Yet the world of quantum physics routinely produces something for nothing. Quantum gravity suggests we might get everything for nothing. Discussing this scenario, the physicist Alan Guth remarked: "It is often said that there is no such thing as a free lunch. The universe, however, is a free lunch.". . . The "free lunch" scenario claims all you need are the laws—the universe can take care of itself, including its own creation.

From *God and the New Physics* (1990).

infinite is a completed totality with an actually infinite number of things.[6] A good example contrasting these two types of infinity is the series of past, present, and future events. For if the universe is eternal, as the atheist claims, then there have occurred in the past an actually infinite number of events. But from any point in the series of events, the number of future (that is, subsequent) events is potentially infinite. Thus, if we pick 1845, the birth year of Georg Cantor, who discovered infinite sets, as our point of departure, we can see that past events constitute an actual infinity while future events constitute a potential infinity. This is because the past is realized and complete, whereas the future is never fully actualized, but is always finite and always increasing. In the following discussion, it is exceedingly important to keep the concepts of actual infinity and potential infinity distinct and not to confuse them.

A second clarification that I must make concerns the word "exist." When I say that an actual infinite cannot exist, I mean "exist in the real world" or "exist outside the mind." I am not in any way questioning the legitimacy of using the concept of actual infinity in the realm of mathematics, for this is a realm of thought only. What I am arguing is that an actual infinite cannot exist in the real world of stars and planets and rocks and men. What I will argue in no way threatens the use of the actual infinite as a concept in mathematics. But I do think it is absurd that an actual infinite could exist in the real world.

I think that probably the best way to show this is to use examples to illustrate the absurdities that would result if an actual infinite could exist in reality. For suppose we have a library that has an actually infinite number of books on its shelves. Imagine furthermore that there are only two colors, black and red, and these are placed on the shelves alternately: black, red, black, red, and so forth. Now if somebody told us that the number of black books and the number of red books is the same, we would probably not be too surprised. But would we believe someone who

6David Hilbert, "On the Infinite," in *Philosophy of Mathematics*, ed. with an Introduction by Paul Benacerraf and Hilary Putnam (Englewood Cliffs, NJ: Prentice-Hall, 1964), pp. 139, 141.

told us that the number of black books is the same as the number of black books *plus* red books? For in this latter collection there are all the black books plus an infinite number of red books as well. Or imagine there are three colors of books, or four, or five, or a hundred. Would you believe someone if he told you that there are as many books in a single color as there are in the whole collection? Or imagine that there are an infinite number of colors of books. You would probably think that there would be one book per color in the infinite collection. You would be wrong. If the collection is actually infinite then, according to mathematicians, there could be for each of the infinite colors an infinite number of books. So you would have an infinity of infinities. And yet it would still be true that if you took all the books of all the colors and added them together, you wouldn't have any more books than if you had taken just the books of a single color.

Suppose each book had a number printed on its spine. Because the collection is actually infinite, that means that *every possible number* is printed on some book. Now this means that we could not add another book to the library. For what number would we give to it? All the numbers have been used up! Thus, the new book could not have a number. But this is absurd, since objects in reality can be numbered. So *if* an infinite library could exist, it would be impossible to add another book to it. But this conclusion is obviously false, for all we have to do is tear out a page from each of the first hundred books, add a title page, stick them together, and put this new book on the shelf. It would be easy to add to the library. So the only answer must be that an actually infinite library could not exist.

But suppose we *could* add to the library. Suppose I put a book on the shelf. According to the mathematicians, the number of books in the whole collection is the same as before. But how can this be? If I put the book on the shelf, there is one more book in the collection. If I take it off the shelf, there is one less book. I can see myself add and remove the book. Am I really to believe that when I add the book there are no more books in the collection and when I remove it there are no less books? Suppose I add an infinity of books to the collection. Am I seriously to believe there are no more books in the collection than before? Suppose I add an infinity of infinities of books to the collection. Is there

not now one single book more in the collection than before? I find this hard to believe.

But now let's reverse the process. Suppose we decide to loan out some of the books. Suppose we loan out book number 1. Isn't there now one less book in the collection? Suppose we loan out all the odd-numbered books. We have loaned out an infinite number of books, and yet mathematicians would say there are no less books in the collection. Now when we loaned out all these books, that left an awful lot of gaps on the shelves. Suppose we push all the books together again and close the gaps. All these gaps added together would add up to an infinite distance. But, according to mathematicians, after you pushed the books together, the shelves will still be full, the same as before you loaned any out! Now suppose once more we loaned out every other book. There would still be no less books in the collection than before. And if we pushed all the books together again, the shelves would still be full. In fact, we could do this an infinite number of times, and there would never be one less book in the collection, and the shelves would always remain full. But suppose we loaned out book numbers 4, 5, 6, . . . out to infinity. At a single stroke, the collection would be virtually wiped out, the shelves emptied, and the infinite library reduced to finitude. And yet, we have removed exactly the same number of books this time as when we first loaned out all the odd numbered books! Can anybody believe such a library could exist in reality?

These examples serve to illustrate that *an actual infinite cannot exist* in the real world. Again I want to underline the fact that what I have argued in no way attempts to undermine the theoretical system bequeathed by Cantor to modern mathematics. Indeed, some of the most eager enthusiasts of transfinite mathematics, such as David Hilbert, are only too ready to agree that the concept of an actual infinite is an idea only and has no relation to the real world.[7] So we can conclude the first step: an actual infinite cannot exist.

The second step is: *a beginningless series of events in time is an actual infinite*. By "event" I mean something that happens. Thus, this step is concerned with change, and it holds that if the series of past events or

---

[7]Hilbert, "On the Infinite," p. 151.

"THE ANTHROPIC PRINCIPLE" ✴ John D. Barrow and Frank J. Tipler

The central problem of science and epistemology is deciding which postulates to take as fundamental. The perennial solution of the great idealistic philosophers has been to regard Mind as logically prior, and even materialistic philosophers consider the innate properties of matter to be such as to allow—or even require—the existence of intelligence to contemplate it; that is, these properties are necessary or sufficient for life. Thus the existence of Mind is taken as one of the basic postulates of a philosophical system. . . . [D]uring the past fifteen years there has grown up amongst cosmologists an interest in a collection of ideas, known as the Anthropic Cosmological Principle, which offer a means of relating Mind and observership directly to the phenomena traditionally within the encompass of physical science.

The expulsion of Man from his self-assumed position at the centre of Nature owes much to the Copernican principle that we do not occupy a privileged position in the Universe. This Copernican assumption would be regarded as axiomatic at the outset of most scientific investigations. However, like most generalizations it must be used with care. Although we do not regard our position in the Universe to be central or special in every way, this does not mean that it cannot be special in *any* way. This "Anthropic Principle" . . .

[is that] *The Universe must have those properties which allow life to develop within it at some stage in its history.*

An implication . . . is that the constants and laws of Nature must be such that life can exist. This speculative statement leads to a number of quite distinct interpretations of a radical nature: firstly, the most obvious is to continue in the tradition of the classical Design Arguments and claim that:

A. *There exists one possible Universe "designed" with the goal of generating and sustaining "observers."*

This view would have been supported by the natural theologians of past centuries . . . [The physicist John Archibald] Wheeler has a second possible interpretation . . . :

B. *Observers are necessary to bring the Universe into being.*

This statement is somewhat reminiscent of the outlook of Bishop Berkeley and we shall see that it has physical content when considered in the light of attempts to arrive at a satisfactory interpretation of quantum mechanics.

From *The Anthropic Cosmological Principle* (1986).

changes just goes back and back and never had a beginning, then, considered all together, these events constitute an actually infinite collection. Let me provide an example. Suppose we ask someone where a certain star came from. He replies that it came from an explosion in a star that existed before it. Suppose we ask again, where did that star come from? Well, it came from another star before it. And where did that star come from?—From another star before it; and so on and so on. This series of stars would be an example of a beginningless series of events in time. Now if the universe has existed forever, then the series of all past events taken together constitutes an actual infinite.

This is because for every event in the past, there was an event before it. Thus, the series of past events would be infinite. Nor could it be potentially infinite only, for we have seen that the past is completed and actual; only the future can be described as a potential infinite. Therefore, it seems pretty obvious that a beginningless series of events in time is an actual infinite.

But that leads us to our conclusion: *therefore, a beginningless series of events in time cannot exist.* We have seen that an actual infinite cannot exist in reality. Since a beginningless series of events in time is an actual infinite, such a series cannot exist. That means the series of all past events must be finite and have a beginning. But because the universe *is* the series of all events, this means that the universe must have had a beginning.

Let me give a few examples to make the point clear. We have seen that if an actual infinite could exist in reality, it would be impossible to add to it. But the series of events in time is being added to every day. Or at least so it appears. If the series were actually infinite, then the number of events that have occurred up to the present moment is no greater than the number of events up to, say, 1789. In fact, you can pick any point in the past. The number of events that have occurred up to the present moment would be no greater than the number of events up to that point, no matter how long ago it might be.

Or take another example. Suppose Earth and Jupiter have been orbiting the sun from eternity. Suppose that it takes the Earth one year to complete one orbit, and that it takes Jupiter three years to complete one orbit. Thus, for every one orbit Jupiter completes, Earth completes three. Now here is the question: if they have been orbiting from eternity, which has completed more orbits? The answer is: they are equal. But this seems absurd, since the longer they went, the farther and farther Jupiter got behind, since every time Jupiter went around the sun once, Earth went around three times. How then could they possibly be equal?

Or, finally, suppose we meet a man who claims to have been counting from eternity, and now he is finishing: −5, −4, −3, −2, −1, 0. Now this is impossible. For, we may ask, why didn't he finish counting yesterday or the day before or the year before? By then an infinity of time had already elapsed, so that he should have finished. The fact is, we could never find anyone completing such a task because at any previous point he would have already finished. But what this means is that there could never be a point in the past at which he finished counting. In fact, we could never find him counting at all. For he would have already finished. But if no matter how far back in time we go, we never find him counting, then it cannot be true that he has been counting from eternity. This shows once more that the series of past events cannot be beginningless. For if you could not count numbers from eternity, neither could you have events from eternity.

These examples underline the absurdity of a beginningless series of events in time. Because such a series is an actual infinite, and an actual infinite cannot exist, a beginningless series of events in time cannot exist. This means that the universe began to exist, which is the point that we set out to prove.

The Second Philosophical Argument

1. The series of events in time is a collection formed by adding one member after another.
2. A collection formed by adding one member after another cannot be actually infinite.
3. Therefore, the series of events in time cannot be actually infinite.

This argument does not argue that an actual infinite cannot exist. But it does argue that an actual infinite cannot come to exist by the members of a collection being added one after the other.

The series of events in time is a collection formed by adding one member after another. This point is pretty obvious. When we consider the collection of all past events, it is obvious that those events did not exist simultaneously—all at once—but they existed one after another in time: we have one event, then another after that, then another, then another, and so on. So when we talk about the collection of "all past events," we are talking about a collection that has been formed by adding one member after another.

The second step is the crucial one: *a collection formed by adding one member after another cannot be actually infinite.* Why? Because no matter how many members a person added to the collection, he could always add one more. Therefore, he would never arrive at infinity. Sometimes this is called the impossibility of counting to infinity. For no matter how many numbers you had counted, you could always count one more. You would never arrive at infinity. Or sometimes this is called the impossibility of traversing the infinite. For you could never cross an infinite distance. Imagine a man running up a flight of stairs. Suppose everytime his foot strikes the top step, another step appears above it. It is clear that the man could run forever, but he would never cross all the steps because you could always add one more step.

Now notice that this impossibility has nothing to do with the amount of time available. It is of the very nature of the infinite that it cannot be formed by adding one member after another, regardless of the amount of time available. Thus, the only way an infinite collection could come to exist in the real world would be by having all the members created simultaneously. For example, if our library of infinite books were to exist in the real world, it would have to be created instantaneously by God. God would say, "Let there be . . . !" and the library would come into existence all at once. But it would be impossible to form the library by adding one book at a time, for you would never arrive at infinity.

Therefore, our conclusion must be: *the series of events in time cannot be actually infinite*. Suppose there were, for example, an infinite number of days prior to today. Then today would never arrive. For it is impossible to cross an infinite number of days to reach today. But obviously, today has arrived. Therefore, we know that prior to today, there cannot have been an infinite number of days. That means that the number of days is finite and therefore the universe had a beginning. Contemporary philosophers have shown themselves to be impotent to refute this reasoning.[8] Thus, one of them asks,

> If an infinite series of events has preceded the present moment, how did we get to the present moment? How could we get to the present moment—where we obviously are now—if the present moment was preceded by an infinite series of events?[9]

Concluding that this difficulty has not been overcome and that the issue is still in dispute, Hospers passes on to another subject, leaving the argument unrefuted. Similarly, another philosopher comments rather weakly, "It is difficult to show exactly what is wrong with this argument," and with that remark moves on without further ado.[10]

Therefore, since the series of events in time is a collection formed by adding one member after another, and since such a collection cannot be actually

infinite, the series of events in time cannot be actually infinite. And once more, since the universe is nothing else than the series of events, the universe must have had a beginning, which is precisely the point we wanted to prove.

The First Scientific Confirmation: The Evidence from the Expansion of the Universe

Prior to the 1920s, scientists assumed that the universe as a whole was a stationary object. But in 1929 an astronomer named Edwin Hubble contended that this was not true. Hubble observed that the light from distant galaxies appeared to be redder than it should be. He explained this by proposing that the universe is expanding. Therefore, the light from the stars is affected since they are moving away from us. But this is the interesting part: Hubble not only showed that the universe is expanding, but that *it is expanding the same in all directions*. To get a picture of this, imagine a balloon with dots painted on it. As you blow up the balloon, the dots get further and further apart. Now those dots are just like the galaxies in space. Everything in the universe is expanding outward. Thus, the relations in the universe do not change, only the distances.

Now the staggering implication of this is that . . . at some point in the past, *the entire known universe was contracted down to a single point*, from which it has been expanding ever since. The farther back one goes in the past, the smaller the universe becomes, so that one finally reaches a point of *infinite density* from which the universe began to expand. That initial event has come to be known as the "big bang."

How long ago did the big bang occur? Only during the 1970s [did] accurate estimates become available. In a very important series of six articles published in 1974 and 1975, Allan Sandage and G. A. Tammann estimate that the big bang occurred about 15 billion years ago.[11] Therefore, according to the big bang model, the universe began to exist with a great explosion from a

---

[8]For an in-depth discussion of this see William Lane Craig, *The Kalam Cosmological Argument* (New York: Macmillan, 1979), App. 1 and 2.

[9]John Hospers, *An Introduction to Philosophical Analysis*, 2nd ed. (London: Routledge & Kegan Paul, 1967), p. 434.

[10]William L. Rowe, *The Cosmological Argument* (Princeton, NJ: Princeton University Press, 1975), p. 122.

[11]Allan Sandage and G. A. Tammann, "Steps Toward the Hubble Constant. I–VI," *Astrophysical Journal* 190 (1974): 525–38; 191 (1974): 603–21; 194 (1974): 223–43, 559–68; 196 (1975): 313–28; 197 (1975): 265–80.

state of infinite density about 15 billion years ago. Four of the world's most prominent astronomers describe that event in these words:

> The universe began from a state of infinite density. Space and time were created in that event and so was all the matter in the universe. It is not meaningful to ask what happened before the big bang; it is somewhat like asking what is north of the north pole. Similarly, it is not sensible to ask where the big bang took place. The point-universe was not an object isolated in space; it was the entire universe, and so the only answer can be that the big bang happened everywhere.[12]

This event that marked the beginning of the universe becomes all the more amazing when one reflects on the fact that a state of "infinite density" is synonymous with "nothing." There can be no object that possesses infinite density, for if it had any size at all, it would not be *infinitely* dense. Therefore, as astronomer Fred Hoyle points out, the big bang theory requires the creation of matter from nothing. This is because as one goes back in time, he reaches a point at which, in Hoyle's words, the universe was "shrunk down to nothing at all."[13] Thus, what the big bang model requires is that the universe had a beginning and was created out of nothing.

Now some people are bothered with the idea that the universe began from nothing. This is too close to the Christian doctrine of creation to allow atheistic minds to be comfortable. But if one rejects the big bang model, he has apparently only two alternatives: the steady state model or the oscillating model. Let's examine each of these.

The steady-state model holds that the universe never had a beginning but has always existed in the same state. Ever since this model was first proposed in 1948, it has never been very convincing. According to S. L. Jaki, this theory never secured "a single piece of

experimental verification."[14] It always seemed to be trying to explain away the facts rather than explain them. According to Jaki, the proponents of this model were actually motivated by "openly antitheological, or rather anti-Christian motivations."[15] A second strike against this theory is the fact that a count of galaxies emitting radio waves indicates that there were once more radio sources in the past than there are today. Therefore, the universe is not in a steady state after all. But the real nails in the coffin for the steady state theory came in 1965, when A. A. Penzias and R. W. Wilson discovered that the entire universe is bathed with a background of microwave radiation. This radiation background indicates that the universe was once in a very hot and very dense state. In the steady-state model no such state could have existed, since the universe was supposed to be the same from eternity. Therefore, the steady-state model has been abandoned by virtually everyone. According to Ivan King, "The steady-state theory has now been laid to rest, as a result of clear-cut observations of how things have changed with time."[16]

But what of the oscillating model of the universe? John Gribbin describes this model,

> The biggest problem with the big bang theory of the origin of the universe is philosophical—perhaps even theological—what was there before the bang? This problem alone was sufficient to give a great initial impetus to the steady-state theory, but with that theory now sadly in conflict with the observations, the best way round this initial difficulty is provided by a model in which the universe expands, collapses back again, and repeats the cycle indefinitely.[17]

According to this model, the universe is sort of like a spring, expanding and contracting from eternity. It is only in the last three or four years that this model has been discredited. The key question here is whether the

[12]J. Richard Gott III, James E. Gunn, David N. Schramm, Beatrice M. Tinsley, "Will the Universe Expand Forever?," *Scientific American*, March 1976, p. 65. This article is a popular rewrite of their article, "An Unbound Universe?" *Astrophysical Journal* 194 (1974): 543–53.
[13]Fred Hoyle, *Astronomy and Cosmology: A Modern Course* (San Francisco: W. H. Freeman, 1975), p. 658.

[14]Stanley L. Jaki, *Science and Creation* (Edinburgh and London: Scottish Academic Press, 1974), p. 347.
[15]Jacki, *Science and Creation*, p. 347.
[16]Ivan R. King, *The Universe Unfolding* (San Francisco: W. H. Freeman, 1976), p. 462.
[17]John Gribbin, "Oscillating Universe Bounces Back," *Nature* 259 (1976): 15.

universe is "open" or "closed." If it is "closed," then the expansion will reach a certain point, and then the force of gravity will pull everything together again. But if the universe is "open," then the expansion will never stop, but will just go on and on forever. Now clearly, if the universe is open, then the oscillating model is false. For if the universe is open, it will never contract again.

Scientific evidence seems to indicate that the universe is open. The crucial factor here is the density of the universe. Scientists have estimated that if there are more than about three hydrogen atoms per cubic meter on the average throughout the universe, then the universe would be closed. That may not sound like very much, but remember that most of the universe is just empty space. I shall not go into all the technicalities of how scientists measure the density of the universe,[18] but let me simply report their conclusions. According to the evidence, the universe would have to be at least ten times denser than it is for the universe to be closed.[19] Therefore, the universe is open by a wide margin. Let me share with you the conclusion of Alan Sandage: (1) the universe is open, (2) the expansion will not reverse, and (3) *the universe has happened only once* and the expansion will never stop.[20]

The evidence therefore appears to rule out the oscillating model, since it requires a closed universe. But just to drive the point home, let me add that the oscillating model of the universe is only a *theoretical* possibility, not a *real* possibility. As Dr. Tinsley of Yale observes, in oscillating models

> even though the mathematics *says* that the universe oscillates, there is no known physics to reverse the collapse and bounce back to a new expansion. The physics seems to say that those

models start from the big bang, expand, collapse, then end.[21]

Hence, it would be impossible for the universe to be oscillating from eternity. Therefore, this model is doubly impossible.

The Second Scientific Confirmation: The Evidence from Thermodynamics

According to the second law of thermodynamics, processes taking place in a closed system always tend toward a state of equilibrium. In other words, unless energy is constantly being fed into a system, the processes in the system will tend to run down and quit. For example, if I had a bottle that was a sealed vacuum inside, and I introduced into it some molecules of gas, the gas would spread itself out evenly inside the bottle. It is virtually impossible for the molecules to retreat, for example, into one corner of the bottle and remain. This is why when you walk into a room, the air in the room never separates suddenly into oxygen at one end and nitrogen at the other. It is also why when you step into your bath you may be confident that it will be pleasantly warm instead of frozen solid at one end and boiling at the other. It is clear that life would not be possible in a world in which the second law of thermodynamics did not operate.

Now our interest in the law is what happens when it is applied to the universe as a whole. The universe is a gigantic closed system, since it is everything there is and there is nothing outside it.[22] What this seems to imply then is that, given enough time, the universe and all its processes will run down and the entire universe will slowly grind to a halt. This is known as the heat death of the universe. Once the universe reaches this state, no further change is possible. The universe is dead.

---

[18]See Gott, et al., "Will the Universe Expand Forever?" for a good synopsis.

[19]J. Richard Gott III and Martin J. Rees, "A Theory of Galaxy Formation and Clustering," *Astronomy and Astrophysics* 45 (1975): 365–76; S. Michael Small, "The Scale of Galaxy Clustering and the Mean Matter Density of the Universe," *Monthly Notices of the Royal Astronomical Society* 172 (1975): 23p–26p.

[20]Sandage and Tammann, "Steps Toward the Hubble Constant. VI," p. 276; Allan Sandage, "The Redshift Distance Relation. VIII," *Astrophysical Journal* 202 (1975): 563–82.

---

[21]Beatrice M. Tinsley, personal letter.

[22]In saying the universe is a closed system, I do not mean it is closed in the sense that its expansion will eventually contract. I rather mean that there is no energy being put into it. Thus, in the thermodynamic sense, the universe is closed, but in the sense of its density the universe is open. One must not confuse "open" and "closed" in thermodynamics with "open" and "closed" in expansion models.

There are two possible types of heat death for the universe. If the universe is "closed," then it will die a hot death. Tinsley describes such a state:

> If the average density of matter in the universe is great enough, the mutual gravitational attraction between bodies will eventually slow the expansion to a halt. The universe will then contract and collapse into a hot fireball. There is no known physical mechanism that could reverse a catastrophic big crunch. Apparently, if the universe becomes dense enough, it is in for a hot death.[23]

If the universe is closed, it is in for a fiery death from which it will never reemerge. But suppose, as is more likely, the universe is "open." Tinsley describes the final state of this universe:

> If the universe has a low density, its death will be cold. It will expand forever, at a slower and slower rate. Galaxies will turn all of their gas into stars, and the stars will burn out. Our own sun will become a cold, dead remnant, floating among the corpses of other stars in an increasingly isolated milky way.[24]

Eventually, equilibrium will prevail throughout, and the entire universe will reach its final state from which no change will occur.

Now the question that needs to be asked is this: If given enough time, the universe will reach heat death, then why is it not in a state of heat death now if it has existed forever, from eternity? If the universe did not begin to exist, then it should now be in a state of equilibrium. Its energy should be all used up. For example, I have a very loud wind-up alarm clock. If I hear that the clock is ticking—which is no problem, believe me—then I know that at some point in the recent past, it was wound up and has been running down since then. It is the same with the universe. Since it has not yet run down, this means, in the words of one baffled scientist, "In some way the universe must have been wound up."[25]

Some scientists have tried to escape this conclusion by arguing that the universe oscillates back and forth from eternity and so never reaches a final state of equilibrium. I have already observed that such a model of the universe is a physical impossibility. But suppose it were possible. The fact is that the thermodynamic properties of this model imply the very beginning of the universe that its proponents seek to avoid. For as several scientists have pointed out, each time the model universe expands it would expand a little further than before. Therefore, if you traced the expansions back in time they would get smaller and smaller and smaller. Therefore, in the words of one scientific team, "The multicycle model has an infinite future, but only a finite past."[26] As yet another writer points out, this implies that the oscillating model of the universe still requires an origin of the universe prior to the smallest cycle.[27]

Traditionally, two objections have been urged against the thermodynamic argument.[28] First, the argument does not work if the universe is infinite. I have two replies to this. (1) The universe is not, in fact, infinite. An actually spatially infinite universe would involve all the absurdities entailed in the existence of an actual infinite. But if space-time is torus-shaped, then the universe may be both open and finite. The objection is therefore irrelevant. (2) Even if the universe were infinite, it would still come to equilibrium. As one scientist explained in a letter to me, if every finite region of the universe came to equilibrium, then the whole universe would come to equilibrium. This would be true even if it had an infinite number of finite regions. This is like saying that if every part of a fence

[23]Beatrice M. Tinsley, "From Big Bang to Eternity?" *Natural History Magazine*, October 1975, p. 103.

[24]Tinsley, "From Big Bang to Eternity?" p. 185.

[25]Richard Schlegel, "Time and Thermodynamics," in *The Voices of Time*, ed. J. T. Fraser (London: Penguin, 1968), p. 511.

[26]I. D. Novikov and Ya. B. Zel'dovich, "Physical Processes Near Cosmological Singularities," *Annual Review of Astronomy and Astrophysics* 11 (1973): 401–2. See also P. C. W. Davies, *The Physics of Time Asymmetry* (London: Surrey University Press, 1974), p. 188. These findings are also confirmed by P. T. Landsberg and D. Park, "Entropy in an Oscillating Universe," *Proceedings of the Royal Society of London* A 346 (1975): 485–95.

[27]Gribbin, "Oscillating Universe," p. 16.

[28]R. G. Swinburne, *Space and Time* (London: Macmillan, 1968), p. 304; Adolf Grunbaum, *Philosophical Problems of Space and Time*, (Boston Studies in the Philosophy of Science), 2nd ed., Vol. 12 (Dordrecht, Neth., and Boston: D. Reidel Publishing, 1973), p. 262.

[29]P. C. W. Davies, personal letter.

is green, then the whole fence is green, even if there are an infinite number of pickets in the fence. Since every single finite region of the universe would suffer heat death, so would the whole universe. Therefore, the objection is unsound.

The second objection is that maybe the present state of the universe is just a fluctuation in an overall state of equilibrium. In other words, the present energy is like just the ripple on the surface of a still pond. But this objection loses all sense of proportion. Fluctuations are so tiny, they are important only in systems where you have a few atoms. In a universe at equilibrium, fluctuations would be imperceptible.[30] A chart showing fluctuations in such a universe would be simply a straight line. Therefore, since the present universe is in *disequilibrium*, what are we to conclude? According to the English scientist P. C. W. Davies, the universe must have been created a finite time ago and is in the process of winding down.[31] He says the present disequilibrium cannot be a fluctuation from a prior state of equilibrium, because prior to this creation event the universe simply did not exist. Thus, Davies concludes, even though we may not like it, we must conclude that the universe's energy "was simply 'put in' at the creation as an initial condition."[32]

Thus, we have two philosophical arguments and two scientific confirmations of the point we set out to defend: the universe began to exist. In light of these four reasons, I think we are amply justified in affirming the first alternative of our first disjunction: *the universe had a beginning.*

2. WAS THE BEGINNING CAUSED?

Having concluded that the evidence points to a beginning of the universe, let's now turn to our second set of alternatives: the beginning of the universe was either caused or not caused. I am not going to give a lengthy defense of the point that the beginning of the universe must have been caused. I do not think I need to. For probably no one in his right mind *sincerely* believes that the universe could pop into ex-

istence uncaused out of nothing. Even the famous skeptic David Hume admitted that it is preposterous to think anything could come into existence without a cause.[33] This is doubly true with regard to the entire universe. As the English philosopher C. D. Broad confessed, "I cannot really *believe in* anything beginning to exist without being caused by something else which existed before and up to the moment when the thing in question began to exist."[34] As still another philosopher has said, "It seems quite inconceivable that our universe could have sprung from an absolute void. If there is anything we find inconceivable it is that something could arise from nothing."[35] The old principle that "out of nothing, nothing comes" is so manifestly true that a sincere denial of this point is practically impossible.

This puts the atheist on the spot. For as Anthony Kenny explains, "A proponent of [the big bang] theory, at least if he is an atheist, must believe that the matter of the universe came from nothing and by nothing."[36] That is a pretty hard pill to swallow. In terms of sheer "believability," I find it intellectually easier to believe in a God who is the cause of the universe than in the universe's popping into existence uncaused out of nothing or in the universe's having existed for infinite time without a beginning. For me these last two positions are intellectually inconceivable, and it would take *more* faith for me to believe in them than to believe that God exists. But at any rate, we are not dependent upon just "believability," for we have already seen that both philosophical and empirical reasoning points to a beginning for the universe. So the alternatives are only two: either the universe was caused to exist or it sprang into existence wholly uncaused out of nothing about fifteen billion years ago. The first alternative is eminently more plausible.

It is interesting to examine the attitude of scientists toward the philosophical and theological implica-

---

[30]P. J. Zwart, *About Time* (Amsterdam and Oxford, Engl.: North Holland Publishing Co., 1976), pp. 117–19.

[31]Davies, *Physics*, p. 104.

[32]Davies, *Physics*, p. 104.

[33]David Hume to John Stewart, February 1754, in *The Letters of David Hume*, Vol. 1, ed. J. Y. T. Greig (Oxford, Engl.: Clarendon Press, 1932), p. 187.

[34]C. D. Broad, "Kant's Mathematical Antinomies," *Proceedings of the Aristotelian Society* 55 (1955): 10.

[35]Zwart, *About Time*, p. 240.

[36]Anthony Kenny, *The Five Ways: St. Thomas Aquinas' Proofs of God's Existence* (New York: Schocken Books, 1969), p. 66.

tions of their own big bang model. It is evident that there are such implications, for as one scientist remarks, "The problem of the origin (of the universe) involves a certain metaphysical aspect which may be either appealing or revolting."[37] Unfortunately, the man of science is, as Albert Einstein once observed, "a poor philosopher."[38] For these implications seem either to escape or not to interest most scientists. Since no empirical information is available about what preceded the big bang, scientists simply ignore the issue. Thus, Hoyle, after explaining that the big bang model cannot inform us as to where the matter came from or why the big bang occurred, comments, "It is not usual in present day cosmological discussions to seek an answer to this question; the question and its answer are taken to be outside the range of scientific discussion."[39] But while this attitude may satisfy the scientist, it can never satisfy the philosopher. For as one scientist admits, the big bang model only *describes* the initial conditions of the universe, but it cannot *explain* them.[40] As yet another astronomer concludes, "So the question 'How was the matter created in the first place?' is left unanswered."[41] Thus, science begs off answering the really ultimate question of where the universe came from. Scientific evidence points to a beginning of the universe; as rigorous scientists we may stop there and bar further inquiry, but as thinking people must we not inquire further until we come to the cause of the beginning of the universe?

Either the universe was caused to exist or it just came into existence out of nothing by nothing. Scientists refuse to discuss the question; but philosophers admit that it is impossible to believe in something's coming to exist uncaused out of nothing. Therefore, I think that an unprejudiced inquirer will have to agree that the beginning of the universe was caused, which is the second point we set out to prove: *the universe was caused to exist.*

Now this is a truly remarkable conclusion. For this means that the universe was caused to exist by something beyond it and greater than it . . .

3. PERSONAL OR IMPERSONAL CREATOR?

I think there is good reason to believe that the cause of the universe is a personal creator. This is our third set of alternatives: *personal or not personal.*

The first event in the series of past events was, as we have seen, the beginning of the universe. Furthermore, we have argued that the event was caused. Now the question is: If the cause of the universe is eternal, then why isn't the universe also eternal, since it is the effect of the cause? Let me illustrate what I mean. Suppose we say the cause of water's freezing is the temperature's falling below 0 degrees. Whenever the temperature is below 0 degrees, the water is frozen. Therefore, if the temperature is always below 0 degrees, the water is always frozen. Once the cause is given, the effect must follow. So if the cause were there from eternity, the effect would also be there from eternity. If the temperature were below 0 degrees from eternity, then any water around would be frozen from eternity. But this seems to imply that if the cause of the universe existed from eternity then the universe would have to exist from eternity. And this we have seen to be false.

One might say that the cause came to exist just before the first event. But this will not work, for then the cause's coming into existence would be the first event, and we must ask all over again for its cause. But this cannot go on forever, for we have seen that a beginningless series of events cannot exist. So there must be an absolutely first event, before which there was no change, no previous event. We have seen that this first event was caused. But the question then is: How can a first event come to exist if the cause of that event is always there? Why isn't the effect as eternal as the cause? It seems to me that there is only one way out of this dilemma. That is to say that the cause of the universe is personal and chooses to create the universe in time. In this way God could exist changelessly from eternity, but choose to create the world in time. By "choose" I do not mean God changes his mind. I mean God intends from eternity to create a world in time. Thus, the

[37]Hubert Reeves, Jean Audouze, William A. Fowler, and David N. Schramm, "On the Origin of Light Elements," *Astrophysical Journal* 179 (1973): 909–30.

[38]Albert Einstein, *Out of My Later Years* (New York: Philosophical Library, 1950), p. 58.

[39]Fred Hoyle, *Astronomy Today* (London: Heinemann, 1975), p. 166.

[40]Adrian Webster, "The Cosmic Background Radiation," *Scientific American*, August 1974, p. 31.

[41]J. V. Narlikar, "Singularity and Matter Creation in Cosmological Models," *Nature: Physical Science* 242 (1973): 136.

cause is eternal, but the effect is not. God chooses from eternity to create a world with a beginning; therefore, a world with a beginning comes to exist. Hence, it seems to me that the only way a universe can come to exist is if a Personal Creator of the universe exists. And I think we are justified in calling a Personal Creator of the universe by the name "God."

I would just like to make a few concluding remarks on God's relationship to time. Many people say God is outside time. But this is not what the Bible says. According to James Barr, in his book *Biblical Words for Time*, the Bible does not make it clear whether God is eternal in the sense that he is outside time or whether he is eternal in the sense of being everlasting throughout all time.[42] Thus, the issue must be decided philosophically. It seems to me that prior to creation God is outside time, or rather there is no time at all. For time cannot exist unless there is change. And prior to creation God would have to be changeless. Otherwise, you would get an infinite series of past events in God's life, and we have seen that such an infinite series is impossible. So God would be changeless and, hence, timeless prior to creation. I think that the doctrine of the Trinity can help us to understand this. Before creation, the Father, Son, and Holy Spirit existed in a perfect and changeless love relationship. God was not lonely before creation. In the tri-unity of his own being, he had full and perfect personal relationships. So what was God doing before creation? Someone has said, "He was preparing hell for those who pry into mysteries." Not at all! He was enjoying the fullness of divine personal relationships, with an eternal plan for the creation and salvation of human persons. The Bible says Christ "had been chosen by God before the creation of the world, and was revealed in these last days for your sake."[43] Nor was this plan decided on several eons ago. It is an eternal plan: The Bible says, "God did this according to his eternal purpose which he achieved through Christ Jesus our Lord."[44] Why did

God do this? Not because he needed us, but simply out of his grace and love.

So in my opinion, God was timeless prior to creation, and He created time along with the world. From that point on God places Himself within time so that He can interact with the world He has created. And someday God will be done with this creation. The universe will not, in fact, suffer cold death, for God will have done with it by then. The Bible says,

> You, Lord, in the beginning created the earth,
> and with your own hands you made the heavens.
> They will all disappear, but you will remain;
>   they will all grow old like clothes.
> You will fold them up like a coat,
>   and they will be changed like clothes.
> But you are always the same,
>   and you will never grow old.[45]

We have thus concluded to a personal Creator of the universe, who exists changelessly and independently prior to creation, and in time subsequent to creation. This is the central idea of what theists mean by "God."

QUESTIONS FOR FURTHER REFLECTION

1. According to many theists, God has always existed. But if God has always existed, why cannot the universe have always existed?

2. Craig defends the personal nature of the cause of the universe by using the notion of agent causation. Does the notion of agent causation depend on the existence of freewill? Why or why not?

3. Are there other models of the origin of the universe that, if true, might help or hurt Craig's argument? What are they and how do they affect his argument?

---

[42]James Barr, *Biblical Words for Time* (London: SCM Press, 1962), pp. 80, 145–47.
[43]I Peter 1:20. (TEV)
[44]Ephesians 3:11. (TEV)

---

[45]Hebrews 1:10–12. (TEV)

14. A CRITICAL EXAMINATION OF THE KALAM COSMOLOGICAL ARGUMENT

Wes Morriston

In 1972, Wes Morriston received his Ph.D. in philosophy from Northwestern University. Since then he has taught philosophy at the University of Colorado–Boulder. He has published on a variety of topics in philosophy of religion. In this selection, Morriston first explains that William Lane Craig's version of the *kalam* cosmological argument tries to establish (1) that the series of all past events must have a beginning; (2) that there is a First Cause of this series of events; (3) that the First Cause is a timeless person; and (4) that this person created the universe out of nothing. Morriston then takes issue with Craig's arguments for all of these conclusions. He tries to show (1) that neither of his philosophical arguments against the infinite past is successful; (2) that it is far from obvious that the beginning of the whole temporal series (even if it has one) must have a cause; (3) that Craig's argument for the claim that the first cause is a person cannot be sustained in the context of the sort of theism that he himself wishes to defend; and (4) that Craig's arguments for creation *ex nihilo* are not cogent. Morriston does not offer an alternative explanation of the universe—suggesting instead that we simply don't have enough to go on to answer all of the hard questions we are capable of asking about the origin of the natural world.

READING QUESTIONS

1. What is Euclid's maxim? How might it be argued that an actually infinite set does not violate this principle?
2. Which premise of Craig's second philosophical argument against the infinite past does Morriston reject, and why?
3. How does Craig distinguish between physical and metaphysical time? How does Morriston use this distinction to show that the two philosophical arguments against the infinite past are indispensable to the *kalam* argument?
4. Craig points out that no one in his right mind would suppose that a tiger couldn't pop into existence "uncaused, out of nothing, in this room right now." Morriston distinguishes between a "top down" and a "bottom up" explanation of this fact. Which explanation does Morriston prefer, and what bearing does this have on premise 1 of the *kalam* argument?
5. Why does Morriston think that the medieval principle, "nothing comes from nothing," provides no support for Craig's claim that the whole natural order (including time itself) must have a cause?
6. Why does Craig think that creation *ex nihilo* follows from the big bang model of the origin of the universe? What are Morriston's main objections to the arguments for this claim?
7. Craig claims that God "intends from eternity" to create a universe in time. He also claims that an eternal cause that is sufficient for its effect must have an eternal effect. Why does Morriston find this combination of claims problematic?

The *kalam*[1] cosmological argument has two parts. The first part attempts to show that there is a First Cause of the universe. It can be conveniently summarized as follows:

1. Everything that begins to exist has a cause of its existence.
2. The universe began to exist.
3. Therefore, the universe has a cause of its existence.

The second (and much less straightforward) part of the argument tries to show that the cause of the universe is a very powerful person—something like the God of classical theism. Only a personal cause, it is said, could have produced a universe with a temporal beginning.

In "Philosophical and Scientific Pointers to Creation *ex Nihilo*"[2], William Lane Craig strongly defends both parts of the *kalam* argument. Believing that premise 1 above is so obviously true that no sane person could doubt it, he concentrates most of his attention on premise 2, offering two philosophical arguments against the possibility of an infinite past. He also points to "scientific confirmation" of the claim that the universe has a beginning. Finally, Craig briefly presents the second part of the *kalam* argument, arguing (1) that the cause of the universe must be eternal, and (2) that an eternal cause of something that begins to exist could only be a person.

In the present essay, I shall raise a number of objections to both parts of the *kalam* argument. I shall try to show (1) that they depend heavily on the two philosophical arguments against the infinite past; (2) that neither of the philosophical arguments against the infinite past is successful; (3) that when it is applied to events happening at the very first moment of time, premise 1 is much more problematic than Craig realizes; (4) that the argument provides no evidence for creation *out of nothing*; and (5) that Craig's argument for the claim that the first cause is a person cannot be

sustained in the context of the sort of theism that he himself wishes to defend.

1. FIRST PHILOSOPHICAL ARGUMENT AGAINST THE INFINITE PAST

If the series of past events had no beginning, then the past would consist in an infinite series of events, all of which have actually happened. Is this possible? Craig thinks that it isn't. An infinite series of past events would be an actually infinite set of events, and he believes that there cannot be an actual infinite in reality.

To convince us that this is so, Craig asks us to imagine a library containing infinitely many books, numbered from zero onwards. Such a library would have some very peculiar properties. For example, one could add infinitely many books to such a library without increasing the number of books in the library. One could remove the first three books, and the library would not have any fewer books. One could even remove every other book, and it would not have any fewer books. Craig thinks it is obvious that such a library could not exist in reality. Even God could not create a library with infinitely many books.

Let's pause for a moment, and try to see what is going on. Why would the library not have any more books, no matter how many were added to its collection? Why would it have no fewer books even if every other book were removed? The reason is that there is a "one-to-one correspondence" between the set of books in the library before and the set of books after the change.

To see how this works, suppose that all the odd-numbered books have been removed. We can map the collection of books after their removal onto the total collection as follows. Let book #0 after the change correspond to book #0 before the change, book #2 after to book #1 before, book #4 after to book #2 before, and so on . . . There is then a one-to-one correspondence between the set of books *before*, and the set of books *after* the removal of all the odd-numbered books.

Now according to the *Principle of Correspondence*, as its mathematicians call it,

PC If two sets can be placed in one-to-one correspondence, they must have the same number of elements.

---

[1] So called in recognition of the Islamic philosophers who first developed this argument for the existence of God. The word "*kalam*" is Arabic for "speech" or "discourse," but it became the name of a school of Islamic theology that flourished in the middle ages.

[2] William Lane Craig, "Philosophical and Scientific Pointers to Creation *ex Nihilo*," in R. Douglas Geivett and Brendan Sweetman, eds., *Contemporary Perspectives on Religious Epistemology*, (New York and Oxford: Oxford University Press, 1992), 185–200.

It follows that there are no *fewer* books after the removal of all the odd-numbered ones.

Craig thinks this is absurd—there ought to be more odd-and-even numbered books altogether than even-numbered alone. So he concludes that there is something wrong with the whole idea of an infinite collection. Such collections simply cannot exist in reality.

Craig's argument at this point assumes the truth of a general principle that is worth stating explicitly. He calls it *"Euclid's maxim"* (after Euclid's fifth axiom).[3]

EM A whole is greater than any of its parts.

Given PC and EM, Craig thinks he can show that there are no actually infinite sets. For suppose there were. Then its members could be placed in one-to-one correspondence with a mere part (a "proper subset"[4]) of itself. By PC, it would then follow that the set has no more members than its part, contrary to EM.

As Craig sees it, both the Principle of Correspondence and Euclid's maxim are intuitively plausible. Both are obviously true of all finite sets. We get into trouble only when we try to apply them to infinite sets. So the reasonable thing to do is simply to deny that there are any actually infinite sets in reality. And since the series of past events exists in reality, Craig concludes that there cannot be infinitely many past events. The past must have a beginning—a very first event before which there were no others.

How strong is Craig's argument against the possibility of an actual infinite? The first thing to see is that Euclid's maxim about wholes and parts says nothing about the *number* of elements in a set. At most, it entails that *taken as a whole*, a set is *greater* than a mere *part* (a "proper subset") of itself. This is important, because Craig's argument turns on the claim that an infinite set would *not* be "greater" than its parts, and because (as we are about to see) there is a perfectly straightforward sense in which an infinite set *is greater* than any one of its proper subsets, even those that also have infinitely many members.

Craig's own example will make this clear. There is an obvious sense in which his imaginary library is "greater" than any of its parts, and this is so even though it does not have a greater *number* of books than some of its parts. For instance, the library as a whole is "greater" ("larger") than the part of the library containing only books numbered 3 and higher *simply in virtue of the fact that it contains books numbered 0, 1, and 2 as well as all the higher numbered books*. This is all by itself a perfectly legitimate sense of the word "greater"— one that is logically independent of the question, "What is the *number* of books in the two sets?"

There is, then, a fairly intuitive sense in which any set—even an infinite one—is "greater" than any of its parts. Not because the *number* of elements in the greater set is necessarily larger than the number of elements in the lesser one—but merely in virtue of the fact that it "contains" all the elements in the lesser set plus some others that the lesser one does not contain. That, all by itself, and without any reference to the *number* of elements in either set, is sufficient to make one "greater" than the other. When the word "greater" is understood this way, Craig's infinite library does *not* violate the principle that the "whole" is greater than its "part."

So EM by itself will not get Craig's argument off the ground. His argument requires something like the following principle:

EM* A set must have a greater *number* of elements than any of its proper subsets.

Now everyone would agree that while EM* is true of finite sets, it cannot be true of infinite sets. But what should we conclude from this? That there can't be any infinite sets? Or merely that while EM* is true of finite sets, but not of *all* sets?

How can we decide? Craig's appeal to the allegedly "absurd" properties of an actually infinite set won't settle the issue, since the "absurdity" of those properties depends on the necessary truth of EM*.

It seems that we have arrived at an impasse. Craig thinks it is obvious that something like EM* must be true of all sets, and that an actual infinite is therefore impossible. His opponents think that an actual infinite is possible, and that EM* is therefore true only of finite sets. Is there any way to decide who is right?

---

[3]William Lane Craig (with Quentin Smith), *Theism, Atheism, and Big Bang Cosmology*, (Oxford: Oxford University Press, 1993), 23ff.
[4]A set A is a proper subset of a set B if every element of A is an element of B, but not every element of B is an element of A.

One way to break the impasse would be to ask whether we know of any sets that really do (or could) have infinitely many members. Several candidates have been proposed.[5] I'll present just one of them.

Consider a finite chunk of spatial extension. It can, as we all know, be divided into subregions, each of which can again be divided into smaller subregions, and so on *ad infinitum*. It seems, then, that within any region of space, there are infinitely many subregions.

Craig is well aware of this objection. His answer is that space is not composed of points.[6] It follows that there are no natural boundaries within a given chunk of space, so that the various subregions do not exist *as* subregions until a division is actually made (at least in thought). Since we never arrive at a point at which all possible divisions have already been made (we can always—at least in principle—divide again), Craig thinks the number of subregions is only *potentially* infinite. It follows that we do not after all have a good example of an actual infinite existing in reality.

I think Craig is wrong about this. While it is true that we cannot actually make an infinite number of subdivisions within a region of space, it doesn't follow that the subregions are not *there* prior to any possible division. Nor does the lack of natural boundaries within a region of space settle this issue in Craig's favor. What follows from the absence of natural boundaries is only that the infinitely many subregions do not exist *apart from a specified way of dividing things up*.

It is not difficult to come up with a specification relative to which the number of coexistent subregions

is infinite. Unlike actually dividing a thing a given number of times, the specification for so dividing it doesn't have to be provided one step at a time—it can be given all at once. Just as we can specify the set of natural numbers all at once by the single rule, "starting with one, add one to the previous sum *ad infinitum*," so too I suggest that we can specify all the subregions of a given region *R* of space *relative to the rule*, "starting with *R* divide the results of the previous division by half *ad infinitum*." We don't have to rely on *natural* points of division within *R* to apply this rule to *R*. Nor do we need to *complete* the series of divisions in order to know that, *relative to this rule*, there is an *actual*—and not merely a potential—infinity of subregions.[7]

2. SECOND PHILOSOPHICAL ARGUMENT AGAINST THE INFINITE PAST

Craig has a second philosophical argument against the infinite past. Even if infinitely many things could exist at the same time, Craig thinks that the series of past events could not be actually infinite. He summarizes this argument as follows.

a. The series of events in time is a collection formed by adding one member after another.
b. A collection formed by adding one member after another cannot be actually infinite.
c. Therefore, the series of events in time cannot be actually infinite.[8]

Probably no one will want to deny the first premise. It just says that in any temporal series of events, the members of the series happen successively, one after the other. One event passes by, then another, and so on, up until the last event in the series. But what about the second premise? Why can't a collection formed in this step-by-step way have infinitely many members? Craig's answer is that an infinite collection could never be completed. No matter how many members have been added to the collection, you could always add one more. No matter how many

[5]Here are some other candidates. (1) Euclidean space contains an infinity of nonoverlapping subregions. Space may not be Euclidean, but it could have been. So an actual infinite is at least possible. (2) There are infinitely many natural numbers. If they are real, then the set of natural numbers is an actual infinite. (3) Craig thinks the future is infinite, and that there is a complete set of facts known to God about this infinite future. He argues that this is a merely potential infinite, on the ground that the future is not "real." This is quite a controversial claim—but even it is granted, it might still seem that Craig is committed to thinking that the set of *facts* about the future is actually infinite. Naturally, Craig has things to say about these candidates for an actual infinite, but limitations of space prevent a full treatment of the issue here.
[6]See William Lane Craig and Michael Tooley, *A Classic Debate on the Existence of God* (http://www.leaderu.com/offices/billcraig/docs/craig-tooley0.html)

[7]For a more thorough treatment of Craig's argument against the possibility of an actual infinite, see Wes Morriston, "Craig on the Actual Infinite," forthcoming in *Religious Studies*.
[8]"Philosophical and Scientific Pointers to Creation *ex Nihilo*," 190.

events have "gone by," the number of past events is only finite. We never arrive at infinity.

The second premise is obviously true of any series *having a temporal beginning*. Consider, for example, the series of years that began exactly one hundred years ago. One hundred of its members have passed by. The hundred and first is on its way. But no matter how many years are added, only finitely many years will have passed by. The collection will never be a completed infinity.

But what about a series *having no temporal beginning*? Why couldn't there be a series of years in which there is no first year? It's true that in such a series we never "arrive" at infinity, but that is only because infinity is, so to speak, "always already there." At every point in the series, infinitely many years have already passed by.

Craig thinks this is impossible. If infinitely many years must have passed by before a given year, then that year could never arrive. Craig illustrates his point as follows:

> . . . suppose we meet a man who claims to have been counting from eternity, and now he is finishing: −5, −4, −3, −2, −1, 0. Now this is impossible. For, we may ask, why didn't he finish counting yesterday or the day before or the year before? By then an infinity of time had already elapsed, so that he should have finished. The fact is, we could never find anyone completing such a task because at any previous point he would have already finished.[9]

This is not a good argument. It confuses "having counted infinitely many numbers" with "having counted all the negative numbers up to zero." The man has indeed always already completed the first of these tasks; but he has not completed the second one until he arrives at zero. When he arrived at −1 he had completed a different task—that of counting all the members in the series < . . , −n, . . , −2, −1 >. When he arrived at −2, he had completed yet another task—that of counting all the members in the series, < . . , −n, . . , −3, −2 >. And so on.

9"Philosophical and Scientific Pointers to Creation *ex Nihilo*," 189–90.

No doubt there *could* have been a beginningless count ending in zero at any time in the infinite past. But Craig gives no good reason for thinking that there *must* have been one or that the infinite counter in his example would have to be the person who had completed it. Consequently, it seems to me that our objection to Craig's defense of premise *b* remains undefeated. This premise holds true for any series *having a beginning*—if you *start out* on an infinite series, you will never complete it. But that tells us nothing at all about whether a *beginningless* series of events is possible.

3. HASN'T GOD ALWAYS EXISTED?

But suppose Craig is right, and the past does have a beginning. You might wonder how long he thinks God has existed. Since God does not begin to exist, mustn't He have existed forever? And wouldn't that be an actual infinite of the very sort that Craig says is impossible? Craig's explanation is interesting.

> God was timeless prior to creation, and He created time along with the world. From that point on God places Himself within time so that He can interact with the world He has created. [198]

This might seem incoherent. If God exists *prior* to creation, mustn't He exist at a *time* prior to creation? How, then, can He be *timeless* prior to creation? Craig's answer is that God is causally, but not temporally, prior. He has the kind of "priority" that any cause has over its effect. Let me explain.

Craig believes that it is possible for a cause and its effect to occur simultaneously. For example, it might be thought that the pressure of a man's posterior on a cushion causes the depression in the cushion, even though these states of affairs obtain simultaneously. But even in cases like this, the causal relation is asymmetrical—the cause is the source of the effect, and not the other way around. In that sense, the cause is "prior" to its effect.

This is how we must understand Craig's claim that God is timeless "prior" to the creation of time. Insofar as he is the *creator* of time, God is "causally prior" to time itself. And this is so even though there is (obviously enough) no time prior to the creation of time. "Prior to" (apart from) the creation of time and the universe, God is timeless.

On the other hand, Craig also insists that in creating time God "places Himself within time so that He can interact with the world He has created." Even though God—*as* creator of the universe and time—is timeless, Craig insists that God's life in relation to the world He creates has temporal duration. God's life in time, so to speak, begins with creation. Subsequent to creation, God has a past and that past has a beginning, since it began with the creation of time and the universe.

There is a small but extremely important qualification that Craig does not mention in "Philosophical and Scientific Pointers to Creation *ex Nihilo*." He wants to leave open the *possibility* that time began prior to the creation of the physical universe. This may surprise you, since the four "prominent astronomers" whose words Craig quotes with so much approval in this essay assert that it is "meaningless" to "ask what happened before the big bang."[10] This might lead one to suppose that Craig agrees that it is meaningless to suggest that there was a time prior to the creation of our physical universe. But this is not his considered view. In another essay, he writes:

> . . . [S]uppose that God led up to creation by counting, "1, 2, 3, . . ., fiat lux!" In that case the series of mental events alone is sufficient to establish a temporal succession prior to the commencement of physical time at t = 0. There would be a sort of metaphysical time based on the succession of contents of consciousness in God's mind prior to the inception of physical time. Thus, it is meaningful to speak both of the cause of the Big Bang and of the beginning of the universe.[11]

In this scenario, the physical time of the universe is created at t = 0 when God says, "fiat lux" ("let there be light"). But the creation of physical time happens within a more fundamental kind of time—"metaphysical time," as Craig calls it. This more fundamental

temporal series also has a beginning, however. For expository purposes, Craig usually operates on the assumption that it is created along with physical time. But in the passage quoted above he acknowledges another possibility—that of a temporal series of events leading up to creation. In Craig's imaginary illustration, metaphysical time begins on the count of "one," and whole series of events between that first moment and the creation of the universe occurs prior to the first moment of physical time.

The nature of metaphysical time and its relation to physical time are large and difficult questions, lying well beyond the scope of this essay.[12] But for reasons that will become apparent in the next section, it is important to see that Craig does allow for the possibility of a series of events that are prior—in metaphysical time—to the beginning of our universe.

4. SCIENTIFIC CONFIRMATION

In sections 1 and 2 I tried to show that Craig's two philosophical arguments against the possibility of an infinite past are unsuccessful. But you might think this doesn't matter very much, since scientists have shown that the universe very likely *did* have a beginning—that it almost certainly began with a very big "bang" about fifteen billion years ago. So doesn't Craig's argument get all the backing it needs even if the two philosophical arguments against the possibility of an infinite past are unsound?

Unfortunately, things are not that simple. What the scientific considerations show is only that our physical universe very likely had a beginning. What, if anything, happened before the beginning of our universe—and even whether or not there was any "before"—is not settled by the scientific evidence. Discoveries in the empirical sciences have not ruled out the possibility that our universe is the product of events that occurred at a time prior to the beginning of our space-time.

It may occur to you to object that it makes no sense to speak of a time prior to the beginning of space-time, since it is created along with the universe. But

---

[10]This is the view of the four "prominent astronomers" whom Craig quotes so approvingly. See "Philosophical and Scientific Pointers to Creation *ex Nihilo*," 192.

[11]"The Origin and Creation of the Universe: A Response to Adolf Grünbaum," *British Journal for the Philosophy of Science* 43 (1992), 233–240.

[12]For more on Craig's view of these matters, see his *Time and Eternity: Exploring God's Relationship to Time* (Wheaton, III: Crossway Books, 2001).

this point is of no use to Craig, since, as we saw at the end of the previous section, he thinks there is another more fundamental kind of time—*metaphysical* time—that does not depend on the existence of our universe. So on Craig's own view, there at least *could* have been a series of events occurring in metaphysical time prior to the beginning of our universe.

This is important, because it means that we have to take into account the logical possibility of a temporal series of causes and effects prior to the beginning of the universe. Perhaps the universe was produced by something else, which in turn was produced by something else, and so on *ad infinitum*. The scientific considerations do not rule this out. To block the possibility of such a regress, Craig must rely on his philosophical arguments against the infinite past. If those arguments are unsound, then the beginning of our universe might (for all Craig has shown) be merely the most recent in a beginningless series of causes and effects.

One much discussed version of this possibility is the so-called "oscillating universe" hypothesis. On this hypothesis, the universe expands and then contracts. Each cycle begins with a "big bang," and ends in a "big crunch." And that's how it is throughout a possibly infinite past.

Craig thinks there is more than enough scientific evidence to refute the oscillating universes hypothesis. For example, he points out that there isn't enough dark matter to reverse the expansion of the universe and bring about a "big crunch."[13] But even if this is correct, it tells us only that the pattern of oscillation is not going to *continue*. It tells us nothing about what, if anything, *preceded* the big bang. Why think that in the previous cycle—if there was one—there was no more dark matter than in ours? Why even think it must have been governed by the same physical laws as ours?

Now Craig would undoubtedly point out that there is no empirical support for saying that the preceding cycles contained more dark matter than ours. For that matter, he could point out that there is no em-

pirical support for any sort of infinite series of past causes and effects. This is undoubtedly true. On the other hand, unless Craig's arguments against the infinite past are better than I think they are, an infinite series of causes and effects in metaphysical time remains one of the logical possibilities. And even if it lacks empirical support, it is not obvious that it has any *less* going for it than Craig's hypothesis—that of a timeless person who somehow managed to create time and put itself into time. One should not overlook the possibility that none of our hypotheses about the origin of the universe is especially likely to be true. Perhaps we just don't have enough to go on to choose among the logical possibilities, and the right thing to say is that we simply do not know how or why the universe came into existence.

5. MUST THE BEGINNING HAVE A CAUSE?

But suppose it is granted that the past is finite, and that there is a very first event in the series of events leading up to the present. For simplicity's sake, let us assume that this first event coincides with the beginning of our universe.

This brings us to our next question. Is premise 1 of the *kalam* argument true? Must everything that begins to exist—even the very first event in the history of time—have a cause? Craig thinks it is unnecessary to give a lengthy defense of this claim. "Does anyone in his right mind," he asks, "really believe that, say, a raging tiger could suddenly come into existence uncaused, out of nothing, in this room right now?"[14] Probably no one does. Craig then invites us to apply this "intuition" to the beginning of the universe, and conclude that it too must have a cause.

But surely this is much too quick. Of course, no one thinks a tiger could just spring into existence "in this room right now." But before we jump to conclusions, we need to ask *why* this is so. What makes this so obvious? Is it, as Craig seems to suppose, that all normal persons believe the first premise of the *kalam* argument, and then apply it to the case of the tiger? Call that the *top-down* explanation. Or is it rather that we have a lot of experience of animals (and other middle-sized

---

[13]Actually, the most recent speculation has it that there is enough "dark matter," but that this is more compensated for by the presence of something called "dark energy." There is, so they say, enough dark energy to resist the pull of gravity, and keep the universe expanding indefinitely. If this is right, then *our* universe is not going to collapse in a "big crunch."

[14]Craig, "the Existence of God and the Beginning of the Universe," *Truth Journal*, v. 3 (http://www.iclnet.org/clm/truth/3truth11.html)

material objects), and we know that popping up like that is just not the way such things come into existence? Call that the *bottom-up* explanation.

The bottom-up explanation takes note of the fact that we are dealing with a familiar *context*—one provided by our collective experience of the world in which we live and of the way it operates. It is our background knowledge of that context—our empirical knowledge of the natural order—that makes it so preposterous to suppose that a tiger might pop into existence uncaused. We *know* where tigers and such come from, and that just isn't the way it happens.

Now contrast the situation with regard to the beginning of time and the universe. There is no familiar law-governed context for it, precisely because there is nothing (read, "there is not anything") prior to such a beginning. We have no experience of the origin of worlds to tell us that *worlds* don't come into existence like that. We don't even have experience of the coming into being of anything remotely analogous to the "initial singularity" that figures in the big bang theory of the origin of the universe. The intuitive absurdity of tigers and the like popping into existence out of nowhere does not entitle us to draw quick and easy inferences about the beginning of the whole natural order.

However, Craig thinks it is, if anything, even *more* obvious that the universe (and time) could not have come into existence uncaused. His reason seems to be that prior to the beginning of an uncaused universe, there would be absolutely nothing. Immediately following the tiger passage quoted above, he writes, "If prior to the existence of the universe, there was absolutely nothing—no God, no space, no time—how could the universe possibly come to exist?[15] Craig thinks this is a straightforward application of the medieval principle that "nothing comes from nothing" (*ex nihilo nihil fit*)—a principle he believes to be so obviously true that no one could sincerely deny it. In another place, he writes:

. . . if originally there were absolutely nothing—no God, no space, no time—then how could the universe possibly come to exist? The truth of the

principle *ex nihilo, nihil fit* is so obvious that I think we are justified in foregoing an elaborate defense of the argument's first premiss.[16]

Let's think about this a bit. It sounds rather as if Craig is saying that if there existed a *situation* in which there was absolutely nothing, then—in that situation—nothing could come into existence. This is nonsense. "Nothing at all" is not a weird sort of "something." It is not a situation "in" which something else "can" or "cannot" come to be. "Nothing" just means "not anything."

What else could Craig mean when he says that "if originally there were absolutely nothing" nothing could come into existence? Perhaps he means no more than this:

(NA) If there had not been anything, then there would not have been anything.

NA is undoubtedly true. If there were "not anything"—*not even time*—then there would not be anything—not even a "coming-into-existence" of the universe. But I doubt if this can be all that Craig has in mind, since nothing of interest follows from so trivial a claim.

It is not surprising, therefore, that Craig sometimes slips into talking as if the issue were whether something could "spring into existence" out of a *temporally prior situation* in which there is nothing at all. In the following passage, for example, he writes:

. . . virtually no one ever challenges the premiss that if *in the past* nothing existed then nothing would exist now. . . . The old principle *ex nihilo nihil fit* appears to be so manifestly true that a sincere denial of this axiom is well-nigh impossible.[17]

Since there can hardly be a *past* state of affairs in which there is *no time*, it looks as if Craig here understands the principle, *ex nihilo nihil fit*, to mean something like the following.

(NT) If, at a given time, there were nothing at all (apart from time itself), then at no later time could anything begin to exist.

---

15 *Reasonable Faith: Christian Truth and Apologetics*, 93.

16"The Existence of God and the Beginning of the Universe." My emphasis.
17 *Theism, Atheism, and Big Bang Cosmology*, 58–59. My emphasis.

But this won't give Craig what he wants, since even if it is true, NT does not entail that the first event—the event before which there was no time—must have a cause.

If neither NA nor NT provides what is needed here, is there anything else Craig might mean by his frequent repetition of the phrase, "from nothing, nothing comes"? I think there is. I suspect that at bottom this is merely a confusing way of saying that whatever begins to exist must have a cause (something "from" which it "comes"). But if that's all it comes to, then the great medieval principle is merely a restatement of premise 1 of the *kalam* argument, and provides no additional support for it. Certainly it tells us nothing useful about the beginning of the whole natural order—or about the need for a cause at a time prior to which there is no time.

There may also be something to be said *against* the claim that there could be a cause of the whole temporal order of events. Many philosophers hold that causes must precede their effects in time. If they are right, then it follows straightaway that a first event *could not* have a cause.

The nature of causation is another large and difficult issue that lies beyond the scope of this essay, but it is interesting to observe that some of the very philosophers Craig cites as favoring his own causal principle also hold that causes must precede their effects in time. For example, David Hume's famous analysis of the causal relation explicitly includes this requirement. And in the very passage quoted by Craig, C. D. Broad says that he cannot believe that anything could begin to exist "without being caused by something else which existed *before and up to* the moment when the thing in question began to exist."[18] This is obviously inconsistent with Craig's account of creation, since according to that account, there is no time prior to the very first event. Its cause cannot therefore have existed "before and up to the moment" at which it occurred.

I am not sure what Hume and Broad and the rest would say if they thought time had a beginning. Would they (like Craig) conclude that some causes do not precede their effects in time? Or would they simply say

that a first event (unlike all later ones) could not have a cause? I won't try to settle that issue here. But it is important to see that in order to get the *kalam* argument off the ground, Craig must take controversial positions on a number of highly debatable issues having to do with the nature of time and of causation. Contrary to what Craig supposes, therefore, a sane adult may have sincere—and quite reasonable—doubts about the scope of premise 1 of the *kalam* argument.

6. CREATION OUT OF NOTHING?

As the title "Philosophical and Scientific Pointers to Creation *ex Nihilo*" suggests, Craig believes he can show, not merely that the universe was created *by* a person, but that it was created *out of* nothing. His argument for the second of these claims appeals to a version of the big bang theory according to which the universe emerged from an infinitely dense particle that exploded some fifteen billion years ago.

> This event that marked the beginning of the universe becomes all the more amazing when one reflects on the fact that a state of "infinite density" is synonymous with "nothing." There can be no object that possesses infinite density, for if it had any size at all, it would not be *infinitely* dense. Therefore, as astronomer Fred Hoyle points out, the big bang theory requires the creation of matter from nothing. This is because as one goes back in time, he reaches a point at which, in Hoyle's words, the universe was "shrunk down to nothing at all." Thus, what the big bang model requires is that the universe had a beginning and was created out of nothing.[19]

The argument Craig presents in this passage can be summarized as follows.

a. According to the big bang theory, the universe was created out of an infinitely dense particle.
b. There can be no object having infinite density.
c. So "infinite density" is synonymous with "nothing."
d. Therefore, the big bang theory entails that the universe was created out of nothing.

---

[18]"Philosophical and Scientific Pointers to Creation *ex Nihilo*," 196. My emphasis.

[19]*Ibid.*, 192.

This argument is extremely confused. For one thing, step *c* of the argument is obviously false. "Infinite density" is not synonymous with "nothing," and the "initial singularity" that figures in the big bang theory is not simply nothing at all. A mere *nothing* could not explode, as the infinitely dense particle is supposed to have done. And even if it lacks spatial and temporal spread, the initial singularity has other properties. For starters, it has the property of "being infinitely dense." It is therefore a quite remarkable *something*, and not a mere nothing.

But this is not all. If premise *b* is true—if it is really true that "there can be no object that possesses infinite density," then this version of the big bang theory is simply false, since it says that there once was such an object.

So far, then, it appears that the big bang model of the origin of our universe provides no support for the claim that the universe was created *out of* nothing. Elsewhere, however, Craig explains his position somewhat differently.

> On such a model the universe originates *ex nihilo* in the sense that at the initial singularity it is true that *There is no earlier space-time point* or it is false that *Something existed prior to the singularity.*[20]

In this passage, Craig does not deny that an infinitely dense particle could exist. Nor does he make the mistake of saying that the "initial singularity" is a mere "nothing." What he says instead is that nothing *preceded* the initial singularity *in time*, and this is somehow supposed to show that the initial singularity was created out of nothing. The argument goes like this:

e. The initial singularity exists at the earliest point of space-time.
f. There is no time prior to the earliest point in space-time.
g. Therefore, there was nothing temporally prior to the initial singularity.
h. So the initial singularity must have been created out of nothing.

There are at least two problems with this argument. For the reasons already given in section 3 above, I do not think the big bang theory entails the truth of premise *f*. Even it is granted that space-time begins at the initial singularity, it does not follow that *metaphysical* time begins with the first moment in space-time. Recall that on Craig's view, God *could have* created time long before creating the space-time of our universe. It follows that there *could have been* something prior to the earliest point in space-time (t = 0), in which case premise *f* would be false. Premise *f may* be true anyway—metaphysical time and space-time *could have* begun together. But since the big bang theory says nothing about metaphysical time, Craig cannot consistently claim that the big bang theory shows this to be so.

But suppose that the first moment of metaphysical time does coincide with t = 0 in the space-time of our universe. That still doesn't give us creation *ex nihilo*. What follows is only that the universe wasn't created out of something *that existed at a time earlier than* t = 0. So step *h* of the argument does not follow from step *g* without an additional premise:

i. If there was nothing temporally prior to the initial singularity, then it must have been created out of nothing.

But why think this additional premise is true? Why couldn't the initial singularity be created out of something that exists timelessly? Whether this is possible depends on what sorts of things exist outside of time. According to Craig we know that God, the first cause of the universe exists outside time "prior" to creating the universe. But why suppose that God is the only being who exists outside time? Why couldn't there also have been a timeless "stuff" that God formed into a universe?

Craig thinks he can rule out this possibility on the ground that physical matter and energy are temporal in nature. But why suppose that these are the only possible "stuffs" out of which God might have made the universe? It's true that we are not acquainted with any timeless "stuffs" that could have played this role. But we don't encounter any timeless persons either, and Craig has no trouble with that idea. So why couldn't there also have been a timeless material "stuff" for God to work with?

---

[20]"The Ultimate Question of Origins: God and the Beginning of the Universe," *Astrophysics and Space Science* 269–270 (1999), 723–740.

I am not putting this forward as a particularly likely hypothesis. It seems to me that we simply don't have enough to go on to decide what (if anything) God (if he exists) might have made the universe out of. As a wise philosopher once said, "Our line is too short to fathom such abysses."[21] What I am sure of is that the big bang theory does not settle the issue in favor of creation *ex nihilo*.

7. MUST THE FIRST CAUSE BE A PERSON?

Our final topic is Craig's argument for saying that the First Cause of the universe must be a person. It is a difficult argument, and Craig's presentation of it is brief. It seems to go something like this.

We know that the cause of the beginning of the universe (or whatever the first event was) must be eternal. Otherwise it would be one of the things that begins to exist, and would be just as much in need of a cause as the universe.

Now natural causes—"mechanical" causes, as Craig sometimes calls them[22]—are *sufficient* for their effects. They produce their effects as soon as all the relevant conditions are in place. It follows that if this sort of cause had no beginning, its effect could not have a beginning either. For example, Craig says, if the temperature is cold enough for long enough, whatever water happens to be around must have turned to ice. So if there had always been water and the temperature had *always* been below zero, all the water would *always* have been frozen.

The general point is that if a cause is sufficient for its effect, and the cause is eternal, then the effect must be eternal too. So if it had that sort of eternal cause the universe would have to be eternal too.

Craig thinks he has shown that the universe isn't eternal—that it has a beginning. How then, he asks, can it have an eternal cause? We have just seen that it couldn't have an eternal "mechanical" cause. But what other sort of eternal cause might there be?

Craig thinks there is another familiar sort of cause that provides the answer to this question. In addition to mechanical causes that automatically produce their effects, he says that there are *personal* causes. Individual persons are free agents who have the power to cause all sorts of things. But they don't have to do so and can exist fully without producing the various effects they are capable of causing.

Suppose, for example, that a man is seated. The man can, at any time, decide to stand up. But he can also choose to remain seated. He has the power to decide either way—it is entirely up to him to determine when or even whether to stand up. If he does decide to stand, then he, and he alone, is the *cause* of his decision. Unlike a merely mechanical cause, the man can exist fully without exercising his power to produce the various effects of which he is the cause.

This is quite a controversial claim. Many philosophers believe that the true cause of a person's decision is not simply the person, but various other psychological factors at work within the person—his beliefs and values and preferences, and that these in turn are the product of other causes. Unlike these philosophers, Craig claims that a person—and not something else happening within the person—is the sole cause of his own decisions. In *exactly the same situation*, with *exactly the same ongoing desires and beliefs*, our seated man could decide either to stand up or to remain seated.

Let's suppose, at least for the sake of argument, that Craig is right about this. It follows that there are at least two radically different kinds of causation in the world. On the one hand, there are mechanical causes that cannot help bringing about their effects; and on the other hand, there are personal causes with the power to bring about various effects, but who are free to determine just how and when and whether they will exercise that power.

Against this theoretical background, we can see why Craig thinks the First Cause must be a person. How is it, he asks, that the cause of the universe is eternal, even though the universe is not? We have already seen that an eternal mechanical cause could have only an eternal effect. But what about an eternal personal cause? Craig thinks that an eternal person could cause a temporal effect. Here is his explanation.

> . . . a man sitting from eternity may will to stand up; hence, a temporal effect may arise from an

---

[21]David Hume, *Enquiry Concerning the Human Understanding*, section vii, part i.
[22]"The Existence of God and the Beginning of the Universe."

eternally existing agent. Indeed, the agent may will from eternity to create a temporal effect, so that no change in the agent need be conceived.[23]

Suppose, then, that the cause of the universe is an eternal person. It does not follow that the universe is eternal—since the personal cause of the universe could have "willed from eternity" to produce a universe with a beginning in time. Craig thinks this is the only possible way to explain why the universe is not eternal: "The only way to have an eternal cause but a temporal effect would seem to be if the cause is a personal agent who freely chooses to create an effect in time."[24]

There are a number of difficult issues here. Does personal causation work the way Craig thinks it does? Or is causation by a person always analyzable in terms of other things happing within the person? Is personal causation the only alternative to mechanical causation? Or might there be some other type of "eternal cause" that wouldn't necessarily produce an eternal effect? I won't pursue these questions further here, but there is another objection to Craig's argument that I would like to develop. To see how this line of criticism goes, we need to back up a bit and take a close look at the way persons are related to the things they cause.

When a person stands up, he makes his body move. But he does that by producing another kind of change in himself—a mental change. He *decides* that now is the time to get up—he forms the intention to get up right away—and it is this mental change that is the immediate cause of the changed position of his body. Granted that a person can sit on a bench for a long time without deciding to get up, once his decision to "get up now" is made, it normally produces its effect straightaway—faster even than a temperature below zero freezes water.

So how does it work with God and creation? Apparently, God must *choose* to create, or nothing will happen. It is God's choosing to create that is the immediate cause of the beginning of the universe. God chooses to create a universe, and the universe comes into being.

You might think that God's choosing is a mental *change* in God. God thinks it over, *and then* decides to create. But Craig denies that this is so.

> By "choose" I do not mean God changes His mind. I mean God intends from eternity to create a world in time.[25]

It is not hard to see why Craig wouldn't want to say that "choosing to create" is a *change* in God. Craig's God is omniscient. He can't arrive at decisions the way you and I do, because He always already knows what He is going to do. (You aren't *arriving at* a decision about what to do if you *already know* what you are going to do.) So naturally Craig concludes that God's decision to create is eternal—that He "intends from eternity to create a world."

But this creates a different problem for Craig's account of creation. We have seen that God's decision to create is the immediate cause of the universe. But now we learn that God's decision to create is eternal. So how, on Craig's principles, can we avoid the conclusion that the universe is just as eternal as God's decision to create it?

To be sure, Craig also says, "God chooses from eternity to create a world *with a beginning*."[26] But it is hard to see how this is possible. You will recall that Craig's argument for saying that the first cause must be a person assumes that:

a. An eternal sufficient cause must have an eternal effect.

But presumably Craig doesn't think God needs any help getting the universe going. So it is natural to suppose that:

b. God's will to create "a world with a beginning" is *sufficient* to produce it.

But we have just learned that:

c. God's will to create "a world with a beginning" is eternal.

---

[23]"The Existence of God and the Beginning of the Universe."
[24]*Ibid.*

[25]"Philosophical and Scientific Pointers to Creation *ex Nihilo*," 197.
[26]*Ibid.*, 197.

From these three premises, it follows that:

d. "A world with a beginning" is eternal.

This conclusion is obviously absurd. A "world with a beginning" cannot be eternal. So, since *d* follows from premises *a*, *b*, and *c*, one of them must be false. But which? Craig's answer appears to be that *b* is false.

> I am inclined simply to deny that God's eternally willing to create the universe, properly understood, is sufficient for the existence of the universe . . .[27]

How could this be? Surely Craig doesn't think God could fail to accomplish what he "eternally wills"! Here is his explanation:

> . . . [I]t is insufficient to account for the origin of the universe by citing simply God, His timeless intention to create a world with a beginning, and His power to produce such a result. There must be an exercise of His causal power in order for the universe to be created. . . . [We must] differentiate between God's timeless intention to create a temporal world and God's undertaking to create a temporal world.[28]

Craig here distinguishes God's eternal will to create a world from his actually exercising the power to do what He thus wills—His eternal intention to create from His "undertaking" to carry out this intention. God's "undertaking" to create the universe is presumably sufficient for the existence of the universe, and the universe begins to exist "as soon as" God "undertakes" to create it. But this doesn't make the universe eternal because the "undertaking" (unlike the original intention) is not eternal. Since God puts Himself into time when He "undertakes" to create the universe, His "undertaking" to create occurs at the very first moment of time. It is, so to speak, the very first of the events that God causes.

But surely this only pushes the question back to the relation between God's eternal will and His "un-

dertaking" to execute His prior intention. If God's will to create is sufficient for His undertaking to create, then on Craig's principles the undertaking must be eternal, in which case, once again, the universe must be eternal. Craig must therefore deny, not only that God's eternal will is sufficient for the existence of the universe, but also that it is sufficient for His *undertaking* to create the universe. Is this at all plausible?

I don't think so. It is easy enough to see that the will of a merely human person is often not sufficient for his actually undertaking to do what he intends to do. There are at least two reasons for this. You and I can intend to do something at a *later time*, but not until that time comes will we *undertake* to do anything about our earlier intention. This afternoon, for example, I plan to go to a certain store to buy some vitamins. I have not—yet—undertaken to do so, because the time I have selected for this activity has not yet arrived. But even when the proper time does arrive, I may change my mind and not go. This is the second reason for saying that a human person's will is not sufficient for his actually undertaking to do what he has willed. Human beings have wills that are changeable and inconstant. Sometimes they even suffer from *weakness* of will, and fail to do what they (perhaps sincerely) intended to do, even when it is long past the time for action.

It is obvious that neither of these explanations of the gap between willing and undertaking can be applied to the sort of God Craig believes in—a God who is omnipotent, omniscient, and timeless. An omnipotent being cannot suffer from weakness of will. An omniscient being cannot change its mind. And a timeless being cannot meaningfully be said to "delay" undertaking to carry out its intentions. So it is very hard indeed to see how God's eternal will to create can fail to be sufficient for His undertaking to do so, in which case it is also sufficient for the beginning of the universe. On Craig's principles, therefore, it ought to follow that the universe is eternal.

8. CONCLUSION

I have tried to show that the *kalam* argument is not a successful argument for the existence of God or for creation *ex nihilo*. This does not mean, of course, that

---

[27]"Must the Beginning of the Universe Have a Personal Cause?: A Rejoinder," forthcoming in *Faith and Philosophy*.
[28]*Ibid*.

I have a better theory of the origin of the universe on offer. My own view is that we simply don't know enough to draw firm conclusions about such matters. It is fun to speculate, but we cannot hope to come up with answers that any honest, reasonable, and well-informed person would be bound to accept. Most of us have different and somewhat conflicting intuitions about time and eternity, causation and agency, about the nature of personhood, and about many other matters. It is an illusion to suppose that there is a single obviously correct way of sorting it all out. That is why the history of philosophy is, and will continue to be, a history of contest and controversy . . . and *fun*.[29]

QUESTIONS FOR FURTHER REFLECTION

1. Although Craig thinks that time will go on forever, he insists that the future is not an actual infinite on the ground that the future does not exist. It is, he says, only a potential infinite. But Craig also claims that there is a complete body

of truth about the future known to God. Are these claims consistent?

2. Consider the following principle:

   At least part of the total cause of any event precedes it in time.

   Can you think of any exceptions? What implications does your answer have for premise 1 of the *kalam* argument?

3. Is creation *out of nothing* any more intelligible than creation *by nothing*? What implications does your answer have for premise 1 of the *kalam* argument?

4. Is Craig's distinction between "mechanical" and "personal" causation sustainable? Or is personal causation at bottom just another sort of mechanical causation?

5. Most physicists believe that there is genuine randomness at the level of subatomic particles. For example, if you ask why a uranium atom disintegrated at a particular moment, the answer is that at any given time the probability is one in 10^{32} that an "alpha particle" will "tunnel out" of the nucleus of that atom. And that is all there is to say. Might this provide a model for the origin of the universe different from any that Craig considers in your reading?

---

[29]I would like to take this opportunity to thank Barbara Morriston, who read an earlier draft of this paper and made many helpful suggestions.

15. THE WATCH AND THE WATCHMAKER

William Paley

William Paley (1743–1805), one of the most influential Christian apologists of his time, taught philosophy at Cambridge University. In 1776, he was ordained in the Church of England and served as a priest in several parishes. In 1872, he became archdeacon of Carlisle. He was a vocal opponent of the slave trade. His most influential work, *Natural Theology, or Evidences of the Existence and Attributes of the Deity Collected from the Appearances of Nature* (1802), from which the following selection is taken, profoundly affected theology during the nineteenth century. Paley is considered by some to have anticipated the utilitarianism of Jeremy Bentham. In what follows, he presents the case for the existence of God based on apparent design in nature.

READING QUESTIONS

1. Why would our conclusion about the watch not be weakened if we had never seen one?
2. Why would an imperfect watch not weaken out the conclusion that the watch had been designed?

3. With what does Paley compare an eye?
4. What two peculiarities are found in the eyes of birds?
5. What is different about the irises of fish eyes and how does that feature suit them to their environment?

1. THE WATCH

In crossing a heath, suppose I pitched my foot against a *stone*, and were asked how the stone came to be there, I might possibly answer, that for any thing I knew to the contrary it had lain there for ever; nor would it, perhaps, be very easy to show the absurdity of this answer. But suppose I had found a *watch* upon the ground, and it should be inquired how the watch happened to be in that place, I should hardly think of the answer which I had before given, that for any thing I knew the watch might have always been there. Yet why should not this answer serve for the watch as well as for the stone; why is it not as admissible in the second case as in the first? For this reason, and for no other, namely, that when we come to inspect the watch, we perceive—what we could not discover in the stone—that its several parts are framed and put together for a purpose, for example that they are so formed and adjusted as to produce motion, and that motion so regulated as to point out the hour of the day; that if the different parts had been differently shaped from what they are, or placed after any other manner or in any other order than that in which they are placed, either no motion at all would have been carried on in the machine, or none which would have answered the use that is now served by it. To reckon up a few of the plainest of these parts and of their offices, all tending to one result: We see a cylindrical box containing a coiled elastic spring, which, by its endeavor to relax itself, turns round the box. We next observe a flexible chain—artificially wrought for the sake of flexure—communicating the action of the spring from the box to the fusee. We then find a series of wheels, the teeth of which catch in and apply to each other, conducting the motion from the fusee to the balance and from the balance to the pointer, and at the same time, by the size and shape of those wheels, so regulating that motion as to terminate in causing an index, by an equable and measured progression, to pass over a given space in a given time. We take notice that the wheels are made of brass, in order to keep them from rust; the springs of steel, no other metal being so elastic; that over the face of the watch there is placed a glass, a material employed in no other part of the work, but in the room of which, if there had been any other than a transparent substance, the hour could not be seen without opening the case. This mechanism being observed—it requires indeed an examination of the instrument, and perhaps some previous knowledge of the subject, to perceive and understand it; but being once, as we have said, observed and understood, the inference we think is inevitable, that the watch must have had a maker—that there must have existed, at some time and at some place or other, an artificer or artificers who formed it for the purpose which we find it actually to answer, who comprehended its construction and designed its use.

2. ANTICIPATED OBJECTIONS

Nor would it, I apprehend, weaken the conclusion, that we had never seen a watch made—that we had never known an artist capable of making one—that we were altogether incapable of executing such a piece of workmanship ourselves, or of understanding in what manner it was performed; all this being no more than what is true of some exquisite remains of ancient art, of some lost arts, and, to the generality of mankind, of the more curious productions of modern manufacture. Does one man in a million know how oval frames are turned? Ignorance of this kind exalts our opinion of the unseen and unknown artist's skill, if he be unseen and unknown, but raises no doubt in our minds of the existence and agency of such an artist, at some former time and in some place or other. Nor can I perceive that it varies at all the inference, whether the question arise concerning a human agent or concerning an agent of a different species, or an agent possessing in some respects a different nature.

Neither, secondly, would it invalidate our conclusion that the watch sometimes went wrong, or that it seldom went exactly right. The purpose of the machinery, the design, and the designer might be evident, and in the case supposed, would be evident, in whatever way we accounted for the irregularity of the movement, or whether we could account for it or not. It is not necessary that a machine be perfect, in order to show with what design it was made: still less necessary, where the only question is whether it were made with any design at all.

Nor, thirdly, would it bring any uncertainty into the argument, if there were a few parts of the watch, concerning which we could not discover or had not yet discovered in what manner they conduced to the general effect; or even some parts, concerning which we could not ascertain whether they conduced to that effect in any manner whatever. For, as to the first branch of the case, if by the loss, or disorder, or decay of the parts in question, the movement of the watch were found in fact to be stopped, or disturbed, or retarded, no doubt would remain in our minds as to the utility or intention of these parts, although we should be unable to investigate the manner according to which, or the connection by which, the ultimate effect depended upon their action or assistance; and the more complex the machine, the more likely is this obscurity to arise. Then, as to the second thing supposed, namely, that there were parts which might be spared without prejudice to the movement of the watch, and that we had proved this by experiment, these superfluous parts, even if we were completely assured that they were such, would not vacate the reasoning which we had instituted concerning other parts. The indication of contrivance remained, with respect to them, nearly as it was before.

Nor, fourthly, would any man in his senses think the existence of the watch with its various machinery accounted for, by being told that it was one out of possible combinations of material forms; that whatever he had found in the place where he found the watch, must have contained some internal configuration or other; and that this configuration might be the structure now exhibited, namely, of the works of a watch, as well as a different structure.

Nor, fifthly, would it yield his inquiry more satisfaction, to be answered that there existed in things a principle of order, which had disposed the parts of the watch into their present form and situation. He never knew a watch made by the principle of order; nor can he even form to himself an idea of what is meant by a principle of order, distinct from the intelligence of the watchmaker.

Sixthly, he would be surprised to hear that the mechanism of the watch was no proof of contrivance, only a motive to induce the mind to think so:

And not less surprised to be informed, that the watch in his hand was nothing more than the result of the laws of *metallic* nature. It is a perversion of language to assign any law as the efficient, operative cause of any thing. A law presupposes an agent; for it is only the mode according to which an agent proceeds: it implies a power; for it is the order according to which that power acts. Without this agent, without this power, which are both distinct from itself, the *law* does nothing, is nothing. The expression, the "law of metallic nature," may sound strange and harsh to a philosophic ear; but it seems quite as justifiable as some others which are more familiar to him, such as "the law of vegetable nature," "the law of animal nature," or, indeed, as "the law of nature" in general, when assigned as the cause of phenomena, in exclusion of agency and power, or when it is substituted into the place of these.

Neither, lastly, would our observer be driven out of his conclusion or from his confidence in its truth, by being told that he knew nothing at all about the matter. He knows enough for his argument; he knows the utility of the end; he knows the subserviency and adaptation of the means to the end. These points being known, his ignorance of other points, his doubts concerning other points, affect not the certainty of his reasoning. The consciousness of knowing little need not beget a distrust of that which he does know. . . .

3. THE EYE. . . .

Every indication of contrivance, every manifestation of design which existed in the watch, exists in the works of nature, with the difference on the side of nature of being greater and more, and that in a degree which exceeds all computation. I mean, that the contrivances of nature surpass the contrivances of art, in the complexity, subtilty, and curiosity of the mechanism; and still more, if possible, do they go beyond them in number and variety; yet, in a multitude of cases, are not less evidently mechanical, not less evi-

"SELF-DUPLICATION AS EVIDENCE OF DESIGN" ✳
Michael Denton

One of the accomplishments of living systems which is, of course, quite without any analogy in the field of our own technology is their capacity for self-duplication. With the dawn of the age of computers and automation after the Second World War, the theoretical possibility of constructing self-replicating automata was considered seriously by mathematicians and engineers. Von Neumann discussed the problem at great length in his famous book *Theory of Self-Reproducing Automata*, but the practical difficulties of converting the dream into reality have proved too daunting. As Von Neumann pointed out, the construction of any sort of self-replicating automaton would necessitate the solution to three fundamental problems: that of storing information; that of duplicating information; and that of designing an automatic factory which could be programmed from the information store to construct all the other components of the machine as well as duplicating itself. The solution to all three problems is found in living things and their elucidation has been one of the triumphs of modern biology.

So efficient is the mechanism of information storage and so elegant the mechanism of duplication of this remarkable molecule that it is hard to escape the feeling that the DNA molecule may be the one and only perfect solution to the twin problems of information storage and duplication for self-replicating automata.

The solution to the problem of the automatic factory lies in the ribosome. Basically, the ribosome is a collection of some fifty or so large molecules, mainly proteins, which fit tightly together. Altogether the ribosome consists of a highly organized structure of more than one million atoms which can synthesize any protein that it is instructed to make by the DNA, including the particular proteins which comprise its own structure—so the ribosome can construct itself! . . .

It is astonishing to think that this remarkable piece of machinery, which possesses the ultimate capacity to construct every living thing that ever existed on Earth, from a giant redwood to the human brain, can construct all its own components in a matter of minutes and weigh less than 10^{-16} grams. It is of the order of several thousand million million times smaller than the smallest piece of functional machinery ever constructed by man.

From Michael Denton, *Evolution:
A Theory In Crisis* (1985).

dently contrivances, not less evidently accommodated to their end or suited to their office, than are the most perfect productions of human ingenuity.

I know no better method of introducing so large a subject, than that of comparing a single thing with a single thing: an eye, for example, with a telescope. As far as the examination of the instrument goes, there is precisely the same proof that the eye was made for vision, as there is that the telescope was made for assisting it. They are made upon the same principles; both being adjusted to the laws by which the transmission and refraction of rays of light are regulated. I speak not of the origin of the laws themselves; but such laws being fixed, the construction in both cases is adapted to them. For instance, these laws require, in order to produce the same effect, that the rays of light, in passing from water into the eye, should be refracted by a more convex surface than when it passes out of air into the eye. Accordingly we find that the eye of a fish, in that part of it called the crystalline lens, is much rounder than the eye of terrestrial animals. What plainer manifestation of design can there be than this difference? What could a mathematical instrument maker have done more to show his knowledge of his principle, his application of that knowledge, his suiting his means to his end? . . .

But this, though much, is not the whole: by different species of animals, the faculty we are describing is possessed in degrees suited to the different range of vision which their mode of life and of procuring their food requires. *Birds*, for instance, in general, procure their food by means of their beak; and the distance between the eye and the point of the beak being small, it becomes necessary that they should have the power of seeing very near objects distinctly. On the other hand, from being often elevated much above the ground, living in the air, and moving through it with great velocity, they require for their safety, as well as for assisting them in descrying their prey, a power of seeing at a great distance—a power of which, in birds of rapine, surprising examples are given. The fact accordingly is, that two peculiarities are found in the eyes of birds, both tending to *facilitate* the change upon which the adjustment of the eye to different distances depends. The one is a bony, yet, in most species, a flexible rim or hoop, surrounding the broadest part of the eye, which confining the action of the muscles to that part, increases the effect of their lateral pressure upon the orb, by which pressure its axis is elongated for the purpose of looking at very near objects. The other is an additional muscle called the marsupium, to draw, on occasion, the crystalline lens *back*, and to fit the same eye for the viewing of very distant objects. By these means, the eyes of birds can pass from one extreme to another of their scale of adjustment, with more ease and readiness than the eyes of other animals.

The eyes of *fishes* also, compared with those of terrestrial animals, exhibit certain distinctions of structure adapted to their state and element. We have already observed upon the figure of the crystalline compensating by its roundness the density of the medium through which their light passes. To which we have to add, that the eyes of fish, in their natural and indolent state, appear to be adjusted to near objects, in this respect differing from the human eye, as well as those of quadrupeds and birds. The ordinary shape of the fish's eye being in a much higher degree convex than that of land animals, a corresponding difference attends its muscular conformation, namely, that it is throughout calculated for *flattening* the eye.

The *iris* also in the eyes of fish does not admit of contraction. This is a great difference, of which the probable reason is, that the diminished light in water is never strong for the retina.

In the *eel*, which has to work its head through sand and gravel, the roughest and harshest substances, there is placed before the eye, and at some distance from it, a transparent, horny, convex case or covering, which, without obstructing the sight, defends the organ. To such an animal could any thing be more wanted or more useful?

Thus, in comparison, the eyes of different kinds of animals, we see in their resemblances and distinctions one general plan laid down, and that plan varied with the varying exigencies to which it is to be applied. . . .

In considering vision as achieved by the means of an image formed at the bottom of the eye, we can never reflect without wonder upon the smallness yet correctness of the picture, the subtilty of the touch, the fineness of the lines. A landscape of five or six square leagues is brought into a space of half an inch diameter, yet the multitude of objects which it contains are all preserved, are all discriminated in their magnitudes, positions, figures, colors. The prospect from Hampstead-hill is compressed into the compass of a sixpence, yet circumstantially represented. A stagecoach, travelling at an ordinary speed for half an hour, passes in the eye only over one-twelfth of an inch, yet is this change of place in the image distinctly perceived throughout its whole progress; for it is only by means of that perception that the motion of the coach itself is made sensible to the eye. If any thing can abate our admiration of the smallness of the visual tablet compared with the extent of vision, it is a reflection which the view of nature leads us every hour to make, namely, that in the hands of the Creator, great and little are nothing.

Sturmius held that the examination of the eye was a cure for atheism. Besides that conformity to optical principles which its internal constitution displays, and which alone amounts to a manifestation of intelligence having been exerted in the structure— besides this, which forms, no doubt, the leading character of the organ, there is to be seen, in every thing belonging to it and about it, an extraordinary degree of care, an anxiety for its preservation, due, it if we may so speak, to its value and its tenderness. It is lodged in a strong, deep, bony socket, composed by the junction of seven different bones, hollowed out at their edges. In some few species, as that of the coatimondi, the orbit is not bony throughout; but whenever this is the case, the upper, which is the deficient part, is supplied by a cartilaginous ligament, a substitution which shows the same care. Within this socket it is embedded in fat, of all animal substances the best adapted both to its repose and motion. It is sheltered by the eyebrows—an arch of hair which, like a thatched penthouse, prevents the sweat and moisture of the forehead from running down into it.

But it is still better protected by its *lid*. Of the superficial parts of the animal frame, I know none which, in it, office and structure, is more deserving of attention than the eyelid. It defends the eye; it wipes it; it closes it in sleep. Are there in any work of art whatever, purposes more evident than those which this organ fulfils; or an apparatus for executing those purposes more intelligible, more appropriate, or more mechanical? If it be overlooked by the observer of nature, it can only be because it is obvious and familiar. This is a tendency to be guarded against. We pass by the plainest instances, while we are exploring those which are rare and curious; by which conduct of the understanding we sometimes neglect the strongest observations, being taken up with others which, though more recondite and scientific, are, as solid arguments, entitled to much less consideration.

In order to keep the eye moist and clean—which qualities are necessary to its brightness and its use—a wash is constantly supplied by a secretion for the purpose; and the superfluous brine is conveyed to the nose through a perforation in the bone as large as a goosequill. When once the fluid has entered the nose, it spreads itself upon the inside of the nostril, and is evaporated by the current of warm air which in the course of respiration is continually passing over it. Can any pipe or outlet for carrying off the waste liquor from a dye-house or distillery, be more mechanical than this is? It is easily perceived that the eye must want moisture; but could the want of the eye generate the gland which produces the tear, or bore the hole by which it is discharged—a hole through a bone? . . .

4. THE ARGUMENT CUMULATIVE

Were there no example in the world of contrivance except that of the *eye*, it would be alone sufficient to support the conclusion which we draw from it, as to the necessity of an intelligent Creator. It could never be got rid of, because it could not be accounted for by any other supposition which did not contradict all the principles we possess of knowledge—the princi-

ples according to which things do, as often as they can be brought to the test of experience, turn out to be true or false. Its coats and humors, constructed as the lenses of a telescope are constructed, for the refraction of rays of light to a point, which forms the proper action of the organ; the provision in its muscular tendons for turning its pupil to the object, similar to that which is given to the telescope by screws, and upon which power of direction in the eye the exercise of its office as all optical instrument depends; the further provision for its defence, for its constant lubricity and moisture, which we see in its socket and its lids, in its glands for the secretion of the matter of tears, its outlet or communication with the nose for carrying off liquid after the eye is washed with it; these provisions compose altogether an apparatus, a system of parts, a preparation of means, so manifest in their design, so exquisite in their contrivance, so successful in their issue, so precious, and so infinitely beneficial in their use, as, in my opinion, to bear down all doubt that can be raised upon the subject. And what I wish, under the title of the present chapter, to observe, is, that if other parts of nature were inaccessible to our inquiries, or even if other parts of nature presented nothing to our examination but disorder and confusion, the validity of this example would remain the same. If there were but one watch in the world, it would not be less certain that it had a maker. If we had never in our lives seen any but one single kind of hydraulic machine, yet if of that one kind we understood the mechanism and use, we should be as perfectly assured that it proceeded from the hand and thought and skill of a workman, as if we visited a museum of the arts, and saw collected there twenty different kinds of machines for drawing water, or a thousand different kinds for other purposes. Of this point each machine is a proof independently of all the rest. So it is with the evidence of divine agency. The proof is not a conclusion which lies at the end of a chain of reasoning, of which chain each instance of contrivance is only a link, and of which, if one link fail, the whole fails; but it is an argument separately supplied by every separate example. An error in stating an example affects only that example. The argument is cumulative in the fullest sense of that term. The eye proves it without the ear; the ear without the eye. The proof in each example is complete; for when the design of the part, and the conduciveness of its

"COMPLEX LIVING SYSTEMS ARE EVIDENCE OF DESIGN" ✳ *Walter Bradley*

The existence of living systems requires the specification of some very complex boundary conditions, such as the sequencing required to get functional biopolymers. As Michael Polanyi noted some years ago, both machines and living systems transcend simple explanations based on the laws of chemistry and physics, requiring as they do highly improbable initial conditions or time independent boundary constraints . . .

Polanyi illustrated his argument with a discussion of an automobile. The operation of every part of the automobile can be fully explained in terms of principles of chemistry and physics. When the piston is lowered, air and vaporized gasoline are drawn into the cylinder. This mixture is subsequently compressed as the piston rises to the top of its stroke. A spark ignites the mixture, allowing the reaction of the oxygen in the air with the gasoline, releasing a large amount of energy. This released energy causes tremendous pressure on the piston, which is then displaced downward. This downward motion is transmitted to the drive shaft as torque, which is then transmitted to the wheels of the car, completing the transformation of chemical energy in the gasoline into kinetic energy of the moving automobile.

Every step can be nicely explained by the laws of chemistry and physics. Yet these laws cannot account for the existence (i.e., origin) of the automobile, but only for its operation. The highly unusual (boundary) conditions under which the chemical energy in the gasoline is converted into kinetic energy in the automobile are the result of careful design of the system and its component parts by a mechanical engineer who subsequently passed the drawings to a skilled machinist who fabricated the pieces and then gave them to a mechanic who assembled the pieces in just the right fashion. Human intelligence is a crucial factor in the existence of a functional automobile. Polanyi argues that living systems are far more complicated than the machines of people and thus provide an even greater challenge to the observer to explain their existence in terms of natural laws alone.

From Walter Bradley, "Designed or Designoid," in *Mere Creation* William Dembski ed., (1998).

structure to that design is shown, the mind may set itself at rest; no future consideration can detract any thing from the force of the example. . . .

5. THE DESIGNER

Contrivance, if established, appears to me to prove every thing which we wish to prove. Among other things, it proves the *personality* of the Deity, as distinguished from what is sometimes called nature, sometimes called a principle which terms, in the mouths of those who use them philosophically, seem to be intended to admit and to express an efficacy, but to exclude and to deny a personal agent. Now, that which can contrive, which can design, must be a person. These capacities constitute personality, for they imply consciousness and thought. They require that which can perceive an end or purpose, as well as the power of providing means and directing them to their end. They require a centre in which perceptions unite, and from which volitions flow; which is mind. The acts of a mind prove the existence of a mind; and in whatever a mind resides, is a person. The seat of intellect is a person. We have no authority to limit the properties of mind to any particular corporeal form, or to any particular circumscription of space. These properties subsist, in created nature, under a great variety of sensible forms. Also, every animated being has its *sensorium*; that is, a certain portion of space, within which perception and volition are exerted. This sphere may be enlarged to an indefinite extent—may comprehend the universe; and being so imagined, may serve to furnish us with as good a notion as we are capable of forming, of the *immensity* of the divine nature, that is, of a Being, infinite, as well in essence as in power, yet nevertheless a person. . . .

Wherever we see marks of contrivance, we are led for its cause to an *intelligent* author. And this transition of the understanding is founded upon uniform experience, We see intelligence constantly contriving; that is, we see intelligence constantly producing effects, marked and distinguished by certain properties—not certain particular properties, but by a kind and class of properties, such as relation to an end, relation of parts to one another and to a common purpose. We see, wherever we are witnesses to the actual formation of things nothing except intelligence producing effects so marked and distinguished. Furnished with this experience, we view the productions of nature. We observe *them* also marked and distinguished in the same manner. We wish to account for their origin. Our experience suggests a cause perfectly adequate to this account. No experience, no single instance or example, can be offered in favor of any other. In this cause, therefore, we ought to rest; in this cause the common sense of mankind has, in fact, rested, because it agrees with that which in all cases is the foundation of knowledge—the undeviating course of their experience. . . .

QUESTIONS FOR FURTHER REFLECTION

1. Paley argues that imperfect design doesn't weaken the conclusion that the watch was designed. But doesn't imperfect design in nature weaken the inference to a *perfect* and *all-knowing* designer of nature? Why or why not?

2. What is "teleology" and what role does it play in Paley's argument?

3. Do examples of "bad design" in nature (e.g., tooth-decay, troglodytes living in caves have useless eyes, women past menopause tend to suffer from osteoporosis) show that the design is either imperfect, or worse, evil?

16. CRITIQUE OF THE DESIGN ARGUMENT
David Hume

David Hume (1711–1776), a Scot, was the last of the three great "British Empiricists." The other two were John Locke and George Berkeley. Hume took the empiricism of Locke and Berkeley to its logical conclusion—skepticism. A sympathetic critic once remarked that by making empiricism consistent, Hume had made it "incredible." In addition to his work in the theory of knowledge, Hume did important work in ethics and the philosophy of religion. The following selection is from his famous *Dialogues Concerning Natural Religion*, which consists of a dialogue between three friends—Demea, a theist who offers a Leibniz-like cosmological argument; Cleanthes, also a theist, who prefers the design argument; and Philo, a skeptic, who may well represent Hume's position. In this selection, Cleanthes presents the design argument and Philo critiques it.

READING QUESTIONS

1. To what does Cleanthes compare the natural world?
2. Why does Philo think we can infer an architect from the existence of a house but we cannot infer God from apparent design in nature?
3. How does the principle "like effects prove like causes" figure in the discussion?
4. Why does Philo argue that Cleanthes cannot ascribe perfection to the designer of the world?
5. Why does Philo contend that even if Cleanthes's design argument proves a designer exists, it does not show that just *one* designer exists?

Cleanthes: Look round the world: contemplate the whole and every part of it: You will find it to be nothing but one great machine, subdivided into an infinite number of lesser machines, which again admit of subdivisions to a degree beyond what human senses and faculties can trace and explain. All these various machines, and even their most minute parts, are adjusted to each other with an accuracy which ravishes into admiration all men who have ever contemplated them. The curious adapting of means to ends, throughout all nature, resembles exactly, though it much exceeds, the productions of human contrivance; of human designs, thought, wisdom, and intelligence. Since, therefore, the effects resemble each other, we are led to infer, by all the rules of analogy, that the causes also resemble; and that the Author of Nature is somewhat similar to the mind of man, though possessed of much larger faculties, proportioned to the grandeur of the work which he has executed. By this argument a posteriori, and by this argument alone, do we prove at once the existence of a Deity, and his similarity to human mind and intelligence. . . .

Philo: What I chiefly scruple in this subject, said Philo, is not so much that all religious arguments are by Cleanthes reduced to experience, as that they appear not to be even the most certain and irrefragable of that inferior kind. That a stone will fall, that fire will burn, that the earth has solidity, we have observed a thousand and a thousand times; and when any new instance of this nature is presented, we draw without hesitation the accustomed inference. The exact similarity of the cases gives us a perfect assurance of a similar event; and a stronger evidence is never desired nor sought after. But wherever you depart, in the least, from the similarity of the cases, you diminish proportionably the evidence; and may at last bring it to a very weak analogy, which is confessedly liable to error and uncertainty. . . .

If we see a house, Cleanthes, we conclude, with the greatest certainty, that it had an architect or builder; because this is precisely that species of effect which we have experienced to proceed from that species of cause. But surely you will not affirm, that the universe bears such a resemblance to a house, that we can with the same certainty infer a similar cause, or that the analogy is here entire and perfect. The dissimilitude is so striking, that the utmost you can here pretend to is a guess, a conjecture, a presumption concerning a similar cause; and how that pretension will be received in the world, I leave you to consider.

Cleanthes: It would surely be very ill received, replied Cleanthes; and I should be deservedly blamed and detested, did I allow, that the proofs of a Deity amounted to no more than a guess or conjecture. But is the whole adjustment of means to ends in a house and in the universe so slight a

---

"WHO DESIGNED THE DESIGNER?" * George Smith

Let us grant the premises of this argument and see where it leads. Order is exhibited in nature; order requires a designer; therefore, God exists. Surely, the wondrous regularity of nature—where acorns grow into trees and planets revolve around the sun—cannot be the result of mere chance. There must be a master planner at work.

It is now up to the theist to answer the question: Who designed God? Surely, nothing as complex and intricate as a supernatural intelligence can be the result of mere "chance." Therefore, there must be a super-designer who designed God. But a super-designer would require a super-super-designer, and so on *ad infinitum*. Thus, by the premises of the teleological argument, we are led to an infinite series of transcendental designers—a "solution" that leaves much to be desired. If an orderly universe requires explanation, the positing of a god does not provide it.

From George Smith, *Atheism: The Case Against God* (1989).

resemblance? The economy of final causes? The order, proportion, and arrangement of every part? Steps of a stair are plainly contrived, that human legs may use them in mounting; and this inference is certain and infallible. Human legs are also contrived for walking and mounting; and this inference, I allow, is not altogether so certain, because of the dissimilarity which you remark; but does it, therefore, deserve the name only of presumption or conjecture? . . .

Philo: Experience alone can point out to him the true cause of any phenomenon. Now, according to this method of reasoning . . . it follows, (and is, indeed, tacitly allowed by Cleanthes himself,) that order, arrangement, or the adjustment of final causes, is not of itself any proof of design; but only so far as it has been experienced to proceed from that principle. For aught we can know a priori, matter may contain the source or spring of order originally within itself, as well as mind does; and there is no more difficulty in conceiving, that the several elements, from an internal unknown cause, may fall into the most exquisite arrangement, than to conceive that their ideas, in the great universal mind, from a like internal unknown cause, fall into that arrangement. The equal possibility of both these suppositions is allowed. But, by experience, we find, (according to Cleanthes), that there is a difference between them. Throw several pieces of steel together, without shape or form; they will never arrange themselves so as to compose a watch. Stone, and mortar, and wood, without an architect, never erect a house. But the ideas in a human mind, we see, by an unknown, inexplicable economy, arrange themselves so as to form the plan of a watch or house. Experience, therefore, proves, that there is an original principle of order in mind, not in matter. From similar effects we infer similar causes. The adjustment of means to ends is alike in the universe, as in a machine of human contrivance. The causes, therefore, must be resembling. . . .

But can you think, Cleanthes, that your usual phlegm and philosophy have been preserved in so wide a step as you have taken, when you compared to the universe houses, ships, furniture, machines, and, from their similarity in some circumstances, inferred a similarity in their causes? Thought, design, intelligence, such as we discover in men and other animals, is no more than one of the springs and principles of the universe, as well as heat or cold, attraction or repulsion, and a hundred others, which fall under daily observation. . . . But, allowing that we were to take the operations of one part of nature upon another, for the foundation of our judgement concerning the origin of the whole, (which never can be admitted,) yet why select so minute, so weak, so bounded a principle, as the reason and design of animals is found to be upon this planet? What peculiar privilege has this little agitation of the brain which we call thought, that we must thus make it the model of the whole universe? Our partiality in our own favour does indeed present it on all occasions; but sound philosophy ought carefully to guard against so natural an illusion. . . .

But to show you still more inconveniences, continued Philo, in your Anthropomorphism, please to take a new survey of your principles. *Like effects prove like causes.* This is the experimental argument; and this, you say too, is the sole theological argument. Now, it is certain, that the liker the effects are which are seen, and the liker the causes which are inferred, the stronger is the argument. Every departure on either side diminishes the probability, and renders the experiment less conclusive. You cannot doubt of the principle; neither ought you to reject its consequences.

Now, Cleanthes, said Philo, with an air of alacrity and triumph, mark the consequences. First, By this method of reasoning, you renounce all claim to infinity in any of the attributes of the Deity. For, as the cause ought only to be proportioned to the effect, and the effect, so far as it falls under our cognisance, is not infinite; what pretensions have we, upon your suppositions, to ascribe that attribute to the Divine Being? . . .

Secondly, You have no reason, on your theory, for ascribing perfection to the Deity, even in his finite capacity, or for supposing him free from every error, mistake, or incoherence, in his undertakings. There are many inexplicable difficulties in the works of Nature, which, if we allow a perfect author to be proved a priori, are easily solved, and become only seeming difficulties, from the narrow capacity of man, who cannot trace infinite relations. But according to your method of reasoning, these difficulties become all real. . . .

But were this world ever so perfect a production, it must still remain uncertain, whether all the excellences of the work can justly be ascribed to the workman. If we survey a ship, what an exalted idea must we form of the ingenuity of the carpenter who framed so complicated, useful, and beautiful a machine? And what surprise must we feel, when we find him a stupid mechanic, who imitated others, and copied an art, which, through a long succession of ages, after multiplied trials, mistakes, corrections, deliberations, and controversies, had been gradually improving? Many worlds might have been botched and bungled, throughout an eternity, ere this system was struck out; much labour lost, many fruitless trials made; and a slow, but continued improvement carried on during infinite ages in the art of world-

making. In such subjects, who can determine, where the truth; nay, who can conjecture where the probability lies, amidst a great number of hypotheses which may be proposed, and a still greater which may be imagined?

And what shadow of an argument, continued Philo, can you produce, from your hypothesis, to prove the unity of the Deity? A great number of men join in building a house or ship, in rearing a city, in framing a commonwealth; why may not several deities combine in contriving and framing a world?

To multiply causes without necessity, is indeed contrary to true philosophy: but this principle applies not to the present case. Were one deity antecedently proved by your theory, who were possessed of every attribute requisite to the production of the universe; it would be needless, I own, (though not absurd,) to suppose any other deity existent. But while it is still a question, Whether all these attributes are united in one sub-

---

"EVOLUTION EXPLAINS APPARENT DESIGN" ✳ *Robin Le Poidevin*

The notion of purpose was, however, more obviously applied to the parts of living things. The parts of the body clearly do have a function: the legs, or wings, for locomotion, the stomach for digestion, the circulatory system for the transport of gases and dissolved nutrients, and so on. Does the fitness of the parts to their ends, and more generally the adaptation of living things to their environment, not indicate the existence of a creator who so constructed them? This rhetorical question, however, highlights the fact that the traditional teleological argument has not survived the advance of science. We now know, or think we know, why life is adapted to its environment: by the production of thousands of variations, some of which will better adapt the organism which has them to its environment and which will therefore provide it with a better chance of survival. Evolution through natural selection is the nontheological account of what, prior to Darwin, seemed an extraor-

dinary fact requiring the hypothesis of a benevolent creator to explain it. The appearance of design, then, may simply be specious. Although we can, at one level, talk of the purpose of the eye—to provide information about the immediate environment—the facts underlying this talk are not themselves purposive. It is not that the eye developed in order that organisms would be all the better at adapting themselves to their environment, but rather that the adaptive consequences of having eyes ensured that the organisms possessing them would be more likely to reproduce. . . .

The analogy between artifacts and sense organs is a weak one, therefore. Although there are no laws which would explain the natural (i.e., nonartificial) production of accurate mechanical time pieces, there are laws which explain the natural development of sense organs.

From Robin Le Poidevin, *Arguing for Atheism* (1996).

ject, or dispersed among several independent beings, by what phenomena in nature can we pretend to decide the controversy? Where we see a body raised in a scale, we are sure that there is in the opposite scale, however concealed from sight, some counterpoising weight equal to it; but it is still allowed to doubt, whether that weight be an aggregate of several distinct bodies, or one uniform united mass. And if the weight requisite very much exceeds any thing which we have ever seen conjoined in any single body, the former supposition becomes still more probable and natural. An intelligent being of such vast power and capacity as is necessary to produce the universe, or, to speak in the language of ancient philosophy, so prodigious an animal exceeds all analogy, and even comprehension. . . .

And why not become a perfect Anthropomorphite? Why not assert the deity or deities to be corporeal, and to have eyes, a nose, mouth, ears, and so on? Epicurus maintained, that no man had ever seen reason but in a human figure; therefore the gods must have a human figure. And this argument, which is deservedly so much ridiculed by Cicero, becomes, according to you, solid and philosophical.

In a word, Cleanthes, a man who follows your hypothesis is able perhaps to assert, or conjecture, that the universe, sometime, arose from something like design: but beyond that position he cannot ascertain one single circumstance; and is left afterwards to fix every point of his theology by the utmost license of fancy and hypothesis. . . .

Questions for Further Reflection

1. What can the defender of the design argument say in response to Philo's charge that the designer is imperfect because his creation is imperfect?
2. Philo contends that, at best, the design argument demonstrated polytheism rather than monotheism. Suppose he is right. Does this fact favor the theist or the atheist?
3. If goal-oriented complexity demands a designer as an explanation, then doesn't God need a designer to explain him? Can the theist reformulate the design argument to avoid this type of objection?
4. Do we typically go beyond agents when giving an explanation? Is an agent a natural stopping point for an explanation? How does this influence Philo's objection, if at all?

17. GOD, DESIGN, AND FINE-TUNING
Robin Collins

Robin Collins is Associate Professor of Philosophy at Messiah College in Grantham, PA. He received undergraduate degrees in mathematics and physics at Washington State University and completed two years of graduate study in theoretical physics at the University of Texas at Austin. In 1993, he received his Ph.D. in Philosophy at the University of Notre Dame, after which he held a postdoctoral fellowship in Philosophy of Science at Northwestern University. He is widely published, with several articles and book chapters specifically addressing the question of "fine-tuning." Currently he is finishing a book, *The Well-Tempered Universe: God, Fine-Tuning, and the Laws of Nature.*

In this selection, Collins defends the fine-tuning design argument for the existence of God. The "fine-tuning" of the cosmos refers to the discovery made by physicists and cosmologists that the fundamental structure of the physical universe is balanced on a razor's edge, seemingly for life to occur; if the structure were slightly different, life would be impossible. In the last thirty years, the argument for the existence of God from the fine-tuning of the cosmos has steadily gained in popularity. It is regarded by many as the strongest single argument for God's existence. In what follows, he first develops this argument for the existence of God, and then responds to the major objections that have been raised against it.

Reading Questions

1. Present two examples of fine-tuning in as much detail as you can.
2. What principle of reasoning does Collins use in his argument that the fine-tuning provides strong evidence in support of theism over the atheistic single-universes hypothesis?
3. What are Collins's arguments for thinking that the fine-tuning is improbable under the atheistic single-universe hypothesis?
4. What is the many-universes hypothesis and how is it supposed to explain the fine-tuning? What is Collins's response to this hypothesis?
5. Does Collins claim that the existence of fine-tuning shows that God's existence is more likely than not? Does he show that we are warranted in believing in God's existence? If not, what does he claim the fine-tuning shows?

1. INTRODUCTION

The Evidence of Fine-Tuning

Suppose we went on a mission to Mars, and found a domed structure in which everything was set up just right for life to exist. The temperature, for example, was set around 70 degrees Farenheit and the humidity was at 50 percent; moreover, there was an oxygen recycling system, an energy gathering system, and a whole system for the production of food. Put simply, the domed structure appeared to be a fully functioning biosphere. What conclusion would we draw from finding this structure? Would we draw the conclusion that it just happened to form by chance? Certainly not. Instead, we would unanimously conclude that it was designed by some intelligent being. Why would we draw this conclusion? Because an intelligent designer appears to be the only plausible explanation for the existence of the structure. That is, the only alternative explanation we can think of—that the structure was formed by some natural process—seems extremely unlikely. Of course, it is *possible* that, for example, through some volcanic eruption various metals and other compounds could have formed, and then separated out in just the right way to produce the "biosphere," but such a scenario strikes us as extraordinarily unlikely, thus making this alternative explanation unbelievable.

The universe is analogous to such a "biosphere," according to recent findings in physics. Almost everything about the basic structure of the universe—for example, the fundamental laws and parameters of physics and the initial distribution of matter and energy—is balanced on a razor's edge for life to occur. As eminent Princeton physicist Freeman Dyson notes, "There are many . . . lucky accidents in physics. Without such accidents, water could not exist as liquid, chains of carbon atoms could not form complex organic molecules, and hydrogen atoms could not form breakable bridges between molecules" (1979, p. 251)—in short, life as we know it would be impossible.

Scientists and others call this extraordinary balancing of the fundamental physical structure of the universe for life the "fine-tuning of the cosmos." It has been extensively discussed by philosophers, theologians, and scientists, especially since the early 1970s, with many articles and books written on the topic. Today, many consider it as providing the most persuasive current argument for the existence of God. For example, theoretical physicist and popular science writer Paul claims that with regard to basic structure of the universe, "the impression of design is overwhelming" (Davies, 1988, p. 203).

Many examples of this fine-tuning can be given.[1] One particularly important category of fine-tuning is that of the *constants* of physics. The constants of physics are a set of fundamental numbers that, when plugged into the laws of physics, determine the basic structure of the universe. An example of such a con-

---

[1] For an up-to-date analysis of the evidence for fine-tuning, with a careful physical analysis of what I consider the six strongest cases, see my "The Evidence for Fine-Tuning," in *God and Design*, Neil Manson (ed), Routledge, forthcoming. More detailed treatments of the cases of fine-tuning cited below are presented in that paper, along with more detailed references to the literature.

stant is the gravitational constant G that is part of Newton's law of gravity, $F = GM_1M_2/r^2$. G essentially determines the strength of gravity between two masses. If one were to double the value of G, for instance, then the force of gravity between any two masses would double.

So far, physicists have discovered four forces in nature—gravity, the weak force, electromagnetism, and the strong nuclear force that binds protons and neutrons together in an atom. Each of these forces has its own coupling constant that determines its strength, in analogy to the gravitational constant G. Using one of the standard dimensionless measures of force strengths (Barrow and Tipler, 1986, pp. 293–295), gravity is the weakest of the forces, and the strong nuclear force is the strongest, being a factor of 10^{40}—or ten thousand billion, billion, billion, billion—times stronger than gravity.

Various calculations show that the strength of each of the forces of nature must fall into a very small life-permitting region for intelligent life to exist. As our first example, consider gravity. If we increased the strength of gravity on earth a billionfold, for instance, the force of gravity would be so great that any land-based organism anywhere near the size of human beings would be crushed. (The strength of materials depends on the electromagnetic force via the fine-structure constant, which would not be affected by a change in gravity.) As astrophysicist Martin Rees notes, "In an imaginary strong gravity world, even insects would need thick legs to support them, and no animals could get much larger." (Rees, 2000, p. 30). Now, the above argument assumes that the size of the planet on which life formed would be an earth-sized planet. Could life forms of comparable intelligence to ourselves develop on a much smaller planet in such a strong-gravity world? The answer is no. A planet with a gravitational pull of a thousand times that of earth—which would make the existence of organisms of our size very improbable—would have a diameter of about 40 feet or 12 meters, once again not large enough to sustain the sort of large-scale ecosystem necessary for organisms like us to evolve. Of course, a billion-fold increase in the strength of gravity is a lot, but compared to the total range of strengths of the forces in nature (which span a range of 10^{40} as we saw above), this still amounts to a fine-tuning of one part in 10^{31}.

On the other hand, if the strong force were slightly increased the existence of complex life would be seriously inhibited, if not rendered impossible. For instance, using the latest equations and codes for stellar evolution and nucleosynthesis, Heinz Oberhummer, et al., showed that a small increase in the strong force—by as little as 1 percent—would drastically decrease, by thirty to a thousandfold, the total amount of oxygen formed in stars (Oberhummer, et al., 2000, p. 88). Since the oxygen on planets comes from previous stars that have exploded or blown off their outer layers, this means that very little oxygen would be available for the existence of carbon-based life. At the very least, this would have a life-inhibiting effect given the many important, and seemingly irreplaceable, roles oxygen plays in living processes, such as that of being essential for water (Denton, 1998, pp. 19–47, 117–140). Other arguments can be given for the other two forces—the electromagnetic force and the weak force—being fine-tuned, but we do not have space to provide the evidence here. (See, however, my "Evidence for Fine-Tuning," in *God and Design*, Neil Manson (ed.), Routledge, Forthcoming.)

There are other cases of the fine-tuning of the constants of physics besides the strength of the forces, however. Probably the most widely discussed among physicists and cosmologists—and esoteric—is the fine-tuning of what is known as the *cosmological constant*. The cosmological constant was a term that Einstein included in his central equation of his theory of gravity—that is, general relativity—which today is thought to correspond to the energy density of empty space. A positive cosmological constant acts as a sort of antigravity, a repulsive force causing space itself to expand. If the cosmological constant had a significant positive value, space would expand so rapidly that all matter would quickly disperse, and thus galaxies, stars, and even small aggregates of matter could never form. The upshot is that it must fall exceedingly close to zero for complex life to be possible in our universe.

Now, the fundamental theories of particle physics set a natural range of values for the cosmological constant. This natural range of values, however, is at least 10^{53}—that is, one followed by fifty three zeros—times the range of life-permitting values. That is, if 0 to L represent the range of life-permitting values, the theoretically possible range of values is at least 0 to 10^{53} L.[2] To intuitively see what this means, consider a dartboard analogy: suppose that we had a dart board that extended across the entire visible galaxy, with a bull's eye on the dart board of less than an inch in diameter. The amount of fine-tuning of the cosmological constant could be compared to randomly throwing a dart at the board and landing exactly in the bull's-eye!

Further examples of the fine-tuning of the fundamental constants of physics can also be given, such as that of mass difference between the neutron and the proton. If, for example, the mass of the neutron were slightly increased by about one part in seven hundred, stable hydrogen burning stars would cease to exist. (Leslie, 1989, pp. 39–40, Collins, EFT, forthcoming.)

Besides the constants of physics, however, there is also the fine-tuning of the laws. If the laws of nature were not just right, life would probably be impossible. For example, consider again the four forces of nature. If gravity did not exist, masses would not clump together to form stars or planets, and hence the existence of complex, intelligent life would be seriously inhibited, if not rendered impossible; if the electromagnetic force didn't exist, there would be no chemistry; if the strong force didn't exist, protons and neutrons could not bind together and hence no atoms with atomic number greater than hydrogen would exist; and if the strong force were a long-range force (like gravity and electromagnetism) instead of a short range force that only acts between protons and neutrons in the nucleus, all matter would either almost instantaneously undergo nuclear fusion and explode or be sucked together forming a black hole.

Similarly, other laws and principles are necessary for complex life: as prominent Princeton physicist Freeman Dyson points out (1979, p. 251), if the Pauli-exclusion principle did not exist, which dictates that no two fermions can occupy the same quantum state, all electrons would occupy the lowest atomic orbit, eliminating complex chemistry; and if there were no quantization principle, which dictates that

particles can only occupy certain discrete allowed quantum states, there would be no atomic orbits and hence no chemistry since all electrons would be sucked into the nucleus.

Finally, in his book *Nature's Destiny*, biochemist Michael Denton extensively discusses various higher-level features of the natural world, such as the many unique properties of carbon, oxygen, water, and the electromagnetic spectrum, that are conducive to the existence of complex biochemical systems. As one of many examples Denton presents, both the atmosphere and water are transparent to electromagnetic radiation in a thin band in the visible region, but nowhere else except radio waves. If instead either of them absorbed electromagnetic radiation in the visible region, the existence of terrestrial life would be seriously inhibited, if not rendered impossible. (pp. 56–57)

Thus, the evidence for fine-tuning is extensive, even if one has doubts about some individual cases. As philosopher John Leslie has pointed out, "clues heaped upon clues can constitute weighty evidence despite doubts about each element in the pile" (1988, p. 300). Imaginatively, one could think of each instance of fine-tuning mentioned above as a radio dial: unless all the dials are set exactly right, complex, intelligent life would be impossible. Or, one could think of the values of the initial conditions of the universe and the constants of physics as coordinates on a dart board that fills the whole galaxy, and the conditions necessary for life to exist as an extremely small target, say less than a trillionth of an inch: unless the dart hits the target, complex life would be impossible. The fact that the dials are perfectly set, or the dart has hit the target, strongly suggests that some intelligent being set the dials or aimed the dart, for it seems enormously improbable that such a coincidence could have happened by chance.

A Preliminary Distinction

Many people take the evidence mentioned above, along with the dart-board analogy, as sufficient reason to infer to theism as the best explanation of the fine-tuning. In this paper, however, I will attempt to make the argument more rigorous. To rigorously develop the fine-tuning argument, we will find it useful to dis-

---

[2]The fine-tuning of the cosmological constant is widely discussed in the literature (e.g., see Davies, 1982, 105–109, Rees, pp. 95–102, 154–155.) For an accessible, current discussion, see Collins, EFT, forthcoming.

tinguish between what I shall call the *atheistic single-universe hypothesis* and the *many-universes hypothesis*.[3] According to the atheistic single-universe hypothesis, there is only one universe, and it is ultimately an inexplicable, "brute" fact that the universe exists and is fine-tuned. Many atheists, however, advocate another hypothesis, one which attempts to explain how the seemingly improbable fine-tuning of the universe could be the result of chance. This hypothesis could be called the *many-worlds hypothesis*, or *the many-universes hypothesis*. According to the most popular version of this hypothesis, there exists some physical process that could be imaginatively thought of as a "universe generator" that produces a very large or infinite number of universes, with each universe having a randomly selected set of initial conditions and values for the constants of physics. Because this generator produces so many-universes, just by chance it will eventually produce one that is fine-tuned for intelligent life to occur.

Given this distinction, we will next attempt to rigorously develop the argument from fine-tuning against the atheistic single universe hypothesis, and then consider four major objections to it. Finally, in section IV we will consider the many-universes hypothesis and some theistic responses to it.

2. ARGUMENT AGAINST ATHEISTIC SINGLE-UNIVERSE HYPOTHESIS

In this section, we will attempt to rigorously develop the argument for preferring theism over the atheistic single-universe hypothesis. It should be stressed, however, that the soundness of the inference to design based on the fine-tuning does not crucially depend on the ability to make this argument rigorous. We accept many inferences in science, yet philosophers have worked without success for over a century in making these inferences philosophically rigorous. Of course, the skeptic might object that scientific theories are testable, whereas the theistic explanation of the fine-

tuning is not. But why should testability be epistemically relevant? After all, testability is about being able to find evidence against a theory in the future. What matters for the likelihood of an hypothesis's truth (or empirical adequacy), however, is the current evidence in its favor, not whether it is possible to find evidence against it in the future.

In order to show inference to design based on the fine-tuning is flawed, skeptics must show that it is based on a manifestly problematic form of reasoning. Indeed, a typical atheist objection against the design argument, going back to the famous Scottish philosopher David Hume, is to cast it as an argument from analogy, and then to argue that arguments from analogy in this context are fatally flawed. As we will show below, however, the argument from fine-tuning can be cast into a form that is very different from the argument from analogy, a form that is difficult to refute. This should go a long way both toward making the argument rigorous and toward answering the criticism of some skeptics that the fine-tuning argument relies on a manifestly flawed form of reasoning.

Although the fine-tuning argument against the atheistic single-universe hypothesis can be cast in several different forms—such as inference to the best explanation—I believe the most rigorous way of formulating the argument is in terms of what I will call the *prime principle of confirmation* (PPC), and which Rudolph Carnap has called the *"increase in firmness"* principle, and others have simply called the *likelihood principle*.[4] The prime principle of confirmation is a general principle of reasoning which tells us when some observation counts as evidence in favor of one hypothesis over another. *Simply put, the principle says that whenever we are considering two competing hypotheses, an observation counts as evidence in favor of the hypothesis under which the observation has the highest probability (or is the least improbable).* (Or, put slightly differently, the principle says that whenever we are considering two competing hypotheses, H_1 and H_2, an observation, O, counts as evidence in favor of H_1 over H_2 if O is more probable under H_1 than it is under H_2.) Moreover, the

---

[3]In this paper, I take atheism as more than simply the denial of the God of traditional theism, but as also involving the denial of any overall intelligence that could be considered responsible for the existence or apparent design of the universe.

[4]See Carnap (1962). For a basic, but somewhat dated, introduction to confirmation theory and the prime principle of confirmation, see Swinburne, (1973). For literature specifically casting design arguments as likelihood comparisons see Edwards (1992).

"ATHEISM BEFORE DARWIN?" ✳ *Richard Dawkins*

One thing I shall not do is belittle the wonder of the living "watches" that so inspired Paley. On the contrary, I shall try to illustrate my feeling that here Paley could have gone even further. When it comes to feeling awe over living "watches" I yield to nobody. I feel more in common with the Reverend William Paley than I do with the distinguished modern philosopher, a well-known atheist, with whom I once discussed the matter at dinner. I said that I could not imagine being an atheist at any time before 1859, when Darwin's *Origin of Species* was published. "What about Hume?" replied the philosopher. "How did Hume explain the organized complexity of the living world?", I asked. "He didn't," said the philosopher. "Why does it need any special explanation?"

Paley knew that it needed a special explanation; Darwin knew it, and I suspect that in his heart of hearts my philosopher companion knew it too. In any case it will be my business to show it here. As for David Hume himself, it is sometimes said that that great Scottish philosopher disposed of the Argument from Design a century before Dar-

win. But what Hume did was criticize the logic of using apparent design in nature as *positive* evidence for the existence of a God. He did not offer any *alternative* explanation for apparent design, but left the question open. An atheist before Darwin could have said, following Hume: "I have no explanation for complex biological design. All I know is that God isn't a good explanation, so we must wait and hope that somebody comes up with a better one." I can't help feeling that such a position, though logically sound, would have left one feeling pretty unsatisfied, and that although atheism might have been *logically* tenable before Darwin, Darwin made it possible to be an intellectually fulfilled atheist. I like to think that Hume would agree, but some of his writings suggest that he underestimated the complexity and beauty of biological design. The boy naturalist Charles Darwin could have shown him a thing or two about that, but Hume had been dead 40 years when Darwin enrolled in Hume's university of Edinburgh.

From Richard Dawkins, *The Blind Watchmaker* (1986).

---

degree to which the evidence counts in favor of one hypothesis over another is proportional to the degree to which the observation is more probable under the one hypothesis than the other.[5] For example, I will argue that the fine-tuning is much, much more probable under the theism than under the atheistic single-universe hypothesis, so it counts as strong evidence for theism over this atheistic hypothesis. In the next ma-

jor subsection, we will present a more formal and elaborated rendition of the fine-tuning argument in terms of the prime principle. First, however, let's look at a couple of illustrations of the principle and then present some support for it.

For our first illustration, suppose that I went hiking in the mountains, and found underneath a certain cliff a group of rocks arranged in a formation that clearly formed the pattern "Welcome to the mountains Robin Collins." One hypothesis is that, by chance, the rocks just happened to be arranged in that pattern—ultimately, perhaps, because of certain initial conditions of the universe. Suppose the only viable alternative hypothesis is that my brother, who was in the mountains before me, arranged the rocks in this way. Most of us would immediately take the arrangements of rocks to be strong evidence in favor of the "brother" hypothesis over the "chance" hypothesis. Why? Be-

---

[5]For those familiar with the probability calculus, a precise statement of the degree to which evidence counts in favor of one hypothesis over another can be given in terms of the odds form of Bayes's Theorem: that is, $P(H_1/E)/P(H_2/E) = [P(H_1)/P(H_2)] \times [P(E/H_1)/P(E/H_2)]$, where $P(/)$ represents the conditional probability of one proposition on another. The general version of the principle stated here, however, does not require the applicability or truth of Bayes's theorem.

cause it strikes us as extremely *improbable* that the rocks would be arranged that way by chance, but *not improbable* at all that my brother would place them in that configuration. Thus, by the prime principle of confirmation we would conclude that the arrangement of rocks strongly supports the "brother" hypothesis over the chance hypothesis.

Or consider another case, that of finding the defendant's fingerprints on the murder weapon. Normally, we would take such a finding as strong evidence that the defendant was guilty. Why? Because we judge that it would be *unlikely* for these fingerprints to be on the murder weapon if the defendant was innocent, but *not unlikely* if the defendant was guilty. That is, we would go through the same sort of reasoning as in the above case.

Finally, several things can be said in favor of the prime principle of confirmation. First, many philosophers think that this principle can be derived from what is known as the *probability calculus*, the set of mathematical rules that are typically assumed to govern probability. Second, there does not appear to be any case of recognizably good reasoning that violates this principle. Finally, the principle appears to have a wide range of applicability, undergirding much of our reasoning in science and everyday life, as the examples above illustrate. Indeed, some have even claimed that a slightly more general version of this principle undergirds all scientific reasoning. Because of all these reasons in favor of the principle, we can be very confident in it.

3. FURTHER DEVELOPMENT OF ARGUMENT

To further develop the core version of the fine-tuning argument, we will summarize the argument by explicitly listing its two premises and its conclusion:

Premise 1. The existence of the fine-tuning is not improbable under theism.

Premise 2. The existence of the fine-tuning is very improbable under the atheistic single-universe hypothesis.[6]

Conclusion: From premises (1) and (2) and the prime principle of confirmation, it follows that the fine-tuning data provides strong evidence to favor of the design hypothesis over the atheistic single-universe hypothesis.

At this point, we should pause to note two features of this argument. First, the argument does not say that the fine-tuning evidence proves that the universe was designed, or even that it is likely that the universe was designed. Indeed, of itself it does not even show that we are epistemically warranted in believing in theism over the atheistic single-universe hypothesis. In order to justify these sorts of claims, we would have to look at the full range of evidence both for and against the design hypothesis, something we are not doing in this paper. Rather, the argument merely concludes that the fine-tuning strongly *supports* theism *over* the atheistic single-universe hypothesis.

In this way, the evidence of fine-tuning argument is much like fingerprints found on the gun: although they can provide strong evidence that the defendant committed the murder, one could not conclude merely from them alone that the defendant is guilty; one would also have to look at all the other evidence offered. Perhaps, for instance, ten reliable witnesses claimed to see the defendant at a party at the time of the shooting. In this case, the fingerprints would still count as significant evidence of guilt, but this evidence would be counterbalanced by the testimony of the witnesses. Similarly the evidence of fine-tuning strongly supports theism over the atheistic single-universe hypothesis, though it does not itself show that everything considered theism is the most plausible explanation of the world.

The second feature of the argument we should note is that, given the truth of *the prime principle of confirmation*, the conclusion of the argument follows from the premises. Specifically, if the premises of the argument are true, then we are guaranteed that the conclusion is true: that is, the argument is what philosophers call *valid*. Thus, insofar as we can show that the premises of the argument are true, we will have shown that the conclusion is true. Our next task, therefore, is to

---

[6]To be precise, the fine-tuning refers to the conjunction of the claim that the range of life-permitting values for the constants of physics is small compared to the "theoretically possible" range R for those values *with* the claim that the values actually fall in the life-permitting range. It is only this latter fact that we are arguing is highly improbable under the atheistic single-universe hypothesis.

attempt to show that the premises are true, or at least that we have strong reasons to believe them.

Support for the Premises

Support for Premise (1)   Premise (1) is easy to support and fairly uncontroversial. The argument in support of it can be simply stated as follows: *since God is an all good being, and it is good for intelligent, conscious beings to exist, it not surprising or improbable that God would create a world that could support intelligent life.* Thus, the fine-tuning is not improbable under theism, as premise (1) asserts.

Support for Premise (2)   Upon looking at the data, many people find it very obvious that the fine-tuning is highly improbable under the atheistic single-universe hypothesis. And it is easy to see why when we think of the fine-tuning in terms of the analogies offered earlier. In the dartboard analogy, for example, the initial conditions of the universe and the fundamental constants of physics are thought of as a dartboard that fills the whole galaxy, and the conditions necessary for life to exist as a small one-foot wide target. Accordingly, from this analogy it seems obvious that it would be highly improbable for the fine-tuning to occur under the atheistic single-universe hypothesis—that is, for the dart to hit the board by chance.

Typically, advocates the fine-tuning argument are satisfied with resting the justification of premise (2), or something like it, on this sort of analogy. Many atheists and theists, however, question the legitimacy of this sort of analogy, and thus find the argument unconvincing. Although a full scale, rigorous justification of premise (2) is beyond the scope of this paper, we will briefly sketch how such a further justification could be given in section III below, under objection (5).

4. SOME OBJECTIONS TO CORE VERSION

As powerful as the fine-tuning argument against the atheistic single-universe hypothesis is, several major objections have been raised to it by both atheists and theists. In this section, we will consider these objections in turn.

Objection 1:
More Fundamental Law Objection

One criticism of the fine-tuning argument is that, as far as we know, there could be a more fundamental law under which the constants of physics *must* have the values they do. Thus, given such a law, it is not improbable that the known constants of physics fall within the life-permitting range.

Besides being entirely speculative, the problem with postulating such a law is that it simply moves the improbability of the fine-tuning up one level, to that of the postulated physical law itself. As astrophysicists Bernard Carr and Martin Rees note "even if all apparently anthropic coincidences could be explained [in terms of some grand unified theory], it would still be remarkable that the relationships dictated by physical theory happened also to be those propitious for life" (1979, p. 612).

A similar sort of response can be given to the claim that the fine-tuning is not improbable because it might be *logically necessary* for the constants of physics to have life-permitting values. That is, according to this claim, the constants of physics must have life-permitting values in the same way 2 + 2 must equal 4, or the interior angles of a triangle must add up to 180 degrees in Euclidian geometry. Like the "more fundamental law" proposal above, however, this postulate simply transfers the improbability up one level: of all the laws and constants of physics that conceivably could have been logically necessary, it seems highly improbable that it would be those that are life-permitting.[7]

Objection 2: Other Forms of Life Objection

Another objection people commonly raise against the fine-tuning argument is that as far as we know,

---

[7]Those with some training in probability theory will want to note that the kind of probability invoked here is what philosophers call *epistemic probability*, which is a measure of the rational degree of belief we should have in a proposition. (See objection [5] below) Since our rational degree of belief in a necessary truth can be less than 1, we can sensibly speak of it being improbable for a given law of nature to exist necessarily. For example, we can speak of an unproven mathematical hypotheses—such as Goldbach's conjecture that every even number greater than 6 is the sum of two odd primes—as being probably true or probably false given our current evidence, even though all mathematical hypotheses are either necessarily true or necessarily false.

other forms of life could exist even if the constants of physics were different. So, it is claimed, the fine-tuning argument ends up presupposing that all forms of intelligent life must be like us. One answer to this objection is that many cases of fine-tuning do not make this presupposition. Consider, for instance, the cosmological constant. If the cosmological constant were much larger than it is, matter would disperse so rapidly that no planets, and indeed no stars, could exist. Without stars, however, there would exist no stable energy sources for complex material systems of any sort to evolve. So, all the fine-tuning argument presupposes in this case is that the evolution of life forms of comparable intelligence to ourselves requires some stable energy source. This is certainly a very reasonable assumption.

Of course, if the laws and constants of nature were changed enough, other forms of embodied intelligent life might be able to exist of which we cannot even conceive. But this is irrelevant to the fine-tuning argument since the judgement of improbability of fine-tuning under the atheistic single-universe hypothesis only requires that, given our current laws of nature, the life-permitting range for the values of the constants of physics (such as gravity) is small compared to the *surrounding* range of non-life-permitting values.

Objection 3: Anthropic Principle Objection

According to the weak version of so-called *anthropic principle*, if the laws of nature were not fine-tuned, we would not be here to comment on the fact. Some have argued, therefore, that the fine-tuning is not really *improbable or surprising* at all under atheism, but simply follows from the fact that we exist. The response to this objection is to simply restate the argument in terms of our existence: our existence as embodied, intelligent beings is extremely unlikely under the atheistic single-universe hypothesis (since our existence requires fine-tuning), but not improbable under theism. Then, we simply apply the prime principle of confirmation to draw the conclusion that *our existence* strongly confirms theism over the atheistic single-universe hypothesis.

To further illustrate this response, consider the following "firing-squad" analogy. As John Leslie (1988, p. 304) points out, if fifty sharp shooters all miss me,

the response "if they had not missed me I wouldn't be here to consider the fact" is not adequate. Instead, I would naturally conclude that there was some reason why they all missed, such as that they never really intended to kill me. Why would I conclude this? Because my continued existence would be very improbable under the hypothesis that they missed me by chance, but not improbable under the hypothesis that there was some reason why they missed me. Thus, by the prime principle of confirmation, my continued existence strongly confirms the latter hypothesis.

Objection 4: The "Who Designed God?" Objection

Perhaps the most common objection that atheists raise to the argument from design, of which the fine-tuning argument is one instance, is that postulating the existence of God does not solve the problem of design, but merely transfers it up one level. Atheist George Smith, for example, claims that

> If the universe is wonderfully designed, surely God is even more wonderfully designed. He must, therefore, have had a designer even more wonderful than He is. If *God* did not require a designer, then there is no reason why such a relatively less wonderful thing as the universe needed one. (1980, p. 56.)

Or, as philosopher J. J. C. Smart states the objection:

> If we postulate God in addition to the created universe we increase the complexity of our hypothesis. We have all the complexity of the universe itself, and we have in addition the at least equal complexity of God. (The designer of an artifact must be at least as complex as the designed artifact). . . . *If the theist can show the atheist that postulating God actually reduces the complexity of one's total world view, then the atheist should be atheist.* (pp. 275–276; italics mine)

The first response to the above atheist objection is to point out that the atheist claim that the designer of an artifact must be as complex as the artifact designed is certainly not obvious. But I do believe that their claim has some intuitive plausibility: for example, in the world we experience, organized complexity seems only to be produced by systems that already possess it, such as the human brain/mind, a factory, or an organisms' biological parent.

The second, and better, response is to point out that, at most, the atheist objection only works against a version of the design argument that claims that all organized complexity needs an explanation, and that God is the best explanation of the organized complexity found in the world. The version of the argument I presented against the atheistic single-universe hypothesis, however, only required that the fine-tuning be more probable under theism than under the atheistic single-universe hypothesis. But this requirement is still met even if God exhibits tremendous internal complexity, far exceeding that of the universe. Thus, even if we were to grant the atheist assumption that the designer of an artifact must be as complex as the artifact, the fine-tuning would still give us strong reasons to prefer theism over the atheistic single-universe hypothesis.

To illustrate, consider the example of the "biosphere" on Mars presented at the beginning of this paper. As mentioned, the existence of the biosphere would be much more probable under the hypothesis that intelligent life once visited Mars than under the chance hypothesis. Thus, by the prime principle of confirmation, the existence of such a "biosphere" would constitute strong evidence that intelligent, extraterrestrial life had once been on Mars, even though this alien life would most likely have to be much more complex than the "biosphere" itself.

The final response theists can give to this objection is to show that a supermind such as God would *not* require a high degree of unexplained organized complexity to create the universe. Although I have presented this response elsewhere (unpublished manuscript), presenting it here is beyond the scope of this paper. Here I simply note that, for reasons entirely independent of the argument from design, God has been thought to have little, if any internal complexity. Indeed, Medieval philosophers and theologians often went as far as advocating the doctrine of Divine Simplicity, according to which God is claimed to be absolutely simple, without any internal complexity. So, atheists who push this objection have a lot of arguing to do to make it stick.

Objection 5: No Probability Objection

Some philosophers object to claim that the fine-tuning is highly improbable under the atheistic single-universe hypothesis (that is, premise (2) above) by arguing that since we only have one universe, the notion of the fine-tuning of the universe being probable or improbable is meaningless. Further, they argue, even if it were meaningful, we would have no way of adequately justifying, besides appealing to intuition, that the fine-tuning is very improbable under the atheistic single-universe hypothesis. Typically, the claim behind the first part of this objection is that probability only makes sense in terms of relative frequency among some reference class. Thus, for instance, the assertion that the probability that a randomly selected male smoker will die of lung cancer is 30 percent means that the 30 percent of the members of the class of male smokers die of lung cancer. But, if there is only one universe, there is no reference class of universes to compare it to, and hence claims regarding the probability or improbability of fine-tuning in this context do not make sense.

The problem with this argument is that it completely ignores other well-developed conceptions of probability. One of these is the epistemic notion of probability. *Epistemic probability* is a widely recognized type of probability that applies to claims, statements, and hypotheses—that is, what philosophers call *propositions*.[8] Roughly, the epistemic probability of a proposition can be thought of as the degree of credence—that is, degree of confidence or belief—we rationally should have in the proposition. Put differently, epistemic probability is a measure of our rational degree of belief under a condition of ignorance concerning whether a proposition is true or false. For example, when one says that the special theory of relativity is probably true, one is making a statement of epistemic probability. After all, the theory is actually either true or false. But, we do not know for sure whether it is true or false, so we say it is probably true to indicate that we should put more confidence in its being true than in its being false.

---

[8] For an in-depth discussion of epistemic probability, see Swinburne (1973), Hacking, (1975), and Plantinga (1993), chapters 8 and 9.

Besides epistemic probability simpliciter, philosophers also speak of what is known as the *conditional* epistemic probability of one proposition on another. (A proposition is any claim, assertion, statement, or hypothesis about the world.) The conditional epistemic probability of a proposition R on another proposition S—written as $P(R/S)$—can be defined as the degree to which the proposition S *of itself* should rationally lead us to expect that R is true. Under the epistemic conception of probability, therefore, the statement that *the fine-tuning of the cosmos is very improbable under the atheistic single-universe hypothesis* makes perfect sense: it is to be understood as making a statement about the degree to which the atheistic single-universe hypothesis would or should, *of itself*, rationally lead us to expect cosmic fine-tuning.

Now that we know what it means to say that the fine-tuning of one of the constants of physics is very unlikely under the atheistic single-universe hypothesis, it is time to briefly outline how such a statement could be justified. Here I think we need to apply what is known as the *principle of indifference*. Applied to the case at hand, the principle of indifference could be roughly stated as follows: *when we have no reason to prefer any one value of a parameter over other, we should assign equal probabilities to equal ranges of the parameter, given that the parameter in question directly corresponds to some physical magnitude.*[9] Specifically, if the "theoretically possible" range (that is, the range allowed by the relevant background theories) of such a parameter is R and the life-permitting range is r, then the probability is r/R. Suppose, for instance, that the "theoretically possible" range, R, of values for the strength of gravity is zero to the strength of the strong nuclear force between those protons—that is, 0 to $10^{40}G_0$, where G_0 represents the current value for the strength of gravity. As we saw above, the life-permitting range r for the strength of gravity is at most 0 to $10^9 G_0$. Now, of itself (specifically, apart from the knowledge that we exist), the atheistic single-universe hypothesis gives us *no* reason to think that the strength of gravity would fall into the life-permitting region instead of any other part of the theoretically possible region. Thus, assuming the strength of the forces constitute a real physical magnitude, the principle of indifference would state that equal ranges of this force should be given equal probabilities, and hence the probability of it the strength of gravity falling into the life-permitting region would be at most $r/R = 10^9/10^{40} = 1/10^{31}$.

One major problem with this rough version of the principle of indifference is the well-known Bertrand Paradoxes (e.g., see Weatherford, 1982, p. 56), in which there are two equally good but conflicting parameters that directly correspond to a physical quantity. A famous example of the Bertrand paradox is that of a factory that produces cubes whose sides vary from zero to two inches, which is equivalent to saying that it produces cubes whose volumes vary from zero to eight cubic inches. Given that this is all we know about the factory, the naive form of the principle of indifference implies that we should assign both equal probabilities to equal ranges of volumes *and* equal probabilities to equal ranges of lengths, since both lengths and volumes correspond to actual physical magnitudes. It is easy to see, however, that this leads to conflicting probability assignments—for example, using lengths, we get a probability of 0.5 of a cube being between zero and one inch in length, whereas using volumes we get a probability of 0.125.

Although many philosophers have taken the Bertrand Paradoxes as constituting a fatal objection to the principle of indifference, one can easily avoid this objection either by restricting the applicability the principle of indifference to those cases in which Bertrand Pardoxes do not arise or by claiming that the probability is somewhere between that given by the two conflicting parameters. This problem of conflicting parameters, however, does not seem to arise for most cases of fine-tuning.

Another problem is the total theoretically possible range R of values a constant of physics could have. This is a difficult issue beyond the scope of this paper to address. Here we simply note that often one can make plausible estimates of a lower bound for the theoretically possible range—for example, since the actual range of forces in nature span a range of 10^{40}, the value

---

[9]As an example of what it means to directly correspond to some physical magnitude, consider the mass of an object. A physical parameter "m" that designates the mass directly corresponds to a physical magnitude, whereas a physical parameter "u" that designates that mass squared ($u = m^2$) does not directly correspond to a physical magnitude but is an artificial variable.

of 10^{40} provides a natural lower bound for the theoretically possible range of forces strengths.[10]

Finally, several powerful reasons can be offered for its soundness of the principle of indifference if it is restricted in the ways explained above. First, it has an extraordinarily wide range of applicability. As Roy Weatherford notes in his book, *Philosophical Foundations of Probability Theory*, "an astonishing number of extremely complex problems in probability theory have been solved, and usefully so, by calculations based entirely on the assumption of equiprobable alternatives [that is, the principle of indifference]" (p. 35). Second, at least for the discrete case, the principle can be given a significant theoretical grounding in information theory, being derivable from Shannon's important and well-known measure of *information*, or *negative entropy* (Sklar, p. 191; van Fraassen, p. 345.). Third, in certain everyday cases the principle of indifference seems the only justification we have for assigning probability. To illustrate, suppose that in the last ten minutes a factory produced the first fifty-sided die ever produced. Further suppose that every side of the die is (macroscopically) perfectly symmetrical with every other side, except for there being different numbers printed on each side. (The die we are imagining is like a fair six-sided die except that it has fifty sides instead of six.) Now, we all immediately know that upon being rolled the probability of the die coming up on any given side is one in fifty. Yet, we do not know this directly from experience with fifty-sided dice, since by hypothesis no one has yet rolled such dies to determine the relative frequency with which they come up on each side. Rather, it seems our only justification for assigning this probability is the principle of indifference: that is, given that every side of the die is macroscopically symmetrical with every other side, we have no reason to believe that the die will land on one side over any

other side, and thus we assign them all an equal probability of one in fifty.[11]

Although we have only had space to provide a brief sketch of how one could go about rigorously defending the claim that the fine-tuning is very improbable under the atheistic single-universe hypothesis, the above brief sketch does show, I believe, that there is an initially plausible method available of rigorously supporting our intuitive judgement of the improbability of fine-tuning under the atheistic single-universe hypothesis. Nonetheless, it should be stressed again that even if ultimately our method of support fails, this is not fatal to the fine-tuning arguments. As with arguments in science, the fine-tuning argument has great initial intuitive plausibility. Accordingly, to defeat this initial plausibility, the burden is on the skeptic to show that the fine-tuning argument rests on a clearly faulty form of reasoning.

5. THE MANY-UNIVERSES HYPOTHESIS

The Many-Universes Hypothesis Explained

In response to this theistic or intelligent design explanation of the fine-tuning, many atheists have offered an alternative explanation, what I will call the *many-universes hypothesis*, but which in the literature goes under a variety of names, such as many-worlds hypothesis, the many-domains hypothesis, the world-ensemble hypothesis, the multi-universe hypothesis, and so on. According to this hypothesis, there are a very large—perhaps infinite—number of universes, with the constants of physics varying from universe to universe.[12] Of course, in the vast majority of these

---

[10]Such plausible lower bounds are provided for each case of fine-tuning that I discuss in my paper "Evidence for Fine-Tuning" (Forthcoming). This issue is also briefly discussed in my "The Fine-Tuning Design Argument" (1999, pp. 69–70) and will be discussed in much more depth in the book I am currently working on entitled *The Well-Tempered Universe: God, Fine-Tuning, and the Laws of Nature*.

[11]A full-scale defense of the principle of indifference is beyond the scope of this paper, but will be provided in the book on the fine-tuning design argument that I am currently working on. Also, see Schlesinger (1985, chapter 5) for a lengthy defense of the principle. A somewhat more in-depth treatment of the justification of premise (2) than offered here is presented in the appendix of Collins, 1999.

[12]I define a "universe" as any region of space-time that is disconnected from other regions in such a way that the constants of physics in that region could differ significantly from the other regions. A more thorough discussion of the many-universes hypothesis is presented in Collins, "The Argument from Design and the Many-Worlds Hypothesis" (2001).

universes the constants of physics would *not* have life-permitting values. Nonetheless, in a small proportion of universes they would, and consequently it is no longer improbable that universes such as ours exist in which the constants of physics have just the right values for intelligent life.

Further, usually these universes are thought to be produced by some sort of physical mechanism, which I call a many-universe generator. The universe generator can be thought of as analogous to a lottery ticket generator: just as it would be no surprise that a winning number is eventually produced if enough tickets are generated, it would be no surprise that a universe fine-tuned for life would occur if enough universes are generated.[13]

---

[13]Some have proposed what could be called a *metaphysical* many-universes hypothesis, according to which universes are thought to exist on their own without being generated by any physical process. Typically, advocates of this view—such as the late Princeton University philosopher David Lewis (1986) and University of Pennsylvania astrophysicist Max Tegmark (1998)—claim that every possible world exists. According to Lewis, for instance, there exists a reality parallel to our own in which I am president of the United States and a reality in which objects can travel faster than the speed of light. Dream up a possible scenario, and it exists in some parallel reality, according to Lewis. Besides being completely speculative (and in many people's mind, outlandish), a major problem with this scenario is that the vast majority of possible universes are ones which are chaotic, just as the vast majority of possible arrangement of letters of a thousand characters would not spell a meaningful pattern. So, the only way that these metaphysical hypotheses can explain the regularity and predictability of our universe, and the fact that it seems to be describable by a few simple laws, is to invoke an "observer selection" effect. That is, Lewis and Tegmark must claim that only universes like ours in this respect could support intelligent life, and hence be observed. The problem with this explanation is that it is much more likely for there to exist local islands of the sort of order necessary for intelligent life than for the entire universe to have such an ordered arrangement. Thus, a randomly selected observer from among the many universes should expect to find herself in a universe with a local island of order surrounded by vast regions of disorder. Accordingly, Lewis and Tegmark's hypotheses do not appear to be able to explain why we *qua* supposedly generic observers, live in a universe that is highly ordered throughout. (Among others, George Schlesinger [1984] has raised this objection against Lewis's hypothesis. This sort of objection was raised against a similar explanation of the high degree of order in our universe offered by the famous physicist Ludwig Boltzman, and has generally been considered fatal to Boltzman's explanation [Davies, 1974, p. 103].)

The Inflationary Many-Universes Model

Most many-universes models are entirely speculative, having little basis in current physics. One many-universes model, however, does have a reasonable basis in current physics—namely, that based on inflationary cosmology. Inflationary cosmology is a currently widely discussed cosmological theory that attempts to explain the origin of the universe. Essentially, it claims that our universe was formed by a small area of pre-space being massively blown up by an hypothesized *inflaton* field, in much the same way as a soup bubble would form in an ocean full of soap. In chaotic inflation models—widely considered the most plausible—various points of the pre-space are randomly blown up, forming innumerable bubble universes. Further, because of the inflaton field, the pre-space expands so rapidly that it becomes a never ending source of bubble universes, much as a rapidly expanding ocean full of soap would become a never ending source of soap bubbles. Thus, inflationary cosmology can naturally give rise to many universes.[14]

In order to get the initial conditions and constants of physics to vary from universe to universe, as they must do if this scenario is going to explain the fine-tuning, there must be a further physical mechanism to cause the variation. Such a mechanism *might* be given by superstring theory, but it is too early to tell. Superstring theory is currently one of the most hotly discussed hypotheses about the fundamental structure of the physical universe (Greene, 1999, p. 214). According to superstring theory, the ultimate constituents of matter are strings of energy that undergo quantum vibrations in a 10 (or 11) dimensional space-time, six or seven dimensions of which are "compactified" to extremely small sizes and are hence unobservable. The shape of the compactified dimensions, however, determines the modes of vibration of the strings, and hence the types and masses of fundamental particles, along with many characteristics of the forces between them. Thus, universes in which compactified dimensions have different shapes will have different constants of

---

[14]For a good, accessible overview of inflationary cosmology, see Guth, 1997.

physics and differing lower-level laws governing the forces. It is presently controversial whether superstring theory allows for significant variation in the shape of the compactified dimensions. If it does, however, it is then possible that an inflationary/superstring scenario could be constructed in which the shape of the compactified dimensions, and hence the constants of physics, underwent enough variation from universe to universe to explain the fine-tuning.[15]

Thus, it is in the realm of real physical plausibility that a viable inflationary/superstring many-universes scenario could be constructed that would account for the fine-tuning of the constants of physics. Nonetheless, it should be noted that despite the current popularity of both inflationary cosmology and superstring theory, both are highly speculative. For instance, as Michio Kaku states in his recent textbook on superstring theory, "Not a shred of experimental evidence has been found to confirm . . . superstrings" (1999, p. 17). The major attraction of string theory is its mathematical elegance and the fact that many physicists think that it is the only game in town that offers significant hope of providing a truly unified physical theory of gravitation with quantum mechanics, the two cornerstones of modern physics (Greene, 1999, p. 214).

It should be stressed, however, that even if superstring theory or inflationary cosmology turn out to be false, they have opened the door to taking the many-universes explanation of the fine-tuning as a serious physical possibility since some other physical mechanisms could give rise to multiple universes with a sufficiently large number of variations in the constants of physics. The only way we could close this door is if we discovered that the ultimate laws of physics did not allow either many-universes or much variation in the constants and laws of physics among universes.

15I am indebted to Gerald Cleaver, a string theorist at Baylor University, for helpful discussions of this issue. The sort of inflationary/superstring many-universes explanations of the fine-tuning discussed above have been suggested by a number of authors, such as Linde, (1990, PP&IC, p. 306; 1990, IQC, p. 6) and Greene (1999, pp. 355–363). To date, however, no one has adequately verified or worked-out the physics of superstring theory or inflationary cosmology, let alone the combination of the two, so this scenario remains highly speculative.

Theistic Responses to Many-Universes Generator Scenario

One major theistic response to the many-universes generator scenario, whether of the inflationary variety or some other type, is that a "many-universes generator" itself it seems to need to be "well-designed" in order to produce life-sustaining universes. After all, even a mundane item like a bread machine, which only produces loaves of bread instead of universes, must be well designed to produce decent loaves of bread. If this is right, then invoking some sort of many-universes generator as an explanation of the fine-tuning only kicks the issue of design up one level, to the question of who designed the many-universes generator.

The inflationary scenario discussed above is a good test case of this line of reasoning. The inflationary/superstring many-universes generator can only produce life-sustaining universes because it has the following "components" or "mechanisms":

(i) *A mechanism to supply the energy needed for the bubble universes:* This mechanism is the hypothesized inflaton field. By imparting a constant energy density to empty space, as space expands the inflaton field can act "as a reservoir of unlimited energy" for the bubbles (Peacock, 1999, p. 26).

(ii) *A mechanism to form the bubbles:* This mechanism is Einstein's equation of general relativity. Because of its peculiar form, Einstein's equation dictates that space expand at an enormous rate in the presence of a field, such as the inflaton field, that imparts a constant (and homogenous) energy density to empty space. This causes both the bubble universes to form and the rapid expansion of the prespace (the "ocean") which keeps the bubbles from colliding.

(iii) *A mechanism to convert the energy of inflaton field to the normal mass/energy we find in our universe.* This mechanism is Einstein's relation of the equivalence of mass and energy combined with an hypothesized coupling between the inflaton field and normal mass/energy fields we find in our universe.

(iv) *A mechanism that allows enough variation in constants of physics among universes:* The most physically viable candidate for this mechanism is superstring theory. As explained above, superstring theory *might* allow enough variation in the variations in the constants of physics among bubble universes to make it reasonably likely that a fine-tuned universe would be produced. The other leading alternatives to string theory being explored by physicists, such as the currently proposed models for Grand Unified Field Theories (GUTS), do not appear to allow for enough variation.[16]

Without all these "components," the many-universes generator would almost certainly fail to produce a single life-sustaining universes. For example, Einstein's equation and the inflaton field harmoniously work together to enormously inflate small regions of space while at the same time both imparting to them the positive energy density necessary for a universe with significant mass-energy and causing the pre-space to expand rapidly enough to keep the bubble universes from colliding. Without either factor, there would neither be regions of space that inflate nor would those regions have the mass-energy necessary for a universe to exist. If, for example, the universe obeyed Newton's theory of gravity instead of Einstein's, the vacuum energy of the inflaton field would at best simply create a gravitational attraction causing space to contract, not to expand.

In addition to the four factors listed above, the inflationary/superstring many-universes generator can only produce life-sustaining universes because the right background laws are in place. For example, as mentioned earlier, without the principle of quantization, all electrons would be sucked into the atomic nuclei and hence atoms would be impossible; without the Pauli-exclusion principle, electrons would occupy the lowest atomic orbit and hence complex and varied atoms would be impossible; without a universally attractive force between all masses, such as gravity, matter would not be able to form sufficiently large material bodies (such as planets) for life to develop or for long-lived stable energy sources such as stars to exist.[17]

In sum, even if an inflationary/superstring many-universes generator exists, it along with the background laws and principles could be said to be an *irreducibly complex* system, to borrow a phrase from biochemist Michael Behe (1996), with just the right combination of laws and fields for the production of life-permitting universes: if one of the components were missing or different, such as Einstein's equation or the Pauli-exclusion principle, it is unlikely that any life-permitting universes could be produced. In the absence of alternative explanations, the existence of such an a system suggests design since it seems very unlikely that such a system would have just the right components by chance. Thus, it does not seem that one can escape the conclusion of design merely by hypothesizing some sort of many-universes generator.

Finally, the many-universes generator hypothesis cannot explain other features of the universe that seem to exhibit apparent design, whereas theism can. For example, many physicists, such as Albert Einstein, have observed that the basic laws of physics exhibit an extraordinary degree of beauty, elegance, harmony, and ingenuity. Nobel Prize winning physicist Steven Weinberg, for instance, devotes a whole chapter of his book *Dreams of a Final Theory* (Chapter 6, "Beautiful Theories") explaining how the criteria of beauty and elegance are commonly used to guide physicists in formulating the right laws. Indeed, one

---

[16]The simplest and most studied GUT, SU(5), allows for three differing sets of values for the fundamental constants of physics when the other non-SU(5) Higgs fields are neglected (Linde, PP&IC, p. 33). Including all th other Higgs fields, the number of variations increases to perhaps several dozen (Linde, IQC, p. 6). Merely to account for the fine-tuning of the cosmological constant, however, which is estimated to be fine-tuned to one part in 10^{53}, would require on the order of 10^{53} variations of the physical constants among universes.

[17]Although some of the laws of physics can vary from universe to universe in string theory, these background laws and principles are a result of the structure of string theory and therefore cannot be explained by the inflationary/superstring many-universes hypothesis since they must occur in all universes. Further, since the variation among universes would consist of variation of the masses and types of particles, and the form of the forces between them, complex structures would almost certainly be atom-like and stable energy sources would almost certainly require aggregates of matter. Thus, the above background laws seem necessary for there to be life in any of the many-universes generated in this scenario, not merely a universe with our specific types of particles and forces.

of most prominent theoretical physicists of this century, Paul Dirac, went so far as to claim that "it is more important to have beauty in one's equations than to have them fit experiment." (1963, p. 47).

Now such beauty, elegance, and ingenuity make sense if the universe was designed by God. Under the atheistic many-universes hypothesis, however, there is no reason to expect the fundamental laws to be elegant or beautiful. As theoretical physicist Paul Davies writes, "If nature is so 'clever' as to exploit mechanisms that amaze us with their ingenuity, is that not persuasive evidence for the existence of intelligent design behind the universe? If the world's finest minds can unravel only with difficulty the deeper workings of nature, how could it be supposed that those workings are merely a mindless accident, a product of blind chance?"(1984, pp. 235–236.)[18]

6. CONCLUSION

In this paper, I have argued that the fine-tuning of the cosmos for life presents provides strong evidence for preferring theism over the atheistic single-universe hypothesis. I then argued that although one can partially explain the fine-tuning of the constants of physics by invoking some sort of many-universes generator, we have good reasons to believe that the many-universes generator itself would need to be well designed, and hence that hypothesizing some sort of many-universes generator only pushes the case for design up one level. The arguments I have offered do not prove the truth of theism, or even show that theism is epistemically warranted or the most plausible position to adopt. To show this would require examining all the evidence both for and against theism, along with looking at all the alternatives to theism. Rather, the arguments in this paper were only intended to show that the fine-tuning of the cosmos offers us significant reasons for preferring theism over atheism, where atheism is understood as not simply the denial of theism, but as also including the denial of any sort of intelligence behind the existence or structure of the universe.

---

[18]For more on the case for design from the simplicity and beauty of the laws of nature, see part II of my "The Argument from Design and the Many-Worlds Hypothesis" (2001).

REFERENCES

Barrow, John and Tipler, Frank. *The Anthropic Cosmological Principle*. Oxford: Oxford University Press, 1986.

Behe, Michael. *Darwin's Black Box: The Biochemical Challenge to Evolution*. New York: The Free Press, 1996.

Carnap, Rudolph. (1962) *The Logical Foundations of Probability*. Chicago: University of Chicago Press, 1962).

Carr, B. J., and Rees, M. J. (April, 1979). "The Anthropic Cosmological Principle and the Structure of the Physical World." *Nature*, Vol. 278, 12 April 1979, pp. 605–612.

Collins, Robin. (1999) "The Fine-Tuning Design Argument" in *Reason for the Hope Within*, Michael Murray (ed.), Grand Rapids, MI: Eerdman's Publishing Company.

———. (2001). "The Argument from Design and the Many-Worlds Hypothesis," in *Philosophy of Religion: A Reader and Guide*, William Lane Craig, editor, Edinburgh: Edinburgh University Press.

———. (Forthcoming). "The Evidence for Fine-Tuning." In *God and Design*, Neil Manson (ed.), Routledge.

Davies, Paul. (1974). *The Physics of Time Asymmetry*. Berekely, CA: University of California Press.

———. *The Accidental Universe*. Cambridge: Cambridge University Press, 1982.

———. *Superforce: The Search for a Grand Unified Theory of Nature*. New York: Simon and Schuster, 1984.

———. *The Cosmic Blueprint: New Discoveries in Nature's Creative Ability to Order the Universe*. New York: Simon and Schuster, 1988.

Denton, Michael. (1998). *Nature's Destiny: How the Laws of Biology Reveal Purpose in the Universe*. New York: The Free Press.

Dirac, P. A. M. "The Evolution of the Physicist's Picture of Nature." *Scientific American*, May 1963.

Dyson, Freeman. (1979). *Disturbing the Universe*. New York: Harper and Row.

Edwards, A. W. F. (1992) *Likelihood*. Baltimore: Johns Hopkins University Press.

Greene, Brian. *The Elegant Universe: Superstrings, Hidden Dimensions, and the Quest for the Ultimate Theory*. New York: W. W. Norton and Company, 1999.

Guth, Alan. *The Inflationary Universe: The Quest for a New Theory of Cosmic Origins*. New York: Helix Books, 1997.

Hacking, Ian. *The Emergence of Probability: A Philosophical Study of Early Ideas About Probability, Induction and Statistical Inference*. Cambridge: Cambridge University Press, 1975.

Kaku, Michio. *Introduction to Superstrings and M-Theory*, Second Edition. New York: Springer-Verlag, 1999.

Leslie, John. "How to Draw Conclusions From a Fine-Tuned Cosmos," In Robert Russell, et. al., eds., *Physics, Philosophy and Theology: A Common Quest for Understanding*. Vatican City State: Vatican Observatory Press, pp. 297–312, 1988.

Lewis, David. *On the Plurality of Worlds*. New York, Basil Blackwell, 1986.

Linde, Andrei. *Particle Physics and Inflationary Cosmology*. Translated by Marc Damashek. Longhorne, PA: Harwood Academic Publishers, 1990.

———. *Inflation and Quantum Cosmology*. New York: Academic Press, Inc., 1990.

Oberhummer, H., Csoto, A., and Schlattl, H. (2000a). "Fine-Tuning of Carbon-Based Life in the Universe by Triple-Alpha Process in Red Giants," *Science*, Vol. 289, No. 5476, 7 July 2000, pp. 88–90.

Peacock, John. (1999). *Cosmological Physics*. Cambridge: Cambridge University Press, 1999.

Rees, Martin. *Just Six Numbers: The Deep Forces that Shape the Universe*. New York: Basic Books, 2000.

Schlesinger, George (1984), "Possible Worlds and the Mystery of Existence," *Ratio*, 26, pp. 1–18.

———. (1985). *The Intelligibility of Nature*. Aberdeen, Scottland: Aberdeen University Press.

Sklar, Lawrence. *Physics and Chance: Philosophical Issues in the Foundation of Statistical Mechanics*. Cambridge: Cambridge University Press, 1993.

Smart, J. J. C. "Laws of Nature and Cosmic Coincidence," *The Philosophical Quarterly*, Vol. 35, No. 140.

Smith, George. "Atheism: The Case Against God," reprinted in *An Anthology of Atheism and Rationalism*, edited by Gordon Stein, Prometheus Press, 1980.

Swinburne, Richard. *An Introduction to Confirmation Theory*. London: Methuen and Co. Ltd, 1973.

Tegmark, Max. "Is 'The Theory of Everything' Merely the Ultimate Ensemble Theory?" *Annals of Physics*, 270, (1998), pp. 1–51.

Van Fraassen, Bas. *Laws and Symmetry*. Oxford: Oxford University Press, 1989.

Weatherford, Roy. *Foundations of Probability Theory*. Boston: Routledge and Kegan Paul, 1982.

Weinberg, Steven. *Dreams of a Final Theory*. New York: Vintage Books, 1992.

QUESTIONS FOR FURTHER REFLECTION

1. If you were an atheist, how would you respond to the fine-tuning argument? Do you think the response is adequate?

2. Does Collins's version of the fine-tuning argument avoid Hume's objections to the argument from design? Why or why not?

3. How plausible do you think the many-universes hypothesis is? Do you find Collins's response to the many-universes hypothesis convincing? Why or why not?

4. In your view, how does the strength of Collins's argument for the existence of God compare with what you consider the strongest argument against the existence of God? Explain your answer.

18. THE MORAL ARGUMENT FOR THE EXISTENCE OF GOD

C. S. Lewis

C. S. Lewis (1898–1963) was a fellow of Magdalen College Oxford and also Professor of Medieval and Renaissance Literature at Cambridge University. Though well published in his own field, he is best known for his popular works, including *The Space Trilogy* and the popular children's series *The Chronicles of Narnia*. Lewis was a friend of fantasy writer J. R. R. Tolkien. Lewis also wrote several widely read works of nonfiction for adults, including *Miracles* and *Mere Christianity*, from which the following selection is taken, in which he argues that there is an objective moral law which implies the existence of a moral law giver.

1. What does Lewis think quarreling shows us?
2. What did the "Law or Rule about Right and Wrong" used to be called?
3. How does Lewis respond to the charge that there is no objective moral law because various cultures have different moral norms?
4. How does Lewis think that moral relativists show that they don't really believe moral relativism?
5. What is the difference between how humans study man and how they study everything else?

Every one has heard people quarrelling. Sometimes it sounds funny and sometimes it sounds merely unpleasant; but however it sounds, I believe we can learn something very important from listening to the kind of things they say. They say things like this: "How'd you like it if anyone did the same to you?"—"That's my seat, I was there first"—"Leave him alone, he isn't doing you any harm"—"Why should you shove in first?"—"Give me a bit of your orange, I gave you a bit of mine"—"Come on, you promised." People say things like that every day, educated people as well as uneducated and children as well as grown-ups.

Now what interests me about all these remarks is that the man who makes them is not merely saying that the other man's behaviour does not happen to please him. He is appealing to some kind of standard of behaviour which he expects the other man to know about. And the other man very seldom replies: "To hell with your standard." Nearly always he tries to make out that what he has been doing does not really go against the standard, or that if it does there is some special excuse. He pretends there is some special reason in this particular case why the person who took the seat first should not keep it, or that things were quite different when he was given the bit of orange, or that something has turned up which lets him off keeping his promise. It looks, in fact, very much as if both parties had in mind some kind of Law or Rule of fair play or decent behaviour or morality or whatever you like to call it, about which they really agreed. And they have. If they had not, they might, of course, fight like animals, but they could not *quarrel* in the human sense of the word. Quarrelling means trying to show that the other man is in the wrong. And there would be no sense in trying to do that unless you and he had some sort of agreement as to what Right and Wrong are; just as there would be

no sense in saying that a footballer had committed a foul unless there was some agreement about the rules of football.

Now this Law or Rule about Right and Wrong used to be called the Law of Nature. Nowadays, when we talk of the "laws of nature" we usually mean things like gravitation, or heredity, or the laws of chemistry. But when the older thinkers called the Law of Right and Wrong "the Law of Nature," they really meant the Law of *Human* Nature. The idea was that, just as all bodies are governed by the law of gravitation and organisms by biological laws, so the creature called man also had *his* law—with this great difference, that a body could not choose whether it obeyed the law of gravitation or not, but a man could choose either to obey the Law of Human Nature or to disobey it.

We may put this another way. Each man is at every moment subjected to several different sets of law but there is only one of these which he is free to disobey. As a body, he is subjected to gravitation and cannot disobey it; if you leave him unsupported in mid-air, he has no more choice about falling than a stone has. As an organism, he is subjected to various biological laws which he cannot disobey any more than an animal can. That is, he cannot disobey those laws which he shares with other things; but the law which is peculiar to his human nature, the law he does not share with animals or vegetables or inorganic things, is the one he can disobey if he chooses.

This law was called the Law of Nature because people thought that every one knew it by nature and did not need to be taught it. They did not mean, of course, that you might not find an odd individual here and there who did not know it, just as you find a few people who are colour-blind or have no ear for a tune. But taking the race as a whole, they thought that the human idea of decent behaviour was obvious to every one. And I believe they were right. If they were not, then all things we said about the war were nonsense. What was the sense in saying the enemy were in the wrong unless Right is a real thing which the Nazis at bottom knew as well as we did and ought to have practised? If they had had no notion of what we mean by right, then, though we might still have had to fight them, we could no more have blamed them for that than for the colour of their hair.

I know that some people say the idea of a Law of Nature or decent behaviour known to all men is unsound, because different civilisations and different ages have had quite different moralities.

But this is not true. There have been differences between their moralities, but these have never amounted to anything like a total difference. If anyone will take the trouble to compare the moral teaching of, say, the ancient Egyptians, Babylonians, Hindus, Chinese, Greeks, and Romans, what will really strike him will be how very like they are to each other and to our own. Some of the evidence for this I have put together in the appendix of another book called *The Abolition of Man*; but for our present purpose I need only ask the reader to think what a totally different morality would mean. Think of a country where people were admired for running away in battle, or where a man felt proud of double-crossing all the people who had been kindest to him. You might just as well try to imagine a country where two and two made five. Men have differed as regards what people you ought to be unselfish to—whether it was only your own family, or your fellow countrymen, or everyone. But they have always agreed that you ought not to put yourself first. Selfishness has never been admired. Men have differed as to whether you should have one wife or four. But they have always agreed that you must not simply have any woman you liked.

But the most remarkable thing is this. Whenever you find a man who says he does not believe in a real Right and Wrong, you will find the same man going back on this a moment later. He may break his promise to you, but if you try breaking one to him he will be complaining "It's not fair" before you can say Jack Robinson. A nation may say treaties do not matter; but then, next minute, they spoil their case by saying that the particular treaty they want to break was an unfair

one. But if treaties do not matter, and if there is no such thing as Right and Wrong—in other words, if there is no Law of Nature—what is the difference between a fair treaty and an unfair one? Have they not let the cat out of the bag and shown that, whatever they say, they really know the Law of Nature just like anyone else?

It seems, then, we are forced to believe in a real Right and Wrong. People may be sometimes mistaken about them, just as people sometimes get their sums wrong; but they are not a matter of mere taste and opinion any more than the multiplication table. Now if we are agreed about that, I go on to my next point, which is this. None of us are really keeping the Law of Nature. If there are any exceptions among you, I apologise to them. They had much better read some other work, for nothing I am going to say concerns them. And now, turning to the ordinary human beings who are left. . . .

I do not succeed in keeping the Law of Nature very well, and the moment anyone tells me I am not keeping it, there starts up in my mind a string of excuses as long as your arm. The question at the moment is not whether they are good excuses. The point is that they are one more proof of how deeply, whether we like it or not, we believe in the Law of Nature. If we do not believe in decent behaviour, why should we be so anxious to make excuses for not having behaved decently? The truth is, we believe in decency so much— we feel the Rule or Law pressing on us so—that we cannot bear to face the fact that we are breaking it, and consequently we try to shift the responsibility. For you notice that it is only for our bad behaviour that we find all these explanations. It is only our bad temper that we put down to being tired or worried or hungry; we put our good temper down to ourselves.

These, then, are the two points I wanted to make. First, that human beings, all over the earth, have this curious idea that they ought to behave in a certain way, and cannot really get rid of it. Secondly, that they do not in fact behave in that way. They know the Law of Nature; they break it. These two facts are the foundation of all clear thinking about ourselves and the universe we live in. . . .

Let us sum up what we have reached so far. In the case of stones and trees and things of that sort, what we call the Laws of Nature may not be anything except a way of speaking. When you say that nature is governed by certain laws, this may only mean that nature does, in fact, behave in a certain way. The so-called laws may not be anything real—anything above and beyond the actual facts which we observe. But in the case of Man, we saw that this will not do. The Law of Human Nature, or of Right and Wrong, must be something above and beyond the actual facts of human behaviour. In this case, besides the actual facts, you have something else—a real law which we did not invent and which we know we ought to obey.

I now want to consider what this tells us about the universe we live in. Ever since men were able to think, they have been wondering what this universe really is and how it came to be there. And, very roughly, two views have been held. First, there is what is called the materialist view. People who take that view think that matter and space just happen to exist, and always have existed, nobody knows why; and that the matter, behaving in certain fixed ways, has just happened, by a sort of fluke, to produce creatures like ourselves who are able to think. By one chance in a thousand something hit our sun and made it produce the planets; and by another thousandth chance the chemicals necessary for life, and the right temperature, occurred on one of these planets, and so some of the matter on this earth came alive; and then, by a very long series of chances, the living creatures developed into things like us. The other view is the religious view. According to it, what is behind the universe is more like a mind than it is like anything else we know. That is to say, it is conscious, and has purposes, and prefers one thing to another. And on this view it made the universe, partly for purposes we do not know, but partly, at any rate, in order to produce creatures like itself—I mean, like itself to the extent of having minds. Please do not think that one of these views was held a long time ago and that the other has gradually taken its place. Wherever there have been thinking men both views turn up. And note this too. You cannot find out which view is the right one by science in the ordinary sense. Science works by experiments. It watches how things behave. Every scientific statement in the long run, however complicated it looks, really means something like, "I pointed the telescope to such and such a part of the sky at 2:20 A.M. on January 15th and saw so-and-so," or "I put some of this stuff in a pot and heated it to such-and-such a tempera-

ture and it did so-and-so." Do not think I am saying anything against science: I am only saying what its job is. And the more scientific a man is, the more (I believe) he would agree with me that this is the job of science—and a very useful and necessary job it is too. But why anything comes to be there at all, and whether there is anything behind the things science observes—something of a different kind—this is not a scientific question. If there is "Something Behind," then either it will have to remain altogether unknown to men or else make itself known in some different way. The statement that there is any such thing, and the statement that there is no such thing, are neither of them statements that science can make. And real scientists do not usually make them. It is usually the journalists and popular novelists who have picked up a few odds and ends of half-baked science from textbooks who go in for them. After all, it is really a matter of common sense. Supposing science ever became complete so that it knew every single thing in the whole universe. Is it not plain that the questions, "Why is there a universe?" "Why does it go on as it does?" "Has it any meaning?" would remain just as they were?

Now the position would be quite hopeless but for this. There is one thing, and only one, in the whole universe which we know more about than we could learn from external observation. That one thing is Man. We do not merely observe men, we *are* men. In this case we have, so to speak, inside information; we are in the know. And because of that, we know that men find themselves under a moral law, which they did not make, and cannot quite forget even when they try, and which they know they ought to obey. Notice the following point. Anyone studying Man from the outside as we study electricity or cabbages, not knowing our language and consequently not able to get any inside knowledge from us, but merely observing what we did, would never get the slightest evidence that we had this moral law. How could he? for his observations would only show what we did, and the moral law is about what we ought to do. In the same way, if there were anything above or behind the observed facts in the case of stones or the weather, we, by studying them from outside, could never hope to discover it.

The position of the question, then, is like this. We want to know whether the universe simply happens to be what it is for no reason or whether there is a power behind it that makes it what it is. Since that power, if it exists, would be not one of the observed facts but a reality which makes them, no mere observation of the facts can find it. There is only one case in which we can know whether there is anything more, namely our own case. And in that one case we find there is. Or put it the other way round. If there was a controlling power outside the universe, it could not show itself to us as one of the facts inside the universe—no more than the architect of a house could actually be a wall or staircase or fireplace in that house. The only way in which we could expect it to show itself would be inside ourselves as an influence or a command trying to get us to behave in a certain way. And that is just what we do find inside ourselves. Surely this ought to arouse our suspicions? In the only case where you can expect to get an answer, the answer turns out to be Yes; and in the other cases, where you do not get an answer, you see why you do not. Suppose someone asked me, when I see a man in a blue uniform going down the street leaving little paper packets at each house, why I suppose that they contain letters? I should reply, "Because whenever he leaves a similar little packet for me I find it does contain a letter." And if he then objected, "But you've never seen all these letters which you think the other people are getting," I should say, "Of course not, and I shouldn't expect to, because they're not addressed to me. I'm explaining the packets I'm not allowed to open by the ones I am allowed to open." It is the same about this question. The only packet I am allowed to open is Man. When I do, especially when I open that particular man called Myself, I find that I do not exist on my own, that I am under a law; that somebody or something wants me to behave in a certain way. I do not, of course, think that if I could get inside a stone or a tree I

should find exactly the same thing, just as I do not think all the other people in the street get the same letters as I do. I should expect, for instance, to find that the stone had to obey the law of gravity—that whereas the sender of the letters merely tells me to obey the law of my human nature, He compels the stone to obey the laws of its stony nature. But I should expect to find that there was, so to speak, a sender of letters in both cases, a Power behind the facts, a Director, a Guide. . . .

[What] I have got to is a Something which is directing the universe, and which appears in me as a law urging me to do right and making me feel responsible and uncomfortable when I do wrong. I think we have to assume it is more like a mind than it is like anything else we know—because after all the only other thing we know is matter and you can hardly imagine a bit of matter giving instructions.

QUESTIONS FOR FURTHER REFLECTION

1. Explain how Lewis's example involving quarreling proves there is an objective moral law. Does the fact that people *behave* as if there is an object moral standard mean there is one?
2. Is Lewis's argument against moral relativism successful? Does the fact that most cultures agree on moral norms undermine relativism? Are there any major moral differences between different cultures and are these enough to undermine Lewis's claim?
3. Lewis argues that we have special access to studying humans because we have "inside knowledge." Why think that our introspective knowledge gives us special access to our internal states? Do I have special access to the PH level of my blood merely because it is internal to me?

19. CRITIQUE OF THE MORAL ARGUMENT

J. L. Mackie

A brief biography of J. L. Mackie occurs on page 77. In this selection, he criticizes several versions of the moral argument for the existence of God.

READING QUESTIONS

1. Does Mackie think that the moral argument is an original ground for religious belief?
2. What, according to Mackie, is the first premise of Newman's argument?

3. Why does Mackie think it is a mistake for Kant to argue from "we ought to seek the highest good" to "it must therefore be possible" to do so?
4. Why do many think that objective values are reason to think that God exists?
5. On what grounds does R. M. Hare reject the argument from objective values?

1. A POPULAR LINE OF THOUGHT

It is often suggested that morality requires and presupposes religion, and that moral thinking will therefore support theistic beliefs. A familiar line of popular thought runs somewhat like this. Moral principles tell us what we must do, whether we like it or not. That is, they are commands, and such commands must have a source, a commander. But the requirements of morality go beyond what any human authority demands of us, and they sometimes require us to resist all human authorities. Moral requirements go beyond, and sometimes against, what the law prescribes, or the state, or our friends, or any organized church, or the public opinion of any community, even a world-wide one. They must therefore be the commands of some more than human, and hence supernatural, authority. Also, if these commands are to overrule, as they claim to do, all other considerations, we must have an adequate motive for obeying them no matter what threats or temptations urge us to disobey. Such a motive can be supplied only by our knowing that there is a being who has both the will and the power to give rewards and to impose penalties which outweigh all worldly losses and gains. Morality needs a god, therefore, both as a supreme source of commands and as an all-powerful wielder of sanctions to enforce them. Besides, moral thinking includes a confident demand for justice, an assurance that what is unfair and unjust cannot in the end prevail, and justice requires that there should be some power which will somehow balance happiness with desert.

Such an argument has, perhaps, seldom served as an original ground of religious belief; but it has seemed to many to be a powerful reinforcement for that belief, and, in particular, a strong reason for continuing to adhere to it when it is threatened in some other way. It is felt that if theistic beliefs are given up, moral convictions will lose their point and their force, and also their determinacy. Religious beliefs that we see some ground for doubting are thus buttressed by the feeling that we can neither abandon morality nor leave it without religious support.

I shall come back later to this popular line of thought. But first I want to examine several different and even incompatible philosophical versions of the argument from morality, each of which can be seen as a development or refinement of some elements in the popular line of thought. These versions are ones put forward by Newman and by Kant, and one that is considered, but not endorsed, by Sidgwick.

2. NEWMAN: CONSCIENCE AS THE CREATIVE PRINCIPLE OF RELIGION

Newman, in A Grammar of Assent, starts from the thesis that "Conscience has a legitimate place among our mental acts"; he compares it in this respect with memory, reasoning, imagination, and the sense of beauty. He claims that "in this special feeling, which follows on the commission of what we call right or wrong, lie the materials for the real apprehension of a Divine Sovereign and Judge." Newman distinguishes two aspects of conscience. On the one hand it is a moral sense which supplies us with "the elements of morals," particular judgements about what we must or must not do, "such as may be developed by the intellect into an ethical code." On the other hand it is a sense of duty which enforces these prescriptions. It is on this second aspect, on conscience as "a sanction of right conduct," that Newman relies. This side of conscience, he suggests, "does not repose on itself, but vaguely reaches forward to something beyond self, and dimly discovers a sanction higher than self for its decisions, as is evidenced in that keen sense of obligation and responsibility which informs them." In this respect it is, he says, quite unlike "taste"—that is, the aesthetic faculty, the sense of beauty—which "is its own evidence, appealing to nothing beyond its own sense of the beautiful or the ugly, and enjoying the specimens of the beautiful simply for their own sake." Pursuing this contrast, he says that "Conscience has an intimate bearing on our affections and emotions." Someone who recognizes that his conduct has not been beautiful does not feel any fear on that account. But someone who recognizes his own conduct as immoral "has a lively sense of responsibility and guilt, though the act be no offence against society—of distress and apprehension, even though it may be of present service to him—of compunction and regret, though in itself it be most pleasurable—of confusion of face, though it may have no witnesses." Such affections, Newman says, "are correlative with persons." "If, as is the case, we feel responsibility, are ashamed, are frightened, at transgressing the voice of conscience, this implies that there is One to whom we are responsible, before whom we are ashamed, whose claims upon us we fear." And equally the enjoyment of a good conscience implies a person in whose approval we are happy. "These feelings in us are such as require for their exciting cause an intelligent being." Yet there is no earthly person who systematically fills this role. Conscience, therefore, must be related to a supernatural and divine person: "and thus the phenomena of Conscience, as a dictate, avail to impress the imagination with the picture of a Supreme Governor, a Judge, holy, just, powerful, all-seeing, retributive, and [are] the creative principle of religion, as the Moral Sense is the principle of ethics."[1]

I suggested above that the popular moral argument is seldom an original ground of religious belief. Newman is not here denying this, but making the rather different suggestion that not the argument but the actual experience of conscience is the original ground of such belief, that the sense of duty and responsibility—that is, answerability—gives rise to religion in much the same way that the other aspect of conscience, the moral sense, gives rise to ethical beliefs. However, he is not only making this genetic claim: he is also saying that the phenomena of conscience are a good reason for theistic beliefs. So understood, his argument rests on three premises: that conscience is legitimate or authoritative; that it looks beyond the agent himself to a further imperative and a higher sanction; and that these must stem from a person, an intelligent being, if they are to arouse powerful emotions with exactly the tone of those that moral

awareness involves. If we grant all three premises, we must admit that the argument is cogent, though the god that it introduces need not have the infinite attributes of Descartes's god, or Anselm's. But must we grant all three premises? In fact this argument faces a dilemma. If we take conscience at its face value and accept as really valid what it asserts, we must say that there is a rational prescriptivity about certain kinds of action in their own right: that they are of this or that kind is in itself a reason for doing them or for refraining from them. There is a to-be-done-ness or a not-to-be-done-ness involved *in that kind of action in itself*. If so, there is no need to look beyond this to any supernatural person who commands or forbids such action. Equally the regret, guilt, shame, and fear associated with the consciousness of having done wrong, although normally such feelings arise only in relations with persons, are in this special case natural and appropriate: what conscience, taken at its face value, tells us is that this is how one should feel about a wrong action simply in itself. That is, if we wholeheartedly accept Newman's first premise, we must reject the second and the third. But if we do not take conscience at its face value, if we seek critically to understand how conscience has come into existence and has come to work as it does, then we do indeed find persons in the background, but human persons, not a divine one. If we stand back from the experience of conscience and try to understand it, it is overwhelmingly plausible to see it as an introjection into each individual of demands that come from other people; in the first place, perhaps, from his parents and immediate associates, but ultimately from the traditions and institutions of the society in which he has grown up, or of some special part of that society which has had the greatest influence upon him. In thus understanding conscience we do, admittedly, look beyond conscience itself and beyond the agent himself, but we look to natural, human, sources, not to a god. We are now in a way accepting Newman's second and third premises, but modifying the first. It is not easy to accept all three. Newman's argument walks, as it were, a tightrope, allowing to conscience, as it claims, an authority and an origin independent of all human feelings and demands, and yet not endorsing its claim to complete autonomy. But it is arbitrary to choose just this degree of critical reinterpretation, no more and no less.

---

[1] J. H. Newman, *A Grammar of Assent* (Longmans, London, 1870), Chapter 5.

Perhaps Newman will rely not on conscience in general, as a mode of thinking almost universal among human beings, but on the particular form of conscience which already ties its moral ideas to belief in a god. If he takes this special form of conscience at its face value, he can indeed assert all three premises; but then his argument will carry conviction only with those who already accept his conclusion. Addressed to a wider public or to an initially open-minded audience, it becomes the hopelessly weak argument that there must be a god because some people believe that there is a god and have incorporated this belief into their moral thought. Something more would be needed to show that this special form of moral thinking is distinctively valid, and this would have to include an independent argument precisely for the existence of a god of the appropriate sort.

This criticism may be restated in terms of the confirmation of hypotheses by evidence, which is undermined by the availability of better rival explanations. The phenomena of conscience to which Newman draws attention could indeed be explained by the hypothesis that there is a supernatural person with the traditional theistic attributes, or some rough approximation to them, of whose presence and demands and attitudes and powers everyone, in thinking morally, is at least dimly aware. But there are at least two rival hypotheses which would explain these phenomena equally well: these are ethical objectivism or intuitionism on the one hand, and the naturalistic, psychological, account of the origin of conscience on the other.[2] Since there are these alternative explanations, of which at least the second is intrinsically less demanding, less metaphysically improbable, than the theistic one, the latter is not significantly confirmed by the phenomena which, I concede, it would explain.

2. KANT: GOD AS A PRESUPPOSITION OF MORALITY

In the *Critique of Pure Reason* Kant argues that there is no sound speculative proof of the existence of a god. We have already referred to his criticisms of the ontological and cosmological arguments, and we shall see what he says against the design argument in Chapter 8. But in the *Critique of Practical Reason* he suggests that moral reasoning can achieve what speculative reasoning cannot, and that the existence of a god, and also affirmative solutions to the other great metaphysical questions of the immortality of the soul and the freedom of the will, can be defended as being necessarily presupposed in moral consciousness.[3]

Kant's view is much further than Newman's from the popular line of thought with which we began. He stresses the autonomy of morality, to which I appealed in the first horn of the dilemma used to criticize Newman's argument. What is morally right and obligatory is so, Kant holds, in itself, and can be rationally seen in itself to be so. Each rational being is, as such, competent to determine the moral law, to prescribe moral commands to himself, and therefore does not need God to command him—or even, it would seem, to advise him. "Moreover, it is not meant by this that it is necessary to suppose the existence of God *as a basis of all obligation in general* (for this rests . . . simply on the autonomy of reason itself)." (267) Moral agents, or rational beings, are the citizens of an ideal commonwealth, making universal laws for themselves and one another. Morality is corrupted if it is derived from prudence and self-interest: divine rewards and punishments, therefore, far from supplying a necessary motive for morality, would introduce heteronomy, substituting an alien and morally worthless motive for the only genuinely valuable one of respect for the moral law.

However, Kant finds another and more appropriate place for a god in the moral universe. His positive argument starts from the notion of the *summum bonum*, the highest good, which, he says, is not merely moral rectitude but also includes happiness. Virtue and happiness together constitute the highest good for a person, and the distribution of happiness in proportion to morality constitutes the highest good for a possible world. Whereas the Epicureans made the mistake of reducing morality to the pursuit of happiness, the Stoics

---

[2]Cf. my *Hume's Moral Theory* (Routledge & Kegan Paul, London, 1980), especially pp. 145–50.

[3]I. Kant, *Critique of Practical Reason*, e.g. in T. K. Abbott, *Kant's Theory of Ethics* (Longmans, London, 1927), especially Part I, Book II, Chapter 2. References in the text to this work and to Kant's *Metaphysic of Morals* are to the pages in the German edition of Rosenkranz and Schubert, given at the top of each page in Abbott.

made the opposite mistake of either leaving happiness out of their conception of the highest good, or—what amounts to the same thing—identifying happiness simply with the consciousness of virtue. In contrast with both these mistakes, an adequate conception of the highest good must include both virtue and happiness, but each in its own right. Now since these two elements in the highest good are independent of one another, there is no logical necessity that they should go together, and hence no a priori guarantee that the realization of this highest good is even possible. Equally, there is no natural, causal, guarantee of this. Happiness (in this life) depends largely on what happens in the natural world, but the moral choices of rational beings are not to any great extent in control of this: our moral efforts cannot causally ensure that those who will and act rightly will be happy. Nor does nature as such conform to a moral standard. But, Kant says, moral thought tells us that we must take the highest good as a supreme end; that is, "we ought to endeavour to promote the highest good, which must, therefore, be possible." He infers that "the existence of a cause of all nature, distinct from nature itself, and containing the principle . . . of the exact harmony of happiness with morality" is *postulated* in moral thought. "The highest good is possible in the world only on the supposition of a Supreme Being having a causality corresponding to moral character"—that is, a god. Since it is for us a duty to promote the highest good, there is "a necessity connected with duty as a requisite, that we should presuppose the possibility of this *summum bonum*: and as this is possible only on condition of the existence of God . . . it is morally necessary to assume the existence of God." But since happiness in this life is pretty plainly not proportioned to morality, it is also necessary to assume that individuals survive in a life after death; Kant has also argued separately for such immortality, again as a presupposition of moral thought, as being necessary to allow for an indefinite progress towards perfection which is involved in the first half of the highest good, complete virtue or "the *perfect accordance* of the mind with the moral law." (265–7)

It is not easy to decide just how Kant meant these conclusions to be interpreted. On the one hand he argues for "the primacy of pure practical reason in its union with the speculative reason," saying that when certain propositions "are *inseparably* attached *to the practical interest* of pure reason," theoretical reason must accept them, and "must try to compare and connect them with everything that it has in its power as speculative reason" (261), and this is plainly intended to apply to the propositions asserting the immortality of the soul and the existence of a god, as well as the freedom of the will. But on the other hand, asking whether our knowledge is "actually extended in this way by pure practical reason," and whether that is "*immanent* in practical reason which for the speculative was only *transcendent*," Kant replies "Certainly, but *only in a practical point of view*"—which seems to take away what it gives. We do not in this way gain knowledge of our souls or of the Supreme Being as they are in themselves. Theoretical reason "is compelled to admit *that there are such objects*, although it is not able to define them more closely"; knowledge of them has been given "only for practical use." In fact speculative reason will work with regard to these objects only "in a negative manner," to remove "*anthropomorphism* as the source of *superstition*, or seeming extension of these conceptions by supposed experience; and . . . *fanaticism*, which promises the same by means of supersensible intuition." (276–9) He seems to be saying that the existence of a god and the immortality of the soul can be established as facts by the arguments from morality, but only in a highly indeterminate form. Yet he hints also at a more sceptical position, that the existence of a god, the freedom of the will, and the immortality of the soul cannot be established as facts, even by reasoning based on the moral consciousness, but can only be shown to be necessarily presupposed in that consciousness, to be, as it were, implicit in its content. In other words, we as rational beings cannot help thinking morally, and if we develop our moral thinking fully and coherently we cannot help supposing that there is a god; but whether in fact there is a god remains an open question. Kant says that "the righteous man may say: I *will* that there be a God, that my existence in this world be also an existence outside the chain of physical causes, and in a pure world of the understanding, and lastly, that my duration be endless; I firmly abide by this, and will not let this faith be taken from me; for in this instance alone my interest, because I *must* not relax anything of it, inevitably determines my judgement," and he speaks of a *faith of pure practical reason*, which, he admits, is an "unusual notion." (289–92)

But in whichever of these ways we interpret his conclusion, Kant's argument is open to criticism. The most glaring weakness is in the step from the proposition that "we ought to seek the highest good" to the claim that it "must therefore be possible." Even if, as Kant argues elsewhere, "ought" implies "can," the thesis that we ought to seek to promote the highest good implies only that we can *seek to promote* it, and perhaps, since rational seeking could not be completely fruitless, that we can to some extent actually *promote* it. But this does not require that the full realization of the highest good should be possible. For example, it is thoroughly rational to try to improve the condition of human life, provided that some improvement is possible; there is no need to entertain vain hopes for its perfection. And even for the *possibility* of that full realization the most that would be needed is the possible existence of a wholly good and all-powerful governor of the world; the actual existence of such a governor would ensure not merely the possibility but the actuality of the highest good. Kant might say that we can and should aspire to the ultimate realization of the highest good, and that a *hope* for such ultimate realization is necessarily involved in moral thought. But he cannot claim that even its possible realization is a necessary postulate of moral thought in general; it is not even a necessary postulate of that particular sort of moral theory which Kant himself developed. The willing of universal laws by and for all rational beings as such could be a strictly autonomous activity.

There are, indeed, recurrent tensions between Kant's theism and his stress on the autonomy of morals. In sharp contrast with the popular view, and with Newman's, Kant holds that neither our knowledge of God and of his will, nor that will itself, is the foundation of the moral law. Yet because (as he thinks) we have to postulate a god who *also* wills these laws, as does every other free and rational will, he still calls them "commands of the Supreme Being," but in a sense which is only a pale shadow of what is intended by most theological moralists. Again, Kant holds that no "desired results" are "the proper motive of obedience" to these laws, indeed that fear of punishment or hope of reward "if taken as principles, would destroy the whole moral worth of actions." Yet his belief that there is something appropriate about the *proportioning* of happiness to morality—a retributive thesis—again

seems to be a pale shadow of the popular reliance on punishments and rewards. Is not this true also of his stress (after all) on happiness, whose conjunction with virtue we are to take not merely as a legitimate hope but as a *postulate* of moral thought? Would not a thoroughgoing recognition of the autonomy of morals lead rather to the Stoic view that morality needs no actual happiness beyond the consciousness of right action itself?

Kant himself seems to have been aware of these difficulties, and a passage in his *Metaphysic of Morals* suggests a quite different proof of God's existence: again a moral proof, but one which anticipates Newman's argument about conscience.

> Now this original intellectual and . . . moral capacity, called *conscience*, has this peculiarity in it, that although its business is a business of man with himself, yet he finds himself compelled by his reason to transact it as if at the command *of another person* . . . in all duties the conscience of the man must regard *another* than himself as the judge of his actions. . . . Now this other may be an actual or a merely ideal person which reason frames to itself. Such an idealized person . . . must be one who knows the heart . . . at the same time he must also be *all-obliging*, that is, must be or be conceived as a person in respect of whom all duties are to be regarded as his commands . . . Now since such a moral being must at the same time possess all power (in heaven and earth), since otherwise he could not give his commands their proper effect, and since such a moral being possessing power over all is called God, hence conscience must be conceived as the subjective principle of a responsibility for one's deeds before God; nay, this latter concept is contained (though it be only obscurely) in every moral self-consciousness. (293–4)

Here Kant is vacillating between the recognition of the merely psychological phenomenon of the setting up of an ideal spectator (Adam Smith's "man within the breast"[4]) and the suggestion that moral thought has at least to postulate the real

---

[4]A. Smith, *The Theory of Moral Sentiments* (Edinburgh, 1808), Part III, Chapter 2, p. 308.

existence of an outside authority—but how weak a reason he offers for the ascription of all power to this moral being! In any case, in so far as this argument anticipates Newman's, it is open to the same criticisms.

We need not labour these internal tensions and vacillations. What is important is that even if moral thought is as Kant describes it, it does not follow that such thought has even to postulate the existence of a god, let alone that we can infer the real existence of a god from the character of that thought . . .

3. GOD AND THE OBJECTIVITY OF VALUE

There is an element in the popular line of thought which has not, as far as I know, been properly examined by philosophers. This is the suggestion that there are objective moral values and prescriptions, but that they are created by God, and indeed require a god to create them.

Philosophers from Plato onwards have repeatedly criticized the suggestion that moral obligations are created by God's commands. The commands of a legitimate human ruler do not *create* obligations: if such a ruler tells you to do X, this makes it obligatory for you to do X only if it is *already* obligatory for you to do whatever the ruler tells you (within the sphere in which X lies). The same applies to God. He can make it obligatory for us to do Y by so commanding only because there is first a general obligation for us to obey him. His commands, therefore, cannot be the source of moral obligation in general: for any obligation that they introduce, there must be a more fundamental obligation that they presuppose. This criticism decisively excludes one way in which it might be thought that God could create morality.

But there is a further problem. On any plausible objectivist view of ethics, moral values, obligations, and the like are held to supervene upon certain nonmoral or "natural" features of situations or actions. If a state of affairs is good or bad, there must be something about it that makes it good or bad, and similarly there must be something other than its rightness or wrongness that makes an action right or wrong. Now what is the logical character of this *supervenience* or *making*? Swinburne takes it to be analytic: "Once one has specified fully what it is that makes the action wrong, then

it will be (given that it is a truth) an analytic truth that an action of that kind is wrong."[5] But this cannot be right. Objective wrongness, if there is such a thing, is intrinsically prescriptive or action-guiding, it in itself gives or constitutes a reason for not doing the wrong action, and this holds also for some, if not all, other moral features. To say that they are intrinsically action-guiding is to say that the reasons that they give for doing or for not doing something are independent of that agent's desires or purposes. But the natural features on which the moral ones supervene cannot be *intrinsically* action-guiding or reason-giving in this way. Supervenience, then, must be a synthetic connection. But, if so, then a god whose power was limited only by logical, analytic, constraints—that is, not really limited at all—could presumably make there to be, or not to be, such and such relations of supervenience. This *creation of supervenient value* is, of course, quite different from the creation of obligation by command that has been rejected, with good reason, by Plato and his many followers. In this sense it is not absurd to suppose that a god could create moral values. Besides, we might well argue (borrowing, perhaps, from my own discussion elsewhere[6]) that objective intrinsically prescriptive features, supervening upon natural ones, constitute so odd a cluster of qualities and relations that they are most unlikely to have arisen in the ordinary course of events, without an all-powerful god to create them. If, then, there are such intrinsically prescriptive objective values, they make the existence of a god more probable than it would have been without them. Thus we have, after all, a defensible inductive argument from morality to the existence of a god. The popular line of thought to which I referred at the beginning of this chapter has regularly included some inkling of this truth.

It might be objected that this argument relies on a perverse and unnecessary formulation of ethical objectivism. Rather than sharply distinguish the "natural" features from the reason-giving moral ones, and see the supervenience of the latter on the former as a puzzling synthetic connection that invites the postulation of a god to explain it, why

---

[5] *The Existence of God*, p. 177.
[6] Cf. my *Ethics: Inventing Right and Wrong* (Penguin, Harmondsworth, 1977). Chapter 1.

should not the objectivist say that certain natural features simply do in themselves constitute reasons for or against the actions that involve them? Objectivism would then be the doctrine that an action's being of a certain naturally identifiable kind may in itself be a reason for doing it or for not doing it: that is, that there may be a fact of a peculiarly moral kind. But this is a mere reformulation, which leaves the substance of the problem unchanged. It will then be this alleged moral fact itself that is the initially puzzling item, which the existence of a god may be postulated to explain.

Some thinkers—R. M. Hare, for example—would reject this argument on the ground that the notion of objective intrinsically prescriptive features, supervening on natural ones and therefore synthetically connected with them, is not merely puzzling but incoherent. However, I have argued elsewhere that it is not incoherent,[7] and the oddity of these features is just what is needed to make their existence count significantly in favour of theism. (Both this objection and this reply can, trivially, be adapted to apply to the reformulation sketched in the last paragraph.)

A third objection: why postulate a god, of all things, to explain this initially puzzling matter? The simple answer to this question is that the more intrinsically puzzling something is, the more it requires, to explain it, something whose power is limited only by logical necessity. But we could add that the way in which intrinsic values are believed to be distributed is, on the whole, in accordance with the supposed purposes of a benevolent god. But a more subtle explanation is this: we can understand a human thinker, either as an agent or as a critic, seeing things as to be done or not to be done, where this is a reflection or projection of his own purposiveness; hence if we are to explain an intrinsic to-be-done-ness or not-to-be-done-ness, which is *not* such a reflection or projection, it is natural to take this as an injection into reality made by a universal *spirit*, that is, something that has some analogue of human purposiveness.

There are, nevertheless, some difficulties for the proposed argument. If we put it in terms of truths of supervenience, are these synthetic truths necessary or contingent? Do they hold in all possible worlds or only in some? Are there other worlds in which there are quite different truths of supervenience—so that radically different sorts of actions are right or wrong—or none at all? If the range of possible worlds is to cover all logical possibilities, there must be such variations. So a rational agent has not only to identify the natural situation in which he finds himself and reason about it; he has also to ascertain which of various possible worlds *with regard to moral supervenience* is the actual one—for example, whether the actual world is one in which pain is *prima facie* to be relieved, or one in which, other things being equal, pain is to be perpetuated. However, this problem only brings into the open the intuitionist moral epistemology which is at least implicit in any coherent doctrine of objective prescriptivity. Moral values, on such a view, are not discoverable by any purely general reasoning based on natural facts, but only by some kind of intuition: the moral thinker has, as it were, to respond to a value-laden atmosphere that surrounds him in the actual world.

In any case, there is available an adequate alternative explanation of moral thinking which does not require the assumption of objective prescriptivity.[8] In consequence, although the objectivity of prescriptive moral values would give some inductive support to the hypothesis that there is a god, it would be more reasonable to reject the kind of moral objectivity that is required for this purpose than to accept it and use it as a ground for theism.

When this moral objectivism is replaced by a subjectivist or sentimentalist theory, there can, indeed, be yet another form of moral argument for theism. Hutcheson, who bases both moral action and moral judgement on instincts, on natural human tendencies to act benevolently and to approve of benevolent action, says that 'this very moral sense, implanted in rational agents, to approve and admire whatever actions flow from a study of the good of others, is one of the strongest evidences of goodness in the Author of na-

[7]*Ethics: Inventing Right and Wrong*, pp. 20–5.

[8]*Hume's Moral Theory* (see n. 2 (p. 106) above), *passim*.

ture'.[9] This really belongs among the arguments for design that we shall consider in Chapter 8; but it is not a strong one, because it is easy to explain this moral sense as a natural product of biological and social evolution, rather than as having been implanted in us by an Author of nature.

Our survey of specific philosophical forms of the moral argument shows both what is wrong and what is right in the popular line of thought with which we began. Morality does not need a god as a supreme source of commands or as a wielder of decisive sanctions. The phenomena of conscience may help causally to produce and maintain theistic belief, but they do not rationally support it. Nor does moral thinking require that the sort of justice incorporated in Kant's highest good should be realized, so it need not postulate a god, or even, more generally, a moral government of the universe, to realize it. There is no good reason for introducing a god even as an essential part of the content of moral thinking. And even if it turned out that firmly held moral—or, more generally, practical—convictions presupposed the existence of a god, such convictions could not be used to show that there is a god: that would have to be shown independently in order to validate those convictions. But if we take a different point of view, and look at moral thinking from the outside, as a phenomenon to be understood and explained, the position is more complicated. If we adopted moral objectivism, we should have to regard the relations of supervenience which connect values and obligations with their natural grounds as synthetic; they would then be in principle something that a god might conceivably create; and since they would otherwise be a very odd

sort of thing, the admitting of them would be an inductive ground for admitting also a god to create them. There would be something here in need of explanation, and a being with the power to create what lies outside the bounds of natural plausibility or even possibility might well be the explanation we require. Moral values, their objectivity and their supervenience, would be a continuing miracle in the sense explained in Chapter I, a constant intrusion into the natural world. But then our post-Humean scepticism about miracles will tell against this whole view. If we adopted instead a subjectivist or sentimentalist account of morality, this problem would not arise. We can find satisfactory biological, sociological, and psychological explanations of moral thinking which account for the phenomena of the moral sense and conscience in natural terms. This approach dissolves away the premiss of our inductive argument, which given that premiss, would have been the one defensible form of moral argument for the existence of a god.

QUESTIONS FOR FURTHER REFLECTION

1. Does Kant take his own argument as establishing the existence of God or merely as showing that we *presuppose* His existence in practical reason? Explain your interpretation of Kant, given what Mackie says about this.
2. Why does Mackie think that Kant cannot argue that "ought implies can"? Is Mackie right?
3. Mackie wonders why one would posit God to explain objective moral values, even if they are odd given a naturalistic world. Why cannot the theist answer that a theistic worldview explains and makes more sense of objective values that naturalism does. Why can't the theist argue that objective morality is more surprising on naturalism then theism?

---

[9] F. Hutcheson, *An Inquiry concerning Moral Good and Evil.* Section VII, in *British Moralists*, edited by L. A. Selby-Bigge (Oxford University Press, 1897), Vol. I, p. 176.

SUGGESTIONS FOR FURTHER READING

Aquinas, Thomas. *Summa Theologiae* I. Q2.A3 in *Basic Writings of Saint Thomas Aquinas*, edited by Anton C. Pegis. Indianapolis: Hackett, 1997.

Barrow, John, and Frank Tipler. *The Anthropic Cosmological Principle*. Oxford: Oxford University Press, 1986.

Clarke, Samuel. *A Demonstration of the Being and Attributes of God and Other Writings*, edited by Ezio Vailati. Cambridge, U. K., and New York: Cambridge University Press, 1998.

Craig, William Lane. *The Cosmological Argument from Leibniz to Plato*. New York: Barnes and Noble, 1980.

———. *The Kalam Cosmological Argument*. New York: Barnes and Noble, 1975.

———. "Design and the Cosmological Argument," *Mere Creation*, edited by William A. Dembski. Downers Grove, IL: InterVarsity Press, 1998, 332–359.

Craig, William Lane, and Quentin Smith. *Theism, Atheism, and Big Bang Cosmology*. Oxford: Oxford University Press, 1993.

Dembski, William, ed., *Mere Creation*. Downers Grove, IL: InterVarsity Press, 1998, 265–288.

Gale, R. *On the Nature and Existence of God*. New York: Cambridge University Press, 1991.

Hick, John. *Arguments for the Existence of God*. London: MacMillan, 1971.

Hume, David. *Dialogues Concerning Natural Religion*, edited by Stanley Tweyman, London: Routledge, 1991.

Mackie, J. L. *The Miracle of Theism*. Oxford: Oxford University Press (Clarendon), 1982.

Martin, M. *Atheism: A Philosophical Justification*. Philadelphia: Temple University Press, 1990.

Matson, Wallace. *The Existence of God*. Ithaca, NY: Cornell University Press, 1965.

Moreland, J. P. *Scaling the Secular City*. Grand Rapids, MI: Baker, 1987

———. *The Creation Hypothesis*. Downers Grove, IL: InterVarsity, 1994.

Morriston, Wes. "Must the Past Have a Beginning?" *Philo*, Vol. 2 (1999), 5–19.

Plantinga, A. *God, Freedom, and Evil*. Grand Rapids, MI: William B. Eerdmans Publishing Co. 1977.

Radhakrishnan, Sarvepalli, and Charles A. Moore, eds. *A Sourcebook in Indian Philosophy*. Princeton, NJ: Princeton University Press, 1957.

Rowe, William. *The Cosmological Argument*. Princeton, NJ: Princeton University Press, 1975.

Smart, Ninian. *Doctrine and Argument in Indian Philosophy*. London: George Allen and Unwin, 1964.

Swinburne, Richard. *The Existence of God*. Oxford and New York: Oxford University Press (Clarendon), 1979; rev. ed. 1991.

Swinburne, R. *Is There a God?* New York: Oxford University Press, 1996.

Taylor, Richard. *Metaphysics*. (Englewood Cliffs, NJ: Prentice Hall, 1983) pp. 91–99.

van Inwagen, Peter. *Metaphysics*. (Boulder: Westview Press, 1993); see Chapter Six.

Yandell, Keith E. *Hume's "Inexplicable Mystery"* (Philadelphia: Temple University Press, 1990)

———. *Philosophy of Religion: A Contemporary Introduction*. (New York: Routledge, 1999).

PART III

FAITH AND REASON

The Evidential Challenge

20. The Presumption of Atheism * *Antony Flew*

Michael Scriven, "Santa Claus and Belief in God"

21. A Pascalian Rejoinder to the Presumption of Atheism * *R. Douglas Geivett*

22. Response to R. Douglas Geivett's "A Pascalian Rejoinder to the Presumption of Atheism" * *Antony Flew*

23. It Is Wrong to Believe without Evidence * *William Clifford*

24. What Should We Expect from Theistic Proofs? * *George I. Mavrodes*

Belief without Evidence: A Defense

25. Pascal's Wager * *Blaise Pascal*

William Lycan and George Schlesinger, "You Bet Your Life"

26. The Will to Believe * *William James*

27. Religious Belief Requires a Leap of Faith * *Søren Kierkegaard*

28. Kierkegaard's Arguments against Objective Reasoning in Religion * *Robert Merrihew Adams*

29. Reformed Epistemology and the Rationality of Theistic Belief * *James F. Sennett*

Alvin Plantinga, "The Aquinas/Calvin Model"

Alvin Plantinga, "The Great Pumpkin Objection"

30. Reformed Epistemology: An Atheist Perspective * *Keith M. Parsons*

Michael Martin, "Son of a Great Pumpkin"

31. Religious Belief for the Rest of us: Reflections on Reformed Epistemology * *Sandra Menssen and Thomas D. Sullivan*

Reason and Revelation

32. Reason and Revelation Compliment Each Other * *Thomas Aquinas*

Suggestions for Further Reading

20. THE PRESUMPTION OF ATHEISM

Antony Flew

Antony Flew (1923–) is professor emeritus of philosophy at the University of Reading. A prominent atheist, he has written or edited dozens of books and many papers. In this selection, he argues that, in the debate over the existence of God, the theist bears the burden of proof. Atheism is, as it were, a default position. If the theist cannot prove that God exists, he claims, then we should be atheists.

READING QUESTIONS

1. What is the difference between a "direct atheological argument" and an "indirect atheological argument"? In what sense is Antony Flew's argument that one should adopt a presumption of atheism an indirect atheological argument?
2. What, according to Flew, is the difference between "positive atheism" and "negative atheism"? How is this distinction important to understanding what Flew means by a "presumption of atheism"? How does he understand "agnostic"?
3. In what ways is a presumption of atheism supposed to be like the presumption of innocence in a court of law, according to Flew?
4. What similarities does Flew think there are between the presumption of atheism and the presumption of theism?

1. INTRODUCTORY

At the beginning of Book X of his last work *The Laws*, Plato turns his attention from violent and outrageous actions in general to the particular case of undisciplined and presumptuous behavior in matters of religion:

> We have already stated summarily what the punishment should be for temple-robbing, whether by open force or secretly. But the punishments for the various sorts of insolence in speech or action with regard to the gods, which a man can show in word or deed, have to be proclaimed af-

ter we have provided an exordium. Let this be it: "No one believing, as the laws prescribe, in the existence of the gods has ever yet performed an impious action willingly, or uttered a lawless word. Anyone acting in such a way is in one of three conditions: either, first, he does not believe the proposition aforesaid; or, second, he believes that though the gods exist they have no concern about men; or, third, he believes that they can easily be won over by the bribery of prayer and sacrifice" (§ 885B).[1]

---

[1] This and all later translations from the Greek and Latin are by me.

So Plato in this notorious treatment of heresy might be said to be rebuking the presumption of atheism. The word "presumption" would then be employed as a synonym for "presumptuousness." But, interesting though the questions here raised by Plato are, the word has in my title a different interpretation. The presumption of atheism which I want to discuss is not a form of presumptuousness; indeed it might be regarded as an expression of the very opposite, a modest teachability. My presumption of atheism is closely analogous to the presumption of innocence in the English Law; a comparison which we shall later find it illuminating to develop. What I want to examine in this paper is the contention that the debate about the existence of God should properly begin from a presumption of atheism, that the onus of proof must lie on the theist.

The word "atheism," however, has in this contention to be construed unusually. Whereas nowadays the usual meaning of "atheist" in English is "someone who asserts that there is no such being as God," I want the word to be understood here much less positively. I want the originally Greek prefix "a" to be read in the same way in "atheist" as it customarily is read in such other Greco-English words as "amoral," "atypical," and "asymmetrical." In this interpretation an atheist becomes: not someone who positively asserts the nonexistence of God; but someone who is simply not a theist. Let us, for future ready reference, introduce the labels "positive atheism" for the former doctrine and "negative atheism" for the latter.

The introduction of this new sense of the word "atheism" may appear to be a piece of perverse Humpty-Dumptyism,[2] going arbitrarily against established common usage. "Whyever," it could be asked, "don't you make it not the presumption of atheism but the presumption of agnosticism?" But this pardonably petulant reaction fails to appreciate just how completely noncommittal I intend my negative atheist to be. For in this context the agnostic—and it was, of course, in this context that Thomas Henry Huxley first introduced the term[3]—is by the same criterion of established common usage someone who, having entertained the existence of God as at least a theoretical possibility, now claims not to know either that there is or that there is not such a being. To be in this ordinary sense an agnostic you have already to have conceded that there is, and that you have, a legitimate concept of God; such that, whether or not this concept does in fact have application, it theoretically could. But the atheist in my peculiar interpretation, unlike the atheist in the usual sense, has not as yet and as such conceded even this.

This point is important, though the question whether the word "agnosticism" can bear the meaning which I want now to give to the word "atheism" is not. What the protagonist of the presumption of atheism, in my sense, wants to show is: that the debate about the existence of God ought to be conducted in a particular way, and that the issue should be seen in a certain perspective. His thesis about the onus of proof involves that it is up to the theist: first, to introduce and to defend his proposed concept of God; and, second, to provide sufficient reason for believing that this concept of his does in fact have an application. It is the first of these two stages which needs perhaps to be emphasized even more strongly than the second. Where the question of existence concerns, for instance, a Loch Ness Monster or an Abominable Snowman this stage may perhaps reasonably be deemed to be more or less complete before the argument begins. But in the controversy about the existence of God this is certainly not so: not only for the quite familiar reason that the word "God" is used—or misused—in more than one way; but also, and much more interestingly, because it cannot be taken for granted that even the would-be mainstream theist is operating with a legitimate concept which theoretically could have an application to an actual being.

[2]See Chapter VI of Lewis Carroll's *Through the Looking Glass*:
"But 'glory' doesn't mean 'a nice knock-down argument,' " Alice objected.
"When I use a word," Humpty Dumpty said in rather a scornful tone, "it means just what I choose it to mean—neither more nor less."
"The question is," said Alice, "whether you can make words mean so many different things."
"The question is," said Humpty Dumpty, "which is to be master—that's all."

[3]See the essay "Agnosticism," and also that on "Agnosticism and Christianity," in Volume 5 of his *Collected Essays* (London: Macmillan, 1894). I may perhaps also refer to my own article on "Agnosticism" for the 1972 revision of the *Encyclopaedia Britannica*.

This last suggestion is not really as newfangled and factitious as it is sometimes thought to be. But its pedigree has been made a little hard to trace. For the fact is that, traditionally, issues which should be seen as concerning the legitimacy or otherwise of a proposed or supposed concept have by philosophical theologians been discussed: either as surely disposable difficulties in reconciling one particular feature of the Divine nature with another; or else as aspects of an equally surely soluble general problem of saying something about the infinite Creator in language intelligible to his finite creatures. These traditional and still almost universally accepted forms of presentation are fundamentally prejudicial. For they assume: that there is a Divine being, with an actual nature the features of which we can investigate; and that there is an infinite Creator, whose existence—whatever difficulties we finite creatures may have in asserting anything else about Him—we may take for granted.

The general reason why this presumption of atheism matters is that its acceptance must put the whole question of the existence of God into an entirely fresh perspective. Most immediately relevant here is that in this fresh perspective problems which really are conceptual are seen as conceptual problems; and problems which have tended to be regarded as advanced and, so to speak, optional extras now discover themselves as both elementary and indispensable. The theist who wants to build a systematic and thorough apologetic finds that he is required to begin absolutely from the beginning; and this absolute beginning is to ensure that the word "God" is provided with a meaning such that it is theoretically possible for an actual being to be so described.

Although I shall later be arguing that the presumption of atheism is neutral as between all parties to the main dispute, inasmuch as to accept it as determining a procedural framework is not to make any substantive assumptions, I must give fair warning now that I do nevertheless believe that in its fresh perspective the whole enterprise of theism appears even more difficult and precarious than it did before. In part this is a corollary of what I have just been suggesting; that certain difficulties and objections, which may previously have seemed peripheral or even factitious, are made to stand out as fundamental and unavoidable. But it is also in part, as we shall be seeing soon, a consequence of the emphasis which it places on the imperative need to produce some sort of sufficient reason to justify theist belief.

2. THE PRESUMPTION OF ATHEISM AND THE PRESUMPTION OF INNOCENCE

One thing which helps to conceal this need is a confusion about the possible varieties of proof, and this confusion is one which can be resolved with the help of the first of a series of comparisons between my proposed presumption of atheism and the legal presumption of innocence. It is frequently said nowadays, even by professing Roman Catholics, that everyone knows that it is impossible to prove the existence of God. The first objection to this putative truism is, as my reference to Roman Catholics should have suggested, that it is not true. For it is an essential dogma of Roman Catholicism, defined as such by the First Vatican Council, that "the one and true God our creator and lord can be known for certain through the creation by the natural light of human reason."[4] So even if this dogma is, as I myself believe, false, it is certainly not known to be false by those many Roman Catholics who remain, despite all the disturbances consequent upon the Second Vatican Council, committed to the complete traditional faith.

To this a sophisticated objector might reply that the definition of the First Vatican Council speaks of knowing for certain rather than of proving or demonstrating; adding perhaps, if he was very sophisticated indeed, that the word "demonstrari" in an earlier draft was eventually replaced by the expression "certo cognosci." But though this is, I am told,[5] correct, it is certainly not enough to vindicate the conventional wisdom. For the word "proof" is not ordinarily restricted in its application to demonstratively valid arguments; arguments, that is, in which the conclusion cannot be denied without thereby contradicting the premises. So it is too flattering to suggest that most of those who make this facile claim, that everyone knows that it is impossible to prove the existence of God, are

---

[4]H. Denzinger, ed., *Enchiridion Symbolorum* (29th rev. Freiburg im Breisgau: Herder, 1953), section 1806.
[5]By Professor P. T. Geach of Leeds.

intending only the strictly limited assertion that one special sort of proof is impossible.

The truth, and the danger, is that wherever there is any awareness of such a limited and specialized interpretation, there will be a quick and illegitimate move to the much wider general conclusion that it is impossible and, furthermore, unnecessary to provide any sufficient reason for believing. It is, therefore, worth underlining that when the presumption of atheism is explained as insisting that the onus of proof must be on the theist, the word "proof" is being used in the ordinary wide sense in which it can embrace any and every variety of sufficient reason. It is, of course, in this and only this sense that the word is interpreted when the presumption of innocence is explained as laying the onus of proof on the prosecution.

A second element of positive analogy between these two presumptions is that both are defeasible; and that they are, consequently, not to be identified with assumptions. The presumption of innocence indicates where the court should start and how it must proceed. Yet the prosecution is still able, more often than not, to bring forward what is in the end accepted as sufficient reason to warrant the verdict "Guilty"; which appropriate sufficient reason is properly characterized as a proof of guilt. The defeasible presumption of innocence is thus in this majority of cases in fact defeated; whereas, were the indefeasible innocence of all accused persons an assumption of any legal system, there could not be within that system any provision for any verdict other than "Not Guilty." To the extent that it is, for instance, an assumption of the English Common

---

"SANTA CLAUS AND BELIEF IN GOD" ✳ *Michael Scriven*

Atheism is obligatory in the absence of any evidence for God's existence.

Why do adults not believe in Santa Claus? Simply because they can now explain the phenomena for which Santa Claus's existence is invoked without any need for introducing a novel entity. When we were very young and naively believed our parents' stories, it was hard to see how the presents could get there on Christmas morning since the doors were locked and our parents were asleep in bed. Someone *must* have brought them down the chimney. And how could the person get to the roof without a ladder and with all those presents? Surely only by flying. And then there is a great traditional literature of stories and songs which immortalize the entity and his (horned) attendants; surely these cannot all be just products of imagination? Where there is smoke there must be fire.

Santa Claus is not a bad hypothesis at all for 6-year-olds. As we grow up, no one comes forward to *prove* that such an entity does not exist. We just come to see that there is not the least reason to think he *does* exist. And so it would be entirely foolish to assert that he does, or believe that he

does, or even think it likely that he does. Santa Claus is in just the same position as fairy godmothers, wicked witches, the devil, and the ether. Each of these entities has some supernatural powers, that is, powers which contravene or go far beyond the powers that we know exist, whether it be the power to levitate a sled and reindeer or the power to cast a spell. Now even belief in something for which there is no evidence, that is, a belief which goes *beyond* the evidence, although a lesser sin than belief in something which is *contrary* to well-established laws, is plainly irrational in that it simply amounts to attaching belief where it is not justified. So the proper alternative, when there is no evidence, is not mere suspension of belief, for example, about Santa Claus, it is *disbelief*: It most certainly is not faith.

The situation is slightly different with the Abominable Snowman, sea serpents, or even the Loch Ness monster. No "supernatural" (by which, in this context, we only mean wholly unprecedented) kinds of powers are involved.

From Michael Scriven, *Primary Philosophy* (1966).

Law that every citizen is cognizant of all that the law requires of him, that law cannot admit the fact that this assumption is, as in fact it is, false.

The presumption of atheism is similarly defeasible. It lays it down that thorough and systematic inquiry must start from a position of negative atheism, and that the burden of proof lies on the theist proposition. Yet this is not at all the same thing as demanding that the debate should proceed on a positive atheist assumption, which must preclude a theist conclusion. Counsel for theism no more betrays his client by accepting the framework determined by this presumption than counsel for the prosecution betrays the state by conceding the legal presumption of innocence. The latter is perhaps in his heart unshakeably convinced of the guilt of the defendant. Yet he must, and with complete consistency and perfect sincerity may, insist that the proceedings of the court should respect the presumption of innocence. The former is even more likely to be persuaded of the soundness of his brief. Yet he too can with a good conscience allow that a thorough and complete apologetic must start from, meet, and go on to defeat, the presumption of atheism.

Put as I have just been putting it, the crucial distinction between a defeasible presumption and a categorical assumption will, no doubt, seem quite obvious. But I know from experience that many do find it difficult to grasp, at least in its application to the present highly controversial case.[6] Theists fear that if once they allow this procedural presumption they will have sold the pass to the atheist enemy. Most especially when the proponent of this procedure happens to be a known opponent of theism, the theist is inclined to mistake it that the procedure itself prejudicially assumes an atheist conclusion. But this, as the comparison with the legal presumption of innocence surely makes clear, is wrong. Such presumptions are procedural and not substantive; they assume no conclusion, either positive or negative.

However, and here we come to a third element in the positive analogy, to say that such presumptions are in themselves procedural and not substantive is not to say that the higher-order questions of whether to follow this presumption or that are trifling and merely formal rather than material and substantial. These higher-order questions are not questions which can be dismissed cynically as "issues of principle as opposed to issues of substance." It can matter a lot which presumption is adopted. Notoriously, there is a world of difference between legal systems which follow the presumption of innocence, and those which do not. And, as I began to indicate at the end of the Introductory, to adopt the presumption of atheism does put the whole argument into a distinctive perspective.

Next, as a fourth element in the positive analogy, it is a paradoxical consequence of the fact that these presumptions are procedural and not substantive that particular defeats do not constitute any sort of reason, much less a sufficient reason, for a general surrender. The fact that George Joseph Smith was in his trial proved guilty of many murders defeats the original presumption of his innocence. But this particular defeat has no tendency at all to show that even in this particular case the court should not have proceeded on this presumption. Still less does it tend to establish that the legal system as a whole was at fault in incorporating this presumption as a general principle. It is the same with the presumption of atheism. Suppose that someone is able to prove the existence of God. This achievement must, similarly, defeat our presumption. But it does not thereby show that the original contention about the onus of proof was mistaken.

One may, therefore, as a mnemonic, think of the word "defeasible" (= defeatable) as implying precisely this capacity to survive defeat. A substantive generalization—such as, for instance, the assertion that all persons accused of murder are in fact innocent—is falsified decisively by the production of even one authentic counterexample. That is part of what is meant by

---

[6]This was brought home to me most forcibly by studying some of the reviews of my *God and Philosophy* (London: Hutchinson; New York: Harcourt Brace, 1966). It can be both interesting and instructive to notice the same confusion occurring in an equally controversial socio-political case. A. F. Young and E. T. Ashton, in their *British Social Work in the Nineteenth Century* (London: Routledge and Kegan Paul, 1956), quote Lord Attlee as reproaching the "general assumption that all applicants are frauds unless they prove themselves otherwise" (p. 111). It should by now be clear that to put the onus of proof of entitlement upon the applicant for welfare payments is emphatically not to assume that all or most of those who apply are in fact cheats.

This last example is the more salutary since the mistake is made by a former leader of the Labour Party who was above suspicion of any dishonourable intention to twist or to misrepresent. Would it were ever thus!

the Baconian slogan: "Magis est vis instantiae negativae."[7] But a defeasible presumption is not shown to have been the wrong one to have made by being in a particular case in fact defeated. What does show the presumption of atheism to be the right one to make is what we have now to investigate.

3. THE CASE FOR THE PRESUMPTION OF ATHEISM

An obvious first move is to appeal to the old legal axiom: "Ei incumbit probatio qui dicit, non qui negat." Literally and unsympathetically translated this becomes: "The onus of proof lies on the man who affirms, not on the man who denies." To this the objection is almost equally obvious. Given just a very little verbal ingenuity, contrary notions can be rendered alternatively in equally positive forms: either "That this house affirms the existence of God," or "That this house takes its stand for positive atheism." So interpreted, therefore, our axiom provides no determinate guidance.[8]

Suppose, however, that we take the hint already offered in the previous paragraph. A less literal but more sympathetic translation would be: "The onus of proof lies on the proposition, not on the opposition." The point of the change is to bring out that this maxim was offered in a legal context, and that our courts are institutions of debate. An axiom providing no determinate guidance outside that framework may nevertheless be fundamental for the effective conduct of orderly and decisive debate. Here the outcome is supposed to be decided on the merits of what is said within the debate itself, and of that alone. So no opposition can set about demolishing the proposition case until and unless that proposition has first provided them with a case for demolition.

Of course our maxim, even when thus sympathetically interpreted, still offers no direction on which

contending parties ought to be made to undertake which roles. Granting that courts are to operate as debating institutions, and granting that this maxim is fundamental to debate, we have to appeal to some further premise principle before we become licensed to infer that the prosecution must propose and the defense oppose. This further principle is, once again, the familiar presumption of innocence. Were we, while retaining the conception of a court as an institution for reaching decisions by way of formalized debate, to embrace the opposite presumption, the presumption of guilt, we should need to adopt the opposite arrangements. In these the defense would first propose that the accused is after all innocent, and the prosecution would then respond by struggling to disintegrate the case proposed.

The first move examined cannot, therefore, be by itself sufficient. To have considered it does nevertheless help to show that to accept such a presumption is to adopt a policy. And policies have to be assessed by reference to the aims of those for whom they are suggested. If for you it is more important that no guilty person should ever be acquitted than that no innocent person should ever be convicted, then for you a presumption of guilt must be the rational policy. For you, with your preference structure, a presumption of innocence becomes simply irrational. To adopt this policy would be to adopt means calculated to frustrate your own chosen ends; which is, surely, paradigmatically irrational. Take, as an actual illustration, the controlling elite of a ruling Leninist party, which must, as such, refuse to recognize any individual rights if these conflict with the claims of the party, and which in fact treats all those suspected of actual or potential opposition much as if they were already known "counterrevolutionaries," "enemies of socialism," "friends of the United States," "advocates of free elections," and all other like things bad. I can, and do, fault this policy and its agents on many counts. Yet I cannot say that for them, once granted their scale of values, it is irrational.

What then are the aims by reference to which an atheist presumption might be justified? One key word in the answer, if not the key word, must be "knowledge." The context for which such a policy is proposed is that of inquiry about the existence of God; and the object of the exercise is, presumably, to discover whether it is possible to establish that the word "God"

---

[7]"The force of the negative instance is greater." For, whereas a single positive, supporting instance can do only a very little to confirm a universal generalization, one negative, contrary example would be sufficient decisively to falsify that generalization.

[8]See the paper "Presumptions" by my former colleague Patrick Day in the *Proceedings of the XIVth International Congress of Philosophy* (Vienna, 1968), Vol. 5, p. 140. I am pleased that it was I who first suggested to him an exploration of this unfrequented philosophical territory.

does in fact have application. Now to establish must here be either to show that you know or to come to know. But knowledge is crucially different from mere true belief. All knowledge involves true belief; not all true belief constitutes knowledge. To have a true belief is simply and solely to believe that something is so, and to be in fact right. But someone may believe that this or that is so, and his belief may in fact be true, without its thereby and necessarily constituting knowledge. If a true belief is to achieve this more elevated status, then the believer has to be properly warranted so to believe. He must, that is, be in a position to know.

Obviously, there is enormous scope for disagreement in particular cases: both about what is required in order to be in a position to know; and about whether these requirements have actually been satisfied. But the crucial distinction between believing truly and knowing is recognized as universally as the prior and equally vital distinction between believing and believing what is in fact true. If, for instance, there is a question whether a colleague performed some discreditable action, then all of us, though we have perhaps to admit that we cannot help believing that he did, are rightly scrupulous not to assert that this is known unless we have grounds sufficient to warrant the bolder claim. It is, therefore, not only incongruous but also scandalous in matters of life and death, and even of eternal life and death, to maintain that you know either on no grounds at all, or on grounds of a kind which on other and comparatively minor issues you yourself would insist to be inadequate.

It is by reference to this inescapable demand for grounds that the presumption of atheism is justified. If it is to be established that there is a God, then we have to have good grounds for believing that this is indeed so. Until and unless some such grounds are produced we have literally no reason at all for believing; and in that situation the only reasonable posture must be that of either the negative atheist or the agnostic. So the onus of proof has to rest on the proposition. It must be up to them: first, to give whatever sense they choose to the word "God," meeting any objection that, so defined, it would relate only to an incoherent pseudo-concept; and, second, to bring forward sufficient reasons to warrant their claim that, in their present sense of the word "God," there is a God. The same applies, with appropriate alterations, if what is to be made out is, not that atheism is known to be true, but only—more modestly—that it can be seen to be at least more or less probable.

4. OBJECTIONS TO THE PRESUMPTION OF ATHEISM

Once the nature of this presumption is understood, the supporting case is short and simple. One reason why it may appear unacceptable is a confusion of contexts. In a theist or posttheist society it comes more easily to ask why a man is not a theist than why he is. Provided that the question is to be construed biographically this is, no doubt, methodologically inoffensive. But our concern here is not at all with biographical questions of why people came to hold whatever opinions they do hold. Rather, it is with the need for opinions to be suitably grounded if they are to be rated as items of knowledge, or even of probable belief. The issue is: not what does or does not need to be explained biographically; but where the burden of theological proof should rest.

A more sophisticated objection of fundamentally the same sort would urge that our whole discussion has been too artificial and too general, and that any man's inquiries have to begin from wherever he happens to be. "We cannot begin," C. S. Peirce wrote, "with complete doubt. We must begin with all the prejudices which we actually have. . . . These prejudices are not to be dispelled by a maxim. . . ."[9] With particular present reference Professor John Hick has urged:

> The right question is whether it is rational for the religious man himself, given that his religious experience is coherent, persistent, and compelling, to affirm the reality of God. What is in question is not the rationality of an inference from certain psychological events to God as their cause; for the religious man no more infers the existence of God than we infer the existence of the visible world around us. What is in question

[9]C. S. Peirce, "Some Consequences of Four Incapacities," pp. 156–57 of Volume 5 of the *Collected Papers* (Cambridge, MA: Harvard University Press, 1934).

is the rationality of the one who has the religious experiences. If we regard him as a rational person we must acknowledge that he is rational in believing what, given his experiences, he cannot help believing.[10]

To the general point drawn from Peirce the answer comes from further reading of Peirce himself. He was, in the paper from which I quoted, arguing against the Cartesian programme of simultaneous, systematic, and (almost) universal doubt. Peirce did not want to suggest that it is impossible or wrong to subject any of our beliefs to critical scrutiny. In the same paragraph he continues: "A person may, it is true, find reason to doubt what he began by believing; but in that case he doubts because he has a positive reason for it, and not on account of the Cartesian maxim." One positive reason for being especially leery towards religious opinions is that these vary so very much from society to society; being, it seems, mainly determined, in Descartes's phrase, "by custom and example."[11]

To Hick it has at once to be conceded: that it is one thing to say that a belief is unfounded or well-founded; and quite another to say that it is irrational or rational for some particular person, in his particular time and circumstances, and with his particular experience and lack of experience, to hold or to reject that belief. Granted that his usually reliable Intelligence were sure that the enemy tank brigade was in the town, it was entirely reasonable for the General also to believe this. But the enemy tanks had in fact pulled back. Yet it was still unexceptionally sensible for the General on his part to refuse to expose his flank to those tanks which were in fact not there. This genuine and important distinction cannot, however, save the day for Hick.

In the first place, to show that someone may reasonably hold a particular belief, and even that he may properly claim that he knows it to be true, is at best still not to show that that belief is indeed well grounded, much less that it constitutes an item of his knowledge.

Nor, second, is to accept the presumption of atheism as a methodological framework, as such: either to deprive anyone of his right "to affirm the reality of God", or to require that to be respectable every conviction should first have been reached through the following of an ideally correct procedure. To insist on the correctness of this presumption as an initial presumption is to make a claim which is itself procedural rather than substantive; and the context for which this particular procedure is being recommended is that of justification rather than of discovery.

Once these fundamentals are appreciated, those for whom Hick is acting as spokesman should at first feel quite content. For on his account they consider that they have the very best of grounds for their beliefs. They regard their "coherent, consistent, and compelling" religious experience as analogous to perception; and the man who can see something with his own eyes and feel it in his own hands is in a perfect position to know that it exists. His position is indeed so perfect that, as Hick says, it is wrong to speak here of evidence and inference. If he saw his wife in the act of intercourse with a lover, then he no longer needs to infer her infidelity from bits and pieces of evidence. He has now what is better than inference; although for the rest of us, who missed this display, his testimony still constitutes an important part of the evidence in the case. The idiomatic expression "the evidence of my own eyes" derives its paradoxical piquancy from the fact that to see for oneself is better than to have evidence.

All this is true. Certainly, too, anyone who thinks that he can, as it were, see God must reject the suggestion that in so doing he infers "from certain psychological events to God as their cause." For to accept this account would be to call down upon his head all the insoluble difficulties which fall to the lot of all those who maintain that what we see, and all we ever really and directly see, is visual sense-data. And, furthermore, it is useful to be re-

---

[10]In his review of *God and Philosophy* in *Theology Today* (1967): 86–87. He makes his point not against the general presumption but against one particular application. (See John Hick's paper, "The Rationality of Religious Belief," in Part IV of this volume, pp. 304–19.)

[11]Rene Descartes, *Discourse on the Method* Part II. It occurs almost immediately after his observation: "I took into account also the very different character which a person brought up from infancy in France or Germany exhibits, from that which . . . he would have possessed had he lived among the Chinese or with savages."

minded that when we insist that knowledge as opposed to mere belief has to be adequately warranted, this grounding may be a matter either of having sufficient evidence or of being in a position to know directly and without evidence. So far, therefore, it might seem that Hick's objection was completely at cross-purposes; and that anyway his protégés have no need to appeal to the distinction between actual knowledge and what one may rationally and properly claim to know.

Wait a minute. The passage of Hick which has been under discussion was part of an attempt to show that criticism of the Argument from Religious Experience is irrelevant to such claims to, as it were, see God. But on the contrary: what such criticism usually challenges is just the vital assumption that having religious experience really is a kind of perceiving, and hence a sort of being in a position to know about its putative object. So this challenge provides just exactly that positive reason, which Peirce demanded, for doubting what, according to Hick, "one who has the religious experiences . . . cannot help believing." If, therefore, he persists in so believing without even attempting to overcome this criticism, then it becomes impossible to vindicate his claims to be harboring rational beliefs; much less items of authentic knowledge.

A third objection, of a different kind, starts from the assumption, mentioned earlier, that any program to prove the existence of God is fundamentally misconceived; that this enterprise is on all fours with projects to square the circle or to construct a perpetual motion machine. The suggestion then is that the territory which reason cannot inhabit may nevertheless be freely colonized by faith: "The world was all before them, where to choose."[12]

Ultimately, perhaps, it is impossible to establish the existence of God, or even to show that it is more or less probable. But, if so, this is not the correct moral: the rational man does not thereby become in this area free to believe, or not to believe, just as his fancy takes him. Faith, surely, should not be a leap in the dark but a leap toward the light. Arbitrarily to plump for some particular conviction, and then stubbornly to cleave to it, would be—to borrow the term which St. Thomas

employed in discussing natural reason, faith, and revelation[13]—frivolous. If your venture of faith is not to be arbitrary, irrational, and frivolous, you must have presentable reasons: first, for making any such commitment in this area, an area in which, by hypothesis, the available grounds are insufficient to warrant any firm conclusion; and, second, for opting for one particular possibility rather than any of the other available alternatives. To most such offerings of reasons the presumption of atheism remains relevant. For though, again by the hypothesis, these cannot aspire to prove their conclusions, they will usually embrace some estimation of their probability. If the onus of proof lies on the man who hopes definitively to establish the existence of

---

[13]St. Thomas Aquinas, *Summa contra Gentiles*, Bk. I, Ch. VI. The whole passage, in which Aquinas gives his reasons for believing that the Christian candidate does, and that of Mohammed does not, constitute an authentic revelation of God, should be compared with some defense of the now widely popular assumption that the contents of a religious faith must be without evidential warrant.

Professor A. C. MacIntyre, for instance, while he was still himself a Christian, argued with great vigor for the Barthian thesis that "belief cannot argue with unbelief: it can only preach to it." Thus, in his paper on "The Logical Status of Religious Belief" in *Metaphysical Beliefs* (London: Student Christian Movement Press, 1957), MacIntyre urged: ". . . suppose religion could be provided with a method of proof . . . since the Christian faith sees true religion only in a free decision made in faith and love, the religion would by this vindication be destroyed. For all possibility of free choice would have been done away. Any objective justification of belief would have the same effect . . . faith too would have been eliminated" (p. 209).

Now first, insofar as this account is correct, any commitment to a system of religious belief has to be made altogether without evidencing reasons. MacIntyre himself concludes with a quotation from John Donne to illustrate the "confessional voice" of faith, commenting: "The man who speaks like this is beyond argument" (p. 211). But this, we must insist, would be nothing to be proud of. It is certainly no compliment, even if it were a faithful representation, to portray the true believer as necessarily irrational and a bigot. Furthermore, second, it is not the case that where sufficient evidence is available there can be no room for choice. Men can, and constantly do, choose to deceive themselves about the most well-evidenced, inconvenient truths. Also, no recognition of any facts, however clear, is by itself sufficient to guarantee one's allegiance and to preclude its opposite. MacIntyre needs to extend his reading of the Christian poets to the greatest of them all. For the hero of Milton's *Paradise Lost* had the most enviably full and direct knowledge of God. Yet Lucifer, if any creature could, chose freely to rebel.

God, it must also, by the same token, rest on the person who plans to make out only that this conclusion is more or less probable.

I put in the qualifications "most" and "usually" in order to allow for apologetic in the tradition of Pascal's Wager.[14] Pascal makes no attempt in this most famous argument to show that his Roman Catholicism is true or probably true. The reasons which he suggests for making the recommended bet on his particular faith are reasons in the sense of motives rather than reasons in our previous sense of grounds. Conceding, if only for the sake of the present argument, that we can have no knowledge here, Pascal tries to justify as prudent a policy of systematic self-persuasion, rather than to provide grounds for thinking that the beliefs recommended are actually true.

Another instructive feature of Pascal's argument is his unwarranted assumption that there are only two betting options, neither of which, on the assumption of total ignorance, can be awarded any measure of positive probability. Granted all this, it then appears compulsively reasonable to wager one's life on the alternative which promises and threatens so inordinately much. But the number of theoretically possible world-systems is infinite, and the subset of those making similar promises and threats is also infinite. The immediate relevance of this to us is that it will not do, without further reason given, to set up as the two mutually exclusive and together exhaustive alternatives (one sort of) theism and (the corresponding sort of) positive atheism; and then to suggest that, since neither position can be definitely established, everyone is entitled simply to take their pick. The objection that this way of constructing the book leaves out a third, agnostic, opinion is familiar; and it is one which Pascal himself tried to meet by arguing that to refuse to decide is in effect to decide against religion. The objection based on the point that the number of theoretically possible Hell-threatening and Heaven-promising world-systems is infinite, is quite different and, against the Wager as

he himself sets it up, decisive. The point is that, on the given assumption of total ignorance, combined with our present recognition of the infinite range of alternative theoretical possibilities; to bet on any one of the, so to speak, positive options, none of which can, by the hypothesis, be awarded any measure of positive probability, must be in the last degree arbitrary and capricious.

5. THE FIVE WAYS AS AN ATTEMPT TO DEFEAT THE PRESUMPTION OF ATHEISM

I have tried, in the first four sections, to explain what I mean by "the presumption of atheism," to bring out by comparison with the presumption of innocence in law what such a presumption does and does not involve, to deploy a case for adopting my presumption of atheism, and to indicate the lines on which two sorts of objection may be met. Now, finally, I want to point out that St. Thomas Aquinas presented the Five Ways in his *Summa Theologica* as an attempt to defeat just such a presumption. My hope in this is both to draw attention to something which seems generally to be overlooked, and, by so doing, to summon a massive authority in support of a thesis which many apparently find scandalous.

These most famous arguments were offered there originally, without any inhibition or equivocation, as proofs, period: "I reply that we must say that God can be proved in five ways"; and the previous second Article, raising the question "Whether the existence of God can be demonstrated" gives the categorical affirmative answer that "the existence of God . . . can be demonstrated."[15] Attention usually and understandably concentrates on the main body of the third Article, which is the part where Aquinas gives his five supposed proofs. But, as so often, it is rewarding to read the entire Article, and especially the second of the two Objections to which these are presented as a reply:

[14]See Blaise Pascal, *Pensées* section 233 in the Brunschvicg arrangement. For a discussion of Pascal's argument see Chapter 6, section 7 of my *An Introduction to Western Philosophy* (London: Thames & Hudson; New York: Bobbs-Merrill, 1971). (See Part V of this volume for a detailed discussion of prudential accounts of religious belief.)

[15]It is worth stressing this point, since nowadays it is frequently denied. Thus L. C. Velecky, in an article in *Philosophy* (1968), asserts: "He did not prove here the existence of God, nor indeed, did he prove it anywhere else, for a very good reason. According to Thomas, God's existence is unknowable and, hence, cannot be proved" (p. 226). The quotations from Aquinas given in my text ought to be decisive. Yet there seems to be quite a school of devout interpretation which waives aside what the Saint straightforwardly said as almost irrelevent to the question of what he really meant.

Furthermore, what can be accounted for by fewer principles is not the product of more. But it seems that everything which can be observed in the world can be accounted for by other principles, on the assumption of the nonexistence of God. Thus natural effects are explained by natural causes, while contrived effects are referred to human reason and will. So there is no need to postulate the existence of God.[16]

The Five Ways are thus, at least in one aspect, an attempt to defeat this presumption of (an Aristotelian) atheist naturalism, by showing that the things "which can be observed in the world" cannot "be accounted for . . . on the assumption of the nonexistence of God," and hence that there is "need to postulate the existence of God."[17] One must never forget that Aquinas composed his own Objections, and hence that it was he who introduced into his formulation here the idea of (this Aristotelian) scientific naturalism. No such idea is integral to the presumption of atheism as that has been construed in the present paper. When the addition is made the presumption can perhaps be labeled "Stratonician." (Strato was the next but one in succession to Aristotle as head of the Lyceum, and was regarded by Bayle and Hume as the archetypal ancient spokesman for an atheist scientific naturalism.)

By suggesting, a century before Ockham, an appeal to an Ockhamist principle of postulational economy, Aquinas also indicates a reason for adopting such a presumption. The fact that the Saint cannot be suspect of wanting to reach atheist conclusions can now be made to serve as a spectacular illustration of a point labored in previously, that to adopt such a presumption is not to make an assumption. And the fact, which has been put forward as an objection to this reading of Aquinas, that "Thomas himself was never in the position of a Stratonician, nor did he live in a milieu in which Stratonicians were plentiful,"[18] is simply irrelevant. For the thesis that the onus of proof lies upon the theist is entirely independent of these biographical and sociological facts.

What is perhaps slightly awkward for present purposes is the formulation of the first Objection: "It seems that God does not exist. For if of two contrary things one were to exist without limit the other would be totally eliminated. But what is meant by this word 'God' is something good without limit. So if God were to have existed no evil would have been encountered. But evil is encountered in the world. Therefore, God does not exist."

It would, from my point of view, have been better had this first Objection referred to possible difficulties and incoherencies in the meaning proposed for the word "God." Unfortunately, it does not, although Aquinas is elsewhere acutely aware of such problems. The changes required, however, are, though important, not extensive. Certainly, the Objection as actually given is presented as one of the God hypothesis falsified by familiar fact. Yet a particular variety of the same general point could be represented as the detection of an incoherence, not in the proposed concept of God as such, but between that concept and another element in the theoretical structure in which it is normally involved.

The incoherence—or perhaps on this occasion I should say only the ostensible incoherence—is between the idea of creation, as necessarily involving complete, continual, and absolute dependence of creature upon Creator, and the idea that creatures may nevertheless be sufficiently autonomous for their faults not to be also and indeed primarily His fault. The former idea, the idea of creation, is so essential that it provides the traditional criterion for distinguishing theism from deism. The latter is no less central to the three great theist systems of Judaism, Christianity, and Islam, since all three equally insist that creatures of the immaculate Creator are corrupted by sin. So where Aquinas put as his first Objection a statement of the traditional Problem of Evil, conceived as a problem of squaring the God hypothesis with certain undisputed facts, a redactor fully

---

[16]St. Thomas Aquinas, *Summa Theologica*, 1, Q2 A3.

[17]In this perspective it becomes easier to see why Aquinas makes so much use of Aristotelian scientific ideas in his arguments. That they are in fact much more dependent on these now largely obsolete ideas is usefully emphasized in Anthony Kenny's *The Five Ways* (London: Routledge & Kegan Paul; New York: Schocken Books, 1969). But Kenny does not bring out that they were deployed against a presumption of atheist naturalism.

[18]Velecky, pp. 225–26.

seized of the presumption of atheism as expounded in the present paper would refer instead to the ostensible incoherence, within the system itself, between the concept of creation by a flawless Creator and the notion of His creatures flawed by their sins.

Questions for Further Reflection

1. Does Flew use traditional definitions of "theism," "atheism," and "agnosticism"? If not, why do you think he doesn't? Does it help his case at all that atheism is understood as a lack of belief?

2. Does the positive atheist, the person who believes there is no God, bear any burden? Does Ockham's Razor, the demand for ontological simplicity, exempt the positive atheist from shouldering the burden of proof?

3. If the theist does not want to convince anyone that God exists, if he "minds his own religious business," does he still bear a burden? Does the theist have to be able to prove to someone else that God exists before the theist is justified in believing that God exists?

21. A PASCALIAN REJOINDER TO THE PRESUMPTION OF ATHEISM

R. Douglas Geivett

R. Douglas Geivett (Ph.D., University of Southern California) is Chair and Professor of Philosophy at Biola University, in California. He is the author of *Evil and the Evidence for God* (Temple University Press, 1993), co-editor with Brendan Sweetman of *Contemporary Perspectives on Religious Epistemology* (Oxford University Press, 1992), and co-editor, with Gary R. Habermas, of *In Defense of Miracles* (InterVarsity Press, 1997).

Reading Questions

1. Why does Geivett hold that even a confident natural theologian should be wary of accepting Flew's presumption of atheism?
2. What, according to Geivett, is a "Pascalian rejoinder" to the presumption of atheism? Why does he adopt this label for his response to Flew's argument for a presumption of atheism?
3. Flew seeks to argue for a presumption of atheism by first asking "What are the aims by reference to which an atheist presumption might be justified?" Why does Geivett hold that this is the wrong question? What is the right question, according to him?
4. What intellectual virtue does Geivett think sheds light on the problem with adopting a presumption of atheism?
5. What is the difference between the ontology of "negative atheism" and the methodology of the "presumption of atheism"? What is the significance of this distinction?

"A true atheist is one who is willing
to face the full consequences
of what it means to say there is no God."
(Buechner 1973, 2)

1. DIRECT AND INDIRECT ATHEOLOGICAL ARGUMENTS

What strategies justify belief of the proposition "God does not exist"? Perhaps none. What strategies have

been attempted by atheists? Several. Most atheological strategies can, I think, be divided conveniently into direct atheological arguments and indirect atheological arguments.

First, it has often been argued *directly* that God does not exist. There have been many varieties of this strategy. Sartre argued, for example, that since humans have free will and free will precludes the existence of God, God does not exist (Sartre 1947). More recently,

Michael Martin has argued, somewhat surprisingly, that the design of the universe implies the nonexistence of God (Martin 1990).

Certainly, the most common kind of direct atheological argument infers the nonexistence of God from the experience of evil in the world. It is now widely acknowledged, even by atheists, that the old strategy of arguing that God and evil are logically incompatible fails. But even probabilistic (or evidential) arguments from evil, which everyone agrees do not demonstrate that God does not exist, are thought by many atheists to show that belief of the proposition "God does not exist" is rational or justified, perhaps more rational or justified than belief of the proposition "God exists" (see, for example, Rowe 1979 and Draper 1989).

Arguments from the incoherence of the theistic conception of God also fall into the general category of direct atheological arguments. If the internal structure of theism is not coherent, then clearly the God of theism does not exist. Indeed, it has been argued that religious language is itself so defective that the very term "God" has no clear referent, with the result that there is no intelligible sense in which one could even think about whether God exists and what attributes He might have.

Second, it has been argued *indirectly* that, in the absence of compelling theistic evidence, belief in the nonexistence of God is rational, even more rational than theistic belief. This strategy takes at least two forms. According to one, the general failure of natural theology,[1] together with the somewhat plausible premise that if God exists then his existence would be manifest, implies the nonexistence of God. This strategy is indirect in the sense that its success depends upon the failure of theistic arguments. Clearly, this type of argument depends upon engagement with the proffered evidence for the existence of God. It is, however, a very strong form of indirect atheological argument, for its premises entail the nonexistence of God. The method, if successful, constitutes what Michael Scriven calls a "complete justification" for the claim that God does not exist (Scriven 1966, 406).

Another type of indirect atheological strategy involves arguing for a weaker conclusion. It is nevertheless potentially quite destructive. This is the strategy of arguing that all inquiry into the question of God's existence ought to begin with a presumption of atheism, that atheism must be the default position of any honest and prudent inquirer. Call this "default atheism." What makes this approach weaker than other indirect atheological arguments is the specific character of the atheism it calls upon one to presume. In fact, atheologians who argue in this manner hold that the presumption of atheism is entirely innocuous, even from the point of view of the theist who believes that there is good evidence for the existence of God.

It is this second type of indirect atheological argument that I wish to address here. In this context, compelling theistic evidence is absent in the special sense that no evidence on either side of the question of God's existence has yet been considered. One is encouraged to adopt a presumption of atheism at the very threshold of inquiry.

I limit my attention here to Antony Flew's version of the argument for the presumption of atheism (Flew 1972).[2] First, I describe Flew's way of presenting the presumption of atheism and state his argument for it (section II). Second, I briefly discuss responses available to the theist (section III). Third, I try to show why even a confident natural theologian should not accept Flew's presumption of atheism (section IV). And finally, I suggest that there are broadly prudential (or Pascalian) reasons for rejecting this presumption (section V).

2. FLEW'S PRESENTATION OF THE PRESUMPTION OF ATHEISM

By way of exposition, I need to comment on three aspects of Flew's proposal: first, his distinction between positive and negative atheism; second, the four

---

[1] I define natural theology as "the systematic formulation of reasons to believe that God exists, that he has a particular nature, and that he stands in relation to the world in certain definite ways, without relying directly upon sacred texts or any prophetic tradition" (Geivett 1993, 90).

[2] Page numbers are to the reprint of Flew 1972 in Geivett and Sweetman 1992. Flew offers what I regard as the most sophisticated defense of a presumption of atheism, depending as it does upon a distinction between positive and negative atheism. Moreover, some atheists (for example, Scriven 1966, Hanson 1972, and Parsons 1989) seem to have something rather different in mind when they assert that there is a presumption of atheism, something akin to the *strong* form of indirect atheological argument I have described above.

parallels he draws between a presumption of atheism in the context of religious inquiry and the presumption of innocence adopted in legal contexts; and, third, his argument for there being a presumption of atheism.

Positive and Negative Atheism

Flew distinguishes between "positive atheism" and "negative atheism."

Positive atheism holds that God does not (or probably does not) exist. Normally, one would suppose, the positive atheist would judge that belief in God is irrational. In a certain sense, negative atheism leaves the question of God's existence open; it does not rule on this question.

Flew says that a negative atheist is "someone who is simply not a theist" (Flew 1972, 20). But this initial characterization is too vague to be helpful. For one thing, it suggests that positive atheists form a special class among negative atheists; but clearly Flew means to distinguish negative atheists from positive atheists. Perhaps the idea is that all there is to being a negative atheist is not being a theist, so that withholding belief in the existence of God without denying the existence of God is both a necessary and a sufficient condition for being a negative atheist. But then theological agnostics would qualify as negative atheists; they may even be indistinguishable from negative atheists. And yet, Flew eventually explicitly distinguishes negative atheists and agnostics.

That there is more to being a negative atheist than being "someone who is simply not a theist" should become clear during the course of this paper. In particular, there are reasons to think that a negative atheist is one who thinks he is justified in withholding belief in the existence of God, even if he does not take the failure of natural theology to be definitive proof that God does not exist. The negative atheist withholds belief of the proposition that God exists until the evidence for the existence of God has been fairly assessed. Upon consideration of the evidence, if it is judged to be adequate the negative atheist is converted to theism. If the evidence is judged to be inadequate, then one's negative atheism may develop into positive atheism. The most characteristic attitude of the negative atheist is that, relative to the question of God's ex-

istence, the burden of proof rests squarely upon the theist's shoulders.

Apparently, then, negative atheism is incompatible with positive atheism: one could not be both a negative atheist and a positive atheist at the same time. Perhaps it would be possible, however, for one to vacillate back and forth between negative and positive atheism as one happened across new evidence for the nonexistence of God, or as one encountered problems with old evidence for the nonexistence of God.

At any rate, the negative atheist does not assert the nonexistence of God. Flew points out that the label "negative atheism" is meant to stand for a "completely noncommittal" point of view or attitude (Flew 1972, 20). One is a negative atheist only if one is not a theist and one does not assert the nonexistence of God. But again, this will hardly serve as a sufficient condition for negative atheism since this condition is also satisfied by theological agnosticism, which is to be contrasted with negative atheism according to Flew. What truly distinguishes the negative atheist from the agnostic is, I believe, a matter of considerable significance.

The Presumption of Atheism and the Presumption of Innocence

To explain what he means by a presumption of atheism, Flew compares his notion with the familiar presumption of innocence adopted in a court of law. He draws four parallels.

First, the presumption of atheism lays it down that the withholding of belief in God's existence is innocent until proven "guilty" by a sufficient reason to believe in God. Just as the presumption of innocence lays a special burden of proof upon a defendant's accusers or prosecutors in a court of law, so the presumption of atheism insists that in the contest between atheism and theism the onus of proof rests squarely upon the shoulders of the theist. Flew qualifies the notion of proof required in the context of religious inquiry by pointing out that the theist may execute his or her duty successfully without actually demonstrating the existence of God, so long as reasonable standards of evidence support the contention that God exists.

Second, both sorts of presumption are defeasible. A presumption of innocence does not entail that an accused party is actually innocent until proven guilty, nor does it follow from a presumption of innocence that the accused is not demonstrably guilty. Defeat of the presumption of innocence will consist in finding enough of the right kind of evidence to convict the party of wrongdoing. *Mutatis mutandis*, defeat of the presumption of atheism depends upon the marshaling of compelling evidence for the existence of God.

Third, in some sense, as a function of the burden of proof owned by the theist, a presumption of atheism sets a greater challenge for the theist than for the atheist. If the theist is unable to present evidence for the existence of God, there is nothing further the atheist need do to justify withholding belief in God. If the theist manages to present evidence for the existence of God, the atheist must do little more than punch holes in the evidence presented. The parallel with the presumption of innocence should be obvious.

Of course, in the legal case one does not go to trial unless there is a suspicion of guilt. During the preliminary hearing the prima facie evidence of guilt is presented in order to justify going to trial. While the prosecution bears the onus of proving guilt, the counsel for the defense must try show that the suspicion of guilt is misplaced. One purpose of a preliminary hearing is to prevent a perfectly gratuitous case from going to trial. Flew never considers whether the two sorts of presumption are parallel in this respect.

Fourth, defeat of the presumption of atheism does not show that it was wrong in the first place to presume atheism. In the parallel case, we do not rule that since in the majority of cases the accused is actually convicted we should henceforth assume that the accused is probably guilty and adopt the converse presumption of guilt during all future trials. The presumption of innocence is appropriate in all future trials regardless of the outcomes of all past trials. Indeed, the presumption of innocence is appropriate in a particular trial regardless of the outcome of that trial itself. This principle holds for inquiry about God's existence. As Flew remarks, if we "suppose that someone is able to prove the existence of God," it does not follow "that the original contention about the onus of proof was mistaken" (Flew 1972, 23).

The Case for the Presumption of Atheism

One must be careful to keep in mind that when Flew draws parallels between the presumption of atheism and the presumption of innocence he is merely engaged in exposition. He is explaining what he means by a presumption of atheism; he is not arguing by analogy for a presumption of atheism. His case for the presumption of atheism does not depend upon the parallels that are thought to exist between the presumption of atheism and the presumption of innocence.

Flew's argument for the presumption of atheism begins with the reminder that "to accept such a presumption is to adopt a policy. And policies have to be assessed by reference to the aims of those for whom they are suggested." Flew then goes on to ask and answer what he takes to be the central question: "What then are the aims by reference to which an atheist presumption might be justified? One key word in the answer, if not the key word, must be 'knowledge'." What one wants to know, in particular, is, first, whether the term "God" is coherent and, second, whether there is a being to which this term refers. But for any true belief to achieve the elevated status of knowledge, "the believer has to be properly warranted so to believe. . . . It is by reference to this inescapable demand for grounds that the presumption of atheism is justified. . . . Until and unless such grounds are produced we literally have no reason at all for believing" (Flew 1972, 24–25).

3. SIMPLE DEFEATERS OF THE PRESUMPTION OF ATHEISM

Theistic responses to Flew's proposal may take one of two forms. First, one may accept the presumption of atheism and seek to defeat it (in the sense Flew himself requires) by pointing to compelling evidence for the existence of God. In the nature of the case, this will require a successful programme of natural theology. Second, a theist who denies the possibility of natural theology, or one who holds that belief in God may be justified quite apart from its being grounded in propositional evidence (such as a Reformed epistemologist), or one who maintains that belief in God does not require justification (a Wittgensteinian fideist, say), must respond directly to Flew's argument for the presumption of atheism.

These different types of theistic responses to Flew's thesis represent different ways of trying to defeat his thesis. The first type of response is offered as a defeater of the presumption of atheism. The second type of response is presented as a defeater, not of the presumption of atheism, but of Flew's argument for the presumption of atheism. For ease of exposition, I shall henceforth refer to defeaters of the first kind as "simple defeaters" and defeaters of the second kind as "rejoinders."

As I have pointed out, *simple defeaters* require a successful programme of natural theology. But what counts as a successful programme of natural theology? Certainly, if God's existence can be demonstrated by one or more of the traditional arguments for the existence of God, that constitutes a successful programme of natural theology. Moreover, I should think that the project of natural theology may be deemed successful if it can show that it is more rational to believe that God exists than it is to believe that God does not exist, even if God's existence cannot be demonstrated.[3]

The question, however, is what to say about a situation where the evidence for God's existence is not weighty enough to compel belief in God but is weighty enough to forbid the assertion that God does not exist. Should one in such a situation simply remain an atheist in the negative sense, that is, go on with the presumption of atheism until something gives? Not clearly. The deadlock between the evidence for theism and the evidence for atheism in such a scenario is due to the partial success of natural theology. Enough evidence has been marshaled on behalf of theism to show that theism is at least on a par epistemically with atheism.

Some philosophers have concluded that when there is enough evidence to achieve epistemic parity between theism and atheism, one ought, on the basis of prudential considerations, to bet on God. This suggestion involves what has been called by Thomas Morris an "epistemically concerned" use of Pascal's Wager. To my mind, it represents the best interpretation of Pascal's own intent in the classic passage on the Wager (see Morris 1986). I also think that this use of the Wager depends upon a moderately successful natural theology.[4]

Thus, a simple defeater of the presumption of atheism may rely wholly or in part on a successful programme of natural theology. A simple defeater of the presumption of atheism will require an epistemically concerned use of Pascal's Wager in combination with natural theology, just in case natural theology alone will not defeat the presumption of atheism. So, much

---

[3]William Rowe has suggested to me that because the latter result is compatible with justifiably *withholding* belief (that is, neither affirming nor denying that God exists), natural theology cannot be deemed successful. It is, of course, true that being more justified in affirming some proposition P than in denying P does not entail that one is more justified in affirming P than in withholding P. In terms of Roderick Chisholm's categories of epistemic appraisal, P may be *merely probable* for some subject S, or even *epistemically in the clear* for S. In either case, while S is more justified in affirming P than in denying P, S may nevertheless be justified in withholding P because P is not quite *beyond reasonable doubt* for S. So S may either be more justified in withholding P than in affirming P, or be equally justified in withholding P as in affirming P—even if we suppose that S is more justified in affirming P than in denying P. (See Chisholm 1989, 16.) Thus, one may be more justified in withholding belief about the existence of God than in affirming the existence of God, or be at least as justified in withholding belief about the existence of God as in affirming the existence of God— even if one is more justified in affirming the existence of God than in denying the existence of God. But does it follow that if natural theology does not make it more reasonable for one to affirm that God exists than either to deny that God exists or *to withhold belief*, natural theology cannot be deemed successful? It does not. For that it is more reasonable to affirm than to deny the existence of God, however reasonable it may be to withhold belief, may be a function of some programme of natural theology. In that event, natural theology enjoys modest success. Furthermore, when it comes to the proposition that God exists, it is perhaps more difficult to remain doxastically neutral and withhold belief than it is to do so for other sorts of propositions. So in the case of the proposition that God ex-

ists, we may have an unusual exception to the epistemic rule that sometimes one ought to withhold belief of P even if it is more reasonable for one to believe P than to deny P. Or, if one will not countenance exceptions to such an epistemic rule, one may see the wisdom of subordinating this particular epistemic rule to prudential constraints on "rational" belief where the proposition that God exists is in question. Finally—and this is more in keeping with the intent of my original proposal about the success of natural theology—a programme of natural theology, patterned after inference to the best explanation, may be so strong that it is far more reasonable to affirm the existence of God than either to deny the existence of God or to withhold belief, even if the proposition that God exists does not enjoy the epistemically exalted status that would accompany a "demonstration" or "proof" of the existence of God.

[4]This is true, I think, whether or not Pascal himself thought so, and whether or not Pascal believed in the prospect of a successful programme of natural theology.

depends upon the fortunes of natural theology. And this is just as Flew would have it.

I have sketched two ways a theist might respond to the presumption of atheism with a simple defeater. Let us now consider them individually, beginning with the case where, because natural theology alone will not defeat the presumption, a bit of Pascalian wagering is required.

Assume that there are resources enough within natural theology to generate rough epistemic parity between theism and atheism. What might Flew have to say about appealing to Pascal's Wager to get people to bet on God? Flew has discussed Pascal's Wager in several places, including the present context. It turns out, however, that he adopts an epistemically unconcerned interpretation of the Wager.

> Pascal makes no attempt in this most famous argument to show that his Roman Catholicism is true or probably true. The reasons which he suggests for making the recommended bet on his particular faith are reasons in the sense of motives rather than reasons in our previous sense of grounds. Conceding, if only for the sake of present argument, that we can have no knowledge here, Pascal tries to justify as prudent a policy of systematic self-persuasion, rather than to provide grounds for thinking that the beliefs recommended are actually true (Flew 1972, 28).

Given this interpretation of Pascal, it is easy to see how the Wager argument can be thought to fail as a simple defeater of the presumption of atheism. To function in that capacity it needs to be united with natural theology.

Flew does not say what force the Wager argument would have if it was offered in an epistemically charged context where natural theology achieves for theism rough epistemic parity vis-à-vis atheism. In such a situation Flew might accept the proposed role for Pascal's Wager and conclude that the theist's success in discharging the burden of proof will then depend upon the natural theologian's success in achieving epistemic parity. In that case, he would perhaps argue against this attempted defeater of the presumption of atheism in the same way that he might argue against natural theology generally: by meeting argument with counterargument, and evidence with counterevidence. (The

suggestion, according to this tactic, is that there simply is no such thing as epistemic parity for the fully informed inquirer.)[5]

On the other hand, Flew might hold for some reason that Pascal's Wager cannot be used in an epistemically concerned setting (where one encounters rough epistemic parity between theism and atheism) to justify betting on God. Since the critical literature on Pascal's Wager tends to assume an epistemically unconcerned version of the Wager, and since I shall assume without argument that most if not all standard objections to this version of the Wager can be avoided if an epistemically concerned version of the Wager is adopted, it is hard to say what objection Flew would offer. This is not, in any case, the type of situation I am most interested in at the moment.[6]

Since it is likely that Flew's reply to the simple defeater consisting of an amalgam of natural theology and Pascalian wagering would focus on the fortunes of natural theology, let us briefly consider the relation between natural theology and Flew's presumption of atheism. Anyone who is familiar with the larger body of Flew's work in the philosophy of religion will know that he takes a rather dim view of the prospects for natural theology. Of course, once the theist has taken it upon herself to answer the presumption of atheism with an appeal to natural theology, the negative atheist

---

[5]Some have argued that it is impossible ever to be in conditions of rough epistemic parity, and so the relevant context for the appropriate application of the Wager never obtains. For a discussion of this claim, see Morris 1986, 263–67. For the purpose of my paper, I shall simply stipulate that a use of the Wager is epistemically concerned if and only if either theism stands in rough epistemic parity with atheism or theism is epistemically justified or warranted to a greater degree than atheism, whether one is fully informed or not.
[6]For arguments along these lines, see Morris 1986. Morris has pointed out that there are two ways that competing beliefs may be in rough epistemic parity for a person. A person finds herself in "epistemically null conditions" when she can see no positive reason to accept either theism or atheism. If she recognizes roughly equally compelling positive reasons for accepting both theism and atheism, then she finds herself in "epistemically ambiguous conditions." Without taking the time to argue for the claim here, I suggest that the typical inquirer finds herself in epistemically null conditions only at the very outset of inquiry into the question of God's existence. But is this really a case of epistemic parity? On the threshold of inquiry no evidence has even been considered. The context is, we might say, epistemically vacuous.

can no longer avoid the rough and tumble of examining evidence for the existence of God and offering counterevidence.

Michael Martin, himself an atheist, has remarked that, even if there is a presumption of atheism, since theists have as a matter of fact put forward arguments both for the cognitive meaningfulness of religious language and for the existence of God, "negative atheists must show that these . . . arguments are inadequate" (Martin 1990, 30).

> Thus even if Flew is right about the burden of proof, this does not affect to any significant extent what negative atheists must do. They must undermine reasons and arguments produced by theists before their position is secure. If they need not make the first move, they must make the second (Martin 1990, 30).

Because atheological apologetics is in this sense unavoidable, Martin chooses "to remain neutral on whether there is a presumption in favor of atheism" (Martin 1990, 30).

4. THE NEED FOR A REJOINDER

It is interesting to consider whether simple defeaters may, even by a confident natural theologian, be considered adequate as rebuttals to Flew's presumption of atheism. As an initial approach to this issue, let us ask, is the presumption of atheism really noncommittal?

Is the Presumption of Atheism Noncommittal?

Michael Martin is right to observe that atheism can only be preserved by engaging the actual arguments of theists. It is wrong, however, to imply (as he does) that the presumption of atheism is *therefore* relatively insignificant. For if there is any sort of presumption of atheism at all, then negative atheism must seem to be the most appropriate attitude for one to take *even beyond the threshold of inquiry*, just so long as compelling reasons for theistic belief are not forthcoming or the best theistic arguments are shown to be defective. And this constitutes a sort of victory for atheism more generally.

Theistic arguments function, for Flew, as potential defeaters of the presumption of atheism. But if theistic

arguments fail, then the presumption of atheism is undefeated. Successful objections to theistic arguments function as defeaters of defeaters for the presumption of atheism. This can hardly be considered a trivial result once one grants that there is a general presumption of atheism. For if there existed no antecedently plausible presumption of atheism, then successful objections to theistic arguments would not in themselves support atheistic belief in any way. The only way the failure of natural theology can tend to preserve (negative) atheism is if there is in fact a justified presumption of atheism. Even if, as Martin thinks, the failure of all of the most plausible theistic arguments to date implies that no successful argument will ever appear on the stage of debate about God's existence, this does not tend to confirm (negative) atheism at all, unless there is a well-established presumption of atheism.

It will have been noticed that when I have here spoken of negative atheism I have placed the term "negative" in parentheses. I have done this because I think there is another strategy available to the atheist which parallels the defense of negative atheism I have just described, but which, if successful, actually constitutes a positive proof of atheism. This strategy assumes that if there are no good arguments for the existence of God, then God does not exist. If this assumption is correct, and if the programme of natural theology fails, then negative atheism rightly gives way to positive atheism. That is, actual engagement with the theistic arguments goes far beyond preserving the presumption of atheism by closing the question of God's existence. Positive atheism supplants negative atheism, *but it is helped along toward this result by an initial posture of negative atheism.*

Still, it must be recognized that this is no part of the *negative* atheist's explicit strategy (though it may be an incentive operating in the background). The point can be brought out best, perhaps, by noting that the preservation of negative atheism (by the method of defeating all natural theology arguments, say) does not permit one to assert the nonexistence of God. (Even a guilty party may be exonerated following "due process.") Flew stresses this point by stating that the presumption of atheism is procedural rather than substantive. But it is hard to believe that the procedure Flew recommends has no substantive significance whatsoever. For while the presumption of atheism is not substantive in the sense of *tout de suite* closing the question of God's existence, this presumption does, as Flew says, "put the whole argument into a distinctive perspective" (Flew 1972, 23). What he means, as we have already seen, is that the presumption of atheism sets a greater challenge for theism vis-à-vis atheism. This differential challenge is not a function of the comparative difficulty of demonstrating the existence of God on the one hand and of demonstrating the nonexistence of God on the other.[7] According to default atheism, even if both God exists and there is plentiful evidence for his existence, withholding belief of the proposition that God exists is the only attitude warranted until that evidence has been compellingly marshaled.

Perhaps this way of stating the default position does not quite express Flew's fondest hopes. Perhaps, as I have already suggested, there is more to adopting the attitude of the negative atheist than just withholding belief of the proposition that God exists. Flew does distinguish between negative atheism and agnosticism. He writes as if the chief difference is that agnosticism assumes the cognitive meaningfulness of religious language, whereas the negative atheist takes even this to be an open question. But there is, I think, another equally important difference between agnosticism and negative atheism, a difference that Flew never makes explicit.

Flew says that the negative atheist is "completely noncommittal" regarding both the legitimacy of the concept of God (that is, the theoretical possibility of the existence of God) and the application of this concept (that is, the actual existence of God). We may think of the theological agnostic as completely noncommittal only with respect to the question of God's actual existence. At first blush it would seem that the negative atheist and the agnostic adopt precisely the same attitude concerning the *being* of God. But this is doubtful. For the agnostic as such makes no general judgment about how the debate about the existence of God ought to be conducted. Moreover, as a rule, the agnostic just finds herself without belief of the proposi-

tion that God exists and thinks of this as the result of lacking evidence which counts decisively either for or against the existence of God. To the agnostic, the inclination to positively deny the existence of God and the inclination to positively assert the existence of God seem equally irresponsible. Agnosticism as such does not embody any claim whatsoever about whether it is the theist or the atheist who owns a special burden of proof. The negative atheist, on the other hand, insists that the theist bears a special burden of proof.

So in a nontrivial sense, agnosticism and negative atheism are not very compatible attitudes. For the negative atheist will recommend a default position of atheism both at the threshold of inquiry and throughout inquiry until (perhaps *per impossibile*) the theist shows either that God exists or that it is rational to believe in the existence of God. Unlike the agnostic, the negative atheist makes a telling procedural commitment which potentially prejudices the case against theism. The negative atheist seeks a superior field position against theism in a totally a priori manner. In contrast, from the agnostic point of view theism and atheism are strictly deadlocked, epistemically and doxastically.

Implications for Natural Theology

If the presumption of atheism makes the sort of commitment just described, what are the implications for natural theology? Flew insists that one of the most celebrated figures of the natural theology tradition, St. Thomas Aquinas himself, acknowledged a presumption of atheism and viewed his Five Ways as various attempts to answer this presumption. My response to Flew's claim regarding St. Thomas is twofold. First, he probably misunderstands what Thomas says. Certainly, nothing in the extended passage cited by Flew justifies his assertion that the Angelic Doctor accepted a presumption of atheism. Second, if St. Thomas did believe that it was innocuous for a natural theologian to assume a presumption of atheism, such a belief represented an unfortunate and potentially disastrous oversight on his part.

Let me concede that I have myself at various turns been sympathetic with the suggestion that a successful programme of natural theology would defeat any presumption of atheism that might be adopted at the outset of religious inquiry. Because I also believe in the

[7]Obviously, one fundamental condition which determines the possibility of a demonstration in either case is the actual truth of the matter. If God exists, then demonstrating his nonexistence will not just be difficult, it will be impossible.

possibility of a successful programme of natural theology (see Geivett 1993, Part II), I have not, in the past, taken the presumption of atheism to be any great threat to the structure or pattern of justified belief in God. But I have reconsidered my position on this. It now seems to me that the possibility of a successful programme of natural theology depends in no small measure upon the attitude one adopts at the very threshold of religious inquiry. Natural theologians, no less than those who view the character of justified belief in God quite differently, need to consider the *possibility* that any inquiry conducted on Flew's terms will tend to perpetuate an attitude of negative atheism, no matter how powerful the evidence may be for the existence of God.

The natural theologian, then, cannot accept with perfect equanimity the terms of religious inquiry set down by Antony Flew. While the procedure he recommends may not prejudicially assume an atheist conclusion in the sense of logically entailing that God does not exist, it does prejudice the way inquiry into the question of God's existence is carried out. Thus, Flew's proposal may have the grave tendency to foreclose prematurely on the question of God's existence.

What seems to be needed, then, is not a defeater of Flew's presumption of atheism in the form of natural theology, but a defeater of Flew's argument for the presumption of atheism which natural theology cannot provide and without which natural theology cannot succeed (in the sense of leading people to belief in God). The sort of defeater needed I have called a *rejoinder* to the presumption of atheism. One might be inclined to think that there are two types of rejoinders to Flew's presumption: a *refuting rejoinder*, which would show that there is no presumption of atheism, and a *rebutting rejoinder*, which would show that Flew's argument for a presumption of atheism does not go through, that his argument does not succeed in showing that there is a presumption of atheism. If there is no good argument for the presumption of atheism, however, then there is no nonarbitrary presumption of atheism. For in the nature of the case, a presumption about how one ought to conduct a certain sort of inquiry cannot exist without a decision to adopt the presumption. The choice, then, is between an arbitrary decision and a reasoned decision to adopt a presumption of atheism. So any rejoinder that shows that extant arguments for a presumption of atheism do not go through also shows that there is, as yet, no nonarbitrary presumption of atheism. A rejoinder is a rejoinder.

5. A PASCALIAN REJOINDER TO THE PRESUMPTION OF ATHEISM

I cannot help believing, then, that Flew's recommendation prejudices religious inquiry unfairly, even dangerously. It seems to me that one should not take his advice about what attitude to adopt during inquiry into the question of God's existence. For one thing, it is very hard to see how one could know, in advance of an examination of the evidence concerning God's existence, that the best policy is to presume that God does not exist. Furthermore, there are reasons for thinking that this policy might be counterproductive given the proper aims or interests of such inquiry. These reasons constitute a rejoinder to the presumption of atheism.

The rejoinder I have in mind I shall call "Pascalian." By "Pascalian" I mean a rejoinder that is broadly prudential. A broadly prudential policy is one that is adopted out of concern for the personal significance of possible outcomes. I take it that the appropriate context for Pascalian wagering (in the broad sense) is one, first, where the evidence on two sides of a question either has not yet come into view or is inconclusive, and second, where there is something at stake which interests the inquirer—that is, where the stakes are so high that the outcome is of such interest to the inquirer that the inquirer is compelled to seek resolution on the question. It needs to be asked whether a presumption of atheism is even compatible with taking a sincere interest in the question of God's existence.

It is noteworthy that Flew takes a presumption of atheism to be appropriate in the special context of *debate* about the existence of God (Flew 1972, 20). But this, surely, is not the only (or even the most important) context in which the question of God's existence may be of legitimate interest to the unbeliever. The question of God's existence is charged with personal significance. It is the significance of this question for human existence which makes disinterested inquiry seem imprudent if not psychologically impossible.

Given the nature of the presumption of atheism and of Flew's argument for it, where aims or interests are central, it would seem that a satisfactory rejoinder to the presumption of atheism must also take aims or interests into account. And it does seem possible to offer a plausible alternative account of those aims that are most relevant at the threshold of inquiry into the question of God's existence. This means, in part, that there are reasons for thinking that adopting a presumption of atheism may be contrary to one's interests. So let us ask, how might the attitude of the negative atheist function in religious inquiry in a way that is counterproductive for the (earnest) inquirer?

Well, we cannot rule out a priori the possibility that God will not be found by one who adopts the presumption of atheism. Within the Christian tradition, at least, that possibility is embodied in dogma: "For whoever would draw near to God must believe that He exists and that He rewards those who seek Him" (Heb. 11:6, RSV). This perspective was also announced by the Hebrew prophet, Jeremiah: "Then you will call upon me and come and pray to me, and I will hear you. You will seek me and find me; when you seek me with all your heart, I will be found by you, says the Lord" (Jer. 29:12–14, RSV). This is significant, for if it is the existence of the Judeo-Christian God that we care to know about, then we need to conduct our inquiry into His existence by methods that are compatible with the way the tradition represents His attitude toward inquiry about His existence.

This suggests that if God exists, there may be considerable risk in presuming atheism. A presumption of atheism may prevent one from noticing relevant positive evidence for the existence of God. Flew does, after all, speak as if, because the theist owns the burden of proof, the negative atheist can simply remain aloof until some candidate for theistic "proof" is offered. A presumption of atheism may also blind one to the significance of the positive evidence which one does notice. One might worry, then, that the evidence for God's existence, powerful though it may be, may not be fully appreciated unless and until one has adopted the right attitude toward inquiry into the possibility of God's existence, a rather different attitude than the one proposed by Flew.

We might say, then, that, precisely at the most crucial point in his argument for a presumption of atheism, Flew begs the question. The real question is, or should be: *What are the aims by reference to which one ought to think about the ideal strategy for resolving the question of God's existence?* This is not quite the question Flew puts for himself. Recall how it is formulated by him: "What then are the aims by reference to which an atheist presumption might be justified?" (Flew 1972, 24). It may be fruitful to pose such a question. Also, it may be that Flew's view, as an answer to this particular question, is exactly right. *That* part of his thesis just may be innocuous. But no answer to that question, even if it is Flew's answer, could tell us that one ought to adopt a presumption of atheism. For it may also be that "the aims by reference to which an atheist presumption might be justified" are not the aims appropriate to religious inquiry. Flew's question simply is not general enough, and consequently his policy is not broad enough. Again, it needs to be asked, are the aims associated with a presumption of atheism the right aims for religious inquiry?

Take the legal case as a parallel. A presumption of innocence, where it is the law, is preferred because of inherent risks embedded in the trial of any accused party. There is, on the one hand, the risk of exonerating a guilty party. On the other hand, there is the risk of convicting the innocent. These risks cannot be ruled out a priori in advance of the actual trial. So the law passes judgment on the comparative value of these two risks. It decides upon the presumption of innocence by virtue of a greater willingness to risk exonerating the guilty than to risk convicting the innocent. While we do not want to exonerate a person who is guilty as charged, we are even less willing to convict the innocent. This preference, we might argue, is tied in some way to a principle of justice. That is, we might reason that it is more just to exonerate a guilty party than to convict an innocent party when we cannot determine on the basis of the evidence whether the party is actually guilty or not. Thus, if we must err (or run the risk of erring), we prefer to do so on the side of exonerating the guilty.

Now there are risks, as well, in the case of inquiry into the existence of God. If it is not possible to adopt a strictly neutral, indifferent attitude about the outcome of such an inquiry, and if some "presumptive closure" on the question of God's existence is required at the threshold of investigation into the evidence, we do well to bear in mind that we want to believe that God exists if He exists, and to believe that God does not exist if He does not exist. However, our cognitive aim in religious matters (or in any other matters, for that matter) is not the reductive one of acquiring knowledge only on the condition that we do not risk falling into error. We do not always have the luxury of avoiding cognitive commitment until we can be sure that we have avoided cognitive error. The venture of cognitive inquiry is quite often attended by the risk of error. And one guideline for how best to conduct inquiry recommends comparing the risk of falling into error upon believing the proposition under consideration with the risk of falling into error upon denying that proposition. A Pascalian will point out that true belief that God exists, at the risk of being mistaken, is more desirable than true belief that God does not exist, if it too is attended by the risk of being mistaken. The supposition that God may exist should lead one to inquire into the question of God's existence in a way that increases the chances that one will eventually come to believe in God if it is the case that God exists. (Can we say, with the same conviction, that the supposition that God may not exist equally motivates and prescribes a way to find out that God does not exist?) The sincere inquirer after truth concerning the existence of God should adopt a policy of inquiry that greatly improves rather than diminishes her chances of sincerely and responsibly believing in God should it be the case that God exists.[8]

Moreover, given the stakes of withholding belief in God should God exist, and the greater chance that one will fail to see that the evidence points to the existence of God if one does adopt a presumption of atheism, there are prudential reasons for conducting inquiry as if God does exist and as if He will make His existence manifest to anyone *in the right passional state*. If one wants to know what is the ideal passional state for conducting inquiry into God's existence, one would be advised to look at the specific content of the theistic hypothesis under investigation. If one really wishes to know whether God exists, why would one adopt a posture which quite possibly diminishes the chances of finding out that there is a God?

Negative atheism, positive atheism, and theism are not the only choices available, so far as attitudes toward religious inquiry are concerned. Another possible attitude is one of genuine openness toward the possibility of God's existence, an attitude of sincere willingness to believe which does not place any special burden of proof upon the theist.

When one suggests that the theist owns a special burden of proof, one assumes that the only suitable context of inquiry into the possibility of God's existence is one of *debate* between two or more parties. But that is not the best way to think about how inquiry into the question of God's existence ought to be conducted. The best context for such an investigation is the highly personal and somewhat individualistic one of engaged interest for the sake of finding out, if God exists, that He exists—accompanied by a sincere willingness to adjust one's beliefs (and one's life, perhaps) accordingly. But in that context there is no point to insisting upon a burden of proof that must be shouldered by someone else. For no one else can be responsible for what another comes to believe. The inquirer simply owes it to himself to find out the truth of the matter if he can. Pursuant to this goal, he should settle on a policy of inquiry that takes comparative risks into consideration. In this respect, if there are any parallels between the jurisprudential presumption of innocence and the policy proper to investigation into God's existence, they are perhaps the reverse of what Flew takes them to be.

---

[8]Dale Cannon, "A Post-Critical Approach to Conceiving and Teaching Introduction to Philosophy," APA Newsletter (Spring 2001), p. 187. In the spirit of William James, the author recommends a convergence of "methodological belief" and "methodological doubt" in his attempt to specify "the process of authentic inquiry," which balances the twin objectives of seeking truth and avoiding error. He says, "the methodological belief is primarily the outgoing, venturesome investment of oneself in following up the hunch and finding out whether and to what extent it is true." Inherent in this approach is a measure of risk-taking. But there is more to support risk-taking in inquiry than the sheer thrill of following up a hunch, I think. Sometimes the focus of inquiry is a matter so momentous that there may seem to be greater risk of an altogether different kind by not taking the cognitive risk of falling into error by pursuing a line of inquiry governed by "methodologi-

cal belief." Inquiry into the question of God's existence is an especially good candidate for this kind of risk-taking through methodological belief. Of course, methodological belief is not itself belief.

Of course, a convinced religious believer may aid the process of inquiry conducted by another by pointing to the evidence he is aware of as such. The prudent inquirer has every reason to welcome the companionship of the convinced theist, for the convinced theist represents the possibility of future rational conviction to the not-yet-convinced. There are indications within the sources of the Christian tradition that when a sincere seeker joins the believing community with honest questions, he is eventually rewarded with an awareness of God attended by faith, and he thereby becomes a bona fide member of that community.

The whole point is that we may have an interest in taking a different view than what Flew recommends given the differential significance of possible outcomes on the adoption of one attitude rather than another. There is no reason to think that reasonable standards of the rational appraisal of theism must begin with a presumption of atheism. A presumption of atheism is not needed as a curb against gullibility except for the most insecure of intellectuals.[9] And even in those cases of extreme insecurity, the proper corrective is not to adopt a presumption of atheism but to look confidently to the evidence with the expectation that one's best efforts at rational inquiry will be rewarded with a glimpse of the truth.

One's "best efforts at rational inquiry" will include exercise of the relevant intellectual virtues. Exercising intellectual virtue in this context will include, for example, setting aside whatever *preference* one may have for positively denying the existence of God, in the interests of believing whatever happens to be true. The desire to know the truth about God's existence, which remains an open question at the outset of inquiry, should, as a matter of intellectual virtue, take precedence over the desire to believe that God does not exist. This suggests that an earnest inquirer after the truth about God's existence ought to adopt a policy that mitigates the influence of a preference for a particular outcome, such as believing that God does not exist. Does Flew's recommended policy of adopting a pre-

sumption of atheism achieve this goal? I confess to being skeptical.

Flew himself has recently remarked, "the more I contemplate the eschatological teachings of Christianity and Islam, the more I wish I could demonstrate their falsity" (Flew 2001). Flew clearly considers the eschatological teachings of Christianity and Islam to be repugnant. Successfully demonstrating that God does not exist would be sufficient for demonstrating the falsity of the eschatological teachings of Christianity and Islam. Perhaps we may discern in the above remark (embedded as it is in a published internet notice titled "Sorry to Disappoint, but I'm Still an Atheist") Flew's preference to be able to prove that God does not exist, and thus his preference for denying the existence of God. If that is so, then we might well be suspicious of Flew's recommended adoption of a presumption of atheism, even if a "presumption of theism," as it were, is not a superior alternative.

Adopting a presumption of atheism is, on one level, supposed to be innocuous, for it is associated with "merely" negative atheism. But negative atheism is still a variety of atheism. Granted, the *ontology* to which one is committed as a negative atheist may seem innocent enough, for negative atheism does not assert the nonexistence of God. But the presumption of atheism has to do with *methodology* rather than ontology. It is a policy about how best to conduct inquiry into the question of God's existence. But a policy about the proper way to conduct inquiry in this matter should include guidance about how to curb the inordinate influence of the preference for a certain outcome. Flew's choice to label his policy "the presumption of atheism" may be thought to signal a preference for a particular outcome, namely, the denial that God exists. For those who doubt that this is a substantial objection to Flew's use of the term, there is an additional reason to worry that more is involved in adopting a presumption of atheism than merely assuming the position of the negative atheist.

Flew's label, "the presumption of atheism," is thought to be meaningful through its analogy with a jurisprudential presumption of innocence. But what is a presumption of innocence? It is a presumption that a defendant in a court of law is "not guilty." In effect, a trial in court begins with the provisional verdict of "not guilty." "Innocent" and "guilty" are two possible

---

[9]If it is possible to be fair-minded and objective about the evidence for or against the existence of God when adopting a presumption of atheism, as Flew seems to think, why shouldn't it be equally possible to remain fair-minded and objective on a contrary presumption?

and contrary verdicts. A judgment of "innocent" is a judgment of "not guilty" (i.e., the negation of guilt) and a judgment of "guilty" is a judgment of "not innocent" (i.e., the negation of innocence). In this respect, a guilty verdict (i.e., the judgment that the defendant is guilty) is the contradictory of a verdict of innocence (i.e., the judgment that the defendant is not guilty; the defendant is innocent).[10]

Mutatis mutandis, a presumption of atheism is a provisional verdict of "not theism." "Theism" and "atheism" are labels for two possible and contrary verdicts. A judgment in favor of theism is a judgment of "not atheism" (i.e., the negation of atheism) and a judgment in favor of atheism is a judgment of "not theism" (i.e., the negation of theism). In this respect, a verdict in favor of theism is the contradictory of a verdict in favor of atheism, and vice versa, of course. But what sort of atheism is the contradictory of theism? It is not "negative atheism." Rather, it is "positive atheism," Flew's label for the positive assertion that God does not exist (see Flew 1972, 20). So the presumption of atheism, if we press its analogy with the jurisprudential presumption of innocence, is a presumption of *positive* atheism. The fact that the atheism in question at this stage is merely presumed and not demonstrated does nothing to change the status of such atheism from positive to negative. Adopting a presumption of atheism is thus incompatible with the posture of negative atheism (whatever merit that posture might have under different circumstances). Thus we see that, if there is a genuine analogy between a presumption of atheism and a presumption of innocence, the "atheism" in "the presumption of atheism" is not itself "negative atheism" but "positive atheism."

Returning now to the general thesis of this section, the policy of diligently seeking God, without positively asserting that He exists, is not clearly compatible with the policy of the negative atheist. But, according to a prominent branch of the Christian tradition at least, that is a condition that God himself has established for finding him: you do not find him without looking. On the other hand, one test of one variety of theism is that if one approaches the question of God's existence without a presumption that the evidence is lacking and with a genuine interest in believing in God if God exists, one will be rewarded with sufficient evidence to justify believing in God.

Let me conclude with two fitting passages from fragment 427 of the *Pensées* (Pascal 1966): (1) "Let them, in short, acknowledge that there are only two classes of persons who can be called reasonable: those who serve God with all their heart because they know him and those who seek him with all their heart because they do not know him"; (2) "I can feel nothing but compassion for those who sincerely lament their doubt, who regard it as the ultimate misfortune, and who, sparing no effort to escape from it, make their search their principle and most serious business."[11]

REFERENCES

Buechner, Frederick. 1973. *Wishful Thinking*. New York: Harper & Row.

Chisholm, Roderick M. 1989. *Theory of Knowledge*. 3rd ed. Englewood Cliffs, NJ: Prentice Hall.

Draper, Paul. 1989. "Pain and Pleasure: An Evidential Problem for Theists." In *The Evidential Argument from Evil*. Ed. Daniel Howard-Snyder. Bloomington, IN: Indiana University Press. Pp. 12–29.

Flew, Antony. 1972. "The Presumption of Atheism." *The Canadian Journal of Philosophy* 2. Reprinted in Geivett and Sweetman 1992, 19–32.

———. 2001. "Sorry to Disappoint, but I'm Still an Atheist." Internet: http://www.secweb.org/asset.asp?AssetID=138.

Geivett, R. Douglas. 1993. *Evil and the Evidence for God*. Philadelphia, PA: Temple University Press.

———, and Brendan Sweetman, eds. 1992. *Contemporary Perspectives on Religious Epistemology*. New York: Oxford University Press.

Hanson, N. R. 1972. "What I Don't Believe." In *What I Do Not Believe and Other Essays*. Ed. Stephen Toulmin and Harry Woolf. Dordrecht, Neth.: D. Reidel.

---

[10]Of course, all this is true, quite apart from whether the defendant is in fact guilty rather than innocent, or innocent rather than guilty. We are concerned here with judgments of guilt or innocence, which may or may not correspond to a defendant's actual condition of being guilty or innocent of the crime with which he is charged.

[11]For helpful comments on various portions of this paper, I wish to thank Christopher Bernard, Thomas Crisp, John Greco, Douglas Groothuis, J. P. Moreland, Paul Moser, William Power, William Rowe, and Brendan Sweetman, as well as participants at the 1996 meeting of the Society for Philosophy of Religion, Atlanta, GA.

Martin, Michael. 1990. "Atheistic Teleological Arguments." In Geivett and Sweetman 1992, 43–57.

Morris, Thomas V. 1986. "Pascalian Wagering." In Geivett and Sweetman 1992, 257–69.

Parsons, Keith. 1989. *God and the Burden of Proof*. Buffalo, NY: Prometheus Books.

Pascal, Blaise. 1966. *Pensées*. Trans. A. J. Krailsheimer. New York, NY: Penguin.

Pojman, Louis P., ed. 1994. *Philosophy of Religion: An Anthology*. 2nd ed. Belmont, CA: Wadsworth.

Rowe, William L. 1979. "The Problem of Evil and Some Varieties of Atheism." In Geivett and Sweetman 1992, 33–42.

Sartre, Jean-Paul. 1947. *Existentialism*. New York, NY: Philosophical Library.

Scriven, Michael. 1966. "The Presumption of Atheism." In Pojman 1994, 403–409.

QUESTIONS FOR FURTHER REFLECTION

1. How would you advise a friend who wanted to know the best way to pursue the question of God's existence? What advice would you give on the basis of this article? What other advice would you want to add?

2. Geivett holds that even if there is very good evidence for the existence of God, a person who adopts the presumption of atheism might not be able to appreciate the strength of that argument. Do you agree? Can you describe other types of situations where an individual might have good evidence for believing some proposition but is unable to accept that proposition either because (1) the individual is using the wrong standards to evaluate the evidence, or (2) the individual has a preference for believing that the proposition is false?

3. Have you ever faced a dilemma where you had strong evidence for a proposition you did not want to believe? How did you resolve the dilemma? How *should* a person resolve a dilemma of this kind? Does it make any difference what the proposition is about?

4. Toward the end of his article, Geivett argues that the presumption of atheism is a presumption of *positive* atheism rather than a presumption of *negative* atheism. What is the significance of this if he is right? How would you evaluate his argument? How might Flew respond?

5. Review the two Pascal quotations in the final paragraph of Geivett's article. Do you agree with Pascal's division of two classes of people? Which of these two classes most closely describes your own position on the question of God's existence? What do you think Pascal would say to you, based on your answer to this question?

22. RESPONSE TO R. DOUGLAS GEIVETT'S "A PASCALIAN REJOINDER TO THE PRESUMPTION OF ATHEISM"

Antony Flew

A brief biography of Antony Flew occurs on page 151. In this selection, Flew responds to Geivett's critique of "The Presumption of Atheism."

READING QUESTIONS

1. What might Flew say to anyone who challenged his use of the word "atheist"?
2. How did Rui Zhu come to learn about the Western theistic conception of God?
3. According to Flew, at what point did Christianity become predestinarian?
4. What, according to Flew, do predestinarians assert?
5. What are Flew's two helpful suggestions?

My paper on 'The Presumption of Atheism' was first printed in 1972, first reprinted in 1976 in a collection entitled *God, Freedom, and Immortality* (Amhest, NY: Prometheus, 1984), and reprinted again in 1997 in the *Journal for the Central Study of Religion* Vol. 2, No. 2. I want to begin by repeating what I said in response to Professor Geivett's paper on its first publication, namely, that "Professor Geivett may be surprised to learn that I found very little in his paper with which to disagree." This was not and is not because in the now 30 years since my paper was first published I have completely changed my mind, nor is it because he has inexcusably misunderstood what I then wrote. Instead it is because I did at that time write about the presumption of atheism as if to be a rational man or a rational woman you would have to start as and to continue to be a negative atheist until and unless someone else provided you with at least strong evidencing reasons for believing in, if not a substantive proof of, the existence of God. In fact I would then have agreed, as I now do still heartily agree, with Geivett's profoundly Protestant insistence that no "no one else can be responsible for what another comes to believe. The inquirer simply owes it to himself to find out the truth of the matter if he can."

T. H. Huxley, who introduced the term "agnosticism" and employed it to describe his own position, which was reached only after sustained inquiry, would have recognized me as a fellow agnostic. At a time when so many people who have never, it seems, given any serious thought to such matters describe themselves as agnostics, I prefer to describe myself, awkwardly and rather more aggressively as a negative atheist, while indicating to anyone challenging my employment of the word "atheist" that my interpretation of the initial "a" in that word is exactly the same as everyone's interpretation of the initial "a's" in "atypical", "amoral", and "asymmetrical."

My purpose in arguing for the presumption of atheism was from the beginning and still remains to try to ensure that we should approach the fundamental questions of the possible existence and nature of God without prejudice. If, that is to say, we want to approach the question of the existence of the God of what Islam knows as "the peoples of the Book" without prejudice, as we should approach all such disputed questions, then we need to try to approach it as if we, as fully grown adults, were meeting the concept of that God, also fully developed, for the first time, and as if we were now, also for the first time, wondering whether that concept does in fact have actual application. For it is, surely, significant that almost everyone who has ever given sustained attention to this question has treated it as being about the concept of the logically presupposed source of a putative self-revelation, and that accounts of those putative self-revelations have been handed down and made familiar to those questioners through generations of parents and pedagogues, of priests and rabbis, of imams and ayatollahs.

Conversations in Beijing with the very able graduate student who served as my "minder" during a 1990 visit to the Institute for Foreign Philosophy in the University of Peking were a great help to me in appreciating how strong and how deeply concealed such prejudices can be. Rui Zhu[1] was of course by that time familiar with that conception of God. But he had met it as today anyone anywhere might happen to come upon the notions of Aphrodite or Poseidon. He had never had occasion to confront it as what William James called a "live option" any more than, for any of our contemporaries anywhere, belief in the real existence of the Olympians constitutes such an option. So, confronted by the question "What if anything caused the Big Bang?" his response would have been—indeed it was—that if physicists cannot find the true physical answer, if there is one, then the Big Bang itself will have to be accepted as for us the ultimate brute fact, which explains but cannot itself be explained. And, having learned from Hume that the sentence "Every event has a cause" is not an expression of a logically necessary truth, he had no inclination to seek a metaphysical cause. He had no inclination, that is to say, to argue—as was argued against me in a Campus Crusade for Christ debate some years later—that "from the very nature of the case, as the cause of space and time, this cause must be uncaused, timeless, changeless, an immaterial being of unimaginable power that created the universe."

---

[1]His name can now be revealed since, having obtained a scholarship to study at a university in the United States, he has since acquired a Ph.D. and is now established on the teaching staff of a state university.

Again, it is only prejudice derived from the three great theistic religions which misleads people that the Aristotelian ideas which Aquinas employed in the constriction of his Five Ways point to the existence of a God with an insistent desire to be obeyed and worshipped by his human creatures.

Surely to anyone who was for the first time and without prejudice entertaining the hypothesis that our Universe is the creation of an omnipotent and omniscient God, it would appear obvious that everything which occurs or does not occur within it must, by the hypothesis, be precisely and only what its Creator wants, indeed causes, to occur or not to occur. What scope is there for creatures in such a Universe to defy the will of their Creator? What room even for a concept of such defiance? For a Creator to punish creatures for what by the hypothesis He necessarily and as such (ultimately) causes them to do would be the most monstrous, perverse, unjust, and sadistic of performances. Absent revelation to the contrary, the expectations of love's natural reason must surely be that such a Creator God would be detached and uninvolved as the gods of Epicurus. Indeed some Indian religious thinkers not prejudiced by any present or previous Mosaic commitments are said to describe their monotheistic God as being, essentially and in the nature of the case, "beyond good and evil."

The writings of Aristotle himself contain no concept of a single omnipotent and omniscient personal Being, making demands on His human beings for our obedience, much less threatening us with an eternity of extreme torture for our (by Him) unforgiven perceived (by Him) disobedience. The closest which Aristotle's God comes in either the *Nicomachean Ethics* or the *Politics*, and it is scarcely close, to prescribing or proscribing any sort of human conduct is when in the former work he tells us that "the divine life, which surpasses all other blessedness, consists in contemplation" (X, viii, 7). So when we find Aquinas concluding, after presenting an Aristotelian argument for a First Cause or a Prime Mover, that "This we call God" we may well agree; but only with the caveat: "Yes, but not in the same sense of the word 'God'."

For the rarely recognized truth would seem to be that Christianity from its beginning and for more than a millennium thereafter was unequivocally predesti-

narian.[2] Its teaching was, that is to say, that God is the ultimate, fully determining cause of all human action: both of these actions and failures to act for which their agents are to be consigned—as a supposedly just punishment—to an eternity of extreme torture; and of the actions and failures to act of those who are to be awarded—not as a deserved reward but as an act of Divine grace—with an eternity of bliss.[3]

Nowadays, as I know from much experience of maintaining the contradictory, it is widely believed that only Calvinists are or ever have been committed to such predestinarian doctrines. Indeed I have had more than once or twice to draw the attention of some otherwise apparently well instructed Roman Catholic student to the article "Concerning Predestination" in the *Summa Theologica*. But I prefer to quote a passage from another work of the Angelic Doctor:

> God alone can move the will, as an agent, without doing violence to it . . . Some people . . . not understanding how God can cause a movement of will in us without prejudicing the freedom of the will, have tried to explain . . . authoritative texts wrongly; that is, they would say that God "works in us, to wish and to accomplish" means that he causes in us the power of willing, but not in such a way that he makes us will this or that. . . . These people are, of course, opposed quite plainly by authoritative texts of Holy Writ. For it says in *Isaiah* (26.2) "Lord, you have worked all our work in us." Hence we receive from God not only the power of willing but its employments also.[4]

Had he been writing for Christians Aquinas would have found his Biblical authority not in *Isaiah* but in St. Paul's Epistle to the Romans; where, of course, in the matter Luther and Calvin also found it:

> For the scripture saith unto Pharaoh, Even for this same purpose have I raised thee up, that I

---

[2]For the relevant teachings of Islam see my "The Terrors of Islam" in Paul Kurtz and Timothy J. Madigan, eds., *Challenges to the Enlightenment* (Buffalo, NY: Prometheus, 1996), pp. 272–83.
[3]Since September 11, 2001 it has become impossible to refrain from pointing out that the nature of this promised bliss is not such as to have much positive appeal to *l'homme moyen sensuel*.
[4]*Summa contra gentiles*, III, 88–89.

might shew my power in thee, and that my name might be declared throughout all the earth. Therefore hath he mercy upon whom he will have mercy, and whom he will he hardeneth. Thou wilt say then unto me, Why doth he yet find fault? For who hath resisted his will? Nay but, O man who art thou that repliest against God? Shall the thing formed say to him that formed it, Why hast thou made me thus? Hath not the potter power over the clay, of the same lump to make one vessel unto honour and another unto dishonour? What if God, willing to show his wrath, and to make his power known, endured with much long suffering the vessels of wrath fitted to destruction: and that he might make known the riches of his glory on the vessels of mercy, which had afore prepared unto glory, even us, whom he hath called, not of the Jews only but also of the Gentiles?[5]

Luther, to his credit, was appalled by the implications of this passage, and in *The Bondage of the Will* he did the best he could to meet the objections of Erasmus:

The highest degree of faith is to believe He is just, though of His own will he makes us . . . proper subjects for damnation, and seems (in the words of Erasmus) "to delight in the torments of poor wretches and to be a fitter object for hate than love." If I could by any means understand how this same God . . . can yet be merciful and just, there would be no need for faith.[6]

Later, Luther addresses himself to the question: "Why then does He not alter those evil wills which He moves?" Understandably, if unsatisfactorily, Erasmus receives no answer:

It is not for us to inquire into these mysteries, but to adore them. If flesh and blood take offense here and grumble, well, let them grumble; they will achieve nothing; grumbling will not change God! And however many of the ungodly stumble and depart, the elect will remain.[7]

But the Reformer, unlike the Angelic Doctor, was no so completely the complacent apparatchik as to proceed to a cool summary of the reasons why—very properly—"the blessed in glory will have no pity for the damned." The relevant passage of Aquinas reads:

In order that the happiness of the saints may be more delightful to them and that they may render more copious thanks to God first, they are allowed to see perfectly the sufferings of the damned . . . the Divine justice and their own deliverance will be the direct cause of the joy of the blessed, while the pains of the damned will cause it indirectly . . . the blessed in glory will have no pity for the damned.[8]

It is important to realize that when believers in Divine predestination—let us call such persons predestinarians—assert that God is the ultimate, fully determining cause of all human actions and refrainings from actions they are precisely not asserting, what is manifestly not true, that no one ever acts of their own freewill, as opposed to under some form and some degree of compulsion or constraint. When people accuse predestinarians of *denying* freewill they are unwittingly displaying a factitious misunderstanding of the ordinary nontechnical meaning of the word "freewill."

What should be meant when someone insists on a uniqueness of our species by asserting that God or Nature has endowed human beings with freewill is that we are all members of a kind of creatures who can and therefore cannot but make choices, some of which are made of the individuals' own freewill and some of which are made under one of many kinds and degrees of coercion or constraint.

The word "freewill" is formed in untechnical colloquial speech only as one term in such expressions "of his," or "of her" or "of their own freewill." But it was later given a use—I would like to discover when and where and by whom this was first done—as a word to refer to some putative characteristic possessed by all human beings the possession of which falsifies predesti-

[5]*Romans*, IX, 17–24.
[6]Martin Luther, *The Bondage of the Will*, in E. G. Rupp, A. N. Marlow, P. S. Watson, and B. Drewery, eds. and trans. *Luther and Erasmus: Freewill and Salvation* (Philadelphia, PA: Westminster, 1969), p. 139.
[7]*Ibid.*, p. 138.

[8]*Summa Theologica*, III Supp. xciv, 1–3. I confess, not very shamefully, that whenever I read this passage I am reminded of what a Sergeant in the Royal Air Force told me on my first day in that Service that the motto of the Royal Air Force was: "F——you, Jack; I'm fireproof!"

narianism. Actually to falsify predestinarianism it would of course be necessary not only to specify what this characteristic is supposed to be but also to demonstrate that it is in fact a characteristic of our species.

Finally, I would like to offer two hopefully helpful suggestions for those wanting to continue discussion on this area. The first is to recommend a very relevant paragraph in the great chapter of "Of Power" in Locke's *Essay Concerning Human Understanding*. In it Locke speaks of putting an end to that

> unreasonable, because unintelligible, Question, viz. *Whether Man's Will be free or no*. For if I mistake it not, it follows from what I have said, that the Question itself is altogether improper, and it is as insignificant to ask whether Man's Will be free, as to ask, whether his Sleep be Swift, or his Vertue square . . . and when anyone well considers it, I think he will as plainly perceive, that *Liberty* which is but a power, belongs only to Agents, and cannot be an attribute or modification of the Will, which is also *but a Power*.[9]

It is here relevant to point out also that that chapter includes extremely valuable suggestions for the elucidation of the closely related ideas of being an agent, of having a choice, and of being in the fundamental sense able to do otherwise than one does actually do.[10] This fundamental sense is that of course that in which it would have been true to say that Martin Luther could have done otherwise than he did, when he said: "Here I stand, I can no other, so help me God." (Had he really been struck with a sudden paralysis making him incapable of flight, his stance would have been no credit to him.)

My second hopefully helpful suggestion for continuing discussion in this area is that we should all take note of a distinction made by Hume in his essay "Of Natural Characters": "By *moral* causes, I mean all circumstances, which are fitted to work on the mind as motives or reasons. . . . By physical causes I mean those qualities of the air and climate, which are supposed to work insensibly on the temper, by altering the tone and habit of the body . . ."[11]

The absolutely fundamental difference between these two kinds of cause, two sense of the word "cause," is that whereas sufficient physical causes necessarily necessitate the occurrence of their effects, correspondingly sufficient moral causes do not. If, for instance, I convey to you some splendid news—news the reception of which, if you decided to celebrate, you and everyone else would point to as the cause of that celebration—then I do not by so doing ensure that you must, whether or not you want to, celebrate. Actions which are thus caused by moral causes are neither uncaused nor necessarily capricious and inexplicable, although, inasmuch as they are indeed actions, it is impossible for them to be physically necessitated. It is equally mistaken to assume—as most professing social scientists, apparently, do assume—that all environmental causes are, in the sense explained, physical and therefore physically necessitating, and therefore, because physically necessitating, excusing.

Corresponding to these two radically different senses of the word "cause" are two similarly different understandings of the term "determinism": what is determined by physical causes *must*, whereas what is determined by moral causes *cannot*, be physically necessitated. These two distinctions are essential for any adequate understanding of the fundamental and irreducible differences between natural and the human sciences, and for an appreciation of what is and is not implied by any discoveries which professors of the latter may claim to have made about the causes of marriage breakdown, war, juvenile or adult delinquency, or any of the other myriad ills to which the flesh is heir. If, having their reasons for acting, people act—whether creditably or discreditably, or neither—then it cannot have been physically impossible for them to have done other than they did. If this was not true of their behaviors, then those behaviors cannot have constituted instances of human action.

QUESTION FOR FURTHER REFLECTION

1. What does Flew think a "moral cause" is? How does this notion fit into what Flew has to say on the topic of free will?

---

[9] Paragraph 14 in Chapter XVI of Book II, in the standard Clarendon Press edition of P. H. Nidditch, p. 240 (emphasis and spelling original).

[10] For more on what can be learnt from this same great chapter see my "Second Thoughts about the First Enquiry" in *Philosophical Writings*, No. 10, Spring 1999.

[11] David Hume, *Essays Moral, Political, and Literary*, edited by Eugene F. Miller (Indianapolis, IN: Liberty, 1985), p. 120 (emphasis original).

23. IT IS WRONG TO BELIEVE WITHOUT EVIDENCE

William Clifford

William K. Clifford (1845–1879) was a mathematician and philosopher. As a student at Trinity College, Cambridge, he was a Catholic interested in the works of Thomas Aquinas. He later became an agnostic and turned against religion. Part of what changed his mind were his reflections on Charles Darwin's new theory of evolution. He developed a scientific theory of knowledge in which he saw knowledge as a biological response to the environment. Subsequently he took a rather extreme stand against faith. In the following selection, he argues that it is morally wrong for anyone, under any circumstances, to believe something without sufficient evidence.

READING QUESTIONS

1. What is Clifford's shipowner example?
2. What is his society of agitators example?
3. What are these examples supposed to show?
4. Where does Clifford think the sense of power comes in to play?
5. What harm does Clifford think the credulity of man brings about?

1. THE SHIPOWNER

A Shipowner was about to send to sea an emigrant-ship. He knew that she was old, and not over-well built at the first; that she had seen many seas and climes, and often had needed repairs. Doubts had been suggested to him that possibly she was not seaworthy. These doubts preyed upon his mind and made him unhappy; he thought that perhaps he ought have her thoroughly overhauled and refitted, even though this should put him to great expense. Before the ship sailed, however he succeeded in overcoming these melancholy reflections. He said to himself that she had gone safely through many voyages and weathered so many storms that it was idle to suppose she would not come safely home from this trip also. He would put his trust in Providence, which could hardly fail to protect all these unhappy families that were leaving their fatherland to seek for better times elsewhere. He would dismiss from his mind all ungenerous suspicions about the honesty of builders and contractors. In such ways he acquired a sincere and comfortable conviction that his vessel was thoroughly safe and seaworthy; he watched her departure with a light heart, and benevolent wishes for the success of the exiles in their strange new home that was to be; and he got his insurance money when she went down in mid-ocean and told no tales.

What shall we say of him? Surely this, that he was verily guilty of the death of those men. It is admitted that he did sincerely believe in the soundness of his ship; but the sincerity of his conviction can in no wise help him, because *he had no right to believe on such evidence as was before him.* He had acquired his belief not by honestly earning it in patient investigation, but by stifling his doubts. And although in the end he may have felt so sure about it that he could not think otherwise, yet inasmuch as he had knowingly and willingly worked himself into that frame of mind, he must be held responsible for it.

Let us alter the case a little, and suppose that the ship was not unsound after all; that she made her voyage safely, and many others after it. Will that diminish the guilt of her owner? Not one jot. When an action is once done, it is right or wrong for ever; no accidental failure of its good or evil fruits can possibly alter that. The man would not have been innocent, he would only have been not found out. The question of right or wrong has to do with the origin of his belief, not the matter of it; not what it was, but how he got it; not whether it turned out to be true or false, but whether he had a right to believe on such evidence as was before him. . . .

It may be said, however, that . . . it is not the belief which is judged to be wrong, but the action following upon it. The shipowner might say, "I am perfectly certain that my ship is sound, but still I feel it my duty to have her examined, before trusting the lives of so many people to her. . . ."

2. BELIEF AND ACTIONS

. . . [I]t is not possible so to sever the belief from the action it suggests as to condemn the one without condemning the other. . . . Nor is that truly a belief at all which has not some influence upon the actions of him who holds it. He who truly believes that which prompts him to an action has looked upon the action to lust after it, he has committed it already in his heart. If a belief is not realized immediately in open deeds, it is stored up for the guidance of the future. It goes to make a part of that aggregate of beliefs which is the link between sensation and action at every moment of all our lives, and which is so organized and compacted together that no part of it can be isolated from the rest, but every new addition modifies the structure of the whole. No real belief, however trifling and fragmentary it may seem, is ever truly insignificant; it prepares us to receive more of its like, confirms those which resembled it before, and weakens others; and so gradually it lays a stealthy train in our inmost thoughts, which may some day explode into overt action, and leave its stamp upon our character for ever.

And no one man's belief is in any case a private matter which concerns himself alone. Our lives are guided by general conception of the course of things which has been created by society for social purposes. Our words, our phrases, our forms and processes and modes of thought, are common property, fashioned and perfected from age to age; an heirloom which every succeeding generation inherits as a precious deposit and a sacred trust to be handed on to the next one, not unchanged but enlarged and purified, with some clear marks of its proper handiwork. Into this, for good or ill, is woven every belief of every man who has speech of his fellows. An awful privilege, and an awful responsibility, that we should help to create the world in which posterity will live.

3. ALL BELIEFS AND BELIEVERS

In the . . . case which [has] been considered, it has been judged wrong to believe on insufficient evidence, or to nourish belief by suppressing doubts and avoiding investigation. The reason of this judgment is not far to seek: it is that . . . the belief held by one man was of great importance to other men. But forasmuch as no belief held by one man, however seemingly trivial the belief, and however obscure the believer, is ever actually insignificant or without its effect on the fate of mankind, we have no choice but to extend our judgment to all cases of belief whatever. Belief, that sacred faculty which prompts the decisions of our will, and knits into harmonious working all the compacted energies of our being, is ours not for ourselves, but for humanity. It is rightly used on truths which have been established by long experience and waiting toil, and which have stood in the fierce light of free and fearless questioning. Then it helps to bind men together, and to strengthen and direct their common action. It is desecrated when given to unproved and unquestioned statements, for the solace and private pleasure of the believer; to add a tinsel splendour to the plain straight road of our life and display a bright mirage beyond it; or even to drown the common sorrows of our kind by a self-deception which allows them not only to cast down, but also to degrade us. Whoso would deserve well of his fellows in this matter will guard the purity of his belief with a very fanaticism of jealous care, lest at any time it should rest on an unworthy object, and catch a stain which can never be wiped away.

It is not only the leader of men, statesman, philosopher, or poet, that owes this bounden duty to mankind. Every rustic who delivers in the village alehouse his slow, infrequent sentences, may help to kill or keep alive the fatal superstitions which clog his race. Every hard-worked wife of an artisan may transmit to her children beliefs which shall knit society together, or rend it in pieces. No simplicity of mind, no obscurity of station, can escape the universal duty of questioning all that we believe.

It is true that this duty is a hard one, and the doubt which comes out of it is often a very bitter thing. It leaves us bare and powerless where we thought that we were safe and strong. To know all about anything is to know how to deal with it under all circumstances. We feel much happier and more secure when we think we know precisely what to do, no matter what happens, than when we have lost our way and do not know where to turn. And if we have supposed ourselves to know all about anything, and to be capable of doing what is fit in regard to it, we naturally do not like to find that we are really ignorant and powerless, that we have to begin again at the beginning, and try to learn what the thing is and how it is to be dealt with—if indeed anything can be learnt about it. It is the sense of power attached to a sense of knowledge that makes men desirous of believing, and afraid of doubting.

4. DUTY TO MANKIND

This sense of power is the highest and best of pleasures when the belief on which it is founded is a true belief, and has been fairly earned by investigation. For then we may justly feel that it is common property, and holds good for others as well as for ourselves. Then we may be glad, not that I have learned secrets by which I am safer and stronger, but that *we men* have got mastery over more of the world; and we shall be strong, not for ourselves, but in the name of Man and in his strength. But if the belief has been accepted on insufficient evidence, the pleasure is a stolen one. Not only does it deceive ourselves by giving us a sense of power which we do not really possess, but it is sinful, because it is stolen in defiance of our duty to mankind. That duty is to guard ourselves from such beliefs as from a pestilence, which may shortly master our own body and then spread to the rest of the town. What would be thought of one who, for the sake of a sweet fruit, should deliberately run the risk of bringing a plague upon his family and his neighbours?

And, as in other such cases, it is not the risk only which has to be considered; for a bad action is always bad at the time when it is done, no matter what happens afterwards. Every time we let ourselves believe for unworthy reasons, we weaken our powers of self-control, of doubting, of judicially and fairly weighing evidence. We all suffer severely enough from the maintenance and support of false beliefs and the fatally wrong actions which they lead to, and the evil born when one such belief is entertained is great and wide. But a greater and wider evil arises when the credulous character is maintained and supported, when a habit of believing for unworthy reasons is fostered and made permanent. If I steal money from any person, there may be no harm done by the mere transfer of possession; he may not feel the loss, or it may prevent him from using the money badly. But I cannot help doing this great wrong towards Man, that I make myself dis-

honest. What hurts society is not that it should lose its property, but that it should become a den of thieves; for then it must cease to be society. This is why we ought not to do evil that good may come; for at any rate this great evil has come, that we have done evil and are made wicked thereby. In like manner, if I let myself believe anything on insufficient evidence, there may be no great harm done by the mere belief; it may be true after all, or I may never have occasion to exhibit it in outward acts. But I cannot help doing this great wrong towards Man, that I make myself credulous. The danger to society is not merely that it should believe wrong things, though that is great enough; but that it should become credulous, and lose the habit of testing things and inquiring into them; for then it must sink back into savagery.

The harm which is done by credulity in a man is not confined to the fostering of a credulous character in others, and consequent support of false beliefs. Habitual want of care about what I believe leads to habitual want of care in others about the truth of what is told to me. Men speak the truth to one another when each reveres the truth in his own mind and in the other's mind; but how shall my friend revere the truth in my mind when I myself am careless about it, when I believe things because I want to believe them, and because they are comforting and pleasant? Will he not learn to cry, "Peace," to me, when there is no peace? By such a course I shall surround myself with a thick atmosphere of falsehood and fraud, and in that I must live. It may matter little to me, in my cloud-castle of sweet illusions and darling lies; but it matters much to Man that I have made my neighbours ready to deceive. The credulous man is father to the liar and the cheat; he lives in the bosom of this his family, and it is no marvel if he should become even as they are. So closely are our duties knit together, that whoso shall keep the whole law, and yet offend in one point, he is guilty of all.

5. THE ETHICS OF BELIEF

To sum up: it is wrong always, everywhere, and for any one, to believe anything upon insufficient evidence.

If a man, holding a belief which he was taught in childhood or persuaded of afterwards, keeps down and pushes away any doubts which arise about it in his mind, purposely avoids the reading of books and the company of men that call in question or discuss it, and regards as impious those questions which cannot easily be asked without disturbing it—the life of that man is one long sin against mankind. . . .

Inquiry into the evidence of a doctrine is not to be made once for all, and then taken as finally settled. It is never lawful to stifle a doubt; for either it can be honestly answered by means of the inquiry already made, or else it proves that the inquiry was not complete.

"But," says one, "I am a busy man; I have no time for the long course of study which would be necessary to make me in any degree a competent judge of certain questions, or even able to understand the nature of the arguments." Then he should have no time to believe.

QUESTIONS FOR FURTHER REFLECTION

1. Can you think of any *noncontroversial* examples in which it is not immoral to believe without evidence?
2. Do you agree with Clifford that the characters in the shipowner example and his society of agitators example were wrong to have believed as they did?
3. If we held strictly to Clifford's standards of appropriate belief, would we end up excluding important beliefs that we all agree we know?

24. WHAT SHOULD WE EXPECT FROM THEISTIC PROOFS?

George I. Mavrodes

A short biography of George Mavrodes appears on page 7. In this selection, he argues that philosophers of religion, whether theist or atheist, have placed too much emphasis on proofs. Proofs, he says, must be taken off of their pedestal and put in their rightful place. They are simply epistemic tools designed to extend our knowledge. We should not expect them to change the mind of a convinced atheist.

READING QUESTIONS

1. Mavrodes lists four possible ways that having and giving could be related. He gives an example where options (a) and (d) only seem to apply; what is that example? What examples does he give where options (b) and (c) seem possibile?
2. Mavrodes distinguishes between three types of proof. What are the three types of proof and with which type is his discussion mainly concerned?
3. Briefly lay out Mavrodes sample argument for the existence of God.
4. Does Mavrodes intend his sample argument to be convincing? If not, why does he lay out the argument?
5. Why does Mavrodes think that neither Hume nor Kant nor any other philosopher has shown that there are no sound arguments for God's existence unless they have shown his sample argument to be unsound?

In a previous section I said that knowing may require having a reason. There is some temptation to convert this statement into the requirement that one should give—or perhaps be able to give—a reason. But it is not at all clear that "having a reason" must mean "being able to give a reason" and it might be wise not to commit ourselves too early to some rigid connection between the two.

HAVING AND GIVING

Suppose that someone asks us whether we *have* a reason for some particular belief and also whether we can *give* a reason for that belief. Abstractly, there seem to be four possibilities:

(a) We have reasons and we can give reasons.
(b) We have reasons but we cannot give any.
(c) We have no reasons but we can give some.
(d) We have no reasons and we cannot give any.

At first sight (a) and (d) may seem to be the only genuine possibilities, with (b) and (c) being absurd. If we have reasons, it might be asked, why should it not be possible to give them? And perhaps (c) is even worse than (b) for how can we give something that we do not have? But if (a) and (d) are the only real possibilities, then it will be the case that we can *give* a reason whenever we *have* a reason and vice versa. If this view were correct, then no harm would be done if we insisted that knowing requires being able to give a reason as well as having a reason.

In spite of the apparent plausibility of this line of reasoning, we may be too hasty in accepting it. Its credibility is derived from the relation between having and giving in certain common cases but it overlooks the quite different relations that can arise between them in other cases.

If I have an apple then I can give an apple to a friend and if I have no apple then I cannot give one to a friend. For apples, then, the analogues of (a) and (d) seem to be the real possibilities and the analogues of (b) and (c) are absurd or impossible. But is having a reason and giving a reason like having an apple and giving an apple? Notice that if I have just one apple and I give that apple to a friend, then I will have no apple at all. Suppose that I have just one reason for my belief and I give that reason to a friend, will it follow that I will then have no reason at all for my belief? If not, then reasons are not exactly like apples, so far as having them and giving them are concerned.

Once we notice that the relations between having and giving are not exactly the same for reasons as for apples, we will be able to think of many other cases in which these relations are widely different. It certainly seems possible, for example, for a person to have a good reputation without his being able to give someone else a good reputation. The same thing also seems to be true of having a headache, a flair for music, and a premonition of disaster. No doubt we could extend this list substantially if we wished. For things of this sort, the analogue of possibility (b) is not absurd but rather very likely to be true. All of these are things that a person could have without being able to give them. Certainly having a reason is not exactly like having a headache or a good reputation, but we have already seen that neither is it like having an apple. We should therefore not be too quick to assume that it is impossible to have a reason without being able to give one.

There seem also to be some things for which the analogue of (c) is true. I may, for example, succeed in giving someone an incentive to study even if I myself have no incentive to study. And I may also be able to give someone a headache or a deep sense of insecurity without having these things myself. So not even (c) is intrinsically absurd as a statement about the possible relations between having and giving.

In the case of reasons, then, it is unwise to assume that the relations between having and giving are just those represented by (a) and (d). In fact, it is equally unwise to assume that the relations between having and giving must be the same for all reasons. Some reasons, after all, may be quite different from others; and therefore the relations between having and giving may also differ. A resolution of these uncertainties probably requires a more detailed analysis of the structure of specific types of reasons. A study of the reasons involved in argument and experience is presented in Chapters II and III.

GIVING "MY" REASON

Suppose it is true that knowing requires having a reason. Suppose also that I know a certain proposition *p*. It thus follows that I must *have* at least one reason for believing *p*. Suppose also that I am able to *give* a reason for *p*. In this case, possibility (a) is fulfilled. Does it follow that the reason which I am able to give is identical with the reason that I have? In the case of apples, of course, what I give will be identical with something that I had before the giving. But I may have a headache or an incentive to study and I may give someone else a headache or an incentive without those headaches or incentives being identical (either numerically or qualitatively). So even for cases in which (a) is fulfilled, it seems rash to assume that the reasons involved must be identical.

A person who receives a challenge of this sort and who really does know the proposition involved may attempt to give *his* reason. That is, he will attempt to give the reason that is related to his own belief in whatever way is required to qualify his belief as knowledge. But perhaps this way of responding to the challenge will fail in one way or other. It may be that the person has a reason that cannot by its very nature be given to another. Or though it is possible to give the reason, the person may be unsuccessful in doing so. Or it may be that he actually does give his reason but fails to convince the questioner. In any of these cases the response—regardless of what other virtues it may have—fails to be effective in meeting the challenge that is posed.

We have already recognized, however, that it may sometimes be possible for one to give a reason that is not *his* reason—in the sense that it does not bear the required relation to his own belief. If this is correct, then it may also be the case that in some circumstances giving that reason would be a more effective response to the challenge than giving one's own reason. Furthermore, this reason may have all of the other virtues that one's own reason possesses. In such a case, it would be unfortunate and unnecessary if one were to restrict his responses to his own reasons, instead of availing himself of this wider range of possible responses.

GIVING AND RECEIVING

Two last questions should be raised here. If I give someone a reason for believing *p*, does it follow that he then has a reason for believing *p*? And if he does have a reason after I give him one—though he had none before—does it follow that the reason that he now has is identical with the reason that I gave him? Or may it be quite different?

Regarding the first question, we may notice that some people apparently believe that one can sometimes give a reason (perhaps one's own reason) by talking. It is possible, however, for a person to talk and for everything that he says to be true and relevant, without his being believed by his hearers. Suppose, then, that I believe *p* and that there is some reason for *p* that I can give by talking. And suppose that I speak to someone who does not believe *p* and who has no reason to believe *p* and I give him this reason. Then suppose that he does not believe what I say when I give him that reason. It is hard to see in what sense that person has any more reason to believe *p* than he had before, merely because he has heard something else that he does not believe.

With respect to the second question, we might consider the following case. I see an auto accident at the corner of State and Liberty streets, and consequently I believe that there has been an accident there. I express this belief to someone who has no reason to believe that there has been such an accident, and he asks how I know, or what my reason is. Apparently, some people believe that I can give my reason by saying "I saw it myself." At any rate, it certainly seems to be the case that by saying this I report or tell him what my reason is. Perhaps my hearer believes me to be a careful observer and a man of good character and so perhaps he comes to have a reason for believing that there was such an accident. But it is clear that the reason that he has is not identical or even very similar to my reason. For his reason seems to involve my report or testimony in a way in which mine does not (notice that whether I am of good character is relevant to *his* having a good reason but not to *my* having a good reason).

People who have an epistemological interest in the philosophy of religion often express that interest in the form of a demand for some *proof*—usually of God's existence. Consequently, there have been a large number of attempts to satisfy that demand, along with a similar number of criticisms of such attempts. A disproportionately large part of the philosophy of religion has thus centered around the problem of proof.

This chapter will discuss the possibility of proving God's existence, the conditions that must be fulfilled for this to be done successfully, and the results that we could reasonably expect from such attempts. The discussion, however, is subject to an important restriction. Since it would be tiresome to repeat the restriction continuously, hopefully it can be made clear here. This chapter will be limited to a consideration of one specific method of proof but it is one that has loomed very large in the history of both philosophy and theology.

Proofs of this sort may be called *discursive*, since the proof consists of an argument, presented entirely by talking or writing. Ordinary English usage, of course, recognizes other senses of the verb "to prove." A boy scout proves that he knows how to tie knots by actually tying them for the scoutmaster rather than by talking to him and, as mentioned before, the attorney proves his point in court partly by argument but also partly by exhibiting photographs, weapons, and other evidence. A consideration of the theological analogues of these latter types of proof will be left to the discussion of the experience of God in Chapter III. Here we will consider only those proofs that are given *entirely* in the form of argument. Furthermore, the discussion will be restricted to considering deductive, rather than inductive, arguments. But I believe that the substantive points made will apply equally well to inductive attempts. It will not be necessary, however, to repeat continuously the qualifying adjectives discursive and deductive.

1. THREE PRELIMINARY QUESTIONS

What Is It Worth?

The first of these three questions is: If it is possible to prove God's existence, would it be worth doing so? We should not be too hasty in giving an affirmative answer to this question. After all, the mere fact that something is possible is not by itself a reason for thinking that it is worthwhile. To commit yourself to doing everything that is possible is almost surely to guarantee that you will do very little that is valuable. Suppose then that I could prove the existence of God and it would take me a year to do it. Would it be worth a year's time? A year's salary? Why? Or why not?

One might reply that God is very important and, therefore, doing anything that is related to Him is very important and worthwhile. I agree that God is very important (although I will not argue for it here), but the argument based on that assumption seems fallacious. The project of proving the existence of God will not inherit any of the importance of God merely by bearing *any* relation to Him; it must be related to Him in an important or worthwhile way. Is it?

Again someone might reply that it would be very worthwhile to know that God exists, and if one *proves* that God exists then people will *know* that God exists.

Such a proof, therefore, would be valuable. This is an interesting suggestion and we will come back to it a later in section.

What If We Fail?

The second question is: If it should happen that God's existence cannot be proved would that be any cause for regret or disappointment? Again we ought not to rush into an affirmative answer. The mere fact that something cannot be done does not seem to be a just cause for regret. I cannot recall, for example, ever feeling any sorrow over the fact that it is not possible to trisect an angle by Euclidian means. Of course, if someone has committed himself to this project he may be disappointed to discover that he cannot succeed, but this seems to be more closely related to his special ambition than to the significance of the project itself. Is there some significance in the project of proving God's existence that would make its impossibility disturbing?

Earlier the following proposition was suggested:

(a) If one proved the existence of God, then people would know that God exists.

We have not yet examined (a) very carefully but it seems to have some plausibility and many people would probably accept it. They might also be inclined to derive from it another proposition:

(b) If one does not prove that God exists, then people would not know that God exists.

Now, if (b) were true it would be an important consequence of failing to prove God's existence, and such a failure might well be a cause of regret. Unfortunately, however, (b) does not follow from (a) and so (a), even if it should be true and we should accept it, does not provide us with a reason for accepting (b).[1]

Of course, if we had some other reason for believing (b), it might still be acceptable and would

---

[1]Consider for example,

(a′) If he jumps he will be injured. from this it does *not* follow that (b′) If he does not jump he will not be injured. For he may well be injured whether or not he jumps. Similarly, nothing in (a) precludes the possibility that there may be other ways of knowing about God. Thus (a) does not entail (b).

support the view that a failure to prove God's existence would be significant and perhaps regrettable. In fact, even the weaker

(b″) If one did not prove God's existence then people *probably* would not know that He exists.

would support the view. Are there reasons to believe either (b) or (b″) or any similar proposition? Or is there any other kind of significance that can be attributed to a failure in proving God's existence? We will come back to this as well.

Must We Know It?

The third question is: Is it possible that someone has proved the existence of God without anyone (even the man who did the proving) knowing that he had done so? Perhaps this question seems absurd. But it might again be best to hesitate a moment before committing ourselves to a negative answer. There are certainly some cases in which it is possible for a person to do something without either his or anyone else's knowing that he has done it. For example, it is possible for a hunter to shoot the largest elephant in Africa without him or anyone else knowing that he has done so. Such an incident might occur because it is possible for an animal to *be* the largest elephant in Africa without anyone knowing it. But is it also possible for something to be a proof of God's existence without anyone knowing that it is? Is it possible for someone to construct such proof (perhaps playfully or by accident) without knowing it himself? If this is not possible, what is it about a proof that renders such an event impossible?

If, on the other hand, we suppose that it is possible to construct such a proof without anyone's knowing it, then we are brought back to something like the first question: What would be the significance or importance of that event? Are we inclined to say that it would have none? But many events can be important even if no one knows they have occurred. If the cook inadvertently poisons the banquet, this is likely to be important, even if neither he nor anyone else knows that it has been done. (In fact, the guests may die from the effects of the poison without knowing the cause of their misfortune and without anyone else knowing it either.) Constructing a proof may, of course, be much

different from poisoning a dinner. But just what is the important difference that is relevant to this question?

Recognizing a Proof

To know (or perhaps to stipulate) answers to these three questions is also to know (or to stipulate) a good deal about what a proof is. The remainder of this chapter is largely a discussion of just this topic. At this point, however, we should take note of an important distinction. Knowing what a proof is may not be quite the same thing as being in a position to recognize a proof, although it may help in such a recognition. For example, I know (in the theoretical sense) what it is to be the oldest man now living in the United States but I am not in a position to recognize reliably such a man. Consequently, I can *understand* the claim that a certain Sioux Indian of North Dakota is the oldest man now living in the United States without being in a position to know whether that claim is *true*. It might, therefore, be possible for a person to know what a proof is while he is unable to determine whether a certain attempt is, in fact, a proof.

2. A SIMPLE ARGUMENT FOR THE EXISTENCE OF GOD

The Argument Stated

Consider the following argument:

I (1a) Either nothing exists or God exists.
   (1b) Something exists.
   (1c) Therefore, God exists.

First, it may be wise to recall that this is not a *proof* of God's existence (that topic is discussed in the following section), but rather an *argument* for the existence of God. It is called an argument for the *existence of God* since "God exists" is its conclusion. In general, an argument will be an argument for *p* if and only if its conclusion is *p*.

The second premise is to be understood in the most prosaic possible sense—that which is entailed by propositions such as "I exist" and "A few eighteenth-century clocks still exist." The first premise is to be understood in its weakest possible sense. The "either . . . or . . ." that occurs in it is to be taken as an inclusive, truth-functional disjunction. That is, the entire statement should be taken to assert merely that one or both of its constituent disjuncts is true, and nothing more. In particular, it should not be taken to assert (or deny) that there is any logical or causal relation between the disjuncts or between the facts or entities to which they refer. It expresses a truth relation only and is noncommittal with respect to other relations. Therefore, it contains *less* information than we might sometimes want to have.[2]

We will now consider three of the most important sorts of criticism that might be urged against this argument. Some other possible criticisms are discussed in succeeding sections.

Is It Valid?

Rather surprisingly, some professional philosophers, on first hearing this argument, have declared it invalid. (Perhaps they were accustomed to hearing invalid arguments for the existence of God.) Its form, however (a disjunctive syllogism), is such that it is logically impossible for the conclusion to be false if the premises are true. If we adopt this usual definition of *validity* (as I will do), then we must accept this argument as valid.

Is It Sound?

Let us follow some logicians in defining a *sound* argument as one that is valid and whose premises are all true. A consequence of this definition, when it is combined with that for validity, is that all sound arguments have true conclusions. Furthermore, the soundness of the argument involved may well be at least a necessary condition for a satisfactory proof.

Since we have already seen that argument (I) is valid, the question of its soundness becomes simply a question about the truth of its premises. The second premise (1b), however, seems obvious. At any rate, if anyone doubts it I will not undertake to convince him of its truth. Such a person, however, may still be able to

construct for himself an analogue of this argument which will have the same important features. If he knows *any* true proposition, let him substitute it for (1b), and let him substitute its denial for the first disjunct in (1a). The resulting argument will function in the same way as mine.

This brings us to (1a). Is it true? I believe that it is, but I will not argue this point here. Instead, note that (1a) is logically entailed by the proposition "God exists" (which is identical with the conclusion). Consequently, (1a) is true if God exists, and false only if there is no God. This fact has at least three consequences.

First, a person who criticizes this argument as unsound and who also wishes to be consistent must either deny its validity or else deny the truth of (1b)—both of which are implausible and unlikely moves—or else he must adopt an explicitly atheistic position. Agnosticism is not enough for it leaves open the possibility of God's existence and thus provides no basis for the charge of unsoundness here. This is one example of the general truth that criticizing an argument—just like defending one—costs something. It requires some positive commitment on the part of the critic; and, in general, the stronger the criticism the stronger (and riskier) must be that commitment. What has been constructed here is an argument that cannot be strongly rejected (declared unsound) except by a person who is willing to risk a strong and positive stand on the metaphysical and theological question of God.

Incidentally, the commitment required here has an interesting corollary. Some people profess to believe that one should always be ready to defend or prove every statement that he makes. I do not hold this principle, for reasons which may become clearer later on. Those who do hold this principle, however, might be expected to apply it to themselves. Therefore, if any of them are inclined to call this argument unsound they should be prepared not only to adopt but also to prove the atheist position.

The second major consequence related to this corollary is that neither Hume nor Kant nor any other philosopher can have shown or proved that there are no sound arguments for God's existence unless he has also proved that there is no God. So far as I know, neither Hume nor Kant even claimed to prove the latter proposition. It is often claimed, however, that in some way one or both of them dealt the-

[2]Some readers may find it easier to follow an equivalent account of statements of this form. When the "or" is taken in the inclusive, truth-functional sense, then an expression of the form "*p* or *q*" is totally equivalent to the longer expression: "The following is a list of propositions, at least one of which is true: (1) *p*, (2) *q*." If anyone prefers this longer form of expression, he may replace (1a) with the corresponding expression of the longer form.

istic argumentation a fatal blow. If that is so, then they must have done it in some way other than by showing there are no sound arguments for God's existence. But it is far from clear what such an alternative might be.

The third consequence is simply that unless argument (I) is sound, no argument for God's existence is sound. There are, no doubt, many arguments for His existence that are far more sophisticated than this one, and some of them may have virtues that this lacks. But none of them can be sound if this one is not. For, as we noted earlier, no argument for God's existence can be sound unless God exists. And if God exists then my argument is sound.

Can (1a) Be Proved?

Now that we have discussed those criticisms that focus upon the logic of my argument or upon the truth of its premises, let us turn to a somewhat different sort of criticism that will direct our attention toward the defects that this argument may really have. In a preliminary way this criticism charges that (1a), though possibly true, has not been *proved* to be true.

If we restrict the range of this charge to what has been proved in this book, the charge is certainly true. I have not even attempted to prove (1a), let alone succeeded in that task. But though the charge is true, the proper initial response to it is, "So what?" This question must not be misunderstood. It has an important answer and that is the very reason why it should be asked.

We might note as a beginning that (1b) has not been proved either; and, in fact, I specifically declined that task. But hardly anyone is likely to charge that not proving the second premise is a defect in the argument. Why not? Premise (1b) is, after all, just as essential to my argument as (1a). Is it because most people already know (1b)? I suspect that it is. But perhaps some people already know (1a) too. (After all, I claim to know it myself.) But the objector may continue to argue that he does not know it. I am prepared to accept that claim as true also but again I want to ask, "So what? How does the fact that he does not know my premise to be true make my argument defective?" The only plausible reply that comes to mind is that this fact will make my

argument useless or ineffective for that objector. This may be true and, if so, it identifies an important defect, provided that the argument is intended to convince that objector.

Can One Prove All His Premises?

Before leaving this general objection, perhaps we ought to explore another variant. Someone may claim, in principle, that any argument for p is defective unless all of its premises are proved. (We might call this the "proved-premise" principle.) And since argument (I) does not conform to this principle it is defective. But how shall we understand the term "proved" which occurs in this principle? Suppose, for the moment, that we understand it as requiring merely the construction of some other sound arguments that have these premises as conclusions.

At this point a further question arises. It is quite possible to construct a series of sound arguments such that the first one has a premise p and a conclusion q, the second one has q for a premise and r for a conclusion, and so on until there is one that has z for a premise and p for its conclusion. We might call this circular chain of argumentation. Supposing that all the arguments in this circle are sound, would the construction of such a circle satisfy the proved-premise principle? If the answer is affirmative, then whatever defect my argument may have along this line can be easily remedied. For (1c) directly entails both (1a) and (1b). The circle can therefore be closed by the construction of a single additional argument embodying this entailment. If anyone believes that there is any benefit to be gained from such a circle, he is free to construct it.

Suppose, however, that such circular chains are rejected as satisfying the proved-premise principle. In that case it will not be possible to satisfy that principle for my argument. But this will not be a special defect of my argument for there will be no argument whatever, theological or otherwise, for which that principle can be satisfied. The reason that no argument could satisfy this requirement is that the proved-premise principle (if circular chains are rejected) demands the construction of an infinite series of arguments, each one of which embodies a proof of the premises of the succeeding argument. But since neither I nor any other philosopher can construct an infinite series of arguments, no argument will satisfy this principle.

Proving Some Premises

The proved-premise principle, which is a universal generalization (and, as we have seen, a self-stultifying or illegitimate one), must not be confused with the demand *in some particular case* for a proof of a certain premise. This latter sort of demand arises in many discussions and need not be stultifying or illegitimate. It will be legitimate if some termination rule for such demands is at least implicitly recognized by the discussants. Such a rule may be formulated something like this: The series of challenges and replies will end when a proof is obtained whose soundness is know to the participants in the discussion. When people use the processes of argument and proof for the sake of extending their own or someone else's knowledge of some subject matter, rather than as mere logical exercises or as demonstrations of technical virtuosity, then they do not demand proofs of what they already know to be true. Under such circumstances the construction of regressive proofs can have a goal that is logically possible to reach and to recognize when it is reached. A man who undertakes the task of supporting a certain argument under this rule can have some hope of completing his task successfully. But if there is no willingness to recognize such a rule, then the task is logically impossible.

The termination rule that has been formulated here contains within it a reference to a certain set of persons—the participants in the discussion. Although this set varies from one discussion to another, for any one application of the rule it identifies certain people whose knowledge is relevant and others whose knowledge is not. Because the set of people involved varies from one application to another, the rule does not determine a fixed termination point for any argument. At most it determines a termination point for a certain argument relative to a certain group of people who are considering it. For another group the termination point may be quite different and may be reached much more easily or with much greater difficulty. This variation is due to the fact that different people bring quite different ranges of initial knowledge with them to the consideration of any question.

Even given that the argument under discussion is in fact sound, the rule does not tell us how to construct a satisfactory support for it. The participants in the discussion know that they will have to find premises that all of them know to be true and a form of argument that they all know to be valid. But the fulfilling of these requirements depends entirely on their own perseverance and ingenuity, which, like initial knowledge, varies from group to group. Consequently, the rule provides no guarantee that, even when the argument under consideration is in fact sound, any particular group will be able to reach the termination point that will convince all the participants. Any teacher presenting an introductory course in geometry faces this problem and very few of them surmount it with respect to the entire class. It is also important to realize that in an undertaking of this sort the successes and failures are independent of each other.

3. WHAT IS A PROOF?

In the preceding section a special point was made of not calling my argument a proof, though I believe it to be both valid and sound. In discussing the last objection, however, it was tentatively suggested that we might construe "proof" merely in terms of sound argument. We must now examine this question directly.

Logic, Truth, and Proof

Many people seem to think that the notion of proof can be defined satisfactorily purely in terms of logic and truth. But there does not seem to be any more stringent logical requirement than that of validity. Nor is there any more stringent truth requirement than the one included in the notion of soundness. Every sound argument, then, involves the strongest logical tie between its premises and its conclusion (the logical impossibility of the conclusion's being false if the premises are true) and the truth of all the statements involved in it. If proof can be characterized purely in terms of truth and logic, then it seems that a sound argument must be a proof of its conclusion.

If this is so, however, then either my argument is a proof of God's existence or else there is no God and there cannot be a proof of His existence. If we are satisfied with a notion of proof given entirely in terms of truth and logic, than we need search no further for a proof of God's existence.

How to "Prove" Everything

This notion of proof has, however, some peculiar consequences. One of them is that it is extremely easy to prove every true proposition. In fact, we can give a general procedure (there will be, of course, indefinitely many general procedures) for constructing proofs and teach it to any reasonably bright fifth-grade child. He will then be as adept at proving as will any expert in the field.

One such simple general procedure, involving the same pattern as my simple argument, is this: To prove any true proposition q choose some other true proposition p and use it as the second premise. For the first premise construct the proposition *not-p or q*. These two premises will both be true and will validly entail q.

It looks as though proof, if it is construed purely in terms of logic and truth, is a project hardly requiring the training of a philosopher, scientist, or theologian.

Proof Without Knowledge

A second peculiar consequence of construing proof in this way is that it will be possible—and indeed easy—to prove something without knowing anything about it either before or after the proof, and without helping anyone else to know anything about it either. For example, suppose that a person is provided with a list of propositions, of which some are true and the others false. (In order to guarantee that some are true and some are false we might make half of them the contradictories of the other half. Anyone can, of course, make up such a list for himself.) Suppose also that he knows nothing about the subject matter involved and has no idea which ones are true. He can nevertheless easily construct an argument of the form described above for each one of these propositions. Some of these arguments—those with the false conclusions—will be unsound (their first premise will be false). But the others will be perfectly sound. According to this interpretation of what a proof is, he will have proved all of the true propositions on his list. It is clear, however, that such a proof neither represents nor contributes to any knowledge of his own and it is quite possible that it contributes to no one else's knowledge either.

If we were to accept this characterization of a proof purely in terms of logic and truth, then the answers to the three questions introduced in Section (1) seem quite straightforward. Taking them in reverse order, it is clear that if a proof of a given proposition is possible at all then it is also possible without knowledge, as an accident, or in jest. If a proof is not possible, however, this can be only because the proposition involved is not true. That is, we would fail to prove the existence of God only if He did not exist. The metaphysical fact that He did not exist might, of course, be a cause of disappointment; but there would seem to be no reason for any further lament over our inability to prove His existence.

On the other hand, it is clear that we could construct proofs without doing ourselves or anyone else any cognitive good. Although we might, perhaps, think of some other noncognitive benefit that a proof of this sort might confer, the construction of arguments that do nothing more than satisfy the requirements of logic and truth, while easy, seems hardly worth the time.

4. COGENT AND CONVINCING ARGUMENTS

The consequences discussed in the preceding section seem entirely paradoxical when compared with more ordinary notions of what a proof is and what it achieves. Perhaps the most prominent feature of these notions is the conviction that the discovery or construction of a proof represents some genuine cognitive advance—an epistemic achievement, an event which is internally and necessarily related to some knowledge-gaining project. This section proposes and discusses two attempts at embodying this cognitive feature in a definition. The second one is successful.

Cogency

Let us introduce a new technical term, analogous to "sound," to be used in the discussion of arguments. Let us say that an argument is *cogent for a certain person N* if and only if (1) It is sound, and (2) N knows it to be sound.[3]

The reference to soundness in this definition is sufficiently clear but we should say something here

---

[3]Strictly speaking, the first clause of this definiens is redundant (given our use of "to know").

about the introduction of a new element—the references to some particular person N. These references relativize the concept being defined in a way that is crucial for everything else that will be said about proving. The technical term that is introduced here is not "cogent" but "cogent for a certain person N." The references to N reflect the fact that "being known to be true" is a person-related and person-variable property of certain statements in just the way that "being a father" is a person-related and person-variable property of some people. No one is a father unless he is the father *of* somebody, and no statement is known to be true unless it is known *by* someone. The fact that a man is the father of someone does not imply that he is the father of everyone, and the fact that the statement is known to someone does not imply that it is known to everyone. Finally, being a father may give a man a certain legitimate authority in the lives of those whose father he is without giving him that authority in everyone's life, and, similarly, being known may give a statement a legitimate effectiveness in the intellectual lives of those to whom it is known without giving it such an effectiveness for those who do not know it.

If knowledge is going to be introduced into the requirements for proving a conclusion, then it seems clear that the proof-generating force of the argument in question must be limited to the persons who are in possession of the requisite knowledge. Imagine, for example, a murder trial that consists of nothing more than the following pair of arguments, presented respectively by the prosecution and the defense.

II (2a) Either the accused did not commit the crime or he should be convicted.
  (2b) The accused committed the crime.
  (2c) Therefore, the accused should be convicted.
III (3a) Either the accused did commit the crime or he should be acquitted.
  (3b) The accused did not commit the crime.
  (3c) Therefore, the accused should be acquitted.

As before, one of these arguments must be sound. In addition, however, of the premises labeled (2b) and (3b) the true one is very likely to be known to be true, by the accused at least, and perhaps also by many other people. But it may not be known to the members of the jury. In that case, regardless of whether one of these arguments proves its conclusion to somebody, it could

not prove it to the jury. Neither argument extends the jury's knowledge as neither argument gives jurors any grounds upon which to base their verdict.

This example calls to our attention the relevance of the question "*To whom* did you prove it?" as a response to a claim to have proved a certain statement. The proving of a statement is supposed to be an epistemically significant event. But there is no epistemic significance *in vacuo*; some person must be involved. Who it is that is involved may be a crucial consideration for the epistemic significance often varies from person to person. Any satisfactory account of what it means to prove something must make a place for this crucial consideration. My account makes a place for it at this point.

This is not to say, however, that we now have a satisfactory account of what it is to prove a statement to someone. For even a cogent argument may not always suffice to prove its conclusion, even to those for whom it is cogent. As an illustration consider the following argument:

IV (4a) Either Jupiter has no satellite or President Nixon is a Republican.
  (4b) Jupiter has a satellite.
  (4c) Therefore, President Nixon is a Republican.

Most of us know this argument to be valid and its premises to be true. It is therefore cogent for us. Does it also prove to us that Mr. Nixon is a Republican?

The crucial point to be considered here is not that we already knew Mr. Nixon to be a Republican before we heard this argument. It is rather that, at least for most of us, our knowledge of the truth of the first premise rests on our knowledge of the truth of the conclusion. We accept (4a) as a true premise only because we know (4c) and we can infer (4a) from (4c). Most of us do not have an independent way of knowing (4a) to be true (though, as we shall see later, it is not impossible that we should have such a way).

It seems implausible and unprofitable to speak of an argument's proving its conclusion to someone who must derive his knowledge of the truth of its premises from his prior knowledge of the truth of its conclusion. For such an argument neither enables him to know a conclusion that he did not know before, nor does it provide him with any new grounds for a piece of knowledge that he may already have had. We can therefore conclude that cogent arguments are not always sufficient to prove their conclusions, even to those for whom they are cogent.

Convincingness

Let us say that an argument is *convincing for N* if and only if (1) it is cogent for N, and (2) N knows that each of its premises is true without having to infer any of them from its conclusion or from any other statement or statements that he knows only by an inference from that conclusion.

This definition does not preclude convincing arguments for conclusions that are already known, but it does require that the person for whom the argument is to be convincing should know its premises to be true without having to infer them from its conclusion. Such an argument will provide new or additional grounds for his knowledge of a statement that he may have already known on other grounds.

We have now defined a type of argument that is sufficiently strong, in an epistemic sense, for it to bear the weight of a definition of "proving." We will have proved a statement to N if and only if we succeed in presenting N with an argument that is convincing for him. (N may, of course, be identical with the person who constructs the argument. We might, that is, extend our own knowledge by means of a proof.) For if we do this we will have taken something that N already knows and will have shown him how to derive some further consequence from it. N will then have just as good grounds for this further consequence as he has for his original knowledge. It seems plausible that providing grounds of this sort for a new cognitive item represents an epistemic or cognitive advance. . . .

6. LIMITATIONS AND EXPECTATIONS

This section discusses some of the consequences that can be drawn from the considerations advanced in the previous section and explores a little further the questions of what we might expect and what we might look for in theological proofs.

Could a Person Learn All He Knows from Proofs?

A prominent requirement for a proof is that the person for whom the proof is to be effective should already know something relevant. Argumentation then,

as a method of proof, is not a substitute for knowledge any more than a hammer is a substitute for lumber or a needle is a substitute for cloth. Like these other tools, the techniques of valid argument are useful only if we are already in possession of something else besides these tools. If we also have lumber, a hammer may be useful in constructing a house but without lumber it is useless. Similarly, if we already have some knowledge, an argument may help us to know something further but if we know nothing to begin with then argument cannot help us. It follows that no one could gain all of his knowledge by means of argument and proof; and from this it follows that if anyone knows anything at all, there must be some means of gaining knowledge other than by proof.

Once we realize this, we will be in a position to take a more realistic attitude toward the significance of proofs for religion and theology. Since there must be some other way of achieving knowledge in general, it is possible that there may be some other way of achieving theological knowledge. Therefore, we need not consider the question of proof as crucial in the theological case unless we discover some special reason for doing so. On the other hand, since proof is one possible method of achieving knowledge in general, it may be one method of achieving theological knowledge. So the question of proof need not be entirely unimportant either.

Is There Something that Cannot Be Proved to Anyone?

There are, no doubt, many true propositions that have never been proved to anyone. There are probably also some propositions that are known to someone, or even widely known, that have never been proved to anyone. But is there some true proposition that by its very nature could not be proved to anyone? This question is not very easy to answer. Since, however, someone might think that a proposition about God's existence might be one of the unprovable ones the question should perhaps be discussed.

If a proposition, though true, is in principle unknowable, it will also be unprovable. I know of no reason to suppose that the truth about God's existence is in principle unknowable. But if someone supposes that it is, then he will also believe it to be unprovable. Perhaps a more interesting supposition, however, is that there may be a proposition—perhaps "God exists"—that is knowable but unprovable. That is, this proposition must be known in some other way. For this supposition to be correct, there must be a certain pair of statements, q and r, such that both of them are true and can be known to be true but r can be known *only* by inferring it from q. We will refer to this condition as the "Condition of Cognitive Order" (CCO). To see the function of this condition, consider a true statement q that *can* be known by N (though, in fact, he *may* not know it) and another true statement p that *is* known to N. Then the following argument is sound:

V (5a) Not-p or q
 (5b) p
 (5c) ∴q

Since it is possible for N to know (5c), it is possible for him to know (5a); and if N knows (5a), the argument is cogent for him. In addition, if he knows (5a) independently of his knowledge of (5c), then the argument is convincing for him. It is this last possibility that the Condition of Cognitive Order (CCO) must preclude if it is to be true that though q can be known, no convincing argument for it is possible. That is, it must be the case that (5a), while it is true and can be known, can be known *only* by inferring it from (5c).

It seems very unlikely that the CCO is ever fulfilled. It might be thought, however, that truth-functional disjunction provides a method of constructing such pairs of statements and that the statements (4a) "Either Jupiter has no satellite, or Mr. Nixon is a Republican," and (4c) "Therefore, Mr. Nixon is a Republican," are such a pair. That is, it might be thought that (4a) could be known only by inferring it from (4c), but this is not the case. An examination of the reason why this pair fails to fulfill the CCO will reveal the difficulty of finding any other pair that does fulfill it.

Though it may not be true, let us suppose that the first person to know (4a) must have come to that knowledge on the basis of his knowledge of (4c). Does it follow that everyone else who knows (4a) must have followed the same path? No. One of the most important and far reaching consequences of the human capacity for rational communication is that the individual does not have to recapitulate in his own intellectual life the intellectual history of the race. For example, the greater part of my knowledge about matters of science and history have usually been gained without my repeating the experiments and observations that first brought that knowledge into human possession. Rather I learned these things from people who knew them. Were this not possible, the extension of human knowledge would long ago have reached its limit.

As a matter of fact, most of the people who know that Mr. Nixon is a Republican were told it by news reporters, political analysts, and writers of campaign literature. Since some people might have come to this knowledge by being assured of this fact by a single competent and reliable authority on the contemporary American political scene, it is possible that someone could come to know (4a) by being assured of its truth by just such an authority. It is highly unlikely, of course, that anyone would undertake to communicate (4a), since the kernel of information that it contains can be communicated in a less circuitous way, merely by asserting that Mr. Nixon is a Republican. But we can imagine cases in which it might even be desirable to communicate a statement from which the desired information could be inferred only with the aid of some other statement. Such a stratagem might serve, for example, in lieu of a pre-arranged code.[4]

What is important for us here, however, is not the likelihood or utility of a person's coming to know (4a) independently of (4c), but rather the *possibility* of it. And the possibility certainly seems open. In fact, a person might come to know (4a) without knowing (4c), and without being immediately able to infer (4c) either, since he might not know enough astronomy to know whether the statement "Jupiter has a satellite," (4b) is true. But having looked that up, he would then be able to infer (4c) and thus to extend his own knowledge on the basis of these two statements. In his case, the more usual ordering of the knowledge of statements (4a) and (4c) would have been reversed, both temporally and logically. Therefore, the CCO would not be fulfilled by statements (4a) and (4c).

_____

[4]This possibility was suggested to me by my colleague, Proffessor Arthur W. Burks.

This possibility of learning by communication, and perhaps by other means as well, defeats any attempt to show that the CCO holds true for any pair of statements. If this is so, then for any statement that can be known to be true an argument that is convincing for someone can be constructed.

This has an interesting consequence for my initial simple argument for God's existence. Assuming that God exists and that some people know it, that argument will be cogent for these people. Is it possible that it is also convincing for someone? It will probably seem unlikely that this argument will be convincing for any particular person, since it is so hard to imagine anyone coming to know "Either nothing exists or God exists," (1a) other than by inferring it from "Therefore, God exists," (1c). But there seems no way of entirely ruling out that unlikely possibility. So perhaps even the absurdly simple argument with which this chapter began [propositions (1a)–(1c)] has some possibility of functioning as a proof for someone.

Is There Some Argument that Will Prove *P* to Everyone?

For there to be such an argument there must be a set of premises that validly entail *p* and that are known to everyone. I do not know whether there is any such argument for any proposition whatever because I do not know whether there are any propositions that are known to everyone. Moreover, even if there do happen to be some such propositions, it remains quite likely that no further interesting consequences follow from them. For the most plausible candidates for things that everyone knows are extremely simple propositions such as "There is a world" or "Some things change." It does not seem, however, that interesting conclusions are likely to follow from a collection of statements of this type. Even the simple argument for the existence of God discussed earlier contained something more complex—a disjunction. Some such "combining" proposition that provides a means, as it were, for propositions to operate on each other seems to be required if the argument itself is to be more than trivial.[5] It is much less plausible, how-ever, to suppose that there is some combining proposition that is universally known.[6]

We are, of course, especially interested in whether there is any argument that will prove God's existence to everyone. Such an argument has apparently not yet been invented. If it is to be invented, there must be some set of propositions that everyone knows and that entail, by logical relations that are also known to everyone, that God exists. The invention of such an argument would, of course, be a wonderful thing, just as would be the development of a drug that would cure all diseases. But there is not much reason to believe that either of these is possible.

It is interesting to note, however, that just this project, or some very similar one, is sometimes demanded (or attempted) as a proof of God's existence. For example, a recent (and in many ways admirable) discussion of some theistic arguments begins by saying

> What the natural theologian sets out to do is to show that some of the central beliefs of theism follow deductively or inductively from propositions that are obviously true and accepted by nearly every sane man (e.g., *Some things are in motion*) together with propositions that are self-evident or necessarily true.[7]

It is perhaps significant, however, that the author gives no reason whatever as to *why* the natural theologian should construe his task in terms of these limitations. So far as I can tell, the vast majority of the things that each of us knows are neither necessary truths nor truths "accepted by nearly every sane man." Why, then, should not each of us make use of his own knowledge, and extend it by argument if he can, even if it happens not to be universally shared? It would seem foolish for anyone else to construe another's ignorance as a limit upon his own intellectual life. Conversely, we should not make anyone else's ignorance a barrier to whatever advance we might be

---

[5]Universal generalizations have the requisite combining power.

[6]For a discussion of Aristotle's attempt to show that some generalizations are universally known, see George I. Mavrodes, "Aristotle and Non-contradiction," *The Southern Journal of Philosophy*, Vol. 3, No. 3 (Fall 1965), pp. 111–114.

[7]Alvin Plantinga, *God and Other Minds* (Ithaca: Cornell University Press, 1967), p. 4.

able to make. The notion of a proof as construed in the previous section takes account of the fact that not every piece of knowledge is universally shared. It also recognizes that one person's knowledge may properly be used as a basis upon which some further advance *for that person* can be built. There is no reason why an advance of that sort should not be a suitable project for a natural theologian.

Is There Something that Can Be Proved to Everyone by Some Argument or Other?

Perhaps there is, though this also seems somewhat unlikely. If "God exists" were to be a proposition of this sort then everyone would have to know something or other (not necessarily the same thing) that entails that God exists, and each person would also have to know the requisite logic. Perhaps everyone does know something of this sort but there is no reason to think so.

The Question of Proof and the Question of God

I want to close this chapter by drawing attention to the way in which the epistemological question about proofs is related to the theological and metaphysical question about the existence of God. If what I have argued above is correct, then the epistemological question depends upon the metaphysical one. It is a mistake to suppose that we can answer the epistemological question prior to answering the other—either the answers are simultaneous or else the metaphysical reply comes first. A person who has settled the metaphysical question can settle the question of proof in the same way. If he is mistaken about God, of course, he will be mistaken in the same way about the general possibility of theological proofs. But while the first mistake might well be lamentable, the second adds nothing substantial to it. A person who has not settled the question about God,

however, cannot settle the general proof question either. And if he tries to do the latter first, then the whole inquiry is liable to be misdirected and distorted.

For this reason it is important for all the participants in a theological inquiry or discussion to remember that proofs and arguments are epistemological tools to be used when and if they can be used. They are not to be prized for their own sakes nor are they the prime subjects of the discussion and dispute. One who finds an argument unconvincing, for whatever reason or even for no reason that he can specify, need not hesitate to say so. He thereby identifies a fatal defect in the argument as it applies to him. The proponent of the argument need not concern himself with defending it. He should ask, rather, whether it can be strengthened to overcome this defect. If it can be strengthened, fine; if not, let it be set aside without discussion. It is a tool that did not work in that particular case. Let him, therefore, cast about for some other tool, whether another argument or some quite different type of approach, might succeed. For the discussants to forget the great question of God while they quibble over some proof would be disastrous. I have discussed the question of proof here in the hope that it can then be transcended in those situations in which the living issues of faith and life come before us.

QUESTIONS FOR FURTHER REFLECTION

1. Explain why Mavrodes thinks that proofs are person-relative? Do you agree with him?
2. How would Mavrodes explain the failure of the theistic proofs to convince someone that God exists?
3. Mavrodes claims that if the notion of proof expressed solely in terms of logic and truth is correct, then one can *very easily* prove every true proposition. Following his example, prove the truth about the existence of intelligent extraterrestrial life on other planets.

25. PASCAL'S WAGER

Blaise Pascal

Blaise Pascal (1623–1662) was born in Auvergne, France. A child genius, he became a theologian, scientist, philosopher, inventor, and mathematician and made important contributions to probability theory, number theory, and geometry. In this selection he argues that, even if there are not good evidential reasons to think that God exists, there are good practical reasons to think that God exists.

READING QUESTIONS

1. Why does Pascal think that we have no choice but to bet on God's existence?
2. What is the expected payoff if God exists?
3. What is the risk if God does not exist but we believe He does?
4. Why does Pascal think that the evidence for God can be extremely scant and it is still rational to believe that God exists?

We know neither the existence nor the nature of God, because He has neither extension nor limits.

But by faith we know His existence; in glory we shall know His nature. Now, I have already shown that we may well know the existence of a thing, without knowing its nature.

Let us now speak according to natural lights.

If there is a God, He is infinitely incomprehensible, since, having neither parts nor limits, He has no affinity to us. We are then incapable of knowing either what He is or if He is. This being so, who will dare to undertake the decision of the question? Not we, who have no affinity to Him.

Who then will blame Christians for not being able to give a reason for their belief, since they profess a religion for which they cannot give a reason? They declare, in expounding it to the world, that it is a foolishness, *stultitiam*; and then you complain that they do not prove it! If they proved it, they would not keep their words; it is in lacking proofs, that they are not lacking in sense. "Yes, but although this excuses those who offer it as such, and takes away from them the blame of putting it forward without reason, it does not excuse those who receive it." Let us then examine this point, and say, "God is, or He is not." But to which side shall we incline? Reason can decide nothing here. There is an infinite chaos which separates us. A game is being played at the extremity of this infinite distance where heads or tails will turn up. What will

you wager? According to reason, you can do neither the one thing nor the other; according to reason, you can defend neither of the propositions.

Do not then reprove for error those who have made a choice; for you know nothing about it. "No, but I blame them for having made, not this choice, but a choice; for again both he who chooses heads and he who chooses tails are equally at fault, they are both in the wrong. The true course is not to wager at all."

—Yes; but you must wager. It is not optional. You are embarked. Which will you choose then; Let us see. Since you must choose, let us see which interests you least. You have two things to lose, the true and the good; and two things to stake, your reason and your will, your knowledge and your happiness; and your nature has two things to shun, error and misery. Your reason is no more shocked in choosing one rather than the other, since you must of necessity choose. This is one point settled. But your happiness? Let us weigh the gain and the loss in wagering that God is. Let us estimate these two chances. If you gain, you gain all; if you lose, you lose nothing. Wager then without hesitation that He is.—"That is very fine. Yes, I must wager; but I may perhaps wager too much."—Let us see. Since there is an equal risk of gain and of loss, if you had only to gain two lives, instead of one, you might still wager. But if there were three lives to gain, you would have to play (since you are under the necessity of playing), and you would be

"YOU BET YOUR LIFE" * *William Lycan and George Schlesinger*

1. "But my beliefs are not under my control; if I don't believe, then I can't believe, any more than I can believe there to be a live swordfish in front of me just because someone offers me $1,000 if I can get myself to believe that." *Reply:* In the long run, most people's beliefs *are* under their control; as Pascal himself emphasized, behavior therapy is remarkably effective even upon intellectuals. Start going to church and observing its rituals; associate with intelligent and congenial religious people; stop reading philosophy and associating with cynics and logical positivists. To quote William James's pungent paraphrase of Pascal, "Go then and take holy water, and have masses said; belief will come and stupefy your scruples." It may be that some people, of an indefatigably analytical and uncredulous temperament, simply cannot let themselves neglect the evidence and acquiesce in faith, just as some people simply cannot let themselves be hypnotized. But this is no reflection on the prudential rationality of the Wager; many people are psychologically incapable of doing what is demonstrably in their interest and known by them to be in their interest.

2. "The Wager is cynical and mercenary; God wouldn't reward a 'believer' who makes it."

Reply: Of course He wouldn't, just like that. Pascal's claim is rather that our interest lies in leaving our cynicism behind and eventually *becoming* believers, if we can. There is no particular reason to think that God would punish a truly sincere and devout believer just because of the historical origins of his or her belief. People are reportedly saved as a result of deathbed conversions, even after lives of the most appalling corruption, if their new belief is sincere and authentic.

3. "Pascal is wrong in conjecturing that the probability of theism is as high as .5. It isn't; it's minuscule." *Reply:* That doesn't matter; even if the probability of theism is .001, the expected payoffs are still infinite. "All right, then, the probability is *zero*. I'm *certain* there is no God." *Reply:* How certain? And on what grounds? We would need to see a very convincing argument that no God of even roughly the traditional sort *could* exist, and it would have to be better than most philosophical arguments. (How many philosophical arguments do we know that confer probability 1 on their conclusions??)

From William Lycan and George Schlesinger
"You Bet Your Life: Pascal's Wager Defended"
in *Reason and Responsibility* (1989).

imprudent, when you are forced to play, not to chance your life to gain three at a game where there is an equal risk of loss and gain. But there is an eternity of life and happiness. And this being so, if there were an infinity of chances, of which one only would be for you, you would still be right in wagering one to win two, and you would act stupidly, being obliged to play, by refusing to stake one life against three at a game in which out of an infinity of chances there is one for you, if there were an infinity of an infinitely happy life to gain. But there is here an infinity of an infinitely happy life to gain, a chance of gain against a finite number of chances of loss, and what you stake is finite. It is all divided; wherever the infinite is and there is not an infinity of chances of loss against that of gain, there is no time to hesitate, you must give all. And thus, when one is forced to play, he must renounce reason to preserve his life, rather than risk it for infinite gain, as likely to happen as the loss of nothingness.

For it is no use to say it is uncertain if we will gain, and it is certain that we risk, and that the infinite distance between the *certainty* of what is staked and the *uncertainty* of what will be gained, equals the finite good which is certainly staked against the uncertain infinite. It is not so, as every player stakes a certainty to gain an uncertainty, and yet he stakes a finite certainty to gain a finite uncertainty, without transgressing against reason.

There is not an infinite distance between the certainty staked and the uncertainty of the gain; that is untrue. In truth, there is an infinity between the certainty of gain and the certainty of loss. But the uncertainty of the gain is proportioned to the certainty of the stake according to the proportion of the chances of gain and loss. Hence it comes that, if there are as many risks on one side as on the other, the course is to play even; and then the certainty of the stake is equal to the uncertainty of the gain, so far is it from the fact that there is an infinite distance between them. And so our proposition is of infinite force, when there is the finite to stake in a game where there are equal risks of gain and of loss, and the infinite to gain. This is demonstrable; and if men are capable of any truths, this is one.

"I confess it, I admit it. But still is there no means of seeing the faces of the cards?"—Yes, Scripture and the rest, and so on—"Yes, but I have my hands tied and my mouth closed; I am forced to wager, and am not free. I am not released, and am so made that I cannot believe. What then would you have me do?"

"True. But at least learn your inability to believe, since reason brings you to this, and yet you cannot believe. Endeavour then to convince yourself, not by increase of proofs of God, but by the abatement of your passions. You would like to attain faith, and do not know the way; you would like to cure yourself of unbelief, and ask the remedy for it. Learn of those who have been bound like you, and who now stake all their possessions. These are people who know the way which you would follow, and who are cured of an ill of which you would be cured. Follow the way by which they began; by acting as if they believe, taking the holy water, having masses said, and so on. Even this will naturally make you believe, and deaden your acuteness.—"But this is what I am afraid of."—And why? What have you to lose?

But to show you that this leads you there, it is this which will lessen the passions, which are your stumbling blocks.

QUESTIONS FOR FURTHER REFLECTION

1. Suppose someone is convinced by Pascal's argument and thinks he should believe that God exists. How can he create genuine belief? If you were offered a million dollars to believe that the president of the United States is juggling candy bars on a unicycle in his office right now, could you do it? Do we have control over our beliefs in such a way that we can start to really believe something is true if we see it is in our interest?
2. Could God be offended if someone believes in Him because it is in their best interest? Does God want belief in Him to be the result of gambling?
3. How does Pascal's argument assume the only choice is between Christianity and atheism?

26. THE WILL TO BELIEVE

William James

William James (1842–1910), the brother of the novelist Henry James, was born in New York City in 1842 and educated at Harvard University. He made important contributions to psychology and philosophy. He is best known in philosophy for the development of pragmaticism. He also did extensive work in the philosophy of religion. In this selection James argues, contrary to Clifford, that under certain conditions which James specifies, it can be rational to believe something, including that God exists, in the absence of evidence.

READING QUESTIONS

1. What three options does James set out as possibilities?
2. What does James mean by a "genuine option"?
3. Give an example of an option that is not "momentous." Give one of an option that is not "forced."
4. What is James's thesis, briefly stated?
5. What is the difference between claims of science, morality, and religion?
6. How does James think people misunderstand faith?

. . . Let us give the same of *hypothesis* to anything that may be proposed to our belief; and just as the electricians speak of live and dead wires, let us speak of any hypothesis as either *live* or *dead*. A live hypothesis is one which appeals as a real possibility to him to whom it is proposed. If I ask you to believe in the Mahdi, the notion makes no electric connection with your nature—it refuses to scintillate with any credibility at all. As an hypothesis it is completely dead. To an Arab, however (even if he be not one of the Mahdi's followers), the hypothesis is among the mind's possibilities: it is alive. This shows that deadness and liveness in an hypothesis are not intrinsic properties, but relations to the individual thinker. They are measured by his willingness to act. The maximum of liveness in an hypothesis means willingness to act irrevocably. Practically, that means belief; but there is some believing tendency wherever there is willingness to act at all.

Next, let us call the decision between two hypotheses an *option*. Options may be of several kinds. They may be—1, *living or dead*; 2, *forced or avoidable*; 3, *momentous or trivial*; and for our purposes we may call an option a *genuine* option when it is of the forced, living, and momentous kind.

1. A living option is one in which both hypotheses are live ones. If I say to you: "Be a theosophist or be a Mohammedan," it is probably a dead option, because for you neither hypothesis is likely to be alive. But if I say, "Be an agnostic or be a Christian," it is otherwise: trained as you are, each hypothesis makes some appeal, however small, to your belief.
2. Next, if I say to you: "Choose between going out with your umbrella or without it," I do not offer you a genuine option, for it is not forced. You can easily avoid it by not going out at all. Similarly, if I say, "Either love me or hate me," "Either call my theory true or call it false," your option is avoidable. You may remain indifferent to me, neither loving nor hating, and you may decline to offer any judgment as to my theory. But if I say, "Either accept this truth or go without it," I put on you a forced option, for there is no standing place outside of the alternative. Every dilemma based on a complete logical disjunction, with no possibility of not choosing, is an option of this forced kind. . . .

The thesis I defend is, briefly stated, this: *Our passional nature not only lawfully may but must, decide an option between propositions, whenever it is a genuine option that cannot by its nature be decided on intellectual grounds; for to say, under such circumstances, "Do not decide, but leave the question open," is itself a passional decision—just like deciding yes or no—and is attended with the same risk of losing the truth.* . . .

Wherever the option between losing truth and gaining it is not momentous, we can throw the chance of *gaining truth* away, and at any rate save ourselves from any chance of *believing falsehood*, by not making up our minds at all till objective evidence has come. In scientific questions, this is almost always the case; and even in human affairs in general, the need of acting is seldom so urgent that a false belief to act on is better than no belief at all. Law courts, indeed, have to decide on the best evidence attainable for the moment, because a judge's duty is to make law as well as to ascertain it, and (as a learned judge once said to me) few cases are worth spending much time over: the great thing is to have them decided on *any* acceptable principle, and got out of the way. But in our dealings with objective nature we obviously are recorders, not makers, of the truth; and decisions for the mere sake of deciding promptly and getting on to the next business would be wholly out of place. Throughout the breadth of physical nature facts are what they are quite independently of us, and seldom is there any such hurry about them that the risks of being duped by believing a premature theory need be faced. The questions here are always trivial options, the hypotheses are hardly living (at any rate not living for us spectators), the choice between believing truth or falsehood is seldom forced. The attitude of sceptical balance is therefore the absolutely wise one if we would escape mistakes. What difference, indeed, does it make to most of us whether we have or have not a theory of the Röntgen rays, whether we believe or not in mind-stuff, or have a conviction about the causality of conscious states? It makes no difference. Such options are not forced on us. On every account it is better not to make them, but still keep weighing reasons *pro et contra* with an indifferent hand. . . .

. . . Religions differ so much in their accidents that in discussing the religious question we must make it very generic and broad. What then do we now mean by the religious hypothesis? Science says things are; morality says some things are better than other things; and religion says essentially two things.

First, she says that the best things are the more eternal things, the overlapping things, the things in the universe that throw the last stone, so to speak, and say the final word. "Perfection is eternal"—this phrase of Charles Secrétan seems a good way of putting this first affirmation of religion, an affirmation which obviously cannot yet be verified scientifically at all.

The second affirmation of religion is that we are better off even now if we believe her first affirmation to be true.

Now, let us consider what the logical elements of this situation are *in case the religious hypothesis in both its branches be really true* (Of course, we must admit that possibility at the outset. If we are to discuss the question at all, it must involve a living option. If for any of you religion be a hypothesis that cannot, by any living possibility be true, then you need go no farther. I speak to the "saving remnant" alone.) So proceeding, we see, first that religion offers itself as a *momentous* option. We are supposed to gain, even now, by our belief, and to lose by our nonbelief, a certain vital good. Secondly, religion is a *forced* option, so far as that good goes. We cannot escape the issue by remaining sceptical and waiting for more light, because, although we do avoid error in that way *if religion be untrue* we lose the good, *if it be true*, just as certainly as if we positively chose to disbelieve. It is as if a man should hesitate indefinitely to ask a certain woman to marry him because he was not perfectly sure that she would prove an angel after he brought her home. Would he not cut himself off from that particular angel-possibility as decisively as if he went and married some one else? Scepticism, then, is not avoidance of option; it is option of a certain particular kind of risk. *Better risk loss of truth than chance of error*—that is your faith-vetoer's exact position. He is actively playing his stake as much as the believer is; he is backing the field against the religious hypothesis, just as the believer is backing the religious hypothesis against the field. To preach scepticism to us as a duty until "sufficient evidence" for religion can be found, is tantamount therefore to telling us, when in presence of the religious hypothesis, that to yield to our fear of its being error is wiser and better than to yield to our hope that it may be true. It is not intellect against all passions, then; it is only intellect with one passion laying down its law. And by what, forsooth, is the supreme wisdom of this passion warranted? Dupery for dupery, what proof is there that dupery through hope is so much worse than dupery through fear? I, for one, can see no proof; and I simply refuse obedience to the scientist's command to imitate his kind of option, in a case where my own stake is important enough to give me the right to choose my own form of risk. If religion be true and the evidence for it be still insufficient, I do not wish, by putting our extinguisher upon my nature (which feels to me as if it had after all some business in this matter), to forfeit my sole chance in life of getting upon the winning side—that chance depending, of course, on my willingness to run the risk of acting as if my passional need of taking the world religiously might be prophetic and right.

All this is on the supposition that it really may be prophetic and right, and that, even to us who are discussing the matter, religion is a live hypothesis which may be true. Now, to most of us religion comes in a still further way that makes a veto on our active faith even more illogical. The more perfect and more eternal aspect of the universe is represented in our religions as having personal form. The universe is no longer a mere *It* to us, but a *Thou*, if we are religious; and any relation that may be possible from person to person might be possible here. For instance, although in one sense we are passive portions of the universe, in another we show a curious autonomy, as if we were small active centres on our own account. We feel, too, as if the appeal of religion to us were made to our own active goodwill, as if evidence might be forever withheld from us unless we met the hypothesis half-way. To take a trivial illustration: just as a man who in a company of gentlemen made no advances, asked a warrant for every concession, and believed no one's word without proof, would cut himself off by such churlishness from all the social rewards that a more trusting spirit would earn—so here, one who should shut himself up in snarling logicality and try to make the gods extort his recognition willy-nilly, or not get it at all, might cut himself off forever from his only opportunity of making the gods' acquaintance. This feeling, forced on us we know not whence, that by obstinately believing that there are gods (although not to do so would be so easy both for our logic and our life) we are doing the universe the deepest service we can, seems part of the living essence of the religious hypothesis. If the hypothesis *were* true in all its parts, including this one, then pure intellectualism, with its veto on our making willing advances, would be an absurdity; and some participation of our sympathetic nature would be logically required. I, therefore, for one, cannot see my way to accepting the agnostic rules for truthseeking, or wilfully agree to keep my willing nature out of the game. I cannot do so for this plain reason, that *a rule of thinking which would absolutely prevent me from acknowledging certain kinds of truth if those kinds of truth were really there, would be an irrational rule*. That for me is the long and short of the formal logic of the situation, no matter what the kinds of truth might materially be.

I confess I do not see how this logic can be escaped. But sad experiences make me fear that some of you may still shrink from radically saying with me, *in abstracto*, that we have the right to believe at our own risk any hypothesis that is live enough to tempt our will. I suspect, however, that if this is so, it is because you have got away from the abstract logical point of view altogether, and are thinking (perhaps without realizing it) of some particular religious hypothesis which for you is dead. The freedom to "believe what we will" you apply to the case of some patent superstition; and the faith you think of is the faith defined by the schoolboy when he said, "Faith is when you believe something that you know ain't true." I can only repeat that this is misapprehension. *In concreto*, the freedom to believe can only cover living options which the intellect of the individual cannot by itself resolve; and

living options never seem absurdities to him who has them to consider. When I look at the religious question as it really puts itself to concrete men, and when I think of all the possibilities which both practically and theoretically it involves, then this command that we shall put a stopper on our heart, instincts, and courage, and *wait*—acting of course meanwhile more or less as if religion were *not* true—till doomsday, or till such time as our intellect and senses working together may have raked in evidence enough—this command, I say, seems to me the queerest idol ever manufactured in the philosophic cave. Were we scholastic absolutists, there might be more excuse. If we had an infallible intellect with its objective certitudes, we might feel ourselves disloyal to such a perfect organ of knowledge in not trusting to it exclusively, in not waiting for its releasing word. But if we are empiricists, if we believe that no bell in us tolls to let us know for certain when truth is in our grasp, then it seems a piece of idle fantasticality to preach so solemnly our duty of waiting for the bell. Indeed we *may* wait if we will—I hope you do not think that I am denying that—but if we do so, we do so at our peril as much as if we believed. In either case we *act*, taking our life in our hands. . . .

QUESTIONS FOR FURTHER REFLECTION

1. How does James's pragmatic defense of religious belief differ from Pascal's?
2. Suppose a 110-pound woman believed on faith that she could bench press 350 pounds. Is James committed to the rationality of this belief?

27. RELIGIOUS BELIEF REQUIRES A LEAP OF FAITH

Søren Kierkegaard

Søren Kierkegaard (1813–1855) was born in Copenhagen, Denmark. His father was a pious Lutheran whose stern religious outlook greatly influenced his son. Kierkegaard studied philosophy and theology at the University of Copenhagen, where he became particularly attracted to the philosophy of Hegel. A substantial inheritance from his father allowed Kierkegaard to devote himself exclusively to writing on philosophical and theological matters. Kierkegaard was a solitary man, who had few friends and only one love affair, with a seventeen-year-old churchgoer named Regina Olson. He became engaged to her, but quickly broke it off, knowing in his heart that he was fit only for solitude and contemplation. Kierkegaard's literary output was enormous. Among his over 20 published works are such classics as, *The Sickness Unto Death*, which deals with the nature of despair and *Fear and Trembling*, which is an exposition on the nature of faith as exemplified by the patriarch Abraham. On November 11, 1855, he died from overwork and exhaustion. His legacy has been enormous, influencing both religious thinkers and the major proponents of twentieth century existentialism. Although he is widely regarded as the father of existentialism, the atheistic despair of a Sartre, or even the ethical humanism of a Camus, was quite alien to him. Kierkegaard was a profoundly religious man, who believed that submission to the will of God was both the highest good, and the only possible escape from despair. He believed that all dogmatic philosophical systems are false because the complex and paradoxical nature of existence cannot be reduced to a neat set of axioms. Rather, he focused on the often tormented nature of individual existence, hence the term *existentialism*. He believed that truth must be experienced subjectively, not just apprehended with the objective discernment of pure reason. In this selection from Kierkegaard's work entitled, *Concluding Unscientific Postscript*, he discusses the relationship between the subjective and the objective. True to his conception that truth must be experienced, not just known, he states that subjectively known truths are truths of relationship rather than truths of objective fact. That is to say, a subjectively held truth is one that breaks down the barrier between the knower and the known, while an objectively held truth only strengthens this barrier. Kierkegaard uses this line of thought to demonstrate that God can be known only subjectively, never objectively.

READING QUESTIONS

1. How does Kierkegaard define subjective reflection?
2. How does Kierkegaard define objective reflection?
3. How does Kierkegaard relate these two forms of reflection to the knowledge of God?
4. In what sense is God a postulate?
5. Why does Kierkegaard state that, "postulation of God is a necessity"?

In an attempt to make clear the difference of way that exists between an objective and a subjective reflection. I shall now proceed to show how a subjective reflection makes its way inwardly in inwardness. Inwardness in an existing subject culminates in passion: corresponding to passion in the subject the truth becomes a paradox; and the fact that the truth becomes a paradox is rooted precisely in its having a relationship to an existing subject. Thus the one corresponds to the other. By forgetting that one is an existing subject, passion goes by the board and the truth is no longer a paradox; the knowing subject becomes a fantastic entity rather than a human being, and the truth becomes a fantastic object for the knowledge of this fantastic entity.

When the question of truth is raised in an objective manner, reflection is directed objectively to the truth, as an object to which the knower is related. Reflection is not focussed upon the relationship, however, but upon the question of whether it is the truth to which the knower is related. If only the object to which he is related is the truth, the subject is accounted to be in the truth. When the question of the truth is raised subjectively, reflection is directed subjectively to the nature of the individual's relationship; if only the mode of this relationship is in the truth, the individual is in the truth even if he should happen to be thus related to what is not true.[1] Let us take as an example the knowledge of God. Objectively, reflection is directed to the problem of whether this object is the true God; subjectively, reflection is directed to the question whether the individual is

---

[1]The reader will observe that the question here is about essential truth, or about the truth which is essentially related to existence, and that it is precisely for the sake of clarifying it as inwardness or as subjectivity that this contrast is drawn.

related to a something *in such a manner* that his relationship is in truth a God-relationship. On which side is the truth now to be found? Ah, may we not here resort to a mediation, and say: It is on neither side, but in the mediation of both? Excellently well said, provided we might have it explained how an existing individual manages to be in a state of mediation. For to be in a state of mediation is to be finished, while to exist is to become. Nor can an existing individual be in two places at the same time—he cannot be an identity of subject and object. When he is nearest to being in two places at the same time he is in passion; but passion is momentary; and passion is also the highest expression of subjectivity.

The existing individual who chooses to pursue the objective way enters upon the entire approximation-process by which it is proposed to bring God to light objectively. But this is in all eternity impossible, because God is a subject, and therefore exists only for subjectivity in inwardness. The existing individual who chooses the subjective way apprehends instantly the entire dialectical difficulty involved in having to use some time, perhaps a long time, in finding God objectively; and he feels this dialectical difficulty in all its painfulness, because every moment is wasted in which he does not have God. That very instant he has God, not by virtue of any objective deliberation, but by virtue of the infinite passion of inwardness. The objective inquirer, on the other hand, is not embarrassed by such dialectical difficulties as are involved in devoting an entire period of investigation to finding God—since it is possible that the inquirer may die tomorrow; and if he lives he can scarcely regard God as something to be taken along if convenient, since God is precisely that which one takes *a tout prix*, which in the understanding of passion constitutes the true inward relationship to God.

It is at this point, so difficult dialectically, that the way swings off for everyone who knows what it means to think, and to think existentially; which is something very different from sitting at a desk and writing about what one has never done, something very different from writing *de omnibus dubitandum* and at the same time being as credulous existentially as the most sensuous of men. Here is where the way swings off, and the change is marked by the fact that while objective knowledge rambles comfortably on by way of the long

road of approximation without being impelled by the urge of passion, subjective knowledge counts every delay a deadly peril, and the decision so infinitely important and so instantly pressing that it is as if the opportunity had already passed.

Now when the problem is to reckon up on which side there is most truth, whether on the side of one who seeks the true God objectively, and pursues the approximate truth of the God-idea; or on the side of one who, driven by the infinite passion of his need of God, feels an infinite concern for his own relationship to God in truth (and to be at one and the same time on both sides equally, is as we have noted not possible for an existing individual, but is merely the happy delusion of an imaginary I-am-I): the answer cannot be in doubt for anyone who has not been demoralized with the aid of science. If one who lives in the midst of Christendom goes up to the house of God, the house of the true God, with the true conception of God in his knowledge, and prays, but prays in a false spirit; and one who lives in an idolatrous community prays with the entire passion of the infinite, although his eyes rest upon the image of an idol: where is there most truth? The one prays in truth to God though he worships an idol; the other prays falsely to the true God, and hence worships in fact an idol.

When one man investigates objectively the problem of immortality, and another embraces an uncertainty with the passion of the infinite: where is there most truth, and who has the greater certainty? The one has entered upon a never-ending approximation, for the certainty of immortality lies precisely in the subjectivity of the individual; the other is immortal, and fights for his immortality by struggling with the uncertainty. Let us consider Socrates. Nowadays everyone dabbles in a few proofs; some have several such proofs, others fewer. But Socrates! He puts the question objectively in a problematic manner: *if* there is an immortality. He must therefore be accounted a doubter in comparison with one of our modern thinkers with the three proofs? By no means. On this "if" he risks his entire life, he has the courage to meet death and he has with the passion of the infinite so determined the pattern of his life that it must be found acceptable—*if* there is an immortality. Is any better proof capable of being given for the immortality of the soul? But those who have the three proofs do not at all determine their lives in conformity therewith; if there is an immortality it must feel disgust over their manner of life: can any better refutation be given of the three proofs? The bit of uncertainty that Socrates had, helped him because he himself contributed the passion of the infinite; the three proofs that the others have do not profit them at all, because they are dead to spirit and enthusiasm, and their three proofs, in lieu of proving anything else, prove just this. A young girl may enjoy all the sweetness of love on the basis of what is merely a weak hope that she is beloved, because she rests everything on this weak hope; but many a wedded matron more than once subjected to the strongest expressions of love, has in so far indeed had proofs, but strangely enough has not enjoyed *quod erat demonstrandum*. The Socratic ignorance, which Socrates held fast with the entire passion of his inwardness, was thus an expression for the principle that the eternal truth is related to an existing individual, and that this truth must therefore be a paradox for him as long as he exists; and yet it is possible that there was more truth in the Socratic ignorance as it was in him, than in the entire objective truth of the System, which flirts with what the times demand and accommodates itself to *Privatdocents*.

The objective accent falls on WHAT is said, the subjective accent on HOW it is said. This distinction holds even in the aesthetic realm, and receives definite expression in the principle that what is in itself true may in the mouth of such and such a person become untrue. In these times this distinction is particularly worthy of notice, for if we wish to express in a single sentence the difference between ancient times and our own, we should doubtless have to say: "In ancient times only an individual here and there knew the truth; now all know it, except that the inwardness of its appropriation stands in an inverse relationship to the extent of its dissemination." Aesthetically the contradiction that truth becomes untruth in this or that person's mouth, is best construed comically: In the ethico-religious sphere, accent is again on the "how." But this is not to be understood as referring to demeanor, expression, or the like; rather it refers to the relationship sustained by the existing individual, in his own existence, to the content of his utterance. Objectively the interest is focussed merely on the thought-content, subjectively on the inwardness. At its maximum this inward "how" is the passion of the

infinite, and the passion of the infinite is the truth. But the passion of the infinite is precisely subjectivity, and thus subjectivity becomes the truth. Objectively there is no infinite decisiveness, and hence it is objectively in order to annul the difference between good and evil, together with the principle of contradiction, and therewith also the infinite difference between the true and the false. Only in subjectivity is there decisiveness, to seek objectivity is to be in error. It is the passion of the infinite that is the decisive factor and not its content, for its content is precisely itself. In this manner subjectivity and the subjective "how" constitute the truth.

But the "how" which is thus subjectively accentuated precisely because the subject is an existing individual, is also subject to a dialectic with respect to time. In the passionate moment of decision, where the road swings away from objective knowledge, it seems as if the infinite decision were thereby realized. But in the same moment the existing individual finds himself in the temporal order, and the subjective "how" is transformed into a striving, a striving which receives indeed its impulse and a repeated renewal from the decisive passion of the infinite, but is nevertheless a striving.

When subjectivity is the truth, the conceptual determination of the truth must include an expression for the antithesis to objectivity, a memento of the fork in the road where the way swings off: this expression will at the same time serve as an indication of the tension of the subjective inwardness. Here is such a definition of truth: *An objective uncertainty held fast in an appropriation-process of the most passionate inwardness is the truth*, the highest truth attainable for an *existing* individual. At the point where the way swings off (and where this is cannot be specified objectively, since it is a matter of subjectivity), there objective knowledge is placed in abeyance. Thus the subject merely has, objectively, the uncertainty; but it is this which precisely increases the tension of that infinite passion which constitutes his inwardness. The truth is precisely the venture which chooses an objective uncertainty with the passion of the infinite. I contemplate the order of nature in the hope of finding God, and I see omnipotence and wisdom; but I also see much else that disturbs my mind and excites anxiety. The sum of all this is an objective uncertainty. But it is for this very reason that the inwardness becomes as intense as it is, for it embraces this objective uncertainty with the entire passion of the infinite. In the case of a mathematical proposition the objectivity is given, but for this reason the truth of such a proposition is also an indifferent truth.

But the above definition of truth is an equivalent expression for faith. Without risk there is no faith. Faith is precisely the contradiction between the infinite passion of the individual's inwardness and the objective uncertainty. If I am capable of grasping God objectively. I do not believe, but precisely because I cannot do this I must believe. If I wish to preserve myself in faith I must constantly be intent upon holding fast the objective uncertainty, so as to remain out upon the deep, over seventy thousand fathoms of water, still preserving my faith.

In the principle that subjectivity, inwardness, is the truth, there is comprehended the Socratic wisdom, whose everlasting merit it was to have become aware of the essential significance of existence, of the fact that the knower is an existing individual. For this reason Socrates was in the truth by virtue of his ignorance, in the highest sense in which this was possible within paganism. To attain to an understanding of this, to comprehend that the misfortune of speculative philosophy is again and again to have forgotten that the knower is an existing individual, is in our objective age difficult enough. But to have made an advance upon Socrates without even having understood what he understood, is at any rate not "Socratic."

Let us now start from this point, and as was attempted in the *Fragments*, seek a determination of thought which will really carry us further. I have nothing here to do with the question of whether this proposed thought-determination is true or not, since I am merely experimenting; but it must at any rate be clearly manifest that the Socratic thought is understood within the new proposal, so that at least I do not come out behind Socrates.

When subjectivity, inwardness, is the truth, the truth becomes objectively a paradox; and the fact that the truth is objectively a paradox shows in its turn that subjectivity is the truth. For the objective situation is repellant; and the expression for the objective repulsion constitutes the tension and the measure of the corresponding inwardness. The paradoxical character of the truth is its objective uncertainty; this uncer-

tainty is an expression for the passionate inwardness, and this passion is precisely the truth. So far the Socratic principle. The eternal and essential truth, the truth which has an essential relationship to an existing individual because it pertains essentially to existence (all other knowledge being from the Socratic point of view accidental, its scope and degree a matter of indifference), is a paradox. But the eternal essential truth is by no means in itself a paradox; but it becomes paradoxical by virtue of its relationship to an existing individual. The Socratic ignorance gives expression to the objective uncertainty attaching to the truth, while his inwardness in existing is the truth. To anticipate here what will be developed later, let me make the following remark. The Socratic ignorance is an analogue to the category of the absurd, only that there is still less of objective certainty in the absurd, and in the repellent effect that the absurd exercises. It is certain only that it is absurd, and precisely on that account it incites to an infinitely greater tension in the corresponding inwardness. The Socratic inwardness in existing is an analogue to faith: only that the inwardness of faith, corresponding as it does, not to the repulsion of the Socratic ignorance, but to the repulsion exerted by the absurd, is infinitely more profound.

Socratically the eternal essential truth is by no means in its own nature paradoxical, but only in its relationship to an existing individual. This finds expression in another Socratic proposition, namely, that all knowledge is recollection. This proposition is not for Socrates a cue to the speculative enterprise, and hence he does not follow it up; essentially it becomes a Platonic principle. Here the way swings off; Socrates concentrates essentially upon accentuating existence, while Plato forgets this and loses himself in speculation. Socrates' infinite merit is to have been an *existing* thinker, not a speculative philosopher who forgets what it means to exist. For Socrates therefore the principle that all knowledge is recollection has at the moment of his leave-taking and as the constantly rejected possibility of engaging in speculation, the following two-fold significance: (1) that the knower is essentially *integer*, and that with respect to the knowledge of the eternal truth he is confronted with no other difficulty than the circumstance that he exists: which difficulty, however, is so essential and decisive for him that it means that existing, the process of transformation to inwardness in existing and by existing, is the truth: (2) that existence in time does not have any decisive significance, because the possibility of taking oneself back into eternity through recollection is always there, though this possibility is constantly nullified by utilizing the time, not for speculation, but for the transformation to inwardness in existing.

The infinite merit of the Socratic position was precisely to accentuate the fact that the knower is an existing individual, and that the task of existing is his essential task. Making an advance upon Socrates by failing to understand this, is quite a mediocre achievement. This Socratic principle we must therefore bear in mind, and then inquire whether the formula may not be so altered as really to make an advance beyond the Socratic position.

Subjectivity, inwardness, has been posited as the truth; can any expression for the truth be found which has a still higher degree of inwardness? Aye, there is such an expression, provided the principle that subjectivity or inwardness is the truth begins by positing the opposite principle: that subjectivity is untruth. Let us not at this point succumb to such haste as to fail in making the necessary distinctions. Speculative philosophy also says that subjectivity is untruth, but says it in order to stimulate a movement in precisely the opposite direction, namely, in the direction of the principle that objectivity is the truth. Speculative philosophy determines subjectivity negatively as tending toward objectivity. This second determination of ours, however, places a hindrance in its own way while proposing to begin, which has the effect of making the inwardness far more intensive. Socratically speaking, subjectivity is untruth if it refuses to understand that subjectivity is truth, but, for example, desires to become objective. Here, on the other hand, subjectivity in beginning upon the task of becoming the truth through a subjectifying process, is in the difficulty that it is already untruth. Thus, the labor of the task is thrust backward, backward, that is, in inwardness. So far is it from being the case that the way tends in the direction of objectivity, that the beginning merely lies still deeper in subjectivity.

But the subject cannot be untruth eternally, or eternally be presupposed as having been untruth; it must have been brought to this condition in time, or here become untruth in time. The Socratic paradox

consisted in the fact that the eternal was related to an existing individual, but now existence has stamped itself upon the existing individual a second time. There has taken place so essential an alteration in him that he cannot now possibly take himself back into the eternal by way of recollection. To do this is to speculate; to be able to do this, but to reject the possibility by apprehending the task of life as a realization of inwardness in existing, is the Socratic position. But now the difficulty is that what followed Socrates on his way as a rejected possibility, has become an impossibility. If engaging in speculation was a dubious merit even from the point of view of the Socratic, it is now neither more nor less than confusion.

The paradox emerges when the eternal truth and existence are placed in juxtaposition with one another; each time the stamp of existence is brought to bear, the paradox becomes more clearly evident. Viewed Socratically the knower was simply an existing individual, but now the existing individual bears the stamp of having been essentially altered by existence.

Let us now call the untruth of the individual *Sin*. Viewed eternally he cannot be sin, nor can he be eternally presupposed as having been in sin. By coming into existence therefore (for the beginning was that subjectivity is untruth), he becomes a sinner. He is not born as a sinner in the sense that he is presupposed as being a sinner before he is born, but he is born in sin and as a sinner. This we might call *Original Sin*. But if existence has in this manner acquired a power over him, he is prevented from taking himself back into the eternal by way of recollection. If it was paradoxical to posit the eternal truth in relationship to an existing individual, it is now absolutely paradoxical to posit it in relationship to such an individual as we have here defined. But the more difficult it is made for him to take himself out of existence by way of recollection, the more profound is the inwardness that his existence may have in existence; and when it is made impossible for him, when he is held so fast in existence that the back door of recollection is forever closed to him, then his inwardness will be the most profound possible. But let us never forget that the Socratic merit was to stress the fact that the knower is an existing individual; for the more difficult the matter becomes, the greater the temptation to hasten along the easy road of speculation, away from fearful dangers and crucial decisions, to the winning of renown and honors and property, and so forth. If even Socrates understood the dubiety of taking himself speculatively out of existence back into the eternal, although no other difficulty confronted the existing individual except that he existed, and that existing was his essential task, now it is impossible. Forward he must, backward he cannot go.

Subjectivity is the truth. By virtue of the relationship subsisting between the eternal truth and the existing individual, the paradox came into being. Let us now go further, let us suppose that the eternal essential truth is itself a paradox. How does the paradox come into being? By putting the eternal essential truth into juxtaposition with existence. Hence when we posit such a conjunction within the truth itself, the truth becomes a paradox. The eternal truth has come into being in time: this is the paradox. If in accordance with the determinations just posited, the subject is prevented by sin from taking himself back into the eternal, now he need not trouble himself about this; for now the eternal essential truth is not behind him but in front of him, through its being in existence or having existed, so that if the individual does not existentially and in existence lay hold of the truth, he will never lay hold of it.

Existence can never be more sharply accentuated than by means of these determinations. The evasion by which speculative philosophy attempts to recollect itself out of existence has been made impossible. With reference to this, there is nothing for speculation to do except to arrive at an understanding of this impossibility; every speculative attempt which insists on being speculative shows *eo ipso* that it has not understood it. The individual may thrust all this away from him, and take refuge in speculation; but it is impossible first to accept it, and then to revoke it by means of speculation, since it is definitely calculated to prevent speculation.

When the eternal truth is related to an existing individual it becomes a paradox. The paradox repels in the inwardness of the existing individual, through the objective uncertainty and the corresponding Socratic ignorance. But since the paradox is not in the first instance itself paradoxical (but only in its relationship to the existing individual), it does not repel with a sufficient intensive inwardness. For without risk there is no faith, and the greater the risk the greater the faith; the more objective security the less inwardness (for inwardness is precisely subjectivity), and the less objective security the more profound the possible inward-

ness. When the paradox is paradoxical in itself, it repels the individual by virtue of its absurdity, and the corresponding passion of inwardness is faith. But subjectivity, inwardness, is the truth: for otherwise we have forgotten what the merit of the Socratic position is. But there can be no stronger expression for inwardness than when the retreat out of existence into the eternal by way of recollection is impossible; and when, with truth confronting the individual as a paradox, gripped in the anguish and pain of sin, facing the tremendous risk of the objective insecurity, the individual believes. But without risk no faith, not even the Socratic form of faith, much less the form of which we here speak.

When Socrates believed that there was a God, he held fast to the objective uncertainty with the whole passion of his inwardness, and it is precisely in this contradiction and in this risk, that faith is rooted. Now it is otherwise. Instead of the objective uncertainty, there is here a certainty, namely, that objectively it is absurd; and this absurdity, held fast in the passion of inwardness, is faith. The Socratic ignorance is as a witty jest in comparison with the earnestness of facing the absurd; and the Socratic existential inwardness is as Greek light-mindedness in comparison with the grave strenuosity of faith.

What now is the absurd? The absurd is—that the eternal truth has come into being in time, that God has come into being, has been born, has grown up, and so forth, precisely like any other individual human being, quite indistinguishable from other individuals.

QUESTIONS FOR FURTHER REFLECTION

1. By proclaiming the ultimate subjectivity of God, does Kierkegaard imply that God doesn't exist objectively?
2. Kierkegaard often speaks of God, but what do you think he means by the term?
3. Would Kierkegaard's concept of God be compatible with traditional monotheism?
4. Why does Kierkegaard seem to feel that objectivity denies the possibility of genuine relationship?
5. Does the necessary postulation of God imply that Man is dependant on God, or does it simply mean that the idea of God is a necessary psychological fixation?

28. KIERKEGAARD'S ARGUMENTS AGAINST OBJECTIVE REASONING IN RELIGION

Robert Merrihew Adams

Robert Merrihew Adams (1937–) is professor of philosophy and Chair of the Department at Yale University. He is also an ordained Presbyterian minister. He has written extensively in metaphysics, ethics, the history of philosophy, and the philosophy of religion. In this selection, he examines three of Kierkegaard's arguments against objective reason in religion and contends that they are problematic.

READING QUESTIONS

1. What is the central question in Kierkegaard's *Postscript*?
2. What is the Approximation Argument?
3. What is the Postponement Argument?
4. What is the Passion Argument?

It is sometimes held that there is something in the nature of religious faith itself that renders it useless or undesirable to reason objectively in support of such faith, even if the reasoning should happen to have considerable plausibility. Søren Kierkegaard's *Concluding Unscientific Postscript* is probably the document most commonly cited as representative of this view. In the present essay I shall discus three arguments for the view. I call them the Approximation Argument, the Postponement Argument, and the Passion Argument; and I suggest they can all be found in the *Postscript*. I shall try to show that the Approximation Argument is a bad argument. The other two will not be so easily disposed of, however. I believe they show that Kierkegaard's conclusion, or something like it, does indeed follow from a certain conception of religiousness—a conception which has some appeal, although for reasons which I shall briefly suggest, I am not prepared to accept it.

Kierkegaard uses the word "objective" and its cognates in several senses, most of which need not concern us here. We are interested in the sense in which he uses it when he says, "it is precisely a misunderstanding to seek an objective assurance," and when he speaks of "an objective uncertainty held fast in the appropriation-process of the most passionate inwardness" (pp. 41, 182).[1] Let us say that a piece of reasoning, R, is *objective reasoning* just in case every (or almost every) intelligent, fairminded, and sufficiently informed person would regard R as showing or tending to show (in the circumstances in which R is used, and to the extent claimed in R) that R's conclusion is true or probably true. Uses of "objective" and "objectively" in other contexts can be understood from their relation to this one; for example, an objective uncertainty is a proposition which cannot be shown by objective reasoning to be certainly true.

1. THE APPROXIMATION ARGUMENT

"Is it possible to base an eternal happiness upon historical knowledge?" is one of the central questions in the *Postscript*, and in the *Philosophical Fragments* to which it is a "postscript." Part of Kierkegaard's answer to the question is that it is not possible to base an eternal happiness on objective reasoning about historical facts.

> For nothing is more readily evident than that the greatest attainable certainty with respect to anything historical is merely an *approximation*. And an approximation, when viewed as a basis for an eternal happiness, is wholly inadequate, since the incommensurability makes a result impossible (p. 25).

[1]Søren Kierkegaard, *Concluding Unscientific Postscript* trans. David F. Swenson: introduction, notes, and completion of translation by Walter Lowrie (Princeton. N.J.: Princeton University Press. 1941). Page references in parentheses in the body of the present paper are to this work.

Kierkegaard maintains that it is possible, however, to base an eternal happiness on a belief in historical facts that is independent of objective evidence for them, and that that is what one must do in order to be a Christian. This is the Approximation Argument for the proposition that Christian faith cannot be based on objective reasoning.[2] (It is assumed that some belief about historical facts is an essential part of Christian faith, so that if religious faith cannot be based on objective historical reasoning, then Christian faith cannot be based on objective reasoning at all.) Let us examine the argument in detail.

Its first premise is Kierkegaard's claim that "the greatest attainable certainty with respect to anything historical is merely an approximation." I take him to mean that historical evidence, objectively considered, never completely excludes the possibility of error. "It goes without saying," he claims, "that it is impossible in the case of historical problems to reach an objective decision so certain that no doubt could disturb it" (p. 41). For Kierkegaard's purposes it does not matter how small the possibility of error is, so long as it is finitely small (that is, so long as it is not literally infinitesimal). He insists (p. 31) that his Approximation Argument makes no appeal to the supposition that the objective evidence for Christian historical beliefs is weaker than the objective evidence for any other historical belief. The argument turns on a claim about *all* historical evidence. The probability of error in our belief that there was an American Civil War in the nineteenth century, for instance, might be as small as $1/10^{2,000,000}$; that would be a large enough chance of error for Kierkegaard's argument.

It might be disputed, but let us assume for the sake of argument that there is some such finitely small probability of error in the objective grounds for all historical beliefs, as Kierkegaard held. This need not keep us from saying that we "know," and it is "certain," that there was an American Civil War. For such an absurdly

small possibility of error is as good as no possibility of error at all, "for all practical intents and purposes," as we might say. Such a possibility of error is too small to be worth worrying about.

But would it be too small to be worth worrying about if we had an *infinite* passionate interest in the question about the Civil War? If we have an infinite passionate interest in something, there is no limit to how important it is to us. (The nature of such an interest will be discussed more fully in section III.) Kierkegaard maintains that in relation to an infinite passionate interest *no* possibility of error is too small to be worth worrying about. "In relation to an eternal happiness, and an infinite passionate interest in its behalf (in which latter alone the former can exist), an iota is of importance, of infinite importance . . ." (p. 28). This is the basis for the second premise of the Approximation Argument, which is Kierkegaard's claim that "an approximation, when viewed as a basis for an eternal happiness, is wholly inadequate" (p. 25). "An approximation is essentially incommensurable with an infinite personal interest in an eternal happiness" (p. 26).

At this point in the argument it is important to have some understanding of Kierkegaard's conception of faith, and the way in which he thinks faith excludes doubt. Faith must be decisive; in fact it seems to consist in a sort of decision-making. "The conclusion of belief is not so much a conclusion as a resolution, and it is for this reason that belief excludes doubt."[3] The decision of faith is a decision to disregard the possibility of error—to act on what is believed, without hedging one's bets to take account of any possibility of error.

To disregard the possibility of error is not to be unaware of it, or fail to consider it, or lack anxiety about it. Kierkegaard insists that the believer must be keenly *aware* of the risk of error. "If I wish to preserve myself in faith I must constantly be intent upon holding fast the objective uncertainty, so as to remain out upon the deep, over seventy thousand fathoms of water, still preserving my faith" (p. 182).

For Kierkegaard, then, to ask whether faith in a historical fact can be based on objective reasoning is to ask whether objective reasoning can justify one in disregarding the possibility of error which (he thinks) his-

[2]The argument is not original with Kierkegaard. It can be found in works of G. E. Lessing and D. F. Strauss that Kierkegaard had read. See especially Thulstrup's quotation and discussion of a passage from Strauss in the commentary portion of Søren Kierkegaard. *Philosophical Fragments.* trans. David F. Swenson, 2d ed., translation revised by Howard V. Hong, with introduction and commentary by Niels Thulstrup (Princeton, N.J.: Princeton University Press, 1962), pp. 149–51.

[3]Kierkegaard. *Philosophical Fragments*, p. 104: cf. pp. 102–3.

torical evidence always leaves. Here another aspect of Kierkegaard's conception of faith plays its part in the argument. He thinks that in all genuine religious faith the believer is *infinitely* interested in the object of his faith. And he thinks it follows that objective reasoning cannot justify him in disregarding *any* possibility of error about the object of faith, and therefore cannot lead him all the way to religious faith where a historical fact is concerned. The farthest it could lead him is to the conclusion that *if* he had only a certain finite (though very great) interest in the matter, the possibility of error would be too small to be worth worrying about and he would be justified in disregarding it. But faith disregards a possibility of error that *is* worth worrying about, since an infinite interest is involved. Thus faith requires a "leap" beyond the evidence, a leap that cannot be justified by objective reasoning (cf. p. 90).

There is something right in what Kierkegaard is saying here, but his Approximation Argument is a bad argument. He is right in holding that grounds of doubt which may be insignificant for most practical purposes can be extremely troubling for the intensity of a religious concern, and that it may require great decisiveness, or something like courage, to overcome them religiously. But he is mistaken in holding that objective reasoning could not justify one in disregarding any possibility of error about something in which one is infinitely interested.

The mistake, I believe, lies in his overlooking the fact that there are at least two different reasons one might have for disregarding a possibility of error. The first is that the possibility is too small to be worth worrying about. The second is that the risk of not disregarding the possibility of error would be greater than the risk of disregarding it. Of these two reasons only the first is ruled out by the infinite passionate interest.

I will illustrate this point with two examples, one secular and one religious. A certain woman has a very great (though not infinite) interest in her husband's love for her. She rightly judges that the objective evidence available to her renders it 99.9 percent probable that he loves her truly. The intensity of her interest is sufficient to cause her some *anxiety* over the remaining 1/1,000 chance that he loves her not: for her this chance is not too small to be worth worrying about. (Kierkegaard uses a similar example to support his Approximation Argument; see p. 511). But she (very reasonably) wants to *disregard* the risk of error, in the sense of not hedging her bets, if he does love her. This desire is at least as strong as her desire not to be deceived if he does not love her. Objective reasoning should therefore suffice to bring her to the conclusion that she ought to disregard the risk of error, since by not disregarding it she would run 999 times as great a risk of frustrating one of these desires.

Or suppose you are trying to base your eternal happiness on your relation to Jesus, and therefore have an infinite passionate interest in the question whether he declared Peter and his episcopal successors to be infallible in matters of religious doctrine. You want to be committed to whichever is the true belief on this question, disregarding any possibility of error in it. And suppose, just for the sake of argument, that objective historical evidence renders it 99 percent probable that Jesus did declare Peter and his successors to be infallible—or 99 percent probable that he did not—for our present discussion it does not matter which. The 1 percent chance of error is enough to make you *anxious*, in view of your infinite interest. But objective reasoning leads to the conclusion that you ought to commit yourself to the more probable opinion, *disregarding* the risk of error, if your strongest desire in the matter is to be so committed to the true opinion. For the only other way to satisfy this desire would be to commit yourself to the less probable opinion, disregarding the risk of error in it. The first way will be successful if and only if the more probable opinion is true, and the second way if and only if the less probable opinion is true. Surely it is prudent to do what gives you a 99 percent chance of satisfying your strong desire, in preference to what gives you only a 1 percent chance of satisfying it.

In this argument your strong desire to be committed to the true opinion is presupposed. The reasonableness of this desire may depend on a belief for which no probability can be established by purely historical reasoning, such as the belief that Jesus is God. But any difficulties arising from this point are distinct from those urged in the Approximation Argument, which itself presupposes the infinite passionate interest in the historical question.

There is some resemblance between my arguments in these examples and Pascal's famous Wager argument. But whereas Pascal's argument turns on weighing an infinite interest against a finite one, mine turn on weighing a large chance of success against a small one. . . .

The reader may well have noticed in the foregoing discussion some unclarity about what sort of justification is being demanded and given for religious beliefs about historical facts. There are at least two different types of question about a proposition which I might try to settle by objective reasoning: (1) Is it probable that the proposition is true? (2) In view of the evidence which I have for and against the proposition, and my interest in the matter, is it prudent for me to have faith in the truth of the proposition, disregarding the possibility of error? Correspondingly, we may distinguish two ways in which a belief can be *based on* objective reasoning. The proposition believed may be the conclusion of a piece of objective reasoning, and accepted because it is that. We may say that such a belief is *objectively probable*. Or one might hold a belief or maintain a religious faith because of a piece of objective reasoning whose conclusion is that it would be prudent, morally right, or otherwise desirable for one to hold that belief or faith. In this latter case let us say that the belief is *objectively advantageous*. It is clear that historical beliefs can be objectively probable; and in the Approximation Argument, Kierkegaard does not deny Christian historical beliefs can be objectively probable. His thesis is, in effect, that in view of an infinite passionate interest in their subject matter, they cannot be objectively advantageous, and therefore cannot be fully justified objectively, even if they are objectively probable. It is this thesis that I have attempted to refute. I have not been discussing the question whether Christian historical beliefs are objectively probable.

2. THE POSTPONEMENT ARGUMENT

The trouble with objective historical reasoning, according to the Approximation Argument, is that it cannot yield complete certainty. But that is not Kierkegaard's only complaint against it as a basis for religious faith. He also objects that objective historical inquiry is never completely finished, so that one who seeks to base his faith on it postpones his religious commitment forever. In the process of historical research "new difficulties arise and are overcome, and new difficulties again arise. Each generation inherits from its predecessor the illusion that the method is quite impeccable, but the learned scholars have not yet succeeded . . . and so forth. . . . The infinite personal passionate interest of the subject . . . vanishes more and more, because the decision is postponed, and postponed as following directly upon the result of the learned inquiry" (p. 28). As soon as we take "an historical document" as "our standard for the determination of Christian truth," we are "involved in a parenthesis whose conclusion is everlastingly prospective" (p. 28)—that is, we are involved in a religious digression which keeps religious commitment forever in the future.[4]

Kierkegaard has such fears about allowing religious faith to rest on *any* empirical reasoning. The danger of postponement of commitment arises not only from the uncertainties of historical scholarship, but also in connection with the design argument for God's existence. In the *Philosophical Fragments* Kierkegaard notes some objections to the attempt to prove God's existence from evidence of "the wisdom in nature, the goodness, the wisdom in the governance of the world," and then says, "even if I began I would never finish, and would in addition have to live constantly in suspense, lest something so terrible should suddenly happen that my bit of proof would be demolished."[5] What we have before us is a quite general sort of objection to the treatment of religious beliefs as empirically testable. On this point many analytical philosophers seem to agree with Kierkegaard. Much discussion in recent analytical philosophy of religion has proceeded from the supposition that religious beliefs are not empirically testable. I think it is far from obvious that that supposition is correct; and it is interesting to consider arguments that may be advanced to support it.

Kierkegaard's statements suggest an argument that I call the Postponement Argument. Its first premise is that one cannot have an authentic religious faith without being totally committed to it. In order to be totally committed to a belief, in the relevant sense, one must be determined not to abandon

---

[4]Essentially the same argument can be found in a plea, which has had great influence among more recent theologians, for making Christian faith independent of the results of critical historical study of the Bible: Martin Kahler's famous lecture, first delivered in 1892, *Der sogenannte historische Jesus und der geschichtliche biblische Christus* (Munich: Christus Kaiser Verlag, 1961), p. 50f.

[5]Kierkegaard, *Philosophical Fragments*, p. 52.

the belief under any circumstances that one recognizes as epistemically possible.

The second premise is that one cannot yet be totally committed to any belief which one bases on an inquiry in which one recognizes any possibility of a future need to revise the results. Total commitment to any belief so based will necessarily be postponed. I believe that this premise, suitably interpreted, is true. Consider the position of someone who regards himself as committed to a belief on the basis of objective evidence, but who recognizes some possibility that future discoveries will destroy the objective justification of the belief. We must ask how he is disposed to react in the event, however unlikely, that the objective basis of his belief is overthrown. Is he prepared to abandon the belief in that event? If so, he is not totally committed to the belief in the relevant sense. But if he is determined to cling to his belief even if its objective justification is taken away, then he is not basing the belief on the objective justification—or at least he is not basing it solely on the justification.[6]

The conclusion to be drawn from these two premises is that authentic religious faith cannot be based on an inquiry in which one recognizes any possibility of a future need to revise the results. We ought to note that this conclusion embodies two important restrictions on the scope of the argument.

In the first place, we are not given an argument that authentic religious faith cannot *have* an objective justification that is subject to possible future revision. What we are given is an argument that the authentic believer's holding of his religious belief cannot *depend* entirely on such a justification.

In the second place, this conclusion applies only to those who *recognize* some epistemic possibility that the objective results which appear to support their belief may be overturned. I think it would be unreasonable to require, as part of total commitment, a determination with regard to one's response to circumstances that one does not recognize as possible at all. It may be,

however, that one does not recognize such a possibility when one ought to.

Kierkegaard needs one further premise in order to arrive at the conclusion that authentic religious faith cannot without error be based on any objective empirical reasoning. This third premise is that in every objective empirical inquiry there is always, objectively considered, some epistemic possibility that the results of the inquiry will need to be revised in view of new evidence or new reasoning. I believe Kierkegaard makes this assumption; he certainly makes it with regard to historical inquiry. From this premise it follows that one is in error if in any objective empirical inquiry one does not recognize any possibility of a future need to revise the results. But if one does recognize such a possibility, then according to the conclusion already reached in the Postponement Argument, one cannot base an authentic religious faith on the inquiry.

Some philosophers might attack the third premise of this argument; and certainly it is controversial. But I am more inclined to criticize the first premise. There is undoubtedly something plausible about the claim that authentic religious faith must involve a commitment so complete that the believer is resolved not to abandon his belief under any circumstances that he regards as epistemically possible. If you are willing to abandon your ostensibly religious beliefs for the sake of objective inquiry, mightn't we justly say that objective inquiry is your real religion, the thing to which you are most deeply committed?

There is also something plausible to be said on the other side, however. It has commonly been thought to be an important part of religious ethics that one ought to be humble, teachable, open to correction, new inspiration, and growth of insight, even (and perhaps especially) in important religious beliefs. That view would have to be discarded if we were to concede to Kierkegaard that the heart of commitment in religion is an unconditional determination not to change in one's important religious beliefs. In fact I think there is something radically wrong with this conception of religious commitment. Faith ought not to be thought of as unconditional devotion to a belief. For in the first place the object of religious devotion is not a belief or attitude of one's own, but God. And in the second place it may be doubted that religious devotion to God can or should be completely unconditional. God's love

[6]Kierkegaard notes the possibility that in believing in God's existence "I make so bold as to defy all objections, even those that have not yet been made." But in that case he thinks the belief is not really based on the evidence of God's work in the world: "It is not from the works that I make my proof" (*Philosophical Fragments*, p. 52).

for sinners is sometimes said to be completely unconditional, not being based on any excellence or merit of
theirs. But religious devotion to God is generally
thought to be based on his goodness and love. It is the
part of the strong, not the weak, to love unconditionally. And in relation to God we are weak.

3. THE PASSION ARGUMENT

In Kierkegaard's statements of the Approximation
Argument and the Postponement Argument it is assumed that a system of religious beliefs might be objectively probable. It is only for the sake of argument,
however, that Kierkegaard allows this assumption. He
really holds that religious faith, by its very nature,
needs objective *im*probability. "Anything that is almost probable, or probable, or extremely and emphatically probable, is something [one] can almost know,
or as good as know, or extremely and emphatically almost *know*—but it is impossible to *believe*" (p. 189).
Nor will Kierkegaard countenance the suggestion
that religion ought to go beyond belief to some
almost-knowledge based on probability. "Faith is the
highest passion in a man. There are perhaps many in
every generation who do not even reach it, but no
one gets further."[7] It would be a betrayal of religion to
try to go beyond faith. The suggestion that faith
might be replaced by "probabilities and guarantees" is
for the believer "a temptation to be resisted with all
his strength" (p. 15). The attempt to establish religious beliefs on a foundation of objective probability
is therefore no service to religion, but inimical to religion's true interests. The approximation to certainty
which might be afforded by objective probability is
rejected, not only for the reasons given in the Approximation Argument and Postponement Argument, but also from a deeper motive, "since on the
contrary it behooves us to get rid of introductory
guarantees of security, proofs from consequences, and
the whole mob of public pawnbrokers and guarantors,
so as to permit the absurd to stand out in all its
clarity—in order that the individual may believe if he

wills it: I merely say that it must be strenuous in the
highest degree so to believe" (p. 190).

As this last quotation indicates, Kierkegaard
thinks that religious belief ought to be based on a
strenuous exertion of the will—a passionate striving.
His reasons for thinking that objective probability is
religiously undesirable have to do with the place of
passion in religion, and constitute what I call the
Passion Argument. The first premise of the argument is that the most essential and the most valuable feature of religiousness is passion, indeed an infinite passion, a passion of the greatest possible
intensity. The second premise is that an infinite passion requires objective improbability. And the conclusion therefore is that that which is most essential
and most valuable in religiousness requires objective
improbability.

My discussion of this argument will have three
parts. (a) First I will try to clarify, very briefly, what it is
that is supposed to be objectively improbable.
(b) Then we will consider Kierkegaard's reasons for
holding that infinite passion requires objective improbability. In so doing we will also gain a clearer understanding of what a Kierkegaardian infinite passion
is. (c) Finally I will discuss the first premise of the
argument—although issues will arise at that point
which I do not pretend to be able to settle by argument.

(a) What are the beliefs whose improbability is
needed by religious passion? Kierkegaard will hardly
be satisfied with the improbability of just any one belief; it must surely be at least an important belief. On
the other hand it would clearly be preposterous to
suppose that every belief involved in Christianity
must be objectively improbable. (Consider, for example, the belief that the man Jesus did indeed live.) I
think that what is demanded in the Passion Argument is the objective improbability of at least one belief which must be true if the goal sought by the religious passion is to be attained.

(b) We can find in the *Postscript* suggestions of several reasons for thinking that an infinite passion needs
objective improbability. The two that seem to be most
interesting have to do with (i) the risks accepted and
(ii) the costs paid in pursuance of a passionate interest.

(i) One reason that Kierkegaard has for valuing
objective improbability is that it increases the *risk* attaching to the religious life, and risk is so essential for

---

[7]Søren Kierkegaard, *Fear and Trembling*, trans. Walter Lowrie,
2d ed. (Princeton, N.J.: Princeton University Press, 1970: published in one volume with *The Sickness unto Death*), p. 131, Cf. *Postscript*, p. 31f.

the expression of religious passion that "without risk there is no faith" (p. 182). About the nature of an eternal happiness, the goal of religious striving, Kierkegaard says "there is nothing to be said . . . except that it is the good which is attained by venturing everything absolutely" (p. 382).

But what then does it mean to venture? A venture is the precise correlative of an uncertainty; when the certainty is there the venture becomes impossible. . . . If what I hope to gain by venturing is itself certain, I do not risk or venture, but make an exchange. . . . No, if I am in truth resolved to venture, in truth resolved to strive for the attainment of the highest good, the uncertainty must be there, and I must have room to move, so to speak. But the largest space I can obtain, where there is room for the most vehement gesture of the passion that embraces the infinite, is uncertainty of knowledge with respect to an eternal happiness, or the certain knowledge that the choice is in the finite sense a piece of madness: now there is room, now you can venture! (pp. 380–82)

How is it that objective improbability provides the largest space for the most vehement gesture of infinite passion? Consider two cases. (A) You plunge into a raging torrent to rescue from drowning someone you love, who is crying for help. (B) You plunge into a raging torrent in a desperate attempt to rescue someone you love, who appears to be unconscious and *may* already have drowned. In both cases you manifest a passionate interest in saving the person, risking your own life in order to do so. But I think Kierkegaard would say there is more passion in the second case than in the first. For in the second case you risk your life on what is, objectively considered, a smaller chance that you will be able to save your loved one. A greater passion is required for a more desperate attempt.

A similar assessment may be made of the following pair of cases. A′) You stake everything on your faith in the truth of Christianity, knowing that it is objectively 99 percent probable that Christianity is true. (B′) You stake everything on your faith in the truth of Christianity, knowing that the truth of Christianity is, objectively, possible but so improbable that its probability is, say, as small as $1/10^{2,000,000}$. There is passion in

both cases, but Kierkegaard will say that there is more passion in the second case than in the first. For to venture the same stake (namely, everything) on a much smaller chance of success shows greater passion.

Acceptance of risk can thus be seen as a *measure* of the intensity of passion. I believe this provides us with one way of understanding what Kierkegaard means when he calls religious passion "infinite." An *infinite* passionate interest in x is an interest so strong that it leads one to make the greatest possible sacrifices in order to obtain x, on the smallest possible chance of success. The infinity of the passion is shown in that there is no sacrifice so great one will not make it, and no chance of success so small one will not act on it. A passion which is infinite in this sense requires, by its very nature, a situation of maximum risk for its expression.

It will doubtless be objected that this argument involves a misunderstanding of what a passionate interest is. Such an interest is a disposition. In order to have a great passionate interest it is not necessary actually to make a great sacrifice with a small chance of success; all that is necessary is to have such an intense interest that one *would* do so if an appropriate occasion should arise. It is therefore a mistake to say that there *is* more passion in case (B) than in case (A), or in (B′) than in (A′). More passion is *shown* in (B) than in (A), and in (B′) than in (A′); but an equal passion may exist in cases in which there is no occasion to show it.

This objection may well be correct as regards what we normally mean by "passionate interest." But that is not decisive for the argument. The crucial question is what part dispositions, possibly unactualized, ought to play in religious devotion. And here we must have a digression about the position of the *Postscript* on this question—a position that is complex at best and is not obviously consistent.

In the first place I do not think that Kierkegaard would be prepared to think of passion, or a passionate interest, as primarily a disposition that might remain unactualized. He seems to conceive of passion chiefly as an intensity in what one actually does and feels. "Passion is momentary" (p. 178), although capable of continual repetition. And what is momentary in such a way that it must be repeated rather than protracted is presumably an occurrence rather than a disposition. It agrees with this conception of passion that Kierkegaard idealizes a life of "persistent striving," and says that the religious task is to "exercise" the God-relationship and to give "existential expression" to the religious choice (pp. 110, 364, 367).

All of this supports the view that what Kierkegaard means by "an infinite passionate interest" is a pattern of actual decision-making in which one continually exercises and expresses one's religiousness by making the greatest possible sacrifices on the smallest possible chance of success. In order to actualize such a pattern of life one needs chances of success that are as small as possible. That is the room that is required for "the most vehement gesture" of infinite passion.

But on the other hand Kierkegaard does allow a dispositional element in the religious life, and even precisely in the making of the greatest possible sacrifices. We might suppose that if we are to make the greatest possible sacrifices in our religious devotion, we must do so by abandoning all worldly interests and devoting all our time and attention to religion. That is what monasticism attempts to do, as Kierkegaard sees it; and (in the *Postscript*, at any rate) he rejects the attempt, contrary to what our argument to this point would have led us to expect of him. He holds that "resignation" (pp. 353, 367) or "renunciation" (pp. 362, 386) of *all* finite ends is precisely the first thing that religiousness requires; but he means a renunciation that is compatible with pursuing and enjoying finite ends (pp. 362–71). This renunciation is the practice of a sort of detachment; Kierkegaard uses the image of a dentist loosening the soft tissues around a tooth, while it is still in place, in preparation for pulling it (p. 367). It is partly a matter of not treating finite things with a desperate seriousness, but with a certain coolness or humor, even while one pursues them (pp. 368, 370).

This coolness is not just a disposition. But the renunciation also has a dispositional aspect. "Now if for any individual an eternal happiness is his highest good, this will mean that all finite satisfactions are volitionally relegated to the status of what may have to be renounced in favor of an eternal happiness" (p. 350). The volitional relegation is not a disposition but an act of choice. The object of this choice, however, appears to be a dispositional state—the state of being such that one *would* forgo any finite satisfaction *if* it *were* religiously necessary or advantageous to do so.

It seems clear that Kierkegaard, in the *Postscript*, is willing to admit a dispositional element at one point in the religious venture, but not at another. It is enough in most cases, he thinks, if one is *prepared* to cease for the sake of religion from pursuing some finite end; but it is not enough that one *would* hold to one's belief in the face of objective improbability. The belief must actually be improbable, although the pursuit of the finite need not actually cease. What is not clear is a reason for this disparity. The following hypothesis, admittedly somewhat speculative as interpretation of the text, is the best explanation I can offer.

The admission of a dispositional element in the religious renunciation of the finite is something to which Kierkegaard seems to be driven by the view that there is no alternative to it except idolatry. For suppose one actually ceases from all worldly pursuits and enters a monastery. In the monastery one would pursue a number of particular ends (such as getting up in the middle of the night to say the offices) which, although religious in a way ("churchy," one might say), are still finite. The absolute *telos* or end of religion is no more to be identified with them than with the ends pursued by an alderman (pp. 362–71). To pretend otherwise would be to make an idolatrous identification of the absolute end with some finite end. An existing person cannot have sacrificed everything by actually having ceased from pursuing *all* ends. For as long as he lives and acts he is pursuing some finite end. Therefore his renouncing *everything* finite must be at least partly dispositional.

Kierkegaard does not seem happy with this position. He regards it as of the utmost importance that the religious passion should come to expression. The problem of finding an adequate expression for a passion for an infinite end, in the face of the fact that in every concrete action one will be pursuing some finite end, is treated in the *Postscript* as the central problem of religion (see especially pp. 386–468). If the sacrifice of everything finite must remain largely dispositional, then perhaps it is all the more important to Kierkegaard that the smallness of the chance for which it is sacrificed should be fully actual, so that the infinity of the religious passion may be measured by an actuality in at least one aspect of the religious venture.

(ii) According to Kierkegaard, as I have argued, the intensity of a passion is measured in part by the smallness of the chances of success that one acts on. It can also be measured in part by its *costliness*—that is, by how much one gives up or suffers in acting on those chances. This second measure can also be made the basis of an argument for the claim that an infinite passion requires objective improbability. For the objective improbability of a religious belief, if recognized, increases the costliness of holding it. The risk involved in staking everything on an objectively improbable belief gives rise to an anxiety and mental suffering whose acceptance is itself a sacrifice. It seems to follow that if one is not staking everything on a belief one sees to be objectively improbable, one's passion is not infinite in Kierkegaard's sense, since one's sacrifice could be greater if one did adhere to an improbable belief.

Kierkegaard uses an argument similar to this. For God to give us objective knowledge of himself, eliminating paradox from it, would be "to lower the price of the God-relationship."

> And even if God could be imagined willing, no man with passion in his heart could desire it. To a maiden genuinely in love it could never occur that she had bought her happiness too dear, but rather that she had not bought it dear enough. And just as the passion of the infinite was itself the truth, so in the case of the highest value it holds true that the price is the value, that a low price means a poor value . . . (p. 207).

Kierkegaard here appears to hold, first, that an increase in the objective probability of religious belief would reduce its costliness, and second, that the value of a religious life is measured by its cost. I take it his reason for the second of these claims is that passion is the most valuable thing in a religious life and passion is measured by its cost. If we grant Kierkegaard the requisite conception of an infinite passion, we seem once again to have a plausible argument for the view that objective improbability is required for such a passion.

(c) We must therefore consider whether infinite passion, as Kierkegaard conceives of it, ought to be part of the religious ideal of life. Such a passion is a striving, or pattern of decision-making, in which, with the greatest possible intensity of feeling, one continually makes the greatest possible sacrifices on the smallest possible chance of success. This seems to me an impossible ideal. I doubt that any human being could have a passion of this sort, because I doubt that one could make a sacrifice so great that a greater could not be made, or have a (nonzero) chance of success so small that a smaller could not be had.

But even if Kierkegaard's ideal is impossible, one might want to try to approximate it. Intensity of passion might still be measured by the greatness of sacrifices made and the smallness of chances of success acted on, even if we cannot hope for a greatest possible or a smallest possible here. And it could be claimed that the most essential and valuable thing in religiousness is a passion that is very intense (though it cannot be infinite) by this standard—the more intense the better. This claim will not support an argument that objective improbability is absolutely required for religious passion. For a passion could presumably be very intense, involving great sacrifices and risks of some other sort, without an objectively improbable belief. But it could still be argued that objectively improbable religious beliefs enhance the value of the religious life by increasing its sacrifices and diminishing its chances of success, whereas objective probability detracts from the value of religious passion by diminishing its intensity.

The most crucial question about the Passion Argument, then, is whether maximization of sacrifice and risk are so valuable in religion as to make objective improbability a desirable characteristic of religious beliefs. Certainly much religious thought and feeling places a very high value on sacrifice and on passionate intensity. But the doctrine that it is desirable to increase without limit, or to the highest possible degree (if there is one) the cost and risk of a religious life is less plausible (to say the least) than the view that *some* degree of cost and risk may add to the value of a religious life. The former doctrine would set the religious interest at enmity with all other interests, or at least with the best of them. Kierkegaard is surely right in thinking that it would be impossible to live without pursuing some finite ends. But even so it would be possible to exchange the pursuit of better finite ends for the pursuit of worse ones—for example, by exchanging the pursuit of truth, beauty, and satisfying personal relationships for the self-flagellating pursuit of pain. And a way of life would be the costlier for requiring such an exchange. Kierkegaard does not, in the *Postscript*, demand it. But the presuppositions of his Passion Argument seem to imply that such a sacrifice would be religiously desirable. Such a conception of religion is demonic. In a tolerable religious ethics some way must be found to conceive of the religious interest as inclusive rather than exclusive of the best of other interests—including, I think, the interest in having well-grounded beliefs.

4. PASCAL'S WAGER AND KIERKEGAARD'S LEAP

Ironically, Kierkegaard's views about religious passion suggest a way in which his religious beliefs could be based on objective reasoning—not on reasoning which would show them to be objectively probable, but on reasoning which shows them to be objectively advantageous. Consider the situation of a person whom Kierkegaard would regard as a genuine Christian believer. What would such a person want most of all? He would want above all else to attain the truth through Christianity. That is, he would desire both that Christianity be true and that he himself be related to it as a genuine believer. He would desire that state of affairs (which we may call S) so ardently that he would be willing to sacrifice everything else to obtain it, given only the smallest possible chance of success.

We can therefore construct the following argument, which has an obvious analogy to Pascal's Wager. Let us assume that there is, objectively, some chance, however small, that Christianity is true. This is an assumption which Kierkegaard accepts (p. 31), and I think it is plausible. There are two possibilities, then: either Christianity is true, or it is false. (Others might object to so stark a disjunction, but Kierkegaard will not.) If Christianity is false it is impossible for anyone to obtain S, since S includes the truth of Christianity.

It is only if Christianity is true that anything one does will help one or hinder one in obtaining S. And if Christianity is true, one will obtain S just in case one becomes a genuine Christian believer. It seems obvious that one would increase one's chances of becoming a genuine Christian believer by becoming one now (if one can), even if the truth of Christian beliefs is now objectively uncertain or improbable. Hence it would seem to be advantageous for anyone who can to become a genuine Christian believer now, if he wants S so much that he would be willing to sacrifice everything else for the smallest possible chance of obtaining S. Indeed I believe that the argument I have given for this conclusion is a piece of objective reasoning, and that Christian belief is therefore *objectively* advantageous for anyone who wants S as much as a Kierkegaardian genuine Christian must want it.

Of course this argument does not tend at all to show that it is objectively probable that Christianity is true. It only gives a practical, prudential reason for believing, to someone who has a certain desire. Nor does the argument do anything to prove that such an absolutely overriding desire for S is reasonable.[8] It does show, however, that just as Kierkegaard's position has more logical structure than one might at first think, it is more difficult than he probably realized for him to get away entirely from objective justification.

QUESTIONS FOR FURTHER REFLECTION

1. What is the significance of Pascal's Wager to what Adams says?
2. What is Adam's example involving the Civil War supposed to show?

---

[8]It is worth noting, though, that a similar argument might still provide some less overriding justification of belief to someone who had a strong, but less overriding, desire for S.

29. REFORMED EPISTEMOLOGY AND THE RATIONALITY OF THEISTIC BELIEF

James F. Sennett

James F. Sennett is professor of philosophy and interdisciplinary studies at Lincoln Christian College and Seminary in Lincoln, Illinois. He earned an M.A. and Ph.D. in philosophy from the University of Nebraska, an M.Div. in Old Testament Studies from Lincoln Christian Seminary (1981), and an A.B. in Christian Ministry from Atlanta Christian College (1977). He did post doctoral work as a National Endowment for the Humanities Fellow at the University of California–Berkeley and as a Pew Charitable Trusts Scholar at Calvin College. He has written one book, edited another, and published numerous articles on various topics in the philosophy of religion.

READING QUESTIONS

1. What is the difference between the *de facto* and *de jure* objections to theistic belief?
2. What are Plantinga's two arguments against classical foundationalism?
3. What are Plantinga's two arguments against Quinn's defeater objection?
4. What is the difference between rationality and warrant?
5. What, according to Sennett, is the most important insight to come out of the Reformed epistemology program?

1. INTRODUCTION

Few developments in twentieth-century philosophy of religion have generated as much attention and controversy as the theory introduced and developed by Alvin Plantinga and dubbed by him "Reformed epistemology." Plantinga is John A. O'Brien Professor of Philosophy and director of the Center for Philosophy of Religion at the University of Notre Dame. He is also widely recognized as the most important American philosopher of religion of the last 50 years.[1]

Reformed epistemology is the simple yet profound idea that theistic belief can be, and typically is, justified without appeal to evidence. (By "theistic belief" I mean any belief that directly entails the existence of the God of theism—the God of Judaism, Christianity, and Islam. An example of a theistic belief would be the belief that God has forgiven my sins.) Rather, theistic belief is typically "properly basic"—deriving its justification immediately from some appropriate experience. Just as perceptual beliefs, for example, are justified immediately by the perceptual experiences that produce them, so theistic beliefs are appropriately produced by certain experiences, and therefore justified. This provocative idea has formed a stimulating counterbalance to the resurgent interests in natural theology and evidentialist apologetics that have characterized much of the Christian philosophy renaissance of the last 30 years.

An important motivation for Plantinga's Reformed epistemology theory is the doctrine of the *sensus divinitatis*, introduced by the father of Reformed theology, the sixteenth-century theologian John Calvin. Calvin argued that human beings have a "sense of the divine" that enables us to perceive God in much the same way that our perceptual senses

[1] In addition to his three-volume work in epistemology cited below, Plantinga's most important books include *God and Other Minds* (Ithaca, NY: Cornell, 1966), *God, Freedom, and Evil* (Grand Rapids, MI: Eerdmans, 1974), and *The Nature of Necessity* (Cambridge: Cambridge University Press, 1974). Many of his most important articles have been anthologized in *The Analytic Theist: An Alvin Plantinga Reader*, ed. James F. Sennett (Grand Rapids, MI: Eerdmans, 1998). A technical study of Plantinga's philosophy of religion can be found in James F. Sennett, *Modality, Probability, and Rationality: A Critical Examination of Alvin Plantinga's Philosophy* (New York: Peter Lang, 1992).

enable us to perceive the world around us. While this faculty has been corrupted and tainted by sin, it nonetheless remains, and enables those willing to recognize its authority to be aware of the presence and work of God in the world. Plantinga's Reformed epistemology project can be seen as an attempt to give a philosophically sophisticated account of Calvin's *sensus divinitatis* doctrine.

2. REFORMED EPISTEMOLOGY, PROPERLY BASIC BELIEF, AND THE *DE JURE* OBJECTION

It is important to begin by distinguishing exactly what Reformed epistemology is saying about theistic belief. Plantinga's most famous claim is that theistic belief is typically *properly basic*. To say that a belief is *basic* is to say that it is not based on any other beliefs one holds. That is, if a person holds a basic belief, then she does not hold it because she has derived it from any of her other beliefs. Now, this person may or may not be *justified* or *rational* in holding her belief basically.[2] That is, it may or may not be epistemically appropriate for her to hold it. If she is justified in holding her belief basically, then the belief is said to be *properly basic* for her.

The question of whether or not a basic belief is *properly* basic is important for two reasons. First, if it is not, then one is open to the charge of *irrationality*—a sort of epistemic sin or misdeed that responsible people would typically want to avoid. Second, epistemologists have long considered justification to be a necessary condition for knowledge. That is, a person *knows* a certain claim only if her belief of that claim is justified. Therefore, the question of whether or not a given basic belief is *properly* basic is directly related to the important question of whether or not the belief constitutes knowledge.

Both of these considerations have motivated Plantinga's arguments on behalf of the Reformed epistemology program. He has argued both that: (1) theists are typically *justified* or *rational* in their basic theistic

beliefs; and (2) basic theistic beliefs typically constitute knowledge for the theist—provided that the beliefs are true.[3] (This essay will concentrate on the first of these two claims, though the second will be addressed briefly near the end.) These claims emphasize a very important fact about the Reformed epistemology program. Plantinga is not arguing that theism is *true*. He is not engaging in apologetics or natural theology. Rather, he is arguing that theistic beliefs are typically justified, even when basic—a separate issue from the question of their truth.

Plantinga clarifies this distinction by identifying two separate objections that have been raised against theistic belief.[4] The first, which he calls the *de facto* objection, is the claim that theistic belief is inappropriate because theism is false. This is the charge raised by classical philosophy of religion arguments like the so-called "Logical Argument from Evil." This argument asserts that the existence of evil is incompatible with the existence of the theistic God. Since it is obvious that there is evil, it follows that the theistic God does not exist. But there is also what Plantinga calls the *de jure* objection. This objection is that it is irrelevant whether or not theism is true, because even if it is true the theist could never *know* that it is true, because theistic belief cannot be justified. The *de jure* objection is aimed not at the question of the truth of theism, but at the question of the epistemic justification of anyone who believes that theism is true.

And here we come to a point that is vital to remember throughout this essay: Plantinga's Reformed epistemology program is a response to the *de jure* objection, not to the *de facto* objection. Plantinga is not concerned in these discussions with the question of whether or not theism is *true*, but with the question of whether or not theistic belief is *justified*. While questions of truth and justification are often closely related, they are also distinct, and must be kept distinct in or-

---

[2]For the purposes of this chapter, I will use the terms *justified* and *rational*, and related terms, synonymously. Much has been made at times in the debate about alleged differences in the concepts, but such concerns are well beyond the scope of this introductory essay.

[3]Truth is typically considered another of the necessary conditions for knowledge. That is, one cannot know something unless it is true. (One may *think* one knows it, but if it is false, then she is mistaken.) So Plantinga's claim here amounts to the assertion that basic theistic belief meets all other criteria for knowledge—so that, if it is also true, then it is knowledge.

[4]Alvin Plantinga, *Warranted Theistic Belief* (New York: Oxford, 2000), viii–ix.

"THE AQUINAS/CALVIN MODEL" * *Alvin Plantinga*

According to the A/C model, this natural knowledge of God is not arrived at by inference or argument (for example, the famous theistic proofs of natural theology) but in a much more immediate way. The deliverances of the *sensus divinitatis* are not quick and *sotto voce* inferences from the circumstances that trigger its operation. It isn't that one beholds the night sky, notes that it is grand, and concludes that there must be such a person as God: an argument like that would be ridiculously weak. It isn't that one notes some feature of the Australian outback—that it is ancient and brooding, for example—and draws the conclusion that God exists. It is rather that, upon the perception of the night sky or the mountain vista or the tiny flower, these beliefs just arise within us. They are *occasioned* by the circumstances; they are not conclusions from them. The heavens declare the glory of God and the skies proclaim the work of his hands: but not by way of serving as premises for an argument. Awareness of guilt may lead me to God; but it is not that in this awareness I have the mate-

rial for a quick theistic argument: I am guilty, so there must be a God. This argument isn't nearly as silly as it looks; but when the operation of the *sensus divinitatis* is triggered by perception of my guilt, it doesn't work by way of an argument. I don't take my guilt as *evidence* for the existence of God, or for the proposition that he is displeased with me. It is rather that in that circumstance—the circumstance of my clearly seeing my guilt—I simply find myself with the belief that God is disapproving or disappointed.

In this regard, the *sensus divinitatis* resembles perception, memory, and *a priori* belief. Consider the first. I look out into the backyard; I see that the coral tiger lilies are in bloom. I don't note that I am being appeared to a certain complicated way (that my experience is of a certain complicated character) and then make an argument from my being appeared to in that way to the conclusion that in fact there are coral tiger lilies in bloom there.

From Alvin Plantinga, *Warranted Christian Belief* (2000).

der to avoid some very perplexing confusions. Later in this essay I will return to the *de facto* objection to make a very important point that is really the crowning conclusion of Plantinga's Reformed epistemology program. But until then I will be concerned almost exclusively with the *de jure* objection. That is, I (like Plantinga) will be concerned with the justification of theistic beliefs, and not with their truth.

3. EVIDENTIALISM AND FOUNDATIONALISM

It would be natural to begin our inquiry into Reformed epistemology with the question, Why should we believe Plantinga's claim that theistic belief can be, and typically is, properly basic? Plantinga, how-

ever, suggests that we begin with a different question: Why *shouldn't* we accept the Reformed epistemology proposal? Why should we balk at the idea of properly basic theistic belief? Plantinga says the major reason people reject Reformed epistemology is because they accept what he calls *evidentialism*. Evidentialism is the view that theistic belief must be based on *evidence* in order to be justified. By "evidence" the evidentialist means *propositional* evidence in the form of other beliefs one holds. In other words, the evidentialist claims that theistic belief is justified only if it is based on other beliefs, and therefore only if it is not basic.

Evidentialism has a long and rich tradition in Western philosophy, and has been embraced by theists and atheists alike. In the modern period, theist John Locke and atheist David Hume both espoused a form of evidentialism. In our own generation, prominent theistic philosopher Richard Swinburne and influential atheistic thinker John Mackie have agreed in their evidentialist sentiments. And in the three centuries separating these thinkers many others have joined their ranks and voiced the position that theistic belief is justified only if it is based on evidence so defined.

But when we define evidentialism as the view that theistic belief is justified only if it is based on other beliefs, we see that evidentialism is simply the *denial* of Reformed epistemology. That is, Reformed epistemology and evidentialism stand as claim and counterclaim. Plantinga says that theistic belief is properly basic. The evidentialist says that it is not. So evidentialism is not in itself a *reason* to reject Reformed epistemology; it is simply the claim that Reformed epistemology is false. But why should we believe the evidentialist rather than the Reformed epistemologist? The answer to this question can be found by examining the answer to another: What kinds of beliefs are properly basic? Is there a criterion by which we can judge whether beliefs can be justified without evidence or require some evidential base in order to be justified?

Notice something very important that these questions imply (and that we have been assuming since the beginning of this essay)—that there are two different ways beliefs are justified. Some beliefs are justified by being based on evidence, while other beliefs are justified even though they are not based on evidence—even though they are basic. This two-fold division of justified beliefs forms the basis for the epistemological theory known as *foundationalism*.

Foundationalism is motivated by the conviction that not all justified beliefs can be based on evidence. To see this, consider the claim that a certain belief B is justified by another belief B^*.[5] Now it seems clear that B can be justified only if B^* is justified. But if all justified beliefs are based on evidence, then B^* must be justified by another belief B^{**}. But B^* can be so justified only if B^{**} is also justified, say by B^{***}, and off we go. Thus if all justified beliefs must be based on other justified beliefs, we fall into an *infinite regression* of justifica-

tion. Thus it seems that one can have a justified belief only if she has an infinite number of justified beliefs. But no one has an infinite number of beliefs *at all*, let alone an infinite number of justified beliefs. So the assumption that only evidentially based beliefs can be justified leads to skepticism—no one is justified in any beliefs. To stop the regression and its skeptical outcome, foundationalists argue that some beliefs are justified without being based on evidence. These beliefs—the *properly basic* ones—form the *basis* or *foundation* on which all evidentially based beliefs are built (hence the name *foundationalism*).

As a theory about the basic structure of justification,[6] foundationalism makes no judgment about what kinds of beliefs are or can be in the foundations—about what beliefs are properly basic. It merely points out that some beliefs *must* be properly basic in order to stop the infinite regression and avoid skepticism. Nonetheless, Plantinga claims that a certain consensus can be established throughout the history of philosophy concerning what kinds of beliefs can be and typically are properly basic. This consensus Plantinga labels *classical foundationalism*.[7] Classical foundationalism is actually a combination of two different views about proper basicality, one arising from modern philosophy and one from Medieval philosophy.

The modern philosophers (Descartes, Leibniz, Locke, Berkeley, Hume, etc.) limited properly basic beliefs to those that are either *self-evident* or *incorrigible* (Plantinga calls this view *modern foundationalism*). Self-evident beliefs are those that we realize cannot possibly be false. (Descartes called these *clear and distinct ideas*.) Simple truths of arithmetic (e.g., $2 + 1 = 3$) and logic (e.g., *if A is taller than B and B is taller than C, then A is taller than C*), as well as

---

[5]Typically, of course, evidential beliefs are not based on a single belief, but on several or many. I assume the simple case here for the sake of clarity.

[6]There is an analogous foundationalist theory of *knowledge*, which is related to but distinct from the foundationalist theory of justification. However, since our primary concern here is the *de jure* objection to theism, we will be concerned only with the latter.

[7]See Plantinga's article "Reason and Belief in God," in *Faith and Rationality: Reason and Belief in God*, ed. Alvin Plantinga and Nicholas Wolterstorff (Notre Dame, IN: University of Notre Dame Press, 1983), 16–93. Reprinted and excerpted in Sennett, *The Analytic Theist*, 102–61. This article is the cornerstone document of Plantinga's Reformed epistemology program and the source for most of my exposition in sections 3–6.

simple definitional truths (e.g., *if John is a bachelor, then John is not married*) are typical examples. We are justified in holding self-evident beliefs basically because merely entertaining the claims forces us to realize that they cannot possibly be false. To know what they mean is to know that they have to be true.

In contrast, incorrigible beliefs are beliefs that can possibly be false. However, they cannot be false *if we believe them*. That is, if we hold the belief, it must be true. Beliefs about our internal psychological states (e.g., *I am hungry; I am angry with my mother*) are typical examples. It is possible that the proposition *I am hungry* be false. I may not be hungry. However, if I *believe* I am hungry, then I am hungry. (Remember—there is a difference between being hungry and needing food. I may believe that I need food and be mistaken. But I cannot believe that I am hungry—i.e., that I feel hunger pains—and be mistaken.)

The motivation behind modern foundationalism is obvious. Self-evident and incorrigible beliefs are *infallible*. That is, it is impossible that they constitute false beliefs. Thus, if properly basic beliefs are limited to these, then there is never any danger of error or falsehood in the foundations. If we can begin with such infallible foundations and build up from them with infallible moves of logic, then we can be certain of all that we believe, whether properly basic or evidential.

However, contemporary epistemologists have been quick to point out that modern foundationalism does not solve the skepticism problem at all. It is not difficult to show that it is impossible to justify much else at all based on these foundations.[8] That is, if only self-evident and incorrigible beliefs are properly basic, then almost nothing we think we are justified in believing (e.g., our perceptual beliefs and our beliefs about the external world) is in fact justified. Hence, if these are the only properly basic beliefs, we are thrown once again into a very disturbing skepticism.

This skepticism may be avoided, however, if we permit some premodern wisdom to enter the picture. Medieval philosophers like St. Thomas Aquinas assumed that perceptual beliefs are properly basic, provided that such beliefs are "evident to the senses."

That is, if a perceptual experience is sharp and vivid, so that a belief arising from that experience is distinctive and irresistible, then that belief may be considered properly basic. The addition of beliefs evident to the senses to the modern foundationalist pair of self-evident and incorrigible beliefs constitutes classical foundationalism. So classical foundationalism is the view that *beliefs are properly basic only if they are self-evident, incorrigible, or evident to the senses*. Notice, by the way, that while the addition of evident sensory beliefs to the catalog of properly basic beliefs does help avoid the wholesale skepticism of modern foundationalism, it does so only at a cost. The infallibility criterion of modern foundationalism must be given up. Evident sensory beliefs are fallible—it is quite possible that one have a clear, vivid, irresistible perceptual experience that leads to a false belief. This concession to fallible foundations will figure prominently in our discussion later.

So at last we have an answer to the question, "Why shouldn't we believe the Reformed epistemology claim?" Why shouldn't we accept that theistic belief is or can be properly basic? Answer: because classical foundationalism is true—because beliefs are properly basic only if they are self-evident, incorrigible, or evident to the senses. Theistic beliefs are not self-evident, incorrigible, or evident to the senses; hence, theistic beliefs are not and cannot be properly basic. This response, or something very much like it, is what Plantinga believes has typically motivated evidentialism. And, of course, if the argument is sound, then Reformed epistemology is false. So in order to defend his claim, Plantinga must first argue that the evidentialist argument from classical foundationalism is unsound.

4. PLANTINGA'S REJECTION OF CLASSICAL FOUNDATIONALISM

Plantinga argues that classical foundationalism cannot be the proper criterion for proper basicality. This argument has two major lines. First, Plantinga argues that classical foundationalism is "self-referentially incoherent"—a charge I will explain in a moment. Second, and ultimately more important, Plantinga argues that classical foundationalism cannot account for the full breadth of obviously properly basic beliefs.

---

[8]See, for example, Keith Lehrer, *Theory of Knowledge* (Boulder, CO: Westview Press, 1990), 39–62.

"THE GREAT PUMPKIN OBJECTION" ✳ *Alvin Plantinga*

If belief in God is properly basic, why can't *just any* belief be properly basic? Couldn't we say the same for any bizarre aberration we can think of? What about voodoo or astrology? What about the belief that the Great Pumpkin returns every Halloween? Could I properly take *that* as basic? And if I can't, why can I properly take belief in God as basic? Suppose I believe that if I flap my arms with sufficient vigor, I can take off and fly about the room; could I defend myself against the charge of irrationality by claiming this belief is basic? If we say that belief in God is properly basic, won't we be committed to holding that just anything, or nearly anything, can properly be taken as basic, thus throwing wide the gates to irrationalism and superstition?

Certainly not. What might lead one to think the Reformed epistemologist is in this kind of trouble? The fact that he rejects the criteria for proper basicality purveyed by classical foundationalism? But why should *that* be thought to commit him to such tolerance of irrationality? Consider an analogy. In the palmy days of positivism, the positivists went about confidently wielding their verifiability criterion and declaring meaningless much that was obviously meaningful. Now suppose someone rejected a formulation of that criterion—the one to be found in the second edition of A. J. Ayer's *Language, Truth, and Logic,* for example. Would that mean she was committed to holding that

> Twas brillig; and the slithy toves did gyre and gymble in the wabe,

contrary to appearances, makes good sense? Of course not. But then the same goes for the Reformed epistemologist; the fact that he rejects the classical foundationalist's criterion of proper basicality does not mean that he is committed to supposing just anything is properly basic.

But what then is the problem? Is it that the Reformed epistemologist not only rejects those criteria for proper basicality, but seems in no hurry to produce what he takes to be a better substitute? If he has no such criterion, how can he fairly reject belief in the Great Pumpkin as properly basic?

This objection betrays an important misconception. How do we rightly arrive at or develop criteria for meaningfulness, or justified belief, or

According to foundationalism per se, a belief is justified only if it is either properly basic or based on other beliefs in a way that is ultimately grounded in properly basic beliefs. When applied to classical foundationalism, this means that a belief is justified only if it is self-evident, incorrigible, evident to the senses, or based on beliefs that are self-evident, incorrigible, or evident to the senses. But, asks Plantinga, what about the belief that classical foundationalism is true? This belief is certainly neither self-evident, incorrigible, nor evident to the senses. It fits none of the typical cases of beliefs that fall into these categories. Nor is it clear how belief in classical foundationalism could be justified on beliefs that are properly basic in one of the approved ways. Certainly no one has ever offered an argument that it is. So if classical foundationalism is true, one cannot be justified in believing it, since it cannot meet its own criterion for justification. If, on the other hand, one can be justified in believing it, it must be false, since it is justified by some criterion that it does not specify as a criterion for justification. So either classical foundationalism is false or one can never be justified in believing it. This unhappy dilemma is what Plantinga calls "self-referential incoherence." When applied to itself, the classical foundationalism test cannot be passed.

But even if self-referential sense could be made out of classical foundationalism, Plantinga argues that it still cannot be the right story about proper basicality. There are, after all, lots of beliefs that we routinely hold in a basic way and consider ourselves fully justified in holding, even though they do not fall into any proper basicality? Where do they come from? Must one have such a criterion before one can sensibly make any judgments—positive or negative—about proper basicality? Surely not . . . But then the same goes for the Reformed epistemologist: the fact that he rejects the criterion of proper basicality purveyed by classical foundationalism. Does not mean that he is committed to supposing that just anything is properly basic. . . . This objection betrays an important misconception. How *do we* rightly arrive at or develop criteria for meaningfulness, or justified belief, or proper basicality? . . . the proper way to arrive at such a criterion is, broadly speaking, *inductive*. We must assemble examples of beliefs and conditions such that the former are obviously properly basic in the latter, and examples of beliefs and conditions such that the former are obviously *not* properly basic in the latter. . . .

Accordingly, criteria for proper basicality must be reached from below rather than above; they should not be presented *ex cathedra* but argued to and tested by a relevant set of examples. But there is no reason to assume, in advance, that everyone will agree on the examples. The Christian will of course suppose that belief in God is entirely proper and rational; if he does not accept this belief on the basis of other propositions, he will conclude that it is basic for him and quite properly so. Followers of Bertrand Russell and Madelyn Murray O'Hare may disagree; but how is that relevant? Must my criteria, or those of the Christian community, conform to their examples? Surely not. The Christian community is responsible to *its* set of examples, not to theirs . . .

So, the Reformed epistemologist can properly hold that belief in the Great Pumpkin is not properly basic, even though he holds that belief in God is properly basic and even though he has no full-fledged criterion of proper basicality. Ofcourse, he is committed to supposing that there is a relevant *difference* between belief in God and belief in the Great Pumpkin if he holds that the former but not the latter is properly basic. But this should prove no great embarrassment; there are plenty of candidates. These candidates are to be found in a neighborhood of the conditions that justify and ground belief in God.

From Alvin Plantinga, "Is Belief in God Properly Basic?" *Nous* (1981) and Alvin Plantinga, "Reason and Belief in God," in *Faith and Rationality,* Alvin Plantinga and Nicholas Wolterstorff ed. (1983)

of the classical foundationalism categories. Consider my belief that I wrote the first section of this chapter. That belief is not based on some inferential process I've gone through (e.g., "My name is on this chapter; typically my name is only on papers if I wrote them; therefore, I must have written the first section of this chapter"). Rather my belief is the result of a very vivid memory experience I have of composing the first section just a few days ago. So my belief is basic—grounded in a memory experience rather than derived from any other beliefs I hold. This belief does not pass the classical foundationalism test for justification, since it is basic and does not fall into one of the properly basic categories. But surely it is a paradigm case of a justified belief. When faced with the choice *either my belief that I wrote the first section of this chapter is unjusti-*

fied or classical foundationalism is false, I will certainly take the latter alternative, and be fully justified in doing so. This is also be the case with beliefs like My *student is confused by what I've said*, which is not derived from other beliefs I have, but formed as an immediate response to seeing a certain expression on my student's face. In short, there are many different kinds of beliefs that may be properly basic in the right circumstances, and neither classical foundationalism nor any such limiting criterion can ever hope to capture them all.[9]

---

[9] See James F. Sennett, "Direct Justification and Universal Sanction," *Journal of Philosophical Review* 23 (1998): 257–287, where I argue that my criterion of universal sanction accounts for all the typical cases of proper basicality that Plantinga is worried about, but still excludes theistic belief.

So classical foundationalism fails. Furthermore, it seems that any attempt to fix it up will ultimately fail as well. Proper basicality appears to be a phenomenon that is much more widespread and endemic to our belief processes than can ever be captured in a simple list of belief kinds. But if this is the case, then any reason for excluding theistic belief would be weak and ad hoc. Why should we be ready to include a wide range of different kinds of beliefs as properly basic, yet draw the line at theistic belief? Classical foundationalism can't proscribe the inclusion. What other possible reason could there be?

5. THE GROUNDING OBJECTION

Plantinga's refutation of classical foundationalism is an important step in his defense of Reformed epistemology, but it is only a negative step. That is, while it removes a reason to think Reformed epistemology *false*, it offers no reason to think it *true*. Are there such reasons? Can Plantinga give reasons for thinking that theistic belief is or can be properly basic? The answer is "yes," but these reasons are best understood by explaining Plantinga's responses to three further objections to Reformed epistemology. The first two objections Plantinga raises himself; the third is offered by his Notre Dame colleague, Philip Quinn. These objections will be examined in this and the following two sections.

One might object that, if theistic belief is not based on evidence, then it is *groundless*—that is, it has no foundation or basis at all. It is as improper as a belief that simply pops into one's head or forms as the result of fevered delirium or aimless conjecture. But Plantinga argues that this charge is no more legitimate against basic theistic belief than it is against any of the obvious cases of properly basic belief. My belief that there is a computer screen before me is not based on evidence, but it is certainly not groundless. It is grounded in a certain kind of perceptual experience. So also with my belief that I wrote the first section of this chapter—it is grounded in a certain kind of memory experience.

So it is with all properly basic beliefs. They result from experiences of certain kinds that form beliefs of certain kinds, such that it is appropriate for those beliefs to be formed in those circumstances. Hence none of them are groundless. There is an important phenomenological and epistemological difference between

such beliefs and beliefs that simply pop into one's head or result from delirium or such like—namely their production by appropriate experiences. It is these experiences, rather than any other beliefs one holds, that ground our properly basic beliefs.

So here we gain an important insight into Plantinga's Reformed epistemology story. Theistic belief can be properly basic if it is appropriately produced by a certain kind of experience. But are there any such experiences? It certainly seems so. If dozens of Christians pray for the healing of a terminal cancer patient and that patient's cancer suddenly disappears, clearly any one of those praying would be justified, upon hearing the news, in forming the belief "God has answered our prayer." True, no atheist would form such a belief, but that need not bother the theist. One might charge that he only formed such a belief because he is a theist. But it is also true that the atheist did *not* form such a belief because he is an atheist. There is no better reason to charge that the theist's theism explains (and therefore invalidates) his formation of theistic belief than there is to charge that the atheist's atheism explains (and therefore invalidates) his failure to form theistic belief. So we are back to the experience, and it seems perfectly natural and above reproach—in a word, *rational*—for the theist to form his belief in these circumstances.

So in response to the grounding objection Plantinga makes an important positive claim about the nature of properly basic theistic belief. Theistic belief is properly basic if it is grounded in an experience that can appropriately produce theistic beliefs. A nonprejudicial examination of ordinary belief-forming experiences of theists would seem to suggest that such experiences abound.

6. THE GREAT PUMPKIN OBJECTION

The grounding objection is the claim that theistic belief not based on evidence is theistic belief that is not grounded. Plantinga's response is that basic theistic belief is grounded in the same way that any properly basic belief is—in appropriate experiences. The Great Pumpkin objection is the claim that, if theistic belief can be properly grounded in appropriate experiences, then any belief at all can be so properly grounded—even, say, Linus Van Pelt's belief that the Great

Pumpkin returns every Halloween to bring gifts to all good boys and girls.

But, Plantinga retorts, there is nothing in the claims of Reformed epistemology that entails or even suggests that any other kinds of beliefs are or can be properly basic. The claim that there are experiences that can properly ground theistic belief does not give any reason to think that there might be grounds that could properly ground Great Pumpkin beliefs, nor is the theist obligated to accept that Great Pumpkin beliefs could be properly basic. For one thing, the theist will hold that Great Pumpkin beliefs are simply false, and no circumstances would ever appropriately give rise to them. (Remember: Reformed epistemology is not a natural theology program—Plantinga does not claim that properly basic theistic belief *proves* the existence of God. Therefore, he does not beg the question by appealing to the truth of theism in support of his Reformed epistemology claims or in rebuttal of objections to them.)

Recall when evident perceptual belief was added to modern foundationalism to avoid skepticism and produce classical foundationalism in section 3 above. There was nothing about that move per se that suggested that the floodgates are open and we must admit any and all beliefs as potentially properly basic. If the addition of perceptual beliefs does not spawn the Great Pumpkin objection, then there's no reason to think that the addition of theistic beliefs would either. The fact that we recognize yet another kind of belief that can be properly basic does not mean that we must now admit belief kinds for which there is no reason whatsoever to think they could ever be properly basic.

Besides, Plantinga points out that one key to proper basicality is that there is an epistemic community that affirms and endorses the beliefs in question as properly basic. Plantinga argues that one reason theistic belief can be understood as properly basic is that there is a natural community within which such beliefs are accepted and condoned. (The fact that this community is not universal is irrelevant—the community that endorses beliefs based on vision is not universal either!) The presence of such a community is important because without it there is no justification for claiming that the beliefs are properly produced by the circumstances that produce them. Without a community

within which such beliefs are produced in such circumstances, the claim would be empty.

Now, when applied to the Great Pumpkin objection, this community requirement is decisive. There *is* no Great Pumpkin community. There is no body of believers that will endorse Linus's belief or give him permission to hold it basically. But clearly there is such a community for the theist. This disanalogy shows the Great Pumpkin objection to be illegitimate and ineffective. So here we have a second positive reason for Reformed epistemology. Basic theistic belief is formed, like other obviously properly basic beliefs, within the context of a community that recognizes and endorses such basic belief formation as proper.

One important point in this rebuttal must be emphasized. Plantinga notes that the theist's conviction that Great Pumpkin beliefs are not true gives her reason to believe they are not properly basic. This suggests that an important reason a theist might be willing to accept theistic belief as properly basic is her prior commitment to the idea that theism is true. So Plantinga's response to the *de jure* objection has here an important link to the *de facto* objection. This link will be explored more closely in section 8 below.

7. QUINN'S DEFEATER OBJECTION

The third objection is by far the most formidable. It was raised by Plantinga's colleague at Notre Dame, Philip Quinn.[10] Quinn argues that a belief (call it "B") cannot be properly basic for someone (call her "S") if there is some other belief (call it "B*") such that all of the following are true: (1) B* is good reason to think B false (i.e., either they are inconsistent or it is highly unlikely that they are both true); (2) S is aware of (1); (3) S has good reason to believe that B* is true. If all of these conditions hold, B* is said to be a *defeater* of B for S. So Quinn's claim is that a belief cannot be properly basic for someone if there is a defeater of the belief for that person. In such a case, Quinn says, the person could be justified in holding the belief only if she had evidence for it that outweighed her reasons for its defeater. But if the belief is justified by evidence, it cannot be properly basic.

[10]Philip Quinn, "In Search of the Foundations of Theism," *Faith and Philosophy* 2 (1985): 468–86.

And, Quinn claims, virtually all theists—or at least all those who are what Quinn calls "intellectually sophisticated adults"—do indeed have a defeater for any theistic belief they hold. One example of such a defeater would be the claim *There is horrendous evil in the world for which we can see no justification.* The problem of evil is as thorny a problem as theism faces. It is safe to say that most intellectually sophisticated theists recognize, or would recognize on proper reflection, that the existence and extent of evil in the world stands as a very good reason to think that theism is false. But, of course, if theism is false, then all theistic beliefs are false. Hence, the problem of evil is a defeater for any theistic belief. So also for the claim *There are many rational, normally functioning human beings—including many of the most brilliant people of the twentieth century, who deny theism.* All things being equal, this undeniable fact must give a theist pause. It, too, may well be a defeater of the sort Quinn claims will disqualify any theistic belief from proper basicality.

Plantinga's response to Quinn is twofold.[11] First, it is not true that one must have evidence *for* theistic belief in order to neutralize a defeater of theistic belief. It is enough to have reason to reject the defeater. In other words, all that's needed is a *defeater-defeater*. And a defeater-defeater will not be evidence *for* the theistic belief; so the theistic belief can still be justified without evidence—hence, properly basic. So, for example, if one understands the free will defense to solve the problem of evil, then the free will defense serves as a defeater-defeater for the problem of evil. But the free will defense is not evidence for theism or for any theistic belief. It is merely an argument that the presence of evil does not prove that God does not exist. (Proof that a claim has not been proven is not proof that the claim is false.) Hence, if one's theistic belief is rational, it is not *based on* the free will defense, and so far forth is still a candidate for proper basicality.

Plantinga's second response to Quinn is that, even if one does not have a defeater-defeater, it might still be more rational to accept a basic belief than to reject it in favor of a defeater.[12] Consider the following scenario. You are accused of stealing something. It is clear that you had ample motive to commit the crime. Furthermore, you are a known thief; on several occasions you have been caught red-handed stealing things for which you had motive to steal. There are even two eyewitnesses—reliable and trustworthy people who have no reason to lie—who testify that they saw you in the proper place at the proper time. Nonetheless, you distinctly remember that you were nowhere near the crime scene on the day in question. You were in fact alone all day in the woods enjoying the beautiful spring weather.

Now, all the evidence against you constitutes a rather formidable defeater for your belief of *I was in the woods all day and did not commit the theft.* And you have no defeater-defeater for this defeater. You cannot deny that you had motive; you cannot deny your proven record of theft; and you have no way of impeaching the reliability of the eyewitnesses. Nonetheless, it would be completely irrational for you to deny your own vivid memory and believe instead that you did commit the crime after all. But your belief that you are innocent is basic—it is based on memory experience, not on any evidence. It is properly basic—and remains properly basic even in the face of a significant defeater for which you have no defeater-defeater.

This illustration shows that the experiences producing properly basic beliefs can provide justification for the beliefs that withstands very strong defeaters, without the aid of any defeater-defeaters, and without the aid of any evidence for the belief in question. So neither defeater-defeaters nor evidence are necessary for the justification of a properly basic belief. Hence, Quinn's objection fails.[13]

---

[11]Alvin Plantinga, "The Foundations of Theism: A Reply," *Faith and Philosophy* 3 (1986): 298–313.

[12]Plantinga actually distinguishes between *extrinsic* defeater-defeaters and *intrinsic* defeater-defeaters. The free will defense is an example of an extrinsic defeater-defeater; it defeats the problem of evil but is not directly related to the theistic belief in question. The present and following paragraphs discuss intrinsic defeater-defeaters; the theistic belief itself serves as the defeater-defeater. While this way of talking is technically more accurate, it is also more confusing for nonphilosophers. Therefore, I will not use this distinction in my discussion.

[13]I have argued elsewhere that Quinn's objection can be revised so as to sidestep Plantinga's objections. See James F. Sennett, "Reformed Epistemology and Epistemic Duty," in *Faith in Theory and*

8. REFORMED EPISTEMOLOGY AND THE *DE FACTO* OBJECTION

At the beginning of this chapter I noted that Plantinga develops his defense of Reformed epistemology in response to two questions: (1) Is theistic belief properly basic? and (2) Does basic theistic belief count as knowledge if it is true? These are importantly different questions. Recent debates in epistemology have demonstrated that it is possible for a belief to be justified or rational in certain senses even though the one holding the belief could not be said to know it, even if it is true. Showing why this is the case would take us too far away from the central concerns of this paper; suffice it to say that Plantinga saw the need to refocus his defense of Reformed epistemology to concentrate on this second question.

Plantinga focuses his attention on that property, whatever it is, that converts true belief into knowledge. He gives this property the name "warrant,"[14] so the second question can be rephrased as, "Does basic theistic belief have warrant?" Plantinga says that, in order to answer this question, we have to have a pretty good idea about what warrant is. In a massive three-volume work Plantinga explores the question of warrant and the question of whether or not basic theistic belief can be shown to have it.[15] I cannot come close to addressing the full extent of his project. Instead, I will speak briefly to the two most important points: what Plantinga thinks constitutes warrant, and how basic theistic belief relates to his analysis of warrant.

In the first volume of his trilogy Plantinga argues that no currently available epistemological theory provides an adequate account of warrant. In the second volume he supplies one. In a nutshell, his account is this: a belief has warrant if it is produced by properly functioning belief-forming faculties in an appropriate environment.[16] That is, warrant is conveyed by epistemic faculties functioning the way they are supposed to. Some of these faculties are supposed to produce beliefs based on reflection on other beliefs that are held. If these faculties are functioning properly, they produce evidentially warranted beliefs. But some faculties (e.g., perception, memory) are supposed to produce beliefs directly from experiences. If these faculties are functioning properly, they will produce warranted basic beliefs. In either case, if the beliefs produced by properly functioning faculties are true, then they constitute knowledge, since they are warranted.

So basic theistic belief has warrant if and only if it is produced by an epistemic faculty that is supposed to produce basic theistic beliefs in proper environments. Essentially, Plantinga argues that, if theism is true, then there is no reason to deny, and good reason to believe, that God would provide human beings with a capacity to know him in a basic way. He develops what he calls the "Aquinas/Calvin Model," based on the work of these two great theologians. This model has at its foundation the *sensus divinitatis* discussed earlier. Plantinga argues that we can make sense of the *sensus divinitatis* as an epistemic faculty on a par with perception, memory, and rational intuition (Plantinga 2000, 167–86).

So, if theism is true, then theistic belief is warranted, and that in a basic way. In other words, the *de jure* objection cannot be separated from the *de facto* objection. It cannot be argued, as many atheists have attempted to do in recent generations, that the truth of

---

Practice: Essays on Justifying Religious Belief, ed. Carol White and Elizabeth Radcliffe (Chicago, IL: Open Court, 1993), 189–207.

[14]In two early papers Plantinga uses the term (borrowed from Roderick Chisholm) "positive epistemic status" to refer to the conversion property. Later he drops this rather unwieldy term in favor of the more euphonistic "warrant." "Positive Epistemic Status and Proper Function," *Philosophical Perspectives 2: Epistemology*, ed. James E. Tomberlin (1989): 1–50; "Justification and Theism," *Faith and Philosophy* 4 (1987): 403–26.

[15]*Warrant: The Current Debate* (New York: Oxford, 1993), *Warrant and Proper Function* (New York: Oxford, 1993), and *Warranted Christian Belief* (New York: Oxford, 2000).

[16]Plantinga's full account is as follows: "A belief has warrant for me only if (1) it has been produced in me by cognitive faculties that are working properly (functioning as they ought to, subject to no cognitive dysfunction) in a cognitive environment that is appropriate for my kinds of cognitive faculties, (2) the segment of the design plan governing the production of that belief is aimed at the production of true beliefs, and (3) there is a high statistical probability that a belief produced under those conditions will be true. Under those conditions, furthermore, the degree of warrant is an increasing function of degree of belief" (*Warrant and Proper Function*, 46f). My thumbnail sketch in the text embraces only the first of these conditions. The others speak to technical aspects of Plantinga's theory that need not concern us here.

falsehood of theism is irrelevant, since it cannot be rationally believed even if it is true. Plantinga's claim is that one can only argue against the rationality or warrant of theistic belief if one is also prepared to argue against its truth. So the *de jure* objection reduces to the *de facto* objection (187–98). The real debate over theism must take place in the realm of natural theology and apologetics—it cannot be settled simply by studying epistemology.

And, regardless of the success of the rest of Plantinga's program, this point seems to be well taken, and is perhaps the most important insight to come out of the Reformed epistemology program. Regardless of whether or not theistic belief is properly basic, one thing seems clear: if the theistic God exists, it only seems obvious that He would form the world and human beings in such a way that they could rationally believe that He exists—indeed, that they could *know* that He exists.[17] True, He would not necessarily make His existence and work *obvious*, but He would certainly make it *available* to properly functioning epistemic faculties. And if this is a sensible conclusion, then Plantinga is correct that theism cannot be attacked on grounds of the *de jure* objection alone. The atheist cannot ignore the arguments over the truth of theism and concentrate solely on the epistemic rationality of the theist.

So Plantinga's project climaxes in a somewhat ironic place. Whether or not we can *know* that theist belief is properly basic (or basically warranted) depends on whether or not there is good evidence for the truth of theism. This is not an inconsistency, however. The believer need not be aware of such evidence in order for her belief to be properly basic. But perhaps the epistemologist must be aware of the evidence in order to be justified in arguing that the believer's belief is properly basic. In other words, while good evidence is not required for basic theistic belief *to be* rational or warranted, good evidence may be required in order for it *to*

be *shown* that basic theistic belief is rational or warranted. The theist requires no evidence for the epistemic pedigree of her own basic theistic belief. But if she wishes to convince anyone else that her basic theistic belief is proper, she (or at any rate, *someone*) must have evidence.[18]

9. APPENDIX: WHAT REFORMED EPISTEMOLOGY IS NOT

My explication and defense of Plantinga's Reformed epistemology program is complete. In this closing section I would like to clarify three common misconceptions about the claims of Reformed epistemology which, if left unchecked, will cause insurmountable difficulties in properly assessing and criticizing this very important development in religious epistemology.

First, it is important to understand that Reformed epistemology is not fideism. Fideism is the doctrine that rationality is irrelevant to theistic belief. (For the sake of simplicity I will speak only of rationality in this section, though it should be understood that, for the most part, the points apply to both rationality and warrant.) For the fideist, any question concerning the rationality of theistic belief is nonsensical. Asking "Is theistic belief rational?" is like asking "Is the number seven blue?" The question cannot be answered "yes" or "no." It is meaningless and has no answer. It is beyond the scope of this paper to explain why fideists hold such a view or to review the many reasons to reject it. Suffice it to say that it should be clear that Plantinga's position is not fideism. Plantinga does not claim that rationality or warrant are irrelevant to theistic belief. He believes that theistic belief can be rational or irrational, and that the preferable state for the conscientious believer is that it be rational. Plantinga argues that the structure of theistic rationality is not what

---

[17]The use of the masculine pronoun is not intended to imply divine gender. I use it, for better or for worse, because there are simply no alternatives that do not detract inexcusably from the flow of the text. They are startling either because of their unconventionality (e.g., use of feminine or neuter pronouns) or because they are simply stylistically reprehensible (e.g., the repeated use of the word "God" without use of any pronouns). I go with convention and let the political correctness chips fall where they may.

[18]This point is reminiscent of a very fine argument by Stephen Wykstra in his article "Toward a Sensible Evidentialism: On the Notion of 'Needing Evidence,' " in *Philosophy of Religion: Selected Readings*, 3rd ed., ed. William Rowe and William Wainwright (New York: Harcourt, Brace, Jovanovich, 1998), 481–91. Wykstra argues that, in order for basic theistic belief to be warranted, evidence for the truth of theism must be available within the Christian community, though not necessarily possessed or understood by the one holding the basic theistic belief.

many people think it is—it does not require evidence. But this is not the same as claiming that rationality does not apply to theistic belief.

Second, Reformed epistemology is not a version of the argument from religious experience. The argument from religious experience is a natural theology argument that focuses on the fact that so many people throughout history and all around the world have reported having experiences that they take to be experiences of God in some way. These experiences may be mystical or mundane. They vary from visions of God or angels to the experiencing of good fortune as a blessing from God. The argument from religious experience is based in the idea that the best explanation for the fact and extent of religious experience is that God does exist and in some way causes or initiates the experiences. Reformed epistemology does not involve the claim that theistic belief producing experiences count as evidence for the existence of God. As I have pointed out several times, Reformed epistemology is not an exercise in natural theology or apologetics. Though the doctrine involves the notion of religious experience, it does not use such experience as evidence of theism. Hence, none of the criticisms and rebuttals that have been aimed at the argument from religious experience have any relevance to Reformed epistemology. Plantinga is simply not employing religious experience the way the natural theologian does.

Finally, Reformed epistemology is not an attack on natural theology or apologetics. The claim that theistic belief is properly basic does not imply or even suggest that the practice of compiling evidence or constructing arguments for theism is unnecessary or illegitimate. In fact, as we saw in the previous section, Reformed epistemology finally calls us back to natural theology and apologetics to make a case for the existence of God, from which warranted basic theistic belief will follow. Far from being opposed to natural theology, Reformed epistemology partners with it for a complete religious epistemology.[19]

QUESTIONS FOR FURTHER REFLECTION

1. Is there something that all obviously properly basic beliefs have in common that theistic belief lacks? If so, what exactly is it? Is this difference enough to justify the claim that theistic belief is not properly basic? Why or why not?

2. Read the story of Jesus healing the blind man in John 9:1–34. Is the blind man's belief that Jesus is a prophet properly basic? How does his inability to answer the questions of the Pharisees compare to Plantinga's rebuttal of Quinn's defeater objection? Who do you think gets the better of this confrontation: the blind man or the Pharisees?

3. Does being rational in holding a certain belief entail that you should be able to convince other people that the belief is true? Why or why not? Give examples to support your response.

4. Sennett reports, "Plantinga argues that, if theism is true, then there is no reason to deny, and good reason to believe, that God would provide human beings with a capacity to know Him in a basic way." Is Plantinga's claim true? Give reasons for your answer. (Note the twofold claim: *to know Him*; and *in a basic way*.)

5. Is it possible to be rational in believing something that is false? Why or why not? Is it possible to be *warranted* in believing something that is false? Give examples to support your responses.

natural theology can provide at best only a tentative and defeasible acceptance of theism, which is much too timid and unsure to bear the weight of commitment and unswerving confidence that genuine Christian faith requires. (Similar arguments have been used by Kierkegaard and others to defend fideism.) Plantinga acknowledges this element in the Reformed tradition and attempts to temper it somewhat in his early papers on Reformed epistemology, "The Reformed Objection to Natural Theology," *Proceedings of the American Catholic Philosophical Association* 54 (1980): 41–51; and "The Reformed Objection Revisited," *Christian Scholars Review* 12 (1983): 57–61. See also "Reason and Belief in God," 63–73 (*Analytic Theist*, 138–48).

---

[19]This point is ironic because much of the Reformed tradition within which Plantinga works has stood in opposition to the practice of natural theology. Many Reformed thinkers have argued that

30. REFORMED EPISTEMOLOGY: AN ATHEIST PERSPECTIVE

Keith M. Parsons

Keith Parsons is Assistant Professor of Philosophy at the University of Houston—Clear Lake. He received his Ph.D. in the history and philosophy of science from the University of Pittsburgh in 1996. He is the author of *God and the Burden of Proof*.

READING QUESTIONS

1. What is the difference between an "internalist" and "externalist" view of epistemology? How do internalism and externalism differ with respect to rational belief?
2. What is an epistemic duty, and how, according to "internalist" views, does it relate to rationality?
3. What is a "natural belief"?
4. What is a "properly basic belief"?
5. What does Plantinga mean by a *sensus divinitatis*?

Philosophical debates sometimes get nasty, most especially perhaps in the philosophy of religion. Atheists have sometimes charged that belief in God is irrational. As we shall see, some people try to turn that accusation back on atheists. It is offensive to be accused of having an irrational belief. We humans regard ourselves as rational creatures, and we like to think that our beliefs and behaviors are reasonable. But unquestionably many people hold irrational beliefs; probably each of us has more than we would want to admit. What does it mean to call a belief "irrational"? Well, it is not the same as saying that the belief is untrue—though this is often implied by someone making the charge of irrationality. One can hold a true belief in an irrational way. For instance, the paranoid irrationally thinks that everyone is out to get him; his obsessive fear of sinister agents is not based on anything reasonable. Still, as the old slogan goes, just because you are paranoid does not mean people aren't out to get you. So the paranoid could irrationally believe something absolutely true!

The really offensive thing about a charge of irrationality is that it usually implies laxness or irresponsibility. American philosopher William Kingdon Clifford argued in a famous essay that we all have responsibilities about how we form our beliefs, just as we have responsibilities to pay our bills and keep our promises (Clifford, 1999). In the technical jargon of philosophy, the responsibilities we have concerning the formation of our beliefs are called "epistemic duties." Epistemic duties are the things we ought to do to make sure we believe what is true and do not believe what is false. If we perform all of our epistemic duties when we acquire a belief, then our belief is rational, and we are said to be within our "epistemic rights" in believing it. If we violate an epistemic duty when we accept a belief, then our belief is irrational and we are not within our epistemic rights in believing it. For instance, suppose that flashy commercials convince me that the "Canyonero" is the vehicle for me. Being overawed by the hype, I do not bother to check the *Consumer Reports* article on SUVs that gives the "Canyonero" a low rating. In this case I have formed my opinion about the "Canyonero" in an irrational, irresponsible manner, and I have no one to blame but myself when I get a shoddy, dangerous, overpriced, gas-guzzler.

By the way, some philosophers now reject the idea of epistemic duties and the definition of rationality in terms of such duties. Philosophers who take an "externalist" approach to epistemology (see below) regard rational beliefs as the product of the proper function of cognitive faculties in the environment in which those faculties were designed to operate. On this view, irrational beliefs are therefore the result of malfunction of those faculties or their operation in circumstances to which they are not suited. However, I think that for many people the account of rationality in terms of epistemic duties will seem more intuitive and closer to commonsense notions. Also, the earlier version of Reformed Epistemology relies on the epistemic duties account of rationality, and, since externalism remains controversial, many might prefer the earlier formulation. Therefore, I shall assume the epistemic duties account of rationality until I explicitly introduce externalism later in the paper.

In general then, what are our epistemic duties? They are hard to state in general since they vary depending on the kind of belief and our particular circumstances. For instance, it is fine to believe some things on the basis of the word of the appropriate authority. If I want to know which countries border on Bhutan, a good atlas is the appropriate authority. On the other hand, some persons or groups have a responsibility to see for themselves whether something is so. For instance, when a new theory is proposed in a scientific field, it cannot be accepted merely on authority. The scientific community has the responsibility to test the theory rigorously before they accept it. So, epistemic duties apply to particular persons in particular circumstances. It can be rational for me to believe something in one circumstance but not in another. For instance, when I see someone that appears to be someone I know well, it is almost always rational for me to believe that that person is present. But if I hear from a reliable source that the person's identical twin is impersonating her, then I should withhold judgment until I can be sure.

What about belief in God? When is it rational to believe that God exists and when not? What epistemic duties do we have in determining whether or not to believe in God? In what circumstances are we within our epistemic rights in having that belief? Some have held that theism—the belief that God exists—is rational if and only if adequate reasons, arguments, or evidence can be given to support that belief. Some atheists have claimed that belief in God is irrational because there are no such adequate grounds. Theists have generally responded by taking up the challenge and attempting to offer such arguments and evidence. In the early 1980's, a number of

philosophers, led by Alvin Plantinga, developed a new approach called "Reformed Epistemology." The central claim of Reformed Epistemology is that it can be rational to believe that God exists even if no argument, evidence, or reasons can be given to support that belief. In other words, Reformed Epistemology rejects the view, which it calls "evidentialism," that theistic belief is rational if and only if adequate argument, evidence, or reasons back it up.

In this essay I give an atheist response to Reformed Epistemology. Since Plantinga has been the main proponent of this view, I examine and evaluate his statements of the claims of Reformed Epistemology. I begin with an early (1983) statement, and focus on the arguments he gives there for a little more than half the paper. I then move to a more recent formulation (1999), which develops a very different epistemological framework. I conclude that Reformed Epistemology, in either its early or later versions, fails to show that theism is rational.

So, should atheists accept the claim of Reformed Epistemology that it can be rational for persons to believe that God exists even if they can give no evidence, logical arguments, or reasons for that belief? Now clearly it is irrational to hold some beliefs unless one has good evidence or reasons for that belief. For instance, members of a jury in a criminal case have the responsibility to refrain from forming the conviction that the accused is guilty until they have carefully weighed the evidence. It is irrational (and wrong) to judge a suspect guilty until such evidence is provided. On the other hand, there are some things that we all believe, and rationally believe, even though we might be hard pressed to state the rational grounds for our beliefs. For instance, we all believe that other people have minds similar to ours. That is, we think that others are not simply zombies or robots, but that they have thoughts, feelings, perceptions, and consciousness as we do. But it is a famous philosophical problem to state just *how* we know that there are other persons like ourselves and not zombies or robots. After all, we have *direct* acquaintance with only one mind—our own!

What we seem to need are some criteria—some standards or rules that would allow us to distinguish between those beliefs which are rational to hold even without supporting evidence or reasons and those which are not. The epistemological theory known as

"Classical Foundationalism" proposed such a set of criteria. Classical Foundationalism developed standards for identifying certain beliefs as "properly basic." A properly basic belief was one that it is rational for someone to accept without supporting reasons or evidence. As characterized by Plantinga (1983, p. 59), Classical Foundationalism recognizes a belief as properly basic if and only if it is one of the following: (a) self-evident, (b) incorrigible, or (c) evident to the senses. Self-evident truths are those that we recognize as true as soon as we understand them. An example would be "$1 + 1 = 2$." Incorrigible beliefs are those that we cannot be wrong about. If I honestly believe I have a bad headache, then I *do* have a bad headache. The objects that we see, hear, taste, smell, and touch— whatever they are; philosophers disagree on this point—are the things that are evident to the senses.

Reformed Epistemologists reject Classical Foundationalism and regard its criteria of proper basicality as too narrow. They want to know why theism cannot be a properly basic belief. Why is it not rational to believe that God exists even if no supporting arguments, reasons, or evidence can be given? What epistemic duty does someone violate if he or she believes in God but can offer no supporting reasons or evidence?

Again, it is obvious that not just any belief can be properly basic, so if we reject the criteria offered by Classical Foundationalism, surely we have a responsibility to justify some other set of such criteria. Plantinga suggests that we formulate such criteria *inductively*, that is, we start with certain *obviously* properly basic beliefs, and generalize from those examples to form a set of criteria (Plantinga, 1983, p. 76). For instance, we would start with such obviously properly basic beliefs as "I have a headache." If someone seriously says "I have a headache," we clearly do not demand of him or her "What is your evidence for that claim?" Clearly, you don't go around gathering *evidence* that you have a headache or *inferring* that you do—you just *feel* your head throbbing. You couldn't want more reason than that to believe you have a headache! We therefore collect as many different examples of obviously properly basic beliefs as we can and then try to categorize them with respect to the type of belief and the precise circumstances in which they are obviously properly basic. Schematically, we would hypothesize that beliefs of type A, B, C, . . . are properly basic for every person P in circumstances E, F, G, . . . and not otherwise. We would then test and refine our proposed criteria for proper basicality. If those criteria exclude a belief that is *obviously* properly basic, or if they permit one that *obviously* is not, then our criteria will need to be modified. Once we are satisfied that we have acceptable criteria, we can consider any belief and see if it measures up by those criteria. If it does, it is properly basic; if it does not, it is not properly basic.

How can theists make sure that "God exists" will be included among our properly basic beliefs? Simple, says Plantinga: Just make "God exists" one of your *obviously* properly basic beliefs! Is "God exists" obviously properly basic? Plantinga realizes that atheists will disagree with Christians about what beliefs are obviously properly basic, but he couldn't care less:

> . . . there is no reason to assume in advance that everyone will agree on the examples [of obviously properly basic beliefs]. The Christian will of course suppose that belief in God is entirely proper and rational; if he does not accept this belief on the basis of other propositions he will conclude that it is basic for him and quite properly so. Followers of Bertrand Russell or Madelyn Murray O'Hare may disagree; but how is that relevant? Must my criteria, or those of the Christian community, conform to their examples? Surely not. The Christian community is responsible to *its* set of examples, not to theirs (Plantinga, 1983, 77).

I regard these statements as cavalier, to say the least— they are the philosophical equivalent of thumbing one's nose and making a razzing noise. After all, it is not just pesky atheists that doubt whether it could be properly basic to believe that God exists. Many theists also do not regard God's existence as properly basic— much less as obviously so. Worse, if persons are responsible only to their own criteria, that is, if their epistemic duty is to be loyal only to their *own* examples of obvious proper basicality, what is to keep people from developing criteria that permit them to believe whatever they want? Plantinga anticipates this criticism of Reformed Epistemology and calls it the "Great Pumpkin" objection. The other "Peanuts" characters ridicule Linus because he believes in the Great Pumpkin. Why can't Linus take inspiration from Professor Plantinga

"SON OF A GREAT PUMPKIN" * Michael Martin

What can one say about Plantinga's ingenious attempt to save theism from the charge of irrationality by making beliefs about God basic?

1. Plantinga's claim that his proposal would not allow just any belief to become a basic belief is misleading. It is true that it would not allow just any belief to become a basic belief *from the point of view of Reformed epistemologists*. However it would seem to allow any belief at all to become basic from the point of view of *some* community. Although reformed epistemologists would not have to accept voodoo beliefs as rational, voodoo followers would be able to claim that insofar as they are basic in the voodoo community they are rational and, moreover, that reformed thought was irrational in this community. Indeed, Plantinga's proposal would generate many different communities that could *legitimately* claim that their basic beliefs are rational and that these beliefs conflict with basic beliefs of other communities. Among the communities generated might be devil worshipers, flat earthers, and believers in fairies just so long as belief in the devil, the flatness of the earth, and fairies was basic in the respective communities.

2. On this view the rationality of any belief is absurdly easy to obtain. The cherished belief that is held without reason by *any* group could be considered properly basic by the group's members. There would be no way to make a critical evaluation of any beliefs so considered. The community's most cherished beliefs and the conditions that, according to the community, correctly trigger such beliefs would be accepted uncritically by the members of the community as just so many more examples of basic beliefs and justifying conditions. The more philosophical members of the community could go on to propose hypotheses as to the necessary and sufficient conditions for inclusion in this set. Perhaps, using this inductive procedure, a criterion could be formulated. However, what examples the hypotheses must account for would be decided by the community. As Plantinga says, each community would be responsible only to its own set of examples in formulating a criterion, and each would decide what is to be in this set.

3. Plantinga seems to suppose that there is a consensus in the Christian community about what beliefs are properly basic and what conditions justify these beliefs. But this is not so . . .

From Michael Martin, *Atheism: A Philosophical Justification* (1990).

and just declare that for him the existence of the Great Pumpkin is obviously properly basic? Worse, what is to keep every kook, crackpot, or fanatic from claiming this for his or her own doctrinal infatuation or occult obsession—vast conspiracies, ghosts, monsters, space aliens, or whatever?

Plantinga replies that just because he accepts God's existence as properly basic, he does not have to accept any and every belief as such (Plantinga, 1983, p. 74). But this reply misses the point. The point is not what Alvin Plantinga does or does not accept as properly basic. The point is, if Christians are within their epistemic rights in basing their criteria of proper basicality on what seems obvious to them, then others have that right too. What then is to keep Muslims, Jews, Hindus, Buddhists—and atheists—from choosing their own examples and formulating their own criteria in a way that will make their beliefs just as rational as those of the Christians? In fact, if Reformed Epistemology does permit such latitude in the formation of criteria of rationality, then it would seem to allow just about anybody to believe just about anything. Well, not just *anything*; surely everyone agrees that any such set of criteria must be consistent, coherent, and not self-refuting. Still, if these are the *only* restrictions, all sorts of very silly and pernicious beliefs could wind up as "rational" for many people in many circumstances. It seems to me that clever enough terrorists, racists, sexists, fascists, communists, fundamentalists, or fanatics could choose examples and formulate criteria that would not be inconsistent, incoherent, or self-refuting. If so, Reformed Epistemology would have to sanction as "rational" all sorts of obviously irrational and morally monstrous beliefs.

Perhaps Reformed epistemologists would bite the bullet and accept this consequence. Perhaps they are willing to accept a very broad relativism about rationality and epistemic duties. That is, except for the duty to avoid inconsistency, incoherence, or self-refutation, different persons or groups can base criteria of proper basicality on whatever examples they happen to find obvious. Their epistemic duty will then be to be loyal to their *own* criteria and their *own* examples. In this case, where criteria of proper basicality are personal or parochial, indefinitely many religious and nonreligious views would be rational. Indeed, what would keep atheists from declaring that for them the *nonexistence* of God is obviously properly basic?

There would be something very odd about the acceptance of such relativism by Christians. After all, Christians have traditionally regarded Christianity not only as true—*the* Truth, in fact—but as so manifestly or clearly true that those who willfully deny it risk eternal damnation. That is, except perhaps for the "invincibly ignorant," there is no excuse for rejection of the Gospel message. Perhaps Christians are now willing to concede that many different beliefs can be justified, and so rationally held, but still insist that only one view—theirs—is actually true. But if you admit that others hold opposing beliefs just as rationally as you hold yours, how *can* you be so sure that yours is the one that is right? Further, if theists claim only rational *parity* with atheists, then it is hard to see how belief can challenge unbelief. Muslim scholar Shabbir Akhtar makes this point eloquently:

Under these circumstances [when theists claim only rational parity with atheists] there is no convincing reason why an atheist or agnostic should come to religious faith nor indeed, more significantly, why a believer should feel morally or religiously obliged to contend indefinitely with doubts he may experience about the authenticity or truth of his convictions. It is not enough that religious practices or experiences provide sustenance to reinforce those who are already *within* the circle of faith: religion must challenge those who are *outside* of it (Akhtar, 1987, p. 197; emphasis in original).

In fact, as we shall see below, Reformed Epistemologists are so far from relativism that they not only regard atheism as wrong, but as irrational. However, to maintain such a view, they adopt an epistemological position very different from the one we have so far been considering. So far we have been considering the earlier (1983) formulation of Reformed Epistemology which was developed along lines laid down by Classical Foundationalism. My argument is that extreme relativism about rational belief seems to follow from that view.

Getting back to the argument at hand, Plantinga denies that Reformed Epistemology closes off all debate about the rationality of theism and atheism (Plantinga, 1983, pp. 82–87). For instance, theists could still argue that atheism is inconsistent, incoherent, or self-refuting. Atheists will blithely defy them to prove this.[1] Anyone claiming to show that a well-entrenched philosophical position is inconsistent, incoherent, or self-refuting has very tough sell. Therefore, unless some tighter restrictions are placed on what can count as a properly basic belief, a very deep relativism seems to follow. In my view, such relativism is bad for a number of reasons, not least because it leads to further fracturing of our already severely balkanized intellectual environment. Each different sect would announce its own criteria of

---

[1]Plantinga has argued that atheism is self-refuting in that it appeals to reason but regards reason as the product of evolution (see Plantinga, 1993). Evolution selects faculties that promote survival rather than truth, and so, says Plantinga, it is unlikely that evolution would produce reliable cognitive functions. Some atheists have argued (e.g., Nielsen, 1973) that theism is incoherent because God-talk does not meet the minimal criteria to count as fact-stating discourse. Here all I have room to say about such efforts, both those of theists and atheists, is that I regard them as wholly wrong-headed. I regard theism and atheism as clearly coherent possibilities which can be stated consistently and which are not self-refuting. The interesting question is which view is *true*.

proper basicality, climb into its own ideological fortress, and damn the other side to prove it wrong. In such an environment, one wonders what use it would be to have such a field as "philosophy of religion."

Classical Foundationalism recognized the dangers of extreme relativism and proposed a very strict set of criteria for proper basicality. Recall that only beliefs that were self-evident, incorrigible, or evident to the senses were recognized as properly basic. This is because such beliefs, and only such sorts, were regarded as the ones we cannot be wrong about. Reformed Epistemology would loosen the criteria and allow other kinds of beliefs to count as properly basic. But how do we keep those criteria from becoming too loose and inviting rampant relativism? The only way seems to be that we limit our examples of obvious proper basicality to the ones that seem obvious to everyone, or—human contrariness being what it is—to almost every one. If we do that, then "God exists" would not be allowed as obviously properly basic since there are very many people—theists as well as atheists—for whom it is simply not obvious.

Perhaps Reformed Epistemologists will argue that we should take as obviously properly basic those examples that are acceptable to just about everybody, and base our criteria of proper basicality on those. Then we shall see that "God exists" meets those criteria and should be counted as properly basic. For instance, perhaps it could be shown that since practically everyone accepts the belief that other minds exist as obviously properly basic, they should also accept "God exists" as properly basic (this, essentially, is just what Plantinga did argue in his book *God and Other Minds*, 1967). But when compared to those beliefs that nearly everyone regards as obviously properly basic, the belief that God exists definitely seems to be the odd one out. For instance, God's existence clearly is not self-evident; we can understand the statement "God exists" without immediately perceiving its truth. Also, theism is not incorrigible, since God's existence certainly seems to be something people could be mistaken about. Further, anyone who claims to see or hear God is usually regarded as a candidate for psychiatric evaluation, so God is not evident to the senses.[2]

What about the comparison of belief in God to the belief in other minds? Some have argued that our belief in other minds is not a basic belief at all, but is a very strong inference to the best explanation (O'Hear, 1984, p. 103). I regard our belief in other minds as properly basic; in fact, the belief in other minds seems to be what the philosopher David Hume called a "natural belief" (see Gaskin 1988, 117–118). A natural belief is one that (a) arises spontaneously and naturally in the course of ordinary life, (b) we hold with a profound sense of conviction that no skepticism can seriously erode, (c) is unavoidable since in order to live a human life we must talk and act in ways that presuppose that belief, and, therefore (d) is a belief all humans share. Clearly, any belief that meets these criteria of natural belief should be accepted as properly basic. Surely, no one could be faulted for having such a belief. Further, the belief that other minds exist certainly seems to meet all of the above criteria for natural beliefs. It certainly seems spontaneous, indubitable, unavoidable, and universal.[3] Now someone might plausibly argue that the belief that God exists meets condition (a) since, for some people anyway, it apparently arises spontaneously and naturally (more on this below). Also, for many people theism certainly meets condition (b); that is, no skeptical arguments can make them seriously doubt that belief. However, it seems quite clear that belief in the existence of God does not meet conditions (c) and (d). It just seems false that theism is somehow presupposed in the ways that we must talk and act to participate in the common life of humans. For instance, the intellectual, artistic, economic, and religious practices of the Greeks of the fifth century BCE did not seem to presuppose the existence of the God of theism. Also, belief in God certainly does not seem universal among human beings.

---

[2]William Alston has argued that it is quite correct to speak of perceiving God (1999), but he does not claim that God is detectable by the five senses, which is what I'm talking about here.

[3]For Descartes, the only things that are strictly indubitable are the awareness of one's own existence, the recognition that one is a thinking being, and certain other "clearly and distinctly perceived" truths. These might seem the only indubitable things when one is meditating alone by a warm fire on a winter day, as Descartes was. Any social interaction, however, draws one into forms of life (to use Ludwig Wittgenstein's term) that presuppose a community of minds. As I argue below, it would be quite literally mad to attempt to maintain serious doubt about other minds.

Prima facie, therefore, the belief in other minds meets the criteria for natural beliefs but the belief that God exists does not. The former belief therefore seems a much better candidate for properly basic status than the latter.

If Hume is right that there are such natural beliefs—and he certainly appears to be—there are only two ways the conclusion of the above paragraph could be wrong: Either the belief in other minds is not a natural belief or, despite appearances, belief in God is. Taking the first option, someone could argue that we do not have to *believe* that other minds exist to participate in the common life of human beings; we need only talk and act *as if* we believed it. We could take what philosophers call an "antirealist" attitude towards belief in other minds; that is, we may admit that we are practically constrained to act and talk as though other minds existed, but we refrain from accepting it as true. Many philosophers take antirealist attitudes towards the entities postulated in scientific theories. For instance, they admit that talk about quarks and quantum fields may help us to organize our data and make accurate predictions, but they think it is going too far to actually believe in such "theoretical entities." But the belief in other minds goes much, much deeper than any scientific theory possibly could. The most basic forms of communication and social interaction presuppose the mutual exchange of thoughts and ideas. The point here is not just that it is psychologically impossible to refrain from belief in other minds. Perhaps it is possible that years of intense brainwashing might derange someone sufficiently to enable him or her to maintain an antirealist attitude about other minds. The point is, that the most basic and universal forms and practices of human life, such as morality, for instance, just make *no sense at all* if other people do not have thoughts and feelings like our own. Unfeeling, unthinking automata have no moral claims on us—or at least not at all the same sort that conscious persons do. If we lived among robots programmed to act as if they had feelings, it might be prudent to interact with them as if they did, but prudence is not the same as morality.

If instead someone were to argue that theism is in fact a natural belief, they would have to show that it meets the above criteria (c) and (d). How could one show that the belief that God exists is unavoidable because in order to live a human life we must talk and act in ways that presuppose such a belief? Worse, how could anyone show, despite appearances very much to the contrary, that all humans actually do believe in God? Anyone who wants to make the former claim, that belief in God is unavoidable because presupposed in our most basic forms of life, has a very big job. Anyone who tried to go through life seriously denying the existence of any minds other than his own would be, or would soon become, quite literally mad. However, very many atheists have led enormously productive, rich, and meaningful lives, lives that embodied high ideals and a degree of moral rectitude that should shame many theists. Such lives indicate that nothing essential to human life, not even spirituality, presupposes the existence of God.

The upshot is that Plantinga's 1983 formulation of Reformed Epistemology runs into trouble whether it directs Christians to begin with their own particular examples of obvious proper basicality, or to begin with those examples acceptable to just about everyone. In the former case, Reformed Epistemology sanctions a deep relativism about epistemic duties that seems very much at odds with a view that regards itself, in the words of its Founder, as The Way, The Truth, and The Life. If all sorts of other views are equally rational, how can salvation be only through Christ? Surely God must open heaven to all of those who honestly believed what it was entirely rational and reasonable for them to accept. Christians will be very surprised to get to heaven and find it full of atheists, Buddhists, Muslims, and pagans! On the other hand, if Christians start with examples that seem obvious to nearly everyone, the belief that God exists seems to wind up as not properly basic. This is because theism just seems very unlike unquestionable examples of properly basic beliefs. For instance, unlike the belief in other minds, it seems not to be what Hume called a natural belief.

The argument need not end here. Perhaps someone would argue that there are no real atheists and that, deep down, everybody believes in God, or that atheists and agnostics are irrational in withholding belief in God. In either case, where nobody really fails to believe in God or only does so irrationally, God's existence could be obvious to every rational creature and surely, therefore, would be properly basic. Now I have heard some people, even philosophers, maintain that there are no real atheists. What I have never heard is anything remotely resembling a good argument for this claim. Usually those who assert such things have given highly idiosyncratic definitions to the key terms. For instance one eminent theologian of the last century said that a true atheist was one who denied that there are any deep meanings in life. You can "prove" anything if, like Humpty Dumpty in *Through the Looking Glass*, you can make words mean whatever you want. On the other hand, you might take the approach of the Apostle Paul who says in the first chapter of *Romans* that God's existence is obvious to everybody and that therefore ungodly persons have no excuse. How is it then that so many intelligent persons have denied or expressed doubt about God's existence, as presumably they would not if they found it obvious? How can anyone, even one bearing apostolic authority, insist that something is obvious for everyone when the words and acts of so many apparently reasonable and honest persons indicate that for them it is not? Plantinga has an answer to this last question, one that Paul would have endorsed with enthusiasm. *Sin* is the reason that some people obstinately deny the obvious (Plantinga, 1999, pp. 291–293). Just as disease or injury can damage the faculty of sight, so that objects that should be obvious are not, so sin corrupts our natural awareness of God.

How did Plantinga arrive at this remarkable conclusion? In his more recent discussions of theism as properly basic, Plantinga has adopted an "externalist" view of epistemology (Plantinga, 1999). Externalism is opposed to more traditional "internalist" views such as Classical Foundationalism. According to internalist epistemologies, a belief is rational if and only if it is justified, and justification is a matter of being aware of reasons, grounds, or evidence that support that belief. In terms of epistemic rights, we have the right to believe something only when we are justified in believing it.[4] For instance, my right to believe that Wordsworth composed "Ode: Intimations of Immortality"—what makes it a rational belief for me—is my memory of justifying grounds for that belief. In particular, I recall

that anthologies, textbooks, and persons who should know consistently identified him as the author of the poem. Plantinga now rejects the idea of justification and the concomitant concepts of epistemic rights and duties (Plantinga, 1999). He regards a belief as rational when it is "warranted." Warrant is an objective matter; it has nothing to do with a subjective awareness of justifying reasons. A belief is warranted when it is produced by the proper functioning of a reliable cognitive faculty in the sort of environment in which that faculty was designed to operate. This sounds like a mouthful, but the idea is really pretty simple. I have a faculty (sight, for example) that provides me with reliable information about my environment in a wide range of circumstances in which it was designed (by God or evolution) to operate. When I think I see Bill Clinton walking down the street shaking hands, my belief that the former president really is walking down the street would normally be warranted. The only things that would keep it from being warranted would be that something has gone wrong with my vision or that I am in some circumstance where such appearances could be unreliable—say the Bill Clinton Impersonators convention was in town.

According to Plantinga, all humans have a natural cognitive faculty that can make them aware of God (Plantinga, 1999, p. 288). When this faculty, the *sensus divinitatis*, is functioning properly, it gives us a warranted and properly basic awareness of God in a wide variety of circumstances. Plantinga gives a number of these circumstances:

> . . . Including in particular some of the glories of nature: the marvelous, impressive beauty of the night sky; the timeless crash and roar of the surf that resonates deep within us; the majestic grandeur of the mountains . . . the ancient, brooding presence of the Australian outback; the roar of a great waterfall . . . there is something like an awareness of divine disapproval upon having done what is wrong, or cheap, and something like a perception of divine forgiveness upon confession and repentance. People in grave danger instinctively turn to the Lord, asking for succor and support, having formed the belief that he can hear and help if he sees fit (Plantinga, 1999, p. 288).

---

[4] I am following Plantinga's (1999) characterization of internalism and externalism and the relationship of justification to epistemic duties. Some philosophers disagree with some of these points. In particular, Evan Fales (private communication) holds that Plantinga wrongly conflates justification with the satisfaction of epistemic duties.

However, the *sensus divinitatis*, like other cognitive faculties, can malfunction:

> . . . this natural knowledge of God has been compromised, weakened, reduced, smothered, overlaid, or impeded by sin and its consequences . . . due to one cause or another, the faculty itself may be *diseased* and thus partly or wholly disabled. There is such a thing as cognitive disease; there is blindness, deafness, inability to tell right from wrong, insanity; and there are analogues to these conditions with respect to the operation of the *sensus divinitatis* . . . the unbeliever . . . displays epistemic malfunction; failing to believe in God is a result of some sort of dysfunction of the *sensus divinitatis* (Plantinga, 1999, p. 291).

Further, like believing, withholding belief can be warranted or unwarranted and so rational or irrational. When we withhold a belief because of the malfunction of a cognitive faculty, which would have induced that belief had it been functioning properly, then our withholding of belief is not warranted and so is irrational. Therefore, when sin corrupts the *sensus divinitatis* of atheists and agnostics and they withhold belief in God, their failure to believe is unwarranted and irrational. Only faith and the working of the Holy Spirit can heal and restore the proper function of the *sensus divinitatis* (Plantinga, 1999, p. 293).

Therefore Plantinga regards atheism as irrational. Sin has so corrupted the atheist's cognitive faculties that he or she is incapable of sensing the divine presence even when contemplating the night sky or feeling guilty. It should come as no surprise that many atheists fully reciprocate these sentiments and are perfectly willing to play hardball if that is what Plantinga wants. In an earlier work I summarized some of the standard Freudian and Marxist reasons that atheists have given for claiming that theism is irrational since theistic belief is produced by malfunctioning cognitive processes:

> The world is a grim and frightening place; it threatens us constantly with pain, sorrow, and death. Nature obeys her own laws, oblivious of the suffering or hardship they might cause us. Further even if we do discover happiness, we know that it will be short-lived and that we will die someday. Surely It would be wonderful if, living in such a world, we could be assured that Someone is ultimately in charge—Someone who loves us and will guide and comfort us through life's travails. . . . Thus does belief in God come about—as a product of hope and fear. . . . Further, . . . an oppressed populace will not so stridently demand justice in the here and now if they can be assured of pie in the sky when they die. Thus, belief in God, with its attendant promises of reward and punishment (safely postponed to the hereafter), is a powerful tool for social control. Recognizing this, those who govern a society will strongly reinforce the approved religious doctrines (Parsons, 1989, pp. 57–58).

In short, wishful thinking and socialization hijack theists' cognitive faculties and make them adopt a fantasy as real.

In my view, anthropologist Stewart Guthrie gives a better argument for a similar conclusion in his book *Faces in the Clouds* (1993). Guthrie provides copious evidence of the universal human tendency to anthropomorphize, that is, to see human features in nonhuman and even inanimate things. He argues that there is an enormous survival advantage in interpreting ambiguous appearances in anthropomorphic ways. It is so important that we detect human presence and influence wherever it occurs, that we are programmed to "see" human features even when the sensory cues are very slight or ambiguous. We are programmed to be hypersensitive to any appearances that are even vaguely human and, in general, to put a human face on impersonal nature. It is far better to "see" a human face that is not there than not to see one that is, or to falsely attribute something to human influence than to fail to recognize its actual occurrence. Therefore, we have a universal tendency to see the world in human terms. It is precisely this anthropomorphizing tendency, Guthrie argues, that causes us to feel an "awareness" of God when we contemplate the starry heavens or the resounding surf or the brooding presence of the outback. The sense of awareness of God we get in those situations is not warranted; it is not caused by the proper working of a reliable cognitive faculty in the circumstances for which it was designed. Instead, such "awareness" is the by-product of an anthropomorphizing tendency that is cognitively unreliable but useful for survival.

Well, which view is correct? Is theistic belief "warrant basic"—warranted because the unimpaired functioning of the *sensus divinitatis* has given theists a properly basic awareness of God? Does it fail to be warrant basic because such "awareness" is a delusion caused by some cognitive malfunction or produced by some faculty not aimed at truth? Plantinga says that the answer depends on whether theism is *true* (Plantinga, 1999, pp. 295–296). If God does not exist, then there is no reliable *sensus divinitatis* and it is very improbable that any other means could warrant belief in God as properly basic. If God does exist, then accounts such as Freud's, Marx's, and Guthrie's cannot be true, and it is very probable that God has given us some direct, reliable means of knowing him and that some people do have warranted properly basic belief in God. Plantinga concludes that nobody can argue that theistic belief is not warrant basic belief without *also* arguing against the truth of theism (Plantinga, 1999, pp. 295–296). The lesson he seems to draw is that much of the sting is taken out of arguments, such as Freud's, Marx's, or Guthrie's, which attempt to impeach the *rationality* of theism rather than its truth. Only arguments that directly challenge the *existence* of God, such as the problem of evil, can pose any real threat to theism (Plantinga, 1999, p. 296).

I draw a different lesson. Plantinga says that it is much more likely that belief in God is warrant basic if in fact there is a God than if there is not. But if we make the probability that belief in God is warrant basic depend on whether or not God exists, then the probability that God exists can be lowered by any independent evidence that belief in God is not warrant basic. This is a simple consequence of the rule of the probability calculus known as Bayes' Theorem.[5] So as not to terrify the mathphobic, I shall illustrate the point with a simple example: Lots of people believe they have seen ghosts. Are these beliefs warranted?

That is, did reliable perceptual processes produce these beliefs? Or were these beliefs the result of mistakes or malfunctions, like hallucinations or overactive imaginations? Suppose there really are ghosts who enjoy a good haunt every now and then. That is, they sometimes amuse themselves by becoming apparitions and scaring the wits out of the living. If there really are such mischievous spirits, then some people are very likely to be warranted in believing that they have seen a ghost. On the other hand, if there are no ghosts, it is very unlikely that the proper functioning of any reliable faculty in the circumstance in which it was designed to operate will convince us that we have seen a ghost. If ghosts do not exist it is very unlikely that anyone will have a warranted belief that he or she has seen a ghost. Suppose now that all previous reports of ghost sightings have been thoroughly debunked; each is shown to be a result of hallucination, perceptual errors, or imagination. Suppose further that neuroscience provides a very convincing explanation of why people sometimes hallucinate ghosts. Such findings should make you more skeptical of the existence of ghosts. The same reasoning applies to God. If sound, arguments such as Guthrie's that belief in God is not warrant basic should make you more skeptical of God's existence. It seems to me therefore that Plantinga's approach makes arguments like Guthrie's *more* dangerous to theism, not less.

So again, *is* there a *sensus divinitatis*? The occurrence of religious or spiritual experience is a human universal, a phenomenon common to all times and places. Encounters with the sacred or the numinous have innumerable literary and artistic expressions, dating back to the beginnings of human culture. Even atheists have such experiences. I have felt the

---

[5]For those who are not mathphobic, let

W = Belief in God is warrant basic.

and

G = God exists.

Then, by Bayes's Theorem, the probability that belief in God is warrant basic given that God exists, $p(W/G)$, is

$$p(W/G) = \frac{p(G/W)}{p(G)} \times p(W)$$

Where $p(G/W)$ is the probability that God exists given that the belief in God is warrant basic, $p(G)$ is the total probability that

God exists, that is, the probability that God exists whether belief in God is warrant basic or not, and $p(W)$ is the background probability that belief in God is warrant basic. Multiplying both sides of the equation by $p(G)$ and then dividing by $p(W/G)$ gives

$$p(G) = \frac{p(G/W)}{p(W/G)} \times p(W)$$

So, the total probability that God exists is lowered if arguments, like Guthrie's, lower $p(W)$, the background probability that belief in God is warrant basic. This means that arguments like Guthrie's are doubly dangerous to theism because they not only threaten to show that theism is not warrant basic, but *ipso facto* they also lower the overall probability that God exists.

profound silence, emptiness, and solitude of the Wyoming high desert and marveled at the shining translucence of the Orion Nebula. In the Galapagos Islands I have seen shafts of sunlight descending into the Pacific depths, illuminating myriad fish of every conceivable hue. Such experiences were of the deepest significance for me, but they were not experiences of God. Rather, I was overwhelmed with a sense of awe and connectedness to all things and of myself as a small though integral part of the whole. There was also an awareness of the preciousness and significance both of my own life and the lives of all the creatures with which we share this planet. Actually, Wordsworth, in "Lines: Composed a Few Miles Above Tintern Abbey," expressed my experiences far better than I can:

> . . . a sense sublime
> Of something far more deeply interfused,
> Whose dwelling is the light of setting suns,
> And the round ocean and the living air,
> And the blue sky, and in the mind of man;
> A motion and a spirit, that impels
> All thinking things, all objects of all thought,
> And rolls through all things. . .

But again, that "something far more deeply interfused" did not seem to be the God of theism; it did not seem to be any sort of encounter with a *personal* being. Rather, it was a discovery of "sacred depths" *within* the universe itself.

My religious or spiritual experiences, and those of very many other people in diverse cultures, present a challenge to theists who believe in a *sensus divinitatis*. Why do so many of those experiences fail to impart an awareness of the theistic deity? Of course, Plantinga could dig in his heels and say that in such cases sin has distorted the experience, but one wonders just how far he is prepared to carry such a claim. It seems that Christians who believe in a *sensus divinitatis* are committed to each of the following claims: (1) The Christian God exists, (2) he has implanted a *sensus divinitatis* in all humans, and (3) the proper functioning of the *sensus divinitatis* in the appropriate circumstances imparts knowledge of the Christian God. The problem is that many persons believe in God but do not believe in the *Christian* God. Jews and Muslims for instance are devout monotheists but do not believe that God is Father, Son, and Holy Spirit as Christians do. How does someone like Plantinga, a Christian who believes in a *sensus divinitatis*, account for this situation? Has sin corrupted the *sensus divinitatis* of Jews and Muslims, as it allegedly has with atheists and agnostics, so that this faculty does not function properly and leaves non-Christian theists with a false or at least incomplete concept of God? Such a view certainly seems unattractive given the ugly history of Christian intolerance and persecution. Besides, what is to keep Jews and Muslims from saying the same thing about Christians? Has the *sensus divinitatis* been designed only to give us a general awareness of a Supreme Being, but not specific knowledge of the Christian God? But why would the Christian God not give us true and complete knowledge, especially when, as orthodox Christians believe, the acknowledgment of the Christian God is necessary for salvation? On the other hand, perhaps the *sensus divinitatis* cannot function properly in persons born into cultures with very strong non-Christian traditions. Perhaps being born into a devoutly Jewish or Muslim environment produces a sort of invincible ignorance that prevents the *sensus divinitatis* from functioning correctly. But why would the Christian God, who, according to scripture, desires that all should be saved, allow his will to be thwarted by accidents of birth? And again, if Christians make charges of invincible ignorance, why cannot Jews and Muslims do the same?

In conclusion, has Reformed Epistemology succeeded in showing that theism is a properly basic belief? Plantinga certainly has not adequately addressed skeptic's qualms about the proper basicality of theistic belief. The belief that God exists does not seem to be like uncontroversial cases of properly basic belief. Further, atheists and agnostics are given no reason to think the proper functioning of a *sensus divinitatis* warrants theistic belief. Instead our doubts on this point are attributed to our unrepentant sinfulness. But perhaps Plantinga's aim has not been to convince us doubters, but only to deflect the arguments we might make against the rationality of theistic belief. Even here his success is equivocal. True, I cannot prove that there is no *sensus divinitatis* any more than I can show that no one possesses psychic powers or can foresee the future. All I can do is point out that the evidence for the claims that such persons do possess such faculties is zero. Further, I can argue, as Guthrie does, that the beliefs people claim to have acquired by the functioning of an occult faculty are much more likely to have other causes. Nothing Plantinga has said shows that arguments such as Guthrie's cannot be sound. Further, even if Plantinga does succeed in insulating theism from being proven irrational in certain ways, this is not the same thing as proving that it is rational. I conclude, therefore, that Reformed Epistemology, both in its internalist and externalist versions, fails to show that theistic belief is rational.

WORKS CITED

Note: Where possible I have drawn on sources readily available to undergraduate students. In particular, I have made use of the widely used anthology *Philosophy of Religion: The Big Questions*, edited by Eleonore Stump and Michael J. Murray, Oxford: Blackwell Publishers (1999).

Akhtar, S., (1987), *Reason and the Radical Crisis of Faith.* New York: Peter Lang.

Alston, W. "Perceiving God," in Stump and Murray, pp. 142–149.

Clifford, W. K., "The Ethics of Belief" in Stump and Murray, pp. 269–273.

Gaskin, J. C. A., *Hume's Philosophy of Religion.* Atlantic Highlands, NJ: Humanities Press International.

Guthrie, S. (1993), *Faces in the Clouds.* Oxford: Oxford University Press.

Nielsen, K. (1973), *Skepticism.* London: The Macmillan Press.

O'Hear, A. (1984), *Experience, Explanation, and Faith.* London: Routledge & Kegan Paul.

Parsons, K. (1989), *God and the Burden of Proof.* Buffalo, NY: Prometheus Books.

Plantinga, A. (1967), *God and Other Minds.* Ithaca, NY: Cornell University Press.

———. (1983), "Reason and Belief in God," in *Faith and Rationality*, Plantinga, A. and Wolterstorff, N., Eds. Notre Dame: Notre Dame University Press, pp. 16–93; an excerpt, "Is Naturalism Irrational?" is in Stump and Murray, pp. 125–138.

———. (1993), *Warrant and Proper Function.* Oxford: Oxford University Press.

———. (1999), "Warranted Belief in God," in Stump and Murray, pp. 285–297.

QUESTIONS FOR FURTHER REFLECTION

1. Consider the following argument against the existence of epistemic duties: "To say that we ought to do something implies that we can. Therefore, when we speak of epistemic duties—which supposedly define what we *ought* to believe—the implication is that our beliefs are subject to our wills, that is, that we can decide what we shall believe. But beliefs are involuntary. No one has any control over what seems right to him or her at any given time. It would be pointless for someone to tell us that we ought not to believe something when in fact we cannot help but believe it." How would you respond to this argument?

2. *Could* Christians embrace relativism? That is, could Christians reject the idea that Christianity is an absolute truth and be happy with the view that there are many "true" religions?

3. There has been much discussion in the media lately of the discovery of the "God part" of the brain. That is, a number of researchers now claim that certain brain functions seem to trigger deep spiritual or religious experiences. Do such discoveries support Plantinga's claims about the existence of a *sensus divinitatis*, or do they indicate the opposite, namely, that the brain itself may be responsible for our "awareness" of God?

4. Consider the following argument for the existence of a *sensus divinitatis*: "All cultures and the overwhelming majority of individual human beings have recognized some conception of the divine. Atheists and agnostics have always been a tiny minority of humans. Such near-universal agreement indicates that humans do indeed possess an innate awareness of the divine. Now humans may have given many different names to God—Zeus, Odin, Brahma, Marduk, Allah, Yahweh, and so on—but these are just different ways of expressing the same truth, namely the existence of a Supreme Being." How do you respond to this argument?

5. Is it even a very interesting issue whether or not theism is rational? Isn't it more appropriate for philosophers to inquire about the *truth* of theism? Would it be more fruitful for philosophers to agree that the existence of God is a question on which entirely rational people can hold opposite views? How would discussion proceed if theists and atheists each conceded that the opposing view was rational?

31. RELIGIOUS BELIEF FOR THE REST OF US

Reflections on Reformed Epistemology

Sandra Menssen and Thomas D. Sullivan

Sandra Menssen is Professor of Philosophy at the University of St. Thomas. She has also taught at St. Olaf College and at the University of Minnesota (where she received her doctorate). Her major interests are in philosophy of religion, metaphysics, and ethics. She is Co-editor of *Logos: A Journal of Catholic Thought and Culture*, published by the University of St. Thomas. Currently she is working on a book entitled *The Agnostic Inquirer: Rethinking the Question of Revelation* (with Thomas D. Sullivan, forthcoming from Ashgate Publishing).

Thomas D. Sullivan is Professor of Philosophy at the University of St. Thomas, where he holds the Aquinas Chair in Philosophy and Theology. He did his doctoral work at St. John's University. His major interests are in philosophy of logic, metaphysics, and ethics. Currently he is working on a book entitled *On Being and Essence: An Exploration of Aquinas's Ontology from a Contemporary Standpoint* (with Russell Pannier), and one entitled *The Agnostic Inquirer: Rethinking the Question of Revelation* (with Sandra Menssen).

How could someone come to believe—confidently—in a revelatory claim, a claim that God has communicated a message of great importance to us? Alvin Plantinga has an answer to this question. It's an answer Menssen and Sullivan can accept only in part. Plantinga proposes a model of warranted Christian belief that, according to Menssen and Sullivan, embeds a weaker thesis and a stronger thesis. The weaker thesis is that Christians who believe in accordance with the model are warranted in resolute religious belief. This Menssen and Sullivan do not dispute. The stronger thesis is that one who does *not* accept Christianity in accord with the model or something much like it cannot know that Christianity is true, or have faith that it is true, or even (merely) believe that it is true. It is this to which Menssen and Sullivan take exception. Two claims generate the stronger thesis. Menssen and Sullivan argue that both of these claims are false, and in the process explain their own answer to the original question.

READING QUESTIONS

1. What is the difference between the "weak" and the "strong" theses of Reformed epistemology, according to Menssen and Sullivan?
2. What are the central or key claims of the essay by Menssen and Sullivan?
3. Menssen and Sullivan set out six arguments in their essay, labeled (A)–(F). Look at each of the six arguments, and explain the *point* of each argument. (For instance: are Menssen and Sullivan endorsing the argument, or are they criticizing it? Is the argument intended to support a premise of some other argument in the essay?)
4. Look at each of the six arguments (A)–(F), and be prepared to explain the *conclusions* of the arguments (in other words, be prepared to reexpress the conclusions in your own words).
5. Look at each of the six arguments (A)–(F), and be prepared to explain the *premises* of the arguments (in other words, be prepared to reexpress the premises in your own words).

1. THE STRONG THESIS OF REFORMED EPISTEMOLOGY

It is at least conceptually possible that there is religious experience so forceful that one no more needs to reason about whether it comes from God than to reason whether light is radiating from the sun. Perhaps Paul on the road to Damascus, or Mohammed, or Arjuna, or Teresa of Avila had such experience. Few believers today claim the dramatic experiences visionaries report. Nevertheless, the Reformed epistemologists suggest, religious believers may know that God exists, and know that Christianity is true, not by inference or argument but in a much more immediate way.

According to Alvin Plantinga, the best known of the Reformed epistemologists, the believer may simply *find* in himself or herself a conviction that there is a God, as one finds oneself perceiving trees, or remembering what one had for breakfast, or realizing that 2 + 2 = 4, or believing in the existence of other persons. The believer's conviction that there is a God may be not only basic—that is, not based on other propositions—but *properly* basic, or justified. Further still, it may be *warranted*: it may be produced by a mechanism designed to produce true beliefs about God, a properly functioning mechanism that generates belief sufficiently strong to count as knowledge. On the extended account of the model, Plantinga suggests, warrant may similarly be provided for specifically Christian beliefs. Plantinga writes:

> We [Christians] read Scripture, or something presenting scriptural teaching, or hear the gospel preached. . . . What is said simply seems right; it seems compelling; one finds oneself saying, "Yes, that's right, that's the truth of the matter; this is indeed the word of the Lord." I read, "God was in Christ, reconciling the world to himself"; I come to think: "Right; that's true; God really was in Christ, reconciling the world to himself!"[1]

Plantinga is clearly committed to the thesis that *some* persons (those who have a belief in God of the

sort the "Aquinas/Calvin" or A/C model[2] describes) are warranted in resolute[3] religious belief. This is a fairly weak thesis. In order for it to be true it's enough if there is *one person* who has the sort of basic belief in God Plantinga describes (logicians typically read "some" as "at least one"). In fact, there doesn't have to be *anybody* who has properly basic belief in God in order for the thesis to be true if it is understood as equivalent to the claim that *if* there is anyone who has a belief in God of the sort the A/C model describes, than that person is warranted in resolute religious belief. We do wonder how often people really have such knockdown certainty about God's existence, but we will not dispute the claim that some people do, or that they are warranted in resolute belief.

We want to note, though, that the weak thesis has limited utility. The A/C model will not demonstrate to *all* Christian believers that their beliefs are warranted or justified. We are Christians, adult converts, as it happens. Along with Plantinga and other prominent representatives of Reformed epistemology, we share belief in central Christian mysteries. However, we do not think we *know* that Christianity is true. (And if our conception here of knowledge is off-base, at least we do not know that we know that Christianity is true. Thus we cannot have the confidence Plantinga's account requires.) Many Christians, unlike Plantinga, do not find the basic truths of Christianity lodged in their epistemic foundations. And Plantinga's account is unlikely to help an inquiring agnostic see the truth of Christianity (as Plantinga might well acknowledge). Agnostics are not conscious of having the sorts of basic beliefs Plantinga reports. Can an agnostic take Plantinga's account as a map for getting Christian beliefs? Perhaps Plantinga means to direct agnostics to read Scripture, and ask

---

[1] Alvin Plantinga, *Warranted Christian Belief*, (New York and Oxford: Oxford University Press, 2000), p. 250.

[2] Plantinga labels his account of warranted Christian belief "the A/C model," after Aquinas and Calvin. We will not pause to consider how his account converges or diverges with those of Aquinas and Calvin.

[3] By a "resolute" belief we mean a belief that is held firmly, with resolve. We don't take resolute belief to be equivalent to knowledge (our reasons will become evident later), but knowing that something is true is sufficient for resolutely believing that it is true. Since anyone whose belief in God is captured by the A/C model *knows* that God exists, they are warranted in believing this resolutely.

for help from the Holy Spirit. But many inquiring agnostics have *already* read parts of Scripture, and, in the manner of the young Charles Ryder in *Brideshead Revisited*, have mustered the sort of prayers an agnostic can offer ("O God, if there is a God, show me the truth of these Scriptures, if they are in fact true"). When an agnostic reads that to Plantinga it "simply seems right" that "God was in Christ reconciling the world to himself," the reaction may well be something like: "That is a beautiful sentiment; I wish Christians could give me reasons for thinking it is true."

Plantinga appears committed to a much stronger thesis. Despite some quick nods in the direction of natural theology, it looks like Plantinga is stuck with the thesis that a person who does not accept Christianity in accord with the A/C model or something much like it cannot know that Christianity is true, or have faith that it is true, or even (merely) believe that it is true. For it looks like Plantinga is committed to the following argument, which we'll call (A):

(A-1) It is impossible to work up a reasoned case that the likelihood that Christianity is true is over .5 because of the principle of declining probabilities.[4]

(A-2) If a person does not accept Christianity in accord with the A/C model or something much like it, then the person could know that Christianity is true, or rationally have faith that it is true, or even (merely) rationally believe it is true *only if* the person could work up a reasoned case for Christianity that is substantially stronger than the case against (a case that the probability is over .5 would not do).

(A-3) So, a person who does not accept Christianity in accord with the A/C model or something much like it cannot know that Christianity is true, or rationally have faith that it is true, or even (merely) rationally believe that it is true.

What are the grounds for attributing (A-1) to Plantinga? Plantinga takes it that the project of the philosophical inquirer into Christianity is to find the probability (given the inquirer's background knowledge) of the claim that Jesus, the incarnate second person of the trinity, atoned for our sin through his suffering and death and enables us to attain eternal salvation. The inquirer arrives at the final probability by first determining the probability that God exists (given background knowledge). Then the inquirer determines the probability that God would make some kind of revelation to humankind (given the probability that God exists, plus the background knowledge). Then the inquirer goes on to assess the probability that Jesus's teachings could sensibly be interpreted to include the claim that Jesus was the incarnate second person of the trinity sent to atone for our sin and save us through his suffering and death (given the probability that God exists, combined with the probability that God would make some kind of revelation to humankind, combined with the background knowledge). And then there are additional probabilities to be figured: the probability that Jesus rose from the dead, and the probability that in raising Jesus from the dead God endorsed Jesus's teachings. Each step one takes in this investigative process knocks the probability down. As Plantinga puts it:

> The main problem for such a historical case, as I see it, is what we can call the principle of dwindling probabilities: the fact that in giving such a historical argument, we can't simply annex the intermediate propositions to K [the background knowledge] (as I'm afraid many who employ this sort of argument actually do) but must instead *multiply* the relevant probabilities.[5]

Perhaps, a careful reader will object, we are being too hasty in attributing to Plantinga the claim that it's *impossible* to work up a reasoned case for Christianity that brings the probability up over .5. Plantinga has been arguing against the plausibility of what he calls "a historical case," a reasoned case for Christianity that combines some traditional natural theology with traditional historical arguments concerning Christianity. Might Plantinga endorse some *other* way of obtaining a reasoned case for Christianity? Well, he doesn't rule it out a priori. But the title of the section in which

---

[4]We may permit ourselves to assign rough numerical values to probability judgments even if quantitative confirmation is strictly speaking impossible. When one says the probability of God's existence can be raised above .5, one means that the case for God's existence can be made the better case.

[5]Plantinga, WCB, p. 280.

Plantinga presents his argument from declining probabilities against a philosophical/historical case for Christianity is: "Why Necessary?" The section apparently is intended to answer the question Plantinga poses in its first sentence: "Why is this elaborate scheme [the scheme described by the A/C model] necessary? Why these supernaturally inspired writings and this individually applied supernatural testimony of the Holy Spirit?" Plantinga immediately indicates that he doesn't think the "necessity" at issue here is of a sort that would have made it impossible for God to set up a different scheme. But in the discussion that follows he takes only *one* alternative seriously, and that is the alternative we've just discussed, the alternative that involves a combined philosophical/historical case for Christianity. The section concludes with the statement: "It is for this reason that some such scheme as proposed in the testimonial model is necessary, if we human beings are to be able to know the great truths of the gospel."[6]

Let us move on to consider grounds for attributing (A-2) to Plantinga. Although there do not exist complete and widely accepted analyses or definitions of the concepts of "knowledge," "faith," and "belief," (or, for that matter, of many of the concepts philosophers discuss), there appears to be something approaching a consensus about some relationships among the concepts. Surely one who does not rationally *believe* that Christianity is true also does not *know* or have a rational *faith* that it is true. (Some philosophers hold that faith without belief is possible. Most philosophers, however, do not take this possibility seriously. We side with the majority here.) So if Plantinga sets out a necessary condition for rationally *believing* that Christianity is true, it will also be a condition for knowing that it is true or rationally having faith that it is true. And he does set out such a condition: he holds that one must know *more* than that the probability of Christian belief is higher than .5:[7]

> But if my only ground for Christian teaching is its probability with respect to *K*, and all I know about that probability is that it is greater than .5, then I can't rationally *believe* that teaching.

How much higher must the probability be pushed for rational belief? It may be hard to say precisely; let's just say it looks like Plantinga thinks a case for Christianity that is "substantially stronger" than the case against (i.e., that has a probability substantially higher than .5) is required.

So it looks like Plantinga is committed to the premises of argument (A), and to its conclusion, which states what we have called the *strong* thesis of Reformed epistemology. Now perhaps texts intimating this strong thesis may be read in a different way than the way in which we read them. If so, that is all to the good. In that case it may turn out that we have no substantive disagreement with the Reformed epistemologists. Still, there is considerable utility in making the stronger thesis explicit if Reformed epistemologists may reasonably be construed as asserting it, even if they do not intend to assert it. For if the stronger thesis is not part of what Reformed epistemologists are intending to say, this can be made explicit in future articulations of an ingenious theory.

2. AVOIDING THE PROBLEM OF DECLINING PROBABILITIES (REJECTING A-1).

We now argue that (A-1) is false. In other words, we argue that it is *not* at all impossible to work up a reasoned case that the likelihood that Christianity is true is over .5. Our argument (B) is as follows:

(B-1) It is not highly implausible that there is an "originator," a certain sort of necessary condition of the existence of the universe.

(B-2) If it is not highly implausible that there is an originator, then it may well be possible to work up a reasoned case for Christianity that avoids the problem of declining probabilities and assigns a likelihood over .5.

(B-3) So, it may well be possible to work up a reasoned case for Christianity that assigns it a probability over .5.

Premise (B-1)

We understand an *originator* to be a cause of the universe—more specifically, a certain sort of necessary condition of the existence of the universe. As we use the term, "originator" does not even imply intellect.

---

[6]Plantinga, *WCB*, p. 280.

[7]Plantinga, *WCB*, p. 274.

Nevertheless, to show that the existence of an originator is not highly implausible may *in one sense* be to show that God's existence is not highly implausible. Consider the discovery of the electron. If you can prove that there is such a thing as an electron, it may be that you've proved there is something with a charge of 1.6021×10^{-19}C (there is no such thing as an electron without that charge). But you may know there is an electron without knowing that there is a thing with a charge of 1.6021×10^{-19}C.

We propose an argument for an originator that is a stripped-down version of a traditional cosmological argument (C):

(C-1) It is plausible that the physical universe came to be (that is, had a beginning).[8]

(C-2) It is plausible that whatever comes to be has a cause (a certain sort of necessary condition).

(C-3) It is plausible that nothing causes itself to come to be.

(C-4) Therefore it is not highly implausible that the universe has a cause distinct from itself (an originator).

For all this argument tells us, there may be more than one cause of the universe, more than one originator.[9] But if the argument is correct, it cannot be claimed that it is known or all but known that there is no creator.

We need not dwell on the claim that the universe came to be. Cosmologists keep telling us that the universe began some 15 billion years ago, and while the big bang may have been preceded by a big crunch, no respectable cosmologist claims it is highly unlikely that the universe is temporally finite. The theory that the world began from an initial singularity has persuaded even many atheists that it is probably true that the world came to be. Now everyone

recognizes that judgments of this sort can quickly be overturned in contemporary physics. But even on a cautious or skeptical assessment of the evidence, it looks like we have no reason to prefer the hypothesis that the world always existed over the hypothesis that it did not always exist. It looks like we can assign the claim that "the world came to be" a probability of *at least* .5. We can make this assignment without trying to work through either the arguments of contemporary physicists *or* the complex philosophical arguments advanced over the past two millennia in support of the claim. (If there were *no* evidence one way or the other, the probability would be inscrutable; we could then judge that the hypothesis that universe began is not less probable than the denial of the hypothesis. Surely the current consensus of scientific opinion pushes the probability of the claim up a bit.)

As for the proposition that whatever comes to be has a cause, few general principles outside of logic and mathematics strike us with the force of this "universal causal principle" (UCP). The great Scottish philosopher Thomas Reid put it this way:

> That neither existence, nor any mode of existence, can begin without an efficient cause is a principle that appears very early in the mind of man; and it is so universal, and so firmly rooted in human nature, that the most determined skepticism cannot eradicate it.[10]

However, after Hume's skeptical teaching on causality, according to which causation is nothing more than the constant conjunction of events, UCP no longer struck everyone as obvious. (Interestingly, Hume himself wrote, "allow me to tell you that I never asserted so absurd a Proposition as that *anything might arise without a cause....*"[11]) So it pays to examine the grounds for UCP.

We will grant that UCP is not self-evident. It is nevertheless possible to produce a strong argument that UCP is plausible indeed. Here is the argument (D):

(D-1) It is false that: everything is such that, if it can come to be at all, it can come to be without a nec-

[8]By "universe" we mean *this* universe, a space that includes all matter and energy, and nothing beyond that space. Controversies concerning alternative understandings of the universe's beginnings do not affect our argument, so long as it is understood that we are not claiming the world came to be in the course of an already-existing time.

[9]Thus when we speak of "the originator" we will *not* mean "the one and only originator or cause." Rather, we mean "either the one and only originator, *or* one of the originators."

[10]Thomas Reid, *Essays on the Active Powers of the Human Mind*, Baruch Brody (ed.) (Cambridge, Massachusetts and London, England: MIT Press, 1969), Essay IV, Ch. II, 267.

[11]*The Letters of David Hume* J.Y.T. Greig (ed.), (Oxford: Clarendon Press, 1932), Vol. I, 187.

essary condition in any situation whatever (in other words, at least one thing has a necessary condition for coming to be).

(D-2) If one holds that while some things cannot come to be without a cause, other things can, there must be a basis for drawing the distinction.

(D-3) There is no basis for saying that while some things cannot come to be without a cause, other things can.

(D-4) So, nothing is such that (if it can come to be at all) it can come to be without a cause in any situation whatever.

Why think (D-3) is true? Might not science provide a basis for saying that while some things cannot come to be without a cause, other things can? Quentin Smith at one point asserted that there is decisive scientific evidence that the universe began causelessly; if true, that would provide a basis for drawing the distinction at issue. But the scientific evidence he supplied at most supports the contention that the world had no physical cause.[12] Smith acknowledged that he had to do much more to show it had no cause at all. The theist will happily receive the news that the world does not have a physical cause. Though it looks to us like UCP is highly likely, let us cautiously assign it a probability of merely .5. At the very least, surely, there is no more reason to reject UCP than to accept it. Given our assignment of a .5 probability to the claim that the world came to be, we get a probability of .25 that the world has a cause (once we multiply the probabilities).

To say that there must *be* some cause for a phenomenon is different from fingering the cause. One may begin to frame in the conditions that must be satisfied if a cause is to be provided, and assert that there must be something that meets the conditions. Imagine a small child sees a magician do a trick for the first time, and says: "The magician is like God; he's making birds!" The parent says: "No, the magician is not making the birds out of thin air, out of nothing." "What *is* the magician doing, then?" asks the child. And the parent responds: "I do not know what he's doing, but I

do know there is a trick involved." The magician is doing something other than making birds *ex nihilo*. The beginning stages of framing in conditions for a causal account of some object or event may be quite modest.

And so, similarly, one might begin to construct an argument that an originator exists. One might say "this universe cannot have existed forever." Then one says certain things about its cause, beginning to frame in the conditions that must be satisfied if there is to be a causal account, and one asserts that there must be something that meets the conditions. In this case one still hasn't said a word about *how* the creation occurs. But one need not hold that the hypothesis about the originator that's made probable is made probable because it is explanatory in some rich sense, or even because it gives a detailed account of the cause of the universe. Overturning the conviction that a secular or materialistic account of the universe is the only possible account may require no more than *beginning* to frame in the conditions a cause of the universe must satisfy.

Smith has recently conceded that it is plausible that if the world came to be, it needed a cause of its existence. But he thinks it is possible that the world caused itself to exist. This brings us to the third of the claims we wish to support in order to establish that it is not highly implausible that there is an originator. Smith offers several arguments intended to open up the possibility of the universe having created itself.[13] But we can put them to one side here, since even if for the sake of discussion every point in all three arguments is conceded, all that follows is that that it is *possible* that the world caused itself. But it is also logically and metaphysically possible that a talking Zebra rules a planet encircling some distant star. Smith points out that the atheist's position cannot be dismissed out of hand. But neither can the theist's. We have good reason to think there is more than just a bare possibility, more than a mere ghost of a chance, that there is a creator, an originator. Based on the very cautious assignments of probability so far to the three propositions we've been defending, their conjunction has a probability no lower than .125. In other words, it is not highly implausible that there is an originator.

---

[12]See Quentin Smith, "The Uncaused Beginning of the Universe," *Philosophy of Science* 55 (1988).

[13]See Quentin Smith, "The Reason the Universe Exists is that it Caused Itself to Exist," *Philosophy* 74 (1999), pp. 579–586.

Premise (B-2)

We now turn to argue that *if* it is not highly implausible that there is an originator, then it may well be possible to work up a reasoned case for Christianity that avoids the problem of declining probabilities. The basic idea here is this. There's a certain kind of evidence available to inquirers (including agnostic inquirers) that should be examined with some care once one realizes it's not highly implausible that the world has an originator or creator. This evidence is typically left out of the picture, left out of the data base that is presented to an agnostic inquirer. When it's brought into the picture, it may well be possible to develop a case for Christianity that has a probability higher than .5.

An objection might be lodged against our general strategy. While a proposition with a probability of .125 is not known or all but known to be false, it may seem far from obvious that the probability is high enough to merit further investigation, even given the high stakes. The objection can be answered in two ways. First, each of the three claims asserted to be "plausible" in argument (C) above is *at least* equiprobable with its contradictory. In our view, however, at least two of the propositions have a probability greater than .5. The proposition that nothing comes to be without a cause is often taken to be self-evident, and the proposition that nothing causes itself to come to be is scarcely ever denied, even by atheists. We would assign the conjunction of the three propositions a probability considerably higher than .125 if we were not bending over backwards to be conservative in our estimates. But we make the conservative estimates, because (and here's the second response to the objection), *even if* the probability of the conjunction is only .125, further investigation might well be in order. Imagine you are in an abandoned mine, a mine nobody knows you have entered, and are suddenly shut off from the entrance by the collapse of the ceilings both in front of and behind you. It seems pretty clear that the oxygen left will last only a short time. As you search in the dark for a way out, you see—or think you see—the faintest line of light passing through what may be a thin passage leading up and out. And you hear—or think you hear—a voice above calling down to you. You have no proof, of course, that by trying to crawl up through the one passage available you would not be disappointed or would

not find yourself wedged in a tight space. But what choice do you have? There may be only a small chance that the passage leads out into the open air, but it is hardly foolish to explore where it leads.

To understand the sort of evidence typically left out of the data base theists offer the agnostic inquirer, recall Plantinga's assessment of the chances of finding a reasoned case for Christianity. His pessimistic assessment of the chances makes a tacit presupposition. The presupposition (which can be found in many accounts of the way to approach investigation of particular religions, accounts by theists and atheists alike) is that one cannot obtain a convincing philosophical case for a particular revelatory claim (such as the Christian claim) without first obtaining a highly plausible case for a good God.

The presupposition may be grounded in the belief that if the truth of a complex proposition (one that embeds other propositions) is at issue, then each embedded subproposition must be established, or at least rendered probable, before the complex proposition is addressed directly. But there are plenty of cases that show it is *not* necessary (or even feasible) to establish the truth of embedded subpropositions before addressing a complex proposition directly. And some of these cases should persuade us that Plantinga's presupposition is false (even if the presupposition does not in fact have the grounding we alluded to in the previous paragraph).

Consider the discovery of Neptune. In 1781 William Hershel discovered Uranus, which he first took to be a comet. Soon a reasonably accurate orbit for Uranus was plotted, but by 1840 a discrepancy of over one arc minute between its predicted and actual orbit was noted. The size of the discrepancy was so great it was conjectured that another object in space might be perturbing Uranus's orbit. J. C. Adams and U. J. Leverrier carried out the laborious calculations pinpointing the part of the sky to be examined. In 1846, astronomers at the Berlin Observatory, responding to Leverrier's request, quickly found Neptune. The statement "There is a heavenly body beyond Uranus that is perturbing its orbit" embeds the substatement "There is a heavenly body beyond Uranus," but it was perfectly rational to try to determine the truth of the embedded statement by determining the truth of the more complex, embedding statement.

Take another case. Imagine that your next-door neighbor says to you: "There's a guy I've never met who has promised to leave me a large fortune. He's some sort of distant admirer and benefactor; he writes me every month to see how my life is going." You are initially skeptical. But one day when you and your neighbor are out collecting your mail, she hands you an envelope that's just arrived, which she says is from the admirer, and tells you to open it. You find a check for $10,000 inside, along with a letter that refers to the sender's recent investment successes, and his admiration for the poetry your friend has been publishing in the local literary review, and his own loneliness and declining health. Now how do you assess the likelihood that there actually is some man that's going to leave your neighbor a large fortune? You may put it at below .5. However, seeing the communication from the alleged benefactor moves the likelihood from the realm of "exceedingly unlikely" to "quite possibly true."

The last example demonstrates an important point: *The existence of a doubtful being may be rendered probable by consulting an alleged communication from the being.* Given that fact, it is counterproductive to exclude from the data base available to the religious inquirer data from putative revelatory claims, putative divine communications. But that is exactly what Plantinga's approach to what he calls "the historical case" for Christianity does. Recognizing this, we suggest, gives one the key to finding the following argument (E) persuasive:

(E-1) The existence of a doubtful being may be rendered probable by consulting an alleged communication from the being.

(E-2) If the existence of a doubtful being may be rendered probable by consulting an alleged communication from the being, then, if it is not highly implausible that there is an originator, it may well be possible to work up a reasoned case for Christianity that assigns Christianity a probability over .5.[14]

(E-3) So, if it is not highly implausible that there is an originator, then it may well be possible to work

up a reasoned case for Christianity that assigns Christianity a probability over .5.

How is an agnostic to evaluate the contents of a revelatory claim, a putative communication from God? One may begin by asking, in Newman's words, whether the contents are "what divine goodness would vouchsafe, did it vouchsafe anything." Does the alleged revelation provide moral guidance? Is it noble and elevated and illuminating? Does it satisfy spiritual hunger and heal the deepest of human wounds? Does it offer a satisfactory (though possibly incomplete) account of evil? The questions are not easy to answer. But that is no reason for leaving them out of the picture altogether. One cannot ignore data about whether a revelatory claim is *fitting* for the human condition and say that one has looked at the total evidential base. Questions beyond those concerning fittingness can and should be raised in evaluating the content of a revelatory claim. Is the content *original?* Is the content of the revelatory claim consistent with what we know about *history and science*—is it free from error on these matters (in those instances where it promises to be free from error)? What are the metaphysical presuppositions of the revelation at issue—is the content of the revelatory claim consistent with *philosophical* knowledge (or, at least, do the metaphysical presuppositions make sense)? Is the claim *self-consistent?* Is the doctrinal content of the putative revelation strikingly *developed* over time, developed in a way that suggests providential guidance through the ages? These are among the questions that can help an agnostic evaluate the contents of an alleged divine communication, in order to form a judgment about the truth of the claim that the communication is in fact from God.

3. AVOIDING THE CONSTRUAL OF FAITH AS KNOWLEDGE (REJECTING A-2).

We now turn to the second premise of Plantinga's reasoning underwriting the strong thesis of Reformed epistemology:

(A-2) If a person does not accept Christianity in accord with the A/C model or something much like it, then the person could know that Christianity is true, or have faith that it is true, or even (merely) rationally believe it is true *only if* the person could

---

[14]For a defense of this premise see our forthcoming book, *The Agnostic Inquirer: A Nonstandard Philosophical Approach to Problems of Evil and Revelation.*

work up a reasoned case for Christianity that is substantially stronger than the case against (a case that the probability is over .5 would not do).

As we noted earlier, Plantinga explicitly states that "if my only ground for Christian teaching is its probability with respect to K, and all I know about that probability is that it is greater than .5, then I can't rationally *believe* that teaching." Why does he think this? Immediately after making the claim we've just quoted, he tells us:[15]

> Suppose I know that the coin you are about to toss is loaded. I don't know just how heavily it is loaded, so I don't know what the probability is that it will come up heads, but I do know that this probability is greater than .5. Under those conditions I do not believe that the next toss of this coin will come up heads. (Of course I also don't believe that it will come up *tails*; and I *suspect* that it will come up heads.)

True, it would not be rational to believe in the imagined situation that the next toss would show heads. *But this does not prove the point at issue.* The example shows that knowing that the probability of some proposition is greater than .5 is not always *sufficient* for believing that the proposition is true. But a proposition may have special features such that when one understands the proposition, and knows (or even merely believes) its probability is greater than .5, one *can* rationally believe the proposition. Or so we will suggest.

We want to offer an argument that it is *reasonable* to believe in the Christian revelatory claim if one has a good case that Christianity is more likely than not true.

The argument we are about to offer *also* establishes that a case for Christianity with a probability above .5 makes it reasonable to *firmly* or *confidently* or *resolutely* believe Christian teaching—in other words, such a case makes *faith* reasonable. If our argument is correct, then (A-2) would have to be revised to read something like this:

If a person does not accept Christianity in accord with the A/C model or something much like it, then the person could know that Christianity is true only if the

person could work up a reasoned case for Christianity that is substantially stronger than the case against.

And, of course, the conclusion of argument (A) would also have to be revised. That is, the "strong" thesis of Reformed epistemology would need to be weakened considerably, to something like the claim that a person who does not accept Christianity in accord with the A/C model or something much like it cannot know that Christianity is true. To weaken the claim in this fashion is to change it radically (in our view, it's to change it from a false to a true proposition).

We offer the following argument (F) as grounds for rejecting the original (*unrevised*) claim labeled (A-2):

(F-1) If a person believes that there is a better case for than against some end being obligatory and some act being indispensable for achieving that end, then the act is obligatory (and hence justified) for that person.

(F-2) If a person believes that there is a better case for than against Christianity, and understands the central teachings of Christianity, then that person believes that there is a better case for than against the end of union with God being obligatory, and the act of resolute belief being indispensable for achieving that end.

(F-3) So if a person believes that there is a better case for than against Christianity, and understands the central teachings of Christianity, then the act of resolute belief is obligatory (and hence justified) for that person—even though the person does not *know* that Christianity is true.

Premise (F-1) seems initially plausible, as examples illustrate. Imagine you are walking by a neighbor's house and, looking over the fence, see what might be the body of an infant floating unattended in a swimming pool. Perhaps it is just a doll—you're not sure. Since you're not sure, you judge (quickly) that there is a better case for than against your having an obligation to at least get a closer look at the pool. Jumping the fence, let us imagine, is the only way to get closer. So it is obligatory for you to jump the fence (and hence you are justified in doing so).

Premise (F-2) is simply an assertion about what Christianity teaches. Christianity teaches that people are obliged to seek union with God, and that resolute belief is required for the union.

---
[15]Plantinga, WCB, p. 274.

Though both premises of (F) are initially plausible, we may strengthen the argument's appeal by reflection on two objections to the first premise.

First Objection to Premise (F-1)

The first objection is as follows. Different people make positive appraisals of the cases for different religions; so, according to (F-1), members of different religions may be obliged resolutely to believe different things. Furthermore, since an atheist may see resolute atheism as an indispensable means to the obligatory end of truth, for some people even resolute atheism is obligatory. So, something is wrong with premise (F-1).

But why should we think that in worshiping according to their lights earnest Christians, Jews, and Muslims are doing anything but carrying out their duties? Why not say that for a conscientious atheist who sees resolute disbelief as indispensable to the end of truth, resolute disbelief is obligatory? (F-1) supports the correctness of believing according to one's lights, not the correctness of the beliefs themselves. (It is worth noting that it is very hard to see how one could arrive at the conclusion that *resolute* disbelief is obligatory. A religious believer who is asked to justify the conviction that resolute belief or faith is required will point to scriptural or ecclesial statements taken to express God's will. But an atheist cannot similarly point to some Bible of Disbelief to justify *resolute* atheism. An atheist can believe that truth is a necessary end, and that since God does not exist, disbelief is obligatory. But nothing in this argues *resolute* disbelief.)

Second Objection to Premise (F-1)

Perhaps a weightier objection to (F-1) is that it somehow dispenses a believer from the obligation to be objective. There are (at least) two essential conditions of objectivity: one must acquire the relevant evidence, and one must weigh the evidence properly (objectively). It might be thought that (F-1) ignores both conditions.

But why should (F-1) constitute an impediment to *acquiring* the relevant evidence? Arguably, a Christian who acts in accordance with (F-1) does better in acquiring the full range of relevant evidence than the nonbeliever. If you are told that the jewel you are examining will appear brilliant and clear if it is moved

out of the artificial light into daylight, the best way to tell whether that is true may be to make the move. Leading Christian theologians have held that evidence of the truth of Christianity, though deriving from many sources, is conveyed through the experience of living it: illumination increases as one prays, reads scripture, receives the sacraments, and performs Christian works of mercy. One who enters the life (or at least tries) has access to a broader range of evidence than one who does not. (Note this does *not* mean that religions cannot objectively be evaluated from the outside. We are suggesting merely that gaining access to *some* of the evidence relevant to determining the truth of a religion may require entering into its practices.)

Perhaps a critic will respond as follows. A resolute religious believer may have access to some evidence the nonbeliever lacks, but a resolute believer also is cut off from acquiring certain evidence. Once one "enters the faith," believes resolutely, one gives up the possibility of acquiring new evidence *that counts against belief*. The resolute Christian believer says that Christian belief cannot conceivably be false.

To reply to the critic we need a distinction. If by "conceivably" one means "it is metaphysically possible that," then the Christian cannot agree that conceivably Christianity is false. For if it is possibly false in this sense, then it *is* false. But if by "conceivably" one just means that for all one *knows*, there could be a contradiction, then the Christian can concede that Christian belief is conceivably false. Perhaps an example outside religion is helpful here. Either there are or there are not infinitesimal quantities, infinite quantities smaller than any finite quantity but not equal to zero. One might have evidence supporting a belief one way or the other, but grant that for all one *knows*, evidence compelling a change in belief could come along. Still, if one believes (with Leibniz) that there are infinitesimal quantities, and the proposition that such quantities exist is in fact true, then it is not metaphysically possible that it is false. Similarly, given the distinction between epistemic and metaphysical "conceivability," there is no incoherence in saying "I believe absolutely that the Christian message is true, but for all I *know* Christianity is false." It is entirely consistent with resolute belief to say one would abandon belief *if* upon mature reflection the case for Christianity were to prove inferior to the case against

Christianity. The key word, of course, is *if*. The faithful Christian is confident the condition will not be satisfied. But that does not mean the faithful Christian is unable honestly to assimilate and examine arguments and new evidence against religious belief.

Weighing the evidence properly is the second condition of objectivity. It's hard to specify exactly what is involved in weighing evidence properly (objectively). One principle sometimes defended by agnostics (famously, by W. K. Clifford) that would seem to tell against (F-1) is a "proportionality precept": when troubled about a proposition, proportion belief in the proposition to the evidence.[16] But it is difficult to formulate a version of the precept that withstands careful scrutiny. As long as one speaks broadly about proportioning belief to evidence, the idea has appeal; but when one gets specific, the precept looks quite strange. Are we at *every moment* to proportion belief to the available evidence? Imagine that as a juror in a trial between Smith and Jones, you first hear Smith tell his tale. Of course he tells it in his way, and so as he finishes, the evidence favors him. Should you then immediately side with Smith, believing him, before Jones gets to tell her side of the story? Clearly not. Since sometimes we are obliged to defer judgment, it cannot be true that immediately proportioning belief to the evidence is obligatory. Can the precept be modified to allow reasonable time for assessment of the essential evidence? When is all the evidence relevant to religious belief in? It's hard to draw the line. According to the Christian, fresh evidence is always opening up to the believer.

4. CONCLUDING REMARKS: A STRATEGY FOR INQUIRERS

Where does all this leave us? Well, it leaves us with a decisive refutation of the "strong" thesis of the Reformed epistemologists: we have argued that each of the two premises of the argument supporting the strong thesis is false. But beyond this, we are left with the possibility of a nonstandard strategy for investigation of theism and of revelatory claims, a strategy that moves investigation of the contents of revelatory claims up towards the beginning of the philosophical inquiry. We say the approach is nonstandard because so far as we know, it is nowhere developed. It deviates appreciably both from the Reformed epistemologists' model of religious belief, and from the natural theologians' strategy (as developed, for instance, by Richard Swinburne) for investigating theistic and revelatory claims. However, in another way the approach is quite standard indeed: it articulates a process that (in its general form) approximates the thinking of many agnostics-turned-believers.

One might expect to find the question of whether a good God has given us a revelation extensively examined in works on the philosophy of religion, but as a matter of fact it is seldom broached directly. Obviously, the question is important. How could it be unimportant whether the revelatory claims of Hinduism, Judaism, Christianity, Islam, or any other religion are true? Since the question is momentous, why is it not commonly confronted by philosophers?

One possible reason for the silence is that it is tacitly assumed that before one asks whether a good God has revealed, one must dispose of a whole list of prior questions about the attributes and existence of God. Is there a being of maximal power? A being of transcendent knowledge? One who is immaterial? One who is perfectly good? And so on. Philosophers do, of course, spend a lot of time on such matters. So it may seem that the question of whether a good God has revealed is approached as fully as it can be from a philosophical standpoint.

We have suggested that the tacit assumption is seriously mistaken. It is unnecessary to settle questions about God's existence and nature before going on to revelation. We think it is a good thing the tacit assumption is false, for if it must first be shown that a good God exists, the inquiry may be all but doomed from the outset. The problem of evil is (we think) insoluble without appeal to an afterlife in which evil is somehow overcome, and natural theology, is the standard approach, hard-pressed to deliver the assurance that there is any such life beyond.

We have argued in preceding sections that it makes sense for an inquirer to investigate revelatory claims if only it first can be shown that the existence of

---

[16]Students of W. K. Clifford will note that this is a more restricted (and more defensible) statement of the precept than the one Clifford himself offered.

a creator of any ilk is not highly improbable, and we have argued that can be shown. Further, we have argued that it makes sense for an inquirer resolutely or confidently to believe the Christian revelatory claim if the total evidence available (including evidence from the content of the revelatory claim) makes it more probable than not that the Christian claim is true.

QUESTIONS FOR FURTHER REFLECTION

1. Are there important theses or claims of Reformed epistemologists not discussed by Menssen and Sullivan? If so, what are they? How would you assess these claims?
2. *Evaluate* each of the five arguments (B)–(F). (Ask about each argument: Are the premises true? Assuming the premises are true, does the conclusion follow? What is the significance of the conclusion?)
3. Compare argument (C), the argument for an "originator," with traditional cosmological arguments you have studied (pay special attention to the "Kalam" argument, if you have studied that). What similarities and differences do you see among these arguments?
4. Menssen and Sullivan suggest that the approach to investigation of revelatory claims that has become standard among philosophers doing "natural theology" leaves important evidence out of the database, evidence that can be gathered by evaluation of the content of revelatory claims. What difficulties do you think an agnostic inquirer would encounter in undertaking the recommended evaluation?
5. What business do philosophers have paying attention to "revelatory claims"? Isn't that the business of theologians? What is the difference between philosophy and theology?

32. REASON AND REVELATION COMPLIMENT EACH OTHER

Thomas Aquinas

A brief biography of Thomas Aquinas occurs on page 5. In this selection, he explains what he takes to be the proper relationship between faith, particularly as disclosed in revelation, and human reason.

READING QUESTIONS

1. What two types of theological truths are there?
2. Why can't humans have knowledge of God's substance?
3. What can we know about God from human reason alone?
4. What three problems would there be if knowledge of God came from human reason alone?
5. What does Aquinas think is the "mother of error"?

The truths that we confess concerning God fall under two modes. Some things true of God are beyond all the competence of human reason, like the trinity. Other things there are to which even human reason can attain, such as the existence and unity of God, which philosophers have proved to a demonstration under the guidance of the light of natural reason. . . . The human understanding cannot go so far of its natural ability as to grasp His substance, since under the conditions of the present life the knowledge of our understanding commences with the senses; and therefore objects beyond senses cannot be grasped by human understanding except so far as knowledge is gathered of them through the senses.

But things of sense cannot lead our understanding to read in them the essence of the Divine Substance, because they are effects inadequate to the power that caused them. Nevertheless we do have some knowledge of God, namely, of His existence and of other attributes that must necessarily be attributed to the First Cause. There are, therefore, some points of intelligibility in God, accessible to human reason, and other points that altogether transcend the power of human reason. . . .

Holy Scripture also bears testimony to this fact. For it is said: *Perchance thou wilt seize upon the traces of God, and fully discover the Almighty* (Job xi, 7). And, *Lo, God is great, and surpassing our knowledge* (Job xxxvi, 26). And, *We know in part* (I Cor. xiii, 9). Not everything, then, that is said of God, even though it be beyond the power of reason to investigate, is at once to be rejected as false.

If a truth of this nature were left to the sole enquiry of reason, three disadvantages would follow. One is that the knowledge of God would be confined to few. The discovery of truth is the fruit of studious enquiry. From this very many are hindered. Some are hindered by a constitutional unfitness, their natures being ill-disposed to the acquisition of knowledge. They could never arrive by study to the highest grade of human knowledge, which consists in the knowledge of God.

Others are hindered by the needs of business and the ties of the management of property. There must be in human society some men devoted to temporal affairs. These could not possibly spend time enough in the learned lessons of speculative enquiry to arrive at the highest point of human enquiry, the knowledge of God. Some again are hindered by sloth. The knowledge of the truths that reason can investigate concerning God presupposes much previous knowledge. Indeed almost the entire study of philosophy is directed to the knowledge of God. Hence, of all parts of philosophy, that part stands over to be learnt last, which consists of metaphysics dealing with points of Divinity. Thus, only with great labour of study is it possible to arrive at the searching out of the aforesaid truth; and this labour few are willing to undergo for sheer love of knowledge.

Another disadvantage is that such as did arrive at the knowledge or discovery of the aforesaid truth would take a long time. . . . Thus, if the only way open to the knowledge of God were the way of reason, the human race would dwell long in thick darkness of ignorance: as the knowledge of God, the best instrument for making men perfect and good, would accrue only to a few, and to those few after a considerable lapse of time.

A third disadvantage is that, because of the weakness of our judgment and the perturbing force of imagination, there is some mixture of error in most of the investigations of human reason. This would be a reason to many for continuing to doubt even of the most accu-

rate demonstrations, not perceiving the force of the demonstration, and seeing the divers judgments of divers persons who have the name of being wise men. Besides, in the midst of much demonstrated truth there is sometimes an element of error, not demonstrated but asserted on the strength of some plausible and sophistic reasoning that is taken for a demonstration. And therefore it was necessary for the real truth concerning divine things to be presented to men with fixed certainty by way of faith. Wholesome therefore is the arrangement of divine clemency, whereby things even that reason can investigate are commanded to be held on faith, so that all might easily be partakers of the knowledge of God, and that without doubt and error. . . .

SOME may possibly think that points which reason is unable to investigate ought not to be proposed to man to believe, since Divine Wisdom provides for every being according to the measure of its nature; and therefore we must show the necessity of things even that transcend reason being proposed by God to man for his belief. . . .

One proof is this. No one strives with any earnestness of desire after anything, unless it be known to him beforehand. Since, then, as will be traced out in the following pages (B.III, Chap.CXLVIII), Divine Providence directs men to a higher good than human frailty can experience in the present life, the mental faculties ought to be evoked and led onward to something higher than our reason can attain at present, learning thereby to desire something and earnestly to tend to something that transcends the entire state of the present life. And such is the special function of the Christian religion, which stands alone in its promise of spiritual and eternal goods, whereas the Old Law, carrying temporal promises, proposed few tenets that transcended the enquiry of human reason. . . .

Also another advantage is thence derived, to wit, the repression of presumption, which is the mother of error. For there are some so presumptuous of their own genius as to think that they can measure with their understanding the whole nature of the Godhead, thinking all that to be true which seems true to them, and that to be false which does not seem true to them. In order then that the human mind might be delivered from this presumption, and attain to a modest style of enquiry after truth, it was necessary for certain things to be proposed to man from God that altogether exceeded his understanding. . . .

There is also another evident advantage in this, that any knowledge, however imperfect, of the noblest objects confers a very high perfection on the soul. And therefore, though human reason cannot fully grasp truths above reason, nevertheless it is much perfected by holding such truths after some fashion at least by faith. . . .

The Divine Wisdom, that knows all things most fully, has deigned to reveal these her secrets to men, and in proof of them has displayed works beyond the competence of all natural powers, in the wonderful cure of diseases, in the raising of the dead, and what is more wonderful still, in such inspiration of human minds as that simple and ignorant persons, filled with the gift of the Holy Ghost, have gained in an instant the height of wisdom and eloquence.

By force of the aforesaid proof, without violence of arms, without promise of pleasures, and, most wonderful thing of all, in the midst of the violence of persecutors, a countless multitude, not only of the uneducated but of the wisest men, flocked to the Christian faith, wherein doctrines are preached that transcend all human understanding, pleasures of sense are restrained, and a contempt is taught of all worldly possessions.

That mortal minds should assent to such teaching is the greatest of miracles, and a manifest work of divine inspiration leading men to despise the visible and desire only invisible goods. Nor did this happen suddenly nor by chance, but by a divine disposition, as is manifest from the fact that God foretold by many oracles of His prophets that He intended to do this. The books of those prophets are still venerated amongst us, as bearing testimony to our faith. . . . This so wonderful conversion of the world to the Christian faith is so certain a sign of past miracles, that they need no further reiteration, since they appear evidently in their effects.

It would be more wonderful than all other miracles, if without miraculous signs the world had been induced by simple and low-born men to believe truths so arduous, to do works so difficult, to hope for reward so high. And yet even in our times God ceases not through His saints to work miracles for the confirmation of the faith. . . . The natural dictates of reason must certainly be quite true: it is impossible to think of their being otherwise. Nor a gain is it permissible to believe that the tenets of faith are false, being so evidently confirmed by God. Since the refore falsehood alone is contrary to truth, it is impossible for the truth of faith to be contrary to principles known by natural reason.

QUESTIONS FOR FURTHER REFLECTION

1. Aquinas gives the Christian doctrine of the trinity as an example of a truth that exceeds human reason. Does this implying anything about differing interpretations of the passages in the Bible that imply a trinity? Can we reason about those Scriptures about the nature of the trinity?
2. Aquinas points to several advantages of this division between truths that can be grasped by reason alone and those that need to be revealed. What disadvantages are there?

SUGGESTIONS FOR FURTHER READING

Alston, William. "Perceiving God," *Journal of Philosophy* 83 (1986): 655–665.

———. "Religious Experience and Religious Belief," *Nous* 6 (1982): 3–12. Reprinted in *Contemporary Perspectives on Religious Epistemology*, edited by R. Douglas Geivett and Brendan Sweetman. New York: Oxford, 1992, pp. 295–304.

Davis, Stephen T. *God, Reason, and Theistic Proofs*, ch. 5. Grand Rapids, MI: Eerdmans, 1997.

Plantinga, Alvin. "The Foundations of Theism: A Reply," *Faith and Philosophy* 3 (1986): 298–313.

———. "Is Belief in God Properly Basic?" *Nous* 15 (1981): 41–51. Reprinted in *Contemporary Perspectives on Religious Epistemology*, edited by R. Douglas Geivett and Brendan Sweetman. New York: Oxford, 1992, pp. 133–42.

———. "Reason and Belief in God." In *Faith and Rationality: Reason and Belief in God*, edited by Alvin Plantinga and Nicholas Wolterstorff, Notre Dame, IN: University of Notre Dame Press,

1983, pp. 16–93. Reprinted and excerpted in *The Analytic Theist: An Alvin Plantinga Reader*, edited by James F. Sennett, Grand Rapids, MI: Eerdmans, 1998, pp. 102–161.

———. *Warranted Christian Belief*. New York and Oxford: Oxford University Press, 2000.

Quinn, Philip. "In Search of the Foundations of Theism," *Faith and Philosophy* 2 (1985): 468-486.

Sennett, James F. "Reformed Epistemology and Epistemic Duty," in *Faith in Theory and Practice: Essays on Justifying Religious Belief,* edited by Carol White and Elizabeth Radcliffe. Chicago: Open Court, 1993, 189–207.

Shalkowski, Scott A. 1989. "Atheological Apologetics," *American Philosophical Quarterly* 26. Reprinted in *Contemporary Perspectives on Religious Epistemology*, edited by R. Douglas Geivett and Brendan Sweetman. New York: Oxford University Press, 1992, 58–73.

Swinburne, Richard. *Revelation: From Metaphor to Analogy*. Oxford: Oxford University Press, 1992.

Wykstra, Stephen. "Toward a Sensible Evidentialism: On the Notion of 'Needing Evidence,' " in *Philosophy of Religion: Selected Readings*, 3rd ed., edited by William Rowe and William Wainwright. New York: Harcourt, Brace, Jovanovich, 1998, 481–491.

Zagzebski, Linda, ed. *Rational Faith: Catholic Responses to Reformed Epistemology*. South Bend, IN: University of Notre Dame Press, 1993.

PART IV

THE PROBLEM OF EVIL

33. EVIL AND THE EXISTENCE OF GOD * *David Hume*

An Author of Genesis, "Abraham and Isaac"

34. SOUL-MAKING THEODICY * *John Hick*

Edward Madden and Peter Hare, "The Torturing Headmaster"

Sarvepalli Radhakrishnan, "Karma and Freedom"

35. THIS IS THE BEST POSSIBLE WORLD * *Gottfried Leibniz*

36. MUST GOD CREATE THE BEST? * *Robert M. Adams*

Tan Tai Wei, "Morality and the God of Love"

37. THE LOGICAL PROBLEM OF EVIL * *J. L. Mackie*

38. THE FREE WILL DEFENSE * *Alvin Plantinga*

Richard Gale, "The Causal Compatibilist Objection"

Richard Swinburne, "Free to Be Responsible for Others"

39. THE EVIDENTIAL ARGUMENT FROM EVIL * *Michael Martin*

William Rowe, "The Inductive Argument from Evil"

Paul Draper, "The Abductive Argument from Evil"

40. INDUCTION, ABDUCTION, AND THE ARGUMENT FROM EVIL * *Christopher Bernard*

SUGGESTIONS FOR FURTHER READING

33. EVIL AND THE EXISTENCE OF GOD

David Hume

A Short biography of David Hume occurs on page 115. In this selection, Hume, speaking through the character Philo, lays out the argument from evil against the existence of God.

READING QUESTIONS

1. With which argument for the existence of God does Philo compare the argument from evil?
2. Does Philo grant that the existence of evil is compatible with the existence of God?
3. What two main sources of misery do Philo and Demea point out?

Philo: I am indeed persuaded, said Philo, that the best, and indeed the only method of bringing every one to a due sense of religion, is by just representations of the misery and wickedness of men. And for that purpose a talent of eloquence and strong imagery is more requisite than that of reasoning and argument. For is it necessary to prove what every one feels within himself? It is only necessary to make us feel it, if possible, more intimately and sensibly.

Demea: The people, indeed, replied Demea, are sufficiently convinced of this great and melancholy truth. The miseries of life; the unhappiness of man; the general corruptions of our nature; the unsatisfactory enjoyment of pleasures, riches, honours; these phrases have become almost proverbial in all languages. And who can doubt of what all men declare from their own immediate feeling and experience?

Philo: In this point, said Philo, the learned are perfectly agreed with the vulgar; and in all letters, *sacred* and *profane*, the topic of human misery has been insisted on with the most pathetic eloquence that sorrow and melancholy could inspire. The poets, who speak from sentiment, without a system, and whose testimony has therefore the more authority, abound in images of this nature. From Homer down to Dr. Young, the whole inspired tribe have ever been sensible, that no other representation of things would suit the feeling and observation of each individual . . .

Observe . . . the curious artifices of Nature, in order to embitter the life of every living being. The stronger prey upon the weaker, and keep them in perpetual terror and anxiety. The weaker too, in their turn, often prey upon the stronger, and vex and molest them without relaxation. Consider that innumerable race of insects, which either are bred on the body of each animal, or, flying about, infix their stings in him. These insects have others still less than themselves, which torment them. And thus on each hand, before and behind, above and below, every animal is surrounded with enemies, which incessantly seek his misery and destruction . . .

[Consider also human society] . . . What woe and misery does it not occasion? Man is the greatest enemy of man. Oppression, injustice, contempt, contumely, violence, sedition, war, calumny, treachery, fraud; by these they mutually torment each other; and they would soon dissolve that society which they had formed, were it not for the dread of still greater ills, which must attend their separation.

Demea: But though these external insults, said Demea, from animals, from men, from all the elements, which assault us, form a frightful catalogue of woes, they are nothing in comparison of those which arise within ourselves, from the distempered condition of our mind and body. How many lie under the lingering torment of diseases? Hear the pathetic enumeration of the great poet.

Intestine stone and ulcer, colic-pangs, Demoniac frenzy, moping melancholy, And moonstruck madness, pining atrophy, Marasmus, and wide-wasting pestilence. Dire was the tossing, deep the groans: *despair* Tended the sick, busiest from couch to couch. And over them triumphant *death* his dart Shook: but delay'd to strike, though oft invok'd With vows, as their chief good and final hope.

The disorders of the mind, continued Demea, though more secret, are not perhaps less dismal and vexatious. Remorse, shame, anguish, rage, disappointment, anxiety, fear, dejection, despair; who has ever passed through life without cruel inroads from these tormentors? How many have scarcely ever felt any better sensations? Labour and poverty, so abhorred by every one, are the certain lot of the far greater number; and those few privileged persons, who enjoy ease and opulence, never reach contentment or true felicity. All the goods of life united would not make a very happy man; but all the ills united would make a wretch indeed; and any one of them almost (and who can be free from every one?) nay often the absence of one good (and who can possess all?) is sufficient to render life ineligible.

Were a stranger to drop on a sudden into this world, I would show him, as a specimen of its ills, a hospital full of diseases, a prison crowded with malefactors and debtors, a field of battle strewed with carcasses, a fleet foundering in the ocean, a nation languishing under tyranny, famine, or pestilence. To turn the gay side of life to him, and give him a notion of its pleasures; whither should I conduct him? to a ball, to an opera, to court? He might justly think, that I was only showing him a diversity of distress and sorrow . . .

Cleanthes: I can observe something like what you mention in some others, replied Cleanthes: but I confess I feel little or nothing of it in myself, and hope that it is not so common as you represent it.

Demea: If you feel not human misery yourself, cried Demea, I congratulate you on so happy a singularity. Others, seemingly the most prosperous, have not been ashamed to vent their complaints in the most melancholy strains. Let us attend to the great, the fortunate emperor, Charles V, when, tired with human grandeur, he resigned all his extensive dominions into the hands of his son. In the last harangue which he made on that memorable occasion, he publicly avowed, *that the greatest prosperities which he had ever enjoyed, had been mixed with so many adversities, that he might truly say he had never enjoyed any satisfaction or contentment.* But did the retired life, in which he sought for shelter, afford him any greater happiness? If we may credit his son's account, his repentance commenced the very day of his resignation.

Cicero's fortune, from small beginnings, rose to the greatest lustre and renown; yet what pathetic complaints of the ills of life do his familiar letters, as well as philosophical discourses, contain? And suitably to his own experience, he introduces Cato, the great, the fortunate Cato, protesting in his old age, that had he a new life in his offer, he would reject the present.

Ask yourself, ask any of your acquaintance, whether they would live over again the last ten or twenty years of their life. No! but the next twenty, they say, will be better: And from the dregs of life, hope to receive What the first sprightly running could not give.

Thus at last they find (such is the greatness of human misery, it reconciles even contradictions), that they complain at once of the shortness of life, and of its vanity and sorrow.

Philo: And is it possible, Cleanthes, said Philo, that after all these reflections, and infinitely more, which might be suggested, you can still persevere in your Anthropomorphism, and assert the moral attributes of the Deity, his justice, benevolence, mercy, and rectitude, to be of the same nature with these virtues in human creatures? His power we allow is infinite: whatever he wills is executed: but neither man nor any other animal is happy: therefore he does not will their happiness. His wisdom is infinite: He is never mistaken in choosing the means to any end: But the course of Nature tends not to human or animal felicity: therefore it is not established for that purpose. Through the whole compass of human knowledge, there are no inferences more certain and infallible than these. In what respect, then, do his benevolence and mercy resemble the benevolence and mercy of men?

Epicurus's old questions are yet unanswered.

Is he willing to prevent evil, but not able? then is he impotent. Is he able, but not willing? then is he malevolent. Is he both able and willing? whence then is evil?

You ascribe, Cleanthes (and I believe justly), a purpose and intention to Nature. But what, I beseech you, is the object of that curious artifice and machinery, which she has displayed in all animals? The preservation alone of individuals, and propagation of the species. It seems enough for her purpose, if such a rank be barely upheld in the universe, without any care or concern for the happiness of the members that compose it. No resource for this purpose: no machinery, in order merely to give pleasure or ease: no fund of pure joy and contentment: no indulgence, without some want or necessity accompanying it. At least, the few phenomena of this nature are overbalanced by opposite phenomena of still greater importance.

Our sense of music, harmony, and indeed beauty of all kinds, gives satisfaction, without being absolutely necessary to the preservation and propagation of the species. But what racking pains, on the other hand, arise from gouts, gravels, megrims, toothaches, rheumatisms, where the injury to the animal machinery is either small or incurable? Mirth, laughter, play, frolic, seem gratuitous satisfactions, which have no further tendency: spleen, melancholy, discontent, superstition, are pains of the same nature. How

then does the Divine benevolence display itself, in the sense of you Anthropomorphites? None but we Mystics, as you were pleased to call us, can account for this strange mixture of phenomena, by deriving it from attributes, infinitely perfect, but incomprehensible.

Cleanthes: And have you at last, said Cleanthes smiling, betrayed your intentions, Philo? Your long agreement with Demea did indeed a little surprise me; but I find you were all the while erecting a concealed battery against me. And I must confess, that you have now fallen upon a subject worthy of your noble spirit of opposition and controversy. If you can make out the present point, and prove mankind to be unhappy or corrupted, there is an end at once of all religion. For to what purpose establish the natural attributes of the Deity, while the moral are still doubtful and uncertain?

Demea: You take umbrage very easily, replied Demea, at opinions the most innocent, and the most generally received, even amongst the religious and devout themselves: and nothing can be more surprising than to find a topic like this, concerning the wickedness and misery of man, charged with no less than Atheism and profaneness. Have not all pious divines and preachers, who have indulged their rhetoric on so fertile a subject; have they not easily, I say, given a solution of any difficulties which may attend it? This world is but a point in comparison of the universe; this life but a moment in comparison of eternity. The present evil phenomena, therefore, are rectified in other regions, and in some future period of existence. And the eyes of men, being then opened to larger views of things, see the whole connection of general laws; and trace with adoration, the benevolence and rectitude of the Deity, through all the mazes and intricacies of his providence.

Cleanthes: No! replied Cleanthes, No! These arbitrary suppositions can never be admitted, contrary to matter of fact, visible and uncontroverted. Whence can any cause be known but from its known effects? Whence can any hypothesis be proved but from the apparent phenomena? To establish one hypothesis upon another, is building entirely in the air; and the utmost we ever attain, by these conjectures and fictions, is to ascertain

---

"ABRAHAM AND ISAAC" ✳ An Author of Genesis

As it came to pass after these things, that God, did tempt Abraham, and said unto him, "Abraham": and he said, "Behold, here I am."

And he said, "Take now thy son, thine only son Isaac, whom thou lovest, and get thee into the land of Moriah; and offer him there for a burnt offering upon one of the mountains which I will tell thee of."

And Abraham rose up early in the morning, and saddled his ass, and took two of his young men with him, and Isaac his son, and clave the wood for the burnt offering, and rose up, and went unto the place of which God had told him.

Then on the third day. Abraham lifted up his eyes, and saw the place afar off.

And Abraham said unto his young men, "Abide ye here with the ass; and I and the lad will go yonder and worship, and come again to you."

And Abraham took the wood of the burnt offering, and laid it upon Isaac his son; and he took the fire in his hand, and a knife; and they went both of them together.

And Isaac spake unto Abraham his father, and said, "My father": and he said, "Here am I, my son." And he said, "Behold the fire and the wood: but where is the lamb for a burnt offering?"

And Abraham said, "My son, God will provide himself a lamb for a burnt offering": so they went, both of them together. . . .

---

the bare possibility of our opinion; but never can we, upon such terms, establish its reality. The only method of supporting Divine benevolence, and it is what I willingly embrace, is to deny absolutely the misery and wickedness of man. Your representations are exaggerated; your melancholy views mostly fictitious; your inferences contrary to fact and experience. Health is more common than sickness; pleasure than pain; happiness than misery. And for one vexation which we meet with, we attain, upon computation, a hundred enjoyments.

Philo: Admitting your position, replied Philo, which yet is extremely doubtful, you must at the same time allow, that if pain be less frequent than pleasure, it is infinitely more violent and durable. One hour of it is often able to outweigh a day, a week, a month of our common insipid enjoyments; and how many days, weeks, and months, are passed by several in the most acute torments? Pleasure, scarcely in one instance, is ever able to reach ecstasy and rapture; and in no one instance can it continue for any time at its highest pitch and altitude. The spirits evaporate, the nerves relax, the fabric is disordered, and the enjoyment quickly degenerates into fatigue and uneasiness. But pain often, good God, how often! rises to torture and agony; and the longer it continues, it becomes still

more genuine agony and torture. Patience is exhausted, courage languishes, melancholy seizes us, and nothing terminates our misery but the removal of its cause, or another event, which is the sole cure of all evil, but which, from our natural folly, we regard with still greater horror and consternation.

But not to insist upon these topics, continued Philo, though most obvious, certain, and important; I must use the freedom to admonish you, Cleanthes, that you have put the controversy upon a most dangerous issue, and are unawares introducing a total scepticism into the most essential articles of natural and revealed theology. What! no method of fixing a just foundation for religion, unless we allow the happiness of human life, and maintain a continued existence even in this world, with all our present pains, infirmities, vexations, and follies, to be eligible and desirable! But this is contrary to every one's feeling and experience: It is contrary to an authority so established as nothing can subvert. No decisive proofs can ever be produced against this authority; nor is it possible for you to compute, estimate, and compare, all the pains and all the pleasures in the lives of all men and of all animals: And thus, by your resting the whole system of religion on a point, which, from its very nature, must for ever be uncertain, you tacitly confess, that that system is equally uncertain.

But allowing you what never will be believed, at least what you never possibly can prove, that animal, or at least human happiness, in this life, exceeds its misery, you have yet done nothing: For this is not, by any means, what we expect from infinite power, infinite wisdom, and infinite goodness. Why is there any misery at all in the world? Not by chance surely. From some cause then. Is it from the intention of the Deity? But he is perfectly benevolent. Is it contrary to his intention? But he is almighty. Nothing can shake the solidity of this reasoning, so short, so clear, so decisive; except we assert, that these subjects exceed all human capacity, and that our common measures of truth and falsehood are not applicable to them; a topic which I have all along insisted on, but which you have, from the beginning, rejected with scorn and indignation.

But I will be contented to retire still from this entrenchment, for I deny that you can ever force me in it. I will allow, that pain or misery in man is *compatible* with infinite power and goodness in the Deity, even in your sense of these attributes: What are you advanced by all these concessions? A mere possible compatibility is not sufficient. You must *prove* these pure, unmixed, and uncontrollable attributes from the present mixed and confused phenomena, and from these alone. A hopeful undertaking! Were the phenomena ever so pure and unmixed, yet being finite, they would be insufficient for that purpose. How much more, where they are also so jarring and discordant!

Here, Cleanthes, I find myself at ease in my argument. Here I triumph. Formerly, when we argued concerning the natural attributes of intelligence and design, I needed all my sceptical and metaphysical subtlety to elude your grasp. In many views of the universe, and of its parts, particularly the latter, the beauty and fitness of final causes strike us with such irresistible force, that all objections appear (what I believe they really are) mere cavils and sophisms; nor can we then imagine how it was ever possible for us to repose any weight on them. But there is no view of human life, or of the condition of mankind, from which, without the greatest violence, we can infer the moral attributes, or learn that infinite benevolence, conjoined with infinite power and infinite wisdom, which we must discover by the eyes of faith alone. It is your turn now to tug the labouring oar, and to support your philosophical subtleties against the dictates of plain reason and experience.

QUESTIONS FOR FURTHER REFLECTION

1. Demea claims that the miseries of life far outweigh the pleasures. Do you think he is right or is he being pessimistic? Do you think you might answer this differently if you lived in Hume's day?

2. Philo compares the argument from evil to the argument from design. If Cleanthes is right and we can learn that God exists and what he is like from nature, doesn't all the suffering in the world show that God is evil? What sort of reply could Cleanthes make?

34. SOUL-MAKING THEODICY

John Hick

John Hick (1922–) was for many years professor of philosophy at the University of Birmingham, in England. In the latter part of his career, he taught at Claremont Graduate School in California. In this selection, Hick explains and defends "soul-making theodicy," according to which God allows evil in order to promote moral and spiritual growth. Hick argues that God wants us to develop character traits that suit us for a relationship with God, as well as with other humans, and that this requires that we live in a morally challenging environment.

READING QUESTIONS

1. What is Stendhal's bombshell?
2. With which Christian church father does Hick associate the soul-making theodicy?
3. Explain the two-stage conception of the creation of humankind.
4. Why does Hick think that God could not just insert the relevant virtues into us at creation?
5. When does Hick think that the soul-making process is complete?
6. How does Hick explain apparently pointless suffering?

Can a world in which sadistic cruelty often has its way, in which selfish lovelessness is so rife, in which there are debilitating diseases, crippling accidents, bodily and mental decay, insanity, and all manner of natural disasters be regarded as the expression of infinite creative goodness? Certainly all this could never by itself lead anyone to believe in the existence of a limitlessly powerful God. And yet even in a world which contains these things innumerable men and women have believed and do believe in the reality of an infinite creative goodness, which they call God. The theodicy project starts at this point, with an already operating belief in God, embodied in human living, and attempts to show that this belief is not rendered irrational by the fact of evil. It attempts to explain how it is that the universe, assumed to be created and ultimately ruled by a limitlessly good and limitlessly powerful Being, is as it is, including all the pain and suffering and all the wickedness and folly that we find around us and within us. The theodicy project is thus an exercise in metaphysical construction, in the sense that it consists in the formation and criticism of large-scale hypotheses concerning the nature and process of the universe.

Since a theodicy both starts from and tests belief in the reality of God, it naturally takes different forms in relation to different concepts of God. In this essay I shall be discussing the project of a specifically Christian theodicy; I shall not be attempting the further and even more difficult work of comparative theodicy, leading in turn to the question of a global theodicy.

The two main demands upon a theodicy hypothesis are (1) that it be internally coherent, and (2) that it be consistent with the data both of the religious tradition on which it is based, and of the world, in respect both of the latter's general character as revealed by scientific enquiry and of the specific facts of moral and natural evil. These two criteria demand, respectively, possibility and plausibility.

Traditionally, Christian theology has centered upon the concept of God as both limitlessly powerful and limitlessly good and loving; and it is this concept of deity that gives rise to the problem of evil as a threat to theistic faith. The threat was definitively expressed in Stendhal's bombshell, "The only excuse for God is that he does not exist!" The theodicy project is the attempt to offer a different view of the universe which is both possible and plausible and which does not ignite Stendhal's bombshell.

Christian thought has always included a certain range of variety, and in the area of theodicy it offers two broad types of approach. The Augustinian approach, representing until fairly recently the majority report of the Christian mind, hinges upon the idea of the fall, which has in turn brought about the disharmony of nature. This type of theodicy is developed today as "the Free Will Defense." The Irenaean approach, representing in the past a minority report, hinges upon the creation of humankind through the evolutionary process as an immature creature living in a challenging and therefore person-making world. I shall indicate very briefly why I do not find the first type of theodicy satisfactory, and then spend the remainder of this essay in exploring the second type.

In recent years the philosophical discussion of the problem of evil has been dominated by the Free Will Defense. A major effort has been made by Alvin Plantinga and a number of other Christian philosophers to show that it is logically possible that a limitlessly powerful and limitlessly good God is responsible for the existence of this world. For all evil may ultimately be due to misuses of creaturely freedom. But it may nevertheless be better for God to have created free than unfree beings; and it is logically possible that any and all free beings whom God might create would, as a matter of contingent fact, misuse their freedom by falling into sin. In that case it would be logically impossible for God to have created a world containing free beings and yet not containing sin and the suffering which sin brings with it. Thus it is logically possible, despite the fact of evil, that the existing universe is the work of a limitlessly good creator.

These writers are in effect arguing that the traditional Augustinian type of theodicy, based upon the fall from grace of free finite creatures—first angels and then human beings—and a consequent going wrong of the physical world, is not logically impossible. I am in fact doubtful whether their argument is sound, and will return to the question later. But even if it should be sound, I suggest that their argument wins only a Pyrrhic victory, since the logical possibility that it would establish is one which, for very many people today, is fatally lacking in plausibility. For most educated inhabitants of the modern world regard the biblical story of Adam and Eve, and their temptation by the devil, as myth rather than as history; and they believe that so far from having been created finitely perfect and then failing, humanity evolved out of lower forms of life, emerging in a morally, spiritually, and culturally primitive state. Further, they reject as incredible the idea that earthquake and flood, disease, decay, and death are consequences either of a human fall, or of a prior fall of angelic beings who are now exerting an evil influence upon the earth. They see all this as part of a prescientific world view, along with the stories of the world having been created in six days and of the sun standing still for 24 hours at Joshua's command. One cannot, strictly speaking, disprove any of these ancient biblical myths and sagas, or refute their confident elaboration in the medieval Christian picture of the universe. But those of us for whom the resulting theodicy, even if logically possible, is radically implausible, must look elsewhere for light on the problem of evil.

I believe that we find the light that we need in the main alternative strand of Christian thinking, which goes back to important constructive suggestions by the early Hellenistic Fathers of the Church, particularly St. Irenaeus (A.D. 120–202). Irenaeus himself did not develop a theodicy, but he did—together with other Greek-speaking Christian writers of that period, such as Clement of Alexandria—build a framework of thought within which a theodicy became possible which does not depend upon the idea of the fall, and which is consonant with modern knowledge concerning the origins of the human race. This theodicy cannot, as such, be attributed to Irenaeus. We should rather speak of a type of theodicy, presented in varying ways by different subsequent thinkers (the greatest of whom has been Friedrich Schleiermacher), of which Irenaeus can properly be regarded as the patron saint.

The central theme out of which this Irenaean type of theodicy has arisen is the two-stage conception of the creation of humankind, first in the "image" and then in the "likeness" of God. Reexpressing this in modern terms, the first stage was the gradual production of homo sapiens, through the long evolutionary process, as intelligent ethical and religious animals. The human being is an animal, one of the varied forms of earthly life and continuous as such with the whole realm of animal existence. But the human being is uniquely intelligent, having evolved a large and immensely complex brain. Further, the human being is ethical—that is, a gregarious as well as an intelligent animal, able to realize and respond to the complex demands of social life. And the human being is a religious animal, with an innate tendency to experience the world in terms of the presence and activity of supernatural beings and powers. This then is early homo sapiens, the intelligent social animal capable of awareness of the divine. But early homo sapiens is not the Adam and Eve of Augustinian theology, living in perfect harmony with self, with nature, and with God. On the contrary, the life of this being must have been a constant struggle against a hostile environment, and capable of savage violence against one's fellow human beings, particularly outside one's own immediate group; and this being's concepts of the divine were primitive and often bloodthirsty. Thus existence "in the image of God" was a potentiality for knowledge of and relationship with one's Maker rather than such knowledge and relationship as a fully realized state. In other words, people were created as spiritually and morally immature creatures, at the beginning of a long process of further growth and development, which constitutes the second stage of God's creative work. In this second stage, of which we are a part, the intelligent, ethical, and religious animal is being brought through one's own free responses into what Irenaeus called the divine "likeness." The human animal is being created into a child of God. Irenaeus' own terminology (*eikon, homoiosis; imago, similitudo*) has no particular merit, based as it is on a misunderstanding of the Hebrew parallelism in Genesis 1:26; but his conception of a two-stage creation of the human, with perfection lying in the future rather than in the past, is of fundamental importance. The notion of the fall was not basic to this picture, although it was to become basic to the great drama of salvation depicted by St. Augustine and accepted within Western Christendom, including the churches stemming from the Reformation, until well into the nineteenth century. Irenaeus himself however could not, in the historical knowledge of his time, question the fact of the fall; though he treated it as a relatively minor lapse, a youthful error, rather than as the infinite crime and cosmic disaster which has ruined the whole creation. But today we can acknowledge that there is no evidence at all of a period in the distant past when humankind was in the ideal state of a fully realized "child of God." We can accept that, so far as actual events in time are concerned, there never was a fall from an original righteousness and grace. If we want to continue to use the term fall, because of its hallowed place in the Christian tradition, we must use it to refer to the immense gap between what we actually are and what in the divine intention is eventually to be. But we must not blur our awareness that the ideal state is not something already enjoyed and lost, but is a future and as yet unrealized goal. The reality is not a perfect creation which has gone tragically wrong, but a still continuing creative process whose completion lies in the eschaton.

Let us now try to formulate a contemporary version of the Irenaean type of theodicy, based on this suggestion of the initial creation of humankind, not as a finitely perfect, but as an immature creature at the beginning of a long process of further growth and development. We may begin by asking why one should have been created as an imperfect and developing creature rather than as the perfect being whom God is presumably intending to create? The answer, I think, consists in two considerations which converge in their practical implications, one concerned with the human's relationship to God and the other with the relationship to other human beings. As to the first, we could have the picture of God creating finite beings, whether angels or persons, directly in God's own presence, so that in being conscious of that which is other than one's self the creature is automatically conscious of God, the limitless divine reality and power, goodness and love, knowledge and wisdom, towering above one's self. In such a situation the disproportion between Creator and creatures would be so great that the latter would have no freedom in relation to God; they would indeed not exist as independent autonomous persons. For what freedom could finite beings have in an immediate consciousness of the presence of the one who has created them, who knows them through and through, who is limitlessly powerful as well as limitlessly loving and good, and who claims their total obedience? In order to be a person, exercising some measure of genuine freedom, the creature must be brought into existence, not in the immediate divine presence, but at a "distance" from God. This "distance" cannot of course be spatial; for God is omnipresent. It must be an epistemic distance, a distance in the cognitive dimension. And the Irenaean hypothesis is that this "distance" consists, in the case of humans, in their existence within and as part of a world which functions as an autonomous system and from within which God is not overwhelmingly evident. It is a world, in Bonhoeffer's phrase, *etsi deus non daretur*, as if there were no God. Or rather, it is religiously ambiguous, capable both of being seen as a purely natural phenomenon and of being seen as God's creation and experienced as mediating God's presence. In such a world one can exist as a person over against the Creator. One has space to exist as a finite being, a space created by the epistemic distance from God and protected by one's basic cognitive freedom, one's freedom to open or close oneself to the dawning awareness of God which is experienced naturally by a religious animal. This Irenaean picture corresponds, I suggest, to our actual human situation. Emerging within the evolutionary process as part of the continuum of animal life, in a universe which functions in accordance with its own laws and whose workings can be investigated and described without reference to a creator, the human being has a genuine, even awesome, freedom in relation to one's Maker. The human being is free to acknowledge and worship God; and is free—particularly since the emergence of human individuality and the

"THE TORTURING HEADMASTER" ✳ *Edward Madden and Peter Hare*

Perhaps an analogy will be helpful. God, as Hick views him, might be described as headmaster to a vast progressive school where the absolute freedom of the students is sacred. He does not want to force any children to read textbooks because, he feels, that will only produce students who are more motivated by fear of punishment than by love of knowledge for its own sake. Every student must be left to educate himself as much as possible. However, it is quite unconvincing to argue that because rigid regulation has horrible consequences, almost no regulation is ideal-there are dangers in either extreme. And it is just as much of a mistake to argue that because the possibility of God's creation of men as pet animals is ghastly to contemplate God's creation of men with the sort of freedom they have now is the best possible choice . . .

This suggests that God has deliberately refrained from giving much knowledge of himself to men for fear that it would jeopardize the development of "authentic fiduciary attitudes" in men. God is fearful (in our analogy) that "spoon-feeding" his creatures will prevent them from developing genuine intellectual curiosity. Because he thinks that constant and thorough spoon-feeding will ruin their intellects, he advocates contact between schoolboy and teacher only once a year.

But we are being too kind in our analogy. God does not even think it wise to deliver a matriculation address to each student. Almost all students must be content with meager historical records of a matriculation address in the distant past and a hope of a commencement speech in the future. It is no wonder there have been student riots. The countless generations before Christ were especially destitute of faculty-student contact. And even now the vas amount of humanity in non-Christian parts of the world find it difficult to be admitted to the soul-making school at all.

Sometimes Hick feels the weakness of the "all or nothing" argument and accordingly shifts to the "it could be worse" strategy. "Christian theodicy must point forward to that final blessedness, am claim that this infinite future good will render worth while all the pain and travail and wickedness that has occurred on the way to it." To be sure, we should be grateful to God for not tormenting us for an eternity, but the question remains of why he is torturing us at all.

From Edward Madden and Peter Hare, *Evil and the Concept of God* (1968).

beginnings of critical consciousness during the first millennium B.C.—to doubt the reality of God.

Within such a situation there is the possibility of the human being coming freely to know and love one's Maker. Indeed, if the end state which God is seeking to bring about is one in which finite persons have come in their own freedom to know and love God, this requires creating them initially in a state which is not that of their already knowing and loving God. For it is logically impossible to create beings already in a state of having come into that state by their own free choices.

The other consideration, which converges with this in pointing to something like the human situation

as we experience it, concerns our human moral nature. We can approach it by asking why humans should not have been created at this epistemic distance from God, and yet at the same time as morally perfect beings? That persons could have been created morally perfect and yet free, so that they would always in fact choose rightly, has been argued by such critics of the Free Will Defense in theodicy as Antony Flew and J. L. Mackie, and argued against by Alvin Plantinga and other upholders of that form of theodicy. On the specific issue defined in the debate between them, it appears to me that the criticism of the Free Will Defense stands. It appears to me that a perfectly good being, although formally free to sin, would in fact never do so. If we imagine such a being in a morally frictionless environment, involving no stresses or temptation, then we must assume that one would exemplify the ethical equivalent of Newton's first law of motion, which states that a moving body will continue in uniform motion until interfered with by some outside force. By analogy, a perfectly good being would continue in the same moral course forever, there being nothing in the environment to throw one off it. But even if we suppose the morally perfect being to exist in an imperfect world, in which one is subject to temptations, it still follows that, in virtue of moral perfection, one will always overcome those temptations—as in the case, according to orthodox Christian belief, of Jesus Christ. It is, to be sure, logically possible, as Plantinga and others argue, that a free being, simply as such, may at any time contingently decide to sin. However, a responsible free being does not act randomly, but on the basis of moral nature. And a free being whose nature is wholly and unqualifiedly good will accordingly never in fact sin.

But if God could, without logical contradiction, have created humans as wholly good free beings, why did God not do so? Why was humanity not initially created in possession of all the virtues, instead of having to acquire them through the long hard struggle of life as we know it? The answer, I suggest, appeals to the principle that virtues which have been formed within the agent as a hard-won deposit of her own right decisions in situations of challenge and temptation, are intrinsically more valuable than virtues created within her ready made and without any effort on her own part. This principle expresses a basic value judgment, which cannot be established by argument but which one can only present, in the hope that it will be as morally plausible, and indeed compelling, to others as to oneself. It is, to repeat, the judgment that a moral goodness which exists as the agent's initial given nature, without ever having been chosen by her in the face of temptations to the contrary, is intrinsically less valuable than a moral goodness which has been built up through the agent's own responsible choices through time in the face of alternative possibilities.

If, then, God's purpose was to create finite persons embodying the most valuable kind of moral goodness, God would have to create them, not as already perfect beings but rather as imperfect creatures who can then attain to the more valuable kind of goodness through

their own free choices as in the course of their personal and social history new responses prompt new insights, opening up new moral possibilities, and providing a milieu in which the most valuable kind of moral nature can be developed.

We have thus far, then, the hypothesis that one is created at an epistemic distance from God in order to come freely to know and love the Maker; and that one is at the same time created as a morally immature and imperfect being in order to attain through freedom the most valuable quality of goodness. The end sought, according to this hypothesis, is the full realization of the human potentialities in a unitary spiritual and moral perfection in the divine kingdom. And the question we have to ask is whether humans as we know them, and the world as we know it, are compatible with this hypothesis.

Clearly we cannot expect to be able to deduce our actual world in its concrete character, and our actual human nature as part of it, from the general concept of spiritually and morally immature creatures developing ethically in an appropriate environment. No doubt there is an immense range of possible worlds, any one of which, if actualized, would exemplify this concept. All that we can hope to do is to show that our actual world is one of these. And when we look at our human situation as part of the evolving life of this planet we can, I think, see that it fits this specification. As animal organisms, integral to the whole ecology of life, we are programmed for survival. In pursuit of survival, primitives not only killed other animals for food but fought other human beings when their vital interests conflicted. The life of prehistoric persons must indeed have been a constant struggle to stay alive, prolonging an existence which was, in Hobbes' phrase, "poor, nasty, brutish and short." And in his basic animal self-regardingness humankind was, and is, morally imperfect. In saying this I am assuming that the essence of moral evil is selfishness, the sacrificing of others to one's own interests. It consists, in Kantian terminology, in treating others, not as ends in themselves, but as means to one's own ends. This is what the survival instinct demands. And yet we are also capable of love, of self-giving in a common cause, of a conscience which responds to others in their needs and dangers. And with the development of civilization we see the growth of moral insight, the glimpsing and gradual assimilation of higher ideals, and tension between our animality and our ethical values. But that the human being has a lower as well as a higher nature, that one is an animal as well as a potential child of God, and that one's moral goodness is won from a struggle with one's own innate selfishness, is inevitable given one's continuity with the other forms of animal life. Further, the human animal is not responsible for having come into existence as an animal. The ultimate responsibility for humankind's existence, as a morally imperfect creature, can only rest with the Creator. The human does not, in one's own degree of freedom and responsibility, choose one's origin, but rather one's destiny.

This then, in brief outline, is the answer of the Irenaean type of theodicy to the question of the origin of moral evil: the general fact of humankind's basic self-regarding animality is an aspect of creation as part of the realm of organic life; and this basic self-regardingness has been expressed over the centuries both in sins of individual selfishness and in the much more massive sins of corporate selfishness, institutionalized in slavery and exploitation and all the many and complex forms of social injustice.

But nevertheless our sinful nature in a sinful world is the matrix within which God is gradually creating children of God out of human animals. For it is as men and women freely respond to the claim of God upon their lives, transmuting their animality into the structure of divine worship, that the creation of humanity is taking place. And in its concrete character this response consists in every form of moral goodness, from unselfish love in individual personal relationships to the dedicated and selfless striving to end exploitation and to create justice within and between societies.

But one cannot discuss moral evil without at the same time discussing the nonmoral evil of pain and suffering. (I propose to mean by "pain" physical pain, including the pains of hunger and thirst; and by "suffering" the mental and emotional pain of loneliness, anxiety, remorse, lack of love, fear, grief, envy, etc.) For what constitutes moral evil as evil is the fact that it causes pain and suffering. It is impossible to conceive of an instance of moral evil, or sin, which is not productive of pain or suffering to anyone at any time. But in addition to moral evil there is another source of pain and suffering in the structure of the physical world, which produces storms, earthquakes, and floods and which afflicts the human body with diseases—cholera, epilepsy, cancer, malaria, arthritis, rickets, meningitis, and so on—as well as with broken bones and other outcomes of physical accident. It is true that a great deal both of pain and of suffering is humanly caused, not only by the "inhumanity of man to man" but also by the stresses of our individual and corporate lifestyles, causing many disorders—not only lung cancer and cirrhosis of the liver but many cases of heart disease, stomach and other ulcers, strokes, and so on—as well as accidents. But there remain nevertheless, in the natural world itself, permanent causes of human pain and suffering. And we have to ask why an unlimitedly good and unlimitedly powerful God should have created so dangerous a world both as regards its purely natural hazards of earthquake and flood, and so on, and as regards the liability of the human body to so many ills, both psychosomatic and purely somatic.

The answer offered by the Irenaean type of theodicy follows from and is indeed integrally bound up with its account of the origin of moral evil. We have the hypothesis of humankind being brought into being within the evolutionary process as a spiritually and morally immature creature, and then growing and developing through the exercise of freedom in this religiously ambiguous world. We can now ask what sort of a world would constitute an appropriate environment for this second stage of creation? The development of human personality— moral, spiritual, and intellectual—is a product of challenge and response. It does not occur in a static situation demanding no exertion and no choices. So far as intellectual development is concerned, this is a well-established principle which underlies the whole modern educational process, from preschool nurseries designed to provide a rich and stimulating environment, to all forms of higher education designed to challenge the intellect. At a basic level the essential part played in learning by the learner's own active response to environment was strikingly demonstrated by the Held and Heim experiment with kittens.[1] Of two litter-mate kittens in the same artificial environment one was free to exercise its

---

[1] R. Held and A. Heim, "Movement-produced stimulation in the development of visually guided behaviour," *Journal of Comparative and Physiological Psychology* 56 (1963): 872–876.

own freedom and intelligence in exploring the environment, while the other was suspended in a kind of "gondola" which moved whenever and wherever the free kitten moved. Thus the second kitten had a similar succession of visual experiences as the first, but did not exert itself or make any choices in obtaining them. And whereas the first kitten learned in the normal way to conduct itself safely within its environment, the second did not. With no interaction with a challenging environment there was no development in its behavioral patterns. And I think we can safely say that the intellectual development of humanity has been due to interaction with an objective environment functioning in accordance with its own laws, an environment which we have had actively to explore and to cooperate with in order to escape its perils and exploit its benefits. In a world devoid both of dangers to be avoided and rewards to be won we may assume that there would have been virtually no development of the human intellect and imagination, and hence of either the sciences or the arts, and hence of human civilization or culture.

The fact of an objective world within which one has to learn to live, on penalty of pain or death, is also basic to the development of one's moral nature. For it is because the world is one in which men and women can suffer harm—by violence, disease, accident, starvation, and so on—that our actions affecting one another have moral significance. A morally wrong act is, basically, one which harms some part of the human community; while a morally right action is, on the contrary, one which prevents or neutralizes harm or which preserves or increases human well-being. Now we can imagine a paradise in which no one can ever come to any harm. It could be a world which, instead of having its own fixed structure, would be plastic to human wishes. Or it could be a world with a fixed structure, and hence the possibility of damage and pain, but whose structure is suspended or adjusted by special divine action whenever necessary to avoid human pain. Thus, for example, in such a miraculously pain-free world one who falls accidentally off a high building would presumably float unharmed to the ground; bullets would become insubstantial when fired at a human body; poisons would cease to poison; water to drown, and so on. We can at least begin to imagine such a world. And a good deal of the older discussion

of the problem of evil—for example in Part xi of Hume's *Dialogues Concerning Natural Religion*—assumed that it must be the intention of a limitlessly good and powerful Creator to make for human creatures a pain-free environment; so that the very existence of pain is evidence against the existence of God. But such an assumption overlooks the fact that a world in which there can be no pain or suffering would also be one in which there can be no moral choices and hence no possibility of moral growth and development. For in a situation in which no one can ever suffer injury or be liable to pain or suffering there would be no distinction between right and wrong action. No action would be morally wrong, because no action could have harmful consequences; and likewise no action would be morally right in contrast to wrong. Whatever the values of such a world, it clearly could not serve a purpose of the development of its inhabitants from self-regarding animality to self-giving love.

Thus the hypothesis of a divine purpose in which finite persons are created at an epistemic distance from God, in order that they may gradually become children of God through their own moral and spiritual choices, requires that their environment, instead of being a pain-free and stress-free paradise, be broadly the kind of world of which we find ourselves to be a part. It requires that it be such as to provoke the theological problem of evil. For it requires that it be an environment which offers challenges to be met, problems to be solved, dangers to be faced, and which accordingly involves real possibilities of hardship, disaster, failure, defeat, and misery as well as of delight and happiness, success, triumph and achievement. For it is by grappling with the real problems of a real environment, in which a person is one form of life among many, and which is not designed to minister exclusively to one's well-being, that one can develop in intelligence and in such qualities as courage and determination. And it is in the relationships of human beings with one another, in the context of this struggle to survive and flourish, that they can develop the higher values of mutual love and care, of self-sacrifice for others, and of commitment to a common good.

To summarize thus far:

1. The divine intention in relation to humankind, according to our hypothesis, is to create perfect fi-

"KARMA AND FREEDOM" ✻ *Sarvepalli Radhakrishnan*

The two pervasive features of all nature, connection with the past and creation of the future, are present in the human level. The connection with the past at the human stage is denoted by the word "Karma" in the Hindu systems. The human individual is a self-conscious, efficient portion of universal nature with his own uniqueness. His history stretching back to an indefinite period of time binds him with the physical and vital conditions of the world. Human life is an organic whole where each successive phase grows out of what has gone before. We are what we are on account of our affinity with the past. Human growth is an ordered one and its orderedness is indicated by saying that it is governed by the law of Karma.

Karma literally means action, deed. All acts produce their effects which are recorded both in the organism and the environment. Their physical effects may be short-lived but their moral effects (samsskāra) are worked into the character of the self. Every single thought, word and deed enters into the living chain of causes which makes us what we are. Our life is not at the mercy of blind chance or capricious fate. The conception is not peculiar to the Oriental creeds. The Christian Scriptures refer to it. "Be not deceived; God is not mocked: for whatsoever a man soweth, that shall he also reap." Jesus is reported to have said on the Mount, "Judge not that ye be not judged, for with what judgment ye judge, ye shall be judged, and with what measure ye mete, it shall be measured to you again."

Karma is not so much a principle of retribution as one of continuity. Good produces good, evil, evil. Love increases our power of love, hatred our power of hatred. It emphasizes the great importance of right action. Man is continuously shaping his own self. The law of Karma is not to be confused with either a hedonistic or a juridical theory of rewards and punishments. The reward for virtue is not a life of pleasure nor is the punishment for sin pain. Pleasure and pain may govern the animal nature of man but not his human. Love which is a joy in itself suffers; hatred too often means a perverse kind of satisfaction. Good and evil are not to be confused with material well-being and physical suffering.

From S. Radhakrishnan's *An Idealist View of Life* (1932).

nite personal beings in filial relationship with their Maker.

2. It is logically impossible for humans to be created already in this perfect state, because in its spiritual aspect it involves coming freely to an uncoerced consciousness of God from a situation of epistemic distance, and in its moral aspect, freely choosing the good in preference to evil.

3. Accordingly the human being was initially created through the evolutionary process, as a spiritually and morally immature creature, and as part of a world which is both religiously ambiguous and ethically demanding.

4. Thus that one is morally imperfect (i.e., that there is moral evil), and that the world is a challenging and even dangerous environment (i.e., that there is natural evil), are necessary aspects of the present stage of the process through which God is gradually creating perfected finite persons.

In terms of this hypothesis, as we have developed it thus far, then, both the basic moral evil in the human heart and the natural evils of the world are compatible with the existence of a Creator who is unlimited in both goodness and power. But is the hypothesis plausible as well as possible? The principal threat to its plausibility comes, I think, from the sheer amount and intensity of both moral and natural evil. One can accept the principle that in order to arrive at a freely chosen goodness one must start out in a state of moral immaturity and imperfection. But is it necessary that there should be the depths of demonic malice and cruelty which each generation has experienced, and which we have seen above all in recent history in the Nazi attempt to exterminate the Jewish population of Europe? Can any future fulfillment be worth such horrors? This was Dostoyevsky's haunting question: "Imagine that you are creating a fabric of human destiny with the object of making men happy in the end, giving them peace and rest at last, but that it was essential and inevitable to torture to death only one tiny creature—that baby beating its breast with its fist, for instance—and to found that edifice on its unavenged tears, would you consent to be the architect on those conditions?"[2] The theistic answer is one which may be true but which takes so large a view that it baffles the imagination. Intellectually one may be able to see, but emotionally one cannot be expected to feel, its truth; and in that sense it cannot satisfy us. For the theistic answer is that if we take with full seriousness the value of human freedom and responsibility, as essential to the eventual creation of perfected children of God, then we cannot consistently want God to revoke that freedom when its wrong exercise becomes intolerable to us. From our vantage point within the historical process we may indeed cry out to God to revoke his gift of freedom, or to overrule it by some secret or open intervention. Such a cry must have come from millions caught in the Jewish Holocaust, or in the yet more recent laying waste of Korea and Vietnam, or from the victims of racism in many parts of the world. And the thought that humankind's moral freedom is indivisible, and can lead eventually to a consummation of limitless value which could never be attained without that freedom, and which is worth any finite suffering in the course of its creation, can be of no comfort to those who are now in the midst of that suffering. But while fully acknowledging this, I nevertheless want to insist that this eschatological answer may well be true. Expressed in religious language it tells us to trust in God even in the midst of deep suffering, for in the end we shall participate in his glorious kingdom.

Again, we may grant that a world which is to be a person-making environment cannot be a pain-free paradise but must contain challenges and dangers, with real possibilities of many kinds of accident and disaster, and the pain and suffering which they bring. But need it contain the worst forms of disease and catastrophe? And need misfortune fall upon us with such heartbreaking indiscriminateness? Once again there are answers, which may well be true, and yet once again the truth in this area may offer little in the way of pastoral balm. Concerning the intensity of natural evil, the truth is probably that our judgments of intensity are relative. We might identify some form of natural evil as the worst that there is—say, the agony that can be caused by death from cancer—and claim that a loving God would not have allowed this to exist. But in a world in which there was no cancer, something else would then rank as the worst form of natural evil. If we then eliminate this; something else; and so on. And the process would continue until the world was free of all natural evil. For whatever form of evil for the time being remained would be intolerable to the inhabitants of that world. But in removing all occasions of pain and suffering, and hence all challenge and all need for mutual care, we should have converted the world from a person-making into a static environment, which could not elicit moral growth. In short, having accepted that a person-making world must have its dangers and therefore also its tragedies, we must accept that whatever form these take will be intolerable to the inhabitants of that world. There could not be a person-making world devoid of what we call evil; and evils are never tolerable—except for the sake of greater goods which may come out of them.

But accepting that a person-making environment must contain causes of pain and suffering, and that no pain or suffering is going to be acceptable, one of the most daunting and even terrifying features of the world is that calamity strikes indiscriminately. There is no justice in the incidence of disease, accident, disaster and tragedy. The righteous as well as the unrighteous are struck down by illness and afflicted by misfortune. There is no security in goodness, but the good are as likely as the wicked to suffer "the slings and arrows of outrageous fortune." From the time of Job this fact has set a glaring question mark against the goodness of God. But let us suppose that things were otherwise. Let us suppose that misfortune came upon humankind, not haphazardly and therefore unjustly, but justly and therefore not haphazardly. Let us suppose that instead

[2]Fyodor Dostoyevsky, *The Brothers Karamozou* trans. Constance Garnett (New York: Modern Library, n.d.), Bk. V, chap. 4, p. 254.

of coming without regard to moral considerations, it was proportioned to desert, so that the sinner was punished and the virtuous rewarded. Would such a dispensation serve a person-making purpose? Surely not. For it would be evident that wrong deeds bring disaster upon the agent whilst good deeds bring health and prosperity; and in such a world truly moral action, action done because it is right, would be impossible. The fact that natural evil is not morally directed, but is a hazard which comes by chance, is thus an intrinsic feature of a person-making world.

In other words, the very mystery of natural evil, the very fact that disasters afflict human beings in contingent, undirected and haphazard ways, is itself a necessary feature of a world that calls forth mutual aid and builds up mutual caring and love. Thus on the one hand it would be completely wrong to say that God sends misfortune upon individuals, so that their death, maiming, starvation or ruin is God's will for them. But on the other hand God has set us in a world containing unpredictable contingencies and dangers, in which unexpected and undeserved calamities may occur to anyone; because only in such a world can mutual caring and love be elicited. As an abstract philosophical hypothesis this may offer little comfort. But translated into religious language it tells us that God's good purpose enfolds the entire process of this world, with all its good and bad contingencies, and that even amidst tragic calamity and suffering we are still within the sphere of God's love and are moving towards God's kingdom.

But there is one further all-important aspect of the Irenaean type of theodicy, without which all the foregoing would lose its plausibility. This is the eschatological aspect. Our hypothesis depicts persons as still in course of creation towards an end state of perfected personal community in the divine kingdom. This end state is conceived of as one in which individual egoity has been transcended in communal unity before God. And in the present phase of that creative process the naturally self-centered human animal has the opportunity freely to respond to God's noncoercive self-disclosures, through the work of prophets and saints, through the resulting religious traditions, and through the individual's religious experience. Such response always has an ethical aspect; for the growing awareness of God is at the same time a growing awareness of the moral claim which God's presence makes upon the way in which we live.

But it is very evident that this person-making process, leading eventually to perfect human community, is not completed on this earth. It is not completed in the life of the individual—or at best only in the few who have attained to sanctification, or moksha, or nirvana on this earth. Clearly the enormous majority of men and women die without having attained to this. As Erich Fromm has said, "The tragedy in the life of most of us is that we die before we are fully born."[3] And therefore if we are ever to reach the full realization of the potentialities of our human nature, this can only be in a continuation of our lives in another sphere of existence after bodily death. And it is equally evident that the perfect all-embracing human community, in which self-regarding concern has been transcended in mutual love, not only has not been realized in this world, but never can be, since hundreds of generations of human beings have already lived and died and accordingly could not be part of any ideal community established at some future moment of earthly history. Thus if the unity of humankind in God's presence is ever to be realized it will have to be in some sphere of existence other than our earth. In short, the fulfillment of the divine purpose, as it is postulated in the Irenaean type of theodicy, presupposes each person's survival, in some form, of bodily death, and further living and growing towards that end state. Without such an eschatological fulfillment, this theodicy would collapse.

A theodicy which presupposes and requires an eschatology will thereby be rendered implausible in the minds of many today. I nevertheless do not see how any coherent theodicy can avoid dependence upon an eschatology. Indeed I would go further and say that the belief in the reality of a limitlessly loving and powerful deity must incorporate some kind of eschatology according to which God holds in being the creatures whom God has made for fellowship with himself, beyond bodily death, and brings them into the eternal fellowship which God has intended for them. I have tried elsewhere to argue that such an eschatology is a necessary corollary of ethical monotheism; to argue for

---

[3]Erich Fromm, "Values, Psychology, and Human Existence," in *New Knowledge of Human Values*, ed. A. Maslow (New York: Harper & Row, 1959), p. 156.

the realistic possibility of an afterlife or lives, despite the philosophical and empirical arguments against this; and even to spell out some of the general features which human life after death may possibly have.[4] Since all this is a very large task, which would far exceed the bounds of this essay, I shall not attempt to repeat it here but must refer the reader to my existing discussion of it. It is that extended discussion that constitutes my answer to the question whether an Irenaean theodicy, with its eschatology, may not be as implausible as an Augustinian theodicy, with its human or angelic fall. (If it is, then the latter is doubly implausible; for it also involves an eschatology!)

There is however one particular aspect of eschatology which must receive some treatment here, however brief and inadequate. This is the issue of "universal salvation" versus "heaven and hell" (or perhaps annihilation instead of hell). If the justification of evil within the creative process lies in the limitless and eternal good of the end state to which it leads, then the completeness of the justification must depend upon the completeness, or universality, of the salvation achieved. Only if it includes the entire human race can it justify the sins and sufferings of the entire human race throughout all history. But, having given human beings cognitive freedom, which in turn makes possible moral freedom, can the Creator bring it about that in the end all his human creatures freely turn to God in love and trust? The issue is a very difficult one; but I believe that it is in fact possible to reconcile a full affirmation of human freedom with a belief in the ultimate universal success of God's creative work. We have to accept that creaturely freedom always occurs within the limits of a basic nature that we did not ourselves choose; for this is entailed by the fact of having been created. If then a real though limited freedom does not preclude our being endowed with a certain nature, it does not preclude our being endowed with a basic Godward bias, so that, quoting from another side of St. Augustine's thought, "our hearts are restless until they find their rest in Thee."[5] If this is so, it can be predicted that sooner or later, in our own time and in our own way, we shall all freely come to God; and universal salvation can be affirmed, not as a logical necessity but as the contingent but predictable outcome of the process of the universe, interpreted theistically. Once again, I have tried to present this argument more fully elsewhere, and to consider various objections to it.[6]

On this view the human, endowed with a real though limited freedom, is basically formed for relationship with God and destined ultimately to find the fulfillment of his or her nature in that relationship. This does not seem to me excessively paradoxical. On the contrary, given the theistic postulate, it seems to me to offer a very probable account of our human situation. If so, it is a situation in which we can rejoice; for it gives meaning to our temporal existence as the long process through which we are being created, by our own free responses to life's mixture of good and evil, into "children of God" who "inherit eternal life."

QUESTIONS FOR FURTHER REFLECTION

1. According to theists, God has the very best quality of virtues. There is no one more loving, for example, than God. But God did not get those virtues through the soul-making process. So, doesn't that mean that one can acquire those virtues without developing in an environment that includes suffering?

2. Hick responds to the criticism that when you look at the world it doesn't seem like much spiritual maturing is going on by claiming that for all we know this present life is just a small segment of our total life. The bulk of soul-making will occur in the "next life." Does this appeal to a possible afterlife satisfactorily answer the criticism?

3. Is Hick committed to claiming that each instance of suffering a person experiences is exactly what that person needed at that time to make progress on the road to spiritual maturity? Why or why not?

[4]John Hick, *Death and Eternal Life* (New York: Harper & Row; and London: Collins, 1976; revised, London: Macmillan, 1987).

[5]*The Confessions of St. Augustine*, trans. F. J. Sheed (New York: Sheed and Ward, 1942), Bk. 1, chap. 1, p. 3.
[6]Hick, *Death and Eternal Life*, chap. 13.

35. THIS IS THE BEST POSSIBLE WORLD

Gottfried Leibniz

Gottfried Leibniz (1646–1714) was learned not only in philosophy, but also in mathematics, logic, theology, history, science, and a wide variety of other disciplines. He invented calculus concurrently with Newton. Born in Leipzig, Germany, he studied at the universities of Leipzig, Jena, and Altdorf, and in 1666 became a lawyer. He then served a number of aristocrats in a variety of capacities. He spent the last 40 years of his life as a librarian at the court of Hanover. Throughout his life, Leibniz demonstrated a personal asceticism, and a single-minded devotion to his labors that left little time for anything else. His *Theodicy* and *Monadology*, are attempts to defend Christian theism by utilizing the rationalist tools of the age of Enlightenment. He became one of the most widely admired men of his day, and remains one of the greatest theistic intellectuals who has ever lived.

In this selection, from his monumental work *Theodicy*, Leibniz argues that this is the best of all possible worlds. Evil in humans is counterbalanced by the good in other forms of life, and the evil that humans experience will surely be counterbalanced by the blessedness of heaven. He also espouses an optimistic universalism that is at variance with the Christian thinkers whom he quotes. Of the non-Christian, Leibniz writes, "if such a man had failed to receive light during his life, he would receive it at least in the hour of death."

READING QUESTIONS

1. What premise does Leibniz deny in objection one?
2. Why does Leibniz think it is wrong to infer that there is more evil than good in the world just because there is more evil than good in intelligent beings?
3. What, according to Leibniz, is true liberty?
4. What, according to Leibniz, is moral necessity?
5. Why does Leibniz think that moral necessity does not destroy moral responsibility?

1. ABRIDGMENT OF THE ARGUMENT REDUCED TO SYLLOGISTIC FORM

Some intelligent persons have desired that this supplement should be made [to the Theodicy], and I have the more readily yielded to their wishes as in this way I have an opportunity to again remove certain difficulties and to make some observations which were not sufficiently emphasized in the work itself.

I. *Objection.* Whoever does not choose the best is lacking in power, or in knowledge, or in goodness.
God did not choose the best in creating this world.
Therefore God has been lacking in power, or in knowledge, or in goodness.

Answer. I deny the minor, that is, the second premise of this syllogism: and our opponent proves it by this.

Prosyllogism. Whoever makes things in which there is evil, which could have been made without any evil, or the making of which could have been omitted, does not choose the best.
God has made a world in which there is evil; a world, I say, which could have been made without any evil, or the making of which could have been omitted altogether.
Therefore God has not chosen the best.

Answer. I grant the minor of this prosyllogism; for it must be confessed that there is evil in the world which God has made, and that it was possible to make a world without evil, or even not to create a world at all, for its creation depended on the free will of God; but I deny the major, that is, the first of the two premises of the prosyllogism, and I might content myself with simply demanding its proof; but in order to make the matter clearer, I have wished to justify this denial by showing that the best plan is not always that which seeks to avoid evil, since it may happen *that the evil be accompanied by a greater good*. For example, a general of the army will prefer a great victory with a slight wound to a condition without wound and without victory. We have proved this more fully in the large work by making it clear, by instances taken from mathematics and elsewhere, that an imperfection in the part may be required for a greater perfection in the whole. In this I have followed the opinion of St. Augustine, who has said a hundred times, that God permitted evil in order to bring about good, that is, a greater good; and that of Thomas Aquinas' (in libr. II sent. dist. 32, qu. I, art. 1), that the permitting of evil tends to the good of the universe. I have shown that the ancients called Adam's fall *felix culpa*, a happy sin, because it had been retrieved with immense advantage by the incarnation of the Son of God, who has given to the universe something nobler than anything that ever would have been among creatures except for this. And in order to a clear understanding, I have added, following many good authors, that it was in accordance with order and the general good that God gave to certain creatures the opportunity of exercising their liberty, even when he foresaw that they would turn to evil, but which he could so well rectify; because it was not right that, in order to hinder sin, God should always act in an extraordinary manner.

To overthrow this objection, therefore, it is sufficient to show that a world with evil might be better than a world without evil; but I have gone even farther in the work, and have even proved that this universe must be in reality better than every other possible universe.

II. *Objection*. If there is more evil than good in intelligent creatures, then there is more evil than good in the whole work of God.

Now, there is more evil than good in intelligent creatures.

Therefore there is more evil than good in the whole work of God.

Answer. I deny the major and the minor of this conditional syllogism. As to the major, I do not admit it at all, because this pretended deduction from a part to the whole, from intelligent creatures to all creatures, supposes tacitly and without proof that creatures destitute of reason cannot enter into comparison nor into account with those which possess it. But why may it not be that the surplus of good in the nonintelligent creatures which fill the world, compensates for, and even incomparably surpasses, the surplus of evil in the rational creatures? It is true that the value of the latter is greater; but, in compensation, the other are beyond comparison the more numerous, and it may be that the proportion of number and of quantity surpasses that of value and of quality.

As to the minor, that is no more to be admitted; that is, it is not at all to be admitted that there is more evil than good in the intelligent creatures. There is no need even of granting that there is more evil than good in the human race, because it is possible, and in fact very probable, that the glory and the perfection of the blessed are incomparably greater than the misery and the imperfection of the damned, and that here the excellence of the total good in the smaller number exceeds the total evil in the greater number. The blessed approach the Divinity, by means of the Divine Mediator, as near as may suit these creatures, and make such progress in good as is impossible for the damned to make in evil, approach as nearly as they may to the nature of demons. God is infinite, and the devil is limited; good may and does advance *ad infinitum*, while evil has its bounds. It is therefore possible, and is credible, that in the comparison of the blessed and the damned, the contrary of that which I have said might happen in the comparison of intelligent and nonintelligent creatures, takes place; namely, it is possible that in the comparison of the happy and the unhappy, the proportion of degree exceeds that of number, and that in the comparison of intelligent and nonintelligent creatures, the proportion of number is greater than that of value. I have the right to suppose that a thing is possible so long as its impossibility is not proved; and indeed that which I have here advanced is more than a supposition.

But in the second place, if I should admit that there is more evil than good in the human race, I have still good grounds for not admitting that there is more evil than good in all intelligent creatures. For there is an inconceivable number of genii, and perhaps of other rational creatures. And an opponent could not prove that in all the City of God, composed as well of genii as of rational animals without number and of infinity of kinds, evil exceeds good. And although in order to answer an objection, there is no need of proving that a thing is, when its mere possibility suffices; yet, in this work, I have not omitted to show that it is a consequence of the supreme perfection of the Sovereign of the universe, that the kingdom of God be the most perfect of all possible states or governments, and that consequently the little evil there is, is required for the consummation of the immense good which is there found. . . .

VIII. *Objection.* He who cannot fail to choose the best, is not free. God cannot fail to choose the best. Hence, God is not free.

Answer. I deny the major of this argument; it is rather true liberty and the most perfect, to be able to use one's free will for the best, and to always exercise this power without ever being turned from it either by external force or by internal passions, the first of which causes slavery of the body, the second, slavery of the soul. There is nothing less servile than to be always led toward the good, and always by one's own inclination, without any constraint and without any displeasure. And to object therefore that God had need of external things, is only a sophism. He created them freely; but having proposed to himself an end, which is to exercise his goodness, wisdom determined him to choose those means best fitted to attain this end. To call this a *need* is to take that term in an unusual sense which frees it from all imperfection, just as when we speak of the wrath of God.

Seneca has somewhere said that God commanded but once but that he obeys always, because he obeys the laws which he willed to prescribe to himself; *semel jussit semper paret.* But he had better have said that God always commands and that he is always obeyed; for in willing, he always follows the inclination of his own nature, and all other things always follow his will. And as this will is always the same, it cannot be said that he obeys only that will which he formerly had.

Nevertheless, although his will is always infallible and always tends toward the best, the evil, or the lesser good, which he rejects, does not cease to be possible in

itself; otherwise the necessity of the good would be geometrical (so to speak), or metaphysical and altogether absolute; the contingency of things would be destroyed, and there would be no choice. But this sort of necessity, which does not destroy the possibility of the contrary, has this name only by analogy; it becomes effective, not by the pure essence of things, but by that which is outside of them, above them,—namely, by the will of God. This necessity is called moral, because, to the sage, *necessity and what ought to be* are equivalent things; and when it always has its effect, as it really has in the perfect sage, that is, in God, it may be said that it is a happy necessity. The nearer creatures approach to it, the nearer they approach to perfect happiness.

Also this kind of necessity is not that which we try to avoid and which destroys morality, rewards and praise. For that which it brings, does not happen whatever we may do or will, but because we will it well. And a will to which it is natural to choose well, merits praise so much the more; also it carries its reward with it, which is sovereign happiness. And as this constitution of the divine nature gives entire satisfaction to him who possesses it, it is also the best and the most desirable for the creatures who are all dependent on God. If the will of God did not have for a rule the principle of the best, it would either tend toward evil, which would be the worst; or it would be in some way indifferent to good and to evil, and would be guided by chance: but a will which would allow itself always to act by chance, would not be worth more for the government of the universe than the fortuitous concourse of atoms, without there being any divinity therein. And even if God should abandon himself to chance only in some cases and in a certain way (as he would do, if he did not always work towards the best and if he were capable of preferring a lesser good to a greater, that is, an evil to a good, since that which prevents a greater good is an evil), he would be imperfect, as well as the object of his choice; he would not merit entire confidence; he would act without reason in such a case, and the government of the universe would be like certain games, equally divided between reason and chance. All this proves that this objection which is made against the choice of the best, perverts the notions of the free and of the necessary, and represents to us even the best as evil; to do which is either malicious or ridiculous.

Questions for Further Reflection

1. Leibniz claims that evil may indeed be necessary in order to secure a greater good in the end. Why is evil necessary? Couldn't God simply create the world perfect in the first place?

2. Leibniz admits that God cannot sin. If God cannot sin, why is He morally praiseworthy? Leibniz says it is because being good comes natural to Him and this in itself is praiseworthy. Is he right? If by nature you have no choice but to do right, are you worthy of moral praise?

36. MUST GOD CREATE THE BEST?

Robert M. Adams

A brief biography of Robert Adams occurs on page 209. In this selection, Adams argues that the ethical views of the Judeo-Christian religious tradition do not require the theist to believe that God would have to create the best possible world.

Reading Questions

1. Does Adams think there is a best possible world?
2. Under what standard of goodness will we have to accept *P*?
3. How does Adams use the distinction between possible beings and actual beings?
4. How does Adams define "grace"? Why, in his view, might a gracious God create less than perfect beings?
5. What two conditions need to be satisfied for a creature to not be wronged by its creator by being created?

Many philosophers and theologians have accepted the following proposition:

(*P*) If a perfectly good moral agent created any world at all, it would have to be the very best world that he could create.

The best world that an omnipotent God could create is the best of all logically possible worlds. Accordingly, it has been supposed that if the actual world was created by an omnipotent, perfectly good God, it must be the best of all logically possible worlds.

In this paper I shall argue that ethical views typical of the Judeo-Christian religious tradition do not require the Judeo-Christian theist to accept *(P)*. He must hold that the actual world is a good world. But he need not maintain that it is the best of all possible worlds, or the best world that God could have made.[1]

The position which I am claiming that he can consistently hold is that *even if* there is a best among possible worlds, God could create another instead of it, and still be perfectly good. I do not in fact see any good reason to believe that there is a best among possible worlds. Why can't it be that for every possible world there is another that is better? And if there is no maximum degree of perfection among possible worlds, it would be unreasonable to blame God, or think less highly of His goodness, because He created a world less excellent than He could have created.[2] But I do not claim to be able to prove that there is no best among possible worlds, and in this essay I shall assume for the sake of argument that there is one.

---

[1]What I am saying in this paper is obviously relevant to the problem of evil. But I make no claim to be offering a complete theodicy here.

[2]Leibniz held (in his *Theodicy*, pt. I. sec. 8) that if there were no best among possible worlds, a perfectly good God would have created nothing at all. But Leibniz is mistaken if he supposes that in this way God could avoid choosing an alternative less excellent than others He could have chosen. For the existence of no created world at all would surely be a less excellent state of affairs than the existence of some of the worlds that God could have created.

Whether we accept proposition (P) will depend on what we believe are the requirements for perfect goodness. If we apply an act-utilitarian standard of moral goodness, we will have to accept (P). For by act-utilitarian standards, it is a moral obligation to bring about the best state of affairs that one can. It is interesting to note that the ethics of Leibniz, the best-known advocate of (P), is basically utilitarian.[3] In his *Theodicy* (Part I, Section 25) he maintains, in effect, that men, because of their ignorance of many of the consequences of their actions, ought to follow a rule-utilitarian code, but that God, being omniscient, must be a perfect act utilitarian in order to be perfectly good.

I believe that utilitarian views are not typical of the Judeo-Christian ethical tradition, although Leibniz is by no means the only Christian utilitarian. In this essay I shall assume that we are working with standards of moral goodness which are not utilitarian. But I shall not try either to show that utilitarianism is wrong or to justify the standards that I take to be more typical of Judeo-Christian religious ethics. To attempt either of these tasks would unmanageably enlarge the scope of the paper. What I can hope to establish here is therefore limited to the claim that the rejection of (P) is consistent with Judeo-Christian religious ethics.

Assuming that we are not using utilitarian standards of moral goodness, I see only two types of reason that could be given for (P). (1) It might be claimed that a creator would necessarily wrong someone (violate someone's rights), or be less kind to someone than a perfectly good moral agent must be, if he knowingly created a less excellent world instead of the best that he could. Or (2) it might be claimed that even if no one would be wronged or treated unkindly by the creation of an inferior world, the creator's choice of an inferior world must manifest a defect of character. I will argue against the first of these claims in the next section. Then I will suggest, in the section that follows that God's choice of a less excellent world could be accounted for in terms of His grace, which is considered a virtue rather than a defect of character in Judeo-Christian ethics. A counterexample, which is the basis for the most persuasive objections to my position that I have encountered, will be considered in the last two sections.

Is there someone *to* whom a creator would have an obligation to create the best world he could? Is there someone whose rights would be violated, or who would be treated unkindly, if the creator created a less excellent world? Let us suppose that our creator is God, and that there does not exist any being, other than Himself, which He has not created. It follows that if God has wronged anyone, or been unkind to anyone, in creating whatever world He has created, this must be one of His own creatures. To which of His creatures, then, might God have an obligation to create the best of all possible worlds? (For that is the best world He could create.)

Might He have an obligation to the creatures in the best possible world, to create them? Have they been wronged, or even treated unkindly, if God has created a less excellent world, in which they do not exist, instead of creating them? I think not. The difference between actual beings and merely possible beings is of fundamental moral importance here. The moral community consists of actual beings. It is they who would have actual rights, and it is to them that there are actual obligations. A merely possible being cannot be (actually) wronged or treated unkindly. A being who never exists is not wronged by not being created, and there is no obligation to any possible being to bring it into existence.

Perhaps it will be objected that we believe we have obligations to future generations, who are not yet actual and may never be actual. We do say such things, but I think what we mean is something like the following. There is not merely a logical possibility, but a probability greater than zero, that future generations will really exist; and *if* they will in fact exist, we will have wronged them if we act or fail to act in certain ways. On this analysis we cannot have an obligation to future generations to bring them into existence.

I argue, then, that God does not have an obligation to the creatures in the best of all possible worlds to create them. If God has chosen to create a world less excellent than the best possible, He has not thereby wronged any creatures whom He has chosen not to create. He has not even been unkind to them. If any creatures are wronged, or treated unkindly, by such a choice of the creator, they can only be creatures that exist in the world He has created.

---

[3]See Gaston Grua, *Jurisprudence universelle et théodicée selon Leibniz* (Paris, 1953), pp. 210–218.

I think it is fairly plausible to suppose that God could create a world which would have the following characteristics:

1. None of the individual creatures in it would exist in the best of all possible worlds.
2. None of the creatures in it has a life which is so miserable on the whole that it would be better for that creature if it had never existed.
3. Every individual creature in the world is at least as happy on the whole as it would have been in any other possible world in which it could have existed.

It seems obvious that if God creates such a world He does not thereby wrong any of the creatures in it, and does not thereby treat any of them with less than perfect kindness. For none of them would have been benefited by His creating any other world instead.[4]

If there are doubts about the possibility of God's creating such a world, they will probably have to do with the third characteristic. It may be worthwhile to consider two questions, on the supposition (which I am not endorsing) that no possible world less excellent than the best would have characteristic (3), and that God has created a world which has characteristics (1) and (2) but not (3). In such a case must God have wronged one of His creatures? Must He have been less than perfectly kind to one of His creatures?

I do not think it can reasonably be argued that in such a case God must have wronged one of His creatures. Suppose a creature in such a case were to complain that God had violated its rights by creating it in a world in which it was less happy on the whole than it would have been in some other world in which God could have created it. The complaint might express a claim to special treatment: "God ought to have created *me* in more favorable circumstances (even though that would involve His creating some *other* creature in less favorable circumstances than He could have created it in)." Such a complaint would not be reasonable, and would not establish that there had been any violation of the complaining creature's rights.

Alternatively, the creature might make the more principled complaint, "God has wronged me by not following the principle of refraining from creating any world in which there is a creature that would have been happier in another world He could have made." This also is an unreasonable complaint. For if God followed the stated principle, He would not create any world that lacked characteristic (3). And we are assuming that no world less excellent than the best possible would have characteristic (3). It follows that if God acted on the stated principle He would not create any world less excellent than the best possible. But the complaining creature would not exist in the best of all possible worlds; for we are assuming that this creature exists in a world which has characteristic (1). The complaining creature, therefore, would never have existed if God had followed the principle that is urged in the complaint. There could not possibly be any advantage to this creature from God's having followed that principle; and the creature has not been wronged by God's not following the principle. (It would not be better for the creature if it had never existed; for we are assuming that the world God created has characteristic [2].)

The question of whether in the assumed case God must have been unkind to one of His creatures is more complicated than the question of whether He must have wronged one of them. In fact it is too complicated to be discussed adequately here. I will just make three observations about it. The first is that it is no clearer that the best of all possible worlds would possess characteristic (3) than that some less excellent world would possess it. In fact it has often been supposed that the best possible world might not possess it. The problem we are now discussing can therefore arise also for those who believe that God has created the best of all possible worlds.

My second observation is that if kindness to a person is the same as a tendency to promote his happiness, God has been less than perfectly (completely, unqualifiedly) kind to any creature whom He could have made somewhat happier than He has made it. (I shall not discuss here whether kindness to a person is indeed the same as a tendency to promote his happiness; they are at least closely related.)

But in the third place I would observe that such qualified kindness (if that is what it is) toward some creatures is consistent with God's being perfectly good, and with His being very kind to all His creatures. It is

---

[4]Perhaps I can have a right to something which would not benefit me (e.g., if it has been promised to me). But if there are such non-beneficial rights, I do not see any plausible reason for supposing that a right not to be created could be among them.

"MORALITY AND THE GOD OF LOVE" * Tan Tai Wei

There is something fundamentally inappropriate in the claim made by many that if God is a being *worthy of our worship* then He must be morally good in the same sense that you and I may be evaluated to be morally good. Surely worship does not arise in the cool and calculated way implied, that is, resulting from a prior examination and evaluation of the divine nature. Such has never been the manifestation of awe. And isn't it inconsistent with the humility and contrition implied in worship to presuppose that we are capable of judging God and this done by independent standards, as the logic of moral appraisal does insist? Isaiah's vision of God that left him humbled and awe-stricken in worship is rather his being immediately confronted by the very paradigm of goodness resulting in his realization of the utter incompatibility of his own being with the divine light. If anything resembling moral evaluation is at all implicit in this realization, it is certainly not done in terms of a standard independent of deity. In some sense, the realization is that he is the very standard: there can be no other. He is that he is and what he is is supremely worthy, and yet the worthiness is inherent in the fact that he is.

Nor does our account amount to the view that we worship God because of the mere fact that he is. Our point is that we respond to his love—"we love him because he first loved us." If he were other than love, creation would probably never be and the question of worship is rendered moot. In any case, Jesus also taught that no man can approach the Father unless the Father himself draws him: we worship him for he is love and draws us to himself, and not merely because he is.

Tan Tai Wei, "Morality and the God of Love," *Sophia* (1987).

consistent with His being very kind to all His creatures because He may have prepared for all of them a very satisfying existence even though some of them might have been slightly happier in some other possible world. It is consistent with His being perfectly good because even a perfectly good moral agent may be led, by other considerations of sufficient weight, to qualify his kindness or beneficence toward some person. It has sometimes been held that a perfectly good God might cause or permit a person to have less happiness than he might otherwise have had, in order to punish him, or to avoid interfering with the freedom of another person, or in order to create the best of all possible worlds. I would suggest that the desire to create and love all of a certain group of possible creatures (assuming that all of them would have satisfying lives on the whole) might be an adequate ground for a perfectly good God to create them, even if His creating *all* of them must have the result that some of them are less happy than they might otherwise have been. And they need not be the best of all possible creatures, or included in the best of all possible worlds, in order for this qualification of His kindness to be consistent with His perfect goodness. The desire to create *those* creatures is as legitimate a ground for Him to qualify His kindness toward some, as the desire to create the best of all possible worlds. This suggestion seems to me to be in keeping with the aspect of the Judeo-Christian moral ideal which will be discussed in the next section.

These matters would doubtless have to be discussed more fully if we were considering whether the *actual* world can have been created by a perfectly good God. For our present purposes, however, enough may have been said—especially since, as I have noted, it seems a plausible assumption that God could make a world having characteristics (1), (2), and (3). In that case He could certainly make a less excellent world than the best of all possible worlds without wronging any of His creatures or failing in kindness to any of them. (I have, of course, *not* been arguing that there is *no* way in which God could wrong anyone or be less kind to anyone than a perfectly good moral agent must be.)

Plato is one of those who held that a perfectly good creator would make the very best world he could. He thought that if the creator chose to make a world less good than he could have made, that could be understood only in terms of some defect in the creator's character. Envy is the defect that Plato suggests.[5] It may be thought that the creation of a world inferior to the best that he could make would manifest a defect in the creator's character even if no one were thereby wronged or treated unkindly. For the perfectly good moral agent must not only be kind and refrain from violating the rights of others, but must also have other virtues. For instance, he must be noble, generous, high-minded, and free from envy. He must satisfy the moral ideal.

There are differences of opinion, however, about what is to be included in the moral ideal. One important element in the Judeo-Christian moral ideal is *grace*. For present purposes, grace may be defined as a disposition to love which is not dependent on the merit of the person loved. The gracious person loves without worrying about whether the person he loves is worthy of his love. Or perhaps it would be better to say that the gracious person sees what is valuable in the person he loves, and does not worry about whether it is more or less valuable than what could be found in someone else he might have loved. In the Judeo-Christian tradition it is typically believed that grace is a virtue which God does have and men ought to have.

A God who is gracious with respect to creating might well choose to create and love less excellent creatures than He could have chosen. This is not to suggest that grace in creation consists in a preference for imperfection as such. God could have chosen to create the best of all possible creatures, and still have been gracious in choosing them. God's graciousness in creation does not imply that the creatures He has chosen to create must be less excellent than the best possible. It implies, rather, that even if they are the best possible creatures, that is not the ground for His choosing them. And it implies that there is nothing in God's nature or character which would require Him to act on the principle of choosing the best possible creatures to be the object of His creative powers.

Grace, as I have described it, is not part of everyone's moral ideal. For instance, it was not part of

Plato's moral ideal. The thought that it may be the expression of a virtue, rather than a defect of character, in a creator, *not* to act on the principle of creating the best creatures he possibly could, is quite foreign to Plato's ethical viewpoint. But I believe that thought is not at all foreign to a Judeo-Christian ethical viewpoint.

This interpretation of the Judeo-Christian tradition is confirmed by the religious and devotional attitudes toward God's creation which prevail in the tradition. The man who worships God does not normally praise Him for His moral rectitude and good judgment in creating *us*. He thanks God for his existence as for an undeserved personal favor. Religious writings frequently deprecate the intrinsic worth of human beings, considered apart from God's love for them, and express surprise that God should concern Himself with them at all.

> When I look at thy heavens, the work of thy fingers, the moon and the stars which thou hast established;
> What is man that thou art mindful of him, and the son of man that thou dost care for him?
> Yet thou hast made him little less than God, and dost crown him with glory and honor.
> Thou hast given him dominion over the works of thy hands; thou hast put all things under his feet [Psalm 8:3–6].

Such utterances seem quite incongruous with the idea that God created us because if He had not He would have failed to bring about the best possible state of affairs. They suggest that God has created human beings and made them dominant on this planet although He could have created intrinsically better states of affairs instead.

I believe that in the Judeo-Christian tradition the typical religious attitude (or at any rate the attitude typically encouraged) toward the fact of our existence is something like the following. "I am glad that I exist, and I thank God for the life He has given me. I am also glad that other people exist, and I thank God for them. Doubtless there could be more excellent creatures than we. But I believe that God, in His grace, created us and loves us; and I accept that gladly and gratefully." (Such an attitude need not be complacent; for the task of struggling against certain evils

[5]*Timaeus*, 29E–30A.

may be seen as precisely a part of the life that the religious person is to accept and be glad in.) When people who have or endorse such an attitude say that God is perfectly good, we will not take them as committing themselves to the view that God is the kind of being who would not create any other world than the best possible. For they regard grace as an important part of perfect goodness.

On more than one occasion when I have argued for the positions I have taken in the two previous sections, a counterexample of the following sort has been proposed. It is the case of a person who, knowing that he intends to conceive a child and that a certain drug invariably causes severe mental retardation in children conceived by those who have taken it, takes the drug and conceives a severely retarded child. We all, I imagine, have a strong inclination to say that such a person has done something wrong. It is objected to me that our moral intuitions in this case (presumably including the moral intuitions of religious Jews and Christians) are inconsistent with the views I have advanced above. It is claimed that consistency requires me to abandon those views unless I am prepared to make moral judgments that none of us are in fact willing to make.

I will try to meet these objections. I will begin by stating the case in some detail, in the most relevant form I can think of. Then I will discuss objections based on it. In this section I will discuss an objection against what I have said previously, and a more general objection against the rejection of proposition (P) will be discussed in the next section.

Let us call this Case (A). A certain couple become so interested in retarded children that they develop a strong desire to have a retarded child of their own—to love it, to help it realize its potentialities (such as they are) to the full, to see that it is as happy as it can be. (For some reason it is impossible for them to *adopt* such a child.) They act on their desire. They take a drug which is known to cause damaged genes and abnormal chromosome structure in reproductive cells, resulting in severe mental retardation of children conceived by those who have taken it. A severely retarded child is conceived and born. They lavish affection on the child. They have ample means, so that they are able to provide for special needs, and to insure that others will never be called on to pay for the child's support. They give themselves unstintedly, and do develop the child's

capacities as much as possible. The child is, on the whole, happy, though incapable of many of the higher intellectual, aesthetic, and social joys. It suffers some pains and frustrations, of course, but does not feel miserable on the whole.

The first objection founded on this case is based, not just on the claim that the parents have done something wrong (which I certainly grant), but on the more specific claim that they have *wronged the child*. I maintained, in effect, in an earlier section that a creature has not been wronged by its creator's creating it if both of the following conditions are satisfied.[6] (4) The creature is not, on the whole, so miserable that it would be better for him if he had never existed. (5) No being who came into existence in better or happier circumstances would have been the same individual as the creature in question. If we apply an analogous principle to the parent-child relationship in Case (A), it would seem to follow that the retarded child has not been wronged by its parents. Condition (4) is satisfied: the child is happy rather than miserable on the whole. And condition (5) also seems to be satisfied. For the retardation in Case (A), as described, is not due to prenatal injury but to the genetic constitution of the child. Any normal child the parents might have conceived (indeed any normal child at all) would have had a different genetic constitution, and would therefore have been a different person, from the retarded child they actually did conceive. But—it is objected to me—we do regard the parents in Case (A) as having wronged the child, and therefore we cannot consistently accept the principle that I maintained in the second section.

My reply is that if conditions (4) and (5) are really satisfied the child cannot have been wronged by its parents' taking the drug and conceiving it. If we think otherwise we are being led, perhaps by our emotions, into a confusion. If the child is not worse off than if it had never existed, and if *its* never existing would have been a sure consequence of *its* not having been brought into existence as retarded, I do not see how *its*

---

[6]I am not holding that these are necessary conditions, but only that they are jointly sufficient conditions, for a creature's not being wronged by its creator's creating it. I have numbered these conditions in such a way as to avoid confusion with the numbered characteristics of worlds in an earlier section.

interests can have been injured, or *its* rights violated, by the parents' bringing it into existence as retarded.

It is easy to understand how the parents might come to feel that they had wronged the child. They might come to feel guilty (and rightly so), and the child would provide a focus for the guilt. Moreover, it would be easy, psychologically, to assimilate Case *(A)* to cases of culpability for prenatal injury, in which it is more reasonable to think of the child as having been wronged.[7] And we often think very carelessly about counterfactual personal identity, asking ourselves questions of doubtful intelligibility, such as, "What if I had been born in the Middle Ages?" It is very easy to fail to consider the objection, "But that would not have been the same person."

It is also possible that an inclination to say that the child has been wronged may be based, at least in part, on a doubt that conditions (4) and (5) are really satisfied in case *(A)*. Perhaps one is not convinced that in real life the parents could ever have a reasonable confidence that the child would be happy rather than miserable. Maybe it will be doubted that a few changes in chromosome structure, and the difference between damaged and undamaged genes, are enough to establish that the retarded child is a different person from any normal child that the couple could have had. Of course, if conditions (4) and (5) are not satisfied, the case does not constitute a counterexample to my claims. But I would not rest any of the weight of my argument on doubts about the satisfaction of the conditions on Case *(A)*, because I think it is plausible to suppose that they would be satisfied in Case *(A)* or in some very similar case.

Even if the parents in Case *(A)* have not wronged the child, I assume that they have done something wrong. It may be asked *what* they have done wrong, or *why* their action is regarded as wrong. And these questions may give rise to an objection, not specifically to what I said in the second section, but more generally to my rejection of proposition *(P)*.

For it may be suggested that what is wrong about the action of the parents in Case *(A)* is that they have violated the following principle:

> *(Q)* It is wrong to bring into existence, knowingly, a being less excellent than one could have brought into existence.[8]

If we accept this principle we must surely agree that it would be wrong for a creator to make a world that was less excellent than the best he could make, and therefore that a perfectly good creator would not do such a thing. In other words, *(Q)* implies *(P)*.

I do not think *(Q)* is a very plausible principle. It is not difficult to think of counterexamples to it.

Case *(B)*: A man breeds goldfish, thereby bringing about their existence. We do not normally think it is wrong, or even prima facie wrong, for a man to do this, even though he could equally well have brought about the existence of more excellent beings, more intelligent and capable of higher satisfactions. (He could have bred dogs or pigs, for example.) The deliberate breeding of human beings of subnormal intelligence is morally offensive; the deliberate breeding of species far less intelligent than retarded human children is not morally offensive.

Case *(C)*: Suppose it has been discovered that if intending parents take a certain drug before conceiving a child, they will have a child whose abnormal genetic constitution will give it vastly superhuman intelligence and superior prospects of happiness. Other things being equal, would it be wrong for intending parents to have normal children instead of taking the drug? There may be considerable disagreement of moral judgment about this. I do not think that parents who chose to have normal children rather than take the drug would be doing anything wrong, nor that they would necessarily be manifesting any weakness or defect of moral character. Parents' choosing to have a normal rather than a superhuman child would not, at any rate, elicit the strong and universal or almost uni-

---

[7]I may be questioned whether even the prenatally injured child is the same person as any unimpaired child that might have been born. I am inclined to think it is the same person. At any rate there is *more* basis for regarding it as the same person as a possible normal child than there is for so regarding a child with abnormal genetic constitution.

[8]Anyone who was applying this principle to human actions would doubtless insert an "other things being equal" clause. But let us ignore that, since such a clause would presumably provide no excuse for an agent who was deciding an issue so important as what world to create.

versal disapproval that would be elicited by the action of the parents in Case (A). Even with respect to the offspring of human beings, the principle we all confidently endorse is not that it is wrong to bring about, knowingly and voluntarily, the procreation of offspring less excellent than could have been procreated, but that it is wrong to bring about, knowingly and voluntarily, the procreation of a human offspring which is deficient by comparison with normal human beings.

Such counterexamples as these suggest that our disapproval of the action of the parents in Case (A) is not based on principle (Q), but on a less general and more plausible principle such as the following:

> (R) It is wrong for human beings to cause, knowingly and voluntarily, the procreation of an offspring of human parents which is notably deficient, by comparison with normal human beings, in mental or physical capacity.

One who rejects (Q) while maintaining (R) might be held to face a problem of explanation. It may seem arbitrary to maintain such a specific moral principle as (R), unless one can explain it as based on a more general principle, such as (Q). I believe, however, that principle (R) might well be explained in something like the following way in a theological ethics in the Judeo-Christian tradition, consistently with the rejection of (Q) and (P).[9]

God, in His grace, has chosen to have human beings among His creatures. In creating us He has certain intentions about the qualities and goals of human life. He has these intentions for us, not just as individuals, but as members of a community which in principle includes the whole human race. And His intentions for human beings as such extend to the offspring (if any) of human beings. Some of these intentions are to be realized by human voluntary action, and it is our duty to act in accordance with them.

It seems increasingly possible for human voluntary action to influence the genetic constitution of human offspring. The religious believer in the Judeo-Christian tradition will want to be extremely cautious about this. For he is to be thankful that we exist as the beings we

are, and will be concerned lest he bring about the procreation of human offspring who would be deficient in their capacity to enter fully into the purposes that God has for human beings as such. We are not God. We are His creatures, and we belong to Him. Any offspring we have will belong to Him in a much more fundamental way than they can belong to their human parents. We have not the right to try to have as our offspring just any kind of being whose existence might on the whole be pleasant and of some value (for instance, a being of very low intelligence but highly specialized for the enjoyment of aesthetic pleasures of smell and taste). If we do intervene to affect the genetic constitution of human offspring, it must be in ways which seem likely to make them *more* able to enter fully into what we believe to be the purposes of God for human beings as such. The deliberate procreation of children deficient in mental or physical capacity would be an intervention which could hardly be expected to result in offspring more able to enter fully into God's purposes for human life. It would therefore be sinful, and inconsistent with a proper respect for the human life which God has given us.

On this view of the matter, our obligation to refrain from bringing about the procreation of deficient human offspring is rooted in our obligation to God, as His creatures, to respect His purposes for human life. In adopting this theological rationale for the acceptance of principle (R), one in no way commits oneself to proposition (P). For one does not base (R) on any principle to the effect that one must always try to bring into existence the most excellent things that one can. And the claim that, because of His intentions for human life, we have an obligation to God not to try to have as our offspring beings of certain sorts does not imply that it would be wrong for God to create such beings in other ways. Much less does it imply that it would be wrong for God to create a world less excellent than the best possible.

In this essay I have argued that a creator would not necessarily wrong anyone, or be less kind to anyone than a perfectly good moral agent must be, if he created a world of creatures who would not exist in the best world he could make. I have also argued that from the standpoint of Judeo-Christian religious ethics, a creator's choice of a less excellent world need not be regarded as manifesting a defect of character. It could

---

[9]I am able to give here, of course, only a very incomplete sketch of a theological position on the issue of "biological engineering."

be understood in terms of his *grace* which (in that ethics) is considered an important part of perfect goodness. In this way I think the rejection of proposition (P) can be seen to be congruous with the attitude of gratitude and respect for human life as God's gracious gift which is encouraged in the Judeo-Christian religious tradition. And that attitude (rather than any belief that one ought to bring into existence only the best beings one can) can be seen as a basis for the disapproval of the deliberate procreation of deficient human offspring.

QUESTIONS FOR FURTHER REFLECTION

1. Assuming that Adams's argument is successful, how might it be used to bolster the design argument?
2. Can God be gracious towards merely possible beings?
3. Is it gracious to create a being who, on balance, lives a pleasant life? Would it be ungracious not to create such a being?

---

37. THE LOGICAL PROBLEM OF EVIL

J. L. Mackie

A brief biography of J. L. Mackie occurs on page 77. In this selection, Mackie argues that the existence of God and the existence of evil are logically inconsistent.

READING QUESTIONS

1. Mackie says the problem of evil is a logical problem. What two kinds of problems does he say the problem of evil is *not*?
2. Name and explain the two broad types of solutions to the problem of evil that he mentions.
3. Give one reason why Mackie rejects the solution: "evil is due to human freewill."
4. What are the two "quasi-logical" rules or principles that Mackie mentions?
5. What, according to Mackie, is the "paradox of omnipotence"?

The traditional arguments for the existence of God have been fairly thoroughly criticised by philosophers. But the theologian can, if he wishes, accept this criticism. He can admit that no rational proof of God's existence is possible. And he can still retain all that is essential to his position, by holding that God's existence is known in some other, nonrational way. I think, however, that a more telling criticism can be made by way of the traditional problem of evil. Here it can be shown, not that religious beliefs lack rational support, but that they are positively irrational, that the several parts of the essential theological doctrine are inconsistent with one another, so that the theologian can maintain his position as a whole only by a much more extreme rejection of reason than in the former case. He must now be prepared to believe, not merely what cannot be proved, but what can be *disproved* from other beliefs that he also holds.

The problem of evil, in the sense in which I shall be using the phrase, is a problem only for someone who believes that there is a God who is both omnipotent and wholly good. And it is a logical problem, the problem of clarifying and reconciling a number of beliefs: it is not a scientific problem that might be solved by further observations, or a practical problem that might be solved by a decision or an action. These points are obvious; I mention them only because they are sometimes ignored by theologians, who sometimes parry a statement of the problem with such remarks as "Well, can you solve the problem yourself?" or "This is a mystery which may be revealed to us later" or "Evil is something to be faced and overcome, not to be merely discussed."

In its simplest form the problem is this: God is omnipotent; God is wholly good; and yet evil exists. There seems to be some contradiction between these three propositions, so that if any two of them were true the third would be false. But at the same time all three are essential parts of most theological positions: the theologian, it seems, at once *must* adhere and *cannot consistently* adhere to all three. (The problem does not arise only for theists, but I shall discuss it in the form in which it presents itself for ordinary theism.)

However, the contradiction does not arise immediately; to show it we need some additional premises, or perhaps some quasi-logical rules connecting the terms "good," "evil," and "omnipotent." These additional principles are that good is opposed to evil, in such a way that a good thing always eliminates evil as far as it can, and that there are no limits to what an omnipotent thing can do. From these it follows that a good omnipotent thing eliminates evil completely, and then the propositions that a good omnipotent thing exists, and that evil exists, are incompatible.

1. ADEQUATE SOLUTIONS

Now once the problem is fully stated it is clear that it can be solved, in the sense that the problem will not arise if one gives up at least one of the propositions that constitute it. If you are prepared to say that God is not wholly good, or not quite omnipotent, or that evil does not exist, or that good is not opposed to the kind of evil that exists, or that there are limits to what an omnipotent thing can do, then the problem of evil will not arise for you.

There are, then, quite a number of adequate solutions of the problem of evil, and some of these have been adopted, or almost adopted, by various thinkers. For example, a few have been prepared to deny God's omnipotence, and rather more have been prepared to keep the term "omnipotence" but severely to restrict its meaning, recording quite a number of things that an omnipotent being cannot do. Some have said that evil is an illusion, perhaps because they held that the whole world of temporal, changing things is an illusion, and that what we call evil belongs only to this world, or perhaps because they held that although temporal things *are* much as we see them, those that we call evil are not really evil. Some have said that what we call evil is merely the privation of good, that evil in a positive sense, evil that would really be opposed to good, does not exist. Many have agreed with Pope that disorder is harmony not understood, and that partial evil is

universal good. Whether any of these views is *true* is, of course, another question. But each of them gives an adequate solution of the problem of evil in the sense that if you accept it this problem does not arise for you, though you may, of course, have *other* problems to face.

But often enough these adequate solutions are only *almost* adopted. The thinkers who restrict God's power, but keep the term "omnipotence," may reasonably be suspected of thinking, in other contexts, that his power is really unlimited. Those who say that evil is an illusion may also be thinking, inconsistently, that this illusion is itself an evil. Those who say that "evil" is merely privation of good may also be thinking, inconsistently, that privation of good is an evil. (The fallacy here is akin to some forms of the "naturalistic fallacy" in ethics, where some think, for example, that "good" is just what contributes to evolutionary progress, and that evolutionary progress is itself good.) If Pope meant what he said in the first line of his couplet, that "disorder" is only harmony not understood, the "partial evil" of the second line must, for consistency, mean "that which, taken in isolation, falsely appears to be evil," but it would more naturally mean "that which, in isolation, really is evil." The second line, in fact, hesitates between two views, that "partial evil" isn't really evil, since only the universal quality is real, and that "partial evil" is really an evil, but only a little one.

In addition, therefore, to adequate solutions, we must recognise unsatisfactorily inconsistent solutions, in which there is only a half-hearted or temporary rejection of one of the propositions which together constitute the problem. In these, one of the constituent propositions is explicitly rejected, but it is covertly reasserted or assumed elsewhere in the system.

2. FALLACIOUS SOLUTIONS

Besides these half-hearted solutions, which explicitly reject but implicitly assert one of the constituent propositions, there are definitely fallacious solutions which explicitly maintain all the constituent propositions, but implicitly reject at least one of them in the course of the argument that explains away the problem of evil.

There are, in fact, many so-called solutions which purport to remove the contradiction without abandoning any of its constituent propositions. These must be fallacious as we can see from the very statement of the problem, but it is not so easy to see in each case precisely where the fallacy lies. I suggest that in all cases the fallacy has the general form suggested above: in order to solve the problem one (or perhaps more) of its constituent propositions is given up, but in such a way that it appears to have been retained, and can therefore be asserted without qualification in other contexts. Sometimes there is a further complication: the supposed solution moves to and fro between, say, two of the constituent propositions, at one point asserting the first of these but covertly abandoning the second, at another point asserting the second but covertly abandoning the first. These fallacious solutions often turn upon some equivocation with the words "good" and "evil," or upon some vagueness about the way in which good and evil are opposed to one another, or about how much is meant by "omnipotence." I propose to examine some of these so-called solutions, and to exhibit their fallacies in detail. Incidentally, I shall also be considering whether an adequate solution could be reached by a minor modification of one or more of the constituent propositions, which would, however, still satisfy all the essential requirements of ordinary theism.

1. "Good cannot exist without evil" or "Evil is necessary as a counterpart to good."

It is sometimes suggested that evil is necessary as a counterpart to good, that if there were no evil there could be no good either, and that this solves the problem of evil. It is true that it points to an answer to the question "Why should there be evil?" But it does so only by qualifying some of the propositions that constitute the problem.

First, it sets a limit to what God can do, saying that God *cannot* create good without simultaneously creating evil, and this means either that God is not omnipotent or that there are *some* limits to what an omnipotent thing can do. It may be replied that these limits are always presupposed, that omnipotence has never meant the power to do what is logically impossible, and on the present view the existence of good without evil would be a logical impossibility. This interpretation of omnipotence may, indeed, be accepted as a modification of our original account which does

not reject anything that is essential to theism, and I shall in general assume it in the subsequent discussion. It is, perhaps, the most common theistic view, but I think that some theists at least have maintained that God can do what is logically impossible. Many theists, at any rate, have held that logic itself is created or laid down by God, that logic is the way in which God arbitrarily chooses to think. (This is, of course, parallel to the ethical view that morally right actions are those which God arbitrarily chooses to command, and the two views encounter similar difficulties.) And *this* account of logic is clearly inconsistent with the view that God is bound by logical necessities—unless it is possible for an omnipotent being to bind himself, an issue which we shall consider later, when we come to the Paradox of Omnipotence. This solution of the problem of evil cannot, therefore, be consistently adopted along with the view that logic is itself created by God.

But, secondly, this solution denies that evil is opposed to good in our original sense. If good and evil are counterparts, a good thing will not "eliminate evil as far as it can." Indeed, this view suggests that good and evil are not strictly qualities of things at all. Perhaps the suggestion is that good and evil are related in much the same way as great and small. Certainly, when the term "great" is used relatively as a condensation of "greater than so-and-so," and "small" is used correspondingly, greatness and smallness are counterparts and cannot exist without each other. But in this sense greatness is not a quality, not an intrinsic feature of anything; and it would be absurd to think of a movement in favour of greatness and against smallness in this sense. Such a movement would be self-defeating, since relative greatness can be promoted only by a simultaneous promotion of relative smallness. I feel sure that no theists would be content to regard God's goodness as analogous to this—as if what he supports were not the *good* but the *better*, and if he had the paradoxical aim that all things should be better than other things.

This point is obscured by the fact that "great" and "small" seem to have an absolute as well as a relative sense. I cannot discuss here whether there is absolute magnitude or not, but if there is, there could be an absolute sense for "great," it could mean of at least a certain size, and it would make sense to speak of all things getting bigger, of a universe that was expanding all over, and therefore it would make sense to speak of promoting greatness. But in *this* sense great and small are not logically necessary counterparts: either quality could exist without the other. There would be no logical impossibility in everything's being small or in everything's being great.

Neither in the absolute nor in the relative sense, then, of "great" and "small" do these terms provide an analogy of the sort that would be needed to support this solution of the problem of evil. In neither case are greatness and smallness *both* necessary counterparts *and* mutually opposed forces or possible objects for support and attack.

It may be replied that good and evil are necessary counterparts in the same way as any quality and its logical opposite: redness can occur, it is suggested, only if nonredness also occurs. But unless evil is merely the privation of good, they are not logical opposites, and some further argument would be needed to show that they are counterparts in the same way as genuine logical opposites. Let us assume that this could be given. There is still doubt of the correctness of the metaphysical principle that a quality must have a real opposite: I suggest that it is not really impossible that everything should be, say, red, that the truth is merely that if everything were red we should not notice redness, and so we should have no word "red"; we observe and give names to qualities only if they have real opposites. If so, the principle that a term must have an opposite would belong only to our language or to our thought, and would not be an ontological principle, and correspondingly, the rule that good cannot exist without evil would not state a logical necessity of a sort that God would just have to put up with. God might have made everything good, though *we* should not have noticed it if he had.

But, finally, even if we concede that this *is* an ontological principle, it will provide a solution for the problem of evil only if one is prepared to say, "Evil exists, but only just enough evil to serve as the counterpart of good." I doubt whether any theist will accept this. After all, the ontological requirement that nonredness should occur would be satisfied even if all the universe, except for a minute speck, were red, and, if there were a corresponding requirement for evil as a counterpart to good, a minute dose of evil would presumably do. But theists are not usually willing to say, in

all contexts, that all the evil that occurs is a minute and necessary dose.

2. "Evil is necessary as a means to good."

It is sometimes suggested that evil is necessary for good not as a counterpart but as a means. In its simple form this has little plausibility as a solution of the problem of evil, since it obviously implies a severe restriction of God's power. It would be a *causal* law that you cannot have a certain end without a certain means, so that if God has to introduce evil as a means to good, he must be subject to at least some causal laws. This certainly conflicts with what a theist normally means by omnipotence. This view of God as limited by causal laws also conflicts with the view that causal laws are themselves made by God, which is more widely held than the corresponding view about the laws of logic. This conflict would, indeed, be resolved if it were possible for an omnipotent being to bind himself, and this possibility has still to be considered. Unless a favourable answer can be given to this question, the suggestion that evil is necessary as a means to good solves the problem of evil only by denying one of its constituent propositions, either that God is omnipotent or that "omnipotent" means what it says.

3. "The universe is better with some evil in it than it could be if there were no evil."

Much more important is a solution which at first seems to be a mere variant of the previous one, that evil may contribute to the goodness of a whole in which it is found, so that the universe as a whole is better as it is, with some evil in it, than it would be if there were no evil. This solution may be developed in either of two ways. It may be supported by an aesthetic analogy, by the fact that contrasts heighten beauty, that in a musical work, for example, there may occur discords which somehow add to the beauty of the work as a whole. Alternatively, it may be worked out in connection with the notion of progress, that the best possible organization of the universe will not be static, but progressive, that the gradual overcoming of evil by good is really a finer thing than would be the eternal unchallenged supremacy of good.

In either case, this solution usually starts from the assumption that the evil whose existence gives rise to the problem of evil is primarily what is called physical evil, that is to say, pain. In Hume's rather half-hearted presentation of the problem of evil, the evils that he stresses are pain and disease, and those who reply to him argue that the existence of pain and disease makes possible the existence of sympathy, benevolence, heroism, and the gradually successful struggle of doctors and reformers to overcome these evils. In fact, theists often seize the opportunity to accuse those who stress the problem of evil of taking a low, materialistic view of good and evil, equating these with pleasure and pain, and of ignoring the more spiritual goods which can arise in the struggle against evils.

But let us see exactly what is being done here. Let us call pain and misery "first order evil" or "evil (1)." What contrasts with this, namely, pleasure and happiness, will be called "first order good" or "good (1)." Distinct from this is "second order good" or "good (2)" which somehow emerges in a complex situation in which evil (1) is a necessary component—logically not merely causally, necessary. (Exactly *how* it emerges does not matter: in the crudest version of this solution good (2) is simply the heightening of happiness by the contrast with misery, in other versions it includes sympathy with suffering, heroism in facing danger, and the gradual decrease of first order evil and increase of first order good.) It is also being assumed that second order good is more important than first order good or evil, in particular that it more than outweighs the first order evil it involves.

Now this is a particularly subtle attempt to solve the problem of evil. It defends God's goodness and omnipotence on the ground that (on a sufficiently long view) this is the best of all logically possible worlds, because it includes the important second order goods, and yet it admits that real evils, namely first order evils, exist. But does it still hold that good and evil are opposed? Not, clearly, in the sense that we set out originally: good does not tend to eliminate evil in general. Instead, we have a modified, a more complex pattern. First order good (*e.g.*, happiness) *contrasts with* first order evil (*e.g.*, misery): these two are opposed in a fairly mechanical way; some second order goods (*e.g.*, benevolence) try to maximize first order good and minimize first order evil; but God's goodness is not this, it is rather the will to maximize *second* order good. We might, therefore, call God's goodness an example of a third order goodness, or

good (3). While this account is different from our original one, it might well be held to be an improvement on it, to give a more accurate description of the way in which good is opposed to evil, and to be consistent with the essential theist position.

There might, however, be several objections to this solution.

First, some might argue that such qualities as benevolence—and *a fortiori* the third order goodness which promotes benevolence—have a merely derivative value, that they are not higher sorts of good, but merely means to good (1), that is, to happiness, so that it would be absurd for God to keep misery in existence in order to make possible the virtues of benevolence, heroism, and so on. The theist who adopts the present solution must, of course, deny this, but he can do so with some plausibility, so I should not press this objection.

Secondly, it follows from this solution that God is not in our sense benevolent or sympathetic: He is not concerned to minimize evil (1), but only to promote good (2); and this might be a disturbing conclusion for some theists.

But, thirdly, the fatal objection is this. Our analysis shows clearly the possibility of the existence of a *second* order evil, an evil (2) contrasting with good (2) as evil (1) contrasts with good (1). This would include malevolence, cruelty, callousness, cowardice, and states in which good (1) is decreasing and evil (1) increasing. And just as good (2) is held to be the important kind of good, the kind that God is concerned to promote, so evil (2) will, by analogy, be the important kind of evil, the kind which God, if he were wholly good and omnipotent, would eliminate. And yet evil (2) plainly exists, and indeed most theists (in other contexts) stress its existence more than that of evil (1). We should, therefore, state the problem of evil in terms of second order evil, and against this form of the problem the present solution is useless.

An attempt might be made to use this solution again, at a higher level, to explain the occurrence of evil (2); indeed the next main solution that we shall examine does just this, with the help of some new notions. Without any fresh notions, such a solution would have little plausibility: for example, we could hardly say that the really important good was a good (3), such as the increase of benevolence in proportion to cruelty, which logically required for its occurrence the occurrence of some second order evil. But even if evil (2) could be explained in this way, it is fairly clear that there would be third order evils contrasting with this third order good: and we should be well on the way to an infinite regress, where the solution of a problem of evil, stated in terms of evil *(n)*, indicated the existence of an evil *(n + 1)*, and a further problem to be solved.

4. "Evil is due to human free will."

Perhaps the most important proposed solution of the problem of evil is that evil is not to be ascribed to God at all, but to the independent actions of human beings, supposed to have been endowed by God with freedom of the will. This solution may be combined with the preceding one: first order evil (*e.g.*, pain) may be justified as a logically necessary component in second order good (*e.g.*, sympathy) while second order evil (*e.g.*, cruelty) is not *justified* but is so ascribed to human beings that God cannot be held responsible for it. This combination evades my third criticism of the preceding solution.

The free will solution also involves the preceding solution at a higher level. To explain why a wholly good God gave men free will although it would lead to some important evils, it must be argued that it is better on the whole that men should act freely, and sometimes err, than that they should be innocent automata, acting rightly in a wholly determined way. Freedom that is to say, is now treated as a third order good, and as being more valuable than second order goods (such as sympathy and heroism) would be if they were deterministically produced, and it is being assumed that second order evils, such as cruelty, are logically necessary accompaniments of freedom, just as pain is a logically necessary precondition of sympathy.

I think that this solution is unsatisfactory primarily because of the incoherence of the notion of freedom of the will: but I cannot discuss this topic adequately here, although some of my criticisms will touch upon it.

First I should query the assumption that second order evils are logically necessary accompaniments of freedom. I should ask this: if God has made men such that in their free choices they sometimes prefer what is good and sometimes what is evil, why could he not

have made men such that they always freely choose the good? If there is no logical impossibility in a man's freely choosing the good on one, or on several, occasions, there cannot be a logical impossibility in his freely choosing the good on every occasion. God was not, then, faced with a choice between making innocent automata and making beings who, in acting freely, would sometimes go wrong: there was open to him the obviously better possibility of making beings who would act freely but always go right. Clearly, his failure to avail himself of this possibility is inconsistent with his being both omnipotent and wholly good.

If it is replied that this objection is absurd, that the making of some wrong choices is logically necessary for freedom, it would seem that "freedom" must here mean complete randomness or indeterminacy, including randomness with regard to the alternatives good and evil, in other words that men's choices and consequent actions can be "free" only if they are not determined by their characters. Only on this assumption can God escape the responsibility for men's actions; for if he made them as they are, but did not determine their wrong choices, this can only be because the wrong choices are not determined by men as they are. But then if freedom is randomness, how can it be a characteristic of *will*? And, still more, how can it be the most important good? What value or merit would there be in free choices if these were random actions which were not determined by the nature of the agent?

I conclude that to make this solution plausible two different senses of "freedom" must be confused, one sense which will justify the view that freedom is a third order good, more valuable than other goods would be without it, and another sense, sheer randomness, to prevent us from ascribing to God a decision to make men such that they sometimes go wrong when he might have made them such that they would always freely go right.

This criticism is sufficient to dispose of this solution. But besides this there is a fundamental difficulty in the notion of an omnipotent God creating men with free will, for if men's wills are really free this must mean that even God cannot control them, that is, that God is no longer omnipotent. It may be objected that God's gift of freedom to men does not mean that he *cannot* control their wills, but that he always *refrains* from controlling their wills. But why, we may ask, should God refrain from controlling evil wills? Why should he not leave men free to will rightly, but intervene when he sees them beginning to will wrongly? If God could do this, but does not, and if he is wholly good, the only explanation could be that even a wrong free act of will is not really evil, that its freedom is a value which outweighs its wrongness, so that there would be a loss of value if God took away the wrongness and the freedom together. But this is utterly opposed to what theists say about sin in other contexts. The present solution of the problem of evil, then, can be maintained only in the form that God has made men so free that he *cannot* control their wills.

This leads us to what I call the Paradox of Omnipotence: can an omnipotent being make things which he cannot subsequently control? Or, what is practically equivalent to this, can an omnipotent being make rules which then bind himself? (These are practically equivalent because any such rules could be regarded as setting certain things beyond his control, and *vice versa*.) The second of these formulations is relevant to the suggestions that we have already met, that an omnipotent God creates the rules of logic or causal laws, and is then bound by them.

It is clear that this is a paradox: the questions cannot be answered satisfactorily either in the affirmative or in the negative. If we answer "Yes," it follows that if God actually makes things which be cannot control, or makes rules which bind himself, he is not omnipotent once he has made them: there are *then* things which he cannot do. But if we answer "No," we are immediately asserting that there are things which he cannot do, that is to say that he is already not omnipotent.

It cannot be replied that the question which sets this paradox is not a proper question. It would make perfectly good sense to say that a human mechanic has made a machine which he cannot control: if there is any difficulty about the question it lies in the notion of omnipotence itself.

This, incidentally, shows that although we have approached this paradox from the free will theory, it is equally a problem for a theological determinist. No one thinks that machines have free will, yet they may well be beyond the control of their makers. The determinist might reply that anyone who makes anything determines its ways of acting, and so determines its subsequent behaviour: even the human mechanic does

this by his *choice* of materials and structure for his machine, though he does not know all about either of these: the mechanic thus determines, though he may not foresee, his machine's actions. And since God is omniscient, and since his creation of things is total, he both determines and foresees the ways in which his creatures will act. We may grant this, but it is beside the point. The question is not whether God *originally* determined the future actions of his creatures, but whether he can *subsequently* control their actions, or whether he was able in his original creation to put things beyond his subsequent control. Even on determinist principles the answers "Yes" and "No" are equally irreconcilable with God's omnipotence.

Before suggesting a solution of this paradox, I would point out that there is a parallel Paradox of Sovereignty. Can a legal sovereign make a law restricting its own future legislative power? For example, could the British parliament make a law forbidding any future parliament to socialise banking, and also forbidding the future repeal of this law itself? Or could the British parliament, which was legally sovereign in Australia in, say, 1899, pass a valid law, or series of laws, which made it no longer sovereign in 1933? Again, neither the affirmative nor the negative answer is really satisfactory. If we were to answer "Yes," we should be admitting the validity of a law which, if it were actually made, would mean that parliament was no longer sovereign. If we were to answer "No," we should be admitting that there is a law, not logically absurd, which parliament cannot validly make, that is, that parliament is not now a legal sovereign. This paradox can be solved in the following way. We should distinguish between first order laws, that is laws governing the actions of individuals and bodies other than the legislature, and second order laws, that is laws about laws, laws governing the actions of the legislature itself. Correspondingly, we should distinguish two orders of sovereignty, first order sovereignty (sovereignty [1]) which is unlimited authority to make first order laws, and second order sovereignty (sovereignty [2]) which is unlimited authority to make second order laws. If we say that parliament is sovereign we might mean that any parliament at any time has sovereignty (1), or might mean that parliament has both sovereignty (1) and sovereignty (2) at present, but we cannot without contradiction mean both that the present parliament has sovereignty (2) and that every parliament at every time has sovereignty (1), for if the present parliament has sovereignty (2) it may use it to take away the sovereignty (1) of later parliaments. What the paradox shows is that we cannot ascribe to any continuing institution legal sovereignty in an inclusive sense.

The analogy between omnipotence and sovereignty shows that the paradox of omnipotence can be solved in a similar way. We must distinguish between first order omnipotence (omnipotence [1]), that is unlimited power to act, and second order omnipotence (omnipotence [2]), that is unlimited power to determine what powers to act things shall have. Then we could consistently say that God all the time has omnipotence (1), but if so no beings at any time have powers to act independently of God. Or we could say that God at one time had omnipotence (2), and used it to assign independent powers to act to certain things, so that God thereafter did not have omnipotence (1). But what the paradox shows is that we cannot consistently ascribe to any continuing being omnipotence in an inclusive sense.

An alternative solution of this paradox would be simply to deny that God is a continuing being, that any times can be assigned to his actions at all. But on this assumption (which also has difficulties of its own) no meaning can be given to the assertion that God made men with wills so free that he could not control them. The paradox of omnipotence can be avoided by putting God outside time, but the free will solution of the problem of evil cannot be saved in this way, and

equally it remains impossible to hold that an omnipotent God *binds himself* by causal or logical laws.

3. CONCLUSION

Of the proposed solutions of the problem of evil which we have examined, none has stood up to criticism. There may be other solutions which require examination, but this study strongly suggests that there is no valid solution of the problem which does not modify at least one of the constituent propositions in a way which would seriously affect the essential core of the theistic position.

Quite apart from the problem of evil, the paradox of omnipotence has shown that God's omnipotence must in any case be restricted in one way or another, that unqualified omnipotence cannot be ascribed to any being that continues through time. And if God and his actions are not in time, can omnipotence, or power of any sort, be meaningfully ascribed to him?

QUESTIONS FOR FURTHER REFLECTION

1. Are there "solutions" to the problem of evil that Mackie has not mentioned that might not be susceptible to his criticisms?
2. Are the "adequate" solutions really adequate? Is a God who is not omnipotent or perfectly good the traditional God of western theism? If the theist concedes either of those two attributes, hasn't the atheist succeeded in showing that the traditional God does not exist?

38. THE FREE WILL DEFENSE
Alvin Plantinga

Alvin Plantinga (1932–) is widely regarded as the most important and influential theistic philosopher of the latter half of the twentieth century. In 1980, *Time* magazine published a cover story about belief in God becoming more respectable among academic philosophers. Plantinga, among others, was credited with this trend. Particularly noteworthy is his work on the problem of evil and on the justification of religious belief without evidence. Currently, he is the John A. O'Brien Professor of Philosophy and Director of the Center for Philosophy of Religion at the University of Notre Dame. He has written thirteen books and over one hundred articles. He has delivered the prestigious Gifford and Wilde lectures and is a founding member of the Society of Christian Philosophers. In this article, he criticizes the logical argument from evil by setting out the Free Will Defense.

1. What three types of inconsistency does Plantinga mention?
2. Which two theists have thought that God's omnipotence means He can even do the logically impossible?
3. What is a necessary truth?
4. What two general strategies can the theist employ for responding to the argument from evil?
5. How does Plantinga's Free Will Defense account for natural evil?

1. ON THE ALLEGED CONTRADICTION IN THEISM

In a widely discussed piece entitled "Evil and Omnipotence" John Mackie makes this claim:

> I think, however, that a more telling criticism can be made by way of the traditional problem of evil. Here it can be shown, not that religious beliefs lack rational support, but that they are positively irrational, that the several parts of the essential theological doctrine are *inconsistent* with one another. . . .[1]

Is Mackie right? Does the theist contradict himself? But we must ask a prior question: just what is being claimed here? That theistic belief contains an inconsistency or contradiction, of course. But what, exactly, is an inconsistency or contradiction? There are several kinds. An *explicit* contradiction is a *proposition* of a certain sort—a conjunctive proposition, one conjunct of which is the denial or negation of the other conjunct. For example:

Paul is a good tennis player, and it's false that Paul is a good tennis player.

(People seldom assert explicit contradictions.) Is Mackie charging the theist with accepting such a contradiction? Presumably not; what he says is

> In its simplest form the problem is this: God is omnipotent; God is wholly good; yet evil exists. There seems to be some contradiction between these three propositions, so that if any two of them were true the third would be false. But at the same

time all three are essential parts of most theological positions; the theologian, it seems, at once *must* adhere and *cannot consistently* adhere to all three.

According to Mackie, then, the theist accepts a group or set of three propositions; this set is inconsistent. Its members, of course, are

1. God is omnipotent
2. God is wholly good

and

3. Evil exists.

Call this set A; the claim is that A is an inconsistent set. But what is it for a *set* to be inconsistent or contradictory? Following our definition of an explicit contradiction, we might say that a set of propositions is explicitly contradictory if one of the members is the denial or negation of another member. But then, of course, it is evident that the set we are discussing is not explicitly contradictory; the denials of (1), (2), and (3), respectively, are

1. God is not omnipotent (or it's false that God is omnipotent)
2. God is not wholly good

and

3. There is no evil

none of which is in set A.

Of course many sets are pretty clearly contradictory, in an important way, but not *explicitly* contradictory. For example, set B:

4. If all men are mortal, then Socrates is mortal
5. All men are mortal
6. Socrates is not mortal.

This set is not explicitly contradictory; yet surely *some* significant sense of that term applies to it. What

---

[1]John Mackie, "Evil and Omnipotence," in *The Philosophy of Religion*, ed. Basil Mitchell (London: Oxford University Press, 1971), p. 92. [See previous reading.]

is important here is that by using only the rules of ordinary logic—the laws of propositional logic and quantification theory found in any introductory text on the subject—we can deduce an explicit contradiction from the set. Or to put it differently, we can use the laws of logic to deduce a proposition from the set, which proposition, when added to the set, yields a new set that is explicitly contradictory. For by using the law *modus ponens* (if *p*, then *q*; *p*; therefore *q*) we can deduce

7. Socrates is mortal

from (4) and (5). The result of adding (7) to B is the set (4), (5), (6), (7). This set, of course, is explicitly contradictory in that (6) is the denial of (7). We might say that any set which shares this characteristic with set B is *formally* contradictory. So a formally contradictory set is one from whose members an explicit contradiction can be deduced by the laws of logic. Is Mackie claiming that set A is formally contradictory?

If he is, he's wrong. No laws of logic permit us to deduce the denial of one of the propositions in A from the other members. Set A isn't formally contradictory either.

But there is still another way in which a set of propositions can be contradictory or inconsistent. Consider set C, whose members are

8. George is older than Paul
9. Paul is older than Nick

and

10. George is not older than Nick.

This set is neither explicitly nor formally contradictory; we can't, just by using the laws of logic, deduce the denial of any of these propositions from the others. And yet there is a good sense in which it is consistent or contradictory. For clearly it is *not possible* that its three members all be true. It is *necessarily true* that

11. If George is older than Paul, and Paul is older than Nick, then George is older than Nick.

And if we add (11) to set C, we get a set that is formally contradictory; (8), (9), and (11) yield, by the laws of ordinary logic, the denial of (10).

I said that (11) is *necessarily true*; but what does *that* mean? Of course we might say that a proposition

is necessarily true if it is impossible that it be false, or if its negation is not possibly true. This would be to explain necessity in terms of possibility. Chances are, however, that anyone who does not know what necessity is, will be equally at a loss about possibility, the explanation is not likely to be very successful. Perhaps all we can do by way of explanation is to give some examples and hope for the best. In the first place many propositions can be established by the laws of logic alone—for example,

12. If all men are mortal and Socrates is a man, then Socrates is mortal.

Such propositions are truths of logic; and all of them are necessary in the sense of question. But truths of arithmetic and mathematics generally are also necessarily true. Still further, there is a host of propositions that are neither truths of logic nor truths of mathematics but are nonetheless necessarily true;

11. would be an example, as well as
13. Nobody is taller than himself
14. Red is a color
15. No numbers are persons
16. No prime number is a prime minister

and

17. Bachelors are unmarried.

So here we have an important kind of necessity—let's call it "broadly logical necessity." Of course there is a correlative kind of *possibility*: a proposition *p* is possibly true (in the broadly logical sense) just in case its negation or denial is not necessarily true (in that same broadly logical sense). This sense of necessity and possibility must be distinguished from another that we may call *causal* or *natural* necessity and possibility. Consider

18. Henry Kissinger has swum the Atlantic.

Although this proposition has an implausible ring, it is not necessarily false in the broadly logical sense (and its denial is not necessarily true in that sense). But there is a good sense in which it is impossible: it is *causally* or *naturally* impossible. Human beings, unlike dolphins, just don't have the physical equipment demanded for this feat. Unlike Superman, furthermore, the rest of us are incapable of leaping tall buildings at a single bound or (without auxiliary power of some kind) traveling faster than a speeding bullet. These things are *impossible* for us—but not *logically* impossible, even in the broad sense.

So there are several senses of necessity and possibility here. There are a number of propositions, furthermore, of which it's difficult to say whether they are or aren't possible in the broadly logical sense; some of these are subjects of philosophical controversy. Is it possible, for example, for a person never to be conscious during his entire existence? Is it possible for a (human) person to exist *disembodied*? If that's possible, is it possible that there be a person who *at no time at all* during his entire existence has a body? Is it possible to see without eyes? These are propositions about whose possibility in that broadly logical sense there is disagreement and dispute.

Now return to set C. . . . What is characteristic of it is the fact that the conjunction of its members—the proposition expressed by the result of putting "and's" between (8), (9), and (10)—is necessarily false. Or we might put it like this: what characterizes set C is the fact that we can get a formally contradictory set by adding a necessarily true proposition—namely (11). Suppose we say that a set is *implicitly contradictory* if it resembles C in this respect. That is, a set S of propositions is implicitly contradictory if there is a necessary proposition p such that the result of adding p to S is a formally contradictory set. Another way to put it: S is implicitly contradictory if there is some necessarily true proposition p such that by using just the laws of ordinary logic, we can deduce an explicit contradiction from p together with the members of S. And when Mackie says that set A is contradictory, we may properly take him, I think, as holding that it is implicitly contradictory in the explained sense. As he puts it:

> However, the contradiction does not arise immediately; to show it we need some additional premises, or perhaps some quasi-logical rules connecting the terms "good" and "evil" and "omnipotent." These additional principles are that good is opposed to evil, in such a way that a good thing always eliminates evil as far as it can, and that there are no limits to what an omnipotent thing can do. From these it follows that a good omnipotent thing eliminates evil completely, and then the propositions that a good

omnipotent thing exists, and that evil exists, are incompatible.[2]

Here Mackie refers to "additional premises"; he also calls them "additional principles" and "quasi-logical rules"; he says we need them to show the contradiction. What he means, I think, is that to get a formally contradictory set we must add some more propositions to set A; and if we aim to show that set A is implicitly contradictory, these propositions must be necessary truths—"quasi-logical rules" as Mackie calls them. The two additional principles he suggests are

19. A good thing always eliminates evil as far as it can.

and

20. There are no limits to what an omnipotent being can do.

And, of course, if Mackie means to show that set A is implicitly contradictory, then he must hold that (19) and (20) are not merely *true* but *necessarily true*.

But, are they? What about (20) first? What does it mean to say that a being is omnipotent? That he is *all-powerful*, or *almighty*, presumably. But are there no limits *at all* to the power of such a being? Could he create square circles, for example, or married bachelors? Most theologians and theistic philosophers who hold that God is omnipotent, do not hold that He can create round squares or bring it about that He both exists and does not exist. These theologians and philosophers may hold that there are no *nonlogical* limits to what an omnipotent being can do, but they concede that not even an omnipotent being can bring about logically impossible states of affairs or cause necessarily false propositions to be true. Some theists, on the other hand—Martin Luther and Descartes, perhaps—have apparently thought that God's power is unlimited even by the laws of logic. For these theists the question whether set A is contradictory will not be of much interest. As theists they believe (1) and (2), and they also, presumably, believe (3). But they remain undis-

_____

[2]Ibid., p. 93. [*Philosophy of Religion: Selected Readings*, Second Edition, p. 224.]

"THE CAUSAL COMPATIBILIST OBJECTION" * Richard Gale

This objection holds that since an action or choice can be both free and causally determined in the sense of admitting of a Hempelian deductive-nomological explanation (i.e., a proposition reporting the action or choice is deducible from the conjunction of causal laws and propositions reporting conditions prior to it, without being entailed by the latter alone), God can make certain that all of the free persons he creates always freely go right by (A) ordaining that certain strict deterministic laws hold, and (B) creating persons in circumstances such that they would be determined by these laws always freely to go right. It takes considerable intelligence to find just the right combination of laws and initial conditions, but this should be no problem for an omniscient being. Once God has done (A) and (B), he can sit back like the God of Deism and just watch the inevitable beneficent unfolding of what their conjunction entails.

Plantinga does not consider the case in which events admit of only a Hempelian inductive-statistical-type explanation, no doubt because such a case could not serve as the basis for an objection to the Free Will Defense. The reason is that if God were to determine that probabilistic laws hold, regardless of how high the probabilities, and determine the initial state of the universe, it would not logically ensure that persons always freely go right. Were God to try to determine this morally desirable situation in this fashion, he could be faulted by the causal compatibilist objector for not availing himself of the better option of laying down strict deterministic laws so as to logically ensure this outcome.

From Richard Gale, *On the Nature and Existence of God* (1991).

turbed by the claim that (1), (2), and (3) are jointly inconsistent—because, as they say, God can do what is logically impossible. Hence He can bring it about that the members of set A are all true, even if that set is contradictory (concentrating very intensely upon this suggestion is likely to make you dizzy). So the theist who thinks that the power of God isn't limited *at all*, not even by the laws of logic, will be unimpressed by Mackie's argument and won't find any difficulty in the contradiction set A is alleged to contain. This view is not very popular, however, and for good reason; it is quite incoherent. What the theist typically means when he says that God is omnipotent is not that there are *no* limits to God's power, but at most that there are no nonlogical limits to what He can do; and given this qualification, it is perhaps initially plausible to suppose that (20) is necessarily true.

But what about (19), the proposition that every good thing eliminates every evil state of affairs that it can eliminate? Is that necessarily true? Is it true at all? Suppose, first of all, that your friend Paul unwisely goes for a drive on a wintry day and runs out of gas on a deserted road. The temperature dips to −10°, and a miserably cold wind comes up. You are sitting comfortably at home (25 miles from Paul) roasting chestnuts in a roaring blaze. Your car is in the garage; in the trunk there is the full five-gallon can of gasoline you always keep for emergencies. Paul's discomfort and danger are certainly an evil, and one which you could eliminate. You don't do so. But presumably you don't thereby forfeit your claim to being a "good thing"—you simply didn't know of Paul's plight. And so (19) does not appear to be necessary. It says that every good thing has a certain property—the property of eliminating every evil that it can. And if the case I described is possible—a good person's failing through ignorance to eliminate a certain evil he can eliminate—then (19) is by no means necessarily true.

But perhaps Mackie could sensibly claim that if you *didn't know* about Paul's plight, then in fact you were *not*, at the time in question, able to eliminate the evil in question; and perhaps he'd be right. In any event he could revise (19) to take into account the kind of case I mentioned:

19a. Every good thing always eliminates every evil that *it knows about* and can eliminate.

{(1), (2), (3), (20), (19a)}, you'll notice is not a formally contradictory set—to get a formal contradiction we must add a proposition specifying that God *knows about* every evil state of affairs. But most theists do believe that God is omniscient or all-knowing; so if this new set—the set that results when we add to set A the proposition that God is omniscient—is implicitly contradictory then Mackie should be satisfied and the theist confounded. (And, henceforth, set A will be the old set A together with the proposition that God is omniscient.)

But is (19a) necessary? Hardly. Suppose you know that Paul is marooned as in the previous example, and you also know another friend is similarly marooned 50 miles in the opposite direction. Suppose, furthermore, that while you can rescue one or the other, you simply can't rescue both. Then each of the two evils is such that it is within your power to eliminate it; and you know about them both. But you can't eliminate *both*; and you don't forfeit your claim to being a good person by eliminating only one—it wasn't within your power to do more. So the fact that you don't doesn't mean that you are not a good person. Therefore (19a) is false; it is not a necessary truth or even a truth that every good thing eliminates every evil it knows about and can eliminate.

We can see the same thing another way. You've been rock climbing. Still something of a novice, you've acquired a few cuts and bruises by inelegantly using your knees rather than your feet. One of these bruises is fairly painful. You mention it to a physician friend, who predicts the pain will leave of its own accord in a day or two. Meanwhile, he says, there's nothing he can do, short of amputating your leg above the knee, to remove the pain. Now the pain in your knee is an evil state of affairs. All else being equal, it would be better if you had no such pain. And it is within the power of your friend to eliminate this evil state of affairs. Does his failure to do so mean that he is not a good person? Of course not; for he could eliminate this evil state of affairs only by bringing about another, much worse evil. And so it is once again evident that (19a) is false.

It is entirely possible that a good person fail to eliminate an evil state of affairs that he knows about and can eliminate. This would take place, if, as in the present example, he couldn't eliminate the evil without bringing about a *greater* evil.

A slightly different kind of case shows the same thing. A really impressive good state of affairs G will *outweigh* a trivial E—that is, the conjunctive state of affairs G and E is itself a good state of affairs. And surely a good person would not be obligated to eliminate a given evil if he could do so only by eliminating a good that outweighed it. Therefore (19a) is not necessarily true; it can't be used to show that set A is implicitly contradictory.

These difficulties might suggest another revision of (19); we might try

19b. A good being eliminates every evil E that it knows about and that it can eliminate without either bringing about a greater evil or eliminating a good state of affairs that outweighs E.

Is this necessarily true? It takes care of the second of the two difficulties afflicting (19a) but leaves the first untouched. We can see this as follows. First, suppose we say that a being *properly eliminates* an evil state of affairs if it eliminates that evil without either eliminating an outweighing good or bringing about a greater evil. It is then obviously possible that a person find himself in a situation where he could properly eliminate an evil E and could also properly eliminate another evil E', but couldn't properly eliminate them *both*. You're rock climbing again, this time on the dreaded north face of the Grand Teton. You and your party come upon Curt and Bob, two mountaineers stranded 125 feet apart on the face. They untied to reach their cigarettes and then carelessly dropped the rope while lighting up. A violent, dangerous thunderstorm is approaching. You have time to rescue one of the stranded climbers and retreat before the storm hits; if you rescue both, however, you and your party and the two climbers will be caught on the face during the thunderstorm, which will very likely destroy your entire party. In this case you can eliminate one evil (Curt's being stranded on the face) without causing more evil or eliminating a greater good; and you are also able to properly eliminate the other evil (Bob's being thus stranded). But you can't properly eliminate

"FREE TO BE RESPONSIBLE FOR OTHERS" * *Richard Swinburne*

It is good that the free choices of humans should include *genuine* responsibility for other humans, and that involves the opportunity to benefit *or* harm them. God has the power to benefit or to harm humans. If other agents are to be given a share in his creative work, it is good that they have that power too (although perhaps to a lesser degree). A world in which agents can benefit each other but not do each other harm is one where they have only very limited responsibility for each other. If my responsibility for you is limited to whether or not to give you a camcorder, but I cannot cause you pain, stunt your growth, or limit your education, then I do not have a great deal of responsibility for you.

A God who gave agents only such limited responsibilities for their fellows would not have given much. God would have reserved for himself the all-important choice of the kind of world it was to be, while simply allowing humans the minor choice of filling in the details. He would be like a father asking his elder son to look after the younger son, and adding that he would be watching the elder son's every move and would intervene the moment the elder son did a thing wrong. The elder son might justly retort that, while he would be happy to share his father's work, he could really do so only if he were left to make his own judgments as to what to do within a significant range of the options available to the father. A good God, like a good father, will delegate responsibility. In order to allow creatures a share in creation, he will allow them the choice of hurting and maiming, of frustrating the divine plan. Our world is one where creatures have just such deep responsibility for each other. I can not only benefit my children, but harm them. One way in which I can harm them is that I can inflict physical pain on them. But there are much more damaging things which I can do to them. Above all I can stop them growing into creatures with significant knowledge, power, and freedom; I can determine whether they come to have the kind of free and responsible choice which I have. The possibility of humans bringing about significant evil is a logical consequence of their having this free and responsible choice. Not even God could give us this choice without the possibility of resulting evil.

From Richard Swinburne, *Is There a God?* (1996).

---

them *both*. And so the fact that you don't rescue Curt, say, even though you could have, doesn't show that you aren't a good person. Here, then, each of the evils is such that you can properly eliminate it; but you can't properly eliminate them both, and hence can't be blamed for failing to eliminate one of them.

So neither (19a) nor (19b) is necessarily true. You may be tempted to reply that the sort of counterexamples offered—examples where someone is able to eliminate an evil A and also able to eliminate a different evil B, but unable to eliminate them both—are irrelevant to the case of a being who, like God, is both omnipotent and omniscient. That is, you may think that if an omnipotent and omniscient being is able to eliminate each of two evils, it follows that he can eliminate them *both*. Perhaps this is so; but it is not strictly to the point. The fact is the counterexamples show that (19a) and (19b) are not necessarily true and hence can't be used to show that set A is implicitly inconsistent. What the reply does suggest is that perhaps the atheologian will have more success if he works the properties of omniscience and omnipotence into (19). Perhaps he could say something like

19c. An omnipotent and omniscient good being eliminates every evil that it can properly eliminate.

And suppose, for purposes of argument, we concede the necessary truth of (19c). Will it serve Mackie's purposes? Not obviously. For we don't get a set that is formally contradictory by adding (20) and (19c) to set A. This set (call it A′) contains the following six members:

1. God is omnipotent
2. God is wholly good
2′. God is omniscient
3. Evil exists
19c. An omnipotent and omniscient good being eliminates every evil that it can properly eliminate

and

20. There are no nonlogical limits to what an omnipotent being can do.

Now if A′ were formally contradictory, then from any five of its members we could deduce the denial of the sixth by the laws of ordinary logic. That is, any five would *formally entail* the denial of the sixth. So if A′ were formally inconsistent, the denial of (3) would be formally entailed by the remaining five. That is, (1), (2), (2′), (19c), and (20) would formally entail

3′. There is no evil.

But they don't; what they formally entail is not that there is no evil *at all* but only that

3″. There is no evil that God can properly eliminate.

So (19c) doesn't really help either—not because it is not necessarily true but because its addition [with (20)] to set A does not yield a formally contradictory set.

Obviously, what the atheologian must add to get a formally contradictory set is

21. If God is omniscient and omnipotent, then he can properly eliminate every evil state of affairs.

Suppose we agree that the set consisting in A plus (19c), (20), and (21) is formally contradictory. So if (19c), (20), and (21) are all necessarily true, then set A is implicitly contradictory. We've already conceded that (19c) and (20) are indeed necessary. So we must take a look at (21). Is this proposition necessarily true?

No. To see this let us ask the following question. Under what conditions would an omnipotent being be unable to eliminate a certain evil E without eliminating an outweighing good? Well, suppose that E is

included in some good state of affairs that outweighs it. That is, suppose there is some good state of affairs G so related to E that it is impossible that G obtain or be actual and E fail to obtain. (Another way to put this: a state of affairs S includes S′ if the conjunctive state of affairs S *but not* S′ is impossible, or if it is necessary that S′ obtains if S does.) Now suppose that some good state of affairs G includes an evil state of affairs E that it outweighs. Then not even an omnipotent being could eliminate E without eliminating G. But *are* there any cases where a good state of affairs includes, in this sense, an evil that it outweighs?[3] Indeed there are such states of affairs. To take an artificial example, let's suppose that E is Paul's suffering from a minor abrasion and G is your being deliriously happy. The conjunctive state of affairs, G and E—the state of affairs that obtains if and only if both G and E obtain—is then a good state of affairs: it is better, all else being equal, that you be intensely happy and Paul suffer a mildly annoying abrasion than that this state of affairs not obtain. So G and E is a good state of affairs. And clearly G *and* F includes E: obviously it is necessarily true that if you are deliriously happy and Paul is suffering from an abrasion, then Paul is suffering from an abrasion.

But perhaps you think this example trivial, tricky, slippery, and irrelevant. If so, take heart; other examples abound. Certain kinds of values, certain familiar kinds of good states of affairs, can't exist apart from evil of some sort. For example, there are people who display a sort of creative moral heroism in the face of suffering and adversity—a heroism that inspires others and creates a good situation out of a bad one. In a situation like this the evil, of course, remains evil; but the total state of affairs— someone's bearing pain magnificently, for example— may be good. If it is, then the good present must outweigh the evil; otherwise the total situation would not be *good*. But, of course, it is not possible that such a good state of affairs obtain unless some evil also obtain. It is a necessary truth that if someone bears pain magnificently, then someone is in pain.

---

[3]More simply, the question is really just whether any good state of affairs includes an evil; a little reflection reveals that no good state of affairs can include an evil that it does *not* outweigh.

The conclusion to be drawn, therefore, is that (21) is not necessarily true. And our discussion thus far shows at the very least that it is no easy matter to find necessarily true propositions that yield a formally contradictory set when added to set A.[4] One wonders, therefore, why the many atheologians who confidently assert that this set is contradictory make no attempt whatever to *show* that it is. For the most part they are content just to *assert* that there is a contradiction here. Even Mackie, who sees that some "additional premises" or "quasi-logical rules" are needed, makes scarcely a beginning towards finding some additional premises that are necessarily true and that together with the members of set A formally entail an explicit contradiction.

2. CAN WE SHOW THAT THERE IS NO INCONSISTENCY HERE?

To summarize our conclusions so far: although many atheologians claim that the theist is involved in contradiction when he asserts the members of set A, this set, obviously, is neither *explicitly* nor *formally* contradictory; the claim, presumably, must be that it is *implicitly* contradictory. To make good this claim the atheologian must find some necessarily true proposition p (it could be a conjunction of several propositions) such that the addition of p to set A yields a set that is formally contradictory. No atheologian has produced even a plausible candidate for this role, and it certainly is not easy to see what such a proposition might be. Now we might think we should simply declare set A implicitly consistent on the principle that a proposition (or set) is to be presumed consistent or possible until proven otherwise. This course, however, leads to trouble. The same principle would impel us to declare the atheologian's claim—that set A is *in*consistent—possible or consistent. But the claim that a given set of propositions is implicitly contradictory, is itself either necessarily true or necessarily false; so if such a claim is *possible*, it is not necessarily false and is, therefore, true (in fact, necessarily true). If we followed the suggested principle, therefore, we

should be obliged to declare set A implicitly consistent (since it hasn't been shown to be otherwise), but we should have to say the same thing about the atheologian's claim, since we haven't shown *that* claim to be inconsistent or impossible. The atheologian's claim, furthermore, is necessarily true if it is possible. Accordingly, if we accept the above principle, we shall have to declare set A both implicitly consistent and implicitly inconsistent. So all we can say at this point is that set A has not been shown to be implicitly inconsistent.

Can we go any further? One way to go on would be to try to *show* that set A is implicitly consistent or possible in the broadly logical sense. But what is involved in showing such a thing? Although there are various ways to approach this matter, they all resemble one another in an important respect. They all amount to this: to show that a set S is consistent you think of a *possible state of affairs* (it needn't *actually obtain*) which is such that if it were actual, then all of the members of S would be true. This procedure is sometimes called *giving a model of S*. For example, you might construct an axiom set and then show that it is consistent by giving a model of it; this is how it was shown that the denial of Euclid's parallel postulate is formally consistent with the rest of his postulates.

There are various special cases of this procedure to fit special circumstances. Suppose, for example, you have a pair of propositions p and q and wish to show them consistent. And suppose we say that a proposition p_1 entails a proposition p_2 if it is impossible that p_1 be true and p_2 false—if the conjunctive proposition p_1 and not p_2 is necessarily false. Then one way to show that p is consistent with q is to find some proposition r whose conjunction with p is both possible, in the broadly logical sense, and entails q. A rude and unlettered behaviorist, for example, might hold that thinking is really nothing but movements of the larynx; he might go on to hold that

P Jones did not move his larynx after April 30

is inconsistent (in the broadly logical sense) with

Q Jones did some thinking during May.

By way of rebuttal, we might point out that P appears to be consistent with

[4]In Plantinga, *God and Other Minds* (Ithaca, N.Y.: Cornell University Press, 1967), chap. 5, I explore further the project of finding such propositions.

R While convalescing from an April 30 laryngotomy, Jones whiled away the idle hours by writing (in May) a splendid paper on Kant's *Critique of Pure Reason.*

So the conjunction of *P* and *R* appears to be consistent; but obviously it also entails *Q* (you can't write even a passable paper on Kant's *Critique of Pure Reason* without doing some thinking); so *P* and *Q* are consistent.

We can see that this is a special case of the procedure I mentioned above as follows. This proposition *R* is consistent with *P*; so the proposition *P* and *R* is possible, describes a possible state of affairs. But *P* and *R* entails *Q*; hence if *P* and *R* were true, *Q* would also be true, and hence both *P* and *Q* would be true. So this is really a case of producing a possible state of affairs such that, if it were actual, all the members of the set in question (in this case the pair set of *P* and *Q*) would be true.

How does this apply to the case before us? As follows, let us conjoin propositions (1), (2), and (2') and henceforth call the result (1):

1. God is omniscient, omnipotent, and wholly good.

The problem, then, is to show that (1) and (3) (evil exists) are consistent. This could be done, as we've seen, by finding a proposition *r* that is consistent with (1) and such that (1) and (*r*) together entail (3). One proposition that might do the trick is

22. God creates a world containing evil and has a good reason for doing so.

If (22) is consistent with (1), then it follows that (1) and (3) (and hence set A) are consistent. Accordingly, one thing some theists have tried is to show that (22) and (1) are consistent.

One can attempt this in at least two ways. On the one hand, we could try to apply the same method again. Conceive of a possible state of affairs such that, if it obtained, an omnipotent, omniscient, and wholly good God would have a good reason for permitting evil. On the other, someone might try to specify *what God's reason is* for permitting evil and try to show, if it is not obvious, that it is a good reason. St. Augustine, for example, one of the greatest and most influential philosopher-theologians of the Christian Church, writes as follows:

. . . some people see with perfect truth that a creature is better if, while possessing free will, it remains always fixed upon God and never sins; then, reflecting on men's sins, they are grieved, not because they continue to sin, but because they were created. They say: He should have made us such that we never willed to sin, but always to enjoy the unchangeable truth.

They should not lament or be angry. God has not compelled men to sin just because He created them and gave them the power to choose between sinning and not sinning. There are angels who have never sinned and never will sin.

Such is the generosity of God's goodness that He has not refrained from creating even that creature which He foreknew would not only sin, but remain in the will to sin. As a runaway horse is better than a stone which does not run away because it lacks self-movement and sense perception, so the creature is more excellent which sins by free will than that which does not sin only because it has no free will.[5]

In broadest terms Augustine claims that God could create a better, more perfect universe by permitting evil than He could by refusing to do so:

Neither the sins nor the misery are necessary to the perfection of the universe, but souls as such are necessary, which have the power to sin if they so will, and become miserable if they sin. If misery persisted after their sins had been abolished, or if there were misery before there were sins, then it might be right to say that the order and government of the universe were at fault. Again, if there were sins but no consequent misery, that order is equally dishonored by lack of equity.[6]

Augustine tries to tell us *what God's reason is* for permitting evil. At bottom, he says, it's that God can create a more perfect universe by permitting evil. A really top-notch universe requires the existence of free, rational, and moral agents; and some of the free creatures

---

[5]*The Problem of Free Choice*, Vol. 22 of *Ancient Christian Writers* (Westminster, Md.: The Newman Press, 1955), bk. 2, pp. 14–15.
[6]Ibid., bk. 3, p. 9.

He created went wrong. But the universe with the free creatures it contains and the evil they commit is better than it would have been had it contained neither the free creatures nor this evil. Such an attempt to specify God's reason for permitting evil is what I earlier called a *theodicy*; in the words of John Milton it is an attempt to "justify the ways of God to man," to show that God is just in permitting evil. Augustine's kind of theodicy might be called a Free Will Theodicy, since the idea of rational creatures with free will plays such a prominent role in it.

A theodicist, then, attempts to tell us why God permits evil. Quite distinct from a Free Will Theodicy is what I shall call a Free Will Defense. Here the aim is not to say what God's reason *is*, but at most what God's reason *might possibly be*. We could put the difference like this. The Free Will Theodicist and Free Will Defender are both trying to show that (1) is consistent with (22), and of course if so, then set A is consistent. The Free Will Theodicist tries to do this by finding some proposition *r* which in conjunction with (1) entails (22); he claims, furthermore, that this proposition is true, not just consistent with (1). He tries to tell us what God's reason for permitting evil *really is*. The Free Will Defender, on the other hand, though he also tries to find a proposition *r* that is consistent with (1) and in conjunction with it entails (22), does *not* claim to know or even believe that *r* is true. And here, of course, he is perfectly within his rights. His aim is to show that (1) is consistent with (22); all he need do then is find an *r* that is consistent with (1) and such that (1) and (*r*) entail (22); whether *r* is *true* is quite beside the point.

So there is a significant difference between a Free Will Theodicy and a Free Will Defense. The latter is sufficient (if successful) to show that set A is consistent; in a way a Free Will Theodicy goes beyond what is required. On the other hand, a theodicy would be much more satisfying, if possible to achieve. No doubt the theist would rather know what God's reason *is* for permitting evil than simply that it's possible that He has a good one. But in the present context (that of investigating the consistency of set A), the latter is all that's needed. Neither a defense or a theodicy, of course, gives any hint to what God's reason for some *specific evil*—the death or suffering of someone close to you, for example—might be. And there is still another

function—a sort of pastoral function[7]—in the neighborhood that neither serves. Confronted with evil in his own life or suddenly coming to realize more clearly than before the *extent* and *magnitude* of evil, a believer in God may undergo a crisis of faith. He may be tempted to follow the advice of Job's "friends"; he may be tempted to "curse God and die." Neither a Free Will Defense nor a Free Will Theodicy is designed to be of much help or comfort to one suffering from such a storm in the soul (although in a specific case, of course, one or the other could prove useful). Neither is to be thought of first of all as a means of pastoral counseling. Probably neither will enable someone to find peace with himself and with God in the face of the evil the world contains. But then, of course, neither is intended for that purpose.

3. THE FREE WILL DEFENSE

In what follows I shall focus attention upon the Free Will Defense. I shall examine it more closely, state it more exactly, and consider objections to it; and I shall argue that in the end it is successful. Earlier we saw that among good states of affairs there are some that not even God can bring about without bringing about evil: those goods, namely, that *entail* or *include* evil states of affairs. The Free Will Defense can be looked upon as an effort to show that there may be a very different kind of good that God can't bring about without permitting evil. These are good states of affairs that don't include evil; they do not entail the existence of any evil whatever; nonetheless God Himself can't bring them about without permitting evil.

So how does the Free Will Defense work? And what does the Free Will Defender mean when he says that people are or may be free? What is relevant to the Free Will Defense is the idea of *being free with respect to an action*. If a person is free with respect to a given action, then he is free to perform that action and free to refrain from performing it; no antecedent conditions and/or causal laws determine that he will perform the action, or that he won't. It is within his power, at the

---

[7] I am indebted to Henry Schuurman (in conversation) for helpful discussion of the difference between this pastoral function and those served by a theodicy or a defense.

time in question, to take or perform the action and within his power to refrain from it. Freedom so conceived is not to be confused with unpredictability. You might be able to predict what you will do in a given situation even if you are free, in that situation, to do something else. If I know you well, I may be able to predict what action you will take in response to a certain set of conditions; it does not follow that you are not free with respect to that action. Secondly, I shall say that an action is *morally significant*, for a given person, if it would be wrong for him to perform the action but right to refrain or *vice versa*, Keeping a promise, for example, would ordinarily be morally significant for a person, as would refusing induction into the army. On the other hand, having Cheerios for breakfast (instead of Wheaties) would not normally be morally significant. Further, suppose we say that a person is *significantly free*, on a given occasion, if he is then free with respect to a morally significant action. And finally we must distinguish between *moral evil* and *natural evil*. The former is evil that results from free human activity; natural evil is any other kind of evil.[8]

Given these definitions and distinctions, we can make a preliminary statement of the Free Will Defense as follows. A world containing creatures who are significantly free (and freely perform more good than evil actions) is more valuable, all else being equal, than a world containing no free creatures at all. Now God can create free creatures, but He can't *cause* or *determine* them to do only what is right. For if He does so, then they aren't significantly free after all; they do not do what is right *freely*. To create creatures capable of *moral good*, therefore, He must create creatures capable of moral evil; and He can't give these creatures the freedom to perform evil and at the same time prevent them from doing so. As it turned out, sadly enough, some of the free creatures God created went wrong in the exercise of their freedom; this is the source of moral evil. The fact that free creatures sometimes go wrong, however, counts neither against God's omnipotence nor against His goodness; for He could have forestalled the occurrence of moral evil only by removing the possibility of moral good.

I said earlier that the Free Will Defender tries to find a proposition that is consistent with

1. God is omniscient, omnipotent, and wholly good

and together with (1) entails that there is evil. According to the Free Will Defense, we must find this proposition somewhere in the above story. The heart of the Free Will Defense is the claim that it is *possible* that God could not have created a universe containing moral good (or as much moral good as this world contains) without creating one that also contained moral evil. And if so, then it is possible that God has a good reason for creating a world containing evil.

Now this defense has met with several kinds of objections. For example, some philosophers say that *causal determinism* and *freedom*, contrary to what we might have thought, are not really incompatible.[9] But if so, then God could have created free creatures who were free, and free to do what is wrong, but nevertheless were causally determined to do only what is right. Thus He could have created creatures who were free to do what was wrong, while nevertheless preventing them from ever performing any wrong actions—simply by seeing to it that they were causally determined to do only what is right. Of course this contradicts the Free Will Defense, according to which there is inconsistency in supposing that God determines free creatures to do only what is right. But is it really possible that all of a person's actions are causally determined while some of them are free? How could that be so? According to one version of the doctrine in question, to say that George acts freely on a given occasion is to say only this: *if George had chosen to do otherwise, he would have done otherwise*. Now George's action A is causally determined if some event E—some event beyond his control—has already occurred, where the state of affairs consisting in E's occurrence conjoined with Geroge's *refraining* from performing A, is a causally impossible state of affairs. Then one can consistently hold both that all of a man's actions are causally determined and that some of them are free in the above sense. For suppose that all of a man's actions are causally determined and that he *couldn't*, on any occasion, have

---

[8]This distinction is not very precise (how, exactly, are we to construe "results from"?), but perhaps it will serve our present purposes.

[9]See, for example, A. Flew, "Divine Omnipotence and Human Freedom," in *New Essays in Philosophical Theology*, eds. A. Flew and A. MacIntyre (London: SCM, 1955), pp. 150–53.

made any choice or performed any action different from the ones he did make and perform. It could still be true that if he *had* chosen to do otherwise, he would have done otherwise. Granted, he couldn't have chosen to do otherwise; but this is consistent with saying that *if* he had, things would have gone differently.

This objection to the Free Will Defense seems utterly implausible. One might as well claim that being in jail doesn't really limit one's freedom on the grounds that if one were *not* in jail, he'd be free to come and go as he pleased. So I shall say no more about this objection here.[10]

A second objection is more formidable. In essence it goes like this. Surely it is possible to do only what is right, even if one is free to do wrong. It is *possible*, in that broadly logical sense, that there would be a world containing free creatures who always do what is right. There is certainly no *contradiction* or *inconsistency* in this idea. But God is omnipotent; his power has no nonlogical limitations. So if it's possible that there be a world containing creatures who are free to do what is wrong but never in fact do so, then it follows that an omnipotent God could create such a world. If so, however, the Free Will Defense must be mistaken in its insistence upon the possibility that God is omnipotent but unable to create a world containing moral good without permitting moral evil. J. L. Mackie . . . states this objection:

> If God has made men such that in their free choices they sometimes prefer what is good and sometimes what is evil, why could he not have made men such that they always freely choose the good? If there is no logical impossibility in a man's freely choosing the good on one, or on several occasions, there cannot be a logical impossibility in his freely choosing the good on every occasion. God was not, then, faced with a choice between making innocent automata and making beings who, in acting freely, would sometimes go wrong; there was open to him the obviously better possibility of making beings who would act freely but always go right. Clearly, his failure to avail himself of this possibility is inconsistent

with his being both omnipotent and wholly good.[11]

Now what, exactly, is Mackie's point here? This. According to the Free Will Defense, it is possible both that God is omnipotent and that He was unable to create a world containing moral good without creating one containing moral evil. But, replies Mackie, this limitation on His power to create is inconsistent with God's omnipotence. For surely it's *possible* that there be a world containing perfectly virtuous persons—persons who are significantly free but always do what is right. Surely there are *possible worlds* that contain moral good but no moral evil. But God, if He is omnipotent, can create any possible world He chooses. So it is *not* possible, contrary to the Free Will Defense, both that God is omnipotent and that He could create a world containing moral good only by creating one containing moral evil. If He is omnipotent, the only limitations of His power are *logical* limitations; in which case there are no possible worlds He could not have created.

This is a subtle and important point. According to the great German philosopher G. W. Leibniz, *this* world, the actual world, must be the best of all possible worlds. His reasoning goes as follows. Before God created anything at all, He was confronted with an enormous range of choices; He could create or bring into actuality any of the myriads of different possible worlds. Being perfectly good, He must have chosen to create the best world He could; being omnipotent, He was able to create any possible world He pleased. He must, therefore, have chosen the best of all possible worlds; and hence *this* world, the one He did create, must be the best possible. Now Mackie, of course, agrees with Leibniz that God, if omnipotent, could have created any world He pleased and would have created the best world he could. But while Leibniz draws the conclusion that this world, despite appearances, must be the best possible, Mackie concludes instead that there is no omnipotent, wholly good God. For, he says, it is obvious enough that this present world is not the best of all possible worlds.

The Free Will Defender disagrees with both Leibniz and Mackie. In the first place, he might say, what is

---

[10]For further discussion of it see Plantinga, *God and Other Minds*, pp. 132–35.

[11]Mackie, in *The Philosophy of Religion*, pp. 100–101.

the reason for supposing that *there* is such a thing as the best of all possible worlds? No matter how marvelous a world is—containing no matter how many persons enjoying unalloyed bliss—isn't it possible that there be an even better world containing even more persons enjoying even more unalloyed bliss? But what is really characteristic and central to the Free Will Defense is the claim that God, though omnipotent, could not have actualized just any possible world He pleased.

4. WAS IT WITHIN GOD'S POWER TO CREATE ANY POSSIBLE WORLD HE PLEASED?

This is indeed the crucial question for the Free Will Defense. If we wish to discuss it with insight and authority, we shall have to look into the idea of *possible worlds*. And a sensible first question is this: what sort of thing is a possible world? The basic idea is that a possible world is a *way things could have been*; it is a *state of affairs* of some kind. Earlier we spoke of states of affairs, in particular of good and evil states of affairs. Suppose we look at this idea in more detail. What sort of thing is a state of affairs? The following would be examples:

> Nixon's having won the 1972 election
> 7 + 5's being equal to 12
> All men's being mortal

and

> Gary, Indiana's, having a really nasty pollution problem.

These are *actual* states of affairs: states of affairs that do in fact *obtain*. And corresponding to each such actual state of affairs there is a true proposition—in the above cases, the corresponding propositions would be *Nixon won the 1972 presidential election, 7 + 5 is equal to 12, all men are mortal*, and *Gary, Indiana, has a really nasty pollution problem*. A proposition *p corresponds* to a state of affairs *s*, in this sense, if it is impossible that *p* be true and *s* fail to obtain and impossible that *s* obtain and *p* fail to be true.

But just as there are false propositions, so there are states of affairs that do *not* obtain or are *not* actual. *Kissinger's having swum the Atlantic* and *Hubert Horatio Humphrey's having run a mile in four minutes* would be

examples. Some states of affairs that do not obtain are *impossible*: for example, *Hubert's having drawn a square circle, 7 + 5's being equal to 75*, and *Agnew's having a brother who was an only child*. The propositions corresponding to these states of affairs, of course, are necessarily false. So there are states of affairs that *obtain* or *are actual* and also states of affairs that don't obtain. Among the latter some are *impossible* and others are possible. And a possible world is a possible state of affairs. Of course not every possible state of affairs is a possible world; *Hubert's having run a mile in four minutes* is a possible state of affairs but not a possible world. No doubt it is an *element* of many possible worlds, but it isn't itself inclusive enough to be one. To be a possible world, a state of affairs must be very large—so large as to be *complete* or *maximal*.

To get at this idea of completeness we need a couple of definitions. As we have already seen . . . a state of affairs A *includes* a state of affairs B if it is not possible that A obtain and B not obtain or if the conjunctive state of affairs A *but not B*—the state of affairs that obtains if and only if A obtains and B does not—is not possible. For example, *Jim Whittaker's being the first American to climb Mt. Everest includes Jim Whittaker's being an American.* It also includes *Mt. Everest's being climbed, something's being climbed, no American's having climbed Everest before Whittaker did*, and the like. Inclusion among states of affairs is like *entailment* among propositions; and where a state of affairs A includes a state of affairs B, the proposition corresponding to A entails the one corresponding to B. Accordingly, *Jim Whittaker is the first American to climb Everest* entails *Mt. Everest has been climbed, something has been climbed*, and *no American climbed Everest before Whittaker did*. Now suppose we say further that a state of affairs A *precludes* a state of affairs B if it is not possible that *both* obtain, or if the conjunctive state of affairs A and B is impossible. Thus *Whittaker's being the first American to climb Mt. Everest* precludes *Luther Jerstad's being the first American to climb Everest*, as well as *Whittaker's never having climbed any mountains*. If A precludes B, than A's corresponding proposition entails the denial of the one corresponding to B. Still further, let's say that the *complement* of a state of affairs is the state of affairs that obtains just in case A does not obtain. [Or we might say that the complement (call it Ā) of A is the state of affairs corresponding to the *denial* or *negation* of the proposition corresponding to A.] Given these definitions, we can say what it is for a state of affairs to be *complete*: A is a complete state of affairs if and only if for every state of affairs B, either A *includes* B or A *precludes* B. (We could express the same thing by saying that if A is a complete state of affairs, then for every state of affairs B, either A includes B or A includes $\bar{B}$ the complement of B.) And now we are able to say what a possible world is: a possible world is any possible state of affairs that is complete. If A is a possible world, then it says something about everything; every state of affairs S is either included in or precluded by it.

Corresponding to each possible world W, furthermore, there is a set of propositions that I'll call the book on W. A proposition is in the book on W just in case the state of affairs to which it corresponds is included in W. Or we might express it like this. Suppose we say that a proposition P *is true in a world W* if and only if *P would have been true if W had been actual*—if and only if, that is, it is not possible that W be actual and P be false. Then the book on W is the set of propositions true in W. Like possible worlds, books are *complete*; if B is a book, then for any proposition P, either P or the denial of P will be a member of B. A book is a *maximal consistent set* of propositions; it is so large that the addition of another proposition to it always yields an explicitly inconsistent set.

Of course, for each possible world there is exactly one book corresponding to it (that is, for a given world W there is just one book B such that each member of B is true in W); and for each book there is just one world to which it corresponds. So every world has its book.

It should be obvious that exactly one possible world is actual. At *least* one must be, since the set of true propositions is a maximal consistent set and hence a book. But then it corresponds to a possible world, and the possible world corresponding to this set of propositions (since it's the set of *true* propositions) will be actual. On the other hand there is at *most* one actual world. For suppose there were two: W and W'. These worlds cannot include all the very same states of affairs; if they did, they would be the very same world. So there must be at least one state of affairs S such that W includes S and W' does not. But a possible world is maximal; W', therefore, includes the complement S of S. So if both W and W' were actual, as we have supposed, then both S and $\bar{S}$ would be actual—which is

impossible. So there can't be more than one possible world that is actual.

Leibniz pointed out that a proposition p is necessary if it is true in every possible world. We may add that p is possible if it is true in one world and impossible if true in none. Furthermore, p *entails* q if there is no possible world in which p is true and q is false, and p *is consistent with q* if there is at least one world in which both p and q are true.

A further feature of possible worlds is that people (and other things) *exist* in them. Each of us exists in the actual world, obviously; but a person also exists in many worlds distinct from the actual world. It would be a mistake, of course, to think of all of these worlds as somehow "going on" at the same time, with the same person reduplicated through these worlds and actually existing in a lot of different ways. This is not what is meant by saying that the same person exists in different possible worlds. What is meant, instead, is this: a person Paul exists in each of those possible worlds W which is such that, if W had been actual, Paul would have existed—actually existed. Suppose Paul had been an inch taller than he is, or a better tennis player. Then the world that does in fact obtain would not have been actual; some other world—W', let's say—would have obtained instead. If W' had been actual, Paul would have existed; so Paul exists in W'. (Of course there are still other possible worlds in which Paul does not exist—worlds, for example, in which there are no people at all.) Accordingly, when we say that Paul exists in a world W, what we mean is that Paul *would have* existed had W been actual. Or we could put it like this: Paul exists in each world W that includes the state of affairs consisting in Paul's existence. We can put this still more simply by saying that Paul exists in those worlds whose books contain the proposition *Paul exists*.

But isn't there a problem here? *Many* people are named "Paul": Paul the apostle, Paul J. Zwier, John Paul Jones, and many other famous Pauls. So who goes with "Paul exists"? Which Paul? The answer has to do with the fact that books contain *propositions*—not sentences. They contain the sort of thing sentences are used to express and assert. And the same sentence—"Aristotle is wise," for example—can be used to express many different propositions. When Plato used it, he asserted a proposition predicating wisdom of his famous pupil; when Jackie Onassis uses it, she asserts a proposition predicating wisdom of her wealthy husband. These are distinct propositions (we might even think they differ in truth value); but they are expressed by the same sentence. Normally (but not always) we don't have much trouble determining which of the several propositions expressed by a given sentence is relevant in the context at hand. So in this case a given person, Paul, exists in a world *W* if and only if *W'* book contains the proposition that says that *he*—that particular person—exists. The fact that the sentence we use to express this proposition can also be used to express *other* propositions is not relevant.

After this excursion into the nature of books and worlds we can return to our question. Could God have created just any world He chose? Before addressing the question, however, we must note that God does not, strictly speaking, *create* any possible worlds or states of affairs at all. What He creates are the heavens and the earth and all that they contain. But He has not created states of affairs. There are, for example, the state of affairs consisting in God's existence and the state of affairs consisting in His nonexistence. That is, there is such a thing as the state of affairs consisting in the existence of God, and there is also such a thing as the state of affairs consisting in the nonexistence of God, just as there are the two propositions *God exists* and *God does not exist*. The theist believes that the first state of affairs is actual and the first proposition true, the atheist believes that the second state of affairs is actual and the second proposition true. But, of course, both propositions *exist*, even though just one is true. Similarly, there are two states of affairs here, just one of which is actual. So both states of affairs *exist*, but only one *obtains*. And God has not created either one of them since there never was a time at which either did not exist. Nor has he created the state of affairs consisting in the earth's existence; there was a time when *the earth* did not exist, but none when the state of affairs consisting in the earth's existence didn't exist. Indeed, God did not bring into existence any states of affairs at all. What He did was to perform actions of a certain sort—creating the heavens and the earth, for example—which resulted in the *actuality* of certain states of affairs. God *actualizes* states of affairs. He actualizes the possible world that does in fact obtain; He does not create it.

And while He has created Socrates, He did not create the state of affairs consisting in Socrates' existence.[12]

Bearing this in mind, let's finally return to our question. Is the atheologian right in holding that if God is omnipotent, then he could have actualized or created any possible world He pleased? Not obviously. First, we must ask ourselves whether God is a *necessary* or a *contingent* being. A *necessary* being is one that exists in every possible world—one that would have existed no matter which possible world had been actual; a contingent being exists only in some possible worlds. Now if God is not a necessary being (and many, perhaps most, theists think that He is not), then clearly enough there will be many possible worlds He could not have actualized—all those, for example, in which He does not exist. Clearly, God could not have created a world in which He doesn't even exist.

So, if God is a contingent being then there are many possible worlds beyond His power to create. But this is really irrelevant to our present concerns. For perhaps the atheologian can maintain his case if he revises his claim to avoid this difficulty; perhaps he will say something like this: if God is omnipotent, then He could have actualized any of these possible worlds *in which He exists*. So if He exists and is omnipotent, He could have actualized (contrary to the Free Will Defense) and of those possible worlds in which He exists and in which there exist free creatures who do no wrong. He could have actualized worlds containing moral good but no moral evil. Is this correct?

Let's begin with a trivial example. You and Paul have just returned from an Australian hunting expedition: your quarry was the elusive double-wattled cassowary. Paul captured an aardvark, mistaking it for a cassowary. The creature's disarming ways have won it a place in Paul's heart; he is deeply attached to it. Upon your return to the States you offer Paul $500 for his aardvark, only to be rudely turned down. Later you ask yourself, "What would he have done if I'd offered him $700?" Now what is it, exactly, that you are asking?

[12]Strict accuracy demands, therefore, that we speak of God as *actualizing* rather than creating possible worlds. I shall continue to use both locutions, thus sacrificing accuracy to familiarity. For more about possible worlds see my book *The Nature of Necessity* (Oxford: The Clarendon Press, 1974), chaps. 4–8.

What you're really asking in a way is whether, under a *specific set of conditions*, Paul would have sold it. These conditions include your having offered him $700 rather than $500 for the aardvark, everything else being as much as possible like the conditions that did in fact obtain. Let S' be this set of conditions or state of affairs. S' includes the state of affairs consisting in your offering Paul $700 (instead of the $500 you did offer him); of course it does not include his *accepting* your offer, and it does not include his *rejecting* it; for the rest, the conditions it includes are just like the ones that did obtain in the actual world. So, for example, S' includes Paul's being free to accept the offer and free to refrain; and if in fact the going rate for an aardvark was $650, then S' includes the state of affairs consisting in the going rate's being $650. So we might put your question by asking which of the following conditionals is true:

23. If the state of affairs S' had obtained, Paul would have accepted the offer
24. If the state of affairs S' had obtained, Paul would not have accepted the offer.

It seems clear that at least one of these conditionals is true, but naturally they can't both be; so exactly one is.

Now since S' includes neither Paul's accepting the offer nor his rejecting it, the antecedent of (23) and (24) does not entail the consequent of either. That is,

25. S' obtains

does not entail either

26. Paul accepts the offer

or

27. Paul does not accept the offer.

So there are possible worlds in which both (25) and (26) are true, and other possible worlds in which both (25) and (27) are true.

We are now in a position to grasp an important fact. Either (23) or (24) is in fact true; and either way there are possible worlds God could not have actualized. Suppose, first of all, that (23) is true. Then it was beyond the power of God to create a world in which (1) Paul is free to sell his aardvark and free to refrain, and in which the other states of affairs included in S'

obtain, and (2) Paul does not sell. That is, it was beyond His power to create a world in which (25) and (27) are both true. There is at least one possible world like this, but God, despite His omnipotence, could not have brought about its actuality. For let W be such a world. To actualize W, God must bring it about that Paul is free with respect to this action, and that the other states of affairs included in S' obtain. But (23), as we are supposing, is true; so if God had actualized S' and left Paul *free* with respect to this action, he would have sold: in which case W would not have been actual. If, on the other hand, God had *brought it about* that Paul didn't sell or had *caused him* to refrain from selling, then Paul would not have been free with respect to this action; then S' would not have been actual (since S' includes Paul's being free with respect to it), and W would not have been actual since W includes S'.

Of course if it is (24) rather than (23) that is true, then another class of worlds was beyond God's power to actualize—those, namely, in which S' obtains and Paul *sells* his aardvark. These are the worlds in which both (25) and (26) are true. But either (23) or (24) is true. Therefore, there are possible worlds God could not have actualized. If we consider whether or not God could have created a world in which, let's say, both (25) and (26) are true, we see that the answer depends upon a peculiar kind of fact; it depends upon what Paul would have freely chosen to do in a certain situation. So there are any number of possible worlds such that it is partly up to Paul whether God can create them.[13]

That was a past tense example. Perhaps it would be useful to consider a future tense case, since this might seem to correspond more closely to God's situation in choosing a possible world to actualize. At some time t in the near future Maurice will be free with respect to some insignificant action—having freeze-dried oatmeal for breakfast, let's say. That is, at time t Maurice will be free to have oatmeal but also free to take something else—shredded wheat, perhaps. Next, suppose we consider S', a state of affairs that is included in the actual world and includes

---

[13]For a fuller statement of this argument see Plantinga, *The Nature of Necessity*, chap. 9, secs. 4–6.

Maurice's being free with respect to taking oatmeal at time *t*. That is, *S'* includes Maurice's being free at time *t* to take oatmeal and free to reject it. *S'* does not include Maurice's taking oatmeal, however; nor does it include his rejecting it. For the rest *S'* is as much as possible like the actual world. In particular there are many conditions that do in fact hold at time *t* and are *relevant* to his choice—such conditions, for example, as the fact that he hasn't had oatmeal lately, that his wife will be annoyed if he rejects it, and the like; and *S'* includes each of these conditions. Now God no doubt knows what Maurice will do at time *t*, if *S* obtains; He knows which action Maurice would freely perform if *S* were to be actual. That is, God knows that one of the following conditionals is true:

28. If *S'* were to obtain, Maurice will freely take the oatmeal

or

29. If *S'* were to obtain, Maurice will freely reject it.

We may not know which of these is true, and Maurice himself may not know; but presumably God does.

So either God knows that (28) is true, or else He knows that (29) is. Let's suppose it is (28). Then there is a possible world that God, though omnipotent, cannot create. For consider a possible world *W'* that shares *S'* with the actual world (which for ease of reference I'll name "Kronos") and in which Maurice does *not* take oatmeal. (We know there is such a world, since *S'* does not include Maurice's taking the oatmeal.) *S'* obtains in *W'* just as it does in Kronos. Indeed, everything in *W'* is just as it is in Kronos up to time *t*. But whereas in Kronos Maurice takes oatmeal at time *t*, in *W'* he does not. Now *W* is a perfectly possible world; but it is not within God's power to create it or bring about its actuality. For to do so He must actualize *S'*. But (28) is in fact true. So if God actualizes *S'* (as He must to create *W'*) and leaves Maurice free with respect to the action in question, then he will take the oatmeal; and then, of course, *W'* will not be actual. If, on the other hand, God causes Maurice to *refrain* from taking the oatmeal, then he is not *free* to take it. That means, once again, that *W'* is not actual; for in *W'* Maurice is free to take the oatmeal (even if he doesn't do so). So if (28) is true, then this world *W'*

is one that God can't actualize; it is not within His power to actualize it even though He is omnipotent and it is a possible world.

Of course, if it is (29) that is true, we get a similar result; then too there are possible worlds that God can't actualize. These would be worlds which share *S'* with Kronos and in which Maurice *does* take oatmeal. But either (28) or (29) *is* true; so either way there is a possible world that God can't create. If we consider a world in which *S'* obtains and in which Maurice freely chooses oatmeal at time *t*, we see that whether or not it is within God's power to actualize it depends upon what Maurice would do if he were free in a certain situation. Accordingly, there are any number of possible worlds such that it is partly up to Maurice whether or not God can actualize them. It is, of course, up to God whether or not to create Maurice and also up to God whether or not to make him free with respect to the action of taking oatmeal at time *t*. (God could, if He chose, cause him to succumb to the dreaded *equine obsession*, a condition shared by some people and most horses, whose victims find it *psychologically impossible* to refuse oats or oat products.) But if He creates Maurice and creates him free with respect to this action, then whether or not he actually performs the action is up to Maurice—not God.[14]

Now we can return to the Free Will Defense and the problem of evil. The Free Will Defender, you recall, insists on the possibility that it is not within God's power to create a world containing moral good without creating one containing moral evil. His atheological opponent—Mackie, for example—agrees with Leibniz in insisting that *if* (as the theist holds) God is omnipotent, then it *follows* that He could have created any possible world He pleased. We now see that this contention—call it "Leibniz' Lapse"—is a mistake. The atheologian is right in holding that there are many possible worlds containing moral good but no moral evil; his mistake lies in endorsing Leibniz' Lapse. So one of his premises—that God, if omnipotent, could have actualized just any world He pleased—is false.

---

[14]For a more complete and more exact statement of this argument see Plantinga, *The Nature of Necessity*, chap. 9, secs. 4–6.

5. COULD GOD HAVE CREATED A WORLD CONTAINING MORAL GOOD BUT NO MORAL EVIL?

Now suppose we recapitulate the logic of the situation. The Free Will Defender claims that the following is possible:

30. God is omnipotent, and it was not within His power to create a world containing moral good but no moral evil.

By way of retort the atheologian insists that there are possible worlds containing moral good but no moral evil. He adds that an omnipotent being could have actualized any possible world he chose. So if God is omnipotent, it follows that He could have actualized a world containing moral good but no moral evil, hence (30), contrary to the Free Will Defender's claim, is not possible. What we have seen so far is that his second premise—Leibniz' Lapse—is false.

Of course, this does not settle the issue in the Free Will Defender's favor. Leibniz' Lapse (appropriately enough for a lapse) is false; but this doesn't show that (30) is possible. To show this latter we must demonstrate the possibility that among the worlds God could not have actualized are all the worlds containing moral good but no moral evil. How can we approach this question?

Instead of choosing oatmeal for breakfast or selling an aardvark, suppose we think about a morally significant action such as taking a bribe. Curley Smith, the mayor of Boston, is opposed to the proposed freeway route; it would require destruction of the Old North Church along with some other antiquated and structurally unsound buildings. L. B. Smedes, the director of highways, asks him whether he'd drop his opposition for $1 million. "Of course," he replies. "Would you do it for $2?" asks Smedes. "What do you take me for?" comes the indignant reply. "That's already established," smirks Smedes; "all that remains is to nail down your price." Smedes then offers him a bribe of $35,000; unwilling to break with the fine old traditions of Bay State politics, Curley accepts. Smedes then spends a sleepless night wondering whether he could have bought Curley for $20,000.

Now suppose we assume that Curley was free with respect to the action of taking the bribe—free to take it and free to refuse. And suppose, furthermore, that he would have taken it. That is, let us suppose that

31. If Smedes had offered Curley a bribe of $20,000, he would have accepted it.

If (31) is true, then there is a state of affairs S' that (1) includes Curley's being offered a bribe of $20,000; (2) does not include either his accepting the bribe or his rejecting it; and (3) is otherwise as much as possible like the actual world. Just to make sure S' includes every relevant circumstance, let us suppose that it is a *maximal world segment*. That is, add to S' any state of affairs compatible with but not included in it, and the result will be an entire possible world. We could think of it roughly like this: S' is included in at least one world W in which Curley takes the bribe and in at least one world W' in which he rejects it. If S' is a maximal world segment, then S' is what remains of W when *Curley's taking the bribe* is deleted; it is also what remains of W' when *Curley's rejecting the bribe* is detected. More exactly, if S' is a maximal world segment, then every possible state of affairs that includes S', but isn't included by S', is a possible world. So if (31) is true, then there is a maximal world segment S' that (1) includes Curley's being offered a bribe of $20,000; (2) does not include either his accepting the bribe or his rejecting it; (3) is otherwise as much as possible like the actual world—in particular, it includes Curley's being free with respect to the bribe; and (4) is such that if it were actual then Curley would have taken the bribe. That is,

32. If S' were actual, Curley would have accepted the bribe is true.

Now, of course, there is at least one possible world W' in which S' is actual and Curley does not take the bribe. But God could not have created W'; to do so, He would have been obliged to actualize S', leaving Curley free with respect to the action of taking the bribe. But under these conditions Curley, as (32) assures us, would have accepted the bribe, so that the world thus created would not have been S'.

Curley, as we see, is not above a bit of Watergating. But there may be worse to come. Of course, there are possible worlds in which he is significantly free (i.e., free with respect to a morally significant action) and never does what is wrong. But the sad truth about

Curley may be this. Consider W', any of these worlds: in W' Curley is significantly free, so in W' there are some actions that are morally significant for him and with respect to which he is free. But at least one of these actions—call it A—has the following peculiar property. There is a maximal world segment S' that obtains in W' and is such that (1) S' includes Curley's being free *re* A but neither his performing A nor his refraining from A; (2) S' is otherwise as much as possible like W' and (3) if S' had been actual, Curley would have gone wrong with respect to A.[15] (Notice that this third condition holds in fact, in the actual world; it does not hold in that world W'.)

This means, of course, that God could not have actualized W'. For to do so He'd have been obliged to bring it about that S' is actual; but then Curley would go wrong with respect to A. Since in W' he always does what is right, the world thus actualized would not be W'. On the other hand, if God *causes* Curley to go right with respect to A or *brings it about that* he does so, then Curley isn't free with respect to A; and so once more it isn't W' that is actual. Accordingly God cannot create W'. But W' was just any of the worlds in which Curley is significantly free but always does only what is right. It therefore follows that it was not within God's power to create a world in which Curley produces moral good but no moral evil. Every world God can actualize is such that if Curley is significantly free in it, he takes at least one wrong action.

Obviously Curley is in serious trouble. I shall call the malady from which he suffers *transworld depravity*. (I leave as homework the problem of comparing transworld depravity with what Calvinists call "total depravity.") By way of explicit definition:

33. A person P *suffers from transworld depravity* if and only if the following holds: for every world W such that P is significantly free in W and P does only what is right in W, there is an action A and a maximal world segment S' such that
1. S' includes A's being morally significant for P
2. S' includes P's being free with respect to A
3. S' is included in W and includes neither P's performing A nor P's refraining from performing A

and

4. If S' were actual, P would go wrong with respect to A.

(In thinking about this definition, remember that (4) is to be true in fact, in the actual world—not in that world W.)

What is important about the idea of transworld depravity is that if a person suffers from it, then it wasn't within God's power to actualize any world in which that person is significantly free but does no wrong—that is, a world in which he produces moral good but no moral evil.

We have been here considering a crucial contention of the Free Will Defender: the contention, namely, that

30. God is omnipotent, and it was not within His power to create a world containing moral good but no moral evil.

How is transworld depravity relevant to this? As follows. Obviously it is possible that there be persons who suffer from transworld depravity. More generally, it is possible that *everybody* suffers from it. And if this possibility were actual, then God, though omnipotent, could not have created any of the possible worlds containing just the persons who do in fact exist, and containing moral good but no moral evil. For to do so He'd have to create persons who were significantly free (otherwise there would be no moral good) but suffered from transworld depravity. Such persons go wrong with respect to at least one action in any world God could have actualized and in which they are free with respect to morally significant actions; so the price for creating a world in which they produce moral good is creating one in which they also produce moral evil.

QUESTIONS FOR FURTHER REFLECTION

1. Would it be better for God to not give humans free will if it meant there would be no suffering? Do you value free will more than you value an absence of suffering? Would you be willing to give up free will if it meant no more rape, cancer, or babies being born addicted to drugs?
2. Suppose free will is objectively not more valuable than an absence of suffering. Does this undermine Plantinga's Free Will Defense? Why or why not?

[15] A person goes wrong with respect to an action if he either wrongfully performs it or wrongfully fails to perform it.

39. THE EVIDENTIAL ARGUMENT FROM EVIL

Michael Martin

Michael Martin, who received a Ph.D. from Harvard University, is Professor of Philosophy Emeritus at Boston University. His central areas of research are the philosophy of religion, the philosophy of law, and the philosophy of social science. He is the author of *Concepts of Science Education*, (1972); *Social Science and Philosophical Analysis*, (1978); *The Legal Philosophy of H.L.A. Hart*, (1987); *Atheism: A Philosophical Justification*, (1990); *The Case Against Christianity*, (1991); *The Big Domino in the Sky*, (1996); *Legal Realism: American and Scandinavian*, (1997); and *Verstehen: The Uses of Understanding in the Social Sciences*, (2000). He is co-editor of *Probability, Confirmation, and Simplicity: Readings in the Philosophy of Inductive Logic*, (1966) and *Readings in the Philosophy of Social Science*, (1994). In addition, he has published numerous articles and reviews on various topics in the philosophy of the social sciences, philosophy of science, philosophy of law, philosophy of religion, philosophy of education, philosophy of sport, and ethics, including more than 20 papers and two debates on the Internet.

In this selection, Martin defends two versions of the evidential argument from evil—direct and indirect. He argues that both versions provide strong, but not irrefutable, evidence for the nonexistence of God. He contends that the Direct Evidential Argument shows that under certain conditions the fact of apparently pointless evil provides a strong reason for not believing in God. In the case of the Indirect Argument, he maintains that the failure of known theodicies provides a powerful reason for nonbelief.

READING QUESTIONS

1. What is the major problem with the Deductive Argument from Evil?
2. Why does the Evidential Argument from Evil not have this problem?
3. What is the difference between the Direct Evidential Argument from Evil and the Indirect Evidential Argument from Evil?
4. What are some objections to these arguments? Can they be answered?
5. What are the Free Will Defense and the Soul Making Defense? What are some objections to these defenses?

1. INTRODUCTION

Historically the Argument from Evil is perhaps the most important argument against the existence of God. The Greek philosopher Epicurus (341–270 B.C.) first formulated the problem that generates this argument:

> God either wishes to take away evil, and is unable, or He is able, and unwilling; or He is neither willing nor able, or He is both willing and able. If He is willing and is unable, He is feeble, which is not in accordance with the character of God; if He is able and unwilling, He is envious, which is equally at variance with God; if He is neither willing nor able, He is both envious and feeble, and therefore not God; if He is both willing and able, which alone is suitable to God, from what source then are evils? or why does He not remove them?

Both believers and nonbelievers have taken the problem of the existence of evil very seriously. On the one hand, theologians have produced what they believe to be adequate solutions ranging from the suggestion that evil is an illusion to the claim that it is the result of free will. On the other hand, religious skeptics have maintained that the problem can be used to support disbelief in God. Arguing that the existence of evil cannot be reconciled with belief in God, they have judged the proposed theological solutions offered inadequate.

The argument itself proceeds as follows: God by definition is all-powerful, all knowing and all good. If God is all-powerful, He can prevent evil. If God is all knowing and can prevent evil, He knows how to prevent it. If God is all good, He would want to prevent evil. But since there is evil God cannot exist.

This argument has usually been construed as one in which the premises provide irrefutable reasons for accepting the conclusion. However, most critics of religion are now skeptical that a viable deductive argument can be constructed. The Deductive Argument from Evil maintains that the conjunction of the following statements is inconsistent:

1. God is all-powerful and all-knowing.
2. God is all good.
3. Evil exists.

If this inconsistency can be shown, then if evil exists, God cannot be all-good and all-powerful and all-knowing. However, God is by definition all good, all-powerful, and all-knowing. Hence, God does not exist.

Most philosophers now believe that there is good reason why the Deductive Argument from Evil fails: it is logically possible that evil can exist even if God exists *if* God has good moral reasons for allowing it. Suppose

4. God could only bring about some great good if He allowed evil or if He could prevent some greater evil only if He allowed some lesser evil.

If (4) were true, then God's existence would not conflict with the existence of evil. Thus, religious believers could admit that some evil *appears* pointless yet hold that this appearance is misleading. They could maintain that, in fact, there might be good reason for this evil.

Consider these two examples:

1. A fawn named Bambi is unable to escape from a forest fire and dies in horrible agony.
2. A 7-year-old girl named Sue is raped, tortured, and killed.

A believer in God might argue either that Bambi's and Sue's suffering and death were necessary in order to bring about some great good, or that if God had prevented Bambi's and Sue's suffering and deaths, He

would have allowed an even greater evil to occur. In other words, God could not have prevented their suffering and death without either sacrificing this good or allowing this greater evil. Thus God would have good reason for allowing these two evils and there would be no inconsistency between belief in God's existence and belief in the existence of evils like Bambi's and Sue's suffering and deaths.

Because of the failure of the Deductive Argument from Evil critics of religion have developed Evidential Arguments from Evil for the nonexistence of God. In these the conclusion that God does not exist is reasonable to hold in the light of the evidence, although not certain. It is helpful to distinguish two kinds of arguments. One kind proceeds directly from the existence of evil to the nonexistence of God whereas as the other is based on refutations of theories known as theodicies that attempt to vindicate God's goodness in the light of the problem of evil. In the remainder of this paper I will expound and defend these two versions of the Evidential Argument from Evil.

2. THE DIRECT EVIDENTIAL ARGUMENT FROM EVIL

Informally stated, the Direct Evidential Argument is this: In the light of our background knowledge—our evidence about good and evil, the way natural laws work in our world, what an omnipotent being is capable of doing and so on—it is sensible to conclude after careful examination that there is pointless evil in the world. This is so because there is no good reason in the light of our background knowledge to suppose that there is a great good or a greater evil that would justify allowing Bambi's and Sue's suffering and death. But then it is reasonable to conclude that God, a being who would not allow pointless evil, does not exist.

Stated more formally, the argument is this:

1. The suffering and death of Bambi and Sue appears to be pointless in that they do not appear necessary to achieve some great good or to prevent a greater evil. (Based on examination of the evidence.)
2. There is no good reason to suppose that this appearance is deceptive. (Based on our background information.)
3. The suffering and death of Bambi and Sue are pointless. (From (1) and (2) and the principle that

unless one has good reason to suppose evidence is deceptive one can reasonably assume it is not.)

4. If there is pointless suffering and death, then God does not exist. (By definition of pointless evil and the meaning of the theistic God.)

5. Therefore, God does not exist. (By deductive inference from [3] and [4].)

The inference from (3) and (4) to (5) is deductive and (5) is certain relative to (3) and (4). But from premises (1) and (2) one cannot deductively infer (3). (1) and (2) only strongly support (3), that is, it is reasonable to believe (3) on the basis of (1) and (2).

Let us now consider the justification of these premises. Premise (1) is certainly true for there *appears* to be no good reason for the suffering of Bambi and Sue and so it *appears* that these are two cases of pointless evil. Is Premise (2) true as well? Although the appearance of pointless evil may sometimes be misleading we have no good reason for supposing that it is so in these cases. Indeed, in the light of our background knowledge and the evidence, the way things appear does not seem misleading. Of course, if we had independent reason to believe that God exists, then we would have good grounds for thinking that no evil is really pointless. But no such independent reason exists. In fact, there are independent reasons for supposing that God does not exist.

The principle that permits the inference to (3) is reasonable. Not only do we rely on this constantly in our ordinary every day practices, it is hard to see how we could proceed without it. Suppose I am home alone at night and entertain the disturbing thought that there is man-eating tiger in my room and consequently that I should leave quickly. I carefully inspect my room and it seems that there is no tiger. I check the newspapers, the zoo, and the police, none of whom report an escaped tiger. I ask my neighbor who is an experienced tiger hunter to inspect my room. He can find no tiger. Given this principle and the fact that there is no good reason to suppose that appearances are deceptive, I can reasonably believe that there is no tiger in my room. If this principle were rejected it would not be reasonable to believe that there is no tiger present. Since countless other examples could be cited in which this premise is assumed, to reject this premise would result in wholesale skepticism: we would not be able to rely on how things appear in our everyday lives even though there is no reason to suppose that appearances are deceptive.

Premise (4) is also justified since if there was pointless evil then God could not be an all good, all powerful being. This is because an all good, all powerful being would by definition prevent the occurrence of any pointless evil.

3. OBJECTIONS TO THE ARGUMENT

One objection to the argument might be this. Suppose we believe that God exists. Surely in this case, it will be said, it will not seem that there is pointless evil even if we do not know what the point is. So Premise (1) is not justified for believers. But the fact that a person believes in God does not mean that Bambi's and Sue's suffering would not seem pointless. Their suffering would indeed *seem* pointless to believers although they would believe that it is not pointless. A religious believer would tend to discount the appearance and believe that the evil is not pointless despite it.

Another objection is that God's reasons for allowing Bambi's and Sue's suffering may be beyond human understanding. So the fact that just because evil appears to be pointless is no reason to believe that it is pointless. God may have reasons beyond our understanding that justify these two cases of evil. Thus, Premise (2) is not justified. However, one can grant that if God exists He *might* have reasons that are beyond our understanding for allowing Bambi's and Sue's suffering. But unless in fact we have good grounds to suppose that there are in fact such reasons, Premise (2) remains untouched. The bare possibility that there could be such reasons carries no weight. Consider an analogous case. Suppose that all known medical indicators make it seem that Bill is going to die in the next week. But it is possible that all medical indicators are misleading and that factors unknowable to medical science are present in Bill's illness that will result in his inexplicable recovery. It would still be reasonable to suppose that Bill will soon die. The mere possibility that there are such factors beyond scientific understanding has no bearing on this case.

"THE INDUCTIVE ARGUMENT FROM EVIL" ✳ *William Rowe*

1. There exist instances of intense suffering which an omnipotent, omniscient being could have prevented without thereby losing some greater good or permitting some equally bad or worse.
2. An omniscient, wholly good being would prevent the occurrence of any intense suffering it could, unless it could not so without thereby losing some greater good or permitting some evil equally bad or worse.
3. There does not exist an omnipotent, omniscient, wholly good being.

Suppose in some distant forest lightning strikes a dead tree, resulting in a forest fire. In the fire a fawn is trapped, horribly burned, and lies in terrible agony for several days before death relieves its suffering. So far as we can see, the fawn's intense suffering is pointless. For there does not appear to be any greater good such that the prevention of the fawn's suffering would require either the loss of that good or the occurrence of an evil equally bad or worse. Nor does there seem to be any equally bad or worse evil so connected to the fawn's suffering that it would have had to occur had the fawn's suffering been prevented. Could an omnipotent, omniscient being have prevented the fawn's apparently pointless suffering? The answer is obvious, as even the theist will insist. An omnipotent, omniscient being could have easily prevented the fawn from being horribly burned, or, given the burning, could have spared the fawn the intense suffering by quickly ending its life, rather than allowing the fawn to lie in terrible agony for several days. Since the fawn's intense suffering was preventable and, so far as we can see, pointless, doesn't it appear that premise (1) of the argument is true, that there do exist instances of intense suffering which an omnipotent, omniscient being could have prevented without thereby losing some greater good or permitting some evil equally bad or worse.

From William Rowe, "The Problem of Evil and Some Varieties of Atheism" *American Philosophical Quarterly* (1979).

Another objection is that there is no justification for accepting the principle that allows us to infer Premise (3). As it stands, it might be said that this principle is arbitrary. So the Evidential Argument from Evil fails. But we have already answered this objection. Since this principle is an assumption that we rely on in all our thinking and action, one whose rejection would result in wholesale skepticism and would paralyze our practical action, it is hardly arbitrary.

4. STRENGTHENING THE ARGUMENT

There are at least two other considerations that strengthen the Direct Evidential Argument from Evil. First, so far I have argued from cases like Bambi's and Sue's is that it is reasonable to suppose that God does not exist. But suppose these particular cases are not examples of pointless evil. This would hardly refute the Direct Evidential Argument from Evil for there are millions of other ones ranging from the Lisbon Earthquake to the Holocaust, from child molestation to AIDS, from severe birth defects to slavery. Religious apologists must show that it is not reasonable to believe that *any* of these are cases of pointless evil. Needless to say it seems unlikely that this could be done.

The second consideration is this. If God is supposed to be good and merciful, why would He not give His creatures some idea of why so much apparently pointless evil exists? If God has reasons for allowing seemingly pointless evils that are beyond His creatures' understanding, He could at least explain that there are reasons beyond His creatures' ken. However, He does not. God is silent. This silence is not only inexplicable but seems to conflict with His purposes. Surely, God wants His creatures to worship and love Him. Yet unexplained seemingly pointless evil is one of the greatest obstacles to these ends. God's silence is precisely what one would not expect if God exists.

5. THE INDIRECT EVIDENTIAL ARGUMENT FROM EVIL

In the Indirect Evidential Argument from Evil one argues not from the existence of apparently pointless evil to the reasonableness of belief in God's nonexistence but from the failure of known theodicies—attempts to vindicate God's goodness in the light of apparently pointless evil—to the reasonableness of belief in the nonexistence of God. The argument proceeds as follows. As we have seen, the following conjunction is not inconsistent:

1. God is all-powerful and all-knowing.
2. God is all good.
3. Evil exists.

This is because it is possible that

4. God allows evil in order to either bring about a great good or to prevent a greater evil.

But if it were reasonable to believe that (4) is false, then one would have good reason to suppose that the existence of evil is incompatible with the existence of God. And it is reasonable to believe that (4) is false since it is reasonable to believe that there are no successful theodicies.

Quite simply, given the fact that there is no positive evidence for the existence of God, it is reasonable to suppose that there are no successful theodicies because all *known* theodicies have failed. Unless we have good reason to suppose otherwise—for example, good reason to suppose that unknown theodicies would be successful—given centuries of failed attempts by the best minds to defend known theodicies, it is reasonable to believe that no theodicy is successful. Indeed, it is safe to say that despite centuries of effort no progress has been made in reconciling evil and God. So it is reasonable to suppose that (4) is false and, consequently, that God does not exist. This inference relies on the following principle: (Principle P) If evidence would falsify some hypothesis unless one makes an assumption and repeated attempts have failed to establish this assumption, and there is no independent reason to suppose that either this assumption is true or that if it is true it is beyond our powers to discover its truth and there is no positive evidence for this hypothesis, then one is rationally justified in assuming that this hypothesis is false.

More formally stated the Indirect Evidential Argument from Evil is this:

1. There is no positive evidence that God exists. (Based on previous refutations.[1])
2. The apparently pointless evil connected with the suffering and death of Bambi and Sue would falsify the existence of God unless one assumed that some theodicy successfully vindicates this suffering and death. (Based on the meaning of successful theodicy and pointless evil.)
3. Despite centuries of trying by the best philosophical minds no progress has been made in developing a theodicy that successfully vindicates the suffering and death of Bambi and Sue. (Based on examination of known theodicies.)
4. There is no independent reason to suppose that unknown successful theodicies exist or that if they do exist, they would be beyond our powers to discover. (Based on our background knowledge.)
5. No theodicy can successfully vindicate the suffering and death of Bambi and Sue. (Inductively inferred from [1], [2], [3], [4] and the Principle P.)
6. There is pointless evil. (From [5] by definition of unsuccessful theodicy.)
7. If there is pointless evil, then God does not exist. (By definition of pointless evil and the meaning of the theistic God.)
8. Therefore, God does not exist. (By deductive inference from [6] and [7].)

The inference from (6) and (7) to (8) is deductive and, given (6) and (7), (8), is certain. The inference from (5) to (6) is also deductive and, given (5) and (6), is certain. However, the inference from (1), (2), (3), and (4) to (5) is inductive. Consequently, (5) is not certain relative to (1), (2), (3), and (4) but merely well supported, that is, it is reasonable to believe (5) on the basis of (1), (2), (3), and (4).

It would be inconsistent to reject the inference from (1), (2), (3), and (4) to (5) and accept this mode of inference in everyday life and science. Consider the following hypothetical case to illustrate the use of this mode of inference in other contexts. Jones is dead and

[1]Michael Martin, *Atheism: A Philosophical Justification* (Temple University Press, 1990), Part 1.

some of his friends suspect foul play. The available evidence is strong against the foul play hypothesis unless the police were involved in a cover-up. However, Jones' friends who are very skillful and dedicated try without success to establish a cover-up theory. Furthermore, there is no independent evidence for the foul-play theory. Surely in this case the general evidential argument outlined above would constitute a strong argument for the falsity of the foul play theory. It is irrelevant that there *could* have been a cover-up. The question is: Was there one? Clearly this is an empirical issue and the failure to establish any cover-up after diligent and skillful effort does provide good, although not irrefutable, evidence that there is no cover-up. In addition, if there were good reason to believe the foul play or to believe that establishing this theory is beyond our powers, then we could not conclude that cover-up theory is false. But we have no reason to suppose this. Countless other examples of the same mode of inference can be found in everyday life and science.

6. OBJECTIONS TO THE ARGUMENT

It may be objected that some known theodicies are successful, hence Premise (3) of the argument is not true. However, as I have argued in detail elsewhere, all of the known major and the important minor theodicies fail.[2] Later on in this article I will critically consider two major theodicies in order to illustrate their problems.

It may also be objected that Principle P used to infer (5) seems arbitrary. Why should we suppose that it is justified? The basic reason is that this principle is widely accepted whether the things under investigation are bats, baboons, beans, babies, or bellows and its acceptance partially defines what we mean by rationality. It would be inconsistent to accept it in general but not with respect to theodicies.

One might object to Premise (4) on the grounds that God has reasons for allowing seemingly pointless evil that are not taken into account by any known theodicies and indeed that are beyond our ken. In response one can admit that this

might be true but insist that we have no good reasons to suppose that it is. Until we have some we are justified in supposing that any unknown theodicy would be no more successful in justifying evil than those provided in known theodicies and that if there were a successful theodicy, diligent effort would have discovered it. To be sure, if we had independent reason to suppose that God exists, perhaps a different belief would be justified. But we do not have such.[3]

7. TWO IMPORTANT THEODICIES

As we have seen, the Indirect Argument from Evil assumes that all known theodicies fail. Although it is impossible to examine all of them here, I will sketch in some of the problems belonging to the two leading theodicies.

The Free Will Defense

Perhaps the most widely used theodicy is that evil is not to be blamed on God but is the result of the misuse by human beings of their free will. Moreover, the defense assumes that this misuse is worth the price since free will is of enormous value. This Free Will Defense has several serious problems.

First of all, at most this theodicy provides an explanation of moral evil; that is, evil deliberately brought about by human beings. For example, it might be argued that Sue's rapist is responsible for her suffering and death and not God. But this theodicy does not explain natural evil; that is, the evil brought about by natural events such as tidal waves, hurricanes, and birth defects. Thus, if the forest fire causing Bambi's suffering and death was started by lightening, the Free Will Defense would not apply to Bambi's suffering and death.

The second problem is that the Free Will Defense presupposes a particular view of human freedom that we have no reason to believe is true. If freedom is compatible with human decisions being caused by events in our brains or nervous systems, then an all powerful God could have created people who never

[2]*Atheism*, Chapters 14–18. See also Theodore M. Drange, *Evil and Nonbelief* (Prometheus Books, 1998).

[3]*Atheism*, Part 1.

"THE ABDUCTIVE ARGUMENT FROM EVIL" ＊ *Paul Draper*

A question that David Hume asked (1980, Part XI, pp. 74–75) but that most contemporary philosophers of religion have ignored, is whether or not any serious hypothesis that is logically inconsistent with theism explains some significant set of facts about evil or about good and evil much better than theism does.

I will argue for an affirmative answer to this question. Specifically, I will compare theism to the following alternative, which I will call "the Hypothesis of Indifference" ("HI" for short):

HI: neither the nature nor the condition of sentient beings on earth is the result of benevolent or malevolent actions performed by nonhuman persons.

Unlike theism, HI does not entail that supernatural beings exist and so is consistent with naturalism. But HI is also consistent with the existence of supernatural beings. What makes HI inconsistent with theism is that it entails that, if supernatural beings do exist, then no action performed by them is motivated by a direct concern for our well-being. Now let "0" stand for a statement reporting both the observations one has made of humans and animals experiencing pain or pleasure and the testimony one has encountered concerning the observations others have made of sentient beings experiencing pain or pleasure. By "pain" I mean physical or mental suffering of any sort. I will argue that the pain and pleasure in our world create an epistemic problem for theists by arguing that:

C: HI explains the facts . . . [of evil] . . . much better than theism does.

One problem with this formulation of C is that the verb "to explain" has a number of distinct but easily confused meanings. For my purposes here, it will suffice to point out that in some instances the claim that one hypothesis explains some observation report much better than another is equivalent in meaning, or at least bears a close conceptual connection, to the claim that the truth of that observation report is much less surprising on the first hypothesis than it is on the second.

From Paul Draper, "Pain and Pleasure:
An Evidential Problem for Theists," *Nous* (1989).

freely choose to do wrong. The Free Will Defense must assume that human decisions are *not* caused by any events in our brains or nervous systems. However, as neuroscience develops there is more and more reason to suppose that human decisions are caused in this way.

The third problem is that God could have created human beings with a tendency to do good. Given this tendency people would produce less evil than they do now.

The fourth problem is that God could have produced human beings who are less vulnerable to physical attack than they in fact are; for example, children who when attacked have great strength. This ability would make it less likely that Sue would be attacked or, if attacked, harmed.

The fifth problem is that God could have created natural laws that would have made it difficult for human beings to inflict harm on one another. For example, there could be laws that tend to bring about heart attacks in rapists while they are attempting rape.

The sixth problem is that the Free Will Defense assumes that the exercise of free will is worth the price of millions of deaths and untold suffering. This is a doubtful assumption.

The seventh problem is that although God is not directly responsible for evil according to the Free Will Defense, He is indirectly responsible. Presumably He has knowledge of the future. Given this foreknowledge God knew that His creatures would misuse their free will and yet He created human beings. If He did not have foreknowledge, He at least knew that this misuse was possible and took no safeguards to prevent it. In the first case God was reckless. In the other He was negligent.

The Soul-Making Defense

Next in importance to the Free Will Defense against the Argument from Evil is the Soul-Making Defense. The basic idea of this defense can be stated very simply. In creating the world God did not make a paradise but rather a place to make souls. Rational agents freely choose to develop certain valuable moral traits of character and to know and to love God. In order to develop moral and spiritual character there must be a struggle and obstacles to overcome. In a world without suffering, natural calamities, disease, and the like there would be no obstacles and no struggle, consequently there would be no soul making. This account thus explains both moral and natural evil. Since soul-making is of unsurpassed value, its value outweighs any moral or natural evil that results from or is a necessary means to it. Thus the Soul-Making Defense purports to justify both moral and natural evil.

However, there are decisive objections against this theodicy. First, given our present laws of nature, one might agree that in a world free of pain and suffering it would be hard to develop moral character. However, it is important to remember that an all powerful God could have created a different world with different laws of nature. It seems plausible to suppose that in some world God might have created the moral character of human beings could be developed without pain and suffering.

Second, although the Soul-Making Defense purports to justify both moral and natural evil, it does not. Natural evil is redundant. There are plenty of evils to develop character without there also being floods, disease, and other natural evils. Since the moral evil brought about by human beings provides abundant material for soul making, natural evil is unnecessary.

Third, in many cases the great amount of evil there is hinders or even completely prevents moral development. In cases of abuse, for example, extreme hardship and suffering do not so much further development of moral character as crush it. In some cases, evil may prevent moral development entirely.

Fourth, in many cases it hard to see how the evil involved could possibly be relevant to moral development. Let us assume that Bambi's suffering and death was unknown to any human being. How then could it possibly be relevant to *human* moral development?

8. THE EVIDENTIAL PROBLEM OF EVIL AND ATHEISM

In this paper I have shown that the Evidential Problem of Evil is one argument for the view that God does not exist. However, this argument is just one aspect of the overall case for atheism. Atheists must show that the Cosmological, Teleological, Ontological Arguments for the existence of God also fail[4] and also endeavor to show that God cannot exist because the concept of God is inconsistent.[5]

QUESTIONS FOR FURTHER REFLECTION

1. Interview a friend, relative, or roommate who believes in God and find out how he or she explains the problem of evil. What are the problems, if any, with his or her explanation?
2. How might a religious believer respond to Martin's criticisms of the Free Will Defense? What might a nonbeliever say to this response?
3. How might a religious believer respond to Martin's criticisms of the Soul-Making Defense? What might a nonbeliever say to this response?
4. Discuss the following argument:
"The fact of evil—suffering and death—is no real problem for Christianity since although people suffer for a brief time in this life and die, they will have eternal bliss and everlasting life in Heaven."
5. Discuss the following argument:
"There is a problem of evil only if evil is real. But evil is an illusion. Once we realize this we will see that really there is no evil and hence there is no problem."

[4]*Atheism*, Part 1.
[5]*Atheism*, Chapter 12.

40. INDUCTION, ABDUCTION, AND THE ARGUMENT FROM EVIL

Christopher Bernard

Christopher Bernard is a graduate student and lecturer at the University of Maryland—College Park. He has a B.A. in philosophy from the University of Minnesota, an M.A. in New Testament from Luther Seminary, and an M.A. in philosophy from the University of Maryland. He was awarded the Distinguished Teaching Assistant Award from the University of Maryland Center for Teaching Excellence. Currently he is pursuing his Ph.D.

READING QUESTIONS

1. What are the three ways or frameworks to describe the argument from evil?
2. What two general kinds of evil are there?
3. What three general types of inference are there?
4. What is a noseeum inference?
5. How might nonpropositional evidence mitigate against the evidential argument from evil?

1. INTRODUCTION

Writing of the hanging of two adults and a child that he witnessed while in a Nazi death camp, holocaust survivor Elie Wiesel relates that the two adults died quickly. The child, on the other hand, took longer: "For more than a half an hour he stayed there, struggling between life and death, dying slowly in agony under our eyes. And we had to look him full in the face. He was still alive when I passed in front of him. His tongue was still red, his eyes were not yet glazed. Behind me, I heard the same man asking: 'Where is God now' " (Wiesel 1992, p.86).

Incidents like this provide the impetus for the most pervasive argument against the existence of God—the argument from evil.[1] It is most often phrased in the form of a question. Why would a perfectly loving, all-powerful, all-knowing God permit the suffering we see all around us? The Scottish philosopher David Hume wrote:

> Epicurus' old questions are yet unanswered. Is he willing to prevent evil, but not able? then he is impotent. Is he able but not willing? then he is malevolent. Is he both able and willing? whence then is evil (Hume 1989, p.84)?[2]

This kind of question is so compelling that, as novelist Peter De Vries puts it, the question mark turns like a fishhook in the human heart (qtd. in Yancey 1990, p.20).

It is a bit misleading, though, to speak of *the* argument from evil. There is not just one argument from evil. What philosophers call "the argument from evil" is really a family of related arguments. In this paper, I shall focus my criticism on evidential forms of the argument. I shall argue that two popular evidential versions of the argument, the inductive and abductive, fail to establish that God does not exist.

---

[1] The word "evil" has several meanings and this is sometimes a source of confusion. Some see how people, like Adolph Hitler, are evil but they don't see how natural events, like an earthquake, is evil. Natural events, like earthquakes, seem to be morally neutral. To avoid this confusion, it is important to understand that philosophers are mainly concerned with the evil of *suffering*. Both persons, like Hitler, and natural events, like earthquakes, seem to be evidence that God does not exist because a completely good, all-powerful God, if he existed, could and should prevent it. The problem really is, in the words of Christian thinker C. S. Lewis, "the problem of pain."

[2] This quote is from a dialogue Hume wrote between three people: Philo, Cleanthes, and Demea. These are the words of Philo, who is widely regarded as representing Hume's position.

First, I shall map out a rough geography of the problem of evil and briefly explain why the logical version of the argument is unpersuasive. Then, I shall set out and criticize the inductive and abductive forms of the evidential argument respectively.

2. THE GEOGRAPHY OF THE ARGUMENT FROM EVIL

The Logical/Evidential Description

Philosophers have described the geography of the problem of evil in at least three different ways. Understanding the different ways to categorize the argument from evil will make the exact nature of the argument clearer.

The first, and most common, way to organize this family of arguments is to divide them into two categories—logical and evidential. According to the logical argument, the existence of evil is logically inconsistent with the existence of God. J. L. Mackie, for instance, writes that the problem of evil "is a logical problem . . . there seems to be some contradiction" (Mackie 1992, p.89).

Traditionally, theists have believed the following five propositions. Let's call this set of propositions the "set of essential theistic beliefs."

Set of essential theistic beliefs:
1. God exists.
2. God is omnipotent.
3. God is omnibenevolent.
4. God is omniscient.
5. Evil exists.

According to advocates of the logical argument from evil, not all of the propositions in the set of essential theistic beliefs can be true. If God were all-powerful, he could destroy evil. If he were all-good he would want to destroy evil. Since evil exists, either God is not all-powerful or he is not all-good, or he just does not exist. As H. J. McCloskey puts it:

> Evil is a problem for the theist in that a contradiction is involved in the fact of evil on the one hand, and the belief in the omnipotence and perfection of God on the other. God cannot be both all-powerful and perfectly good if evil is real (McCloskey 1997, p.203).

Thus, it appears that the set of essential theistic beliefs is a logically inconsistent set. The first four propositions in the set are essential elements of classical theism. If anyone of them is false, then classical theism is false. The fifth proposition, though not essential to a more austere version of theism, is essential to traditional theistic religions like Judaism, Christianity, and Islam and is hardly deniable. So, to remain consistent, it looks like the theist has to either give up his belief in God or has to give up his belief that there is suffering in the world.

Another way to understand this is by introducing the notions of logical impossibility, possibility, and necessity. Something is logically impossible if it involves a contradiction. It is logically impossible, for example, for a physical object to be both a square and a circle. What it means for something to be a square is logically incompatible with what it means for something to be a circle. Something is logically possible if it does not involve a contradiction. It is logically possible that Al Gore won the 2000 presidential election, even though he lost. Something is logically necessary if it *has* to be true as a matter of logic. It is logically necessary that a bachelor is a male. If someone is not a male, then that person is not a bachelor. Put in these terms, Mackie and McCloskey are arguing that claiming that God and evil both exist is logically impossible. It is akin to saying that a certain object is both a square and a circle.

The evidential argument, by contrast, contends that although the existence of evil is logically consistent with the existence of God, it is, nonetheless, strong evidence against it. It is logically possible for those five key propositions to be true, but, according to advocates of the evidential argument, it is unlikely.

The A *Priori*/Empirical Description

There are two other ways to classify arguments from evil. The arguments can be categorized as either *a priori* or empirical. *A priori* knowledge is knowledge that is justified prior to and independent of experience. It is sometimes referred to as "armchair knowledge" because it can be justified without the need to get up from one's armchair to inspect the world. Arithmetic, for instance, is often cited as an example of *a priori* knowledge because one can know that $1 + 1 = 2$ by reason alone. One need not look around the world to know it is true. One doesn't need to do an experiment to confirm it. In fact, we would think it bizarre if some mathematician told us he discovered $1 + 1 = 2$ by putting one apple on a table and then later putting another apple on the same table and then noticing that he had two apples.

Empirical knowledge, by contrast, is gained through experience. Science is empirical. Scientists gain knowledge by going out into the field or into a lab and making observations about the actual world. Marine biologists acquire knowledge about dolphins by studying dolphins in the ocean or in a tank. Unlike the mathematician, the marine biologist cannot study his subject matter from his armchair.

The logical argument from evil is an *a priori* argument because it does not depend upon empirical inspection of the world to establish the truth of the conclusion. According to the logical argument, the five propositions that comprise the set of essential theistic beliefs cannot all be true because they are inconsistent. If this is true, we can know it by reasoning from the comfort of our armchair. We do not need to do experiments and make observations of actual squares and circles to know that something cannot be a square circle and we don't need to observe the world to see that God and evil cannot both exist. The evidential argument,

by contrast, *is* empirical. According to the evidential argument, it is only upon inspecting the world that we see that much of the pain and suffering is pointless and hence unjustified.

The Inference Description: Deduction, Induction, and Abduction

The last way to categorize the argument from evil is in terms of the form of inference the argument takes. According to philosophers, there are three basic types of argument or inference: deduction, induction, and abduction. The logical argument is often referred to as the deductive argument from evil. The evidential argument can be further divided into two kinds, corresponding to the two types of empirical inference—induction and abduction. I shall say more about the various types of inferences and their relation to the argument from evil as the paper unfolds.

In summation, the argument from evil can be divided into roughly two types. One form is deductive, *a priori*, and claims a logical inconsistency in the set of essential theistic beliefs. The other form is inductive or abductive, empirical, and claims that evil is evidence which makes the existence of God unlikely. The geography of the argument from evil can be mapped thus:

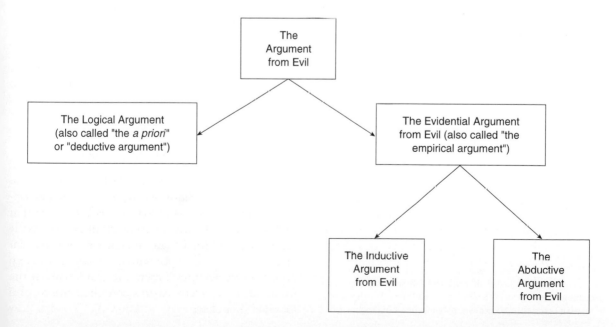

The Demise of the Deductive Argument

For the logical argument to be successful, it has to be logically impossible for God to have a morally sufficient reason to permit evil. Alvin Plantinga, however, is widely regarded as having shown that God *could* have a good reason to allow suffering. He calls this possibility the "Free Will Defense." According to the Free Will Defense, it is logically possible that:

> A world containing creatures who are significantly free (and freely perform more good than evil actions) is more valuable, all else being equal, than a world containing no free creatures at all (Plantinga 1977, p. 30).[3]

Plantinga's work has shifted attention from the logical argument from evil to the evidential argument. The atheist philosopher William Rowe writes:

> Some philosophers have contended that the existence of evil is *logically inconsistent* with the existence of the theistic God. No one, I think, has succeeded in establishing such an extravagant claim. Indeed, granted incompatibilism,[4] there is a fairly compelling argument for the view that the existence of evil is logically consistent with the existence of God . . . there remains, however, what we may call the *evidential* form—as opposed to the *logical* form—of the problem of evil (Rowe 1996, p.10).

Paul Draper, also an atheist, agrees "with most philosophers of religion that theists face no serious logical problem of evil" (Draper 1996, p. 26). Rather than argue that it is a necessary truth that God has no morally justified reason for permitting evil and that we can know this *a priori*, they argue it is a contingent truth that can be established empirically.

3. THE INDUCTIVE ARGUMENT FROM EVIL

Earlier I mentioned that philosophers distinguish between three general types of inference: deduction, induction, and abduction, and that for each type of inference there is a corresponding form of the problem of evil. In the last section, I briefly explained the deductive or logical argument from evil and Plantinga's critique of it. In this section, I shall lay out and criticize the inductive argument.

Induction

In a sound deductive argument, the conclusion is implicitly contained in the premises. *Induction*, by contrast, is a form of inference in which the conclusion goes beyond the premises. It is sometimes referred to as an "ampliative" inference because the conclusion amplifies and expands the premises.

Inductive reasoning is reasoning of the following sort: if a large number of A's have been observed and found to possess the property B, without exception, under a wide variety of conditions, then we can infer that all A's possess the property B. Consider the following example. Suppose I didn't know much about ravens and that I decided to start observing them. Suppose further that I see a raven and notice that it is black. I write this observation down in my notepad of observations and continue. I see another raven and notice that it is also black. I continue to see ravens and every one I see is black. Later, when I review my notebook, I notice that every raven I saw was black and I conclude that all ravens are black:

Observations of Ravens:
Observation 1. Raven$_1$ is black.
Observation 2. Raven$_2$ is black.
Observation 3. Raven$_3$ is black.
Observation 4. Raven$_4$ is black.
Observation n. Raven$_n$ is black.
Therefore: all Ravens are black.

Every observed A, in this case a raven, has the property B, the property of being black. So, I infer that all A's are B, or, that all ravens are black.

Inductive inferences consist in taking a description of some sample and extending that description to things outside the sample. In the case of the ravens, I generalized from observations of particular ravens to a universal conclusion about all ravens, even unobserved ones. I drew a conclusion about the whole class of ravens based upon observations of a subset of that class:

---

[3]For details see Plantinga's argument in chapter 38 of this book.
[4]Incompatibilism is the view that free will and determinism are not compatible. Some determinists are incompatibilists but the term is often, as in this case, used as a synonym for (libertarian) "free will."

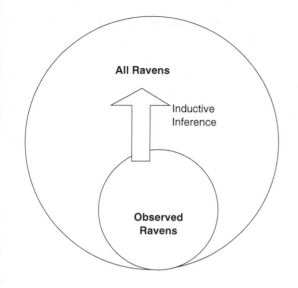

Not all inductive arguments are good ones. A good inductive argument has two qualities. First, it must be drawn from a representative sample. Suppose I wanted to determine what percentage of Americans are Republicans. If I had the resources, I would commission a poll. The pollsters would call a small subset of Americans, usually less than 1000 people, and ask them what their party affiliation is.

We would generalize from the small subset of Americans we polled to the set of all Americans only if we thought that sample was representative of the whole. If, by some accident, everyone polled lived in New York City and the results showed only 10 percent of those polled are Republican, we could not properly infer that only 10 percent of Americans are Republican. With respect to party affiliation, New York is not a snapshot of America. There are five times more registered Democrats than Republicans in New York City. Thus, the political views of people who live in New York City are not representative of the country as a whole and any poll based on that sample would be skewed.

Second, a good inductive inference must be based on a large sample size. If we took the same poll above but only called one person, who said he was a Republican, we could not properly conclude that 100 percent of Americans are Republican. We don't have a large enough sample size to make a proper inference.

Induction differs from deduction in another important way. If a deductive argument is sound, the conclusion *must* be true. The conclusion of a good inductive argument, on the other hand, is only probably true. Recall the induction about ravens. Since we have not seen every raven it is possible that there is a raven, which we have not yet come across, that is not black. It is *unlikely*, given all our observations about ravens, but not impossible.

The Inductive Argument from Evil

In "The Problem of Evil and Some Varieties of Atheism," William Rowe sets out the inductive version of the argument from evil. Rowe's argument comes in two phases. The first stage is deductive, the second is inductive. The deductive portion of Rowe's argument can be simplified as follows:

Premise 1. There is some morally unjustified, or pointless, suffering.
Premise 2. If God exists, there would be no morally unjustified, or pointless, suffering.
Conclusion: Therefore, God does not exist.

This argument is logically valid. If both premises are true, the conclusion has to be true. Premise 2 is true. If God permits evil that serves no purpose and is completely pointless, he is not completely good and, hence, not the God of traditional theism. So, whether Rowe's argument is successful or not depends on the truth of Premise 1.

Rowe gives several closely related arguments in support of premise 1. I will focus on two. Both revolve around the following case:

> Suppose in some distant forest lightning strikes a dead tree, resulting in a forest fire. In the fire a fawn is trapped, horribly burned, and lies in terrible agony for several days before death relieves its suffering. So far as we can see, the fawn's intense suffering is pointless. For there does not appear to be any greater good such that the prevention of the fawn's suffering would require either the loss of that good or the occurrence of an evil equally bad or worse (Rowe 1996, p.4).

If this is a case of pointless suffering, then Rowe's argument goes through.

Rowe's first argument for premise 1 involves a type of deductive inference that logicians call "existential generalization." Existential generalization is any inference of the form x has property F; therefore at least one thing has the property F. This type of inference is clearly valid. If my car is red, then there is at least one thing that is red. Rowe's argument is that the suffering of the fawn is pointless, so there is at least one instance of suffering that is pointless and if there is one case of pointless suffering, then premise 1 is true.

Rowe's second argument is inductive. For an instance of suffering to *not* be pointless there would have to be some greater good that justifies it. During the Civil War, for example, when there was no anesthesia, the suffering caused by a surgeon amputating a leg was morally justified because if the leg was not amputated the soldier would most likely die from gangrene. The greater good of surviving an infection outweighs the suffering caused by amputation.

Rowe argues inductively for premise 1 by arguing that there is no greater good that justifies the kind of horrible suffering experienced by the fawn burned in the forest fire:

> . . . we are justified in making this inference in the same way we are justified in making the many inferences we constantly make from the known to the unknown. All of us are constantly inferring from the A's we know of to the A's we don't know of. If we observe many A's and all of them are B's we are justified in believing that the A's we haven't seen are also B's (Rowe 1988, pp. 123–124).

Rowe's inductive argument looks something like this:

Observations of Goods:
Observation 1. Good$_1$ does not justify the kind of suffering experienced by the fawn.
Observation 2. Good$_2$ does not justify the kind of suffering experienced by the fawn.
Observation 3. Good$_3$ does not justify the kind of suffering experienced by the fawn.
Observation 4. Good$_4$ does not justify the kind of suffering experienced by the fawn.
Observation n. Good$_n$ does not justify the kind of suffering experienced by the fawn.
Therefore: no good justifies the kind of suffering experienced by the fawn.

Critique of the Inductive Argument from Evil

Rowe's inductive argument from evil tries to establish empirically what the defender of the logical argument could not establish *a priori*, namely, that God has no morally sufficient reason to permit suffering. The theist has two general strategies he can employ to counter the inductive argument from evil—theodicy and defense. The term "theodicy" was first coined by the German philosopher Gottfried Leibniz and comes from the Greek words for "God" and "justification." John Milton described a theodicy as an attempt to "justify the ways of God to man." A theodicy is any response to the problem of evil that purports to tell us *why* God permits evil. A defense is any response to the problem of evil that *does not* try to tell us why God permits evil.

If the theist gives a theodicy, he is maintaining that God does, in fact, have a good reason to permit evil and that reason is spelled out by a theodicy. If the theist gives a defense, he is contending that even though he doesn't know why God permits evil, the empirical argument to establish that there is pointless suffering, fails.

Theodicy Theodicies can be divided into two types—local and global. A local theodicy is meant to explain why God permits *some* evil. A global theodicy is intended to justify God's permitting all evil. In what follows, I will briefly explain four local theodicies and five global theodicies and let the reader decide whether they serve as sufficient reason for God to permit evil.

In the biblical book of Job, we read of the sufferings of a man by the same name. Job loses his entire family, all his property, and comes down with a painful disease. His friends come to console him and one of them, Eliphaz, tries to explain Job's suffering as punishment for sin:

> Consider now: Who, being innocent, has ever perished? Where were the upright ever destroyed? As I have observed, those who plow evil and those who sow trouble reap it. At the breath of God, they are destroyed; at the blast of his anger, they are destroyed (Job 4:7–9 NIV).

Like Eliphaz, many theists believe that God is justified in permitting suffering as a punishment for sin. There are two versions of the punishment theodicy. According to the first version it is just to permit Adolph Hitler and Joseph Stalin to suffer because they are such evil people.

The main criticism of this version of the theodicy is that so many innocents suffer. Eliphaz's question "who, being innocent, has ever perished" has an obvious answer: infants and young children. Surely, a baby born addicted to crack did nothing worthy of punishment. If suffering is punishment for sin, it should be distributed proportionately to the sinfulness of the sufferer but this is not the case. Many basically good people seem to suffer far more than many evil people. Rabbis at Auschwitz suffered more than Hitler. The people of Afghanistan do not seem more sinful than the people of Switzerland but Afghanis have suffered far more in the twentieth century than the Swiss.

The punishment theodicy also comes in a second form according to which disease, physical hardship, natural disasters, and death entered the world as a result of the sin of the first humans. This theodicy depends upon a particular view of the Bible and the history of humankind. If someone doesn't take the biblical account of the fall of man seriously, they will not find this theodicy very plausible. This version of the punishment theodicy also suffers from some of the same problems of the first version.

A second theodicy is the counterpart theodicy. According to this theodicy, good and evil are metaphysical compliments or counterparts. One cannot exist without the other. God is justified in permitting evil because without evil there could be no good. One criticism of this theodicy is that it limits God's power. Even God cannot create good without creating evil. Second, it assumes that if two properties are opposites, then one cannot exist unless the other does. This assumption is false. There are many properties that are instantiated in the world while their corresponding compliment is not. Consider the property of being a non-unicorn. Everything in the world has that property. Surely this does not mean that its opposite, the property of being a unicorn must exist?

A third local theodicy is the contrast theodicy. This theodicy is closely related to the previous one. According to this theodicy, evil is an important contrast with good. We would not know what good was if there were no evil. The contrast theodicy makes a claim about *knowledge* while the counterpart theodicy makes a claim about the *world*. Critics have pointed out two problems with this theodicy. First, even if the contrast theodicy is right, we don't need *so much* evil to understand goodness. Second, Michael Martin contends that we could learn about evil without there actually being evil. We could learn about evil from novels, movies, and art (Martin 1990, p. 450).

A fourth theodicy is the natural law theodicy. According to this theodicy God created the world to work according to natural laws and rules. Much suffering, like drowning or falling from a cliff, is the result of the laws of nature. These physical laws create the possibility of natural evil but we need regular and systematic natural laws to farm, plan ahead, build, and invent. The same water that quenches thirst can also drown. Detractors of this theodicy point out that an all-powerful God could make regular natural laws that do not result in suffering. Further, they contend that even with natural laws that have the potential to inflict suffering, God could intervene to prevent *some* suffering without rendering the laws of nature so unpredictable that we could not survive and thrive in our environment.

Some critics of these four theodicies point out that even if we grant that they explain and justify some suffering, they don't explain all suffering. This objection, however, is misguided. Local theodicies are only intended to explain some cases of suffering. The punishment theodicy, for example, cannot explain why infants suffer but it can explain why Stalin suffered. The natural law theodicy cannot explain why people murder each other but perhaps it can explain why people drown in swimming pools. Surely this is something.

Theists have also offered several global theodicies.[5] The most popular global theodicy is the free will theodicy. According to the free will theodicy, a world with free will is better than a world without free

---

[5]Two global theodicies I don't discuss are the process theodicy and the protest theodicy. I don't discuss them because I am not convinced they are theodicies. Oversimplifying things a bit, the process theodicy says that God is not all powerful and the protest theodicy says he is not all good. While these replies might explain suffering, they do so by conceding that the God of traditional theism does not exist.

will. But free will requires the possibility of doing morally wrong acts.[6] Suffering is the result of people abusing their free will. God is morally justified in permitting suffering because free will is so valuable. The main objection to the free will theodicy is that God should be able to create a world where people have free will and always freely choose the good.

This assumes, however, that if God is omnipotent he can do anything he pleases. Theists have traditionally understood God's omnipotence to mean that God can do anything logically possible, not anything whatsoever. Omnipotence means that God's power is unlimited. Some limits, though, are not imposed by a lack of power. Even God, for example, cannot make a square circle because that involves a contradiction. I cannot squat 500 pounds, but if I had more strength I could. In principle, I could incrementally add strength until I was able to squat that much weight. Could I, even in principle, increase my knowledge and drawing ability to the point where I could draw a square circle? It doesn't seem so. My inability to draw a square circle has nothing to do with my lack of intelligence, artistic ability, or power. The same is true of God. His inability to make a square circle has nothing to do with a lack of power. It is not the case that if God had just a little more power he could create a square circle.

Likewise, God can create people with free will or he can create people who always choose the good. He cannot create people with free will and then guarantee that they always choose to do good. Anything that God did to assure that they always choose to do good would violate their free will. The best he can do is create people with free will and hope they always choose to do good.[7]

Another objection to the free will theodicy is that at best it explains moral evil but not natural evil. Theists have offered two ways of understanding the free will theodicy so that it can also account for natural evil. Some have suggested that it is possible that all natural evil is caused by demons. If this is true, then all natural evil is just a type of moral evil and the free will defense explains moral evil nicely. Others, like Richard

Swinburne, argue that to truly have the freedom to bring about evil or good we would have to have knowledge of how to bring about evil. We gain such knowledge, he thinks, by observing natural evil. He also maintains that natural evil creates additional opportunities for making moral choices. Cancer provides us with the opportunity to help a person suffering from cancer (Swinburne 1996, pp. 107–109).

A second global theodicy is John Hick's soul-making theodicy (Hick 1977). Hick thinks that God allows evil in order to promote moral and spiritual maturity. God wants us to develop character traits that suit us for a relationship with Him and others. We develop such character by making free choices in challenging situations. The world we inhabit is an environment designed to promote God's plan of soul-making. God permits evil in that environment because a world without suffering would not be conducive to spiritual growth.

Third, some theists, like Gottfried Leibniz, argue that this is the best of all possible worlds. God could not have created a better world than the actual world because there is no better world. Among other criticisms, many seriously doubt that the world we live in is the best God could have created.

Fourth, the great North African bishop Augustine offered a theodicy in which he maintained that evil isn't really a "thing" but rather a lack of a thing. According to the Augustinian theodicy, evil is a privation. It is similar to blindness. Blindness isn't a thing. It is the absence of something, namely, the ability to see. He thinks goodness is a thing but evil is just the lack of goodness. This theodicy, and the version of the problem of evil it addresses, assumes a Neo-Platonic view of the world that almost no philosopher today accepts.

The last theodicy we will consider is the disjunctive theodicy. According to the disjunctive theodicy, there is no one reason why God permits evil. A realistic theodicy should link partially successful theodicies together with the disjunction "or." So, when Rowe asks why God allows the fawn to suffer, the advocate of the disjunctive theodicy says "it is either as punishment for sin, or to provide a contrast with good, or because regular natural laws are necessary and they permit forest fires, or because of the free will of men or demons, or to provide an environment for soul-making, or . . ."

---

[6]The sense of "free will" here is metaphysical libertarian freedom.
[7]For more on this see Plantinga (1977) and Mavrodes, G. (1963). "Some Puzzles Concerning Omnipotence." *Philosophical Review* 72: 221–223.

Defense Suppose that none of the theodicies we have reviewed provide a good reason for God's permitting evil. The theist is not without recourse. He can attempt to undermine Rowe's argument without saying why God allows evil. It is possible that God has good reason to permit suffering but we don't know what those reasons are.

Recall that Rowe offered two very closely related arguments in defense of the first premise of the deductive portion of his argument. First, he argues that the suffering of the fawn is pointless, so there is at least one case of pointlessness. Second, he argues inductively that no observed good justified the kind of suffering experienced by the fawn, so no good does. I will limit my comments to one criticism.

Rowe's arguments depend on an inference of the follow sort: it appears that ~P, therefore ~P. He argues that it *appears* that there is no good reason to let the fawn suffer, therefore there *is* no good reason to let the fawn suffer. Stephen Wykstra calls this type of inference a "noseeum inference" (pronounced, noh-see-um) because it moves from the fact that we "no see" P to the fact that there is no P (Wykstra 1996). Sometimes noseeum inferences are legitimate and sometimes they are not. To determine whether Rowe's noseeum inference is a good one, we need to determine under what conditions noseeum inferences can properly be made and whether his inference meets those conditions.

Suppose you walked into a classroom and the professor told you that for all he knows there could be a flea egg in the classroom. You are not allowed to with a magnifying glass search the room by crawling around on your knees. You can only look around the room from your desk. Looking around the room, you do not see a flea egg. Clearly, you cannot legitimately infer that there is not a flea egg in the room because you don't see one. It would be a mistake to make a noseeum inference in this case.

Now suppose you walk into a classroom and the professor informs you that there is a normal sized adult elephant in the room. You look around and you do not see an elephant. In this case, it looks like one can legitimately make a noseeum inference. The fact that you cannot see the elephant is reason to infer that there is no elephant.

What is the difference between the two cases? In the second case, if there were an elephant in the room we are in a position to know it. We would see the elephant if he were there. Because we do not see an elephant, we are entitled to conclude that there is no elephant in the room. In the first case, however, if there were a flea egg in the room we would not be in a position to see it. We cannot tell just by casually glancing around the room that it lacks flea eggs. These cases show us that inferences from "it appears that ~P" to "~P" are good only when it is reasonable to believe that we would see P, if P were true.

We need to determine, then, whether God's reasons for permitting evil, if he exists and has any, are more like the elephant or the flea egg. If they are more like the case of the elephant and we would expect to know what they were, then Rowe's noseeum inference is a good one. If it is more like the case of the flea egg, then it is not.

Rowe has not provided any reason to think that if God has good reason to permit evil, we would be the first to know them. So, at best, his argument is incomplete. Alternatively, we do seem to have reason to think that if God did have good reasons for permitting evil, we would probably not know them. Consider one such reason.

Given the enormous difference between how much we know and how much God knows, it seems unlikely that we would know his reasons for permitting evil. God, if he exists, knows *everything*. What percent of *everything* do we know? Not much. Suppose the relationship between God's knowledge and our knowledge can be represented like this:

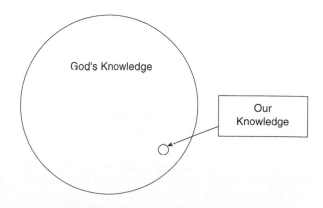

God knows everything we know and we know very little of what he knows.

Now suppose that the greater good that justifies God permitting evil is somewhere in the circle of God's knowledge.[8] What is the likelihood that it is also in our little sphere of knowledge? To make an estimate, assume the drawing above represents a dartboard. If you randomly threw a dart at the dartboard and it hit the board, how likely is it that it would hit inside the smaller circle? It isn't very likely. Stephan Wykstra writes:

> . . . the outweighing good at issue is of a special sort: one proposed by the Creator of all that is, whose vision and wisdom are therefore somewhat greater than ours. How much greater? A modest proposal might be that his wisdom is to ours, roughly as an adult human's is to a one-month-old infant's . . . that we should discern most of them seems about as likely as that a one-month-old should discern most of his parents' purpose for those pains they allow him to suffer—which is to say, it is not likely at all (Wykstra 1990, pp. 155–156).

Rowe's noseeum inference is akin to inferring that there is no intelligent extraterrestrial life because we have not seen any. Given the vast amount of space and the tiny sliver of the sky we have been able to examine, it is unlikely that we would have evidence of intelligent extraterrestrial life, if it existed.

4. THE ABDUCTIVE ARGUMENT FROM EVIL

Abduction

Abduction is inference to the best explanation. Abductive reasoning consists in formulating a hypothesis that best explains some relevant data. Suppose, for example, that several members of your family become ill. If you wanted to understand what explained their illness, you would collect as many relevant facts as you could and try to come up with a hypothesis that makes sense of those facts. You might infer that the illness is caused by food poisoning or, perhaps, the flu.

Whatever you ended up concluding, your reasoning would be abductive because you are trying to draw an inference to the best explanation.

Suppose that, while investigating the matter, you found that the symptoms of the illness include nausea and stomach cramps. Nobody has a fever. Nobody has a cough or runny nose. Everyone who became ill did so shortly after dinner. Everyone who ate meat at dinner became ill and those who did not eat meat remained healthy. You would probably infer that the best explanation of those observations is that the illness was brought on by food poisoning caused by tainted meat:

Observations of Facts Surrounding Family Illness:
Observation 1. The symptoms of the illness include nausea and stomach cramps.
Observation 2. Nobody has a fever.
Observation 3. Nobody has a cough or runny nose.
Observation 4. People became ill shortly after dinner.
Observation 5. Everyone who ate meat at dinner became ill and those who did not eat meat remained healthy.
Therefore: the illness was brought on by food poisoning caused by tainted meat.

It is instructive to compare this list of observations with the one involving the ravens. In the case of induction, the observations are almost identical. The only difference is the particular raven observed. In the case of abduction, the observations are diverse and varied. This highlights the differences between induction and abduction. Induction extends a description of a property from a representative sample to a whole. Abduction postulates a hypothesis that best ties together and explains a variety of different facts:

Abduction typically involves evaluating several competing hypotheses. So, we have to be able to decide when a fact is reason to prefer one explanation over another. In general, we can say that a piece of evidence favors one hypothesis over another when the truth of that hypothesis makes the evidence more probable than the competing explanation does. One way to be more specific without going into the complexities of probability theory is to follow the lead of Elliott Sober.[9] Sober proposes the "Surprise Principle"

---

[8]We need to also assume that knowledge of goods is even distributed. This is to prevent that odd situation that all goods are within our circle of knowledge.

[9]Philosophers typically distinguish between three notions of probability: possibility theory, relative frequencies, and epistemic proba-

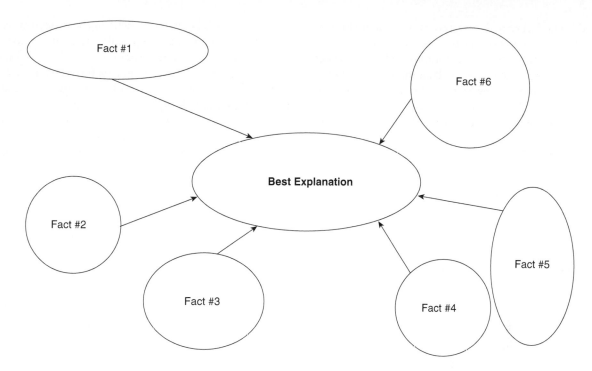

to decide when a piece of evidence strongly favors one hypothesis over another:

> *The Surprise Principle*: An observation O strongly supports hypothesis H_1 over hypothesis H_2 if both the following conditions are satisfied, but not otherwise: (1) if H_1 were true, O is to be expected: and (2) if H_2 were true, O would have been unexpected (Sober 2001, p. 30).

Consider the case of the family illness. We mentioned two possible explanations.

H_1. The illness was caused by food poisoning.
H_2. The illness was caused by a flu virus.

Which hypothesis explains the evidence best? According to the Surprise Principle, we should assume each hypothesis is true for the sake of argument and decide which theory makes the relevant observations less sur-

prising.[10] For brevity's sake, we will consider only one of the five observations.

Suppose that the illness was caused by food poisoning. Is it surprising that all and only those who ate the meat became ill? No, it is not. One would expect that the food poisoning was caused by some tainted food and that those who ate the tainted food would become ill while those who did not eat it would remain healthy. Suppose, on the other hand, that the illness was caused by the flu. Is it surprising that all and only those who ate the meat became ill? Yes, it is more surprising. There is no reason to think that the flu is caused by eating meat. So, the observation that all and only those who ate the meat became ill is evidence for hypothesis H_1 over H_2 because H_1 makes the observation less surprising than H_2 does.

For evidence to be useful in making abductive inferences, it has to be discriminating evidence. By "discriminating evidence," I mean evidence that one hypothesis explains or makes less surprising than the

bility. The relevant notion of probability in this context is epistemic probability. Sober's Surprise Principle provides a simple and intuitive way of employing the notion of epistemic probability without having to explain it.

---

[10]The sense of "surprise" here is epistemic not merely psychological.

other. The fact that the symptoms of the family illness include nausea and stomach cramps does not discriminate between our two competing hypotheses. It is not surprising that those who are ill are nauseous and have stomach cramps if they have food poisoning *or* if they have the flu.

A moment's reflection should make the importance and pervasiveness of abduction apparent. Much, if not a majority, of the reasoning we use in everyday life is abductive. The kind of reasoning that lawyers and juries use in courts of law, for example, is abductive. Prosecutors and defense lawyers set out the evidence of a particular case and they offer competing hypotheses to explain the evidence. The prosecution argues the best explanation of the evidence is that the defendant is guilty. The defense argues that the best explanation is that the defendant is not guilty.[11] Criminal investigators try to develop a theory that explains the evidence they have developed in their investigation. In fact, the most famous investigator of all, the fictional Sherlock Holmes, described his method as the "science of deduction." It would have been more accurate to call it the "science of abduction." Much scientific reasoning is also abductive.

The Abductive Argument from Evil

In "Pain and Pleasure: An Evidential Problem for Theists," Paul Draper lays out an abductive version of the argument from evil (Draper 1996). He argues that the facts about pain and suffering are better explained by atheism[12] than by theism, and hence, evil is abductive evidence against the existence of God.

Draper contends that all our observations about pain and pleasure can be reduced to three facts: First, moral agents experience pain and pleasure that we know to be biologically useful. A moral agent is any being that is morally responsible for his actions. What makes someone a morally responsible agent is something like the ability to understand moral reasons and

to control one's behavior in light of those reasons. A typical adult is a morally responsible agent but a newborn infant is not. Draper defines something as biologically useful if it is part of an organism and it contributes to the biological goals (i.e. survival and reproduction) of that organism.[13]

Second, sentient beings, that are not also moral agents, experience pain and pleasure that we know to be biologically useful. A sentient being is any being that is capable of conscious experience. All moral agents are sentient beings but not all sentient beings are moral agents. A typical adult is a moral agent *and* a sentient being. A dog is not a moral agent but is a sentient being because dogs are capable of sensory experiences.[14]

Third, moral agents and sentient beings experience pain and pleasure that we do not know to be biologically useful. Each of these three observations, he argues, is less surprising if atheism is true than if theism is true. Thus, according to the Surprise Principle, the facts about pain and suffering are strong evidence for atheism over theism.

We can summarize his argument thus:

Observations of Pain and Pleasure:

Observation 1. Moral agents experience pain and pleasure that we know to be biologically useful.

Observation 2. Sentient beings, that are not also moral agents, experience pain and pleasure that we know to be biologically useful.

Observation 3. Moral agents and sentient beings experience pain and pleasure that we do not know to be biologically useful.

Therefore: God does not exist.

Let's consider each observation in its turn. First, Draper argues that if there is no God, it is not surprising that moral agents experience biologically useful pain and pleasure. Independent of our observations about pain and pleasure, we know that moral agents, like humans, are biological organisms

---

[11]Or the defense argues that the prosecution has failed to prove beyond a reasonable doubt that its hypothesis is the best explanation.
[12]In this article, Draper argues that what he calls "the hypothesis of indifference" better explains the facts of suffering than theism. In another article, he sets theism and naturalism up as the views competing to explain evil. For didactic purposes, I have chosen to use the term "atheism" rather than naturalism.

[13]He actually uses the term "biological system" rather than "organism," presumably because a biological system is broader and can include things like whole species. I use the term "organism" for simplicity's sake.
[14]From this point on, for brevity's sake, I shall use the term "sentient being" to mean "sentient being that is not also a moral being."

that have biological goals like survival and reproduction. The various parts of those organisms, like kidneys, lungs, and the reproductive system, contribute to those biological goals. It shouldn't be surprising, then, that the part of the organism responsible for pain and pleasure also contributes to survival and reproduction.

Given theism, though, it would be surprising that pain has biological utility. An omnipotent God could create beings that survive, reproduce, and even thrive without using pain. He could, because he is all-powerful and all-knowing, have created us so that we knew to avoid touching excessively hot objects without having to experience the intense pain associated with burns. If God could create moral agents that achieved their biological goals without experiencing pain, he would do so because he is completely good. All things being equal, only a cruel person would see two equally effective ways to teach someone not to touch hot objects and purposely choose the one that involves the most pain. So, Observation 1 seems to be evidence against the existence of God because it is surprising on theism but not on atheism.

Second, sentient beings are biologically very similar to moral agents. This, he maintains, gives us reason to predict, in an atheistic universe, that sentient beings would experience pain and pleasure that we know to be biologically useful. Any reason we have to expect that moral agents would experience biologically useful pain and pleasure also gives us reason to expect the same of sentient beings.[15]

If theism is true, he contends, we have two reasons to be surprised if sentient beings experienced biologically useful pain. First, we have the same reason in this case as in the case of moral agents. If God is all-powerful, he could create sentient beings, say dogs, that survived and reproduced without using pain. If God is moral, he would create dogs that way. Imagine a dog owner who could teach his dog to behave either by kicking it senseless when it disobeyed or by rewarding

it when it obeyed. Suppose both methods were equally effective. If he chose the kicking method, he would not be a very good person. Second, the case of sentient creatures seems to bode even worse for the theist because in the case of moral agents it might be that pain and pleasure play a moral role in addition to a biological one. Sentient beings are not moral agents, so pain can only play a biological role. So, Observation 2 seems to be more surprising on theism than atheism.

Third, Draper argues that it should not surprise us, if there is no God, that both moral agents and sentient beings experience pain that does not contribute to survival or reproduction.[16] Given what we know about the world, biologically useless pain is unsurprising because we would expect that the processes that brought about our nervous system would not be perfect. The same pain that teaches me to avoid a hot stove continues to hurt days after I remove my hand. This pain doesn't contribute to my survival or reproduction. It just makes me miserable. This lack of fine-tuning of our nervous system is not surprising given atheism. But if we were created by an omnipotent and wholly good God, we would expect all biological pain to be perfectly fine-tuned. This is even more surprising in the case of merely sentient beings.

Thus, Draper concludes, our observations about evil can be broken down into three types. Each of these kinds of observations are more surprising if theism were true than if atheism is true. Thus, evil is strong abductive evidence against atheism rather than theism.

Critique of the Abductive Argument from Evil

I shall divide my criticism of this argument into two parts. In the first part, I shall quickly address two specifics of Draper's abductive argument. In the second part, I will outline five *general* strategies the theist can employ to respond to this type of argument.

Criticism of Draper's Argument There are several problems with Draper's argument. First, it is not clear that Draper's three observations *are* more probable

---

[15]Draper points out that, given a particular theorem of probability calculus that relates to epistemic probability, the probability of Observation 2 is, technically, $P(O2/HI \& O1)$. So, we what we are really doing is determining how likely Observation 2 is given atheism *and* Observation 1 (Draper 1996, p. 16).

[16]Again, technically, Draper is arguing that $P(O3/HI \& O1 \& O2) > P(O3/T \& O1 \& O2)$.

given atheism than theism. Consider Draper's argument that it is more surprising on theism than atheism that moral agents experience biologically useful pain and pleasure.

If atheism is true, should we really expect pain and pleasure would be biologically useful? So many areas of human life, like morality and altruism, don't play much of a biological role, why shouldn't pain and pleasure be like them? As Alvin Plantinga puts it:

> There are many other characteristically human activities and phenomena that apparently do not (or do not apparently) contribute to those biological goals. Literature, poetry, music, art, mathematics, logic, philosophy, nuclear physics, evolutionary biology, play, humor, exploration, and adventure—these are phenomena of enormous significance in human life. Indeed they are among the most important and significant of all things we human beings do. But again, they don't seem in any direct way to contribute to survival and reproduction (Plantinga 1996, p. 253).

Shouldn't we expect pain and pleasure to be like much of human life and lack biological utility as well? Of course, some people argue that those endeavors do contribute to survival and reproduction but evolutionary explanations of morality, altruism, and art, for example, are speculative at best.

Second, Draper claims that atheism explains suffering better than theism does. But atheism doesn't explain suffering as well as one might expect because it is not clear that it explains suffering at all. Theism and atheism are just too general to explain much. Theism is the view that God exists. Atheism is the negative view that something, namely God, does not exist. How does either of these views *explain why* there is suffering in the world? Saying that theism explains suffering is, as William Alston points out, like saying that the sun explains the growth of plants. It is just too general to illuminate or explain much. Atheism is in an even worse situation because it just tells us what doesn't explain suffering, namely God (Alston 1996, p.329).

General Strategies for Replying to the Abductive Argument

Given the nature of the abductive argument, the theist has five strategies available to him for criticizing the abductive argument. The theist can argue that:

1. Atheism doesn't explain suffering as well as one might expect.
2. Theism can explain suffering better than one might expect.
3. There is other relevant evidence that theism explains better than atheism and it explains that evidence better than atheism explains suffering.
4. Contrary to initial appearances, we are not in a position to judge whether atheism or theism explains suffering better.
5. Theism is not a bad explanation because it is not an explanation period.

The first option is the most difficult and least promising. One criticism in this vein is the sort offered by Alston above. Atheism doesn't explain suffering as well as one might expect because it isn't clear that it explains suffering at all.

The second strategy is the project of giving theodicies. The goal of a theodicy is to tell a story that, if true, makes suffering less surprising given theism. I quickly reviewed the nine most common theodicies in my discussion of the inductive argument. I leave it to the reader to decide how well they fare.

The third option involves giving stronger reasons to think that God exists than suffering provides reason to think he does not exist. If the evidence for the existence of God outweighs the evidence against the existence of God, the *total evidence* favors the existence of God. Any proper abduction is made from *all* relevant evidence.

During the O. J. Simpson murder trial, for example, the defense argued that an LAPD detective, Mark Fuhrman, lied about using racist terms to refer to African Americans. They argued that this piece of evidence best fit their theory that Simpson was framed by a racist police officer. The prosecution pointed out that although the defense's theory makes *that* fact less surprising, the prosecution's theory makes *all the other* evidence less surprising. When the total evidence is taken into account, they argued, it favors the view that Simpson is guilty.

Broadly speaking, the evidence for the existence of God can be divided into two sorts. First, there is propositional or inferred evidence, the arguments for the existence of God. This includes the ontological, cosmological, teleological and moral arguments. The example of the O. J. Simpson trial shows that some inferential evidence can outweigh other inferential evidence.

There is, though, another relevant type of evidence—nonpropositional or noninferential evidence. Suppose I know that nine out of ten Germans cannot swim. This piece of evidence makes it unlikely that Fritz, a German, can swim. Now suppose I see Fritz swim. My seeing Fritz swim justifies my belief that he can swim in the face of some propositional evidence that makes Fritz's being able to swim unlikely. It doesn't do so indirectly through reasoning, inference, or argument but directly. Upon seeing Fritz swim, I immediately form the belief that he can swim. Religious experience and related grounds, like those urged by Reformed epistemologists, may provide reason to believe in God despite some facts that make it unlikely that God exists.

Peter Van Inwagen employs the fourth strategy. Van Inwagen argues that although suffering is a difficulty for theism it is not a serious enough difficulty to be considered evidence against theism. Evil, he thinks, is not all that surprising given theism because we are not in a position to know what to expect if theism is true.

Van Inwagen maintains that in order to make decisions about how likely evil is if God exists, we need to be able to make two types of judgments—modal and moral. He argues that our cognitive abilities are such that we can make modal and moral judgments about situations that do not stray too far from everyday life. We know whether it is possible for the table to be a different shape or a different color. We know that the act of helping an old lady across the street is more valuable than murdering an innocent child. But when we start making abstract modal and moral judgments about distant possible worlds, our cognitive abilities fail us. And it is precisely these remote judgments that we need to be able to make in order to know what to expect if God exists (Van Inwagen 1996).

Fifth, the theist can argue that theism is not a bad explanation because it is not an explanation at all and shouldn't be viewed as one. Theists don't typically think of belief in God as some explanatory hypothesis competing with rival scientific hypotheses to account for aspects of the natural world. People don't believe in God because they think it explains the world better than other theories. Some theists argue that it misconstrues belief in God to understand it as an explanatory hypothesis. It is even worse to then turn around and criticize it for not being a good hypothesis.

5. CONCLUSION

Why does the problem of evil seem like such a persuasive argument, and yet, under philosophical scrutiny, turn out otherwise? The answer can be found by realizing that there are two ways to view an argument that leads to a problematic conclusion from *prima facie* plausible premises. On the one hand, one can accept that the argument is good and acknowledge the truth of the conclusion, even though it is surprising. On the other hand, one can reject the conclusion and be left with the problem of explaining how the plausible premises and inferences which lead to that conclusion are, in fact, mistaken. The difference of approach is the difference between seeing an argument as a *disproof* and seeing it as *generating a puzzle*.

The history of philosophy affords many examples of arguments that lead to problematic conclusions from plausible premises: Zeno's paradoxes, the problem of induction, skeptical arguments against the existence of a physical world, and so on. In each case, philosophers have taken both approaches. Some have accepted these counterintuitive conclusions and rejected motion or the existence of a physical world. Most, though, have looked at these arguments as creating problems to be solved with philosophical analysis and careful thought. In fact, some of the best philosophy has been produced by efforts to diagnose where these arguments go wrong.

If my argument in this essay is correct, the problem of evil generates a puzzle for theists, not a disproof of theism. It seems persuasive to us simply because it really *is* difficult for us to understand why a good God permits many instances of suffering. As Marilyn Adams points out, taken this way "the argument is constructive: it is an invitation to probe more deeply into the logical relations among these propositions, to offer more rigorous and subtle analyses of the divine perfections" (Adams 1999, p. 8).

References

Adams, M. M. (1999). *Horrendous Evils and the Goodness of God*. Ithaca, Cornell University Press.

Alston, W. (1996). Some (Temporarily) Final Thoughts on Evidential Arguments from Evil. *The Evidential Argument from Evil*. D. Howard-Snyder. Bloomington, Indiana University Press: 311–332.

Draper, P. (1996). Pain and Pleasure: An Evidential Problem for Theists. *The Evidential Argument from Evil*. D. Howard-Snyder. Bloomington, Indiana University Press: 12–29.

Hick, J. (1977). *Evil and the God of Love*. New York, Harper and Row.

Hume, D. (1989). *Dialogues Concerning Natural Religion*. Amherst, Prometheus Books.

Mackie, J. L. (1992). Evil and Omnipotence. *The Problem of Evil: Selected Readings*. M. Peterson. Notre Dame, University of Notre Dame Press: 89–101.

Martin, M. (1990). *Atheism: A Philosophical Justification*. Philadelphia, Temple University Press.

Mavrodes, G. (1963). "Some Puzzles Concerning Omnipotence." *Philosophical Review* 72: 221–223.

McCloskey, H. J. (1997). God and Evil. *Critiques of God: Making the Case Against Belief in God*. P. Angeles. Amherst, Prometheus Books: 203–224.

Plantinga, A. (1977). *God, Freedom, and Evil*. Grand Rapids, William B. Eerdmans Publishing Co.

Plantinga, A. (1996). On Being Evidentially Challenged. *The Evidential Argument from Evil*. D. Howard-Snyder. Bloomington, Indiana University Press: 244–261.

Rowe, W. (1988). "Evil and Theodicy." *Philosophical Topics* XVI(2): 119–132.

Rowe, W. (1996). The Problem of Evil and Some Varieties of Atheism. *The Evidential Argument from Evil.*

D. Howard-Snyder. Bloomington, Indiana University Press: 1–11.

Sober, E. (2001). *Core Questions in Philosophy: A Text with Readings*. Upper Saddle River, Prentice Hall.

Swinburne, R. (1996). *Is There a God?* New York, Oxford University Press.

Van Inwagen, P. (1996). The Problem of Evil, the Problem of Air, and the Problem of Silence. *The Evidential Argument from Evil*. D. Howard-Snyder. Bloomington, Indiana University Press: 151–174.

Wiesel, E. (1992). Night. *The Problem of Evil: Selected Readings*. M. Peterson. Notre Dame, University of Notre Dame Press: 79–86.

Wykstra, S. J. (1990). The Human Obstacle to Evidential Arguments from Suffering: On Avoiding the Evils of 'Appearance.' *The Problem of Evil*. M. M. Adams and R. M. Adams. New York, Oxford Universaity Press: 138–160.

Wykstra, S. J. (1996). Rowe's Noseeum Argument from Evil. *The Evidential Argument from Evil*. D. Howard-Snyder. Bloomington, Indiana University Press: 126–150.

Yancey, P. (1990). *Where is God When It Hurts?* Grand Rapids, Zondervan.

Questions for Further Reflection

1. What are the two characteristics of a good inductive argument? Does Rowe's argument have those two characteristics?
2. What other reasons might we have to think that we would probably not know God's reason for permitting evil?
3. Are there any facts about pain and pleasure that are more surprising on atheism than on theism? If so, what are they?

Suggestions for Further Reading

Adams, M. M. *Horrendous Evils and the Goodness of God*. Ithaca, NY: Cornell University Press, 1999.

Adams M. M., and R. M. Adams. *The Problem of Evil*. New York: Oxford University Press, 1990.

Drange, T. *Evil and Nonbelief*. Prometheus Books, 1998.

Draper, P. "Pain and Pleasure: An Evidential Problem for Theists." *The Evidential Argument from Evil*, edited by D. Howard-Snyder. Bloomington, IN: Indiana University Press, 1996.

Gale, R. *On the Nature and Existence of God*. New York: Cambridge University Press, 1991.

Hick, J. *Evil and the God of Love*. New York: Harper and Row, 1977.

Howard-Snyder, D. *The Evidential Argument from Evil*. Bloomington, IN: Indiana University Press, 1996.

Hume, D. *Dialogues Concerning Natural Religion*. Amherst, MA: Prometheus Books, 1989.

Mackie, J. L. "Evil and Omnipotence," *The Problem of Evil: Selected Readings*, edited by M. Peterson. Notre Dame, University of Notre Dame Press, 1992, pp. 89–101.

Martin, M. *Atheism: A Philosophical Justification*. Philadelphia: Temple University Press, 1990.

McCloskey, H. J. "God and Evil," *Critiques of God: Making the Case Against Belief in God*, edited by P. Angeles. Amherst, MA: Prometheus Books, 1997, pp. 203–224.

Plantinga, A. *God, Freedom, and Evil*. Grand Rapids, MI: William B. Eerdmans Publishing, 1977.

Plantinga, A. "On Being Evidentially Challeneged," *The Evidential Argument from Evil*, edited by D. Howard-Snyder. Bloomington, IN: Indiana University Press, 1996, pp. 244–261.

Rowe, W. "Evil and Theodicy," *Philosophical Topics* XVI 1988, 119–132.

PART V

RELIGIOUS EXPERIENCE

41. VARIETIES OF RELIGIOUS EXPERIENCE * *William James*

Shankara, "The Mind"

Laozi, "Dao De Jing"

42. IS NUMINOUS EXPERIENCE EVIDENCE THAT GOD EXISTS? * *Keith Yandell*

Walpola Rahula, "Nirvana"

43. PERCEIVING GOD * *William P. Alston*

44. CRITIQUE OF THE ARGUMENT FROM RELIGIOUS EXPERIENCE * *Michael Scriven*

SUGGESTIONS FOR FURTHER READING

41. VARIETIES OF RELIGIOUS EXPERIENCE

William James

A brief biography of William James occurs on page 199. *The Varieties of Religious Experience*, from which this selection is taken, is widely regarded as the most important work on the topic of religious experience ever written. In this selection, James defines and catalogues various types of religious experiences and argues that such experiences may justify the mystical beliefs of the person who had them.

READING QUESTIONS

1. What are the four marks of religious experience?
2. What is the simplest rudiment of mystical experience?
3. What type of religious experience does public opinion and ethical philosophy brand as pathological?
4. For whom does James think religious experience is authoritative?
5. Why does James think that the subject of religious experience cannot claim that we ought to accept the deliverances of his mystical experience?

1. LECTURES XVI AND XVII: MYSTICISM

Over and over again in these lectures I have raised points and left them open and unfinished until we should have come to the subject of Mysticism. Some of you, I fear, may have smiled as you noted my reiterated postponements. But now the hour has come when mysticism must be faced in good earnest, and those broken threads wound up together. One may say truly, I think, that personal religious experience has its root and centre in mystical states of consciousness; so for us, who in these lectures are treating personal experience as the exclusive subject of our study, such states of consciousness ought to form the vital chapter from which the other chapters get their light. Whether my treatment of mystical states will shed more light or darkness, I do not know, for my own constitution shuts me out from their enjoyment almost entirely, and I can speak of them only at second-hand. But though forced to look upon the subject so externally, I will be as objective and receptive as I can; and I think I shall at least succeed in convincing you of the reality of the states in question, and of the paramount importance of their function.

First of all, then, I ask, What does the expression "mystical states of consciousness" mean? How do we part off mystical states from other states?

The words "mysticism" and "mystical" are often used as terms of mere reproach, to throw at any opinion which we regard as vague and vast and sentimental, and without a base in either facts or logic. For some writers a "mystic" is any person who believes in thought-transference, or spirit-return. Employed in this way the word has little value: there are too many less ambiguous synonyms. So, to keep it useful by restricting it, I . . . propose to you four marks which, when an experience has them, may justify us in calling it mystical for the purpose of the present lectures. In this way we shall save verbal disputation, and the recriminations that generally go therewith.

1. *Ineffability*—The handiest of the marks by which I classify a state of mind as mystical is negative. The subject of it immediately says that it defies expression, that no adequate report of its contents can be given in words. It follows from this that its quality must be directly experienced; it cannot be imparted or transferred to others. In this peculiarity mystical states are more like states of feeling than like states of intellect. No one can make clear to another who has never had a certain feeling, in what the quality or worth of it consists. One must have musical ears to know the value of a symphony; one must have been in love one's self to understand a lover's state of mind. Lacking the heart or ear, we cannot interpret the musician or the lover justly, and are even likely to consider him weak-minded or absurd. The mystic finds that most of us accord to his experiences an equally incompetent treatment.

2. *Noetic quality*—Although so similar to states of feeling, mystical states seem to those who experience them to be also states of knowledge. They are states of insight into depths of truth unplumbed by the discursive intellect. They are illuminations, revelations, full of significance and importance, all inarticulate though they remain; and as a rule they carry with them a curious sense of authority for after-time.

These two characters will entitle any state to be called mystical, in the sense in which I use the word. Two other qualities are less sharply marked, but are usually found. These are:

3. *Transiency*—Mystical states cannot be sustained for long. Except in rare instances, half an hour, or at most an hour or two, seems to be the limit beyond which they fade into the light of common day. Often, when faded, their quality can but imperfectly be reproduced in memory; but when they recur it is recognized; and from one recurrence to another it is susceptible of continuous development in what is felt as inner richness and importance.

4. *Passivity*—Although the oncoming of mystical states may be facilitated by preliminary voluntary operations, as by fixing the attention, or going through certain bodily performances, or in other ways which manuals of mysticism prescribe; yet when the characteristic sort of consciousness once has set in, the mystic feels as if his own will were in abeyance, and indeed sometimes as if he were grasped and held by a superior power. This latter peculiarity connects mystical states with certain definite phenomena of secondary or alternative personality, such as prophetic speech, automatic writing, or the mediumistic trance. When these latter conditions are well pronounced, however, there may be no recollection whatever of the phenomenon, and it may have no significance for the subject's usual inner life, to which, as it were, it makes a mere interruption. Mystical states, strictly so called, are never merely interruptive. Some memory of their content always remains, and a profound sense of their importance. They modify the inner life of the subject between the times of their recurrence. Sharp divisions in this region are, however, difficult to make, and we find all sorts of gradations and mixtures.

These four characteristics are sufficient to mark out a group of states of consciousness peculiar enough to deserve a special name and to call for careful study. Let it then be called the mystical group.

Our next step should be to gain acquaintance with some typical examples. Professional mystics at the height of their development have often elaborately organized experiences and a philosophy based thereupon. But you remember what I said in my first lecture: phenomena are best understood when placed within their series, studied in their germ and in their overripe decay, and compared with their exaggerated and degenerated kindred. The range of mystical experience is very wide, much too wide for us to cover in the time at our disposal. Yet the method of serial study is so essential for interpretation that if we really wish to reach conclusions we must use it. I will begin, therefore, with phenomena which claim no special religious significance, and end with those of which the religious pretensions are extreme.

The simplest rudiment of mystical experience would seem to be that deepened sense of the significance of a maxim or formula which occasionally sweeps over one. "I've heard that said all my life," we exclaim, "but I never realized its full meaning until now." . . . This sense of deeper significance is not confined to rational propositions. Single words,[1] and conjunctions of words, effects of light on land and sea, odors and musical sounds, all bring it when the mind is tuned aright. Most of us can remember the strangely moving power of passages in certain poems read when we were young, irrational doorways as they were through which the mystery of fact, the wildness and the pang of life, stole into our hearts and thrilled them. The words have now perhaps become mere polished surfaces for us; but lyric poetry and music are alive and significant only in proportion as they fetch these vague vistas of a life continuous with our own, beckoning and inviting, yet ever eluding our pursuit. We are alive or dead to the eternal inner message of the arts according as we have kept or lost this mystical susceptibility.

A more pronounced step forward on the mystical ladder is found in an extremely frequent phenomenon, that sudden feeling, namely, which sometimes sweeps over us, of having "been here before," as if at some indefinite past time, in just this place, with just these people, we were already saying just these things. As Tennyson writes:

> Moreover, something is or seems,
> That touches me with mystic gleams,
> Like glimpses of forgotten dreams—
>
> Of something felt, like something here;
> Of something done, I know not where;
> Such as no language may declare.[2]

Sir James Crichton-Browne has given the technical name of "dreamy states" to these sudden invasions of vaguely reminiscent consciousness.[3] They bring a sense of mystery and of the metaphysical duality of things, and the feeling of an enlargement of perception which seems imminent but which never completes itself. In Dr. Crichton-Browne's opinion they connect themselves with the perplexed and scared disturbances of self-consciousness which occasionally precede epileptic attacks. I think that this learned alienist takes a rather absurdly alarmist view of an intrinsically insignificant phenomenon. He follows it along the downward ladder, to insanity; our path pursues the upward ladder chiefly. The divergence shows how important it is to neglect no part of a phenomenon's connections, for we make it appear admirable or dreadful according to the context by which we set if off.

Somewhat deeper plunges into mystical consciousness are met with in yet other dreamy states. Such feelings as these which Charles Kingsley describes are surely far from being uncommon, especially in youth:

> When I walk the fields, I am oppressed now and then with an innate feeling that everything I see has a meaning, if I could but understand it.

---

[1] "Mesopotamia" is the stock comic instance. An excellent old German lady, who had done some traveling in her day, used to describe to me her *Sehnsucht* that she might yet visit "Philadelphia," whose wondrous name had always haunted her imagination. . . .

[2] The Two Voices. In a letter to Mr. B. P. Blood. Tennyson reports of himself as follows:

"I have never had any revelations through anaesthetics, but a kind of waking trance—this for lack of a better word—I have frequently had, quite up from boyhood, when I have been all alone. This has come upon me through repeating my own name to myself silently, till all at once, as it were out of the intensity of the consciousness of individuality, individuality itself seemed to dissolve and fade away into boundless being, and this not a confused state but the clearest, the surest of the surest, utterly beyond words—where death was an almost laughable impossibility—the loss of personality (if so it were) seeming no extinction, but the only true life. I am ashamed of my feeble description. Have I not said the state is utterly beyond words?"

Professor Tyndall, in a letter, recalls Tennyson saying of this condition: "By God Almighty! there is no delusion in the matter! It is no nebulous ecstasy, but a state of transcendent wonder, associated with absolute clearness of mind." Memoirs of Alfred Tennyson. ii. 473.

[3] The Lancet, July 6 and 13, 1895, reprinted as the Cavendish Lecture, on Dreamy Mental States, London, Baillière, 1895. . . .

And this feeling of being surrounded with truths which I cannot grasp amounts to indescribable awe sometimes. . . . Have you not felt that your real soul was imperceptible to your mental vision, except in a few hallowed moments?[4]

A much more extreme state of mystical consciousness is described by J. A. Symonds: and probably more persons than we suspect could give parallels to it from their own experience.

. . . One reason why I disliked this kind of trance was that I could not describe it to myself. I cannot even now find words to render it intelligible. It consisted in a gradual but swiftly progressive obliteration of space, time, sensation, and the multitudinous factors of experience which seem to qualify what we are pleased to call our Self. In proportion as these conditions of ordinary consciousness were subtracted, the sense of an underlying or essential consciousness acquired intensity. At last nothing remained but a pure, absolute, abstract Self. The universe became without form and void of content. But Self persisted, formidable in its vivid keenness, feeling the most poignant doubt about reality, ready, as it seemed, to find existence break as breaks a bubble round about it. And what then? The apprehension of a coming dissolution, the grim conviction that this state was the last state of the conscious Self, the sense that I had followed the last thread of being to the verge of the abyss, and had arrived at demonstration of eternal Maya or illusion, stirred or seemed to stir me up again. The return to ordinary conditions of sentient existence began by my first recovering the power of touch, and then by the gradual though rapid influx of familiar impressions and diurnal interests. At last I felt myself once more a human being; and though the riddle of what is meant by life remained unsolved, I was thankful for this return from the abyss—this deliverance from so awful an initiation into the mysteries of skepticism.

"This trance recurred with diminishing frequency until I reached the age of 28. It served to impress upon my growing nature the phantasmal unreality of all the circumstances which contribute to a merely phenomenal consciousness. Often have I asked myself with anguish, on waking from that formless state of denuded, keenly sentient being, Which is the unreality?—the trance of fiery, vacant, apprehensive, skeptical Self from which I issue, or these surrounding phenomena and habits which veil that inner Self and build a self of flesh-and-blood conventionality? Again, are men the factors of some dream, the dream-like unsubstantiality of which they comprehend at such eventful moments? What would happen if the final stage of the trance were reached?"[5]

In a recital like this there is certainly something suggestive of pathology.[6] The next step into mystical states carries us into a realm that public opinion and ethical philosophy have long since branded as pathological, though private practice and certain lyric strains of poetry seem still to bear witness to its ideality. I refer to the consciousness produced by intoxicants and anæsthetics, especially by alcohol. The sway of alcohol over mankind is unquestionably due to its power to stimulate the mystical faculties of human nature, usually crushed to earth by the cold facts and dry criticisms of the sober hour. Sobriety diminishes, discriminates, and says no; drunkeness expands, unites, and says yes. It is in fact the great exciter of the *Yes* function in man. It brings its votary from the chill periphery of things to the radiant core. It makes him for the moment one with truth. Not through mere perversity do men run after it. To the poor and the unlettered it stands in the place of symphony concerts and of literature; and it is part of the deeper mystery and tragedy of

[4]Charles Kingsley's Life. i. 55, quoted by Inge: Christian Mysticism, London, 1899, p. 341.

[5]H. F. Brown: J. A. Symonds, a Biography, London, 1895, pp. 29–31, abridged.

[6]Crichton-Browne expressly says that Symonds's "highest nerve centres were in some degree enfeebled or damaged by these dreamy mental states which afflicted him so grievously." Symonds was, however, a perfect monster of many-sided cerebral efficiency, and his critic gives no objective grounds whatever for his strange opinion, save that Symonds complained occasionally, as all susceptible and ambitious men complain, of lassitude and uncertainty as to his life's mission.

life that whiffs and gleams of something that we immediately recognize as excellent should be vouchsafed to so many of us only in the fleeting earlier phases of what in its totality is so degrading a poisoning. The drunken consciousness is one bit of the mystic consciousness, and our total opinion of it must find its place in our opinion of that larger whole.

Nitrous oxide and ether, especially nitrous oxide, when sufficiently diluted with air, stimulate the mystical consciousness in an extraordinary degree. Depth beyond depth of truth seems revealed to the inhaler. This truth fades out, however, or escapes, at the moment of coming to; and if any words remain over in which it seemed to clothe itself, they prove to be the veriest nonsense. Nevertheless, the sense of a profound meaning having been there persists; and I know more than one person who is persuaded that in the nitrous oxide trance we have a genuine metaphysical revelation.

Some years ago I myself made some observations on this aspect of nitrous oxide intoxication, and reported them in print. One conclusion was forced upon my mind at that time, and my impression of its truth has ever since remained unshaken. It is that our normal waking consciousness, rational consciousness as we call it, is but one special type of consciousness, whilst all about it, parted from it by the filmiest of screens, there lie potential forms of consciousness entirely different. We may go though life without suspecting their existence; but apply the requisite stimulus, and at a touch they are there in all their completeness, definite types of mentality which probably somewhere have their field of application and adaptation. No account of the universe in its totality can be final which leaves these other forms of consciousness quite disregarded. How to regard them is the question—for they are so discontinuous with ordinary consciousness. Yet they may determine attitudes though they cannot furnish formulas, and open a region though they fail to give a map. At any rate, they forbid a premature closing of our accounts with reality. Looking back on my own experiences, they all converge towards a kind of insight to which I cannot help ascribing some metaphysical significance. The keynote of it is invariably a reconciliation, it is as if the opposites of the world, whose contradictoriness and conflict make all our difficulties and troubles, were melted into unity. Not only do they, as contrasted species, belong to one and the same genus, but *one of the species*, the nobler and better one, *is itself the genus, and so soaks up and absorbs its opposite into itself.* This is a dark saying, I know, when thus expressed in terms of common logic, but I cannot wholly escape from its authority. I feel as if it must mean something, something like what the Hegelian philosophy means, if one could only lay hold of it more clearly. Those who have ears to hear, let them hear; to me the living sense

---

"THE MIND" * Shankara

With a controlled mind and an intellect which is made pure and tranquil, you must realize the Atman directly, within yourself. Know the Atman as the real I. Thus you cross the shoreless ocean of worldliness, whose waves are birth and death. Live always in the knowledge of identity with Brahman, and be blessed.

Man is in bondage because he mistakes what is non-Atman for his real Self. This is caused by ignorance. Hence follows the misery of birth and death. Through ignorance, man identifies the Atman with the body, taking the perishable for the real.

Therefore he nourishes this body, and anoints it, and guards it carefully. He becomes enmeshed in the things of the senses like a caterpillar in the threads of its cocoon.

Deluded by his ignorance, a man mistakes one thing for another. Lack of discernment will cause a man to think that a snake is a piece of rope. When he grasps it in this belief he runs a great risk. The acceptance of the unreal as real constitutes the state of bondage. Pay heed to this, my friend.

From Shankara, *The Crest-Jewel of Discrimination* (1970).

of its reality only comes in the artificial mystic state of mind. . . .[7]

In India, training in mystical insight has been known from time immemorial under the name of yoga. Yoga means the experimental union of the individual with the divine. It is based on persevering exercise; and the diet, posture, breathing, intellectual concentration, and moral discipline vary slightly in the different systems which teach it. The yogi, or disciple, who has by these means overcome the obscurations of his lower nature sufficiently, enters into the condition termed *samâdhi*, "comes face to face with facts which no instinct or reason can ever know." He learns—

> That the mind itself has a higher state of existence, beyond reason, a superconscious state, and that when the mind gets to that higher state, then this knowledge beyond reasoning comes. . . . All the different steps in yoga are intended to bring us scientifically to the superconscious state or samâdhi. . . . Just as unconscious work is beneath consciousness, so there is another work which is above consciousness, and which, also, is not accompanied with the feeling of *I*, and yet the mind works, desireless, free from restlessness, objectless, bodiless. Then the Truth shines in its full effulgence, and we know ourselves—for samâdhi lies potential in us all—for what we truly are, free, immortal, omnipotent, loosed from the finite, and its contrasts of good and evil altogether, and identical with the Atman or Universal Soul.[8]

The Vedantists say that one may stumble into superconsciousness sporadically, without the previous discipline, but it is then impure. Their test of its purity, like our test of religion's value, is empirical: its fruits must be good for life. When a man comes out of samâdhi, they assure us that he remains "enlightened, a

sage, a prophet, a saint, his whole character changed, his life changed, illumined."[9]

The Buddhists use the word "samâdhi" as well as the Hindus; but "dhyâna" is their special word for higher states of contemplation. There seem to be four stages recognized in dhyâna. The first stage comes through concentration of the mind upon one point. It excludes desire, but no discernment or judgment: it is still intellectual. In the second stage the intellectual functions drop off, and the satisfied sense of unity remains. In the third stage the satisfaction departs, and indifference begins, along with memory and self-consciousness. In the fourth stage the indifference, memory, and self-consciousness are perfected. [Just what "memory" and "self-consciousness" mean in this connection is doubtful. They cannot be the faculties familiar to us in the lower life.] Higher stages still of contemplation are mentioned—a region where there exists nothing, and where the meditator says: "There exists absolutely nothing," and stops. Then he reaches another region where he says: "There are neither ideas nor absence of ideas," and stops again. Then another region where, "having reached the end of both idea and perception, he stops finally." This would seem to be, not yet Nirvâna, but as close an approach to it as this life affords.[10]

In the Mohammedan world the Sufi sect and various dervish bodies are the possessors of the mystical tradition. The Sufis have existed in Persia from the earliest times, and as their pantheism is so at variance with the hot and rigid monotheism of the Arab mind, it has been suggested that Sufism must have been inoculated into Islam by Hindu influences. We Christians know little of Sufism, for its secrets are disclosed only to those initiated. To give its existence a certain liveli-

[7]What reader of Hegel can doubt that that sense of a perfected Being with all its otherness soaked up into itself, which dominates his whole philosophy, must have come from the prominence in his consciousness of mystical moods like this, in most persons kept subliminal? . . .

[8]My quotations are from Vivekananda, Raja Yoga, London, 1896. The completest source of information on Yoga is the work translated by Vihari Lala Mitra: Yoga Vasishta Maha Ramayana. 4 vols., Calcutta 1891–99.

[9]A European witness, after carefully comparing the results of Yoga with those of the hypnotic or dreamy states artificially producible by us, says: "It makes of its true disciples good, healthy, and happy men. . . . Through the mastery which the yogi attains over his thoughts and his body, he grows into a 'character.' By the subjection of his impulses and propensities to his will, and the fixing of the latter upon the ideal of goodness, he becomes a 'personality' hard to influence by others, and thus almost the opposite of what we usually imagine a 'medium' so-called, or 'psychic subject' to be, "Karl Kellner: Yoga: Eline Skizze. München, 1896, p. 21.

[10]I follow the account in C. F. Koeppen: Die Religion des Buddha, Berlin, 1857, i. 585 ff.

ness in your minds, I will quote a Moslem document, and pass away from the subject.

Al-Ghazzali, a Persian philosopher and theologian, who flourished in the eleventh century, and ranks as one of the greatest doctors of the Moslem church, has left us one of the few autobiographies to be found outside of Christian literature. Strange that a species of book so abundant among ourselves should be so little represented elsewhere—the absence of strictly personal confessions is the chief difficulty to the purely literary student who would like to become acquainted with the inwardness of religions other than the Christian.

M. Schomölders has translated a part of Al-Ghazzali's autobiography into French:[11]

> "The Science of the Sufis," says the Moslem author, "aims at detaching the heart from all that is not God, and at giving to it for sole occupation the meditation of the divine being. Theory being more easy for me than practice, I read [certain books] until I understood all that can be learned by study and hearsay. Then I recognized that what pertains most exclusively to their method is just what no study can grasp, but only transport, ecstasy, and the transformation of the soul. How great, for example, is the difference between knowing the definition of health, of satiety, and their causes and conditions, and being really healthy or filled. How different to know in what drunkenness consists—as being a state occasioned by a vapor that rises from the stomach—and *being* drunk effectively. Without doubt, the drunken man knows neither the definition of drunkenness nor what makes it interesting for science. Being drunk, he knows nothing; whilst the physician, although not drunk, knows well in what drunkenness consists, and what are its predisposing conditions. Similarly there is a difference between knowing the nature of abstinence, and *being* abstinent or having one's soul detached from the world—thus I had learned what words could teach of Sufism, but what was left could be

learned neither by study nor through the ears, but solely by giving one's self up to ecstasy and leading a pious life.

> "Reflecting on my situation, I found myself tied down by a multitude of bonds—temptations on every side. Considering my teaching, I found it was impure before God. I saw myself struggling with all my might to achieve glory and to spread my name. [Here follows an account of his six months' hesitation to break away from the conditions of his life at Bagdad, at the end of which he fell ill with a paralysis of the tongue.] Then, feeling my own weakness, and having entirely given up my own will. I repaired to God like a man in distress who has no more resources. He answered, as he answers the wretch who invokes him. My heart no longer felt any difficulty in renouncing glory, wealth, and my children. So I quitted Bagdad, and reserving from my fortune only what was indispensable for my subsistence, I distributed the rest. I went to Syria, where I remained about two years, with no other occupation than living in retreat and solitude, conquering my desires, combating my passions, training myself to purify my soul, to make my character perfect, to prepare my heart for meditating on God—all according to the methods of the Sufis, as I had read of them.

> "This retreat only increased my desire to live in solitude, and to complete the purification of my heart and fit it for meditation. But the vicissitudes of the times, the affairs of the family, the need of subsistence, changed in some respects my primitive resolve, and interfered with my plans for a purely solitary life. I had never yet found myself completely in ecstasy, save in a few single hours; nevertheless, I kept the hope of attaining this state. Every time that the accidents led me astray, I sought to return; and in this situation I spent ten years. During this solitary state things were revealed to me which it is impossible either to describe or to point out. I recognized for certain that the Sufis are assuredly walking in the path of God. Both in their acts and in their inaction, whether internal or external, they are illumined by the light which proceeds from the prophetic source. The first condition for a Sufi is

---

[11]For a full account of him, see D. B. Macdonald: The Life of Al-Ghazzali, in the Journal of the American Oriental Society, 1899, vol. xx, p. 71.

to purge his heart entirely of all that is not God. The next key of the contemplative life consists in the humble prayers which escape from the fervent soul, and in the meditations on God in which the heart is swallowed up entirely. But in reality this is only the beginning of the Sufi life, the end of Sufism being total absorption in God. The intuitions and all that precede are, so to speak, only the threshold for those who enter. From the beginning, revelations take place in so flagrant a shape that the Sufis see before them, whilst wide awake, the angels and the souls of the prophets. They hear their voices and obtain their favors. Then the transport rises from the perception of forms and figures to a degree which escapes all expression, and which no man may seek to give an account of without his words involving sin.

"Whoever has had no experience of the transport knows of the true nature of prophetism nothing but the name. He may meanwhile be sure of its existence, both by experience and by what he hears the Sufis say. As there are men endowed only with the sensitive faculty who reject what is offered them in the way of objects of the pure understanding, so there are intellectual men who reject and avoid the things perceived by the prophetic faculty. A blind man can understand nothing of colors save what he has learned by narration and hearsay. Yet God has brought prophetism near to men in giving them all a state analogous to it in its principal characters. This state is sleep. If you were to tell a man who was himself without experience of such a phenomenon that there are people who at times swoon away so as to resemble dead men, and who [in dreams] yet perceive things that are hidden, he would deny it [and give his reasons]. Nevertheless, his arguments would be refuted by actual experience. Wherefore, just as the understanding is a stage of human life in which an eye opens to discern various intellectual objects uncomprehended by sensation: just so in the prophetic the sight is illumined by a light which uncovers hidden things and objects which the intellect fails to reach. The chief properties of prophetism are perceptible only during the transport, by those who embrace the Sufi life. The prophet is endowed with qualities to which you possess nothing analogous, and which consequently you cannot possibly understand. How should you know their true nature, since one knows only what one can comprehend? But the transport which one attains by the method of the Sufis is like an immediate perception, as if one touched the objects with one's hand."[12]

This incommunicableness of the transport is the keynote of all mysticism. Mystical truth exists for the individual who has the transport, but for no one else. In this, as I have said, it resembles the knowledge given to us in sensations more than that given by conceptual thought. Thought, with its remoteness and abstractness, has often enough in the history of philosophy been contrasted unfavorably with sensation. It is a commonplace of metaphysics that God's knowledge cannot be discursive but must be intuitive, that is, must be constructed more after the pattern of what in ourselves is called immediate feeling, than after that of proposition and judgment. But *our* immediate feelings have no content but what the five senses supply; and we have seen and shall see again that mystics may emphatically deny that the senses play any part in the very highest type of knowledge which their transports yield.

In the Christian church there have always been mystics. Although many of them have been viewed with suspicion, some have gained favor in the eyes of the authorities. The experiences of these have been treated as precedents, and a codified system of mystical theology has been based upon them, in which everything legitimate finds its place.[13] The basis of the system is "orison" or meditation, the methodical elevation of the soul towards God. Through the practice of orison the higher levels of mystical experience may be attained. It is odd that Protestantism, especially evangelical Protestantism, should seemingly have abandoned everything methodical in this line. Apart from what prayer may lead to, Protestant mystical experi-

---

[12]A. Schmölders: Essai sur les ecoles philosophiques chez les Arabes, Paris, 1842, pp. 54–68, abridged.
[13]Görres's Christliche Mystik gives a full account of the facts. So does Ribet's Mystique Divine, 2 vols., Paris, 1890. . . .

ence appears to have been almost exclusively sporadic. It has been left to our mind-curers to reintroduce methodical meditation into our religious life.

The first thing to be aimed at in orison is the mind's detachment from outer sensations, for these interfere with its concentration upon ideal things. Such manuals as Saint Ignatius's Spiritual Exercises recommend the disciple to expel sensation by a graduated series of efforts to imagine holy scenes. The acme of this kind of discipline would be a semi-hallucinatory monoideism—an imaginary figure of Christ, for example, coming fully to occupy the mind. Sensorial images of this sort, whether literal or symbolic, play an enormous part in mysticism.[14] But in certain cases imagery may fall away entirely, and in the very highest raptures it tends to do so. The state of consciousness becomes then insusceptible of any verbal description. Mystical teachers are unanimous as to this. Saint John of the Cross, for instance, one of the best of them, thus describes the condition called the "union of love," which, he says, is reached by "dark contemplation." In this the Deity compenetrates the soul, but in such a hidden way that the soul—

finds no terms, no means, no comparison whereby to render the sublimity of the wisdom and the delicacy of the spiritual feeling with which she is filled. . . . We receive this mystical knowledge of God clothed in none of the kinds of images, in none of the sensible representations, which our mind makes use of in other circumstances. Accordingly in this knowledge, since the senses and the imagination are not employed, we get neither form nor impression, nor can we give any account or furnish any likeness, although the mysterious and sweet-tasting wisdom comes home so clearly to the inmost parts of our soul. Fancy a man seeing a certain kind of thing for the first time in his life. He can understand it, use and enjoy it, but he cannot apply a name to it, nor communicate any idea of it, even though all the while it be a mere thing of sense.

How much greater will be his powerlessness when it goes beyond the senses! This is the peculiarity of the divine language. The more infused, intimate, spiritual, and supersensible it is, the more does it exceed the senses, both inner and outer, and impose silence upon them. . . . The soul then feels as if placed in a vast and profound solitude, to which no created thing has access, in an immense and boundless desert, desert the more delicious the more solitary it is. There, in this abyss of wisdom, the soul grows by what it drinks in from the wellsprings of the comprehension of love . . . and recognizes, however sublime and learned may be the terms we employ, how utterly vile, insignificant, and improper they are, when we seek to discourse of divine things by their means.[15]

I cannot pretend to detail to you the sundry stages of the Christian mystical life.[16] Our time would not suffice, for one thing; and moreover, I confess that the subdivisions and names which we find in the Catholic books seem to me to represent nothing objectively distinct. So many men, so many minds: I imagine that these experiences can be as infinitely varied as are the idiosyncrasies of individuals.

The cognitive aspects of them, their value in the way of revelation, is what we are directly concerned with, and it is easy to show by citation how strong an impression they leave of being revelations of new depths of truth. Saint Teresa is the expert of experts in describing such conditions, so I will turn immediately to what she says of one of the highest of them, the "orison of union."

---

[14]M. Récéjac, in a recent volume, makes them essential. Mysticism he defines as "the tendency to draw near to the Absolute morally, *and by the aid of Symbols.*" See his Fondements de la Connaissance mystique, Paris, 1897, p. 66. But there are unquestionably mystical conditions in which sensible symbols play no part.

[15]Saint John of the Cross: The Dark Night of the Soul, book ii. ch. xvii., in Vie et Œuvres, 3me edition, Paris. 1893, iii. 428–432. Chapter xi. of book ii. of Saint John's Ascent of Carmel is devoted to showing the harmfulness for the mystical life of the use of sensible imagery.

[16]In particular I omit mention of visual and auditory hallucinations, verbal and graphic automatisms, and such marvels as "levitation," stigmatization, and the healing of disease. These phenomena, which mystics have often presented (or are believed to have presented), have no essential mystical significance, for they occur with no consciousness of illumination whatever, when they occur, as they often do, in persons of nonmystical mind. Consciousness of illumination is for us the essential mark of "mystical" states.

"DAO DE JING" ✳ *Laozi*

The Tao that can be told of is not the eternal Tao;
The name that can be named is not the eternal name.
The Nameless is the origin of Heaven and Earth;
The Named is the mother of all things.
Therefore let there always be nonbeing, so we may see
their subtlety,
And let there always be being, so we may see their
outcome.

The two are the same,
But after they are produced, they have different names.
They both may be called deep and profound.
Deeper and more profound,
The door of all subtleties!

From *A Source Book of Chinese Philosophy*, translated by Wing-tsit Chan. Princeton University Press (1963).

"In the orison of union," says Saint Teresa, "the soul is fully awake as regards God, but wholly asleep as regards things of this world and in respect of herself. During the short time the union lasts, she is as it were deprived of every feeling, and even if she would, she could not think of any single thing. Thus she needs to employ no artifice in order to arrest the use of her understanding: it remains so stricken with inactivity that she neither knows what she loves, nor in what manner she loves, nor what she wills. In short, she is utterly dead to the things of the world and lives solely in God. . . . I do not even know whether in this state she has enough life left to breathe. It seems to me she has not; or at least that if she does breathe, she is unaware of it. Her intellect would fain understand something of what is going on within her, but it has so little force now that it can act in no way whatsoever. So a person who falls into a deep faint appears as if dead. . . .

"Thus does God, when he raises a soul to union with himself, suspend the natural action of all her faculties. She neither sees, hears, nor understands, so long as she is united with God. But this time is always short, and it seems even shorter than it is. God establishes himself in the interior of this soul in such a way, that when she returns to herself, it is wholly impossible for her to doubt that she has been in God, and God in her. This truth remains so strongly impressed on her, that, even though many years should pass without the condition returning, she can neither forget the favor she received, nor doubt of its reality. If you, nevertheless, ask how it is possible that the soul can see and understand that she has been in God, since during the union she has neither sight nor understanding. I reply that she does not see it then, but that she sees it clearly later, after she has returned to herself, not by any vision, but by a certitude which abides with her and which God alone can give her. I knew a person who was ignorant of the truth that God's mode of being in everything must be either by presence, by power, or by essence, but who, after having received the grace of which I am speaking, believed this truth in the most unshakable manner. So much so that, having consulted a half-learned man who was as ignorant on this point as she had been before she was enlightened, when he replied that God is in us only by "grace," she disbelieved his reply, so sure she was of the true answer; and when she came to ask wiser doctors, they confirmed her in her belief, which much consoled her. . . .

"But how, you will repeat, *can* one have such certainty in respect to what one does not see? This question, I am powerless to answer. These are secrets of God's omnipotence which it does not appertain to me to penetrate. All that I know is that I tell the truth; and I shall never believe that any soul who does not possess this certainty has ever been really united to God."[17]

---

[17]The Interior Castle, Fifth Abode, ch. i., in Œuvres, translated by Bouix. iii. 421–424.

The kinds of truth communicable in mystical ways, whether these be sensible or supersensible, are various. Some of them relate to this world—visions of the future, the reading of hearts, the sudden understanding of texts, the knowledge of distant events, for example; but the most important revelations are theological or metaphysical.

Saint Ignatius confessed one day to Father Laynez that a single hour of meditation at Manresa had taught him more truths about heavenly things than all the teachings of all the doctors put together could have taught him. . . . One day in orison, on the steps of the choir of the Dominican church, he saw in a distinct manner the plan of divine wisdom in the creation of the world. On another occasion, during a procession, his spirit was ravished in God, and it was given him to contemplate, in a form and images fitted to the weak understanding of a dweller on the earth, the deep mystery of the holy Trinity. This last vision flooded his heart with such sweetness, that the mere memory of it in after times made him shed abundant tears.[18]

Similarly with Saint Teresa. "One day, being in orison," she writes, "it was granted me to perceive in one instant how all things are seen and contained in God. I did not perceive them in their proper form, and nevertheless the view I had of them was of a sovereign clearness, and has remained vividly impressed upon my soul. It is one of the most signal of all the graces which the Lord has granted me. . . . The view was so subtile and delicate that the understanding cannot grasp it."[19]

She goes on to tell how it was as if the Deity were an enormous and sovereignly limpid diamond, in which all our actions were contained in such a way that their full sinfulness appeared evident as never before. On another day, she relates, while she was reciting the Athanasian Creed—

> Our Lord made me comprehend in what way it is that one God can be in three Persons. He made me see it so clearly that I remained as extremely surprised as I was comforted, . . . and now, when I think of the holy Trinity, or hear It spoken of, I understand how the three adorable Persons form only one God and I experience an unspeakable happiness.

On still another occasion, it was given to Saint Teresa to see and understand in what wise the Mother of God had been assumed into her place in Heaven.[20]

The deliciousness of some of these states seems to be beyond anything known in ordinary consciousness. It evidently involves organic sensibilities, for it is spoken of as something too extreme to be borne, and as verging on bodily pain.[21] But it is too subtle and piercing a delight for ordinary words to denote. God's touches, the wounds of his spear, references to ebriety and to nuptial union have to figure in the phraseology by which it is shadowed forth. Intellect and senses both swoon away in these highest states of ecstasy. "If our understanding comprehends," says Saint Teresa, "it

---

[18]Bartoli-Michel: Vie de Saint Ignace de Loyola. i. 34–36. Others have had illuminations about the created world. Jacob Boehme, for instance. At the age of twenty-five he was "surrounded by the divine light, and replenished with the heavenly knowledge; insomuch as going abroad into the fields to a green, at Görlitz, he there sat down, and viewing the herbs and grass of the field, in his inward light he saw into their essences, use, and properties, which was discovered to him by their lineaments, figures, and signatures." Of a later period of experience he writes: "In one quarter of an hour I saw and knew more than if I had been many years together at an university. For I saw and knew the beings of all things, the Byss and the Abyss, and the eternal generation of the holy Trinity, the descent and original of the world and of all creatures through the divine wisdom. I knew and saw in myself all the three worlds, the external and visible world being of a procreation or extern birth from both the internal and spiritual worlds; and I saw and knew the whole working essence, in the evil and in the good, and the mutual original and existence; and likewise how the fruitful bearing womb of eternity brought forth. So that I did not only greatly wonder at it, but did also exceedingly rejoice, albeit I could very hardly apprehend the same in my external man and set it down with the pen. For I had a thorough view of the universe as in a chaos, wherein all things are couched and wrapt up, but it was impossible for me to explicate the same." Jacob Boehme's Theosophic Philosophy, etc., by Edward Taylor, London, 1691, pp. 425, 427, abridged. . . .

[19]Vie. pp. 581, 582.

[20]Loc. cit., p. 574.

[21]Saint Teresa discriminates between pain in which the body has a part and pure spiritual pain (Interior Castle, 6th Abode, ch. xi.). As for the bodily part in these celestial joys, she speaks of it as "penetrating to the marrow of the bones, whilst earthly pleasures affect only the surface of the senses. I think," she adds, "that this is a just description, and I cannot make it better." Ibid., 5th Abode, ch. i.

is in a mode which remains unknown to it, and it can understand nothing of what it comprehends. For my own part. I do not believe that it does comprehend, because, as I said, it does not understand itself to do so. I confess that it is all a mystery in which I am lost."[22] In the condition called *raptus* or ravishment by theologians, breathing and circulation are so depressed that it is a question among the doctors whether the soul be or be not temporarily dissevered from the body. One must read Saint Teresa's descriptions and the very exact distinctions which she makes, to persuade one's self that one is dealing, not with imaginary experiences, but with phenomena which, however rare, follow perfectly definite psychological types.

To the medical mind these ecstasies signify nothing but suggested and imitated hypnoid states, on an intellectual basis of superstition, and a corporeal one of degeneration and hysteria. Undoubtedly these pathological conditions have existed in many and possibly in all the cases. but that fact tells us nothing about the value for knowledge of the consciousness which they induce. To pass a spiritual judgment upon these states, we must not content ourselves with superficial medical talk, but inquire into their fruits for life.

Their fruits appear to have been various. Stupefaction, for one thing, seems not to have been altogether absent as a result. You may remember the helplessness in the kitchen and schoolroom of poor Margaret Mary Alacoque. Many other ecstatics would have perished but for the care taken of them by admiring followers. The "otherworldliness" encouraged by the mystical consciousness makes this over-abstraction from practical life peculiarly liable to befall mystics in whom the character is naturally passive and the intellect feeble; but in natively strong minds and characters we find quite opposite results. The great Spanish mystics, who carried the habit of ecstasy as far as it has often been carried, appear for the most part to have shown indomitable spirit and energy, and all the more so for the trances in which they indulged.

Saint Ignatius was a mystic, but his mysticism made him assuredly one of the most powerfully practical human engines that ever lived. Saint John of the Cross, writing of the intuitions and "touches" by which God reaches the substance of the soul, tells us that—

They enrich it marvelously. A single one of them may be sufficient to abolish at a stroke certain imperfections of which the soul during its whole life had vainly tried to rid itself, and to leave it adorned with virtues and loaded with supernatural gifts. A single one of these intoxicating consolations may reward it for all the labors undergone in its life—even were they numberless. Invested with an invincible courage, filled with an impassioned desire to suffer for its God, the soul then is seized with a strange torment—that of not being allowed to suffer enough.[23]

Saint Teresa is as emphatic, and much more detailed. You may perhaps remember a passage I quoted from her in my first lecture.[24] There are many similar pages in her autobiography. Where in literature is a more evidently veracious account of the formation of a new centre of spiritual energy than is given in her description of the effects of certain ecstasies which in departing leave the soul upon a higher level of emotional excitement?

Often, infirm and wrought upon with dreadful pains before the ecstasy, the soul emerges from it full of health and admirably disposed for action . . . as if God had willed that the body itself, already obedient to the soul's desires, should share in the soul's happiness. . . . The soul after such a favor is animated with a degree of courage so great that if at that moment its body should be torn to pieces for the cause of God, it would feel nothing but the liveliest comfort. Then it is that promises and heroic resolutions spring up in profusion in us, soaring desires, horror of the world, and the clear perception of our proper nothingness. . . . What empire is comparable to that of a soul who, from this sublime summit to which God has raised her, sees all the things of earth beneath her feet, and is captivated by no one of them? How ashamed she is of her former attachments! How amazed at her blindness! What lively pity she

---

[22]Vie, p. 198.

[23]Œuvres, ii. 320.
[24]Above, p. 34 [1902 edition].

feels for those whom she recognizes still shrouded in the darkness! . . . She groans at having ever been sensitive to points of honor, at the illusion that made her ever see as honor what the world calls by that name. Now she sees in this name nothing more than an immense lie of which the world remains a victim. She discovers, in the new light from above, that in genuine honor there is nothing spurious, that to be faithful to this honor is to give our respect to what deserves to be respected really, and to consider as nothing, or as less than nothing, whatsoever perishes and is not agreeable to God. . . . She laughs when she sees grave persons, persons of orison, caring for points of honor for which she now feels profoundest contempt. It is suitable to the dignity of their rank to act thus, they pretend, and it makes them more useful to others. But she knows that in despising the dignity of their rank for the pure love of God they would do more good in a single day than they would effect in ten years by preserving it. . . . She laughs at herself that there should ever have been a time in her life when she made any case of money, when she ever desired it. . . . Oh! if human beings might only agree together to regard it as so much useless mud, what harmony would then reign in the world! With what friendship we would all treat each other if our interest in honor and in money could but disappear from earth! For my own part, I feel as if it would be a remedy for all our ills.[25]

Mystical conditions may, therefore render the soul more energetic in the lines which their inspiration favors. But this could be reckoned an advantage only in case the inspiration were a true one. If the inspiration were erroneous, the energy would be all the more mistaken and misbegotten. So we stand once more before that problem of truth which confronted us at the end of the lectures on saintliness. You will remember that we turned to mysticism precisely to get some light on truth. Do mystical states establish the truth of those theological affections in which the saintly life has its root?

In spite of their repudiation of articulate self-description, mystical states in general assert a pretty distinct theoretic drift. It is possible to give the outcome of the majority of them in terms that point in definite philosophical directions. One of these directions is optimism, and the other is monism. We pass into mystical states from out of ordinary consciousness as from a less into a more, as from a smallness into a vastness, and at the same time as from an unrest to a rest. We feel them as reconciling, unifying states. They appeal to the yes-function more than to the no-function in us. In them the unlimited absorbs the limits and peacefully closes the account. Their very denial of every adjective you may propose as applicable to the ultimate truth—He, the Self, the Atman, is to be described by "No! no!" only, say the Upanishads,[26] though it seems on the surface to be a no-function, is a denial made on behalf of a deeper yes. Whoso calls the Absolute anything in particular, or says that it is *this*, seems implicitly to shut it off from being *that*—it is as if he lessened it. So we deny the "this," negating the negation which it seems to us to imply, in the interests of the higher affirmative attitude by which we are possessed. The fountainhead of Christian mysticism is Dionysius the Areopagite. He describes the absolute truth by negatives exclusively.

"The cause of all things is neither soul nor intellect; nor has it imagination, opinion, or reason, or intelligence; nor is it reason or intelligence; nor is it spoken or thought. It is neither number, nor order, nor magnitude, nor littleness, nor equality, nor inequality, nor similarity, nor dissimilarity. It neither stands, nor moves, nor rests. . . . It is neither essence, nor eternity, nor time. Even intellectual contact does not belong to it. It is neither science nor truth. It is not even royalty or wisdom; not one; not unity; not divinity or goodness; nor even spirit as we know it," etc., *ad libitum*.[27]

But these qualifications are denied by Dionysius, not because the truth falls short of them, but because it so infinitely excels them. It is above them. It is *super*-lucent, *super*-splendent, *super*-essential, *super*-sublime, *super* everything that can be named. Like Hegel in his

[25]Vie, pp. 200, 229, 231–233, 243.

[26]Muller's translation, part ii, p. 180.
[27]T. Davidson's translation, In Journal of Speculative Philosophy, 1893, vol. xxii. p. 399.

logic, mystics journey towards the positive pole of truth only by the "Methode der Absoluten Negativität."[28]

Thus come the paradoxical expressions that so abound in mystical writings. As when Eckhart tells of the still desert of the Godhead. "where never was seen difference, neither Father, Son, nor Holy Ghost, where there is no one at home, yet where the spark of the soul is more at peace than in itself."[29] As when Boehme writes of the Primal Love, that "it may fitly be compared to Nothing, for it is deeper than any Thing, and is as nothing with respect to all things, forasmuch as it is not comprehensible by any of them. And because it is nothing respectively, it is therefore free from all things, and is that only good, which a man cannot express or utter what it is, there being nothing to which it may be compared, to express it by."[30] . . .

To this dialectical use, by the intellect, of negation as a mode of passage towards a higher kind of affirmation, there is correlated the subtlest of moral counterparts in the sphere of the personal will. Since denial of the finite self and its wants, since asceticism of some sort, is found in religious experience to be the only doorway to the larger and more blessed life, this moral mystery intertwines and combines with the intellectual mystery in all mystical writings.

"Love," continues Behmen, is Nothing, for "when thou art gone forth wholly from the Creature and from that which is visible, and art become Nothing to all that is Nature and Creature, then thou art in that eternal One, which is God himself, and then thou shalt feel within thee the highest virtue of Love. . . . The treasure of treasures for the soul is where she goeth out of the Somewhat into that Nothing out of which all things may be made. The soul here saith. *I have nothing*, for I am utterly stripped and naked; *I can do nothing*, for I have no manner of power, but am as water poured out: *I am nothing*, for all that I am is no more than an image of Being, and only God is to me I AM; and so, sitting down in my own

Nothingness, I give glory to the eternal Being, and *will nothing* of myself, that so God may will all in me, being unto me my God and all things."[31]

In Paul's language, I live, yet not I, but Christ liveth in me. Only when I become as nothing can God enter in and no difference between his life and mine remain outstanding.[32]

This overcoming of all the usual barriers between the individual and the Absolute is the great mystic achievement. In mystic states we both become one with the Absolute and we become aware of our oneness. This is the everlasting and triumphant mystical tradition, hardly altered by differences of clime or creed. In Hinduism, in Neoplatonism, in Sufism, in Christian mysticism, in Whitmanism, we find the same recurring note, so that there is about mystical utterances an eternal unanimity which ought to make a critic stop and think, and which brings it about that

---

[31]Op. cit., pp. 42. 74, abridged.

[32]From a French book I take this mystical expression of happiness in God's indwelling presence:

"Jesus has come to take up his abode in my heart. It is not so much a habitation, as association, as a sort of fusion. Oh, new and blessed life! life which becomes each day more luminous. . . . The wall before me, dark a few moments since, is splendid at this hour because the sun shines on it. Wherever its rays fall they light up a conflagration of glory: the smallest speck of glass sparkles, each grain of sand emits fire: even so there is a royal song of triumph in my heart because the Lord is there. My days succeed each other: yesterday a blue sky: to-day a clouded sun: a night filled with strange dreams; but as soon as the eyes open, and I regain consciousness and seem to begin life again, It is always the same figure before me, always the same presence tilling my heart. . . . Formerly the day was dulled by the absence of the Lord. I used to wake invaded by all sorts of sad impressions, and I did not find him on my path. Today he is with me; and the light cloudiness which covers things is not an obstacle to my communion with him. I feel the pressure of his hand. I feel something else which tills me with a serene joy: shall I dare to speak it out? Yes, for it is the true expression of what I experience. The Holy Spirit is not merely making me a visit: it is no mere dazzling apparition which may from one moment to another spread its wings and leave me in my night, it is a permanent habitation. He can depart only if he takes me with him. More than that: he is not other than myself: he is one with me. It is not a juxtaposition, it is a penetration, a profound modification of my nature, a new manner of my being." Quoted from the MS. "of an old man" by Wilfred Monod: II Vit: six meditations sur le mystere chretien, pp. 280–283.

---

[28]"Deus propter excellentiam non immerito Nihil vocatur." Scotus Erigena, quoted by Andrew Seth: Two Lectures on Theism, New York, 1897, p. 55.

[29]J. Royce: Studies in Good and Evil. p. 282.

[30]Jacob Boehme's Dialogues on the Supersensual Life, translated by Bernard Holland. London, 1901, p. 48.

the mystical classics have, as has been said, neither birthday nor native land. Perpetually telling of the unity of man with God, their speech antedates languages, and they do not grow old.[33]

"That art Thou!" say the Upanishads, and the Vedantists add: "Not a part, not a mode of That, but identically That, that absolute Spirit of the World." "As pure water poured into pure water remains the same, thus, O Gautama, is the Self of a thinker who knows. Water in water, fire in fire, ether in ether, no one can distinguish them; likewise a man whose mind has entered into the Self."[34] " 'Every man,' says the Sufi Gulshan-Râz, 'whose heart is no longer shaken by any doubt, knows with certainty that there is no being save only One. . . . In his divine majesty the *me* the *we* the *thou*, are not found, for in the One there can be no distinction. Every being who is annulled and entirely separated from himself, hears resound outside of him this voice and this echo: *I am God*: he has an eternal way of existing, and is no longer subject to death.' "[35] In the vision of God, says Plotinus, "what sees is not our reason, but something prior and superior to our reason. . . . He who thus sees does not properly see, does not distinguish or imagine two things. He changes, he ceases to be himself, preserves nothing of himself. Absorbed in God, he makes but one with him, like a centre of a circle coinciding with another centre."[36] "Here," writes Suso, "the spirit dies, and yet is all alive in the marvels of the Godhead . . . and is lost in the stillness of the glorious dazzling obscurity and of the naked simple unity. It is in this modeless *where* that the highest bliss is to be found."[37] "Ich bin so gross als Gott," sings Angelus Silesius again, "Er ist als ich so klein; Er kann nicht über mich, ich unter ihm nicht sein."[38]

In mystical literature such self-contradictory phrases as "dazzling obscurity," "whispering silence," "teeming desert," are continually met with. They prove that not conceptual speech, but music rather, is the el-ement through which we are best spoken to by mystical truth. Many mystical scriptures are indeed little more than musical compositions.

He who would hear the voice of Nada, "the Soundless Sound," and comprehend it, he has to learn the nature of Dhâranâ. . . . When to himself his form appears unreal, as do on waking all the forms he sees in dreams; when he has ceased to hear the many, he may discern the ONE—the inner sound which kills the outer. . . . For then the soul will hear, and will remember. And then to the inner ear will speak THE VOICE OF THE SILENCES. . . . And now thy *Self* is lost in SELFS, *thyself* unto THYSELF, merged in that SELF from which thou first didst radiate. . . . Behold! thou hast become the Light, thou hast become the Sound, thou art the Master and thy God. Thou art THYSELF the object of thy search: the VOICE unbroken, the resounds throughout eternities, exempt from change, from sin exempt, the seven sounds in one, the VOICE OF THE SILENCE. *Om tat Sat.*[39]

These words, if they do not awaken laughter as you receive them, probably stir chords within you which music and language touch in common. Music gives us ontological messages which nonmusical criticism is unable to contradict, though it may laugh at our foolishness in minding them. There is a verge of the mind which these things haunt; and whispers therefrom mingle with the operations of our understanding, even as the waters of the infinite ocean send their waves to break among the pebbles that lie upon our shores.

> *Here begins the sea that ends not till the world's end.*
>   *Where we stand,*
> *Could we know the next high sea-mark set beyond*
>   *these waves that gleam,*
> *We should know what never man hath known, nor*
>   *eye of man hath scanned. . . .*

---

[33]Compare M. Maeterlinck: L'Ornement des Noces spirituelles de Ruysbroeck, Bruxelles, 1891. Introduction, p. xix.

[34]Upanishads, M. Muller's translation, ii. 17, 334.

[35]Schmolders: Op. cit., p. 210.

[36]Enneads. Bouillier's translation. Paris. 1861. iii. 561. Compare pp. 473–477, and vol. i. p. 27.

[37]Autobiography, pp. 309, 310.

[38]Op. cit., Strophe 10.

---

[39]H. P. Blavatsky: The Voice of the Silence.

Ah, but here man's heart leaps, yearning towards the
    gloom with venturous glee,
From the shore that hath no shore beyond it, set in all
    the sea.[40]

That doctrine, for example, that eternity is time-less, that out "immortality," if we live in the eternal, is not so much future as already now and here, which we find so often expressed today in certain philosophic circles, finds its support in a "hear, hear!" or an "amen," which floats up from that mysteriously deeper level.[41] We recognize the passwords to the mystical region as we hear them, but we cannot use them ourselves; it alone has the keeping of "the password primeval."[42]

I have now sketched with extreme brevity and in-sufficiency, but as fairly as I am able in the time al-lowed, the general traits of the mystic range of con-sciousness. *It is on the whole pantheistic and optimistic, or at least the opposite of pessimistic. It is anti-naturalistic, and harmonizes best with twice-bornness and so-called otherworldly states of mind.*

My next task is to inquire whether we can invoke it as authoritative. Does it furnish any *warrant for the truth* of the twice-bornness and supernaturality and pantheism which it favors? I must give my answer to this question as concisely as I can.

In brief my answer is this—and I will divide it into three parts:

1. Mystical states, when well developed, usually are, and have the right to be, absolutely authoritative over the individuals to whom they come.
2. No authority emanates from them which should make it a duty for those who stand outside of them to accept their revelations uncritically.
3. They break down the authority of the nonmystical or rationalistic consciousness, based upon the understanding and the senses alone. They show it to be only one kind of consciousness. They open out the possibility of other orders of truth, in which, so far as anything in us vitally responds to them, we may freely continue to have faith.

I will take up these points one by one.

As a matter of psychological fact, mystical states of a well-pronounced and emphatic sort *are* usually authoritative over those who have them.[43] They have been "there," and know. It is vain for ra-tionalism to grumble about this. If the mystical truth that comes to a man proves to be a force that he can live by, what mandate have we of the major-ity to order him to live in another way? We can throw him into prison or a madhouse, but we can-not change his mind—we commonly attach it only the more stubbornly to its beliefs.[44] It mocks our ut-most efforts, as a matter of fact, and in point of logic it absolutely escapes our jurisdiction. Our own more "rational" beliefs are based on evidence ex-actly similar in nature to that which mystics quote for theirs. Our senses, namely, have assured us of certain states of fact; but mystical experiences are as direct perceptions of fact for those who have them as any sensations ever were for us. The records show that even though the five senses be in abeyance in them, they are absolutely sensational in their epistemological quality, if I may be par-doned the barbarous expression—that is, they are face to face presentations of what seems immedi-ately to exist.

The mystic is, in short, *invulnerable*, and must be left, whether we relish it or not, in undisturbed enjoy-ment of his creed. Faith, says Tolstoy, is that by which men live. And faith-state and mystic state are practi-cally convertible terms.

But I now proceed to add that mystics have no right to claim that we ought to accept the deliverance of their peculiar experiences, if we are ourselves out-siders and feel no private call thereto. The utmost they

---

[40]Swinburne: On the Verge, in "A Midsummer Vacation."
[41]Compare the extracts from Dr. Bucke, quoted on p. 136.
[42]As serious an attempt as I know to mediate between the mystical region and the discursive life is contained in an article on Aristo-tle's Unmoved Mover, by F. C. S. Schiller, in Mind, vol. ix., 1900.

[43]I abstract from weaker states, and from those cases of which the books are full, where the director (but usually not the subject) re-mains in doubt whether the experience may not have proceeded from the demon.
[44]Example: Mr. John Nelson writes of his imprisonment for preach-ing Methodism: "My soul was as a watered garden, and I could sing praises to God all day long; for he turned my captivity into joy, and gave me to rest as well on the boards, as if I had been on a bed of down. Now could I say, 'God's service is perfect freedom,' and I carried out much in prayer that my enemies might drink of the same river of peace which my God gave so largely to me." Journal, London, no date, p. 172.

can ever ask of us in this life is to admit that they establish a presumption. They form a consensus and have an unequivocal outcome; and it would be odd, mystics might say, if such a unanimous type of experience should prove to be altogether wrong. At bottom, however, this would only be an appeal to numbers, like the appeal of rationalism the other way: and the appeal to numbers has no logical force. If we acknowledge it, it is for "suggestive," not for logical reasons: we follow the majority because to do so suits our life.

But even this presumption from the unanimity of mystics is far from being strong. In characterizing mystic states as pantheistic, optimistic, and so on. I am afraid I over-simplified the truth. I did so for expository reasons, and to keep the closer to the classic mystical tradition. The classic religious mysticism, it now must be confessed, is only a "privileged case." It is an *extract*, kept true to type by the selection of the fittest specimens and their preservation in "schools." It is carved out from a much larger mass: and if we take the larger mass as seriously as religious mysticism has historically taken itself, we find that the supposed unanimity largely disappears. To begin with, even religious mysticism itself, the kind that accumulates traditions and makes schools, is much less unanimous than I have allowed. It has been both ascetic and antinomianly self-indulgent within the Christian church.[45] It is dualistic in Sankhya, and monistic in Vedanta philosophy. I called it pantheistic; but the great Spanish mystics are anything but pantheists. They are with few exceptions nonmetaphysical minds, for whom "the category of personality" is absolute. The "union" of man with God is for them much more like an occasional miracle than like an original identity.[46] How different again, apart from the happiness common to all, is the mysticism of Walt Whitman, Edward Carpenter, Richard Jefferies, and other naturalistic pantheists, from the more distinctively Christian sort.[47] The fact is that the mysti-

cal feeling of enlargement, union, and emancipation has no specific intellectual content whatever of its own. It is capable of forming matrimonial alliances with material furnished by the most diverse philosophies and theologies, provided only they can find a place in their framework for its peculiar emotional mood. We have no right, therefore, to invoke its prestige as distinctively in favor of any special belief, such as that in absolute idealism, or in the absolute monistic identity, or in the absolute goodness, of the world. It is only relatively in favor of all these things—it passes out of common human consciousness in the direction in which they lie.

So much for religious mysticism proper. But more remains to be told, for religious mysticism is only one half of mysticism. The other half has no accumulated traditions except those which the textbooks on insanity supply. Open any one of these, and you will find abundant cases in which "mystical ideas" are cited as characteristic symptoms of enfeebled or deluded states of mind. In delusional insanity, paranoia, as they sometimes call it, we may have a *diabolical* mysticism, a sort of religious mysticism turned upside down. The same sense of ineffable importance in the smallest events, the same texts and words coming with new meanings, the same voices and visions and leadings and missions, the same controlling by extraneous powers; only this time the emotion is pessimistic: instead of consolations we have desolations; the meanings are dreadful; and the powers are enemies to life. It is evident that from the point of view of their psychological mechanism, the classic mysticism and these lower mysticisms spring from the same mental level, from that great subliminal or transmarginal region of which science is beginning to admit the existence, but of which so little is really known. That region contains every kind of matter: "seraph and snake" abide there side by side. To come from thence is no infallible credential. What comes must be sifted and tested, and run the gauntlet of confrontation with the total context of experience, just like what comes from the outer world of sense. Its value must be ascertained by empirical methods, so long as we are not mystics ourselves.

Once more, then, I repeat that nonmystics are under no obligation to acknowledge in mystical states a

---

[45]Ruysbroeck, in the work which Maeterlinck has translated, has a chapter against the antinomianism of disciples. . . .

[46]Compare Paul Rousselot: Les Mystiques Espagnols, Paris, 1869, ch. xii.

[47]See Carpenter's Towards Democracy, especially the latter parts, and Jefferies's wonderful and splendid mystic rhapsody. The Story of my Heart.

superior authority conferred on them by their intrinsic nature.[48]

Yet, I repeat once more, the existence of mystical states absolutely overthrows the pretension of nonmystical states to be the sole and ultimate dictators of what we may believe. As a rule, mystical states merely add a supersensuous meaning to the ordinary outward data on consciousness. They are excitements like the emotions of love or ambition, gifts to our spirit by means of which facts already objectively before us fall into a new expressiveness and make a new connection with our active life. They do not contradict these facts as such, or deny anything that our senses have immediately seized.[49] It is the rationalistic critic rather who plays the part of denier in the controversy, and his denials have no strength, for there never can be a state of facts to which new meaning may not truthfully be added, provided the mind ascend to a more enveloping point of view. It must always remain an open question whether mystical states may not possibly be such superior points of view, windows through which the mind looks out upon a more extensive and inclusive world. The difference of the views seen from the different mystical windows need not prevent us from entertaining this supposition. The wider world would in that case prove to have a mixed constitution like that of this world, that is all. It would have its celestial and its infernal regions, its tempting and its saving moments, its valid experiences and its counterfeit ones, just as our world has them; but it would be a wider world all the same. We should have to use its experiences by selecting and subordinating and substituting just as is our custom in this ordinary naturalistic world; we should be liable to error just as we are now; yet the counting in of that wider world of meanings, and the serious dealing with it, might, in spite of all the perplexity, be indispensable stages in our approach to the final fullness of the truth.

In this shape, I think, we have to leave the subject. Mystical states indeed wield no authority due simply to their being mystical states. But the higher ones among them point in directions to which the religious sentiments even of nonmystical men incline. They tell of the supremacy of the ideal, of vastness, of union, of safety, and of rest. They offer us *hypotheses*, hypotheses which we may voluntarily ignore, but which as thinkers we cannot possibly upset. The super-naturalism and optimism to which they would persuade us may, interpreted in one way or another, be after all the truest of insights into the meaning of this life.

"Oh, the little more, and how much it is; and the little less, and what worlds away!" It may be that possibility and permission of this sort are all that the religious consciousness requires to live on. In my last lecture I shall have to try to persuade you that this is the case.

QUESTIONS FOR FURTHER REFLECTION

1. James argues that religious experience undermines the pretension that other more conventional ways of knowing are the only ways of knowing. Does the fact that people believe things based upon a religious experience, which others cannot refute, show that religious experience is a path to genuine knowledge?

2. Are there simpler explanations for why people have religious experiences than that they are in contact with some higher reality? If we can explain these experiences without positing God, angels, the One, and so on, should we do so?

3. Does the fact that the adherents of many different, and mutually exclusive, religions have religious experiences show that religious experience does not give us genuine knowledge of God because they each claim their religion is justified by their experience?

---

[48]In chapter i, of book ii, of his work Degeneration, "Max Nordau" seeks to undermine all mysticism by exposing the weakness of the lower kinds. Mysticism for him means any sudden perception of hidden significance in things. He explains such perception by the abundant uncompleted associations which experiences may arouse in a degenerate brain. These give to him who has the experience a vague and vast sense of its leading further, yet they awaken no definite or useful consequent in his thought. The explanation is a plausible one for certain sorts of feeling of significance. . . . But the higher mystical flights, with their positiveness and abruptness, are surely products of no such merely negative condition. It seems far more reasonable to ascribe them to inroads from the subconscious life, of the cerebral activity correlative to which we as yet know nothing.

[49]They sometimes add subjective *audita et visa* to the facts, but as these are usually interpreted as transmundane, they oblige no alteration in the facts of sense.

42. IS NUMINOUS EXPERIENCE EVIDENCE THAT GOD EXISTS?

Keith Yandell

Keith E. Yandell is Professor of Philosophy at the University of Wisconsin in Madison where he also teaches in the Religious Studies Program. He has published over 70 articles and book chapters, as well as *Basic Issues in the Philosophy of Religion*, (1971); *Christianity and Philosophy* (1984); *Hume's "Inexplicable Mystery"*, (1990); *The Epistemology of Religious Experience*, (1993); and *Philosophy of Religion*, (1999). Currently he is completing three additional books: *Comparative Philosophy of Religion; The Soul*; and *History of Modern Philosophy*.

In this selection, Yandell argues that the present widespread acceptance of materialism is not based on powerful arguments in its favor, but on current intellectual fashion. He further contends that the "big" question as to whether (numinous) religious experience provides evidence for religious belief can be properly answered only if one first answers some other questions. He states and answers these questions and then answers the "big" questions affirmatively: experiences of subject/consciousness/object form, or structure, provide evidence for the existence of what seems to be their object, and (numinous) religious experience is of that form. This evidence is not undercut by the sorts of considerations that can cancel experiential evidence.

READING QUESTIONS

1. What are the difficulties with the view that we can reasonably believe only what science tells us?
2. Do explanations of religious experiences, from the social sciences, undermine any evidence such experiences might provide?
3. What is it to have an experience and what sorts of experiences are there?
4. In what ways can an experience be discovered not to provide reliable evidence?
5. How can one tell whether or not (numinous) religious experience is evidence that God exists?

1. "SCIENTIFIC" MATERIALISM AND ITS DISCONTENTS

Pat: In the secular atmosphere of academia, religious experiences aren't going to be taken seriously as evidence for anything except the weird psychological state of the people who have them. I accept what science tells us. It doesn't tell us about God. So I don't think there is a God and I don't think that there is any evidence that God exists.[1]

Kim: It seems to me that there are *sciences* in the plural, that they differ, that within the scientific disciplines there are different and often competing theories, and that not only do these different

---

[1]This question is discussed in several recent books. William Alston, *Perceiving God* (Ithaca: Cornell University Press, 1991) favors a "doxastic" (belief-forming) practice approach. Carolyn Franks Davis, *The Evidential Force of Religious Experience* (Oxford: Clarendon Press, 1989) contains an excellent discussion of social science explanations of religious experience, but assumes—against powerful evidence—that religious experiences that seem quite diverse are all of the same thing. C. D. Broad presented an early version of the argument from religious experience in *Religion, Philosophy, and Psychical Research* (London: Routledge and Kegan Paul, 1953). C. B. Martin's *Religious Belief* (Ithaca: Cornell U. Press, 1989) presents a case against the argument and George Mavrodes, *Belief in God: A Study in the Epistemology of Religion* (New York: Random House, 1970) discusses Martin's views. The present author has discussed the argument in *The Epistemology of Religious Experience* (Cambridge: Cambridge University) Press, 1993) and *Philosophy of Religion* (London: Routledge, 1999).

disciplines use different methods but they support somewhat different views of how the world is.[2] But even if you are right it is one thing to accept what science says, and quite another to accept *only* what it says. Science doesn't say that *only what science says is true or something exists only if science says it does.*[3]

Pat: Perhaps not, but some philosophers say it for them.

Kim: So much the worse for those philosophers. How reasonable is it to follow the rule *Believe only what science says* when the sciences themselves (or science itself) doesn't say *Believe only what science says*? Such philosophers violate their own rule; they hold an inconsistent position of the form *we ought only to believe what science tells us, and science does not tell us that we ought only to believe what science tells us.*

Pat: Actually, I know some scientists who do say science tells us that.

Kim: In every field, you find people who sometimes confuse bits of their own autobiographies with what their disciplines teach. Such confusion doesn't turn autobiography into science or philosophy.

Pat: Let's turn to the fact that the only things we know to exist are material things. This is a view that science has established. It leaves no room for God.

Kim: The view that there are only material things isn't any part of science. When did any of the sciences establish it? What was the great experiment that shows that everything that exists is material? Materialism is a philosophical view that has taken credit for the successes of science, a claim that has the advantage of theft over honest labor. Many of the leaders of what historians call the Scientific Revolution believed in God and didn't find the slightest conflict between that belief and the belief that there is a material universe that manifests sufficient order to make both the sciences and everyday life possible.[4] In fact, they held that God was responsible for there being a natural order that is accessible to us and that makes life possible. After all, there are lots of ways the physical world might be that would not permit life and that would not be orderly in ways that are accessible to us.[5] The idea that the sciences presuppose, or that they support, materialism is one of the grand myths of the modern academy. It should be part of getting an education that one escapes this sort of mythology.

Pat: Perhaps you are right that materialism is philosophy, not science, and isn't either presupposed or supported by science. But tell me one case in which there is any reason to think that anything exists that isn't physical.

Kim: I'll give you an example that is accepted even by many materialists.[6] A proposition is anything that is true or false. Declarative sentences, used as we usually do use them, express propositions. The same proposition can be expressed in various sentences in the same language, and by sentences in different languages. Further, propositions bear logical relations to one another. A proposition is logically inconsistent with its denial and logically independent of propositions about entirely different things. A proposition entails some other propositions and in turn is entailed by some other propositions.[7]

Pat: I know all that. *Cheryl is taller than Tom and Tom is taller than Sue* entails *Cheryl is taller than Sue* because the latter can't be false when the former is true. So what?

Kim: Take your example: *Cheryl is taller than Tom and Tom is taller than Sue* entails *Cheryl is taller than Sue.* This true proposition says that one proposition entails another. Further, it is a *necessarily* true proposition. It is true that *Necessarily, Cheryl is taller than Tom and Tom is taller than Sue* entails

[2]See John Dupre', *The Disorder of Things* (Cambridge: Harvard U. Press, 1993).

[3]While his forays into philosophy seem to me sometimes dubious, the writings of physicist John Polkinghorne interestingly relate science and theology.

[4]On theism and the Scientific Revolution, see the writings of Stanley L. Jaki.

[5]For a brief discussion of the "fine-tuning" needed for life to occur, see John Polkinghorne, *Beyond Science* (Cambridge: Cambridge U. Press, 1996).

[6]See, for example, the article on Physicalism—another name for materialism—in Jaegwon Kim and Ernest Sosa, *A Companion to Metaphysics* (Oxford: Basil Blackwell, 1995), 391–393.

[7]On there being propositions, see Alvin Plantinga, *The Nature of Necessity* (Oxford: Clarendon Press, 1973).

Cheryl is taller than Sue. This is true in all possible worlds, and no matter what.[8]

Pat: You are making a lot of a little. We have (consciously or not) adopted certain conventions in virtue of which some propositions entail others. Perhaps the matter goes a little deeper and there is something in the structure of the human psyche that thinks in such a way that if one believes that *Cheryl is taller than Tom* and *Tom is taller than Sue* one also believes *Cheryl is taller than Sue.* Perhaps the human brain just works that way.

Kim: You're confusing two very different things. One concerns *how we come to see that entailments hold.* The other concerns *that in virtue of which entailments do hold.* It is the latter that is relevant here. If an entailment holds, it holds necessarily. Nothing that holds necessarily can hold in virtue of anything that might not have existed. There might not have been any people, any conventions, any human psyches, or any human brains. So it can't be the case that entailments hold in virtue of there being people, conventions, human psyches, or brains. Further, for anything at all that is material, it might not have existed. So it cannot be in virtue of anything material that entailments hold.

Pat: So what do you propose, to use your language, as "that in virtue of which entailments hold"?

Kim: So far as I know, there are just two candidates. One is that there are abstract objects. An abstract object is an item that exists necessarily, in all possible worlds, and no matter what. It lacks spatial position—it does not exist in, or any number of miles from, Cleveland. Some philosophers think that abstract objects are timeless or eternal, others think that they are everlasting or both beginningless and endless. For our purposes, it doesn't matter which view one takes. Further, an abstract object is not a person, is not conscious or self-conscious, and lacks causal powers—it can't bring it about that something occurs or prevent something from occurring by exercising some ability or capacity it has. Some contemporary materialists have qualified their position so as to say that there are abstract objects as well as material things because they have recognized that only in this way can there be necessary truths. After all, every correct rule of inference is correct because there is a corresponding necessarily true proposition.

Pat: Granting that there are immaterial abstract objects is a big qualification to materialism, even if it is made in order to allow for necessity in one's view of the world. Why not just deny that there is any such thing as necessity?

Kim: "Necessity" here is a matter of there being necessary truths. Our example has been a proposition that says, correctly, that a certain entailment holds. Other examples of necessary truths are *There are prime numbers greater than 17, If Sharon smiles then her smile has shape,* and *No world can contain dinosaurs without its containing living things.* To deny that there are necessary truths is to deny what is obviously so.

Pat: Just what are these supposed abstract objects? Can you give me an example?

Kim: The simplest answer is that it is propositions themselves that are the abstract objects. There are other proposed sorts of abstract objects—Plato's Forms, Frege's concepts, states of affairs, sets, numbers, and so on. It doesn't matter for our purposes exactly what abstract objects there are, important though this is in some contexts. The point is that there seems to be good reason to think there are such things, and that even some materialists grant that there are.

Pat: You said there were two candidates. Abstract objects gives us one. What is the other?

Kim: The thoughts of a necessarily existing God.

Pat: Somehow there being abstract objects sounds more attractive now than it did a moment ago. Can we go back to the question of how we can recognize entailments if they hold in virtue of there being abstract objects? It seems a bit much that our conventions, our psyches, or our brains just happen to accord with the ways in which abstract objects are related.

Kim: Plato, Augustine, Aquinas, and Leibniz, for example, were worried about the same question. Each held, in his own way, that if human beings were purely material then they would not be

---

[8]For more on propositions, see Arthur Pap, *Semantics and Necessary Truth* (New Haven: Yale University Press, 1963), Chapter Seven: The Linguistic Theory of the *A Priori.*

capable of recognizing such things. They inferred that persons are not purely material.

Pat: For a time, behaviorism was a popular view about so-called human thought. John B. Watson suggested that the brain secretes thought as the liver secretes bile, and that thought is simply the silent movement of the larynx. But the basic idea was that human thought is really nothing more than overt behavior, including linguistic behavior, and dispositions to behave. On that account, where is your supposed knowledge of entailments? [9]

Kim: Watson's claim about silent movement of the larynx ran straight into the simple fact that people whose larynx has been removed can do mathematics, which obviously involves thinking. The idea that thought is just actual and potential behavior ran into three basic problems. An analysis of the sort behaviorism proposes has a certain form or structure: A reduces without remainder into B. This requires that: *Necessarily, A is true if and only if B is true.* So behaviorism requires, for example, that (A) *John is thinking of baseball* if and only if (B) *John is behaving in a baseball way and would behave in different baseball ways if the occasion arose.* One problem is that John can simply not be behaving in any overt way and yet be thinking about baseball, and John can be thinking about baseball and sham behavior that suggests he is doing something else, say by pretending to take careful notes in a history class. So (A) can be true when (B) is false, and (B) can be true when (A) is false, and so the behaviorist analysis fails. A second problem is that in order for a proposed behaviorist analysis to be even remotely plausible, typically it has to refer to other mental states than the one being analyzed. A behaviorist analysis of *Ruth believes her dress is on fire* will refer only to Ruth's actual and potential behavior, but what that behavior will be will depend on Ruth's other beliefs and Ruth's desires. If Ruth has typical beliefs, she will dowse her dress with water or roll over and over to try to put out the flames. But if she believes that the dress won't really burn or that she is fireproof, or desires to be rescued by someone else, then she may behave quite differently. If John has unusual beliefs about baseball, he may break out into singing the Portuguese national anthem, falsely thinking it is sung before every National League game. But then the behaviorist has to introduce reference to other beliefs and desires and to "analize them out" in terms of behavior. To do that with any plausibility, still other mental states will have to be referred to, and the process never ends. There is a third problem, namely that a zombie—something without any mental states at all—could emit the behavior that supposedly was identical to thought. Finally, when you proposed behaviorism as a possibility, was all that was going on with you just your exhibiting a bit of linguistic behavior with perhaps a gesture or two thrown in, or did your words express a thought with which they weren't identical?

Pat: You know as well as I do that I wasn't just saying something that didn't express thoughts.

Kim: That is part of my point.

Pat: I can see why behaviorism has pretty much been abandoned. But isn't behaviorism an old view now, and hasn't it been replaced by other views? Functionalism, for example, says that to be a mental state is just to play a certain sort of causal role, and in order to play that role it needn't even be a conscious state.

Kim: That's right. So we are offered a view on which "having a mind" is characterized in such a way that even a creature completely without consciousness—a zombie, for example—can have an active mental life. Functionalism insists that there are things going on "in the head" when we think, and that thought is not reducible to behavior, but it adds that these things need not involve consciousness.[10] It claims that *being conscious*, let alone *being self-conscious*, is inessential, and can be fully absent, from *having a mind* and *being in a mental state.* Functionalism is more complex than its

[9]On Watson's views, see Brand Blanshard, *The Nature of Thought* (New York: Macmillan, 1939, 1940; 2 vols.), Chapter 27. See also, on behaviorism, James W. Cornman and Keith Lehrer, *Philosophical Problems and Arguments* (New York: Macmillan, 1974).

[10]See David Chalmers, *The Conscious Mind: In Search of a Fundamental Theory* (New York: Oxford University Press, 1996).

"NIRVANA" ✳ *Walpola Rahula*

Elsewhere the Buddha unequivocally uses the word Truth in place of Nibbāna: "I will teach you the Truth and the Path leading to the Truth." Here Truth definitely means Nirvāna.

Now, what is Absolute Truth? According to Buddhism, the Absolute Truth is that there is nothing absolute in the world, that everything is relative, conditioned and impermanent, and that there is no unchanging, everlasting, absolute substance like Self, Soul or Ātman within or without. This is the Absolute Truth. Truth is never negative, though there is a popular expression as negative truth. The realization of this Truth, that is, to see things as they are (*yathābhūtam*) without illusion or ignorance (*avijjā*), is the extinction of craving "thirst" (*Tanhakkhaya*), and the cessation (*Nirodha*) of *dukkha*, which is Nirvāna. It is interesting and useful to remember here the Mahāyāna view of Nirvāna as not being different from *Samsāra*. The same thing is Samsāra or Nirvāna according to the way you look at it—subjectively or objectively.

It is incorrect to think that Nirvāna is the natural result of the extinction of craving. Nirvāna is not the result of anything. If it would be a result, then it would be an effect produced by a cause. It would be *samkhata* "produced" and "conditioned." Nirvāna is neither cause nor effect. It is beyond cause and effect. Truth is not a result nor an effect. It is not produced like a mystic, spiritual, mental state, such as *dhyāna* or *samādhi*. TRUTH IS. NIRVĀNA IS. The only thing you can do is to see it, to realize it. There is a path leading to the realization of Nirvāna. But Nirvāna is not the result of this path. You may get to the mountain along a path, but the mountain is not the result, not an effect of the path. You may see a light, but the light is not the result of your eyesight.

From Walpola Rahula, *What the Buddha Taught* (1974).

---

predecessor, behaviorism, but it doesn't seem much more plausible.

Pat: To discuss whether or not persons are purely material beings will draw us into talking about contemporary philosophy of mind with all its complexities. Let's instead go back to your comment about different methods in science (or, if you want, the sciences). There is still a basic method in science, and central to it is a focus on what can be tasted, felt, heard, or smelled—on sensory experience. Confirmation or disconfirmation by sensory experience is the name of the game in evaluating scientific theories.

Kim: *Whatever we know is confirmed by sensory experience* isn't itself confirmed by sensory experience. It isn't a claim that *could* be confirmed, or disconfirmed, by sensory experience. Philosophers such as David Hume and A. J. Ayer held a view that asserted *Statements that are either true or false are either reports of sensory or introspective experience, definitions, or follow from reports and definitions* but, notoriously, this claim itself isn't a report of sensory or introspective experience. It isn't true in terms of any definition we typically accept, and while one could just stipulate a definition that made it true one could also just stipulate a definition that made it false. Views of this sort keep coming up in philosophy, and they keep getting shot down.

Pat: I wasn't trying to limit our overall knowledge, or even our scientific knowledge, to what can be confirmed by sensory experience. I was simply stressing its importance for science.

Kim: That I grant. Having a sensory experience is a matter of its sensorily seeming that there is something which, if it really exists, does so independent of being experienced.

Pat: I take it that you've been trying to convince me that there is something to knowledge beyond what science gives us and that there seem to be some things in our world that science doesn't discuss but philosophy does. Maybe you are right about these things. But it does not follow that God exists or that religious experience provides evidence that God exists. Can we turn to that?

2. EXPERIENTIAL EVIDENCE

Kim: Yes. I want to focus on one sort of religious experience. By an experience I mean a conscious state—to have an experience is a matter of being conscious in some manner. Suppose one feels depressed—not depressed *at* or *by* something, but subject to generalized depression. One feels a certain way; one is aware of being depressed. We might call this a *subject-awareness* experience. Contrast this to watching a tree bend in the wind. Here one is aware of something that exists independent of one's experiencing it. This is a *subject-consciousness-object* or SCO experience. Constrast this with one's wondering what the sum of 1007 and 2942 is, doing the addition in one's head, and coming to see that the answer is 3949. This we can call a *cognitive experience*. Experiences of each sort has its importance for religious traditions, but we'll concentrate on SCO experiences.

Pat: You want to contrast things like having a headache or feeling dizzy with sensory experiences. Having a headache or feeling dizzy isn't a matter of at least seeming to sense something that is "out there" independent of one's experience. Having a headache or feeling dizzy is a *way of experiencing* one's own condition but not even apparently *experiencing something external to oneself*. I assume you take experiences in which someone at least seems to experience God to be SCO experiences. But doesn't that assume that God exists?

Kim: I do take conscious states that, if they are reliable, are experiences of God to be SCO experiences. This doesn't assume that God exists or that religious experiences are reliable. Seeing an oasis and having a mirage are both SCO experiences. They are both experiences in which it at least *seems* to the subject that something exists, and if there is that something, it exists independent of its being experienced. The *structure* of the experi-

ence is internal to the experience, and the structure is SCO.

Pat: Couldn't one think of things like this: if someone has an experience in which it seems that there is something X, and there is an X, then the experience is SCO. But if there isn't any X, then the experience isn't SCO after all.

Kim: On this account, there can't be an *unreliable* SCO experience, and this seems false. We also can't tell whether an experience is SCO until we know whether it is reliable or not. I stick to my view that being SCO in structure is an internal feature of an experience, and (as logic texts say) I'll leave working out what my argument would look like on your proposal "as an exercise for the reader." I do want to add this: when one has an experience in which one seems to encounter something distinct from oneself, having that experience is *evidence* for the existence of that something. Sensory experiences are one sort of experience that is subject-consciousness-object in its very structure. But any sort of SCO experience is evidence for its apparent object.

Pat: I take it that this is going to be a crucial point in your overall argument. Suppose I seem to see an elephant in a room where I know there aren't any—the room is well known to me, has no secret entrances, has no doors or windows an elephant could come through, is well guarded against intruders, and so on. So I know things can't be the way they seem. Maybe I'm seeing an elephant hologram, or an elephant-shaped balloon, but I'm not actually seeing an elephant. What about your claim that *any SCO experience is evidence for its apparent object* then?

Kim: One way to deal with the sort of case you describe—it isn't the only one but it's the one that I prefer—is to say that if a person has an SCO experience in which it seems to her that she encounters some item X, she has *presumptive* evidence that there is an X. If you prefer, she has *prima facie* or *defeasible* evidence in favor of X's existence— evidence that is overturnable but real. Evidence typically is overturnable. In your elephant case, the observer has evidence that there is an elephant in the room. But he has better evidence that there isn't—strong enough evidence to think that things are not as they seem regarding the elephant. The pro-elephant evidence is defeated by other matters. But if evidence was defeated, then there was evidence to defeat.

Pat: There is another way of putting things here. One could say, as you do, that the evidence in favor of an elephant being present was canceled. Couldn't one also say that a person hasn't got evidence until she has reason to think that nothing cancels it? Then one would have to wait and see if anything occurred to one that did cancel the apparent evidence one had.

Kim: There are at least two problems with this way of approaching things. One is this: we've noted that it is always possible that experiential evidence of the sort we are concerned with may be evidence for a false claim. We should also note that it is always possible that it is evidence for a true claim. That it is possible that things aren't as they seem isn't a positive reason to doubt our experiential evidence, just as its being possible that things are as they seem isn't a positive reason to think things really are as they seem. If we take a "presumed guilty unless proved innocent" approach here, we are mistakenly supposing that *possibility of being defeated* is reason for taking an experience *to be defeated*. The other problem is simply that the reason to think things are as they seem is just that they do seem that way. If it looks as if there is an elephant there, that is (defeatable) reason to think there is.

Pat: I understand that some philosophers have developed an argument that appeals to doxastic or belief-forming practices, claiming that we work within a sensory practice in which we develop beliefs regarding the existence and properties of physical objects and within a religious practice in which we develop beliefs concerning God. Our perceptual practice assumes that there are physical objects and monotheistic religious practice assumes that God exists. Each practice has a complex system of possible defeaters that can bring us to revise our beliefs, so that we are not simply prisoners of how things initially seem to us. As the

British say, at the end of the day we then assess the degree to which a practice is successful or defensible. This assessment is particularly important in the religious case, since there are diverse and apparently logically independent religious practices, and not all of them are monotheistic. Will you take this route?

Kim: No. If it is true that SCO experiences provide presumptive evidence for the existence of their apparent objects, we don't need to complicate matters by talking about practices. Nor do we have to assume that there are physical objects or that God exists in order to claim that sensory and religious experiences are evidence that there are physical objects and God, respectively. We will consider ways in which presumptive evidence can be defeated.

This is important to our argument. I won't argue for this here, but I suspect that if one takes the units of evaluation in the theory of knowledge to be practices, one will end up with pragmatic considerations playing a determinative role in their assessment. Pragmatic considerations, it seems to me, don't justify claims that some proposition is true. But even considering all that would take us far afield. For now, I'll just take the belief-forming practice approach as a friendly path that I'm not going to take here.

Pat: Some appeals to N-experiences argue that the best explanation of their occurrence is that God causes them. Is this going to be your line of reasoning?

Kim: No. One could argue as follows: we seem to see buildings; the best explanation of our seeming to see buildings is that there are buildings; it is reasonable to accept the best explanation of things we know occur; so it is reasonable to believe that there are buildings. If reasonable beliefs are likely to be true, our belief that there are buildings is likely to be true.

Pat: But your argument that religious experience is evidence for God's existence isn't going to go like that?

Kim: No. I want to contrast that line of reasoning with the view I'll defend. We don't typically argue that it is reasonable to think that there are buildings because *there being buildings* is the best explanation of our seeming to see buildings. Our sensory experiences include our at least apparently seeing buildings, and we take those experiences as (sufficient) evidence that there are such things. More carefully, we take it that we do see what we seem to see. So, I'll view the best explanation approach as another friendly alternative that I'll not take here.

Pat: But whatever approach you take, the fact is that sometimes things are not as they seem—there isn't a patch of water that stays the same distance ahead of our car on the highway in the Summer, straight sticks dipped in water look bent when they aren't, and there are various illusions and hallucinations. Maybe seeing is believing, but believing isn't always being right.

Kim: Here we agree. SCO experiences provide evidence that their apparent objects exist, but we need to consider whether that evidence is defeated in some way.

Pat: Isn't it about time that you tell me exactly what sort of SCO religious experiences you have in mind?

Kim: The experiences that I have in mind have occurred to famous as well as very ordinary people. Here are some famous examples.

> Experience 1: Moses, tending the flock of his father-in-law Jethro, sees a bush that apparently is burning and not consumed by the fire. Then, the text of Exodus tells us: "And Moses said, 'I will turn aside and see this great sight, why the bush is not burnt.' When the Lord saw that he turned aside to see, God called to him out of the bush, 'Moses, Moses!' And he said, 'Here am I.' The he [God] said, 'Do not come near; put off your shoes from your feet, for the place on which you are standing is holy ground.' And he said, 'I am the God of your Father, the God of Abraham, the God of Isaac, the God of Jacob.' And Moses hid his face, for he was afraid to look at God." [Exodus 3:3–6]

> Experience 2: In the year that King Uzziah died I saw the Lord, high and holy and lifted up; and his train filled the temple. Above him stood the seraphim; each had six wings: with two he covered his face, and with two he covered his feet, and with two he flew. And one called to another and said: "Holy, holy, holy is the Lord of Hosts; the whole earth is full of His glory." And the foundations of the thresholds shook at the voice of him who called, and the house was filled with smoke. And I said: "Woe is me! For I am lost; for I am a man of unclean lips and I dwell in the midst of a people of unclean lips; for my eyes have seen the king, the Lord of hosts!" Then flew one of the seraphims to me, having in his hand a burning coal which he had taken with tongs from the altar. And he touched my mouth, and said: Behold, this has touched your lips; your guilt is taken away, and your sin forgiven.' And I heard the Lord saying, "Whom shall I send, and who will go for us?" Then I said, "Here I am! Send me." And he said, "Go. . .". (Isaiah 6:1–9)

> Experience 3: I [John] was in the Spirit on the Lord's day, and I heard behind me a loud voice like a trumpet saying, "Write what you see in a book and send it to the seven churches. . . . Then I turned to see the voice that was speaking to me, and on turning I saw seven golden lampstands, and in the midst of the lampstands one like a son of man, clothed with a long robe and with a golden girdle round his breast; his head and his hair were white as wool, white as snow; his eyes were like a flame of fire, his feet were like burnished bronze, refined as in a furnace, and his voice was like the sound of many waters; in his right hand he held seven stars, from his mouth issued a sharp two-edged sword, and his face was like the sun shining in full strength. When I saw him, I fell at his feet as though dead. But he laid his right hand upon me, saying "Fear not, I am the first and the last, and the living one; I died, and behold I am alive forevermore, and I have the keys of Death and Hades." [Revelation 1:10–18]

Of course not all apparent experiences of God are so "electric" as these, and apparently lots of people have them sometime or other during their lifetimes.[11] Roughly, having an experience of this sort is a matter of at least seeming to be in the presence of a holy, living, majestic, powerful being on whom one is dependent and before whom one is awed. Due to Rudolph Otto, these have come to be called "numinous" experiences—experiences of the holy. In order to have a convenient term, let's call them "N-experiences."

Pat: What are we to make of the visual and auditory language in these descriptions, since God is not supposed to have a body.

Kim: The usual view is that the visual and auditory imagery are a means by which God communicates with human beings—not that God actually sits on a throne, for example, but that God is a powerful being.

Pat: The phenomenological content of these experiences suggests a being like God, but not necessarily God—not necessarily a being that is omnipotent and omniscient, let alone creator and providence and savior and judge.

Kim: You are right that N-experiences suggest a being who is powerful, majestic, holy, living, and the like, but the idea that this being is omnipotent or omniscient goes beyond anything that is experientally given. In fact, it isn't clear what it would be for either omnipotence or omniscience to be experientially given. This is another case of what philosophers of science have called "underdetermination." Once the content of experience is accurately described, there remain different ways to proceed theoretically. The theoretical concepts of science, and the doctrinal concepts of theology, develop in the context of further considerations besides experiential content. So far as I know, this is a matter that deserves much fully and richer dis-

cussion, both in philosophy of science and in theology, than it has thus far received.

3. DISANALOGIES BETWEEN SENSORY AND NUMINOUS EXPERIENCE

Pat: I'm surprised that you suggest that such experiences are evidence for God's existence. Just stop and think of the ways in which sensory experience differs from religious experience. Suppose you and I are sitting down and relaxing after an exam. You suddenly have what you think of as a sense of the presence of God, whatever that is. I don't feel anything. My not feeling anything isn't supposed to be evidence that you aren't sensing the presence of God. But if I were to at least seem to see a collie run across the grass of a fenced-in yard and you seem to see just an empty lawn, either I'm hallucinating a collie or you are collie-blind. Not so in the experiencing God case. In the collie case, we can see if there is a collie somewhere inside the fence, which is too high for it to get away, so if the collie was really here, we can tell because then we'll find it. If we look carefully and find no dogs here, when there was no way for a dog to get out if one was here, I'll have to conclude I didn't really see a collie running after all. Not so with God. We can run tests, if we like, to find out what collies look like when they run, and make predictions as to what we'll see, and find out whether they come true or not. Not so with God. In places where there are collies, everyone sees them. Not so with God. If we doubt the deliverances of our sight regarding collies, we can scratch behind their ears, hear them bark, smell their wet fur—there are multiple senses through which we can detect the presence of collies. There isn't anything like multiple sensory modalities for experiencing God. How many disanalogies do you need before you grant that while sensory experience is evidence for the existence of what one seems to sense, religious experience isn't evidence for God's existence?

Kim: There are all of the disanalogies you point out. The question is whether your conclusion follows from there being those disanalogies. Let's look at them one by one. First, religious experience is not

---

[11]The classic discussion of such experiences is Rudolph Otto, *The Idea of the Holy* (Oxford: Oxford U. Press, 1936); for some reservations about some of Otto's discussion, see Keith E. Yandell, *Basic Issues in the Philosophy of Religion* (Boston: Allyn and Bacon, 1971). Examples of more ordinary religious experiences can be found in William James, *Varieties of Religious Experience* (Glasgow: Collins Fount Paperbacks, 1977), Alasdair Hardy, *The Spiritual Nature of Man* (Oxford: Clarendon Press, 1979), and Timothy Beardsworth, *A Sense of Presence* (Oxford: Religious Experience Research Unit, 1977). Oxford's Religious Experience Research Unit has collected a large number of descriptions of religious experience.

public in this sense: if one person at some time and in some place has an experience of God, the reliability of that experience—its actually being an experience of God—isn't called in question simply because someone else at the same time and in the same place does not even seem to have an experience of God. How does that show that the person who has the religious experience does not thereby have evidence that God exists? That such experience is not public in the sense just defined entails that one sort of check on the reliability of the experience is not available. But that is not at all the same thing as the experience not being evidence. You need some such claim as this: *one person's experience of something at some time and in some place cannot be evidence for the existence of that something unless another person in the same place and at the same time also experiences that something.* Roughly, this seems right about physical somethings. Why suppose it is right about God? Why suppose that if God causes one person to have an experience of God at some time and place, God must cause everyone in that place at that time to have an experience of God?

Pat: Perhaps that deals with one disanalogy. What about the others?

Kim: You point out that there don't seem to be a variety of capacities or modalities of experiencing God, whereas one can, say, see, touch, taste, and smell a chocolate mint, hear the sound it makes if you drop it one the table. But that is important only if one cannot in some way or other check one experience of God against another. In fact, we have descriptions of religious experience from different times and cultures, and when we compare them there is a surprising uniformity. The philosophical interest of various sorts of sensory access comes simply in terms of their providing relevant comparisons—something available in the case of religious experiences in another way. We can, of course, compare sensory experiences too; that is a similarity between sensory and religious experiences.

Kim: Another disanalogy concerns possible disconfirmation: *you can't experientially disconfirm that God was present.* Some philosophers will take this as decisive, arguing that if you can have experiential

evidence for the existence of something then, in principle anyway, you could have experiential evidence against its existence. If you accept that idea, and there can't be experiential disconfirmation of God's existence, then there can't be experiential evidence for God's existence.

Pat: That would end our discussion. Let me suggest that there is evidence against the existence of God, namely the existence of evil. When we experience evil, we have experiential evidence against God's existence. So the principle that if you can have experiential evidence for the existence of something, then in principle you can have experiential evidence against its existence, is satisfied in God's case after all.

Kim: This is a possible line of reply and I appreciate your mentioning it. I don't, though, accept it. For one thing, I don't think that the existence, or the experience, of evil does provide evidence against the existence of God, though that is another story. More importantly for present purposes, I think the challenge can be met more directly, to the degree that it is a correct challenge in the first place.

Pat: What, exactly, is your reservation about the challenge?

Kim: My reservation is this. Suppose there are some very tiny particles that appear only entirely randomly and so unpredictably. These particles, let's suppose, are postulated in a theory—*shyness theory*, let's call it—that explains some newly noticed energy changes that occur randomly. It dawns on some particularly creative physicist that these shy particles occur under conditions that are enormously costly to produce. Since these conditions are being produced for other reasons anyway, the physicist produces a shymeter that itself operates randomly, this being the only sort of instrument that will register the presence of shy particles. Given the odds against such particles occurring are already incredibly high, and the odds against the shymeter detecting them even if they are there are also high, there is little hope for positive results. But the nearly impossible happens and the shymeter reliably detects the presence of shy particles. There is a crucial asymmetry here: *that there are shy particles* is confirmable but not disconfirmable. *Not* observing any shy particles is just what one would expect, even if there are such items. If this sort of scenario is possible, then the idea that if there can be experiential evidence for the existence of something then, in principle, there can be experiential evidence against its existence is false.

Pat: And if there is some subtle reason why this sort of scenario isn't possible? We are supposed to be discussing the view that if it is impossible to have experiential evidence of a given kind *against* the existence of something it is also impossible to have experiential evidence *for* its existence. Unanswered prayer and evil aren't supposed to be evidence against God's existence and I suspect you don't think there is, or even could be, *any* experiential evidence against God's existence. So, if those philosophers are right, there can't be any evidence for God's existence.

Kim: Their view is controversial, but for now I'll just grant it for the sake of the argument. So far as I know there isn't any experiential evidence against God's existence. But it does not follow that there couldn't be such evidence. We need to note that there are two distinct ways in which one can have evidence against the existence of something. Here is one way: you find some circumstance in which, if something X exists, X will show up. Here is another way: you find a circumstance in which something Y exists, where Y's existence is evidence against X's existence.

Pat: What good will that distinction do you?

Kim: Suppose everybody who held some position of responsibility in any monotheistic religious community—every bishop, pastor, rabbi, priest, imam, nun, and so on all around the world—had an experience that I'll call a *Great Deception Experience*. Each of them was outdoors, suspended ten feet in the air to get their attention, and subjected to an experience in which they alternately seemed to undergo an N-experience of a certain sort followed by a terrifying laughter and a voice saying "I caused that experience, and it was a deception." So a priest or nun or rabbi or the pope would be suspended in the air, have an experience like Moses had at the burning bush, and then there would be that terrifying laughter and voice, and then they'd have an experience like Isaiah's vi-

sion, followed by the laughter and voice, and so on. The experiences would reflect the phenomenologies of Indian monotheistic experiences, African monotheistic experiences, and so on through all the world's monotheisms. These experiences would be, so to speak, *bad* N-experiences. They would provide evidence against God's existence, since they would provide evidence of the existence of a being who caused sham experience of God which has played an important role in the development of monotheism around the world. It is at least very plausible that if God exists, God will not allow that to happen.

Pat: Maybe God would have sufficient reason to allow even that. Maybe God is testing people's faith, or allowing the Devil to cause such experiences to test their faith.

Kim: That is logically possible. But the fact that it is logically possible doesn't entail that, if the Great Deception Experience occurred, its occurrence would be at least some evidence against the existence of God. So it is *possible* that there be experiences of the same sort as N-experiences that provided evidence against God's existence. So if negative evidence must be possible if positive evidence is to exist, that is consistent with my argument.

Pat: Perhaps we can say "so far, so good." But what about other ways in which whatever evidence N-experiences provide for God's existence can be defeated?

Kim: We can take our cue from the ways in which sensory experience can "go wrong." Suppose the water we drink today contains a pigeon hallucinogen so that, if we've drunk any of it, we'll seem to see pigeons whether there are any around or not. This will defeat apparent pigeon sightings as evidence for there being pigeons in the neighborhood. If we are aware of this feature of the water, we won't suppose that our at least seeming to see pigeons to be evidence that there are some around. Or suppose the pigeon hallucinogen works exactly half the time. The same things applies. We'd seem to see pigeons whether there are any around or not.

Pat: So if we learn that an N-experience is caused by a God-hallucinogen, that defeats it as evidence for God?

Kim: I'll agree to not appeal to any such N-experiences as evidence. But notice that if a person has an N-experience that they have no reason to suppose is caused by an N-hallucinogen, then so far the N-experience holds up as evidence.

Pat: Let's be sure we understand each other here. Suppose a brainometer chip is constructed that records the states a brain is in at each given time, and a chip is implanted in the brain of each of millions of volunteers. Some of the volunteers have N-experiences and we discover that the brain of each person who has an N-experience is in a state G when the experience occurs. Finally, we find a way of bringing it about that a person's brain is in state G, so that we can produce N-experiences in people whenever we want. If these conditions were satisfied, wouldn't we know that N-experiences weren't evidence for God's existence?

Kim: Suppose that an imageometer chip is constructed that records the images that occur on the retina at each given time, and a chip is implanted in the brain of each of millions of volunteers. Some of the volunteers have experiences in which they at least seem to see a chair and we discover that every person who comes to believe that she is seeing a chair has a retinal image of a chair. Finally, we discover a way to bring it about that a person's retina contains an image of a chair. If these conditions were satisfied, would we know that at least seeing a chair is not evidence that there is a chair to be seen?

Pat: You've changed things with your story. A retinal image of a chair is typically produced by a causal chain that includes a chair. So to talk about a retinal image of a chair is to introduce what we might call pro-evidence regarding there being a chair. The brain being in some "X state" isn't analogous to there being a retinal image.

Kim: I see why you say that. But we need to fine-tune your story a bit. Your "G state" in the brain is either, on your view, correlated with an N-experience—one's brain being in an X state is sufficient for one's having an N-experience—or (if you are a materialist) it is identical to an N-experience. But an N-experience has a certain phenomenology—having it is a matter of seeming to see God.

Pat: Still, your analogy introduces a new element. There being a retinal image is part of a causal process that leads to one's having the visual experience we call seeing a chair; at least this is so according to our best current theory. Reference to retinal images in your analogy beings in theoretical considerations you don't want to have a role in the line of reasoning you are developing.

Kim: You are right about that; I withdraw any reference to retinal images. Suppose, then, we stick with your brainometer. It tells us that when people see chairs, their brains are in a brain state of sort C. Then we discover how to produce C states whether there are chairs around or not. Does this bring into doubt whether we see chairs or whether experiences in which we at least seem to see them are typically evidence that there are chairs to be seen?

Pat: Don't we have to make exceptions of the cases in which C states are, so to speak, artificially produced?

Kim: Yes, but not the ones that are not artificially produced. Similarly, we make exceptions of the cases in which G states are, so to speak, artificially produced, but not the ones that aren't. That those who suffer from delirium tremens often seem to see insects that aren't there does not endanger the science of entomology. If a human being is experiencing having something, presumably the brain will be in some active state or other. Your assumption is that if two persons are experiencing God, or a chair, their brains will be in the same sort of state—each will be in its own G state or its own C state. I don't know whether that is right or not, but suppose it is. Suppose, further, we learn how to put brains in C states—you just implant a little chip in someone's brain, and activate it by pressing an electronically sensitive spot on a thing that looks like a credit card. Suppose we all agree to activate the chip only when there is no chair around, so we won't have a case in which a C state is overdetermined—caused both by seeing chair and by the chip being activated. So if you are chatting with Merritt, in whose brain the chip has been planted, then if you like you can cause Merritt to seem to see a chair by pressing a spot on a piece of plastic, even though there is no chair in the vicinity.

Pat: Right, and we have learned how to cause G-experiences at will, and we do it by another chip, and that chip was also implanted in Merritt's brain, you can cause Merritt to have an N-experience by pressing on another spot on another piece of plastic, quite independent of whether God is around or not.

Kim: Let's take the cases one at a time. If we cause Merritt's brain to be in a C state, Merritt presumably will think there is a chair around. Further, given that Merritt does not know about the chip having been implanted, Merritt will believe that there is a chair around, and will be justified in having that belief. But the belief won't be favored by any evidence—it will just seem to Merritt that it is.

Pat: Right, and the same thing will be true in the case of our causing Merritt to have a G experience.

Kim: It is less clear here. A monotheist who understand monotheism well will hold that whatever exists, even though it might not have existed, and *can* be caused to exist, is caused to exist by God. Further, she will believe that every such thing is sustained in existence by God so long as it exists at all. There isn't any such thing as "God not being around" and God might use G state in the brain, caused by us, to be a genuine revelation to Merritt—to be an experience in which we played a role in a causal chain in which God also played a role and which provided true information to Merritt.

Pat: That complicates things considerably. It even raises the question as to whether there could be an at least apparant experience of God that was not also a genuine experience of God.

Kim: We can simplify things. Suppose we agree to simply set aside experiences correlated with G states of the brain if they are at least in part caused by activating chips implanted in someone's brain. Let's also set aside drug-induced G states. In both cases, I'll not appeal to them as evidence. Most N-experiences aren't drug-induced and of course aren't caused by activating chips that have been placed in people's brains. The point to be remembered here is that when we have discovered how certain sorts of brain states can be artificially produced—for example, in persons suffering from delirium tremens—we rightly haven't concluded

that similar states not artificially produced are not evidence.

Pat: So where does this leave us.

Kim: If every N-experience is accompanied by a G state in the brain of the person who has it, and we learn how to produce G state in brains, this won't call into question the evidential worth of N-experiences *not* produced by us any more than the fact that one can produce insect hallucination by getting delirium tremens challenges our experience of insects as evidence for claims about insects.

Pat: Fair enough. Next question: I don't think anyone has held this about the concept of a pigeon, but people have held that the concept of God is logically inconsistent. If they are right, won't that make actual experience of God impossible?

Kim: Yes. Further, some concepts of God are inconsistent. For example, if one holds that God is omnipotent in the sense of doing the logically impossible, that notion of omnipotence is inconsistent. Thus, so is any concept of God which includes it. But there are other concepts of omnipotence that are not inconsistent. All I require is that there be some concept of God that is logically consistent and religiously adequate in the sense of expressing monotheistic belief concerning the supreme being.

Pat: These days social scientists—in particular, those who do sociology, psychology, or anthropology of religion—emphasize that their work is neutral regarding the reliability of religious experience. In earlier day, social scientists often offered explanations that were intended to explain religious experiences in ways that rendered these experiences unreliable. What do you think about social-science explicability of religious experience?

Kim: Anyone who has a sensory or religious experience will be a member of some culture and some society, and will be in some psychological state. They will also be in some physiological state. In principle at least, any experience can be "explained" in terms of a social science explanation in the sense of specifying the cultural, social, psychological, and physiological conditions under which it occurred. That there be some such conditions may be a necessary condition of the experience in question occurring, and typically this does not in any way negate whatever evidential force the experience has. If it did, then, since social science explanations can be given of the experiences social scientists have in their professional capacities, social science explanations would undercut their own credibility.

Pat: What if I have an N-experience and I also have a knock-down proof that there is no God.

Kim: Then you have conflicting evidence, which sometimes happens. Either your experience is not reliable or your proof is subtly mistaken. But I'll bet you don't have any such proof.

Pat: Neither have I had an N-experience, and it would be irrational of me to accept anyone else's N-experience as evidence that God exists.

Kim: I don't see the irrationality there. I haven't seen the Great Wall of China, and until recently I hadn't seen the Liffey River in Ireland. But I had good reason to think there are such things, though maybe I've got better reason regarding the Liffey since I've seen it myself. A great many of the things we believe, we accept on the testimony of others. I have never understood why the N-experiences of others cannot be evidence for me. Suppose you sincerely reported that you had an N-experience, and described it to me, and we both agreed it was an N-experience. Then even if you didn't take it as evidence that God exists, I think your not so taking it would be a mistake and I don't see any good reason that I shouldn't take it as evidence.

Pat: So what is the upshot of your argument?

Kim: Typically people who have had N-experiences don't have them in contexts where they've reason to suppose they'd have them even if God did not exist, or that the experience has been produced in some manner that defeats its evidential force. The concept of God does not seem to be contradictory. The content of N-experiences does not seem to lead to conflicting views concerning the nature of the being apparently experienced. So N-experiences provide evidence that God exists.

4. LANGUAGE ABOUT GOD

Pat: Even philosophers and theologians who believe in God are hesitant about the adequacy of their language about God. They have claimed that God cannot be spoken of literally, but only analogically, metaphorically, or the like. If this is so, doesn't it interfere with exactly what we can experiential evidence for, even if there is such evidence? If God is so very hard to describe, doesn't this make it hard to tell what would even count as experiential evidence for the existence of God?

Kim: Various thinkers have made things needlessly hard for themselves here. One source of the problem has been the baseless assumption *All language is metaphorical*, which is a counterexample to itself. Another is the idea that we can't talk clearly about the nonphysical and nonsensory, which ignores the fact that logic and mathematics are our best models of clarity and discourse concerning abstract objects is perfectly intelligible. Still another is the idea that God does not share a genus or kind with anything else, and words mean something different when applied to things of different kinds. This seems false regarding such terms as *is holy* and *is self-conscious*, and concerning such actions as *making a promise*.[12]

Pat: I assume that you have the same view regarding such terms as *majestic*, *living*, and the other terms involved in describing the phenomenology of N-experiences.

Kim: Right. There is a further point here. Consider these (rough) definitions:

God is *omnipotent* if and only if, for any proposition P, neither P itself, nor *God makes P true*, is necessarily false.

God is *omniscient* if and only if, for any proposition P, if P is true, and *God knows that P* is not necessarily false, then God knows that P.

God is *independent* if and only if there is no X such that X is distinct from God and God depends for existence on X.

God is *necessarily independent* if and only if it is necessarily true that theres no X such that X is distinct from God and God depends for existence on X.

This is a short list of claims that monotheists believe to be true about God, and each is literal. Fur-

[12]See William P. Alston, *Divine Nature and Human Language* (Ithaca: Cornell U. Press, 1989).

ther, the notions of omnipotence and omniscience don't apply to anything but God, so there is no question of cross-genus ambiguity here. As to *independence* and *necessary independence*, if they apply to both God and abstract objects, they bear the same sense in both cases.

Pat: The natures of particles and fields as described by physical theory is quite different from the way physical things appear to us. On your account, theology might well give us a more accurate account of God than common sense beliefs give us of the physical world.

Kim: This may be correct.

Pat: What would happen to your argument if sensory experience turned out to be unreliable?

Kim: My argument has relied on the claim that if one has an SCO experience whose apparent object is X, that is presumptive evidence that X exists, and that N-experiences are SCO in structure. Further, I've claimed that the evidence that N-experiences

provide is not defeated. Suppose it turned out that the evidence supplied by sensory experience were somehow defeated. Nothing would change regarding the evidence N-experiences provide.

QUESTIONS FOR FURTHER REFLECTION

1. What sorts of evidence other than religious experience is there regarding the existence of God?
2. Does that other evidence support or conflict with the evidence provided by religious experience?
3. Does religious experience that is not subject-consciousness-object in structure provide evidence for religious beliefs?
4. Can one person's religious experience provide evidence to someone else?
5. What sorts of considerations are involved in making a belief that is underdetermined by experience more determinate?

43. PERCEIVING GOD

William P. Alston

William Alston (1922–   ) is Professor of Philosophy Emeritus at Syracuse University. He has written extensively in the philosophy of language, epistemology, and the philosophy of religion. The editor and author of many books, he is also the author of more than 150 journal articles, many anthologized, 18 articles in the Encyclopedia of Philosophy (1967), and numerous reviews. Two collections of his essays have been published by Cornell University Press (1989): *Epistemic Justification: Essays in Epistemology* and *Divine Nature and Human Language: Essays in Philosophical Theology*. His most recent books are *Perceiving God: A Study in the Epistemology of Religious Experience*, (1991); *The Reliability of Sense Perception*, (1993); *A Realist Conception of Truth*, (1995); and *Illocutionary Acts and Sentence Meaning*, (2000). In the following selection, Alston argues that religious experience provides *prima facie* justification for belief in God.

READING QUESTIONS

1. Which two types of perception does Alston compare?
2. What is the possibility Alston wants to explore?
3. What are "M-beliefs"?
4. Why does Alston think that Objection III assumes a double standard?
5. Why does he think that Objection VI assumes epistemic chauvinism?

I want to explore and defend the idea that the experience, or, as I shall say, the *perception* of God plays an epistemic role with respect to beliefs about God importantly analogous to that played by sense perception with respect to beliefs about the physical world. The nature of that latter role is, of course, a matter of controversy, and I have no time here to go into those controversies. It is admitted, however, on (almost) all hands that sense perception provides us with knowledge (justified belief) about current states of affairs in the immediate environment of the perceiver and that knowledge of this sort is somehow required for any further knowledge of the physical world. The possibility I wish to explore is that what a person takes to be an experience of God can provide him/her with knowledge (justified beliefs) about what God is doing, or how God is "situated," *vis-à-vis* that subject at that moment. Thus, by experiencing the presence and activity of God, S can come to know (justifiably believe) that God is sustaining her in being, filling her with His love, strengthening her, or communicating a certain message to her. Let's call beliefs as to how God is currently related to the subject M-*beliefs* (M for manifestation); these are the "perceptual beliefs" of the theological sphere. I shall suppose that here too the "perceptual" knowledge one acquires from experience is crucial for whatever else we can learn about God, though I won't have time to explore and defend that part of the position; I will have my hands full defending the claim that M-beliefs are justified. I will just make two quick points about the role of M-beliefs in the larger scheme. First, just as with our knowledge of the physical world, the recognition of a crucial role for perceptual knowledge is compatible with a wide variety of views as to just how it figures in the total system and as to what else is involved. Second, an important difference between the two spheres is that in the theological sphere perceptual beliefs as to what God has "said" (communicated, revealed) to one or another person play a major role.

I have been speaking alternatively of perceptual *knowledge* and of the *justification* of perceptual beliefs. In this paper I shall concentrate on justification, leaving to one side whatever else is involved in knowledge. It will be my contention that (putative) experience of God is a source of justification for M-beliefs, somewhat in the way that sense experience is a source of justification for perceptual beliefs. Again, it is quite controver-

sial what this latter way is. I shall be thinking of it in terms of a direct-realist construal of sense perception, according to which I can be justified in supposing that my dog is wagging his tail just because something is visually presenting itself to me as (looks like) my dog wagging his tail; that is, it looks to me in such a way that I am thereby justified in thereby supposing it to be my dog wagging his tail. Analogously I think of the "experience of God" as a matter of something's presenting itself to one's experience as God (doing so and so); so that here too the subject is justified in believing that God is present to her, or is doing so and so *vis-à-vis* her, just because that is the way in which the object is presented to her experience. (For the purposes of this paper let's focus on those cases in which this presentation is not via any *sensory* qualities or sensorily perceivable objects. The experience involved will be nonsensory in character.) It is because I think of the experience of God as having basically the same structure as the sense perception of physical objects that I feel entitled to speak of "perceiving God." But though I construe the matter in direct-realist terms, most of what I have to say here will be relevant to a defense of the more general claim that the experiential justification of M-beliefs is importantly parallel to the experiential justification of perceptual beliefs about the physical environment, on any halfway plausible construal of the latter, at least on any halfway plausible realist construal.

I shall develop the position by way of responding to a number of objections. This procedure reflects my conviction that the very considerable incidence of putative perceptions of God creates a certain initial presumption that these experiences are what they seem to be and that something can thereby be learned about God.

OBJECTION I

What reason do we have for supposing that anyone ever does really perceive God? In order for S to perceive God it would have to be the case that (1) God exists, and (2) God is related to S or to his experience in such a way as to be perceivable by him. Only after we have seen reason to accept all that will we take seriously any claim to perceive God.

Answer. It all depends on what you will take as a reason. What you have in mind, presumably, are reasons drawn from some source other than perceptions of God, for example metaphysical arguments for the existence and nature of God. But why do you think you are justified in that restriction? We don't proceed in this way with respect to sense perception. Although in determining whether a particular alleged perception was genuine we don't make use of the results of *that* perception, we do utilize what has been observed in many other cases. And what alternative is there? The conditions of veridical sense perception have to do with states of affairs and causal interactions in the physical world, matters to which we have no cognitive access that is not based on sense perception. In like fashion, if there is a divine reality, why suppose that the conditions of veridically perceiving it could be ascertained without relying on perceptions of *it*? In requiring external validation in this case but not the other you are arbitrarily imposing a double standard.

OBJECTION II

There are many contradictions in the body of M-beliefs. In particular, persons report communications from God that contradict other reported communications. How, then, can one claim that all M-beliefs are justified?

Answer. What is (should be) claimed is only *prima facie* justification. When a person believes that God is experientially present to him, that belief is justified *unless* the subject has sufficient reasons to suppose it to be false or to suppose that the experience is not, in these circumstances, sufficiently indicative of the truth of the belief. This is, of course, precisely the status of individual perceptual beliefs about the physical environment. When, seeming to see a lake, I believe there to be a lake in front of me, my belief is thereby justified unless I have sufficient reason to suppose it false or to suppose that, in these circumstances, the experience is not sufficiently indicative of the truth of the belief.

OBJECTION III

It is rational to form beliefs about the physical environment on the basis of the way that environment appears to us in sense experience (call this practice of belief formation *SP*) because that is a generally reliable mode of belief formation. And it is reliable just

because, in normal conditions, sense experience varies concomitantly with variations in what we take ourselves to be perceiving. But we have no reason to suppose any such regular covariation for putative perception of God. And hence we lack reason for regarding as rational the parallel practice of forming M-beliefs on the basis of what is taken to be a perception of God (call that practice *RE*).

Answer. This is another use of a double standard. How do we know that normal sense experience varies concomitantly with perceived objects? We don't know this *a priori*. Rather, we have strong empirical evidence for it. That is, by relying on sense perception for our data we have piled up evidence for the reliability of *SP*. Let's call the kind of circularity exhibited here *epistemic circularity*. It is involved whenever the premises in an argument for the reliability or rationality of a belief-forming practice have themselves been acquired by that practice.[1] If we allow epistemically circular arguments, the reliability of *RE* can be supported in the same way. Among the things people have claimed to learn from *RE* is that God will enable people to experience His presence and activity from time to time in a veridical way. By relying on what one learns from the practice of *RE*, one can show that *RE* is a reliable belief-forming practice. On the other hand, if epistemically circular arguments are not countenanced, there can be no significant basis for a reliability claim in either case.

OBJECTION IV

A claim to perceive X, and so to form reliable perceptual beliefs about X on the basis of this, presupposes that the experience involved is best explained by the activity of X, *inter alia*. But it seems that we can give adequate explanations of putative experiences of God in purely naturalistic terms, without bringing God into the explanation at all. Whereas we can't give adequate explanations of normal sense experience without bringing the experienced external objects into the explanation. Hence *RE*, but not *SP*, is discredited by these considerations.

---

[1]See my "Epistemic Circularity," *Philosophy and Phenomenological Research*, 47, 1 (September 1986): pp. 1–30.

Answer. I do not believe that much of a case can be made for the adequacy of any naturalistic explanation of experiences of God. But for present purposes I want to concentrate on the way in which this objection once more depends on a double standard. You will have no case at all for your claim unless you, question-beggingly, restrict yourself to sources of evidence that exclude *RE*. For from *RE* and systems built up on its output we learn that God is involved in the explanation of every fact whatever. But you would not proceed in that way with *SP*. If it is a question of determining the best explanation of sense experience you will, of course, make use of what you think you have learned from *SP*. Again, you have arbitrarily applied different standards to the two practices.

Here is another point. Suppose that one could give a purely psychological or physiological explanation of the experiences in question. That is quite compatible with God's figuring among their causes and, hence, coming into an ideally complete explanation. After all, it is presumably possible to give an adequate causal explanation of sense experience in terms of what goes on within the skull, but that is quite compatible with the external perceived objects' figuring further back along the causal chain.

OBJECTION V

You have been accusing me of *arbitrarily* employing a double standard. But I maintain that *RE* differs from *SP* in ways that make different standards appropriate. *SP* is a pervasive and inescapable feature of our lives. Sense experience is insistent, omnipresent, vivid, and richly detailed. We use it as a source of information during all our waking hours. *RE*, by contrast, is not universally shared; and even for its devotees its practice is relatively infrequent. Moreover, its deliverances are, by comparison, meager, obscure, and uncertain. Thus when an output of *RE* does pop up, it is naturally greeted with more skepticism, and one properly demands more for its validation than in the case of so regular and central part of our lives as *SP*.

Answer. I don't want to deny either the existence or the importance of these differences. I want to deny only that they have the alleged bearing on the epistemic situation. Why should we suppose that a cognitive access enjoyed only by a part of the population is less likely to be reliable than one that is universally distributed? Why should we suppose that a source that yields less detailed and less fully understood beliefs is more suspect than a richer source? A *priori* it would seem just as likely that some aspects of reality are accessible only to persons that satisfy certain conditions not satisfied by all human beings as that some aspects are equally accessible to all. A *priori* it would seem just as likely that some aspects of reality are humanly graspable only in a fragmentary and opaque manner as that some aspects are graspable in a more nearly complete and pellucid fashion. Why view the one sort of cognitive claim with more suspicion than the other? I will agree that the spotty distribution of *RE* calls for explanation, as do the various cognitively unsatisfactory features of its output. But, for that matter, so does the universal distribution and cognitive richness of *SP*. And in both cases explanations are forthcoming, though in both cases the outputs of the practices are utilized in order to achieve those explanations. As for *RE*, the limited distribution may be explained by the fact that many persons are not prepared to meet the moral and other "way of life" conditions that God has set for awareness of Himself. And the cognitively unsatisfactory features of the doxastic output are explained by the fact that God infinitely exceeds our cognitive powers.

OBJECTION VI

When someone claims to see a spruce tree in a certain spot, the claim is checkable. Other people can take a look, photographs can be taken, the subject's condition can be diagnosed, and so on. But there are no comparable checks and tests available in *RE*. And how can we take seriously a claim to have perceived an objective state of affairs if there is, in principle, no intersubjective way of determining whether that claim is correct?

Answer. The answer to this objection is implicit in a point made earlier, viz. that putative experience of God yields only *prima facie* justification, justification (unqualifiedly) provided there are no sufficient overriding considerations. This notion has a significant application only where there is what we may call an *overrider system*, that is, ways of determining whether the facts are such as to indicate a belief from the range in question to be false and ways of determining whether conditions are such that the basis of the belief is sufficiently indicative of its truth. SP does contain such a system. What about RE? Here we must confront a salient difference between the two spheres. If we consider the way in which a body of beliefs has been developed on the basis of SP we find pretty much the same system across all cultures. But our encounters with God have spawned a number of different religious communities with beliefs and practices of worship which are quite different, though with some considerable overlap. These differences carry with them differences in overrider systems. But it remains true that if we consider any particular religious community which exhibits a significant commonality in doctrine and worship it will feature a more or less definite overrider system. For concreteness let's think of what I will call the *mainline Christian community*. (From this point onward I will use the term "RE" for the practice of forming M-beliefs as it goes on in this community.) In that community a body of doctrine has developed concerning the nature of God, His purposes, and His interactions with mankind, including His appearances to us. If an M-belief contradicts this system that is a reason for deeming it false. Moreover there is a long and varied history of experiential encounters with God, embodied in written accounts as well as oral transmission. This provides bases for regarding particular experiences as more or less likely to be veridical, given the conditions, psychological or otherwise, in which they occurred, the character of the subject, and the effects in the life of the subject. Thus a socially established religious doxastic practice like RE will contain a rich system of overriders that provides resources for checking the acceptability of any particular M-belief.

But perhaps your point is rather that there are no *external* checks on a particular report, none that do not rely on other claims of the same sort. Let's agree that this is the case. But why suppose that to be any black mark against RE? Here is the double standard again. After all, particular claims within SP cannot be checked without relying on what we have learned from SP. Suppose I claim to see a fir tree in a certain spot. To check on this one would have to rely on other persons' perceptual reports as to what is at that spot, our general empirical knowledge of the likelihood of a fir tree in that locality, and so on. Apart from what we take our-

selves to have learned from SP, we would have nothing to go on. One can hardly determine whether my report was accurate by intuiting self-evident truths or by consulting divine revelation. But if SP counts as having a system of checks even though this system involves relying on some outputs of the practice in order to put others to the test, why should RE be deemed to have no such system when its procedures exhibit the same structure? Once more you are, arbitrarily, setting quite different requirements for different practices.

Perhaps your point was that RE's system of checks is unlike SP's. In particular, the following difference can be discerned. Suppose I report seeing a morel at a certain spot in the forest. Now suppose that a number of qualified observers take a good look at that spot at that time and report that no morel is to be seen. In that case my report would have been decisively disconfirmed. But nothing like that is possible in RE. We can't lay down any conditions (of a sort the satisfaction of which we can determine) under which a properly qualified person will experience the presence of God if God is "there" to be experienced. Hence a particular report cannot be decisively disconfirmed by the experience of others.

But what epistemic relevance does this difference have? Why should we suppose that RE is rendered dubious for lacking checkability of this sort? Let's consider what makes this kind of intersubjective test possible for SP. Clearly it is that we have discovered fairly firm regularities in the behaviour of physical things, including human sense perception. Since there are stable regularities in the ways in which physical objects disclose themselves to our perception, we can be assured that if X exists at a certain time and place and if S satisfies appropriate conditions then S is sure to perceive X. But no such tight regularities are discoverable in God's appearances to our experience. We can say something about the way in which such matters as the distribution of attention and the moral and spiritual state of the subject are conducive to such appearances; but these most emphatically do not add up to the sort of lawlike connections we get with SP. Now what about this difference? Is it to the epistemic discredit of RE that it does not enable us to discover such regularities? Well, that all depends on what it would be reasonable to expect if RE does put us into effective cognitive contact with God. Given what we have learned about

God and our relations to Him (from *RE*, supplemented by whatever other sources there be), should we expect to be able to discover such realities if God really exists? Clearly not. There are several important points here, but the most important is that it is contrary to God's plans for us to give us that much control, cognitive and practical. Hence it is quite understandable, if God exists and is as *RE* leads us to suppose, that we should not be able to ascertain the kinds of regularities that would make possible the kinds of intersubjective tests exhibited by *SP*. Hence, the epistemic status of *RE* is in no way diminished by its lack of such tests. Once more *RE* is subjected to an inappropriate standard. This time, however, it is not a double standard, but rather an inappropriate single standard. *RE* is being graded down for lacking positive features of other practices, where these features cannot reasonably be supposed to be generally necessary conditions of epistemic excellence, even for experiential practices. Thus my critic is exhibiting what we might term *epistemic chauvinism*, judging alien forms of life according to whether they conform to the home situation, a procedure as much to be deplored in the epistemic as in the political sphere.

OBJECTION VII

How can it be rational to take *RE* as a source of justification when there are incompatible rivals that can lay claim to that status on exactly the same grounds? M-beliefs of different religious communities conflict to a considerable extent, particularly those concerning alleged divine messages, and the bodies of doctrine they support conflict even more. We get incompatible accounts of God's plans for us and requirements on us, of the conditions of salvation, and so on. This being the case, how can we pick out just one of these communal practices as yielding justified belief?

Answer. I take this to be by far the most serious difficulty with my position. I have chosen to concentrate on what I take to be less serious problems, partly because their consideration brings out better the main lineaments of the position, and partly because any serious treatment of this last problem would spill beyond the confines of this paper.[2] Here I shall have

to content myself with making one basic point. We are not faced with the necessity of choosing only one such practice as yielding *prima facie* justified M-beliefs. The fact that there are incompatibilities between systems of religious beliefs, in M-beliefs and elsewhere, shows that not all M-beliefs can be true, but not that they cannot all be *prima facie* justified. After all, incompatible beliefs *within* a system can all be *prima facie* justified; that's the point of the *prima facie* qualification. When we are faced with a situation like that, the hope is that the overrider system and other winnowing devices will weed out the inconsistencies. To be sure, intersystem winnowing devices are hazier and more meager than those which are available within a system; but consistency, consonance with other well-entrenched beliefs and doxastic practices, and general reasonability and plausibility give us something to go on. Moreover, it may be that some religious ways of life fulfill their own promises more fully than others. Of course, there is never any guarantee that a unique way of resolving incompatibilities will present itself, even with a system. But where there are established practices of forming beliefs on the basis of experience, I believe the rational course is to regard each such belief as thereby *prima facie* justified, hoping that future developments, perhaps unforeseeable at present, will resolve fundamental incompatibilities.

In conclusion I will make explicit the general epistemological orientation I have been presupposing in my defense of *RE* I take our human situation to be such that we engage in a plurality of basic doxastic practices, each of which involves a distinctive sort of input to belief-forming "mechanisms," a distinctive range of belief contents (a "subject matter" and ways of conceiving it), and a set of functions that determine belief contents as a function of input features. Each practice is socially established: socially shared, inculcated, reinforced, and propagated. In addition to experiential practices, with which we have been concerned in this paper, there are, for example, inferential practices, the input of which consists of beliefs, and the practice of forming memory beliefs. A doxastic practice is not restricted to the formation of first-level beliefs; it will also typically involve criteria and procedures of criticism of the beliefs thus formed; here we will find the

---

[2]For an extended treatment of this issue see my "Religious Experience and Religious Diversity," forthcoming in *Christian Scholars' Review*.

"overrider systems" of which we were speaking earlier. In general, we learn these practices and engage in them long before we arrive at the stage of explicitly formulating their principles and subjecting them to critical reflection. Theory is deeply rooted in practice.

Nor, having arrived at the age of reason, can we turn our back on all that and take a fresh start, in the Cartesian spirit, choosing our epistemic procedures and criteria anew, on a purely "rational" basis. Apart from reliance on doxastic tendencies with which we find ourselves, we literally have nothing to go on. Indeed, what Descartes did, as Thomas Reid trenchantly pointed out, was arbitrarily to pick one doxastic practice he found himself engaged in—accepting propositions that seem self-evident—and set that as a judge over all the others, with what results we are all too familiar. This is not to say that we must acquiesce in our prereflective doxastic tendencies in every respect. We can tidy things up, modify our established practices so as to make each more internally consistent and more consistent with the others. But, on the whole and for the most part, we have no choice but to continue to form beliefs in accordance with these practices and to take these ways of forming beliefs as paradigmatically conferring epistemic justification. And this is the way that epistemology has in fact gone, except for some arbitrary partiality. Of course it would be satisfying to economize our basic commitments by taking one or a few of these practices as basic and using them to validate the others; but we have made little progress in this enterprise over the centuries. It is not self-evident that sense perception is reliable, nor can we establish its reliability if we restrict ourselves to premises drawn from introspection; we cannot show that deductive reasoning is valid without using deductive reasoning to do so; and so on. We are endowed with strong tendencies to engage in a number of distinct doxastic practices, none of which can be warranted on the basis of others. It is clearly the better part of wisdom to recognize beliefs that emerge from these practices to be rational and justified, at least once they are properly sifted and refined.

In this paper I have undertaken to extend this account to doxastic practices that are not universally practiced. Except for that matter of distribution and the other peripheral matters mentioned in Objection V and except for being faced with actually existing rivals, a religious experiential doxastic practice like *RE* seems to me to be on all fours with *SP* and other universal practices. It too involves a distinctive range of inputs, a range of belief contents, and functions that map features of the former on to contents of the latter. It is socially established within a certain community. It involves higher-level procedures of correction and modification of its first-level beliefs. Though it *may* be acquired in a deliberate and self-conscious fashion, it is more typically acquired in a practical, prereflective form. Though it is obviously evitable in a way *SP*, for example, is not, for many of its practitioners it is just about as firmly entrenched.

These similarities lead me to the conclusion that if, as it seems we must concede, a belief is *prima facie* justified by virtue of emerging from one of the universal basic practices, we should also concede the same status to the products of *RE*. I have sought to show that various plausible-sounding objections to this position depend on the use of a double standard or reflect arbitrary epistemic chauvinism. They involve subjecting *RE* to inappropriate standards. Once we appreciate these points, we can see the strength of the case for *RE* as one more epistemically autonomous practice of belief formation and source of justification.

QUESTIONS FOR FURTHER REFLECTION

1. Which objection do you think is the most serious objection to Alston's thesis? Explain why you think it is the most serious and why you think Alston's answer is not satisfactory.
2. Alston calls Objection VII the most serious objection. Lay out his answer to this objection, explaining the significance of *prima facie* justification, and assess it.
3. Is there some other important objection to religious experience that Alston has not considered in this selection?

44. CRITIQUE OF THE ARGUMENT FROM RELIGIOUS EXPERIENCE

Michael Scriven

Michael Scriven is Professor of Psychology at Claremont Graduate University. He has been a professor of philosophy at several universities, including the University of California at Berkeley. He has authored or co-authored 14 books and numerous articles. In this selection, Scriven criticizes religious experience as a reason for believing in God.

READING QUESTIONS

1. Why does Scriven think that agreement is not the only requirement for avoiding error?
2. What does Scriven think the difference is between scientific beliefs and commonly agreed upon religious beliefs?
3. Why does Scriven think that it is not surprising that millions of people have religious experiences?

We must now contend with the suggestion that reason is irrelevant to the commitment to theism because this territory is the domain of another faculty: the faculty of faith. It is sometimes even hinted that it is morally wrong and certainly foolish to suggest we should be reasoning about God. For this is the domain of faith or of the "venture of faith," of the "knowledge that passeth understanding," of religious experience and mystic insight.

Now the normal meaning of *faith* is simply "confidence"; we say that we have great faith in someone or in some claim or product, meaning that we believe and act as if they were very reliable. Of such faith we can properly say that it is well founded or not, depending on the evidence for whatever it is in which we have faith.[1] So there is no incompatibility between this kind of faith and reason; the two are from different families and can make a very good marriage. Indeed if they do not join forces, then the resulting ill-based or inadequate confidence will probably lead to disaster. So

faith, in this sense, means only a high degree of belief and may be reasonable or unreasonable.

But the term is sometimes used to mean an *alternative to reason* instead of something that should be founded on reason. Unfortunately, the mere use of the term in this way does not demonstrate that faith is a possible route to truth. It is like using the term "winning" as a synonym for "playing" instead of one possible outcome of playing. This is quaint, but it could hardly be called a satisfactory way of proving that we are winning; any time we "win" by changing the meaning of winning, the victory is merely illusory. And so it proves in this case. To use "faith" *as if* it were an alternative way to the truth cannot bypass the crucial question whether such results really have any likelihood of being true. A rose by any other name will smell the same, and the inescapable facts about "faith" in the new sense are that it is still *applied to* a belief and is still supposed to imply *confidence in* that belief: the belief in the existence and goodness of God. So we can still ask the same old question about that belief: Is the confidence justified or misplaced? To say we "take it on faith" does not get it off parole.

Suppose someone replies that theism is a kind of belief that does not need justification by evidence. This means either that no one cares whether it is correct or not or that there is some other way of checking that it is correct besides looking at the evidence for it, that is, giving rea-

---

[1] For faith to be well founded, especially faith in a person, it is not required that the evidence available at a particular moment justify exactly the degree of confidence one exhibits. There may be overriding reasons for retaining trust beyond the first point of rationally defensible doubt (see the discussion of attitude inertia in the *Morality* chapter). But this minor divergence does not seriously affect the discussion here.

sons for believing it. But the first alternative is false since very many people care whether there is a God or not; and the second alternative is false because any method of showing that belief is likely to be true is, by definition, a justification of that belief, that is, an appeal to reason. You certainly cannot show that a belief in God is likely to be true just by having confidence in it and by saying this is a case of knowledge "based on" faith, any more than you can win a game just by playing it and by calling that winning.

It is psychologically possible to have faith in something without any basis in fact, and once in a while you will turn out to be lucky and to have backed the right belief. This does not show you "really knew all along"; it only shows you cannot be unlucky all the time. But, in general, beliefs without foundations lead to an early grave or to an accumulation of superstitions, which are usually troublesome and always false beliefs. It is hardly possible to defend this approach just by *saying* that you have decided that in this area confidence is its own justification.

Of course, you might try to *prove* that a feeling of great confidence about certain types of propositions is a reliable indication of their truth. If you succeeded, you would indeed have shown that the belief was justified; you would have done this by justifying it. To do this you would have to show what the real facts were and show that when someone had the kind of faith we are now talking about, it usually turned out that the facts were as he believed, just as we might justify the claims of a telepath. The catch in all this is simply that you have got to show what the real facts are in some way *other* than by appealing to faith, since that would simply be assuming what you are trying to prove. And if you can show what the facts are in this other way, you do not need faith in any new sense at all; you are already perfectly entitled to confidence in any belief that you have shown to be well supported.

How are you going to show what the real facts are? You show this by any method of investigation that has itself been tested, the testing being done by still another tested method, and so on, through a series of tested connections that eventually terminates in our ordinary everyday reasoning and testing procedures of logic and observation.

Is it not prejudiced to require that the validation of beliefs always involve ultimate reference to our ordinary logic and everyday-plus-scientific knowledge? May not faith (religious experience, mystic insight) give us access to some new domain of truth? It is certainly possible that it does this. But, of course, it is also possible that it lies. One can hardly accept the reports of those with faith or, indeed, the apparent revelations of one's own religious experiences on the ground that they *might* be right. So *might* be a fervent materialist who saw his interpretation as a revelation. Possibility is not veracity. Is it not of the very greatest importance that we should try to find out whether we really can justify the use of the term "truth" or "knowledge" in describing the content of faith? If it is, then we must find something in that content that is known to be true in some other way, because to get off the ground we must first push off against the ground—we cannot lift ourselves by our shoelaces. If the new realm of knowledge is to be a realm of knowledge and not mythology, then it must tell us something which relates it to the kind of case that gives meaning to the term "truth." If you want to use the old word for the new events, you must show that it is applicable.

Could not the validating experience, which religious experience must have if it is to be called true, be the experience of others who also have or have had religious experiences? The religious community could, surely, provide a basis of agreement analogous to that which ultimately underlies scientific truth. Unfortunately, agreement is not the only requirement for avoiding error, for all may be in error. The difficulty for the religious community is to show that its agreement is not simply agreement about a shared mistake. If agreement were the only criterion of truth, there could never be a shared mistake; but clearly either the atheist group or the theist group shares a mistake. To decide which is wrong must involve appeal to something other than mere agreement. And, of course, it is clear that particular religious beliefs are mistaken, since religious groups do not all agree and they cannot all be right.

Might not some or all scientific beliefs be wrong, too? This is conceivable, but there are crucial differences between the two kinds of belief. In the first place, any commonly agreed religious beliefs concern only one or a few entities and their properties and histories. What for convenience we are here calling "scientific belief" is actually the sum total of all conventionally founded human knowledge, much of it not part of any science, and it embraces billions upon billions of facts, each of them perpetually or frequently subject to checking by independent means, each connected with a million others. The success of *this* system of knowledge shows up every day in everything that we do: we eat, and the food is not poison; we read, and the pages do not turn to dust; we slip, and gravity does not fail to pull us down. We are not just relying on the existence of agreement about the interpretation of a certain experience among a small part of the population. We are relying directly on our extremely reliable, nearly universal, and independently tested senses, and each of us is constantly obtaining independent confirmation for claims based on these, many of these confirmations being obtained for many claims, independently of each other. It is the wildest flight of fancy to suppose that there is a body of common religious beliefs which can be set out to exhibit this degree of repeated checking by religious experiences. In fact, there is not only gross disagreement on even the most fundamental claims in the creeds of different churches, each of which is supported by appeal to religious experience or faith, but where there is agreement by many people, it is all too easily open to the criticism that it arises from the common cultural exposure of the child or the adult convert and hence is not independent in the required way.

This claim that the agreement between judges is spurious in a particular case because it only reflects previous common indoctrination of those in agreement is a serious one. It must always be met by direct disproof whenever agreement is appealed to in science, and it is. The claim that the food is not poison cannot be explained away as a myth of some subculture, for anyone, even if told nothing about the eaters in advance, will judge that the people who ate it are still well. The whole methodology of testing is committed to the doctrine that any judges who could have learned what they are expected to say about the matter they are judging are completely valueless.[2] Now anyone ex-

posed to religious teaching, whether a believer or not, has long known the standard for such experiences, the usual symbols, the appropriate circumstances, and so on. These suggestions are usually very deeply implanted, so that they cannot be avoided by good intentions, and consequently members of our culture are rendered entirely incapable of being independent observers. Whenever observers are not free from previous contamination in this manner, the only way to support their claims is to examine independently testable *consequences* of the novel claims, such as predictions about the future. In the absence of these, the religious-experience gambit, whether involving literal or analogical claims, is wholly abortive.

A still more fundamental point counts against the idea that agreement among the religious can help support the idea of faith as an alternative path to truth. It is that every sane theist also believes in the claims of ordinary experience, while the reverse is not the case. Hence, the burden of proof is on the theist to show that the *further step* he wishes to take will not take him beyond the realm of truth. The two positions, of science and religion, are not symmetrical; the adherent of one of them suggests that we extend the range of allowable beliefs and yet is unable to produce the same degree of acceptance or "proving out" in the ordinary field of human activities that he insists on before believing in a new instrument or source of information. The atheist obviously cannot be shown his error in the way someone who thinks that there are no electrons can be shown his, *unless some of the arguments for the existence of God are sound*. Once again, we come back to these. If some of them work, the position of religious knowledge is secure; if they do not, nothing else will make it secure.

In sum, the idea of separating religious from scientific knowledge and making each an independent realm with its own basis in experience of quite different kinds is a counsel of despair and not a product of true sophistication, for one cannot break the connection between everyday experience and religious claims, for purposes of defending the latter, without eliminating the consequences of religion for everyday life.

---

[2]More precisely, a judge is said to be "contaminated" if he could know which way his judgment will count insofar as the issue at

stake is concerned. The famous double-blind experimental design, keystone of drug research, achieves reliability by making it impossible for either patient or nurse to know when the real drug, rather than the dummy drug or placebo, is being judged.

There is no way out of this inexorable contract: if you want to support your beliefs, you must produce some experience which can be shown to be a reliable indicator of truth, and that can be done only by showing a connection between the experience and what we know to be true in a previously established way.

So, if the criteria of religious truth are not connected with the criteria of everyday truth, then they are not criteria of truth at all and the beliefs they "establish" have no essential bearing on our lives, constitute no explanation of what we see around us, and provide no guidance for our course through time.

STATEMENT OF THE ARGUMENT

The argument may be stated defensively or aggressively, either as the claim to a private experience from which no conclusions are supposed to follow for anyone else or as the claim that there are certain gifted people in this field, as in music or the other arts, who should be believed because of their conviction, the agreement between them, or the reliability with which they are able to tell us about some aspect of life.

ASSESSMENT OF THE ARGUMENT

Supporters of the argument often think that doubting it is like doubting the word of an otherwise honest person; after all, if someone you trust tells you that he has seen an ivory-billed woodpecker during a trip deep into the swamps of Florida, who are you to be sure he was mistaken, even though the species is known to be very rare? But there is no similarity between the cases. What one sees in the swamps is seen with one's eyes, and the reliability of one's eyes is constantly being checked. We would certainly not believe a person's report if he were known to be half blind. Furthermore, the specific skill of recognizing birds would need and can be given definite, positive support. Is it absolutely certain that your friend would not take a pileated for an ivory-billed woodpecker, which, after all, he had never seen previously? We would expect him to be highly reliable in identifying unmarked photographs of the two species, for example. Much of this implicit testing we forget because much of it is so well entrenched in the ordinary procedure of survival in our daily life that we do not think of it as a part of a testing program. But it is an essential part of the grounds for accepting visual reports of unusual experiences.

When it comes to accepting reports that involve some alleged *new* sense that has never been tested in the routine of daily life, special tests must be passed before *anyone* has any grounds for thinking the reports reliable. It is easy for someone to imagine that he saw something he did not see; it is even easier for him to "sense that some presence is nigh," to use a common description of the religious experience, for the sense that gives him this report is not one with the built-in training of our usual senses and is all the easier for the emotions to use as a projection screen.

That the millions who are brought up in a nervous and stress-provoking world and taught the tradition of religious experience and symbolism should produce thousands who claim to have had religious experiences is not surprising but entirely to be expected. Such experiences do not confirm each other in the way that the reports of independent judges do, for each of the people involved has a background containing the same elements which are projected into the emotional religious experience just as into the dreams, art, and literature of that culture. In the old days, the days of the Old Testament, those who saw God brought back a prophecy, and the children of Israel knew they spoke truly, for their prophecies were fulfilled, according to Scripture. But the God of those tales, if ever He was here, is not dispensing prophecies now; so the success of His prophets no longer provides any reason to think He is here. Therefore, we cannot suppose that those who think they have experienced His presence are any more reliable guides than those who have seen the great vision of the Universe as a mighty engine at last delivering itself of man, who turns to drive it faster still, a noble and natural conception.

QUESTIONS FOR FURTHER REFLECTION

1. Many think that we establish the reliability of sense perception in an epistemically circular manner. We use sense perception to establish that sense perception is a reliable belief-forming process. Can religious experience be shown to be a reliable knowledge-forming process by using religious experience?

2. Some claim that in order to take a religious perception seriously, we would have to rule out the possibility of hallucination. Is "ruling out" hallucination too strong a requirement? Do sense perceptions meet this strict standard? What if we can show that it is more likely than not that some experience is not a hallucination? Would that be enough? Why or why not?

3. Suppose a mystic is sane and mentally healthy in every area of life and that the only thing that distinguishes him from nonmystics is his claim to have mystical experience. How reasonable is it for the nonmystic to think that mystics like that are crazy?

Suggestions for Further Reading

Alston, William P. *Perceiving God*. Ithaca, NY: Cornell University Press, 1991.

Davis, Caroline Franks. *The Evidential Force of Religious Experience*. New York: Oxford University Press, 1989.

Gellman, Jerome. *Experience of God and the Rationality of Theistic Belief*. Ithaca, NY: Cornell University Press, 1997.

Mavrodes, George. *Belief in God: The Epistemology of Religious Experience*. New York: Macmillan, 1970.

Yandell, Keith E. *The Epistemology of Religious Experience*. New York: Cambridge University Press, 1993.

———. *Philosophy of Religion*. New York: Routledge, 1969.

PART VI

✧ MIRACLES ✧

45. OF MIRACLES • *David Hume*
46. ON HUME'S PHILOSOPHICAL CASE AGAINST MIRACLES • *Daniel Howard-Snyder*
C. S. Lewis, "Hume Begs the Question"
47. HISTORIANS ON MIRACLES • *Raymond Martin*
Morton Smith, "Historical Method in the Study of Religion"
Nancy Murphy, "The Historian as Philosopher"

SUGGESTIONS FOR FURTHER READING

45. OF MIRACLES

David Hume

A brief biography of David Hume occurs on page 115. In this selection, from *An Inquiry Concerning Human Understanding*, Hume argues that the occurrence of miracles is unlikely given the uniform experience of the laws of nature as without exception.

READING QUESTIONS

1. How does Hume define a miracle?
2. What reason to we have to think that the laws of nature are unalterable?
3. Why is no testimony sufficient to establish a miracle?

Though experience be our only guide in reasoning concerning matters of fact; it must be acknowledged, that this guide is not altogether infallible, but in some cases is apt to lead us into errors. One, who in our climate, should expect better weather in any week of June than in one of December, would reason justly, and conformably to experience: but it is certain, that he may happen, in the event, to find himself mistaken. However, we may observe, that, in such a case, he would have no cause to complain of experience; because it commonly informs us beforehand of the uncertainty, by that contrariety of events, which we may learn from a diligent observation. All effects follow not with like certainty from their supposed causes. Some events are found, in all countries and all ages, to have been constantly conjoined together: Others are found to have been more variable, and sometimes to disappoint our expectations; so that, in our reasonings concerning matter of fact, there are all imaginable degrees of assurance, from the highest certainty to the lowest species of moral evidence.

A wise man, therefore, proportions his belief to the evidence. In such conclusions as are founded on an infallible experience, he expects the event with the last degree of assurance, and regards his past experience as a full *proof* of the future existence of that event. In other cases, he proceeds with more caution: He weighs the opposite experiments: He considers which side is supported by the greater number of experiments: To that side he inclines, with doubt and hesitation; and when at last he fixes his judgment, the evidence exceeds not what we properly call *probability*. All probability, then, supposes an opposition of experiments and observations, where the one side is found to overbalance the other, and to produce a degree of evidence, proportioned to the superiority. A hundred instances or experiments on one side, and fifty on another, afford a doubtful expectation of any event; though a hundred uniform experiments with only one that is contradictory, reasonably beget a pretty strong degree of assurance. In all cases, we must balance the opposite experiments, where they are opposite, and deduct the smaller number from the greater in order to know the exact force of the superior evidence.

To apply these principles to a particular instance; we may observe, that there is no species of reasoning more common, more useful, and even necessary to human life, than that which is derived from the testimony of men, and the reports of eyewitnesses and spectators. This species of reasoning, perhaps, one may deny to be founded on the relation of cause and effect. I shall not dispute about a word. It will be sufficient to observe, that our assurance in any argument of this kind is derived from no other principle than our observation of the variety of human testimony, and of the usual conformity of facts to the reports of witnesses. It being a general maxim, that no objects have any discoverable connexion together, and that all the inferences, which we can draw from one to another, are founded merely on our experience of their constant and regular conjunction, it is evident, that we ought not to make an exception to this maxim in favour of human testimony, whose connexion with any event seems, in itself, as little necessary as any other. Were not the memory tenacious to a certain degree; had not men commonly an inclination to truth and a principle of probity; were they not sensible to shame, when detected in a falsehood: Were not these, I say, discovered by *experience* to be qualities, inherent in human nature, we should never repose the least confidence in human testimony. A man delirious, or noted for falsehood and villany, has no manner of authority with us.

And as the evidence, derived from witnesses and human testimony, is founded on past experience, so it varies with the experience, and is regarded either as a *proof* or a *probability*, according as the conjunction between any particular kind of report and any kind of object has been found to be constant or variable. There are a number of circumstances to be taken into consideration in all judgments of this kind; and the ultimate standard, by which we determine all disputes, that may arise concerning them, is always derived from experience and observation. Where the experience is not entirely uniform on any side, it is attended with an unavoidable contrariety in our judgments, and with the same opposition and mutual destruction of argument as in every other kind of evidence. We frequently hesitate concerning the reports of others. We balance the opposite circumstances, which cause any doubt or uncertainty; and when we discover a superiority on any side, we incline to it; but still with a diminution of assurance, in proportion to the force of its antagonist.

This contrariety of evidence, in the present case, may be derived from several different causes; from the opposition of contrary testimony; from the character or number of the witnesses; from the manner of their delivering their testimony; or from the union of all these circumstances. We entertain a suspicion concerning any matter of fact, when the witnesses contradict each other; when they are but few, or of doubtful character; when they have an interest in what they affirm; when they deliver their testimony with hesitation, or on the contrary, with too violent asseverations. There are many other particulars of the same kind, which may diminish or destroy the force of any argument, derived from human testimony.

Suppose, for instance, that the fact, which the testimony endeavours to establish, partakes of the extraordinary and the marvellous; in that case, the evidence, resulting from the testimony, admits of a diminution, greater or less, in proportion as the fact is more or less unusual. The reason, why we place any credit in witnesses and historians, is not derived from any *connexion*, which we perceive *a priori*, between testimony and reality, but because we are accustomed to find a conformity between them. But when the fact attested is such a one as has seldom fallen under our observation, here is a contest of two opposite experiences; of which the one destroys the other, as far as its force goes, and the superior can only operate on the mind by the force, which remains. The very same principle of experience, which gives us a certain degree of assurance in the testimony of witnesses, gives us also, in this case, another degree of assurance against the fact, which they endeavour to establish; from which contradiction there necessarily arises a counterpoise, and mutual destruction of belief and authority. . . .

But in order to increase the probability against the testimony of witnesses, let us suppose, that the fact, which they affirm, instead of being only marvellous, is really miraculous: and suppose also, that the testimony, considered apart and in itself, amounts to an entire proof: in that case, there is proof against proof, of which the strongest must prevail, but still with a diminution of its force, in proportion to that of its antagonist.

A miracle is a violation of the laws of nature; and as a firm and unalterable experience has established these laws, the proof against a miracle, from the very nature of the fact, is as entire as any argument from experience can possibly be imagined. Why is it more than probable, that all men must die; that lead cannot, of itself, remain suspended in the air; that fire consumes wood, and is extinguished by water; unless it be, that these events are found agreeable to the laws of nature, and there is required a violation of these laws, or in other words, a miracle to prevent them? Nothing is esteemed a miracle, if it ever happen in the common course of nature. It is no miracle that a man, seemingly in good health, should die on a sudden: because such a kind of death, though more unusual than any other, has yet been frequently observed to happen. But it is a miracle, that a dead man should come to life; because that has never been observed, in any age or country. There must, therefore, be a uniform experience against every miraculous event, otherwise the event would not merit that appellation. And as an uniform experience amounts to a proof, there is here a direct and full *proof*, from the nature of the fact, against the existence of any miracle; nor can such a proof be destroyed, or the miracle rendered credible, but by an opposite proof, which is superior.[1]

The plain consequence is (and it is a general maxim worthy of our attention), "That no testimony is sufficient to establish a miracle, unless the testimony be of such a kind, that its falsehood would be more miraculous, than the fact, which it endeavours to establish: And even in that case there is a mutual destruction of arguments, and the superior only gives us an assurance suitable to that degree of force, which remains, after deducting the inferior." When any one tells me, that he saw a dead man restored to life, I immediately consider with myself, whether it be more probable, that this person should either deceive or be deceived, or that the fact, which he relates, should really have happened. I weigh the one miracle against the other; and according to the superiority, which I discover, I pronounce my decision, and always reject the greater miracle. If the falsehood of his testimony would be more miraculous, than the event which he relates; then, and not till then, can he pretend to command my belief or opinion.

In the foregoing reasoning we have supposed, that the testimony, upon which a miracle is founded, may possibly amount to an entire proof, and that the falsehood of that testimony would be a real prodigy: But it is easy to shew, that we have been a great deal too liberal in our concession, and that there never was a miraculous event established on so full an evidence.

For *first*, there is not to be found in all history, any miracle attested by a sufficient number of men, of such unquestioned good-sense, education, and learning, as to secure us against all delusion in themselves; of such undoubted integrity, as to place them beyond all suspicion of any design to deceive others; of such credit and reputation in the eyes of mankind, as to have a great deal to lose in case of their being detected in any falsehood; and at the same time, attesting facts, performed in such a public manner, and in so celebrated a part of the world, as to render the detection unavoidable: All which circumstances are requisite to give us a full assurance in the testimony of men.

Secondly, We may observe in human nature a principle, which, if strictly examined, will be found to diminish extremely the assurance, which we might, from human testimony, have, in any kind of prodigy. The maxim, by which we commonly conduct ourselves in our reasonings, is, that the objects, of which we have no experience, resemble those, of which we have; that what we have found to be most usual is always most probable; and that where there is an opposition of arguments, we ought to give the preference to such as are founded on the greatest number of past observations.

[1] Sometimes an event may not in itself, *seem* to be contrary to the laws of nature, and yet, if it were real, it might, by reason of some circumstances, be denominated a miracle; because, in fact, it is contrary to these laws. Thus if a person, claiming a divine authority, should command a sick person to be well, a healthful man to fall down dead, the clouds to pour rain, the winds to blow, in short, should order many natural events which immediately follow upon his command; these might justly be esteemed miracles, because they are really, in this case, contrary to the laws of nature. For if any suspicion remain, that the event and command concurred by accident, there is no miracle and no transgression of the laws of nature. If this suspicion be removed, there is evidently a miracle, and a transgression of these laws; because nothing can be more contrary to nature than that the voice or command of a man should have such an influence. A miracle may be accurately defined, *a transgression of a law of nature by a particular volition of the Deity or by the interposition of some invisible agent.* A miracle may either be discoverable by men or not. This alters not its nature and essence. The raising of a house or ship into the air is a visible miracle. The raising of a feather, when the wind wants ever so little of a force requisite for that purpose, is as real a miracle, though not so sensible with regard to us.

But though, in proceeding by this rule, we readily reject any fact which is unusual and incredible in an ordinary degree; yet in advancing farther, the mind observes not always the same rule; but when anything is affirmed utterly absurd and miraculous, it rather the more readily admits of such a fact, upon account of that very circumstance, which ought to destroy all its authority. The passion of *surprise* and *wonder* arising from miracles, being an agreeable emotion, gives a sensible tendency towards the belief of those events, from which it is derived. And this goes so far, that even those who cannot enjoy this pleasure immediately, nor can believe those miraculous events, of which they are informed, yet love to partake of the satisfaction at second-hand or by rebound, and place a pride and delight in exciting the admiration of others.

With what greediness are the miraculous accounts of travellers received, their descriptions of sea and land monsters, their relations of wonderful adventures, strange men, and uncouth manners? But if the spirit of religion join itself to the love of wonder, there is an end of common sense; and human testimony, in these circumstances, loses all pretensions to authority. A religionist may be an enthusiast, and imagine he sees what has no reality: He may know his narrative to be false, and yet persevere in it, with the best intentions in the world, for the sake of promoting so holy a cause: Or even where this delusion has not place, vanity, excited by so strong a temptation, operates on him more powerfully than on the rest of mankind in any other circumstances: and self-interest with equal force. His auditors may not have, and commonly have not, sufficient judgment to canvass his evidence: What judgment they have, they renounce by principle, in these sublime and mysterious subjects: Or if they were ever so willing to employ it, passion and a heated imagination disturb the regularity of its operations. Their credulity increases his impudence: And his impudence overpowers their credulity. . . .

Thirdly, it forms a strong presumption against all supernatural and miraculous relations, that they are observed chiefly to abound among ignorant and barbarous nations; or if a civilized people has ever given admission to any of them, that people will be found to have received them from ignorant and barbarous ancestors, who transmitted them with that inviolable sanction and authority, which always attend received opinions. When we peruse the first histories of all nations, we are apt to imagine ourselves transported into some new world; where the whole frame of nature is disjointed, and every element performs its operations in a different manner, from what it does at present. Battles, revolutions, pestilence, famine, and death, are never the effect of those natural causes, which we experience. Prodigies, omens, oracles, judgments, quite obscure the few natural events, that are intermingled with them. But as the former grow thinner every page, in proportion as we advance nearer the enlightened ages, we soon learn, that there is nothing mysterious or supernatural in the case, but that all proceeds from the usual propensity of mankind towards the marvellous, and that, though this inclination may at intervals receive a check from sense and learning, it can never be thoroughly extirpated from human nature. . . .

I may add as a *fourth* reason, which diminishes the authority of prodigies, that there is no testimony for any, even those which have not been expressly detected, that is not opposed by an infinite number of witnesses; so that not only the miracle destroys the credit of testimony, but the testimony destroys itself. To make this the better understood, let us consider, that, in matters of religion, whatever is different is contrary; and that it is impossible the religions of ancient Rome, of Turkey, of Siam, and of China should, all of them, be established on any solid foundation. Every miracle, therefore, pretended to have been wrought in any of these religions (and all of them abound in miracles), as its direct scope is to establish the particular system to which it is attributed; so has it the same force, though more indirectly, to overthrow every other system. In destroying a rival system, it likewise destroys the credit of those miracles, on which that system was established; so that all the prodigies of different religions are to be regarded as contrary facts, and the evidences of these prodigies, whether weak or strong, as opposite to each other. According to this method of reasoning, when we believe any miracle of Mahomet or his successors, we have for our warrant the testimony of a few barbarous Arabians: And on the other hand, we are to regard the authority of Titus Livius, Plutarch, Tacitus, and in short, of all the authors and witnesses, Grecian, Chinese, and Roman Catholic, who have related any miracle in their particular religion; I say, we are to regard their testimony in the same light as if they had mentioned that Mahometan miracle, and had in express terms contradicted it, with the same certainty as they have for the miracle they relate. This argument may appear over subtile and refined; but is not in reality different from the reasoning of a judge, who supposes, that the credit of two witnesses, maintaining a crime against any one, is destroyed by the testimony of two others, who affirm him to have been two hundred leagues distant, at the same instant when the crime is said to have been committed. . . .

Upon the whole, then, it appears, that no testimony for any kind of miracle has ever amounted to a probability, much less to a proof; and that, even supposing it amounted to a proof, it would be opposed by another proof; derived from the very nature of the fact, which it would endeavour to establish. It is experience only, which gives authority to human testimony; and it is the same experience, which assures us of the laws of nature. When, therefore, these two kinds of experience are contrary, we have nothing to do but substract the one from the other, and embrace an opinion, either on one side or the other, with that assurance which arises from the remainder. But according to the principle here explained, this substraction, with regard to all popular religions, amounts to an entire annihilation; and therefore we may establish it as a maxim, that no human testimony can have such force as to prove a miracle, and make it a just foundation for any such system of religion.

I beg the limitations here made may be remarked, when I say, that a miracle can never be proved, so as to be the foundation of a system of religion. For I own, that otherwise, there may possibly be miracles, or violations of the usual course of nature, of such a kind as to admit of proof from human testimony; though, perhaps, it will be impossible to find any such in all the records of history. Thus, suppose, all authors, in all languages, agree, that, from the first of January 1600, there was a total darkness over the whole earth for eight days: Suppose that the tradition of this extraordinary event is still strong and lively among the people: That all travellers, who return from foreign countries, bring us accounts of the same tradition, without the least variation or contradiction: It is evident, that our present philosophers, instead of doubting the fact, ought to receive it as certain, and ought to search for the causes whence it might be derived. The decay, corruption,

and dissolution of nature, is an event rendered probable by so many analogies, that any phænomenon, which seems to have a tendency towards that catastrophe, comes within the reach of human testimony, if that testimony be very extensive and uniform.

But suppose, that all the historians who treat of England, should agree, that, on the first of January 1600, Queen Elizabeth died; that both before and after her death she was seen by her physicians and the whole court, as is usual with persons of her rank; that her successor was acknowledged and proclaimed by the parliament; and that, after being interred a month, she again appeared, resumed the throne, and governed England for three years: I must confess that I should be surprized at the occurrence of so many odd circumstances, but should not have the least inclination to believe so miraculous an event. I should not doubt of her pretended death, and of those other public circumstances that followed it: I should only assert it to have been pretended, and that it neither was, nor possibly could be real. You would in vain object to me the difficulty, and almost impossibility of deceiving the world in an affair of such consequence; the wisdom and solid judgment of that renowned queen; with the little or no advantage which she could reap from so poor an artifice: All this might astonish me; but I would still reply, that the knavery and folly of men are such common phænomena, that I should rather believe the most extraordinary events to arise from their concurrence, than admit of so signal a violation of the laws of nature.

But should this miracle be ascribed to any new system of religion; men, in all ages, have been so much imposed on by ridiculous stories of that kind, that this very circumstance would be a full proof of a cheat, and sufficient, with all men of sense, not only to make them reject the fact, but reject it without farther examination. Though the Being to whom the miracle is ascribed, be, in this case, Almighty, it does not, upon that account, become a whit more probable; since it is impossible for us to know the attributes or actions of such a Being, otherwise than from the experience which we have of his productions, in the usual course of nature. This still reduces us to past observation, and obliges us to compare the instances of the violation of truth in the testimony of men, with those of the violation of the laws of nature by miracles, in order to judge which of them is most likely and probable. As the violations of truth are more common in the testimony concerning religious miracles, than in that concerning any other matter of fact; this must diminish very much the authority of the former testimony, and make us form a general resolution, never to lend any attention to it, with whatever specious pretence it may be covered. . . .

I am the better pleased with the method of reasoning here delivered, as I think it may serve to confound those dangerous friends or disguised enemies to the *Christian Religion*, who have undertaken to defend it by the principles of human reason. Our most holy religion is founded on *Faith*, not on reason; and it is a sure method of exposing it to put it to such a trial as it is, by no means, fitted to endure. To make this more evident, let us examine those miracles, related in scripture; and not to lose ourselves in too wide a field, let us confine ourselves to such as we find in the *Pentateuch*, which we shall examine, according to the principles of those pretended Christians, not as the word or testimony of God himself, but as the production of a mere human writer and historian. Here then we are first to consider a book, presented to us by a barbarous and ignorant people, written in an age when they were still more barbarous, and in all probability long after the facts which it relates, corroborated by no concurring testimony, and resembling those fabulous accounts, which every nation gives of its origin. Upon reading this book, we find it full of prodigies and miracles. It gives an account of a state of the world and of human nature entirely different from the present; of our fall from that state; of the age of man, extended to near a thousand years; of the destruction of the world by a deluge; of the arbitrary choice of one people, as the favourites of heaven; and that people the countrymen of the author; of their deliverance from bondage by prodigies the most astonishing imaginable. I desire any one to lay his hand upon his heart, and after a serious consideration declare, whether he thinks that the falsehood of such a book, supported by such a testimony, would be more extraordinary and miraculous than all the miracles it relates; which is, however, necessary to make it to be received, according to the measures of probability above established.

What we have said of miracles may be applied, without any variation, to prophecies; and indeed, all prophecies are real miracles, and as such only, can be admitted as proofs of any revelation. If it did not exceed the capacity of human nature to foretell future events, it would be absurd to employ any prophecy as an argument for a divine mission or authority from heaven. So that, upon the whole, we may conclude, that the *Christian Religion* not only was at first attended with miracles, but even at this day cannot be believed by any reasonable person without one. Mere reason is insufficient to convince us of its veracity: And whoever is moved by *Faith* to assent to it, is conscious of a continued miracle in his own person, which subverts all the principles of his understanding, and gives him a determination to believe what is most contrary to custom and experience.

QUESTIONS FOR FURTHER REFLECTION

1. Some have interpreted Hume to be arguing that we should always believe what is more probable. Do you agree with this interpretation? If so, suppose you are sitting at a bridge table and observe that a perfect bridge hand has been dealt. According to this interpretation of Hume, should you believe that a perfect bridge hand was dealt?

2. Given Hume's argument, could there ever be evidence for a miracle in principle? Explain your answer.

3. In other places of the *Inquiry*, Hume raises the problem of induction, according to which the past is not a reliable guide to the future. He is even skeptical about whether we are justified inferring from past observations of the sun rising that the sun will rise tomorrow. Is his skepticism about relying on the past as a guide to the future inconsistent with what he has to say about that practice when he discusses miracles?

46. ON HUME'S PHILOSOPHICAL CASE AGAINST MIRACLES

Daniel Howard-Snyder

Daniel Howard-Snyder is Associate Professor of Philosophy at Western Washington University. He received his Ph.D. from Syracuse University in December, 1992. He is the editor or co-editor of three volumes: *The Evidential Argument from Evil* (1996); *Faith, Freedom, and Rationality* (1996); and *Divine Hiddenness* (2002). His publications appear in several books, including those just mentioned, as well as *Reason for the Hope Within* (1999); *Philosophy of Religion: The Big Questions* (1999); *God and the Problem of Evil* (2001); and *Readings in the Philosophy of Religion* (2001). Currently he is enjoying life with his wife and twin 2-year-old sons, and thankful for a year-long remission from Burkit's Lymphoma—a remission which he hopes will continue indefinitely.

Hume is commonly thought to have provided two arguments against the reasonableness of believing in any miracle and in particular the Resurrection of Jesus Christ; arguments that show that it is unreasonable to believe that the Resurrection occurred despite how strong the testimonial evidence might be. In this essay, Howard-Snyder assesses those two arguments, and concludes that they fail.

READING QUESTIONS

1. What two claims do some discern in Hume?
2. What is a counterinstance?
3. What two pictures are there of natural laws?
4. What does Howard-Snyder think we should infer from the array of various definitions of "miracle"?
5. What does Howard-Snyder say is Hume's view of a proof?

For our sake he was crucified under
Pontius Pilate; He suffered death and
was buried. On the third day he rose again
—The Nicene Creed

1. INTRODUCTION

As I understand the Christian faith, if certain events did not occur in human history, then many of its distinctive claims are false. What I have to say below concerns one such (alleged) event, an event affirmed in the earliest Christian creeds.[1] It is known as "the Resurrection of Jesus Christ." I choose this event as my focus not because I believe it occurred but because the great eighteenth century Scottish philosopher, David Hume contends that it did not occur, or at least that it is beyond credibility, and hundreds of intelligent and admirable men and women like him

One of the earliest Christian creeds that affirms the Resurrection was cited by Paul in his first letter to the Corinthian church (circa 55AD): "For what I have received I passed on to you as of first importance: that Christ died for our sins . . . , that he was buried, that he was raised on the third day, . . . and that he appeared to Peter, and then to the Twelve. After that, he appeared to more than five hundred of the brothers at the same time . . ." (15:3ff). The bishops gathered at the first ecumenical council (Nicea, 325AD) reaffirmed this event in the words quoted at the beginning of this paper.

---

[1]From this point on, I will stop using the parenthetical qualifier "alleged," but I want my readers to insert it whenever it might otherwise seem that I am affirming that some miracle occurred, or that some text accurately reported one. What I have to say here is perfectly at home with denying that any miracle has ever occurred.

concur.[2] In one of the most stirring and impassioned pieces of prose written in the English language, Hume summarizes his contention in these words:

> [U]pon the whole, we may conclude, that the *Christian Religion* not only was at first attended with miracles, but even at this day cannot be believed by any reasonable person without one. Mere reason is insufficient to convince us of its veracity: And whoever is moved by *Faith* to assent to it, is conscious of a continued miracle in his own person, which subverts all the principles of his understanding, and gives him a determination to believe what is most contrary to custom and experience. (131)

As it turns out, Hume's reasons for drawing this conclusion are perfectly general; if they apply to the Resurrection, they apply to any event that a religious adherent might regard as a miracle. (I invite the reader to substitute for the Resurrection whatever event they wish, so long as it is widely regarded as a miracle by adherents of a theistic religious tradition. The parting of the Red Sea would be a good example.)

Now, why should we care about why Hume thought that Jesus did not rise from the dead? Well, in a word, I take it that whether Hume is right is *important*. If Jesus did not rise from the dead, we can pretty much ignore his claims and the claims of his associates that he was the Son of God, the Messiah, Emmanuel; and along with them, we can pretty much dismiss the Christian faith too, or at least its distinctive doctrines.[3] However, if Jesus did rise from the dead, then we would be most foolish to dismiss these claims. If Jesus was crucified, suffered death and was buried, and on the third day rose again, then, on the face of it, a supernatural explanation of the latter event is by far the likeliest, and his explanation of it becomes a live option, one that we would be most unwise simply to ignore.

Here enters Hume. I would have thought that to investigate whether Jesus rose from the dead, we would need to do some historical research: we would need to assess the reliability of the New Testament documents and related manuscripts; we would need to look into the credibility of the witnesses to his post-mortem appearances, the empty tomb, and the like. The task looks rather daunting.[4] But, according to Hume, we don't have to do anything of the kind. For no matter how strong the testimony in favor of a miracle is—indeed, even if we "suppose . . . that the testimony considered apart and in itself, amounts to an entire proof" (114)—we have at our disposal a "full *proof* . . . against the existence of any miracle" (115). So we can avoid all that tedious historical work. We can simply use Hume's shortcut, a proof against the existence of *any* miracle, and hence a proof against the Resurrection.

So Hume has a "a decisive argument," "an everlasting check to all kinds of superstitious delusion," superstitious delusions like the Resurrection. There is good news and bad news in Hume's proclamation. The good news is that he really has *two* arguments, not just one—or, at any rate, many scholars discern in his writings two arguments. The bad news is that neither succeeds; at any rate, try as *I* might, I can't see how they do.

2. ON THE IMPOSSIBILITY OF MIRACLES

Everyone discerns in Hume's writings the claim that there is good reason to believe that miracle claims are

---

[2]"Of Miracles," section X, *An Enquiry Concerning Human Understanding*, in *Enquiries Concerning Human Understanding and Concerning the Principles of Morals*, ed. L. A. Selby-Bigge, 2nd ed. (Oxford: Clarendon Press, 1902). I quote from the 3rd edition (1975), ed. P. H. Nidditch. Parenthetical page references in the body of my paper are to this work.

[3]We are strongly encouraged to draw these inferences by the earliest Christians, for example Paul, in the aforementioned letter: "if Christ has not been raised, your faith is futile; you are still in your sins. . . . If only for this life we have hope in Christ, we are to be pitied more than all men" (15: 17,19).

[4]I do not mean to imply that historical research of the sort envisaged here is the *only* way in which one could justifiably believe that Jesus rose from the dead. Perhaps one could justifiably believe that Jesus rose from the dead on the basis of the testimony of some authoritative community, or of the Holy Spirit, or a little of both, and so on. All I mean to imply is that you would have thought that it was about as likely that we could arrive at a negative verdict on the Resurrection by *a priori* philosophizing of the sort Hume engages in as you would that we could arrive at a positive verdict by the same means—which is to say it isn't likely at all. Nevertheless, that's the strategy Hume holds out to us.

not credible, reason that is at least good enough to counterbalance or outweigh the strongest testimony for a miracle. Many discern a different claim, however, namely that miracles are absolutely impossible, impossible no matter what. It is this latter claim, and the argument for it, that I will assess first.

Now, on the face of it, this claim is rather astonishing. While many of us may well think that Jesus did not *in fact* rise from the dead, or that the total available evidence for his having done so is 50-50, so to speak, none of us—I dare say—think that he *could not* have arisen from the dead *no matter what*. After all, "no matter what" includes "no matter if there is an omnipotent and omniscient God," and it seems quite incredible that if there is such a God, *He* could not have miraculously raised Jesus from the dead if He had wanted to. But that's what Hume says.

I should note immediately that scholars disagree as to whether Hume says that. The argument I will evaluate in this section may not have been intended by Hume. So, in order to avoid getting embroiled in a textual dispute, I will call the argument I will assess *the Humean argument*, the argument inspired by Hume. And I will speak of its advocate as *the Humean*, the one inspired to defend the argument.[5] Before I assess the Humean argument, however, I need to address a popular objection to it.

"So What? With God All Things Are Possible"

The conclusion of the Humean argument is that miracles are impossible. Many a Christian believer, well-versed in the gospels, will have a ready response to this line of thought. They will say, "So what? So what if miracles are absolutely impossible? What's that got to do with whether God could perform one? *God* can do the impossible. After all, as Jesus said, with God *all* things are possible."

As plausible and pious as this response might initially appear, it is neither. For even if God is omnipotent and omniscient, He cannot do the impossible. Thus, *if* miracles really are absolutely impossible, then not even God can perform one. And *if* God cannot perform a miracle, then He could not have miraculously raised Jesus from the dead.

Many people of a traditional religious persuasion have a difficult time with sentences that begin "God cannot. . . ." Two points might be helpful here. First, to say that God cannot do something is not to say God's power is limited to what *we are able to do*, or to what *we think* is possible. Rather, it is to say that no matter what degree of power a being has—even omnipotence—that being cannot do what is *absolutely impossible*. Second, very few religiously inclined thinkers have been willing to say that it is possible for God both to exist and not exist at the very same time, or that it is possible for a man to be a bachelor and married at once, or that the number 2 can be the only whole number between 1 and 3 and be odd—and for good reason. Such things are absolutely impossible. This is the answer that traditional believers usually give to questions like "Why can't God bring it about that He breaks a promise?" or "Why can't God fulfill His purposes without permitting evil?" God can't do these things because, well, they are absolutely impossible. Just as there is nothing impious in answering these questions in this way, so there is nothing impious in saying that God cannot perform a miracle—*if* miracles are absolutely impossible.

But that's a big *if*. Instead of piously proclaiming that God can perform a miracle even if miracles are absolutely impossible, the religious believer would do

---

[5]See, for example Alastair McKinnon, " 'Miracle' and 'Paradox,' " *American Philosophical Quarterly*, 4 (1967), 308–14, and Nicholas Everitt, "The Impossibility of Miracles," *Religious Studies*, 23 (1987), 347–9. As J. L. Mackie notes, *The Miracle of Theism* (Oxford: Clarendon Press, 1982), 19, Hume *seems* to disagree with McKinnon, Everitt, and their ilk. Hume *seems* to use the word "miracle" in such a way that miracles are possible. In "Of Miracles" (127), the paragraph beginning "I beg the limitations . . . ," Hume says that, by his lights, "there may possibly be miracles, or violations of the usual course of nature," and then describes such a hypothetical possibility, the case of eight consecutive days of darkness. Someone who thinks that miracles are impossible would not say such things, unless he was confused. Unfortunately, we must take the latter alternative seriously. After all, Hume does say "a miracle is a violation of a law of nature," an exception to it, and he notoriously held that laws of nature are nothing but exceptionless regularities. Of course, nothing can be an exception to an exceptionless regularity.

better to inquire into what argument the Humean offers on behalf of the astonishing claim that miracles are impossible.[6]

The Humean Argument for the Impossibility of the Resurrection

So how, exactly, does the argument go? I think that it can be fairly expressed like this:

> One of the main aims of science is to discover the laws of nature. Whether scientists have succeeded is a matter of dispute, but that there are such laws and that their discovery is an aim of science is beyond dispute. Now, whatever the laws are exactly, let's suppose that one of them is this: *Nothing travels faster than the speed of light*, that is, nothing travels faster than about 186,000 miles per second. A simple question arises: could it be a law of nature that nothing travels faster than the speed of light even though something has travelled or will travel faster than the speed of light? The answer, of course, is "no." It is a law of nature that nothing travels faster than the speed of light only if it is *true* that nothing travels faster than the speed of light; and it is true that nothing travels faster than the speed of light only if *in fact* nothing travels faster than the speed of light. Thus, if it is a law of nature that nothing travels faster than the speed of light, then in fact nothing travels faster than the speed of light. If it is a law of nature that nothing travels faster than the speed of light, then

it is *false* that there has been or ever will be something—say, a photon—that travels faster than the speed of light.

> We can put the point this way: if something were to travel faster than the speed of light, it would run counter to the claim that nothing travels faster than the speed of light; it would be a *counterinstance* to it. But no law of nature has a counterinstance. That's because, as J. L. Mackie puts it, "a law of nature is, by definition, a regularity—or a statement of a regularity—about what happens, about the way the world works."[7] A statement of such a regularity is what philosophers call a true *universal generalization*.[8] Universal generalizations are statements of the form *Every F is a G*, or *No F is a G*. Thus, presumably, the statement *Every piece of copper can conductes electricity* is a law of nature, as is the statement *Nothing travels faster than the speed of light*. It simply is not possible that (a) *Every piece of copper can conduct electricity* is a law of nature, and yet (b) the copper wire in my house was unable to conduct electricity on Thanksgiving Day, 2001. Things can't take a holiday from the laws of nature.

> Now, what is a miracle? As Hume put it, "A miracle is a violation of the laws of nature" (114). But what is a violation of a law of nature but a counterinstance to it? Indeed, don't those who use miracles as evidence for their beliefs rely on this fact? For example, the Resurrection is supposed to be weighty evidence for the existence of the supernatural, in general, or for Jesus' religious authority in particular. But how could that be unless it's a violation of a law of nature? If it were merely unusual for dead men to rise again, the Resurrection would not pack the wallop it is supposed to. Only if it is a violation of a

---

[6]They would also do better to read phrases such as "with God all things are possible" in context. The passage from which this phrase comes is Matthew 19, the story of the rich man who could not give up his wealth to follow Jesus:

> Then Jesus said to his disciples, "I tell you the truth, it is hard for a rich man to enter the kingdom of heaven. Again I tell you, it is easier for a camel to go through the eye of a needle than for a rich man to enter the kingdom of God." When the disciples heard this, they were greatly astonished and asked, "Who then can be saved?" Jesus looked at them and said, "With man this is impossible, but with God all things are possible." (23–26)

You don't need a Ph.D. in literary criticism to see that Jesus is not teaching here that God can do the absolutely impossible. The contrast is between what man can't do and what God can do—that's all.

[7]*The Miracle of Theism*, 19.

[8]Laws are not identical with true universal generalizations since there can be true universal generalizations that are only *accidentally true* and hence not laws, for example all humans are born on earth. If there is a truth lurking nearby, it is that laws of nature *imply* true universal generalizations. Nothing would be lost in the argument I am representing here if we replaced "laws of nature *are* true universal generalizations" with "laws of nature *imply* true universal generalizations."

law of nature—say, a violation of the generalization that all dead men stay dead—can the Resurrection be evidence for the supernatural or Jesus' authority.

We can summarize the two points of the last two paragraphs like this:

1. It is a necessary truth that, if a miracle m occurs, then there is a law of nature, L, such that m is a counterinstance to L.
2. It is a necessary truth that, if L is a law of nature, then there are no counterinstances to L.

With these two points in hand, the argument for the impossibility of miracles is as simple as counting to five. Suppose, for *reductio*,[9] that

3. It is possible that a miracle m occurs.

It follows from 1 and 3 that

4. It is possible for there to be a law of nature, L, such that m is a counterinstance to L.

But, on reflection, if 2 is true, then so is

5. It is impossible for there to be a law of nature, L, such that m is a counterinstance to L.

And the conjunction of 4 and 5 is a contradiction. Thus, by *reductio*, 3 is false; and it doesn't take much ingenuity to see that it follows God could not have miraculously raised Jesus from the dead.

What should we make of this argument?

We certainly cannot fault its inferences; the logic is impeccable. So if there is anything wrong with it, either premise 1 or 2 is false or undeserving of our assent. Let's examine premise 2 first.

Must a Law of Nature Have No Counterinstances?

To get at the question of whether premise 2 is true or false, we need to consider two very different pictures of what a law is, Prescriptivism and Descriptivism. In this section, I'll briefly sketch the difference between these two pictures, then I'll fill in the Prescriptivist picture with a bit more detail, and explain how it portrays the laws of nature. We will then be in a better position to assess premise 2.

Two Pictures of Laws   The slogan for Prescriptivism reads, "Laws prescribe, not describe"; the slogan for Descriptivism reads, "Laws describe, not prescribe." That is, according to Prescriptivism, a law tells someone or something how to act; it prescribes behavior. "Do this . . . Don't do that"—that's what a law looks like, that's the form that a law takes, according to Prescriptivism. According to Descriptivism, however, a law states how someone or something acts; it describes behavior. "It did this . . . It didn't do that"—that's what a law looks like, that's the form a law takes, according to Descriptivism. So, in broad strokes, the two pictures come to this:

	SLOGAN	FORM OF A LAW
PRESCRIPTIVISM	Laws prescribe, not describe	"Do this" "Don't do that"
DESCRIPTIVISM	Laws describe, not prescribe	"It does this" "It doesn't do that"

As with most big pictures, the broad strokes of these two need filling in, and may even be somewhat misleading as they stand. This is especially the case for the picture of Prescriptivism.

Prescriptivism   According to the prescriptivist slogan, a law prescribes, it does not describe. Strictly speaking, that slogan does not represent Prescriptivism accurately. While it's accurate in saying that laws do not describe, it is inaccurate in saying that laws prescribe. That's because, strictly speaking, only persons or groups of persons can prescribe, and no law is a person. Still, a law is a prescription, in the sense that it is the result or consequence or upshot of somebody with the relevant authority prescribing something. But here we must take care to understand what the prescriptivist means by the words "prescribe" and "prescription."

---

[9]*Reductio ad absurdum* is a form of argument where you suppose something is true in order to show that it's false—since an absurdity, like a contradiction, follows from the supposition. Any elementary logic textbook will explain it in more detail.

On the one hand, to *prescribe* something is to stipulate how things are to behave; it is to impose, order, or command something. When the state says, "Pay your taxes by April 15," it prescribes certain behavior for taxpayers, behavior indicated in the resulting prescription, and the very act of the state's prescribing it makes it a law. A *prescription*—that is, a law—is what results from the proper authority prescribing something. This is what the prescriptivist means by the words "prescribe" and "prescription."

On the other hand, to prescribe something is to recommend or advise it. This may well be what, nowadays, we mean typically by the words "prescribe" and "prescription." But it is *not* what the prescriptivist means. When a doctor writes on a slip of paper, "Take 50 mg of Zoloft each night for 6 months," and hands it to her patient, she advises him—very strongly, perhaps—to do something. But her prescribing it does not make it a law. A mere recommendation—no matter how firmly or wisely given—is not a law. We might express the difference this way. When a patient does not do what his doctor properly prescribes, does she have the authority to punish him? No. When a citizen does not do what the state (properly) prescribes, does it have the authority to punish him? Yes. That's the difference between a prescription that is a strong recommendation and a prescription that is a law. The state, unlike the doctor, has the authority to makes its prescriptions *laws*.

So, according to the prescriptivist, although laws, strictly speaking, do not prescribe, they are prescriptions, but not recommendations, that is, they are the result of someone with the proper authority performing a certain sort of act, namely prescribing. We might pose a question for the prescriptivist at this juncture: why suppose that there is something that is distinct

HUME BEGS THE QUESTION   *   C. S. *Lewis*

Now of course we must agree with Hume that if there is absolutely "uniform experience" against miracles, if in other words they have never happened, why then they never have. Unfortunately we know the experience against them to be uniform only if we know that all the reports of them are false. And we can know all the reports to be false only if we know already that miracles have never occurred. In fact, we are arguing in a circle.

There is also an objection to Hume which leads us deeper into our problem. The whole idea of Probability (as Hume understands it) depends on the principle of the Uniformity of Nature. Unless Nature always goes on in the same way, the fact that a thing had happened ten million times would not make it a whit more probable that it would happen again. And how do we know the Uniformity of Nature? A moment's thought shows that we do not know it by experience. We observe many regularities in Nature. But of course all the observations that men have made or will make while the race lasts cover only a minute fraction of the events that actually go on. Our observations would therefore be of no use unless we felt sure that Nature when we are not watching her behaves in the same way as when we are: in other words, unless we believed in the Uniformity of Nature. Experience therefore cannot prove uniformity, because uniformity has to be assumed before experience proves anything. And mere length of experience does not help matters. It is no good saying, "Each fresh experience confirms our belief in uniformity and therefore we reasonably expect that it will always be confirmed"; for that argument works only on the assumption that the future will resemble the past—which is simply the assumption of Uniformity under a new name. Can we say that Uniformity is at any rate very probable? Unfortunately not. We have just seen that all probabilities depend on *it*. Unless Nature is uniform, nothing is either probable or improbable. And clearly the assumption which you have to make before there is any such thing as probability cannot itself be probable.

From C. S. Lewis, *Miracles* (1947).

from the performance of a linguistic act (a particular occurrence of a prescribing), something that comes into existence as a result of performing that act? An authority prescribes; but there aren't, *in addition*, prescriptions, the results of an authority's prescribing. It seems to me that a start at answering this question would include the following thought. Suppose my wife and I enter the kitchen only to see standing on the counter reaching for the cookie jar our 2-year-old boys. (They're doing a lot of that sort of thing these days.) We both say, simultaneously, "Get off the counter *now!*" There are clearly two particular occurrences of prescribing here—my wife's, on the one hand, and mine, on the other—but, equally clearly, there is a sense in which my wife and I *prescribed the same thing.* What is that "same thing"? It is neither of our acts of prescribing, for they are two things, not one and the same thing. The prescriptivist says that it is a prescription; something distinct from the acts of prescribing but which results from such acts. Considerations such as these—and there are others, specifically those that parallel considerations offered on behalf of the theory of propositions—lend some support at least to the prescriptivist's claim.[10]

Our excursion from the slogan "Laws prescribe" to the more accurate "Laws are prescriptions," and our clarification of the meaning of "prescribe" and "prescription," allows us to understand a point the prescriptivist wants to make, a point that is so important that it is best to regard it as an axiom of Prescriptivism:

Axiom 1. There *cannot* be a prescription without a prescriber.

Now, if you are at all like me, this hardly sounds surprising. After all, if no state had ever stipulated "Don't drive on the left-hand side of the road, except to pass," it would be silly to suppose that, nevertheless, there was a *law* that would be properly expressed by these words.

We are now in a position to see a second important point. The state says "Pay your taxes by April 15."

Later, for one reason or another, it says "You don't need to pay your taxes by April 15; pay them by April 30." The original law is repealed, and a new one is decreed. Even though you can't, the state can prescribe, cancel the prescription, give a new one, and so on. We have, then, a second axiom of Prescriptivism:

Axiom 2. If one has the authority to prescribe something, then one has the authority to repeal and replace that prescription.[11]

Again, this sounds like a platitude.

Now let's take a closer look at another feature of the big picture sketch of Prescriptivism. It says that a law has the form of an imperative, "Do this" and "Don't do that." As it turns out, things may be a bit more complicated than this. To see why, consider the fact that sometimes when someone exercises their authority, the result is a change in the socio-legal status of something else. So, for example, when a priest or pastor or justice of the peace says, "By the authority invested in me, I pronounce you husband and wife," she thereby alters the socio-legal status of those on whose behalf her pronouncement is made. When a judge says, "I hereby sentence you to two years in prison," you become a convict. When your boss screams, "You're fired!" you become unemployed. And when the Department of the Treasury stipulates that certain pieces of paper shall have a certain value, tens, twenties, and fifties come into existence! An act that alters the socio-legal status of something is called an *exercitive.*[12] Exercitives include pronouncing, stipulating, sentencing, pardoning, appointing, hiring, and firing, among other things. Our interest here, however, is in a certain sort of exercitive act, one that we might call *decreeing.* Decreeing, however—and this is the main point I want to make here—does not take the form of an imperative. So the big picture sketch of Prescriptivism isn't quite accurate. Decreeing takes the form of, well, decreeing: "*Let it be the case that* thus-and-so" or, perhaps

---

[10]For considerations in defense of the theory of propositions, which are analogous to considerations in response to the question raised in this paragraph, see Michael Loux, *Metaphysics* (New York: Routledge, 1993), chapter 4.

[11]My friends, Jan Cover and Hud Hudson, suggest this isn't quite right. Couldn't a law-giver prescribe a law and then decree that she shall never repeal or replace it? I invite the reader to rephrase Axiom 2 so as to avoid this minor worry.
[12]The lingo isn't mine, it's William Alston's. See *Illocutionary Acts and Sentence Meaning* (Ithaca, New York: Cornell University Press, 2000), 33ff.

more commonly, "Things of such-and-such a sort *shall* do this or that."[13] A law, on this way of thinking about laws, is the upshot, result, or consequence of the relevant authority's decreeing that something or someone behave a certain way or that something be the case.[14]

It is not important for our purposes to decide whether laws are prescriptions or decrees, or whether some laws are prescriptions and others are decrees, or whether there really is no difference at all. What is of utmost importance, however, is that whether laws are prescriptions or decrees or both, *they are not descriptions.* To see just how absurd it is, from the point of view of Prescriptivism, to think of laws as describing how things in the world work, or must work, consider the following illustration. Suppose some new state initiates a tax law. "Pay your taxes by April 15," or, alternatively, "Every taxpayer shall pay her taxes by April 15." For ease of reference, call this *The Tax Law.* And suppose every taxpayer obeys it, all the time. In that case, the following is a true universal generalization, something of the form *All Fs are Gs:*

All taxpayers pay their taxes by April 15.

For ease of reference, call this *The Tax Generalization.* Now, according to Prescriptivism, one would display massive confusion if one were to suggest that The Tax Law just is The Tax Generalization. Prescriptions and decrees do not describe how things are; true universal generalizations do. Prescriptions and decrees are neither true nor false; universal generalizations are one or the other. To suppose that prescriptions and decrees just are true universal generalizations is as bizarre as supposing that questions, expletives, and congratulations just are true universal generalizations. You simply

don't understand what a prescription or decree (or question, or expletive, or congratulation) is if you think that it is something that can be true or false.

Prescriptivism and "Laws of Nature"   According to the prescriptivist, the laws of nature—or, as she would be more inclined to say, the natural laws[15]—are, fundamentally, no different than the laws of the state. They are either general prescriptions or decrees. They are, for example, prescriptions like, "Be conductive (addressed, say, to copper)," or "Copper shall be conductive" or "Let it be the case that copper is conductive." Such things as these do not describe regularities in nature. They are neither true nor false. They could not exist if there were no law-giver. If there is a law-giver (and there is if there are any natural laws), he has the authority to rescind them when and where he likes and for whatever purposes he pleases. If, however, there is no law-giver—no one who has laid it down how natural objects shall be—then there are no natural laws. There are just regularities or powers in things. There are just universal generalizations or descriptions of the powers of things. None of these things add up to a *law*, however.

Prescriptivists will differ over what it is about, say, copper that makes it conductive. Ultimately, they will agree, the explanation is the same: someone with the authority laid it down that copper shall be conductive. But what is it about *copper*—the stuff—that makes it the case that *it* "obeys" that law? What is it about those copper *wires* inside the walls of my home that makes them get in line with "Copper shall be conductive"? Here prescriptivists diverge. One natural thing to propose is that it is by virtue of copper having a certain microstructure that it is conductive. God—or whoever the law-giver is—says "Let there be copper," and there is copper, and it is endowed with a certain structure in virtue of which it is conductive. On one model, the law-giver does this moment by moment, continuously

---

[13]Do not confuse decreeing—for example, "Every *F shall G*"—with predicting—for example, "Every *F will be* a *G*"—or asserting—for example, "Every *F ought to G.*" If you are prone to such confusion, use "Let it be the case that *Fs are Gs.*" You won't be tempted at all to confuse the latter with predicting or asserting.

[14]Two notes. First, The noun "decree" was once a common synonym for "law," both of which, on the prescriptivist view, refer to what results from an act of decreeing. Second, probably the most famous (alleged) act of decreeing in all of western literature can be found in the first book of *Genesis:*

And God said, "Let there be light," and there was light. (1:3)

The remaining verses of the first chapter consist in a series of divine decrees.

[15]The name "laws of nature" has a descriptivist ring to it, as though the laws are "out there," "in nature." Nothing could be more inaccurate, on Prescriptivism. If anything of this sort is appropriate, "laws *governing* nature" or "laws *about* nature" would be better than "laws *of* nature." But "natural laws" is best. Just as nobody would be tempted to think that something called a "tax law" is "out there," "in the citizenry," so nobody should be tempted to think that something called a "natural law" is "out there," "in nature."

decreeing that copper exist and that it have whatever structure it has in virtue of which it is conductive. On another model, the law-giver issues his decree just once, and that's enough for copper to exist and have whatever structure it has in virtue of which it is conductive. Of course, on either model, copper will behave in a regular fashion, perhaps even an exceptionlessly regular fashion. But no such regularity—and no description of such a regularity, and no description of the structure of copper, and no description of the powers copper has in virtue of having that structure—should be confused with the natural *law, Copper shall be conductive*, which the law-giver lays down.

A more accurate sketch of Prescriptivism can be expressed in the table below:

Now, our first question is this: *if* Prescriptivism is true, what does that imply for Premise 2 of the Humean argument? Premise 2, recall, is this:

2. It is a necessary truth that, if *L* is a law of nature, then there are no counterinstances to *L*.

Prescriptivism and Counterinstances To answer this question, let's suppose that Prescriptivism is true, just to see what follows. And, for the sake of illustration, suppose that it is a law of nature that *Copper shall be conductive*. It follows from these two supposi-

tions and Axiom 1 that there is a law-giver—say, God—who exercised His authority to bring about such states of affairs just by prescribing or decreeing them. Moreover, it follows from Axiom 2 that God can rescind and/or replace this law as He pleases. Suppose it suits His purposes on some occasion to do so. Suppose He decrees, "Let the copper in the Howard-Snyder home stop being conductive on Thanksgiving Day, 2001." Well, that's His prerogative, and if God decrees something, that's how it is. Consequently, the copper in my house takes a holiday (unlike me!). We have here, then, an exception to the law *Copper shall be conductive*, a counterinstance to it.

Here's another illustration. Suppose, as David Hume did, that there is a law of nature that has to do with dead men staying dead. If Prescriptivism is true, this law will *not*, contrary to Hume, be an exceptionless regularity or a true universal generalization like *All dead men stay dead*. Rather, it will be something like *Dead men shall stay dead*, where this is understood as the upshot of an authoritative act of decreeing, not a predicting or asserting. It follows from this supposition and Axiom 1 that there is a law-giver—say, God—who exercised His authority to bring about such a state of affairs. And from this and Axiom 2 it follows that He can revoke His decree. Suppose His purposes call for such a revocation. Then, I suppose, He can bring it about that some dead

	SLOGAN	FORM OF A LAW	NATURAL LAWS	AXIOMS
PRESCRIPTIVISM	Laws are prescriptions or decrees, not descriptions	Imperative: "Do this," "Don't do that"	[To the void] *Be conductive (in this sort of way, here and there)*	No prescription without a prescriber
		Decree: "Let it be the case that . . ." "*Fs* shall be *Gs*"	*Let it be the case that copper is conductive* *Copper shall be conductive*	Prescribers and law-givers may repeal and replace prescriptions & decrees as they please

man is no longer dead. If He does, the raised man is an exception to (what, at any rate, once was) the law.

It seems we must conclude that *if* Prescriptivism is true, Premise 2 of the Humean argument is false.

Of course, the million dollar question is this: *is* Prescriptivism true? I suspect that I am like most of my readers. Prescriptivism holds a certain plausibility for us; it's not an unnatural way to think about laws in general or natural laws in particular. Even so, we must investigate it more thoroughly before we endorse it.[16] In the meantime, however, provided that nothing we reasonably believe *rules it out*, then, wouldn't it be unwise to affirm that laws of nature can have no counterinstances? If so, we can't affirm the impossibility of miracles—or the Resurrection—on the basis of the Humean argument.

Let us turn now to an assessment of Premise 1. In the remainder of section 2, I will assume—just for the sake of argument—that Prescriptivism is false and that Descriptivism is true.

Must a Miracle Be a Counterinstance to a Law of Nature?

Recall that Premise 1 of the Humean argument says this:

1. It is a necessary truth that, if a miracle m occurs, then there is a law of nature, L, such that m is a counterinstance to L.

We might adopt one of two strategies in assessing this premise. First, we might press on what a law of nature is, and discover that a miracle is not a counterinstance to a *law of nature*, properly understood. Second, we might press on what a miracle is, and discover that a *miracle*, properly understood, need not be a counterinstance to a law of nature. I shall approach each strategy in the order mentioned.

Laws of Nature, the Goals of Science, and Implicit Restrictions According to the Humean, laws of nature are (or are expressed by, or imply) true universal generalizations of the form *All Fs are Gs*.[17] Now, suppose our best scientists developed the wisdom and technology to discover all the laws of nature, every last one of them—and suppose they succeeded. Then, according to the Humean, we would have a list of true universal generalizations, call it *The List*. Of course, many of the items on The List would be full of mathematical equations and technical jargon that very few people could understand. But many of them would be more homely, like this:

1. All copper is conductive.
2. Nothing travels faster than the speed of light.
3. All water freezes at temperatures below 32 degrees Fahrenheit.

---

[16]Here's one objection: the prescriptive force of an imperative or command cannot have the *descriptive* content that we take laws of nature to in fact have. See Jan Cover, "Miracles and (Christian) Theism," in *Philosophy of Religion: The Big Questions*, eds. Eleonore Stump and Michael Murray (Malden, Massachusetts: Blackwell, 1999), 343. At first glance, this seems to be little more than the question-begging assertion that laws are descriptions. On closer inspection, however, perhaps Cover means to argue (1) laws have content, but (2) prescriptions don't, so (3) laws aren't prescriptions. The prescriptivist may well deny (1), but that would be desperate. After all, people obey prescriptions because they understand them, and they understand them because they have content. It seems to me that (2) is false, however. Here are two (incompatible) ways to argue for (2)'s falsity; I'm not sure which is correct, but I'm sure one of them is. Way 1. Prescriptions have *prescriptive* content. When I command my 2-year-old sons, "Stay off the street!" the prescriptive content of my command is that *They shall stay off the street* (which, again, is neither a prediction nor a moral assertion). Way 2. Prescriptions have the same content as descriptions. When I command my sons, "Stay off the street!" the content of my linguistic act is that

They stay off the street. When I command my sons, I prescribe a certain state of affairs to them, *Their staying off the street.* Suppose they obey, and a passerby notices it. She might describe my sons behavior with "They stay off the street," the content of her linguistic act is that *They stay off the street.* When she describes my sons, she describes a certain state of affairs, *Their staying off the street.* Perhaps Cover meant a different argument, say this: (1′) laws have *descriptive* content, but (2′) prescriptions don't, so (3) laws aren't prescriptions. The proponent of Way 1 will say (1′) is nothing but the implicit question-begging conjunction *laws are descriptions and their content is descriptive.* The proponent of Way 2 will, first, distinguish a speech act—like, prescribing and describing—from its content, and note that the content of two distinct speech acts can be the very same, as I illustrated with my command and the passerby's description. She'll then say that the phrase "descriptive content" is, strictly speaking, ill-formed. If it means "content of a description," then (2′) is the false claim that prescriptions don't have *the content* of a description. If it does not mean that, then (1′) is the question-begging assertion the proponent of Way 1 noticed.

[17]I'll leave this parenthetical remark tacit from here on out, but I do mean it to be understood.

Let's imagine, then, that we have The List before us. I want to make an observation about the particular items on it.

Note that items 1 and 3 of the portion in view before us are about copper and water. Other items on The List are about more exotic things: muons, gluons, fields of force (perhaps). But what is 2 about? Certainly not nothing! Well, then, what is it about? Presumably, *everything*. Item 2 is equivalent to the statement "Everything travels no faster than the speed of light." What can we infer from this? We can infer that no copper penny, no molecule of water, no photon, *absolutely nothing*, travels faster than the speed of light. Right?

Well, not exactly. Let me explain. Suppose a note is taped to my office door when I arrive back from class: "Dan, Frances wants you to come home quickly." I race home, run in the door, and shriek, "Is everything alright?" My wife responds, "Yes, everything's fine; sorry to alarm you. Peter just got a bloody nose. I thought it was broken." No one would mistake her for having claimed that—strictly speaking—*everything* is fine. There are still wars, famines, droughts, diseases, abused women and children, and so on. Everything—strictly speaking—is *not* fine. Or suppose you're the janitor at a high school, and, after a basketball game, you clean up the mess in the gym. Your boss says to you the next day, "The gym sure was a mess last night. Did you clean up everything?" You answer, "Yep. It's all gone; nothing's left." Obviously, you don't mean the bleachers and backboards and banners are gone. You don't even mean that there aren't several scuff marks here or there, and a bit of dust in the corners. In everyday life, we invariably use the words "everything" and "nothing" with certain goals and restrictions in mind, indicated by contextual clues. Given the goal of getting the gym ready for the next game, none of the mess from the night before is left. Everything within the scope of my wife's immediate concern is fine. The moral here is this: we need to understand a universal generalization as it is intended in the context in which it is put forward.

So let's return to The List and our hypothetical scientists who put it together. What do they intend by those universal generalizations? Well, what is the goal of science? Presumably, one of them is to understand how things in the *natural world* work. In that case,

when they write down item 2 on The List—"Nothing travels faster than the speed of light"—they do not mean to pronounce on how things go in a *supernatural world*, if such there be. Item 2 is not intended as a quasi-theological claim, one that should get Jerry Falwell and Pat Robertson upset, one that implies that no angel, if such there be, can travel from here to there in, say, twice the speed of light. That's not the business of science.[18] Rather, scientists mean something like "Nothing travels faster than the speed of light, supernatural objects aside (if such there be)." And a similar point applies to the other items on The List. Take, for example, item 1—"All copper is conductive." Like item 2, it is not intended as a quasi-theological claim, one that implies, say, that no supernatural being, if such there be, can prevent the copper pipes in my home from conducting electricity for a day. Rather, item 2 is to be understood along the lines of "All copper is conductive, supernatural intervention aside (if there is any)." So, strictly speaking, given the goals of science, the universal generalizations that scientists say are (or are implied by) the laws of nature do not take the unrestricted form

All Fs are Gs,

but rather have implicit restrictions, something like this:

All Fs are Gs, supernatural objects and intervention aside (if such there be).

We are now in a position to see that Premise 1 is false.

Suppose that a miracle occurs: say, a man rises from the dead. According to Hume, this occurrence is a counterinstance to a law of nature, something like the universal generalization that

All dead men stay dead.

We now see, however, that this expression of the relevant law is, strictly speaking, incorrect, and that the correct expression is that

All dead men stay dead, supernatural intervention aside (if such there be).

Of course, this law of nature is compatible with some dead man getting up from his grave. For it does not

---

[18]Lest I be misunderstood, I am not implying that science and religion *could not* conflict.

speak to dead men a supernatural being raises from the dead. If there is such a being, and he raises some man from the dead, the man who is raised is no counterinstance to the generalization that *All dead men stay dead, supernatural intervention aside*; that event, after all, would be a case of supernatural intervention.

So, once we get clear on what the laws of nature are about (the natural world, not supernatural goings on), then—even if the laws are (or imply) universal generalizations—we can see that they must be implicitly restricted in such a way that no miracle is a counterinstance to the laws of nature. Premise 2 is, therefore, false. It is based on a misunderstanding of what a law of nature is.

Of "Miracles" Suppose that Premise 2 of the Humean argument is true: necessarily, if *L* is a law of nature, then there are no counterinstances to *L*. And suppose that, contrary to what I affirmed in the last section, laws of nature are true *unrestricted* universal generalizations of the form *All Fs are Gs*. Given these suppositions, how does the Humean argument fare? Not well, or it seems to me. To see why, let's press on the word "miracle." What does it mean?

Hume, like many of his academic contemporaries, insisted that the word "miracle" was "accurately defined" as "[i] *a transgression of a law of nature* [ii] *by a particular volition of the Deity, or by the interposition of some invisible agent*" (115). It is not uncommon for academics to agree with Hume.[19] Many, however, do not agree. Some drop [i] but insist on [ii].[20] Others drop [ii] but insist on [i].[21] Yet others drop [i]

and [ii].[22] And if you look at the English dictionary in the library closest to you, I'll bet my house that it offers *several* definitions of the term "miracle," some of which imply only [i], some of which imply only [ii], some of which imply neither [i] nor [ii], and *none* of which imply both [i] and [ii].

What should we make of this (dis)array of definitions? Well, the first thing to note is that it doesn't mean that anything goes. You and I cannot just stipulate what the term "miracle" means however we please; not, that is, if we intend to be using it as it is used in the English language.

The second thing to note is that, even if not anything goes, considerable variance is permitted, as we just saw. This leads to a very awkward question for the Humean: why should we believe his Premise 1? Premise 1 says that

1. It is a necessary truth that, if a miracle *m* occurs, then there is a law of nature, *L*, such that *m* is a counterinstance to *L*.

But why should we believe it?

It won't do to argue for it on the grounds that the concept of a miracle implies that a miracle is a counterinstance to a law of nature. For, as we've just seen, there doesn't seem to be any such thing as *the* concept of a miracle; apparently, there are several concepts, some of which do not have that implication.

Neither will it do to argue that if Premise 1 is false, then there is no distinction between a miracle and a coincidence, which obviously there is.[23] For even if Premise 1 is false, a miracle can be distinguished from a coincidence by, for example, its having a supernatural cause, or, alternatively, its being a violation of what

---

[19]Martin Curd, "Miracles as Violations of Laws of Nature," *Faith, Freedom, and Rationality*, eds. Daniel Howard-Snyder and Jeff Jordan (Totowa, New Jersey: Rowman and Littlefield, 1996), 171, says that "According to the standard modern concept of a miracle . . . there are at least two necessary conditions for an event to be miraculous:

M1. E violates at least one law of nature, and
M2. E is caused directly by God or some other supernatural agent."
[20]Thomas Aquinas says "those things are properly called miracles which are done by divine agency beyond the order commonly observed in nature." See *Summa Contra Gentiles*, III. No violation of a law of nature here.
[21]David Johnson, *Hume, Holism, and Miracles* (Ithaca, New York: Cornell University Press, 1999), 9, says an "[event] *m* is a miracle for [person] *x* at [time] *t* if and only if *m* actually occurs at some time and *m* is a violation of (an exception to) something which is

for *x* at *t* exceedingly well established, relative to a body of inductive evidence, as being a law of nature." No violation of a law of nature here, only a violation of what one has excellent reason to believe is law of nature; and nothing at all about a supernatural cause.
[22]Harold Clark Kee, "Miracles," *The Oxford Companion to the Bible*, eds. Bruce Metzger and Michael Coogan (New York: Oxford University Press, 1993), 519, says "A miracle is an extraordinary event, perceived to be the result of the direct, purposeful action of a god or the agent of a god."
[23]William Rowe, *Philosophy of Religion*, 2nd ed. (Belmont, California: Wadsworth, 1993), 120

one had thought, for very good reason, to be a (Humean) law of nature.

And the Humean (surely!) won't argue for Premise 1 by offering us a representative sampling of miracles, all of which are known to be counterinstances to some law of nature, and bid us to infer inductively that miracles are (must be?) counterinstances to such laws. So why believe Premise 1?

Some people say that if Premise 1 is false, then miracles cannot be strong evidence for the supernatural, or the authority of some religious figure.[24] To test this contention, let us imagine that we have just arrived at the scene of a horrifying traffic accident. A body has been separated into several, large pieces, strewn about the street. We get out of our car, careful to avoid an arm here, a leg there, and we check the inside of the smashed truck to see whether there are any survivors. There's no one there. We turn back to our car and, as we walk toward it, the body parts begin to move together so that, in a minute or so, a woman arises from the ground, rubbing her head, but otherwise looking perfectly fine. Now, suppose that Premise 1 is false. That is, suppose that it's possible for a miracle to occur even though it is not a violation of a Humean law of nature. And suppose that, *unbeknownst to us*, the event we just witnessed is not such a violation, say, because long ago some dead man didn't stay dead. Still, prior to witnessing what we just saw, the proposition that *All dead men stay dead* was exceedingly well-established for us by a large body of inductive evidence as being a law of nature, evidence that surpassed the most rigorous criteria for inductive evidence that you

please. In those circumstances and given these suppositions, *might not* the event we just witnessed be strong evidence for some sort of supernatural intervention? I should hope so.

So we're left with a question: why should we believe that it is a necessary truth that a *miracle* is a violation or a counterinstance of a law of nature? Since we have no satisfactory answer to that question, we would be most unwise to affirm Premise 1 of the Humean argument. Let's now turn to Hume's second argument against miracles, and the Resurrection in particular.

3. ON THE UNREASONABLENESS OF BELIEVING THE RESURRECTION OCCURRED

The most salient portions of Hume's "proof against proof" argument against the Resurrection occur in these three passages:

> In order to encrease the probability against the testimony of witnesses, let us suppose, that the fact, which they affirm, instead of being only marvellous, is really miraculous; and suppose also, that the testimony considered apart and in itself, amounts to an entire proof; in that case, there is proof against proof, of which the strongest must prevail. (114)
>
> A miracle is a violation of the laws of nature; and as a firm and unalterable experience has established these laws, the proof against a miracle, from the very nature of the fact, is as entire as any argument from experience can possibly be imagined. (114)
>
> And as a uniform experience amounts to a proof, there is here a direct and full *proof*, from the very nature of the fact, against the existence of any miracle; nor can such a proof be destroyed, or the miracle rendered credible, but by an opposite proof, which is superior. (115)

To get clear on Hume's contention here, we need first to understand what Hume regarded as a "proof."

What's a "Proof" According to Hume?

Hume tells us that "we ought to divide arguments into *demonstrations, proofs, and probabilities*."[25] A demonstration is a deductively valid argument with

[24]Antony Flew seems to be such a person. See, among other things, "Neo-Humean Arguments About the Miraculous," In Defense of Miracles, eds. Doug Geivett and Gary Habermas (Downer's Grove, Illinois: InterVarsity Pres, 1997), 46, where he says that in order for a miracle to serve as a "demonstration" that "the Christian revelation, or any rival candidate, constitutes an authentic self-revelation of the true God,"

> the word *miracle* has to be construed (as both Hume himself and all his contemporary opponents did construe it) in a very strong sense. It must involve an overriding of a law of nature, a doing of what is known to be naturally impossible by a Power which is, by this very overriding, shown to be supernatural.

Only if this is given can the occurrence of a miracle under the auspices of some particular system of belief constitute an inexpungible divine endorsement of that system.

[25]*Enquiry*, 56, note 1.

known premises. A probability is a statistical induction with known premises. And a proof is a nonstatistical induction with known premises.[26] Let me explain the latter a bit, as it is Hume's main concern.

A proof, according to Hume, is an argument that has the *form* of a nonstatistical induction. The form of a nonstatistical induction is this:

1. All hitherto observed (i.e., examined) As have been Bs.
2. So, all As are Bs.

In addition, the premise of every proof is *known*. So, for example, this is a proof, according to Hume:

1. All hitherto observed (i.e., examined) water has been composed of H_2O.
2. So, all water is composed of H_2O.

It has the form of a nonstatistical induction, and its premise is known.

There are three things to keep in mind about nonstatistical induction. First, we reason in this way frequently, and such reasoning sometimes provides very strong grounds for believing the conclusion to be true. Second, the premise of a nonstatistical induction is not intended to guarantee the truth of the conclusion; it is intended only to make the conclusion likely to one degree or another. So we can't write off some particular nonstatistical induction by saying that even if all the As we've observed are Bs, some A that we haven't observed *might not* be a B. That's true but irrelevant to the strength of any such induction; for even the strongest one has that feature. Third, there are several standard criteria for assessing nonstatistical inductions. The two most important are sample size and sample representation. That is, the more As we've observed that are Bs, the more likely it is that all As are Bs, given the truth of the premise; and the more that the As we've observed differ in other respects, the more likely it is that all As are Bs, given the truth of the premise. Of course, the premise should be true as well.

So, with these things in mind, what, *exactly*, is Hume's argument?

Hume's "Proof against Proof" Argument

Hume has in mind two proofs, one based on "testimony" in favor of a miracle and the Resurrection in particular, and the other based on "uniform experience" (115) against any miracle and the Resurrection in particular. At the most general level, the idea is that, no matter how strong the first proof is, the second cancels it out; "there is a mutual destruction of arguments" (116). Consequently, "no testimony is sufficient to establish a miracle" (115–6), and a miracle "cannot be believed by any reasonable person" (131). So it's not reasonable to believe the Resurrection occurred.[27] But how exactly do these proofs go? And how do they cancel each other out? And how are we supposed think of testimony as a proof, anyway?

Of course, testimony isn't the sort of thing that can *be* a proof, in Hume's sense of the term—a nonstatistical induction with a known premise. Suppose you tell me today that you turned 20 last week; naturally enough, I believe you. But how can we regard your testimony—that particular act at that particular place and time, or its content, that you turned 20 last week—as a nonstatistical induction with a known premise? We can't. In all fairness, Hume does not ask us to consider a case in which testimony *is* a proof; he asks us to consider a case in which testimony "*amounts* to an entire proof" (114, my emphasis). But if we're really going to have "proof against proof" so that "there is a mutual destruction of arguments," we can't have on the one side a proof and on the other side something that just "amounts" to a proof, something perhaps that isn't even an argument at all. If we are going to take Hume seriously, we're going to have to fill in the blanks for him.

Here's how to fill in the blanks.[28] On the one side, the side in favor of a miracle—the Resurrection, say—

---

[26]See 110–11, "A wise man . . . observations," and consult David Johnson, *Hume, Holism, and Miracles*, 11–16, for textual evidence. Consult a logic textbook for more information about these kinds of arguments.

[27]Hume says that his argument has only to do with testimony considered as an "external evidence," something publically available. Whether in jest or in earnest, I'm not sure, he explicitly states that his argument has no bearing on the (alleged) testimony of the Holy Spirit, whereby the truth of some proposition is "brought home . . . by the immediate operation of the Holy Spirit" (109). For extensive treatment of this idea, see Alvin Plantinga, *Warranted Christian Belief* (New York: Oxford University Press, 2000).

[28]Here I rely on David Johnson, *Hume, Holism, and Miracles*, 17–18.

we have the following argument, the first two premises of which constitute a proof, in Hume's sense of the term:

1. All hitherto observed (that is, tested for accuracy) witnesses with such-and-such credentials[29] are completely accurate reporters.
2. So, all witnesses with such-and-such credentials are completely accurate reporters. (from 1, nonstatistical induction)
3. Some witness with such-and-such credentials reported that Jesus died, and on the third day rose again.
4. So, Jesus did not stay dead. (from 2 and 3, deduction)

On the other side, the side against the Resurrection, we have this argument, the first two premises of which constitute a proof, in Hume's sense of the term:

5. All hitherto observed dead men have stayed dead.
6. So, all dead men stay dead. (from 5, nonstatistical induction)
7. So, Jesus stayed dead. (from 6, deduction)

Hume's contention is that the second proof cancels out the first. Thus, it is unreasonable to believe that the Resurrection occurred. Now, we might wonder why he affirms premise 5, which, as he sees things, describes "a firm and unalterable experience." What he offers is this: "because that has never been observed in any age or country" (115).

What should we make of this argument? I can best explain my take on it by relating a story that was reported recently in my local newspaper, the *Bellingham Gazette*. But first I must give some background.

The Fourth of July Bellingham Salmon Derby

Out here in Bellingham, Washington, where I live, there are salmon derbies about every other week during the summer. These derbies are taken very seriously (I'd say way *too* seriously), as there are large cash prizes for whoever catches the largest salmon during a derby, which usually lasts a whole weekend; occasionally, the prize is $2,500 in the king salmon category, if there is an unusually large number of registrants.

Now, salmon get pretty big, especially the kings. The world-record—or, at any rate, the record presently recognized by the *Guiness Book of World Records*—is 143 pounds, caught in 1976, near Glasgow, Scotland. The typical king out here in the Pacific Northwest is quite a bit smaller than that. Most weigh in between 30 and 50 pounds, and winners of our derbies these days sometimes come in between 70 and 80 pounds, but only very rarely. The all-time best was 103 pounds, caught back in 1953. Now, a fish can lose up to *two percent* of its body weight within an hour of being caught, and when you're dealing with fish the size of a king, well, you get the picture: if you catch one that might be a contender, you want to get it weighed lickety-split. To facilitate matters, the Bellingham City Council, which sponsors these derbies, has arranged for four, huge yachts, carrying three judges apiece (usually Council members or civic dignitaries), to cruise the area being fished, which usually spans 100 square miles. Each yacht is responsible for about a quarter of the area, and each is kitted out with three state-of-the-art co-calibrated Konisberg scales, so that fishermen don't have to go all the way back to the marina to get their salmon weighed, losing precious time . . . or, more importantly, precious ounces. (Some fishermen carry syringes in their boats. Fortunately, the Council has developed a pretty reliable procedure for detecting fish that have been "pumped"; moreover, the penalty, if you're caught, is a $5,000 fine, a life-time ban from the derbies, and your face on a "wanted" poster in the *Gazette*. These things add up to a pretty strong deterrent.) At any rate, what I recount here was reported in an article in the *Gazette* on November 22, 2001.

During the Fourth of July Weekend Derby, 2001, a local, Manuel Kont, an engineer at Georgia Pacific, won with a Derby- and *world*-record 178-pound king salmon. (I can remember the *Gazette* and local television stations making a big fuss about it.) Of course, no salmon can win a derby, or even place second or third, if it isn't weighed on an official scale, witnessed by three judges. In this case, however, given that the world-record was at stake, all four yachts weighed the monster, with a difference of only two ounces between them, and all twelve judges witnessed the weighings. Unfortunately, after the final weighing, as the king was being transferred back to Mr. Kont's

---

boat, it slipped into the Bay; before anyone could find a net big enough to scoop it up, it swam away. One week after the Derby, the City Council notified the Guiness Foundation, located in Edinburgh, Scotland, which publishes the well-known *Guiness Book of World Records*, of Mr. Kont's catch. The Council sent an affidavit, signed by each of the twelve judges, and some material about the Derby's history and, most importantly, weighing procedures and scales. A reply was returned quickly, the substance of which was recounted in the article as follows: "The officials at the Guiness Foundation said that they 'cannot accept the claim that Mr. Kont caught a 178-pound king salmon' on the grounds that 'the affidavit and other materials that were sent to the Foundation are insufficient evidence.' " Upon inquiring what further evidence was needed, the Council received another letter, quoted in full in the article:

3 August 2001

Dear Sirs and Madams,

The Foundation has reconsidered the case of Mr. Kont in light of your letter of 29 July 2001. Unfortunately, we still find the evidence for the claim that he caught a 178-pound king salmon, on 4 July 2001, insufficient. Furthermore, upon consultation with the Department of Philosophy at the University of Edinburgh, we have determined that, even if the affidavit we received from you amounted to an entire proof, we could not find the claim credible. We therefore regret to inform you that the case has been closed. We realize that Mr. Kont and the City of Bellingham must be deeply disappointed. We hope, however, that you will appreciate the Foundation's insistence on the highest principles of evidence.

Sincerely,
The Guiness Foundation

Upon receiving this letter, the Bellingham City Council consulted its own local Department of Philosophy, at Western Washington University. Subsequently, the following letter was sent by the Council to the Foundation:

August 13, 2001

Dear Administrators,

We are perplexed by your letter of August 3, 2001. It states that "even if the affidavit . . . amounted to an entire proof, we could not find the claim credible." But how can that be? Upon consulting the Department of Philosophy at Western Washington University, we are curious as to why it is that you cannot find the claim credible in light of the following proof:

1. All hitherto observed (that is, tested for accuracy) witnesses with such-and-such credentials are completely accurate reporters.
2. So, all witnesses with such-and-such credentials are completely accurate reporters. (from 1, nonstatistical induction)
3. The twelve judges of the Bellingham Annual Salmon Derby have such-and-such credentials—as do the 500 or more fishermen, carpenters, etc. who have signed the enclosed affividat—and they all report that Mr. Manuel Kont caught a 178-pound king salmon, on July 4, 2001.
4. So, Mr. Manuel Kont caught a 178-pound king salmon, on July 4, 2001. (from 2 and 3, deduction)

We would be most grateful for a response.

Sincerely,
The Bellingham City Council

After a month or so, the Council received the following communication from the Guiness Foundation:

7 September 2001

Dear Sirs and Madams,

Although we have closed the case of Mr. Manuel Kont, and although it is not our usual practice to respond to inquiries such as yours after a case has been closed, we feel that your kind-spirited letter, of 13 August 2001, is worthy of a response. Our response is this: the proof that you have provided is cancelled out by the following proof, which is based on a uniform experience.

5. All hitherto observed (that is, tested for accuracy) king salmon that have been caught weigh less than 178-pounds.
6. So, all king salmon that are caught weigh less that 178-pounds. (from 5, nonstatistical induction)
7. So, Mr. Manuel Kont did not catch a 178-pound king salmon, on 4 July 2001. (from 6, deduction)

This full proof is founded on an infallible experience, and its premise—which, no doubt, you wonder why we affirm—describes a firm and unalterable experience, namely this: a 178-pound king salmon has *never* been observed in *any* age or country, or in *any* sea.

We hope this settles the matter for you, as it should for any reasonable man. And we also hope you appreciate—perhaps more fully now—why the Guiness Foundation is respected round the globe for its insistence on the highest principles of reason and understanding.

Sincerely, and with utmost best wishes,
The Guiness Foundation

The Bellingham City Council, upon further consultation, drafted the following letter, and sent it by registered mail on the date indicated:

September 21, 2001

Dear Administrators,

Thank you for your response of September 7, 2001, regarding the case of Mr. Manuel Kont. We realize (all too well, now) that you must receive countless complaints about your decisions, and we are most grateful that you found our query worthy of such a generous response. We wish only to raise three brief questions about it.

First, might something in addition to the affidavits be relevant to your judgment? If so, perhaps the enclosed photos, local press clippings, and video of the event will be of use.

Second, if your proof cancels ours, then no world-record can be reasonably believed to be broken—a rather odd consequence, don't you think?

Third, the premise of your proof states that "All hitherto observed (that is, tested for accuracy) king salmon that have been caught were less than 178-pounds." With all due respect, we are perplexed by the reason you gave for this premise, namely this: "a 178-pound king salmon has *never* been observed in *any* age or country, or in *any* sea." For when you say "a 178-pound king salmon has *never* been observed in *any* age or country, or in *any* sea," either you mean to include the observations of the 512-plus, or you don't. If you do, then doesn't your reason presuppose the *denial* of what is precisely at issue, namely whether the 512-plus *really did* witness Mr. Kont's 178-pound king salmon—in which case your argument begs the question? (Of course, if you have some independent reason to deny the report of the 512-plus, we would be most anxious to hear it; but, as it stands, you profess your proof cancels ours without considering any other independent reason.) If you do not, however, why not? After all, you claim to have given us a non-statistical induction with a *known* premise. But you know the premise only if you have taken into consideration *all* the information available to you, including the affidavits and supporting material from us (which, we remind you, you have said "amounts to a proof"). And if you take it into consideration, wouldn't you agree—at the very least—that it is not at all clear that "a 178-pound king salmon has *never* been observed in *any* age or country, or in *any* sea"? Consequently, wouldn't you agree that you don't know your premise, after all?

If the Foundation would be so kind as to clarify these matters for us, we would be in their debt.

Sincerely,
The Bellingham City Council

As of November 22—two months after this letter was sent—the Council has yet to receive a response, despite several queries and phone calls.[30]

QUESTIONS FOR FURTHER REFLECTION

1. What's the point of each of the questions presented to the Guiness Foundation? Do the same points apply to Hume's "proof against proof" argument? If so, how? If not, why not?

2. Assess the following argument:
   If Prescriptivism is true, then it is a necessary truth that, if L is a law of nature, L is not a claim. But it is also a necessary truth that, if L is not a claim, then there are no counterinstances to L, since something can be a counterinstance only if it runs counter to a claim. Thus, if Prescriptivism is true, then it is a necessary truth that, if L is a law of nature, there are no counterinstances to L. That is to say, if Prescriptivism is true, then Premise 2 of the Humean argument for the impossibility of miracles is *true*—contrary to what Howard-Snyder says.

3. Suppose that the property of *being conductive* is an *essential* property of copper, i.e., that it is absolutely impossible for something to be copper and lack conducivity. In that case, given Prescriptivism, could God decree that the copper wires in the Howard-Snyder house stop being conductive, as Howard-Snyder claims?

---

[30]I leave as homework to the reader the application of this story to Hume's "proof against proof" argument for the unreasonableness of believing in the Resurrection. A hint can be found in Jan Cover, "Miracles and (Christian) Theism," in eds. Michael Murray and Eleonore Stump, *Philosophy of Religion: The Big Questions* (Blackwell, 1999).

For an extensive bibliography on contemporary philosophical literature on miracles, see Michael Levine, "Miracles," in the *Stanford Encyclopedia of Philosophy*, online at http:/plato.stanford.edu. Also, see David Johnson's *Hume, Holism, and Miracles* (note 19)—upon which I have relied heavily—and John Earman's *Hume's Abject Failure* (New York: Oxford University Press, 2000).

Thanks to Jan Cover, Frances Howard-Snyder, Hud Hudson and Michael Murray for comments on earlier drafts of this paper, the most important of which remain to be addressed.

47. HISTORIANS ON MIRACLES

Raymond Martin

Raymond Martin has taught philosophy at the University of Maryland and now teaches at Union College, where he is chair of the department. He writes in the areas of personal identity theory, philosophy of history, philosophy of religion, and history of philosophy. He is the author of *The Past Within Us: An Empirical Approach to Philosophy of History* (1989); *Self-Concern: An Experiential Approach to What Matters in Survival* (1998); and *The Elusive Messiah: A Philosophical Overview of the Quest for the Historical Jesus* (1999). He is co-author of *Naturalization of the Soul: Self and Personal Identity in the Eighteenth Century* (2000). Two additional books of his are forthcoming: *The Rise and Fall of Soul and Self* (co-authored) and *Philosophy of History from the Bottom Up: An American Revolution*. The selection that follows was written exclusively for this volume, but is based on *The Elusive Messiah*, where the issues under consideration are discussed in greater depth. The main question at issue is whether it is possible to do historical studies responsibly while allowing for the real possibility, not only that a miracle has occurred, but that the evidence might support that one has occurred.

READING QUESTIONS

1. What is "methodological naturalism"?
2. How would the arguments of Spinoza and Hume, if accepted, support methodological naturalism in historical studies?
3. Martin claims that historians of Jesus, such as E. P. Sanders, are committed to certain conclusions in advance of their study of the evidence. What sort of conclusions does he have in mind? Why does he think that historians are committed to these conclusions?
4. Does Meier, in doing his history of Jesus, reject the possibility of miracles?
5. Crossan, in doing his history, has tried "to move behind the screen of creedal interpretation and, without in any way denying or negating the validity of faith, give an accurate but impartial account of the historical Jesus." Has he succeeded?
6. Why does Martin think that "methodological naturalism" implies "methodological atheism"?
7. What is "faith history"? In what ways is it an alternative to "methodological naturalism"?

The Dutch rationalist philosopher, Baruch (or Benedict) Spinoza (1632–1677) denied the reality of miracles, reasoning as follows: a miracle, were one to occur, would "by Divine decree" be a violation of a law of nature; a law of nature must be necessarily true; anything necessarily true must be "by Divine decree," that is, follow "from the necessity and perfection of the Divine nature"; so, a miracle, were one to occur, would both be by Divine decree and violate laws of nature that are also by Divine decree; hence, a miracle, were one to occur, would involve God's acting against His own nature, that is, acting inconsistently. It is absurd to suppose that God could or would act inconsistently.[1]

Spinoza's argument against miracles, unlike the arguments of many who would come later, was based not on atheism, but on theism—at least on pantheism. He argued that miracles cannot occur not because there is no God, but because there is one. His aim, however,

---

[1]Benedict de Spinoza, *Theological-Political Treatise*, 1670, in *The Chief Works of Benedict de Spinoza*, 2 vols., trans. R.H.M. Elwes (New York: Dover, 1951), vol. I, p. 83.

was not primarily to make a positive contribution to theology, but to lay the foundations for a naturalistic approach to historical studies. To do that, he thought, miracle stories had to be discredited. He tried to discredit them, not one at a time, but all at the same time. The idea that this could be done was his great contribution to the philosophical discussion of miracles. In his view, historians who employ proper methods do not *emerge from* the examination of history with the *discovery* that no miracles have occurred. Rather, they *bring to* the study of history the certain knowledge that none has occurred. Hence, in his view, any claims made by ancient authors that miracles have occurred should be rejected out of hand and explained naturalistically. The important question historically, he said, is not whether a miracle story is true, but why an ancient author would report a false story. Was the ancient author deluded? Was he credulously passing on something he had read or heard? Was the story his mythical way of saying something that could be understood, in different terms, naturalistically?

Subsequently the Scottish philosopher and historian David Hume (1711–1776) argued against miracles, not on theistic grounds, as had Spinoza, but on the basis of an assessment of what would have to obtain *evidentially* for anyone to be rationally entitled to conclude that a miracle had occurred. As a philosopher, Hume is renowned primarily for developing the empirical philosophies of John Locke and George Berkeley to their logical, skeptical conclusions. As a historian, he is renowned for writing a famous history of England. So far as his thoughts on miracles are concerned, he conceded that a miracle might occur, but denied that anyone could ever have good reason to believe that one had occurred. For someone to have good reason, Hume argued, he would have to know that the law of nature that the so-called miraculous event supposedly violated really was a law of nature, and to know that he would have to have a great deal of evidence that nature, without exception, works contrary to the supposed miracle. But, his evidence that nature works contrary to the supposed miracle would then count against its being true that there was a miraculous exception to the law of nature.

Hume's argument has been so enormously influential that it is worth pausing briefly to illustrate what he had in mind. Imagine, for instance, that someone reports that through prayer and faith she has been cured of a supposedly incurable disease, say, advanced cancer of some sort. Initially, a Humean might be skeptical that the report is true, that is, that the alleged faith-healing actually occurred. However, were the evidence very strong that it did occur, then the Humean would deny that we know that the supposed laws of nature that allegedly were violated by the faith-healing are genuine laws of nature. In other words, he would admit that the unusual event—the faith-healing—occurred, but deny that its occurring is evidence of God's intervention in the natural world. Rather, he would argue, its occurring is either a coincidence or else evidence of the extraordinary power of mind over matter, a natural phenomenon that some day may be scientifically understood. What the Humean would never admit is that we have adequate evidence that a law of nature had actually been violated.

Hume, thus, claimed that on the basis of evidence alone, we are never entitled to conclude that a genuine miracle has occurred, and that we can know this in advance of examining the evidence for an alleged miracle. Hence, it follows from his argument (as it had also from Spinoza's) that no one needs to examine the historical evidence for some miracle story in order to determine whether the story is worthy of being believed. On the assumption that genuine prophesies, were they to occur, would be miracles, Hume's argument is also an argument against the validity of prophesies. Over the years, Hume's argument has been extremely influential. To this day, there are philosophers and historians who staunchly defend it.[2]

Such arguments as those of Hume and Spinoza pose a problem for educated believers. On the one hand, it seems obvious that not all miracle stories are worthy of being believed—the evidence for most of them is skimpy. On the other hand, it seems obvious that professional academic historians ought to be the best judges of which stories are worthy of being believed. But if, as Spinoza and Hume recommended, historians *bring to* their examination of the evidence the certain conviction that no miracle story can ever be shown to be true, then what sort of examination of the evidence can historians conduct? So, the

---

[2]A good selection of contributions to this debate may be found in Richard Swinburne, ed., *Miracles* (New York: Macmillan, 1989).

question arises of whether there isn't a way of being as responsible in examining the evidence for a miracle as any academic historian would be in examining the evidence for any other sort of past happening, and yet leave it an open question whether one's examination of the evidence would support the miracle story. In the present paper, I want to suggest an answer to this question. But, first, I want to look briefly at how several prominent contemporary academic historians have actually dealt with the question of miracles. For this purpose, I shall consider academic historians of Jesus.

1. HISTORIANS OF JESUS

Since the seventeenth century, scholars have aspired to write objective histories of religious figures, such as Jesus. It has been hard for them to do. One major obstacle, even in accounts that have achieved the status of standard texts, has been overcoming ordinary bias. W. Boussett, for instance, is a case in point. His widely used text was published originally in 1913 and reprinted as recently as 1966. In it, he contrasted Jesus and Judaism as follows:

> On the one hand was the artificiality of a hair-splitting and barren erudition, on the other the fresh directness of the layman and the son of the people; here was the product of long generations of misrepresentation and distortion, there was simplicity, plainness, and freedom; here a clinging to the petty and the insignificant, a burrowing in the dust, there a constant dwelling upon the essential and a great inward sense of reality; here the refinement of casuistry, formula- and phrase-mongering, there the straightforwardness, severity, and pitilessness of the preacher of repentance; here a language which was scarcely to be understood, there the inborn power of the mighty orator; there the letter of the law and here the living God.[3]

E. P. Sanders, a distinguished contemporary New Testament historian, has called these remarks of Bousett "a fairy tale." Sanders said that Bousett's comparison was motivated by his religious views and has little to do with historical scholarship.[4]

Understandably, contemporary academic historians of the origins of religious traditions, such as Sanders, have wanted to distance themselves not only from such apologetics, but from theology altogether. Many of them, especially recently, believe that they have done so. Sanders too, as we shall see, believes that he has done so. But, as I shall now attempt to show, on the plausible assumption that the denial of a theological claim itself involves a theological commitment, Sanders is mistaken. And so are the others mistaken.

E. P. Sanders

Sanders has been Dean Ireland's Professor of Exegesis at Oxford University and has twice won a National Religious Book Award. His portrait of Jesus appears primarily in two books: *Jesus and Judaism* (1985) and *The Historical Figure of Jesus* (1993).[5] In an earlier book on how to study the synoptic gospels that he wrote with Margaret Davies, he stresses that secular historians study the New Testament not to proclaim or denounce the Christian faith, and not for purposes of worship, but objectively. They aim, he says, "at *disinterested* inquiry," where "disinterested" means "not [being] committed to conclusions in advance of the study of the evidence." Hence, he continues, they cannot aim "to establish the truth of Christianity" or to establish "the truth of one version of it over another," but "must study with open minds."[6]

What I want to suggest is that Sanders (and virtually all other secular historians) are in fact committed to conclusions in advance of their study of the evidence. I say this not as a criticism, but merely because

[3]W. Boussett, *Kyrios Christos* (Göttingen: Vandenhoeck and Ruprech, 1913 [trans. 1970]); quoted in E. P. Sanders, *Jesus and Judaism* (Philadelphia: Fortress Press, 1985), p. 25. For an explanation of why Boussett was so respected, see Stephen Neill and Tom Wright, *The Interpretation of the New Testament: 1861–1986*, New Edition, (New York: Oxford University Press, 1988; [1st ed., 1966]), pp. 175-8.

[4]Sanders, *Jesus and Judaism*, p. 24.
[5]E. P. Sanders, *Jesus and Judaism* (Philadelphia: Fortress Press, 1985); *The Historical Figure of Jesus* (New York: Penguin Books, 1993).
[6]E. P. Sanders and Margaret Davies, *Studying the Synoptic Gospels* (Philadelphia: Trinity Press International, 1989), p. 45. In *The New Testament and the People of God* (London: SPCK, 1992), N. T. Wright chastens Sanders for what Wright takes to be Sanders' naive commitment to positivist assumptions, p. 82, n. 3.

it is a fact that needs to be taken into account in assessing the relative merits of secular and religious histories of Jesus. Secular historians, like all historians, bring to their study of the historical evidence a certain framework of real possibilities. It is only within this framework, if anywhere, that they are genuinely open-minded. What lies outside their frameworks has already been excluded from serious consideration.

Sanders, for instance, is a methodological naturalist. That is, he thinks of the world as a closed causal system that is not subject to any "other-worldly" interferences. On the question of miracles, he says that he fully shares Cicero's view that there are none.[7] The modern historian, he says, wants to know such things as the circumstances in which Jesus worked, why his efforts sometimes succeeded and sometimes failed, and why the Christian movement developed as it did. The gospels, he says, answer by saying that God, through Jesus, culminated a process of salvation that God started with the call of Abraham. Sanders says that the plan of God is "difficult" for the historian to study and that while historians have to take into account that the Gospel writers had theological views, the further question of whether those views are true is "essentially beyond the scope of historical inquiry" and, hence, one with which "we cannot deal."[8] But in saying this, Sanders leaves a basic question unanswered. By "cannot deal," does he mean that he cannot decide one way or the other whether these theological views are true, or that in order to do history "objectively" he has to assume that the views are false?

One of the theological views of the authors of the New Testament gospels was that Jesus was God or divinely empowered. Does Sanders leave it an open question whether that claim is true? In my view, he does not—at least, he does not for the purpose of his historical study. Instead, he denies that Jesus was God or divinely empowered, as, for instance, in the following remarks:

- "The view that Jesus died for grace thus ends with sheer invention about what would constitute an issue in first-century Judaism. . . .

[It] is basically opposed to seeing Jesus as a first-century Jew, who thought like others, spoke their language, was concerned about things which concerned them, and got into trouble over first-century issues. It is thus bad history. Though I am no theologian I suspect that it is bad theology."[9]

- "Jesus did not expect the end of the world in the sense of destruction of the cosmos. He expected a divine, transforming miracle. As a devout Jew, he thought that God had previously intervened in the world in order to save and protect Israel."[10]

- "These partial overlaps between Jesus and other Jews of his time . . . help us understand Jesus."[11]

- "Everyone, including Jesus and his followers, believed that God gave the law to Moses and that he had inspired the other scriptures as well."[12]

- "My own assumption about such [miracle] stories is that many of the 'incredible' ones are based on wishful thinking, others on exaggeration, and only a very few on the conscious wish to deceive."[13]

Obviously, Sanders has assumed, in the absence of evidence to the contrary, that Jesus believed whatever most other Jews in his time and circumstances believed. And he has assumed that the miracle stories are false. But if Sanders had left open the real possibility that Jesus was either God or divinely empowered, there would be no nontheological reason to make such assumptions. So, Sanders must have assumed that Jesus was neither God nor divinely empowered.

John Meier

Meier, a Catholic priest, is Professor of New Testament at the Catholic University of America and an editor of the *Catholic Biblical Quarterly*. His portrait

[7]Ibid., pp. 136, 143.
[8]Ibid., p. 91.

[9]E. P. Sanders, *Jesus and Judaism* (Philadelphia: Fortress Press, 1985), p. 331.
[10]Sanders, *The Historical Figure of Jesus*, p. 183.
[11]Ibid., p. 187.
[12]Ibid., 1993, p. 225.
[13]Ibid., 1993, p. 136; see also p. 143.

HISTORICAL METHOD
IN THE STUDY OF RELIGION ✳ *Morton Smith*

The science of religion, for which these histories of particular religions are prerequisites, is still far in the future. But, when and if it comes, both it, and the individual histories already developing, will be shaped by a basic supposition of sound historical method.

This supposition, in classical terms, is "atheism." I say "in classical terms" because the adjective "atheist" was regularly used in classical times to describe, for instance, the Epicureans, who insisted that there were gods, but denied that they ever descended to any special intervention in the world's affairs. It is precisely this denial which is fundamental to any sound historical method. Whether or not supernatural beings exist is a question for metaphysics. Even if they exist and exercise some regular influence on the world, some influence of which the consequences are taken to be a part of the normal course of natural events—let us say, for instance, that they determine the motion of the sphere of fixed stars, or that the whole of nature,

including its regular operation, is a manifestation of some unchanging divine nature or will—even this is of no concern to history, since it is not history's task to inquire into the causes of the normal phenomena of nature. But the historian does require a world in which these normal phenomena are not interfered with by arbitrary and *ad hoc* divine interventions to produce abnormal events with special historical consequences. This is not a matter of personal preference, but of professional necessity, for the historian's task, . . . is to calculate the most probable explanation of the preserved evidence. Now the minds of the gods are inscrutable and their actions, consequently, incalculable. Therefore, unless the possibility of their special intervention be ruled out, there can be no calculation of most probable causes—there would always be an unknown probability that a deity might have intervened.

From *History and Theory* (1968).

---

of Jesus appears in two volumes of *A Marginal Jew* (1991/94), the first of which is concerned mainly with sources and methods and the second with Jesus' words and deeds.[14] Meier says that his entire study is animated by a single, "central question": Who did Jesus think he was?[15] His point of departure is to ask us to imagine that a Catholic, a Protestant, a Jew, and an agnostic, all honest, competent historians of first century religious movements, were locked up together "in the bowels of the Harvard Divinity School library" and "not allowed to emerge until they had hammered out a consensus document on who Jesus of Nazareth was and what he intended in his own time and place." He says that "an essential

requirement of this document would be that it be based on purely historical sources and arguments." His book is what he thinks that document would reveal. In other words, he intends to write a secular history of Jesus, free of theology and parochial points of view.[16]

Meier insists on the importance of distinguishing among "the real Jesus," "the historical Jesus," and "the theological Jesus." It is hard to make sense of his distinctions as he draws them.[17] A way of understanding them that would allow him to say what he wants to say is that the *real* Jesus is simply Jesus: whoever he was (or is); the *historical* Jesus is that same Jesus, subject to this constraint: his properties are only those that we are justified in attributing to him on the basis of secular his-

---

[14]John P. Meier, *A Marginal Jew*, 2 vols (New York: Doubleday, 1991–4).

[15]Meier, *A Marginal Jew*, vol. II, p. 1046.

[16]Ibid., vol. I, p. 1; vol. II, pp. 4–5.

[17]Ibid., vol. I, p. 124–7.

torical research alone; and the theological Jesus is that same Jesus, however now his properties are those we are justified in attributing to him on the basis of historical scholarship supplemented by theology.

An important respect in which Meier differs from Sanders, as well as from most of the other historians whose views we shall consider, is that he bends over backwards not to step on anyone's toes theologically, particularly with respect to the question of miracles and the toes of those who, like himself, are believing Christians. It is not that, as a historian, he accepts the miracle stories. Rather, he thinks it is incompatible with his job *as a historian* either to accept *or* to reject them. However one feels about this objective, it is another question whether he actually succeeds in leaving the question open. He says, for instance:

- "It is not my intention here or elsewhere in this book to make the theological claim that Jesus actually worked miracles. It is sufficient for the historian to know that Jesus performed deeds that many people, both friends and foes, considered miracles."[18]
- "My major point is that a decision such as 'God has worked a miracle in this particular healing' is actually a theological, not a historical, judgment. A historian may examine claims about miracles, reject those for which there are obvious natural explanations, and record instances where the historian can find no natural explanation. Beyond that, a purely historical judgment cannot go."[19]
- "Just as a historian must reject credulity, so a historian must reject an *a priori* affirmation that miracles do not or cannot happen. That is, strictly speaking, a philosophical or theological proposition, not a historical one."[20]

In sum, in Meier's view, the historian must leave it an open question whether Jesus performed miracles. He thinks that in deciding this question *either* way, one ceases to be a historian pure and simple and becomes a

part-time theologian. However, it is not clear that Meier avoids mixing these two roles.[21]

Consider, first, Meier's hope to know what Jesus' baptism by John meant to Jesus. He says that it surely meant that Jesus saw himself as a part of the people of Israel. Further, in Jesus' accepting John's baptism as a "divinely appointed means of passage from this sinful Israel to a group of Israelites promised salvation on the day of judgment," Jesus was accepting an unofficial, charismatic ritual. Meier says, "Jesus would have been a very strange first-century Jew if he had rejected all religious ritual."[22] The clear implication is that Jesus was not "a very strange first-century Jew." But, of course, if Jesus were God or divinely empowered—even if Jesus in some other way had *genuinely* miraculous powers—then he would have been a very strange first-century Jew. Similarly, Meier says that "there is every reason to suppose" that Jesus thought that certain religious texts, such as the Five Books of Moses and the Prophets, were "authoritative" since "the divine authority of the core of the canon was a given for devout Jews [and, hence, for Jesus] by the time of Jesus."[23] And Meier says that it was "quite natural" for Jesus, "as a first-century Jew," to understand that he was performing exorcisms, which "simply underscores the obvious: Jesus was a man and a Jew of his times."[24] But, obviously God or one who was divinely empowered would not necessarily be a man or a Jew of Jesus' times.

The inescapable conclusion is that, in composing his historical account, Meier did, in fact, take what by his own admission is a theological stand. He assumed that Jesus was neither God nor divinely empowered—or, more precisely, that if Jesus was God or divinely empowered, his being exceptional in either of these ways did not extend to the cases considered. But if Jesus was neither God nor divinely empowered, then it would seem that the odds decline rather sharply that Jesus

---

[18]Ibid., vol. II., p. 11.
[19]Ibid.
[20]Ibid.; see also vol II, p. 788.

[21]More precisely: In the context of writing a history of Jesus, it is natural to suppose that if Jesus could perform miracles, then it is because he is God or he was divinely empowered. As a historian, Meier clearly wants to remain neutral on the question of whether Jesus is God or he was divinely empowered. Does he succeed in remaining neutral?
[22]Meier, *A Marginal Jew*, vol. II, pp. 106, 110; see also vol. II, p. 175.
[23]Ibid., vol. II, p. 253.
[24]Ibid., vol. II, p. 407.

was a genuine miracle-worker, say, that he could actually walk on water or raise the dead.

J. D. Crossan

Crossan, who received his doctorate from the National University of Ireland, has been co-chair of the Jesus Seminar and chair of the Historical Jesus Section of the Society of Biblical Literature. From 1969 until his retirement in 1995, he was a professor of Religious Studies at DePaul University, in Chicago. A gifted writer, his account of Jesus may be found primarily in *The Historical Jesus* (1992), which is regarded by many scholars as one of the most important twentieth-century contributions to historical Jesus studies, and his shorter and more popular, *Jesus: A Revolutionary Biography* (1995).[25]

Crossan follows the same supposedly secular approach in both of his books. In the latter book, he asks you, the reader, to suppose that you wanted to know not what early Christians wrote about Jesus, but what you would have seen and heard, if you had been there as a more or less neutral observer of Jesus. What, he asks, if you wanted "to move behind the screen of creedal interpretation and, without in any way denying or negating the validity of faith, give an accurate, but impartial account of the historical Jesus as distinct from the confessional Christ?" That, he says, is his goal.[26]

Has Crossan succeeded in writing about Jesus "without in any way denying or negating the validity of faith"? In *Jesus: A Revolutionary Biography*, he makes the following remarks:

- "I understand the virginal conception of Jesus to be a confessional statement about Jesus' status and not a biological statement about Mary's body."[27]
- "Since between 95 and 97 percent of the Jewish state was illiterate at the time of Jesus, it must be presumed that Jesus also was illiterate."[28]

- "The divine origins of Jesus are, to be sure, just as fictional or mythological as those of Octavius."[29]
- "I presume that Jesus, who did not and could not cure that disease or any other one, healed the poor man's illness by refusing to accept the disease's ritual uncleanness and social ostracization."[30]
- "I propose that other [miracle] stories in the gospels are not about Jesus' physical power over the world but about the apostles' spiritual power over the community."[31]

In my view, in assuming that Jesus could not have been born of a virgin, was probably illiterate, and could not have performed miracles, Crossan, in effect, has assumed that Jesus was neither God nor divinely empowered. If Jesus had been God or divinely empowered, then he might have been able to do the things that Crossan assumes he could not do. If I am right about this, then the question is whether in Crossan's assuming that Jesus could not do any of these things, and thus was neither God nor divinely empowered, he has in *any way* denied or negated "the validity of faith."

How one answers will depend on what one means by *denying or negating the validity of faith*. I assume that if a person of faith, because of her faith, assumes, asserts, or implies one thing—say, that Jesus was God or divinely empowered—and someone else either by assumption, assertion, or implication denies that very same thing, then the person who does the denying has in some way denied or negated the validity of the other's faith. Granted, the denier may have denied or negated the other's faith only temporarily and/or methodologically, say, for the purpose of composing a secular history of Jesus. Even so, the anti-faith person has *in some way*, and it would seem in a pretty important way, denied or negated the validity of the other's faith. Thus, Crossan has not succeeded in doing what he set out to do.

Assume, for the sake of argument, that some historian has denied or negated the validity of someone's faith only temporarily and methodologically, for the

---

[25]J. D. Crossan, *The Historical Jesus* (San Francisco: HarperSan-Francisco, 1991) and *Jesus: A Revolutionary Biography* (San Francisco: HarperSan Francisco, 1994).

[26]Crossan, *Jesus: A Revolutionary Biography*, p. xi.

[27]Ibid., p. 23.

[28]Ibid., p. 26.

[29]Ibid., pp. 26–7.

[30]Ibid., p. 82.

[31]Ibid., p. 170.

purpose of composing a secular history of Jesus, and that the historian leaves open the option of letting that person's faith back in later. This seems to be what Crossan wants to do. For instance, in his remarks on the uses to which he thinks Christians should put secular histories of Jesus, including his own history, which come as addenda at the very end of each of his two books, he says, in brief, that Christian belief is "an act of faith in the historical Jesus as the manifestation of God."[32] He assumes that there will always be divergent accounts of the historical Jesus and that there will always be divergent Christs built upon these accounts. But, he says, "the structure of Christianity will always be: this is how we see Jesus-then as Christ-now." He concludes that each generation of Christians must "make its best historical judgment about who Jesus was then and, *on that basis*, decide what that reconstruction means as Christ now."[33]

The key words in these remarks of Crossan are: *on that basis*. His view is, first, that whatever ideas the best secular historians have about who Jesus *was* as a historical person should be the point of departure for Christians' views about who Jesus *is* as Christ and, second, that the transition from Jesus to Christ is the work of faith, which Crossan allows may be perfectly valid. But these sentiments, which seem meant to be conciliatory, leave a crucial question unanswered: What role, if any, should the secular quest for the historical Jesus play in determining Christians' views about the historical Jesus—that is, about Jesus-then? Crossan suggests that secular historians should produce candidate portraits of Jesus-then, and that these should then exercise some sort of *constraint* on what sort of Christ-now Christians make out of Jesus-then. But it is not obvious that Christians should go to secular historians for their portraits of Jesus-then or, even if they do, that these should *constrain* them in any way in elaborating a Christ as the focus of their religious belief. I am not saying that Crossan is wrong in his apparent view about how Christians ought to proceed, but merely

that it is not obvious that he is right. And while he may be right, he has not given us any reason for thinking that he is right. That is, he has not argued for his view, but merely asserted it.[34]

2. METHODOLOGICAL NATURALISM

We have seen that even with the best of intentions it is difficult for historians of Jesus to avoid being methodological *naturalists* (which implies that they are methodological *atheists* as well). Why is it so difficult? Other secular scientists, it may seem, can be theologically neutral. Why must only secular historians be closet methodological atheists? The answer is that other scientists also are closet methodological atheists.

If this is not obvious, go back mentally to the earliest beginning of scientific philosophy in the west. Consider the first steps that were taken toward what today we would call a *scientific approach*. One of the very first steps was taken by the Greek philosopher, Heraclitus (c. 540–470 B.C.E.), when he began using the Greek word, *kosmos*, in a new way. He was followed in this by the *physiologoi*, who were sixth and fifth century B.C.E. philosophers from Greece and Asia Minor.[35] Previously *kosmos* had meant an arranged, beauty-enhancing order. Heraclitus, and then the physiologoi, used it to mean a natural system that is closed to supernatural interference. Along with other thinkers of the time, they believed that the *physis* of a thing, that is, its

---

[32]Crossan, *The Historical Jesus*, pp. 423–6; *Jesus: A Revolutionary Biography*, pp. 199–201. Crossan's formula is sometimes quoted favorably by others; see, for instance, Stephen J. Patterson, *The God of Jesus: The Historical Jesus & the Search for Meaning* (Harrisburg: Trinity Press International, 1998), p. 48.

[33]Crossan, *Jesus: A Revolutionary Biography*, p. 200, emphasis added.

[34]In *The Historical Jesus*, p. 426, Crossan reminded Christians that they should not reject the results of secular historical scholarship, presumably including the results of his own scholarship, merely because those results are reconstructions, "as if reconstruction invalidated somehow the entire project. Because there is only reconstruction. For a believing Christian both the life of the Word of God and the text of the Word of God are alike a graded process of historical reconstruction." So, "if you cannot believe in something produced by reconstruction, you may have nothing left to believe in." But however respectable on secular grounds such a view may be, it begs the question against certain sorts of believing Christians. For even if every account is a reconstruction, it may be that some accounts, such as Crossan's, are *mere* reconstructions and, hence, dismissible, while others, such as those of Mark, Matthew, Luke, and John, are *divinely-inspired* reconstructions and, hence, the word of God. I do not say that this is so, but only that Crossan has not explained why he is entitled to assume that it is not so.

[35]The *physiologoi* included most of those who historians of philosophy usually think of as the "pre-Socratics."

stable characteristics, set limits both on what it can do and also on what can happen to it. These other thinkers made an exception in the case of supernatural intervention. The physiologoi refused to make this exception. That is, they made the world into a cosmos by retaining the physis of things and eliminating everything else. Historians of science often characterize that decision, which was crucial to the origins of science, in heroic terms. Gregory Vlastos, for instance, said of it that "for the first time in history man had achieved a perception of a rational universe" in which the destiny of everything is determined solely by its physis. On this point, he continued, the physiologoi stood united, "a handful of intellectuals against the world."[36]

No doubt it did not occur to the physiologoi to adopt their secular point of view only methodologically. Surely they also adopted it substantively. That is, in all likelihood, they did not just adopt it for the purpose of studying the world purely naturalistically. Rather, they believed that only what is revealed from such a perspective is real. Admittedly, their having adopted a secular point of view, even if only methodologically, was a big advance toward natural science. Even so, as a substantive thesis, their postulate went well beyond anything they could prove. There were many things the physiologoi could not explain. For all they knew, some of these unexplained happenings resulted from "supernatural" intervention. As a matter of *secular faith*, they believed that none of them did. But that was something they merely believed, not something they had good reason to think was actually true. The physiologoi were, thus, the first authors of a kind of secular, antitheological faith. The first, but, as we have seen, not the last. Ever since, scientists and scientifically minded historians, at least for the purpose of doing science and history, have excluded supernatural intervention from the world. The question I want to consider is whether this is the only responsible way for scientists, in general, and scientifically minded historians, in particular, to proceed.

Many feel strongly that it is the only responsible way for scientists and historians to proceed.[37] Yet even though today we know a great deal more than the physiologoi knew about the natural world, we are not even close to being able to explain everything. The merest glance at any of countless controversies in the sciences or in historical studies will quickly confirm this. Thus, as a substantive thesis, even today the view that everything can be explained naturalistically still goes well beyond anything we can prove.[38] Some might argue that our success in explaining naturalistically so much of what previously was unexplained gives us good inductive grounds for claiming that everything *can* be explained naturalistically. But such arguments always depend on the assumption that everything we cannot explain is analogous in all relevant respects to whatever we can explain. There is no non-question-begging reason I can think of to make this assumption.

Consider, for instance, faith healings. At the shrine of Lourdes in France, teams of doctors of various theological and secular views have conducted before-and-after examinations of scores of people many of whom claim that they were suddenly cured by divine power. In many cases, these doctors have determined to their own satisfaction that people who claimed to have been cured were once seriously ill and, for reasons that currently cannot be explained scientifically, have suddenly overcome their illnesses.[39] Or, to take another example, consider so-called interactions with "the spirit world" that are regularly reported to have occurred in the context of Native American spiritual rituals. Allegedly neutral observers have substantiated the claim that bizarre things for which we currently have no "natural" explanation have happened there also.[40] One can and, I think, should admit that a great many, perhaps most, stories both of faith healings and

---

[36]I am indebted throughout this paragraph to Gregory Vlastos, *Plato's Universe*, (Seattle: University of Washington Press, 1975), Chs. 1–3.

[37]See, for example, the views of George M. Marsden's critics, as quoted by him in his, *The Outrageous Idea of Christian Scholarship* (New York: Oxford University Press, 1997). For a discussion of similar issues in a Jewish context, see David Weiss Halivni, *Revelation Restored: Divine Writ and Critical Responses* (Boulder: Westview Press, 1997).

[38]I am assuming, for the sake of this discussion, that we know what it means to explain naturalistically.

[39]Meier, *A Marginal Jew*, vol. II, pp. 515–17.

[40]For example, Wallace Black Eik and William S. Lyon, *Black Elk: The Sacred Ways of a Lakota* (San Francisco: HarperSanFrancisco, 1995).

THE HISTORIAN AS PHILOSOPHER * *Nancy Murphy*

The historian is consciously or unconsciously a philosopher. It is quite obvious that every task of the historian beyond the finding of facts is dependent on evaluations of historical factors, especially the nature of man, his freedom, his determination, his development out of nature, and so on. It is less obvious but also true that even in the act of finding historical facts philosophical presuppositions are involved. This is especially true in deciding, out of the infinite number of happenings in every infinitely small moment of time, which facts shall be called historically relevant facts. The historian is further forced to give his evaluation of sources and their reliability, a task which is not independent of his interpretation of human nature. Finally, in the moment in which a historical work gives implicit or explicit assertions about the meaning of historical events for human existence, the philosophical presuppositions of history are evident.

From *Theology in the Age of Scientific Reasoning* (1990).

---

of interactions with the spirit world are based on incidents that have "naturalistic" explanations, whether or not anyone will ever discover what they are. But do we have reason to believe that the incidents reported in *all* such stories can be explained naturalistically? Methodologically, for the purpose of doing history and anthropology, we may be entitled to act as if they all have naturalistic explanations. Substantively, too, we may be entitled to believe that they all have naturalistic explanations. But, substantively, do we have so much reason to believe that they all have naturalistic explanations that it would not *also* be rationally *permissible* for someone to leave the matter open? If we do, I, for one, cannot imagine what that reason might be.

Suppose we were all to agree that, as a substantive thesis, one is rationally entitled to leave it an open question whether everything that occurs can be explained naturalistically. Even so, we might still doubt whether, methodologically, for the purpose of doing science and, in particular, for the purpose of doing so-called secular histories of Jesus, one can and/or should leave it an open question. Many, probably most, academic historians believe that historians cannot leave this question open. According to Morton Smith, for instance, a renowned New Testament historian, whether "supernatural beings exist is a question for metaphysics." But, he said, even if they do exist "and exercise some regular influence on the world," with consequences that "are taken to be a part of the normal course of natural events," the historian requires "a world in which these normal phenomena are not interfered with by arbitrary and ad hoc divine interventions to produce abnormal events with special historical consequences." Smith said that "this is not a matter of personal preference, but of professional necessity." In his view, the historian's job "is to calculate the most probable explanation of the preserved evidence." "The minds of the gods are inscrutable and their actions, consequently, incalculable." So, Smith concluded, unless the possibility of their special intervention is ruled out, there "would always be an unknown probability that a deity might have intervened." And so long as there is that unknown probability, "there can be no calculation of most probable causes."[41]

Smith is wrong. Historians do not have to assume that God does not (or the gods do not) intervene ad hoc in the human world. They can get along with weaker assumptions. Before explaining how, I want to show that the problem under consideration is not just one for historians, such as Crossan and Sanders, who would write the history of Jesus in a purely secular way, but also one for some of their most intelligent and well-meaning critics who advocate that the history of Jesus should be written on the basis of theological presuppositions.

---

[41]Morton Smith, "Historical Method in the Study of Religion," *History and Theory*, vol. 8, 1968, pp. 12–14.

C. Stephen Evans

Evans, a professor of philosophy at Calvin College, is a philosophically sophisticated and well-informed critic of secular historical Jesus studies. As a religiously conservative Christian, he has tried to answer the challenge that such studies pose for Christian beliefs. In his view, a basic problem with all such studies is that their authors are closet philosophers. That, he seems to think, rather than slim and ambiguous evidence and the demand for full-fledged interpretations of Jesus, is what explains disagreement in historical Jesus studies.

To explain what he means, Evans imagines someone—he calls him, *James*—who, by hypothesis, lacks the professional expertise of trained historians. In Evans' view, a good deal of disagreement among secular historians of Jesus is rooted in assumptions—"philosophical, theological, and literary"—that they have made, about which they "may not have any special expertise." So, with respect to views so rooted, "James may be competent to evaluate the views of the scholars."[42] One such philosophical assumption is a prejudice that Evans says many secular historians have against the miraculous and, in general, against any supernatural intervention into the natural world, including prophecy.[43] In his view, one "cannot begin by ruling out as impossible any supernatural knowledge or insight on the part of Jesus, if one wishes fairly to test the claim that God was at work in Jesus in a special way, or that Jesus was actually God incarnate."[44] But then Evans says almost nothing about how an enlightened historian is supposed to deal with the possibility that Jesus may have had foreknowledge.

This silence on Evans' part causes problems. For instance, he endorses enthusiastically an interpretation offered by the philosopher Eleanor Stump of the story of the raising of Lazarus. According to Evans' presentation of Stump's interpretation, in the story, "Jesus may be seen as delaying his coming partly so as to reward the faith of the sisters with a glorious miracle." However, "when he arrives, the distress of the sisters reveals that his plans have not proceeded precisely as he wished and expected."[45] Thus, in the interpretation that Evans endorses, on the occasion under discussion Jesus expected one thing and something else happened. What, then, of Jesus' supposed divine foreknowledge? Does it come and go? Does it come into play only on certain kinds of issues? Is his foreknowledge normally reliable, but simply failed him this time? The closest Evans comes to even raising such questions, let alone answering them, is to say that "it is thus quite coherent with the story to see Jesus as empowered with supernatural insight at times."[46] True enough, but even conceding that it is coherent, we are still left with a huge question about how, as historians, we should proceed.

J. D. G. Dunn

Dunn is Professor of Divinity at the University of Durham, in England, and the author of several books on the history of early Christianity.[47] In one of these, *The Evidence for Jesus* (1985), he addresses the quest for the historical Jesus. Dunn makes no bones about the fact that he is a believing Christian. And he admits that he wrote this particular book to quiet the fears of other Christians about historical Jesus studies. Like Evans, he makes the point that Christians have "nothing to fear from scholarship." However, unlike Evans, he makes this point not by trying to put historians down, but by arguing that Christians "should welcome the critically inquiring and investigative skills of scholars." He thinks that Christians should

---

[42]C. Stephan Evans, *The Historical Christ and the Jesus of Faith* (Oxford: Oxford University Press, 1996), p. 332.

[43]Evans points out, for instance, that many secular historians of Jesus date Acts after the fall of Jerusalem because they think that otherwise they would have to admit that the author of Acts had prophetic powers. Evans argues for an earlier dating, noting that "it is important to challenge the implicit assumption that any accurate 'prophecy' must have been made after the events in question" since "such an assumption makes it impossible to give the incarnational narrative, with its ineradicable miraculous elements, a fair historical test." Ibid., p. 33.

[44]Ibid., p. 332.

[45]Ibid., p. 341.

[46]Ibid., pp. 333–4.

[47]J. D. G. Dunn, *Baptism in the Holy Spirit* (London: SCM, 1970); *Jesus and the Spirit: A Study of the Religious and Charismatic Experience of Jesus and the First Christians as Reflected in the New Testament* (London: SCM, 1975); *The Evidence for Jesus* (Louisville, Kentucky: The Westminster Press, 1985).

welcome them partly because he thinks that eventually scholars will arrive at results that are congenial to Christians, but also partly for theological reasons: "liberty of opinion, genuine respect for those who differ and a reverent agnosticism in many matters of secondary importance is a wholly proper and indeed essential response of faith"; "since we walk by faith and not by light, our confidence should be in the God and Father of our Lord Jesus Christ, rather than in what we can see and handle and control. 'Let him who boasts, boast of the Lord!' "[48]

Needless to say, Dunn's methods differ sharply from those of Crossan and Sanders. They are closer to those of Meier. But whereas Meier thinks that it is no part of the historian's task to assess the plausibility of claims that God intervened in the natural world, Dunn thinks that it is part of the historian's task. He agrees with other New Testament scholars that the authors of the New Testament gospels were often inventive. But he trusts the New Testament authors to reveal what really happened *much* more often than liberal historians trust them, and he puts a different spin than do liberal historians on those passages from the New Testament that he admits are inventive. For instance, in response to the question, "Has New Testament scholarship undermined the ordinary Christian's belief that the Gospels are historically trustworthy and accurate in what they tell about Jesus," he answers, "Yes and No." Yes, in that New Testament scholars agree that the authors of the Gospels did not just report, but also interpreted. "*No*, in that when the Gospel writers intended to provide historical information, that information *can* be trusted as reliable."[49] In explaining what he means, Dunn never mentions the birth narratives, which almost all academic historians regard as mythological, but instead mentions only examples from New Testament accounts of Jesus' public career and his resurrection.

In the case of the resurrection, Dunn says that the claim that God raised Jesus from the dead is of "fundamental importance to Christian faith," and that if this claim is false, or only vaguely true, many basic Christian doctrines would have to be revised, including Christian understandings of who Jesus was and is, of the significance of his death, and the hopes which Christians entertain for themselves and others. He says that the question of whether modern scholarship has "disproved the resurrection of Jesus, or even made belief in his resurrection more difficult," is as important for Christians "as any question can be."[50]

Dunn begins his account of the resurrection by saying that we should start by recognizing that we cannot get back directly to the resurrection itself since it belongs to "the irretrievable pastness of history."[51] Even so, he continues, we have five sorts of historical evidence that it actually occurred: reports of Jesus' tomb being found empty; reported "sightings" of Jesus after his death; the transformation of the first disciples and the subsequent initial spread of the new faith; the very high regard in which Christians soon came to hold Jesus; and claims of believers since the beginning of Christianity to encounter Jesus alive here and now.[52]

Dunn says that many Christians want to include as basic data the testimony of believers today. He concedes that "in a full scale evaluation of the evidence such testimonies would have to be examined with care" and that their potential value, "as 'eyewitness' reports," is considerable. He says, however, that he is going to pass over this evidence since such testimonies "almost always depend to an important extent on the [witnesser's] prior beliefs." In other words, he explains, it is because Christians already believe that Jesus rose from the dead that they can recognize their experience in prayer or devotion as an encounter with Jesus.[53] Dunn says that the same is true of the previous two sorts of evidence that he listed: the transformation of the disciples and high opinion that early Christians had of Jesus.

Dunn's reason for dismissing reports in our own times of people having seen Jesus is curious since it is obviously false. Surely many contemporary "experiences of Jesus" are had by people who are not already Christians. In our own times, there must be hundreds of reported cases of people who in the throes of a *conversion* experience to Christianity came to believe

---

[48]Dunn, *The Evidence for Jesus*, pp. 103, 107.
[49]Ibid., p. 1.
[50]Ibid., pp. 53–4.
[51]Ibid., p. 56.
[52]Ibid., pp. 56–63.
[53]Ibid.

that Jesus is alive. Are *their* experiences evidence that Jesus is alive, or not? If they are, then why don't they count importantly in favor of the New Testament reports that Jesus rose from the dead? I shall return to these questions.

Dunn rests his case for the veracity of the resurrection reports on his first two sorts of evidence: reports of the empty tomb; and early "sightings" of Jesus.[54] So far as the empty tomb reports are concerned, he says there are two kinds of evidence that the reports are not reliable: the reports are conflicting; and Paul, in 1 Cor. 15, does not say anything about an empty tomb. Counterbalancing these negative considerations, he claims, are four sources of evidence in favor of the reliability of the empty tomb reports: all four gospels attribute the discovery of the empty tomb to women; the confusion between the different accounts of the resurrection in the Gospels; archaeological evidence; and the lack of any indications that Christians regarded the place where Jesus had been buried as having any special significance.

Regarding the first of these positive considerations, Dunn says that in first century Judea, since women did not have much status they "were probably regarded as unreliable witnesses." So, the fact that they were reported to be the primary witnesses is evidence that the reports are factual. In his view, the only good reason for attributing the empty tomb reports to women is that this is how it was remembered as having actually happened. Regarding the confusion between different accounts, Dunn says that it is a "a mark of the sincerity of those from whom the testimony was derived" and shows that "we cannot plausibly regard [the reports] as deriving from a single source." In particular, he adds, "the fact that the earliest Gospel (Mark) ends without any record of a 'resurrection appearance' [Dunn accepts that the original version of Mark ended at 16:8] has to be matched with the fact that the earliest account of 'resurrection appearances' (I Cor. 15) has no reference to the tomb being empty." Dunn says that there is nothing to indicate that one was contrived to bolster the other, and that this "speaks favourably for the value of each."

The archeological evidence, Dunn says, shows "that at the time of Jesus, a popular understanding of

resurrection in Palestine would have involved some 're-use' of the dead body." Thus, "a claim made in Jerusalem within a few weeks of [Jesus'] crucifixion, that God had raised Jesus—that is, the body of Jesus—from death, would not have gained much credence had his tomb been undisturbed or the fate of his body known to be otherwise. The absence of any such counter claim in any available literature of the period, Christian or Jewish, he says, is important. Finally, there is no evidence that the first Christians regarded the place where Jesus had been laid as having any special significance. This "strange silence," which Dunn says was exceptional in view of the religious practice of the time, "has only one obvious explanation": the first Christians did not regard Jesus' grave as having any special significance because it was empty. Dunn concludes that on the whole the evidence points firmly to the conclusion that Jesus' tomb was found empty and that its emptiness was a factor in the first Christians' belief in the resurrection of Jesus.[55]

Dunn's account of the "resurrection appearances," while shorter, follows a similar pattern. As evidence against the veracity of the reports, he mentions again conflicts in the New Testament accounts. As evidence in favor, he mentions the "testimony of I Cor: 15:3–8," which Dunn says "goes back to within two or three years of the events described." The prominence of women in the records of the first sightings and the absence of any indication that the reports are contrived are also significant, he claims. In his view, the most plausible alternative explanation is that "the witnesses were deluded"—"not deceitful, but deceived"—in which case, the "resurrection appearances" would simply be hallucinations, perhaps born of frustrated hopes, "visions begotten of hysteria." It counts again this alternative explanation, he says, that the experiences reported by the early Christians were unexpected and that their reports differ from other life-after-death visions from the same period. In no other case, he says, did the person who saw the vision conclude, "This man has been raised from the dead."[56]

Dunn cautions that while historians have good evidence that the resurrection took place, they do not know in what it consisted. Not only do we lack any

_____
[54]Ibid., pp. 62–3.

[55]Ibid., pp. 65–8.
[56]Ibid., pp. 71–2.

record that anyone actually witnessed it, but we cannot be sure that it could be witnessed. However, he says, we can say that by "resurrection," these earliest Christian witnesses meant that something had happened to Jesus and not just to themselves. God had raised *him*, not merely reassured *them*. "He was alive again, made alive again with the life which is the climax of God's purpose for humankind, not merely retrieved from the jaws of death, but conqueror over death, 'exalted to God's right hand.' " Dunn says that it was this glowing conviction that lay at the heart of the chain reaction which began Christianity.[57]

Clearly Dunn, unlike Meier, thinks that it is professionally appropriate for a historian to conclude that God intervened in the natural world. Even more clearly, he does not, as Crossan and Sanders did, rule out *in advance* divine intervention as a possible explanation. Still, it is hard to believe that his assessment of the plausibility of competing accounts of the evidence is not influenced by his extra-historical conviction that Jesus did rise from the dead. For instance, does the lack of evidence that the first Christians regarded the place where Jesus had been laid as having any special significance have as the "only obvious explanation" that Jesus' tomb was empty? For the early Christians, wouldn't the fact that Jesus rose from the dead out of that tomb have itself given the tomb quite a bit of special significance? If, in fact, Dunn's assessment of the evidence is influenced by his extra-historical conviction that Jesus rose from the dead, then he joins Crossan and Sanders, in that all of them are interpreting the historical evidence against the backdrop of controversial and perhaps even question-begging extra-historical convictions. In the cases of Crossan and Sanders, these background convictions rule out the miraculous. In the case of Dunn, they seem to make it more likely, at least in connection with Jesus. Also, Dunn's refusal to consider contemporary reports of "experiences of Jesus" suggests that, like Meier, he recognizes that certain issues fall beyond the purview of the historian, even though he and Meier have different ideas about which issues those are.

When we considered Evans view, it turned out that what we needed to know from him—or

from someone—is how the assumption that Jesus (or anyone else) sometimes has foreknowledge and sometimes does not is supposed to enter into the project of deciding among competing interpretations. Evans did not tell us—in fact, did not even raise the question. His not raising it left open the possibility that the kind of historical research that he endorses is a game without rules. I have the same worry about Dunn's account, though admittedly others may feel differently about it. The assumptions of Crossan and Sanders that nonnatural intervention into the natural world is out of the question may be highhanded and arbitrary, but at least we know the basis on which they are going to proceed. In my view, one cannot say the same about either Evans or Dunn. Should we conclude, then, that Morton Smith was right after all, and that historians must assume that God does not intervene ad hoc into human affairs? I don't think so. Rather, what we should conclude is that historical research must proceed under the rubric of some rules *or other*. It is not proceeding under *any* appropriate rules, rather than not proceeding under the particular rules favored by Crossan, Sanders, and Smith, that leads to methodological chaos. Methodological naturalism is only one among a large number of possible ways for historians to generate appropriate rules for interpreting evidence.

3. FAITH-HISTORY

What I am suggesting, in effect, is that there is unexplored middle ground between Smith's overly restrictive approach to historical research and Evans' and Dunn's overly permissive ones. What this middle ground is can be stated quite simply. It consists in three steps: first, except in certain kinds of circumstances, proceed on the basis of ordinary secular historical methodology, that is, on the basis of methodological naturalism; second, specify which kinds of circumstances are the exceptions; and, third, explain which alternative methodology is going to be followed in these kinds of circumstances. I call the product of following these rules, a *faith-history*.

So far as I know, in writing a faith-history, no historian has ever been explicit about which methodological rules she has followed (but I have not surveyed all of the attempts). Typically, what would-be faith-historians do is either to throw ordinary historical methodology to the winds or use ordinary historical methodology and

[57]Ibid., pp. 74–5.

then drop it, willy-nilly, without explaining the basis for their doing so or even responding to the worry that they may be proceeding arbitrarily. Sometimes historians who are at least trying to make room for exceptions to naturalism proceed more consistently, as Dunn and Meier surely have, but still without ever being explicit about which background assumptions are guiding their historical accounts or how these assumptions are affecting their assessments of the relative merits of competing interpretations. So, to the best of my knowledge, faith-historians (to whatever degree) have not done particularly well at explaining what they are doing.[58]. Even so, faith-history is clearly a possible option.

How should faith-historians proceed? I would suggest that the basic thing faith-historians have to do is to explain, presumably on theological grounds, the ways in which some historical figures, such as Jesus, are more than human or have more than ordinary human powers. And they have to do this in a way which makes nonnatural influences in the natural world the exception, rather than the rule, so that, for the most part, historians can proceed on the assumption that what happens can be explained naturalistically. How might they do this?

Consider, first, a limiting case, so far as the quest for the historical Jesus is concerned. It is a way in which Jesus might have been more than human that would not make any difference at all to historical methodology. Suppose, for instance, that a theologically oriented historian believes that while God has intervened in the natural world, God did so only once, by manifesting as Jesus. That would secure the doctrine of the incarnation, which, for Christians, is no small matter theologically. Suppose our historian also believes that, in manifesting as Jesus, God manifested as a human that is subject to *all* of the limitations of ordinary humans. In that case, except for the incarnation, which may have involved just a miraculous intervention in the physiological processes that led to Jesus' conception, a matter about which historians rarely comment anyway, the task of such a theologically oriented historian would be the same as that of wholly secular historians. So, Smith is wrong. Without un-

leashing methodological chaos, one can believe that God has intervened in the natural world, even that God has intervened miraculously.

What about historians of Jesus who take a more robust view of God's interventions? How should they proceed? One way would be to start from the limiting case scenario just sketched and then to make exceptions to it. For instance, it might be the historian's view that God, in manifesting as Jesus, manifested as a human that is subject to all of the limitations of ordinary humans except for this one: that whereas in the case of ordinary humans biological death ends all of their activity on Earth, in the case of Jesus it did not; rather, without Jesus' having the slightest idea in advance that it would happen, he rose from the dead in some sort of human form and subsequently had augmented powers. So, in the pre-Easter part of such a historians' study, his methodology would be the same as that of wholly secular historians. In the post-Easter part, it would be different. To be methodologically transparent, the historian would have to specify the scope and limits of these differences, which would involve specifying the scope and limits of Jesus' post-Easter augmented powers. Put to one side, for the moment, the question of how he might do this. There is no reason that I know of to think that it could not be done. And, if it were done successfully, the historian would then have made quite a bit of room for Christian theology. He would have made room for the incarnation and also for the claim that Jesus rose from the dead with augmented human powers. And he would have made this room for Christian theology without having unleashed methodological chaos, at least in the pre-Easter part of his story.

Finally, how are historians of Jesus who take an even more robust view about God's interventions to proceed in a way that allows them to continue to do history? The answer, I think, is that it all depends. Clearly, however, one could continue, step by step, in the way I have just illustrated, without necessarily being methodologically irresponsible, to enrich dramatically the scope of one's taking into account what one assumes to be God's interventions in the world. Equally clearly, at some point in such a step by step progression, if one kept going, eventually one would have gone too far. Probably, if one proceeded by small steps, and just kept going, methodological chaos

[58]In *The Elusive Messiah*, Chs. 7 and 9, I discuss the interesting possibility that N. T. Wright is an exception to this rule.

would creep back in gradually, in a variety of ways. There is no point in trying to enumerate them. That theology can undermine secular historical methodology is noncontroversial. The controversial question is whether theology, if it were allowed to exert its influence on an otherwise secular historical inquiry, would *necessarily* undermine it. Many, perhaps most, secular historians believe that it would. I have argued that they are wrong.

It may seem that in opting for the procedure I have sketched, faith-historians are stuck with an impossibly daunting task—that of describing their alternative historical methodologies. But they would not have to describe their alternative methodologies in any more detail than secular historians—who I have been arguing are really faith-historians of a different stripe—describe their secular historical methodologies, which is not in much detail at all. So, the faith-historian's task may not be so daunting after all. Even so, the task is not nothing. And until some faith-historian tries to perform it, the rest of us are stuck with an unpleasant choice: either so-called secular history, with its methodological naturalism, or theologically inspired history, played by unspoken rules.

QUESTIONS FOR FURTHER REFLECTION

1. In trying to decide on the basis of good historical evidence whether a miracle has occurred, is there any point in reading the New Testament?

2. Is there any conceivable circumstance in which on the basis of the testimony of others, you would have good reason to believe that a miracle has occurred? If there is, since historians might be in the same sort of position that you are in, shouldn't historians at least be open to the possibility that a miracle has occurred? If they should, how should historians change their approach to the past?

3. Based on the quotations provided in this essay, would you think that in addition to having a methodological prejudice against miracles, secular historians would also have one against weird phenomena, such as ESP?

4. If you were going to write a "faith-history," how would you explain how you were going to proceed methodologically?

SUGGESTIONS FOR FURTHER READING

Curd, Martin. "Miracles as Violations of Laws of Nature," in *Faith, Freedom, and Rationality*, edited by Daniel Howard-Snyder and Jeff Jordan. Totowa, NJ: Rowman and Littlefield, 1996.

Flew, Antony. "Miracles," in *The Encyclopedia of Philosophy*, edited by Paul Edwards New York: Macmillan, 1967, 5:351.

Geivett, Doug and Gary Habermas. eds, *In Defense of Miracles*. Downer's Grove, IL: InterVarsity Press, 1997.

Johnson, David. *Hume, Holism, and Miracles*. (Ithaca, NY: Cornell University Press, 1999.

Lewis, C. S. *Miracles*. New York: Macmillan, 1947.

Mackie, J. L. *The Miracle of Theism*. Oxford: Oxford University Press, 1982.

McKinnon, Alastair. " 'Miracle' and " 'Paradox,' " *American Philosophical Quarterly*, 4 (1967): 308–14.

McKinnon, Alastair and Nicholas Everritt, "The Impossibility of Miracles," *Religious Studies*, 23 (1987): 347–9.

Swinburne, Richard. *The Concept of Miracle*. London: Macmillan, 1989.

———. *Miracles*. New York: Macmillan, 1989.

PART VII

EVOLUTION

48. SCIENCE REFUTES RELIGION * *Richard Dawkins*
Daniel Dennett, "Darwin's Dangerous Idea"
49. DARWINIST RELIGION * *Phillip E. Johnson*
Alvin Plantinga, "The Grand Evolutionary Myth"
50. EVOLUTION IS NOT A THREAT TO RELIGION * *Philip and Patricia Kitcher*

SUGGESTIONS FOR FURTHER READING

48. SCIENCE REFUTES RELIGION

Richard Dawkins

Richard Dawkins (1941–   ) an evolutionary biologist and zoologist, was educated at Oxford University and has taught zoology at the Universities of Oxford and California. In 1995, he became the first holder of the newly endowed Charles Simonyi Chair of Public Understanding of Science at Oxford University. He is the author of *The Selfish Gene* (1976), *The Extended Phenotype* (1999), *The Blind Watchmaker* (1986), *River Out of Eden* (1995), and *Climbing Mount Improbable* (1996). In the following selection, Dawkins argues that when science and religion make conflicting claims on the same topic, science is right. This is because science has a superior method of producing knowledge.

READING QUESTIONS

1. What is Stephan J. Gould's opinion on whether science and religion conflict?
2. How does Dawkins describe the "God of the Old Testament"?
3. How does Dawkins represent the Pope's view of the relation between God and evolution?
4. What other religious doctrines does Dawkins think conflict with science?
5. Why does Dawkins think that it is dishonest and self-serving to claim that religious beliefs are outside the domain of science?

A cowardly flabbiness of the intellect afflicts otherwise rational people confronted with long-established religions (though, significantly, not in the face of younger traditions such as Scientology or the Moonies). S. J. Gould, commenting . . . on the Pope's attitude to evolution, is representative of a dominant strain of conciliatory thought, among believers and nonbelievers alike:

> Science and religion are not in conflict, for their teachings occupy distinctly different domains . . . I believe, with all my heart, in a respectful, even *loving* concordat [my emphasis]. . . .

Well, what are these two distinctly different domains, these "Nonoverlapping Magisteria" which should snuggle up together in a respectful and loving concordat? Gould again:

> The net of science covers the empirical universe: what is it made of (fact) and why does it work this way (theory). The net of religion extends over questions of moral meaning and value.

Would that it were that tidy. In a moment I'll look at what the Pope actually says about evolution, and then at other claims of his church, to see if they really are so neatly distinct from the domain of science. First though, a brief aside on the claim that religion has some special expertise to offer us on moral questions. This is often blithely accepted even by the nonreligious, presumably in the course of a civilized "bending over backwards" to concede the best point your opponent has to offer—however weak that best point may be.

The question, "What is right and what is wrong?" is a genuinely difficult question which science certainly cannot answer. Given a moral premise or a priori moral belief, the important and rigorous discipline of secular moral philosophy can pursue scientific or logical modes of reasoning to point up hidden implications of such beliefs, and hidden inconsistencies between them. But the absolute moral premises themselves must come from elsewhere, presumably from unargued conviction. Or, it might be hoped, from religion—meaning some combination of authority, revelation, tradition and scripture.

Unfortunately, the hope that religion might provide a bedrock, from which our otherwise sand-based morals can be derived, is a forlorn one. In practice no civilized person uses scripture as ultimate authority for moral reasoning. Instead, we pick and choose the nice bits of scripture (like the Sermon on the Mount) and blithely ignore the nasty bits (like the obligation to stone adulteresses, execute apostates, and punish the grandchildren of offenders). The God of the Old Testament himself, with his pitilessly vengeful jealousy, his racism, sexism, and terrifying bloodlust, will not be adopted as a literal role model by anybody you or I would wish to know. Yes, *of course* it is unfair to judge the customs of an earlier era by the enlightened standards of our own. But that is precisely my *point!* Evidently, we have some alternative source of ultimate moral conviction which overrides scripture when it suits us.

That alternative source seems to be some kind of liberal consensus of decency and natural justice which changes over historical time, frequently under the influence of secular reformists. Admittedly, that doesn't sound like bedrock. But in practice we, including the religious among us, give it higher priority than scripture. In practice we more or less ignore scripture, quoting it when it supports our liberal consensus, quietly forgetting it when it doesn't. And, wherever that lib-

eral consensus comes from, it is available to all of us, whether we are religious or not.

Similarly, great religious teachers like Jesus or Gautama Buddha may inspire us, by their good example, to adopt their personal moral convictions. But again we pick and choose among religious leaders, avoiding the bad examples of Jim Jones or Charles Manson, and we may choose good secular role models such as Jawaharlal Nehru or Nelson Mandela. Traditions too, however anciently followed, may be good or bad, and we use our secular judgment of decency and natural justice to decide which ones to follow, which to give up.

But that discussion of moral values was a digression. I now turn to my main topic of evolution, and whether the Pope lives up to the ideal of keeping off the scientific grass. His Message on Evolution to the Pontifical Academy of Sciences begins with some casuistical doubletalk designed to reconcile what John Paul is about to say with the previous, more equivocal pronouncements of Pius XII whose acceptance of evolution was comparatively grudging and reluctant. Then the Pope comes to the harder task of reconciling scientific evidence with "revelation."

> Revelation teaches us that [man] was created in the image and likeness of God . . . if the human body takes its origin from preexistent living matter, the spiritual soul is immediately created by God . . . Consequently, theories of evolution which, in accordance with the philosophies inspiring them, consider the mind as emerging from the forces of living matter, or as a mere epiphenomenon of this matter, are incompatible with the truth about man . . . With man, then, we find ourselves in the presence of an ontological difference, an ontological leap, one could say.

To do the Pope credit, at this point he recognizes the essential contradiction between the two positions he is attempting to reconcile:

> However, does not the posing of such ontological discontinuity run counter to that physical continuity which seems to be the main thread of research into evolution in the field of physics and chemistry?

DARWIN'S DANGEROUS IDEA ✳ *Daniel Dennett*

Let me lay my cards on the table. If I were to give an award for the single best idea anyone has ever had, I'd give it to Darwin, ahead of Newton and Einstein and everyone else. In a single stroke, the idea of evolution by natural selection unifies the realm of life, meaning, and purpose with the realm of space and time, cause and effect, mechanism and physical law. But it is not just a wonderful scientific idea. It is a dangerous idea. My admiration for Darwin's magnificent idea is unbounded, but I, too, cherish many of the ideas and ideals that it *seems* to challenge, and want to protect them. For instance, I want to protect the campfire song, and what is beautiful and true in it, for my little grandson and his friends, and for their children when they grow up. There are many more magnificent ideas that are also jeopardized, it seems, by Darwin's idea, and they, too, may need protection. The only good way to do this—the only way that has a chance in the long run—is to cut through the smokescreens and look at the idea as unflinchingly, as dispassionately, as possible.

On this occasion, we are not going to settle for "There, there, it will all come out all right." Our examination will take a certain amount of nerve. Feelings may get hurt. Writers on evolution usually steer clear of this apparent clash between science and religion. Fools rush in, Alexander Pope said, where angels fear to tread. Do you want to follow me? Don't you really want to know what survives this confrontation? What if it turns out that the sweet vision—or a better one—survives intact, strengthened and deepened by the encounter? Wouldn't it be a shame to forgo the opportunity for a strengthened, renewed creed, settling instead for a fragile, sickbed faith that you mistakenly supposed must not be disturbed?

There is no future in a sacred myth. Why not? Because of our curiosity. Because, as the song reminds us, *we want to know why*. We may have outgrown the song's answer, but we will never outgrow the question. What ever we hold precious, we cannot protect it from our curiosity, because being who we are, one of the things we deem precious is the truth. Our love of truth is surely a central element in the meaning we find in our lives. In any case, the idea that we might preserve meaning by kidding ourselves is a more pessimistic, more nihilistic idea than I for one can stomach. If that were the best that could be done, I would conclude that nothing mattered after all.

From Daniel Dennett, *Darwin's Dangerous Idea* (1995).

Never fear. As so often in the past, obscurantism comes to the rescue:

> Consideration of the method used in the various branches of knowledge makes it possible to reconcile two points of view which would seen irreconcilable. The sciences of observation describe and measure the multiple manifestations of life with increasing precision and correlate them with the time line. The moment of transition to the spiritual cannot be the object of this kind of observation, which nevertheless can discover at the experimental level a series of very valuable signs indicating what is specific to the human being.

In plain language, there came a moment in the evolution of hominids when God intervened and injected a human soul into a previously animal lineage. (When? A million years ago? Two million years ago? Between Homo erectus and Homo sapiens? Between "archaic" Homo sapiens and H. sapiens sapiens?) The sudden injection is necessary, of course, otherwise there would be no distinction upon which to base Catholic morality, which is speciesist to the core. You can kill adult animals for meat, but abortion and euthanasia are murder because *human* life is involved.

Catholicism's "net" is not limited to moral considerations, if only because Catholic morals have scientific implications. Catholic morality demands the presence of a great gulf between Homo sapiens and the rest of the animal kingdom. Such a gulf is fundamentally antievolutionary. The sudden injection of an immortal soul in the time-line is an antievolutionary intrusion into the domain of science.

More generally it is completely unrealistic to claim, as Gould and many others do, that religion keeps itself away from science's turf, restricting itself to morals and values. A universe with a supernatural presence would be a fundamentally and qualitatively different kind of universe from one without. The difference is, inescapably, a scientific difference. Religions make existence claims, and this means scientific claims.

The same is true of many of the major doctrines of the Roman Catholic Church. The Virgin Birth, the bodily Assumption of the Blessed Virgin Mary, the Resurrection of Jesus, the survival of our own souls after death: these are all claims of a clearly scientific nature. Either Jesus had a corporeal father or he didn't. This is not a question of "values" or "morals," it is a question of sober fact. We may not have the evidence to answer it, but it is a scientific question, nevertheless. You may be sure that, if any evidence supporting the claim were discovered, the Vatican would not be reticent in promoting it.

Either Mary's body decayed when she died, or it was physically removed from this planet to Heaven. The official Roman Catholic doctrine of Assumption, promulgated as recently as 1950, implies that Heaven has a physical location and exists in the domain of physical reality—how else could the physical body of a woman go there? I am not, here, saying that the doctrine of the Assumption of the Virgin is necessarily false (although of course I think it is). I am simply rebutting the claim that it is outside the domain of science. On the contrary, the Assumption of the Virgin is transparently a scientific theory. So is the theory that our souls survive bodily death and so are all stories of angelic visitations, Marian manifestations, and miracles of all types.

There is something dishonestly self-serving in the tactic of claiming that all religious beliefs are outside the domain of science. On the one hand miracle stories and the promise of life after death are used to impress simple people, win converts, and swell congregations. It is precisely their scientific power that gives these stories their popular appeal. But at the same time it is considered below the belt to subject the same stories to the ordinary rigors of scientific criticism: these are religious matters and therefore outside the domain of science. But you cannot have it both ways. At least, religious theorists and apologists should not be allowed to get away with having it both ways. Unfortunately all too many of us, including nonreligious people, are unaccountably ready to let them get away with it.

I suppose it is gratifying to have the Pope as an ally in the struggle against fundamentalist creationism. It is certainly amusing to see the rug pulled out from under the feet of Catholic creationists such as Michael Behe. Even so, given a choice between honest-to-goodness fundamentalism on the one hand, and the obscurantist, disingenuous doublethink of the Roman Catholic Church on the other, I know which I prefer.

QUESTIONS FOR FURTHER REFLECTION

1. What other reasons might lead one to think that science "defeats" religion?
2. Dawkins considers two models of how science and religion relate. He thinks science refutes religion. Gould thinks they don't conflict because they are concerned with different domains. What other models are there?

49. DARWINIST RELIGION

Phillip E. Johnson

Phillip Johnson is a professor of law at the University of California, Berkeley. A graduate of Harvard University and the University of Chicago, he was a law clerk for Chief Justice Earl Warren. He is the author of *Darwin on Trial* (1993), *Reason in the Balance* (1995), *Defeating Darwinism by Opening Minds* (1997), and *The Wedge of Truth: Splitting the*

Foundations of Naturalism (2000). In the following selection, he argues that Darwinism is not religiously neutral. It is often the foundation of a broader naturalistic worldview and plays a quasi-religious role in the thinking of many evolutionists.

READING QUESTIONS

1. What is the fact-value distinction?
2. Does Johnson think that scientific naturalist believe that science and religion are of equal dignity and importance?
3. What, according to Johnson, is "compatiblism"?
4. Name someone that Johnson thinks tried to fashion a scientific religion?
5. In what sense does Johnson think Darwinism has a "mythical dimension"? What sense of the word "myth" is he employing?

The preface to the 1984 pamphlet *Science and Creationism: A View from the National Academy of Sciences*, signed by the Academy's president, Frank Press, assured the nation that it is "false . . . to think that the theory of evolution represents an irreconcilable conflict between religion and science." Dr. Press explained:

> A great many religious leaders accept evolution on scientific grounds without relinquishing their belief in religious principles. As stated in a resolution by the Council of the National Academy of Sciences in 1981, however, "Religion and science are separate and mutually exclusive realms of human thought whose presentation in the same context leads to misunderstanding of both scientific theory and religious belief."

The Academy's concern was only to justify its opposition to creation-science, and it did not feel obliged to explain what "religion" might be, or under what circumstances the religious realm might be entitled to protection from incursions by science. Stephen Jay Gould had somewhat more to say on this subject, however, in his rebuttal to Irving Kristol's charge that neo-Darwinism as currently taught incorporates "an ideological bias against religious belief." Gould responded that most scientists show no hostility to religion, because their subject "doesn't intersect the concerns of theology."

Science can no more answer the question of how we ought to live than religion can decree the age of the earth. Honorable and discerning scientists (most of us, I trust) have always understood that the limits to what science can answer also describe the power of its methods in their proper domain. Darwin himself exclaimed that science couldn't touch the problem of evil and similar moral conundrums: "A dog might as well speculate on the mind of Newton. Let each man hope and believe what he can."

The Gould-Darwin disclaimer contains an important ambiguity. If science can tell us nothing about how we ought to live, does this mean that knowledge about this subject can be obtained through religion, or does it mean that we can know no more about good and evil than a dog knows about the mind of Newton? Each man may hope and believe as he can, but there are some who would say that hopes and beliefs are mere subjective expressions of feeling, little more than sentimental nonsense, unless they rest upon the firm foundation of scientific knowledge.

One Darwinist who says exactly this is Cornell University Professor William Provine, a leading historian of science. Provine insists that the conflict between science and religion is inescapable, to the extent that persons who manage to retain religious beliefs while accepting evolutionary biology "have to check [their] brains at the church-house door." Specifically:

> Modern science directly implies that the world is organized strictly in accordance with mechanistic principles. There are no purposive principles whatsoever in nature. There are no gods and no designing forces that are rationally detectable. . . .
>
> Second, modern science directly implies that there are no inherent moral or ethical laws, no absolute guiding principles for human society.

Third, human beings are marvelously complex machines. The individual human becomes an ethical person by means of two primary mechanisms: heredity and environmental influences. That is all there is.

Fourth, we must conclude that when we die, we die and that is the end of us. . . .

Finally, free will as it is traditionally conceived—the freedom to make uncoerced and unpredictable choices among alternative possible courses of action—simply does not exist. . . . There is no way that the evolutionary process as currently conceived can produce a being that is truly free to make choices.

Gould had assured Kristol that among evolutionary biologists there is "an entire spectrum of religious attitudes—from devout daily prayer and worship to resolute atheism." I have myself noticed a great deal more of the latter than the former, and Provine agrees with me. He reports that most evolutionary biologists are atheists, "and many have been driven there by their understanding of the evolutionary process and other science." The few who see no conflict between their biology and their religion "are either obtuse or compartmentalized in their thinking, or are effective atheists without realizing it." Scientific organizations hide the conflict for fear of jeopardizing the funding for scientific research, or because they feel that religion plays a useful role in moral education. According to Provine, who had the Academy's 1984 statement specifically in mind, "These rationalizations are politic but intellectually dishonest."

It is not difficult to reconcile all these statements, once we untangle the confusing terminology. The Academy is literally correct that there is no incompatibility between "evolution" and "religion." When these terms are not defined specifically, neither has enough content to be incompatible with anything else. There is not even any conflict between evolution and *theistic* religion. God might very well have "created" by gradually developing one kind of creature out of other kinds. Evolution of that sort is not what the scientists have in mind, but they have nothing to gain from making this clear to the public.

Gould's remark is similarly misleading. Most scientific naturalists accept what is called the "fact-value distinction," and do not claim that a scientific description of what "is" can lead directly to a theory of what we "ought" to do. On the other hand, they do not consider all statements about ethics to be equally rational. A rational person starts with what is known and real rather than what is unknown and unreal. As George Gaylord Simpson explained the matter:

> Of course there are some beliefs still current, labelled as religious and involved in religious emotions, that are flatly incompatible with evolution and therefore are intellectually untenable in spite of their emotional appeal. Nevertheless, I take it as now self-evident, requiring no further special discussion, that evolution and *true* religion are compatible.

A scientific doctrine that sets the boundary between true and false religion is certainly not "antireligious," but it directly contradicts the Academy's assurance that religion and science are separate and mutually exclusive realms of human thought.

Scientific naturalists do not see a contradiction, because they never meant that the realms of science and religion are of equal dignity and importance. Science for them is the realm of objective knowledge; religion is a matter of subjective belief. The two should not conflict because a rational person always prefers objective knowledge to subjective belief, when the former is available. Religions which are based on intellectually untenable ideas (such as that there is a Creator who has somehow communicated His will to humans) are in the realm of fantasy. Naturalistic religion, which looks to science for its picture of reality, is a way of harnessing irrational forces for rational purposes. It may perform useful service by recruiting support for scientific programs in areas like environmental protection and medical research.

The American Scientific Affiliation (ASA) incurred the wrath of Darwinists for mixing the wrong kind of religion with science. The ASA's membership is made up of science teachers and others who identify themselves as evangelical Christians committed both to Jesus Christ and to a scientific understanding of the natural world. The fundamentalist creation-scientists split from the ASA years ago in disgust at its members' willingness to accept not only the geological evidence that the earth is very old, but also the theory of biological evolution.

The ASA leadership has generally embraced "compatibilism" (the doctrine that science and religion do not conflict because they occupy separate realms) and "theistic evolution." Theistic evolution is not easy to define, but it involves making an effort to maintain that the natural world is God-governed while avoiding disagreement with the Darwinist establishment on scientific matters. Because the Darwinists have become increasingly explicit about the religious and philosophical implications of their system, this strategy led the theism in the ASA's evolution to come under ever greater pressure.

Compatibilism has its limits, however, and some ASA leaders were prodded into action by the strong naturalistic bias of the National Academy's 1984 pamphlet, which tried to give the public the impression that science has all the major problems of evolution well in hand. With foundation support, the ASA produced its own 48-page illustrated booklet, titled *Teaching Science in a Climate of Controversy: A View from the American Scientific Affiliation* and mailed it to thousands of school teachers. The general tenor of the booklet was to encourage open-mindedness, especially on such "open questions" as whether life really arose by chance, how the first animals could have evolved in the Cambrian explosion, and how human intelligence and upright posture evolved.[1]

---

[1] The following paragraphs reflect the general theme of *Teaching Science*:

Many aspects of evolution are currently being studied by scientists who hold varying degrees of belief or disbelief in God. No matter how those investigations turn out, most scientists agree that a "creation science" based on an earth only a few thousand years old provides no theoretical basis sound enough to serve as a reasonable alternative.

Clearly, it is difficult to teach evolution—or even to avoid teaching it—without stepping into a controversy loaded with all kinds of implications: scientific, religious, philosophical, educational, political and legal. Dogmatists at either extreme who insist that theirs is the only tenable position tend to make both sides seem unattractive.

Many intelligent people, however, who accept the evidence for an earth billions of years old and recognize that life-forms have changed drastically over much of that time, also take the Bible seriously and worship God as their Creator. Some (but not all) who affirm creation on religious grounds are able to envision *macro*-evolution as a possible explanation of how God has created new life-forms.

In other words, a broad middle ground exists in which creation and evolution are not seen as antagonists.

The ASA members who wrote *Teaching Science* naively expected that most scientists would welcome their contribution as a corrective to the overconfidence that evolutionary science tends to project when it is trying to persuade the public not to entertain any doubts. The official scientific organizations, however, are at war with creationism, and their policy is to demand unconditional surrender. Persons who claim to be scientists, but who try to convince school teachers that there are "open questions" about the naturalistic understanding of the world, are traitors in that war.

Retribution quickly followed. A California "science consultant" named William Bennetta, who makes a career of pursuing creationists, organized a posse of scientific heavyweights to condemn the ASA's pamphlet as "an attempt to replace science with a system of pseudoscience devoted to confirming Biblical narratives." A journal called *The Science Teacher* published a collection of essays edited by Bennetta, titled "Scientists Decry a Slick New Packaging of Creationism." Nine prominent scientists, including Gould, Futuyma, Eldredge, and Sarich, contributed heavy-handed condemnations of *Teaching Science*. The pervasive message was that the ASA is a deceitful creationist front which disguises its Biblical literalist agenda under a pretence of scientific objectivity.

The accusations bewildered the authors of *Teaching Science*, and were so far off the mark that persons familiar with the ASA might easily have mistaken them for intentional misrepresentations. It would be a mistake to infer any intent to deceive, however, because really zealous scientific naturalists do not recognize subtle distinctions among theists. To the zealots, people who say they believe in God are either harmless sentimentalists who add some vague God-talk to a basically naturalistic worldview, or they are creationists. In either case they are fools, but in the latter case they are also a menace.

From a zealot's viewpoint, the ASA writers had provided ample evidence of a creationist purpose. Why would they harp on "open questions" except to imply that God might have taken a hand in the appearance of new forms? That suggestion is creationism by definition, and the ASA admits to being an organization of Christians who accept the authority of the Bible. Their true reason for rejecting scientific evolution must therefore be that it contradicts the Biblical narrative. What other reason could they have?

THE GRAND EVOLUTIONARY MYTH * *Alvin Plantinga*

Consider the Grand Evolutionary Myth (GEM). According to this story, organic life somehow arose from nonliving matter by way of purely natural means and by virtue of the workings of the fundamental regularities of physics and chemistry. Once life began, all the vast profusion of contemporary flora and fauna arose from those early ancestors by way of common descent. The enormous contemporary variety of life arose, basically, through natural selection operating on such sources of genetic variability as random genetic mutation, genetic drift and the like. I call this story a myth not because I do not believe it (although I do not believe it) but because it plays a certain kind of quasi-religious role in contemporary culture. It is a shared way of understanding ourselves at the deep level of religion, a deep interpretation of ourselves to ourselves, a way of telling us why we are here, where we come from, and where we are going . . .

So suppose we separate off this thesis about the origin of life. Suppose we use the term "evolution" to denote the much weaker claim that all contemporary forms of life are genealogically related. According to this claim, you and the flowers in your garden share common ancestors, though we may have to go back quite a ways to find them. Many contemporary experts and spokespersons—Francisco Ayala, Richard Dawkins, Stephen Gould, William Provine, and Philip Spieth, for example—unite in declaring that evolution is no mere theory, but established fact. According to them, this story is not just a virtual certainty, but a real certainty. Now why do they think so? . . . The answer can be seen, I think, when we realize that what you properly think about these claims of certainty depends in part on how you think about theism. If you reject theism in favor of naturalism, this evolutionary story is the only game in town, the only visible answer to the question: Where did all this enormous variety of flora and fauna come from? How did it all get here? Even if the fossil record is at best spotty and at worst disconfirming, this story is the only answer on offer (from a naturalistic perspective) to these questions.

From Alvin Plantinga, "Methodological Naturalism?" in Philosophical Analysis *Origins & Design* (1997).

Mixing religion with science is obnoxious to Darwinists only when it is the wrong religion that is being mixed. To prove the point, we may cite two of the most important founders of the modern synthesis, Theodosius Dobzhansky and Julian Huxley. Julian Huxley's religion of "evolutionary humanism" offered humanity the "sacred duty" and the "glorious opportunity" of seeking "to promote the maximum fulfillment of the evolutionary process on the earth." That did not mean merely working to ensure that the organisms that have the most offspring continue to have the most offspring, but rather promoting the "fullest realization" of mankind's "inherent possibilities." Inspired by the same vision, the American philosopher and educational reformer John Dewey launched a movement in 1933 for "religious humanism," whose Manifesto reflected the assumption current among scientific naturalists at the time that the final demise of theistic religion would usher in a new era of scientific progress and social cooperation for mankind. Soon thereafter, Hitler and Stalin provided a stunning realization of some of mankind's inherent possibilities. Dewey's successors admitted in 1973 that a new Manifesto was needed because the events of the previous forty years had made the original statement "seem far too optimistic."

The revised Manifesto makes some unenthusiastic concessions to reality, such as that "Science has sometimes brought evil instead of good," and "Traditional religions are surely not the only obstacle to human progress." The overall message is as before. It is that salvation comes through science:

Using technology wisely, we can control our environment, conquer poverty, markedly reduce disease, extend our life-span, significantly modify our behavior, alter the course of human evolution and cultural development, unlock vast new powers, and provide humankind with unparalleled opportunity for achieving an abundant and meaningful life.

The scientist-philosopher who went farther than anybody else in drawing a message of cosmic optimism from evolution was Pierre Teilhard de Chardin, the unorthodox Jesuit paleontologist who played an important role in the Piltdown and Peking Man discoveries. Teilhard aimed to bring Christianity up to date by founding it squarely upon the rock of evolution rather that upon certain events alleged to have occurred in Palestine nearly two thousand years ago. The more rigorously materialistic Darwinists dismissed Teilhard's philosophy as pretentious claptrap, but it had a strong appeal to those of a more spiritual cast of mind, such as Theodosius Dobzhansky.

In his reply to Irving Kristol, Gould cited Dobzhansky, "the greatest evolutionist of our century and a lifelong Russian Orthodox," to illustrate the compatibility of evolution and religion. For Dobzhansky the two were a good deal more than compatible, for he wrote in his book *Mankind Evolving* that Darwin had healed "the wound inflicted by Copernicus and Galileo." This wound was the discovery that the earth, and therefore man, is not the physical center of the universe. Darwinism had healed it by placing mankind at the *spiritual* center of the universe, because man now understands evolution and has the potential capacity to take control of it. Dobzhansky exulted that "Evolution need no longer be a destiny imposed from without; it may conceivably be controlled by man, in accordance with his wisdom and his values." For further detail he referred his readers to the following quotations, which encapsulate Teilhard's "inspiring vision":

Is evolution a theory, a system, or a hypothesis? It is much more—it is a general postulate to which all theories, all hypotheses, all systems must henceforth bow and which they must satisfy in order to be thinkable and true. Evolution is a light which illuminates all facts, a trajectory which all lines of thought must follow—this is what evolution is.

Evolution is, in short, the God we must worship. It is taking us to heaven, "The Point Omega" in Teilhard's jargon, which is:

a harmonized collectivity of consciousness, equivalent to a kind of superconsciousness. The earth is covering itself not only by myriads of thinking units, but by a single continuum of thought, and finally forming a functionally single Unit of Thought of planetary dimensions. The plurality of individual thoughts combine and mutually reinforce each other in a single act of unanimous Thought. . . . In the dimension of Thought, like in the dimension of Time and Space, can the Universe reach consummation in anything but the Measureless?

The naive optimism of these attempts to fashion a scientific religion survives in the contemporary "New Age" movement, but the trend among Darwinists today is to take a more somber view of humanity's prospects. Writing in 1989, Maitland Edey and Donald Johanson speculate that Homo sapiens may be about to make itself extinct, as a result of nuclear war or ecological catastrophe. This depressing situation is the result of a runaway technology that produces enormous quantities of toxic waste, destroys the jungle and the ozone layer, and permits unrestrained population growth. We are unable to deal intelligently with these problems because "in our guts we are passionate stone age people" who are capable of creating technology but not controlling it. Edey and Johanson think that science is about to develop the technical capacity to design "better people" through genetic engineering. If humanity is to avoid extinction, it must summon the political will to take control of evolution, and make it in the future a matter of human choice rather than blind selection.

The continual efforts to base a religion or ethical system upon evolution are not an aberration, and practically all the most prominent Darwinist writers have tried their hand at it. Darwinist evolution is an imaginative story about who we are and where we came from, which is to say it is a creation myth. As such it is an obvious starting point for speculation about how we ought to live and what we ought to value. A creationist appropriately starts with God's creation and God's will for man. A scientific naturalist just as appropriately starts with evolution and with man as a product of nature.

In its mythological dimension, Darwinism is the story of humanity's liberation from the delusion that its destiny is controlled by a power higher than itself.

Lacking scientific knowledge, humans at first attribute natural events like weather and disease to supernatural beings. As they learn to predict or control natural forces they put aside the lesser spirits, but a more highly evolved religion retains the notion of a rational Creator who rules the universe.

At last the greatest scientific discovery of all is made, and modern humans learn that they are the products of a blind natural process that has no goal and cares nothing for them. The resulting "death of God" is experienced by some as a profound loss, and by others as a liberation. But liberation to what? If blind nature has somehow produced a human species with the capacity to rule earth wisely, and if this capacity has previously been invisible only because it was smothered by superstition, then the prospects for human freedom and happiness are unbounded. That was the message of the Humanist Manifesto of 1933.

Another possibility is that purposeless nature has produced a world ruled by irrational forces, where might makes right and human freedom is an illusion. In that case the right to rule belongs to whoever can control the use of science. It would be illogical for the rulers to worry overmuch about what people say they *want* because science teaches them that wants are the product of irrational forces. In principle, people can be made to want something better. It is no kindness to leave them as they are, because passionate stone age people can do nothing but destroy themselves when they have the power of scientific technology at their command.

Whether a Darwinist takes the optimistic or the pessimistic view, it is imperative that the public be taught to understand the world as scientific naturalists understand it. Citizens must learn to look to science as the only reliable source of knowledge, and the only power capable of bettering (or even preserving) the human condition. That implies, as we shall see, a program of indoctrination in the name of public education.

QUESTIONS FOR FURTHER REFLECTION

1. Can a worldview, or philosophy of life, be considered religious if it lacks belief in a God?
2. Is Darwinism, or, more broadly speaking, evolution, an all encompassing worldview? Is it just a narrowly defined scientific theory? Explain your answer.
3. Does science assume that there is no God? Does it assume, at least for methodological purposes that there is no God? If there were a God that interfered with nature, would that make nature impossible to study and systematize?

50. EVOLUTION IS NOT A THREAT TO RELIGION

Philip and Patricia Kitcher

Philip and Patricia Kitcher are professors of philosophy at Columbia University. After graduating in mathematics from Cambridge University and in philosophy from Princeton University, Philip taught at Vassar College, the University of Vermont, the University of Minnesota, the University of California at San Diego, and finally Columbia. His books include *Abusing Science: The Case Against Creationism* (1982), *The Nature of Mathematical Knowledge* (1983), and *Vaulting Ambition: Sociobiology and the Quest for Human Nature* (1985). Patricia taught for 13 years at the University of California San Diego before coming to Columbia. Her books include *Kant's Transcendental Psychology* (1990), *Freud's Dream: A Complete Interdisciplinary Science of Mind* (1992), and *Kant's Critique of Pure Reason: Critical Essays* (1998). In the following selection, the Kitchers argue that evolution is not a threat to religion even though it conflicts with a literal interpretation of Genesis.

READING QUESTIONS

1. What, according to the Kitchers, is the "forced choice"?
2. What do the Kitchers think is at the heart of the creationist opposition to evolution?
3. What is the obvious response to the charge that all "Bible-believing Christians" must abandon evolutionary theory?
4. What do the Kitchers say is the believers understanding of how the Bible was written?
5. What, according to Freud, are the three great blows that humankind took to its self-esteem?

A FORCED CHOICE

Evolution is the root of atheism, of communism, nazism, behaviorism, racism, economic imperialism, militarism, libertinism, anarchism, and all manner of anti-Christian systems of belief and practice.

Morris 1972, 75

We come, at last, to the real problem. Creationists are not down on Darwin because the methodology of evolutionary biology offends their scientific sensibilities. They are not clamoring for reform in biology because they think that important theoretical and empirical breakthroughs await us if we adopt their preferred perspective. The root of the trouble is that the theory of evolution contradicts a literal reading of the first eleven chapters of Genesis. However, contemporary Creationists do not present the issue in quite this way. Their basic strategy is to portray evolutionary theory as opposed to a vast array of valued institutions: family, morality, religion, even science itself. The rationale for this strategy is obvious. By depicting evolution as opposed, not just to a particular doctrine of a particular sect, but to a large number of institutions that are cherished by a large number of people, they make it "easier" for their audience to choose sides in the genuine conflict between evolution and Creationist fundamentalism.

Although this strategy is unavailable in the official debate about what to teach in high school courses, there is no point in pretending that it lacks influence. When all the diatribes about thermodynamics, falsifiability, and the fossil record have been forgotten, the suggestion that evolutionary thinking leads to degeneracy and the dissolution of society may capture the heart. Those who have been beguiled into thinking that a high school course in evolutionary biology is the gateway to a life of violence and depravity are not likely to ponder the scientific credentials of the theory of evolution.

There are numerous passages in Creationist literature that portray evolutionary theory as opposed to morality and religion and that emphasize the evil consequences of teaching evolution. Morris elaborates the theme at great length, holding "evolutionary philosophy" responsible for promiscuity, pornography, and perversion (Morris 1974b, 166–168). In similar vein, Watson claims that the "new cosmology" lays a firm foundation for "the new theology and new morality" (Watson 1976, 37), and Hiebert asserts that there is an "irreconcilable difference between the Bible and evolutionary dogma" (Hiebert 1979, 145, and see also 17–18). The Gablers complain that textbooks that teach evolution "undermine the faith of thousands of students"; one of their allies, the newspaper editor Reuel Lemmons, suggests that adoption of books presenting evolutionary theory would "entrench sheer atheism" in the classroom (citations from Hefley 1974, 44). Finally, John Moore draws up a table to show how the evil tentacles of evolutionary theory have crept into all corners of modern thought; the sins of Marx, Keynes, Freud, Dewey, Frankfurter, Nietzsche, Camus, and Sartre (among others) are all to be laid at Darwin's door (Moore 1974, 27).

Anxiety about evolutionary theory is coeval with the theory itself. Shortly after the *Origin* was published, the wife of an Anglican bishop expressed the hope that, even if the theory of evolution was true, it would not become widely known. Such muddled nervousness persists, and the Creationists are adept at exploiting it. It would be impossible to consider all the accusations that evolutionary theory fosters evil. However, we shall consider the two most central attacks: the claim that one cannot accept Darwin's theory and be a good Christian and the claim that the theory of evolution purveys an "animalistic amorality."

We should emphasize that the charges about to be examined are not part of the "scientific" defenses of

Creationism. The bullying from the pulpit is reserved for the pulpit (whether found in a church or a television studio), campaign fliers, and the "general" (nonscientific) works written by Creationists. The "public school" edition of *Scientific Creationism* contains only the "scientific" arguments lately considered. But other books mix such arguments with religious exhortations. The short popularization of Creationism, distributed by the Old Time Gospel Hour, is quite explicit on the point that the scientific evidence is only one source of support for Creationism: "The discussion is primarily approached from the Biblical point of view, and assumes throughout that the Bible is the Word of God, divinely inspired and, therefore, completely reliable and authoritative on every subject with which it deals" (Morris 1972, v). But the appeal to scripture does not just provide extra support for Creationism, it seals the case: "We are forced to the conclusion, as Bible believing Christians, that the earth is really quite young after all, regardless of the contrary views of evolutionary geologists. This means then that all the uranium-lead measurements, the potassium-argon measurements and all similar measurements which have shown greater ages have somehow been misinterpreted" (Morris 1972, 89).

Of course, there is an obvious response to the charge that "Bible-believing Christians" must abandon evolutionary theory. Within Christianity, there is a long tradition of liberal interpretation of the Bible. Many Christian denominations, including some fundamentalist groups, do not insist that every sentence in the Bible should be read literally. They are aware of the difficulties involved in a literal reading, and, while they maintain that the Bible is a divinely inspired document, they are prepared for the possibility that, on a literal construction, the Genesis story is inaccurate.

Some passages in the Bible are obviously perplexing. There are lines in the Psalms suggesting that the earth is the center of the universe. Creationists feel that they are able to read *these* in a nonliteral way, because the Psalms are obviously poetry. The Creationist writings that we have read do not explicitly discuss the verse that gave the original Copernicans the most trouble: the description of how Joshua "commanded the sun to stand still" (Joshua 10:12–14). Watson claims that Galileo's claims conflicted only with "a few words of Bible poetry" (Watson 1976, 46); he does not

deal with Galileo's (or the Church's?) major problem. (We understand from conversations with people who favor literal reading that Joshua's command should be regarded as requiring the cessation of *relative* motion and that this was simply expressed from a "human point of view.")

In any case, Creationists are not about to permit a liberal interpretation of the early chapters of Genesis. They regard this attitude as pernicious, or confused, or un-Christian (or all three). The Christian who would go down this path is solemnly warned that it "inevitably leads eventually to complete apostasy" (Morris 1974a, 247). Insofar as an argument is offered, it consists in pointing out that the early chapters of Genesis are written in the style of a historical narrative and that some New Testament writers (including Apostles) treat them as offering a historical narrative:

> This type of Biblical exegesis [not treating Genesis as "true history"] is out of the question for any real believer in the Bible. It is the method of so-called "neo-orthodoxy," though it is neither new nor orthodox. It cuts out the foundation of the entire Biblical system when it expunges Genesis 1–11. The events of these chapters are recorded in simple narrative form, as though the writer or writers fully intended to record a series of straightforward historical facts; there is certainly no internal or exegetical reason for taking them in any other way. (Morris 1974a, 244)

Here the main thrust is clearly that someone who is prepared to abandon a literal reading of Genesis has no basis for taking any part of the Bible seriously. Watson makes the same point in a revealing way:

> "Mommy, if God did not mean what He said, why did He not say what He *did* mean?"
> The little girl's question highlights a problem that has faced every teacher of Genesis over the past hundred years. (Watson 1976, 11)
> The only God worthy of mankind's trust and adoration is the God who can accurately describe the world's past, as a basis for predicting the world's future. (Watson 1976, 13)

So if one is to take the Bible as the Word of God, one must accept every word in it as literally true, including the beginning of Genesis. It is all very simple and convincing. Undoubtedly, this line has convinced many a sincere Christian to take a rosy view of Creation "science." But if the theological argument for Creationism is so straightforward, how can liberal theologians be so obtuse as to have missed it? As we have seen so many times before, matters are much more complex than the Creationists would like to think.

We begin with an obvious fact. The words in the Bible were written down by human beings. From the believer's perspective the writers were divinely inspired. But what exactly does this mean? There are two possible answers. First, the writers were simply *transcribers*. Their function was simply to write down words previously uttered or written by God—as, in the Mormon account, Joseph Smith had the function of transcribing and translating the tablets brought by the angel Moroni. Second, the writers were *authors*, composers of original words, who reported their experiences. If one accepts the first answer, then in the Bible God has literally spoken. Hence it would be possible to ask—like Watson's little girl—why God did not say what He meant. However, given the second view, that question does not arise. The Genesis account of creation is not God's description of historical events. It is a narrative offered by human authors, people who may have been blessed with exceptional experiences, but who, nonetheless, were human.

We know of no compelling theological reason for preferring the first answer to the second. Certainly none is offered by the Creationists, whose arguments blur the distinction. Anybody who makes the distinction, and who accepts the second answer, can easily turn back the arguments that Morris and others offer. It is possible to accept the idea that the writers of Genesis *intended* to relate the true history of the origin of life, and to deny that their history is accurate. Nor do we discredit them by refusing to accept their narrative at face value. Human authors are fallible, and the works they write can mix important religious truth with factual error. (We can even accept the idea that the authors of the New Testament, themselves fallible humans, incorrectly believed that the Genesis narrative is accurate.) A religious person can accept evolutionary theory by elaborating further the idea of the Bible as *inspired* by God but *written* by humans. From this person's perspective, God originally created the

universe, leaving it to evolve according to natural law. After the evolution of *Homo sapiens*, God chose to reveal Himself and some of His purposes to some of His creatures. The group of people in question, and some of their descendants (who may themselves also have had direct experiences of God), wrote books in which the important messages of the Creator are sometimes intertwined with highly inaccurate views about the workings of nature. As we discover things that they were in no position to know, we are able to identify places in which their primitive conceptions of the world overlay important truths. But to correct for these inadequacies should not diminish our respect for them or for the vital religious truths that their writings convey.

Yet it may seem that a residue of Watson's question remains. If the Bible does not record the true history of creation, why did the Creator allow the inspired people who wrote it to put forward so mistaken a picture of their origins? Why did God abstain from correcting their errors? These questions do not threaten the position of the religious evolutionist. Any theist will agree that God might have created wiser, more discerning creatures than *Homo sapiens*, or that God might have shared more knowledge with us. (Perhaps laypeople can even be excused for thinking that this is one message of the Book of Job.) For the religious evolutionist, the Bible contains information that God has chosen to transmit. There is no more reason to wonder why God did not clear up our confusion about the origin of the universe than to ask why God did not enlighten us about many issues on which we have only partial information. The believer maintains that God has made us aware of the important truths. But it has always been clear that we have not been told everything. Some things, like the true origin of life, we have to discover for ourselves.

Creationist arguments, such as they are, trade on linking the idea of the Bible as a divinely inspired document to the claim that every sentence it contains has to be taken literally. It is important to see that there is no tight connection here, and that the idea that religious evolutionists are compelled to deny the significance of the Bible is simply an attempt to bully Christians into accepting a doctrine for which there is not a shred of evidence.

Another Creationist tactic portrays the theory of evolution as severing the special relation between God and human beings. From an evolutionary point of view, we are a very recent development in the history of life. So why would an omniscient Creator choose so inefficient a method as evolution to achieve His purposes? As Morris asks, "If the goal of the evolutionary process was man, why did God take so long to get to the business at hand?" (Morris 1972, 73). A short answer to the question would be that God's purposes are not always apparent. Yet there is a serious worry, produced by reflection on the vastness of time, that the short answer does not touch. Evolutionary theory reveals *Homo sapiens* as simply one of the latest stages in a long process of development of living forms. There is no suggestion that humans are privileged, that our species is the focal point of divine concern. We have occupied the earth for a relatively short time, and, if we manage not to destroy it, our planet *may* one day provide a home for organisms who are our evolutionary descendants. Do not these evolutionary observations threaten religion by denying that there is a special relationship between humans and their Creator?

Freud claimed that humanity had suffered three great blows to its self-esteem. The first came when Copernicus declared that the earth is not the center of the universe and Galileo concluded that the universe is vastly larger than had hitherto been thought. The second was Darwin's proposal that living forms have evolved from common ancestors and that humans are descendants of animals who also gave rise to the contemporary apes. Freud thought that he himself had administered the third blow; by uncovering the workings of the unconscious, he had exposed us as far less rational than we had taken ourselves to be.

Whether Freud was correct to identify exactly these three incidents as critical in transforming our conception of ourselves, there is something acute in his characterization of them. They are indeed *blows to our self-esteem*. It is hard today to recapture the sense of uncertainty and loss that pervades some seventeenth-century writings. Donne remarks that "the new philosophy casts all in doubt," and Pascal reacts in horror to the infinite space of the universe. We have come to terms with the idea that our planet is not the physical center of a cozy Aristotelian cosmos. But, 125 years after Darwin, human vanity is still sometimes wounded by the thought of our kinship with the apes.

Yet, however much they may hurt our pride, Copernicanism and Darwinism are alike in that they do not question the possibility of a special relationship between God and humanity. Special relationships need not be exclusive. If, as some seventeenth-century cosmologists feared, the immensity of the universe suggests that we are not its only rational inhabitants, then that, in and of itself, need not diminish God's concern for us. If we are simply one among innumerable species who have occupied and will occupy our planet, then we are not compelled to conclude that we are not the focus of a special care. Religious belief is not threatened by the discovery that our part in the cosmic drama is confined to a single scene, unless we suppose that any object of divine concern will hog the stage throughout the entire play. Or, to switch metaphors, the religious believer should not behave like an eldest child who concludes that his parents no longer love him when he acquires a baby sister. To conceive of God as a Father, we need not suppose that we are His *only* children. It is enough to suppose that He cares for all His creatures and that He cares for each in ways that are appropriate to its abilities and needs.

Once we have adopted this perspective, we can see that the Creationist attempt to diagnose evolution as inefficient is based on a vain anthropocentrism. Evolutionary theory emphasizes our kinship with nonhuman animals and denies that we were created separately. But it does not interfere with the central Judaeo-Christian message that we are objects of special concern to the Creator. It simply denies us an exclusive right to that title.

In conclusion, let us look briefly at one of the more bizarre passages in the Creationist literature. Creationists could surely force Christians to choose between science and religion if they could successfully conclude that evolutionary theory is the invention of the Devil and specifically designed to overthrow the church of Christ. Henry Morris has suggested that this conclusion is literally true. Since 1859, many people have believed that Charles Darwin was the father of evolutionary theory. Morris thinks that they are quite wrong. Evolutionary theory was really devised by the Father of Lies Himself.

Creationists not only have their own "science." They also have their own "history of ideas," based on a surprising conspiracy theory. Morris claims that evolutionary theory is the outgrowth of an old movement, launched by the Forces of Darkness, that aims to overthrow Christianity. The movement includes an odd mixture of coconspirators: Immanuel Kant, for example, whose piety one might have taken to be beyond reproach, is accused of reviving "pagan philosophies" (Morris 1974b, 65). However, the main point of the history seems to be to trace evolutionary ideas to the early Greek atomists. After noting that the Greek atomists held that the order of the universe "arises out of a blind interplay of atoms" (Munitz 1957, 63; quoted in Morris 1974b, 66), Morris concludes triumphantly, "Modern evolutionary materialists are not so modern after all. Their system is essentially the same as the pre-Socratic Greek cosmology of 2500 years ago!" (Morris 1974b, 67). With this connection firmly in place, he goes on to appeal to an "unanswered" "classic work" (*The Two Babylons* by Alexander Hislop) that traces the early pagan ("evolutionary") philosophies back to Babylon. Now the stage is set. After assuming that "the Babylonian mysteries were originally established by Nimrod and his followers at Babel" (Morris 1974b, 73), Morris unmasks the horrible truth: "It therefore is a reasonable deduction, even though hardly capable of proof, that the entire monstrous complex was revealed to Nimrod at Babel by demonic influences, perhaps by Satan himself" (Morris 1974b, 74). Initially, Morris treats his hypothesis cautiously—claiming only that his account seems to be the best available treatment of the "known facts of the history of religions." But after a brief investigation of Satanic psychology, Morris becomes more confident. The discussion ends with a full-blown statement of the conspiracy theory: "[Satan] then brought about man's fall with the same deception ('ye shall be as gods') and the long sad history of the outworking of human unbelief as centered in the grand delusion of evolution has been the result" (Morris 1974b, 76).

We find it hard to believe that anybody—including Morris himself—accepts this shaggy-dog story. (One could make a far better case for tracing thermodynamics—specifically, the kinetic theory of heat—to the early Greek atomists. Are we then to think that this science too was inspired by the Devil?) We mention this curiosity only because it shows the lengths to which a prominent Creationist will go to attack the theory of evolution.

References

Hefley, l. C. *Are Textbooks Harming Your Children*. Milford, MI: Mott Media, 1979.

Hempel, C. G. "Problems and Changes in the Empiricist Criterion of Meaning," In *Aspects of Scientific Explanation*, Glencoe: The Free Press, 1965,

Hiebert, H. *Evolution: Its Collapse in Viewl*. Camp Hill, PA: Horizon Books, 1979,

Moore, J. *Should Evolution Be Taught?* San Diego: Creation-Life Publishers, 1974.

Morris, H. M. *The Remarkable Birth of Planet Earth*. San Diego: Creation-Life Publishers, 1972.

Morris, H. M. *Scientific Creationism* (general edition). San Diego: Creation-Life Publishers, 1974a.

Morris, H. M. *The Troubled Waters of Evolution*. San Diego: Creation-Life Publishers, 1974b.

Munitz, M. K. *Theories of the Universe*. Glencoe: The Free Press, 1957.

Watson, D. C. C. *The Great Brain Robbery*. Chicago: Moody Press, 1976.

QUESTIONS FOR FURTHER REFLECTION

1. Do you think that evolution threatens religion? Explain your answer.
2. The Kitchers attack the view that if one is going to take the Bible as divinely inspired, you must interpret everything in it literally. Do you agree or disagree with this position? Explain your answer.

SUGGESTIONS FOR FURTHER READING

Behe, Michael. *Darwin's Black Box*. New York: The Free Press, 1996.

Dawkins, Richard. *The Blind Watchmaker: Why the Evidence of Evolution Reveals a Universe Without Design*. reissue edition, New York: Norton, 1996.

Dembski, William. *Mere Creation: Science, Faith, and Intelligent Design*. Downers Grove, IL: IVP, 1998.

Dennett, Daniel. *Darwin's Dangerous Idea: Evolution and the Meanings of Life*. New York: Simon & Schuster, 1995.

Johnson, Philip. *Darwin on Trial*. Downers Grove, IL: IVP, 1991.

Kitcher, Philip. *Abusing Science*. Cambridge, MA: MIT Press, 1982.

Ruse, Michel. *But Is It Science?* Buffalo, NY: Prometheus, 1988.

PART VIII

✦ SURVIVAL OF BODILY DEATH ✦

51. DEATH AND IMMORTALITY ✳ *Plato*
Sri Aurobindo, "The Nature of the Self"
Shunryu Suzuki, "Zen Mind, Beginner's Mind"
52. EXPLORING THE CASE FOR LIFE AFTER DEATH ✳ *J. P. Moreland*
Peter van Inwagen, "Resurrection"
Thomas Nagel, "Death"
C. J. Ducasse, "REMEMBRANCES OF PAST LIVES"

SUGGESTIONS FOR FURTHER READING

51. DEATH AND IMMORTALITY

Plato

Plato was born in Athens about 427 B.C. to a prominent aristocratic family. Around 387 B.C. he founded the first university, which he named after Academus; it lasted more than a thousand years. Plato wrote philosophy, poetry, and drama, worked as a politician, and was a champion wrestler. He is one of the most influential persons in history; one prominent twentieth-century philosopher has called all Western philosophy merely "a series of footnotes to Plato." Plato lived to be eighty.

In the following selection, from *Phaedo*, Plato recounts the conversation that took place in Socrates' prison cell on the day that he was put to death. According to Plato, Socrates spent this day with some of his closest students, discussing the immortality of the soul. Socrates argued that the soul is immortal. His students disagreed. To a modern reader, it may seem ungracious of Socrates's students to have pressed the case for the finality of death to Socrates on the very day that he would die. But their doing this was a compliment. For Socrates did not want any of his students to believe something just because he believed it. He had no use for that sort of disciple. Instead, he encouraged his students to question, especially everything that he himself believed.

Reading Questions

1. Why does Socrates think that true philosophers should welcome death?
2. Souls aside, Socrates thinks that whereas some things are changeable, others are unchangeable. Give examples of each. Why does he think that the soul is more like these unchangeable things than it is like changeable things?
3. Does Socrates believe in the transmigration of souls?

In this present life, I reckon that we make the nearest approach to knowledge when we have the least possible intercourse or communion with the body, and are not surfeited with the bodily nature, but keep ourselves pure until the hour when God himself is pleased to release us. And thus having got rid of the foolishness of the body we shall be pure and hold converse with the pure, and know of ourselves the clear light everywhere, which is no other than the light of truth. For the impure are not permitted to approach the pure. These are the sort of words, Simmias, which the true lovers of knowledge cannot help saying to one another, and thinking. You would agree; would you not?

Undoubtedly, Socrates.

But, O my friend, if this be true, there is great reason to hope that, going whither I go, when I have come to the end of my journey, I shall attain that which has been the pursuit of my life. And therefore I go on my way rejoicing, and not I only, but every other man who believes that his mind has been made ready and that he is in a manner purified.

Certainly, replied Simmias.

And what is purification but the separation of the soul from the body, as I was saying before; the habit of the soul gathering and collecting herself into herself from all sides out of the body; the dwelling in her own place alone, as in another life, so also in this, as far as she can—the release of the soul from the chains of the body?

Very true, he said.

And this separation and release of the soul from the body is termed death?

To be sure, he said.

And the true philosophers, and they only, are ever seeking to release the soul. Is not the separation and release of the soul from the body their especial study?

That is true.

And, as I was saying at first, there would be a ridiculous contradiction in men studying to live as nearly as they can in a state of death, and yet repining when it comes upon them.

Clearly.

And the true philosophers, Simmias, are always occupied in the practice of dying, wherefore also to them least of all men is death terrible. Look at the matter thus: if they have been in every way the enemies of the body, and are wanting to be alone with the soul, when this desire of theirs is granted, how inconsistent would they be if they trembled and repined, instead of rejoicing at their departure to that place where, when they arrive, they hope to gain that which in life they desired—and this was wisdom—and at the same time to be rid of the company of their enemy. Many a man has been willing to go to the world below animated by the hope of seeing there an earthly love, or wife, or son, and conversing with them. And will he who is a true lover of wisdom, and is strongly persuaded in like manner that only in the world below he can worthily enjoy her, still repine at death? Will he not depart with joy? Surely he will, O my friend, if he be a true philosopher. For he will have a firm conviction that there, and there only, he can find wisdom in her purity. And if this be true, he would be very absurd, as I was saying, if he were afraid of death. . . .

1. RECOLLECTION

. . . And shall we proceed a step further, and affirm that there is such a thing as equality, not of one piece of wood or stone with another, but that, over and above this, there is absolute equality? Shall we say so?

Say so, yes, replied Simmias, and swear to it, with all the confidence in life.

And do we know the nature of this absolute essence?

To be sure, he said.

And whence did we obtain our knowledge? Did we not see equalities of material things, such as pieces of wood and stones, and gather from them the idea of an equality which is different from them? For you will acknowledge that there is a difference. Or look at the matter in another way: Do not the same pieces of wood or stone appear at one time equal, and at another time unequal?

That is certain.

But are real equals ever unequal? or is the idea of equality the same as of inequality?

Impossible, Socrates.

Then these (so-called) equals are not the same with the idea of equality?

I should say, clearly not, Socrates.

And yet from these equals, although differing from the idea of equality, you conceived and attained that idea?

Very true, he said.

Which might be like, or might be unlike them?

Yes.

But that makes no difference: whenever from seeing one thing you conceived another, whether like or unlike, there must surely have been an act of recollection?

Very true.

But what would you say of equal portions of wood and stone, or other material equals? and what is the impression produced by them? Are they equals in the same sense in which absolute equality is equal? or do they fall short of this perfect equality in a measure?

Yes, he said, in a very great measure too.

And must we not allow, that when I or any one, looking at any object, observes that the thing which he sees aims at being some other thing, but falls short of, and cannot be, that other thing, but is inferior, he who

THE NATURE OF THE SELF * *Sri Aurobindo*

The old Indian thinkers—I am not speaking of the popular belief which was crude enough and thought not at all about the matter—the old Buddhistic and Vedantist thinkers surveyed the whole field from a very different standpoint. They were not attached to the survival of the personality; they did not give to that survival the high name of immortality; they saw that personality being what it is, a constantly changing composite, the survival of an identical personality was nonsense, a contradiction in terms. They perceived indeed that there is a continuity and they sought to discover what determines this continuity and whether the sense of identity which enters into it is an illusion or the representation of a fact, of a real truth, and, if the latter, then what that truth may be. The Buddha denied any real identity. There is, he said, no self, no person; there is simply a continuous stream of energy in action like the continuous flowing of a river or the continuous burning of a flame. It is this continuity which creates in the mind the false sense of identity. I am not now the same person that I was a year ago, not even the same person that I was a moment ago, any more than the water flowing past yonder ghaut is the same water

that flowed past it a few seconds ago; it is the persistence of the flow in the same channel that preserves the false appearance of identity. Obviously, then, there is no soul that reincarnates, but only Karma that persists in flowing continuously down the same apparently uninterrupted channel. It is Karma that incarnates; Karma creates the form of a constantly changing mentality and physical bodies that are, we may presume, the result of that changing composite of ideas and sensations which I call myself. The identical "I" is not, never was, never will be. Practically, so long as the error of personality persists, this does not make much difference and I can say in the language of ignorance that I am reborn in a new body; practically, I have to proceed on the basis of that error. But there is this important point gained that it is all an error and an error which can cease; the composite can be broken up for good without any fresh formation, the flame can be extinguished, the channel which called itself a river destroyed. And then there is nonbeing, there is cessation, there is the release of the error from itself.

From Sri Aurobindo, *The Problem of Rebirth* (1952).

---

makes this observation must have had a previous knowledge of that to which the other, although similar, was inferior?

Certainly.

And has not this been our own case in the matter of equals and of absolute equality?

Precisely.

Then we must have known equality previously to the time when we first saw the material equals, and reflected that all these apparent equals strive to attain absolute equality, but fall short of it?

Very true.

And we recognize also that this absolute equality has only been known, and can only be known, through the medium of sight or touch, or of some other of the senses, which are all alike in this respect?

Yes, Socrates, as far as the argument is concerned, one of them is the same as the other.

From the senses then is derived the knowledge that all sensible things aim at an absolute equality of which they fall short?

Yes.

Then before we began to see or hear or perceive in any way, we must have had a knowledge of absolute equality, or we could not have referred to that standard the equals which are derived from the senses? For to that they all aspire, and of that they fall short.

No other inference can be drawn from the previous statements.

And did we not see and hear and have the use of our other senses as soon as we were born?

Certainly.

Then we must have acquired the knowledge of equality at some previous time?

Yes.

That is to say, before we were born, I suppose?

True.

And if we acquired this knowledge before we were born, and were born having the use of it, then we also knew before we were born and at the instant of birth not only the equal or the greater or the less, but all other ideas; for we are not speaking only of equality, but of beauty, goodness, justice, holiness, and of all which we stamp with the name of essence in the dialectical process, both when we ask and when we answer questions. Of all this we may certainly affirm that we acquired the knowledge before birth?

We may.

But if, after having acquired, we have not forgotten what in each case we acquired, then we must always have come into life having knowledge, and shall always continue to know as long as life lasts—for knowing is the acquiring and retaining knowledge and not forgetting. Is not forgetting, Simmias, just the losing of knowledge?

Quite true, Socrates.

But if the knowledge which we acquired before birth was lost by us at birth, and if afterwards by the use of the senses we recovered what we precisely knew, will not the process which we call learning be a recovering of the knowledge which is natural to us, and may not this be rightly termed recollection? . . .

2. THE SOUL'S KINSHIP WITH THE DIVINE

Then now let us return to the previous discussion. Is that idea or essence, which in the dialectical process we define as essence or true existence—whether essence of equality, beauty, or anything else—are these essences, I say, liable at times to some degree of change? or are they each of them always what they are, having the same simple self-existent and unchanging forms, not admitting of variation at all, or in any way, or at any time?

They must be always the same, Socrates, replied Cebes.

And what would you say of the many beautiful—whether men or horses or garments or any other things which are named by the same names and may be called equal or beautiful—are they all unchanging and the same always, or quite the reverse? May they not rather be described as almost always changing and hardly ever the same, either with themselves or with one another?

The latter, replied Cebes; they are always in a state of change.

And these you can touch and see and perceive with the senses, but the unchanging things you can only perceive with the mind—they are invisible and are not seen?

That is very true, he said.

Well then, added Socrates, let us suppose that there are two sorts of existences—one seen, the other unseen.

Let us suppose them.

The seen is the changing, and the unseen is the unchanging?

That may be also supposed.

And, further, is not one part of us body, another part soul?

To be sure.

And to which class is the body more alike and akin?

Clearly to the seen—no one can doubt that.

And is the soul seen or not seen?

Not by man, Socrates.

And what we mean by "seen" and "not seen" is that which is or is not visible to the eye of man?

Yes, to the eye of man.

And is the soul seen or not seen?

Not seen.

Unseen then?

Yes.

Then the soul is more like to the unseen, and the body to the seen?

That follows necessarily, Socrates.

And were we not saying long ago that the soul when using the body as an instrument of perception, that is to say, when using the sense of sight or hearing or some other sense—for the meaning of perceiving through the body is perceiving through the senses—were we not saying that the soul too is then dragged by the body into the region of the changeable, and wanders and is confused; the world spins round her, and she is like a drunkard, when she touches change?

Very true.

But when returning into herself she reflects, then she passes into the other world, the region of purity, and eternity, and immortality, and unchangeableness, which are her kindred, and with them she ever lives, when she is by herself and is not let or hindered; then she ceases from her erring ways, and being in communion with the unchanging is unchanging. And this state of the soul is called wisdom?

That is well and truly said, Socrates, he replied.

And to which class is the soul more nearly alike and akin, as far as may be inferred from this argument, as well as from the preceding one?

I think, Socrates, that, in the opinion of every one who follows the argument, the soul will be infinitely more like the unchangeable—even the most stupid person will not deny that.

And the body is more like the changing?

Yes.

Yet once more consider the matter in another light: When the soul and the body are united, then nature orders the soul to rule and govern, and the body to obey and serve. Now which of these two functions is akin to the divine? and which to the mortal? Does not the divine appear to you to be that which naturally orders and rules, and the mortal to be that which is subject and servant?

True.

And which does the soul resemble?

The soul resembles the divine, and the body the mortal—there can be no doubt of that, Socrates.

Then reflect, Cebes: of all which has been said is not this the conclusion? That the soul is in the very likeness of the divine, and immortal, and intellectual, and uniform, and indissoluble, and unchangeable; and that the body is in the very likeness of the human, and mortal, and unintellectual, and multiform, and dissoluble, and changeable. Can this, my dear Cebes, be denied?

It cannot.

But if it be true, then is not the body liable to speedy dissolution? and is not the soul almost or altogether indissoluble?

Certainly.

And do you further observe, that after a man is dead, the body, or visible part of him, which is lying in the visible world, and is called a corpse, and would naturally be dissolved and decomposed and dissipated, is not dissolved or decomposed at once, but may remain for some time, nay even for a long time, if the constitution be sound at the time of death, and the season of the year favourable? For the body when shrunk and embalmed, as the manner is in Egypt, may remain almost entire through infinite ages; and even in decay, there are still some portions, such as the bones and ligaments, which are practically indestructible. Do you agree?

Yes.

And is it likely that the soul, which is invisible, in passing to the place of the true Hades, which like her is invisible, and pure, and noble, and on her way to the good and wise God, whither, if God will, my soul is also soon to go—that soul, I repeat, if this be her nature and origin, will be blown away and destroyed immediately on quitting the body, as the many say? That can never be, my dear Simmias and Cebes. The truth rather is, that the soul which is pure at departing and draws after her no bodily taint, having never voluntarily during life had connection with the body, which she is ever avoiding, herself gathered into herself—and making such abstraction her perpetual study—which means that she has been a true disciple of philosophy; and therefore has in fact been always engaged in the practice of dying? For is not philosophy the study of death?

Certainly.

That soul, I say, herself invisible, departs to the invisible world—to the divine and immortal and rational: thither arriving, she is secure of bliss and is released from the error and folly of men, their fears and wild passions and all other human ills, and for ever dwells, as they say of the initiated, in company with the gods. Is not this true, Cebes? . . .

3. TRANSMIGRATION

. . . the soul which has been polluted, and is impure at the time of her departure, and is the companion and servant of the body always, and is in love with and fascinated by the body and by the desires and pleasures of the body, until she is led to believe that the truth only exists in a bodily form, which a man may touch and see and taste, and use for the purposes of his lusts—the soul, I mean, accustomed to hate and fear and avoid the intellectual principle, which to the bodily eye is dark and invisible, and can be attained only by philosophy—do you suppose that such a soul will depart pure and unalloyed?

ZEN MIND, BEGINNER'S MIND * *Shunryu Suzuki*

When we practice zazen our mind always follows our breathing. When we inhale, the air comes into the inner world. When we exhale, the air goes out to the outer world. The inner world is limitless, and the outer world is also limitless. We say "inner world" or "outer world," but actually there is just one whole world. In this limitless world, our throat is like a swinging door. The air comes in and goes out like someone passing through a swinging door. If you think, "I breathe," the "I" is extra. There is no you to say "I." What we call "I" is just a swinging door which moves when we inhale and when we exhale. It just moves; that is all. When your mind is pure and calm enough to follow this movement, there is nothing: no "I," no world, no mind nor body; just a swinging door.

From *Zen Mind, Beginner's Mind* (1970)

Impossible, he replied.

She is held fast by the corporeal, which the continual association and constant care of the body have wrought into her nature.

Very true.

And this corporeal element, my friend, is heavy and weighty and earthy, and is that element of sight by which a soul is depressed and dragged down again into the visible world, because she is afraid of the invisible and of the world below—prowling about tombs and sepulchres, near which, as they tell us, are seen certain ghostly apparitions of souls which have not departed pure, but are cloyed with sight and therefore visible.

That is very likely, Socrates.

Yes, that is very likely, Cebes; and these must be the souls, not of the good, but of the evil, which are compelled to wander about such places in payment of the penalty of their former evil way of life; and they continue to wander until through the craving after the corporeal which never leaves them, they are imprisoned finally in another body. And they may be supposed to find their prisons in the same natures which they have had in their former lives.

What natures do you mean, Socrates?

What I mean is that men who have followed after gluttony, and wantonness, and drunkenness, and have had no thought of avoiding them, would pass into asses and animals of that sort. What do you think?

I think such an opinion to be exceedingly probable.

And those who have chosen the portion of injustice, and tyranny, and violence, will pass into wolves, or into hawks and kites—whither else can we suppose them to go?

Yes, said Cebes; with such natures, beyond question.

And there is no difficulty, he said, in assigning to all of them places answering to their several natures and propensities?

There is not, he said.

Some are happier than others; and the happiest both in themselves and in the place to which they go are those who have practised the civil and social virtues which are called temperance and justice, and are acquired by habit and attention without philosophy and mind.

Why are they the happiest?

Because they may be expected to pass into some gentle and social kind which is like their own, such as bees or wasps or ants, or back again into the form of man, and just and moderate men may be supposed to spring from them.

Very likely.

No one who has not studied philosophy and who is not entirely pure at the time of his departure is allowed to enter the company of the Gods, but the lover of knowledge only. And this is the reason, Simmias and Cebes, why the true votaries of philosophy abstain from all fleshly lusts, and hold out against them and refuse to give themselves up to them—not because they fear poverty or the ruin of their families, like the lovers of money, and the world in general; nor like the lovers of power and honour, because they dread the dishonour or disgrace of evil deeds.

No, Socrates, that would not become them, said Cebes.

4. THE BODY AS THE SOUL'S PRISON

. . . they who have any care of their own souls, and do not merely live moulding and fashioning the body, say farewell to all this; they will not walk in the ways of the blind: and when philosophy offers them purification and release from evil, they feel that they ought not to resist her influence, and whither she leads they turn and follow.

What do you mean, Socrates?

I will tell you, he said. The lovers of knowledge are conscious that the soul was simply fastened and glued to the body—until philosophy received her, she could only view real existence through the bars of a prison, not in and through herself; she was wallowing in the mire of every sort of ignorance, and by reason of lust had become the principal accomplice in her own captivity. This was her original state; and then, as I was saying, and as the lovers of knowledge are well aware, philosophy, seeing how terrible was her confinement, of which she was to herself the cause, received and gently comforted her and sought to release her, pointing out that the eye and the ear and the other senses are full of deception, and persuading her to retire from them, and abstain from all but the necessary use of them, and be gathered up and collected into herself, bidding her trust in herself and her own pure apprehension of pure existence, and to mistrust whatever comes to her through other channels and is subject so variation; for such things are visible and tangible, but what she sees in her own nature is intelligible and invisible. And the soul of the true philosopher thinks that she ought not to resist this deliverance, and therefore abstains from pleasures and desires and pains and fears, as far as she is able; reflecting that when a man has great joys or sorrows or fears or desires, he suffers from them, not merely the sort of evil which might be anticipated—as for example, the loss of his health or property which he has sacrificed to his lusts—but an evil greater far, which is the greatest and worst of all evils, and one of which he never thinks.

What is it, Socrates? said Cebes.

The evil is that when the feeling of pleasure or pain is most intense, every soul of man imagines the objects of this intense feeling to be then plainest and truest: but this is not so, they are really the things of sight.

Very true.

And is not this the state in which the soul is most enthralled by the body?

How so?

Why, because each pleasure and pain is a sort of nail which nails and rivets the soul to the body, until she becomes like the body, and believes that to be true which the body affirms to be true; and from agreeing with the body and having the same delights she is obliged to have the same habits and haunts, and is not likely ever to be pure at her departure to the world below, but is always infected by the body; and so she sinks into another body and there germinates and grows, and has therefore no part in the communion of the divine and pure and simple. . . .

. . . A man of sense ought not to say, nor will I be very confident, that the description which I have given of the soul and her mansions is exactly true. But I do say that, inasmuch as the soul is shown to be immortal, he may venture to think, not improperly or unworthily, that something of the kind is true. The venture is a glorious one, and he ought to comfort himself with words like these, which is the reason why I lengthen out the tale. Wherefore, I say, let a man be of good cheer about his soul, who having cast away the pleasures and ornaments of the body as alien to him and working harm rather than good, has sought after the pleasures of knowledge; and has arrayed the soul, not in some foreign attire, but in her own proper jewels, temperance, and justice, and courage, and nobility, and truth—in these adorned she is ready to go on her journey to the world below, when her hour comes. You, Simmias and Cebes, and all other men, will depart at some time or other. Me already, as a tragic poet would say, the voice of fate calls. . . .

5. THE SOUL'S RELEASE

. . . We will do our best, said Crito: And in what way shall we bury you?

In any way that you like; but you must get hold of me, and take care that I do not run away from you. Then he turned to us, and added with a smile: I cannot make Crito believe that I am the same Socrates who has been talking and conducting the argument; he fancies that I am the other Socrates whom he will soon see, a dead body—and he asks, How shall he bury me? And though I have spoken many words in the endeavour to show that when I have drunk the poison I shall leave you and go to the joys of the blessed—these words of mine, with which I was comforting you and myself, have had, as I perceive, no effect upon Crito. And therefore I want you to be surety for me to him now, as at the trial he was surety to the judges for me: but let the promise be of another sort; for he was surety for me to the judges that I would remain, and you must be my surety to him that I shall not remain, but go away and depart; and then he will suffer less at my death, and not be grieved when he sees my body being burned or buried. I would not have him sorrow at my hard lot, or say at the burial, Thus we lay out Socrates, or, Thus we follow him to the grave or bury him; for false words are not only evil in themselves, but they infect the soul with evil. Be of good cheer then, my dear Crito, and say that you are burying my body only, and do with that whatever is usual, and what you think best. . . .

QUESTIONS FOR FURTHER REFLECTION

1. Some regard the passages in this selection as the origin of a dualistic view, according to which reality comprises two radically different sorts of things, one of which is immaterial and the other of which is material. Is that view actually expressed in these passages? Does Socrates commit himself to the view that humans have an immaterial part?

2. Suppose you have an immaterial soul and that it persists after your bodily death. How much, if any, of your psychology—your beliefs, memories, likes and dislikes, and so on—would have to go along with your soul in order to satisfy your desire for survival of bodily death?

52. EXPLORING THE CASE FOR LIFE AFTER DEATH

J. P. Moreland

J. P. Moreland is Professor of Philosophy at Talbot School of Theology, Biola University in La Mirada, California. He has four earned degrees: a B.S. in chemistry from the University of Missouri, a Th.M. in theology from Dallas Seminary, an M.A. in philosophy from the University of California–Riverside, and a Ph.D. in philosophy from the University of Southern California. Among his books are *Scaling the Secular City* (1987), *Christianity and the Nature of Science* (1989), *Does God Exist?* (1993), *The Creation Hypothesis* (1994), and *Body & Soul: Human Nature and the Crisis in Ethics* (2000). In the following selection, he sets out the case for life after death.

READING QUESTIONS

1. Into what categories does Moreland divide the argument for life after death?
2. Briefly list the empirical arguments.
3. Briefly list the nonempirical arguments.
4. What does "simplicity" refer to in this context?
5. What is substance dualism?

French philosopher Blaise Pascal once remarked that the immortality of the soul is something of such vital importance to us that one must have lost all feeling not to care about knowing the facts of the matter. Throughout history, the overwhelming majority of people have longed for and believed in some sort of immortality. Conceptions of the afterlife vary, ranging from the mere continuation of one's memory in one's work, the survival of one's ancestral line, the loss of personal identity through union with being, to full-blown post-mortem personal survival. The great theistic religions have advocated the more robust notion of life after death. According to the Judeo-Christian tradition, the human soul, while not by nature immortal, is nevertheless, capable of entering an intermediate disembodied state upon death and, eventually, being reunited with a resurrected body. On this view, the soul is immortal, not in the sense that it exists on its own forever without the sustaining power of God, but in the sense that once created, the individual person will never cease to be.

Is it reasonable to believe in life after death in this more robust sense? Can a case be made for it? I think the answer is yes, but before I present the broad contours of such a case, we need to get clear on the epistemological task involved. Sometimes people ask if there are proofs for the existence of God, immortality, and so forth, where by "proof" they mean something akin to mathematical certainty. So understood, there most likely is no "proof" for immortality, but this does not matter. The majority of things people know or justifiably believe fail to enjoy that degree of support and are none the worse for it.

In my view, the task before us is to assess the evidence for life after death to see how strong that evidence is. I believe that, apart from accepting the existence of God, there is evidence for an afterlife that is suggestive, but it falls short of placing an intellectual obligation on someone to believe in it. Put differently, apart from accepting the existence of God, there is some presumption in favor of an afterlife but it would be more reasonable to suspend judgment about life after death than to accept it. However, if the existence of the God of traditional theism is granted (and God's existence can itself be supported with rational arguments and evidence that do not require faith for their justification), then life after death is justified beyond reasonable doubt.

In what follows, I will present, in a brief and introductory way, some of the main pieces of evidence for immortality as defined above. Because this is an essay in philosophical argumentation, I shall limit the evidence to be considered to nonempirical philosophical considerations. I shall divide these philosophical considerations into two sorts of nonempirical evidence—theistic dependent and theistic independent arguments.

Before we proceed, I should mention briefly two sorts of empirical evidence that are often marshaled on behalf of life after death—Near Death Experiences (NDEs) and the historical evidence for the Resurrection of Jesus. First, consider the evidence of NDEs. A growing body of cases exists in which many people have, apparently, died in the medical sense, left their bodies, remained conscious and acquired knowledge while disembodied, and returned to their bodies to resume normal, bodily life.[1] Less than a month ago, one of my own students had a grandfather who died, saw and heard from a vantage point near the ceiling of the hospital room two doctors disagreeing about whether or not to attempt resuscitation, observed his own body, returned to that body and, upon awakening, began to argue fiercely with the doctor who was contending against resuscitation! During the experience he saw his own dead body on the operating table.

The evidence for life after death from NDEs is considerable. Critics respond to it by attempting to explain such experiences in naturalistic terms, for example, as mere results of oxygen depravation of the brain. While this may explain some of the cases, it clearly fails to account for those in which the disembodied person gains knowledge that simply could not have been obtained in normal ways. In one such case, a girl named Katie watched and reported minute particulars about what her family members were doing at home while she was comatose in the hospital.[2] These details were corroborated by family members.

Cases like these simply defy naturalistic explanation. Others argue that, even if real, NDEs only justify belief in life after death for a very short period after leaving the body, they do not justify everlasting life. Strictly speaking, this rebuttal is correct. On the other hand, if the self is capable of surviving such a traumatic event as biological death, then it could survive forever and, moreover, it is not clear what would cause it to cease to exist, once it was disembodied. In any case, the evidence of NDEs is crucial to the case for life after death, but I shall not consider them in more detail,

---

[1] For a presentation and assessment of the evidence from NDEs, see Gary R. Habermas, J. P. Moreland, *Beyond Death* (Wheaton, Illinois: Crossway, 1998), chapters 7–9.
[2] Ibid., pp. 187–188.

RESURRECTION ✳ *Peter van Inwagen*

It is part of the Christian faith that all men who share in the sin of Adam must die. What does it mean to say that I must die? Just this: that one day I shall be composed entirely of nonliving matter; that is, I shall be a corpse. It is not part of the Christian faith that I must at any time be totally annihilated or disintegrate. (One might note that Christ, whose story is supposed to provide the archetype for the story of each man's resurrection, became a corpse but did not, even in His human nature, cease to exist.) It is of course true that men apparently cease to exist: those who are cremated, for example. But it contradicts nothing in the creeds to suppose that this is not what really happens, and that God preserves our corpse contrary to all appearance. . . . Perhaps at the moment of each man's death, God removes his corpse and replaces it with a simulacrum which is what is burned or rots. Or perhaps God is not quite so wholesale as this: perhaps He removes for "safekeeping" only the "core person"—the brain and central nervous system—or even some special part of it. These are details.

I take it that this story shows that the resurrection is a feat an almighty being *could* accomplish. . . . Of course one might wonder *why* God would go such lengths to make it look as if most people not only die but pass into complete nothingness. This is a difficult question. I think it can be given a plausible answer, but not apart from a discussion of the nature of religious belief. I will say just this. If corpses inexplicably disappeared no matter how carefully they were guarded, or inexplicably refused to decay and were miraculously resistant to the most persistent and ingenious attempts to destroy them, then we should be living in a world in which observable events that were *obviously* miraculous, *obviously* due to the intervention of a power beyond Nature, happened with monotonous regularity. In such a world we should all believe in the supernatural: its existence would be the best explanation for the observed phenomena. If Christianity is true, God wants us to believe in the supernatural. But experience shows us that, if there is a God, He does not do what He very well *could* do: provide us with a ceaseless torrent of public, undeniable evidence of a power outside the nature order. And perhaps it is not hard to think of good reasons for such a policy.

From "The Possibility of Resurrection," *International Journal for Philosophy of Religion*, 1978.

preferring instead to focus on distinctively philosophical issues.

The second empirical argument for life after death centers on making a historical case for the literal, bodily resurrection of Jesus of Nazareth from the dead, and arguing that since he rose from the dead, this qualifies him to speak authoritatively about life after death because his resurrection (1) provides evidence that he was the Son of God and (2) means that he has been to the afterlife, returned, and told us about what is there. Again, the details of this argument must be set aside.[3]

However, one point must be made clear about the way the argument is presented by its defenders. They do not start by assuming the Bible is true or a revelation from God. Rather, they use general historical arguments to justify the claim that the New Testament documents are generally reliable, that there is sufficient historical evidence to establish beyond reasonable doubt certain facts about Jesus that are best explained by His literal resurrection from the dead. Obviously, assessing the strength of this argument would require, among other things, analyzing the his-

---

[3] For more on this, see Michael Wilkins, J. P. Moreland, eds., *Jesus Under Fire* (Grand Rapids: Zondervan, 1995; Paul Copan, Ronald

Tacelli, eds., *Jesus' Resurrection: Fact or Figment?* (Downers Grove, Illinois: Inter Varsity Press, 2000).

torical evidence, discussing arguments for and against belief in miracles, and so forth.

1. THEISTIC DEPENDENT NONEMPIRICAL EVIDENCE

When most of us wonder about life after death, we find ourselves thinking about God as well. This attitude is quite natural and proper, for while it is possible to believe in God without believing in life after death (and conversely), the two notions do fit together in a rational, mutually reinforcing way. In fact, if we grant the existence of a theistic God, especially the Judeo-Christian God, then belief in immortality is overwhelmingly probable, beyond a reasonable doubt. Consider the arguments.

Kinship with the Divine

Take the argument from kinship with the divine. It has at least three forms. First, humans are made in the image of God and are like God in many ways: We can transcend our bodies by thinking, loving, feeling, and willing. One of the ways we resemble God is in possessing a form of immortality.

Unfortunately, this argument is not a good one. According to theism, only God possesses a natural immortality in himself. Everything else, including the human body and human soul, is sustained in existence by God. Immortality is not a natural aspect of what we are—instead, it flows from what God does on our behalf. He holds us (and the entire universe) in existence.

On the other hand, the kinship-with-the-divine type of argument might be used in another way. God is a pure, unchanging spirit and is suited for life in a place like heaven (more accurately, heaven is a suitable place for a being like God). Humans are like God in this respect. Perhaps we are like God in this respect. We were meant to live a type of life suited for a heavenly mode of existence.

This idea is certainly plausible. Most of us have experienced periodic longings for a different world, and these longings may be indicators of our kinship with the divine in this sense. Still, while suggestive, the argument is far from conclusive.

There is yet a third way our kinship with God might be used to argue for life after death. If we are made in God's image, we have an incredible degree of intrinsic value as persons. From this notion, the following moral principle seems reasonable: It is wrong, all things being equal, to annihilate or extinguish something with intrinsic value, especially of the sort possessed by God and those made in his image.

Consider things with lesser intrinsic value than humans, say a work of art. All things being equal, it is wrong to destroy a work of art and take it out of existence, because, among other things, the universe loses something of value. Similarly, it would be wrong for anyone, even God, to annihilate a creature made in God's image, for such an act would remove the value sustained in being by that creature's existence, and it would treat the person as a mere means to an end (say, of getting rid of him) instead of as an end in himself.

> This argument was stated nicely by philosopher Geddes MacGregor: If there is a Creator God who is infinitely benevolent as well as the source of all values, then he must be committed to the conservation of values. The highest values we know are experiences of the fulfillment of ideal purposes by individual persons. The existence of these values depends upon persons. God must, therefore, be the conserver of persons. Every argument for theism is an argument for the preservation of all persons whose extinction would seem to entail a failure on God's part in his benevolent purpose.[4]

This last argument seems to be a strong one. If the theistic God exists and has created us in His image, it seems unreasonable to think that God would fail to conserve those made in His image whom He loves.

Divine Justice

A second major argument flows from our sense of justice. It is obvious that in this life goods and evils, rewards and punishments, are not evenly distributed. Inequities abound. Good people often live miserable lives, and evil people often prosper. If God is infinitely just, as theism affirms, he must rectify these injustices. Because that rectification does not take place in this life, it must take place in the life to come.

[4] Geddes McGregor, *Introduction to Religious Philosophy* (Washington, D.C.: University Press of America, 1981), p. 206.

This argument has some force, but it is inconclusive for at least two reasons. It would not apply to those who have not suffered serious inequities in this life (if there are such people!). Further, it does not prove that the afterlife is unending. Perhaps life's inequities could be balanced in a finite period of life after death.

Divine Love

This third argument goes like this: As infinite, pure love, God intends the highest good for his creatures. Humans has been made for communion with God, and the highest good would be for that communion between finite lovers and the infinite lover to be endless. Further, God has placed in our hearts a desire for eternity, and it would be cruel for him to frustrate that desire. The same love that moved Him to create in the first place, and to place in us a desire to live forever with God, that same love is what guarantees our eternal, face-to-face communion with God for eternity.

Although these arguments are based on theism, if theism *is* rational they hold a lot of weight. In fact, some philosophers and theologians have argued that the only reason for believing in life after death is that it follows from a prior belief in theism. Whether or not this statement is too strong, it seems true that if belief in the theistic God, especially the Christian God, is rational, then so is believe in life after death relative to that prior belief.

2. THEISTIC INDEPENDENT NONEMPIRICAL EVIDENCE

Two general arguments for life after death have been offered that do not depend epistemologically on a prior belief in the existence of God: the argument from desire and arguments from the nature of consciousness and the human self.

The Argument from Desire

Briefly put, the argument from desire looks like this:

1. The desire for life after death is a natural desire.
2. Every natural desire corresponds to some real state of affairs that can fulfill it.
3. Therefore, the desire for life after death corresponds to some real state of affairs—namely life after death—that fulfills it.

Let's consider two elaborations of this basic argument by two of its most famous advocates—Thomas Aquinas and C. S. Lewis. We will begin with Aquinas.[5]

According to Aquinas, things in the world have natures that define what those things are. Fido is in the class of dogs because he possesses dogness. Beatrice is in the class of humans because she possesses humanness. Dogness and humanness are the natures of Fido and Beatrice, respectively. Now a thing has a set of natural tendencies, aspirations, and desires—conscious or unconscious—grounded in its nature. Dogs have a natural tendency to bark; humans have a natural tendency to acquire knowledge and use language.

Now, Aquinas continues, a thing has a natural tendency to maintain itself in existence in a manner natural and appropriate to the kind of thing it is. Furthermore, among the things that have knowledge, desires naturally arise according to the type of knowledge possessed. An apple does not possess knowledge. On the other hand various mammals, such as dogs, possess sensory knowledge; they have sensory experiences of particular things immediately present before them. And humans have intellectual knowledge; they can contemplate general ideas, such as the class of dogs, triangles, or even existence itself.

When we apply these different kinds of knowledge to the knowledge of existence, animals only know existence here and now because that is the only notion of existence of which they can have a particular sensory awareness. But humans are intellectual creatures and, as such, have an intellectual understanding of everlasting life. Since natural desires ensue upon, or flow from, the knowledge possessed by a living thing, then humans have a natural desire for everlasting life.

Finally, according to Aquinas, natural desires are not in vain. For every natural desire there is a real state of affairs that has the potential to respond to or fulfill that desire. Therefore, there is such a thing as everlasting life.

C. S. Lewis offered a different form of the argument from desire.[6] He claims that it is not necessarily egoistic to desire our own good and hope for happiness;

---

[5] Thomas Aquinas, *Summa Theologica*, Pt. 1, Q. 75, Art. 6.
[6] C. S. Lewis, *The Weight of Glory* (Grand Rapids, MI: Eerdmans, 1949), pp. 1–15.

indeed, it can be quite appropriate. This is because there are different kinds of rewards, and some are proper because they have a natural connection with the things we do to earn them. Money is not the natural reward for love (one is mercenary to marry for money) because money is foreign to the desires that ought to accompany love. By contrast, victory is a natural reward for battle. It is a proper reward because it is not tacked onto the activity for which the reward is given, but rather victory is the consummation of the activity itself.

A third case is a schoolboy enjoying Greek poetry. In the beginning, he works at grammar as a mercenary (to get good grades, avoid punishment, etc.) because he has no idea what the enjoyment of Greek poetry would be like. The reward he will get (enjoying Greek poetry) will, in fact, be the proper reward for his activities, but he does not know that at the beginning.

Believers are like the schoolboy. Those who have attained heaven or who mature as believers desire everlasting communion with God as a proper reward for the consummation of our efforts on earth. But when we begin the religious life, we often obey God for other reasons (to please others, out of fear of punishment, and so on).

Now, according to Lewis, we all desire heaven, although that desire can be hidden from us. Sometimes we desire lesser, finite goods (such as beauty), but these are symbols of and pointers to the transtemporal, transfinite good that is our real destiny. The desire for heaven is a desire that no natural happiness will satisfy.

Furthermore, our natural desires are indicators of what the world is like. If we have a natural desire for something, then that thing must exist. We may desire food and not get it, but we would not be hungry in a world where food and eating did not exist. Again, a man may love a woman and not win her, but falling in love would not occur in a sexless world. By the same token, someone may desire heaven and not obtain it, but such a desire would not occur in a world where heaven was not real. Therefore, life after death must be real.

As you might imagine, the argument from desire has had its critics. First, some claim that the desire for heaven is just an example of ethical egoism: the view that an act or desire is right if and only if it is in the person's own self-interest. But Lewis's argument appears to answer this objection. Some desires are proper for humans, and seeking to meet them is part of what we ought to do, part of what it is supposed to mean to be human in the first place. Additionally, one could desire heaven for other reasons besides self-interest. We might desire it because it is simply right to seek the type of life heaven offers. Finally, the desire for heaven can be an expression of the fact that a person views himself/herself as an intrinsically valuable end. Since a person sees himself/herself as a creature of intrinsic value, one's desire for heaven is a way of treating oneself as a person of value, as an intrinsically valuable end. So this first objection fails.

A second objection is this: We simply don't desire heaven, or at least many people do not. But this objection does not appear decisive either. One could reply that abnormal people do not desire what they ought to. For instance, anorexic people lose their desire for food, which is self-destructive. One could also argue that people who desire finite goods are really desiring in them, or at least in addition to them, an eternal good.

It must be admitted that both of these points, while plausible, are nevertheless controversial. In support of the first point, one could note that the vast majority of people throughout history have desired an afterlife of some type. Even those who have claimed not to desire it have found themselves with such a desire in unguarded moments, especially when close to death. Regarding the second point, one could make a case that finite goods leave people unsatisfied. No matter how many finite goods people accumulate, they still have a longing for something more, something that, in fact, only eternity with God and others could satisfy. But neither of these responses is conclusive against this criticism, though they do place it in some doubt.

A third criticism against the argument from desire is that even if there are such things as natural desires, and even if people have a desire for heaven, the desire is not a natural one but a learned one. But this objection is problematic also. The widespread endurance of the desire—it seems present wherever humans live, regardless of the period in history or the culture—lends support to the idea that it is natural. Furthermore, a case could be made that the loss of the desire is a learned response, perhaps a defense mechanism of repression or suppression. But again, it is hard to weigh the strength of this third criticism.

A fourth criticism points out that there is no natural desire for heaven for the simple reason that there are no natural desires because there are no natures (e.g., a human nature) to have them. This criticism raises a plethora of difficult issues that are well beyond the scope of this chapter. But suffice it to say that if the notion of a nature, in this case *human* nature, is a reasonable one, then this objection loses its force, and a number of philosophers and theologians have believed that natures exist.

A final criticism is the claim that even if there are natural desires, they are, in fact, sometimes frustrated. There is no necessary connection between a desire and what the world is like. A response to this objection could go something like this: There is, in fact, a very large correlation between what appear to be natural desires and the existence of objects that could potentially satisfy them. Think of what human life would be like if, in the majority of cases, nothing existed that answered to the basic, natural desires humans have. Therefore, it is wrong to say that no evidence exists to show that our natural desires are in vain. In fact, the majority of human experience indicates that this principle is true. Our natural desires are, in fact, good indicators that objects really exist to satisfy those desires.

Where does this leave us? In my opinion, the argument from desire is suggestive, but it is inconclusive. The criticisms just listed indicate that the argument has problems, and one would not be foolish in rejecting it. On the other hand, one would not be irrational to accept it either, for the argument is plausible and answers do exist for the criticisms listed above. The value of the argument from desire will comedown to one's assessment of the strength of the criticisms of the argument vs. the argument itself and the responses to those criticisms.

Arguments from Mind/Body Dualism

Some have offered arguments for immortality from the nature of consciousness and the self. In this section, we shall state and reject one such argument from the alleged simplicity of the self. This will be followed by a brief presentation of some important arguments for the immateriality of mental properties and consciousness, and of the substantial self or ego that has consciousness, along with an assessment of the role that property and substance dualism play in the case for life after death.

Arguments from the Simplicity of the Soul Quite a number of thinkers have argued that there is something about the very nature of the human self that implies or supports life after death. The most prominent is the argument based on the alleged simplicity of the soul. Advocates of this approach include Plato and G. M. E. McTaggart. *Simplicity* in this case means that the soul has no parts; it is not a complex entity that can lose parts and still remain a soul. For example, a human being can lose an arm or leg and still be human. A soul has no parts as human bodies do, therefore, all a soul can lose is *all* it is. The argument looks like this:

1. There are two ways for something to be destroyed: annihilation (something simply pops out of existence, as it were, all at once) and through separation and loss of parts.
2. Science does not give examples of annihilation. Rather, physical objects are destroyed through the loss of their parts as they leave or rearrange to form new things. For example, a chair ceases to be when its legs, seat, and back are torn apart and shredded. In general, our experience does not give us examples of annihilation. Thus, the most reasonable way to understand a case of ceasing-to-be is to treat it as an example of disassociation of parts.
3. Physical objects are complex entities in that they are complex wholes composed of a number of different parts. We know from intuition and our experience of the unity of consciousness that the soul, being an immaterial, spiritual substance, is a basic, simple entity—that is, it is not a heap or complex of parts as a chair or computer is.
4. Therefore, the soul is immortal, because there is no good reason to believe it can be annihilated or can lose parts.

How should we evaluate this argument? Premise 1 seems reasonable enough. It accounts for the vast majority, and perhaps all, of the cases of ceasing to exist that we encounter in daily life, so let us agree to accept it.

Similarly, let us agree to accept premise 2. In science, one of the main points of advocating the exis-

DEATH * *Thomas Nagel*

There will be a last day, a last hour, a last minute of consciousness, and that will be it. Off the edge.

To grasp this it isn't enough to think only of a particular stream of consciousness coming to an end. The external view of death is psychological as well as physical: it includes the idea that the person who you are will have no more thoughts, experiences, memories, intensions, desires, and so on. That inner life will be finished. But the recognition that the life of a particular person in the world will come to an end is not what I am talking about. To grasp your own death from within you must try to look *forward* to it—to see it as a *prospect*.

Is this possible? It might seem that there could be no form of thought about your own death except either an external view, in which the world is pictured is continuing after your life stops, or an internal view that sees only this side of death—that includes only the finitude of your expected future consciousness. But this is not true. There is also something that can be called the expectation of nothingness, and though the mind tends to veer away from it, it is an unmistakable experience, always startling, often frightening, and very different from the familiar recognition that your life will go on for only a limited time—that you probably have less than thirty years and certainly less than a hundred. The positive prospect of the end of subjective time, though it is logically inseparable from these limits, is something distinct.

From *Mortal Questions* (1979).

tence of atoms is to explain change in terms of the separation and recombination of those atoms. For example, when a piece of paper is burned up, this change is viewed as a chemical rearrangement of the atoms that make up the paper. They rearrange and combine with oxygen in the process of burning, and they form new chemical compounds.

The main problem with the argument is found in premise 3. The argument assumes the soul is a simple, noncomplex entity, but there are good reasons for rejecting this assumption. It is true that ordinary physical objects (e.g., tables) are not simple, but complex. One reason for this is that these objects are extended throughout a region of space. Consider a round, five-inch disk. The left half of the disk cannot be identical to the right half, or else the disk would not have *two* halves. In general, physical objects must be complex, because they must have different parts to occupy different points of space throughout the region they occupy.

On the other hand, assuming a traditional view of the soul for the sake or argument, some people have thought that the soul is simple because it is not a spatially extended entity. Unfortunately, while it is true that all spatially extended things are nonsimple (i.e., composed of parts), it is not true that all nonspatially extended things, such as the soul, are simple. In fact, we can reject the soul's simplicity on grounds other than its relation to spatial extension. As we shall see shortly, the soul is capable of having desires, beliefs, thoughts, sensations of color, sound, and so forth. A thought of love is not the same thing as a sensation of red. Further, the soul contains various capacities that differ from each other—a vast array of intellectual, emotional, and volitional capacities. These capacities are contained within the soul itself and they differ from each other. Thus, the soul contains internal differences, which means it could not be simple. Tables are composed of separable parts, parts such as the legs that can exist outside the wholes of which they are parts. Assuming the existence of the soul as traditionally conceived, it is not composed of separable parts, but it does seem to have various inseparable parts within it—parts that cannot exist outside the wholes of which they are parts for example, various intellectual, emotional, and volitional capacities.

Therefore, as it stands, the argument from simplicity does not work. However, good arguments exist that justify belief that consciousness and mental properties are immaterial, and that the ego or self is immaterial. The former belief is called property dualism and the latter is substance dualism. In what follows, arguments for the nonphysical nature of consciousness and the self are offered and an assessment is provided of the contribution to a case for life after death from the truth of property and substance dualism.

Property Dualism   Dualists disagree with physicalists. According to dualists, genuinely mental entities are real. As with matter, it is hard to give a *definition* of mental entities. But *examples* of mental entities are easy to supply. First, there are various kinds of *sensations*: experiences of colors, sounds, smells, tastes, textures, pains, and itches. Sensations are individual things that occur at particular times. One can have a sensation of red after looking in a certain direction or by closing one's eyes and daydreaming. An experience of pain will arise at a certain time, say, after one is stuck with a pin.

Further, sensations are natural kinds of things that have, as their very essence, the felt quality or sensory property that makes them what they are. Part of the very essence of a pain is the felt quality it has; part of the very essence of a red sensation is the presentation of a particular shade of color to one's consciousness. Sensations are not identical to things outside a person's body—for instance, a feeling of pain is not the same thing as being stuck with a pin and shouting, "Ouch!" Sensations are essentially characterized by a certain conscious feel, and thus, they presuppose consciousness for their existence and description. If there were no conscious beings, there would be no sensations.

Second, there are things called *propositional attitudes*: having a certain mental attitude involving a proposition that is part of a that-clause. For example, one can hope, desire, fear, dread, wish, think, believe that P where P may be the proposition "The Royals are a great baseball team." Propositional attitudes include at least two components. First, there is the attitude itself. Hopes, fears, dreads, wishes, thoughts, and so on are all different attitudes, different states of consciousness, and they are all different from each other based on their conscious feel. A hope is a different form of consciousness from an episode of fear. A hope that it will rain is different from a fear that it will rain. What's the difference? A hope has a very different conscious feel from a fear.

Second, they all have a content or a meaning embedded in the propositional attitude—namely, the propositional content of one's consciousness while one is having the propositional attitude. One's hope that P differs from one's hope that Q because P and Q are different propositions or meanings in one's consciousness. If there were no conscious selves, there would be no propositional attitudes. One's hope that it will rain is different from one's hope that taxes will be cut. The contents of these two hopes have quite different meanings.

Third, there are *acts of free will or purposings*. What is a purposing? If, unknown to me, my arm is tied down and I still try to raise it, then the purposing is the "trying to bring about" the event of raising my arm. Intentional actions are episodes of volition, exercises of active power, by conscious selves wherein and whereby they do various actions for the sake of certain ends. They are acts of will performed by conscious selves.

The following argument has been proffered for property/event dualism: Once one gets an accurate description of consciousness (see above), it becomes clear that mental properties/events are not identical to physical properties/events. Mental states are characterized by their intrinsic, subjective, inner, private, qualitative feel, made present to a subject by first person introspection. For example, a pain is a certain felt hurtfulness. Mental states cannot be intrinsically described by physical language, even if through study of the brain one can discover the causal/functional relations between mental and brain states.

In general, mental states have some or all of the following features, none of which is a physical feature of anything: Mental states like pains have an intrinsic, raw conscious feel. There is a "what-it-is-like" to a pain. Most, if not all mental states have intentionality, that is, they are of or about things, but ofness is not a physical attribute and no purely physical state has intentionality. Mental states are inner, private, and known by first person, direct introspection. Any way one has of knowing about a physical property of a physical entity is available to everyone else, including ways of knowing about the physical attributes in one's brain. But a subject has a way of knowing about his mental properties/states not available to others—through introspection.

Mental states are constituted by self-presenting properties. One can be aware of the external, physical world only by means of one's mental states, but one need not be aware of one's mental states by means of anything else. For example, it is by way of a sensation of red that one is aware of an apple, but one need not be aware of the sensation of red by way of another sensation. Mental states are necessarily owned, and, in fact, one's mental states could not have belonged to someone else. However, no physical state is necessarily owned, much less necessarily owned by a specific subject.

Some sensations are vague, for example, a sensation of a object may be fuzzy or vague, but no physical state is vague. Some sensations are pleasurable or unpleasurable, but nothing physical has these properties. A cut in the knee is, strictly speaking, not unpleasurable. It is the pain event caused by the cut that is unpleasurable. Mental states can have the property of familiarity (e.g., when a desk looks familiar to someone), but familiarity is not a feature of a physical state.

Since mental states have these features and physical states do not, then mental states are not identical to physical states. Some physicalists have responded by denying that consciousness has the features in question. For example, dualists have argued that thinking events are not spatially located even though the brain event associated with them is. Physicalists counter that thoughts are, after all, located in certain places of the brain. But there is no reason to accept this claim, since dualists can account for all the spatial factors in terms of the brain events causally related to thoughts. Moreover, through introspection subjects seem to know quite a bit about the features of their thoughts and spatial location is not one of them. Similar responses are offered by dualists for physicalist claims about the other features of consciousness.

Substance Dualism One argument for substance dualism derives from what we seem to know about ourselves from first person introspection. It can be summarized in this manner. When we reflect upon ourselves, certain things become evident to us. First, we know that we *have* a body but are not the same thing as our body. Also, even though my self contains a plurality of contents—different thoughts, pains, feelings, desires, sensory experiences, episodes of willing—I am not identical to a bundle of those contents, nor am I a combination of those contents. My thoughts, feelings, and so on could not exist without me. But my being as known to me in introspection could not be due to a certain combination of the contents that compose me.

Moreover, the unity of consciousness cannot be treated as a collective unity of separate entities for the following reason. Consider one's awareness of a complex fact, say one's own visual field consisting of awareness of several objects at once, including a number of different surface areas of each object. Now one may claim that such a unified awareness of one's visual field consists in the fact that there are a number of different (gross or spiritual) physical parts each of which is aware only of part of and not the whole of the complex fact. However, this will not work, because it cannot account for the fact that there is a single, unitary awareness of the entire visual field. Only a single, uncomposed mental substance can account for the unity of one's visual field or, indeed, the unity of consciousness in general. I am not a heap or combination of anything. Instead, I am a *center* of consciousness, an irreducible *I*, an *ego* that has my various mental contents but is different from them and more basic than they. I could exist without any one of them, but they could not exist without me.

These basic intuitions about the self can be strengthened with a thought experiment. Suppose it becomes possible someday to perform a brain operation upon a person in such a way that exactly half of his/her brain is transplanted into each of two different brainless bodies. The person operated on, we'll call Sally. Let's imagine that the left hemisphere of her brain is placed in body 1, and the right hemisphere of her brain goes into body 2.

Suppose further that, upon recovery, each of the two previously brainless bodies manifest the same character traits and have the same memories as Sally did. After transplantation, there are two persons, but Sally cannot be identical to both of them because one thing cannot be the same as two things. It may be that Sally ceased to exist, and the two other entities are two to-tally new people. Or it may be that Sally survived and is now identical to the brain-filled body 1 (or vice versa), so that only one new person—the brain-filled body 2 (or vice versa)—came into being as a result of the operation.

We learn two things from the example. First, a person is not identical to her brain, body or to her memories and character traits. Persons *have* these things, they are not *identical to* them or to a collection of them. In this thought experiment, we know all the facts about where the relevant brains and bodies are and the various memories and character traits, but we do not know where Sally is. Therefore, there is more to Sally than her brain, body, and mental states. Substance dualists claim that this "more" resides in a substantial soul that has a body and that contains mental states.

The second lesson is this: Persons are not capable of partial identity and survival as are physical objects. If you break a table in half and use each half to build two new tables, it makes sense to say that the original table partially survives and is partly present in each of the new tables. But in our brain operation example, the following four options are the only possible ways to understand what happened: (1) Sally ceases to be and two new persons come to be; (2) Sally survives and is identical to body 1, and a new person, body 2, comes to be; (3) Sally survives and is identical to body 2, and a new person, body 1, comes to be; (4) Sally partially survives in bodies 1 and 2. Although option 4 may make sense of physical objects like tables, it is not a reasonable option with regard to persons.

To see why option 4 is not a good one, consider another experiment. Suppose a mad surgeon captures you and announces that he is going to transplant the left hemisphere of your brain into one body and the right hemisphere into another body. After surgery, he is going to torture one of the resultant persons and re-ward the other one with a gift of a million dollars. You can choose which of the two persons, A or B, will be tortured and which will be rewarded. It is clear that whichever way you choose, your choice would be a risk. Perhaps you will cease to exist and be neither A nor B. But it is also possible that you will be either A or B. However, one thing does not seem possible—your being partially A and partially B. For in that case

you would have reason to approach the surgery with both a feeling of joyous expectation and horrified dread! Why? After the operation you would simulta-neously experience torture and reward because you yourself would partially be A and partially be B! But it is hard to make sense of such a mixed anticipation be-cause *there will be no person after the surgery who will experience such a mixed fate.* Partial survival, at least when it comes to persons, does not seem to make sense. No sense can be given to the notion that a per-son is partly in that body and partly in this one. Per-sons are deep unities, not mere collections or combi-nations of things that admit of partial survival like physical objects.

Our basic awareness of ourselves and the nature of the unity of consciousness, as illustrated in the two thought experiments above, indicate that there is more to a person than his/her body, brain and consciousness. And as Richard Swinburne has argued, "My conclu-sion—that truths about persons are other than truths about their bodies and parts thereof—is, I suggest, forced upon anyone who reflects seriously on the fact of the unity of consciousness over time and at a time. A framework of thought which makes sense of this fact is provided if we think of a person as body plus soul, such that the continuing of the soul alone guarantees the continuing of the person."[7]

Thought experiments have rightly been central to debates about personal identity. For example, we are often invited to consider a situation in which two per-sons switch bodies, brains, or personality traits or in which a person exists disembodied. In these thought experiments, someone argues in the following way: Be-cause a certain state of affairs S (e.g., Smith existing disembodied) is conceivable, this provides justification for thinking that S is metaphysically possible. Now if S is possible, then certain implications follow about what is/is not essential to personal identity (e.g., Smith is not essentially a body). To be sure, judgments that a state of affairs is possible/impossible grounded in con-ceivability are not infallible. They can be wrong. Still, they provide strong evidence for genuine possibility/ impossibility.

---

[7] Richard Swinburne, *The Evolution of the Soul* (Oxford: Clarendon, 1986), p. 160.

REMEMBRANCES OF PAST LIVES * *C.J. Ducasse*

Moreover, there is occasional testimony of recollection of a previous life, where the recollection is quite circumstantial and even alleged to have been verified. One such case may be cited here without any claim that it establishes preexistence, but only to substantiate the assertion that specific testimony of this kind exists. . . .

It is that of "The Rebirth of Katsugoro," recorded in detail and with many affidavits respecting the facts, in an old Japanese document translated by Lafcadio Hearn. [L. Hearn, *Gleanings in Buddha Fields*, Chap. X.] The story is, in brief, that a young boy called Katsugoro, son of a man called Genzo in the village of Nakanomura, declared that in his preceding life a few years before he had been called Tozo; that he was then the son of a farmer called Kyubei and his wife Shidzu in a village called Hodokubo; that his father had died and had been replaced in the household by a man called Hanshiro; and that he himself, Tozo, had died of small-pox at the age of six, a year after his father. He described his burial, the appearance of his former parents, and their house. He eventually was taken to their village, where such persons were found. He himself led the way to their house and recognized them; and they confirmed the facts he had related. Further, he pointed to a shop and a tree, saying that they had not been there before; and this was true.

Testimony of this kind is directly relevant to the question of rebirth. The recollections related in this case are much too circumstantial to be dismissed as instances of the familiar and psychologically well-understood illusions of *déja vu*, and although the testimony that they were verified is not proof that they were, it cannot be rejected *a priori*. Its reliability has to be evaluated in terms of the same standards by which the validity of testimonial evidence concerning anything else is appraised.

From *Nature, Mind and Death* (1951).

Let us apply these insights about conceivability and possibility to a second argument for substance dualism, called the modal argument. The argument comes in many forms, but it may be fairly stated as follows:

1. The law of identity: If x is identical to y, then whatever is true of x is true of y and vice versa.
2. I can conceive of myself as existing disembodied.
3. If I can conceive of some state of affairs S that S possibly obtains, then I have good grounds for believing of S that S is possible.
4. Therefore, I have good grounds for believing of myself that it is possible for me to exist and be disembodied.
5. If some entity x is such that it is possible for x to exist without y, then x is not identical to y and y is not essential to x.
6. My body is not such that it is possible to exist disembodied, that is, my body is essentially a body.
7. Therefore, I have good grounds for believing of myself that I am not identical to my body and that my physical body is not essential to me.

A parallel argument can be advanced in which the notions of a body and disembodiment are replaced with the notions of physical objects. So understood, the argument would imply the conclusion that I have good grounds for thinking that I am not identical to a physical particular nor is any physical particular essential to me. A parallel argument can also be developed to show that possessing the ultimate capacities of sensation, thought, belief, desire, and volition are essential to me, that is, I am a substantial soul or mind.

I cannot undertake a full defense of the argument here, but it would be useful to a say a bit more regarding (2). There are a number of things about ourselves and our bodies of which we are aware that ground the conceivability expressed in (2). I am aware that I am unextended (I am "fully present" at each location in my body as Augustine claimed), that I am not a complex aggregate of separable parts nor am I the sort of thing that can be composed of physical parts, but rather, that I am a basic, unity of inseparable faculties (of mind, volitions, emotion, etc.) that sustains absolute sameness through change, and that I am not capable of gradation (I cannot become two-thirds a person). In near death experiences, people report themselves to have been disembodied. They are not aware of having bodies in any sense. Rather, they are aware of themselves as unified egos that exemplify sensations, thoughts, and so forth.

All of these factors imply that people can conceive of themselves as existing in a disembodied state, that this provides grounds for thinking that this is a real possibility, and, thus, I cannot be my body nor is my body essential to me, regardless of whether or not there is life after death. Note carefully, that if successful, taken alone this argument does not provide grounds for life after death; it provides evidence that a person is not identical to his body.

Dualism and Life After Death   Property and substance dualism lends support to belief in life after death for at least three reasons.

First, property/substance dualism makes eternal life more *plausible* and *intelligible* than does physicalism. If physicalism were true, then with the death of the body, the person would become extinct. The most likely way eternal life could be possible would be for God to recreate an individual out of nothing at the final resurrection, or to reconstruct the resurrected body around some preserved body part. While not impossible, this physicalist view is hard to harmonize with the traditional theist commitment to a disembodied intermediate state between death and the final resurrection. It also has difficulties accounting for personal identity in the afterlife. What, exactly, would make the re-created person identical to the individual who had died years earlier? When we ponder eternal life, we are interested in a survival where I am literally the same person who survives death and exists in the afterlife. We are not interested in becoming extinct at death and having a double recreated who looks like us or has our memories or character traits. What we want to know is whether we ourselves will live on after the death of our bodies.

The substance dualist has a way of making sense out of my literal survival of death. The person who lives in the afterlife will be the same person as I am now, because that person will have my soul. Sameness of soul is what constitutes personal identity through change, even death. I am the same person I was at childhood and who will be in the afterlife because the very same soul will exist at all those times. Some physicalists believe that they can answer these objections and provide an account of literal personal identity in an afterlife.[8] The issues in this discussion are beyond the scope of this essay, but suffice it to say that many thinkers have held that a dualist understanding of the self is easier to harmonize with literal personal identity in the afterlife than is physicalism, though not all agree with them.

Second, the nature of the human soul *lends more support to* the notion of eternal life than merely making it plausible and intelligible. Throughout the history of traditional theism, the classic understanding of living things has included the notion that animals, as well as humans, have souls. On this view, animals are not merely automatons, capable of exhaustive description in terms of the laws of chemistry and physics. Rather, animals are living things with a principle of life in them (an animal soul), and they have sensory awarenesses, feel pain, and enjoy a certain form of sentient life.

Even though traditional theism has been quite clear about the existence of animal souls, there has been no consensus about the existence of animals in the afterlife, some theists favoring the idea, some arguing against it, some remaining agnostic. Thus, the mere presence of dualism regarding animals has not been sufficient, by itself to carry clear conviction regarding animal immortality. An important reason for this ambivalence is that, while traditional theists have held that animals have souls, they have also thought that animal souls are different in nature from human souls and that there is something about human souls that makes them better candidates for eternal life than animal souls.

Thomas Aquinas advanced this type of argument in the thirteenth century. To fully evaluate his argu-

---

[8] See Trenton Merricks, "The Resurrection of the Body and the Life Everlasting," in *Reason for the Hope Within*, ed. by Michael J. Murray (Grand Rapids: Eerdmans, 1999), pp. 261–286)

ment would require a detailed treatment of his meta-physics, which is not possible here. But his case is worth pondering.

Aquinas argued, reasonably enough, that animal souls function in clear dependence on the animal body. For example, animals' functions are tied to sensory experiences and these, in turn, depend upon the sense organs of sight, smell, and so on. However, the human soul gives evidence of being self-subsistent, of existing in its own right apart from the body. Why? Aquinas' main premise seems to be this: Because certain functions of the human soul appear to be independent of the body, therefore, the existence of the human soul can be independent of the body. The human soul has certain abilities that rise above a dependence upon a specific body organ, and the exercise of these abilities requires that the human soul have a foothold in being all its own, independent of the body.

For example, the human soul can engage in abstract reflection about broad concepts that do not depend upon any specific sense organ. Some of these concepts would be existence in general, truth, causation, mathematics, and morality. An animal, on the other hand, can sense a specific shade of red, but it cannot contemplate redness or color in general, much less the notion of a property or existence. These latter abilities require the soul to transcend the body. Moreover, the human soul has freedom and that requires the soul to act independently of the body in the sense that the conditions in the body are insufficient to cause the self to act in a certain way. If the self is free, it must be self-subsistent in order to be a free self-mover. Thus, these features of the human soul give some indication that the human soul can survive apart from the body.

Aquinas' argument does lend some support to belief in the survival of the human soul after the death of the body. But how much support is hard to say, so his argument is inconclusive by itself. The most we can say is that it contributes to the case for life after death.

There is a third contribution of dualism to belief in eternal life: *Dualism supports belief in a nonphysical realm of reality and the existence of God and, thus, contributes indirectly to the case for life after death by providing evidence against naturalism and for theism which, in turn, reinstates theistic dependent arguments for life after death.* Dualism breaks the stranglehold of naturalism (the physical cosmos studied by the hard sciences is all

there is) and supports belief in God and a nonphysical dimension of reality. The main reason modern people do not believe in eternal life is that they explicitly or implicitly embrace the worldview of naturalism: The sensible, spatiotemporal, physical world that science investigates is all there is to reality. Both property and substance dualism provide evidence that everything, specifically consciousness and the soul, is not physical.

They also provide grounds for belief in the existence of God. To see this, consider the following statement form naturalist Paul Churchland:

> The important point about the standard evolutionary story is that the human species and all of its features are the wholly physical outcome of a purely physical process. . . . If this is the correct account of our origins, then there seems neither need, nor room, to fit any nonphysical substances or properties into our theoretical account of ourselves. We are creatures of matter. And we should learn to live with that fact.[9]

Many have agreed with Churchland. On this view, if naturalism is true, then the history of the cosmos is a story of strictly physical events causing physical events to occur according to physical law. On this view, mental properties/substances cannot come into existence out of nothing nor can the emerge from strictly physical entities. For this reason, some have argued that if finite mental properties/substances are real, the best explanation of their existence is that they were created by a Mind. William Lyons statement is representative of most naturalists on this point: "[Physicalism] seem[s] to be in tune with the scientific materialism of the twentieth century because it [is] a harmonic of the general theme that all there is in the universe is matter and energy and motion and that humans are a product of the evolution of species just as much as buffaloes and beavers are. Evolution is a seamless garment with no holes wherein souls might be inserted from above."[10] Lyons's reference to souls being "inserted from above"

9 Paul Churchland, *Matter and Consciousness* (Cambridge, Mass.: MIT Press, 1984), p. 21.
10 William Lyons, "Introduction," in *Modern Philosophy of Mind*, ed. by William Lyons, (London: Everyman, 1995), p. lv. In context, Lyons remark is specifically about the identity thesis, but he clearly intends it to cover physicalism in general.

appears to be a veiled reference to the explanatory power of theism given the existence of the mental. Dualism provides evidence for a nonphysical realm of reality and for the existence of God. Eternal life is at home in a worldview that embraces both these notions, but it is alien in a worldview that denies a nonphysical realm of being and the existence of God.

3. SUMMARY

In general, it can be said that, given the truth of traditional theism, life everlasting is beyond reasonable doubt. But, granting that there may be some positive evidence for life after death that does not require assuming some form of theism, that evidence is far from conclusive. Thus, justification of an afterlife seems to be theistic dependent. If the empirical evidence from NDEs and the resurrection of Jesus are added, the case for life after death is stronger still. This chapter has provided only a surface examination of some of the main issues. However, I hope the reader is stimulated to study this most important question further. For as Pascal noted, the immortality of the soul is something of such vital importance to us that one must have lost all feeling not to care about knowing the facts of the matter.

Questions for Further Reflection

1. Read the Churchland and Lyons quotes in the chapter. Each is claiming that the existence of genuinely mental properties and substances provides evidence against a purely naturalistic evolutionary account of the origin of conscious living things and for the existence of God. What, exactly, is the problem that consciousness presents to a purely naturalistic evolutionary account of origins? How would you respond to this problem?

2. The following argument (called the Knowledge argument) has been offered for property dualism: Mary, a brilliant scientist blind from birth, knows all the physical facts relevant to acts of perception. When she suddenly gains the ability to see, she gains knowledge of new facts. Since she knew all the physical facts before recovery of sight, and since she gains knowledge of new facts, these facts must not be physical facts and, moreover, given Mary's situation, they must be mental facts. How would you strengthen the argument? How would you criticize it?

3. What do you make of NDEs? Do you know anyone personally who has been through such an experience? How would you argue for and against the use of NDEs as part of a case for life after death? Include in your answer an assessment of cases such as the one about Katie mentioned in the reading.

4. How would a substance dualist respond to the following argument: "while advances in science do not prove that substance dualism is false, they do show that it is a position with incredibly weak justification. This is because physicalism is not primarily a philosophical thesis, but the hard core of a scientific research program for which there is ample evidence. This evidence consists in the fact that biology, neuroscience, and cognitive science have provided accounts of the dependence on physical processes of specific faculties once attributed to the soul. Dualism cannot be proven false—a dualist can always appeal to correlations or functional relations between soul and brain/body—but advances in science make it a view with little justification."

5. Assess the following argument: "Bestowing eternity on an empty life does not make it meaningful. It only yields an eternity of emptiness. Adding more meaningless days to an already meaningless existence does not provide meaning to life. Thus, life after death is not enough make life itself meaningful." In your assessment, state the difference between a necessary and a sufficient condition. Granting the argument is successful, does it show that life after death is not necessary for a meaningful life or not sufficient for a meaningful life? In light of your answer to this last question, state what you take to be the limits of the argument.

SUGGESTIONS FOR FURTHER READING

Cooper, John W. *Body, Soul, and Life Everlasting*. Grand Rapids, MI: Eerdmans, 1989.

Davis, Stephen T., ed. *Death and Afterlife*. New York: St. Martin's Press, 1989.

Edwards, Paul, ed. *Immortality*. New York: Macmillan, 1992.

Fisher, John Martin, ed. *The Metaphysics of Death*. Stanford, CA: Stanford University Press, 1993.

Gauld, Alan. *Mediumship and Survival*. London: Paladin Books, 1993.

Glover, Johathan. *I: The Philosophy and Psychology of Personal Identity*. London: Penquin Books, 1998

Habermas, Gary, and J. P. Moreland. *Beyond Death*. Wheaton, IL: Crossway Books, 1998.

Hasker, William. *The Emergent Self*. Ithaca, NY: Cornell University Press, 1999.

Hick, John H. *Death and Eternal Life*. San Francisco: Harper & Row, 1976.

Kolak, Daniel. *In Search of Myself: Life, Death, and Personal Identity*. Belmont, CA: Wadsworth, 1999.

Martin, Raymond. *Self-Concern: An Experiential Approach to What Matters in Survival*. New York: Cambridge University Press, 1998.

Martin, Raymond, and John Barresi. *Naturalization of the Soul: Self and Personal Identity in the Eighteenth Century*. London: Routledge, 2000.

Martin, Raymond, and John Barresi, eds. *Personal Identity*. New York: Blackwell, 2003.

Martin, Raymond, and John Barresi, *The Rise and Fall of Soul and Self*. forthcoming.

Moreland, J. P., and Scott B. Rae. *Body and Soul*. Downers Grove, IL: InterVarsity Press, 2000.

Perry, John. *A Dialogue on Personal Identity and Survival*. Indianapolis, IN: Hackett, 1978.

Swinburne, Richard. *The Evolution of the Soul*, rev.ed. Oxford: Oxford University Press, 1997.

Tipler, Frank J. *The Physics of Immortality*. New York: Doubleday, 1994.

PART IX

RELIGION, ETHICS, AND THE MEANING OF LIFE

53. THE EUTHYPHRO DILEMMA * *Plato*

Jiddu Krishnamurti, "Religion and Spirituality"

54. IS GOD THE SOURCE OF MORALITY? * *Sharon M. Kaye and Harry J. Gensler*

55. MY CONFESSION * *Leo Tolstoy*

Adrienne Rich, "The Liar Fears the Void"

56. THE MYTH OF SISYPHUS * *Albert Camus*

Robert Nozick, "Why Are Traces Important?"

SUGGESTIONS FOR FURTHER READING

53. THE EUTHYPHRO DILEMMA

Plato

Plato was born in Athens about 427 B.C. to a prominent aristocratic family. Around 387 B.C. he founded the first university, which he named after Academus; it lasted more than a thousand years. Plato wrote philosophy, poetry, and drama, worked as a politician, and was a champion wrestler. He is one of the most influential persons in history; one prominent twentieth-century philosopher has called all Western philosophy merely "a series of footnotes to Plato." Plato lived to be eighty.

Many people consider religion and morality to be inseparable. In the following dialogue, however, Plato attempted to sever ethics from theology with one penetrating question: Is an act right because God approves of it, or does God approve of it because it is right?

READING QUESTIONS

1. What does Socrates mean by "piety"? Why does Euthyphro have such a difficult time trying to define this term?
2. What is the significance of the "disagreement" between the gods? Can you translate this "disagreement" into contemporary terms?
3. How would you describe, using your own words, the "method" Socrates uses against Euthyphro? What is Socrates trying to do? Does he succeed?
4. Why is Socrates being prosecuted?
5. List Euthyphro's definitions of piety and Socrates' objections to each one.
6. What is Socrates' definition of piety, and his objection to his own definition?

Euth.: But what is the charge which he [Meletus] brings against you?

Soc.: What is the charge? Well, rather a grand one, which implies a degree of discernment far from contemptible in a young man. He says he knows how the youth are corrupted and who are their corruptors. I fancy that he must be a wise man, and seeing that I am the reverse of a wise man, he has found me out, and is going to accuse me of corrupting his generation. And of this our mother the state is to be the judge. Of all our political men he is the only one who seems to me to begin in the right way, with the cultivation of virtue in youth; like a good husbandman, he makes the young shoots his first care, and clears away us whom he accuses of destroying them. This is only the first step; afterwards he will assuredly attend to the elder branches; and if he goes on as he has begun, he will be a very great public benefactor.

Euth.: I hope that he may; but I rather fear, Socrates, that the opposite will turn out to be the truth. My opinion is that in attacking you he is simply aiming a blow at the heart of the state. But in what way does he say that you corrupt the young?

Soc.: In a curious way, which at first hearing excites surprise: he says that I am a maker of gods, and that I invent new gods and deny the existence of the old ones; this is the ground of his indictment.

Euth.: I understand, Socrates; he means to attack you about the familiar sign which occasionally, as you say, comes to you. He thinks that you are a neologian, and he is going to have you up before the court for this. He knows that such a charge is readily received by the world, as I myself know too well; for when I speak in the assembly about divine things, and foretell the future to them, they laugh at me and think me a madman. Yet every word that I say is true. But they are jealous of us all; and we must be brave and go at them.

Soc.: Their laughter, friend Euthyphro, is not a matter of much consequence. For a man may be thought clever; but the Athenians, I suspect, do not much trouble themselves about him until he begins to impart his wisdom to others; and then for some reason or other, perhaps, as you say, from jealousy, they are angry.

Euth.: I have no great wish to try their temper towards me in this way.

Soc.: No doubt they think you are reserved in your behaviour, and unwilling to impart your wisdom. But I have a benevolent habit of pouring out myself to everybody, and would even pay for a listener, and I am afraid that the Athenians may think me too talkative. Now if, as I was saying, they would only laugh at me, as you say that they laugh at you, the time might pass gaily enough with jokes and merriment in the court; but perhaps they may be in earnest, and then what the end will be you soothsayers only can predict.

Euth.: I dare say that the affair will end in nothing, Socrates, and that you will win your cause; and I think that I shall win my own.

Soc.: And what is your suit, Euthyphro? are you the pursuer or the defendant?

Euth.: I am the pursuer.

Soc.: Of whom?

Euth.: When I tell you, you will perceive another reason why I am thought mad.

Soc.: Why, has the fugitive wings?

Euth.: Nay, he is not very volatile at his time of life.

Soc.: Who is he?

Euth.: My father.

Soc.: My dear Sir! Your own father?

Euth.: Yes.

Soc.: And of what is he accused?

Euth.: Of murder, Socrates.

Soc.: Good heavens! How little, Euthyphro, does the common herd know of the nature of right and truth! A man must be an extraordinary man, and have made great strides in wisdom, before he could have seen his way to bring such an action.

Euth.: Indeed, Socrates, he must.

Soc.: I suppose that the man whom your father murdered was one of your family—clearly he was; for if he had been a stranger you would never have thought of prosecuting him.

Euth.: I am amused, Socrates, at your making a distinction between one who is a member of the family and one who is not; for surely the pollution is the same in either case, if you knowingly associate with the murder when you ought to clear yourself and him by proceeding against him. The real question is whether the murdered man has been justly slain. If justly, then your duty is to let the matter alone; but if unjustly, then proceed against the murderer, if, that is to say, he lives under the same roof with you and eats at the same table. In fact, the man who is dead was a poor dependant of mine who worked for us as a field labourer on our farm in Naxos, and one day in a fit of drunken passion he got into a quarrel with one of our domestic servants and slew him. My father bound him hand and foot and threw him into a ditch, and then sent to Athens to ask an expositor of religious law what he should do with him. Meanwhile he never attended to him and took no care about him, for he regarded him as a murderer; and thought that no great harm would be done even if he did die. Now this was just what happened. For such was the effect of cold and hunger and chains upon him, that before the messenger returned from the expositor, he was dead. And my father and family are angry with me for taking the part of the murderer and prosecuting my father. They say that he did not kill him, and that if he did, the dead man was but a murderer, and I ought not to take any notice, for that son is impious who prosecutes a father for murder. Which shows, Socrates, how little they know what the gods think about piety and impiety.

Soc.: Good heavens, Euthyphro! and is your knowledge of religion, and of things pious and impious so very exact, that, supposing the circumstances to be as you state them, you are not afraid lest you too may be doing an impious thing in bringing an action against your father?

Euth.: The best of Euthyphro, that which distinguishes him, Socrates, from the common herd, is his exact knowledge of all such matters. What should I be good for without it?

Soc.: Rare friend! I think that I cannot do better than be your disciple. . . . And therefore, I adjure you to tell me the nature of piety and impiety, which you said that you knew so well, in their bearing on murder and generally on offenses against the gods. Is not piety in every action always the same? and impiety, again—is it not always the opposite of piety, and also the same with itself, having, as impiety, one notion or form which includes whatever is impious?

Euth.: To be sure, Socrates.

Soc.: And what is piety, and what is impiety?

Euth.: Piety is doing as I am doing; that is to say, prosecuting anyone who is guilty of murder, sacrilege, or of any similar crime—whether he be your father or mother, or whoever he may be—that makes no difference; and not to prosecute them is impiety. And please to consider, Socrates, what a notable proof I will give you that this is the law, a proof which I have already given to others—of the principle, I mean, that the impious, whoever he may be, ought not to go unpunished. For do not men acknowledge Zeus as the best and most righteous of the gods? And yet they admit that he bound his father (Cronos) because he wickedly devoured his sons, and that he too had punished his own father (Uranus) for a similar reason, in a nameless manner. And yet when I proceed against my father, they are angry with me. So inconsistent are they

in their way of talking when the gods are concerned, and when I am concerned.

Soc.: May not this be the reason, Euthyphro, why I am charged with impiety—that I cannot accept these stories about the gods? that, I suppose is where people think I go wrong. But as you who are well informed about them approve of them, I cannot do better than assent to your superior wisdom. What else can I say, confessing as I do, that I know nothing about them? Tell me, for the love of Zeus, whether you really believe that they are true.

Euth.: Yes, Socrates; and things more wonderful still, of which the world is in ignorance.

Soc.: And do you really believe that the gods fought with one another, and had dire quarrels, battles, and the like, as the poets say, and as you see represented in the works of great artists? The temples are full of them; and notably the robe of Athene, which is carried up to the Acropolis at the great Panathenaea, is embroidered with them throughout. Are all these tales of the gods true, Euthyphro?

Euth.: Yes, Socrates; and, as I was saying, I can tell you, if you would like to hear them, many other things about the gods which would quite amaze you.

Soc.: I dare say; and you shall tell me them at some other time when I have leisure. But just at present I would rather hear from you a more precise answer, which you have not as yet given, my friend, to the question, "What is 'piety'?" When asked, you only replied, "Doing as you do, charging your father with murder."

Euth.: And what I said was true, Socrates.

Soc.: No doubt, Euthyphro; but you would admit that there are many other pious acts?

Euth.: There are.

Soc.: Remember that I did not ask you to give me two or three examples of piety, but to explain the general form which makes all pious things to be pious. Do you not recollect saying that one and the same form made the impious impious, the pious pious?

Euth.: I remember.

Soc.: Tell me what is the nature of this form, and then I shall have a standard to which I may look, and by which I may measure actions, whether yours or those of anyone else, and then I shall be able to say that such and such an action is pious, such another impious.

Euth.: I will tell you, if you like.

Soc.: I should very much like.

Euth.: Piety, then, is that which is dear to the gods, and impiety is that which is not dear to them.

Soc.: Very good, Euthyphro; you have now given me the sort of answer which I wanted. But whether what you say is true or not I cannot as yet tell, although I make no doubt that you will go on to prove the truth of your words.

Euth.: Of course.

Soc.: Come, then, and let us examine what we are saying. That thing or person which is dear to the gods is pious, and that thing or person which is hateful to the gods is impious, these two being the extreme opposites of one another. Was not that said?

Euth.: It was. . . .

Soc.: And further, Euthyphro, the gods were admitted to have enmities and hatreds and differences?

Euth.: Yes, that was also said.

Soc.: And what sort of difference creates enmity and anger? Suppose for example that you and I, my good friend, differ on the question which of two groups of things is more numerous; do differences of this sort make us enemies and set us at variance with one another? Do we not proceed at once to counting, and put an end to them?

Euth.: True.

Soc.: Or suppose that we differ about magnitudes, do we not quickly end the difference by measuring?

Euth.: Very true.

Soc.: And we end a controversy about heavy and light by resorting to a weighing machine?

Euth.: To be sure.

Soc.: But what are the matters about which differences arise that cannot be thus decided, and therefore make us angry and set us at enmity with one another? I dare say the answer does not occur to you at the moment, and therefore I will suggest that these enmities arise when the matters of difference are the just and unjust, good and evil, honourable and dishonourable. Are not these the subjects about which men differ, and about which when we are unable satisfactorily to decide our differences, you and I and all of us quarrel, when we do quarrel?

Euth.: Yes, Socrates, the nature of the differences about which we quarrel is such as you describe.

Soc.: And the quarrels of the gods, noble Euthyphro, when they occur, are of a like nature?

Euth.: Certainly they are.

Soc.: They have differences of opinion, as you say, about good and evil, just and unjust, honourable and dishonourable: there would be no quarrels among them, if there were not such differences—would there now?

Euth.: You are quite right.

Soc.: Does not each party of them love that which they deem noble and just and good, and hate the opposite? . . .

Then the same things are hated by the gods and loved by the gods, and are both hateful and dear to them?

Euth.: It appears so.

Soc.: And upon this view the same things, Euthyphro, will be pious and also impious?

Euth.: So I should suppose.

Soc.: Then, my friend, I remark with surprise that you have not answered the question which I asked. For I certainly did not ask you to tell me what action is both pious and impious; but now it would seem that what is loved by the gods is also hated by them. And therefore, Euthyphro, in thus chastising your father you may very likely be doing what is agreeable to Zeus but disagreeable to Cronos or Uranus, and what is acceptable to Hephaestus but unacceptable to Hera, and there may be other gods who have similar differences of opinion.

Euth.: But I believe, Socrates, that all the gods would be agreed as to the propriety of punishing a murderer: there would be no difference of opinion about that.

Soc.: Well, but speaking of men, Euthyphro, did you ever hear anyone arguing that a murderer or any sort of evil-doer ought to be let off?

Euth.: I should rather say that these are the questions which they are always arguing, especially in courts of law: they commit all sorts of crimes, and there is nothing which they will not do or say in their own defence.

Soc.: But do they admit their guilt, Euthyphro, and yet say that they ought not to be punished?

Euth.: No; they do not.

Soc.: Then there are some things which they do not venture to say and do: for they do not venture to

RELIGION AND SPIRITUALITY ✳ *Jiddu Krishnamurti*

Because you have placed beliefs before life, creeds before life, dogmas before life, religions before life, there is stagnation. Can you bind the waters of the sea or gather the winds in your fist? Religion, as I understand it, is the frozen thought of men out of which they have built temples and churches. The moment you attribute to external authority a spiritual and divine law and order, you are limiting, you are suffocating, that very life that you wish to fulfill, to which you would give freedom. If there is limitation, there is bondage and hence suffering. The world at present is the expression of life in bondage. So, according to my point of view, beliefs, religions, dogmas, and creeds, have nothing to do with life, and hence have nothing to do with truth.

From *Life the Goal*, (1928).

---

argue that if guilty they are to go unpunished, but they deny their guilt, do they not?

Euth.: Yes.

Soc.: Then they do not argue that the evil-doer should not be punished, but they argue about the fact of who the evil-doer is, and what he did and when?

Euth.: True.

Soc.: And the gods are in the same case, of as you assert they quarrel about just and unjust, and some of them say while others deny that injustice is done among them. For surely neither god nor man will ever venture to say that the doer of injustice is not to be punished?

Euth.: That is true, Socrates, in the main.

Soc.: But they join issue about the particulars—gods and men alike, if indeed the gods dispute at all; they differ about some act which is called in question, and which by some is affirmed to be just, by others to be unjust. Is not that true?

Euth.: Quite true.

Soc.: Well then, my dear friend Euthyphro, do tell me, for my better instruction and information, what proof have you that in the opinion of all the gods a servant who is guilty of murder, and is put in chains by the master of the dead man, and dies because he is put in chains before he who bound him can learn from the expositors of religious law what he ought to do with him, is killed unjustly; and that on behalf of such a one a son ought to proceed against his father and accuse him of murder. How would you show that all the gods absolutely agree in approving of his act? Prove to me that they do, and I will applaud your wisdom as long as I live.

Euth.: No doubt it will be a difficult task; though I could make the matter very clear indeed to you.

Soc.: I understand; you mean to say that I am not so quick of apprehension as the judges: for to them you will be sure to prove that the act is unjust, and hateful to all the gods.

Euth.: Yes indeed, Socrates; at least if they will listen to me.

Soc.: But they will be sure to listen if they find that you are a good speaker. There was a notion that came into my mind while you were speaking; I said to myself: "Well, and what if Euthyphro does prove to me that all the gods regarded the death of the serf as unjust, how do I know anything more of the nature of piety and impiety? for granting that this action may be hateful to the gods, still piety and impiety are not adequately defined by these distinctions, for that which is hateful to the gods has been shown to be also dear to them." And therefore, Euthyphro, I do not ask you to prove this; I will suppose, if you like, that all the gods condemn and abominate such an action. But I will amend the definition so far as to say that what all the gods hate is impious, and what they love pious or holy; and what some of them love and others hate is both or neither. Shall this be our definition of piety and impiety?

Euth.: Why not, Socrates?

Soc.: Why not! certainly, as far as I am concerned, Euthyphro, there is no reason why not. But whether this premise will greatly assist you in the task of instructing me as you promised, is a matter for you to consider.

Euth.: Yes, I should say that what all the gods love is pious and holy, and the opposite which they all hate, impious.

Soc.: Ought we to inquire into the truth of this, Euthyphro, or simply to accept it on our own authority and that of others—echoing mere assertions? What do you say?

Euth.: We should inquire; and I believe that the statement will stand the test of inquiry.

Soc.: We shall soon be better able to say, my good friend. The point which I should first wish to understand is whether the pious or holy is beloved by the gods because it is holy, or holy because it is beloved of the gods.

Euth.: I do not understand your meaning, Socrates.

Soc.: I will endeavour to explain: . . . is not that which is beloved distinct from that which loves?

Euth.: Certainly. . . .

Soc.: And what do you say of piety, Euthyphro: is not piety, according to your definition, loved by all the gods?

Euth.: Yes.

Soc.: Because it is pious or holy, or for some other reason?

Euth.: No, that is the reason.

Soc.: It is loved because it is holy, not holy because it is loved?

Euth.: Apparently.

Soc.: And it is the object of the gods' love, and is dear to them, because it is loved of them?

Euth.: Certainly.

Soc.: Then that which is dear to the gods, Euthyphro, is not holy, nor is that which is holy dear to the gods, as you affirm; but they are two different thing. . . .

Euth.: Yes.

Soc.: But that which is dear to the gods is dear to them because it is loved by them, not loved by them because it is dear to them.

Euth.: True.

Soc.: But, friend Euthyphro, if that which is holy were the same with that which is dear to the gods, and

were loved because it is holy, then that which is dear to the gods would be loved as being dear to them; but if that which is dear to them were dear to them because loved by them, then that which is holy would be holy because loved by them. But now you see that the reverse is the case, and that the two things are quite different from one another. For one is of a kind to be loved because it is loved, and the other is loved because it is of a kind to be loved. Thus you appear to me, Euthyphro, when I ask you what is the nature of holiness, to offer an attribute only, and not the essence—the attribute of being loved by all the gods. But you still do not explain to me the nature of holiness. And therefore, if you please, I will ask you not to hide your treasure, but to start again, and tell me frankly what holiness or piety really is, whether dear to the gods or not (for that is a matter about which we will not quarrel); and what is impiety?

Euth.: I really do not know, Socrates, how to express what I mean. For somehow or other the definitions we propound, on whatever bases we rest them, seem always to turn round and walk away from us. . . .

Soc.: Then we must begin again and ask. What is piety? That is an inquiry which I shall never be weary of pursuing as far as in me lies; and I entreat you not to scorn me, but to apply your mind to the utmost, and tell me the truth. For, if any man knows, you are he; and therefore I must hold you fast, like Proteus, until you tell. If you had not certainly known the nature of piety and impiety, I am confident that you would never, on behalf of a serf, have charged your aged father with murder. You would not have run such a risk of doing wrong in the sight of the gods, and you would have had too much respect for the opinions of men. I am sure, therefore, that you know the nature of piety and impiety. Speak out then, my dear Euthyphro, and do not hide your knowledge.

Euth.: Another time, Socrates; for I am in a hurry, and must go now.

Soc.: Alas! my friend, and will you leave me in despair? I was hoping that you would instruct me in the nature of piety and impiety; and then I might have cleared myself of Meletus and his indictment. I would have told him that I had been enlightened by Euthyphro, and had given up rash innovations and speculations in which I had indulged only through ignorance, and that now I am about to lead a better life.

QUESTIONS FOR FURTHER REFLECTION

1. State in your own words what the problem is with supposing "an act is right *because* God approves of it." State what the problem is with supposing that "God approves of an act *because* it is right." How might a religious person respond? You might, as an exercise, go to a religious authority and pose the question to him or her. What answer do you get? What happens when you keep asking the question?
2. Why do you suppose that, in our society and in others, morality is widely considered to be the domain of religion? Do you think this is appropriate? Why or why not?
3. How might Socrates, were he alive, respond to the "religious moral authorities" of today? What would he say, for instance, to the way the Pope justifies a particular view, say the one against the use of artificial birth control?
4. If Socrates is right that morality is independent of the will of the gods, why then have so many societies, past and present, insisted on justifying morality on the grounds that it came from the accepted gods or God? What is their intent?
5. Socrates believed in subjecting all of his beliefs to rational scrutiny and in abandoning those that could not be supported by good reasons. Do you think this is how a person ought to live?

54. IS GOD THE SOURCE OF MORALITY?

By Sharon M. Kaye and Harry J. Gensler

Sharon M. Kaye is Assistant Professor of Philosophy at John Carroll University in Cleveland. She has a special interest in medieval philosophy and is co-author of *On Ockham* (2001) and *On Augustine* (2001). Harry J. Gensler, S.J., is Professor of Philosophy at John Carroll University. He has a special interest in logic and ethics. His recent books include *Formal Ethics* (1996), *Ethics: A Contemporary Introduction* (1998), and *Introduction to Logic* (2002).

In this chapter, Kaye and Gensler explore God's relation to moral obligation in light of the Euthyphro question: Is a right thing right because God commands it, or does God command it because it's already right? Kaye argues for the first alternative; she develops a version of the divine command theory, which holds that God's will creates moral obligations. Gensler argues for the second alternative; he sees most duties as existing independently of God. The authors raise objections against each other.

READING QUESTIONS

1. How do the authors see the Euthyphro question: more as an objection to the divine command theory (DCT), or as a dilemma that both sides must deal with?
2. Explain the difference between the DCT and the independent-duty view. What is one objection to the latter?
3. How, according to Gensler, does the Bible enter into the moral life of the believer?
4. Name one or two objections to DCT?
5. How, according to Gensler, can atheists defend morality?

Imagine that everyone gave up believing in God. Stores replace churches, ministers disappear, and any remaining bibles are tucked away in dusty libraries. Everyone—including you—sees religion as a thing of the past. What would happen to morality? If we gave up believing in God, would we have to give up believing in moral obligation?

Many people say "Yes." In their minds, God is the source of moral obligation. Without God, we'd have no duty to be kind or avoid cruelty. We might, to be sure, be kind and avoid cruelty out of habit, social pressure, or personal preference. But there'd be no genuine duty.[1] As Dostoyevsky remarked, "If there is no God, all things are permitted." Philosophers call this view *the divine command theory*: what makes a right act right is that it is commanded by God, and what makes a wrong act wrong is that it is forbidden by God.

Many other people, including religious ones, disagree with this. They claim that God is not the source of moral obligation. There's an independent right and wrong, not based on God's will. If there were no God, we'd still have a duty to do the right thing and avoid the wrong thing—and the distinction between right and wrong wouldn't vanish.

So, is God the source of moral obligation? The two co-authors of this paper disagree: one says "Yes," the other says "No." We'll try to give you both sides of the story.

1. THE EUTHYPHRO QUESTION

Socrates, the first major philosopher of ancient Greece, was a religious person. His *Apology* defended his philosophical life as an act of obedience to God. But he rejected the divine command theory (DCT)—largely on the basis of a penetrating question raised in the *Euthyphro*. Since then, "the Euthy-

phro question" has been a central part of the DCT debate. We'll ask Socrates's question in our own way.

Let's suppose that there is a God and he commands what is right. We ask:

Is a right thing right *because* God commands it? Or does God command it *because* it is right?

Let's assume that kindness is right and God commands it. Which is based on which? Is kindness right because God commands it? Or does God command it because it's already right? This is the Euthyphro question.

DCT supporters take the first alternative: kindness is right because God commands it. Kindness wouldn't be right if God didn't command it. Independently of God's will, kindness is neither right nor wrong. God's will makes kindness a moral obligation.

Socrates and many others take the second alternative: God commands kindness because he knows it's right. His commands don't make it right; instead, he wouldn't command it if it weren't already right. So kindness is right independently of God's will. It would be right even if there were no God. This alternative involves giving up DCT.

We can ask the Euthyphro question in another way. Let's assume that cruelty is wrong and God forbids it. Is cruelty wrong because God forbids it? Or does God forbid cruelty because it's already wrong? Which alternative do *you* agree with? DCT supporters think cruelty is wrong because God forbids it. Socrates thinks God forbids cruelty because it's already wrong.

Socrates presented the Euthyphro question as an objection to DCT. If a wrong thing is wrong simply because God forbids it, then seemingly whatever God forbids would have to be wrong. So kindness would be wrong if God forbade it! The objection is that DCT makes morality arbitrary, meaning that it could be the opposite of what it is. Socrates concluded that the first way of answering the Euthyphro question was incorrect.

DCT supporters charge that Socrates's answer is at least as objectionable. If cruelty is already wrong, why does God need to forbid it? The objection is that Socrates's answer makes religion morally redundant, meaning that belief in God is unnecessary for belief in morality.

From this perspective, the Euthyphro question presents a dilemma for believers. They seem to run

---

[1] Some atheists agree, including Jean-Paul Sartre, in *Existentialism and Human Emotions* (New York: Wisdom Library, 1957), and J. L. Mackie, in Chapter 1 of *Ethics: Inventing Right and Wrong* (London: Penguin, 1977). Both say objective moral duties are possible only if based on God's will; since they reject God, they reject objective duties. In contrast, C. S. Lewis argues that there must be a God— since we have objective duties and these require a divine source; see the beginning of his *Mere Christianity* (London: Geoffrey Bles, 1952).

into trouble no matter how they answer it. If something is right because God commands it, then morality becomes arbitrary. If God commands something because it's already right, then religion becomes morally redundant. Hence, it seems, believers have to accept one of two things: *either morality is arbitrary or religion is morally redundant.*

Believers give two main responses to this dilemma:

1. DCT response: "Something is right because God commands it (so God is the source of obligation); but this doesn't make morality arbitrary in any objectionable way."
2. Independent-duty response: "God commands something because it's already right (so God isn't the source of obligation); but this doesn't make religion morally redundant in any objectionable way."

The two co-authors will each defend one of the responses—and try to criticize the other.

2. DCT (KAYE)

I'm a supporter of DCT. Over the last forty years, DCT supporters have developed a number of ways to deal with the objection that this approach makes morality arbitrary. There are two main strategies.

One strategy simply denies that God could command cruelty and forbid kindness; there's a principle of goodness within God that makes it impossible for him to command other than he does.[2] Although this solves the problem, it sacrifices a very important feature of God, namely, freedom. If it's impossible for God to command cruelty and forbid kindness, then God isn't even as free as human beings are! Supporters of the strategy can claim that "true freedom" doesn't involve the ability to do otherwise. I believe, however, that this is an implausible account of freedom, and so I will pass over this strategy.

The other strategy is to develop an account of DCT that admits God could command cruelty or forbid kindness.[3] I'll sketch the essentials of such an account.

---

[2]This strategy is often traced to Thomas Aquinas. See also Mark D. Linville, "On Goodness: Human and Divine," *American Philosophical Quarterly* 27 (1990): 143–52.

[3]This strategy is often traced to John Duns Scotus and William of Ockham. See also Paul Rooney, "Divine Commands and Arbitrariness," *Religious Studies* 31 (1995): 149–65.

Most people recognize that objects in the world have inherent value. For example, horses and rocks are inherently good. Furthermore, most people recognize a hierarchy among such goods. For example, horses are more valuable than rocks.

Suppose it's true that each object in the world possesses a certain degree of inherent value. Where does this value come from? Some theists claim that God gives things their value at will. They say that horses are more valuable than rocks simply because God wants them to be. If he wanted to, God could make rocks more valuable than horses. Supporters of this view seem to be concerned that we will be limiting God's freedom if we deny him this ability.

But this view is implausible. If value is an inherent property, then it's essential to the object, and it's logically impossible for it to be otherwise. Consider the following example. Water is essentially wet. This means that if someone took the wetness out of water, it wouldn't be water any more. You can freeze water or boil it, but when you do so it stops being water and becomes ice or steam. Not even God can make water that isn't wet. The reason is that wetness is essential to water. Water possesses wetness simply in virtue of being what it is.

Likewise, if objects in the world really do possess specific degrees of inherent value, as they seem to, then this value is part of their essence. If God creates a horse, then he creates an object that necessarily possesses a certain degree of value. This doesn't limit God's freedom because God doesn't have to create any horses if he doesn't want to.

The thesis that each object in the world possesses its own degree of inherent value is very plausible. It does not, however, imply anything about moral obligation. The fact that horses are necessarily more valuable than rocks does not tell me that I should treat horses better than rocks. Suppose I enjoy kicking horses around. Nothing in any horse can tell me that this is wrong.

Nevertheless, all normal human beings feel that it *is* wrong to kick horses around. We experience a sense of shame (sometimes called a pang of conscience) when we don't treat things according to their inherent value. Unless this experience is some kind of illusion, a moral obligation must be present. Where does it come from? What makes it wrong for us to disregard the value of things?

This is a very difficult question that philosophers have struggled with for centuries. DCT provides a clear and straightforward answer: moral obligation comes from God's will. Our sense of shame at the idea of kicking a horse around comes from our awareness that the horse's creator does not want it treated that way.

What is distinctive about DCT is that it holds that God's caring about how the objects in the world are treated is a matter of his free choice. He need not have made any rules against kicking things around at all. In fact, he was perfectly free to *encourage* people to kick things around. But he chose not to: he wants everything to be treated according to its inherent value. Supporters of DCT believe this shows that he truly loves us. If there were some necessity in his attitude toward the world then it wouldn't be true love. True love presupposes free choice.

This very freedom is what leads to the charge that DCT makes morality arbitrary. God is free to command cruelty, so it seems that he could make cruelty morally obligatory. Although this is often considered an insurmountable problem for DCT, the version of DCT I have outlined above provides a solution.

Before explaining the solution a distinction should be made. Supporters of DCT are *not* forced to admit that God ever does command cruelty. On the contrary, we can maintain that God always commands kindness. Nevertheless, we must face the question: What would happen if God did command cruelty? This is a hard question for supporters of DCT because we are forced to admit that God *could* do this even though he never does. If God commanded me to slaughter an innocent child in a painful way, would I be obligated to do so?[4]

In answer to this question, it should first be noted that the ability to do something bad is not itself a bad thing. My mother *could* have slaughtered me in a painful way the day she took me home from the hospital. This undeniable fact does not make her a bad mother. On the contrary, the fact that she could *but didn't* shows that she loves me. Likewise in the case of

God. The fact that he could command cruelty *but never does* demonstrates his perfect love for human beings.

Second, the DCT supporter need not even concede that I would be morally obligated to slaughter an innocent child in a painful way if God commanded this. The version of DCT developed above provides an alternative. It can maintain that, although divine command is a necessary condition for obligation, it is not sufficient: inherent value is a necessary condition as well. If God issued commands inversely proportionate to the objective value scale, then he could not be said to love us. So, like a bad parent, he would loose his authority. This relieves DCT of having to accept that God could make cruelty morally obligatory.

3. INDEPENDENT DUTY (GENSLER)

In contrast to my colleague, I reject DCT and I claim that most duties are independent of religion. God's will reflects, but doesn't create, the moral order. Cruelty isn't wrong because God forbids it; rather, God forbids it because it's already wrong.

In this section, I'll defend my independent-duty view against two objections that could be raised from DCT perspective. In a later section, I'll raise two objections to DCT.

One objection is that the independent-duty view makes religion morally redundant, since God isn't needed for morality. But, while I concede that God isn't needed for morality as such, I do claim that he's needed for a fuller morality.

On my view, atheists can have a genuine morality. Atheists can accept that kindness is right and cruelty is wrong, as truths based on reason.[5] And atheists can do the right thing, for either lower motives (like habit and social approval) or higher motives (like concern for others and a desire to do the right thing for its own sake).

---

[4]Some people believe that the Bible reports such an incident in Genesis 22, where God commands Abraham to sacrifice his son Isaac. But some scripture scholars interpret the story differently, as a criticism of human sacrifice.

[5]How does reason in ethics work? The short answer is that it requires at least three things: factual understanding, imagination (role reversal—visualizing ourselves in the other person's position), and consistency (which requires making similar judgments about similar cases and treating others only as we're willing to be treated in the same situation). Both atheists and believers can use reason in ethics. For a fuller account of reason in ethics, see Chapters 7 to 9 of my *Ethics: A Contemporary Introduction* (London: Routledge, 1998).

Believers can have a fuller and deeper morality—since they have all this plus the religious dimension. First, believers have additional ways to know right from wrong—including the Bible, church teaching, and prayer; these are useful because human reason is often clouded. Second, believers have additional motives to do the right thing—motives like gratitude to God and love for his creatures; so doing the right thing is linked to our personal relationship to God. Finally, believers have a world-view that better supports morality. Believers see our origin and purpose in moral terms; God created us so that our minds can know the good and our wills can freely choose it—and he intends that our moral struggles purify us and lead us toward our ultimate goal, which is eternal happiness with him.

So religion makes possible, not morality itself (which can exist without belief in God), but the religious dimension that makes morality so much richer and more meaningful.

A second objection is that the independent-duty view limits God's sovereignty (his power and authority). Surely God must be in absolute control of everything; so all basic laws of every sort must depend on God's will. But then all basic *moral* laws must depend on God's will.

The problem here is that it's doubtful that all basic laws depend on God's will. Is "$x = x$" true because of God's will—so it would have been false had God willed otherwise? This law seems true of its very nature, and not true because God made it true. Maybe basic moral laws are the same. Maybe cruelty is evil in itself, and not just evil because God made it so.

So I do limit God's power. God can't bring about square circles or other self-contradictions. God can't make $2 + 2$ equal to 5, he can't make $x \neq x$, he can't bring it about that he never existed, he can't believe falsehoods, and he can't make cruelty right. But God *can* do whatever doesn't involve violating a necessary truth or violating his perfect nature. This is power and authority enough. The abilities that God lacks (like the ability to make square circles or to make cruelty right) are silly abilities that aren't worth having.

And so I argue that the independent-duty view doesn't make God morally redundant or limit God's sovereignty in any objectionable way.

4. OBJECTIONS TO THE INDEPENDENT-DUTY VIEW (KAYE)

Although I find my colleague's independent-duty view interesting, I'm not persuaded by it. Let me explain my two most pressing concerns.

First, it deprives God of freedom, and therefore love. Dr. Gensler compares moral laws to logical laws. So, in the same way that God necessarily judges that $x = x$, he necessarily cares how the objects in the world are treated. I agree that God necessarily judges that $x = x$. This is because logical laws necessitate the intellect. Once you understand what the equation means you will necessarily see that it's true. But I disagree that God necessarily cares about how the objects in the world are treated. One can understand the value of something without caring about it. This is because caring is a function of the will, not the intellect, and the will is free.

The idea of necessarily caring about something is actually very peculiar. The following example shows why. Imagine one year your cousin surprises you with a really nice birthday present. At first you're very touched. Then you find out your cousin gave you this present because someone was forcing him at gunpoint to do so. Would you still be touched? Suppose, alternatively, you found out that there was a law of nature that says: Every 500 years, every human being with a specific type of genetic predisposition gives really nice birthday presents to all of his or her cousins. Would you be touched then?

I wouldn't. In my view, necessity, regardless of what kind of necessity it is, changes the nature of the act. So, if God necessarily cares about the world, then it isn't genuine care after all. Philosophers have often argued that true love is inconsistent with necessity. If they're right, then the independent-duty view can't be correct.

My second worry is that the independent-duty view makes it impossible for atheists to be fully moral. The Euthyphro question raised the problem that a religious person seemingly cannot reject DCT without making God morally redundant. To address this problem, Dr. Gensler introduces two levels of morality: "fuller morality" requires belief in God; "minimal morality" does not. God is not redundant on the independent-duty view because religion is a necessary condition for fuller morality.

Dr. Gensler regards it as an advantage of his view that it allows atheists to have minimal morality. I agree that any plausible moral theory must recognize the existence of moral atheists—and immoral theists, for that matter! But my version of DCT goes further than the independent-duty view: it allows atheists to be *fully* moral.

As I indicated above, human beings become aware of moral obligation through a feeling that it would be wrong not to treat objects in the world according to their inherent value. This feeling occurs in theists and atheists alike. The only difference is that theists believe this feeling comes from God. Atheists don't share this belief. They are therefore disinclined to interpret their feeling as a divine command. Nevertheless, the supporter of DCT can maintain that anyone who is motivated by the feeling that it would be wrong not to treat things according to their inherent value is fully moral, whether or not the individual happens to believe that the feeling has a supernatural source.

My version of DCT not only makes it possible for atheists to be fully moral, it does so without making God morally redundant. God plays an important role, on this view, in explaining where our moral feelings come from and why these feelings, unlike other feelings, create obligations. But this role is purely theoretical. Since it makes no difference in practice, there is no moral difference between moral theists and moral atheists.

For these and other reasons, I believe my version of DCT shares the same advantages as my colleague's independent-duty view, while avoiding some of its problems.

5. OBJECTIONS TO DCT (GENSLER)

I promised earlier to give two objections to DCT. My first objection is that DCT makes morality arbitrary. I'll discuss this in general terms and then examine Dr. Kaye's response.

Suppose that the standard version of DCT is correct. Then kindness is right simply because God commands it—and cruelty is wrong simply because God forbids it. There's no preexisting moral order; instead, God's will creates the distinction between right and wrong. Now imagine that a God, bound by no preex-

isting right and wrong, created the world and commands cruelty.[6] He commands, not just that we be cruel on rare occasions, but that we be cruel always—for the sake of being cruel. Would we have a duty to obey such a God? The standard DCT has to say "Yes." But this is absurd; such a God would be evil, and his commands would merit, not obedience, but disobedience.

I can express my objection as an argument:

If DCT is true, then we'd have a duty to be cruel if God commanded cruelty.
But it's false that we'd have a duty to be cruel if God commanded cruelty.
Therefore, DCT isn't true.

To keep their view, DCT supporters must reject one of the premises. They have two choices.

The standard choice rejects the second premise and says: "Yes, we *would* have a duty to be cruel." I don't think this response is plausible—and neither does my colleague Dr. Kaye.

Another choice rejects the first premise and refines DCT to avoid the implication about cruelty. While there are various ways to do this, I'll focus on Dr. Kaye's approach. On her view:

1. There are truths about what is good (inherently valuable) that are independent of God's will.
2. Duty depends partly on God's will. An act is a duty if and only if (*a*) God commands it and (*b*) it treats things according to their inherent value.

On Dr. Kaye's DCT, we *wouldn't* have a duty to be cruel if God commanded cruelty—since God can create a duty only by commanding according to inherent value (as cruelty isn't). So her view avoids the stated objec-

---

[6] I hold that our God, being *morally good*, wouldn't command such cruelty; to call God *morally good* in a significant way requires that we recognize independent moral truths (like the moral goodness of kindness and the moral evil of cruelty) with which God is in harmony. I'm inclined to go further and claim that God, not only is good, but is so good that he's *incapable* of doing evil. Dr. Kaye objects that this makes God unfree and thus incapable of true love. I'm not quite sure how to respond. Which is greater, a God who is good of necessity (and not of free choice)—or a God who is good of free choice (and not of necessity)? I'm not ready to accept the latter alternative (which is that of Dr. Kaye); but I think I could switch to it without giving up my belief in independent duties.

tion. But another objection emerges: on her view, there's nothing wrong with obeying a God who commands continual cruelty. On her DCT, such cruelty would be *permissible* (wouldn't violate duty) if God commanded it. This strikes me as implausible.

Another problem is the two parts of her view seem to clash. On her view, (1) God desires a good thing because it's already good, but (2) a right action is right because God commands it. She takes one side of the Euthyphro dilemma for "good," and the other for "right"; "good" is independent of God, but "right" isn't. This is a difficult combination to defend. Wouldn't the reasons for accepting one half of her view also be reasons for rejecting the other half?

Supporters of the standard DCT would see Dr. Kaye's approach as an unhappy mixture. They'd insist that what is good depends on what God desires; prior to God's desires, things have no value. They'd also complain that Dr. Kaye limits God's sovereignty—since God is limited by independent values and can create duties only if his commands accord with these values.

We who accept objective duties have problems with the other half of her view. If we have grounds to accept value as independent of God, don't we have similar grounds to accept right as independent of God? Why think that goodness is essential to horses but wrongness isn't essential to cruelty? Let's grant that "most people recognize that objects in the world have inherent value" is a reason to take value as objective. Then wouldn't "most people recognize objective right and wrong" be a reason to take right and wrong as objective?

So I don't think Dr. Kaye's response to the arbitrariness objection totally succeeds. My second objection is that DCT has difficulty explaining the meaning and status of its central claim, "Nothing can be wrong unless God forbids it":

1. What does "wrong" here mean? Is "wrong" definable using religious concepts (perhaps as "forbidden by God")? Or is it an objective but indefinable notion? Or is "wrong" to be understood in some third way?
2. How do we know that nothing can be wrong unless God forbids it? Is this claim true-by-definition? Or is it based on sense experience? Or is it self-evident—or perhaps known by moral intuitions?

DCT supporters tend to be evasive on answering these questions.

DCT could define "wrong" as "forbidden by God"—and then see "Nothing can be wrong unless God forbids it" as true-by-definition. But this approach has an implausible consequence: it makes it impossible for atheists to have moral beliefs. If "wrong" means "forbidden by God," then atheists can't coherently believe that cruelty is wrong. So the first view is implausible.

Or DCT might take "wrong" as indefinable—and then see "Nothing can be wrong unless God forbids it" as a self-evident truth that isn't true-by-definition. But this approach has a similarly implausible consequence. If it's self-evident that nothing can be wrong unless God forbids it, then again atheists can't intelligently believe that cruelty is wrong.

So I don't think we have a plausible explanation of "Nothing can be wrong unless God forbids it"—what it means, how we know it, and how it permits atheists to have moral beliefs.

Let me sum up. On my view, there's an independent right and wrong. Being all-knowing and all-good, God knows what is right and wrong—and thus he commands the right and forbids the wrong. So God's will reflects, but doesn't create, the moral order. The contrary DCT view seems to me to have serious flaws.

While this is what I believe, several of my friends, including Dr. Sharon Kaye, believe something different. We are both happy to have had this opportunity to explain our views about the relationship between ethics and religion.

QUESTIONS FOR FURTHER REFLECTION

1. One of the co-authors sees the Euthyphro question more as an objection to DCT, while the other sees it more as a dilemma that both sides must deal with. How do you see it—and why?
2. Do most of your religious friends base ethics on religion? Would they tend to favor DCT or the independent-duty view?
3. Does the Bible take a stand on this dispute between DCT and the independent-duty view? Explain and justify your answer.
4. Explain where you stand on this issue—and why.
5. In general terms, how would you defend morality from an atheistic perspective?

55. MY CONFESSION

Leo Tolstoy

Count Leo Tolstoy (1828–1910) was born, educated, and lived almost all of his life in Russia. At the age of 50, after writing some of the greatest novels ever written, including *War and Peace* and *Anna Karenina*, Tolstoy experienced a religious crisis, described in the following selection, in which he sought the meaning of life and found it in faith. Tolstoy's discovery led him to advocate humility, nonviolence, vegetarianism, the moral value of manual labor, the avoidance of luxury, and sexual abstinence. After his conversion, he continued to write prolifically. He produced *The Death of Ivan Ilyich* during this latter period of his life.

READING QUESTIONS

1. What is the "strange thing" that began to happen to Tolstoy?
2. What perplexity is he evoking with the phrase, "Why? Well, and then?"
3. Why does he feel as if somebody had played a mean trick on him by creating him?
4. What is the "cruel truth" of life?
5. What are the two drops of honey in Tolstoy's life, and why are they no longer sweet to him?
6. When Tolstoy says that he can no longer keep himself from seeing the truth, "and the truth is death," what does he mean? Is he just making the mistake of supposing that to be valuable at all, something must last forever? Or is he trying to convey a deeper insight?
7. How did Tolstoy resolve his crisis? Did he resolve it by taking refuge in a system of beliefs that he accepted on faith, or did he solve it by having a genuine insight he had previously overlooked? (Or are these two the same?)

Although I regarded authorship as a waste of time, I continued to write during those fifteen years. I had tasted of the seduction of authorship, of the seduction of enormous monetary remunerations and applauses for my insignificant labour, and so I submitted to it, as being a means for improving my material condition and for stifling in my soul all questions about the meaning of my life and life in general.

In my writings I advocated, what to me was the only truth, that it was necessary to live in such a way as to derive the greatest comfort for oneself and one's family.

Thus I proceeded to live, but five years ago something very strange began to happen with me: I was overcome by minutes at first of perplexity and then of an arrest of life, as though I did not know how to live or what to do, and I lost myself and was dejected. But that passed, and I continued to live as before. Then those minutes of perplexity were repeated oftener and oftener, and always in one and the same form. These arrests of life found their expression in ever the same questions: "Why? Well, and then?"

At first I thought that those were simply aimless, inappropriate questions. It seemed to me that that was all well known and that if I ever wanted to busy myself with their solution, it would not cost me much labour—that now I had no time to attend to them, but that if I wanted to I should find the proper answers. But the questions began to repeat themselves oftener and oftener, answers were demanded more and more persistently, and, like dots that fall on the same spot, these questions, without any answers, thickened into one black blotch.

There happened what happens with any person who falls ill with a mortal internal disease. At first there appear insignificant symptoms of indisposition, to which the patient pays no attention; then these symptoms are repeated more and more frequently and blend into one temporally indivisible suffering. The suffering keeps growing, and before the patient has had time to look around, he becomes conscious that what he took for an indisposition is the most significant thing in the world to him—is death.

The same happened with me. I understood that it was not a passing indisposition, but something very important, and that, if the questions were going to repeat themselves, it would be necessary to find an answer for them. And I tried to answer them. The questions seemed to be so foolish, simple, and childish. But the moment I touched them and tried to solve them. I became convinced, in the first place, that they were not childish and foolish, but very important and profound questions in life, and, in the second, that, no matter how much I might try, I should not be able to answer them. Before attending to my Samara estate, to my son's education, or to the writing of a book, I ought to know why I should do that. So long as I did not know why, I could not do anything. I could not live. Amidst my thoughts of farming, which interested me very much during that time, there would suddenly pass through my head a question like this: "All right, you are going to have six thousand desyatínas of land in the Government of Samára, and three hundred horses—and then?" And I completely lost my senses and did not know what to think farther. Or, when I thought of the education of my children, I said to myself: "Why?" Or, reflecting on the manner in which the masses might obtain their welfare, I suddenly said to myself: "What is that to me?" Or, thinking of the fame which my works would get me, I said to myself: "All right, you will be more famous than Gógol, Púshkin, Shakespeare, Molière, and all the writers in the world—what of it?" And I was absolutely unable to make any reply. The questions were not waiting, and I had to answer them at once; if I did not answer them, I could not live. . . .

All that happened with me when I was on every side surrounded by what is considered to be complete happiness. I had a good, loving, and beloved wife, good children, and a large estate, which grew and increased without any labour on my part. I was respected by my neighbours and friends, more than ever before, was praised by strangers, and, without any self-deception, could consider my name famous. With all that, I was not deranged or mentally unsound—on the contrary, I was in full command of my mental and physical powers, such as I had rarely met with in people of my age: physically I could work in a field, mowing, without falling behind a peasant; mentally I could work from eight to ten hours in succession, without experiencing any consequences from the strain. And while in such condition I arrived at the conclusion that I could not live, and, fearing death, I had to use cunning against myself, in order that I might not take my life.

This mental condition expressed itself to me in this form: my life is a stupid, mean trick played on me by somebody. Although I did not recognize that "somebody" as having created me, the form of the conception that some one had played a mean, stupid trick on me by bringing me into the world was the most natural one that presented itself to me.

Involuntarily I imagined that there, somewhere, there was somebody who was now having fun as he looked down upon me and saw me, who had lived for thirty or forty years, learning, developing, growing in body and mind, now that I had become strengthened in mind and had reached that summit of life from which it lay all before me, standing as a complete fool on that summit and seeing clearly that there was nothing in life and never would be. And that was fun to him.

But whether there was or was not that somebody who made fun of me, did not make it easier for me. I could not ascribe any sensible meaning to a single act, or to my whole life. I was only surprised that I had not understood that from the start. All that had long ago been known to everybody. Sooner or later there would come diseases and death (they had come already) to my dear ones and to me, and there would be nothing left but stench and worms. All my affairs, no matter what they might be, would sooner or later be forgotten, and I myself should not exist. So why should I worry about all these things? How could a man fail to see that and live—that was surprising! A person could live only so long as he was drunk; but the moment he sobered up, he could not help seeing that all that was only a deception, and a stupid deception at that! Really, there was nothing funny and ingenious about it, but only something cruel and stupid.

Long ago has been told the Eastern story about the traveller who in the steppe is overtaken by an infuriated beast. Trying to save himself from the animal, the traveller jumps into a waterless well, but at its bottom he sees a dragon who opens his jaws in order to swallow him. And the unfortunate man does not dare climb out, lest he perish from the infuriated beast, and does not dare jump down to the bottom of the well, lest he be devoured by the dragon, and so clutches the twig of a wild bush growing in the cleft of the well and holds on to it. His hands grow weak and he feels that soon he shall have to surrender to the peril which awaits him at either side; but he still holds on and sees two mice, one white, the other black, in even measure making a circle around the main trunk of the bush to which he is clinging, and nibbling at it on all sides. Now, at any moment, the bush will break and tear off, and he will fall into the dragon's jaws. The traveller sees that and knows that he will inevitably perish; but while he is still clinging, he sees some drops of honey hanging on the leaves of the bush, and so reaches out for them with his tongue and licks the leaves. Just so I hold on to the branch of life, knowing that the dragon of death is waiting inevitably for me, ready to tear me to pieces, and I cannot understand why I have fallen on such suffering. And I try to lick that honey which used to give me pleasure; but now it no longer gives me joy, and the white and the black mouse day and night nibble at the branch to which I am holding on. I clearly see the dragon, and the honey is no longer sweet to me. I see only the inevitable dragon and the mice, and am unable to turn my glance away from them. That is not a fable, but a veritable, indisputable, comprehensible truth.

The former deception of the pleasures of life, which stifled the terror of the dragon, no longer deceives me. No matter how much one should say to me, "You cannot understand the meaning of life, do not think, live!" I am unable to do so, because I have been doing it too long before. Now I cannot help seeing day and night, which run and lead me up to death. I see that alone, because that alone is the truth. Everything else is a lie.

The two drops of honey that have longest turned my eyes away from the cruel truth, the love of family and of authorship, which I have called an art, are no longer sweet to me.

"My family," I said to myself, "but my family, my wife and children, they are also human beings. They are in precisely the same condition that I am in; they must either live in the lie or see the terrible truth. Why should they live? Why should I love them, why guard, raise, and watch them? Is it for the same despair which is in me, or for dullness of perception? Since I love them, I cannot conceal the truth from them—every step in cognition leads them up to this truth. And the truth is death."

"Art, poetry?" For a long time, under the influence of the success of human praise, I tried to persuade myself that that was a thing which could be done, even though death should come and destroy everything, my deeds, as well as my memory of them; but soon I came to see that that, too, was a deception. It was clear to me that art was an adornment of life, a decoy of life. But life lost all its attractiveness for me. How, then, could I entrap others? So long as I did not live my own life, and a strange life bore me on its waves; so long as I believed that life had some sense, although I was not able to express it—the reflections of life of every description in poetry and in the arts afforded me pleasure, and I was delighted to look at life through this little mirror of art; but when I began to look for the meaning of life, when I experienced the necessity of living myself, that little mirror became either useless, superfluous, and ridiculous, or painful to me. I could no longer console myself with what I saw in the mirror, namely, that my situation was stupid and desperate. . . .

By abandoning myself to the bright side of knowledge I saw that I only turned my eyes away from the question. No matter how enticing and clear the horizons were that were disclosed to me, no matter how enticing it was to bury myself in the infinitude of this knowledge, I comprehended that these sciences were the more clear, the less I needed them, the less they answered my question.

"Well, I know," I said to myself, "all which science wants so persistently to know, but there is no answer to the question about the meaning of my life." But in the speculative sphere I saw that, in spite of the fact that the aim of the knowledge was directed straight to the answer of my question, or because of that fact, there could be no other answer than what I was giving to myself: "What is the meaning of my life?" "None." Or, "What will come of my life?" "Nothing." Or, "Why does everything which exists exist, and why do I exist?" "Because it exists."

Putting the question to the one side of human knowledge, I received an endless quantity of exact answers about what I did not ask; about the chemical composition of the stars, about the movement of the sun toward the constellation of Hercules, about the origin of species and of man, about the forms of infinitely small, imponderable particles of ether; but the answer in this sphere of knowledge to my question what the meaning of my life was, was always: "You are what you call your life; you are a temporal, accidental conglomeration of particles. The interrelation, the change of these particles, produces in you that which you call life. This congeries will last for some time; then the interaction of these particles will cease, and that which you call life and all your questions will come to an end. You are an accidentally cohering globule of something. The globule is fermenting. This fermentation the globule calls its life. The globule falls to pieces, and all fermentation and all questions will come to an end." Thus the clear side of knowledge answers, and it cannot say anything else, if only it strictly follows its principles.

With such an answer it appears that the answer is not a reply to the question. I want to know the meaning of my life, but the fact that it is a particle of the infinite not only gives it no meaning, but even destroys every possible meaning. . . .

I lived for a long time in this madness, which, not in words, but in deeds, is particularly characteristic of us, the most liberal and learned of men. But, thanks either to my strange, physical love for the real working class, which made me understand it and see that it is not so stupid as we suppose, or to the sincerity of my conviction, which was that I could know nothing and that the best that I could do was to hang myself—I felt that if I wanted to live and understand the meaning of life, I ought naturally to look for it, not among those who had lost the meaning of life and wanted to kill themselves, but among those billions of departed and living men who had been carrying their own lives and ours upon their shoulders. And I looked around at the enormous masses of deceased and living men, not learned and wealthy, but simple men, and I saw something quite different. I saw that all these billions of men that lived or had lived, all, with rare exceptions,

did not fit into my subdivisions, and that I could not recognize them as not understanding the question, because they themselves put it and answered it with surprising clearness. Nor could I recognize them as Epicureans, because their lives were composed rather of privations and suffering than of enjoyment. Still less could I recognize them as senselessly living out their meaningless lives, because every act of theirs and death itself was explained by them. They regarded it as the greatest evil to kill themselves. It appeared, then, that all humanity was in possession of a knowledge of the meaning of life, which I did not recognize and which I condemned. It turned out that rational knowledge did not give any meaning to life, excluded life, while the meaning which by billions of people, by all humanity, was ascribed to life was based on some despised, false knowledge.

The rational knowledge in the person of the learned and the wise denied the meaning of life, but the enormous masses of men, all humanity, recognized this meaning in an irrational knowledge. This irrational knowledge was faith, the same that I could not help but reject. That was God as one and three, the creation in six days, devils and angels, and all that which I could not accept so long as I had not lost my senses.

My situation was a terrible one. I knew that I should not find anything on the path of rational knowledge but the negation of life, and there, in faith, nothing but the negation of reason, which was still more impossible than the negation of life. From the rational knowledge it followed that life was an evil and men knew it—it depended on men whether they should cease living, and yet they lived and continued to live, and I myself lived, though I had known long ago that life was meaningless and an evil. From faith it followed that, in order to understand life, I must renounce reason, for which alone a meaning was needed.

There resulted a contradiction, from which there were two ways out: either what I called rational was not so rational as I had thought; or that which to me appeared irrational was not so irrational as I had thought. And I began to verify the train of thoughts of my rational knowledge.

In verifying the train of thoughts of my rational knowledge, I found that it was quite correct. The deduction that life was nothing was inevitable; but I saw

THE LIAR FEARS THE VOID * *Adrienne Rich*

The liar lives in fear of losing control. She cannot even desire a relationship without manipulation, since to be vulnerable to another person means for her the loss of control.

The liar has many friends, and leads an existence of great loneliness.

The liar often suffers from amnesia. Amnesia is the silence of the unconscious.

To lie habitually, as a way of life, is to lose contact with the unconscious. It is like taking sleeping pills, which confer sleep but blot out dreaming. The unconscious wants truth. It ceases to speak to those who want something else more than truth.

In speaking of lies, we come inevitably to the subject of truth. There is nothing simple or easy about this idea. There is no "the truth," "a truth"—truth is not one thing, or even a system. It is an increasing complexity. The pattern of the carpet is a surface. When we look closely, or when we become weavers, we learn of the tiny multiple threads unseen in the overall pattern, the knots on the underside of the carpet.

This is why the effort to speak honestly is so important. Lies are usually attempts to make everything simpler—for the liar—than it really is, or ought to be.

In lying to others we end up lying to ourselves. We deny the importance of an event, or a person, and thus deprive ourselves of a part of our lives. Or we use one piece of the past or present to screen out another. Thus we lose faith even with our own lives.

The unconscious wants truth, as the body does. The complexity and fecundity of dreams comes from the complexity and fecundity of the unconscious struggling to fulfill that desire. The complexity and fecundity of poetry come from the same struggle.

An honorable human relationship—that is, one in which two people have the right to use the word "love"—is a process, delicate, violent, often terrifying to both persons involved, a process of refining the truths they can tell each other.

It is important to do this because it breaks down human self-delusion and isolation.

It is important to do this because in so doing we do justice to our own complexity.

It is important to do this because we can count on so few people to go that hard way with us. . . .

The liar is afraid.

But we are all afraid: without fear we become manic, hubristic, self-destructive. What is this particular fear that possesses the liar?

She is afraid that her own truths are not good enough.

She is afraid, not so much of prison guards or bosses, but something unnamed within her. . . .

The liar fears the void.

From *On Lies, Secrets, and Silence*. Norton, 1986.

---

a mistake. The mistake was that I had not reasoned in conformity with the question put by me. The question was, "Why should I live?" that is, "What real, indestructible essence will come from my phantasmal, destructible life? What meaning has my finite existence in this infinite world?" And in order to answer this question, I studied life.

The solutions of all possible questions of life apparently could not satisfy me, because my question, no matter how simple it appeared in the beginning, included the necessity of explaining the finite through the infinite, and vice versa.

I asked, "What is the extra-temporal, extra-causal, extra-spatial meaning of life?" But I gave an answer to the question, "What is the temporal, causal, spatial meaning of my life?" The result was that after a long labour of mind I answered, "None." . . .

When I saw that [. . . for philosophy the solution remains insoluble] I understood that it was not right for me to look for an answer to my question in rational knowledge, and that the answer given by rational knowledge was only an indication that the answer might be got if the question were differently put, but only when into the discussion of the question should be introduced the question of the relation of the finite to the infinite. I also understood that, no matter how irrational and monstrous the answers might be that faith gave, they had this advantage that they introduced into each answer the relation of the finite to the infinite, without which there could be no answer.

No matter how I may put the question, "How must I live?" the answer is, "According to God's law." "What real result will there be from my life?" "Eternal torment or eternal bliss." "What is the meaning which is not destroyed by death?" "The union with infinite God, paradise."

Thus, outside the rational knowledge, which had to me appeared as the only one, I was inevitably led to recognize that all living humanity had a certain other irrational knowledge, faith, which made it possible to live.

All the irrationality of faith remained the same for me, but I could not help recognizing that it alone gave to humanity answers to the questions of life, and in consequence of them, the possibility of living.

The rational knowledge brought me to the recognition that life was meaningless—my life stopped, and I wanted to destroy myself. When I looked around at people, at all humanity, I saw that people lived and asserted that they knew the meaning of life. I looked back at myself: I lived so long as I knew the meaning of life. As to other people, so even to me, did faith give the meaning of life and the possibility of living.

Looking again at the people of other countries, contemporaries of mine and those passed away, I saw again the same. Where life had been, there faith, ever since humanity had existed, had given the possibility of living, and the chief features of faith were everywhere one and the same.

No matter what answers faith may give, its every answer gives to the finite existence of man the sense of the infinite—a sense which is not destroyed by suffering, privation, and death. Consequently in faith alone could we find the meaning and possibility of life. What, then, was faith? I understood that faith was not merely an evidence of things not seen, and so forth,

not revelation (that is only the description of one of the symptoms of faith), not the relation of man to man (faith has to be defined, and then God, and not first God, and faith through him), not merely an agreement with what a man was told, as faith was generally understood—that faith was the knowledge of the meaning of human life, in consequence of which man did not destroy himself, but lived. Faith is the power of life. If a man lives he believes in something. If he did not believe that he ought to live for some purpose, he would not live. If he does not see and understand the phantasm of the finite, he believes in that finite; if he understands the phantasm of the finite, he must believe in the infinite. Without faith one cannot live. . . .

In order that all humanity may be able to live, in order that they may continue living, giving a meaning to life, they, those billions, must have another, a real knowledge of faith, for not the fact that I, with Solomon and Schopenhauer, did not kill myself convinced me of the existence of faith, but that these billions had lived and had borne us, me and Solomon, on the waves of life.

Then I began to cultivate the acquaintance of the believers from among the poor, the simple and unlettered folk, of pilgrims, monks, dissenters, peasants. The doctrine of these people from among the masses was also the Christian doctrine that the quasi-believers of our circle professed. With the Christian truths were also mixed in very many superstitions, but there was this difference; the superstitions of our circle were quite unnecessary to them, had no connection with their lives, were only a kind of an Epicurean amusement, while the superstitions of the believers from among the labouring classes were to such an extent blended with their life that it would have been impossible to imagine it without these superstitions—it was a necessary condition of that life. I began to examine closely the lives and beliefs of these people, and the more I examined them, the more did I become convinced that they had the real faith, that their faith was necessary for them, and that it alone gave them a meaning and possibility of life. In contradistinction to what I saw in our circle, where life without faith was possible, and where hardly one in a thousand professed to be a believer, among them there was hardly one in a thousand who was not a believer. In contradistinction to what I saw in our circle, where all life passed in idleness, amusements, and tedium of life, I saw that the whole life of these people was passed in hard work, and that they were satisfied with life. In contradistinction to the people of our circle, who struggled and murmured against fate because of their privations and their suffering, these people accepted diseases and sorrows without any perplexity or opposition, but with the calm and firm conviction that it was all for good. In contradistinction to the fact that the more intelligent we are, the less do we understand the meaning of life and the more do we see a kind of a bad joke in our suffering and death, these people live, suffer, and approach death, and suffer in peace and more often in joy. In contradistinction to the fact that a calm death, a death without terror or despair, is the greatest exception in our circle, a restless, insubmissive, joyless death is one of the greatest exceptions among the masses. And of such people, who are deprived of everything which for Solomon and for me constitutes the only good of life, and who withal experience the greatest happiness, there is an enormous number. I cast a broader glance about me. I examined the life of past and present vast masses of men, and I saw people who in like manner had understood the meaning of life, who had known how to live and die, not two, not three, not ten, but hundreds, thousands, millions. All of them, infinitely diversified as to habits, intellect, culture, situation, all equally and quite contrary to my ignorance knew the meaning of life and of death, worked calmly, bore privations and suffering, lived and died, seeing in that not vanity, but good.

I began to love those people. The more I penetrated into their life, the life of the men now living, and the life of men departed, of whom I had read and heard, the more did I love them, and the easier it became for me to live. Thus I lived for about two years, and within me took place a transformation, which had long been working within me, and the germ of which had always been in me. What happened with me was that the life of our circle—of the rich and the learned—not only disgusted me, but even lost all its meaning. All our acts, reflections, sciences, arts—all that appeared to me in a new light. I saw that all that was mere pampering of the appetites, and that no meaning could be found in it; but the life of all the working masses, of all humanity, which created life, presented itself to me in its real significance. I saw that that was life itself and that the meaning given to this life was truth, and I accepted it.

QUESTIONS FOR FURTHER REFLECTION

1. It is hard to read Tolstoy's account without being moved. If you were moved, what moved you? His beliefs, or the beautiful way he expresses them, or the simple humanity with which he lived his life? Did you like best those parts of his account that agree with what you already believe? Or were you led to see something that you hadn't seen before? If the latter, what? If you were charmed by Tolstoy, was it by the beautiful way he expressed himself or by what he expressed?

2. When you read an essay like this one, do you look for new insight or merely a beautiful expression of what you already believe? What can you learn about yourself from the way you answer this question? Can you learn whether you are searching for truth or just for confirmation?

56. THE MYTH OF SISYPHUS

Albert Camus

French essayist, novelist, and playwright Albert Camus was born in Algeria in 1913. After studying philosophy at the University of Algiers, he worked as meteorologist, stockbroker's agent, civil servant, journalist, and actor and director in an amateur theatrical company. During World War II, he joined the French resistance movement. As a journalist, he often got into trouble with authorities by campaigning for economic and social reforms on behalf of Algerians. He died in an automobile accident in 1960.

Camus expressed his theme of the absurd and irrational nature of the world in various forms. Among his best: a collection of essays, *The Myth of Sisyphus* (1942); the novels, *The Stranger* (1946), *The Plague* (1948), and *The Fall* (1957); and the play, *Caligula* (1944). He won the Nobel Prize for literature in 1957.

READING QUESTIONS

1. Why does Camus think the world is absurd? What does he mean by this? Do you agree?
2. Camus seems to suggest that while the world does not have any meaning, your individual life *can* have meaning. How?
3. How do human beings "secrete the inhuman"?
4. What does Camus mean by "living without appeal"?

All great deeds and all great thoughts have a ridiculous beginning. Great works are often born on a streetcorner or in a restaurant's revolving door. So it is with absurdity. The absurd world more than others derives its nobility from that abject birth. In certain situations, replying "nothing" when asked what one is thinking about may be pretense in a man. Those who are loved are well aware of this. But if that reply is sincere, if it symbolizes that odd state of soul in which the void becomes eloquent, in which the chain of daily gestures is broken, in which the heart vainly seeks the link that will connect it again, then it is as it were the first sign of absurdity.

It happens that the stage sets collapse. Rising, streetcar, four hours in the office or the factory, meal, streetcar, four hours of work, meal, sleep, and Monday Tuesday Wednesday Thursday Friday and Saturday according to the same rhythm—this path is easily followed most of the time. But one day the "why" arises and everything begins in that weariness tinged with amazement. "Begins"—this is important. Weariness comes at the end of the acts of a mechanical life, but at the same time it inaugurates the impulse of consciousness. It awakens consciousness and provokes what follows. What follows is the gradual return into the chain or it is the definitive awakening. . . .

Likewise and during every day of an unillustrious life, time carries us. But a moment always comes when we have to carry it. We live on the future: "tomorrow," "later on," "when you have made your way," "you will understand when you are old enough." Such irrelevancies are wonderful, for, after all, it's a matter of dying. Yet a day comes when a man notices or says that he is thirty. Thus he asserts his youth. But simultaneously he situates himself in relation to time. He takes his place in it. He admits that he stands at a certain point on a curve that he acknowledges having to travel to its end. He belongs to time, and by the horror that seizes him, he recognizes his worst enemy. Tomorrow, he was longing for tomorrow, whereas everything in him ought to reject it. That revolt of the flesh is the absurd.

A step lower and strangeness creeps in: perceiving that the world is "dense," sensing to what a degree a stone is foreign and irreducible to us, with what intensity nature or a landscape can negate us. At the heart of all beauty lies something inhuman, and these hills, the softness of the sky, the outline of these trees at this very minute lose the illusory meaning with which we had clothed them, henceforth more remote than a lost paradise. The primitive hostility of the world rises up to face us across millennia. For a second we cease to understand it because for centuries we have understood in it solely the images and designs that we had attributed to it beforehand, because henceforth we lack the power to make use of that artifice. The world evades us because it becomes itself again. That stage scenery masked by habit becomes again what it is. It withdraws at a distance from us. Just as there are days when under the familiar face of a woman, we see as a stranger her we have loved months or years ago, perhaps we shall come even to desire what suddenly leaves us so alone. But the time has not yet come. Just one thing: that denseness and that strangeness of the world is the absurd.

Men, too, secrete the inhuman. At certain moments of lucidity, the mechanical aspect of their gestures, their meaningless pantomime makes silly everything that surrounds them. A man is talking on the telephone behind a glass partition; you cannot hear him, but you see his incomprehensible dumb show: you wonder why he is alive. This discomfort in the face of man's own inhumanity, this incalculable tumble before the image of what we are, this "nausea," as a writer of today calls it, is also the absurd. Likewise the stranger who at certain seconds comes to meet us in a mirror, the familiar and yet alarming brother we encounter in our own photographs is also the absurd. . . .

Let us insist again on the method: it is a matter of persisting. At a certain point on his path the absurd man is tempted. History is not lacking in either religions or prophets, even without gods. He is asked to leap. All he can reply is that he doesn't fully understand, that it is not obvious. Indeed, he does not want to do anything but what he fully understands. He is assured that this is the sin of pride, but he does not understand the notion of sin; that perhaps hell is in store, but he has not enough imagination to visualize that strange future; that he is losing immortal life, but that seems to him an idle consideration. An attempt is made to get him to admit his guilt. He feels innocent. To tell the truth, that is all he feels—his irreparable innocence. This is what allows him everything. Hence, what he demands of himself is to live *solely* with what he knows, to accommodate himself to what is, and to bring in nothing that is not certain. He is told that nothing is. But this at least is a certainty. And it is with this that he is concerned: he wants to find out if it is possible to live *without* appeal.

THE MYTH OF SISYPHUS

The gods had condemned Sisyphus to ceaselessly rolling a rock to the top of a mountain, whence the stone would fall back of its own weight. They had thought with some reason that there is no more dreadful punishment than futile and hopeless labor.

If one believes Homer, Sisyphus was the wisest and most prudent of mortals. According to another tradition, however, he was disposed to practice the profession of highwayman. I see no contradiction in this. Opinions differ as to the reasons why he became the futile laborer of the underworld. To begin with, he is accused of a certain levity in regard to the gods. He stole their secrets. Ægina, the daughter of Æsopus, was carried off by Jupiter. The father was shocked by that disappearance and complained to Sisyphus.

He, who knew of the abduction, offered to tell about it on condition that Æsopus would give water to the citadel of Corinth. To the celestial thunderbolts he preferred the benediction of water. He was punished for this in the underworld. Homer tells us also that Sisyphus had put Death in chains. Pluto could not endure the sight of his deserted, silent empire. He dispatched the god of war, who liberated Death from the hands of her conqueror.

It is said also that Sisyphus, being near to death, rashly wanted to test his wife's love. He ordered her to cast his unburied body into the middle of the public square. Sisyphus woke up in the underworld. And there, annoyed by an obedience so contrary to human love, he obtained from Pluto permission to return to earth in order to chastise his wife. But when he had seen again the face of this world, enjoyed water and sun, warm stones and the sea, he no longer wanted to go back to the infernal darkness. Recalls, signs of anger, warnings were of no avail. Many years more he lived facing the curve of the gulf, the sparkling sea, and the smiles of earth. A decree of the gods was necessary. Mercury came and seized the impudent man by the collar and, snatching him from his joys, led him forcibly back to the underworld, where his rock was ready for him.

You have already grasped that Sisyphus is the absurd hero. He *is*, as much through his passions as through his torture. His scorn of the gods, his hatred of death, and his passion for life won him that unspeakable penalty in which the whole being is exerted toward accomplishing nothing. This is the price that must be paid for the passions of this earth. Nothing is told us about Sisyphus in the underworld. Myths are made for the imagination to breathe life into them. As for this myth, one sees merely the whole effort of a body straining to raise the huge stone, to roll it and push it up a slope a hundred times over, one sees the face screwed up, the check tight against the stone, the shoulder bracing the clay-covered mass, the foot wedging it, the fresh start with arms outstretched, the wholly human security of two earth-clotted hands. At the very end of his long effort measured by skyless space and time without depth, the purpose is achieved. Then Sisyphus watches the stone rush down in a few moments toward that lower world whence he will have to push it up again toward the summit. He goes back down to the plain.

WHY ARE TRACES IMPORTANT? ✳ *Robert Nozick*

When people desire to leave a trace behind, they want to leave a certain kind of trace. We all do leave traces, causal effects reverberate down: our voices move molecules which have their effects, we feed the worms, and so on. The kind of trace one wishes to leave is one that people know of in particular and that they know is due to you, one due (people know) to some action, choice, plan of yours, that expresses something you take to be important about the kind of person you are, such that people respect or positively evaluate both the trace and that aspect of yourself. We want somehow to live on, but not as an object lesson for others. Notice also that wanting to live on by leaving appropriate traces need not involve wanting continuous existence; you want there to be some time after which you continue to leave a mark, but this time needn't be precisely at your death. Artists as well as those who anticipate resurrection are quite willing to contemplate and tolerate a gap.

Why are traces important? There are several possibilities. First, the importance of traces might lie not in themselves but (only) in what they indicate. Traces indicate that a person's life had a certain meaning or importance, but they are not infallible signs of this—there may be traces without meaning, or meaning without traces. For instance, to "live on" in the memory of others indicates one's effect on these others. It is the effect that matters; even if each of them happened to die first, there still would have been that effect. On this first view, it is a mistake to scrutinize traces in an attempt to understand how life has or can have meaning, for at best traces are a symptom of a life's meaning. Second, traces might be an expression of something important about a life, but it might be important and valuable in addition that this be expressed.

Third, it might be thought that the leaving of traces is intrinsically important. A philosophical tradition going back to Plato holds that the permanent and unchanging is more valuable by virtue of being permanent and unchanging.

From *Philosophical Explanations*, 1981.

It is during that return, that pause, that Sisyphus interests me. A face that toils so close to stones is already stone itself! I see that man going back down with a heavy yet measured step toward the torment of which he will never know the end. That hour like a breathing-space which returns as surely as his suffering, that is the hour of consciousness. At each of those moments when he leaves the heights and gradually sinks toward the lairs of the gods, he is superior to his fate. He is stronger than his rock.

If this myth is tragic, that is because its hero is conscious. Where would his torture be, indeed, if at every step the hope of succeeding upheld him? The workman of today works every day in his life at the same tasks, and this fate is no less absurd. But it is tragic only at the rare moments when it becomes conscious. Sisyphus, proletarian of the gods, powerless and rebellious, knows the whole extent of his wretched condition: it is what he thinks of during his descent.

The lucidity that was to constitute his torture at the same time crowns his victory. There is no fate that cannot be surmounted by scorn. . . .

If the descent is thus sometimes performed in sorrow, it can also take place in joy. This word is not too much. Again I fancy Sisyphus returning toward his rock, and the sorrow was in the beginning. When the images of earth cling too tightly to memory, when the call of happiness becomes too insistent, it happens that melancholy rises in man's heart: this is the rock's victory, this is the rock itself. The boundless grief is too heavy to bear. These are our nights of Gethsemane. But crushing truths perish from being acknowledged. Thus, Œdipus at the outset obeys fate without knowing it. But from the moment he knows, his tragedy begins. Yet at the same moment, blind and desperate, he realizes that the only bond linking him to the world is the cool hand of a girl. Then a tremendous remark rings out: "Despite so many ordeals, my advanced age and the nobility of my soul make me conclude that all is well." Sophocles' Œdipus, like Dostoevsky's Kirilov, thus gives the recipe for the absurd victory. Ancient wisdom confirms modern heroism.

One does not discover the absurd without being tempted to write a manual of happiness. "What! by such narrow ways—?" There is but one world, however. Happiness and the absurd are two sons of the same earth. They are inseparable. It would be a mistake to say that happiness necessarily springs from the absurd discovery. It happens as well that the feeling of the absurd springs from happiness. "I conclude that all is well," says Œdipus, and that remark is sacred. It echoes in the wild and limited universe of man. It teaches that all is not, has not been, exhausted. It drives out of this world a god who had come into it with dissatisfaction and a preference for futile sufferings. It makes of fate a human matter, which must be settled among men.

All Sisyphus's silent joy is contained therein. His fate belongs to him. His rock is his thing. Likewise, the absurd man, when he contemplates his torment, silences all the idols. In the universe suddenly restored to its silence, the myriad wondering little voices of the earth rise up. Unconscious, secret calls, invitations from all the faces, they are the necessary reverse and price of victory. There is no sun without shadow, and it is essential to know the night. The absurd man says yes and his effort will henceforth be unceasing. If there is a personal fate, there is no higher destiny, or at least there is but one which he concludes is inevitable and despicable. For the rest, he knows himself to be the master of his days. At that subtle moment when man glances backward over his life, Sisyphus returning toward his rock, in that slight pivoting he contemplates that series of unrelated actions which becomes his fate, created by him, combined under his memory's eye and soon sealed by his death. Thus, convinced of the wholly human origin of all that is human, a blind man eager to see who knows that the night has no end, he is still on the go. The rock is still rolling.

I leave Sisyphus at the foot of the mountain! One always finds one's burden again. But Sisyphus teaches the higher fidelity that negates the gods and raises rocks. He too concludes that all is well. This universe henceforth without a master seems to him neither sterile nor futile. Each atom of that stone, each mineral flake of that night-filled mountain, in itself forms a world. The struggle itself toward the heights is enough to fill a man's heart. One must imagine Sisyphus happy.

Questions for Further Reflection

1. In what sense are we like Sisyphus? In what sense are we different?
2. Why, according to Camus, must we imagine Sisyphus happy? Do you agree? Why?

Suggestions for Further Reading

Frankl, Victor. *Man's Search for Meaning*. Boston: Beacon Press, 1963.

Garner, Richard. *Beyond Morality*. Philadelphia: Temple University Press, 1994.

Klemke, E. D., ed. *The Meaning of Life*. New York: Oxford University Press, 1991.

Kluge, Eike-Henner W. *The Practice of Death*. New Haven, CT: Yale University Press, 1975.

Lao Tzu. *The Way of Life*. Witter Bynner trans. New York: Perigee Books, 1944, 1972.

Russell, Bertrand. *The Conquest of Happiness*. New York: New American Library, 1930.

Taylor, Richard. *Good and Evil*. Buffalo, NY: Prometheus Books, 1984.

Twain, Mark. *Letters from the Earth*. New York: Fawcett Crest, 1962.

Sanders, Steven, and David Cheney, eds. *The Meaning of Life*. Englewood Cliffs, NJ: Prentice-Hall, 1980.

PART X

RELIGIOUS PLURALISM

57. RELIGIOUS PLURALISM • *John Hick*

Nancy Hartsock, "Feminist Revolution"

Jiddu Krishnamurti, "Revolution"

58. A DEFENSE OF RELIGIOUS EXCLUSIVISM • *Alvin Plantinga*

Peter van Inwagen, "Born into the Right Religion?"

59. EXCLUSIVISM, PLURALISM, AND ANARCHY • *Kevin Meeker*

Ralph Waldo Emerson, "Choices"

60. RELIGIOUS DIVERSITY AND RELIGIOUS BELIEF • *Allen Stairs*

Jane Flax, "Patriarchy"

Naomi Goldenberg, "Women Priests"

61. RELIGION FROM AN AFRICAN PERSPECTIVE • *Kwasi Wiredu*

SUGGESTIONS FOR FURTHER READING

57. RELIGIOUS PLURALISM

John Hick

A brief biography of Hick can be found on p. 265. In the following selection, he claims that each major religion has been a different interpretation of the same God, or Ultimate Reality. Currently, he argues, members of different religions should engage in interreligious dialogue so that they may discover their common bonds and foster mutual respect and tolerance.

READING QUESTIONS

1. How does Hick define *religion*?
2. What does Hick mean by *natural religion*? What is his account of the growth of natural religions?
3. Why does Hick think that the major religions should not be seen as rivals to each other?
4. How does Hick deal with what he takes to be "nontheistic religions"?

Let me begin by proposing a working definition of religion as an understanding of the universe, together with an appropriate way of living within it, which involves reference beyond the natural world to God or gods or to the Absolute or to a transcendent order or process. Such a definition includes such theistic faiths as Judaism, Christianity, Islam, Sikhism; the theistic Hinduism of the Bhagavad Gītā; the semi-theistic faith of Mahayana Buddhism and the nontheistic faiths of Theravada Buddhism and nontheistic Hinduism. It does not however include purely naturalistic systems of belief, such as communism and humanism, immensely important though these are today as alternatives to religious life.

When we look back into the past we find that religion has been a virtually universal dimension of human life—so much so that man has been defined as the religious animal. For he has displayed an innate tendency to experience his environment as being religiously as well as naturally significant, and to feel required to live in it as such. To quote the anthropologist, Raymond Firth, "religion is universal in human societies."[1] "In every human community on earth today," says Wilfred Cantwell Smith, "there exists something that we, as sophisticated observers, may term religion, or a religion. And we are able to see it in each case as the latest development in a continuous tradition that goes back, we can now affirm, for at least one hundred thousand years."[2] In the life of primitive man

---

[1] *Elements of Social Organization*, 3rd ed. (London: Tavistock Publications, 1969) p. 216.
[2] *The Meaning and End of Religion* (New York: Mentor Books, 1963) p. 22.

this religious tendency is expressed in a belief in sacred objects endowed with *mana*, and in a multitude of nature and ancestral spirits needing to be carefully propitiated. The divine was here crudely apprehended as a plurality of quasi-animal forces which could to some extent be controlled by ritualistic and magical procedures. This represents the simplest beginning of man's awareness of the transcendent in the infancy of the human race—an infancy which is also to some extent still available for study in the life of primitive tribes today.

The development of religion and religions begins to emerge into the light of recorded history as the third millennium B.C. moves towards the period around 2000 B.C. There are two main regions of the earth in which civilisation seems first to have arisen and in which religions first took a shape that is at least dimly discernible to us as we peer back through the mists of time—these being Mesopotamia in the Near East and the Indus valley of northern India. In Mesopotamia men lived in nomadic shepherd tribes, each worshipping its own god. Then the tribes gradually coalesced into nation states, the former tribal gods becoming ranked in hierarchies (some however being lost by amalgamation in the process) dominated by great national deities such as Marduk of Babylon, the Sumerian Ishtar, Amon of Thebes, Jahweh of Israel, the Greek Zeus, and so on. Further east in the Indus valley there was likewise a wealth of gods and goddesses, though apparently not so much tribal or national in character as expressive of the basic forces of nature, above all fertility. The many deities of the Near East and of India expressed man's awareness of the divine at the dawn of documentary history, some four thousand years ago. It is perhaps worth stressing that the picture was by no means a wholly pleasant one. The tribal and national gods were often martial and cruel, sometimes requiring human sacrifices. And although rather little is known about the very early, pre-Aryan Indian deities, it is certain that later Indian deities have vividly symbolised the cruel and destructive as well as the beneficent aspects of nature.

These early developments in the two cradles of civilisation, Mesopotamia and the Indus valley, can be described as the growth of natural religion, prior to any special intrusions of divine revelation or illumination. Primitive spirit-worship expressed man's fears of unknown forces; his reverence for nature deities expressed his sense of depencence upon realities greater than himself; and his tribal gods expressed the unity and continuity of his group over against other groups. One can in fact discern all sorts of causal connections between the forms which early religion took and the material circumstances of man's life, indicating the large part played by the human element within the history of religion. For example, Trevor Ling points out that life in ancient India (apart from the Punjab immediately prior to the Aryan invasions) was agricultural and was organised in small village units; and suggests that "among agricultural peoples, aware of the fertile earth which brings forth from itself and nourishes its progeny upon its broad bosom, it is the mother-principle which seems important."[3] Accordingly God the Mother, and a variety of more specialised female deities, have always held a prominent place in Indian religious thought and mythology. This contrasts with the characteristically male expression of deity in the Semitic religions, which had their origins among nomadic, pastoral, herd-keeping peoples in the Near East. The divine was known to the desert-dwelling herdsmen who founded the Israelite tradition as God the King and Father; and this conception has continued both in later Judaism and in Christianity, and was renewed out of the desert experience of Mohammed in the Islamic religion. Such regional variations in our human ways of conceiving the divine have persisted through time into the developed world faiths that we know today. The typical western conception of God is still predominantly in terms of the male principle of power and authority; and in the typical Indian conceptions of deity the female principle still plays a distinctly larger part than in the west.

Here then was the natural condition of man's religious life: religion without revelation. But sometime around 800 B.C there began what has been called the golden age of religious creativity. This consisted in a remarkable series of revelatory experiences occurring during the next five hundred or so years in different parts of the world, experiences which deepened and purified men's conception of the ultimate, and which religious faith can only attribute to the pressure of the divine Spirit upon the human spirit. First came the

---

[3]*A History of Religion East and West* (London: Macmillan and New York: St. Martin's Press, 1968) p. 27.

early Jewish prophets, Amos. Hosea and first Isaiah, declaring that they had heard the Word of the Lord claiming their obedience and demanding a new level of righteousness and justice in the life of Israel. Then in Persia the great prophet Zoroaster appeared; China produced Lao-tzu and then Confucius; in India the Upanishads were written, and Gotama the Buddha lived, and Mahavira, the founder of the Jain religion and, probably about the end of this period, the writing of the Bhagavad Gītā,[4] and Greece produced Pythagoras and then, ending this golden age, Socrates and Plato. Then after the gap of some three hundred years came Jesus of Nazareth and the emergence of Christianity; and after another gap the prophet Mohammed and the rise of Islam.

The suggestion that we must consider is that these were all moments of divine revelation. But let us ask, in order to test this thought, whether we should not expect God to make his revelation in a single mighty act, rather than to produce a number of different, and thereiore presumably partial, revelations at different times and places? I think that in seeing the answer to this question we receive an important clue to the place of the religions of the world in the divine purpose. For when we remember the facts of history and geography we realise that in the period we are speaking of, between two and three thousand years ago, it was not possible for God to reveal himself through any human mediation to all mankind. A world-wide revelation might be possible today, thanks to the inventions of printing, and even more of radio, TV and communication satellites. But in the technology of the ancient world this was not possible. Although on a time scale of centuries and millennia there has been a slow diffusion and interaction of cultures, particularly within the vast Euro-Asian land mass, yet the more striking fact for our present purpose is the fragmented character of the ancient world. Communications between the different groups of humanity was then so limited and slow that for all practical purposes men inhabited different worlds. For the most part people in Europe, in India, in

Arabia, in Africa, in China were unaware of the other's existence. And as the world was fragmented, so was its religious life. If there was to be a revelation of the divine reality to mankind it had to be a pluriform revelation, a series of revealing experiences occurring independently within the different streams of human history. And since religion and culture were one, the great creative moments of revelation and illumination have influenced the development of the various cultures, giving them the coherence and impetus to expand into larger units, thus creating the vast, many-sided historical entities which we call the world religions.

Each of these religio-cultural complexes has expanded until it touched the boundaries of another such complex spreading out from another centre. Thus each major occasion of divine revelation has slowly transformed the primitive and national religions within the sphere of its influence into what we now know as the world faiths. The early Dravidian and Aryan polytheisms of India were drawn through the religious experience and thought of the Brahmins into what the west calls Hinduism. The national and mystery cults of the mediterranean world and then of northern Europe were drawn by influences stemming from the life and teaching of Christ into what has become Christianity. The early polytheism of the Arab peoples has been transformed under the influence of Mohammed and his message into Islam. Great areas of Southeast Asia, of China, Tibet and Japan were drawn into the spreading Buddhist movement. None of these expansions from different centres of revelation has of course been simple and uncontested, and a number of alternatives which proved less durable have perished or been absorbed in the process—for example. Mithraism has disappeared altogether; and Zoroastrianism, whilst it greatly influenced the development of the Judaic-Christian tradition, and has to that extent been absorbed, only survives directly today on a small scale in Parseeism.

Seen in this historical context these movements of faith—the Judaic-Christian, the Buddhist, the Hindu, the Muslim—are not essentially rivals. They began at different times and in different places, and each expanded outwards into the surrounding world of primitive natural religion until most of the world was drawn up into one or other of the great revealed faiths. And once this global pattern had become established it

---

[4]The dating of the Bhagavad Gītā, has been a matter of much debate; but R. C. Zaehner in his recent monumental critical edition says that "One would probably not be going far wrong if one dated it as some time between the fifth and second centuries B.C." *The Bhagavad Gītā*, (Oxford: Clarendon Press, 1969) p. 7.

has ever since remained fairly stable. It is true that the process of establishment involved conflict in the case of Islam's entry into India and the virtual expulsion of Buddhism from India in the medieval period, and in the case of Islam's advance into Europe and then its retreat at the end of the medieval period. But since the frontiers of the different world faiths became more or less fixed there has been little penetration of one faith into societies moulded by another. The most successful missionary efforts of the great faiths continue to this day to be "downwards" into the remaining world of relatively primitive religions rather than "sideways" into territories dominated by another world faith. For example, as between Christianity and Islam there has been little more than rather rare individual conversions; but both faiths have successful missions in Africa. Again, the Christian population of the Indian subcontinent, after more than two centuries of missionary effort, is only about 2.7 percent; but on the other hand the Christian missions in the South Pacific are fairly successful. Thus the general picture, so far as the great world religions is concerned, is that each has gone through an early period of geographical expansion, converting a region of the world from its more primitive religious state, and has thereafter continued in a comparatively settled condition within more of less stable boundaries.

Now it is of course possible to see this entire development from the primitive forms of religion up to and including the great world faiths as the history of man's most persistent illusion, growing from crude fantasies into sophisticated metaphysical speculations. But from the standpoint of religious faith the only reasonable hypothesis is that this historical picture represents a movement of divine self-revelation to mankind. This hypothesis offers a general answer to the question of the relation between the different world religions and of the truths which they embody. It suggests to us that the same divine reality has always been self-revealingly active towards mankind, and that the differences of human response are related to different human circumstances. These circumstances—ethnic, geographical, climatic, economic, sociological, historical—have produced the existing differentiations of human culture, and within each main cultural region the response to the divine has taken its own characteristic forms. In each case the post-primitive response has been initi-

ated by some spiritually outstanding individual or succession of individuals, developing in the course of time into one of the great religio-cultural phenomena which we call the world religions. Thus Islam embodies the main response of the Arabic peoples to the divine reality; Hinduism, the main (though not the only) response of the peoples of India; Buddhism, the main response of the peoples of Southeast Asia and parts of northern Asia; Christianity, the main response of the European peoples, both within Europe itself and in their emigrations to the Americas and Australasia.

Thus it is, I think, intelligible historically why the revelation of the divine reality to man, and the disclosure of the divine will for human life, had to occur separately within the different streams of human life. We can see how these revelations took different forms related to the different mentalities of the peoples to whom they came and developed within these different cultures into the vast and many-sided historical phenomena of the world religions.

But let us now ask whether this is intelligible theologically. What about the conflicting truth claims of the different faiths? Is the divine nature personal or nonpersonal; does deity become incarnate in the world; are human beings born again and again on earth; is the Bible, or the Koran, or the Bhagavad Gītā, the Word of God? If what Christianity says in answer to these questions is true, must not what Hinduism says be to a large extent false? If what Buddhism says is true, must not what Islam says be largely false?

Let us begin with the recognition, which is made in all the main religious traditions, that the ultimate divine reality is infinite and as such transcends the grasp of the human mind. God, to use our Christian term, is infinite. He is not a thing, a part of the universe, existing alongside other things; nor is he a being falling under a certain kind. And therefore he cannot be defined or encompassed by human thought. We cannot draw boundaries around his nature and say that he is this and no more. If we could fully define God, describing his inner being and his outer limits, this would not be God. The God whom our minds can penetrate and whom our thoughts can circumnavigate is merely a finite and partial image of God.

From this it follows that the different encounters with the transcendent within the different religious traditions may all be encounters with the one infinite

FEMINIST REVOLUTION ✳ *Nancy Hartsock*

Feminists, in making theory, take up and examine what we find within ourselves; we attempt to clarify for ourselves and others what we already, at some level, know. Theory itself, then, can be seen as a way of taking up and building on our experience. This is not to say that feminists reject all knowledge that is not firsthand, that we can learn nothing from books or from history. But rather than read a number of sacred texts we make the practical questions posed for us in everyday life the basis of our study. Feminism recognizes that political philosophy and political action do not take place in separate realms. On the contrary, the concepts with which we understand the social world emerge from and are defined by human activity.

For feminists, the unity of theory and practice refers to the use of theory to make coherent the problems and principles expressed in our practical activity. Feminists argue that the role of theory is to take seriously the idea that all of us are theorists. The role of theory, then, is to articulate for us what we know from our practical activity, to bring out and make conscious the philosophy embedded in our lives. Feminists are in fact creating social theory through political action. We need to conceptualize, to take up and specify what we have already done, in order to make the next steps clear. We can start from common sense, but we need to move on to the philosophy systematically elaborated by traditional intellectuals.

A third factor in making feminism a force for revolution is that the mode of analysis I have described leads to a transformation of social relations. This is true first in a logical sense. That is, once social relations are situated within the context of the social formation as a whole, the individual phenomena change their meanings and forms. They become something other than they were. For example, what liberal theory understands as social stratification becomes clearer when understood as class. But this is not simply a logical point. As Lukacs has pointed out, the transformation of each phenomenon through relating it to the social totality ends by conferring "reality on the day to day struggle by manifesting its relation to the whole. Thus it elevates mere existence to reality." This development in mass political consciousness, the transformation of the phenomena of life, is on the one hand a profoundly political act and on the other, a "point of transition." Consciousness must become deed, but the act of becoming conscious is itself a kind of deed.

From "Feminist Theory and the Development of Revolutionary Strategy," in Z. R. Eisenstein, ed., *Capitalistic Patriarchy and the Case for Socialistic Feminism* (1979).

reality; though with partially different and overlapping aspects of that reality. This is a very familiar thought in Indian religious literature. We read, for example, in the ancient Rig-Vedas, dating back to perhaps as much as a thousand years before Christ:

They call it Indra, Mitra, Varuna, and Agni
And also heavenly, beautiful Garutman:
The real is one, though sages name it variously.[5]

We might translate this thought into the terms of the faiths represented today in Britain:

They call it Jahweh, Allah, Krishna, Param Atma,
And also holy, blessed Trinity:
The real is one, though sages name it differently.

And in the Bhagavad Gītā, the Lord Krishna, the personal God of love, says, "However men approach me, even so do I accept them: for, on all sides, whatever path they may choose is mine."[6]

[5]I 164.

[6]IV II.

Again, there is the parable of the blind men and the elephant, said to have been told by the Buddha. An elephant was brought to a group of blind men who had never encountered such an animal before. One felt a leg and reported that an elephant is a great living pillar. Another felt the trunk and reported that an elephant is a great snake. Another felt the tusk and reported than an elephant is like a sharp ploughshare. And so on. And then they all quarrelled together, each claiming that his own account was the truth and therefore all the others false. In fact of course they were all true, but each referring only to one aspect of the total reality and all expressed in very imperfect analogies.

Now the possibility, indeed the probability, that we have seriously to consider is that many different accounts of the divine reality may be true, though all expressed in imperfect human analogies, but that none is "the truth, the whole truth, and nothing but the truth." May it not be that the different concepts of God, as Jahweh, Allah, Krishna, Param Atma, Holy Trinity, and so on: and likewise the different concepts of the hidden structure of reality, as the eternal emanation of Brahman or as an immense cosmic process culminating in Nirvana, are all images of the divine, each expressing some aspect or range of aspects and yet none by itself fully and exhaustively corresponding to the infinite nature of the ultimate reality?

Two immediate qualifications however to this hypothesis. First, the idea that we are considering is not that any and every conception of God or of the transcendent is valid, still less all equally valid; but that every conception of the divine which has come out of a great revelatory religious experience and has been tested though a long tradition of worship, and has sustained human faith over centuries of time and in millions of lives, is likely to represent a genuine encounter with the divine reality. And second, the parable of the blind men and the elephant is of course only a parable and like most parables it is designed to make one point and must not be pressed as an analogy at other points. The suggestion is not that the different encounters with the divine which lie at the basis of the great religious traditions are responses to different *parts* of the divine. They are rather encounters from different historical and cultural standpoints with the same infinite divine reality and as such they lead to differently focused awareness of the reality. The indications of this

are most evident in worship and prayer. What is said about God in the theological treatises of the different faiths is indeed often widely different. But it is in prayer that a belief in God comes alive and does its main work. And when we turn from abstract theology to the living stuff of worship we meet again and again the overlap and confluence of faiths.

Here, for example, is a Muslim prayer at the feast of Ramadan:

> Praise be to God, Lord of creation, Source of all livelihood, who orders the morning, Lord of majesty and honour, of grace and beneficence. He who is so far that he may not be seen and so near that he witnesses the secret things. Blessed be he and for ever exalted.[7]

And here is a Sikh creed used at the morning prayer:

> There is but one God. He is all that is.
> He is the Creator of all things and He is all-pervasive.
> He is without fear and without enmity.
> He is timeless, unborn and self-existent.
> He is the Enlightener
> And can be realised by grace of Himself alone.
> He was in the beginning; He was in all ages.
> The True One is, was, O Nanak, and shall forever be.[8]

And here again is a verse from the Koran:

> To God belongs the praise. Lord of the heavens and Lord of the earth, the Lord of all being. His is the dominion in the heavens and in the earth: he is the Almighty, the All-wise.[9]

Turning now to the Hindu idea of the many incarnations of God, here is a verse from the Rāmāyana:

> Seers and sages, saints and hermits, fix on Him their reverent gaze,

---

[7]Kenneth Cragg, *Alive to God: Muslim and Christian Prayer* (London and New York: Oxford University Press, 1970) p. 65.
[8]Harbans Singh, *Guru Nanak and Origins of the Sikh Faith* (Bombay, London and New York: Asia Publishing House, 1969), pp. 96–7.
[9]*Alive to God*, p. 61 (Surah of the Kneeling, v. 35).

And in faint and trembling accents, holy scripture hymns His praise.
He the omnipresent spirit, lord of heaven and
earth and hell,
To redeem His people, freely has vouchsafed with
men to dwell.[10]

And from the rich literature of devotional song here
is a Bhakti hymn of the Vaishnavite branch of Hinduism:

Now all my days with joy I'll fill, full to the brim
With all my heart to Vitthal cling, and only Him.
He will sweep utterly away all dole and care;
And all in sunder shall I rend illusion's snare.
O altogether dear is He, and He alone.
For all my burden He will take to be His own.
Lo, all the sorrow of the world will straightway
cease,
And all unending now shall be the reign of
peace.[11]

And a Muslim mystical verse:

Love came a guest
Within my breast,
My soul was spread,
Love banqueted.[12]

And finally another Hindu (Vaishnavite) devotional
hymn:

O save me, save me, Mightiest,
Save me and set me free.
O let the love that fills my breast
Cling to thee lovingly.
Grant me to taste how sweet thou art:
Grant me but this, I pray.
And never shall my love depart
Or turn from thee away.
Then I thy name shall magnify
And tell thy praise abroad.
For very love and gladness I
Shall dance before my God.[13]

---

[10]*Sacred Books of the World*, edited by A. C. Bouquet (London:
Pelican Books, 1954) p. 226 (The Rāmāvana of Tulsi Das. Canto 1.
Chandha 2, translated by F. S. Growse).
[11]Ibid., p. 245 (A Hymn of Namdev, translated by Nicol MacNicol).
[12]*Alive to God*, p. 79 (From Ibn Hazm, "The Ring of the Dove").
[13]*Sacred Books of the World*, p. 246 (A Hymn of Tukaram).

Such prayers and hymns as these must express,
surely, diverse encounters with the same divine reality.
These encounters have taken place within different human cultures by people of different ways of thought and
feeling, with different histories and different frameworks of philosophical thought, and have developed
into different systems of theology embodied in different
religious structures and organisations. These resulting
large-scale religiocultural phenomena are what we call
the religions of the world. But must there not lie behind
them the same infinite divine reality, and may not our
divisions into Christian, Hindu, Muslim, Jew, and so
on, and all that goes with them, accordingly represent
secondary, human, historical developments?

There is a further problem, however, which now
arises. I have been speaking so far of the ultimate reality in a variety of terms—the Father, Son and Spirit of
Christianity, the Jahweh of Judaism, the Allah of Islam, and so on—but always thus far in theistic terms,
as a personal God under one name or another. But
what of the nontheistic religions? What of the nontheistic Hinduism according to which the ultimate reality, Brahman, is not He but it; and what about Buddhism, which in one form is agnostic concerning the
existence of God even though in another form it has
come to worship the Buddha himself? Can these nontheistic faiths be seen as encounters with the same divine reality that is encountered in theistic religion?

Speaking very tentatively, I think it is possible
that the sense of the divine as nonpersonal may indeed reflect an aspect of the same infinite reality that
is encountered as personal in theistic religious experience. The question can be pursued both as a matter of
pure theology and in relation to religious experience.
Theologically, the Hindu distinction between Nirguna Brahman and Saguna Brahman is important and
should be adopted into western religious thought. De-
taching the distinction, then from its Hindu context
we may say that Nirguna God is the eternal self-
existent divine reality, beyond the scope of all human
categories, including personality; and Saguna God is
God in relation to his creation and with the attributes
which express this relationship, such as personality,
omnipotence, goodness, love and omniscience. Thus
the one ultimate reality is both Nirguna and nonpersonal, and Saguna and personal, in a duality which is
in principle acceptable to human understanding.

REVOLUTION ✳ *Jiddu Krishnamurti*

Now, society is always trying to control, to shape, to mould the thinking of the young. From the moment you are born and begin to receive impressions, your father and mother are constantly telling you what to do and what not to do, what to believe and what not to believe; you are told that there is God, or that there is no God but the State and that some dictator is its prophet. From childhood these things are poured into you, which means that your mind—which is very young, impressionable, inquisitive, curious to know, wanting to find out—is gradually being encased, conditioned, shaped so that you will fit into the pattern of a particular society and not be a revolutionary. Since the habit of patterned thinking has already been established in you, even if you do "revolt" it is within the pattern. It is like prisoners revolting in order to have better food, more conveniences—but always within the prison. When you seek God, or try to find out what is right government, it is always within the pattern of society, which says, "This is true and that is false, this is good and that is bad, this is the right leader and these are the saints." So your revolt, like the so-called revolution brought about by ambitious or very clever people, is always limited in the past. That is not revolt, that is not revolution: it is merely heightened activity, a more valiant struggle within the pattern. Real revolt, true revolution is to break away from the pattern and to inquire outside of it.

From *Think on These Things*, 1964.

When we turn to men's religious awareness of God we are speaking of Saguna God, God in relation to man. And here the larger traditions of both east and west report a dual experience of the divine as personal and as other than personal. It will be a sufficient reminder of the strand of personal relationship with the divine in Hinduism to mention Iswaru, the personal God who represents the Absolute as known and worshipped by finite persons. It should also be remembered that the characterisation of Brahman as *satcitananda*, absolute being, consciousness and bliss, is not far from the conception of infinitely transcendent personal life. Thus there is both the thought and the experience of the personal divine within Hinduism. But there is likewise the thought and the experience of God as other than personal within Christianity. Rudolph Otto describes this strand in the mysticism of Meister Eckhart. He says:

> The divine, which on the one hand is conceived in symbols taken from the social sphere, as Lord, King, Father, Judge—a person in relation to persons—is on the other hand denoted in dynamic symbols as the power of life, as light and life, as spirit ebbing and flowing, as truth, knowledge, essential justice and holiness, a glowing fire that penetrates and pervades. It is characterized as the principle of a renewed, supernatural Life, mediating and giving itself, breaking forth in the living man as his nova vita, as the content of his life and being. What is here insisted upon is not so much an immanent God, as an "experienced" God, known as an inward principle of the power of new being and life. Eckhart knows this *deuteros theos* besides the personal God . . . [14]

Let me now try to draw the threads together and to project them into the future. I have been suggesting that Christianity is a way of salvation which, beginning some two thousand years ago, has become the principal way of salvation in three continents. The other great faiths are likewise of salvation, providing the principal path to the divine reality for other large sections of humanity. I have also suggested that the idea that Jesus proclaimed himself as God incarnate, and as the sole point of saving contact between God

---

[14]Rudolph Otto, *Mysticism East and West*, trans. Bertha L. Bracey and Richenda C. Payne (New York: Meridian Books, 1957), p. 131.

and man, is without adequate historical foundation and represents a doctrine developed by the church. We should therefore not infer, from the christian experience of redemption through Christ, that salvation cannot be experienced in any other way. The alternative possibility is that the ultimate divine reality—in our christian terms, God—has always been pressing in upon the human spirit, but in ways which leave men free to open or close themselves to the divine presence. Human life has developed along characteristically different lines in the main areas of civilisation, and these differences have naturally entered into the ways in which men have apprehended and responded to God. For the great religious figures through whose experience divine revelation has come have each been conditioned by a particular history and culture. One can hardly imagine Gotama the Buddha except in the setting of the India of his time, or Jesus the Christ except against the background of Old Testament Judaism, or Mohammed except in the setting of Arabia. And human history and culture have likewise shaped the development of the webs of religious creeds, practices and organisations which we know as the great world faiths.

It is thus possible to consider the hypothesis that they are all, at their experiential roots, in contact with the same ultimate reality, but that their differing experiences of that reality, interacting over the centuries with the different thought-forms of different cultures, have led to increasing differentiation and contrasting elaboration—so that Hinduism, for example, is a very different phenomenon from Christianity, and very different ways of conceiving and experiencing the divine occur within them.

However, now that the religious traditions are consciously interacting with each other in the "one world" of today, in mutual observation and dialogue, it is possible that their future developments may be on gradually converging courses. For during the next few centuries they will no doubt continue to change, and it may be that they will grow closer together, and even that one day such names as "Christianity," "Buddhism," "Islam," "Hinduism," will no longer describe the then current configurations of men's religious experience and belief. I am not here thinking of the extinction of human religiousness in a universal wave of secularisation. This is of course a possible future; and

indeed many think it the most likely future to come about. But if man is an indelibly religious animal he will always, even in his secular cultures, experience a sense of the transcendent by which he will be both troubled and uplifted. The future I am thinking of is accordingly one in which what we now call the different religions will constitute the past history of different emphases and variations within a global religious life. I do not mean that all men everywhere will be overtly religious, any more than they are today. I mean rather that the discoveries now taking place by men of different faiths of central common ground, hitherto largely concealed by the variety of cultural forms in which it was expressed, may eventually render obsolete the sense of belonging to rival ideological communities. Not that all religious men will think alike, or worship in the same way or experience the divine identically. On the contrary, so long as there is a rich variety of human cultures—and let us hope there will always be this—we should expect there to be correspondingly different forms of religious cult, ritual and organisation, conceptualised in different theological doctrines. And so long as there is a wide spectrum of human psychological types—and again let us hope that there will always be this—we should expect there to be correspondingly different emphases between, for example, the sense of the divine as just and as merciful, between *karma* and *bhakti*; or between worship as formal and communal and worship as free and personal. Thus we may expect the different world faiths to continue as religio-cultural phenomena, though phenomena which are increasingly influencing one another's development. The relation between them will then perhaps be somewhat like that now obtaining between the different denominations of Christianity in Europe or the United States. That is to say, there will in most countries be a dominant religious tradition, with other traditions present in varying strengths, but with considerable awareness on all hands of what they have in common; with some degree of osmosis of membership through their institutional walls; with a large degree of practical cooperation; and even conceivably with some interchange of ministry.

Beyond this the ultimate unity of faiths will be an eschatological unity in which each is both fulfilled and transcended—fulfilled in so far as it is true, transcended in so far as it is less than the whole truth. And indeed even such fulfilling must be a transcending; for the function of a religion is to bring us to a right relationship with the ultimate divine reality, to awareness of our true nature and our place in the Whole, into the presence of God. In the eternal life there is no longer any place for religions; the pilgrim has no need of a way after he has finally arrived. In St. John's vision of the heavenly city at the end of our christian scriptures it is said that there is no temple—no christian church or chapel, no jewish synagogue, no hindu or buddhist temple, no muslim mosque, no sikh gurdwara. . . . For all these exist in time, as ways through time to eternity.

QUESTIONS FOR FURTHER REFLECTION

1. Think of some dogma of one major religion that is flatly contradicted by a dogma of another major religion? Can such dogmas both be true? Can they be different interpretations of the *same* Ultimate Reality? How would Hick answer? How would you answer?
2. What is Hick's vision of the future of religious belief? First, criticize this vision as effectively as you can and then, on behalf of Hick, respond as plausibly as you can to your criticisms.

58. A DEFENSE OF RELIGIOUS EXCLUSIVISM

Alvin Plantinga

A brief biography of Plantinga can be found on p. 295. Alvin Plantinga (1932–   ) is John A. O'Brien Professor of Philosophy at the University of Notre Dame. One of the leading religious philosophers of our times, his books include *God and Other Minds* (1967), *The Nature of Necessity* (1974), *God, Freedom, and Evil* (1974), *Does God Have a Nature?* (1980), *Warrant: The Current Debate* (1993), *Warrant and Proper Function* (1993), and *Warranted Christian Belief* (2000). In the following selection, he argues (contrary to the view of John Hick in the previous selection) that religious exclusivism is neither morally wrong nor rationally unjustifiable. In fact, he claims, some exclusivism in our beliefs is inevitable.

READING QUESTIONS

1. What does Plantinga take to be the main *moral* criticisms of exclusivism? How does he respond to these criticisms?
2. What does Plantinga take to be the main *epistemic* criticisms of exclusivism? How does he respond to these criticisms?
3. What does Plantinga mean by an *epistemic* duty?
4. What distinctions does Plantinga draw between different kinds, or senses, of rationality? To what uses does he put these distinctions?
5. How does Plantinga respond to the charge that the exclusivist does not have enough warrant for knowledge for his or her exclusivist views?

When I was a graduate students at Yale, the philosophy department prided itself on diversity, and it was indeed diverse. There were idealists, pragmatists, phenomenologists, existentialists. Whiteheadians, historians of philosophy, a token positivist, and what could only be described as observers of the passing intellectual scene. In some ways, this was indeed something to take pride in; a student could behold and encounter real, live representatives of many of the main traditions in philosophy. However, it also had an unintended and unhappy side effect. If anyone raised a philosophical question inside, but particularly outside, of class, the typical response would be to catalog some of the various different answers the world has seen: There is the Aristotelian answer, the existentialist answer, the Cartesian answer, Heidegger's answer, perhaps the Buddhist answer, and so on. But the question "What is the truth about this matter?"

was often greated with disdain as unduly naive. There are all these different answers, all endorsed by people of great intellectual power and great dedication to philosophy; for every argument *for* one of these positions, there is another *against* it; would it not be excessively naive, or perhaps arbitrary, to suppose that one of these is in fact true, the others being false? Or, if even there really is a truth of the matter, so that one of them is true and conflicting ones false, wouldn't it be merely arbitrary, in the face of this embarrassment of riches, to *endorse* one of them as the truth, consigning the others to falsehood? How could you possibly know which was true?

A similar attitude is sometimes urged with respect to the impressive variety of religions the world displays. There are theistic religions but also at least some nontheistic religions (or perhaps nontheistic strands) among the enormous variety of religions going under the names Hinduism and Buddhism; among the theistic religions, there are strands of Hinduism and Buddhism and American Indian religion as well as Islam, Judaism, and Christianity; and all differ significantly from each other. Isn't it somehow arbitrary, or irrational, or unjustified, or unwarranted, or even oppressive and imperialistic to endorse one of these as opposed to all the others? According to Jean Bodin, "each is refuted by all";[1] must we not agree? It is in this neighborhood that the so-called problem of pluralism arises. Of course, many concerns and problems can come under this rubric; the specific problem I mean to discuss can be thought of as follows. To put it in an internal and personal way, I find myself with religious beliefs, and religious beliefs that I realize aren't shared by nearly everyone else. For example, I believe both

1. The world was created by God, an almighty, all-knowing, and perfectly good personal being (one that holds beliefs; has aims, plans, and intentions; and can act to accomplish these aims).
2. Human beings require salvation, and God has provided a unique way of salvation through the incar-

nation, life, sacrificial death, and resurrection of his divine son.

Now there are many who do not believe these things. First, there are those who agree with me on (1) but not (2): They are non-Christian theistic religions. Second, there are those who don't accept either (1) or (2) but nonetheless do believe that there is something beyond the natural world, a something such that human well-being and salvation depend upon standing in a right relation to it. Third, in the West and since the Enlightenment, anyway, there are people—*naturalists*, we may call them—who don't believe any of these three things. And my problem is this: When I become really aware of these other ways of looking at the world, these other ways of responding religiously to the world, what must or should I do? What is the right sort of attitude to take? What sort of impact should this awareness have on the beliefs I hold and the strength with which I hold them? My question is this: How should I think about the great religious diversity the world in fact displays? Can I sensibly remain an adherent of just one of these religions, rejecting the others? And here I am thinking specifically of *beliefs*. Of course, there is a great deal more to any religion or religious practice than just belief, and I don't for a moment mean to deny it. But belief is a crucially important part of most religions; it is a crucially important part of *my* religion; and the question I mean to ask here is. What does the awareness of religious diversity mean or should mean for my religious beliefs?

Some speak here of a *new* awareness of religious diversity and speak of this new awareness as constituting (for us in the West) a crisis, a revolution an intellectual development of the same magnitude as the Copernican revolution of the sixteenth century and the alleged discovery of evolution and our animal origins in the nineteenth.[2] No doubt there is at least some truth to this. Of course, the fact is all along many Western Christians and Jews have known that there are other religions and that not nearly everyone shares

---

[1] *Colloquium Heptaplomeres de Rerum Sublimium Arcanis Abditis*, written by 1593 but first published in 1857. English translation by Marion Kuntz (Princeton, N.J.: Princeton Univ. Press, 1975), p. 256.

[2] Joseph Runzo "Today, the impressive piety and evident rationality of the belief systems of other religious traditions, inescapably confronts Christians with a crisis—and a potential revolution." "God, Commitment, and Other Faiths: Pluralism vs. Relativism," *Faith and Philosophy* 5, no. 4 (October 1988):343f. (Reading VIII.5 in this book.)

their religion. The ancient Israelites—some of the prophets, say—were clearly aware of Canaanite religion; and the apostle Paul said that he preached "Christ crucified, a stumbling block to Jews and folly to the Greeks" (1 Corinthians 1:23). Other early Christians, the Christian martyrs, say, must have suspected that not everyone believed as they did; and the church fathers, in offering defenses of Christianity, were certainly apprised of this fact. Thomas Aquinas, again, was clearly aware of those to whom he addressed the *Summa Contra Gentiles*: and the fact that there are non-Christian religions would have come as no surprise to the Jesuit missionaries of the sixteenth and seventeenth centuries or to the Methodist missionaries of the nineteenth. To come to more recent times, when I was a child, *The Banner*, the official publication of my church, contained a small column for children; it was written by "Uncle Dick" who exhorted us to save our nickels and send them to our Indian cousins at the Navaho mission in New Mexico. Both we and our elders knew that the Navahos had or had had a religion different from Christianity, and part of the point of sending the nickels was to try to rectify that situation.

Still, in recent years, probably more of us Christian Westerners have become aware of the world's religious diversity; we have probably learned more about people of other religious persuasions, and we have come to see that they display what looks like real piety, devoutness, and spirituality. What is new, perhaps, is a more widespread sympathy for other religions, a tendency to see them as more valuable, as containing more by way of truth, and a new feeling of solidarity with their practitioners.

Now there are several possible reactions to awareness of religious diversity. One is to continue to believe what you have all along believed; you learn about this diversity but continue to believe—that is, take to be true—such propositions as (1) and (2) above, consequently taking to be false any beliefs, religious or otherwise, that are incompatible with (1) and (2). Following current practice. I will call this *exclusivism*; the exclusivist holds that the tenets or some of the tenets of *one* religion—Christianity, let's say—are in fact true; he adds, naturally enough, that any propositions, including other religious beliefs, that are incompatible with those tenets are false. And there is a fairly widespread

apprehension that there is something seriously wrong with exclusivism. It is irrational, or egotistical and unjustified,[3] or intellectually arrogant,[4] or elitist,[5] or a manifestation of harmful pride,[6] or even oppressive and imperialistic.[7] The claim is that exclusivism as such is or involves a vice of some sort: It is wrong or deplorable. It is this claim I want to examine. I propose to argue that exclusivism need not involve either epistemic or moral failure and that, furthermore, something like it is wholly unavoidable, given our human condition.

These objections, of course, are not to the *truth* of (1) or (2) or any other proposition someone might accept in this exclusivist way (although objections of that sort are also put forward); they are instead directed to the *propriety or rightness* of exclusivism. There are

---

[3]Gary Gutting: "Applying these considerations to religious belief, we seem led to the conclusion that, because believers have many epistemic peers who do not share their belief in God . . . , they have no right to maintain their belief without a justification. If they do so. They are guilty of epistemological egoism." *Religious Belief and Religious Skepticism* (Notre Dame, Ind.: Univ. of Notre Dame Press, 1982), p. 90 (but see the following pages for an important qualification).

[4]Wilfred Cantwell Smith: "Here my submission is that on this front the traditional doctrinal position of the Church has in fact militated against its traditional moral position, and has in fact encouraged Christians to approach other men immorally. Christ has taught us humility, but we have approached them with arrogance. . . . This charge of arrogance is a serious one." *Religious Diversity* (New York: Harper & Row, 1976), p. 13.

[5]Runzo: "Ethically, Religious Exclusivism has the morally repugnant result of making those who have privileged knowledge, or who are intellectually astute, a religious elite, while penalizing those who happen to have no access to the putatively correct religious view, or who are incapable of advanced understanding." Op. cit., p. 348.

[6]John Hick: "But natural pride, despite its positive contribution to human life, becomes harmful when it is elevated to the level of dogma and is built into the belief system of a religious community. This happens when its sense of its own validity and worth is expressed in doctrines implying an exclusive or a decisively superior access to the truth or the power to save." "Religious Pluralism and Absolute Claims." *Religious Pluralism* (Notre Dame, Ind.: Univ. of Notre Dame Press, 1984), p. 197.

[7]John Cobb: "I agree with the liberal theists that even in Pannenberg's case, the quest for an absolute as a basis for understanding reflects the long tradition of Christian imperialism and triumphalism rather than the pluralistic spirit." "The Meaning of Pluralism for Christian Self-Understanding," *Religious Pluralism*, ed. Leroy Rouner (Notre Dame, Ind.: Univ. of Notre Dame Press, 1984), p. 171.

initially two different kinds of indictments of exclusivism: broadly moral, or ethical, indictments and other broadly intellectual, or epistemic, indictments. These overlap in interesting ways as we will see below. But initially, anyway, we can take some of the complaints about exclusivism as *intellectual* criticisms: It is *irrational* or *unjustified* to think in an exclusivistic way. The other large body of complaint is moral: There is something *morally* suspect about exclusivism—it is arbitrary, or intellectually arrogant, or imperialistic. As Joseph Runzo suggests, exclusivism is "neither tolerable nor any longer intellectually honest in the context of our contemporary knowledge of other faiths."[8] I want to consider both kinds of claims or criticisms: I propose to argue that the exclusivist as such is not necessarily guilty of any of these charges.

1. MORAL OBJECTIONS TO EXCLUSIVISM

I turn to the moral complaints: that the exclusivist is intellectually arrogant, or egotistical or self-servingly arbitrary, or dishonest, or imperialistic, or oppressive. But first, I provide three qualifications. An exclusivist, like anyone else, will probably be guilty of some or of all of these things to at least some degree, perhaps particularly the first two. The question, however, is whether she is guilty of these things just by virtue of being an exclusivist. Second, I will use the term *exclusivism* in such a way that you don't count as an exclusivist unless you are rather fully aware of other faiths, have had their existence and their claims called to your attention with some force and perhaps fairly frequently, and have to some degree reflected on the problem of pluralism, asking yourself such questions as whether it is or could be really true that the Lord has revealed Himself and His programs to us Christians, say, in a way in which He hasn't revealed Himself to those of other faiths. Thus, my grandmother, for example, would not have counted as an exclusivist. She had, of course, *heard* of the heathen, as she called them, but the idea that perhaps Christians could learn from them, and learn from them with respect to religious matters, had not so much as entered her head; and the fact that it *hadn't* entered

her head, I take it, was not a matter of moral dereliction on her part. This same would go for a Buddhist or Hindu peasant. These people are not, I think, properly charged with arrogance or other moral flaws in believing as they do.

Third, suppose I am an exclusivist with respect to (1), for example, but nonculpably believe, like Aquinas, say, that I have a knock-down, drag-out argument, a demonstration or conclusive proof of the proposition that there is such a person as God: and suppose I think further (and nonculpably) that if those who don't believe (1) were to be apprised of this argument (and had the ability and training necessary to grasp it and were to think about the argument fairly and reflectively), *they* too would come to believe (1)? Then I could hardly be charged with these moral faults. My condition would be like that of Gödel, let's say, upon having recognized that he had a proof for the incompleteness of arithmetic. True, many of his colleagues and peers didn't believe that arithmetic was incomplete, and some believed that it *was* complete; but presumably Gödel wasn't arbitrary or egotistical in believing that arithmetic is in fact incomplete. Furthermore, he would not have been at fault had he nonculpably but *mistakenly* believed that he had found such a proof. Accordingly, I will use the term *exclusivist* in such a way that you don't count as an exclusivist if you nonculpably think you know of a demonstration or conclusive argument for the beliefs with respect to which you are an exclusivist, or even if you nonculpably think you know of an argument that would convince all or most intelligent and honest people of the truth of that proposition. So an exclusivist, as I use the term, not only believes something like (1) or (2) and thinks false any proposition incompatible with it; she also meets a further condition C that is hard to state precisely and in detail (and in fact any attempt to do so would involve a long and presently irrelevant discussion of *ceteris paribus clauses*). Suffice it to say that C includes (*a*) being rather fully aware of other religions, (*b*) knowing that there is much that at the least looks like genuine piety and devoutness in them, and (*c*) believing that you know of no arguments that would necessarily convince all or most honest and intelligent dissenters.

Given these qualifications then, why should we think that an exclusivist is properly charged with these moral faults? I will deal first and most briefly with charges of oppression and imperialism: I think we must say that they are on the face of it wholly implausible. I daresay there are some among you who reject some of the things I believe: I do not believe that you are thereby oppressing me, even if you do not believe you have an argument that would convince me. It is conceivable that exclusivism might in some way *contribute* to oppression, but it isn't in itself oppressive.

The more important moral charge is that there is a sort of self-serving arbitrariness, an arrogance or egotism, in accepting such propositions as (1) or (2) under condition C; exclusivism is guilty of some serious moral fault or flaw. According to Wilfred Cantwell Smith, ". . . except at the cost of insensitivity or delinquency, it is morally not possible actually to go out into the world and say to devout, intelligent, fellow human beings: '. . . we believe that we know God and we are right; you believe that you know God, and you are totally wrong.' "[9]

So what can the exclusivist have to say for himself? Well, it must be conceded immediately that if he believes (1) or (2), then he must also believe that those who believe something incompatible with them are mistaken and believe what is false. That's no more than simple logic. Furthermore, he must also believe that those who do not believe as he does—those who believe neither (1) nor (2), whether or not they believe their negations—*fail* to believe something that is deep and important and that he *does* believe. He must therefore see himself as *privileged* with respect to those others—those others of both kinds. There is something of great value, he must think, that *he* has and *they* lack. They are ignorant of something—something of great importance—of which he has knowledge. But does this make him properly subject to the above censure?

I think the answer must be no. Or if the answer is yes, then I think we have here a genuine moral dilemma; for in our earthly life here below, as my Sunday School teacher used to say, there is no real alternative; there is no reflective attitude that is not open to the same strictures. These charges of arrogance are a philosophical tar baby: Get close enough to them to use them against the exclusivist and you are likely to

find them stuck fast to yourself. How so? Well, as an exclusivist, I realize that I can't convince others that they should believe as I do, but I nonetheless continue to believe as I do. The charge is that I am, as a result, arrogant or egotistical, arbitrarily preferring my way of doing things to other ways.[10] But what are my alternatives with respect to a proposition like (1)? There seem to be three choices. I can continue to hold it; I can withhold it, in Roderick Chisholm's sense, believing neither it nor its denial, and I can accept its denial. Consider the third way, a way taken by those pluralists who, like John Hick, hold that such propositions as (1) and (2) and their colleagues from other faiths are literally false, although in some way still valid responses to the Real. This seems to me to be no advance at all with respect to the arrogance or egotism problem; this is not a way out. For if I do this, I will then be in the very same condition as I am now: I will believe many propositions others don't believe and will be in condition C with respect to those propositions. For I will then believe the denials of (1) and (2) (as well as the denials of many other propositions explicitly accepted by those of other faiths). Many others, of course, do not believe the denials of (1) and (2) and in fact believe (1) and (2). Further, I will not know of any arguments that can be counted on to persuade those who do believe (1) or (2) (or propositions accepted by the adherents of other religions). I am therefore in the condition of believing propositions that many others do not believe and furthermore am in condition C. If, in the case of those who believe (1) and (2), that is sufficient for intellectual arrogance or egotism, the same goes for those who believe their denials.

So consider the second option: I can instead *withhold* the proposition in question. I can say to myself: "The right course here, given that I can't or couldn't convince these others of what *I* believe, is to believe neither these propositions nor their denials." The pluralist objector to exclusivism can say that the right course, under condition C, is to abstain from believing the offending proposition and also abstain from believing its denial: call him, therefore, "the abstemious plu-

[9]Smith, op. cit., p. 14.

[10]John Hick: ". . . the only reason for treating one's tradition differently from others is the very human but not very cogent reason that it is one's own!" *An Interpretation of Religion*, loc. cit.

BORN INTO THE RIGHT RELIGION? ✱ *Peter van Inwagen*

"Well, isn't it fortunate for you that you just happen to be a member of this 'unique instrument of salvation.' I suppose you realize that if you had been raised among Muslims, you would make similar claims for Islam?" Yes, it is fortunate for me, very fortunate indeed. And I concede that if I and some child born in Cairo or Mecca had been exchanged in our cradles, very likely I should be a devout Muslim. (I'm not so sure about the other child, however. I was not raised a Christian.) But what is supposed to follow from this observation? If certain people claim to be the members of a body that is the unique instrument of God's salvation, who is supposed to defend their claim? Those who are not members of that body?

It should be noted, moreover, that this style of argument (whatever its merits) can hardly be confined to religion. Consider politics. As is the case with religious options, a multitude of political options faces the citizens of any modern nation. Tell the Marxist or the liberal or the Burkean conservative that if only he had been raised in Nazi Germany he would probably have belonged to the Hitler Youth, and he will answer that he is well aware of this elementary fact, and ask what your point is. No one I know of supposes that the undoubted fact that one's adherence to a system of political thought and action is conditioned by one's upbringing is a reason for doubting that the political system one favors is—if not the uniquely "correct" one—clearly and markedly superior to its available rivals. And yet any argument to show that the Church's belief in her own uniqueness was arrogant would apply a fortiori to this almost universally held belief about politics. The members of the Church can, as I have remarked, take no pride in her unique relation to God, for that relation is His doing and not theirs. But the superiority of one's own political party to all others must be due to the superiority of the knowledge, intelligence, wisdom, courage, and goodness of one and one's colleagues to the knowledge, intelligence, wisdom, courage, and goodness collectively embodied in any other political party.

From van Inwagen, "Non Est Hick,"
in *God, Knowledge, and Mystery* (1995).

ralist." But does he thus really avoid the condition that, on the part of the exclusivist, leads to the charges of egotism and arrogance in this way? Think, for a moment, about disagreement. Disagreement, fundamentally, is a matter of adopting conflicting propositional attitudes with respect to a given proposition. In the simplest and most familiar case. I disagree with you if there is some proposition p such that I believe p and you believe $-p$. But that's just the simplest case: there are also others. The one that is presently of interest is this: I believe p and you withhold it, fail to believe it. Call the first kind of disagreement "contradicting"; call the second "dissenting."

My claim is that if contradicting others (under the condition C spelled out above) is arrogant and egotistical, so is dissenting (under that same condition). Suppose you believe some proposition p but I don't; perhaps you believe that it is wrong to discriminate against people simply on the grounds of race, but I, recognizing that there are many people who disagree with you, do not believe this proposition. I don't disbelieve it either, of course, but in the circumstances I think the right thing to do is to abstain from belief. Then am I not implicitly condemning your attitude, your *believing* the proposition, as somehow improper—naive, perhaps, or unjustified, or in some other way less than optimal? I am implicitly saying that my attitude is the superior one; I think my course of action here is the right one and yours somehow wrong, inadequate, improper, in the circumstances at best second-rate. Of course, I realize that there is no question, here, of *showing* you that your attitude is wrong or improper or naive; so am

I not guilty of intellectual arrogance? Of a sort of egotism, thinking I know better than you, arrogating to myself a privileged status with respect to you? The problem for the exclusivist was that she was obliged to think she possessed a truth missed by many others; the problem for the abstemious pluralist is that he is obliged to think that he possesses a virtue others don't or acts rightly where others don't. If, in condition C, one is arrogant by way of believing a proposition others don't, isn't one equally, under those reflective conditions, arrogant by way of withholding a proposition others don't?

Perhaps you will respond by saying that the abstemious pluralist gets into trouble, falls into arrogance, by way of implicitly saying or believing that his way of proceeding is better or wiser than other ways pursued by other people; and perhaps he can escape by abstaining from *that* view as well. Can't he escape the problem by refraining from believing that racial bigotry is wrong and also refraining from holding the view that it is *better,* under the conditions that obtain, to withhold that proposition than to assert and believe it? Well, yes he can; then he has no *reason* for his abstention; he doesn't believe that abstention is better or more appropriate; he simply does abstain. Does this get him off the egotistical hook? Perhaps. But then he can't, in consistency, also hold that there is something wrong with *not* abstaining, with coming right out and *believing* that bigotry is wrong; he loses his objection to the exclusivist. Accordingly, this way out is not available for the abstemious pluralist who accuses the exclusivist of arrogance and egotism.

Indeed, I think we can show that the abstemious pluralist who brings charges of intellectual arrogance against exclusivism is hoist with his own petard, holds a position that in a certain way is self-referentially inconsistent in the circumstances. For he believes

3. If S knows that others don't believe *p* and that he is in condition C with respect to *p*, then S should not believe *p*.

This or something like it is the ground of the charges he brings against the exclusivist. But the abstemious pluralist realizes that many do not accept (3); and I suppose he also realizes that it is unlikely that he can find arguments for (3) that will convince them; hence, he knows that condition C obtains. Given his acceptance of (3), therefore, the right course for him is to abstain from believing (3). Under the conditions that do in fact obtain—namely, his knowledge that others don't accept it and that condition C obtains—he can't properly accept it.

I am therefore inclined to think that one can't, in the circumstances, properly hold (3) or any other proposition that will do the job. One can't find here some principle on the basis of which to hold that the exclusivist is doing the wrong thing, suffers from some moral fault—that is, one can't find such a principle that doesn't, as we might put it, fall victim to itself.

So the abstemious pluralist is hoist with his own petard; but even apart from this dialectical argument (which in any event some will think unduly cute), aren't the charges unconvincing and implausible? I must concede that there are a variety of ways in which I can be and have been intellectually arrogant and egotistic; I have certainly fallen into this vice in the past and no doubt am not free of it now. But am I really arrogant and egotistic just by virtue of believing what I know others don't believe, where I can't show them that I am right? Suppose I think the matter over, consider the objections as carefully as I can, realize that I am finite and furthermore a sinner, certainly no better than those with whom I disagree; but suppose it still seems clear to me that the proposition in question is true. Can I really be behaving immorally in continuing to believe it? I am dead sure that it is wrong to try to advance my career by telling lies about my colleagues; I realize there are those who disagree; I also realize that in all likelihood there is no way I can find to show them that they are wrong; nonetheless I think they *are* wrong. If I think this after careful reflection, if I consider the claims of those who disagree as sympathetically as I can, if I try my level best to ascertain the truth here, and it *still* seems to me sleazy, wrong, and despicable to lie about my colleagues to advance my career, could I really be doing what is immoral by continuing to believe as before? I can't see how. If, after careful reflection and thought, you find yourself convinced that the right propositional attitude to take to (1) and (2) in the face of the facts of religious pluralism is abstention from belief, how could you properly be taxed with egotism, either for so believing or for so abstaining? Even if you knew others did not agree with you?

2. EPISTEMIC OBJECTIONS TO EXCLUSIVISM

I turn now to *epistemic* objections to exclusivism. There are many different specifically epistemic virtues and a corresponding plethora of epistemic vices. The ones with which the exclusivist is most frequently charged, however, are *irrationality* and *lack of justification* in holding his exclusivist beliefs. The claim is that as an exclusivist he holds unjustified beliefs and/or irrational beliefs. Better, *he* is unjustified or irrational in holding these beliefs. I will therefore consider those two claims, and I will argue that the exclusivist views need not be either unjustified or irrational. I will then turn to the question whether his beliefs could have *warrant*—that property, whatever precisely it is, that distinguishes knowledge from mere true belief—and whether they could have enough warrant for knowledge.

3. JUSTIFICATION

The pluralist objector sometimes claims that to hold exclusivist views, in condition C, is *unjustified*—*epistemically* unjustified. Is this true? And what does he mean when he makes this claim? As even a brief glance at the contemporary epistemological literature will show, justification is a protean and multifarious notion. There are, I think, substantially two possibilities as to what he means. The central core of the notion, its beating heart, the paradigmatic center to which most of the myriad contemporary variations are related by way of analogical extension and family resemblance, is the notion of *being within one's intellectual rights*, having violated no intellectual or cognitive duties or obligations in the formation and sustenance of the belief in question. This is the palimpsest, going back to René Descartes and especially John Locke, that underlies the multitudinous battery of contemporary inscriptions. There is no space to argue that point here; but chances are, when the pluralist objector to exclusivism claims that the latter is unjustified, it is some notion lying in this neighborhood that he has in mind. (Here we should note the very close connection between the moral objections to exclusivism and the objection that exclusivism is epistemically unjustified.)

The duties involved, naturally enough, would be specifically *epistemic* duties: perhaps a duty to propor-

tion degree of belief to (propositional) evidence from what is *certain*, that is, self-evident or incorrigible, as with Locke, or perhaps to try one's best to get into and stay in the right relation to the truth, as with Chisholm, the leading contemporary champion of the justificationist tradition with respect to knowledge. But at present there is widespread (and as I see it, correct) agreement that there is no duty of the Lockean kind. Perhaps there is one of the Chisholmian kind: but isn't the exclusivist conforming to that duty if, after the sort of careful, indeed prayerful consideration I mentioned in the response to the moral objection, it still seems to him strongly that (1), say, is true and he accordingly still believes it? It is therefore very hard to see that the exclusivist is necessarily unjustified in this way.

The second possibility for understanding the charge—the charge that exclusivism is epistemically unjustified—has to do with the oft-repeated claim that exclusivism is intellectually *arbitrary*. Perhaps the idea is that there is an intellectual duty to treat similar cases similarly; the exclusivist violates this duty by arbitrarily choosing to believe (for the moment going along with the fiction that we *choose* beliefs of this sort) (1) and (2) in the face of the plurality of conflicting religious beliefs the world presents. But suppose there is such a duty. Clearly you do not violate it if you nonculpably think the beliefs in question are *not* on a par. And as an exclusivist, I *do* think (nonculpably, I hope) that they are not on a par: I think (1) and (2) *true* and those incompatible with either of them *false*.

The rejoinder, of course, will be that it is not alethic parity (their having the same truth value) that is at issue: it is *epistemic* parity that counts. What kind of epistemic parity? What would be relevant, here, I should think, would be *internal* or internalist epistemic parity: parity with respect to what is internally available to the believer. What is internally available to the believer includes, for example, detectable relationships between the belief in question and other beliefs you hold; so internal parity would include parity of propositional evidence. What is internally available to the believer also includes the *phenomenology* that goes with the beliefs in question: the *sensuous* phenomenology but also the nonsensuous phenomenology involved, for example, in the belief's just having the feel of being *right*. But once more, then, (1) and (2) are not on an internal par, for the exclusivist, with beliefs that are incompatible with them. (1) and (2), after all, seem to me to be true; they have for me the phenomenology that accompanies that seeming. The same cannot be said for propositions incompatible with them. If, furthermore, John Calvin is right in thinking that there is such a thing as the *Sensus Divinitatis* and the Internal Testimony of the Holy Spirit, then perhaps (1) and (2) are produced in me by those belief-producing processes and have for me the phenomenology that goes with them; the same is not true for propositions incompatible with them.

But then the next rejoinder: Isn't it probably true that those who reject (1) and (2) in favor of other beliefs have propositional evidence for their beliefs that is on a par with mine for my beliefs? And isn't it also probably true that the same or similar phenomenology accompanies their beliefs as accompanies mine? So that those beliefs really are epistemically and internally on a par with (1) and (2), and the exclusivist is still treating like cases differently? I don't think so; I think there really are arguments available for (1), at least, that are not available for its competitors. And as for similar phenomenology, this is not easy to say; it is not easy to look into the breast of another; the secrets of the human heart are hard to fathom; it is hard indeed to discover this sort of thing even with respect to someone you know really well. I am prepared, however, to stipulate both sorts of parity. Let's agree for purposes of argument that these beliefs are on an epistemic par in the sense that those of a different religious tradition have the same sort of internally available markers—evidence, phenomenology and the like—for their beliefs as I have for (1) and (2). What follows?

Return to the case of moral belief. King David took Bathsheba, made her pregnant, and then, after the failure of various stratagems to get her husband Uriah to think the baby was his, arranged for him to be killed. The prophet Nathan came to David and told him a story about a rich man and a poor man. The rich man had many flocks and herds: the poor man had only a single ewe lamb, which grew up with his children, "ate at his table, drank from his cup, lay in his bosom, and was like a daughter to him." The rich man had unexpected guests. Rather than slaughter one of his own sheep, he took the poor man's single ewe lamb, slaughtered it, and served it to his guests. David ex-

ploded in anger: "The man who did this deserves to die!" Then, in one of the most riveting passages in all the Bible, Nathan turns to David and declares. "You are that man!" And then David sees what he has done.

My interest here is in David's reaction to the story. I agree with David: Such injustice is utterly and despicably wrong; there are really no words for it. I believe that such an action is wrong, and I believe that the proposition that it *isn't* wrong—either because really *nothing* is wrong, or because even if *some* things are wrong, *this* isn't—is false. As a matter of fact, there isn't a lot I believe more strongly. I recognize, however, that there are those who disagree with me; and once more, I doubt that I could find an argument to show them that I am right and they wrong. Further, for all I know, their conflicting beliefs have for them the same internally available epistemic markers, the same phenomenology, as mine have for me. Am I then being arbitrary, treating similar cases differently in continuing to hold, as I do, that in fact that kind of behavior *is* dreadfully wrong? I don't think so. Am I wrong in thinking racial bigotry despicable, even though I know that there are others who disagree, and even if I think they have the same internal markers for their beliefs as I have for mine? I don't think so. I believe in serious actualism, the view that no objects have properties in worlds in which they do not exist, not even nonexistence. Others do not believe this, and perhaps the internal markers of their dissenting views have for them the same quality as my views have for me. Am I being arbitrary in continuing to think as I do? I can't see how.

And the reason here is this: in each of these cases, the believer in question doesn't really think the beliefs in question *are* on a relevant epistemic par. She may agree that she and those who dissent are equally convinced of the truth of their belief and even that they are internally on a par, that the internally available markers are similar, or relevantly similar. But she must still think that there is an important epistemic difference, she thinks that somehow the other person has *made a mistake*, or *has a blind spot*, or hasn't been wholly attentive, or hasn't received some grace she has, or is in some way epistemically less fortunate. And, of course, the pluralist critic is in no better case. He thinks the thing to do when there is internal epistemic parity is to withhold judgment; he knows that there are others who don't think so, and for all he knows that belief has internal parity with his; if he continues in that belief, therefore, he will be in the same condition as the exclusivist; and if he doesn't continue in this belief, he no longer has an objection to the exclusivist.

But couldn't I be wrong? Of course I could! But I don't avoid that risk by withholding all religious (or philosophical or moral) beliefs; I can go wrong that way as well as any other, treating all religions, or all philosophical thoughts, or all moral views as on a par. Again, there is no safe haven here, no way to avoid risk. In particular, you won't reach a safe haven by trying to take the same attitude toward all the historically available patterns of belief and withholding; for in so doing, you adopt a particular pattern of belief and withholding, one incompatible with some adopted by others. "You pays your money and you takes your choice," realizing that you, like anyone else, can be desperately wrong. But what else can you do? You don't really have an alternative. And how can you do better than believe and withhold according to what, after serious and responsible consideration, seems to you to be the right pattern of belief and withholding?

Irrationality

I therefore can't see how it can be sensibly maintained that the exclusivist is unjustified in his exclusivist views; but perhaps, as is sometimes claimed, he or his view is *irrational*. Irrationality, however, is many things to many people; so there is a prior question: What is it to be irrational? More exactly, precisely what quality is it that the objector is attributing to the exclusivist (in condition C) when the former says the latter's exclusivist beliefs are irrational? Since the charge is never developed at all fully, it isn't easy to say. So suppose we simply consider the main varieties of irrationality (or, if you prefer, the main senses of "irrational") and ask whether any of them attach to the exclusivist just by virtue of being an exclusivist. I believe there are substantially five varieties of rationality, five distinct but analogically connected senses of the term *rational*; fortunately not all of them require detailed consideration.

Aristotelian Rationality   This is the sense in which man is a rational animal, one that has *ratio*, one that can look before and after, can hold beliefs, make inferences and is capable of knowledge. This is perhaps

the basic sense, the one of which the others are analogical extensions. It is also, presumably irrelevant in the present context; at any rate I hope the objector does not mean to hold that an exclusivist will by that token no longer be a rational animal.

The Deliverances of Reason   To be rational in the Aristotelian sense is to possess reason: the power or thinking, believing, inferring, reasoning, knowing. Aristotelian rationality is thus *generic*. But there is an important more specific sense lurking in the neighborhood; this is the sense that goes with reason taken more narrowly, as the source of a priori knowledge and belief. An important use of *rational* analogically connected with the first has to do with reason taken in this more narrow way. It is by reason thus construed that we know *self-evident beliefs*—beliefs so obvious that you can't so much as grasp them without seeing that they couldn't be false. These will be among the *deliverances of reason*. Of course there are other beliefs—$38 \times 39 = 1482$, for example—that are not self-evident but are a consequence of self-evident beliefs by way of arguments that are self-evidently valid; these too are among the deliverances of reason. So say that the deliverances of reason is the set of those propositions that are self-evident for us human beings, closed under self-evident consequence. This yields another sense of rationality: a belief is *rational* if it is among the deliverances of reason and *irrational* if it is contrary to the deliverances of reason. (A belief can therefore be neither rational nor irrational, in this sense.) This sense of *rational* is an analogical extension of the fundamental sense, but it is itself extended by analogy to still other senses. Thus, we can broaden the category of reason to include memory, experience, induction, probability, and whatever else goes into science; this is the sense of the term when reason is sometimes contrasted with faith. And we can also soften the requirement for self-evidence, recognizing both that self-evidence or a priori warrant is a matter of degree and that there are many propositions that have a priori warrant, but are not such that no one who understands them can fail to believe them.[11]

---

[11]*An Interpretation of Religion* (New Haven, Conn.: Yale Univ. Press, 1989), p. 2.

Is the exclusivist irrational in *these* senses? I think not: at any rate, the question whether he is isn't the question at issue. His exclusivist beliefs are irrational in these senses only if there is a good argument from the deliverances of reason (taken broadly) to the denials of what he believes. I do not believe that there are any such arguments. Presumably, the same goes for the pluralist objector: at any rate, his objection is not that (1) and (2) are demonstrably false or even that there are good arguments against them from the deliverances of reason; his objection is instead that there is something wrong or subpar with believing them in condition C. This sense too, then, is irrelevant to our present concerns.

The Deontological Sense

This sense of the term has to do with intellectual *requirement*, or *duty*, or *obligation*; a person's belief is irrational in this sense if in forming or holding it she violates such a duty. This is the sense of *irrational* in which according to many contemporary evidentialist objectors to theistic belief, those who believe in God without propositional evidence are irrational. Irrationality in this sense is a matter of failing to conform to intellectual or epistemic duties; the analogical connection with the first. Aristotelian sense is that these duties are thought to be among the deliverances of reason (and hence among the deliverances of the power by virtue of which human beings are rational in the Aristotelian sense). But we have already considered whether the exclusivist is flouting duties; we need say no more about the matter here. As we say, the exclusivist is not necessarily irrational in this sense either.

Zweckrationalität

A common and very important notion of rationality is *means-end rationality*—what our continental cousins, following Max Weber, sometimes call *Zweckrationalität*, the sort of rationality displayed by your actions if they are well calculated to achieve your goals. (Again, the analogical connection with the first sense is clear: The calculation in question requires the power by virtue of which we are rational in Aristotle's sense.) Clearly, there is a whole constellation of notions lurking in the nearby bushes: What would *in fact* contribute to your goals? What you *take* it would contribute to your goals? What you *would* take it would contribute to your goals if you

were sufficiently acute, or knew enough, or weren't distracted by lust, greed, pride, ambition, and the like? What you would take it would contribute to your goals if you weren't thus distracted and were also to reflect sufficiently? and so on. This notion of rationality has assumed enormous importance in the last 150 years or so. (Among its laurels, for example, is the complete domination of the development of the discipline of economics.) Rationality thus construed is a matter of knowing how to get what you want; it is the cunning of reason. Is the exclusivist properly charged with irrationality in this sense? Does his believing in the way he does interfere with his attaining some of his goals, or is it a markedly inferior way of attaining those goals?

An initial *caveat*; it isn't clear that this notion of rationality applies to belief at all. It isn't clear that in *believing* something, I am acting to achieve some goal. If believing is an action at all, it is very far from being the paradigmatic kind of action taken to achieve some end; we don't have a choice as to whether to have beliefs, and we don't have a lot of choice with respect to which beliefs we have. But suppose we set this *caveat* aside and stipulate for purposes of argument that we have sufficient control over our beliefs for them to qualify as actions. Would the exclusivist's beliefs then be irrational in this sense? Well, that depends upon what his goals *are*: if among his goals for religious belief is, for example, not believing anything not believed by someone else, then indeed it would be. But, of course, he needn't have *that* goal. If I do have an end or goal in holding such beliefs as (1) and (2), it would presumably be that of believing the truth on this exceedingly important matter or perhaps that of trying to get in touch as adequately as possible with God, or more broadly with the deepest reality. And if (1) and (2) are *true*, believing them will be a way of doing exactly that, it is only if they are *not* true, then, that believing them could sensibly be thought to be irrational in this means-ends sense. Because the objector does not propose to take as a premise the proposition that (1) and (2) are false—he holds only that there is some flaw involved in *believing* them—this also is presumably not what he means.

Rationality as Sanity and Proper Function

One in the grip of pathological confusion, or flight of ideas, or certain kinds of agnosia, or the manic phase of manic-depressive psychosis will often be said to be irrational; the episode may pass, after which he has regained rationality. Here *rationality* means absence of dysfunction, disorder, impairment, or pathology with respect to rational faculties. So this variety of rationality is again analogically related to Aristotelian rationality; a person is rational in this sense when no malfunction obstructs her use of the faculties by virtue of the possession of which she is rational in the Aristotelian sense. Rationality as sanity does not require possession of particularly exalted rational faculties; it requires only normality (in the nonstatistical sense) or health, or proper function. This use of the term, naturally enough, is prominent in psychiatric discussions—Oliver Sack's male patient who mistook his wife for a hat, for example, was thus irrational. This fifth and final sense of rationality is itself a family of analogically related senses. The fundamental sense here is that of sanity and proper function, but there are other closely related senses. Thus, we may say that a belief (in certain circumstances) is irrational, not because no sane person would hold it, but because no person who was sane and had also undergone a certain course of education would hold it or because no person who was sane and furthermore was as intelligent as we and our friends would hold it; alternatively and more briefly, the idea is not merely that no one who was functioning properly in those circumstances would hold it, but rather no one who was functioning *optimally*, as well or nearly as well as human beings ordinarily do (leaving aside the occasional great genius) would hold it. And this sense of rationality leads directly to the notion of *warrant*; I turn now to that notion; in treating it, we will also treat *ambulando*—this fifth kind of irrationality.

Warrant

So we come to the third version of the epistemic objection: that at any rate the exclusivist doesn't have warrant, or anyway *much* warrant (enough warrant for knowledge) for his exclusivistic views. Many pluralists—for example, Hick, Runzo, and Cantwell Smith—unite in declaring that, at any rate, the exclusivist certainly can't *know* that his exclusivistic views are true. But is this really true? I will argue

briefly that it is not. At any rate, from the perspective of each of the major contemporary accounts of knowledge, it may very well be that the exclusivist knows (1) or (2) or both. First, consider the two main internalistic accounts of knowledge: the justified true belief accounts and the coherentist accounts. As I have already argued, it seems clear that a theist, a believer in (1) could certainly be *justified* (in the primary sense) in believing as she does: she could be flouting no intellectual or cognitive duties or obligations. But then on the most straightforward justified true belief account of knowledge, she can also *know* that it is true—if, that is, it *can* be true. More exactly, what must be possible is that both the exclusivist is justified in believing (1) and/or (2) and they be true. Presumably, the pluralist does not mean to dispute this possibility.

For concreteness, consider the account of justification given by the classical foundationalist Chisholm. On this view, a belief has warrant for me to the extent that accepting it is apt for the fulfillment of my epistemic duty, which (roughly speaking) is that of trying to get and remain in the right relation to the truth. But if after the most careful, thorough, open, and prayerful consideration, it still seems to me—perhaps more strongly than ever—that (1) and (2) are true, then clearly accepting them has great aptness for the fulfillment of that duty.

A similarly brief argument can be given with respect to *coherentism*, the view that what constitutes warrant is coherence with some body of belief. We must distinguish two varieties of coherentism. On the one hand, it might be held that what is required is coherence with some or all of the other beliefs I actually hold; on the other, that what is required is coherence with my *verific* noetic structure (Keith Lehrer's term): the set of beliefs that remains when all the false ones are deleted or replaced by their contradictories. But surely a coherent set of beliefs could include both (1) and (2) together with the beliefs involved in being in condition C; what would be required, perhaps, would be that the set of beliefs contain some explanation of why it is that others do not believe as I do. And if (1) and (2) *are* true, then surely (and a fortiori) there can be coherent verific noetic structures that include them. Hence, neither of these versions of coherentism rule out the possibility that the exclusivist in condition C could know (1) and/or (2).

And now consider the main externalist accounts. The most popular externalist account at present would be one or another version of *reliabilism*. And there is an oft-repeated pluralistic argument that seems to be designed to appeal to reliabilist intuitions. The conclusion of this argument is not always clear, but here is its premise, in Hick's words:

> For it is evident that in some ninety-nine percent of cases the religion which an individual professes and to which he or she adheres depends upon the accidents of birth. Someone born to Buddhist parents in Thailand is very likely to be a Buddhist, someone born to Muslim parents in Saudi Arabia to be a Muslim, someone born to Christian parents in Mexico to be a Christian, and so on.

As a matter of sociological fact, this may be right. Furthermore, it can certainly produce a sense of intellectual vertigo. But what is one to do with this fact, if fact it is, and what follows from it? Does it follow, for example, that I ought not to accept the religious views that I have been brought up to accept, or the ones that I find myself inclined to accept, or the ones that seem to me to be true? Or that the belief producing processes that have produced those beliefs in me are unreliable? Surely not. Furthermore, self-referential problems once more loom; this argument is another philosophical tar baby.

For suppose we concede that if I had been born of Muslim parents in Morocco rather than Christian parents in Michigan, my beliefs would have been quite different. (For one thing, I probably wouldn't believe that I was born in Michigan.) The same goes for the pluralist. Pluralism isn't and hasn't been widely popular in the world at large; if the pluralist had been born in Madagascar, or medieval France, he probably wouldn't have been a pluralist. Does it follow that he shouldn't be a pluralist or that his pluralist beliefs are produced in him by an unreliable belief producing process? I doubt it. Suppose I hold the following, or something similar:

4. If S's religious or philosophical beliefs are such that if S had been born elsewhere and elsewhen, she wouldn't have held them, then those beliefs are produced by unreliable belief producing mechanisms and hence have no warrant.

Once more I will be hoist with my own petard. For in all probability, someone born in Mexico to Christian parents wouldn't believe (4) itself. No matter what philosophical and religious beliefs we hold and withhold (so it seems), there are places and times such that if we have been born there and then, then we would not have displayed the pattern of holding and withholding of religious and philosophical beliefs we *do* display. As I said, this can indeed be vertiginous; but what can we make of it? What can we infer from it about what has warrant and how we should conduct our intellectual lives? That's not easy to say. Can we infer *anything at all* about what has warrant or how we should conduct our intellectual lives? Not obviously.

To return to reliabilism then: For simplicity, let's take the version of reliabilism according to which S knows p if the belief that p is produced in S by a reliable belief producing mechanism or process. I don't have the space here to go into this matter in sufficient detail, but it seems pretty clear that if (1) and (2) are true, then it *could be* that the beliefs that (1) and (2) be produced in me by a reliable belief-producing process. For either we are thinking of *concrete* belief producing processes, like your memory or John's powers of a priori reasoning (tokens as opposed to types), or else we are thinking of *types* of belief producing processes (type reliabilism). The problem with the latter is that there are an enormous number of *different* types of belief producing processes for any given belief, some of which are reliable and some of which are not; the problem (and a horrifying problem it is) is to say which of these is the type the reliability of which determines whether the belief in question has warrant. So the first (token reliabilism) is a better way of stating reliabilism. But then clearly enough if (1) or (2) *are* true, they could be produced in me by a reliable belief-producing, process. Calvin's *Sensus Divinitatis*, for example, could be working in the exclusivist in such a way as to reliably produce the belief that (1) is true; Calvin's Internal Testimony of the Holy Spirit could do the same for (2). If (1) and (2) are true, therefore, then from a reliabilist perspective there is no reason whatever to think that the exclusivist might not know that they are true.

There is another brand of externalism which seems to me to be closer to the truth than reliabilism: call it *(faute de mieux)* "proper functionalism." This view can be stated to a first approximation as follows: S knows *p* if (1) the belief that *p* is produced in S by cognitive faculties that are functioning properly (working as they ought to work, suffering from no dysfunction), (2) the cognitive environment in which *p* is produced is appropriate for those faculties, (3) the purpose of the module of the epistemic faculties producing the belief in question is to produce true beliefs (alternatively, the module of the design plan governing the production of *p* is aimed at the production of true beliefs), and (4) the objective probability of a belief's being true, given that it is produced under those conditions, is high. All of this needs explanation, of course; for present purposes, perhaps, we can collapse the account into the first condition. But then clearly it *could* be, if (1) and (2) are true, that they are produced in me by cognitive faculties functioning properly under condition C. For suppose (1) is true. Then it is surely possible that God has created us human beings with something like Calvin's *Sensus Divinitatis*, a belief producing process that in a wide variety of circumstances functions properly to produce (1) or some very similar belief. Furthermore it is also possible that in response to the human condition of sin and misery, God has provided for us human beings a means of salvation, which he has revealed in the Bible. Still further, perhaps he has arranged for us to come to believe what he means to teach there by way of the operation of something like the Internal Testimony of the Holy Spirit of which Calvin speaks. So on this view, too, if (1) and (2) are true, it is certainly possible that the exclusivist *know* that they are. We can be sure that the exclusivist's views are irrational in this sense, then, only if they are false: but the pluralist objector does not mean to claim that they *are* false; this version of the objection, therefore, also fails. The exclusivist isn't necessarily irrational, and indeed might *know* that (1) and (2) are true, if indeed they *are* true.

All this seems right. But don't the realities of religious pluralism count for anything at all? Is there nothing at all to the claims of the pluralists? Could that really be right? Of course not. For many or most exclusivists, I think, an awareness of the enormous variety of

human religious response functions as a *defeater* for such beliefs as (1) and (2)—an *undercutting* defeater, as opposed to a rebutting defeater. It calls into question, to some degree or other, the sources of one's belief in (1) or (2). It doesn't or needn't do so by way of an *argument*: and indeed there isn't a very powerful argument from the proposition that many apparently devout people around the world dissent from (1) and (2) to the conclusion that (1) and (2) are false. Instead, it works more directly; it directly reduces the level of confidence or degree of belief in the proposition in question. From a Christian perspective, this situation of religious pluralism and our awareness of it is itself a manifestation of our miserable human condition; and it may deprive us of some of the comfort and peace the Lord has promised his followers. It can also deprive the exclusivist of the *knowledge* that (1) and (2) are true, if even they *are* true and he *believes* that they are. Because degree of warrant depends in part on degree of belief, it is possible, though not necessary, that knowledge of the facts of religious pluralism should reduce an exclusivist's degree of belief and hence of warrant for (1) and (2) in such a way as to deprive him of knowledge of (1) and (2). He might be such that if he *hadn't* known the facts of pluralism, then he would have known (1) and (2), but now that he *does* know those facts, he doesn't know (1) and (2). In this way, he may come to know less by knowing more.

Things *could* go this way with the exclusivist. On the other hand, they *needn't* go this way. Consider once more the moral parallel. Perhaps you have always believed it deeply wrong for a counselor to use his position of trust to seduce a client. Perhaps you discover that others disagree; they think it more like a minor peccadillo, like running a red light when there's no traffic; and you realize that possibly these people have the same internal markers for their beliefs that you have for yours. You think the matter over more fully, imaginatively recreate and rehearse such situations, become more aware of just what is involved in such a situation (the breach of trust, the breaking of implied promises, the injustice and unfairness, the nasty irony of a situation in which someone comes to a counselor seeking help but receives only hurt), and come to believe even more fully that such an action is wrong— and indeed to have more warrant for that belief. But something similar can happen in the case of religious beliefs. A fresh or heightened awareness of the facts of religious pluralism could bring about a reappraisal of one's religious life, a reawakening, a new or renewed and deepened grasp and apprehension of (1) and (2). From Calvin's perspective, it could serve as an occasion for a renewed and more powerful working of the belief-producing processes by which we come to apprehend (1) and (2). In that way, knowledge of the facts of pluralism could initially serve as a defeater, but in the long run have precisely the opposite effect.

QUESTIONS FOR FURTHER REFLECTION

1. Did Plantinga make any points in his paper that caused you to change your views? Why or why not?
2. Put yourself in the place of John Hick, the author of the previous selection, and respond to Plantinga's arguments as effectively as you can. Then explain how you think Plantinga could most plausibly respond to Hick. Which, if either, wins this exchange?

59. EXCLUSIVISM, PLURALISM, AND ANARCHY
Kevin Meeker

Kevin Meeker is assistant professor of philosophy at the University of South Alabama, in Mobile. He is the co-editor of *The Philosophical Challenge of Religious Diversity* (Oxford, 2000) and the author of several papers, published in such journals as *Australasian Journal of Philosophy, International Journal for Philosophy of Religion, Philosophia, Journal of the History of Philosophy*, and *Hume Studies*. In this essay, he distinguishes between two types of pluralism and argues that the most thoroughgoing pluralistic theory is unacceptable. He further argues that the more plausible forms of religious pluralism are plausible, ironically, because they surreptitiously adopt a version of the exclusivistic stance that they officially despise. In an important sense, he claims, there is no choice between exclusivism and pluralism; rather, we must choose among kinds of exclusivism.

READING QUESTIONS

1. What is the similarity between culinary pluralism and religious pluralism?
2. What is the difference between selective pluralism and anarchist pluralism?
3. What are two problems with anarchist pluralism?
4. Why does the author claim that selective pluralism is a type of religious exclusivism?
5. How does Meeker's argument threaten to upset the traditional categories of exclusivism, inclusivism, and pluralism?

1. INTRODUCTION

An attractive aspect of most large metropolitan areas is the diversity of restaurants. In many places one can choose, say, Chinese, Ethiopian, French, Greek, Indonesian, Italian, Mexican, Middle Eastern, or Thai fare. In addition to these international options, one can taste favorite local foods, which often differ dramatically from city to city even within a single culture or country. Taking the United States as an example, one can sample the seafood cooked Cajun-style in New Orleans, Chicago-style pizzas in the Windy City, or steak and cheese sandwiches in Philadelphia. And we could add to such lists almost indefinitely. Of course not everyone will enjoy all of the menu options at all of these types of restaurants. But most consider those who *exclusively* cling to only one type of food, and doggedly refuse to try—or recognize the allure of—any other type, suspect or dull. After all, variety is the spice of life.

Let us call those who celebrate the plethora of recipes that tempt our collective palates *culinary pluralists*.

What precisely do culinary pluralists believe? In brief, they hold that all of these different ways of eating are more or less equally efficacious ways of being physically nourished. To elaborate, they maintain that because these different foods are all constituted by the same basic building blocks of carbohydrates, enzymes, fats, minerals, proteins, vitamins, and the like, they can all nourish us. As long as one is getting the proper amounts of essential nutrients, it does not matter how the food is put together, so to speak. Of course, many do not have access to, or even much knowledge of, a rich variety of foods and must exclusively rely on a local diet, through no fault of their own. Such people can still receive the essential nutrients for living. It would be odd, though, if people with the means to try other food not only refused to do so but also proclaimed that their culinary way was the only way to achieve physical nourishment. Suppose, for instance, that some people proclaimed that French food was the only beneficial way to nourish the body and ruled out all other types of food as unhealthy. Culinary pluralists would understandably protest that such an exclusive approach is grievously incorrect: although one can gain proper nutrition from French food, it is irresponsible to claim that this type of food is the only healthy alternative for humans and thereby *exclude* other types of food from consideration.[1]

Many people, including philosophers, adopt a similar stance toward religion. *Religious Pluralists* claim, roughly speaking, that all the great world religions are equally efficacious in helping one to achieve spiritual nourishment[2] or salvation. To them, it does not matter which religion one holds dear because they are all rooted in the same essential teachings. As long as one is getting the proper amounts of spiritual nutrients, it does not matter how the doctrinal package is put together. Just as it is untoward for someone to claim that, say, Indonesian food is the only way to obtain physical nourishment, so too it is unconscionable that anyone would claim that a particular religion is the only way to achieve spiritual nourishment. In other words, religious pluralists strongly oppose *Religious Exclusivism*, which, roughly speaking, is the view that only one religion provides salvation or essential spiritual nourishment. To religious pluralists such a view's exclusive nature is too narrow-minded.

Although religious pluralism is widely accepted and seems to many to be as obviously true as culinary pluralism, in this essay I shall turn the tables on pluralism. That is, I shall distinguish between two types of pluralism and argue that the most thoroughgoing pluralistic theory is too unpalatable to swallow. Moreover, I shall also show that the more plausible forms of religious pluralism really are, ironically enough, plausible because they (surreptitiously?) adopt a version of the exclusivistic stance that they officially despise. So I shall argue that in an important sense, there is no choice between exclusivism and pluralism; rather we must choose among the various types of exclusivism. To build this case for the near inevitably of some type of exclusivism, I shall first examine John Hick's version of religious pluralism, which is the most sophisticated and well-developed pluralistic theory currently discussed. After explaining Hick's position in the second section, I shall point out one of its major flaws in the third section. This flaw provides the basis for a general argument supporting exclusivism, which the fourth section develops in some detail. The fifth section will provide some important qualifications and amendments to deepen our understanding of the issues under discussion.

2. HICK'S PLURALISTIC THEORY OF RELIGIONS[3]

Hick argues that his theory is the best explanation of the religious diversity present in the world. His

---

[1]Note that I am not discussing those who claim that one type of food tastes better to them. Rather, this is a dispute about how *beneficial* the food is for humans.

[2]I am not here tackling the issue of whether or not we have a soul or spirit, which would be a separate *substance* from the body. I am merely assuming, for the sake of the argument, that there is a spiritual *aspect* to human beings. Mormons, for instance, talk about their spiritual teachings despite the fact that they believe that everything, including God, is a material substance. I hope that my way of speaking will not be too distracting and will not require us to enter the deep and controversial debates about human nature and the relationship between the body and mind.

[3]Sections two and three derive in large measure from my "Religious Diversity, Ethics, and Epistemic Arbitrariness" (forthcoming).

reasoning is roughly as follows.[4] Although religious experience justifies religious adherents in believing that there is a divine reality, the different conceptions of this divine reality in the world religions pose a perplexing problem. For, according to Hick, it is arbitrary to consider one's own religion as the only true religion in light of religious diversity. Despite the doctrinal differences among religions, Hick maintains that ". . . at the level of their most basic moral insights the great traditions use a common criterion. For they agree in giving a central and normative role to the unselfish regard for others we call love or compassion. This is commonly expressed in the principle of valuing others as we value ourselves, and treating them accordingly."[5] In his famous pluralistic vein, Hick contends that following any of these great world religions is a promising way to transform one's life from self-centeredness to an appropriate Reality-centeredness (i.e., a life devoted to compassion). In other words, he insists that, so far as we can tell, all of the great world religions are equally efficacious spheres of salvation. As a result, he argues that it is most reasonable to postulate an Ultimate Reality, which he often calls "the Real," that is experienced in different ways by those in various traditions. Moreover, although the followers of the different religious traditions experience the Real in various ways, on Hick's view the unknowable divine reality for the most part exceeds human conceptualization. That is, the Real is neither good nor evil, neither personal nor nonpersonal, neither one nor many, and so on. In short, religious adherents are correct to believe that there is an Ultimate Reality to which they are responding, but mistaken to believe that their particular religion embodies the only correct possible way to respond to that Ultimate Reality.

So why precisely does Hick claim that exclusivism is so mistaken? He argues that if we consider our own religious experiences as cognitive re-

sponses to a divine reality, we must place the religious experiences of others on an equal footing. According to Hick:

> In acknowledging this we are obeying the intellectual Golden Rule of granting to others a premise on which we rely ourselves. Persons living within other traditions, then, are equally justified in trusting their own distinctive religious experience in forming their beliefs on the basis of it. For the only reason for treating one's tradition differently from others is the very human, but not very cogent, reason that it is one's own![6]

Hick emphasizes the arbitrariness of exclusivistic religious beliefs by arguing that they are highly conditioned by upbringing and culture. After all, those born into Christian homes in the United States ordinarily adopt the Christian beliefs of their environment. Likewise, those born into Hindu homes in India normally follow the Hindu beliefs of their culture. Hick contends that if an exclusivist Christian had been born in a Hindu environment, then it seems very likely that the person would have embraced Hindu thought in such circumstances. One's religion thus appears to be merely an accident of when and where one was born. Hick is thus suspicious of those who maintain their exclusivistic beliefs despite being aware of how arbitrary such beliefs appear.

To gain a better understanding of the nature of Hick's pluralism, it will be helpful to examine his response to some points advanced by Gavin D'Costa that are similar to mine. While I shall contend that there are two types of pluralism, and the only plausible type is a form of exclusivism, D'Costa pushes an even more radical conclusion that pluralism can only exist as a form of exclusivism.[7] More exactly, he maintains that to construct a theory of religious pluralism one *must* employ some criterion to distinguish the great world religions from the others; because employing a criterion is an exclusivistic procedure, he concludes that pluralism itself is a type of exclu-

[4]For a concise summary of Hick's views on these matters, see John Hick, "Religious Pluralism and Salvation," in *The Philosophical Challenge of Religious Diversity*, edited by Philip L. Quinn and Kevin Meeker (New York: Oxford University Press, 2000), pp. 54–66. Originally published in *Faith and Philosophy* 5, 4 (October 1988), pp. 365–377.

[5]Hick, "Religious Pluralism and Salvation," p. 56.

[6]John Hick, *An Interpretation of Religion* (New Haven: Yale University Press, 1989), p. 235.

[7]Gavin D'Costa, "The Impossibility of a Pluralist View of Religions," *Religious Studies* 32 (June 1997), p. 232.

sivism.[8] When he focuses specifically on Hick, he points out that Hick must make

> . . . very specific truth claims that are also exclusive truth claims. For example, it is claimed that the Real cannot be known in itself and when any religion claims that the Real has revealed itself, then such claims are false. Such pluralism cannot tolerate alternative claims and is forced to deem them as mythical. The irony about tolerant pluralism is that it is eventually intolerant towards most forms of orthodox religious belief, Christian or otherwise. Hence . . . [Hick] is an exclusivist and not a pluralist as he claims. I hope that I have shown in this case that pluralism must always logically be a form of exclusivism and that nothing called pluralism really exists.[9]

Hick, needless to say, is not very receptive to this suggestion:

> . . . to think that using criteria, as such, constitutes exclusivism, although intelligible in a purely notional and trivial sense, is much more misleading than helpful . . . For to make an assertion about anything is to deny its contrary, and to propose a theory or view about anything is to reject alternative views. But to label all judgments, all proposing of theories and hypotheses, all expressions of opinion, as exclusivist would be to empty the term of any useful meaning. For there could then be no nonexclusivist statements, so that the term would cease to mark any distinction.[10]

I suggest that Hick is able to deflect D'Costa's criticism because D'Costa only seems to be talking about *doctrinal exclusivism*. A doctrinal exclusivist holds that the *doctrines* or *propositional content* of only one religion

are true. On the other hand, Hick concentrates (as we shall concentrate) on the *salvific efficacy* of religions. In other words, for Hick doctrines are not that important to salvation (unless we are talking about the doctrine of altruism); practicing selflessness is the key to salvation. So Hick is advocating what is sometimes called *soteriological pluralism* in opposition to *soteriological exclusivism*. Hick apparently agrees with D'Costa in one abstract sense: namely, that one (or a small set of) religions might have more true doctrines than most of the others. In fact, he seems to believe that he has the most "true" description of religion. But because Hick is concerned with soteriological pluralism and not doctrinal pluralism, he dismisses D'Costa's point as trivial.[11]

Perhaps D'Costa might argue that his critique works because the claim that the great world religions are salvifically effective is itself a doctrine. But Hick tries to block this maneuver by making the following distinction: ". . . religious exclusivism and religious pluralism are of *different logical kinds* [emphasis added], the one being a self-committing affirmation of faith and the other a philosophical hypothesis."[12] What exactly does Hick mean? His point, I think, is as follows. Let us call "regular" religious beliefs, such as *Moses was a prophet of God*, first-order beliefs. Hick's theory of religious pluralism is not a *first-order* belief, but a *meta-theory* that attempts to explain *first-order* beliefs. That is to say, the *first-order* beliefs of the religious believers are what the *meta-theory* (or *second-order* belief) is trying to explain.[13] Because pluralism and exclusivism are of different logical kinds, it is presumably mistaken to say, as D'Costa does, that pluralism is a type of exclusivism; this would be akin to classifying apples as a type of orange.

[8]D'Costa, "The Impossibility of a Pluralist View of Religions," pp. 223-232. Hick summarizes D'Costa's idea simply: "D'Costa's thesis is that to use a criterion is to be an exclusivist" (John Hick, "The Possibility of Religious Pluralism: A Reply to Gavin D'Costa," *Religious Studies* 33, 2 [June 1997], p. 161).
[9]D'Costa, "The Impossibility of a Pluralist View of Religion," p. 229.
[10]"The Possibility of Religious Pluralism: A Reply to Gavin D'Costa," p. 162.
[11]In light of these distinctions, consider Peter van Inwagen's complaint: "Professor Hick is himself a religious exclusivist . . . practically everyone in the world believes something inconsistent with his Anglo-American academic religious pluralism. . . . 'Religious pluralism' is not the contradictory of religious exclusivism, but one more case of it" ["A Reply to Professor Hick," *Faith and Philosophy* 14, 3 (July 1997), p. 300]. If I understand Hick, he would probably agree with van Inwagen, but, as he said with D'Costa, claim that this is a trivial form of (doctrinal) religious exclusivism.
[12]"The Possibility of Religious Pluralism: A Reply to Gavin D'Costa," p. 163.
[13]See Hick, "The Possibility of Religious Pluralism: A Reply to Gavin D'Costa," p. 163.

So does this distinction allow Hick to escape the general charge that his (soteriological) pluralism is a type of exclusivism? One might question the legitimacy of Hick's distinction. After all, some religions adopt pluralism as a type of self-committing affirmation of faith. Presumably the contents of such pluralistic *first-order* beliefs are the same as Hick's *second-order* beliefs. Does Hick's adoption of these beliefs qua philosopher change their logical status? It is difficult to see how. Moreover, many exclusivists have built-in explanations for religious diversity that are part of their religious creed.[14] Such *second-order* beliefs appear to be self-committing affirmations of faith. In such cases, the distinction between *first-order* beliefs and *meta-theories* (or *second-order* beliefs) seems to break down. Of course, pursuing these issues would lead us into deep and difficult questions about the nature of knowledge, belief, faith, and explanation. Fortunately, we can isolate a major flaw in Hick's position even if we grant him this distinction.

3. PLURALISM AND MORALITY

Let us consider the story of Sophia, a very open-minded agnostic who is herself trying to make sense of religious diversity. She draws on exclusivistic creeds to construct an exclusivistic *meta-theory* to explain this diversity. (It is very important to note that because she is not a religious believer, her views cannot be regarded as *first-order* beliefs.) She also reads Hick's account and dubs it the *Altruistic Pluralism* meta-theory. Particularly interesting to her is the argument that the *first-order* beliefs of religious exclusivists are arbitrary from this *meta-theoretical* vantage point.

During further study, Sophia reads the following accounts of the Thugs in India:

> The Thugs . . . made it plain that to destroy life, not to rob it for their own gain, had been their first aim. They explained how although, for the Hindu, God was both creator and destroyer, the goddess Kali, seeing that the forces of destruction were losing, came down to earth to teach the Thugs their craft and to promise to act as their

guardian . . . They believed that their mission was divine and would be rewarded by a place in their own special heaven.[15]

When faced with the report of these practices, she begins to wonder if *all* behavior, not just following the Golden Rule, will lead one to salvation/liberation. So she constructs an hypothesis that all religious experiences are veridical and cognitive responses to the Real. On this hypothesis, moreover, *all* religious faiths, and not just the "great" world religions, are equally efficacious in helping their followers lead Reality-centered lives. This theory she dubs *Anarchist Pluralism*. By adopting this term, Sophia does not mean to imply that anyone who adopts it will flout all rules. She simply means that those who adopt this position must concede that, when it comes to religion, literally "anything goes."

After further thought, Sophia realizes that Hick could not accept the veridicality of the Thugs' religious experience. For he has argued that "It is important to recognize that religious experience and its fruits . . . cohere together; for if the fruits . . . were hatred, misery, aggression, unkindness, impatience, violence, and lack of self-control this would lead us to deny the authenticity of the experience."[16] But now Sophia is puzzled. How is she to choose between Hick's altruistic pluralism and anarchist pluralism? Hick justifies his own preference for the "great" world religions in the following passage:

> But why select *these* particular traditions in the first place, rather than Satanism, Nazism, the Order of the Solar Temple, and so on, as providing

---

[14]For a discussion of some of these explanations, see Kelly James Clark, "Perils of Pluralism," *Faith and Philosophy* 14, 3 (July 1997), pp. 303–320.

[15]Nigel Davies, *Human Sacrifice in History and Today* (New York: William Morrow and Company, 1981), p. 92. A few pages later, Davies comments:

> At the crucial point in India's great epic [the Bhagavad-Gita] the supreme deity is thus revealed as . . . being both the creator and the destroyer of all that exists . . . [and] if God is both good and evil, man does not have to be good, but is free to copy either side of God's nature. . . . If anything the cruel side of the gods was easier to copy and the results were more spectacular. Why should anyone have qualms about killing a fellow human being in a colorful ceremony when the great Shiva and his wife delighted in destruction, bore in their hands the instruments of death, and fed on human flesh (p. 96)?

[16]Hick, "The Possibility of Religious Pluralism: A Reply to Gavin D'Costa," p. 164.

the right criterion? The answer arises out of the route by which the pluralistic hypothesis is arrived at . . . The hypothesis . . . originates within a particular religious tradition—in my own case Christianity. As a Christian, then, one accepts that the sense of the presence of God within the Christian community is indeed an awareness of a divine presence; and one sees a confirmation of the self-evidently valuable and desirable "fruit of the Spirit" which St. Paul listed as "love, joy, peace, patience, kindness, goodness, faithfulness, gentleness, self-control" (Galatians 5:22).[17]

The problem with Hick's justification is that it relies on an ethical criterion that is as arbitrary as religious exclusivism allegedly is. For Hick's hypothesis is meant to explain the apparent moral progress of believers in all of the great world religions. But his observations of moral progress are based on *first-order* moral beliefs that arise from his commitment to Christianity. And these ethical beliefs are presumably highly contingent on one's upbringing. If Hick had been born in the Indian Thug culture or had been raised in a Nietzschean spirit to loathe Christian morality, then he presumably would not have viewed aggression as inferior to loving kindness. Although he is entitled to his *first-order* belief in the superiority of the Golden Rule, from the *meta-theoretical* perspective it is arbitrary and unjustified. To paraphrase Hick: the only reason for treating one's moral tradition differently from others is the very human, but not very cogent, reason that it is one's own. But if we jettison this belief, then he cannot even propose his altruistic pluralism because what it purports to explain can no longer be taken for granted. In the end, then, Hick seems to compromise his adherence to the intellectual Golden Rule "of granting to others a premise on which we rely ourselves."[18] As a result, he *excludes* certain religious traditions as legitimate ways to approach the "Real" in violation of his own principles. That is to say, although Hick's pluralism includes the great world religions, it excludes many others. Perhaps the claim that Hick's pluralism is, in an important

and nontrivial way, a type of exclusivism is not so far-fetched when put in this light.

4. TWO TYPES OF PLURALISM AND THE ARGUMENT FOR EXCLUSIVISM

We are now in a position to move beyond our discussion of Hick and construct a more general argument for exclusivism. If one holds to a pluralist view of religions, then one must either hold (1) that *all* religions lead to salvation/liberation or (2) that *only some* religions lead to salvation/liberation. Let us call (2) *Selective Pluralism*. Hick's altruistic pluralism is clearly a type of selective pluralism. Of course, those, like Hick, who hold to (2) usually say that the great world religions can help to put one in touch with the "divine" (which Hick prefers to call the "Real") because they share common ethical teachings. Others may opt for some other nonethical way to sift the efficacious religions from the ineffective ones. But in affirming selective pluralism, one is affirming exclusivism. For by definition, if only some religions are effective, then some are not and are thus *excluded* from the category of effective religions. As we have seen, even Hick, the most sophisticated advocate of religious pluralism, cannot escape this classification.

Some may object that exclusivism is usually associated with religious traditions that claim that only *one* religion can provide us with salvation/liberation while selective pluralists are not that restrictive; for they allow that *many* (though not all) religions are salvifically fruitful. And there is a big difference between one and many, as there would be between one wife and many wives. This difference between exclusivism and pluralism is quite significant—significant enough to show that selective pluralism is really not in any nontrivial way a type of exclusivism. But this difference is not so great as it might first appear. To take Hick as an example, he allows *only one* basic ethical principle (altruism) as the correct principle (although many different religions promote this principle). In other words, for Hick there is only one (ethical) way and any way that conflicts with it is excluded.

Although I think that this objection to exclusivism fails, a major insight is lurking beneath its surface. Typically, exclusivism is defined in terms of the truth or salvific efficacy of *one* religion. For example, in recently defending religious exclusivism, Alvin

---

[17]Hick, "The Possibility of Religious Pluralism: A Reply to Gavin D'Costa," p. 164.

[18]*An Interpretation of Religion*, p. 235.

CHOICES * *Ralph Waldo Emerson*

God offers to every mind its choice between truth and repose. Take which you please—you can never have both. Between these, as a pendulum, man oscillates. He in whom the love of repose predominates will accept the first creed, the first philosophy, the first political party he meets—most likely his father's. He gets rest, commodity and reputation; but he shuts the door of truth. He in whom the love of truth predominates will keep himself aloof from all moorings, and afloat. He will abstain from dogmatism, and recognize all the opposite negations between which, as walls, his being is swung. He submits to the inconvenience of suspense and imperfect opinion, but he is a candidate for truth, as the other is not, and respects the highest law of his being.

From Ralph Waldo Emerson, *Progress of Culture* (1867).

Plantinga has offered the following definition: "Following current practice, I shall call [exclusivism the view] . . . that the tenets or some of the tenets of *one* religion—Christianity, let's say—are in fact, true . . . [and] any propositions, including other religious beliefs, that are incompatible with those tenets are false."[19] I have provided such a similar definition in the introduction of this essay and elsewhere.[20] But I have come to think that this definition, like many academic definitions, does not accurately represent the reality it is seeking to describe. To explain what I mean, let us hearken back to the culinary example in the introduction. There I proposed for consideration "some people [who] proclaimed that French food was the only beneficial way to nourish the body and ruled out all other types of food as unhealthy." While such culinary exclusivists tout the benefits of French cuisine, they would surely allow that because French culture has spread through different parts of the world, some types of, say, Canadian or Carribean food might be sufficiently similar to count as nourishing as well—but only insofar as it closely resembles French food. By the same token, many exclusivists would presumably qualify their stances. For example, it seems that even the most exclusivistic versions of Christianity

do not hold that a universally necessary condition for salvation is some adoption of explicitly Christian belief. More specifically, many exclusivist Christians believe not only that infants who perish go to heaven but also that many pre-Christian figures, such as Abraham, Rahab, David, and Jeremiah are in heaven as well despite the fact that none explicitly held to Christian doctrine. Their faith, while not explicitly Christian, was salvifically efficacious because it was sufficiently similar to Christianity. Of course spelling all of this out is a complicated story; but such qualifications seem at the very least to require us to modify our definition of religious exclusivism. Let us say that *Religious Exclusivism* is the view that only one religion—*or a set of closely related religions or practices*—provides salvation or essential spiritual nourishment.

With this definition of exclusivism, the one/many contrast between exclusivism and pluralism evaporates. And we have a more accurate definition to boot. Now some might worry that this switch is simply made to bolster the argument that I am making: that pluralism is a type of exclusivism. But this worry would be unfounded. For the main detractors of exclusivism do not focus on exclusivism restricting salvation to one religion; rather they attack the claim that some religions are salvifically fruitful and *some are not*. To illustrate this point, let us examine two further representative critics of exclusivism. Wilfred Cantwell Smith has lodged the following complaint: "except at the cost of insensitivity or delinquency, it is morally not possible actually to go out into the world and say to devout, in-

---

[19] Alvin Plantinga, *Warranted Christian Belief* (New York: Oxford University Press, 2000), p. 440. Note that Plantinga is really only defending *doctrinal exclusivism*.

[20] See Kevin Meeker and Philip L. Quinn, "Introduction," in *The Philosophical Challenge of Religious Diversity*, edited by Philip L. Quinn and Kevin Meeker (New York: Oxford University Press, 2000), p. 3.

telligent, fellow human beings: 'we believe that we know God and we are right; you believe that you know God, and you are totally wrong.' "[21] Similarly, Joseph Runzo has argued that: "Ethically, Religious Exclusivism has the morally repugnant result of making those who have privileged knowledge, or who are intellectually astute, a religious elite, while penalizing those who happen to have no access to the putatively correct religious view, or who are incapable of advanced understanding."[22] Note that both Smith and Runzo find it objectionable simply to exclude other religions. Note also that such complaints are equally applicable to selective pluralism. For the selective pluralist would presumably say to adherents from those religions that are not selected: "we believe that we know God and we are right; you believe that you know God, and you are totally wrong." By the same token, selective pluralism generates a religious elite insofar as it does not allow that all religions are salvifically beneficial. In short, if one objects to excluding any religion, then one cannot accept traditional exclusivism or selective pluralism.

An implication of my argument is that the difference between religious exclusivism and selective pluralism is at best a difference in degree, not in kind. For both theories exclude a certain set of religions. That is, both claim that some religions are not salvifically fruitful. The debate, then, is not about the propriety of excluding some religion; instead the debate is over which religion(s) should be excluded. In other words, a debate about how exclusive one should be will be quite different from disparaging any form of exclusivism whatsoever on the grounds that it is exclusive. Needless to say, part of my contention is that pluralists have been dismissing exclusivism because it is exclusive, when they themselves are exclusive as well.

At this point, those with pluralistic proclivities might understandably reject both the traditional forms of exclusivism, and the implicit exclusivism of selective pluralism, as equally narrow-minded. Just as culinary pluralists might say that it is wrong to reject any

type of food (Greek, for example), such pluralists would claim that it is wrong to exclude any religion. This stance leads us to option (1). And now we have returned to the anarchist pluralism discussed in the previous section. Anarchist pluralism, unlike selective pluralism, certainly seems to possess the potential to avoid exclusivistic tendencies. Even here, though, exclusivistic leanings are difficult to eradicate entirely. For pluralistic theories as we have been discussing them are theories about *religion* and *salvation/liberation*. So if anarchist pluralists say that *all* religions are spiritually nourishing or lead to salvation/liberation, then they must face the following question: what about nonreligious philosophies or outlooks on life? If one says that they are *excluded* from spiritual benefits, then anarchist pluralism is clearly exclusive as well and does not separate itself in this respect from traditional exclusivism or selective pluralism. But typically those who are willing to traverse the anarchist pluralist route so despise exclusivistic thought that they will say that even nonreligious people can achieve salvation/liberation. Such people are truly devoid of exclusivistic thought. But they face two other daunting problems.

The first problem is that such a theory is implausible in the extreme. At the risk of being redundant, recall again that we are discussing theories of *religion*. Selective pluralists, like Hick, claim that different *religions* provide the means to salvation. An anarchist pluralist, then, would hold that *every* religion provides one with salvation/liberation. So while Hick claims that Nazism (or Satanism) does not provide one with salvation/liberation, anarchist pluralists will deride such exclusion as narrow-minded. But it is quite implausible to say Nazism is spiritually nourishing or edifying. Of course, even some exclusivists might hold that *Nazis* can achieve salvation, *but not in virtue of following Nazism* (more on this point in the next section). But anarchist pluralism holds that Nazis are saved in virtue of following Nazism. Granted, I cannot *prove* that someone is not saved simply in virtue of following Nazism (or Satanism).[23] But this claim is about as implausible as any claim that I have encountered. Some anarchist pluralists might respond by asking: on what

[21]Wilfred Cantwell Smith, *Religious Diversity* (New York: Harper and Row, 1976), p. 14.
[22]"God, Commitment, and Other Faiths: Pluralism vs. Relativism" *Faith and Philosophy* 5 (1988), 348.

[23]Of course, if Hick is correct in defining salvation in terms of becoming more other-centered, loving individuals, then it seems quite obvious that Nazism does not produce loving individuals.

basis can one exclude Nazism? After all, different exclusivists (be they traditional exclusivists or selective pluralists) will give different answers to this question. And the anarchist pluralist may ask how we are to pick the correct answer. This is a good question; but no matter how difficult it is to tackle this question, it seems more plausible and worthwhile to search for such an answer than to acquiesce to the implausible claim that Nazis are saved/liberated in virtue of being Nazis. I suspect that most would agree with this claim.[24]

A second problem with anarchist pluralism is that it seems to make religion pointless. For what is religion? This is a vexing and difficult question, to be sure. Yet, it seems that we can provide a rough characterization. As a first approximation, one might say that religions seek to provide salvation. But some think that this is too Western or Christian of a notion. So many use the hybrid term "salvation/liberation": while Christianity, for example, talks of salvation from sin, many Hindu and Buddhist religions talk of liberation from the wheel of becoming or rebirth. In most cases, though, it seems that religions offer solutions or remedies to some problem (although the solutions and conceptualizations of the problem vary enormously). For example, in Zen Buddhism koans (part of the solution) are provided to help break one's dualistic thinking (the problem). If we think of "problem" and "solution" broadly enough, I suggest that this is a helpful way to think of religion[25] (though I am not claiming that it is a characterization without problems). On the anarchist pluralist view, though, we have to ask: what is the point of religion? If one obtains a correct solution no matter what one tries, then in what sense can we say that there is a problem? And if there is no problem, then religion is not needed to solve it. Religion is pointless. Consider an analogy. When the famous words "Houston, we have a problem" were uttered, the

gravity of the situation was evident (no pun intended). If the astronauts could not perform the right set of actions, or if they did nothing at all, then they would die. If they would have survived no matter what course of action they pursued, or even if they did nothing at all, then one could legitimately ask: "In what sense is there a problem?" In sum, a problem, even in its most abstract sense, seems to suggest that there is a possibility of failure, of not reaching one's goal or proper destination. If there is no possibility of failure, then there is no problem; and this is true whether we are discussing extraterrestrial journeys or spiritual journeys.

Initially anarchist pluralism might look appealing because it seems so similar to culinary pluralism. But now that we have examined the problems with anarchist pluralism, it is clear that culinary pluralists are not really open to any dietary option either. For not all food promotes life. Portabella mushrooms might be nutritious, but some mushrooms are lethally poisonous. A culinary pluralist who said that you could eat anything, poisonous mushrooms included, is surely incorrect. Some might retort that poisonous mushrooms are not food; so the position of culinary pluralist that one should not exclude any *food* remains intact. But even if we ignore this kind of exclusion, it seems obvious that some types of food are more nourishing than others. The typical American diet (if one can talk about such a thing) seems to be lacking nutritionally when compared to the diets of many other cultures; this is supported by the fact that so many Americans (61 percent according to some statistics that I have seen) are overweight. Perhaps the culprit is the fast food and junk food consumed in large quantities. In any event, it does not seem inherently wrong to think that some food in some cultures might be more beneficial than in other cultures. But this would seem to support a selective pluralist approach in which some foods (junk food, fast food?) are *properly excluded* as unhealthy.

Of course some might retort that there is a disanalogy between anarchist culinary pluralism and anarchist religious pluralism; in the former case one can empirically test whether a substance is unhealthy. For if you eat enough of a poisonous mushroom then you will die. If there are some religions that are not spiritually nourishing, then it is difficult to tell empirically

---

[24]D. Z. Phillips once asked me if anyone really held such a view as anarchist pluralism. While no philosopher comes to mind here, I have met some nonphilosophers who hold such a view. So while I am convinced that some hold to anarchist pluralism, I am equally convinced that most people would find it inordinately implausible.

[25]In a very broad sense, of course, for culinary pluralists food is a solution to a problem. This is not to say that the need for food is a disease. The problem is that without food one will die.

which ones those would be. But this disanalogy does not affect my point. After all, I have argued on independent grounds that anarchist pluralism is unacceptable. Here I am merely undermining the suggestion that the analogy between culinary pluralism and religious pluralism might support the anarchist version of pluralism. This disanalogy will simply exacerbate the difficulty of trying to use the analogy to support anarchist pluralism.

In sum, then, I have presented pluralists with a dilemma: either one chooses selective pluralism and automatically excludes some religions as spiritually unhealthy or one adopts the implausible anarchist pluralism. Most clearly adopt the more plausible selective pluralism. But this plausibility is bought at a steep price. That is, its plausibility derives from its *exclusion* of religions like Satanism. While selective pluralism may not exclude to the same degree as traditional exclusivism, it still excludes and is thus properly called a type of religious exclusivism. Because the only plausible approaches to religious diversity are exclusivistic to some extent, traditional forms of exclusivism cannot be dismissed simply because there is something inherently wrong with being exclusive.

5. AMENDMENTS AND QUALIFICATIONS

My defense of exclusivism has been generic. Many types of exclusivism populate the present scene: Christian versions, Islamic versions, and so on. I have not been arguing that any one of these is true; rather I have been contending that these cannot be branded as implausible responses to religious diversity simply in virtue of the fact that they exclude other religions. Different versions of exclusivism might also introduce other subjects that require further discussion. For instance, many exclusivists hold that those who do not adhere to the healthy religion(s) will receive everlasting punishment. So those who reject the notion of everlasting punishment also sometimes automatically reject exclusivism.[26] But these are separate issues. One could be an exclusivist and reject the notion of everlasting punishment. For example, one could hold that salvation is obtained only through the Roman Catholic Church; those who are not members will go to purgatory after death and all those in purgatory will eventually accept the Catholic way and make it to heaven.[27] Or one could hold that following some version of Hinduism is the only correct way to achieve liberation. Those who reject this way in this life could be reincarnated over and over again until they follow the correct path. On both such exclusivistic views, there is no notion of eternal punishment; at least there is no claim that anyone would suffer eternal punishment. In this sense, some exclusivists might hold that even Nazis could eventually be saved or liberated, but not in virtue of following Nazism: they must, say, repent in purgatory or adopt Hinduism in another lifetime.

Of course some might say that my defense has been *too* generic. For I've really only ruled out anarchist pluralism; but all other options are still on the table as types of exclusivism. So have we made any advances? I suggest that we have because my aim has been to level the playing field and propose that traditional exclusivism and selective pluralism, properly understood, are both exclusive to some extent. In other words, I have tried to blur the lines somewhat and suggest that we are faced with a continuum of possible positions. Of course my suggestion might upset some conventional categories. Customarily, philosophers have categorized three types of approaches to religious diversity: exclusivism, inclusivism, and pluralism. On this schema, exclusivism is usually defined on terms of the truth or salvific efficacy of one religion. I've defined it as the view that one religion—*or a set of closely related religions or practices*—provide salvation or essential spiritual nourishment. This definition encroaches on inclusivistic territory. Inclusivism is difficult to define; but perhaps this rough characterization will suffice. Inclusivists are, generally speaking, doctrinal exclusivists. That is, they hold that one religion *correctly describes* the process by which we are saved/liberated. Although only one religion expresses the entire *propositional truth* about the divine, salvation, and so forth, it is still possible that those outside of the one true particular religion will be *saved/liberated* even if they are unaware of

[26]See William Lane Craig, " 'No Other Name': A Middle Knowledge Perspective on the Exclusivity of Salvation through Christ" in *The Philosophical Challenge of Religious Diversity*, pp. 38–53.

[27]I am not suggesting that this is "official" Catholic doctrine. I am merely suggesting that some people might hold to such a position.

the fact that the process by which they are saved is correctly described in the one true tradition. So a Christian inclusivist might say that sincere Jainists, for example, can be saved; but their salvation is possible because of the sacrifice of Christ. Presumably inclusivists are exclusivists too: they exclude some religions such as Nazism. If they did not exclude any religion, then this position would inherit the many problems of anarchist pluralism while still clinging to some vestiges of (doctrinal) exclusivism. In general, though, inclusivists seem more willing to allow that adherents of other religions can be saved/liberated than exclusivists; but they are more restrictive than pluralists. Because inclusivism seeks to occupy a middle ground between what I have called the continuum between exclusivism and pluralism, I do not think that we need to abandon this type of classification altogether, even if it is difficult to draw distinct boundaries. But I would suggest that this classification not be taken so literally that it covers up the exclusive aspects of all these positions.

With these distinctions in hand, we can address another type of pluralistic concern. Some might argue for selective pluralism over traditional exclusivism on the grounds that it allows more people to be saved or liberated. If Islamic exclusivism is true, for example, then the vast majority of people are going to miss out on spiritual nourishment. As we have seen, of course, some forms of exclusivism could hold that everyone will eventually achieve salvation/liberation. This point notwithstanding, though, it seems that this type of concern for numbers or percentages is irrelevant. For suppose that Germany had won World War II and Hitler was able to exterminate vast numbers of people. If the majority of the world then followed Nazism, would someone like Hick agree that Nazism is salvifically efficacious on the grounds that denying such a claim would mean that the vast majority of the world is lacking in spiritual nourishment? I doubt it. Hick, and most others, would still hold that there is good reason to exclude Nazism, independent of the percentage of the world population that affirmed it. So the real issue is this: given that we need to exclude, on what basis should we exclude?

One final important qualification: my argument is admittedly conditional. One will accept its full implications on the condition that one holds, roughly, that there is a spiritual dimension to human life that needs to be addressed. My argument, for example, will doubtless not convince any agnostics or atheists to become religious exclusivists of one sort or another. That is, those who doubt or deny the existence of a spiritual aspect to human beings or the existence of God—or any Transcendent entity—will not be impressed. After all, one response to the diversity of religions is to be skeptical about the whole notion of religion. Here the analogy between, say, culinary pluralism and religious pluralism breaks down to some extent. For I don't know of anyone who denies the existence of physical nourishment; but there are plenty who deny, say, the existence of God or any need for spiritual nourishment. But *if* one is inclined to believe in "religious" or "spiritual" things, then the question becomes this: what is the most plausible way to think about the diversity of religions that offer us solutions to our problems? I have argued that if one is searching for a religious answer to this question, then the only plausible candidates are ones that exclude one religion or another. Pluralists, selective ones at any rate, do not advertise this exclusionary aspect; but it is present nonetheless. One must decide the best way to exclude; it is not plausible to assume that one can opt out of excluding.

6. CONCLUSION

In this essay I have tried to show that any plausible view of religions needs to be exclusivistic to some extent. Even John Hick, the most sophisticated of pluralists, cannot escape this problem. So if one must exclude, then initially any type of exclusivism, even traditional exclusivism, is as defensible as selective pluralism. The real debate is not whether we should exclude, but what type of exclusion is defensible. Selective pluralists will doubtless continue to argue that their way of excluding is superior; but this is a different debate from simply saying that it is wrong to exclude. In short, there is no sharp dividing line between exclusivism and pluralism; so we are faced with a continuum of options. The real question, then, is this: where does one draw the line between salvifically effective and ineffective religions?[28]

---

[28]For helpful comments on earlier versions of this paper, I am grateful to John Coker, William Lane Craig, Kyle Meeker, Patricia Meeker, and Christian Miller.

QUESTIONS FOR FURTHER REFLECTION

1. Is the analogy between religious pluralism and culinary pluralism a good one?
2. Is the author's revised definition of exclusivism better than the original definition?
3. Is selective pluralism really a type of religious ex-clusivism? If so, does this selectivity undermine the spirit of pluralism?
4. Can anything be said on behalf of anarchist pluralism? Does it make religion pointless? Is it that implausible?
5. On what basis should we judge the salvific efficacy of a religion?

60. RELIGIOUS DIVERSITY AND RELIGIOUS BELIEF

Allen Stairs

Allen Stairs is a member of the philosophy department at the University of Maryland, where he has taught since 1979. Although most of his publications have been in the foundations of quantum mechanics, he has had a long-standing interest in the philosophy of religion. Aside from his philosophical interests, Stairs is an avid dancer and writes occasional essays on American roots music.

John Hick claims that most people's religious beliefs are determined by accidents of birth. Stairs surveys a number of responses to this fact: religious skepticism, exclusivism, inclusivism, and pluralism. He points out that all of these are defensible as philosophical theses, but adds that this doesn't help the typical believer, who is likely to be an exclusivist and who is not equipped to give a philosophical defense of her beliefs. Plantinga's version of exclusivism seems to provide a solution since he defends the claim that believers are entitled without offering arguments or evidence to hold their specific religious beliefs. Stairs argues that there are problems with Plantinga's position, not least because typical believers are in no position to know that they aren't missing something that members of other traditions see. Stairs then offers a possible attitude towards one's exclusivist beliefs that might provide a way around the objections.

READING QUESTIONS

1. Stairs distinguishes three kinds of exclusivism. What are they?
2. Why is inclusivism a special case of exclusivism?
3. Explain the difference between inclusivism and pluralism.
4. What is a basic belief? Give some examples of beliefs that you think most people would regard as *properly* basic.
5. What does Plantinga *mean* by the word "warranted"? What does he think that warrant *amounts* to? (Note: these are not the same question.)
6. What does Stairs mean by calling a belief *conditionally self-warranting*? Try to come up with examples—even if they seem a bit artificial—of beliefs that might count as conditionally self-warranting.

Chances are you've met people whose religious beliefs and backgrounds are very different from your own. Chances are, however, that if you were a Muslim or a Buddhist or a Christian before, you haven't taken up a new faith.

John Hick puts it this way:

For it is evident that in some ninety-nine percent of cases the religion which an individual professes and to which he or she adheres depends upon the accidents of birth. Someone born to Buddhist parents in Thailand is very likely to be a Buddhist, someone born to Muslim parents in Saudi Arabia to be a Muslim, someone born to Christian parents in Mexico to be a Christian, and so on. [Quoted in Plantinga 1995, p. 211]

For some people this is an unsettling observation. But what should we say?

1. RESPONSES TO DIVERSITY

Before we survey some responses, an apology. Not all religions are theistic, and certainly not all are Christian. Nonetheless, much of what we'll discuss bears most clearly on theistic religions and most of the examples come from Christianity. Two reasons: first, we'll spend a lot of time discussing Alvin Plantinga, whose defense of religious exclusivism is explicitly Christian. Second, Christianity is the tradition I understand the best and feel most confident describing. Nonetheless, the intent is to say things of more general interest.

Skepticism

One *might* say: all religions are false—the theistic ones *and* the nontheistic ones. Or better: all the religions that go beyond naturalism are false. A weaker version of skepticism would be *agnostic* about all non-naturalist religion.

There are also religious responses to religious diversity. The three most common are *exclusivism, inclusivism,* and *pluralism.*

Exclusivism

Here's Alvin Plantinga's version of exclusivism:

> [T]he exclusivist holds that the tenets or some of the tenets of *one* religion—Christianity, let's say—are in fact true; he adds, naturally enough, that any propositions, including other religious beliefs, that are incompatible with those tenets are false. [Plantinga 1995, p. 194]

Plantinga's definition deals with truth, but there's another issue: salvation or liberation or ultimate fulfillment. That gives us subtypes of exclusivism.

If bumper stickers are any indication, what we'll call *hyper-exclusivism* is a popular view: salvation is open only to members of the "true religion"—the one that the hyper-exclusivist believes; everyone else will be consigned to Hell for eternity.

Backing off one step from hyper-exclusivism, we come to what we'll call *strong exclusivism:* salvation/liberation (John Hick's term) requires accepting the right religion, but not everyone else is eternally damned. People who believe the wrong religion may simply be extinguished at death, or, on one variant, punished for their earthly sins and then extinguished.

Inclusivism

On many people's usage, exclusivism *means* hyper-exclusivism or strong exclusivism. We'll treat *inclusivism* as a distinct position, but given Plantinga's definition above, inclusivism is a variety of exclusivism.

According to inclusivists, the True Religion identifies the *source* of salvation/liberation, but people who don't realize this can still be saved/liberated even though they don't understand how it happens. One statement of a Christian version of inclusivism comes from a recent Vatican document (incorporated almost verbatim into Pope John Paul II's general audience in St. Peter's Square, Sept. 9, 1998.)

> Concretely, it will be in the sincere practice of what is good in their own religious tradition and by following the dictates of their conscience that the members of other religions respond positively to God's invitation and receive salvation in Jesus Christ, even while they do not recognize or acknowledge him as their Saviour [From "Dialogue and Proclamation: Reflections and Orientations on Interrelgious Dialogue and the Proclamation of the Gospels of Jesus Christ"; quote reprinted in Dupuis 1997, p. 178]

It would clearly be possible to formulate similar doctrines for Islam, Sikhism, and so on.

Pluralism

There's a popular image that conveys the central idea of *pluralism:* the different religions as paths up the same mountain. Like inclusivists, pluralists don't believe that salvation/liberation is tied to a *single* religion. According to the pluralist, however, no religion has a lock on the truth. Religious claims are "reflections" or "symbols" of the Divine or the Ultimate, but not literal descriptions; our encounter with the Ultimate is filtered through the set of concepts, stories and symbols that our culture and experience provide us with. John Hick is perhaps the foremost contemporary defender of pluralism.

2. RESPONSES TO DIVERSITY: A PRELIMINARY EVALUATION

These are the most common positions for dealing with religious diversity. What can be said for them?

Skepticism

Religious skepticism is an honorable option, but it's not obligatory. There are enough sophisticated defenses of religion that it would be hard to argue that religious belief is simply indefensible. In any case, I will take the following modest claim for granted: rejecting religious skepticism is among the reasonable options open to thoughtful people. This is quite different from saying that *every* religious point of view is reasonable or that religious skepticism is *un*reasonable.

Pluralism

In Hick's version, pluralism is the product of two somewhat different ideas. One is that we are entitled to trust our religious experiences—to treat them as "cognitively significant" responses to what Hick calls The Real. By calling them "cognitively significant" Hick means at least that they shouldn't be thought of as delusions, though exactly what to make of their content is more complicated. In any case, this doesn't just apply to members of some privileged religion. Hick speaks of an "intellectual golden rule" of "granting to others premises that we rely on." He writes:

> . . . let us avoid the implausibly arbitrary dogma that religious experience is all delusory with the single exception of the particular form enjoyed by the one who is speaking. [Hick 1989, p. 235]

This generosity comes at a price: it must accommodate the wide variety of apparently conflicting religious views. Here Hick points out that within most

of the major religions there is a strand that distinguishes between the Ultimate as it is in itself and as we *experience* it. Mystics urge this distinction, but Hick insists that even mystics filter their experience of the Ultimate through the categories available to them. The Real is ultimately beyond literal description, indeed, unknowable as it is in itself, but religious claims can have *mythological truth*, which Hick understands as a sort of "practical" truth; they can put us in right relationship with Ultimate Reality.

One complaint against pluralism is that even though it *aims* to take the various religions more seriously than inclusivism does, it doesn't succeed. Contrary to the popular cant, the religions *don't* see themselves as different paths to the same destination; there are wide divergences in how the various religions understand religious fulfillment. If pluralism is right, the truth about salvation/liberation is hidden in the mystery of the unknowable Real. That means that pluralism doesn't acknowledge the concrete claims and aims of the religions. (See Heim 2000.) However, if Pluralism is the best hypothesis, it's not clear that this complaint bears on anything other than good manners.

Inclusivism

Inclusivism is a special case of exclusivism. As such, it inherits some of the complaints against exclusivism, most notably the one that asks how anyone can be justified in claiming that *their* religion is the right one. Some people also accuse inclusivists of a condescending attitude towards other religions. Why should we expect a Hindu to be pleased to hear that it is really the death and resurrection of Jesus or the mercy of Allah that is the true source of his own religious fulfillment?

Of course, what the inclusivist says could be *true* even if others don't like to hear it, though whether the inclusivist could *know* this is another matter. In any case, inclusivism is a religious improvement over hyper-exclusivism and strong exclusivism.

Why? Start with hyper-exclusivism. Set aside the question of whether *any* finite amount of sin could call for eternal damnation. Simply think about a pious member of some religion other than your own. This person knows of your religion, but—not surprisingly, given her upbringing—hasn't been persuaded to abandon her own tradition. Still, by our usual standards she is a good and decent person who tries to do her religious duty and to stay in right relation with the Ultimate, even though, like everyone else, she fails to do this fully. What sort of a God would consign her to Hell for eternity? How could that God be worthy of our worship?

For me, these are rhetorical questions. I can't even dimly imagine what it would be like to think that the "sin" of honestly believing the wrong religion should damn someone—even when coupled with the usual run of human failings. Strong exclusivism is more complicated and in the interests of time I'll leave it aside, except to comment that I think it's also implausible on religious grounds. It's too hard to reconcile with the view that God loves us in anything like the way a Father loves His children.

3. EXCLUSIVISM

Exclusivism in Plantinga's version calls for an extended treatment. Following Plantinga, we said that an exclusivist accepts some or all tenets of a *particular* religion, and believes that the contrary claims of other religions are false. Plantinga adds an important qualification:

> . . . an exclusivist, as I use the term, not only [holds such beliefs as "The world was created by God . . ."] and thinks false any proposition incompatible with [them]; she also meets a further condition C that is hard to state precisely and in detail . . . Suffice it to say that C includes (1) Being rather fully aware of other religions, (2) knowing that there is much that at the least looks like genuine piety and devoutness in them, and (3) believing that you know of no arguments that would necessarily convince all or most honest and intelligent dissenters of your own religious allegiances. [Plantinga 1995 p. 196]

Here is how Plantinga frames his defense of exclusivism:

> I propose to argue that exclusivism need not involve either epistemic or moral failure and that furthermore, something like it is wholly unavoidable given our human condition. [*ibid*. p. 195]

"Epistemic" here means, roughly, having to do with the rules of reasonable belief. As for moral failures, Plantinga has in mind sins such as imperialism and intellectual arrogance or egotism.

Philosophical Exclusivism?

There's something odd about the way Plantinga states his aim. *Of course* it's possible to be an exclusivist without committing any moral or intellectual sin. If this weren't true, philosophy itself would be in trouble. My comments here owe quite a bit to Plantinga, though I'm not sure he'd like my way of making the point.

Philosophical claims are inherently contentious, most aren't susceptible of proof and even the best philosopher should admit that philosophers who disagree with her aren't automatically fools. That means that the typical philosopher satisfies an analogue of condition C: she is aware of the diversity of philosophical positions, realizes that they contain much that looks like the product of serious thought, and knows that she doesn't have an argument that would persuade all or most philosophers to adopt her view; that doesn't mean she should abandon her position. But it's possible to argue for religious positions in the way that philosophers argue, and it's possible to do this at an intellectual level that calls for serious attention and respect.

This may suggest that to be entitled to religious belief, a person needs to be able to make a philosophical case for it. I think we don't need to say this; I'll say why later on. Nonetheless, the alternative seems disturbing. Most of us have met people who stand on "faith" when anyone challenges any of their religious beliefs. On the one hand, faith isn't exclusive to exclusivism; a pluralist would probably claim it too. But the pluralist's faith is more diffuse and he isn't likely to say that his commitment to *pluralism* is a matter of faith. More specific sorts of exclusivists—say, Islamic or Christian—tend to make much more specific and contentious claims that they "justify" by appeal to faith. This seems troubling: why is the Christian's or Muslim's unreasoned faith any better than the Hindu's or the Sikh's?

This is what makes Plantinga's position intriguing. He argues that the believer is entitled to her beliefs without reasons or arguments at all.

Plantinga and Properly Basic Belief

When Plantinga says that the believer doesn't need evidence or arguments, he is *not* saying that the beliefs are simply baseless. I believe that I had a bagel for breakfast; I *remember* eating it. But I don't treat the proposition that I have a memory experience as a basis for an inference; I just have the memory and form the belief. The memory experience is my *ground*, in Plantinga's terms, but not my *evidence*. (*Evidence* for Plantinga is *propositional;* experiences aren't propositions.) More generally, certain experiences call forth certain beliefs. These beliefs are *basic* beliefs. And in some cases—memory, perception, and so on,—they can be *properly* basic; *legitimately* held without evidence.

Most philosophers would agree. However, according to Plantinga, belief in God can also be properly basic. Someone looks at the starry sky, or contemplates the wonders of nature and finds himself spontaneously believing "God created all this." On Plantinga's view, such beliefs are *properly basic.*

Is this worrisome? Plenty of people don't find themselves believing in God when they gaze at the starry sky. Still, it's possible to perceive things that others can't. Chinese speakers hear phonetic distinctions that elude me utterly; it's *very* hard to look at a young chick and tell whether it's male or female, even if you know what you're looking for. But a skilled chicken sexer can sort up to 800 chicks an hour.

Of course, we have ways of checking Chinese speakers' discriminations and chicken sexers' sortings. But consider another sort of example. I believe the mural that Jackson Pollock painted for the entranceway to Peggy Guggenheim's house is—among other things—extraordinarily, fiercely beautiful. I know there are people who think the painting looks like a giant drop cloth; it's clear to me that they're missing something. And I don't think I need to convince *them* in order to be entitled to my view.

Plantinga makes a great deal of examples like this. And he insists: if, on sober reflection, it really seems to the believer that she sees something that not everyone sees, she isn't obliged to give up her belief.

Plantinga applies this to specifically *Christian* belief. The believer reads the Gospels, hears their message and becomes convinced. Call this *basic Christian belief*. Plantinga claims that basic Christian belief is

properly basic and provides a theory of knowledge to account for this.

Plantinga's Theory of Knowledge and Basic Belief: Exposition

Plantinga uses the term "warrant" for whatever it is that true belief needs in order to count as knowledge. In Plantinga's view S's belief is warranted if it's

> . . . produced in S by cognitive faculties functioning properly (subject to no dysfunction) in a cognitive environment that is appropriate for S's kind of cognitive faculties, according to a design plan that is successfully aimed at truth. [Plantinga 2000 p. 156]

That's a mouthful; an example should help.

When my memory is functioning properly, and when there's nothing around to trick it or trip it up (that's the bit about the "suitable environment"), remembering something is highly likely to yield the truth about what happened. (That's the bit about "successfully aimed at truth"; notice that it doesn't mean "guaranteed to produce true beliefs.") This is a matter of the proper function or "design plan" of memory, whether this design plan comes from God or evolution. The same goes for seeing, hearing and the other senses.

We can say similar things about typical cases of testimony. Suppose you tell me that Joan was at work today and I believe you. Assuming you're generally honest, and assuming you actually know she was there, I now know it too. Our tendency to accept testimony has a proper function: acquiring knowledge about things we didn't see ourselves.

How does this apply to religious belief? First, according to Plantinga, God endowed each of us with a *sensus divinatus*—a sense of the divine. It leads us spontaneously to form beliefs about God in response to various experiences—for example, seeing the majesty of the heavens.

As for specifically Christian belief, Plantinga believes that at some point, humanity fell into sin. One of the consequences was that our *sensus divinatus* was clouded. But God instituted a plan for reconciling us to Himself. This plan is found in scripture, authored by God through the intermediary of the Bible's human authors. When we read the Bible, we don't go through some complex process of historical/inductive reasoning. Rather, if we are

PATRIARCHY * *Jane Flax*

Feminist theory is based on a series of assumptions. First, it assumes that men and women have different experiences; that the world is not the same for men and women. Some women think the experiences of women should be identical to the experiences of men. Others would like to transform the world so that there are no such dichotomous experiences. Proponents of both views, however, assume that women's experiences differ from men's, and that one task of feminist theory is to explain that difference.

Secondly, feminist theory assumes that women's oppression is not a subset of some other social relationship. Some argue that if the class system were destroyed, then women would not be oppressed—I don't classify that as feminist theory. Feminist theory assumes that women's oppression is a unique constellation of social problems and has to be understood in itself, and not as a subset of class or any other structure.

It also assumes that women's oppression is not merely a case of what the Chinese call "bad attitudes." I have problems with the word "sexism," because the term implies that women's oppression will disappear when men become more enlightened. On the contrary, I think feminist theory assumes that the oppression of women is part of the way the structure of the world is organized, and that one task of feminist theory is to explain how and why this structure evolved.

Feminist theory names this structure "patriarchy," and assumes that it is a historical force that has a material and psychological base. What I mean by "patriarchy" is the system in which men have more power than women, and have more access to whatever society esteems. What society esteems obviously varies from culture to culture; but if you look at the spheres of power, you'll find that all who have it are male. This is a long-term historical fact rooted in real things. It's not a question of bad attitudes; it's not a historical accident—there are real advantages to men in retaining control over women. Feminist theorists want to explain why that's so.

Patriarchy works backwards as well. It affects the way men and women feel about themselves, and is so deeply internalized that we can't imagine a world without gender. As much as we talk about androgyny, or some situation in which gender isn't so significant, I don't think any of us could imagine a world in which gender would not bring with it many special meanings. We may still want to attach special meanings to gender, but a feminist theory would argue that the power attached to gender should disappear; it should not determine whether a person is excluded or included in whatever is esteemed by society.

From "Women Do Theory," *Quest* (1979).

open to it, the Holy Spirit works within us—Plantinga talks of the *internal instigation of the Holy Spirit*—and we come to believe. When this happens, our beliefs are warranted: our belief-forming mechanism is behaving as it should. As Plantinga sees it, we are dealing with something rather like the way that we properly form beliefs in response to testimony—say, a letter from a friend. In this case, however, the Holy Spirit is the testifier and also intervenes to help us come to belief.

Plantinga isn't trying to convince us that Christianity is true. He's offering a model of how knowledge of Christianity could work *if* Christianity is true. In his view, the most important thing about the model is that if classical Christianity is true, this model or something close to it would hold as well. The role of the Holy Spirit in curing us of our spiritual blindness and leading us to Christian belief is *part of Christian doctrine*.

Plantinga thinks this implies something very important: it won't do to object to Christianity by saying:

"I can't *prove* that it's false, but even if it's true, it's irrational to believe it." The model is intended to tell us why Christian belief would be *warranted* if true and hence *known*.

Plantinga's Theory of Knowledge and Basic Belief: Assessment

Plantinga's account of warrant, sketched above, is a "proper function" account. Let's call beliefs that fit the account *functionally sound* (my term; not Plantinga's.) Plantinga is trying to convince us that Christian belief can be *properly basic*. What he actually argues is that Christian belief, held in the basic way, is functionally sound if it's true, and he maintains that warrant *is* functional soundness. Call a belief that would be warranted if true *conditionally self-warranting*. What are the relationships among functional soundness, conditional self-warrant and being properly basic?

Plantinga seems to be saying that conditional self-warrant is *sufficient* to make a belief properly basic. He argues that it would be wrong to object to *basic* Christian belief by saying that even if it's true it's irrational, because if basic Christian belief is true, it is functionally sound and hence, on his view, *warranted*.

This seems wrong. Consider the fanatical religious believer. By "fanatical," I mean someone whose beliefs are widely agreed even by members of his own religion to be well beyond the pale of the reasonable—Osama bin Laden, perhaps. *If* Osama bin Laden's beliefs are true and if he comes by them in the basic way (say, by meditating on the Koran) then they are functionally sound. (I'm assuming an account of how God inspires readers of the Koran.) That would make them warranted on Plantinga's account. But they seem to be the very paradigm of beliefs that *no one* should hold in the basic way; they seem the very paradigm of beliefs that should be subjected to long, hard critical reflection before being accepted and, by the way, would fail that test.

There's an implicit criticism of Plantinga's account of warrant here, but it would take time to develop it in detail. In any case, it's by no means clear from Plantinga's argument that conditional self-warrant—or more accurately, conditional functional soundness—is enough to make a basic belief *properly* basic.

Religious Knowledge and Religious Diversity

Suppose nonetheless that Plantinga's account of warrant is correct. And suppose that if a basic belief has conditional warrant, it's *properly* basic. It's *still* doubtful that one can *know* the truths of Christianity or Hinduism or . . . in the basic way.

Muslims presumably believe that by reading the Koran, they are inspired to believe the truth. If Islam is true, they're no doubt right. Other sorts of believers could make similar claims. The problem is that in addition to whatever reliable belief-producing mechanism may go with the true religion (if there is one) there is another sort of mechanism that regularly produces *false* religious belief: being brought up in a religion, hearing its stories, participating in its rituals, living amongst its adherents. This is a powerful force for producing religious conviction. Nonetheless, there being no majority religion, the usual output is *false* belief.

Recall that for Plantinga, it's not enough that the belief be produced by a mechanism reliably aimed at the truth. Suppose, to take a famous example, I am driving through Barn County, where the locals have scattered lots of fake barn fronts, set up to look real from the road. Among these fakes, there are a few actual barns. Suppose I drive by and happen to notice one of the real ones. Even if my eyes are fine, even if I'm looking at a real barn and even if I *believe* it's a real barn, I don't *know* this, as Plantinga agrees. The problem is that I can't make the right discriminations in this environment.

Why isn't the real world of religions a sort of theological Barn County? There may be a true religion out there; clearly there are many decoys. But given the way we're wired, there's a very good chance that even if we grew up with a decoy, we'll come to think it's real.

Plantinga might reply that in Barn County, the same mechanism—my healthy visual system—is at work whether I see a "barn" or a barn. It's just that the mechanism isn't capable of detecting the difference. In the case of the religions, Plantinga might insist, the Holy Spirit *isn't* at work when I'm faced with the "wrong" one; I *don't* get the belief *via* an otherwise reliable mechanism.

Even if this is true, it's not clear that it's relevant. Suppose I'm in an environment where the conditions tend to produce optical illusions, and they do this partly by interfering with the proper operation of my visual system. If I *think* I see a pool of water, it's most likely an illusion. As it happens, however, what I see before me is a real pool of water and in this instance, by luck, my visual system is functioning properly. It *still* seems clear that I'm not warranted in believing I see a pool of water; just by looking, I can't discriminate between real pools and the illusions that local conditions usually produce.

The facts of religious diversity don't mean that there is *no* way to make a reasonable judgment that a particular religion is true and its rivals false. Perhaps the right kind of properly informed theological argument can, for example. But it's hard to see how a *basic belief* could do the job.

There is a related point. As we noted earlier, sometimes it's reasonable to think you're seeing something that other people are missing. But there's a flip side to this thought: sometimes it's reasonable to think *you* might be missing something that someone else is seeing. An example: I'm not fond of Wagner. I have a colleague who tells me that he once felt this way. Then a friend sat him down in front of the stereo and pointed out various features of Wagner's music. My colleague was converted. He heard what he hadn't heard before.

I take this seriously. My colleague is musically sophisticated. I believe that he almost certainly came to hear something that I haven't heard yet but that's really there. In any case, I certainly don't think I'm in a good position to judge Wagner's music. It sometimes takes time and effort to appreciate a work of art; superficial judgments aren't worth much. If someone who seems otherwise aesthetically competent thinks well of a work of art, and if my casual reaction is to disagree, then I shouldn't give this reaction very much weight. The deeper his acquaintance with the work and the more superficial mine is, the stronger my reason for thinking I may be missing something.

This is relevant to Plantinga's own account of exclusivism. Plantinga insists that religious faith is an affair of the heart as well as the mind. He's surely right. Even the most intellectual of believers probably doesn't believe for purely intellectual reasons; for many people, coming to believe is more like falling in love. The would-be believer feels attracted, drawn in, seduced, even overwhelmed; believers faced with a non-

believer's demand for arguments may feel as though they've been asked to justify their feelings for their lover or their spouse.

Plantinga has a good deal to say about the role of the affections in religious belief. He writes strikingly about the erotic quality of the love of God and the believer's love for God. And he talks of the role that our sense of beauty may have in coming to believe. If he's right, one of reasons that the Christian believes is her perception of the beauty of what she finds in the Gospels. Plantinga points to a secular analogue. He quotes Steven Weinberg, who recalls that the beauty of the general theory of relativity convinced him of its truth well before the evidence from radio and radar astronomy was in. Plantinga writes

> Indeed, there is a connection between belief and perception of beauty . . . that goes much deeper than Weinberg suggests . . . [T]here are ordinarily many different theories or beliefs compatible with our evidence. Why do we accept the hypotheses we do? . . . Why do we [accept] simple hypotheses rather than complex ones? . . . Because we find simple beliefs more natural and compelling than complex beliefs. [*ibid.* pp. 207–208]

The point is that our sense of beauty may have a *proper* role to play in our coming to believe what we believe. In the case of Christianity, Plantinga thinks that this perception of beauty may be what brings the believer to the belief itself; it may be that rather than coming to believe and then seeing the beauty of what I believe, it's the other way around: seeing the beauty calls forth the belief. In that case, if the rest of Plantinga's story is right, affective responses would be part of the mechanism for coming to warranted religious beliefs.

This doesn't give the Christian any less reason to think that non-Christians have missed something she has seen; it does give her a serious reason to think that *she* may have missed something that *they* have seen. No doubt the Muslim or the Hindu claims to find as much beauty in those traditions as Plantinga finds in Christianity. But most members of a given tradition have a relatively shallow acquaintance with other traditions. As someone brought up within Christianity, I know I have only a superficial idea of how Muslims or Hindus see things. In the case of Judaism, I think I have a better understanding—enough to be suspicious of the phrase "Judeo-Christian," which blurs too many distinctions. As a result, I've come to admire Judaism and even, I think, to glimpse its beauty, but I also realize that I'm unlikely ever to get beyond a sympathetic outsider's understanding.

For all I can say for sure, it's possible that if I immersed myself in Islam, its glory would bring me to conclude that it, and not my own tradition, is the right one. Knowing as little as I do about how things look to Muslims and Hindus and even Jews, the idea that I could confidently claim that they're wrong and I'm right seems wrong to me. Perhaps "arrogant" isn't quite the right word, but it's something in that neighborhood.

Plantinga addresses the complaint that exclusivism is a form of arrogance. His response runs like this: the exclusivist believes things that she can't expect to convince most people to believe. If *that's* what makes her arrogant, then there's no hope for anyone who has opinions at all—even the opinion that he shouldn't have first-level religious opinions. So the charge of arrogance is a "tar baby," to use Plantinga's expression. [Plantinga 1995 pp. 194–195] But that doesn't help. The holding of opinions per se isn't the issue. It's the idea that one can say with great conviction that other sorts of believers are wrong without ever having made a serious effort to see how they see things. *This* complaint is hardly a tar baby.

4. PLURALIST EXCLUSIVISM?

Before going on, a bit of stock-taking. Inclusivist exclusivism and pluralism are both defensible in the way that philosophical views are defensible; one can make serious cases for them. Typical believers hold exclusivist views, or so my unscientific sample suggests. However, the average believer is not a philosopher or a theologian. This raises the question of where *these* believers are left. Plantinga has argued that they are entitled to hold their beliefs as *basic* beliefs, their knowledge of religious diversity notwithstanding, and may even *know* what they believe, The argument so far has been that Plantinga's case is problematic. First, the fact that if the beliefs are true, they would meet his conditions for warrant doesn't clearly make it reasonable to hold them in the basic way. Second, the facts of religious diversity and the power

of religious practice to create belief make it doubtful that the basic believer is in a suitable environment for his beliefs to be warranted. Finally, some features of Plantinga's own discussion suggest that without serious acquaintance with other faiths, the believer is not in a position to know that she isn't missing something by rejecting them.

The first two points hinge on the details of Plantinga's theory of knowledge and my discussion is too brief to do them real justice. The third point seems to stand on its own. For all the Plantinga-style exclusivist knows, she would find some other faith just as attractive as her own, just as plausible and in just the same ways if she were more deeply acquainted with it; for all she knows, *she* is missing something herself.

Plantinga says that his exclusivist is "rather fully aware of other religions" but there's no reason to think he means "aware enough to know how things look from their point of view." Most believers—even thoughtful, educated believers—have a limited knowledge of other faiths. This may cast some doubt on the exclusivist's claim to *know* what she believes, but does it mean that she isn't *entitled* to her beliefs—that she is being negligent or irrational in holding them?

Plantinga would certainly say no. I'd like to agree, but I think the problem is harder than Plantinga credits. A good deal of religious belief *is* unreasonable; some of it is harmful, and *some* of it is downright dangerous. The problems of line-drawing here are not trivial and I don't have a general solution. Instead, I'd like to offer a portrait of a certain sort of believer who seems to me to represent one way of solving the problem.

Our believer couldn't make a very powerful philosophical case for what she believes; after all, most people couldn't. She knows there are other religions, but like most people, her knowledge of them isn't deep. She sees real good in many of them, and she doesn't think that these people are facing damnation just because they don't believe "the truth." Nonetheless, her own religious beliefs are deeply important to her—as important as anything else in her life. Even though she knows she couldn't convince nonbelievers, she really does *believe* the central things her religion claims and can't exactly imagine not believing them. It's not that she never has moments of doubt, but on the whole, her religious beliefs and her religious practice make a sort of sense of things that she finds deeply satisfying.

We said that our believer's beliefs are beyond her ability to argue for. That may seem troublesome, but we need to tread carefully here. Most of us, philosophers included, believe things we can't begin to prove. I have no refutation of moral skepticism, for example; that doesn't keep me from having serious moral commitments.

Still, there are many alternatives to our believer's beliefs, and their merits aren't obviously less than the ones she prefers. Here I'd like to suggest a distinction between two broadly different ways of disbelieving. If X and Y are inconsistent with each other and I believe X, then at least implicitly, I don't believe Y. But implicit lack of belief is one thing; active disbelief is another. For example: suppose Paul accepts the doctrine of transubstantiation: he believes that the bread and wine really become the body and blood of Christ during the Mass. Nonetheless, he know that most people, including many Christians, believe otherwise. I think the following is perfectly possible: actively believing this is deeply important to Paul's religious identity. At the same time, actively *disbelieving* contrary doctrines isn't important to him at all. The fact that most people don't accept the doctrine doesn't bother him; he doesn't feel the need to persuade them to see things his way. From one point of view, he takes the doctrine very seriously—seriously enough that if he stopped accepting it, he would see this as a major change in himself. From another point of view, he holds the belief lightly. Disagreement about it simply doesn't worry him.

One the one hand, for any given proposition, I either (1) believe it, (2) disbelieve it or (3) neither believe nor disbelieve. That said, this way of carving things up doesn't take account of the variety of ways we can believe things. For example: one alternative to the doctrine of Transubstantiation is the common Protestant view that when Christians participate in the ritual recreation of the Last Supper—what Catholics call the Mass—all that is going on is a memorial; the bread and wine are simply bread and wine. If we asked Paul whether this is how he understands the Mass, he would say no. But he might *not* be willing to say that people with this Protestant view are making a *mistake*, and if asked whether he thinks they are *wrong*, he might reply that the question seems beside the point for him; saying "no" would do a bad job of capturing his attitude, but so would saying "yes." We might say that Paul's *belief* is important to him, but being *right* about it isn't.

So far, all I've done is characterize a complex set of attitudes. Here are some pieces of a *rationale* for the attitudes.

First, the truth about God or the Ultimate is not likely to be simple. For example, God's relationship with time is hardly straightforward. Is God *in* time? Even if the nature of time depends on the physical make-up of the universe? Or to take another example, does the average Christian *really* know what she means when she says that God is a Trinity—three persons in one being? And could the believer's fate really turn on getting such things right?

This isn't to say that details never matter. The sort of believer I have in mind would *actively* reject the belief that the Jews are responsible for the death of Christ, or that atheists are automatically bound for eternal torture. It's not just that she doesn't believe those things; she thinks they are positively harmful beliefs—spiritually harmful to the person who holds them and potentially harmful to others in less direct ways because of the effect they may have on the behavior of someone who believes them.

The question of just which details matter doesn't have a simple answer. I won't suggest one, except to say that for the sort of believer I have in mind, beliefs that make the Ultimate morally ugly won't make the grade.

The second part of the rationale is that it's not just that it's hard to get the details right; we're almost certainly wrong about some of our own beliefs.

There's really no paradox here. We believe every one of our beliefs, taken one at a time. (How could we not?) But, fallible creatures that we are, it's virtually certain that some of our beliefs are false, even though we don't know which ones. Given the mystery of the Ultimate, it would be surprising if this didn't apply to religious beliefs. Isn't it likely that you're wrong about at least *some* of them? But can't you have faith that you'll be forgiven for this?

Part of Plantinga's condition C is that the exclusivist recognizes that "there is much that at the least looks like genuine piety and devoutness" in other religions. And we already quoted Hick's admonition to "avoid the implausibly arbitrary dogma that religious experience is all delusory with the single exception of the particular form enjoyed by the one who is speak-

WOMEN PRIESTS * *Naomi Goldenberg*

Conservative leaders of contemporary religious institutions understand that allowing women access to top positions of authority threatens the age-old composition of the institutions themselves.

In January 1977, Pope Paul VI issued a declaration affirming the Vatican's ban on allowing women to be ordained as Catholic priests. The document states that because Christ was a man and because he chose only male disciples, women can never serve as chief officials in the Catholic hierarchy.

Pope Paul used an impressive knowledge of how image and symbol operate in the human mind to build his case against female priests. "The priest," he explained, "is a sign . . . a sign that must be perceptible and which the faithful must be able to recognize with ease. The whole sacramental economy is in fact based upon natural signs, on symbols imprinted upon the human psychology. . . ."

Pope Paul reasoned that because the priest must represent Christ, that is, God, the priest must resemble God. If the priest looked very different from Christ, a follower would not feel immediate connection between God and the priest who was supposed to embody *Him*. The Pope realized that people experience God through *His* representatives. If one were to change the sex of God's representatives, one would be changing the nature of God *Himself*. As the chief guardian of the Catholic faith, the Pope understood that he could not allow any serious tampering with the image of God. . . .

However, we must ask ourselves what will happen to Christianity when women do succeed in changing traditions so that they are treated as the equals of men. Will not this major departure from the Christian view of women radically alter the religion? Pope Paul knew it would. The Pope understood that representatives of Christianity mirror the image of God by calling to mind the male figure of Jesus Christ. If women play at being priests, they would play at being God; and Christianity, he insisted, can only afford to have men in that role.

From *Changing of the Gods* (1979).

ing." This brings us to point three. The believer I imagine allows that other traditions might embody real insight. It's even possible from her point of view that other traditions may provide *more* insight into *some* of the Truth than her own tradition does.

The fourth rationale is more speculative. It's related to the idea of Divine Plenitude—the fullness of Divine being. Perhaps this fullness is the source of religious paradox; perhaps its impossible for any one coherent narrative to capture the Ultimate. This wouldn't make it plausible that all religions are right about everything. But it suggests that tensions among the claims of different religions don't always have to amount to outright contradiction—even when they superficially appear to.

There's another important feature of the attitude I have in mind—not a *rationale*, but part of the attitude itself. The sort of believer I'm thinking of mostly isn't very concerned with whether she *knows* what she believes and for the most part wouldn't be inclined to claim that she did. This makes sense in light of our first rationale: the truth about the Ultimate isn't likely to be simple and no one is likely to get all the details right. Nonetheless, the believer I'm imagining *does* have faith in a fairly traditional sense of that word. She has a deep *trust* in the Real—a strong sense that in some way that she may not understand, all *will* be well. And at times she has a strong sense of the *presence* of the Ultimate— of the nearness of God, in the language of the theist.

I've mentioned this feature last, but it's the most important part. Without this underlying sense that there *is* something Ultimate and that it is to be trusted or even loved, our believer would not *be* a believer. In fact, this is where she would be willing to say that nonbelievers have missed something. But notice how this differs from active disbelief in a doctrine of some other religion. There, she's in a diminished epistemic position unless she has a serious understanding of the scriptures, traditions and practices of the religion where the doctrine resides. But when it comes to general religious skepticism, our believer quite plausibly takes herself to be acquainted with the general run of things that nonbelievers know. She believes she can see what they see, but—along with a cloud of many witnesses—can also sense more.

Still, why wouldn't my believer settle for a vague, free-floating theism?

One might. But our believer finds herself with more detailed beliefs. Her believing them is not a sham; she thinks they might really be true and that even if they aren't fully true, they capture something important about the Ultimate. They also flesh out her more diffuse sense of the Ultimate into something that can form the basis for a religious practice. Being in what Hick calls "right relationship" with this Ultimate is deeply important to her; her religious tradition is her means for achieving that relationship. Her trust that from the Ultimate standpoint, it's not important to get the details right means that honest mistakes made in good faith won't be punished. This liberates our believer to *believe* the things she's drawn to while infusing those same beliefs with the sort of lightness that we've tried to describe.

Hick writes

> . . . it is rationally appropriate for those who experience their life in relation to the transcendent to trust their own experience, together with that of the stream of religious life in which they participate and of the great figures who are its primary experiential witnesses, and to proceed to live and believe on that basis. [Hick 1989, p. 13]

Plantinga would agree, but Plantinga takes religious belief at face value; Hick maintains that *all* specific religious belief is strictly speaking false. The view we're considering isn't like either of these. It agrees that, broadly speaking, the believer is entitled to trust her sense that the skeptic is wrong. It allows that *perhaps* some one religion captures The Truth, and *perhaps* the Ultimate is a Kantian noumenon, entirely beyond our

cognitive grasp. At the level of practice, however, the view is more like exclusivism; the Hindu will believe as a Hindu does; the Christian will believe like a Christian. But behind the belief there will be a higher-level lightness; not an ironic attitude, but trust coupled with a deep sense of epistemic humility.

This view—this *attitude*—doesn't have a name. For want of a better label, we'll call it pluralist exclusivism: pluralist in allowing from a *religious* standpoint that there might be real merit in other faiths; exclusivist in that such believers make their homes in their own traditions.

Are there such people? I think I know quite a few. Are most believers like this? Probably not. Many of the believers I meet are more convinced that they're right than seems remotely reasonable and more bound by their beliefs than seems good for the soul. As I've already noted, the problem of line-drawing here is hard; much harder than Plantinga allows. It seems likely to me, however, that the issue has as much to do with attitudes as with exercises in epistemology and settling metaphysical accounts.

The reader might have one more question: have I been describing myself? The answer is: not quite. I'm a bit more of a spiritual orphan than the believers I've described. But that's not something I count to my credit, and certainly not to their blame.

References

Dupuis, Jacques. *Toward a Christian Theology of Religious Pluralism*. Maryknoll, Orbis Books, 1997.

Heim, S. Mark. *Salvations: Truth and Difference in Religion*. Maryknoll, Orbis Books, 1995.

Hick, John. *An Interpretation of Religion: Human Responses to the Transcendent*. New Haven and London: Yale University Press, 1989.

Plantinga, Alvin. "Pluralism: A Defense of Religious Exclusivism," in *The Rationality of Belief and the Plurality of Faith*, ed. Thomas D. Senor, Ithaca and London, Cornell University Press, 1995.

———. *Warranted Christian Belief*. New York, Oxford University Press, 2000.

QUESTIONS FOR FURTHER REFLECTION

1. Stairs identifies skepticism, exclusivism, inclusivism, and pluralism as the main responses to

religious pluralism. Do you think there are any other important alternatives that he has missed?
2. Stairs gives a brief argument against hyper-exclusivism. But suppose someone responded by saying: "God *could* be like that. The fact that this might mean that God would not be worthy of our worship doesn't prove that hyper-exclusivism is false." How do you think Stairs would respond? How would you respond?
3. Do you think Plantinga's account of warrant is adequate? Can you think of an example (imaginary if you like) of a belief that would be warranted according to Plantinga's account but still wouldn't amount to knowledge?
4. The range of properly basic belief seems pretty wide. Is it wide enough to accommodate some religious beliefs? If not, why not? If so, are the limits to the kinds of religious beliefs that could be properly basic?
5. Stairs ends his paper by characterizing a certain attitude that a religious believer might take. He presents this as an acceptable form of exclusivism. What do you think? *Is* it acceptable? Explain. He also suggests that much religious belief is *not* reasonable. Do you agree? If so, do you have any suggestions for distinguishing the reasonable from the unreasonable?

61. RELIGION FROM AN AFRICAN PERSPECTIVE
Kwasi Wiredu

Kwasi Wiredu, a professor of philosophy at the University of South Florida, was formerly professor and head of the Department of Philosophy at the University of Ghana. Educated at the Universities of Ghana and Oxford, he has been a visiting professor at the University of California–Los Angeles, and Duke University. He has received fellowships from the Woodrow Wilson Center and the National Humanities Center. His publications are primarily in the areas of philosophy of logic and African philosophy and include his book *Philosophy and an African Culture* (Cambridge University Press, 1980). In the selection that follows, he explains that the word *religion* may not be properly applicable to many traditional African cultures.

READING QUESTIONS

1. What are Wiredu's reasons for questioning whether traditional African thought is "religious"?
2. With respect to questions of so-called religious attitudes and ethics, how does he say that the Akans differ from typical European believers in a Supreme Being?
3. What is the attitude among Akans toward their dead ancestors? How does it differ from typical Christian attitudes toward the dead?
4. With respect to the ideas of (1) a transcendent being, (2) the supernatural, (3) the spiritual, and (4) creation, how do the Akans differ from European religious believers?

Two assumptions that may safely be made about the human species are one, that the entire race shares some fundamental categories and criteria of thought in common and two, that, nevertheless, there are some very deep disparities among the different tribes of humankind in regard to their modes of conceptualization in some sensitive areas of thought. The first accounts for the possibility of communication among different peoples, the second for the difficulties and complications that not infrequently beset that interaction.

Is religion a field of convergence or divergence of thought among the peoples and cultures of the world? The obvious answer, in alignment with our opening reflection, is that religion is both. There is also an obvious sequel: What are the specifics? But here an obvious answer is unavailable, at least, as concerns Africa vis-à-vis, for instance, the West. In fact, it is not at all obvious in what sense the English word "religion" is applicable to any aspect of African life and thought.

This last remark, of course, amounts to discounting the frequent affirmations, in the literature of African studies, of the immanent religiosity of the African mind. What exactly are the features of life and thought that are appealed to in that characterization? In investigating this issue I am going to have to be rather particularistic. I am going to have particular, though not exclusive, recourse to the Akans of West Africa, for the considerations to be adduced presuppose a level of cultural and linguistic insight to which I cannot pretend in regard to any African peoples except that particular ethnic group which I know through birth, upbringing, reading and deliberate reflective observation. This particularism has, at least, the logical potential of all counterexamples against universal claims.

Let us return to the word "religion." It has been suggested, even by some authors by whose reckoning African life is full of religion, that there is no word in many African languages which translates this word. Whether this is true of all African languages or not I do not know, but it is certainly true of Akan, in the traditional use of that language, that is. Not only is there no single word for religion but there is also no periphrastic equivalent. There is, indeed, the word "Anyamesom" which many translators might be tempted to proffer. But the temptation ought to be resisted. The word is a Christian invention by which the missionaries distinguished, in Akan speech, between their own religion and what they perceived to be the religion of the indigenous "pagans." Thus, it means, not religion, pure and simple, but Christianity. Ironically, in this usage the Christian missionaries were constrained by linguistic exigencies to adapt a word which the Akans use for the Supreme Being. "Onyame" is one among several names for the Supreme Being in Akan. Another very frequent one is "Onyankopon" which literally means The Being That Is Alone Great, in other words, That Than Which a Greater Cannot Be Conceived (with apologies to Saint Anselm). The remaining component of the word "Anyamesom" is "som" which means "to serve," so that the whole word

means, literally, "the service of the Supreme Being" or, if you follow Christian methods of translation, "the service of God." In turn, this was taken to mean the *worship* of God.

By way of a designation for what they saw as indigenous religion, the Christians used the word "Abosomsom." This is a combination of two words "Obosom" and "Som." Etymologically, "obosom" means the service of stones. Thus, literally, the barbarism means the service of stone service! Still, it served its Christian purpose. But why stones? That is an allusion to the fact that the Akans traditionally believe that various objects, such as certain special rocks, trees and rivers, are the abode of extra-human forces and beings of assorted grades.

Having gathered from the foregoing remarks that the Akans, in fact, believe in the existence of a supreme being and a variety of extra-human forces and beings, the reader might be disposed to wonder why I make any issue of the sense in which "religion" might be applied to any aspect of Akan culture. If so, let him or her attend to the following considerations. To begin with, religion, however it is defined, involves a certain kind of attitude. If a given religion postulates a supra-human supreme being, that belief must, on any common showing, necessarily be joined to an attitude not only of unconditional reverence but also of worship. Some will go as far as to insist that this worshipful attitude will have to be given practical expression through definite rituals, especially if the being in question is supposed to be the determiner or controller of human destiny. There is a further condition of the utmost importance; it is one which introduces an ethical dimension into the definition. Essential to any religion in the primary sense is a conception of moral uprightness. If it involves supra-human beliefs, the relevant ethic will be based logically or psychologically on the "supra" being or beings concerned. Typically, but by no means invariably, a religion will have a social framework. In that case, it will have organized hortatory and other procedures for instilling or revivifying the commitment to moral virtue.

Consider, now, the character of the Akan belief in the Supreme Being. There is, indeed, generally among the Akans a confirmed attitude of unconditional reverence for *Onyankopon*, the Supreme Being. However, there is, most assuredly, no attitude or ritual of worship directed to that being either at a social or an individual level. They regard Him as good, wise and powerful in the highest. He is the determiner of human destiny as of everything else. But in all this they see no rationale for worship. Neither is the Akan conception or practice of morality based logically or even psychologically on the belief in the Supreme Being. Being good in the highest. He disapproves of evil; but, to the Akan mind, the reason why people should not do evil is not because he disapproves of it but rather because it is contrary to human well-being, which is why He disapproves of it, in the first place.

The early European visitors to Africa, especially the missionaries, were quick to notice the absence of any worship of God among the Akans and various other African peoples. They were hardly less struck by the fact that God was not the foundation of Akan morals. On both grounds they deduced a spiritual and intellectual immaturity in the African. Notice the workings here of a facile universalism. It seems to have been assumed that belief in God must move every sound mind to worship. Perhaps, even now, such an assumption might sound plausible to many Western ears. It is, of course, not likely in this day and age that many can be found to suppose that any person of a sound mind must necessarily embrace belief in God. But given the prevailing tendencies in Western and even some non-Western cultures, it might be tempting to think that if people believe in God, then the *natural* thing for them to do is to worship Him. Yet, consider the notion of a perfect being. Why would he (she, it) need to be worshipped? What would be the point of it? It is well-known that the Judeo-Christian God *jealously* demands to be worshipped—witness The Ten Commandments—but, from an Akan point of view, such clamoring for attention must be paradoxical in the extreme in a perfect being, and I confess to being an unreconstructed Akan in this regard.

There is, in their resort to the word "Abosomsom" (the worship of stones) to name what they took to be Akan religion, an odd manifestation of the special importance that the Christian missionaries attached to worship. Having seen that the Akans did not worship God, they were keen to find out what it was that they worshipped, for surely a whole people must worship something. They quickly settled on the class of what I have called extra-human forces and beings, which, as I

have already hinted, is a feature of the Akan worldview. There is, indeed, a great variety of such entities postulated in the Akan ontology (as in any other African ontology that I know of). Some are relatively person-like; others somewhat automatic in their operation. The former can, it is believed, be communicated with through some special procedures, and are credited with a moral sense. Commonly, a being of this sort would be believed to be localized at a household "shrine" from where it would protect the given group from evil forces. More person-like still are the ancestors who are thought to live in a realm closely linked with the world of the living.

Actually, the ancestors are conceived of as persons who continue to be members of their premortem families, watching over their affairs and generally helping them. They are regarded as persons, but not as mortal persons; for they have tasted death and transcended it. Accordingly, they are not thought to be constrained by all the physical laws which circumscribe the activities of persons with fully physical bodies. For this reason, they are supposed to be more powerful than mortals. Additionally, they are considered to be more irreversibly moral than any living mortal. All these attributes are taken to entitle the ancestors to genuine reverence. Not quite the same deference is accorded to the first group of beings, but in view of their presumed power to promote human well-being, they are approached with considerable respect.

More types of extra-human forces and beings are spoken of in the Akan ontology than we have mentioned, but these are among the most relevant, and they will suffice for the impending point: which is this: The Akan attitude to the beings in question bears closer analogy to secular esteem than religious worship. The reverence given to the ancestors is only a higher degree of the respect that in Akan society is considered to be due to the earthly elders. For all their postmortem ontologic transformation, the ancestors are, let it be repeated, regarded as members of their families. The libations that are poured to them on ceremonial and other important occasions are simply invitations to them to come and participate in family events. Moreover, everybody hopes eventually to become an ancestor, but this is not seen as a craving for self-apotheosis. Ancestorship is simply the crowning phase of human existence.

The nonreligious character of the Akan attitude to the nonancestral forces is even more clear. Real religious devotion to a being must be unconditional. But that is the one thing that the Akan approach to those beings is not; it is purely utilitarian: if they bring help, praise be to them, and other things besides. On the other hand, if they fail, particularly if that happens consistently, they can fall into disrepute or worse. K. A. Busia and J. B. Danquah, the two most celebrated expositors of Akan thought, have borne unambiguous and, as it seems to me, reliable testimony to this fact. Busia says, "The gods are treated with respect if they deliver the goods, and with contempt if they fail. . . . Attitudes to [the gods] depend on their success, and vary from healthy respect to sneering contempt." Danquah goes somewhat further: ". . . the general tendency is to sneer at and ridicule the fetish and its priest." There is an even more radical consideration. According to popular belief, these "gods" are capable of dying. Of a "god" who is finished the Akans say *nano atro*, that is, its powers have become totally blunted. This may happen through unknown causes, but it may also happen through human design. People can cause the demise of a "god" simply by permanently depriving it of attention. Or, for more rapid results, apply an antithetical substance to its "shrine." Such antidotes are known for at least some of these "gods," according to popular belief. It ought, perhaps, to be emphasized that in this matter the thought is not that a "god" has betaken itself elsewhere, but rather that it has ceased to be a force to be reckoned with at all. In light of all this, it is somewhat of a hyperbole to call the procedures designed for establishing satisfactory relations with the beings in question religious worship.

The considerations rehearsed so far should be enough, I think, to suggest the need for a review of the enthusiastic, not to say indiscriminate, attributions of religiosity to African peoples. But there are deeper reasons of the same significance. And in studying them we will see the role which the hasty universalization of certain Western categories of thought have played in the formation of the misapprehensions under scrutiny. Take, then, the Akan belief in the Supreme Being. In English discourse about Akan thought the word "God" is routinely used to refer to this being. This has led, or has been due, to the supposition that both the Akans and the Christians are talking of the same being when they speak of the Supreme Being, notwithstanding any divergences of cultural perception. This supposed identity of reference has come in handy to Christianized Africans wishing to demonstrate that they can profess Christianity and still remain basically true to their indigenous religions: There is, after all, only one God, and we are all trying to reach Him.

Yet, in spite of any apparent similarities, such as the postulation of That Than Which a Greater Cannot Be Conceived in both traditions of thought, the Akan supreme being is profoundly different from the Christian one. The Christian God is a creator of the world out of nothing. In further philosophical characterization. He is said to be transcendent, supernatural and spiritual in the sense of immaterial, nonphysical. In radical contrast, the Akan supreme being is a kind of cosmic architect, a fashioner of the world order, who occupies the apex of the same hierarchy of being which accommodates, in its intermediate ranges, the ancestors and living mortals and, in its lower reaches, animals, plants and inanimate objects. This universe of being is ontologically homogenous. In other words, everything that exists exists in exactly the same sense as everything else. And this sense is empirical, broadly speaking. In the Akan language to exist is to "wo ho" which, in literal translation, means to be at some place. There is no equivalent, in Akan, of the existential "to be" or "is" of English, and there is no way of pretending in that medium to be speaking of the existence of something which is not in space. This locative connotation of the Akan concept of existence is irreducible except metaphorically. Thus you might speak of there existing an explanation for something (*ne nkyerease wo ho*) without incurring any obligation of spatial specification, because an explanation is not an object in any but a metaphorical sense; and to a metaphorical object corresponds only a metaphorical kind of space. The same applies to the existence of all so-called abstract entities. In the Akan conceptual framework, then, existence is spatial. Now, since, whatever transcendence means in this context, it implies existence beyond space, it follows that talk of any transcendent being is not just false, but unintelligible, from an Akan point of view.

But not only transcendence goes by the board. Neither the notion of the supernatural nor that of the spiritual can convey any coherent meaning to an Akan understanding in its traditional condition. No line is drawn in the Akan worldview demarcating one area of being corresponding to nature from another corresponding to supernature. Whatever is real belongs to one or another of the echelons of being postulated in that worldview. In that context it has all the explanation that is appropriate to it. An important axiom of Akan thought is that everything has its explanation. *biribiara wo nenkyerease*—a kind of principle of sufficient reason; and a clear presupposition of Akan explanations of phenomena is that there are interactions among all the orders of existents in the world. Accordingly, if an event in human affairs, for instance, does not appear explicable in human terms, there is no hesitation in invoking extra-human causality emanating from the higher or even the lower rungs of the hierarchy of beings. In doing this there is no sense of crossing an ontological chasm; for the idea is that there is only one universe of many strata wherein God, the ancestors, humans, animals, plants and all the rest of the furniture of the world have their being.

In this last connection, it might, perhaps, enhance understanding to regiment our terminology a little. Suppose we use the term "the world" to designate the totality of ordered existents fashioned out by God in the process of "creation," then, of course, God, being the author of the world, is not a part of it, in the Akan scheme of things. But we might, then, reserve the term "universe" for the totality of absolutely all existents. In this sense God would be part of the universe. Apart from regimenting our terminology, this gives us the opportunity to reinforce the point regarding the Akan sense of the inherent law-likeness of reality. And the crucial consideration is that God's relationship with the rest of the universe, that is, the world, is also conceived to be inherently law-like. This is the implication of the Akan saying that "The Creator created Death and Death killed the Creator," *Odomankoma boo Owuo na Owuo kum Odomankoma*, which, in my opinion, is one of the profoundest in the Akan corpus of metaphysical aphorisms.

But though God's relation with the world is conceived to be law-like, He is not made the basis of the explanation of any specific phenomenon, for since everything is ultimately traceable to Him, *Biribiara ne Nyame*, references to Him are incapable of helping to explain why any particular thing is what it is and not

another thing. Divine law-likeness only ensures that there will be no arbitrary interferences in the course of the world-process. Thus the reason why Akan explanations of specific things do not invoke God is not because He is thought to be transcendent or supernatural or anything like that, but rather because He is too immanently implicated in the nature and happening of things to have any explanatory value.

Still, however, in facing the cognitive problems of this world all the mundane theaters of being, human and extra-human, are regarded as *equally* legitimate sources of explanation. Thus, if an Akan explains a mysterious malady in terms of, say, the wrath of the ancestors, it makes little sense to ascribe to him or her a belief in the supernatural. That characterization is intelligible only in a conceptual framework in which the natural/supernatural dichotomy has a place. But the point is that it has no place in the Akan system of thought. We may be sure, then, that the widespread notion that Africans are given to supernatural explanations is the result of the superimposition of alien categories of thought on African thought-structures, in the Akan instance, at least. There is nothing particularly insidious in the fact that Western writers on African thought have generally engaged in this practice; for, after all, one thinks most naturally in terms of the conceptual framework of one's intellectual upbringing, and the natural/supernatural distinction is very endemic, indeed, in Western thought. I do not mean by this, of course, that there is a universal belief in the supernatural in the West. The suggestion is only that this concept together with its logical complement is a customary feature of Western conceptualizations; so much so, that even the Western philosophical naturalist, in denying the existence of anything supernatural, does not necessarily dispute the coherence of that concept. It is a more striking fact that many contemporary African expositors of their own traditional systems of thought yield no ground to their Western colleagues in stressing the role of belief in the supernatural in African thinking. It is hard not to see this as evidence of the fact that in some ways Christian proselytization and Western education have been over-successful in Africa.

But an interesting and important question arises. Suppose it granted that, as I have been arguing, the natural/supernatural dichotomy has no place in Akan and, perhaps, African thought generally. Does that not still leave the question of its objective validity intact? And, if it should turn out to be objectively valid, would it not be reasonable to think that it would be a good thing for Africans to learn to think along that line? My answer to both questions is affirmative; which implies a rejection of relativism. This disavowal is fully premeditated and is foreshadowed in the opening paragraph of this essay. However, for reasons of the division of preoccupation, I cannot try to substantiate my anti-relativism here.

Stated baldly, my thesis is that there is such a thing as the objective validity of an idea. Were it not for the recent resurgence of relativism in Philosophy, this would have been too platitudinous for any words. Furthermore, and rather less obviously, if an idea is objectively valid (or invalid or even incoherent) in any given language or conceptual framework, both the idea and its status can, in principle, be *represented* in, if not necessarily translated into, any other language or conceptual framework.

A corollary of the foregoing contention is that, however natural it may be to think in one's native framework of concepts, it is possible for human beings to think astride conceptual frameworks. In the absence of extended argumentation for this general claim, I will content myself with an illustration with respect to the idea of the supernatural. A relevant question, then, is: "Do the Akans need to incorporate the natural/supernatural distinction into their modes of thought?" I think not; for not only is Akan thought inhospitable to this distinction but also the distinction is, in my opinion, objectively incoherent. If this is so, it follows from our principle that it ought to be demonstrable (to the extent that such speculative matters are susceptible of demonstration) in any language and, in particular, in English. In fact, a simple argument suffices for this purpose.

In the sense pertinent to our discussion, the supernatural is that which surpasses the order of nature. In other words, a supernatural event is one whose occurrence is contrary to the laws of nature. But if the event actually happens, then any law that fails to reckon with its possibility is inaccurate and is in need of some modification, at least. However, if the law is suitably amended, even if only by means of an exceptive rider, the event is no longer contrary to natural law. Hence no event can be consistently described as supernatural.

What of the notion of the spiritual? Again, I begin with a disclaimer on behalf of Akan ontological thinking. As can be expected from the spatial character of the Akan concept of existence, the radical dualism of the material and the spiritual can find no home in the Akan scheme of reality. All the extra-human beings and powers, even including God, are spoken of in language irreducibly charged with spatial imagery. It is generally recognized by students of African eschatology that the *place* of the dead, the *abode* of the ancestors, is almost complete modelled on the world of living mortals. If the replication is not complete, it is only because the ancestors are not thought of as having *fully* material bodies. Some analogue of material bodies they surely must be supposed to have, given the sorts of things that are said about them. For example, a postulated component of a person that is supposed to survive death and eventually become an ancestor, all things being equal, is believed soon after death to travel *by land and by river* before arriving at the abode of the ancestors. For this reason in traditional times coffins were stuffed with travel needs such as clothing and money for the payment of ferrying charges. I have never heard it suggested in traditional circles that this practice was purely symbolic. If it were a purely symbolic gesture, that, certainly, would have been carrying symbolism rather far. But, in any case, the practice was of a piece with the conception, and the conception is decidedly quasi-material.

I use the term "quasi-material" to refer to any being or entity conceived as spatial but lacking some of the properties of material objects. The ancestors, for instance, although they are thought of as occupying space, are believed to be invisible to the naked eye and inaudible to the normal ear, except rarely when they choose to *manifest* themselves to particular persons for special reasons. On such occasions they can, according to very widely received conceptions among the Akans, appear and disappear at will unconstrained by those limitations of speed and impenetrability to which the gross bodies of the familiar world are subject. This is held to be generally true of all the relatively personalized forms of extra-human phenomena.

It is apparent from what has just been said that if the extra-human beings of the Akan worldview are not fully material, they are not fully immaterial either. Further to confirm this last point, we might note that, although the beings in question are not supposed to be generally visible to the *naked* eye, they are widely believed to be perceivable to the superior eyes of certain persons of special gift or training. People reputed to be of this class will sometimes tell you. "If you had but eyes to see, you would be amazed at what is going on right here around where you are standing." And here imagery tends to be so lustily spatial that, but for their selective invisibility, one would be hard put to distinguish between the quasi-material apparitions and the garden variety objects of the material world. Descriptions of human-like creatures gyrating on their heads are not unknown in such contexts. Whatever one may think of such claims, the conceptual point itself is clear, namely, that the extra-human existents of the Akan ontology do not belong to the category of the spiritual in the Cartesian sense of nonspatial, unextended. The category itself is conceptually inadmissible in this system of thought. Should the reader be curious at this stage as to whether mind too is quasi-material in the Akan way of thinking, the short answer is that mind is not thought of as an entity at all but rather simply as the *capacity*, supervenient upon brain states and processes, to do various things. Hence the question whether mind is a spiritual or material or quasi-material entity does not arise.

The Akan worldview, then, involves no sharp ontological cleavages such as the Cartesian dichotomy of the material and the spiritual; what difference in nature there is between ordinary material things and those extra-human beings and forces so often called "spirits" in the literature is the difference between the fully material and the partially material. I ought, by the way, to stress that the absence of the spiritual, in the metaphysical sense, from the Akan conceptual framework does not imply the absence of spirituality, in the popular sense, from Akan life. In the latter sense spirituality is sensitivity to the less gross aspects of human experience.

But let us return to the class of quasi-material entities. A legitimate question is whether there is adequate evidence that such entities exist. Actually, this is not a question which faces Akan thought alone. All cultures, East, West and Central, abound in stories of quasi-material goings-on. In the West investigating the veridity and theoretical explicability of such stories is one of the main concerns of Parapsychology. In Africa there are any number of people who would be willing to bet their lives on the reality of such things, on the basis, reputedly, of first hand experience. Basically, the issue is an empirical one, though probably not completely; for if such phenomena were to be definitively confirmed, their explanation would be likely to have conceptual reverberations. Speaking for myself, I would say that neither in Africa nor elsewhere have I seen compelling evidence of such things; though dogmatism would be ill-advised. At all events, it is worth noting that the plausibility of specific quasi-material claims tends to dwindle in the face of advancing scientific knowledge, a consideration which any contemporary African would need to take to heart.

It is, however, interesting to note that the waning, in Africa, of belief in extra-material entities and forces would leave the indigenous orientation thoroughly empirical; for the African worldview, at any rate, the Akan one, makes room for only material and quasi-material existents. The contrary seems to be the case in the West. Here any reduction in quasi-material beliefs has not automatically resulted in gains for empirical thinking in the minds of a large mass of people; for in addition to the categories of material and quasi-material, there is that of the spiritual, that is, the immaterial, which exercises the profoundest influence in philosophic and quasi-philosophic speculation. Not only is actual belief in immaterial entities widespread in the West but also the intelligibility of the material/immaterial contrast seems to be taken for granted even more widely. Moreover, in spite of the fact that, to say the least, quasi-material beliefs are not at all rare in the West, the tendency is for thinking to be governed by an exclusive disjunction of the material with the immaterial. Thus, for many, though, of course, not everybody, in the West, if a thing is not supposed to be material, it is necessarily immaterial. The Europeans who imposed on themselves the "burden" of bringing "salvation" to the souls of the peoples of Africa certainly had this particular either-or fixation. Consequently, those of them who made sympathetic, though not necessarily empathetic, studies of African thought could not but formulate their results in terms of that and cognate schemes of thought. A visible outcome of their assiduous evangelism is the great *flock* of faithful African converts who think in the same language, proudly attributing to their own peoples belief in sundry things spiritual and supernatural.

Yet, not only is the notion of the spiritual unintelligible within a thought system such as that of the Akans, but also it is objectively a very problematic one. One searches in vain for a useful definition of the spiritual. The sum total of the information available from Cartesian and many other spiritually dedicated sources is that the spiritual is that which is nonmaterial. But, definition by pure negation, such as this, brings little enlightenment. The word "that" in the definition suggests that one is envisaging some *sort* of a referent, but this possibility of reference is given absolutely no grounding. How are we to differentiate between the spiritual and the void, for instance? Some negative definitions can be legitimate, but only if their context provides suitable information. In the present case the context seems to be a veritable void!

An even more unfortunate definition of the spiritual than the foregoing is sometimes encountered. It is explained that the spiritual is the unperceivable, the invisible, or, to adapt a phrase of Saint Paul's, the unseen. The problem with this definition is not its apparent negativeness, for the conditions of unperceivability are concrete enough; the problem is that it is so broad as to make gravity, for example, spiritual. It is, of course, not going to help to protest that although gravity is unseen, its effects are seen and felt; for exactly the same is what is claimed for the spiritual. Nor would it be of greater avail to add the condition of nonspatiality to that of invisibility, for something like the square root of four is neither spatial nor visible, and yet one wonders how spiritual it is.

Of the material/spiritual (immaterial) dichotomy, then, we can say the following. It is not a universal feature of human thinking, since the Akans, at least, do not use it. And, in any case, its coherence is questionable. It is not to be assumed though, that if a mode of conceptualization is universal among humankind, then it is, for that reason, objectively valid. Belief in quasi-material entities, for example, seems to be universal among cultures (though not among all individuals) but the chances are that the concepts involved denote nothing.

After all the foregoing the reader is unlikely to be surprised to learn that the idea of creation out of nothing too does not make sense in the Akan framework of thinking. Avenues to that concept are blocked in Akanland from the side both of the concept of creation and that of nothingness. To take the latter first: Nothingness in the Akan language is relative to location. The idea is expressed as the absence of anything at a given location, *se whee nni ho*, literally, the circumstance of there not being something there. Note here the reappearance of the locative conception of existence. If you subtract the locative connotation from this construal of nothingness, you have exactly nothing left, that is, nothing of the conception remains in your understanding.

The concept of creation in the Akan language is similarly non-transcendent. To create is to *bo*, and the most self-explanatory word in Akan for the creator is *Obooade*, *Ade* means thing, and bo means to make in the sense of to fashion out, which implies the use of raw materials. Any claim to *bo* and *ade* without the use of absolutely any raw material would sound decidedly self-contradictory in the language. Thus the Akan Supreme Being is a maker of things, but not out of nothing; so that if the word "Creator" is used for him, it should be clearly understood that the concept of creation involved is fundamentally different from that involved in, say, orthodox Christian talk of creation. The Akan creator is the architect of the world order, but not the *ex nihilo* inventor of its stuff.

Interestingly, even within Western philosophy the concept of *ex nibilo* creation was not in the conceptual vocabulary of some of the greatest thinkers. It is well known, for example, that neither Plato nor Aristotle made use of any such concept. Of course, whether it is intelligible is a separate question. On the face of it, at least, there are tremendous paradoxes in that concept, and unless its exponents can offer profound clarifications, its absence from a conceptual framework can hardly be taken as a mark of insufficiency. Be that as it may, it is clear that the word "creation" should not be used in the context of Akan cosmology without due caution. It should be apparent also that considerable semantical circumspection is called for in using the word "God" for the Akan Supreme Being. Any transcendental inferences from that usage are misplaced.

So, then, we have the following picture of the outlook of the Akans. They believe in a supreme being, but they do not worship Him. Moreover, for conceptual reasons, this being cannot be said to be a spiritual or supernatural being. Nor is He a creator out of nothing. Furthermore, the foundations of Akan ethical life and thought have no necessary reference to Him. It will be recalled also that although the Akans believe in the existence of a whole host of extra human beings and forces, they view these as regular resources of the world order which can be exploited for good or, sometimes for ill, given appropriate knowledge and the right approach. To all this we might add the fact that the customary procedures in Akan society pertaining to important stages in life, such as naming, marriage and death, which are well-structured, elaborate and highly cherished as providing concrete occasions for the manifestation of communal caring and solidarity, have no necessary involvement with the belief in the Supreme Being. These considerations, by the way, explain why some early European students of African cosmology called the African God an absentee God. In my opinion those visitors to Africa had their finger on something real, but the pejorative tenor of the observation can only be put down to a universalistic conceit. As for the ancestors, they are called upon to come and participate in all these ceremonies, but as revered members of the family, not as gods.

If we now renew the question of the applicability of the concept of religion to any aspect of Akan culture, we must be struck by the substantial disanalogies between the Akan setup of cosmological and moral ideas viewed in relation to practical life on the one hand, and Western conceptions of reality and the good life viewed in the same relation. For the purpose of this discussion the most important disparity revolves round the slicing up of human experience into the categories of the religious and the secular. To start from the Western end of the comparison: whether we interpret the concept of the religious in a supernatural or nonsupernatural sense, it is not a simple matter to discover an analogue of it in the traditional Akan context.

It might be thought that there is substantial common ground between Akan life and thought and that of, say, the Christian religion, since, even if the Akan Nyame is not thought of as supernatural, he is still re-garded as in some sense the author of the world and determiner of its destiny. But conceptions or beliefs that do not dovetail into the fabric of practical life can hardly constitute a religion in the primary sense.

That the belief in Nyame has no essential role in the conduct of Akan life can be seen from a little exercise of the imagination. Imagine the belief in Nyame to be altogether removed from the Akan consciousness. What losses will be incurred in terms of sustenance for any institutions or procedures of practical life? The answer is, "Exactly zero." Customs and moral rules relating to the critical (or even noncritical) stages and circumstances in the lives of individuals do not have their basis in the belief in Nyame. The same is true of the institutions of traditional Akan public life. Thus neither the pursuit of moral virtue and noble ideals by individuals nor the cooperative endeavors of the community towards the common good can be said to stand or fall with the belief in Nyame; they all have a solid enough basis in considerations of human well-being, considerations, in other words, which are completely "this-worldly."

To elaborate a little on this last point: to the traditional Akan what gives meaning to life is usefulness to self, family, community and the species. Nothing transcending life in human society and its empirical conditions enters into the constitution of the meaning of life. In particular, there is not, in Akan belief, in contrast, for instance, to Christian belief, any notion of an afterlife of possible salvation and eternal bliss; what afterlife there is thought to be is envisaged very much on the model of this life, as previously hinted. More importantly, that afterlife is not pictured as a life of eternal fun for the immortals but rather as one of eternal vigilance—vigilance over the affairs of the living with the sole purpose of promoting their well-being within the general constraints of Akan ethics. Indeed, this is what is taken to give meaning to their survival. From everything said (to my knowledge) about the ancestors, they are generally believed never to relent in this objective; which is one reason why they are held in such high esteem. The inhabitants of the world of the dead, then, are themselves thoroughly "this-worldly" in their orientation, according to Akan traditional conceptions.

Basically the same considerations would seem to discourage attributing to the Akans any sort of nonsupernaturalistic religiosity. One great difficulty would be how to articulate such a notion within the Akan conceptual framework. Suppose we construe religion as life and thought impregnated by a sense of the sacred. Then, since the primary meaning of the word "sacred" presupposes some conception of deity, we would be in duty bound to give some notification of a broadening of meaning. Accordingly, the sacred might be understood as that in ethical life most worthy of respect, reverence, and commitment. But this, in turn, would presuppose a system of values and ideals, and, in the case of the Akans, would bring us back to their irreducibly "this-worldly" ethic. Now, the remarkable thing is that in this ethic a demonstrated basic commitment to the values and ideals of the society is a component of the very concept of a person. An individual is not a person in the fullest sense unless he or she has shown a responsiveness to those ideals in confirmed habits of life. Not, of course, that an individual failing this test is denuded of human rights; for every individual, simply on the grounds of being human, is regarded as a center of quite extensive rights. On the other hand, there is a prestige attached to the status of personhood, or more strictly, superlative personhood—for indeed the status is susceptible of degrees—to which all Akans of sound mind aspire. But this is simply the aspiration to become a responsible individual in society, an individual who, through intelligent thinking, judicious planning and hard work, is able to carve out an adequate livelihood for himself and family and make significant contributions to the well-being of the community. The problem, now, is that if this is what, in the specific context of Akan culture, living a life informed by a sense of the sacred means, then applying the concept of religion to it would scarcely pick out anything in the culture corresponding to what in, say, Western culture might be called a nonsupernaturalistic religion. In Western society there are historical as well as conceptual reasons why one might want to organize one's life on the lines of what might be called a nonsupernaturalist religion. In Akan society there are really none. In the West, loss of the belief in God, for example, usually results in disengagement from certain well-known institutions and practices. The consequent psychological or social void might be filled for some by a "nontheistic" religion. In the Akan situation, on the other hand, no such void is to be antici-

pated from a comparable belief mutation. Speaking from my own experience, failure to retain the belief in *Nyame*—I make no mention here of the Christian God, the conception of whom registers no coherent meaning upon my understanding—has caused me not the slightest alienation from any of the institutions or practices of Akan culture.

Not unexpectedly, what has cost me some dissonance with the culture is my skepticism regarding the continued existence of our ancestors. The pouring of libation, for example, is a practice in which, as previously hinted, the Akans call upon the ancestors to come and participate in important functions and lend their good auspices to any enterprise launched. This is a significant and not infrequent ceremony in Akan life. But obviously, if one does not believe that the ancestors are actually there, one cannot pretend to call them, or, what is the same thing, one can only pretend to do so. I cannot personally, therefore, participate in a custom like this with any total inwardness. In this, by the way, I do not stand alone. Any Akan Christian—and there are great numbers of them—is logically precluded from believing such things as the Akan doctrine of ancestors, for it does not cohere with Christian eschatology. As far as I am concerned, however, there is a saving consideration. This custom of libation, and many other customs of a like quasi-material basis, can be retained by simply reinterpreting the reference to the ancestors as commemoration rather than invocation. That, of course, would entail obvious verbal reformulations, but it should present no problem. What of customs that prove not to be susceptible to such revisions in the face of advancing skepticism? One hopes that they would eventually be abandoned. The culture is rich enough not to suffer any real existential deficit from such a riddance. Nor is the atrophy of custom under the pressure of changing times at all rare in the history of culture.

Be that as it may, the fact remains that as already argued, the Akan belief in the existence and power of such beings as the ancestors, and the procedures associated with that belief do not constitute a religion in any reliable sense. We are now, therefore, brought to the following conclusion: The concept of religion is not unproblematically applicable within all cultures, and Akan culture is a case in point. Nevertheless, there may be some justification for speaking of Akan religion in a broadened sense of the word "religion." In this sense the word would refer simply to the fact that the Akans believe in Nyame, a being regarded as the architect of the world order. Certainly, this is an extremely attenuated concept of religion. As pointed out already, religion in the fullest sense, whether it be supernaturalistic or not, is not just a set of beliefs and conceptions but also a way of life based on those ideas. What we have seen, however, is that the Akan way of life is not based on the belief in Nyame. Hence, if we do use the word "religion" in the Akan context on the grounds of the belief in Nyame, we should evince some consciousness of the fact that we have made a considerable extension of meaning; otherwise we propagate a subtle misunderstanding of Akan and cognate cultures under the apparently widespread illusion that religion is a cultural universal.

Yet, surely, something must be universal. Consider the case with which Christian missionaries have been able to convert large masses of Africans to Christianity by relaying to them "tidings" which are in some important parts most likely conceptually incoherent or, at any rate, incongruous with categories deeply embedded in indigenous ways of thinking. To be sure, it cannot be assumed that in the large majority of cases conversion has been total in terms of moral and cosmological outlook. Still there are impressive enough numbers of African converts, some in the high reaches of ecclesiastical authority, whose understanding of and dedication to the Christian religion challenges the severest comparisons among the most exalted practitioners of the same faith in the West. I take this as testimony to the malleability of the human mind which enables the various peoples of the world to share not only their insights but also their incoherences. This characteristic of the mind, being fundamental to the human status, makes our common humanity the one universal which potentially transcends all cultural particularities.

QUESTIONS FOR FURTHER REFLECTION

1. Wiredu questions whether "the English word "religion" is applicable to any aspect of African life and thought." Having read his paper, what is your opinion?
2. Besides the notion of religion, can you think of any other ways in which people, by trying to understand another culture in terms of the same categories they use to understand their own culture, misunderstand the other culture?

SUGGESTIONS FOR FURTHER READING

Abraham, W. E. *The Mind of Africa*. Chicago: The University of Chicago Press, 1962.

Black Elk, Wallace, and William S. Lyon. *Black Elk: The Sacred Ways of a Lakota*. San Francisco: HarperSanFrancisco, 1991.

Dupuis, Jacques. *Toward a Christian Theology of Religious Pluralism*. Maryknoll, New York: Orbis Books, 1997.

Graham. A. C. *Disputers of the Tao: Philosophical Argument in Ancient China*. La Salle, New York: Open Court, 1989.

Heim, S. Mark. *Salvations: Truth and Difference in Religion*. Maryknoll, New York: Orbis Books, 1995.

Koller, John M., and Patricia Koller, eds. *A Sourcebook in Asian Philosophy*. New York: Macmillan, 1981.

Martin, Raymond. *On Krishnamurti*. Belmont, CA: Wadsworth, 2002.

Mbiti, John S. *African Religion and Philosophy*. London: Heinemann, 1969.

Serequeberhan, Tsenay, ed. *African Philosophy: The Essential Readings*. New York: Paragon House, 1991.

Smith, Huston. *The World's Religions*. San Francisco: Harper Collins, 1991.

CREDITS

1. From Thomas Aquinas, *Summa Theologica*. Second and revised edition, translated by Fathers of the English Dominican Province (1920).
2. From *Philosophical Review* 72 (1963). Copyright 1963 Cornell University. Reprinted by permission of the publisher.
3. From Thomas Aquinas, *Summa Theologica*. Second and revised edition, translated by Fathers of the English Dominican Province (1920).
4. © 2002 by Scott Davison. Used by kind permission of the author.
5. From Boethius, *The Consolation of Philosophy*, translated by W. V. Cooper (1902).
6. Eleanor Stump and Norman Kretzmann, *The Journal of Philosophy*, 78 (1981). Used by permission of the authors and the publisher.
7. From *Compete Philosophical and Theological Treatises of Anselm of Canterbury*, translated by Jasper Hopkins and Herbert W. Richardson. Minneapolis: Banning Press, 2000 [pp. 9395 and 117–118].
8. From Immanuel Kant, *The Critique of Pure Reason*, translated by J. M. D. Meiklejohn (1990), with emendations by the editors.
9. From *Philosophical Review* 69 (1960). © 1960 Cornell University. Reprinted by permission of the publisher.
10. From Thomas Aquinas, *Summa Theologica*. Second and revised edition, translated by Fathers of the English Dominican Province (1920).
11. © 2002 by David Yandell and Keith Yandell. Used by kind permission of the authors.
12. © John Mackie 1982. Reprinted from *The Miracle of Theism: Arguments for and against the Existence of God*, by J. L. Mackie (1982), by permission of Oxford University Press.
13. From *Journal of the American Scientific Affiliation* 32 (1980). Revised by the author. Used by kind permission of the author.
14. © 2002 by Wes Morriston. Used by kind permission of the author
15. From William Paley, *Natural Theology* (1802).
16. From David Hume, *Dialogues Concerning Natural Religion* (1776).
17. © by Robin Collins. Used by kind permission of the author.
18. *Mere Christianity* by © C. S. Lewis. © C. S. Lewis Pte. Ltd. 1942, 1943, 1944, 1952. Extract reprinted by permission.
19. © John Mackie 1982. Reprinted from *The Miracle of Theism: Arguments for and against the existence of God*, by J. L. Mackie (1982), by permission of Oxford University Press.